International Organization and Global Governance

W9-BZK-969

Completely revised and updated for the second edition, this textbook continues to offer the most comprehensive resource available for all interested in international organization and global governance.

The book offers:

- In-depth and accessible coverage of the history and theories of international organization and global governance.
- Discussions of the full range of state, intergovernmental, and non-state actors.
- Examinations of key issues in all aspects of contemporary world politics.

New additions to this edition include:

- New and revised chapters on theories of international organization and global governance.
- New substantive chapters on global corporations, China, financial markets, terrorist organizations, governing global energy, and the Internet.
- Updated contributions to reflect the changing nature of world politics.

The book comprises fifty-four chapters arranged in seven parts and woven together by a comprehensive introduction to the field, along with separate introductions to each part to guide students and faculty, and helpful pointers to further reading.

International Organization and Global Governance is a self-contained resource enabling readers to comprehend more fully the role of myriad actors in the governance of global life as well as to assemble the many pieces of the contemporary global governance puzzle.

Thomas G. Weiss is Presidential Professor of Political Science at The Graduate Center and Director Emeritus of the Ralph Bunche Institute for International Studies, The City University of New York.

Rorden Wilkinson is Deputy Pro-Vice-Chancellor for Education and Innovation and Professor of Global Political Economy at the University of Sussex.

Praise for the Second Edition

"*International Organization and Global Governance* is an excellent one-stop resource that simultaneously offers a thorough and broad theoretical understanding and empirical insight into a wide array of important issue areas in international relations. It has been an indispensable core text book in my course on global governance for years, and has been highly valued by the students for its clarity and ability to explain complex matters. This second edition provides up-to-date insights into the rapidly evolving field."

—Benedicte Bull, University of Oslo

"*International Organization and Global Governance* is remarkable not just for the breadth and depth of its coverage, but for its ability to stretch our understandings of both organization and governance. It covers classic theories and established institutions (such as the UN and regional organizations) while illuminating the sometimes obscure powers of nongovernmental and "private" entities (ranging from human rights groups to bond rating agencies). This is an indispensable resource for the field."

—Michael Doyle, Columbia University

"An indispensable resource for any student of contemporary global affairs. This latest edition of a now-classic volume balances breadth of coverage with conceptual depth and sophisticated analysis. The editors here have assembled a top-notch team to write an outstanding collection of insightful, accessible essays that span the enormous range of challenges and changes in global governance today."

—Martha Finnemore, George Washington University

"The onset of globalization has led to dramatic shifts in the way the world is organized, with the emergence of new actors, rules, and structures. Weiss and Wilkinson have assembled a wonderful team of authors that allows a reader to navigate the new twenty-first century landscape of global governance. Conceptually rich and thematically comprehensive, the articles go beyond boilerplates to see the politics that are shaping this new landscape."

—Sakiko Fukuda-Parr, The New School

"Never before has a book so comprehensively and rigorously appraised the complex human condition under contemporary world order. This epic 54-chapter volume invites leading experts to grapple with the challenges and opportunities for making international organization and global governance fit-for-purpose. If you seek to inspire your students to be critically minded difference-makers in the world, this is essential reading."

—Erin Hannah, University of Western Ontario

"Motivated by an acute awareness of both the failure and successes of global governance, this comprehensive volume explores the place of international organizations in contemporary world order. With essays from leading writers on international affairs,

it covers an impressive breadth of topics with nuance and sensitivity, from refugees to public health to global corporations. It deserves to be required reading for students and scholars of international politics."

—Ian Hurd, Northwestern University

"The first edition of this volume was a landmark so this second, much-updated volume is most welcome. The editors and authors are all leading authorities on their topics. Highly recommended."

—David Malone, UN University, Tokyo

"Weiss and Wilkinson have comprised another comprehensive and cutting-edge collection of essays on international organizations and global governance. This outstanding volume will quickly become—once again—a standard reference for understanding world politics in contemporary times."

—Susanne Soederberg, Queen's University

"In a fracturing world, international cooperation is looking fragile. This book provides a useful overview of how international organizations can help, where they fail, and with what consequences."

—Ngaire Woods, University of Oxford

Praise for the First Edition

"*International Organization and Global Governance* should have a place on any international relations scholar's shelf. In addition to its sheer comprehensiveness as a reference work, it takes the crucial conceptual leap of focusing not on organizations, institutions, regimes, or any other piece of international order, but instead on the presence or absence of actual governance: the successful exercise of power to achieve outcomes. As one important chapter asks, who are the actual governors of the international system? The answers, with respect to many areas of international life, are surprising."

—Anne-Marie Slaughter, Princeton University

"It is impossible to understand global governance without recognizing the important roles played by international organizations and non-state actors. This volume brings together cutting edge work by experts in their various fields to synthesize actor based and issue based insights about global governance."

—Peter M. Haas, University of Massachusetts Amherst

"A comprehensive survey of the theory and practice of global governance in the modern world. Comprised of outstanding essays by acknowledged experts and filled with important insights, *International Organization and Global Governance* is essential reading for scholars and students as well as practitioners."

—David A. Lake, University of California, San Diego

"Never before has a book demonstrated so systematically that 'global governance' offers a useful lens to analyze world politics. Extraordinarily comprehensive, it will become a vital reference for academics and practitioners."

—Jean-Philippe Thérien, Université de Montréal

"This volume brings together contributions from an outstanding group of scholars. It is an indispensable guide for understanding the full range of contemporary challenges of global governance and international organizations, from a variety of perspectives."

—Keith Krause, Graduate Institute of International and Development Studies, Geneva

"This comprehensive collection, which includes contributions from many of the leading figures in the field, is sure to be the principal reference work on international organizations and global governance for many years to come."

—John Ravenhill, Australian National University

"Weiss and Wilkinson have assembled a magnificent set of chapters from leading scholars that simultaneously provides a tour de force of international organizations and a clear guide to conceptualizing and understanding global governance. This persuasive account of the history, power and authority of international organizations should be required reading for all students, professors and practitioners of global governance and international relations."

—Catherine Weaver, The University of Texas at Austin

"A tour de force. This meticulously conceived textbook on global governance and international organizations with essays by some of the world's finest experts will be a classic for scholars and practitioners from day 1."

—Jan Wouters, Director of the Leuven Centre for Global Governance Studies, KU Leuven

"Kofi Annan was right: we are creating a global village. Hence, the need for stronger global village councils becomes more pressing day by day. Despite this, few understand how spectacularly global governance—in all its manifestations—has grown and why it needs to keep growing to keep the world safe. Weiss and Wilkinson have done us a remarkable service by producing this volume now: it provides an indispensable guide to the fastest growing global industry. And it will be read and studied for several decades as the world continues to converge."

—Kishore Mahbubani, National University of Singapore

"The fifty chapters in this book, written by scholars from around the world, provide a comprehensive overview of the expanding agenda and participation in global governance. All readers will become aware of how they are involved in global governance, and how they might respond."

—Chadwick F. Alger, Ohio State University

"The reach and scope of this collection renders it invaluable for situating the study of international organizations in the broader field of IR."

—Thomas Biersteker, The Graduate Institute, Geneva

INTERNATIONAL ORGANIZATION AND GLOBAL GOVERNANCE

Second Edition

**Edited by
Thomas G. Weiss and
Rorden Wilkinson**

 Routledge
Taylor & Francis Group

LONDON AND NEW YORK

Second edition published 2018
by Routledge
2 Park Square, Milton Park, Abingdon, Oxon OX14 4RN

and by Routledge
711 Third Avenue, New York, NY 10017

Routledge is an imprint of the Taylor & Francis Group, an informa business

First edition published by Routledge 2014

British Library Cataloguing-in-Publication Data
A catalogue record for this book is available from the British Library

Library of Congress Cataloging-in-Publication Data
Names: Weiss, Thomas G. (Thomas George), 1946– editor. | Wilkinson,
    Rorden, 1970– editor.
Title: International organization and global governance / edited by Thomas G.
    Weiss and Rorden Wilkinson.
Description: Second edition. | Milton Park, Abingdon, Oxon ; New York, NY :
    Routledge, 2018. | Includes bibliographical references and index.
Identifiers: LCCN 2017036083 | ISBN 9781138236578 (hardback) |
    ISBN 9781138236585 (pbk.) | ISBN 9781315301914 (ebook)
Subjects: LCSH: International organization. | International agencies. |
    International relations. | Globalization.
Classification: LCC JZ5566 .I59 2018 | DDC 341.2—dc23
LC record available at https://lccn.loc.gov/2017036083

ISBN: 978-1-138-23657-8 (hbk)
ISBN: 978-1-138-23658-5 (pbk)
ISBN: 978-1-315-30191-4 (ebk)

Typeset in Times New Roman
by Apex CoVantage, LLC

Contents

Part V Non-state actors in global governance 337

Part VI Securing the world, governing humanity 451

Part VII Governing the economic and social world 587

Contents

Acknowledgements

We first began thinking about this volume more than fifteen years ago, as part of a first discussion about what became our Routledge book series, "Global Institutions." As the series' tenth anniversary approached, we put together a proposal that contained what we thought a book on international organization and global governance should look like if we were given *carte blanche*. Craig Fowlie and Nicola Parkin at Routledge were enthusiastic about our idea and promptly sent the proposal to ten referees. We were pleasantly surprised when not too long thereafter ten glowing endorsements for the proposal came back. The feedback we received in each of those reviews helped us refine aspects of the proposal for what became the first edition of this book in 2014. We were grateful to those reviewers for their support and constructive criticisms then, and to another football team assembled by Craig and Nicola in 2016 to provide feedback from users about the good, the bad, and the (as it turns out, not so very) ugly of that first attempt.

A decade and a half of collaborating closely on the Global Institutions Series, among other projects, has been fruitful and rewarding, providing us with our own ideas about additions and subtractions. The resultant book represents the recommendations from all sides.

The current edition would not have come together without the first-rate support provided by Nicholas Micinski, an advanced PhD candidate in Political Science at the City University of New York's Graduate Center. With good humor and uncommon common sense, Nick helped make the trains run on time and improve the presentation and the contents of these pages—just as he has as the Managing Editor for the book series.

For the first edition, Oliver Turner helped organize and oversee the delivery of the manuscript from the moment that the chapters started coming in to the correction of the final anomaly in the proverbial last endnote. His industry, willingness, and attention to detail improved the quality of the first edition. A rising young academic star in his own right, we are delighted that he is a contributor to this second edition as he was to the first. The first edition also benefitted from the insights of Erin Hannah, Craig Murphy, and Tim Sinclair. The Brooks World Poverty Institute—now part of the Global Development Institute—at the University of Manchester was the foundry in which we forged the first edition, an endeavor that we could not have achieved without the help, support, and friendship of David Hulme and Denise Redston.

That first edition was also improved by Martin Burke's assistance when it was on the drawing boards, as he had done for the Global Institutions Series. That thirty-three of the contributors to fifty-four of the chapters in this second edition also have books in our series is a source of pride.

Tom was able to devote so much time to this second edition because he was the beneficiary of two-years as an Andrew Carnegie Fellow. Rorden did so while serving as a departmental chair amid the drama and beauty of the Sussex Downs.

T.G.W. and R.W.

New York and Brighton, August 2017

ABBREVIATIONS

AoA	Agreement on Agriculture
ABM	Anti-Ballistic Missile Treaty
ACSRT	African Union's African Center for Study and Research on Terrorism
ACTA	Anti-Counterfeiting Trade Agreement
ADB	Asian Development Bank
AfDB	African Development Bank
AFISMA	African-led International Support Mission to Mali
AG	Australia Group
AIDS	Acquired Immune Deficiency Syndrome
AIIB	Asian Infrastructure Investment Bank
ALAC	At-Large Advisory Committee
ALBA	Bolivarian Alternative of the Americas
AMR	antimicrobial resistance
ANSI	American National Standards Institute
APEC	Asia-Pacific Economic Cooperation
ASEAN	Association of Southeast Asian Nations
ASEM	Asia–Europe Meeting
ASIS	American Society for Industrial Security
ASP	Assembly of States Parties
AU	African Union
BASIC	Brazil, South Africa, India, and China
BI	Brookings Institution
BITs	bilateral investment treaties
BIAC	Business and Industry Advisory Committee
BOAD	West African Development Bank
BoP	base of the pyramid
BPA	Beijing Platform for Action
BRAC	Bangladesh Rehabilitation Assistance Committee (superseded by the abbreviation alone)
BRIC	Brazil, Russia, India, and China
BRICS	Brazil, Russia, India, China, and South Africa
BTWC	Biological and Toxin Weapons Convention
BWC	Biological Weapons Convention
BWIs	Bretton Woods Institutions
CABEI	Central American Bank for Economic Integration
CAN	Andean Community of Nations
CAT	Convention Against Torture
CBDR	common but differentiated responsibilities
CCS	carbon capture and storage
CD	Conference on Disarmament
CDB	Caribbean Development Bank

CEB	UN Chief Executives Board
CEDAW	Committee on the Elimination of Discrimination Against Women
CEIP	Carnegie Endowment for International Peace
CERD	Committee on the Elimination of Racial Discrimination
CERDI	Center for Studies and Research on Development at the University of Auvergne
CFA	Comprehensive Framework for Action
CFCs	chlorofluorocarbons
CFS	Committee on World Food Security
CFSP	Common Foreign and Security Policy
CGIAR	Consultative Group on International Agricultural Research
CHR	Commission on Human Rights
CIC	Center on International Cooperation
CIMMYT	International Maize and Wheat Improvement Center
CIS	Commonwealth of Independent States
CITES	Convention on International Trade in Endangered Species of Fauna and Flora
CMS	Convention for the Conservation of Migratory Species
COMECON	Council for Mutual Economic Assistance
CONGO	Conference of Non-Governmental Organizations in Consultative Relationship with the United Nations
COP21	Conference of the Parties (21)
CRA	Currency Reserve Agreement
CRC	Committee on the Rights of the Child
CRPD	Committee on the Rights of Persons with Disabilities
CRS	Catholic Relief Services
CSD	United Nations Commission on Sustainable Development
CSR	corporate social responsibility
CSDP	Common Security and Defence Policy
CTAG	Counterterrorism Action Group
CTBT	Comprehensive Test Ban Treaty
CTC	Counterterrorism Committee
CTED	Counterterrorism Executive Directorate
CTITF	United Nations Counterterrorism Implementation Taskforce
CVE	countering violent extremism
CWC	Chemical Weapons Convention
DAC	Development Assistance Committee
DARPA	Defense Advanced Research Projects Agency
DESA	Department of Economic and Social Affairs
DFS	Department of Field Support
DfID	Department for International Development (UK)
DNS	Domain Name System
DPA	Department of Political Affairs
DPI	Department of Public Information
DPKO	Department of Peacekeeping Operations

DPRK	Democratic People's Republic of Korea
DRC	Democratic Republic of the Congo
EADB	East African Development Bank
EBRD	European Bank for Reconstruction and Development
EC	European Community
ECJ	European Court of Justice
ECOSOC	Economic and Social Council
ECOWAS	Economic Community of West African States
ECSC	European Coal and Steel Community
EDB	Eurasian Development Bank
EEA	European Economic Area
EEC	European Economic Community
EFTA	European Free Trade Association
EITI	Extractive Industries Transparency Initiative
ELCI	Environment Liaison Centre International
EMs	emerging market economies
ENDA	Environnement et Développement du Tiers-Monde
EP	European Parliament
ERSG	Executive Representatives of the Secretary-General
ETUC	European Trade Union Council
EU	European Union
EULEX KOSOVO	European Union Rule of Law Mission in Kosovo
EUPM	European Union Police Mission in Bosnia and Herzegovina
EUPOL COPPS	European Union Police Mission for the Palestinian Territories
Euratom	European Atomic Energy Community
FAC	Food Aid Convention
FACI	forensic accounting and corporate investigations
FAO	Food and Agriculture Organization
FATF	Financial Action Task Force
FCL	flexible credit line
FCTC	Framework Convention on Tobacco Control
FDI	foreign direct investment
FES	Friedrich Ebert Stiftung
FIFA	Fédération Internationale de Football Association
FIU	financial intelligence unit
FMCT	Fissile Material Cutoff Treaty
FOCAC	Forum on China Africa Cooperation
FSAP	Financial Sector Assessment Program
FSB	Financial Stability Board
FSC	Forest Stewardship Council
FTAA	Free Trade Area of the Americas
FTF	foreign terrorist fighters
FUNDS	Future UN Development System Project
G-7	Group of Seven
G-8	Group of Eight
G-20	Group of 20

G-77	Group of 77
GAIN	Global Alliance for Improved Nutrition
GATT	General Agreement on Tariffs and Trade
GAVI	Global Alliance for Vaccination and Immunization
GCERF	Global Community Engagement and Resilience Fund
GCTF	Global Counterterrorism Forum
GDP	gross domestic product
GECF	Gas Exporting Countries Forum
GEF	Global Environment Facility
GEI	Green Economy Initiative
GFATM	Global Fund to Fight AIDS, Tuberculosis and Malaria
GFC	global financial crisis
GHGs	greenhouse gases
GPN	global production networks
GRI	Global Reporting Initiative
GUF	Global Union Federation
GVC	global value chain
GWOT	global war on terrorism
HCNs	host-country nationals
HEW	hypermasculine Eurocentric whiteness
HIPC	heavily indebted poor country
HIPPO	High-level Independent Panel on Peace Operations
HIV	Human Immunodeficiency Virus
HLP	High-level Panel
HLPE	High-level Panel of Experts
HLPF	High-level Political Forum
HLTF	High-level Task Force on the Food Security Crisis
HRC	Human Rights Council
HST	hegemonic stability theory
IAEA	International Atomic Energy Agency
IANA	Internet Assigned Numbers Authority
IAVI	International AIDS Vaccine Initiative
IBRD	International Bank for Reconstruction and Development
IBSA	India, Brazil, and South Africa
ICANN	Internet Corporation for Assigned Names and Numbers
ICAO	International Civil Aviation Organization
ICC	International Criminal Court
ICCPR	International Covenant on Civil and Political Rights
ICEM	Intergovernmental Committee for European Migration
ICESCR	International Covenant on Economic, Social and Cultural Rights
ICFTU	International Confederation of Free Trade Unions
ICG	International Crisis Group
ICIS	Interpol Criminal Information System
ICISS	International Commission on Intervention and State Sovereignty
ICJ	International Court of Justice
ICM	Intergovernmental Committee for Migration

TTIP	Transatlantic Trade and Investment Partnership
TUAC	Trade Union Advisory Committee
TUCA	Trade Union Confederation of the Americas
UCLG	United Cities and Local Governments
UK	United Kingdom
UN	United Nations
UNAIDS	Joint United Nations Program on HIV/AIDS
UNAMID	United Nations Hybrid Operation in Darfur
UNAMIR	United Nations Assistance Mission for Rwanda
UNAMSIL	United Nations Mission in Sierra Leone
UNAVEM	United Nations Angola Verification Mission
UNCCT	United Nations Counterterrorism Centre
UNCED	United Nations Conference on Environment and Development
UNCHE	United Nations Conference on the Human Environment
UNCLOS	UN Conference on the Law of the Sea
UNCTAD	United Nations Conference on Trade and Development
UNDHR	Universal Declaration of Human Rights
UNDP	United Nations Development Programme
UNEF	United Nations Emergency Force
UNEP	United Nations Environment Programme
UNESCO	United Nations Educational, Scientific and Cultural Organization
UNFCCC	UN Framework Convention on Climate Change
UNFICYP	United Nations Peacekeeping Force in Cyprus
UNFPA	United Nations Population Fund
UNHABITAT	United Nations Habitat
UNHCR	Office of the UN High Commissioner for Refugees
UNICEF	United Nations International Children's Emergency Fund
UNIDO	United Nations Industrial Development Organization
UNITAF	Unified Task Force
UNGC	United Nations Global Compact
UNMA	United Nations Mine Action
UNMIL	United Nations Mission in Liberia
UNMIS	United Nations Mission in Sudan
UNMIS(S)	United Nations Mission in South Sudan
UNMOGIP	United Nations Military Observer Group in India and Pakistan
UNOCI	United Nations Mission in Côte d'Ivoire
UNODC	United Nations Office on Drugs and Crime
UNOPS	United Nations Office for Projected Services
UNOSOM	United Nations Operation in Somalia
UNRRA	United Nations Relief and Rehabilitation Agency
UNRWA	United Nations Relief and Works Agency for Palestine Refugees
UNSCOB	United Nations Special Committee on the Balkans
UNSD	United Nations Statistics Division
UNSMS	United Nations Security Management System
UNSOA	UN Support Office for the African Union Mission in Somalia
UNTSO	United Nations Truce Supervision Organization

UNWOMEN	United Nations Women
UNWTO	United Nations World Tourism Organization
UPU	Universal Postal Union
US	United States of America
USAID	United States Agency for International Development
USSR	Union of Soviet Socialist Republics
USTR	United States Trade Representative
W3C	World Wide Web Consortium
WBG	World Bank Group
WCIT	World Conference on International Telecommunications
WCL	World Confederation of Labour
WEO	World Energy Outlooks
WEU	Western European Union
WFC	World Food Council
WFP	World Food Programme
WFTO	World Fair Trade Organization
WFTU	World Federation of Trade Unions
WHA	World Health Assembly
WHO	World Health Organization
WIPO	World Intellectual Property Organization
WMD	weapons of mass destruction
WMO	World Meteorological Organization
WSSD	World Summit on Social Development
WTO	World Trade Organization

ILLUSTRATIONS

Figures

Tables

Boxes

ABOUT THE CONTRIBUTORS

Michael Barnett is University Professor of International Affairs and Political Science at George Washington University.

Alex J. Bellamy is Director of the Asia-Pacific Centre for the Responsibility to Protect and Professor of Peace and Conflict Studies at the University of Queensland, Australia.

James Brassett is Reader in International Political Economy at the University of Warwick. He works on the politics of globalization with a focus on questions of ethics, governance, crisis, and resistance.

Shaun Breslin is Professor of Politics and International Studies at the University of Warwick, and Co-Editor of the *Pacific Review*.

Gülay Çağlar is Professor of Political Science with a focus on Gender and Diversity at Freie Universität Berlin, Germany.

Madeline Carr is Associate Professor in International Relations and Cyber Security, Department of Science, Technology, Engineering and Public Policy (STEaPP), University College London.

Jason Charrette is Assistant Professor of Political Science at Casper College in Wyoming.

Simon Chesterman is Dean of the National University of Singapore Faculty of Law and also Editor of the *Asian Journal of International Law* and Secretary-General of the Asian Society of International Law.

Jennifer Clapp is a Canada Research Chair and Professor in the School of Environment, Resources and Sustainability at the University of Waterloo.

Roger A. Coate is Paul D. Coverdell Professor of Public Policy at Georgia College & State University, Distinguished Professor Emeritus of Political Science at the University of South Carolina.

Andrew F. Cooper is Professor, Balsillie School of International Affairs and the Department of Political Science, University of Waterloo, Canada, and Associate Research Fellow-UNU CRIS (Institute on Comparative Regional Integration), Bruges, Belgium.

Graciana del Castillo is Senior Fellow at the Ralph Bunche Institute for International Studies; a co-founding partner of Macroeconomics Advisory Group; and a member of the Council on Foreign Relations.

Elizabeth R. DeSombre is the Camilla Chandler Frost Professor of Environmental Studies and Director of the Environmental Studies Program at Wellesley College.

Raymond Duvall is Special Assistant to the Provost for Grand Challenges Research and Distinguished University Teaching Professor of Political Science, the University of Minnesota.

David P. Forsythe is University Professor and Charles J. Mach Distinguished Professor, Emeritus, at the University of Nebraska in Lincoln.

Julian Germann is Lecturer in International Relations and Director for the Centre for Global Political Economy (CGPE) at the University of Sussex.

Richard J. Goldstone is a retired justice of the Constitutional Court of South Africa and the former chief prosecutor of the United Nations International Criminal Tribunals for the former Yugoslavia and Rwanda.

Leon Gordenker is Emeritus Professor of Politics at Princeton University.

Sophie Harman is a Reader in International Politics at Queen Mary University of London.

Nigel Haworth is Professor of Human Resource Development at the University of Auckland.

Andrew Heiss is Visiting Assistant Professor of Public Management at the George W. Romney Institute of Public Management at Brigham Young University.

David Held is Master of University College and Professor of Politics and International Relations, Durham University.

Mônica Herz is an associate professor at the Catholic University of Rio de Janeiro Institute of International Relations.

Harald Heubaum is Assistant Professor of Global Energy and Climate Policy at the Centre for International Studies and Diplomacy, SOAS, University of London.

Bernard Hoekman is a Professor and Director of Global Economics, Robert Schuman Centre for Advanced Studies, European University Institute, Florence, Italy.

Peter J. Hoffman is Assistant Professor of International Relations in the Graduate Program in International Affairs at the New School.

Matthew J. Hoffmann is a Professor of Political Science at the University of Toronto Scarborough and Co-Director of the Environmental Governance Lab at the Munk School of Global Affairs.

Steve Hughes is Professor of International Organizations at Newcastle University Business School.

David Hulme is Executive Director of the Global Development Institute and CEO of the DAMS 2.0 Research Centre at the University of Manchester, UK.

Tana Johnson is a faculty member in the Sanford School of Public Policy and the Department of Political Science at Duke University.

Christer Jönsson is Professor Emeritus of Political Science at Lund University and a member of the Royal Swedish Academy of Sciences.

Jacquelin Kataneksza is a PhD candidate in Public and Urban Policy at the Milano School of International Affairs, Management and Urban Policy at the New School.

W. Andy Knight is Professor of International Relations in the Department of Political Science at the University of Alberta and past Director of the Institute of International Relations (IIR) at the University of the West Indies.

Khalid Koser is Executive Director of the Global Community Engagement and Resilience Fund and editor of the *Journal of Refugee Studies*.

Charlotte Ku is Professor of Law and Associate Dean for Global Programs at the Texas A&M University School of Law.

Angelina H. Li is an economics major at Wellesley College. She has worked on several research projects on aspects of global environmental governance in recent years.

L.H.M. Ling is Professor of International Affairs in the Milano School of International Affairs, Management and Urban Policy at the New School.

S. Neil MacFarlane is Lester B. Pearson Professor of International Relations and Fellow at St Anne's College, University of Oxford.

Frank G. Madsen is a lecturer at the Centre for Development Studies, Department of Political Science and International Studies at the University of Cambridge.

Katherine Marshall is Professor of the Practice of Development, Religion, and Conflict Resolution at Georgetown University's School of Foreign Service and Senior Fellow at the Berkley Center for Religion, Peace, and World Affairs.

Christopher May is Professor of Political Economy at Lancaster University.

James G. McGann is Senior Lecturer of International Studies at the Lauder Institute, Director of the Think Tanks and Civil Societies Program and Senior Fellow, Fels Institute of Government at the University of Pennsylvania.

Bessma Momani is Professor at the University of Waterloo and the Balsillie School of International Affairs, a Senior Fellow at the Centre for International Governance and Innovation.

Michael Moran is Lecturer and Discipline Leader (Social Impact) in the Faculty of Business and Law, Swinburne University of Technology, Australia.

Craig N. Murphy is Betty Freyhof Johnson '44 Professor of Political Science at Wellesley College and Research Professor of Global Governance at the University of Massachusetts, Boston.

Stefanie Neumeier is a PhD student in Political Science and International Relations at the University of Southern California.

Susan Park is an Associate Professor of International Relations at the University of Sydney.

M.J. Peterson is Professor of Political Science at the University of Massachusetts Amherst (USA). She is the author of *The UN General Assembly* (2006) and *The General Assembly in World Politics* (1986).

Elisabeth Prügl is Professor of International Relations and Director of the Gender Centre at the Graduate Institute, Geneva.

Mark Raymond is the Wick Cary Assistant Professor of International Security in the Department of International and Area Studies at the University of Oklahoma.

Peter Romaniuk is Associate Professor of Political Science at John Jay College of Criminal Justice and the Graduate Center, CUNY, and a Senior Fellow at the Global Center on Cooperative Security.

Ben Rosamond is Professor of Political Science at the University of Copenhagen.

Jan Aart Scholte is Professor of Peace and Development in the School of Global Studies at the University of Gothenburg.

Susan K. Sell is Professor at the School of Regulation and Global Governance, College of Asia and the Pacific, the Australian National University, and Professor Emerita of Political Science and International Affairs at the George Washington University.

Sara Shroff is a PhD candidate in Public and Urban Policy at the Milano School of International Affairs, Management and Urban Policy at the New School.

Waheguru Pal Singh (W.P.S.) Sidhu is Clinical Associate Professor at New York University's Center for Global Affairs, nonresident senior fellow for foreign policy at Brookings Institution, and an associate fellow at the Geneva Centre for Security Policy.

Timothy J. Sinclair is Associate Professor of International Political Economy in the Department of Politics and International Studies at the University of Warwick.

Duncan Snidal is Professor of International Relations and Fellow at Nuffield College, University of Oxford.

Jennifer Sterling-Folker is the Alan R. Bennett Honors Professor of Political Science at the University of Connecticut.

Jonathan R. Strand is Professor of Political Science at the University of Nevada, Las Vegas.

Henning Tamm is Lecturer in the School of International Relations at the University of St Andrews.

Ian Taylor is Professor in International Relations and African Political Economy at the University of St Andrews and also Chair Professor in the School of International Studies, Renmin University of China

Ramesh Thakur is professor in the Crawford School of Public Policy, Australian National University.

Oliver Turner is lecturer in International Relations at the University of Edinburgh.

Thomas G. Weiss is Presidential Professor of Political Science at the Graduate Center and Director Emeritus of the Ralph Bunche Institute for International Studies, The City University of New York.

Fabrice Weissman is Director of the Centre de Réflexion sur l'Action et les Savoirs Humanitaires at the Médecins sans Frontières Foundation.

Rorden Wilkinson is Deputy Pro-Vice-Chancellor for Education and Innovation and Professor of Global Political Economy at the University of Sussex.

Paul D. Williams is Associate Professor in the Elliott School of International Affairs at the George Washington University.

Ren Xiao is Professor of International Politics and Director of the Center for the Study of Chinese Foreign Policy at Fudan University, Shanghai, China.

Susanne Zwingel is Associate Professor of International Relations at Florida International University, Miami, USA.

PART I
INTRODUCTION

From international organization to global governance

Thomas G. Weiss and Rorden Wilkinson

Few things point to the importance of understanding international organization (IO) and global governance more than their stark failings. The capacity of global humanitarian instruments to protect the lives of the world's "at-risk" populations has repeatedly been called into question, with the all-too-harrowing images of past failures in Rwanda and Somalia still searing our memories and Syria's ongoing agony an ever-present daily media bill-of-fare.[1]

The continuing absence of a robust global regulatory regime governing financial transactions and innovations helped heighten the effects of the 2007–2008 global economic meltdown, plunging Western economies into more than half a decade of recession and sparing little of the rest of the world. Just a decade earlier, the Asian Financial Crisis of 1997–1998 had also drawn attention to the inadequacies of global financial governance, including to the International Monetary Fund's (IMF) role in exacerbating the crisis.[2] "Spurning" lessons rather than "learning" from them seems to be the human fate, and often for students of IO and global governance.

While the global development architecture has presided over modest reductions in the proportion of the world's population living in extreme poverty, an unprecedented gap has grown more generally between the global "haves" and "haves not." On the eve of the 2016 World Economic Forum in Davos, Switzerland, the poverty-fighting organization Oxfam released data showing that the combined wealth of the world's 62 richest individuals was greater than that of the poorest 3.5 billion people—a shade under half of the world's entire population. Moreover, the richest one percent of the world's population owned more than the bottom ninety-nine percent. Meanwhile, more than one billion people continue to live in extreme deprivation and poverty—defined as \$1.90 per day.[3] As David Hulme summarizes: "[O]ur world is organized in such a way that around 1.5 to 2.5 billion people (depending on how you define poverty) have little or no access to the most basic needs."[4]

In the field of trade, global governance has fared little better. In December 2015, fourteen years of torturous negotiations finally ended when World Trade Organization (WTO) members agreed that the Doha round was no longer fit for purpose, and that their endeavors had come to naught.[5] In drawing a line under the round, they also set aside hopes that a far-reaching trade deal might be negotiated that would genuinely benefit the world's poor, and that trade liberalization and associated rulemaking would act as an engine for accelerated development worldwide.

Elsewhere, the picture has hardly proved any brighter. Existing intergovernmental mechanisms for dealing with infectious disease have fallen short in coping with cholera, HIV/AIDS, Ebola, Zika, and dengue fever, among others.[6] Meanwhile, global development programs have been associated with the stagnation and decline of the health of populations on the periphery of the world economy.[7]

Despite numerous institutions, much activity, and well-publicized negotiations, the pace of climate change, species loss, and desertification continues to call into question intergovernmental mechanisms for dealing with the deteriorating condition of the global environment. Efforts to stem the rate of growth of greenhouse gas (GHG) emissions continue to be frustrated by a lack of political will among the politicians in leading industrialized countries and their newly "emerging" counterparts, as well as among officials from the private sector and indeed citizens everywhere.[8] The celebration of the much heralded 2015 Paris Agreement on Climate Change, which lasted until only a few months after Donald Trump's inauguration in 2017, provides just one compelling illustration.

In short, a well-populated institutional terrain should not hide the reality that we are treading water, at best, in creating adequate global governance. Indeed, we are perhaps drifting farther out to sea and wasting the energy and time necessary to move toward safety and onwards to somewhere less precarious.

It is not just these shortcomings that point to the importance of understanding IO and global governance. It is the increasingly pluralistic nature of global politics and the changing roles of myriad actors therein. States have experimented with alternative intergovernmental arrangements—such as the current profusion of "groups," with the Group of 7/8 (G-7/G-8) and the Group of 20 (G-20) being the most prominent—to coordinate policy in key areas. Regional arrangements continue to drive forward economic integration and sometimes peace operations; and states have taken on the role of managers of global interdependence.

A burgeoning nongovernmental sector is engaged in myriad activities ranging from familiar roles in disaster relief and poverty alleviation through to the implementation of microcredit and microfinance programs, to shaping global policy frameworks in development and health.[9] Knowledge networks and knowledge management[10] play an important role in policy formulation and dissemination.[11] At the same time, other less salubrious actors have become embroiled in the governance of global affairs. Private military and security companies (PMSCs) are increasingly prominent in almost all arenas of conflict.[12] Criminal gangs organize and traffic indentured workers, women, and children from the borderlands of the industrialized world to the plantations of the southern United States and the sex industries of Western Europe and Asia. Terrorist groups and networks have become more active and lethal across the globe, generating and fueling instability and raising questions over the capacity of international mechanisms—among many others—to control their spread.[13]

Credit rating agencies, multinational corporations, and financial markets are key to the functioning of the global economy often intruding into the pockets of everyday life.[14] Transnational religious movements—some interfaith, many not—have come to be seen as important development actors setting the pace for some initiatives while acting to block others.[15] Moreover, it is not just the number of actors involved in the governance of the globe that also requires us to develop a keen sense of the way in which the world is organized. We also need to get a better grip on the role that flows of information facilitated by digital communications, electronic transactions, and the Internet are increasingly shaping life on the planet.

Strikingly, the way that these actors and mechanisms are arranged in relationship to one another, the power that underpins them, and the ideas and ideologies that drive their overall assemblage are not as central to the study of international relations (IR) as they ought to be. While they are concerns within all the major approaches, within the wider IR discipline, IO and global governance are often treated as subfields and commonly as synonyms for each another. More often than not, only one element or issue area—for instance, the United Nations or the multilateral trading system—is engaged, frequently in isolation from others thereby ensuring that the relationship between them is seldom fully diagnosed and understood. Yet for us, they are not merely curious and divisible phenomena but rather essential elements of the form and function of world order; this chapter and the 54 others that follow demonstrate why.

We aim to correct this misrepresentation in the remainder of this chapter and in our further introductions that begin each of the six subsequent parts of the book. Certainly, others have written important interpretations that shed light on the global governance puzzle,[16] but none has done so in way that attempts to grapple with its complexity in the way that the sum of the following chapters do. We made that claim in the first edition of this book; it is even more accurate here with thoroughly revised and expanded contributions from our stable of authors and new additions—conceptual as well as empirical—that expand the breadth of subject matter. The centrality of questions about how the world is organized and governed—and a better understanding of the role myriad actors play in the governance of global life—offers an intriguing framework for what we believe continues to be the most comprehensive guide yet published to help readers assemble the many pieces of the contemporary global governance puzzle.

The remainder of this introduction spells out what matters and why with an overview of the field that we see as expansive and indicative of the broad terrain with which we grapple. We also say a little about why we as a community of scholars have not really put IO and global governance together very well. Thereafter, we explain why the book's contents are essential reading, and we parse briefly the substance of its seven main parts. In addition, we provide more detailed introductions at the beginning of each of the subsequent sections of the book that guide reading and aid understanding.

Bringing international organization and global governance to the fore

As indicated, international relations—as a field of study and as a real-world pursuit—has always been concerned with IO and global governance. Indeed, it could be argued that understanding how the world is governed—of which an appreciation of how relations between states are organized is key—has always been and remains one of the primary concerns of IR scholars.[17] Yet, the central relationship of IO and global governance to the study and practice of IR is rarely appropriately acknowledged and understood.

Rather, and much to the detriment of comprehending better how the world is ordered, IO and global governance have tended to be a combination of all or some of the following elements:

- the activities of the UN and other major international organizations;
- subsets of the broader field of IR;
- the preserve of normative and idealistic projects concerned with making the world a better place;
- the low politics of mundane bureaucracies working on more technical economic, environmental, and social issues and not the high politics of security, warfare and defense; and
- conspiracies about world government.

Yet to present IO and global governance in these terms means misunderstanding that the questions with which they are concerned are actually core endeavors of the major intellectual traditions in IR. A brief *tour d'horizon* illustrates why.

Realism, in both its classical and neorealist variants, has as a constitutive tenet an assumption of how the world is organized. Hans J. Morgenthau was concerned, among other things, with varying forms of international order—imperialism, world government, alliances, and self-determination; and mechanisms of governance—balance of power, international law, and supranational forms of arms control. Moreover, he examined (but did not necessarily advocate) alternative "future" forms of global governance—world state, world community, and the politics of accommodation.[18] Kenneth Waltz's neorealist formulation posits the international system as comprising a structure and a set of interacting units.[19] As in the classical earlier formulation, there is no central authority that orders the units; instead, their relations *vis-à-vis* one another are determined by their relative power capabilities. In both variants, realism has a clear idea of the overall structure of how the world is governed, and the primary task to deal with the negative effects of this form of organization.

Liberal internationalists and their modern (neo)liberal institutionalist, neofunctionalist, cosmopolitan, and constructivist counterparts also recognize the pernicious aspects of the way world politics is organized. However, rather than focusing on the development of self-help manuals designed to bolster state power in the face of changes in relative power capabilities, they emphasize moments of common interest in which cooperation between and among states occurs, and in which such cooperation becomes institutionalized and regularized. These moments of cooperation shape and constrain state behavior via systems of rules, norms, practices, and decision-making procedures that may or may not be guided by progressive ideas and ideologies.[20] The result is a focus on possibility, wherein questions not only focus on how the world is governed but also on how it *ought* to be governed.[21]

More critical traditions too have ideas of world order as central tenets in their intellectual canon. Marxist approaches understand transnational and global organizations as institutional responses to the exigencies of capitalist expansion.[22] Feminist scholars see forms of organization, institutionalization, and regularization as shaped by and helping perpetuate unequal gender relations between women and men, and between girls and boys, irrespective of what might look like progressive policies and elements.[23] Post-structural approaches demonstrate a concern for the way that the world is governed through discourse and practice.[24] And decolonial scholars reflect on the historical processes that have ensured that Western European (including US) imperial orders and patriarchal and heteronormative systems continue to serve as dominant modes of subordinating Others.[25]

Yet for all their (albeit largely unrecognized) centrality to the core intellectual traditions of IR, IO and global governance are hardly unproblematic, neither is the relationship between them uncomplicated. Partly because IO and global governance are often taught as IR subfields rather than as primary concerns in and of themselves, little clarity exists about their core meanings, overlaps, and contradictions let alone how individual theoretical approaches understand and interpret them. In some instances, IO and global governance are treated synonymously; in others, they relate only to what international organizations "do"; in others still, such variance exists in what is treated as the intellectual and empirical terrain as to render both of the terms meaningless.

International organization and global governance: One to another

At its most basic, international organization refers to an instance—or, in an historical sense, a moment—of institutionalization in relations among states. Inis Claude's formulation makes that point distinctly: "International *organization* is a process; international *organizations* are representative aspects of the phase of that process which has been reached at a given time."[26] His and other classic definitions of IO are inexorably bound up with a normative desire to see existing organizations as moments in a progressive march toward growing global institutionalization and order. We tend thus to use IO to refer to formal interstate institutions that are, or have the potential to be, planetary in reach, such as the United Nations (UN) or the World Trade Organization (WTO), although any regional, less formal interstate arrangement can be and often is classified in this way as well. Indeed, analyses of the European Union (EU) are often features of North American classes on international organization; whereas in Europe, supranational European institutions and their relationship to the post-war political economy of that continent are usually viewed as distinct enough to merit separate courses from the treatment of other international organizations.

That said, such an approach may change in the United Kingdom should its divorce from the EU put it sufficiently outside of Europe's institutional sphere to encourage a different analytical emphasis.

Confusing matters further for students, at least initially, is the seeming conflation of the term "IO" with "institutions" and "regimes." Although they are not the same, the family relationship requires further explanation. Strictly speaking, international organizations (as opposed to IO as a process) are formal intergovernmental bureaucracies. They have a legal standing, physical headquarters, executive head, staff, and substantive focus for their operations. Hence, the World Intellectual Property Organization (WIPO) is a UN specialized agency that exists to coordinate and entrench in international legal frameworks the protection of intellectual property rights worldwide; its headquarters are in Geneva; it has 185 member states; and its secretariat is overseen by a director-general. Other organizations might also be considered to be "international" in their focus and remit—such as the World Economic Forum that meets yearly in Davos, Switzerland—but are not intergovernmental and are better described as "institutions"—forums, semi-permanent gatherings, or transnational arrangements depending on their specific character.

An international institution is broader. Whereas international organizations are formalized bureaucracies (and again it is worth bearing in mind that the "s" not only pluralizes the word but refers to specific entities and not a process), international institutions can be both formal and informal manifestations of regularized interstate behavior. So, while international organizations are also international institutions, a moment of regularized interstate behavior that does not have a legal personality, a headquarters, a secretariat, and an executive head is not. Here we can think of a range of institutions, including, but not limited to, semi-formalized groups of states—the G-7/G-8, or Group of 77 (G-77) developing countries—and regularized balances of power between states, including the nineteenth-century Concert of Europe and the twentieth-century Cold War. Thus, international institutions are instances of international organization, but they are not necessarily international organizations. As such, we tend to define them—as Robert Keohane does—as "persistent and connected sets of rules (formal and informal) that prescribe behavioral roles, constrain activity, and shape expectations."[27]

An international regime is slightly different again, although there is a relationship between both international organizations and international institutions, on the one hand, and international regimes, on the other hand. Stephen Krasner's formulation remains the most widely accepted: "Implicit or explicit principles, norms, rules and decision-making procedures around which actors' expectations converge in a given area of international relations."[28] Despite this commonly accepted definition—which suggests they are synonyms of international institutions—international regimes are more accurately viewed as the range of activities that are, in part, created by the behavior-shaping effects of international organizations and institutions.

We have in mind, for example, an area of activity such as the international trade regime. Even in the absence of current global, regional, and national rules, systems of regulation, and organizational structures, international trade would have taken place. Today's international trade regime is distinct because of the behavioral rules, practices, norms, and decision-making procedures of the WTO; myriad regional trade arrangements such as the North American Free Trade Agreement (NAFTA); research by and conversations in such UN bodies as the UN Conference on Trade and Development (UNCTAD) and the International Trade Centre (ITC); and an even greater number of bilateral agreements. In addition, there are also national trade policies, the behavioral practices of private firms, and the lobbying efforts (effective or otherwise) of various nongovernmental actors.[29]

A key concern of scholars is to understand how power is embedded in the way that the behavior of states—and their economic and political agents, including firms that may be multinational but which nonetheless emanate from and retain an organic connection to their states of origin—is shaped by international organizations, institutions, and regimes. Work by Robert Cox and Craig Murphy, for instance, has explored organic connections between dominant states and the creation and evolution of international institutions.[30] Robert Keohane, Robert Wade, and Rorden Wilkinson have examined how the interests of powerful states are embedded in the very design of institutions and their effect on institutional and regime development over time.[31] Catherine Weaver has explored how institutional development can reinforce a form of organization that perpetuates dominant relations of power.[32] Kenneth Abbott and Duncan Snidal's work on principal–agent theory likewise has examined how state imperatives are manifest in organizational behavior and the deviations that occur therefrom.[33] Thomas G. Weiss has probed the relationship between ideas and the creation and development of international organizations.[34] And Susan Park and Antje Vetterlein have examined the role norms play in shaping state behavior and the construction of economic regimes.[35]

Although insightful work continues within the confines of traditional IO studies, it requires a specific recognition of greater global complexity and ongoing changes (technological, economic, political, and ethical) that demonstrate how the world is governed in a multidimensional fashion. Part of this evolution was foreshadowed by work being carried out under the auspices of international institutions and regimes; but the end of the Cold War really shined a spotlight fully on the range of actors operating across borders—and increasingly globally—that needed explaining. Regimes and institutions provided a partial analytical solution, as did attempts to refresh multilateralism as a specific organizational type.[36]

However, it was the emergence of the term "global governance" in the 1990s—with the publication of James Rosenau and Ernst-Otto Czempiel's edited volume, the report by the Commission on Global Governance, and the first issue of a new journal[37]—that really captured the post-Cold War *Zeitgeist* and that has enabled IR scholars to begin to grapple more fully with how the world is organized in all of its complexity. Nonetheless, and as we argue below, the analytical utility of the term "global governance" has not yet been fully realized.

Suffice to say, global governance is different from IO and related work on international institutions and regimes. The core idea is still one of organization—in the sense of the structure and order of things—but the scale and level are different, as is the understanding of the specific forms of organization. Scale wise, global governance refers to the totality of the ways, formal and informal, the world is governed. The emergence and widespread recognition of transnational issues that circumscribe state capacity along with the proliferation of non-state actors responding to perceived shortfalls in national capabilities and a willingness to address them in the context of a perceived crisis of multilateralism combined to stimulate new thinking.

The imperative is to establish the general character of global governance and to identify the dominant actors and mechanisms. Critics have suggested that it is little more than a kitchen-sink approach with an all-too-fuzzy grasp of the way that the world works.[38] While containing elements of apparent accuracy, this characterization misses the importance of struggling to capture more fully the totality of ways life on the planet is ordered. It has encouraged investigators to ask questions not only about who and what were involved in governing the world but also about how any particular form of organization came about and the results of its particular mechanisms of control.

However, it is not just this scale and comprehensive embrace that make global governance distinct. It is also the manner and the value of global governance as an optic for encompassing interactions at all levels of life. What happens in one corner or at any level (local, national, or regional) can have repercussions in all other corners and at all levels. Global governance is thus not just about relations among states—although they remain a crucial aspect of the wider puzzle. It is also about the relationship between global policy-making processes and its implementation in particular localities, the effects of local actions on global life, and the interrelationships that exist between institutions, actors, and mechanisms at every level in between. As James Rosenau noted, inevitably in this mix are countervailing tendencies. He referred to "fragmegration" as a way to capture the centripetal and centrifugal, integration versus fragmentation, tendencies toward lower and higher levels of the contemporary order.[39] However, the continued compartmentalization of global social life into easily consumable levels of analysis actually hinders our digestion of how the world is governed.

This simplification tells us that there is an obvious relationship between IO and global governance—because international organizations are essential and visible aspects of how the world is currently governed—but the terms are not synonymous and certainly not coterminous. Moreover, whereas IO points primarily toward states and emphasizes intergovernmental organizations (IGOs), global governance is far more encompassing. Clearly the UN Security Council and its members (especially its five permanent ones) are important in the arena of international peace and security; but so too are multinational corporations (MNCs), private security firms, transnational criminal networks, terrorist organizations, the media, private regulators, and nongovernmental organizations (NGOs).

Equally, the range of mechanisms by which governance is exercised dramatically increases in moving from IO to global governance. "International" governance (by which we mean "interstate") is limited to those structures that can be agreed by member states to operate under the auspices of a given organization. International legal frameworks are the most common, occasionally backed by some kind of enforcement mechanism—as in the case of the WTO's dispute settlement body, the International Criminal Court's (ICC) pursuit of perpetrators of mass atrocities, or the Security Council's authorization of sanctions, international judicial pursuit, and military force. *Ad hoc* instances of states acting in concert (for example, in coalitions of the willing) also are part of the picture and a common bill-of-fare in foreign policy.

In the realm of global governance more broadly, however, a range of other mechanisms are sometimes equally or even more influential. Financial markets perhaps provide the most prominent illustration. The mechanisms for buying and selling, and the commercial innovations that they drive and encourage, can have dramatic effects, as Jennifer Clapp and Eric Helleiner's work on the financialization of global food markets shows.[40]

Moreover, an exclusive emphasis on states misses numerous examples of steps in issue-specific global governance—for instance, the International Committee of the Red Cross (ICRC) for the laws of war and humanitarian principles; the Fédération Internationale de Football Association (or FIFA, its familiar abbreviation) for the world's most popular sport (football/soccer); and by the Internet Corporation for Assigned Names and Numbers (ICANN) for the Internet. Increasingly, private-sector standard setting is becoming a foundation for addressing global food and hunger problems, with representatives of industry, unions, NGOs, and multi-stakeholder coalitions determining policies and compliance as much or more than many governments; meanwhile, public–private partnerships are being forged between state and non-state actors at all levels.[41]

Less obvious structures of global governance are found not only in the standard-setting activities of IGOs such as the International Organization of Standardization (ISO) but also in the lobbying activities for commercial interests trying to get particular sizes, shapes, weights, and others accepted as standards.[42] Other sources of governance can be found in fledgling and evolving electronic and social media regimes,[43] and in the activities of the super-rich, not only in their consumption patterns but also in their philanthropic activities.[44]

Similarly, Moody's Investors Service and Standard & Poor's Ratings Group render judgments that are authoritative enough to cause substantial market responses.[45] Private regulatory initiatives govern supply chains across the globe to set environmental, food safety, and social standards to such an extent that private not public standards are the prime determinants of access to most western markets.[46] Even for a security issue like piracy, a hybrid private–public initiative seems at least as likely to help forge agreement on the parameters of addressing that global problem as governments by themselves or shipping and insurance companies on their own.[47]

Thinking differently about global governance

"Global governance" is, of course, not an unproblematic label. Many criticisms arise because of its apparent catch-all quality and of the refusal of those who engage in its study to ask new questions, and who often find it useful to confine their intellectual remit to a static and known range. Yet global governance's primary utility lies not only in working out theoretical and empirical parameters but rather in reorienting the way that we ask questions about the world around us. It behooves us to ask and answer questions about how the world is governed, ordered, and organized. These questions not only give us an insight into the way, as John Ruggie remarked, the "world hangs together,"[48] but they also have the potential to overcome some of the fragmentation that IR as a scholarly pursuit has suffered over recent decades.

Increasingly IR has come to consist of a set of separate and discrete intellectual endeavors that make it possible to develop sophisticated frameworks, but which have tended to generate introspective debate among a limited group of advocates rather than a more open-ended conversation among scholars with disparate views to find fertile common ground to be plowed for the field as a whole. The transatlantic divide in international political economy (IPE) is one example of such a division. The gulf between positivist and anti-foundationalist approaches to world politics is another. Refocusing on questions of how the world is organized and governed has the potential to restrain further intellectual fragmentation and reinvigorate the discipline as a whole precisely because—as we illustrated earlier—it has been a preoccupation of all of IR's major theoretical traditions.

There is, however, a need to address a related problem first if global governance is to realize its potential as a core rather than a peripheral IR pursuit. The paucity of existing IR frameworks to explain adequately changes ushered in by the end of the Cold War and the emergence of a host of new actors on the world stage were key factors leading to the emergence of the term "global governance" and the accompanying cottage analytical industry that has grown over the last quarter-century. One consequence in capturing growing global complexity has been to encourage an overly close association between the term and the specific post-Cold War moment in which it emerged. A related consequence has been a failure by analysts to rescue the term from this narrow historical association and to test its utility as a lens through which to view past and future world orders in addition to better understanding the one in which we currently reside.

If global governance provides a helpful perspective for today, it should also help to understand the relations that were maintained by, and the systems of governance between and among, a variety of actors in other eras: the Greek city states; China and its tributaries; various Indian empires and states and other regimes across the Middle East, Asia and Central and Southern America; the empires of Rome, Persia, and Egypt, as well as the kingdoms and empires of pre-colonial Africa; the Islamic caliphates and non-Muslim empires; and the European papal and non-papal states and imperial systems. The framework should also shed light on Cold War bipolarity, the immediate post-Cold War's unipolar moment, or what today appears to be an emerging multipolar order despite continuing US preponderance.

In short, global governance should provide ample insights into the differing forms of overarching world orders that have existed—and which need further investigation to unravel the full range of means by which they were and are held together. Global governance thus should help us understand where we came from and why we have got to where we are, as well as a way to develop strategies for where we should be going. We have begun this task in a number of essays,[49] which we continue in a dedicated book.[50]

The term "global governance" was and continues to be deployed as a means of capturing the pluralization on the world's political stage that has been manifest since the end of the Cold War. Even skeptics would not dispute that large MNC, transnational religious institutions, global NGOs, and credit rating agencies—among many others—are significant in influencing how the world is governed; they would not argue that financial markets and transnational legal frameworks have a negligible passing effect on how the world "hangs together." What we have come to realize also is that a range of actors operate in concert—international organizations along-side labor groups and global corporations in the UN Global Compact, private sector security and logistic firms in humanitarian operations, and nongovernmental relief agencies working alongside the UN and military forces in complex humanitarian emergencies, to name but a few. These ensembles also have important effects on the overall shape of how well or poorly the world currently is governed. Moreover, we have become increasingly sensitive to the role played by ideas, ideologies, norms, and knowledge in global governance; we have come to see states as important global governance actors directing, transmitting, receiving, and holding together forms of organization.

Yet few scholarly works have attempted to offer a complete overview of the actors, institutions, and mechanisms that constitute contemporary global governance. In light of what we have just said, it would be immodest to claim that these pages capture contemporary global governance in its entirety, or that they present readers with every conceivable conceptualization of early twenty-first-century world order. Our aim here, however, has been to compile the best attempt yet.

About the book

The following chapters provide a comprehensive overview of the historical founda-tions of the current world order's evolution as well as its key dynamics; the major conceptual and theoretical approaches to the study of IO and global governance; and the role of states, their coalitions, and IGOs as well as important non-state humanitar-ian, security, and economic actors. They also explore in detail how global governance is manifest in economic and social arenas. We have sought, simultaneously, to end the separation and confusion between the way that we conceptualize and study IO and global governance, to examine the role of many major actors, and to explore the differential manifestations of governance in particular fields while not losing sight of the big picture.

In designing, commissioning, and arranging the contributions, we wanted to bring together as many of the pieces of the IO and global governance puzzle as we could between two covers. Our aim was not only to be as comprehensive as possible. We also sought to enable course leaders to design classes around the issues that they wanted to highlight, while providing a one-stop resource for further reading and wider contextualization. So, classes emphasizing the security, economic, social, legal, or other aspects of IO and global governance are able to select chapters from each of the book's parts, while simultaneously pointing students to other related and seemingly not-so-related topics for further investigation. Likewise, more intro-ductory classes could be designed around the empirical aspects of IO and global governance with a bit of theory added into the mix to help make sense of the material. More advanced classes will inevitably make greater use of the full range of contextualization and theory chapters as well as a broader slew of the empirical contributions. To guide readers, all contributors have suggested "additional reading" at the end of their chapters, pointing to sources to begin reading in more specialized publications.

How the book is arranged

Part II of this book has five chapters that launch this inquiry by "Contextualizing international organization and global governance." We begin with essays that provide the backdrop for reading the rest of the book. Craig N. Murphy (Chapter 1) shows that moves to formalize institutional relations have been much longer lived than many suppose and that these were inevitably tied up with developments in an industrializing and globalizing world economy. Charlotte Ku (Chapter 2) explores a key building block, the development of public international law across the *longue durée*. Michael Barnett and Raymond Duvall (Chapter 3) examine power in the broadest sense, including in IO and global governance, and not simply that emanating from a barrel of a gun, while David Held (Chapter 4) turns to the diffusion of authority. Susan K. Sell (Chapter 5) asks the question that few remember to ask (and many forget to answer), namely which agents actually govern the world.

The ten chapters that comprise Part III deal with "Theories of international organization and global governance." All too often works on IO and global governance have provided only cursory accounts of theory and the tools that different approaches have to offer, or else they have omitted discussions altogether. We strongly believe that readers should understand the dominant and emerging as well as previously popular ways that key schools of thought have tried to make sense of the way that the world is governed before attempting their own original syntheses. These essays look at how we have come to understand the way that the world is governed since the beginning of the Westphalian order with some useful pointers that lead us to ask questions further back in time: "Realism" (Jason Charrette and Jennifer Sterling-Folker, Chapter 6); "Classical liberal internationalism" (Christer Jönsson, Chapter 7); "Liberal institutionalism" (Tana Johnson and Andrew Heiss, Chapter 8); "Rational choice and principal–agent theory" (Duncan Snidal and Henning Tamm, Chapter 9); "Constructivism" (Susan Park, Chapter 10); "Critical theory" (Robert W. Cox, Chapter 11); "Marxism" (Julian Germann, Chapter 12); "Feminism" (Susanne Zwingel, Elisabeth Prügl, and Gülay Çağlar, Chapter 13); "Post-structuralism" (James Brassett, Chapter 14); and "Decoloniality: (Re)making worlds" (Jacquelin Kataneksza, L.H.M. Ling, and Sara Shroff, Chapter 15). This part aims to see how key approaches can lend clarity to understanding IO and global governance. Many of the contributions explore how each can be reformulated and, in some instances, combined to bring the normative project underlying many of the "isms" back into clearer focus and break new ground. Some have been adapted from dominant IR perspectives. Others have been tailored to look specifically at the subject matter at hand. That said, as an intellectual community we have yet to develop anything approximating specific theories of global governance.

Part IV of the book contains eight chapters that explore "States and international institutions in global governance." As indicated, international organizations have often been seen to be the main pillars undergirding the way the world is governed, and so this part examines some of the main units around which the field has revolved, including of course the role that states and the institutions that they have created play in contemporary global governance: "The UN system" (Leon Gordenker, Chapter 16); "The UN General Assembly" (M.J. Peterson, Chapter 17); "Regional governance and regional organizations" (Mônica Herz, Chapter 18); "The European Union" (Ben Rosamond, Chapter 19); "The BRICS: The evolving architecture of global governance" (Andrew F. Cooper and Ramesh Thakur, Chapter 20); "The Global South" (Ian Taylor, Chapter 21); "US hegemony" (W. Andy Knight, Chapter 22); and "China and global governance" (Shaun Breslin and Ren Xiao, Chapter 23).

The eight chapters of Part V move beyond state-centrism to cover "Non-state actors in global governance." As indicated, the proliferation of actors and the scope of their activities have been central to explaining the burgeoning field of global governance, and so this part seeks to probe the implications for IO and global governance of many of the key actors: "Global corporations" (Christopher May, Chapter 24); "Civil society and NGOs" (Jan Aart Scholte, Chapter 25); "Labor" (Nigel Haworth and Steve Hughes, Chapter 26); "Credit rating agencies" (Timothy J. Sinclair, Chapter 27); "Think tanks and global policy networks" (James G. McGann, Chapter 28); "Global philanthropy" (Michael Moran, Chapter 29); "Private military and security companies" (Peter J. Hoffman, Chapter 30); and "Transnational criminal networks" (Frank G. Madsen, Chapter 31). We look at non-state actors, those bodies often added into the IO and global governance mix and then stirred, because all too often they appear as afterthoughts to books that are otherwise really just about intergovernmental organizations. Our aim is to examine these actors as more mainstream components of IR courses and research, introducing them before exploring how they contribute to global governance across issues.

Part VI contains ten chapters on "Securing the world, governing humanity." One of the main explanations for human efforts to better govern the world has been the need to foster international peace and security, and so the reader encounters first what undoubtedly are four familiar topics: "The UN Security Council and peace operations" (Paul D. Williams and Alex J. Bellamy, Chapter 32); "Regional organizations and global security governance" (S. Neil MacFarlane, Chapter 33); "Weapons of mass destruction" (Waheguru Pal Singh Sidhu, Chapter 34); and "Counterterrorism cooperation and global governance" (Peter Romaniuk, Chapter 35). In most texts, these would be the "no questions asked" security institutions. However, given how wide we believe that it is necessary to cast the IO and global governance net, it is essential to explore issues across areas in ways that offer a more complete and complex picture of how the world is governed: "Human rights" (David P. Forsythe, Chapter 36); "The pursuit of international justice" (Richard J. Goldstone, Chapter 37); "Humanitarian intervention and R2P" (Simon Chesterman, Chapter 38); "Crisis and humanitarian containment" (Fabrice Weissman, Chapter 39); "Post-conflict peacebuilding" (Graciana del Castillo, Chapter 40); and "Human security as a global public good" (Mark Raymond and Stefanie Neumeier, Chapter 41).

The thirteen chapters of Part VII, the final in the book, attempt the impossible task of surveying what passes for "Governing the economic and social world." Whatever we mean by "peace," it certainly entails more than the absence of war and large-scale organized violence, and so the book concludes by examining the various components of a fairer world order, including several pressing issues that many would also characterize as "security" challenges: "Global financial governance" (Bessma Momani, Chapter 42); "Global trade governance (Bernard Hoekman, Chapter 43); "Global development governance" (Katherine Marshall, Chapter 44); "Global environmental governance" (Elizabeth R. DeSombre and Angelina H. Li, Chapter 45); "Regional development banks and global governance" (Jonathan R. Strand, Chapter 46); "Climate change" (Matthew J. Hoffmann, Chapter 47); "Sustainable development governance" (Roger A. Coate, Chapter 48); "Global energy governance" (Harald Heubaum, Chapter 49); "Poverty reduction" (David Hulme and Oliver Turner, Chapter 50); "Food and hunger" (Jennifer Clapp, Chapter 51); "Global health governance" (Sophie Harman, Chapter 52); "Refugees and migrants" (Khalid Koser, Chapter 53); and "Global Internet governance (Madeline Carr, Chapter 54).

Conclusion: Moving forward

By disaggregating topics in the way that we have and then putting them back together, we can better understand the complexity, the range of sources of authority, and the multiple ways that power and authority are exercised. This approach provides building blocks for the way that we need to think about world order today, and in the future. What becomes clear is that the field of IR should be widened and deepened. We are proud in these pages to have assembled a strikingly diverse and impressive team of authors whose essays—which we discuss in more detail in separate introductions to the parts that follow—help all of us to continue the unfinished journey toward a better understanding of global governance.

We nonetheless have a long way to go.

Notes

1 Peter J. Hoffman and Thomas G. Weiss, *War, Politics, and Humanitarianism: Solferino to Syria and Beyond* (Lanham, MD: Rowman & Littlefield, 2017).
2 Jonathan Michie and John Grieve Smith, eds., *Global Instability: The Political Economy of World Economic Governance* (London: Routledge, 1999); Joseph E. Stiglitz, *Globalization and Its Discontents* (New York: W. W. Norton & Company, 2002).
3 Oxfam, *An Economy for the 1%*, Oxfam Briefing Paper 2010, 18 January 2016, www.oxfam.org/sites/www.oxfam.org/files/file_attachments/bp210-economy-one-percent-tax-havens-180116-en_0.pdf.
4 David Hulme, *Global Poverty: How Global Governance Is Failing the Poor* (London: Routledge, 2010), 1. See also Erik S. Reinert, *How Rich Countries Got Rich and Why Poor Countries Stay Poor* (London: Public Affairs, 2007).
5 Rorden Wilkinson, "Back to the Future: "Retro" Trade Governance and the Future of the Multilateral Order," *International Affairs* 93, no. 5 (2017): 1131–1147.
6 Sophie Harman, *Global Health Governance* (London: Routledge, 2012); Kelley Lee, *The World Health Organization* (London: Routledge, 2009); Ilari Regondi and Alan Whiteside,

"Global Development Goals and the International HIV Response: A Chance for Renewal," in *The Millennium Development Goals and Beyond: Global Development After 2015*, eds. Rorden Wilkinson and David Hulme (London: Routledge, 2012), 174–191.

7 Jim Yong Kim, Joyce V. Millen, Alec Irwin, and John Gershman, eds., *Dying for Growth: Global Inequality and the Health of the Poor* (Monroe, ME: Common Courage Press, 2000); James Orbinski, *An Imperfect Offering: Humanitarian Action in the Twenty-First Century* (New York: Random House, 2008).

8 Elizabeth R. DeSombre, *Global Environmental Institutions* (London: Routledge, 2006); Harriet Bulkeley and Peter Newell, *Governing Climate Change* (London: Routledge, 2010); Peter Newell, *Globalization and the Environment* (Cambridge: Polity Press, 2012).

9 Jonathan A. Fox and L. David Brown, eds., *The Struggle for Accountability: The World Bank, NGOs and Grassroots Movements* (Cambridge, MA: MIT Press, 1998); Jan Aart Scholte with Albrecht Schnabel, eds., *Civil Society and Global Finance* (London: Routledge, 2002).

10 Nanette Svenson, *The United Nations as a Knowledge System* (London: Routledge, 2016).

11 Diane Stone, "Introduction: Global Knowledge and Advocacy Networks," *Global Networks: A Journal of Transnational Affairs* 2, no. 1 (2002): 1–11.

12 Peter Singer, *Corporate Warriors: The Rise of the Privatized Military Industry* (Ithaca, NY: Cornell University Press, 2003).

13 Peter Romaniuk, *Multilateral Counterterrorism: The Global Politics of Cooperation and Contestation* (London: Routledge, 2010).

14 Timothy J. Sinclair, "Round up the Usual Suspects: Blame and the Subprime Crisis," *New Political Economy* 15, no. 1 (2010): 91–107.

15 Katherine Marshall, "Governance and Inequality: Reflections on Faith," in *Global Governance, Poverty and Inequality*, eds. Jennifer Clapp and Rorden Wilkinson (London: Routledge, 2010), 295–313.

16 Anthony McGrew and David Held, eds., *Governing Globalization* (Cambridge: Polity Press, 2002); Margaret P. Karns and Karen Mingst, *International Organizations: The Politics and Processes of Global Governance* (Boulder, CO: Lynne Rienner, 2009); Deborah D. Avant, Martha Finnemore, and Susan Sell, eds., *Who Governs the Globe?* (Cambridge: Cambridge University Press, 2010).

17 Mark Mazower, *Governing the World: The History of an Idea* (New York: Penguin, 2012).

18 Hans J. Morgenthau, *Politics Among Nations: The Struggle for Power and Peace*, 6th ed. (New York: McGraw-Hill, 1985).

19 Kenneth Waltz, *Theory of International Politics* (New York: Addison-Wesley, 1979).

20 Robert O. Keohane, *After Hegemony: Cooperation and Discord in the World Political Economy* (Princeton, NJ: Princeton University Press, 1984).

21 For example, David Held, *Global Covenant: The Social Democratic Alternative to the Washington Consensus* (Cambridge: Polity Press, 2004).

22 See Paul Cammack, "The Governance of Global Capitalism: A New Materialist Perspective," in *The Global Governance Reader*, ed. Rorden Wilkinson (London: Routledge, 2005), 156–173; Stephen Gill, "New Constitutionalism, Democratisation and Global Political Economy," *Pacifica Review: Peace, Security & Global Change* 10, no. 1 (1998): 23–38; Craig N. Murphy, *International Organization and Industrial Change: Global Governance Since 1850* (Cambridge: Polity Press, 1994).

23 See Shirin Rai and Georgina Waylen, *Global Governance: Feminist Perspectives* (Basingstoke: Palgrave Macmillan, 2008); Gülay Çağlar, Elisabeth Prügl, and Susanne Zwingel, *Feminist Strategies in International Governance* (London: Routledge, 2013).

24 Heikki Patomäki, "Problems of Democratising Global Governance: Time, Space and the Emancipatory Process," *European Journal of International Relations* 9, no. 34 (2003): 347–376; Luigi Pellizzoni, "Governing through Disorder: Neoliberal Environmental Governance and Social Theory," *Global Environmental Change* 21, no. 3 (2011): 795–803.

25 See, for example, Himadeep Muppidi, "Colonial and Postcolonial Global Governance," in *Power in Global Governance*, eds. Michael Barnett and Raymond Duvall (Cambridge: Cambridge University Press, 2005), 273–293; Cynthia Weber, *Queer International Relations: Sovereignty, Sexuality and the Will to Knowledge* (Oxford: Oxford University Press, 2016).

26 Inis L. Claude, Jr., *Swords into Plowshares*, 3rd edition (New York: Random House, 1964), 4.

27 Robert O. Keohane, "International Institutions: Two Approaches," *International Studies Quarterly* 32, no. 4 (1988): 383.

28 Stephen D. Krasner, "Structural Causes and Regime Consequences: Regimes as Intervening Variables," *International Organization* 36, no. 2 (1982): 185.

29 Erin Norma Hannah, "NGOs and the European Union: Examining the Power of Epistemes in the EC's TRIPS and Access to Medicines Negotiations," *Journal of Civil Society* 7, no. 2 (2011): 179–206.

30 Robert W. Cox, ed., *The New Realism: Perspectives on Multilateralism and World Order* (London: Palgrave Macmillan for the United Nations University, 1997); Murphy, *International Organization and Industrial Change*.

31 Robert O. Keohane, *Power and Governance in a Partially Globalized World* (London: Routledge, 2002); Robert Hunter Wade, "What Strategies Are Viable for Developing Countries Today? The World Trade Organization and the Shrinking of 'Development Space,'" *Review of International Political Economy* 10, no. 4 (2003): 621–644; Rorden Wilkinson, *The WTO: Crisis and the Governance of Global Trade* (London: Routledge, 2006).

32 Catherine Weaver, *The Hypocrisy Trap: The World Bank and the Poverty of Reform* (Princeton, NJ: Princeton University Press, 2008).

33 Kenneth W. Abbott and Duncan Snidal, "Why States Act through Formal International Organizations," *Journal of Conflict Resolution* 42, no. 1 (1998): 3–32; Darren Hawkins, David A. Lake, Daniel L. Nielson, and Michael J. Tierney, eds., *Delegation under Agency: States, International Organizations, and Principal–Agent Theory* (Cambridge: Cambridge University Press, 2006).

34 Thomas G. Weiss, *Global Governance: Why? What? Whither?* (Cambridge: Polity Press, 2013); Thomas G. Weiss and Ramesh Thakur, *Global Governance and the UN: An Unfinished Journey* (Bloomington: Indiana University Press, 2010); Richard Jolly, Louis Emmerij, and Thomas G. Weiss, *UN Ideas That Changed the World* (Bloomington: Indiana University Press, 2009).

35 Susan Park and Antje Vetterlein, eds., *Owning Development: Creating Policy Norms in the IMF and World Bank* (Cambridge: Cambridge University Press, 2010).

36 Yoshikazu Sakamoto, ed., *Global Transformations: Challenges to the State System* (Tokyo: United Nations University Press, 1992); Keith Krause and W. Andy Knight, eds., *State, Society and the UN System: Changing Perspectives on Multilateralism* (Tokyo: United Nations University Press, 1995); Robert W. Cox, ed., *The New Realism: Perspectives on Multilateralism and World Order* (Basingstoke: Macmillan, 1997); Stephen Gill, ed., *Globalization, Democratization and Multilateralism* (London: Macmillan, 1997); Michael G. Schechter, ed., *Future Multilateralism: The Political and Social Framework* (London: Macmillan, 1999) and *Innovation in Multilateralism* (London: Macmillan, 1999).

37 James N. Rosenau and Ernst-Otto Czempiel, eds., *Governance without Government: Order and Change in World Politics* (Cambridge: Cambridge University Press, 1992); Commission on Global Governance, *Our Global Neighbourhood* (Oxford: Oxford University Press, 1995); (since 1995) the quarterly *Global Governance: A Review of Multilateralism and International Organizations*.

38 Lawrence Finkelstein, "What Is Global Governance?," *Global Governance* 1, no. 3 (1995): 367–372.

39 James N. Rosenau, "Governance in the Twenty-First Century," in *The Global Governance Reader*, ed. Wilkinson, 45–67.

40 Jennifer Clapp and Eric Helleiner, "Troubled Futures? The Global Food Crisis and the Politics of Agricultural Derivatives Regulation," *Review of International Political Economy* 19, no. 1 (2012): 181–207.

41 Benedicte Bull, "The Global Elite, Public–Private Partnerships and Multilateral Governance," in *Global Governance, Poverty and Inequality*, eds. Clapp and Wilkinson, 209–234.

42 Craig N. Murphy and JoAnne Yates, *The International Organization for Standardization (ISO): Global Governance through Voluntary Consensus* (London: Routledge, 2009).

43 John Mathiason, *Internet Governance: The New Frontier of Global Institutions* (London: Routledge, 2009).

44 Michael Moran, *Private Foundations and Development Partnerships: American Philanthropy and Global Development Agendas* (London: Routledge, 2013).

45 Timothy J. Sinclair, *The New Masters of Capital: American Bond Rating Agencies and the Politics of Creditworthiness* (Ithaca, NY: Cornell University Press, 2005).

46 Axel Marx, et al., eds., *Private Standards and Global Governance: Economic, Legal and Political Perspectives* (Cheltenham: Edward Elgar, 2012).

47 Danielle Zach, Conor Seyle, and Jens Vestergaard Madsen, *Globalizing Governance: The Case of the Contact Group on Piracy off the Coast of Somalia* (Broomfield, CO: OneEarthFuture Foundation, 2013).

48 John Gerard Ruggie, *Constructing the World Polity* (London: Routledge, 1998), 2.

49 Thomas G. Weiss and Rorden Wilkinson, "Rethinking Global Governance? Complexity, Authority, Power and Change," *International Studies Quarterly* 58, no. 2 (2014): 207–215; "Continuity and Change in Global Governance," in *Rising Powers, Global Governance, and Global Ethics*, ed. Jamie Gaskarth (London: Routledge, 2015), 41–56; "Change and Continuity in Global Governance," *Ethics & International Affairs* 29, 4 (2015): 391–395, 397–406; "The Globally Governed—Everyday Global Governance," *Global Governance* 24, no. 3 (2018): forthcoming.

50 Thomas G. Weiss and Rorden Wilkinson, *Rethinking Global Governance* (Cambridge: Polity, 2019).

PART II
CONTEXTUALIZING INTERNATIONAL ORGANIZATION AND GLOBAL GOVERNANCE

Part introduction

Students are often poorly serviced when it comes to the background of—or what might better be thought of as the "back stories to"—international organization (IO) and global governance. All too often accounts of the formation of particular international organizations are prefaced with ready-made accounts of the end of war and an aspiration to avert the possibility of a slide back into hostilities as the engine for a bout of institution building. Certainly there is merit in these interpretations. Often, however, they do not offer a sufficiently rounded account of the slow and incremental struggles and processes that lie behind the emergence of international organizations or of the dramatic accelerators of transformational moments in history.

Part of our willingness to consume easily digestible pieces of history as substitutes for more involved stories results from our natural eagerness to become familiar with an entire terrain of study as quickly as possible. Part of it results from the limitations of space in any publication. Part of it reflects the fact that these stories are not straightforward, and that their content is often contested—potted introductions find it impossible to convey nuances.

We do not claim to have a monopoly of insights into contemporary global governance or the role of international organizations therein. We have, however, tried to be as extensive in our coverage as our limitations of space allow. And we have done so by bringing together five chapters by some of the academy's leading scholars.

Contextualizing international organization and global governance: Chapter synopses

We asked authors to write only on those areas in which they are expert, to build on but also take forward their existing work, and to offer as robust an account as they could of one particular aspect of the formation of, and dynamics within, the way that the world is currently organized. The chapters are arranged so that this part of the book begins with an exploration of the evolution of global governance as a phenomenon before unpacking in further detail some of its constitutive aspects: Law, power, authority, and agents. Thus, the chapters focus on driving impulses and incremental developments that ushered forth a global institutional complex (Craig N. Murphy, Chapter 1); the evolution of an international legal apparatus as both a necessity for states—and other actors—to manage their relations, as well as a vehicle pressing for change (Charlotte Ku, Chapter 2); the manner in which power is diffused and concentrated among international organizations as core components of contemporary global governance (Michael Barnett and Raymond Duvall, Chapter 3); the forces and tendencies that have led to a diffusion of authority across the globe and the resulting challenges (David Held, Chapter 4); and the identity of the governors in this complex, multilayered, multifaceted, and multi-actor system (Susan K. Sell, Chapter 5).

In Chapter 1, "The emergence of global governance," Murphy outlines the private, hidden, and seldom acknowledged origins of contemporary global governance beginning in the "inter-imperial world" (the term he uses for the nineteenth century, in which international organization was predicated on managing relations between the colonial powers), where technical standards helped spread industrial capitalism and soothe the tensions that its spread necessarily created. This world of "creeping" global governance begins with seemingly inconsequential agreements on such things as common chemical and electrical units. However, they paved the way for companies to exploit new markets and for ever greater numbers of new consumers to acquire goods that previously had been unavailable while simultaneously bringing them into an expanding market system. Alongside these technical developments went progressive social agendas driven forward by constellations of civil society actors, interstate conferences on human health, among others, and transnational associations dealing with working conditions and the plight of industrial labor. But he also shows how states were important components of this nascent system. Such incremental global governance nonetheless set the stage for a step-change in world order under US leadership after World War II, generating, among other things, the UN system; and it has helped create the kind of world economy that we currently have, which undoubtedly will survive the onslaught by the Trump administration.

Murphy's chapter offers an insight into the incrementalism that lies behind today's forms of IO and global governance. Locking in the developments that this incrementalism generated in the form of transnational, international, and global legal frameworks is also a key part of the story, which Ku picks up and explores in "The evolution of international law" as a complex and multifaceted system in Chapter 2. She shows how, since the 1648 Treaty of Westphalia, a body of international agreements, norms, declarations, interstate concordats, and public and private arrangements have all combined to generate an international legal regime that, despite lacking the enforcement capabilities of its domestic counterpart, mediates state behavior, helping promote peace, human rights, and other progressive social agendas. Moreover, the evolution of international law has imbued it with a dynamism that enables it to respond to stakeholder needs and continue to, as she writes "address the wellbeing and safety of individuals, provide order for the collective political and economic interests of states, and facilitate increased levels of cross-border/ transnational activity." Crucially, she shows how the kind of global governance that we had—the strictly interstate system of the post-Westphalian era—has generated forms of international law that have also fundamentally changed that system into the multivariate incarnation of today.

In tandem, Murphy and Ku show how incremental developments in forms of regulation at multiple levels—movements in which international organizations have played key roles—have been major drivers in establishing today's complex system of global governance. In Chapter 3, Barnett and Duvall add power into the mix by exploring how international organizations can act simultaneously to reinforce existing—that is, status quo—power relations among member states, as well as to help diffuse power among state and non-state actors. Their "International organizations and the diffusion of power" explores the means by which institutions enable power to be used, and they can act as progressive forces mediating the capacity of powerful states and elites. And Barnett and Duvall lay the ground for the exploration of existing theoretical approaches to IO and global governance discussed in the following part of the book by showing how power is understood by each of the schools of thought that are covered.

Held further develops the back stories to IO and global governance in his Chapter 4 on "The diffusion of authority." His aim is to take in not just international organizations but also a range of transnational and other actors active in shaping the way that the world is currently governed. Yet, for all the diffusion and positive elements that it has brought—particularly in constraining the capacity of states to exercise power in illegitimate ways—his argument resembles that of Barnett and Duvall. Even in a complex multilayered, multisector, and multi-actor system of global governance, state sovereignty remains a stumbling block to the realization of many agendas, particularly on climate change.

In Chapter 5, the final one in this part, Sell asks a question that is so often missing from debates about the way the world is organized: "Who governs the globe?" Set against an account of the development of IO and global governance literatures, Sell illuminates those agents able to exercise power across borders, set agendas, influence policy, establish rules, implement programs, and evaluate and adjudicate outcomes. Importantly, she notes, despite the range of agents involved in the governance of world affairs, and the vast capabilities of some, none is able to govern alone—a realization that some major powers continue to ignore. Moreover, the means by which representation, accountability, and legitimacy result are far from straightforward.

Where to now?

Each of these chapters is essential reading, helping us get a better grip on the origins of, key aspects within, and principal questions pertaining to contemporary IO and global governance. For extensive investigations into the shape of the current global order, none is dispensable. For time-pressured introductions on IO alone, Ku, and Barnett and Duvall are essential. More wide-ranging classes on global governance should begin with Murphy and examine at least Held and Sell. Once they have been read, readers should turn to explore the lengthening list of main theoretical traditions in the field that are surveyed in Part III.

CONTENTS

The emergence of global governance

Craig N. Murphy

Most things exist long before they are named. So it is with global governance. A century ago, before World War I, the globe was already governed by a thin network of public and private international organizations linking the industrial core countries of the mainly European empires that had so recently succeeded in conquering and divvying up the entire world. The organizations served a small but crucial part of the new imperial economies: Their fundamentally new industries—electrical power, pharmaceuticals, and various new consumer products—were the economic engines of the second Industrial Revolution.

This particular moment in the globalization of industrial capitalism ended with the Great War, the inter-war depression, and the war's more horrible successor. Yet even throughout that dark thirty-year period, activists and statesmen tried to form new international institutions that could rebuild the prewar global economy on a more secure, more peaceful foundation. The League of Nations failed, but its experiment with enlarging international peace was more successfully replicated in the United Nations, the center of a new global system of public and private organizations that also helped foster a second age of rapid economic transformation—the automobile and jet age of economic growth from the 1940s into the 1970s.

By the mid-1990s, this mid-twentieth-century world economy was changing once again, in part because China and the former socialist bloc countries were clamoring for deeper integration into the international economy and in part because this dominant and Western-centered economy had been stagnant for twenty years even while it was being transformed by revolutions in global communications, transportation, and trade—transformations that mid-twentieth-century international institutions had fostered but were unable to control. It was in this context of a global manufacturing economy emerging outside the confines of existing international regulations that the phrase "global governance" was first heard. The phrase referred to something that existed, yet something that needed to be reformed, something that demanded as much creative attention of the world's leaders as their predecessors had devoted to the inter-imperial institutions that they built in the 1880s and 1890s, and to the UN system in the 1940s.

The unsolved problems of global governance that existed when the term was first used are still with us. They define a large part of the field that this volume addresses. A related second large part of the field is connected to what global governance has done so successfully: Fostering the internationalization (now, the globalization) of industrial capitalism. This chapter describes the nineteenth-century origins of global governance and the later rise of the UN system. It then outlines the more recent crises that led to the development of the term "global governance," identifies the most fruitful ways the term has been used by activists and scholars, and concludes with some questions to keep in mind when studying and reflecting on global governance.

Global governance before the Great War

Looking back to the world before World War I at the time of the 1929 Wall Street crash, a young American economist, Robert Brady, wrote about the consequences of the late nineteenth-century expansion of Japan, the United States, and at least eight European powers:

> All of these are, of course, matters of common knowledge to any schoolboy. But their significance lies in this—for the first time in many centuries, the known world was politically organized into definite imperial states whose political, military, and naval power depended directly upon their respective industrial resources. The greatest market areas in human history were open for exploitation. Science, invention, and the machine process had made mineral and chemical resources the key to power and placed the wellbeing of the peoples within national[/imperial] borders. In other words, the world was organized on the basis of mass markets, mass production, and mass distribution. In the task of exploiting the resources of national and dependent territories, of refining, transporting, fabricating, and distributing products, machine technology played a dominant role.[1]

The part of the world in which the machines were made, where most of the machines lay, and where the overwhelming bulk of the trade in industrial goods took place was held together by the strong but thin threads of international institutions: The score or so public international unions and the hundreds of international nongovernmental organizations (NGOs) created in the last third of the nineteenth century.

The public international unions linked together the communication and transportation systems of separate empires (the International Telegraph Union was established in 1865 and the International Railway Congress Association in 1885). They established necessary industrial standards and inter-imperial rules governing intellectual property (the International Bureau of Weights and Measures was established in 1875 and the International Bureau for the Protection of Intellectual Property in 1893). They also administered aspects of the inter-imperial monetary system and helped maintain rules of trade (the Latin Monetary Union was established in 1865 and the Brussels Tariff Union in 1890). Of course, the Bank of England and the British government (the putative nineteenth-century hegemonic power) played central roles in these aspects of early global governance, too.

In addition, a few international organizations supported large groups within the industrial core of the inter-imperial world that were likely to be harmed by the growing trade in industrial products fostered by the other public international unions. The International Association for Labor Legislation, established in 1889, attempted to end the race to the bottom in wages and labor standards that had begun when low-wage newly industrialized countries entered the inter-imperial trading system, a system of relatively free trade in industrial goods. Today it may seem ironic that the major concern was the relative poverty of workers in places such as Norway and Sweden. The International Institute of Agriculture was established in 1905 and aimed to redress the information imbalance between, on the one hand, shippers and agricultural cartels, who had a great deal of knowledge about both agricultural supply and demand, and, on the other hand, small European and American farmers, who had little knowledge of either.

The Labor Association, which began as a cooperative project of labor unions and concerned citizens, is typical of global governance in the inter-imperial world: Some of it was done by private international NGOs. This was especially true when it came to creating essential measurement and interoperability standards for the new industries of the second Industrial Revolution. Late nineteenth-century international conferences of scientists and engineers reached agreement on common chemical and electrical units and measurement systems. Electrical engineers established their major industrial standard setting body, the International Electrotechnical Commission, in 1906. Chemists and chemical engineers created the predecessor of today's International Union of Pure and Applied Chemistry in 1911, institutionalizing a chemical standards regime that they had established in 1892.

NGOs and the international social movements that they helped institutionalize played an additional important role by broadly championing the internationalization of the economy that the public international unions would secure. The Free Trade Movement—which included working class consumers and homemakers throughout the industrialized world as well as the more often remembered manufacturers who benefited from lower tariffs—gave many governments the political will to extend the most favored nation trading system that was pioneered by Britain and France in 1860. The Red Cross Movement, the International Labor Movement, International Law Movement, and the Peace Movement all worked for progressive social measures that directly helped secure the newly internationalized economic order.

They and other international social movement organizations also helped secure the new economy indirectly by promoting "internationalism" in general. In case after

THE EMERGENCE OF GLOBAL GOVERNANCE

case, international NGOs used the political space created by the unions to argue that it was only right for similar forms of international cooperation to be tried in the various social fields, as well.

The UN era

The eminent global historian Akira Iriye writes about how the prewar experience of international NGOs began to shape the world that the US government tried to create first through the League of Nations and then through the UN:

> In a book published during the [first] war, Mary Follett, an American political scientist, wrote that "association is the impulse, the core of our being," and since "the creative characteristic of war is doing things together," it was imperative to "begin to do things together in peace" through the efforts of people united not by herd instinct but by group conviction.

Iriye argues that Follett:

> [M]ay well have had in mind the American Friends Service Committee and other organizations established during the war when she noted, "the modern hero goes out to disarm his enemy through creating a mutual understanding." The American Century was beginning to be defined . . . through the spread of NGOs, both domestic and international.[2]

In 1933, Robert Brady wrote that the new associations—whether made up of engineers, workers, or social reformers—all looked forward to a world economy of the greatest possible engineering efficiency: The production of the greatest number of useful goods with the least waste of resources and labor. Such an economy required regulation, *global* regulation, because "*national* regulation is largely, and in some cases, completely ineffective in the modern world."[3]

Yet, ironically, Brady argued, the desire to achieve the greatest possible engineering efficiencies initially only gained ground as part of a struggle to create ever more efficient *national* economies, a struggle initiated by the shortsightedness of the Treaty of Versailles:

> The reparation debts to be paid by Germany to the Allies . . . called for an export value surplus, which Germany could achieve only by underselling its commercial rivals—Britain, France, Italy, and the United States. These countries, the future recipients of the reparations, in order to protect their own disorganized industries and markets, imposed

tariff barriers against the flood of cheap German goods. Needless to say, this action necessitated still cheaper production in Germany in order that its goods might climb over the tariff walls. . . . Meanwhile, international competition took the form of concerted national movements to regain markets formerly held and to keep present markets by producing cheaply at home—and, under large-scale industry, that means by realizing the economies of mass production by rigid standardization and simplification. . . . The rapid growth of trade associations and industrial mergers in this country [the United States] and the renewal of the cartel movement in Europe, made possible standardization and simplification throughout entire industries.[4]

Long before European butchery resumed in 1939, mixed economies of capitalist enterprises regulated by private associations and the state to achieve engineering efficiencies existed throughout the industrialized world. The exception was the Soviet Union, where the state attempted to follow a more thoroughgoing form of planning directed toward the same end.

As World War II wound down, the Franklin D. Roosevelt administration remained committed to creating the foundation of world peace on which a *global* system of regulation could ensure the prosperity that could come from production of the greatest number of useful goods with the least waste of resources and labor. The administration's chosen instrument for achieving this end was the wartime alliance, which Roosevelt had named "the United Nations." The allies reconfigured the world organization into the peace-maintaining instrument of the Security Council supplemented by a universal membership General Assembly, which was given light oversight over the central administration (the Secretariat), and a smaller Economic and Social Council (ECOSOC) with similarly light oversight over a system of relatively autonomous UN specialized agencies, most of which were direct descendants of the public international unions. A few new ones—the International Civil Aviation Organization (ICAO), the International Monetary Fund (IMF), the World Bank, and a stillborn International Trade Organization (ITO), which generated the General Agreement on Tariffs and Trade (GATT)—were designed to play critical roles in the new postwar world economy.

The Security Council was a substantial innovation in global governance. Recent research, however, suggests that the UN system has contributed more through peace-making between adversaries (especially before they engage in all-out war) through peacekeeping and through peacebuilding via the work of the UN development system. Joshua Goldstein's book that documents this impact, *Winning the War on War*, also points to the postwar role of the international peace movement and of its close allies in international peace research. Above the title on the cover of the book's paperback edition, celebrated psychologist Steven Pinker writes, "The greatest untold story of the last two decades."[5] It certainly is, although the story really begins in 1946 when the postwar UN first opened shop.

Beyond contributing to this foundation of peace, the UN system has played roles similar to those that the public international unions played before World War I: Supporting the communication and transportation infrastructures that link the world economy, maintaining global rules governing intellectual property, working with the complex system of standard-setting bodies united under the International Organization for Standardization (ISO), established in 1946 to maintain necessary industrial standards and to establish them in the new industries of the postwar automobile age and jet age. It worked with key national governments and private international associations to support and regulate the global monetary and financial system, and maintaining the rules for international trade.

When it came to supporting groups that could have been harmed by a growing international industrial economy, the postwar global governance system included fundamentally new activities and practices. Labor was in part protected by standards established by the International Labour Organization (ILO, the UN's first specialized agency and the continuation of the organization with the same name from the League of Nations, and successor to the nineteenth-century International Association of Labour Legislation). However, the more important protections for workers and farmers through the non-communist industrialized world came from formal and informal agreements among Western powers to protect their growing welfare states and the domestic class compromises on which they were based. As the levelheaded international political economist and sometime senior UN official John G. Ruggie has long argued, the postwar international economic order involved embedding a system of increasingly free trade in industrialized goods within a larger set of social norms. The GATT actually protected Western and Japanese farmers *from* international *laissez faire* by keeping their products off the negotiating table and by facilitating a host of other domestic social policies throughout the industrialized world.[6]

The other great innovation came in the way that the UN system treated the less industrialized peripheries of the prewar empires, the peoples of what was first known as the "Third World" and now the "Global South." People there, just like farmers in the industrialized world, had reason to fear a more deeply integrated but unregulated global capitalist economy. The postwar system did not give the Global South the prosperity of the growing industrial economies of the North or the protections offered to farmers and industrial workers there, far from it. The GATT provided no exception (implicit or explicit) for the agricultural products of the Global South and parts of the UN system (especially the IMF and the World Bank) were always ready to oppose new welfare policies in Africa, Asia, Latin America, or the Caribbean. Nevertheless, the UN system *did* provide significant support for decolonization and for a limited form of economic development: Something short of catch-up with the industrialized world.

Support for decolonization began as early as 1946 and increased as the former colonial majority of the UN grew. From its beginning the world organization provided technical assistance and humanitarian support that has strengthened state institutions in every part of the developing world. In fact, since the 1970s, the vast majority of the UN system's staff and resources have been devoted to its country offices throughout the Global South. From the point of view of staff time and expenditures, the "UN system" and the "UN development system" are both service providers that operate in the developing world, and both are quite different from the image of the UN gleaned by observing the goings on in the multilateral talking shops in New York and Geneva.[7]

Of course, the system's role as an interlocking set of ongoing conversations matters a great deal; and just as in prewar public international unions, some of the most important talking has always been done by NGOs, especially social movement organizations pushing for global attention to social and environmental issues. The relatively constant postwar expansion of international human rights law and of the UN system's human rights activities reflects the longstanding process of NGOs using the political space created by organizations that promote the internationalization of the economy to demand international cooperation in other fields as well.

The UN's environmental work differs only slightly. The global environmental harms that have been the focus of the UN's environmental conferences, the UN Environment Programme (UNEP), and the environmental assistance provided by the UNDP and the World Bank are all consequences of the type of economy that global governance always fostered.

Late twentieth-century crises and "global governance"

The environmental agenda became a permanent part of the UN's work with the 1972 Stockholm Conference on the Human Environment, when governments affirmed 26 principles. Over half were concerned with adding support for national environmental problems to the agenda of the UN development system. Six referred to the degradation of parts of the global commons. Included were specific references to biological diversity ("wildlife" in the outdated and imprecise terms of the day) and the oceans. The remaining items included a "polluter pays" principle and support for more environmental education and research to be undertaken by international organizations.[8] In keeping with this declaration, the main result of the Stockholm conference was a UN system committed to aiding developing countries with *all* their environmental problems, and to studying and proposing ways to deal with those *few* environmental problems of a truly global nature. Those problems, especially the consequences of pollution of the atmosphere, along with species depletion and pollution of the oceans, became the first of four long-term crises of international governance.

The second crisis emerged at almost the same time. With their proposals for a New International Economic Order (NIEO), governments of developing countries began demanding that global economic governance be reformed to ensure that their countries actually caught up with the industrialized world. Some governments hoped to achieve this through a kind of general strike by raw materials producers. When Arab oil producers successfully carried out a producers' strike against the United States and some Western European countries as part of Arab strategy in the 1973 war against Israel, many in the North saw that action and the subsequent worldwide recession as causing the end of the long period of postwar growth. While that conclusion may be unfounded, the crisis in North–South relations certainly has continued throughout the decades of relatively slow growth in Western economies that started in the 1970s.

At the beginning of that era, first the United Kingdom, then the United States, and then many other Western countries turned away from welfare-oriented policies based on constant increases in productivity (ever greater engineering efficiency), to *laissez faire*-oriented policies of limited government and reliance on the market to lower the prices of labor and raw materials. To use the words of Thorstein Veblen, the economist who had inspired the young Robert Brady, governments and business elites stopped relying on the efficiencies provided by "the engineers" to ensure prosperity; they turned instead to "the price system"—in the same way that Veblen described their predecessors as having done after World War I,[9] and with similar results. The fact that the economic policies of the 1980s onward led to greater income inequality and income stagnation for most wage earners in the industrialized world created the third long crisis. Income inequality across countries also increased as lenders (especially the IMF and World Bank) imposed the new Western economic orthodoxy on much of the developing world.

Many early analyses of this economic shift overlooked the degree to which a further internationalization of industrial capitalism underlay the observed crisis—a further internationalization supported by revolutions in communication, transportation, and industrial standards that had been fostered by global governance in the UN era. The latest communication revolution began with the fantastic increase in available bandwidth for intercontinental messages provided by early communication satellites. In the first year that we had such a satellite, 1962, it carried about 400 such messages. Today, every person who reads this book probably uses more intercontinental bandwidth every week; one needs only to think of the sources of the Internet pages that people typically access, and how frequently they do so. A major source of all that bandwidth is the satellites maintained by Intelsat, a hybrid organization whose original members included both governments and private companies. Similarly, consider the clothes people today typically wear and the objects they have around them; most of these things travel great distances before they get to the people who use them, something that would not have been possible forty years ago. This is a consequence of the global manufacturing economy, a precondition for which was the tremendous reduction in intercontinental shipping costs that came with containerized shipping, which only took off after the ISO established a shipping container standard in 1968.[10] Of course, a second key element in the making of the contemporary world was China's initially cautious entry into the global economy beginning in 1978, something facilitated by UN technical assistance.[11]

With the fall of the socialist bloc regimes of Eastern Europe a decade later, the UN system faced a fourth crisis: The massive increase in demands for peacemaking and peacekeeping services in conflicts that became resolvable because the sides were no longer supported by competing superpowers (as in Central America and Southern Africa) and those that flared up because the control imposed by the Cold War balance of forces was lifted (as in the Caucasus and the former Yugoslavia).

The end of the Cold War also provided new opportunities for global governance. The promoters of the more integrated global manufacturing economy—especially major companies and the US government—used the opening provided by the evaporation of the major alternative to global capitalism to promote stronger rules for liberalizing international trade and investment. The vehicles were through the World Trade Organization (WTO) and the Agreement on Trade Related Investment Measures (TRIMs) and for increasing the power of owners of patents and copyright through the Agreement on Trade Related Aspects of Intellectual Property (TRIPs). Of course, the critics of a more powerful, less regulated global capitalism saw in these developments a deepening of the third crisis, the turn away from welfare-oriented economic policies to a kind of liberal fundamentalism that increased inequality. In Ruggie's terms, by the early 1990s, the challenge of embedding global markets in a system of larger social norms had become much greater than ever before.

It was in the context of these four crises that an independent commission supported by the UN secretary-general and chaired by then Swedish prime minister, Ingvar Carlsson, and former Commonwealth secretary-general Shridath Ramphal coined the current usage of the term "global governance." The 1995 report of the self-named "Global Governance Commission" proposed reforms in international institutions and some national policies to: Address global environmental problems; respond to the demands of developing countries for a more equitable and less hypocritical global economic order; restart a global industrial economy focused on real increases in productivity and strong commitments to sharing the benefits of growth; and strengthen the UN system to deal with all the new demands for its peacekeeping and humanitarian services.[12] In the same year, the Academic Council on the UN System launched a new journal called *Global Governance: A Review of Multilateralism and International Organizations*. In 1999, the fifth year that the phrase was used, Google Scholar reports that there were over 1,000 articles and books published that used it. Twelve years later, there were about ten times that number, about the same number that used "international security," and more than twice the number that refer to "international political economy." The use of "global governance" continues to grow faster than that of either of these other terms.

What the phrase denotes

Obviously, scholars have found "global governance" to be a useful term, but perhaps activists have found it even more useful. If Google Scholar gives us about 15,000 new citations to "global governance" in the last year, Google *per se* gives us 250,000, most of them from advocacy organizations or individuals who want to change some aspect of the way the world is governed. The term is used in a multitude of different, if related, ways across these many thousands of sources. It may be helpful to close this opening chapter to the subject by suggesting that the most fruitful use of the term has been contributing to our understanding of how the world works and what we might do to change that.

In that context, any definition that pulls us toward treating global governance as "all kinds of governance, everywhere" should probably be avoided because such definitions (and they exist) give us little opportunity to say anything that we could not say just by referring to "governance." "*Global* governance" more reasonably refers to a kind of governance—or at least, to attempts to establish governance—at a particular level.

Miles Kahler has observed that some of the most useful literature on global governance seems to embed within it a preference for "subsidiarity," an idea that collective problems are best solved at the lowest level at which they can be solved. Therefore, the best form of global governance would be limited to collective problems that could not be solved by organizations at any lower level, for example by national governments (individually or in coalition) or by international professional associations and the like.[13] Kishore Mahbubani, a founder of one of the first public policy graduate programs that focuses on global governance, expressed this view when he wrote:

> Mao Zedong was right. We should always focus on the primary, not secondary, contradictions. And right now, our primary global contradiction is painfully obvious: the biggest challenges of governance are global in origin, but all the politics that respond to them are local. There are many wise leaders around the world, but there is not enough global leadership.[14]

Arguably, we can still point to some successful forms of governance at the global level; we can, for example, point to the decreasing frequency and violence of war that Goldstein attributes to the governance provided by the UN and the peace and peace research movements.

Yet, even if we embrace the desirability of subsidiarity, we need to recognize that organizations or coalitions often try to exercise governance at a global level, even if it is unwarranted. The contrarian Andrew M. Scott was deeply convinced that all the attempts to increase the world's many channels of communication, lower the costs of travel and transportation, and otherwise facilitate trade and interaction did more harm than good. From Scott's point of view, the ISO, the WTO, TRIPs, TRIMs, and the International Civil Aviation Organization (ICAO) are all global governance, but they *create* global problems rather than solve them.[15]

It may be worthwhile remaining agnostic about that point, but there is less reason to be agnostic about Scott's (or Mahbubani's) conclusion about industrial capitalism and economic globalization. They are fostered by the standards and controls exercised by the governments and organizations promoting an unregulated liberal world economy, and they create global problems that are dealt with by relatively ineffective structures of global governance. The late Susan Strange, one of the founders of the field of international political economy and someone suspicious of the notion of global governance, pointed in her last article, "The Westfailure System," to three global problems of this sort, problems about which both Mahbubani and Scott would agree: The limited number of truly global environmental problems created by two centuries of industrial economies in a world in which no one has effective responsibility for maintaining the various global commons; the regular recurrence of international financial crises created by the vested interest of most of the relevant actors in maintaining geographic spaces in which the main rules do not apply; and persistent and sometimes growing inequalities across classes and regions, a problem of capitalism at all levels, but one that becomes increasingly global as economies become more integrated.[16]

Strange relates these three core global problems to another small set of problems that some analysts might want to consider separately: Pandemics such as HIV/AIDS (which during Strange's lifetime was the subject of global governance as ineffective as that now directed toward climate change); transnational organized crime (TOC) and the particular fields in which it tends to operate (drugs, human trafficking, and the arms trade); and the connected problem of internationalized terrorism (made possible by unregulated global finance and the arms trade). Scholars and policymakers might want to add to this list. For example, in thinking about the sources of the power of TOC, the persistence of the unregulated arms trade, and problems created by dictators and warlords, we need to add a global tendency to overvalue the military. Nevertheless, the number of such issues will still be small.

Even when we add all the fields in which there is some kind of global governance that is not needed—such as in encouraging economic globalization—the entire field of "global governance" is not a large one. However, it is of great significance.

Conclusion

If the approach to global governance suggested here is appealing, it would be worthwhile to ask of anything written on the subject, including the chapters in this volume: "Is this a field in which there should be global governance? Is it a field in which problems exist at a global level that cannot be solved at any other level? If not, and if some kind of system of global governance does exist or is being attempted, then why is that the case? Who is being served by this unnecessary global governance, how and why has this happened, and is there anything that can be done about it?" If it is a field in which there should be effective global governance, but none exists, it is necessary to ask: "Why not? Who is being served by this lack of governance, why and how has this happened, and is there anything that can be done about it?"

After all, whether or not global governance, in itself, exists (as this chapter argues that it has for more than a century), the concept of "global governance" exists. And it does so for a particular purpose: To help us think critically about problems that humanity (and even the whole planet) shares that cannot be solved by individuals, families, private organizations, states, or traditional international relations alone.

Additional reading

Daniel Deudney, "The Great Descent: 'Global Governance' in Historical and Theoretical Perspective," in *Why Govern? Rethinking Demand and Progress in Global Governance*, ed. Amitav Acharya (Cambridge: Cambridge University Press, 2016).

Douglas R. Howland, "An Alternative Mode of International Order: The International Administrative Union in the Nineteenth Century," *Review of International Studies* 41, no. 2 (2014): 161–183.

Mark Mazower, *Governing the World: The History of an Idea, 1815 to the Present* (New York: Penguin, 2012).

Craig N. Murphy, *International Organization and Industrial Change: Global Governance since 1850*, 2nd edition (Cambridge: Polity Press, 2005).

Dan Plesch, *America, Hitler and the UN: How the Allies Won World War II and Forged Peace* (London: IB Tauris, 2011).

Dan Plesch and Thomas G. Weiss, eds., *Wartime Origins and the Future United Nations* (London: Routledge, 2015).

Bob Reinalda, *Routledge History of International Organizations: From 1815 to the Present Day* (London: Routledge, 2009).

Quinn Slobodian, *Globalists: The End of Empire and the Birth of Neoliberalism* (Cambridge, MA: Harvard University Press, forthcoming).

Thomas G. Weiss, *Global Governance: What? Why? Whither?* (Cambridge: Polity Press, 2013).

Notes

1 Robert A. Brady, *Industrial Standardization* (New York: National Industrial Conference Board, 1929), 8.

2 Akira Iriye, "A Century of NGOs," *Diplomatic History* 23, no. 3 (1999): 425–426, quoting Mary Parker Follett, *The New State: Group Organization the Solution of Popular Government* (New York: Longmans, Green), 193–195.

3 Robert A. Brady, *The Rationalization Movement in German Industry: A Study in the Evolution of Economic Planning* (Berkeley: University of California Press, 1933), 395.

4 Brady, *Industrial Standardization*, 14.

5 Steven Pinker, on the cover of Joshua S. Goldstein, *Winning the War on War: The Decline of Armed Conflict Worldwide* (New York: Plume [Penguin], 2012).

6 One of the best assessments of the continuing value of Ruggie's analysis is Andrew T. F. Lang, "Reconstructing Embedded Liberalism: John Gerard Ruggie and Constructivist Approaches to the Study of International Trade," in *Embedding Global Markets: An Enduring Challenge*, ed. John Gerard Ruggie (Aldershot: Ashgate, 2008), 13–45.

7 Two recent empirical studies of these roles are Craig N. Murphy, *The UN Development Programme: A Better Way?* (Cambridge: Cambridge University Press, 2006), and Stephen Browne, *UN Development Programme and System* (Abingdon: Routledge, 2011). Murphy's "Foreword" to Browne's book, xix–xx, provides the data for the assertion about UN system staff and expenditures.

8 "Declaration of the United Nations Conference on the Human Environment," 15 June 1972, www.unep.org/Documents.Multilingual/Default.asp?documentid=97&articleid=1503.

9 Thorstein Veblen, *The Engineers and the Price System* (New York: B. W. Huebsch, Inc., 1921).

10 A clear introduction to Intelsat's organizational history and impact is Patricia McCormick, "The Privatization of Intelsat: The Transition of an Intergovernmental Organization to Private Equity Ownership," in *Telecommunications Research Trends*, eds. Hans F. Erlich and Ernst P. Lehrmann (New York: Nova Science Publishers, 2008), 45–74. On containerized shipping, see Marc Levinson, *The Box: How the Shipping Container Made the World Smaller and the World Economy Bigger* (Princeton, NJ: Princeton University Press, 2006).

11 Murphy, *The UN Development Programme*, 177–181.

12 Commission on Global Governance, *Our Global Neighbourhood* (Oxford: Oxford University Press, 1995).

13 Miles Kahler, "Global Governance Redefined," in *Challenges of Globalization: Immigration, Social Welfare, Global Governance*, ed. A.C. Sobel (London: Routledge, 2009), 174–198.

14 Kishore Mahbubani, "The Problem with Presidents," *Newsweek*, 30 August 2010.

15 Andrew M. Scott, *The Dynamics of Interdependence* (Chapel Hill: University of North Carolina Press, 1982).

16 Susan Strange, "The Westfailure System," *Review of International Studies* 25, no. 3 (1999): 345–354.

The evolution of international law

Charlotte Ku

The international legal system comprises norms, processes, and institutions.[1] The interaction of these elements creates international law's authority, legitimacy, and effectiveness. International law is therefore implemented and given effect less through the threat of sanctions than through the cumulative actions of the system's stakeholders. This self-enforcing characteristic is often regarded as a weakness or flaw in international law as a legal system, but in fact it provides international law the opportunity to grow and to develop as it responds to changing needs and values.

The cumulative effect of this process produced revolutionary developments that today address the wellbeing and safety of individuals, provide order for the collective political and economic interests of states, and facilitate increased levels of cross-border and transnational activity. And the process continues. International law now covers environmental protection, family relations, and criminal activities that were little covered or even recognized as subject to international law only decades ago. It also has a robust operating platform to facilitate the development, implementation, and assessment of international norms. Nevertheless, international law faces the same challenges that all institutions confront in moving toward global governance, including multiple sources of authority, complex interrelated and multi-jurisdictional issues, and short time horizons.

As an institution and factor in international relations, international law predated both international organizations and global governance. As this chapter shows, it has nevertheless played a crucial role in the development of both by facilitating their creation and by drawing on their capacities to meet its own objectives of recognizing individual human dignity and responsibility, of elaborating the scope of state responsibility, and of finding effective pathways to give life to international obligations. Having met these needs, however, international law struggles in a global political environment in which its hold on regulating international behavior and its coherence as a legal system are challenged. International law has not yet conceived or operationalized a framework that effectively harnesses sub-national activities and players. As a result, it has under-recognized and underused the resulting nuances and opportunities in the implementation of international obligations.

International organizations and other institutions or processes of global governance therefore play increasingly central roles in international law's further development as they provide the venues and tools to assess whether local or private actions meet the object and purpose of international obligations. At the same time, global governance provides the necessary normative and political input to keep international law dynamic and relevant. The chapter examines this relationship and its implications for the future.

The status of international law today

The process of development, implementation, and evaluation of international law occurs over large numbers of transactions in numerous locations and settings. The volume of activity is impressive, with one study accounting for 82,000 publicized international agreements and as many as 100,000 additional interstate agreements negotiated since the beginning of diplomatic history.[2] These agreements are supplemented by numerous other "atypical" instruments that include multilateral frameworks and general declaratory instruments in treaty form; soft law in nontreaty form, such as codes of conduct, guidelines, and statements of principles; memoranda of understanding and other informal implementation instruments; political accords; the implementation activities of nongovernmental organizations; UN General Assembly resolutions of a lawmaking quality; UN Security Council resolutions; resolutions of other international organizations with lawmaking capacity; and declarations of intergovernmental conferences.[3] To this list, we might now add private standards and principles and practices agreed on by states, international organizations, nongovernmental organizations, and other non-state actors, such as corporations. To be sure, not all international agreements or actions are of equal importance—for example, the significance of the UN Charter as compared to the International Convention for the Unification of Methods of Sampling and Analyzing Cheeses—or involve the same number of states or parties.[4] The overall volume of activity generated by these treaty and nontreaty forms of international cooperation is nevertheless significant and has contributed to developing the capacity of international law to function.

Lawmaking is a competitive process in which conflicting values or approaches vie for adoption as a prevailing norm. The competition can be played out in actual state practice that may give rise to customary practice or in negotiations that produce a treaty or some other forms of international agreement. The formation of a new rule of customary international law requires that: "State practice, including that of States whose interests are directly affected, should have been both extensive and virtually uniform . . . and should moreover have occurred in such a way as to show a general recognition that a rule of law or legal obligation is involved."[5] The same criteria apply to any exception to general practice that is claimed. See, for example, the *Fisheries Case* (*United Kingdom v. Norway*, 1951), where the International Court of Justice ruled:

> [T]hat the method of straight baselines [as differing from the general practice of following the contours and indentations of the coastline], established in the Norwegian system, was imposed by the peculiar geography of the Norwegian coast; that even before the dispute arose, this method had been consolidated by a constant and sufficiently long practice, in the face of which the attitude of governments bears witness to the fact that they did not consider it to be contrary to international law.[6]

The opportunity to express consent and to see the obligations incurred by parties is key to the importance of international agreements. Contemporary practice, however, shows that it is less the form of an agreement than the implementation of an obligation and the ability to assess its effect on international behavior that is significant. The 1975 Helsinki Final Act of the Conference on Security and Cooperation in Europe, for example, was a political statement rather than a legal instrument. Nevertheless, the system of follow-up conferences generated by this Act gave effect to international human rights standards and provided the opportunity for political activism and networking by nongovernmental organizations within the Warsaw Pact that contributed to the collapse of the Soviet Union and an end to the Cold War.[7] Close attention must therefore now be given to the institutional frameworks—international and domestic, public and private—available to parties to carry out international obligations as well as their capacity to do so. As Rosalyn Higgins describes it, "international law is a continuing process of authoritative decisions."[8] Given this, where and when authoritative decisions can be made and who can make them is important.

Authoritative decision making

A key milestone in international relations was also for the development of international law: 1648, when the Peace of Westphalia concluded the Thirty Years War. Although the war itself was of greatest immediate significance for Europe, the Peace of Westphalia's global order legacy was even more far reaching: It provided the foundation for authoritative decision making in modern international law. It did so by confirming an international order based on a multiplicity of states with responsibilities to each other and to the people and resources that they govern. In the four centuries since the conclusion of the Peace of Westphalia, both the breadth and depth of those responsibilities and the modes of discharging them have undergone substantial change. Although states remain sovereign within their territories, they have also come to accept levels of scrutiny and intrusion that would have been unthinkable only a few decades ago.[9] More significantly, the legitimacy of domestic actions such as decisions to use military force is now increasingly judged based on consistency with international standards, practices, and policies.[10] This includes the requirement for some form of collective authorization and review of any use of military force.

Authority today, whether international or domestic, public or private, is no longer a given, but it must be earned with an increased emphasis on performance as a basis for legitimacy. Individuals are more vocal about what they like or dislike about governments or other institutions, and they use technology to connect with like-minded individuals to create networks to pursue their agendas.[11] Facilitating the creation of authoritative channels for ongoing validation and assessment of individual actions is therefore an important characteristic and function of international law today. As the Westphalian state form was a response to the domestic and political needs of seventeenth-century Europe that required a distinct locus of authority, by the late twentieth century states began to respond to complex cross-border issues that involved a range of emerging authorities and governing capacities.[12] State authority and order remain vital today, but flexibility and agility are now also the hallmarks of statehood operating within a complex governance environment of international organizations and private entities. Multiple authorities are now routinely involved, even within one government, to pursue a policy.

What we have seen in the centuries since the 1648 Peace of Westphalia, and particularly for the past century, is a state governance framework—including international law—responding to the adaptations and adjustments made by states to fulfill their new responsibilities to people in their jurisdictions, stewardship of their territory and resources, and multilateral coordination and cooperation. The state may no longer be the only broker of power and interests; but it remains the most widely recognized actor that, since the seventeenth century, has already proved its own capacity to adapt to the changing needs of domestic and international governance. One manifestation of this adaptability is the establishment of international organizations to enhance the capacity of the state to provide for the wellbeing of its citizens and global economic development. The state originally emerged as a dominant governing form following a competitive exercise, war. The state form triumphed because it best served the organizing needs of the time, and it provided the financial and political resources to field the armies needed to protect and to advance elites' interests. Once they were established, state leaders undertook to mutually empower other entities that most closely resembled their own, thereby squeezing out alternative forms of governance over time. International law was used to express and to validate the characteristics of the state—capacity to control people and territory and to carry out international obligations.

In contemporary terms, mutual empowerment of the state took place in the 1950s and 1960s with the increasing intensity of calls for an end to colonialism that came from the concerted efforts of newly independent states. On attaining their own membership in the United Nations, these states worked assiduously through the General Assembly to maintain a focus on the issue of independence, to pressure states into decolonization, and ultimately to vilify and to shun states that failed to conform. The colonial empire chapter of world history came to a dramatic end with the actions taken by the United Nations against South Africa to advance both the causes of human rights and decolonization. The UN's end of South African control over South West Africa (originally a mandate of the League of Nations) ultimately led to the independence of Namibia in 1988, the ending of apartheid in South Africa, and the election of Nelson Mandela as president of South Africa in 1994.

That a forum such as the UN was available to new states to set and pursue their decolonization agenda shows how the existence of a structure created by states under classical Westphalian international law facilitated the pursuit of a new agenda and substantive norms. International organizations (IOs) originally were created to help states meet their own objectives, but they developed independent capacities—including secretariats and other derivative organizations or emanations. Each such step introduces a new dynamic and potentially a new actor to the international system that can provide new capacity, but may also complicate the political environment in which international law functions.

That the privilege of self-government came with burdens, including the responsibility to protect (R2P) populations from mass violence and brutality, shows that the development of norms and institutions does not stand still. Once adopted, new norms and practices become part of international law and international relations. And the modes used to achieve this level of acceptance are also strengthened and made available for use on other issues. Working in the UN General Assembly to advance a particular agenda, for example, would be one such pathway. The practice of using the infrastructure, staff, and knowhow of international organizations to facilitate treaty making, and the number of multilateral treaties that have now been concluded under the auspices of IOs, have provided them with a stature and possibly even authority that states did not foresee at their founding. Jonathan Charney notes that: "[International organizations] contribute to the coordination and facilitation of contemporary international relations on the basis of legal principles."[13] They do so by providing an established venue in which to take decisions that may have legal effect. In so doing, they supplement the traditional modes of international lawmaking, state practice, and *ad hoc* bilateral and multilateral negotiations and treaty making, and provide the secondary rules of recognition that international law is said to lack.[14]

International law and the global political environment

The enhanced role of individuals and private enterprises, for example, in the international arena has created a post-Westphalian environment in which the international level can join directly with the local, private, or individual level without a state or public intermediary.[15] These developments create a form of cosmopolitan democracy in which individuals may have direct access to international activities and may even be able to assert rights and challenge their own government's actions either in court or through institutions like the World Bank Inspection Panels. For this more active role, individuals have also now acquired direct international responsibility and can be held accountable for mass violations of human rights, as in the case of the indictment of Sudan's president Omar al-Bashir for crimes against humanity, war crimes, and genocide in Darfur.[16]

Historically, international law prescribed conduct between states. As such, it reflected the interests and values of the states involved. Obligations were undertaken only through an expression of state consent. Enforcement of the obligations, if necessary, was based on self-help, with reciprocity serving as both carrot and stick. Where disputes occurred, they might be referred for resolution to a fellow sovereign or other mutually acceptable third party such as the pope. Failure of a state to perform could trigger some form of retaliation on the part of the allegedly injured state, if it had the capability to do so. As international society and international life have become more complicated, international law has also become more complex. Its present scope reflects the reality that states' responsibilities are now more extensive than they were even in the middle of the twentieth century.

Today, states are expected to provide for their people, safeguard their environment, and generally enhance wellbeing through productive interactions within their own societies and transnationally across borders. As governments have become more involved in more aspects of life and responsible for more tasks, the apparatus of government has grown, with an increasing number of cabinet-level ministries and offices reflecting new tasks that citizens expect them to accomplish. The nature of the issues and the variety of people and institutions that are now affected by and crucial to its effective functioning have profoundly changed international law. It is now a dense system of legal interactions with connections to national and subnational institutions, IOs, and a host of private actors.

José Alvarez notes that: "[T]he age of global compacts is not coincidentally the age of IOs."[17] There are now multiple venues for treaty making that can determine the scope and content of an agreement. State power is also altered in these settings, with smaller states able to wield influence that may be disproportionate to their size.[18] An example is the United Nations Conference on the Law of the Sea, inspired by Malta, whose representative, Arvid Pardo, coined the phrase "common heritage of mankind," which appears in Article 136 of the 1982 United Nations Convention on the Law of the Sea (UNCLOS). An equally significant move made in the UN General Assembly by Trinidad and Tobago in 1989 led to efforts in 1990 to establish an International Criminal Court. These efforts culminated in the signing of the Rome Statute of the International Criminal Court in July 1998.[19]

IOs generally provide publicly accessible venues with copious amounts of information available to those interested in initiating a treaty or in participating in the treaty-making process. The 1998 Rome Conference that completed the Statute of the International Criminal Court (ICC), for example, recorded participation from representatives of 160 states, thirty-three IOs, over 200 NGOs, and more than 400 journalists.[20] We should contrast this participation with the 1899 Hague Peace Conference, which included 100 delegates from twenty-four countries, with little press access to the delegates, even though journalists were in attendance and there was great public interest in the Conference proceedings.[21] The existence of IOs can lower the costs of undertaking international treaty making because the mechanisms, structures, and personnel needed to support such efforts are now permanently available through UN organs and those of the UN specialized agencies, as well as regional organizations. Used over time, these institutions and procedures have become well established and can take actions with international legal effect.

Douglas Johnston's overview of international agreement activity included a group of "atypical instruments" that can also be grouped under the heading of "soft law." The spectrum of arrangements that might fall under a soft law heading is wide, and the term has created controversy because it blurs the distinction between binding and non-binding commitment.[22] It includes political instruments like the 1945 Yalta Agreement and the 1975 Final Act of the Conference on Security and Cooperation in Europe, and statements and practices undertaken to supplement or to correct a treaty are another form of soft law. The 1987 Montreal Protocol to the 1985 Vienna Convention for the Protection of the Ozone Layer provided for a non-compliance procedure worked out by a working party and subsequently adopted by a meeting of the parties to the protocol in 1992. Resolutions, declarations, codes of conduct, and guidelines of IOs, including those for World Bank operations, are yet another form of soft law, as are world conference declarations, agendas, programs, and platforms for action.[23] Norm making also occurs through "statements of principle from individuals in a nongovernmental capacity, texts prepared by expert groups, the establishment of 'peoples' tribunals, and self-regulating codes of conduct for networks of professional peoples and multinational corporations," such as the MacBride and Sullivan Principles.[24]

A growing body of empirical work shows that such informal mechanisms do influence state behavior.[25] Of further relevance is work showing that norms have influence if the organizational culture at both the national and international level supports them. In this approach, compliance can be achieved regardless of whether the norm is hard or soft as long as there is a culture that encourages adherence to the norm. Bolstered now by the concept of acculturation advanced by Ryan Goodman and Derek Jinks, we find that "global- and regional-level institutions systematically influence state-level legal and policy choices."[26] One key factor of influence was common membership in an international organization.[27]

Soft law fills a gap in norm creation and implementation when formal agreements are not possible. An executive might choose to circumvent a disagreement with the state's legislative or judicial branch through soft international law. For example, entering commodity agreements, including those on the marketing of specific products such as breast milk substitutes, provides a way to monitor and regulate domestic behavior of international concern without resorting to a treaty on the subject of milk substitutes.[28] Similarly, soft law is a vehicle to link international law to private entities regulated principally by domestic law, such as individuals and transnational corporations. The codes of practice of corporate social responsibility are an example of how corporations doing business across borders adhere to good labor practices and environmental protection by complying with domestic law in their worldwide operations.[29]

States also adopt soft international law provisions as an interim step in areas where they have not yet produced hard law, albeit without the same obligations for compliance (or penalties and responsibilities for non-compliance). A good example of this is preservation of the world's forests through the Forest Stewardship Council (FSC). Formed in 1993 by loggers, foresters, environmentalists, and sociologists, its purpose is to provide an international forum for dialogue on what constitutes a sustainable forest and to set forth principles and standards to guide "forest management towards sustainable outcomes." FSC standards are now in use in over fifty-seven countries around the world, including the United States.[30] The FSC goal is to certify twenty percent of the world's forest-based world trade by 2020.[31] Such soft law provides states great flexibility, as they do not risk creating institutions that turn out to be costly and possibly inappropriate, ineffective, or difficult to adapt or eliminate over time.[32] Soft law institutions and processes can enable states to work on compliance first and to develop an appreciation of the costs and benefits of creating formal mechanisms before entering a formal agreement in the future.[33]

In these ways, the present globalized legal environment provides an opportunity for global actors to draw on the strongest operating capacity, whether that is national or international. International soft law can draw on hard national institutions to strengthen it, and soft private sector practices might harden by virtue of their incorporation into a hard law international instrument like a treaty. The key is that global actors seek to promote orderly and reliable behavior, and that they look to law and legal institutions to help shape those expectations. This has enriched international law's capacity to address global needs, but the resulting complexity in its normative and institutional structure has not yet been fully appreciated, especially by critics of international law, most notably at the national level.

Globalizing international law

Interactions and connections among institutions and structures of global order, including law, have been the focus of this chapter. These interactions developed in response to specific needs and together have generated new capacities that in turn have changed the governance environment by producing new governing institutions, norms, structures, partnerships, and relationships. These have empowered new actors and recognized new values that form the basis of global governance today. They have also created new expectations, responsibilities and obligations. The cumulative effects of these interactions have contributed to globalization.

Governance today occurs in a much more open and participatory environment than it did only a few decades ago. The move towards greater openness and participation is occurring at all levels of government, within international institutions, and throughout the private sector in corporate and other non-state entities. There are three key developments: the building of international institutions and structures that may constrain certain state behaviors in the short run, but are likely to contribute to a more stable and secure order in the long run; the reliance on reporting and monitoring procedures as well as follow-up conferences in order to make states and other responsible parties review compliance with their obligations and publicly assess progress toward stated objectives; and the culture of civil society, mass media, and early warning that is becoming more and more effective at putting the spotlight on emerging areas of potential international concern.

From 1648 to 1918, the principal focus of international activity was on the development and strengthening of the state. Global governance in the Westphalian order was one of facilitating the relations among sovereigns and sovereign states. To the extent people benefited from any privileges, for example freedom of religion, it was as a by-product of state interest. The privilege won in the 1555 Peace of Augsburg provided for *cuius regio, eius religio*, which allowed religious freedom, albeit for the monarch or sovereign and not necessarily for their subjects. In fact, the Latin maxim provided that the people would follow the religion of their ruler.[34] The sovereign would therefore dictate the religion of the realm without consideration as to the wishes or traditions of the people of that realm. Indeed, dissent from the established religion could result in persecutions, including deprivation of property rights, lower status, expulsion, and, on occasion, pogroms or mass killings.

Early treaty making reflects this focus on the state, with a substantial portion of treaty activity devoted to such state interests as alliances, trade, and war.[35] These interests created the state values that became the values of global order: autonomy, mutual respect, and non-interference. The Westphalian system focused on a balance of power among the most powerful states in order to maintain order and to preserve peace. When interests fell out of balance, a state could seek to redress that balance by military force. Individual quality of life and livelihood were determined by state authorities. To the extent that the treatment of people was an issue, it was subject to the domestic values and policies of each individual country and its ruler.

As long as the effects of a state's actions did not spill over into another state, its rulers generally were free to govern within their territory as they deemed appropriate. This practice changed in the late nineteenth and twentieth centuries as the requirements of industrialization forced states to act effectively across borders and as governments were increasingly expected to respond to and to provide for their citizens. As Louis Henkin observes, in the course of the twentieth century, the international system turned its attention from state values to human values in its diplomatic activity and treaty making.[36] IOs were at the center of this shift starting with the UN General Assembly's adoption of the Universal Declaration of Human Rights in 1948.

International organizations were created to enhance the ability of states to pursue their interests and to carry out their responsibilities. Starting with structured, but noninstitutionalized meetings, groups of states would gather to address problems of common concern. It seems commonplace today for an IO like the UN to call attention to an area of international concern, but the creation of such a voice independent of states in the early twentieth century was accepted only with extreme caution and skepticism. The political environment created by the presence of an IO was something on which other actors such as NGOs capitalized. IOs provided a readily accessible platform and connection to a worldwide audience to promote their agendas. International lawmaking and implementation have become more generally accessible and participatory than at any other time since the advent of international political institutions, and the process is ongoing.

Emergence of interstitial norms as a blend of existing and potentially conflicting norms demonstrates the growing complexity of international life and the issues international law addresses. Vaughan Lowe coined the term "interstitial norm" to describe a connective norm that draws together differing norms from hard and soft law as well as domestic and transnational law.[37] The 1997 International Court of Justice (ICJ) ruling in the Gabcikovo case between Hungary and Slovakia illustrates Lowe's point when the two objectives of economic development and environmental protection collided. The outcome was a resort to the principle of sustainable development.[38] However, as Lowe noted, there was insufficient state practice to support the position that sustainable development had acquired the status of a norm of customary international law.[39] Another example of an interstitial norm is the principle of the responsibility to protect that attempts to balance the norm of nonintervention in the internal affairs of a state with that of the norm to protect the human rights of people.

Adding complexity to the current normative environment is the growing body of international law related to and produced by IOs themselves. The 1948 ICJ Advisory Opinion on the *Reparation for Injuries Suffered in the Service of the United Nations* was a milestone, because it recognized that the UN possessed sufficient international legal personality to pursue a claim against a state for harm done to one of its agents. As the UN has become more operational, it has found itself incurring legal responsibility and liability although it still struggles with its inherent lack of capacity to discharge legal obligations in the same way that states do.[40] This lack of capacity was one reason why the UN did not formally tie itself to international humanitarian law until 1999.[41] IOs have become legislators by requiring certain behavior as was the case when in 2001 the Security Council adopted resolution 1373 directing all states to take actions against the financing of terrorism and terrorist activities. IOs have also long provided guidance to national legislatures or regulators through model laws and operating standards. This system of interaction through which legal norms become institutionalized has been described as a transnational legal order of which international law is a part.[42]

Characteristic of today's more globalized international law is a less hierarchical lawmaking and implementation process. Law and regulated behavior can develop through networks and social movements rather than exclusively through institutions or governments. Movements may come and go, but their normative legacies are important, as was the case with the movement to end the use of landmines. Globalized international law functions in an environment that is shaped by ongoing interactions rather than abrupt system-wide changes.[43] These interactions create denser and denser political and normative connections between the local and global, the individual and the institutional, and the national and transnational. As diverse forces that add capacity and depth to international norms, global politics enriches international law. But these forces can also create confusion as to the authority or content of a norm, with negative consequences for global order and governance.

International law is now called on to address multidimensional, multisector, and multi-level issues like sustainable development, environmental protection, and the economic and other wellbeing of individuals. This requires a specialization and focus that have raised questions in the international law community about the ongoing coherence of international law as a legal system. The ILC described the problem as follows:

> The fragmentation of the international social world has attained legal significance especially as it has been accompanied by the emergence of specialized and (relatively) autonomous rules or rule-complexes, legal institutions and spheres of legal practice. . . . The result is conflicts between rules or rule systems, deviating institutional practices and, possibly, the loss of an overall perspective on the law.[44]

This fragmentation is further accentuated by the emergence of an increasingly complex global political environment where authoritative international action may come from multiple sources including subnational or private entities.

Conclusion

Despite the pressures of various needs and competing lawmaking authorities today, international law remains a separate legal system with its own unique functions and purposes. The challenge is to ensure recognition and understanding of the principles and structure of international law that enable international and transnational relations and interactions even as these principles change and develop. Further, meeting this challenge requires understanding at the domestic level that international norms and practices are part of all legal systems and need to be understood and integrated. The relationship between international, national, and subnational legal systems is less a hierarchical one than a partnership among systems that connect with each other to give life to global norms and to transform national norms and local practices into global norms.

International organizations exist today because of a perceived need to address cross-border issues. States used international law to create them; and IOs, in turn, have increased the capacity of international law to meet its objectives by organizing permanent staffs, creating venues for legal interaction, and for ongoing development. These connections and relationships will deepen as international norm development and implementation connect increasingly with domestic political discourse and norm development. As they do, new capacities are generated, new challenges will emerge, and the evolution of international law within the multifaceted global legal system that it helped create will continue.

Additional reading

José E. Alvarez, *International Organizations as Law-Makers* (New York: Oxford University Press, 2005).
Paul F. Diehl and Charlotte Ku, *The Dynamics of International Law* (Cambridge: Cambridge University Press, 2010).
Ryan Goodman and Derek Jinks, *Socializing States: Promoting Human Rights Through International Law* (New York: Oxford University Press, 2013).

Terence C. Halliday and Gregory Shaffer, eds., *Transnational Legal Orders* (New York: Cambridge University Press, 2015).

David Held, *Democracy and the Global Order: From the Modern State to Cosmopolitan Governance* (Stanford, CA: Stanford University Press, 1995).

Charlotte Ku, *International Law, International Relations, and Global Governance* (London: Routledge, 2012).

Beth A. Simmons, *Mobilizing for Human Rights: International Law in Domestic Politics* (New York: Cambridge University Press, 2009).

Notes

1 Portions of this essay are adapted from Charlotte Ku, *International Law, International Relations, and Global Governance* (London: Routledge, 2012).

2 Douglas M. Johnston, *Consent and Commitment in the World Community* (Irvington-on-Hudson, NY: Transnational Publishers, Inc., 1997), 8–9.

3 Ibid., 25.

4 Example provided by Lauren Kolb, Research Assistant, Behrend College, Pennsylvania State University, Comprehensive Statistical Database of Multilateral Treaties (CSDMT) Project, August 2012.

5 ICJ Reports, *North Sea Continental Shelf Cases*, Judgment of 20 February 1969, 75.

6 ICJ Reports, *Fisheries Case (United Kingdom v. Norway)*, Judgment of 18 December 1951, 27.

7 Daniel Thomas, *The Helsinki Effect: International Norms, Human Rights, and the Demise of Communism* (Princeton, NJ: Princeton University Press, 2001).

8 Rosalyn Higgins, "Policy Considerations and International Judicial Process," *International and Comparative Law Quarterly* 17, no. 1 (1968): 58–59.

9 The US Department of State, for example, listed fifty separate transactions and reports—often book length—completed and submitted to United Nations human rights treaty bodies to fulfill a variety of reporting requirements. See www.state.gov/j/drl/hr/treaties.

10 See Charlotte Ku and Harold K. Jacobson, "Conclusion: Toward a Mixed System of Democratic Accountability," in *Democratic Accountability and the Use of Force in International Law*, eds. Charlotte Ku and Harold K. Jacobson (Cambridge: Cambridge University Press, 2002), 349–383.

11 James N. Rosenau, *Turbulence in World Politics: A Theory of Change and Continuity* (Princeton, NJ: Princeton University Press, 1990), 195.

12 Hendrik Spruyt, *The Sovereign State and Its Competitors* (Princeton, NJ: Princeton University Press, 1994), 6.

13 Jonathan I. Charney, "Universal International Law," *American Journal of International Law* 87, no. 4 (1993): 529.

14 Ibid., 547.

15 David Held, *Democracy and the Global Order: From the Modern State to Cosmopolitan Governance* (Palo Alto, CA: Stanford University Press, 1995).

16 *The Prosecutor v. Omar Hassan Ahmad Al Bashir*, www.icc-cpi.int/menus/icc/situations%20and%20cases/situations/situation%20icc%200205/related%20cases/icc02050109/icc02050109?lan=en-GB.

17 José E. Alvarez, "The New Treaty-Makers," *Boston College of International and Comparative Law Review* 25, no. 2 (2002): 217.

18 Ibid., 223–232.

19 See Christiane E. Philipp, "The International Criminal Court—A Brief Introduction," in *Max Planck Yearbook of United Nations Law*, vol. 7, eds. A. von Bogdandy and R. Wolfrum (Amsterdam: Koninklijke Brill NV, 2003), 331–339.

20 Alvarez, "The New Treaty-Makers," 220.

21 Arthur Eyffinger, *The 1899 Hague Peace Conference: The Parliament of Man, the Federation of the World* (The Hague: Kluwer Law International, 1999).

22 Dinah Shelton, "Introduction: Law, Non-Law and the Problem of Soft Law," in *Commitment and Compliance: The Role of Non-Binding Norms in the International Legal System*, ed. Dinah Shelton (Oxford: Oxford University Press, 2000), 8.

23 See Michael G. Schechter, "Conclusions," in *United Nations-Sponsored World Conferences: Focus on Impact and Follow Up*, ed. Michael G. Schechter (Tokyo: United Nations University Press, 2001), 218–222.

24 Christine Chinkin, "Normative Development in the International Legal System," in *Commitment and Compliance: The Role of Non-Binding Norms in the International Legal System*, ed. Dinah Shelton (Oxford: Oxford University Press, 2000), 29.

25 Xinyuan Dai, *International Institutions and National Policies* (Cambridge: Cambridge University Press, 2007).

26 Ryan Goodman and Derek Jinks, *Socializing States: Promoting Human Rights Through International Law* (New York: Oxford University Press, 2013), 12.

27 See Goodman and Jinks, *Socializing States*, 58–60.

28 Christine Chinkin, "The Challenge of Soft Law: Development and Change in International Law," *International and Comparative Law Quarterly* 38, no. 4 (1989): 850–866.

29 See Isabella D. Bunn, "Global Advocacy for Corporate Accountability," *American University International Law Review* 19, no. 6 (2004): 1265–1306.

30 See Forest Stewardship Council United States, www.fscus.org.

31 Forest Stewardship Council International, *FSC Global Strategic Plan 2015–2020*, https://ic.fsc.org/en/fsc-global-strategic-plan-2015–2020.

32 Andrew Guzman, *How International Law Works* (Oxford: Oxford University Press, 2005).

33 See Richard L. Williamson, Jr., "International Regulation of Land Mines," in *Commitment and Compliance: The Role of Non-Binding Norms in the International Legal System*, ed. Dinah Shelton (Oxford: Oxford University Press, 2000), 505–521.

34 See Leo Gross, "The Peace of Westphalia, 1648–1948," *American Journal of International Law* 42, no. 1 (1948): 22.

35 See CSDMT as cited in Charlotte Ku, "Global Governance and the Changing Face of International Law," 2001 John W. Holmes Memorial Lecture, ACUNS Reports & Papers no. 2 (2001), 4.

36 See Louis Henkin, *International Law: Politics & Values* (Dordrecht: Martinus Nijhoff Publishers, 1995).

37 Vaughan Lowe, "The Politics of Law-Making," in *The Role of Law in International Politics*, ed. Michael Byers (Oxford: Oxford University Press, 2000), 212–221.

38 See International Court of Justice, Judgment of 25 September 1997, Gabcikovo-Nagymaros Project (Hungary/Slovkia), www.icj-cij.org/docket; Nico Schrijver, *Development without Destruction: The UN and Global Resource Management* (Bloomington and Indianapolis: Indiana University Press, 2010).

39 Lowe, "The Politics of Law-Making," 216.

40 See the class-action suit against the UN for starting the cholera epidemic in Haiti in 2010. See "UN Sued over Haiti Cholera Epidemic," *The Guardian* 9 October 2013, www.theguardian.com/world/2013/oct/09/un-sued-haiti-cholera-epidemic. See also actions taken to address accounts of sexual abuses committed by UN peacekeepers at un.org.apps/news/story.asp?NewsID=56854#.WS4oPy-cHs1.

41 UN, "Secretary-General's Bulletin on the Observance by United Nations Forces of International Humanitarian Law," UN document ST/SGB/1999/13, 6 August 1999, http://hrlibrary.umn.edu/instree/unobservance1999.pdf.

42 Terence C. Halliday and Gregory Shaffer, eds., *Transnational Legal Orders* (New York: Cambridge University Press, 2015), 16.

43 See Margaret E. Keck and Kathryn Sikkink, *Activists Beyond Borders: Advocacy Networks in International Politics* (Ithaca, NY: Cornell University Press, 1998), 213. See also Halliday and Shaffer, *Transnational Legal Orders.*

44 UN, International Law Commission, "Fragmentation of International Law: Difficulties Arising from the Diversification and Expansion of International Law," Report of the Study Group of the International Law Commission Finalized by Martti Koskenniemi, UN document A/CN.4/L/682, 13 April 2006, 10.

International organizations and the diffusion of power

Michael Barnett and Raymond Duvall

At the risk of simple-mindedness, there are two schools of thought regarding the relationship between international organizations (IOs) and the diffusion of power.[1] One school suggests that IOs are conservative organizations that are designed to freeze existing configurations of power. If they are doing their job, then they are not diffusing power. The other is that IOs are expected to pluralize power. The world is constituted by radical inequalities of power, with some states having an abundance and others a scarcity, and the United Nations and other IOs essential to global governance help to level the playing field by giving an opportunity for the weak to have a voice and neglected issues to be seen. Both camps are right: IOs can be defenders of the powerful and agents of reform. In fact, individual IOs such as the United Nations can function in both capacities. The UN Security Council, for instance, is a bastion of privilege reflecting the distribution of power in the international system seven decades ago, while many of the UN's specialized agencies seat NGOs from the Global South and powerful states at the same table.

This chapter offers one way of thinking about how IOs might be simultaneously reform-minded and defenders of the status quo. We begin by briefly discussing several prominent theories of international organizations and their depiction of the role that IO plays in the global order. While several of the best known theories see IOs as preserving the existing distribution of power and interests, constructivist and critical approaches to IOs offer several reasons why they might also be intended and accidental agents of inclusion and empowerment. Specifically, our discussion of the diffusion of power focuses on how IOs might potentially reshape the social relations that affect the ability of actors to control the conditions of their future. Simplistically asked: How might IOs further the conditions that allow actors to speak for themselves and to act in ways that further their interests? In order to provide a partial answer, we observe that the ability of IOs to have this intended effect can be accomplished via two different kinds of power—compulsory and institutional. Compulsory power highlights how IOs can take direct action to alter the conditions of existence for actors, for instance when peacekeeping forces defend the lives of civilians in the Congo. Institutional power emphasizes how IOs can work indirectly to guide action in directions that potentially improve the positions and ability of once marginalized and vulnerable actors; for instance, former UN Secretary-General Boutros Boutros-Ghali's *Agenda for Peace* drastically altered how the international community defined international peace and security and debated the kinds of tool that were needed for the post-Cold War system. These mechanisms of power highlight how IOs might be able to shape the conditions of existence of other actors, not whether that effect of their actions ultimately preserves or diffuses power. To fill in the blanks, we return to theories of IOs for guidance, because different theories make different claims regarding the likelihood of whether IOs will defend or assail the status quo. Our takeaway line is this: Modern IOs are often designed by (the most powerful) states to advance their interests, which can have the principal effect of reproducing the existing distribution of power; but IOs also have certain qualities and characteristics that can lead them to act in ways that improve the capacity of actors to shape the conditions of their fate.

Theories of IOs

The literature identifies two primary reasons why states create international organizations. The first is to help stabilize an international order and a set of political arrangements. Put more accurately, the most powerful states in the international system have the most say over the design and function of IOs; and since their primary goal is to preserve power, they are likely to design IOs as instruments of their foreign policy goals, ensuring that they can block action that they perceive to be counter to their interests. In this view, most closely associated with realist international relations theory, IOs are accomplices of powerful states and serve an essential function in freezing the existing international order, defending the privileges of the powerful, and making sure that the weak continue to suffer what they must. Specifically, the most powerful states decide which IOs are created, what they are, how they make decisions, and how they operate. In order to ensure their dominance, powerful states constrain IOs in various ways, including making them dependent on states for financing and establishing decision-making procedures that give powerful states preferential treatment. If we want to know what IOs do, we should look to what the most powerful states allow and want them to do.

The second reason, found in institutionalist theories, offers a slightly less severe but nonetheless rather button-down view. These approaches argue that states create institutions to enhance the prospects of cooperation, overcome problems associated with collective choice, and increase individual and collective wellbeing. In other words, states have an interest in creating the conditions for cooperation and mutual welfare gains, and institutions are invaluable in that regard. Institutionalized cooperation is no guarantee that all will benefit equally. In fact, the most powerful states are likely to benefit more than the least powerful, with the important consequence that institutions might well be responsible for widening existing asymmetries of power. For all their disagreements regarding whether IOs matter, realists and institutionalists largely concur that IOs are either conservatives or compassionate conservatives, but in either case they are largely sympathetic to (or captured by) the existing distribution of power. Radical theories of international organizations, including Marxist approaches, also see IOs as defenders of privilege, although in most analyses the real beneficiaries are not states but rather elites or dominant classes at the expense of workers, migrants, peasants—that is, most of the world's population. In general, these approaches give little reason for hope that IOs provide the have-nots of the world with the ability to improve the conditions that shape their lives as they see fit.

Yet other schools of thought can imagine IOs not just as defenders of the *ancien régime* but also as levelers of privilege. Both constructivism and critical theory shift attention away from interests toward culture, norms, ideas, rules, and discourse, demonstrating that the "social" features of life play a primary role in shaping how the world is understood, how actors understand themselves and others, and what sorts of practices and arrangements are considered legitimate.

In so doing, they make three valuable moves, which combine to generate a more nuanced understanding of the simultaneously conservative and reformist tendencies of IOs. First, these theories move us away from actors and toward underlying structures, thus enabling us to better understand how the already existing global culture shapes what IOs are and what they do. In this respect, they are like Marxist theories, but with an important difference: Whereas Marxist theories typically reduce the underlying structure to economics and property relations, constructivist and critical theories are more attentive to the presence of multiple, and not always consistent, cultural fragments. For instance, important elements of contemporary global culture include liberalism, rationality, and technocracy.

Second, the presence of these overlapping and sometimes contradictory cultures will give IOs relative autonomy. In other words, it is not accurate to argue that IOs are merely playthings of states; or to claim that IOs are free to do as they will. IOs, like most actors, have some relative autonomy. But the fact that they have some relative autonomy does not tell us what they will do with that autonomy. They might use their relative autonomy to act in ways that are consistent with the underlying rules of the game, or they might use their autonomy to challenge those rules.

Third, constructivist and critical approaches to the study of IOs point to two culturally inscribed reasons why they might, however unwittingly, diffuse power. To begin with, IOs seek legitimacy. In many respects, legitimacy is the IO's fuel and currency of power. Because IOs are viewed as legitimate, member states are willing to support IO activities and rely on the resulting legitimacy to persuade other states and non-state actors to defer to their decisions. In short, IOs will be effective, and others will defer to them, to the extent that they and their decisions are viewed as legitimate. Legitimacy has procedural and substantive dimensions. Procedural legitimacy refers to the process by which decisions are made. Although there are lots of ways to make decisions, in contemporary affairs modern governance is seen as legitimate to the extent that it operates according to basic principles of fairness and rationality. While great powers might establish IOs to reflect their interests, to the extent that international organizations are viewed as their instrument they may suffer a deficit of fairness and lose legitimacy in the eyes of many. A consequence of this "unmasking" is that it will become more difficult for powerful states to rule without coercion. IOs, therefore, need to appear to be inclusive rather than exclusive, which often means practicing the principles they preach and operating in subtle ways that level power.

IOs are valued to the extent that they operate with efficiency, impartiality, and objectivity, values that are prized in all modern organizations. Although IOs are often a far cry from the idealized image of a well-oiled machine, they aspire to have various qualities that are associated with the best features of bureaucracy: Control on the basis of expert knowledge; the division of the organization into spheres of competence and specialization; the establishment of procedures that standardize responses to the environment; and the creation of a decision process that is driven not by politics but rather by the objective application of rules in a fair-minded way. These organizing principles are technical and political. The rise of the bureaucratic ideal in the nineteenth century was seen as a way of removing existing advantages and power because decisions would now be made on rational, objective criteria and not on the basis of who has influence and connections. In general, IOs that tip their hand to the principles of fairness and rationality are less likely to include "who wins and who loses" as defining criteria of their decision-making procedures.

IOs also need substantive legitimacy. That is, their decisions need to be seen as broadly consistent with the values of the community. Substantively many of these values have a decidedly liberal quality, which brings us to a second factor that potentially pluralizes power. The contemporary global order has a liberal character; and IOs are constituted by that order, which contains a paradox that is central to understanding IOs and their relationship to processes of diffusion. The liberal states that shape the existing world order and its defining institutions imprint that order on the identity and interests of existing international organizations. In other words, many IOs have a defining liberal quality, and this characteristic is likely to lead them to act in ways that protect and preserve the existing liberal order. Yet some of liberalism's values also provide opportunities to level existing power inequalities.

IOs, in the liberal view, are valued because they help to bring about liberal progress—that is, they nurture development, security, justice, and protect individual autonomy. Liberalism is characterized by a concern with the concentration of power and the need to protect the liberal rights of individuals, and these concerns have translated into a strong preference for institutions that honor the rule of law, democracy, and markets. Accordingly, liberal institutions operate in ways that are intended, at least nominally, to ensure individual freedoms. These virtues are among the reasons why liberals have been the most ardent and longstanding champions of IOs. Importantly, many IOs are established not only to protect the interests of the most powerful states but also to help diffuse values that can constrain their ability to act with arbitrary power. Liberally oriented IOs often work to ensure that even small and weak states have their interests represented in international policy discussions (but still acceptable to a liberal world order) and to promote the establishment of markets, democracy and human rights. In general, IOs often oppose the old order; they are champions of those whose voices might otherwise not be heard; and they are promoters of global and domestic institutions that advance equality and inclusion.

In sum, because international organizations are frequently created by powerful states to preserve their interests, the reasonable expectation is that they will serve the status quo and work against any sort of redistribution, diffusion, or pluralization of power. Yet because IOs require legitimacy to be effective, because they are generally advocates of a liberal world view, and because they are supposed to operate according to rule-governed principles, they also can be expected to work against the status quo and toward the conditions that enable states and non-state actors to have a greater say over their lives. IOs not only demonstrate both tendencies, but individual IOs are often at war within themselves, simultaneously championing and critiquing the power distributions underlying the existing world order.

Power and IOs

Power is the production, in and through social relations, of effects on actors that shape their capacity to control their fate. This definition is broader than the one favored by international relations theorists, which is normally taken to be the ability of A to get B to do something it would rather not do. In that standard approach, generally associated with realist international relations theory, power is largely limited to how one state is able to use resources to force another state to do something against its will.

Yet power is not only overt; it can be covert as well. We inhabit structures, institutions, and other social spaces that limit our ability to influence decisions that matter to us. They do so through formal politics and informal governance. For instance, one way institutions exercise power is by keeping items off the agenda. If they are off the agenda, they cannot be discussed. And if they cannot be discussed, then those who care about them have been effectively silenced and disempowered.

Power not only shapes what we can do but also how we see the world, how we see ourselves, how we define our interests, and what we believe is possible and even qualifies as a problem to be addressed. In other words, the effects of power are evident not only in terms of acting but also in terms of constituting, comprehending, and interpreting the world. Democracy might be seen as the great leveler of power, but the rising rates of inequality and disenfranchisement worldwide suggest that the marginalized members of society invariably have a hard time making their voices heard. We inhabit structures, such as capitalism, replete with mechanisms that help to produce the rich and poor, and convince the poor that this system of inequality is in their interest. We also exist in a world in which various kinds of discourse— including racism, civilization, and gender—have lasting effects on the identity, interests, and practices of everyone involved. The standard realist approach articulates only one way to conceptualize how our ability to shape our future is limited; we need to imagine the existence of other kinds of global relations that can be disempowering or empowering.

In a previous effort to demonstrate the many ways power exists in international affairs, we defined power as premised on two analytical dimensions: The kinds of social relation through which power works (in relations of interaction or in social relations of constitution); and the specificity of social relations through which effects are produced (specific/direct or diffuse/indirect). These distinctions draw our attention to the question of whether power operates through actions (e.g., the ability by some actors to keep issues off the agenda) or structures (e.g., the underlying distribution of wealth that allocates privilege and vulnerability); or whether these effects are easily traceable to an identifiable source (e.g., the person holding the gun) or diffuse and not traceable to an identifiable source (e.g., discourses of civilization that produce the categories of civilized and uncivilized). We used these different analytical dimensions (actions and structure; direct and diffuse) to generate four concepts of power: Compulsory, institutional, structural, and productive. These different conceptualizations provide different answers to the fundamental question: In what respects are actors able to control their own fate, and how is that ability limited or enhanced through social relations with others?

To explore how IOs diffuse power entails situating IOs in relationship to these different kinds of power, and examining how they might be directly and indirectly implicated in altering the social relations that enhance the ability of actors to control their fate. Simply put, how do IOs enable or constrain the ability of actors to shape the circumstances of their lives? Compulsory, institutional, structural, and productive power point to different mechanisms whereby these effects are accomplished—with the first two pointing to interactions and the last two to structures. Although all four kinds of power are relevant to this discussion, we focus on compulsory and institutional power, arguably the most important forms through which IOs affect the diffusion or concentration of power.

Compulsory power

This first and most infamous kind of power concerns a situation in which one actor behaves in a way that forces another actor to do something that the latter does not believe is in its interests. Quite often, this form of power is written as the ability of A to get B to do something that B would not do otherwise. *Intentionality* is often treated as an important element of this form of power. What counts is that A wants B to alter its actions in a particular direction. Although sympathetic to this formulation, we want to insist that compulsory power also exists even without intentionality on the part of A. When states use force, people get killed. Some of these people are intended, but quite a few are unintended, euphemistically known as "collateral damage." Unintended does not make it any less compulsory, as we define it. What this suggests is that perhaps the best way to assess the existence of power is from those on the receiving and not the giving end. Another characteristic of compulsory power is a *conflict* of desires to the extent that B now feels compelled to alter its behavior. A and B want different outcomes, and B loses. Three, A is successful because it has material and ideational *resources* at its disposal that lead B to alter its actions. Scandinavian countries arguably are able to influence global outcomes because they have a perceived quality of character and not because these thinly populated countries are closer to the Arctic and go months without daylight. Nongovernmental organizations (NGOs) use normative resources to compel targeted states to alter their policies through a strategy of "naming and shaming."

IOs exhibit compulsory power if their actions directly shape the circumstances of another, if there is a conflict between what the IO wants and what the other actor wants, and if a particular IO's material and ideational resources account for the change in circumstances and actions of another. This is not an uncommon occurrence. IOs often have interests that are aligned against those of another state or non-state actor, and they often attempt to deploy material and ideational resources to compel a target actor to change its ways.

Although IOs might not have the same recourse to material resources as states, they are not without these methods of persuasion. International financial institutions such as the World Bank and the International Monetary Fund (IMF) are able to use their capital to force borrowing states to adopt "best practices," slash budgets, and redirect economic resources. The Office of the UN High Commissioner for Refugees (UNHCR) can shape the life chances of refugees and other displaced peoples by giving them strong incentives to return home by decreasing their rations. Peacekeeping troops, at times, use force to deter would-be violators of the ceasefire and protect civilians from gangs and thugs. Yet when IOs do exercise compulsory power, it is often through symbolic and normative resources rather than material ones. Because of its administrative and bureaucratic role, UNHCR has the power to determine who gets legal protection as a refugee and who does not. The International Criminal Court (ICC) has the power to indict government officials, but because this capacity is not backed by any real enforcement mechanisms, the primary effect is to create global *personae non grata*. But the fact that the ICC lacks compulsory power does not mean it is absent power, for the very ability to create such legal and political categories can have powerful effects, as we will now see.

Institutional power

Institutional power highlights how actors are able to guide, steer, and constrain the actions and circumstances of others through the rules that exist in structural positional differences in formal and informal institutions. Institutional power differs from compulsory power in various ways, but two are most important for this discussion. Whereas compulsory power entails the direct control of one actor over the conditions and actions of another, institutional power reflects *indirect* control. Specifically, the conceptual focus is on the formal and informal institutions that mediate between A and B. Working through the rules and procedures that define those institutions, A can guide, steer, and constrain the actions (or non-actions) and conditions of existence of others. Institutions are nothing if not bundles of rules that specify who is admitted to the club, who can talk, whose voice carries weight and counts, and what can be discussed and when. While often the rules were originally formulated by those with the most compulsory power, few institutions remain the instrument of a single actor or coalition. It is certainly possible that a dominant actor maintains total control over an institution. If so, then it is arguably best to conceptualize that institution as possessed by the actor, and with its compulsory power. But rarely is the institution completely dominated by one actor. Instead, most institutions have some independence from even the most specific resource-laden actors; rules that can take on a life of their own; and even their own independent institutional identity and range of action to the point of frustrating their original creators.

Second, institutional power also highlights the sometimes hidden power at work even without an obvious struggle between two actors. Institutional power considers how power can operate *indirectly*. Compulsory power looks for a chain of events like: "Do it!" "No." "If you don't, we will deny you what you need." "OK." But institutional power acknowledges the existence of power even when there is no observable action, and when power works through institutions that have the effect of obscuring its presence. Compulsory power looks for dogs that bark and bite. But rules, for instance, can create the proverbial dogs that do not bark but nevertheless have a chilling effect and advantage some and disadvantage others. Rules for determining what is on the agenda, for example, mean that some topics are never discussed. There are lots of international crises, but the great powers determine which ones are discussed by the Security Council. Rules also determine who gets to discuss an issue. Only states can be members of the UN. While other international organizations have been more welcoming of NGOs, the United Nations too is making more room for civil society and the private sector. Such venues have enabled disadvantaged populations to ensure that the issues that they care about—including human rights—are discussed. There are rules to determine when votes are cast and whose vote counts. There are voting procedures, including weighted voting and the existence of veto power reserved for special states. This institutional context, moreover, lingers into the future, thus constraining action in ways that might not have been intended but nevertheless limit choice and shape results. Accordingly, even those institutions that are established for the ostensible purpose of producing cooperation create winners and losers and even stack the deck so that some actors potentially win all the time.

IOs often exhibit this form of power, possessing the formal and informal capacity to determine the agenda at forums, meetings, and conferences. This capacity gives them a substantial role in determining what is and is not discussed. The UN secretary-general, for instance, frequently structures the options for particular peacekeeping operations and therefore establishes the parameters of Security Council deliberations. Secretary-General Kofi Annan's decision to make humanitarian intervention a defining theme of his 1999 address to the General Assembly had a decisive impact on all subsequent discussions; and arguably it helped pave the way for the subsequent development of the doctrine of the responsibility to protect. European Union (EU) officials are renowned for possessing this sort of influence. UNHCR and World Bank or IMF officials are directly involved in drawing up the agenda for meetings. In this significant way, IO staff can help to orient discussions and actions in some directions and away from others.

Although IOs might use material resources to have these kinds of effect, it is their position as authorities and use of symbolic resources such as frames that give them the ability to steer action in some directions and away from others. As Michael Barnett and Martha Finnemore have argued, IOs are both of authority and in authority.[2] In addition to authority delegated from states, IOs have authority because they embody rational–legal principles that modern societies value and that are identified with liberal values viewed as legitimate and "progressive." There are many different kinds of authority in social relations, and many organizations are viewed as authorities because they are seen as experts of their domain. One important reason why states create bureaucracies is that states want important social tasks to be executed by individuals with detailed, specialized knowledge. Derived from training or experience, such knowledge persuades us to confer on experts, and the bureaucracies that house them, the power to make judgments and solve problems. Deployment of specialized knowledge is central to the very rational–legal authority which constitutes bureaucracy in the first place since what makes such authority rational is, at least in part, the use of socially recognized relevant knowledge to carry out tasks.

Expertise thus makes IOs authoritative and also shapes their behavior. Just as those organizations authorized by a moral principle must serve that principle and make their actions consistent to remain legitimate and authoritative, so too IOs with authorized expertise must serve that specialized knowledge and ensure that their actions are consistent with it. The IMF cannot authoritatively propose policies beyond those supported by the economic knowledge that its staff deploys. Professional training, norms, and occupational cultures strongly shape the way in which experts view the world. They influence what problems are visible to staff and what range of solutions are entertained. Expert authority also creates the appearance of de-politicization. By emphasizing the "objective" nature of their knowledge, international organizations are able to present themselves as technocrats whose advice is unaffected by partisan squabbles. The greater the appearance of de-politicization, the greater the power of the expertise.

IOs, like all other actors using rhetoric to shape the behavior of others, can and do use a variety of techniques for this purpose. They may "frame" issues in particular ways so that desired choices seem particularly compelling, or so that the sanctions and penalties associated with particular policies are excessively high. They may manipulate emotions of decision makers and publics, creating empathy for landmine victims, refugees, and genocide survivors. They may use information strategically, gathering some kinds of information but not others. They may manipulate audiences strategically, inviting or including only some participants in their bureaucratic processes—for instance, bankers not peasants sit at financial and diplomatic high tables.

IOs also guide behavior through classificatory practices. An elementary feature of bureaucracies is that they classify and organize information and knowledge. Such a process is a form of power because it constitutes a way of "making, ordering, and knowing social worlds" by "mov[ing] persons among social categories or by inventing and applying such categories."[3] The ability to classify objects, to shift their very definition and identity, is one of the bureaucracy's greatest sources of power. This power is frequently treated by the objects of that power as accomplished through caprice and without regard to their circumstances, but it is legitimated and justified by bureaucrats with reference to any number of rules and regulations. The IMF has a particular way of categorizing economies and determining whether they are on the "right track," defined in terms of their capital accounts, balance of payments, budget deficits, and reserves. To be categorized as not "on track" can have massive detrimental consequences for external financing at reasonable rates, access to IMF funds, and conditionality. The world is filled with individuals who have either been forced or chosen to flee their homes, and the UNHCR, working with laws that have been passed by states, imposes a classification scheme that distinguishes between refugees, migrants, and internally displaced persons. Similarly, classification of a conflict as a "civil war" or "genocide" triggers one set of responses by international actors rather than another. The important point is that IOs can have institutional power that operates indirectly because it can help shift how we make sense of the world, what we count as a problem, and how a problem is understood.

Not only do IOs help identify problems, but they also help solve them by crafting particular solutions and persuading others to accept them. Identifying a particular solution from a range of options is consequential and an important exercise of power. The next logical step is to identify a set of actors that should take responsibility for implementing the solution. Authorities, including IOs, once again step into the breach as they are viewed as qualified to manage these solutions to already identified problems.

Diffusing power

We have argued that IOs can be relatively autonomous actors that can directly and indirectly shape the conditions of existence for other actors, and that exhibit these effects through compulsory or institutional power. Moreover, because of their organizational characteristics (both internally and in their relationship to states), they are more likely to exhibit institutional than compulsory power. These claims, however, say nothing about the substance of their actions—that is, whether they preserve the existing distribution of power or attempt to diffuse the underlying conditions that enable actors to determine their fates. The earlier discussion of theories of IOs can help address this issue. To repeat, realist, institutionalist, and Marxist theories assume that IOs will act in ways that are intended to preserve the existing distribution of privileges. Realists see IOs as the playthings of states and Marxists as instruments of capitalism; and even institutionalists, who grant that IO staff have some relative autonomy and discretion, believe that IOs are limited in their ability or desire to effect real change.

Critical and constructivist theories acknowledge that IOs mainly are defenders of the status quo, but they also provide theoretical and conceptual grounds for observing appreciable independence in the attempt to provide greater equality of opportunities for other actors. This dynamic results not only because these theories are better able to imagine IOs as relatively independent actors, but also because they recognize that IOs are actors that are potentially constituted by broader global cultural forces, such as liberalism and rationalism, and by the desire to be seen as legitimate by states and non-state actors. IOs constituted by global liberalism are defenders of an international order that contains the ingredients for the diffusion of power. Most IOs express a strong commitment to the existing liberal international order and the desire to spread, defend, and protect liberalism's values. They are committed to the existing order, whose values include equality, liberty, and autonomy. These are values that create a strong cultural disposition for institutions of the rule of law, democracy, and markets. Such institutions are interested in preserving the existing order but whose individualism nevertheless is designed (at least rhetorically and sometimes actually) to ensure that basic political rights are observed; and the commitment to rights has the potential of creating the conditions for individuals to at least have some measure of self-determination even if that disrupts the status quo.

IOs are shaped not only by the liberal world order but also by a commitment to basic principles of rationality. IOs are constituted by rules, which are designed to standardize the world and a particular IO's response to it; ensure a continuity and consistency in action; divide the organization into areas of competence and specialization to improve the efficiency and predictability of action; and minimize the costs of action and maximize the benefits. The rules associated with rationality are intended to be objective. Unlike the rules of non-rational organizations (such as premodern bureaucracies), the rules are supposed to treat everyone equally because all humans are juridically equal—again, liberalism is important. IOs, like all modern bureaucracies, are not supposed to have one set of rules for the powerful and another for the powerless. Fair is fair. Of course, gaps invariably exist between theory and reality, but the theory can have a disciplinary effect. These rules also are intended to remove politics from decision making. Rather than make decisions based on who is likely to win and who is likely to lose, rules are applied on the basis of technical criteria. Although such de-politicization does not automatically mean that the powerless will always be heard, or be heard in the same way as the powerful, at least it gives them a fighting chance. Because liberalism and rationality, in short, are supposed to dilute power and politics, they potentially help diffuse power. To the extent that IO staff see these values as their own, they may act accordingly.

Even if not all IO staff are liberal bureaucrats, the desire for legitimacy is likely to encourage them to at least play the role. The ability of IOs to survive and be effective is dependent on their legitimacy. In the modern international order, their legitimacy is dependent on their being seen as acting on behalf of the international community of states, which gives them an incentive, in turn, to operate according to rules that can be traced to principles and not politics. These rules are not only substantive but also procedural. IOs are supposed to be moving toward an inclusive decision-making process—although they may not always do so—making decisions on the basis of objective knowledge and expertise, and orienting themselves toward values that favor all rather than some.

Conclusion

This chapter has briefly explored how compulsory and institutional power illuminate the relationship between IOs and the diffusion of power. We repeat three earlier items. IOs are two-faced: They can either preserve or diffuse power, altering the underlying social relations that limit or enhance the ability of actors to control the circumstances of their lives. They also are relatively autonomous. They can be linked to the diffusion and preservation of power in and through their position in existing structures, but they also can be linked to these effects through their actions.

The worldwide cultural values of democracy and technocracy can help diffuse power, but we want to close with a word of warning: These values can operate at cross-purposes. A classic dilemma of modern liberal governance is the presumed tradeoff between democracy and technocracy. In democracy (or the rule of the people), there is deference to respect the "general will," the "majority," and the "will of the people" on various grounds, including autonomy, liberty, and the belief that the people know best. In technocracy (or the rule of experts), there is deference to those who have specific knowledge. The immediate implication is that the rule of experts can be antidemocratic. Experts are not expected to always respect the preferences of the people, but instead they are supposed to use their presumably objective judgment. In these and other instances, outsiders feel justified in ignoring or dismissing the stated needs of the "people." For instance, peacebuilders often argue that they cannot practice the democracy that they preach because war-torn societies do not have the institutions to enable them to debate and aggregate preferences, and because listening to the "people" might mean privileging the powerful and thus reproducing existing societal inequalities. This suggests the possibility that moral progress might depend not on the revolutionary character of the "people" but rather on the role of morally minded elites. Regardless of whether one thinks that elitism has its positive qualities, it is indisputably antidemocratic. In the race between technocracy and democracy, arguably technocracy seems to be winning. If so, IOs might be diffusing and conserving power—for themselves.

By the same token, if democracy continues to express itself in many states as nationalist-populist campaigns to shield themselves from an integrated international order, then IOs might become largely irrelevant to future discussions of the conservation and diffusion of power in a much changed global governance. Growing nationalism and populism means that states will be much more suspect about the presumed benefits of globalization; will be much more suspicious of distant bureaucracies that pledge fealty to rules rather than people; will question the legitimacy of IOs and the world they represent; and might begin to deny them the necessary resources to operate. In other words, the last half century has unleashed various societal, state, and transnational forces that have made IOs critical players in global governance, we might be entering a new chapter.

Additional reading

Michael Barnett and Raymond Duvall, eds., *Power in Global Governance* (Cambridge and New York: Cambridge University Press, 2004).

Michael Barnett and Martha Finnemore, *Rules for the World: International Organizations in World Politics* (Ithaca, NY: Cornell University Press, 2004).

Iver Neumann and Ole Jacob Sending, *Governing the Global Polity: Practice, Mentality, and Rationality* (Ann Arbor: University of Michigan Press, 2010).

Thomas G. Weiss and Ramesh Thakur, *Global Governance and the UN: An Unfinished Journey* (Bloomington: Indiana University Press, 2010).

Notes

1   This chapter relies heavily on previous work by Michael Barnett and Raymond Duvall, "Power in International Politics," *International Organization* 59, no. 1 (2005): 39–75, and Michael Barnett and Martha Finnemore, "The Power of Liberal International Organizations," in *Power in Global Governance*, eds. Michael Barnett and Raymond Duvall (Cambridge: Cambridge University Press, 2004), 161–184.

2   Michael Barnett and Martha Finnemore, *Rules for the World: International Organizations in World Politics* (Ithaca, NY: Cornell University Press, 2004).

3   Don Handelman, "Comment," *Current Anthropology* 36, no. 2 (1995): 280–281.

CONTENTS

The diffusion of authority

David Held

This chapter examines the impact of the growth of multilateral and transnational governance on sovereignty and the diffusion of political authority.[1] It begins by exploring the legacy of World War II and the building of the UN system. The rise of intergovernmentalism and transnational governance arrangements are examined, followed by an assessment of some of the leading changes in the postwar global politics landscape. These issues are explored in greater depth across two cases: Security and the environment. The chapter concludes by drawing together the threads of the discussion.

World War II and the building of the UN system

World War II created conflict and violence on a scale that had never been witnessed before, and was an experience that drastically reshaped the global order. As Hobsbawm put it, World War II was a "global human catastrophe."[2] The scale of the war effort, of destruction and of human suffering, was historically unprecedented. As war embraced Europe and East Asia, military hostilities raged across almost every single continent and ocean, excepting Latin America and southern Africa. Few of those states not engaged directly or indirectly in military combat could effectively remain neutral, since supplying the war effort of both the Axis (Germany, Italy, and Japan) and the Allied powers (United States, United Kingdom, and France) required extensive sourcing. As William McNeill notes, "transnational organization for war . . . achieved a fuller and far more effective expression during the Second World War than ever before".[3] But one of the most profound consequences of the war was the resultant transformation in the structure of world power. The year 1945 marked the end of Europe's global hegemony and confirmed the United States and the Soviet

Union as global superpowers. This structural transformation heralded dramatic consequences for the pattern of postwar global political and security relations.

Against this backdrop, the UN's mandate could not be clearer. Article 1 of its Charter explicitly states that the purpose of the UN is to "maintain international peace and security, and to that end: to take effective collective measures for the prevention and removal of threats to the peace." Moreover, that same article stresses that peace would be sought and protected through principles of international law. It concludes with the position that the UN is to be "a centre for harmonizing the actions of nations in the attainment of these common ends." This is particularly important for the purposes of this chapter since it speaks to the deliberate, facilitated interdependence that was sought by the UN. Where preceding efforts failed (e.g., the League of Nations), the UN aimed for inclusive buy-in from world powers in order to maintain global peace and security. Through centralized coordination and cooperation, the UN created mechanisms that established mutual accountability between states, governed by growing and increasingly entrenched principles of international law. Moreover, the focus on principles of international law emphasized the significance of the formal institutionalization of such prevention and mitigation mechanisms. By facilitating integration in this way, the UN sought to replace the tendency toward unilateral military action with collective action that could still preserve central aspects of state sovereignty. The UN Charter's Article 2 enshrined state sovereignty, but it also planted the seeds of qualification and conditionality; seeds that have grown in certain respects over the last seven decades such that sovereignty is increasingly understood as legitimate, or rightful, authority; an authority that is qualified by human rights and humanitarian principles, as well as both recognized and regulated by the international community of states.

The titanic struggles of World Wars I and II led to a growing acknowledgment that the nature and process of global governance (the manner in which global actors, ranging from states to multinational corporations and civil society organizations, cooperate formally and informally on global collective action problems) would have to change if the most extreme forms of violence against humanity were to be outlawed, and the growing interconnectedness and interdependence of countries recognized. Slowly, the subject, scope, and very sources of the Westphalian conception of international regulation, particularly its conception of international law, were all called into question.[4] The image of international regulation projected by the UN Charter (and related documents) was one of "states still jealously 'sovereign'" but now linked together in "a myriad of relations [sic]"; under pressure to resolve disagreements by peaceful means and according to legal criteria; subject in principle to tight restrictions on the resort to force; and constrained to observe "certain standards" with regard to the treatment of all persons in their territory, including their own citizens.[5] Of course, how restrictive the provisions of the Charter have been to states, and to what extent they have been actually operationalized, remain important issues.

The rise of intergovernmentalism and transnationalism

It is commonplace to criticize the UN for the many ways in which it and the member states that created it have fallen short of its ideals. Yet it would be utterly mistaken to underestimate the successes wrought by the UN system overall and the geopolitical stability that followed its foundation. The decades after World War II were marked by peace between the great powers, although there were many proxy wars fought out in the Global South. This relative stability created the conditions for what now can be recognized as the almost unprecedented period of prosperity that characterized the 1950s onward.[6] The UN is central to this story, although it is by no means the only important institutional innovation of the postwar settlement. A year prior to the founding of the UN, the Bretton Woods institutions were established in an effort to foster economic cooperation and a prosperous global economy: The International Monetary Fund (IMF) and the World Bank. The former focused on exchange rate stability and balance-of-payments assistance, the latter on long-term economic development. A sister, but not constitutionally related, institution, the General Agreement on Tariffs and Trade (GATT), which in 1995 became the World Trade Organization (WTO), committed countries to open their borders to foreign trade. All of these institutions lay at the heart of what we now call postwar "economic globalization"—the growing enmeshment of economies across the world through trade, finance, and foreign direct investment and a slew of policies that facilitate economic interdependence. While the economic record of the postwar years varies by country, many experienced significant economic growth and living standards rose rapidly across large parts of the world. It was not just the West that was redefined by these developments; a global division of labor emerged that linked economic flows across large swathes of the world. In the wake of these changes, the world began, slowly at first, but later more rapidly to shift—from a bipolar toward a multipolar structure. By the late 1980s a variety of East Asian countries were beginning to grow at an unprecedented speed, and by the late 1990s countries such as China, India, and Brazil had gained significant economic momentum, a process that continues to this day.

The geopolitical stability engendered throughout the postwar years was a precondition for economic globalization, which subsequently transformed the way business and commerce were organized. Markets that were first and foremost domestic networks increasingly took on global dimensions. National economies became heavily enmeshed in the global system of production and exchange. Multinational corporations, many of which came to enjoy turnovers that dwarfed the gross domestic product (GDP) of even medium sized countries, expanded across the globe. Financial markets exploded into a world of twenty-four-hour trading, aided by competition between states eager to attract increasingly mobile capital flows. Economic globalization, with all its benefits and costs, winners and losers, came to embrace all regions and continents, and global interdependence deepened to a hitherto unknown degree.[7]

Meanwhile, international cooperation proceeded at an impressive pace. Whereas once participation in the multilateral order was sporadic and tenuous, it became both more entrenched and regularized. The most obvious illustration of this is the rapid emergence of diverse multilateral organizations and transnational agencies. New forms of multilateral and global politics became established, involving states, intergovernmental organizations (IGOs), international nongovernmental organizations (INGOs), and a wide variety of pressure groups. The numbers of active IGOs and INGOs increased exponentially. There was substantial growth in the number of international treaties in force, as well as the number of international regimes, formal and informal, altering the political and legal context in which states operated. To this dense web of mechanisms of coordination and collaboration can be added the routine meetings and activities of the key international policymaking bodies, including not only the UN and Bretton Woods organizations, but also the various G-groups (the G-5, Group-7, G-8, Group-20, among others). Whereas in the middle of the nineteenth century there were just one or two interstate conferences or congresses per annum, the numbers increased to the many thousands each year.[8] Accordingly, states became enmeshed in an array of global governance systems and arrangements.

At the same time, new kinds of institutional arrangement have emerged alongside formal intergovernmental bodies. Networks of ostensibly "domestic" government officials now link with their peers across borders.[9] Different kinds of actor, public and private, form partnerships with each other to tackle issues of mutual concern. Moreover, purely private actors have created an array of their own governance institutions, ranging from voluntary regulations to private arbitral tribunals.[10] In some ways, these new institutions reveal the adaptability and flexibility of global governance. But they also face, as the sections below show, significant limitations.

As forums for collaboration and engagement multiplied, they facilitated direct links between world powers, regardless of how explosive the rhetoric between them sometimes became, and opened the door for peripheral states to participate in the global order. Significantly, however, these institutions also embedded in their infrastructures and *modus operandi* the privileged positions of the 1945 victors. This was, arguably, a compromise needed to give incentives for great powers to participate in the new multilateral order.

The changed landscape of global politics

A number of trends can be identified within the changed landscape of world politics. First, there has been a general trend of integration between national and international political arenas.[11] The relationship between national governments and international bodies is not unilinear, but rather overlapping and reflexive to pressures coming from all sides (domestic constituencies, IGOs, global civil society, and so on). The two distinct spheres of traditional politics—national and international—have merged in some key respects. From global trade rules to intellectual property rights, from the global financial crisis to climate change, issues are posed for all levels of politics. A significant variety of institutional arrangements have been created in response to this trend, and this has included substantial innovation and change resulting in diverse forms of multi-actor, multisector, and multilevel governance.

However, the integration of national and international politics has also had an impact on our understanding of politics. The manner in which politics is conceived in the contemporary world can no longer be focused only on realist state-centric modes of analysis. While this shift in perception has had its critics, the realities of politics today give little support for seeing the nature and form of global governance through the lens of the unitary state acting alone, despite the resilience of great power politics. The greatest issues now confronting the world are not delineated and distributed neatly along national boundaries, and neither is the debate on how to solve them. The diffusion and growth of transborder governance arrangements reflect this integration of politics in significant ways. Any other starting point simplifies the character of the form and nature of global politics and masks the nature of political relationships in the contemporary world.

A second trend that can be observed since 1945 is the emergence of powerful non-state actors in the development of transborder governance. Non-state actors such as INGOs, multinational corporations (MNCs), and even individuals have always been active agents in political debate, but the manner in which they influence international politics has changed in significant ways. While these actors had varying degrees of influence in international politics in earlier periods, their impact came largely through lobbying their national governments. In this mode of political influence, non-state actors aggregate and articulate domestic interests to the state, shaping the preferences of a state, which in turn determine the state's behavior in international politics.

Although the direct relationship between non-state actors and states remains an important link for political participation, non-state actors now also influence international politics directly.[12] Through direct lobbying of global governance bodies, non-state actors shape political debate internationally, in turn impacting on the behavior of states from above and below. The process that led to the Ottawa Treaty (concerning the ban of landmines) is perhaps the most prominent example of non-state actors participating in security governance with marked success.[13] This trend in general is strongest, however, in environmental governance, where INGOs have become such important actors that their influence has been called "functionally equivalent to diplomats" since they perform "many of the same functions as state delegates," such as interest aggregation and articulation, negotiation, and submitting policy recommendations.[14] The emergence of non-state actors certainly creates a more complex governance system than one comprised of traditional principal–agent relationships between states and purely intergovernmental organizations. This can pose potential problems of governance fragmentation, but it also broadens the platform for political deliberation and debate.[15]

Third, there has been a shift in how regulation and governance are enforced. The diverse forms of global governance produce equally diverse regulation that is intended to shape the behavior of states. This requires, first and foremost, the participation of states in regulatory structures, but it also requires that states comply with the result of negotiations even if it is against their own self-interest. Traditionally, compliance in international agreements is linked to the possibility of punitive measures (i.e., sanctions) that penalize violators in order to ensure appropriate conduct. Increasingly, however, trends can be detected that ensure that rules are enforced through alternative means such as voluntary-based arrangements and initiatives, as well as international standards that are adhered to by actors because of their reputational and coordinative effects.[16]

Norm diffusion and capacity building can be an even more powerful tool for behavioral change than punitive measures.[17] This approach seeks to do more than just punish violators by building the capacity and incentives for actors to comply with established international standards. Institutions such as the UN Global Compact and the International Network for Environmental Compliance and Enforcement are good examples of the voluntary and informal regulation that is growing in global governance bodies.[18] These innovations in compliance schemes are positive steps in developing more effective governance; they indicate a range of productive experiments in new methods of creating rules and systems of enforcement which a diversity of public and private actors can both engage with and uphold. However, they are not sufficient in and of themselves to solve the problem of compliance and enforcement as a spiral of global "bads," from global financial market instability to climate change, continues to form.

Fourth, overlapping with the trends mentioned above, there has been a proliferation of new types of global governance institution in the postwar era, and especially since the end of the Cold War.[19] These are not multilateral, state-to-state institutions, but instead combine various actors under varying degrees of institutionalization. In some areas of global governance these kinds of institutions rank among the most important. The case of global finance stands out in this regard (e.g., the Basel Committee on Banking Supervision, the Financial Stability Forum),[20] but other examples include global health governance (e.g., the Global Fund, the GAVI alliance, and polio eradication efforts)[21] and standard setting.[22]

In aggregate, these new institutions have contributed to the growing polycentricism observed in many areas of global governance. A polycentric approach can have advantages and disadvantages. On the one hand, it can mean that more issues are addressed in meaningful ways—through specialized bodies qualified to regulate and govern a specific issue area. On the other hand, it can exacerbate institutional fragmentation. More importantly, in many areas of global governance it is by no means clear that institutional innovation alone is sufficient to fill the governance gap created by new global challenges such as global economic imbalances and climate change. At best, these new institutional forms represent a partial solution.[23]

The complex architecture of global governance

The contemporary global governance system has features of both complexity and polycentricity. It can be usefully characterized as a multilayered, multisectoral, and multi-actor system in which institutions and politics matter in important ways to the determination of global policy outcomes; that is, to who gets what, when, and why.

Global governance is multilayered insofar as the making and implementation of global policies can involve a process of political cooperation and coordination among suprastate, national, transnational, and often sub-state agencies. Humanitarian relief operations, for example, often require the coordinated efforts of global, regional, national, and local agencies. In this respect, global governance is not so much hierarchical (command and control from the top) as horizontal: A process that involves coordination and cooperation among agencies across various levels, from the local to the global. However, the configuration of power and politics differs from sector to sector and from issue to issue, such that policy outcomes are not readily controlled by the same groups; interests and influence may vary from issue to issue. For instance, in the December 2012 climate negotiations in Qatar, poor countries formed a strong lobbying coalition to establish the prospect, in principle, of rich nations having to compensate poorer nations for material losses resulting from climate change. In the

Doha trade round, coordinated developing-country action by the Group of 77 (G-77) has essentially blocked progress in the negotiations by insisting that the trade-distorting effects of industrialized agriculture subsidies be addressed at least along with issues such as services and further tariff reductions. Outcomes can be contingent, in other words, on bargaining, coalition politics, consensus, and compromise, rather than on deference to hegemonic power, significant though this may be.[24] The politics of global governance is, thus, significantly differentiated: The politics of global trade regulation is quite, for instance, distinct from the politics of climate or peacekeeping. Rather than being monolithic or unitary, the system is best understood as sectoral or segmented.

Finally, many of the agencies of, and participants in, the global governance complex are no longer simply public bodies. There is considerable involvement of representatives from transnational civil society, from Greenpeace to Oxfam and an array of NGOs; of the corporate sector, from Monsanto to British Petroleum and trade or industrial associations; and of mixed public–private organizations such as the International Organization of Security Commissions (IOSCO). In addition to being multilayered and multisectoral, global governance is a multi-actor complex in which diverse agencies participate in the formulation and conduct of global public policy.

A polycentric conception of global governance does not imply that all states or agencies have an equal voice or input into—let alone an equal influence over—its agenda or programs. On the contrary, there is a recognition that the system is institutionally biased or distorted in favor of powerful states and vested interests: It is not by chance that in recent years the promotion of the global market has taken priority over tackling poverty, reducing inequality, and achieving the UN's Millennium Development Goals (MDGs) more broadly, and continuing with the successor Sustainable Development Goals (SDGs). Yet the very nature of economic globalization is such that in weaving, however unevenly, thickening webs of world-wide interconnectedness, hierarchical and hegemonic forms of governance become more costly and demanding to pursue and less effective and legitimate.

A notion of shared or common global problems ensures that multilateralism can work to moderate (albeit not to eliminate) power asymmetries.[25] Even the most powerful recognize that without, at least, the formal participation and tacit agreement of the weak or marginalized, effective and especially legitimate solutions to global problems—whether terrorism or money laundering, which directly impinge on their own welfare—would be impracticable. In these new circumstances of "complex interdependence," in which the returns to hierarchy are outweighed generally by the benefits of multi-lateral cooperation, traditional "hard" power instruments—military force or economic coercion—have a more circumscribed influence. This too creates new political opportunities for private actors and the forces of transnational civil society, which can mobilize considerable "soft power" resources in the pursuit of diverse objectives.[26]

Sovereignty and the limits to the diffusion of authority

To further understand the impact of intergovernmentalism and transnational governance on sovereignty and political authority, it is important to reflect more closely on how, and to what extent, the former reshapes the latter. In this regard, it is possible to formulate a hypothesis that illuminates the willingness of states to share and diffuse their authority to other agencies in the global governance complex. It could be put thus: When international and transnational agencies pursue policy agendas that are congruent with state interests, states are more likely to comply with policy outcomes and regulatory standards. When this is not the case, however, and states are confronted with policy outcomes and standards contrary to their interests, principles of sovereignty are typically evoked as a means to trump the agenda of global collaboration and coordination. Moreover, this will more commonly occur among those states able to challenge and ignore international and transnational pressures and forces. Again, it is useful to examine the areas of security and environment as examples.

Security

At the core of the postwar multilateral security order sits the UN Security Council and various disarmament treaties. These are two domains in which problems of great power politics and the forces of growing multi-polarity meet with complex ramifications. Both domains fundamentally reflect the postwar balance of power, which is simultaneously a source of their historical effectiveness and an impediment to addressing emergent security challenges. The need to foster great power inclusion in the UN system at the end of World War II led to the arrangement whereby permanent positions on the Security Council—and a veto—were granted to China, France, the Soviet Union (now Russia), the United Kingdom, and the United States (the P-5). This system has remained intact across socioeconomic and political transformations in the global order and now inhibits progress on some of the most pressing security concerns.

The historical use of the Security Council veto illustrates how the five permanent members have operated to protect and further their interests. The United States has consistently exercised its veto on questions pertaining to Israel; and, more recently, Russia and China have invoked theirs against Security Council resolutions concerning the Syrian state's violent attacks on its civilians, the Sudanese government's brutality in Darfur, and in other similar cases. Attempts at reforming the Security Council veto have failed, with the result that the threats facing the world, especially with the rise of intrastate conflict, are infrequently and ineffectively addressed by the very institution responsible for maintaining global peace and security. Dominant interests have, in short, continued to trump the reform of security arrangements and multilateral approaches to security challenges.

Similar problems of institutional intransigence and increasing multi-polarity are found in the disarmament regimes and concomitant efforts made to contain and reduce the most deadly weapons ever created. The Nuclear Non-Proliferation Treaty (NPT) is the primary mechanism intended to prevent the spread and use of nuclear weapons; the three principle goals of the NPT are non-proliferation, disarmament, and the management of pacific nuclear capacities. While it can be argued that the NPT and related bilateral agreements (such as the Strategic Arms Limitation Talks and Strategic Arms Reduction Treaties between Moscow and Washington) have been successful in helping to prevent the use of nuclear weapons, weaknesses in the regime are apparent when one considers the path that North Korea has taken to develop nuclear weapons: By developing the capacity allowed under Article IV, then by withdrawing from the treaty as allowed by Article X. Similar concerns now exist over Iran's nuclear program, with widespread speculation over its ambitions to develop weapons grade enrichment. India, Pakistan, and Israel simply never joined the treaty, exempting themselves from its requirements.

These examples notwithstanding, "horizontal" proliferation has been largely avoided (e.g., in South Africa, South America, and East Asia). The same cannot be said, however, about "vertical" proliferation and disarmament—evidenced by the vast nuclear stockpiles that were developed by the Soviet Union/Russia and the United States in the postwar years. Continued bilateral agreements between these two countries have been celebrated as successes, yet they have not amounted to actual disarmament by any significant measure. The vested interests of these states, and the structural protections they enjoy in the NPT and UN systems, have allowed them to sustain arsenals capable of global destruction should they ever be operationalized. While the staggered and incremental successes of great power negotiation are important steps, they fall far short of a robust and effective multilateral system capable of eliminating nuclear threats.

Additionally, harder and more complex problems have emerged in the global security arena. A primary example of this can be seen in the contemporary terrorism threat faced by the world community. Terrorism itself is not a new threat but in many ways it has changed, as have the strategies employed to mitigate it. It is a threat that requires effective coordination at the global level engaging multilevel partners, including states, regional bodies, and financial organizations, to name a few.

While multilateral efforts to deal with terrorism have been multifaceted, they have been limited in effect. Perhaps the greatest success has occurred in the tracking and freezing of terrorists' finances through bodies such as the Financial Action Task Force (FATF), and the Basel Committee on Banking Supervision.[27] Having said this, the UN Global Counter-Terrorism Strategy has two different bureaucracies: A Counterterrorism Committee, which exists within the Security Council, and the "Ad Hoc Sixth Committee," which operates within the General Assembly to focus on legal issues. Although the UN has been able to agree to some specific conventions aimed at particular aspects of terrorism, it still cannot agree on a basic definition of terrorism itself. This lack of basic agreement highlights just how challenging it has been for the multilateral order to form and implement coordinated global responses to terrorist threats.

In the absence of a robust global anti-terror regime, dominant states have filled the void with national strategies and policies. In this arena, US president Barack Obama drastically accelerated the use of armed unmanned aerial vehicles (i.e., drones) as a favored tool in US anti-terror strategy, a policy that President Donald Trump has continued. With active drone operations in Afghanistan, Iraq, Pakistan, Somalia, and Yemen, Washington has instituted a policy that is increasingly calling into question the efficacy of international law and emerging security principles. US drone strikes have recently drawn sharp criticism from both the international community,[28] as well as from national leaders—for example, from Pakistan.[29]

Despite widespread criticism, the United States shows no sign of changing its course. Given its power in the international system, the US unilateral abrogation of international law undermines the potential for and effectiveness of a rule-based multilateral system. This is, of course, also true of Russia's contribution to the international system in recent years: The annexation of Crimea, military intervention in Ukraine by proxy, and extensive engagement in Syria have all weakened the possibility of cooperation at the global level. These developments risk deepening the institutional stagnation currently found in global security governance because it subverts effective transborder cooperation on pressing security issues.

Environment

Although the environment was not a significant policy concern when the postwar institutions were established in the 1940s, it has emerged as one of the most developed areas of global politics. Today there are over 200 multilateral environmental agreements and scores of specialized international organizations covering issues ranging from trans-boundary air pollution, to desertification, biodiversity, and the ozone layer.[30] There are also several IGOs that act as focal points for the broader environmental regime, namely the United Nations Environment Programme (UNEP—an international organization), the Commission on Sustainable Development (a UN-based intergovernmental forum), and the Global Environment Facility (GEF—a World Bank-housed specialized fund for environmental projects).

Despite this plethora of institutions, global environmental governance remains fragmented, disjointed and, ultimately, weak. Successful environmental regimes—such as the one limiting ozone-depleting substances—are rare. In turn, failures—deforestation, biodiversity, fisheries, and climate change—are all too common. In response, a wide array of new forms of global governance has emerged, and private firms and civil society groups have played a leading, even dominant role in creating and sustaining these initiatives. Yet despite this intense activity, stalemate all too often pervades environmental politics. Climate change politics is indicative.

Climate change provides perhaps the starkest example of how new levels of interdependence and the interplay between leading and emerging powers can overwhelm the capacity of existing institutions to resolve global collective action problems. Climate change is a quintessentially global issue, as greenhouse gas emissions anywhere have impacts everywhere. Furthermore, the impacts are large. The 2006 Stern Report estimated, among other things, that climate change could reduce global GDP by up to twenty percent compared to what it otherwise would be. We are thus all deeply affected by the carbon usage of all other inhabitants of the planet—a remarkable degree of interconnectedness and interdependence.

Equally troubling, the costs of mitigating climate change, although much smaller than the costs of allowing it to occur, are substantial, and have decisive distributional impacts for countries, industries, firms, and individuals. Rich countries have created the majority of carbon in the atmosphere, and continue to have significantly higher per capita emissions rates than emerging economies, especially in North America, Australia, and the Persian Gulf. However, the majority of future emissions will come from the developing world, meaning that the participation of countries such as China, India, and Brazil is essential for any effort to mitigate climate change to succeed. In sum, climate change has created perhaps unprecedented levels of interdependence even as the power to stop it diffuses to a range of different actors.

Cooperation, then, is necessary, but in short supply. Since the 1992 Rio Summit almost every country in the world has met annually to discuss how to mitigate and adapt to climate change. The objective has been to create a global treaty specifying binding emissions reductions, along the lines of the successful ozone regime. Two decades of negotiations have yielded exactly one treaty requiring reductions in greenhouses gases (GHGs), the 1997 Kyoto Protocol that committed rich nations to a tiny five percent average reduction in emissions below 1990 levels by 2012. Even this weak target proved unacceptable to the United States, which refused to implement the treaty. Indeed, it proved even too ambitious for many signatories, such as Canada, which are on track to violate their commitments (and will face no penalty for doing so). Developing countries, which will produce the lion's share of future emissions, accepted no commitments at all under Kyoto. The Protocol was meant, of course, as a building block toward future commitments. A similar incremental approach had, after all, succeeded within the ozone regime. As the fateful 2009 Copenhagen summit demonstrated, where world leaders were unable (or unwilling) to produce an agreement on climate change, no global deal is likely any time soon.

Instead, the world has turned to a more piecemeal approach. Robert Keohane and David Victor describe a "regime complex" for climate change that includes the United Nations Framework Convention on Climate Change but also an array of other intergovernmental bodies like the G-20 and the international financial institutions.[31] Unable to reach an agreement on a global treaty in the UN process, states increasingly turn to other, more fragmented forums.

In this context, the Paris Agreement in 2015 is especially important. It was animated by the common objective of limiting temperature change to two degrees centigrade, or 1.5 degrees in this century. This objective is translated into the aims of many political and social agents, deploying various instruments. The latter include a pledge and review process with a ratchet mechanism that kicks into place every five years, technical support for countries implementing climate policies, orchestration of climate action by transnational networks of sub- and non-state actors—that aim to strengthen support for pro-climate policies in countries over time.

In the Paris Agreement, domestic policy plays a large role. Individual governmental commitments to reduce emissions, like those implemented by the European Union or various US states, seek to make a major contribution to resolving the problem. Some of these measures are significant. In the United States, for example, one study has estimated that the commitments of seventeen states and 684 cities (representing fifty-three percent of the US population and forty-three percent of its emissions) could stabilize the nation's emissions at 2010 levels by 2020.[32] Other types of policy, such as China's ambitious energy intensity targets, also have important effects. Yet, unlike many areas of environmental politics (forestry, fishing, and biodiversity), climate change is an "all or nothing" collective action problem. Here it is the case that the altruistic initiatives of some actors will matter little unless all the major emitters control their greenhouse gases. The fragmented, domestic, and transnational climate initiatives thus face the enormous challenge of reaching a scale where they can have a meaningful impact.[33] Runaway climate change remains the prospect unless the United States, China, and India, among other major emitters, become genuine partners in a new climate regime. The Trump administration's announcement in June 2017 that the United States would withdraw from the Paris Agreement cast a long shadow.

Conclusion

The proliferation of intergovernmentalism and transnational governance mechanisms in the postwar period is a striking trend. While the complex global governance system has characteristics of a multilayered, multisector, and multi-actor system, the question remains how far political authority has been diffused, in practice, throughout the global order. The global political agenda is increasingly shaped by a diversity of voices and agents, but sovereignty remains a powerful obstacle to the development and execution of policy in areas sensitive to the interests of leading states. Breakthroughs in postwar nuclear disarmament, along with significant progress by the major emitters of GHGs, still seems some distance from the cooperative world envisaged by many of the architects of the postwar multilateral order and of the complex transnational institutions that now struggle to govern it.

The risks that follow from this are all too obvious. To prevent runaway environmental destruction, rein in nuclear proliferation, or confront other global challenges, we must cooperate. But many of the existing tools for global policy making are breaking down or inadequate—chiefly, state-to-state negotiations over treaties and international institutions—at a time when our fate and fortunes are acutely interwoven.[34] These are dangerous trends, but we need to surmount them in the decades ahead if peace and sustainability are to be more common features of the twenty-first century.

Additional reading

Thomas Hale, David Held, and Kevin Young, *Gridlock: Why Global Cooperation Is Failing When We Need It Most* (Cambridge: Polity Press, 2013).
Thomas Hale and David Held, et al., *Beyond Gridlock* (Cambridge: Polity Press, 2017).
David Held and Thomas Hale, eds., *Handbook of Transnational Governance* (Cambridge: Polity Press, 2011).
Anne-Marie Slaughter, *A New World Order* (Princeton, NJ: Princeton University Press, 2004).
Thomas G. Weiss and Ramesh Thakur, *Global Governance and the UN: An Unfinished Journey* (Bloomington: Indiana University Press, 2010).

Notes

1 Many of the themes of this article are explored in Thomas Hale, David Held, and Kevin Young, *Gridlock: Why Global Cooperation Is Failing When We Need It Most* (Cambridge: Polity Press, 2013). I am indebted to my coauthors for our many discussions.

2 Eric Hobsbawm, *Age of Extremes: The Short Twentieth Century 1914–1991* (London: Michael Joseph, 1994), 52.

3 William McNeill, *The Pursuit of Power* (Oxford: Blackwell, 1982), 356.

4 Hedley Bull, *The Anarchical Society* (London: Macmillan, 1977), 6; David Held, *Democracy in the Global Order* (Cambridge: Polity Press, 1995), 4.

5 Antonio Cassese, "Violence, War and the Rule of Law in the International Community," in *Political Theory Today*, ed. David Held (Cambridge: Polity Press, 1991): 255–275.

6 Hale, Held, and Young, *Gridlock*.

7 David Held, et al., *Global Transformations: Politics, Economics and Culture* (Cambridge: Polity Press, 1999).

8 Union of International Associations, *Yearbook of International Organizations* (Leiden: Brill, 2012).

9 Robert Keohane and Joseph Nye, *Power and Interdependence: World Politics in Transition* (Boston, MA: Little Brown, 1977); Anne-Marie Slaughter, *A New World Order* (Princeton, NJ: Princeton University Press, 2004).

10 Tim Büthe, "Private Regulation in the Global Economy: A (P)review," *Business and Politics* 12, no. 3 (2010): 1–38.

11 Helen Milner, *Interests, Institutions and Information* (Princeton, NJ: Princeton University Press, 1997); Slaughter, *A New World Order.*

12 Peter M. Haas, "Policy Responses to Stratospheric Ozone Depletion," *Global Environmental Change* 1, no. 3 (1991): 224–234; Margaret Keck and Kathryn Sikkink, *Activists Beyond Borders* (Ithaca, NY: Cornell University Press, 1998).

13 David Held and Kevin Young, "Crisis in Parallel Worlds: The Governance of Global Risks in Finance, Security, and the Environment," in *The Deepening Crisis: Governance Challenges after Neoliberalism*, eds. Craig Calhoun and Georgi Derluguian (New York: New York University Press, 2011): 19–42.

14 David Held and Thomas Hale, eds., *Handbook of Transnational Governance* (Cambridge: Polity Press, 2011); Michelle Betsill and Elisabeth Corell, eds., *NGO Diplomacy: The Influence of Nongovernmental Organization in International Environmental Negotiations* (Cambridge, MA: MIT Press, 2008).

15 Thomas Risse-Kappen, *Bringing Transnational Relations Back In: Non-State Actors, Domestic Structures and International Institutions* (Cambridge: Cambridge University Press, 1995).

16 Dieter Kerwer, "Rules That Many Use: Standards and Global Regulation," *Governance* 18, no. 4 (2005): 611–632.

17 Abram Chayes and Antonia H. Chayes, *The New Sovereignty: Compliance with International Regulatory Agreements* (Cambridge, MA: Harvard University Press, 1995).

18 Held and Hale, *Handbook of Transnational Governance.*

19 Ibid.

20 Held and Young, "Crisis in Parallel Worlds."

21 Johanna Hanefield, "The Global Fund to Fight AIDS, Malaria, and Tuberculosis," and Mathias Koenig-Archibugi, "Global Polio Eradication Initiative," in *Handbook of Transnational Governance*, eds. Held and Hale, 161–165, 166–175.

22 Tim Büthe, *The New Global Rulers: The Privatization of Regulation in the World Economy* (Princeton, NJ: Princeton University Press, 2011).

23 Thomas Hale and David Held, "Gridlock and Innovation in Global Governance: The Partial Transnational Solution," *Global Policy* 3, no. 2 (2012): 169–181.

24 Robert Keohane, "Governance in a Partially Globalized World," *American Political Science Review* 95, no. 1 (2001): 1–13.

25 John Ikenberry, *After Victory* (Princeton, NJ: Princeton University Press, 2001).

26 Thomas Risse, ""Let's Argue!": Communicative Action in World Politics," *International Organization* 54, no. 1 (2000): 1–39.

27 John Taylor, *Global Financial Warriors: The Untold Story of International Finance in the Post-9/11 World* (London: W. W. Norton & Company, 2007); and Elini Tsingou, "Global Financial Governance and the Developing Anti-Money Laundering Regime: What Lessons for International Political Economy?" *International Politics* 47, no. 6 (2010): 617–637.

28 Owen Bowcott, "Drone Strikes Threaten 50 Years of International Law, Says UN Rapporteur," *The Guardian*, 21 June 2012.

29 Qasim Nauman, "Pakistan Condemns US Drone Strikes," *Reuters*, 4 June 2012, www.reuters.com/article/2012/06/04/us-pakistan-usa-drones-idUSBRE8530MS20120604

30 Held, et al., *Global Transformations*.

31 Robert Keohane and David G. Victor, "The Regime Complex for Climate Change," Discussion Paper 2010–33, Harvard Project on International Climate Change Agreements (Cambridge, MA: Harvard University Press, 2010); Thomas Hale, "A Climate Coalition of the Willing," *Washington Quarterly* 34, no. 1 (2011): 89–101.

32 Nicholas Lutsey and Daniel Sperling, "America's Bottom-up Climate Change Mitigation Policy," *Energy Policy* 36, no. 2 (2008): 673–685.

33 Bruce Au, et al., *Beyond a Global Deal: A UN+ Approach to Climate Governance* (Berlin: Global Governance 2020, 2011).

34 Thomas Hale, David Held, and Kevin Young, *Gridlock: Why Global Cooperation is Failing When We Need It Most* (Cambridge: Polity Press, 2013).

CONTENTS

Who governs
the globe?

Susan K. Sell

Scholars of international politics have long been interested in global governance. It is easy to think of global problems that overwhelm the capacities of individual states to solve them. Climate change, nuclear proliferation, financial crises, disease, and hunger come readily to mind. Many scholars conceive of the international system as a system of sovereign states that answer to no higher authority. States differ in their resources and capacities; they may be equally sovereign but are not equally capable of tackling global problems. Beyond trying to understand global governance, scholars seek to devise strategies for addressing global problems and imagine possibilities for an alternative future.

At the same time, analysts have observed increasing stalemate and a decline in norm setting in multilateral governance organizations such as the World Trade Organization (WTO) and the World Intellectual Property Organization (WIPO). Two recent exceptions to this trend include the Paris Agreement on climate change and the Marrakesh Treaty on copyright limitations and exceptions for the visually impaired.[1] Episodes such as the UK referendum on Brexit and the US election that resulted in Donald Trump reveal apparently reduced appetites for postwar liberal internationalism. Multilateral interstate treaty making seems to be on the decline, with bilateral, regional, and plurilateral initiatives gaining ground. Some scholars have suggested that international law has stagnated and others point out that traditional interstate multilateral governance plays a much smaller role than one might expect. Recent scholarship in political science, sociology, and law is addressing this arc of change and exploring alternative forms and processes of global governance.[2]

The proliferation of new actors and new forms and processes of global governance raises important questions. Who are the global governors? What do they do? Why does anyone defer to them? What are the relationships between various governors? Since no governor governs alone, relationships between them will have an impact on processes and outcomes. What are the relationships between the governors and the governed? In a world lacking a global *demos*, to whom exactly are governors accountable? Whom do they represent? On what basis can one evaluate their legitimacy?

This chapter tackles these questions. It proceeds in four sections. First, it offers a brief overview of the development of global governance literature. Second, the chapter examines the actors, their activities, their bases of authority, and their relationships with each other. Third, it addresses the relationships between the governors and the governed and some of the relevant challenges for accountability, representation, and legitimacy. The chapter concludes with suggestions for further research and development of the ideas presented.

History and development

During the Cold War American neorealist Kenneth Waltz argued that the world was anarchic, and that the distribution of capabilities across states was the most analytically fruitful way to think about the international system.[3] Anarchy simply meant the absence of world government. This perspective has remained influential, and has informed mainstream American scholarship on international cooperation. Studies of the problem of cooperation under anarchy have informed much of the contemporary scholarship on global governance. With anarchy as the central trope, scholars of international politics have explored the concept of governance without government.[4]

In the 1980s international relations scholars focused on international regimes, "principles, norms, rules and decision-making procedures around which actor expectations converge in a given issue area."[5] Stephen Krasner's volume on regimes featured analytic variety, with realists, constructivists, and functionalists weighing in on the sources and contours of international cooperation.[6] Realists focused on power, constructivists on ideas and identity, and functionalists on institutions. However, Robert Keohane's rationalist functionalism, that global needs gave rise to governance arrangements, came to dominate the literature on cooperation and international institutions. He argued that, despite anarchy, states cooperated because institutions provided them with benefits. International institutions reduced transaction costs, provided information, and, if well designed, discouraged cheating and freeriding. Thereafter, the literature on institutions, international regimes, and international organizations dominated mainstream American scholarship on international cooperation. Interstate dynamics, treaty making and international law occupied much of the analytic terrain in studies of global governance.

Produced during an era of the perceived hegemonic decline of the United States in the 1980s, Keohane's analysis foregrounded stability as the chief normative value. The question was how the United States could maintain its "benign" hegemony while losing power relative to other states. Many related analyses were statist and functionalist. They focused on structures or forms of cooperation and downplayed both the contestation and the politics animating international relationships. They exhibited a static conservative bias intended to preserve a particular US-led international order. Susan Strange offered a trenchant critique of this approach, pointing out its inherent normative bias, its preoccupation with stasis, and the limits of its state-centric paradigm.[7]

Subsequent development of this strand of theorizing addressed questions of institutional design, such as membership and decision rules.[8] Ample scholarship on global governance has focused on the forms or structures of governance. This literature focused on intergovernmental interactions and technocratic, managerial, approaches to global governance. Yet just because some problems were global, this did not mean that global governance arrangements would arise. This line of work implicitly assumed that international cooperation and global governance were inherently good. Cooperation was good; more cooperation was better. Governance was good; more governance was better. Even analysts of sub-state actors coordinating across borders emphasized a benign, managerial style of governance.[9] As Ronen Palan argues:

> The results are theories of form without substance. Regime theories are theories about coordination problems that states are facing with no particular reasons or cause for coordination besides some vague notion that those states that join regimes have a reason for doing so. Regime theory supposedly tells us about the impact of coordination, but has little to say about the substance of the regime as such.[10]

Not only did this rationalist functionalist approach say little about substance, it provided little insight into whose needs were being met by governance arrangements. International politics is largely about who gets what, who benefits, how costs and benefits are distributed, who pays adjustment costs, and contestation over all of these. By downplaying these central issues the functionalist approach failed to address some of the more fraught elements of international politics.

Four important developments in the 1980s and 1990s prompted new thinking about international cooperation and led scholars to question this mainstream approach. First, the rapid pace of economic globalization more tightly connected people across space and time. This triggered shifts in thinking from the local and national scales to the global scale. Second, economic privatization and deregulation increased the social power of private actors, especially globally engaged multinational enterprises and titans of global finance. Third, the development of new information and communication technologies radically compressed space and time, and provided both new opportunities for, and constraints on, conflict and cooperation. Fourth, the end of the Cold War ushered in a period of renewed commitment to and optimism about international cooperation. In response to these developments, scholars such as James Rosenau and Philip Cerny explored analytic territory that sought to better capture these momentous changes.[11]

They highlighted the ways globalization strained state capacity. They revealed the poor fit between a system of territorially based sovereign states and rapid processes of globalization that both overwhelmed and undermined that system. Newly connected networks of actors both disaggregated and transcended the state. Rosenau highlighted turbulence in world politics coupled with an increasingly skilled global citizenry. Cerny and Rosenau emphasized the bigger role that private actors were playing. Cerny argued that states were repurposing themselves to compete in global markets and globalization had produced the "competition state" that undermined domestic welfare bargains.

Many scholars focus on international organizations, treaties, and international law, yet these governance foundations are based on thin state consent. For instance, international treaties only require that states agree to them: "[I]nternational law is agnostic on how this agreement was reached (process), who participated in its establishment (actors), what form it takes (instrument) and what is actually agreed on (substance)."[12] Multilateral treaty making in international organizations features high transaction costs and "once concluded is hard to adapt to changing circumstances."[13] Miles Kahler and David Lake have found that this traditional supranational governance structure "plays a less central role than many believe or expect."[14] Joost Pauwelyn, Ramses Wessel, and Jan Wouters have noted the increasing stagnation of international law and the simultaneous emergence of new actors, new outputs, and new processes that have led to a much broader range of governance practices.

Many global governors operate in the space between thin state consent and "thick stakeholder" consensus. Sovereign states are just one constituency. Stakeholders include the rule makers, the governors, and the rule takers, the governed. More informal processes, non-state actors, and networks that strive for more robust, or thick, stakeholder consensus are edging out the traditional state-centric modes of global governance. Globalization has strained more traditional governance mechanisms. As Pauwelyn, Wessel, and Wouters point out:

> The state remains a pivotal entity of interest aggregation, legitimation and control. Yet it is supplemented, assisted, corrected and continuously challenged by a variety of other actors be they regulators, national and international agencies, city mayors, businesses or NGOs who can make cooperation not only more legitimate but also more effective.[15]

Hybrid coalitions and networks of state and non-state actors have emerged as prominent sources of global governance and regulatory change.

Governors and their authority

In the 1990s analysts such as Claire Cutler, Virginia Haufler, Tony Porter, Thomas Biersteker, Rodney Hall, Margaret Keck, and Kathryn Sikkink established the prominence of a variety of non-state actors in global governance.[16] They highlighted the proliferation of potential governors, ranging from business firms, social movements, and NGOs. Scholars began to look more deeply into *who* governs the globe and began to analyze the agency of global governors: "Global governors are authorities who exercise power across borders for purposes of affecting policy. Governors thus create issues, set agendas, establish and implement rules or programs, and evaluate and/or adjudicate outcomes."[17] Global governors can be NGOs, civil society campaigns, experts, intergovernmental organizations, states, regulators, judges, lobbyists, business firms, and hybrid networks blending multiple types of actors.

Global governors engage in numerous tasks, including: Agenda setting, negotiation, decision making, implementation, monitoring, and enforcement. Global governors' activities vary depending on what resources they bring to bear. For example, at the agenda-setting stage NGOs, transnational advocacy networks, and experts may play prominent roles. They work to engage decision makers by defining and framing issues, and advocating for particular approaches to the problem at hand. For example, environmental scientists have played a significant role in defining climate change. Transnational advocacy networks championed the ban on landmines. Hybrid networks of NGOs, experts, and states pressed for access to generic antiretroviral medicines to address the HIV/AIDS pandemic.

Governors play different roles: They may act as "lobbyists, acting as interest groups; partners, providing expertise or participat[ing] in common projects; adversaries, blaming and shaming governmental authorities; and functional substitutes for states, performing regulatory functions."[18] Clifford Bob offers an adversarial example in the role of the National Rifle Association mobilizing to oppose UN efforts to regulate the small arms trade; the result has been stalemate, or, as Bob puts it, "zombie policy."[19]

Different types of global governors' roles vary according to policy stages and issue areas. For traditional interstate multilateral negotiations, states may want to include experts or firms for advice, but states are less likely to invite transnational advocacy networks to participate in negotiations. Alexander Cooley and James Ron have analyzed the substantial role that non-state actors such as accounting firms and humanitarian aid organizations play in policy implementation in economic reform and relief work.[20] Jönsson and Tallberg have found that states are less likely to include transnational actors in decision making and enforcement.[21] Overall, existing work in this area tells us that transnational advocacy networks are less likely to be included in finance and security policy, yet are more likely to be included in human rights, environment, and development issues.

Global governors' bases of authority, the ability to induce deference in others, are varied and are not mutually exclusive.[22] Authority may be institutional. A global governor's authority may derive from her position in an organizational structure, such as a multinational corporation or an international organization. Such a global governor is both empowered and constrained by the institution's rules and mandates. Authority can be delegated; states often delegate authority to international organizations or firms. Some global governors are recognized for their expertise in complex or technical areas. Environmental scientists, economists, and development professionals are examples of governors whose authority is a product of their education and training. Principle-based authority derives from service to some widely accepted principles, morals, or values. These principles may be either religious or secular and may include commitments to peace, human rights, a nuclear-free world, ending global hunger or ending gender-based violence. Global governors frequently promote principles such as liberty, dignity, security, and prosperity. Amnesty International's commitment to human rights and Greenpeace's promotion of environmental preservation are examples of principled authority. Finally, capacity-based authority arises from perceived competence. This is related to expert authority, but tilts toward a known track record for problem solving. This may be more about experience or performing an action effectively rather than professional training, education, or epistemic certification.

In global governance, no governor governs alone. Foregrounding agency and its authoritative bases offers insights into relationships among the governors themselves and the presence or lack of synergistic partnerships. Highlighting agency and relationships allows us to analyze synergies and conflicts across competencies. For example, governors face dilemmas when their delegated authority is in tension with their expertise. The economists at the International Monetary Fund (IMF) are experts in financial stability, not poverty reduction; yet the IMF was charged, along with more development-oriented organizations, with addressing the Millennium Development Goals (MDGs) and now the Sustainable Development Goals (SDGs). Such mismatches can result in poor performance and reduced authority over time.

Kenneth Abbott and Duncan Snidal identified multiple combinations of types of governor in their "governance triangle" to capture interactions and partnerships between the three points of the triangle: NGOs, firms, and states.[23] Distilling potential global governors into three types, they map out a variety of governance arrangements into seven zones defined by the relative participation of combinations of governors. For example, one zone captures governance by states alone, a second by NGOs alone, and a third by firms alone. The other four represent various mixtures, such as NGOs partnering with firms; NGOs partnering with states; states partnering with firms; and a relatively balanced blend of all three types of governor participating in governance (e.g., the International Labour Organization). Whether or not these partnerships will be synergistic and constructive depends, in part, on how well their respective competencies complement each other and whether or not they compete or conflict with one another.

Governors' relationships between each other and to their institutional environment can shape outcomes. Cooley and Ron have demonstrated that at the implementation stage of governance these factors can cause suboptimal outcomes.[24] In their cases—accounting consultancies for market reforms in Eastern Europe and humanitarian aid provision in Rwanda—would-be governors compete in bidding on short-term contracts. This competitive bidding with short time-horizons ensures that implementation and delivery of services will be suboptimal because providers are motivated to secure the next contract. To do so they will be particularly motivated to secure a positive report, which can exacerbate tensions between the purported mission and the wishes of the recipients. For instance, while the mission may be to implement thorough economic liberalization, the local government may wish to drag its heels. Therefore the local government will be disposed to produce the most positive report for the provider that gives it the most latitude in implementation. The provider then may be inclined to exaggerate progress in order to secure the next contract.

While acting in an institutional environment, global governors may exercise considerable agency. At times they can bypass established institutions to achieve desired governance outcomes. As Jakobi suggests:

> Actors on the periphery of a field are more likely to innovate given that they are less bound to the fields [sic] dominant logic of action. . . . Central actors usually have more resources and contacts to help innovate. . . . [But marginal actors] can overcome barriers through inter organizational networking and through networking with higher status organizations, groups and individuals.[25]

Actors at the periphery of powerful institutions have been able to use their networking and technological skills to alter governance outcomes. One important example comes from the regulatory field of intellectual property. The United States Trade Representative's Office (USTR) and global business firms have driven the movement toward higher international standards of property protection and enforcement. The tight relationship between USTR and private global firms largely has kept civil society actors, consumers, and transnational advocacy networks out of the policymaking process. In 2006 the United States pressed for an Anti-Counterfeiting Trade Agreement (ACTA), with Japan and the European Union, as a plurilateral treaty to adopt and promote protection and enforcement standards well above and beyond the WTO standards. The official negotiations began in 2008; they were secret and not transparent. Only global business firms were consulted and kept abreast of developments. Transnational advocacy networks, civil society actors, and consumers learned of the substance of the negotiations only through leaked documents, and only after much of the process had taken place. On 4 October 2011 the United States and seven other countries signed ACTA. The European Union signed in 2012.

Meanwhile, in the United States, two domestic laws aimed at foreign websites that hosted copyright-infringing material were moving through Congress. In the fall of 2011, the two bills were Protect Intellectual Property Act (PIPA) in the Senate, and Stop Online Piracy Act (SOPA) in the House of Representatives. If passed, the bills would block US Internet users from accessing foreign websites such as Pirate Bay and would block US Internet users' payments through services, such as PayPal, to foreign sites hosting copyright-infringing content. Given their deep entrenchment in USTR and generosity toward members of Congress, rights holders, representing the motion picture and sound recording industries, fully expected to secure support for the legislation. As powerful political players they had grown accustomed to getting what they wanted.

However, this time a transnational hybrid coalition of outsiders and Internet users exercised agency by mobilizing protest against SOPA and PIPA. They deployed their considerable technical skills to scale up protest and got millions of users to participate in protesting the proposed bills. Internet activism has lowered the costs of collective action. Using a combination of blogs, denial of service attacks, electronic petitions, and website postings informing users of the dangers of SOPA and PIPA, this coalition mobilized millions of people to try to "kill the bills." They organized a coordinated web blackout. On 18 January 2012, more than 15,000 websites went dark for 24 hours, including Wikipedia, Mozilla, and Reddit, to protest against the legislation and underscore the consequences if the bills were passed. Throughout the day an increasing number of members of Congress renounced their support of the bills, and by 20 January the bills were dead.

This hybrid transnational coalition of hackers, Internet users, consumers, and anticensorship groups won an unexpected victory over rights holders. Inspired by the successful anti-SOPA/PIPA campaign in the United States, hundreds of thousands of Europeans took to the streets to protest the Anti-Counterfeiting Trade Agreement that the EU had negotiated and signed. The transnational coalition of Internet users now mobilized to kill ACTA, and in February 2012 Bulgaria, the Czech Republic, Germany, Cyprus, Latvia, Romania, Estonia, Austria, the Netherlands, and Slovakia suspended ACTA ratification. On 4 July 2012, the Members of the European Parliament voted 478 against and thirty-nine in favor of ACTA (165 abstained), rendering ACTA effectively moribund. The scale shifting that the Internet facilitated between transnational, international, plurilateral, and domestic scales, and the offline mobilization of anti-ACTA forces halted the policy trajectory of locking in higher standards that rights holders had considered a sure thing. With low barriers to entry, and a nimble and fluid digital network, these global governors successfully challenged those governors who had been more deeply entrenched in core institutions in this policy area.

Governors and the governed: Accountability and legitimacy

The previous section examined governors' diverse bases of authority to understand why the governed defer to the governors and to answer the question: "Why are they in charge?" Amitav Acharya examined the demand side of global governance to further explore the rationale behind governance across a number of issue areas. He and the contributors to his edited volume find increased complexity and fragmentation as well as uneven support for global governance.[26] Unavoidably global governance is contested as it is shot through with strategic, political and normative considerations.

Examining relationships between the governors and the *governed* raises important normative issues. Global governors must be attentive to their audiences and constituents. They must manage and adapt to constant change. As Jakobi points out, "although power is important, it also involves partnerships, cooperation and coalitions, material and discursive interventions. Institutional change is a social enterprise, and any activity of an institutional entrepreneur or political leader is targeted to a reaction of others."[27]

Global governance raises particular challenges for accountability, representation and legitimacy. Richard Mulgan offers this definition of accountability:

> Accountability, the obligation to be called "to account," is a method of keeping the public informed and powerful in check. It implies a world which is at once complex, where experts are needed to perform specialized tasks, but still fundamentally democratic in aspiration, in that members of the public assert their right to question the experts and exercise ultimate control over them.[28]

The inherent tension between independence of action required for governors to be effective in governance tasks, and the accountability required to limit their power poses another set of dilemmas. By what metric should global governors be held to account? What mechanisms can enhance accountability? To whom should governors be accountable? Inspired by democratic theory, many commentators suggest that transparency and participation can facilitate accountability. In response to complaints about non-transparency, both the WTO and WIPO have begun to post many more reports and documents on their websites and to make them available with far less delay than in the past. Yet transparency is not enough. In response to pressure for broader stakeholder participation, a number of international organizations have opened up their processes to transnational advocacy groups and civil society actors. Exceptions to this include the IMF, and to some degree the WTO. The extent to which stakeholder participation shapes policy is an empirical question that an exclusive focus on formal institutional design can obscure.

Using participation as a yardstick raises additional questions about representation. Since we have no global democracy, how do we determine who should be represented? Jens Bartelson points out that "there is no *demos* at the global level that could endow global political authorities with the kind of legitimacy that supposedly derives from popular consent."[29] The fragile nexus between the authority of those who make law and the question of who is subject to law "certainly does not vanish in the context of transnational governance regimes."[30]

Scholars have suggested a number of ways to address the unwieldiness of representing the whole world. One approach is to include, or represent the interests of, those who would be most affected by the decision or policy. Who should be at the table when decisions are made, the regulators, the regulated, or both? This is even more contested at a global level than it is in domestic democratic politics. Those who have a bigger stake should have a bigger voice. However, in the case of the IMF, who has the bigger stake? Should it be the donors or the citizens who will experience structural adjustment first hand? Furthermore, it is often not immediately obvious who will, in fact, be affected. For instance, at the time of the WTO negotiations on an Agreement on Trade Related Aspects of Intellectual Property (TRIPs), no one foresaw how much the Agreement would affect the millions of sub-Saharan African and Thai and Brazilian HIV/AIDS patients who needed access to generic antiretroviral medicines. As such, defining the "all affected" political community is hardly a straightforward exercise. Relevant political communities are not static.

In response to these problems, some scholars have offered an alternative "discursive representation" approach to democracy. Rather than worrying about *numbers* of citizens represented, "all the relevant political discourses ought to get represented, regardless of how many people subscribe to each."[31] However, this approach begs the question of who gets to identify and present "all the relevant political discourses." Whose expertise and whose empathy would determine this? Who is the expert? In the case of intellectual property protection, what range of discourses would be provided? Would trade, investment, and rights holders' interests be represented? Or would public health, open science, education, and agriculture also be included? Would this devolve into a kind of tyranny of expertise or a contest over moral righteousness and more far-flung representation? Advocating discursive representation hardly dodges the political contestation at the heart of global governance.

Legitimacy is a social relationship; to be legitimate is to be "*socially recognized as rightful*"[32] by those over whom global governors claim authority. This immediately raises thorny normative issues. As Regine Kreide asks: "What normative demands must transnational governance comply with? And when is transnational governance legitimate?"[33] One prominent approach to thinking about legitimacy and supranational governance comes from the European Union literature; Fritz Scharpf, for instance, has focused on "input" and "output" legitimacy.[34] Briefly, input legitimacy refers to participation and representation in the process of defining policy goals, and output legitimacy refers to the translation of these goals into policy. While complications of participation and representation were discussed above, output legitimacy raises a different set of challenges.

Many scholars have tried to derive checklists of criteria for legitimacy that are informed by democratic theory and then applied to the global level. Yet critics point out that *ex ante* checklists tend to be ahistorical and inattentive to social context. For instance, a legitimate participation norm did not always include women; and one should expect legitimacy to vary according to cultural and social context. Daniel Mugge argues that "assessments of legitimacy have to focus on the actual workings of institutions, not on formal flows of authority, information and accountability."[35] This concern with substance over form underscores the fact that legitimacy is not static; it involves continual interaction between governors and the governed. As Steven Bernstein points out: "[W]hat constitutes legitimacy results from an interaction of the community of actors affected by the regulatory institution, i.e. the public who grant legitimacy, with broader institutionalized norms—or social structure—that prevail in the relevant issue area."[36]

In developing a more dynamic way of thinking about legitimacy Calliess and Zumbansen argue that it is implausible to separate "the sphere where official authorities decide over law or non-law from the societal sphere in which the relevant actors recognize legal norms, by the authority these norms exercise over their lives or actions."[37] Authority, procedure, and substance map onto "actors," "processes," and "outputs" as well as to the benchmark of thick consensus. Pauwelyn and his colleagues endorse procedural integrity rooted in checks and balances that examine the following three elements: "(i) the source, respectability of the norm-creating body, (ii) transparency, openness and neutrality in the norm's procedural elaboration and (iii) the substantive quality, consistency and overall acceptance (consensus) of the norm."

Calliess and Zumbansen propose a "rough consensus and running code" approach to governance. The "rough consensus" applies to the front end of the policy process and would feature "*ex ante* controls (such as setting a clear mandate or benchmark against which actors can be held accountable; guidelines; appointments; or rules on conflicts of interest) and *ex post* controls (such as readjustment of guidelines; financial accountability or complaint mechanisms)."[38]

Thus, legitimacy might better be conceptualized as an ongoing *process* of legitimation. As a process, one important criterion for legitimacy would be the extent to which policy, or output, is open to contestation.[39] This is an important criterion that could address the flexibility and responsiveness that global governors and the governed need to have. Many issues in global governance, such as intellectual property, finance, and the environment exhibit a huge discrepancy between the narrow representation and technical focus of global governors and the huge societal footprint of these policy areas.[40] Finding ways to recognize and institutionalize the ongoing processes of legitimation and interaction of governance policies with communities "on the ground" is a worthwhile goal. This might help to allow for adjustments when communities whose interests were never considered when devising the policy are suddenly deeply affected. For instance, intellectual property rules came to sharply affect HIV/AIDS patients in the developing world. Global governance processes must try to address such unintended consequences in a systematic way.

Notions of legitimacy are bound to change as the governed experience the big societal footprint in unexpected or unintended ways. This evolving process requires an explicitly normative statement of the social purpose of the policy. Focusing on institutional legitimacy alone is insufficient; analysts must squarely face the question of substantive legitimacy. This brings us back to Susan Strange's emphasis on winners and losers in governance contests. What substantive benefits do we want to achieve and for whom? And how shall we do it? Distributional consequences lie at the heart of contestation over global governance and cannot be ignored.

Conclusion

This chapter has presented an account of the evolution of the literature on global governance. Global governance is a dynamic interactive process. Focusing on agency and the bases of global governors' authority allows us to better understand what global governors do. Focusing on relationships between global governors that have to work together can reveal sources of dysfunctional outcomes and constructive collaboration. Looking ahead, one of the trickiest analytic issues is to define clearly the boundaries of global governance. How do we know governance when we see it? Having opened up the analysis to focus on a much larger range of global governors, who is and who is not a global governor? Issues of scope and boundaries will benefit from more empirical research and further conceptual development.

Further research is needed to develop a more precise account of the conditions that lend themselves to better and worse outcomes. Highlighting relationships between the governors and the governed directs our attention to crucial considerations of accountability, representation, and legitimacy. Scholars who dodge explicitly normative issues about substance run the risk of "uncritically adopting dominant notions of the 'public good' that policy should provide."[41] The study of global governance must include more empirical research on the fortunes of the governed. It must uncover unintended consequences and suboptimal outcomes to inform policy going forward.

Additional reading

Amitav Acharya ed., *Why Govern? Rethinking Demand and Progress in Global Governance* (Cambridge: Cambridge University Press, 2016).

Deborah Avant, Martha Finnemore, and Susan K. Sell, eds., *Who Governs the Globe?* (Cambridge: Cambridge University Press, 2010).

Gralf-Peter Calliess and Peer Zumbansen, *Rough Consensus and Running Code: A Theory of Transnational Private Law* (Oxford: Hart Publishing, 2012).

Christer Jönsson and Jonas Tallberg, eds., *Transnational Actors in Global Governance: Patterns, Explanations, and Implications* (New York: Palgrave Macmillan, 2010).

Jonathan Koppell, *World Rule: Accountability, Legitimacy, and the Design of Global Governance* (Chicago: University of Chicago Press, 2010).

Joost Pauwelyn, Ramsel Wessel, and Jan Wouters, "The Stagnation of International Law," Working Paper No. 97, Leuven Centre for Global Governance Studies (October 2012): 1–40.

Notes

1 The Paris Agreement, unfccc.int/paris_agreement/items/9485.php; The Marrakesh Treaty, www.wipo.int/treaties/en/ip/marrakesh/.

2 Gralf-Peter Calliess and Peer Zumbansen, *Rough Consensus and Running Code: A Theory of Transnational Private Law* (Oxford: Hart Publishing, 2012); Christer Jönsson and Jonas Tallberg, eds., *Transnational Actors in Global Governance: Patterns, Explanations, and Implications* (New York: Palgrave Macmillan, 2010); Anja Jakobi, "Leadership in World Society: Power and Change from the Perspective of Sociological Institutionalism," *Peace Research Institute Frankfurt,* Working Paper No. 10, December 2011; Walter Mattli and Ngaire Woods, eds., *The Politics of Global Regulation* (Princeton, NJ: Princeton University Press, 2009); Deborah Avant, Martha Finnemore, and Susan K. Sell, eds., *Who Governs the Globe?* (Cambridge: Cambridge University Press, 2010).

3 Kenneth Waltz, *Theory of International Politics* (Reading, MA: Addison-Wesley, 1979).

4 James Rosenau and Ernst-Otto Czempiel, eds., *Governance without Government: Order and Change in World Politics* (New York: Cambridge University Press, 1992).

5 Stephen D. Krasner, "Structural Causes and Regime Consequences: Regimes as Intervening Variables," *International Organization* 36, no. 2 (1982): 185.

6 Stephen Krasner, ed., *International Regimes* (Ithaca, NY: Cornell University Press, 1983).

7 Susan Strange, "*Cave! Hic Dragones*: A Critique of Regime Analysis," *International Organization* 36, no. 2 (1982): 479–498.

8 Barbara Koremenos, Charles Lipson, and Duncan Snidal, eds., *The Rational Design of International Institutions* (Cambridge: Cambridge University Press, 2004).

9 Anne-Marie Slaughter, *A New World Order (*Princeton, NJ: Princeton University Press, 2005).

10 Ronen Palan, "Cave! Alius Draco: There Was a Sixth Dragon!," www.e-ir.info/2012/09/21/cave-alius-draco-there-was-a-sixth-dragon/.

11 Philip Cerny, "Neomedievalism, Civil War and the New Security Dilemma: Globalization as Durable Disorder," *Civil Wars* 1, no. 1 (1998): 36–64; Philip Cerny, "Globalization and the Changing Logic of Collective Action," *International Organization* 49, no. 4 (1995): 595–625; James Rosenau, *Turbulence in World Politics: A Theory of Change and Continuity* (Princeton, NJ: Princeton University Press, 1990).

12 Joost Pauwelyn, "Informal International Lawmaking: Framing the Concept," in *Informal International Lawmaking*, eds. Joost Pauwelyn, Ramses A. Wessel, and Jan Wouters (Oxford: Oxford University Press, 2012): 20.

13 Ibid., 26.

14 Miles Kahler and David Lake, "Economic Integration and Global Governance: Why So Little Supranationalism?," in *Politics of Regulation*, eds. Mattli and Woods, 274.

15 Joost Pauwelyn, "An Introduction to Informal International Lawmaking," in *Informal International Lawmaking*, eds. Pauwelyn, Wessel, and Wouters, 11.

16 A. Claire Cutler, Virginia Haufler, Tony Porter, eds., *Private Authority and International Affairs* (Albany: State University of New York Press, 1999); Thomas Biersteker and Rodney Hall, eds., *The Emergence of Private Authority in Global Governance* (Cambridge: Cambridge University Press, 2002); Margaret Keck and Kathryn Sikkink, *Activists Beyond Borders: Advocacy Networks in International Politics* (Ithaca, NY: Cornell University Press, 1998).

17 Avant, Finnemore, and Sell, eds., *Who Governs the Globe?* 2.

18 Christer Jönsson, "Capturing the Transnational: A Conceptual History," in *Transnational Actors*, eds. Jönsson and Tallberg, 36.

19 Clifford Bob, "Packing Heat: Pro-Gun Groups and the Governance of Small Arms," in *Who Governs the Globe?* eds. Avant, Finnemore, and Sell, 183–201.

20 Alexander Cooley and James Ron, "The NGO Scramble: Organizational Insecurity and the Political Economy of Transnational Action," *International Security* 27, no. 1 (2002): 5–39; Alexander Cooley, "Outsourcing Authority: How Project Contracts Transform Global Governance Networks," in *Who Governs the Globe?*, eds. Avant, Finnemore, and Sell, 238–265.

21 Jönsson and Tallberg, "Transnational Access: Findings and Future Research," in *Transnational Actors*, eds. Jönsson and Tallberg, 237–246.

22 Avant, Finnemore, and Sell, eds., *Who Governs the Globe?* 9. This discussion of authority is based on the discussion on pp. 9–14.

23 Kenneth Abbott and Duncan Snidal, "The Governance Triangle: Regulatory Standards Institutions and the Shadow of the State," in *The Politics of Global Regulation*, eds. Walter Mattli and Ngaire Woods (Princeton, NJ: Princeton University Press, 2009): 50.

24 Cooley and Ron, "NGO Scramble."

25 Jakobi, "Leadership in World Society," 7.

26 Amitav Acharya, ed., *Why Govern? Rethinking Demand and Progress in Global Governance* (Cambridge: Cambridge University Press, 2016).

27 Jakobi, "Leadership in World Society", 8.

28 Richard Mulgan, *Holding Power to Account: Accountability in Modern Democracies* (New York: Palgrave Macmillan, 2003): 1, quoted in *Informal International Lawmaking*, eds. Pauwelyn, Wessel, and Wouters, 20.

29 Jens Bartelson, "Beyond Democratic Legitimacy: Global Governance and the Promotion of Liberty," in *Transnational Actors*, eds. Jönsson and Tallberg, 226.

30 Calliess and Zumbansen, *Rough Consensus*, 125.

31 Sofia Naastrom, "Democracy Counts: Problems of Equality in Transnational Advocacy," in *Transnational Actors*, eds. Jönsson and Tallberg, 210.

32 Bartelson, "Beyond Democratic Legitimacy," 219, emphasis in original.

33 Regine Kreide, "The Ambivalence of Juridification: On Legitimate Governance in the International Context," *Global Justice: Theory, Practice and Rhetoric* 2 (2009): 19.

34 Fritz Scharpf, *Governing in Europe: Effective and Democratic?* (Oxford: Oxford University Press, 1999).

35 Daniel Mugge, "Limits of Legitimacy and the Primacy of Politics in Financial Governance," *Review of International Political Economy* 18, no. 1 (2011): 54.

36 Steven Bernstein, "Legitimacy in Intergovernmental and Non-State Global Governance," *Review of International Political Economy* 18, no. 1 (2011): 19.

37 Calliess and Zumbansen, *Rough Consensus*, 129.

38 Pauwelyn, Wessel, and Wouters, eds., *Informal International Lawmaking*, quotes from pp. 34, 33, and 25.

39 Bartelson, "Beyond Democratic Legitimacy," 220.

40 Mugge, "Limits of Legitimacy," 68.

41 Ibid., 68.

PART III
THEORIES OF INTERNATIONAL ORGANIZATION AND GLOBAL GOVERNANCE

Part introduction

Much of the way that we think theoretically about international organization (IO) and global governance is derived from broader approaches to the study of international relations (IR). This fact may be unsurprising—as we outlined in the introduction—given that all of the major theoretical traditions in IR are concerned with understanding the way the world is governed and organized as a central feature of their respective endeavors. But it is also why we—as a scholarly community—have seldom ventured beyond our comfortable intellectual silos to develop unconventional explanations of forms of world organization (past and present), and why we have, in turn, so few approaches specifically tailored to understanding global governance.

In the ten chapters in this part of the book some of the world's leading authorities spell out the major theoretical approaches to IO and global governance. In each case, we asked authors to refrain from merely describing the general tenets of an approach but instead to tailor their accounts to engage specifically with the subject matter at hand, and to tease out the implications of a particular theory for the advance or retreat of our dual focus. Thus, this next part of the book comprises one of the few dedicated chapters on "Realism" and IO and global governance, a compelling piece by Jason Charrette and Jennifer Sterling-Folker (Chapter 6); a meticulous full-length treatment of "Classical liberal internationalism" by Christer Jönsson (Chapter 7); an incisive account of one of the most influential approaches in the field—liberal institutionalism—by Tana Johnson and Jason Heiss (Chapter 8); a *tour de force* of rational choice and principal–agent theory by Duncan Snidal and Henning Tamm (Chapter 9); a first-rate synopsis of a current favorite of the field—"Constructivism"—by Susan Park (Chapter 10); a significant challenge to mainstream thinking on international organization and global governance by one of its leading proponents, "Critical theory" by Robert W. Cox (Chapter 11); a stellar account of Marxist approaches by Julian Germann (Chapter 12); the power of "Feminism" as an explanatory framework by three of the best scholars working in the field today, Susanne Zwingel, Elisabeth Prügl, and Gülay Çağlar (Chapter 13); and finally two essential additions to this second edition: Perceptive and discerning accounts of "Post-structuralism" by James Brassett (Chapter 14), and of "Decoloniality: Re(making) worlds" by Jacquelin Kataneksza, L.H.M. Ling, and Sara Shroff (Chapter 15).

None of these approaches is dispensable in pursuit of a clear view of paradigmatic thinking in the field. The dominant approaches fall in the first five chapters in this part of the book (Chapters 6–10); while more critical heterodox perspectives comprise the five that follow (Chapters 11–15). A different way of distinguishing between them would be, on the one hand, to conceive of Chapters 6–10 as dealing with frameworks designed to understand international organization and global governance as it exists (and what might be termed "status quo observing"); and, on the other hand, Chapters 11–15 as seeking to change the forms of international organization and global governance that we currently have (which could be referred to as "status quo transforming").

Introductory classes on international organization would most likely take in Chapters 6 ("Realism"), 7 ("Classical liberal internationalism"), 12 ("Marxism"), and 13 ("Feminism"). The focus would be on understanding core pillars of the discipline's intellectual canon, taking in two chapters on status quo observing and two on status quo transforming approaches. More advanced courses would supplement these with further investigations into liberal approaches ("Liberal institutionalism," Chapter 8), the rational methodology that underpins much contemporary mainstream research ("Rational choice: From principal–agent to orchestration theory" Chapter 9), "Constructivism" (Chapter 10), the rebuke of orthodoxy by "Critical theory" (Chapter 11), and alternative ways of thinking about world order (in the form of "Post-structuralism" and "Decoloniality: Re(making) worlds" in Chapters 14 and 15).

In order to facilitate reading, we offer synopses of each chapter. We spend comparatively longer introducing the content of these chapters than we do for subsequent chapters because of the difficulty and sometimes reticence that some readers have in grasping theory. For us a solid theoretical foundation is an essential component of understanding contemporary IO and global governance.

Theories of international organization and global governance: Chapter synopses

In Chapter 6, Jason Charrette and Jennifer Sterling-Folker show how, contrary to conventional wisdom, IO is actually a central concern for realist thinkers. They detail how the distribution of relative power capabilities in the international system and the forms of order that result shape the kind of global governance that we have. In this account— unlike with most caricatures of realism—they argue that this basic starting point for IR actually accounts for the multiplicity of actors in the current system, the relatively prolonged periods of peace and international cooperation that are associated with it, and the kind of global governance that is contingent on state power in general, and US power in particular. Charrette and Sterling-Folker's contribution goes a long way to addressing some of the misconceptions about realism in relation to IO and global governance. The manner in which realism views moments of relative peace and cooperation nonetheless suggests that stability is a precarious phenomenon, with shifts in relative power distributions having historically generated painful and violent upheavals.

In contrast, classical liberal internationalism focuses very much on the art of the possible, rather than the pessimism of the inevitable. In Chapter 7, Christer

Jönsson explores its foundations, whose importance for IO and global governance should not be underestimated. Although unfairly pilloried for being out of touch with "reality" by a new generation of realist scholars after World War II (WWII), classical liberal internationalism was clear about how the world ought to be organized. Unfettered commerce and the right of all peoples to self-determination were broad organizing principles that were thought to be the appropriate foundations on which a more just form of world order would exist. Early liberal thinking did not, however, focus on the construction of grand international organizations, but instead sought to generate a more progressive world order organically nurtured through the extension of peaceful ties among peoples. It was only with the onset of a more interventionist form of liberal internationalism that top-down initiatives were proposed and advocated to assist in the creation of a more just world order. In their classical formulation, however, these ideas were not always devoid of hierarchical understandings of race and "civilization"—as Article 22 of the Covenant of the League of Nations amply demonstrates.

Jönsson offers a masterly overview of the many varieties of classical liberal internationalism that serves as an important resource for understanding why liberal ideas and ideologies continue to have a purchase in debate about IO and global governance. Yet, as he illustrates, in its classic form liberalism itself was severely damaged by the horrors of WWII, which then lays the groundwork for the next two chapters.

In Chapter 8, Tana Johnson and Jacob Heiss explore the many forms in which liberalism was resurrected and in which the evolved canon has come to be applied to IO and global governance—liberal institutionalism. They guide readers through the main tenets of the approach, contrasting it with neorealism—the modern-day, rationalist variant of classical realism—as well as other approaches as they emerge along the way. In taking this intellectual journey, they guide readers through the evolution of liberal institutionalist thinking taking in functionalism, neo-functionalism, neoliberal institutionalism, and regime theory before setting out how contemporary approaches combine and collide with rationalist and constructivist understandings of IR and the world polity.

Classical realism, liberal internationalism, and elements of early liberal institutionalist thinking draw their analytical purchase from philosophical understandings of human nature—for realists humans are inherently untrustworthy, whereas for liberals humanity has the capacity to exist in a harmonious and cooperative state. What "revolutionized" the study of IR in the 1950s and 1960s was the shift away from these more abstract assertions about human nature as the bases of these approaches toward a more "scientific" foundation. Drawing heavily from work in economics that assumed the preferences of each actor could be determined and the behavior they engaged in predicted, IR scholars began to develop analyses of state behavior drawn from understandings of what might be "rational" as a course of action in a given situation and what a set of national preferences might look like. While the normative character of realism and liberalism did not change—they still assumed the worst (realism) or hoped for the best (liberalism)—the means by which analyses were conducted changed dramatically. And this change has had a profound impact on the way we think about IO and global governance.

In Chapter 9, Duncan Snidal and Henning Tamm explore the rational foundations of recent work on international organization. They explore the way that scholars have sought to answer such questions as "Why do states create and work with international organizations?" They draw on understandings of the preferences and foreign policy objectives that states have. In so doing, they also unpack simple and more complex variants of "principal–agent" (PA) theory as an approach for understanding why states operate in the way that they do. This form of analysis starts from the assumption that in particular instances "principals"—not only states but also non-state actors, voters, agencies, and the like—delegate responsibilities for certain tasks to various "agents"—which again range across international, transnational, national, and local agencies, among others. Here, not only is the nature of the relationship between principals and agents able to be better understood, attention can be directed at instances when problems arise, in which agents lose an element of control in the fulfillment of tasks, where chains of delegation become too extended and unstable, as well as about the value and social purpose of a principal–agent relationship. As they note, while PA theory has most often been applied to the relationship between states and international organizations as their agents, it has explanatory purchase for myriad principal–agent relationships among the full range of global governance actors.

Chapter 10 switches the focus away from the rational bases of much mainstream thinking to the explanatory power of "constructivism"—an approach that sees knowledge about the world as socially constructed. In this chapter, Susan Park examines constructivist approaches to IO and global governance and illustrates how they have informed and stimulated others. She illustrates how constructivism has helped plow new intellectual furrows, illustrating with clear examples its malleability and explanatory utility. Park also surveys current debates and research in the field; she points to areas of convergence and fusion between constructivist and rationalist understandings as part of the wider movement away from "isms" currently animating the field.

Chapter 11 begins Part III's move away from mainstream thinking about IO and global governance—what some would consider the "canon"—towards more heterodox thinking that challenges the longstanding assumptions and purported results of more traditional IR theories. In the first of the five chapters that comprise critiques of the mainstream, we republish the original of a chapter from the first edition by Robert W. Cox, who offers a synopsis of his major contribution to the study of world politics in Chapter 11. With characteristic clarity and insight, Cox offers a perspective that views processes of international organization and formations of global governance over time. This perspective, which he terms "critical theory," differs from mainstream approaches to IO and global governance—which he characterizes as "problem solving"—in that it stands back from the existing order and asks how it came about. But his focus is not just on understanding—it is also concerned with bringing about change. Cox focuses on "inside" aspects of how we have come to the forms of order that we currently have—the "thought, reasoning and emotion that 'makes' history"—so that they can be understood and changed in a way that overcomes instances of dominance and subordination as well as averting crises more effectively, such as climate change. Cox's approach is thus a holistic view of the evolution of international organization and formations of global governance rather than one that is focused on specific aspects or events related to individual international organizations (albeit that these are not unimportant).

In Chapter 12, Julian Germann offers a crystal clear and concise account of the explanatory power of "Marxism" as it relates to IO and global governance. He shows how Marxist approaches make sense of global governance through their capacity to identify a logic and a project at its heart. In so doing, he explores the development of different strands of thinking and how they have tackled questions of who governs and how they do so. But his contribution is about more than just asserting that global governance is best understood as a transnational and global means of facilitating the spread of capitalism worldwide. He also explores the transformative potential of global governance, its capacity to be democratized, and the better service to which it can be put.

Like Cox and Germann, the authors of Chapter 13—Susanne Zwingel, Elisabeth Prügl, and Gülay Çağlar—also focus on advancing an alternative means of understanding that is designed to bring about change. In their chapter on "feminism," they survey efforts to create an agenda for change that has sought to bring about gender equality and the challenges that these efforts have encountered. They examine existing and emerging approaches and debate current issues in feminist scholarship focusing on the translation of international gender norms within and beyond global governance structures; research on the disciplinary and governmental character of international discourses; and approaches that challenge the hegemonic focus on gender as locked into a heteronormative logic. Their purpose throughout is to encourage "an interest in emancipatory knowledge that helps overcome the seemingly endless continuation of gender subordination and gender-based violence . . . [and] to harness power and turn institutions that perpetuate masculine rule into enablers of gender justice."

In Chapter 14, James Brassett draws attention to what "post-structuralism" offers by way of understanding IO and global governance. He shows how post-structural approaches bring a focus on the significance of discourse and what he terms "the mutual entwinement between discourse and political subjects" as key components of understanding what global governance is and the normative projects that are often entailed. Brassett introduces three significant elements of post-structuralism that inform the theory and practice of IO and global governance: Deconstruction, governmentality, and performativity. And he shows how there is a continual process of change and adaptation in the way we understand global governance that augments its purposes and auspices.

Part III concludes with Chapter 15, a contribution from Jacquelin Kataneksza, L.H.M. Ling, and Sara Shroff, "Decoloniality: (Re)making worlds." By introducing decoloniality and its implications for global governance, they explain what decoloniality is, how it differs from post-coloniality, and why decolonizing IO and global governance is an essential endeavor. In pursuit of their aims, they focus on three types of global institution: IR, liberal capitalism, and modern love. They argue that each communicates a colonial narrative that informs action, knowledge, and being; and they illustrate how decoloniality encourages a greater emphasis on justice and a progressive agenda for change.

Where to now?

In surveying the content of the chapters that follow, we have purposely sought to guide readers because theory is often the most challenging component—to teach as well as to understand—of any IO and global governance class. We have pointed not only to how these chapters might be read, but also the order in which they could be consulted, what they contain, and how they can help us better understand IO and global governance. And we have sought to provide a solid foundation on which readers can embark on their more empirical investigations of world order in the chapters that follow in the subsequent sections.

Realism

Jason Charrette and Jennifer Sterling-Folker

The literature on international organization (IO) and global governance gives the impression that realism contributes very little to the topic. Many critics treat it as a nemesis to be defeated before analysis can proceed, rather than as an approach with something important to say in its own right about these subjects. Yet realists have always contributed to discussions of IO and global governance. How realism defines these terms may be part of the reason it is often given short shrift. From a realist perspective, the term "IO" is a reference to the Westphalian system comprised of sovereign states. The system does not exist in a vacuum and the component states interact in predictable ways that generate patterns of order and disorder in world politics.

Central to these patterns is the relative power of states. This is because in an anarchic environment in which there is no world government to impose order and stability, states engage in self-help behavior to ensure their own survival. Anarchy heightens the stakes of state interaction so that competing interests have the potential to escalate into military conflict. Thus, states are concerned with relative power, as power capabilities become the central means within anarchy of obtaining self-interests and defending against other states. In such an environment, relative power—or the distribution of capabilities—determines outcomes. Periods of relative peace or violence are traceable to the interactions of the relatively more powerful states in the system. From a realist perspective, then, the term IO is a reference to the specific patterns of order that can arise from great power self-interests and interaction.[1]

While never fully divorced from patterns of disorder, periods of relatively greater order, organization, and management have existed. Realism explains these periods by focusing on the interactions and efforts of relatively powerful states. These patterns of order do not displace the significance of relative power to global affairs or states as its constitutive unit. Patterns of IO are instead *contingent* on the interests of powerful states. Hence, if there appear to be patterns of authority, control, and legitimacy in contemporary world politics—global governance in common parlance—it is because of the relative power and ongoing interactions among powerful states.

Realist insistence that states and power remain fundamental to the subject of IO and global governance is an important contribution to our understanding of order, organization, and management in world affairs. Realist claims are also essential for understanding the arguments and concerns of many other approaches to IO and global governance, which often contrast themselves to realist explanations. The next section of this chapter reviews the historical development of IO from a realist perspective, with a focus on the implications of polarity and hegemonic stability for contemporary world order. We then discuss a number of current debates among realists involving balancing and power transitions that involve the future of contemporary IO. Because these debates reflect realism's ongoing skepticism about some of the bolder claims in the IO and global governance literature about the future, we then consider how realism addresses key criticisms and emerging issues. In so doing, we argue that the ethical concerns evoked by realism's ongoing pessimism serve as an important check against an undue optimism that masks deep inequalities and exploitations. These can generate backlash both between and within states that have serious ramifications for the sustainability of the current world order. In this respect, realism provides not only a compelling explanation for IO and global governance, but also a basis from which to consider how the normative biases of other perspectives leads them to miss such possibilities.

IO from a realist perspective

Because states are suspicious of one another's intentions in an anarchic environment, relative harmony among powerful states has been historically rare. Cooperation does occur but it has usually been when a collection of states have faced a common threat and have pooled their relative power to defend against it. These dynamics account for the coalitions against Napoleon in the early nineteenth century, as well as opposing alliances during World Wars I and II. Such cooperation can be difficult to achieve and sustain, however, as states are just as suspicious of the intentions of potential alliance partners, and these suspicions reassert themselves after the common enemy has been vanquished.

The contemporary international system is remarkable for the extensiveness of cooperation, as well as for the relatively lengthy period of peace among the great powers. While interstate violence and warfare continue to be endemic to many parts of the globe, their centrality to great power politics declined in the latter half of the twentieth century. A variety of analytical perspectives have tried to explain why contemporary international relations (IR) appear to be qualitatively different from the past. Many of these theories highlight the role of democracy, economic interdependence, and international organizations (whether intergovernmental, IGOs, or nongovernmental, NGOs) as the progenitors of international peace and cooperation.[2] The term "global governance" is often preferred because global politics is seen as the sum of all global actors, their interests and their practices, not just state interests, as the term IO implies. Thus, global governance is sometimes defined as the management of this decentralized web of interdependent transnational actors through public–private partnerships, network entanglements, and institutions that enable increasing cooperation despite the anarchic environment.[3] From a realist perspective, however, the term "global governance" misdirects attention from deeper structures of power that shape patterns of global management by implying that these activities occur independently of states.

Realism, by way of contrast, is suspicious of claims about international institutional causality and it argues that global governance is a phenomenon contingent on power politics. To account for the extensiveness of cooperation today, realists argue that while an anarchic, self-help environment makes suspicion endemic and hence a severe inhibitor to cooperation, these dynamics may be overcome on an ongoing—albeit impermanent—basis if particular circumstances related to relative power occur. Beyond security alliances there are two other circumstances in which more extensive forms of cooperation, organization, and order may be achieved. Both involve the presence of exceptionally powerful states whose interactions shape global interactions in ways that conform to their own interests and values.

The first circumstance involves the concept of polarity, which is the relative distribution of capabilities in the international system during particular time periods. Realists argue that distributional changes affect system stability by producing different patterns of behavior and hence the probability and scale of international violence.[4] Distributional changes also have consequences for international order and management. According to Randall Schweller and David Priess, a multipolar system, which consists of many great powers, can produce two different forms of IO and global governance.[5] If some states are "revisionist," they will be dissatisfied with existing arrangements and seek to dominate the system. This makes other states wary of the existing balance of power so they prefer a freer hand to react to changes in relative power differentials. The resulting international management will be shallow, temporary, and spontaneous, as managing the global space through formal institutions takes a back seat to the needs of survival. Examples of this form of management include Europe during the Napoleonic era and interstate relations prior to WWI. Conversely, in a multipolar system with no revisionist states and in which defensive weaponry has the advantage, more formal, permanent, and negotiated modes of organization among the great powers are likely. States can afford to be relatively less worried about survival and more concerned with peacefully solving differences. An example of this system is the Concert of Europe after Napoleon's defeat in the early nineteenth century.

In a system with two great powers—referred to as "bipolarity"—organization will be a by-product of relations between the two superpowers. The example of this type of IO is the US and Soviet spheres of influence during the Cold War. According to Kenneth Waltz, the two states learned "to behave as sensible duopolists" by "moderating the intensity of their competition and cooperating at times to mutual advantage while continuing to eye each other warily."[6] The resulting pattern of bipolar systemic organization had two characteristics according to Randall Schweller and David Priess. First, there were explicit and implicit arrangements, of an informal, spontaneous nature, between the two superpowers to respect each other's spheres of influence and avoid unnecessary conflict. Second, within each sphere of influence, behavior conformed to the organization found in unipolarity (or one great power), with each superpower either imposing or negotiating an order within its sphere of influence.

In a unipolar system, the most powerful state attempts to establish rules that benefit itself, and its internal characteristics shape the organizational choices it pursues. Although domination alone can be used to establish and enforce the rules of the game in its favor, unipoles will often rely on a combination of domination and negotiated consent. This condition is often referred to as "hegemonic stability." Although the resulting system reflects that hegemon's preferences, it also provides other goods that make its rule attractive to weaker states and thus hegemonic unipolarity can result in a negotiated form of IO. The hegemon uses its greater capabilities to shape international politics for the promotion of more order, stability, and cooperative behavior within the system. Schweller and Priess argue that such a hegemon is the "ideal" realist state in that it "understands the limits of coercive power and so promotes legitimacy and emulation of its values while tolerating pluralism and diversity."[7]

To be clear, as Elke Krahmann notes, "unipolarity does not necessarily entail hegemony; nor can hegemony only be found in unipolar structures."[8] Thus not all unipoles or great powers are hegemons, and most scholars identify just three periods of hegemonic stability: The Netherlands in the seventeenth century, the United Kingdom in the late nineteenth century, and the United States after WWII. What distinguishes hegemony is the great power's desire to promote international trade and investment with other states, which can only be done effectively by encouraging regularized, cooperative relationships.[9]

This does not mean that coercion is absent from how these hegemonic "goods" are spread among participants, but it is the combination of a single state's relatively greater capability *and* the existence of collective self-interests in economic exchange that differentiates hegemony from imperialism and unipolarity. In a period of hegemonic stability "the distribution of power among states is the primary determinant of the character of the international economic system" and it explains "patterns of economic relations among the advanced capitalist countries."[10] It also accounts for the relatively greater cooperation and order we see in contemporary world affairs.

Most of the IGOs that serve as the backbone for contemporary international cooperation can be traced to US hegemony in the immediate aftermath of WWII. The United States emerged from that conflict as the most powerful state in the international system, and its reliance on formal institutions and international law is a distinguishing feature of its hegemony. It promoted the creation of the UN as an umbrella organization for treaty-based cooperation in a variety of global concerns and issue areas. It also oversaw the creation of the International Monetary Fund (IMF), the World Bank, and the General Agreement on Tariffs and Trade (GATT), with the express goal of encouraging cooperative economic exchange. In so doing, the United States rewarded cooperation, punished defectors, and served as a guarantor for the international economic system it shared with its allies. Its presence, combined with the common threat posed by the Soviet Union, was also an inducement to avoid warfare among the states within its alliance system. Hence the term *Pax Americana* is often used to indicate the post-WWII period of US hegemonic stability.

While there are clear differences between a hegemonic stability and a purely polarity perspective, both assume that contemporary world order can be traced to and remains contingent on the current distribution of capabilities. That distribution involves the relatively greater power of the United States and its continued willingness to support an extensively formal and legalized cooperative world order in order to obtain its own economic and military interests. This means that if US relative power or its willingness to support cooperation were to change, then so too would existing patterns of organization and management. In other words, if contemporary world order is sustained through a particular distribution of power, there are significant implications for IO when that distribution changes. Because realists are pessimistic that US primacy can be maintained in the face of rising powers and increased economic and military competition, they are also skeptical about the preservation of the current liberal international order. This has led to debate among realists over whether the United States is in decline and what that would mean for world affairs.

Current debates

There are a variety of reasons why powerful states cannot count on a lasting favorable distribution of capabilities. One reason is that anarchy induces a competitive drive among states to balance unchecked power as a potential threat to their survival.[11] States try to increase their own military capability (internal balancing) or ally with other states to benefit from their pooled military capability (external balancing). Unipolarity is expected to be short lived in such a context, since states face a security risk from the unipole's potential military aggression and are therefore more likely to balance against it—especially if the threat is existential. As a result, realists anticipate that a challenger or group of challengers faced with the presence of a single great power and dissatisfied with its international order will eventually balance against it. Such moments of power transition are often fraught with interstate violence and—at the very least—the system will revert to multipolarity, which is associated with higher levels of warfare among the great powers. This is why realists are concerned with the rise of China as a potential challenger to US dominance. Historical patterns indicate an increased risk for interstate violence in moments of power transition, and it is unclear what sort of IO and patterns of global governance would evolve from an international system dominated by China.

A second reason why particular distributions of capability do not last relates to technological advances that may contribute to the rapid rise of potential challengers, particularly in strategic planning and warfare.[12] Rapid shifts in technology can make weapons systems obsolete almost overnight and, in an environment in which other states have an incentive to compete to acquire more power, the maintenance of relative power is precarious. Even in economic affairs, a hegemonic state cannot expect to dominate the global market indefinitely. The very states that benefit from its international order will also innovate and may eventually prove to be its greatest economic challengers.

A third reason why relative power does not last is because hegemony comes at a high price. To ward off potential challengers to its world order, the hegemon must constantly stay economically and militarily ahead. However, the maintenance of its order inflicts an inescapable and eventually fatal "economic drain" on the hegemon.[13] Since its own economy is critical to the health of the global economy, the hegemon must remain open to commerce and trade—even if it hurts its own people. Thus, it risks domestic backlash against the very policies necessary to maintain its hegemony *vis-à-vis* other states. It must also commit itself to pay for the defense of far-flung allies that are a part of its system—even when its own country is not directly threatened. It might even need to share its military technology with other allies, allowing those states to erode its own military advantage. Put simply, the greater a state's reach and influence, the more territory and core interests it is forced to defend. Eventually, the hegemon will suffer "imperial overstretch," exhaustion and decline, ending the world order that was dependent on it. Whatever order might replace it will be contingent on an entirely new distribution of capabilities, with no guarantee that a hegemon will emerge to encourage and support a system of economic exchange.

If we consider US pre-eminence and decline from either a unipolar or hegemonic perspective, pessimism about the preservation of contemporary world order is warranted. However, not everyone believes the United States is destined to decline, and some realists argue that the United States is categorically different from previous hegemons.[14] For example, rather than exhaust its own resources to maintain its global order, Michael Mastanduno argues that the United States is a "system-maker and privilege-taker," because it pays a lot to maintain its world order but also gets a disproportionate share of the benefits.[15] Moreover, as the most powerful state, the United States sets the international rules for finance and security, thus allowing it to enable some foreign policies while constraining others. Despite potential challenges to its dominance from global financial crises, recessions, and alternative currencies, the US dollar remains the top international currency, and it can slant the rules of international trade in its favor, including using access to its huge consumer market as both a carrot and a stick.[16]

Such realist scholars as Stephen Brooks, William Wohlforth, Barry Posen, and Paul Kennedy, have argued that US military capabilities are without peer.[17] The material gap between the United States and all other countries is so large that the traditional systemic boundaries no longer apply. Similarly, US military capabilities can weaken an adversary's economic and military capabilities as soon as the United States perceives it to be a potential threat. What is more, it has attained this capability without breaking the bank, spending only 4.8 percent of its GDP on military expenditures in 2012 for example, so that, as Paul Kennedy has observed, "being Number One at great cost is one thing; being the world's single superpower on the cheap is astonishing."[18]

Of course, even if the United States is not in decline, its own behavior may provoke balancing against it. Thus one of the key debates within realism about the future of IO concerns how we are to see balancing against the United States as a result of its own behavior. US unilateralism in its invasion of Iraq and the Global War on Terror is often cited as confirmation of the existential danger of a unipole aspiring to global hegemony, leading Waltz (among others) to argue that, "even if a dominant power behaves with moderation, restraint, and forbearance, weaker states will worry about its future behavior."[19]

Other realists disagree that we should expect to see balancing behavior, because if a hegemon becomes too powerful, the cost of both external and internal balancing against it grows enormously.[20] If both the immensity and projection capabilities of US military power can diffuse challenges before they even occur, then states would have considerable difficulty creating an alliance against the United States. What, after all, is to stop it from picking off potential balancers one by one in the formative stage of any grand balancing coalition?

Additionally, Schweller argues that the costs of internally balancing against a country as powerful as the United States make it difficult for foreign leaders to convince an often fragmented domestic constituency to undertake the burden.[21] Few states are single minded enough to pursue such a strategy, and if given a choice many smaller states will bandwagon with the United States, rather than challenge it.

Finally, as G. John Ikenberry and Stephen Walt have argued, a benign foreign policy will mitigate the imperative to balance the United States.[22] They argue that as long as it pursues liberal hegemonic rather than imperial policies to support the current international order, there should be no reason for other states to challenge that order. In other words, if the unipole remains reasonable and respectfully distant in its policies, its order can be maintained. It remains an open question, however, how long the United States will be willing or able to pursue such policies given the internal costs and external difficulties of maintaining hegemony. In the absence of such policies, the imperative for other states to balance it would return and have significant ramifications for the established world order. Yet as all these arguments indicate, from a realist perspective balance of power politics remains central to international order, even in one dominated by liberal processes and preferences.

Key criticisms and emerging issues

Realism is concerned with the effect of relative power on contemporary world order. Because states are the central actors in world affairs, it is the distribution of capabilities among them that sets the stage for patterns of global authority, control, and legitimacy. States should not be analyzed as first among equals in relation to non-state actors (NSAs), such as IGOs, NGOs, transnational corporations, activists, or transnational civil society. No realist scholar would deny that these actors exist, are currently engaged in governance of some sort, or can make a difference to the quality of some people's daily lives. However, their existence does not grant them status as a primary driver of world order. Rather, this web of formal and informal actors, institutions, and arrangements is contingent on the authority and legitimacy of the state. Far from displacing the preeminence of states, there is considerable evidence that non-state actor activities actually reinforce it.[23]

NSAs are important not because they are independent of states but because they allow states to more efficiently achieve their state interests and so are useful to powerful states. Institutions and NSAs "enable great powers to rule others and to manage regional and world affairs more effectively and efficiently than would be possible in their absence," while international law "direct(s) great power behavior in accordance with the established rules of the game."[24] States can, if they wish, halt increasing governance regardless of how binding or permanent it may seem since global governance is an inherently contingent condition. Even the strongest institutions for governing a global space can be fractured once they no longer serve a state's interests, and dense, entrenched networks of capital and trade can be insufficient for preventing management collapse.[25]

Realism's critics often suggest that it fails to read contemporary international order correctly. They argue that it *a priori* privileges the state, misses the importance of NSAs, fails to recognize the social construction of IR because of its rationalist assumptions, and its fatalistic tendencies counsel conservative foreign policies that reinforce power politics and hence its own explanations for world affairs. The result is a widespread accusation that it is realism's hold on policymaker imaginations, not power politics itself, which stands in the way of achieving greater progress in world affairs.[26] Certainly its assumptions can lead realists to make predictions that appear to be wrong and its analyses can also have significant blind spots regarding the actual processes that comprise the daily activities of global management. Moreover, because realism suggests that activism separated from the distribution of capabilities will be ineffective, its underlying fatalism raises serious ethical questions about whether it is suggesting resignation to the oppression and exploitation associated with all power politics. In a liberal world order, realism appears to be out of step with the ideals and aspirations of the majority of its participants.

It is at this juncture, however, that realism makes one of its most important contributions to the discussion of contemporary IO and global governance. Realism's pessimistic reading of the contemporary world order is shaped by its understanding of human history, in which patterns of competition and violence have continually reflected the unfortunate truism that "might makes right." Powerful entities throughout history have always determined what was politically, economically, socially, and ethically acceptable. In so doing, they shaped the boundaries of thought and behavior for the actors and individuals that existed under their exigencies.[27] This is just as true for the contemporary world order, in which "right" is derived from the "might" of the powerful states in the system, among whom a set of Western ideals (involving the desirability of democracy, capitalism, and state sovereignty) shape what international order should look like. The have-nots are well aware that power determines outcomes in this system and that they are not necessarily beneficiaries of it. Yet much of the IO and global governance literature would have one believe that relative power is superfluous because there is an obvious "rightness" to the liberal world order that is globally recognized and shared.

Realism serves as an important corrective for this contemporary tendency to equate liberal ideals, global reach, and normative desirability without also acknowledging the relative power (both among and of states) that necessarily and coercively supports this equation. As Martin Griffiths has observed: "[R]ealists in the US are at the forefront of contemporary debates about the future of US foreign policy," because they recognize the "close nexus between political and economic stability at the global level" and "between power, authority and legitimacy."[28] International organization is dependent on and a reflection of the interests and preferences of the most powerful states in the system. We should not be surprised, then, to discover that the world order they have created supports their continued dominance over others. Hence, realism draws attention to the error of what Duncan Bell (drawing on the work of C.A.J. Coady) calls "the moralism of imposition," in which we "seek to impose values (even if we think they are universally applicable in principle) on other people and communities" without also recognizing that doing so "almost always requires the use of coercion, disrespect or force."[29]

In addition, the most powerful states in the contemporary system have created a liberal world order that generates significant global inequalities and externalities not only for weaker states but also for populations within their own borders. As a result, contemporary IO is increasingly subject to backlash from external groups, such as Al-Qaeda and the Islamic State of Iraq and the Levant/Syria (ISIL, ISIS or Da'esh), and from internal groups, with the rise of far-right populist nationalism in the United States and Europe. The latter development raises serious questions about the long-term sustainability of the liberal consensus shared by the hegemon and other relatively powerful states from which contemporary international cooperation and management derives. Should that consensus shift or decline, so too will the liberal world order that has been built on it.

Conclusion

Despite the contemporary rhetoric about global governance, we do not live in a brave new world in which old ways of thinking and behaving have become irrelevant. Our world continues to be dominated—for better or worse—by the preferences, values, and goals of relatively powerful states. While contemporary world order is character-ized by relatively extensive cooperation, management, and NSA involvement, using the term "global governance" to describe this order is highly problematic. The term suggests that management occurs independently of its deep structural foundations, instead of as a contingent pattern arising from great power interactions. Hence, the term "IO" is still a more appropriate signifier for contemporary world order. Other analytical perspectives prefer the term "global governance" because they divorce the study of systemic organization and governance from these overt and implicit power structures. In doing so, they unnecessarily disconnect the study of world order from the study of IR more broadly. The consequence of so doing is an ever present risk of getting lost in the novelty of a particular international moment and reading its durability with undue sanguinity.

This is hardly a new phenomenon. Remarking about the typical pre-WWI London inhabitant, who could engage in international commerce at home using cutting-edge communications technology, John Maynard Keynes noted that such an individual "regarded this state of affairs as normal, certain, and permanent, except in the direction of further improvement, and any deviation from it as aberrant, scandalous, and avoidable."[30] With little modification, such a statement could describe many contemporary explanations for IO and global governance. Alternatively, the enduring contribution of the realist tradition is both to contextualize the current management of the international environment within the larger sweep of history and to provide a check on the blind optimism that assumes the hegemony of liberal ideas and institu-tions is natural and inevitable. Realism provides a critical voice to the larger debate about IO and global governance by drawing attention to power politics—reminding the discipline that, despite the fluidity of international politics, some things never change.

Additional reading

Michael E. Brown, et al., eds., *Primacy and Its Discontents: American Power and International Stability* (Cambridge, MA: MIT Press, 2008).

Robert Gilpin, "A Realist Perspective on International Governance," in *Governing Globalization: Power, Authority and Global Governance*, eds. Anthony McGrew and David Held (Oxford: Polity Press, 2002): 237–248.

John J. Mearsheimer, "Imperial by Design," *The National Interest* 111 (2011): 16–34.

Jennifer Sterling-Folker, "Realist Global Governance: Revisiting *Cave! Hic Dragones* and Beyond," in *Contending Perspectives on Global Governance: Coherence, Contestation, and World Order*, eds. Matthew Hoffmann and Alice Ba (London: Routledge, 2000): 17–38.

Notes

1 Robert Gilpin, *War and Change in World Politics* (New York: Cambridge University Press, 1981), 1–32; Kenneth Waltz, *Theory of International Politics*, (New York: McGraw-Hill, 1979).

2 Helen V. Milner and Andrew Moravcsik, eds., *Power, Interdependence, and Nonstate Actors in World Affairs* (Princeton, NJ: Princeton University Press, 2009); Bruce Russett and John Oneal, *Triangulating Peace: Democracy, Interdependence, and International Organizations* (New York: W.W. Norton & Company, 2001).

3 James N. Rosenau and Ernst-Otto Czempiel, eds., *Governance without Government: Order and Change in World Politics* (Cambridge: Cambridge University Press, 1992); Jim Whitman, ed., *Global Governance* (Basingstoke: Palgrave Macmillan, 2009).

4 Paul Kennedy, *The Rise and Fall of the Great Powers: Economic Change and Military Conflict from 1500 to 2000* (New York: Vintage Books, 1987).

5 The following discussion is drawn from Randall L. Schweller and David Priess, "A Tale of Two Realisms," 18–21, Gilpin, *War and Change*, ch. 2; Waltz, *Theory of International Politics*, ch. 9.

6 Waltz, *Theory of International Politics*, 203.

7 Schweller and Priess, "A Tale of Two Realisms," 18.

8 Elke Krahmann, "American Hegemony or Global Governance? Competing Visions of International Security," *International Studies Review* 7, no. 4 (2005): 533.

9 Christopher Chase-Dunn, et al., "The Forum: Hegemony and Social Change," *Mershon International Studies Review* 38, no. 2 (1994): 361–376; David Lake, "Leadership, Hegemony, and the International Economy: Naked Emperor or Tattered Monarch with Potential?," *International Studies Quarterly* 37, no. 4 (1993): 459–489; David Wilkinson, "Unipolarity without Hegemony," *International Studies Review* 1, no. 2 (1999): 141–172.

10 Michael C. Webb and Stephen D. Krasner, "Hegemonic Stability Theory: An Empirical Assessment," *Review of International Studies* 15, no. 2 (1989): 183.

11 Christopher Layne, "The Unipolar Illusion Revisited," *International Security* 31, no. 2 (2006): 7–41; Jack S. Levy and William R. Thompson, "Hegemonic Threats and Great-Power Balancing in Europe, 1945–1999," *Security Studies* 14, no. 1 (2005): 29–30;

John J. Mearsheimer, *The Tragedy of Great Power Politics* (New York: W. W. Norton & Company, 2001), 139, 156–157; Robert Pape, "Soft Balancing against the United States," *International Security* 30, no. 1 (2005): 7–45; Stephen Walt, *Taming American Power: The Global Response to US Primacy* (New York: W. W. Norton & Company, 2005), 132.

12 Michael C. Horowitz, *The Diffusion of Military Power: Causes and Consequences for International Politics* (Princeton, NJ: Princeton University Press, 2010); João Resende-Santos, *Neorealism, States, and the Modern Mass Army* (Cambridge: Cambridge University Press, 2007).

13 Gilpin, *War and Change*, 156–157, 175–185; Kennedy, *The Rise and Fall*, xvi; Charles P. Kindleberger, "Dominance and Leadership in the International Economy: Exploitation, Public Goods, and Free Riders," *International Studies Quarterly* 25, no. 2 (1981): 246–248;

14 Ewan Harrison, "The Contradictions of Unipolarity," in *Rethinking Realism in International Relations: Between Tradition and Innovation*, eds. Annette Freyberg-Inan, Ewan Harrison, and Patrick James (Baltimore, MD: Johns Hopkins University Press, 2009), 76–102; Krahmann, "American Hegemony"; Christopher Layne, "The Waning of US Hegemony—Myth or Reality? A Review Essay," *International Security* 34, no. 1 (2009): 147–172;.

15 Michael Mastanduno, "System Maker and Privilege Taker: US Power and the International Political Economy," *World Politics* 61, no. 1 (2009): 121–154.

16 Carla Norrlof, *America's Global Advantage* (Cambridge, MA: Cambridge University Press, 2009), ch. 4; Susan Strange, "The Persistent Myth of Lost Hegemony," *International Organization* 41, no. 4 (1987): 551–574.

17 Stephen Brooks and William Wohlforth, *World Out of Balance* (Princeton, NJ: Princeton University Press, 2008); Paul Kennedy, "The Greatest Superpower Ever," *New Perspectives Quarterly* 19, no. 2 (2002): 8–18; Barry Posen, "Command of the Commons: The Military Foundations of US Hegemony," *International Security* 28, no. 1 (2003): 5–46.

18 The World Bank, *World Development Indicators* (Washington, DC: World Bank, 2012), 310; Kennedy, "The Greatest Superpower," 13.

19 Waltz, "Structural Realism," 27–28. See also Christopher Layne, "The War on Terrorism and the Balance of Power," in *Balance of Power: Theory and Practice in the 21st Century*, eds. T. V. Paul, James J. Wirtz, and Michel Fortmann (Stanford, CA: Stanford University Press, 2004); Pape, "Soft Balancing."

20 Posen, "Command of the Commons"; Brooks and Wohlforth, *World Out of Balance*, 23.

21 Randall L. Schweller, *Unanswered Threats: Political Constraints on the Balance of Power* (Princeton, NJ: Princeton University Press, 2006).

22 G. John Ikenberry, *Liberal Leviathan: The Origins, Crisis, and Transformation of the American World Order* (Princeton, NJ: Princeton University Press, 2011); Walt, *Taming American Power*, 119–120.

23 Kim D. Reimann, "A View from the Top: International Politics, Norms and the Worldwide Growth of NGOs," *International Studies Quarterly* 50, no. 1 (2006): 45–67; Anna Stavrianakis, "Missing the Target: NGOs, Global Civil Society and the Arms Trade," *Journal of International Relations and Development* 15, no. 2 (2011): 224–249; Randall W. Stone, *Controlling Institutions: International Organizations and the Global Economy* (Cambridge: Cambridge University Press, 2011).

24 Schweller and Priess, "Tale of Two Realisms," 3–4.

25 Jervis, "Realism, Neoliberalism, and Cooperation," 56–7; Jeffry Frieden, *Global Capitalism: Its Fall and Rise in the Twentieth Century* (New York: W. W. Norton & Company, 2006).

26 For example, Beverly Crawford, "Toward a Theory of Progress in International Relations," in *Progress in Postwar International Relations*, eds. Emanuel Adler and Beverly Crawford (New York: Columbia University Press, 1991): 440–444.

27 Iver B. Neumann and Ole Jacob Sending, *Governing the Global Polity: Practice, Mentality, and Rationality* (Ann Arbor: University of Michigan Press, 2010); Christian

Reus-Smit, *The Moral Purpose of the State: Culture, Social Identity, and Institutional Rationality in International Relations* (Princeton, NJ: Princeton University Press, 1999).

28 Martin Griffiths, *Rethinking International Relations Theory* (Basingstoke: Palgrave Macmillan, 2011).

29 Duncan Bell, "Political Realism and the Limits of Ethics," in *Ethics and World Politics*, ed. Duncan Bell (Oxford: Oxford University Press, 2010), 100.

30 John Maynard Keynes, *Economic Consequences of the Peace* (New York: Harcourt, Brace & Howe, 1919), 6.

Classical liberal internationalism

Christer Jönsson

As none of the three terms in the title of this chapter is self-explanatory or uncontroversial, each warrants some clarification. "Internationalism" has been described succinctly as "the ideology of international bonding" or "the idea that we both are and should be part of a broader community than that of the nation or the state." As such, it has a range of overlapping meanings, all revolving around attempts to regulate political life at the global level in the pursuit of peace. Internationalism can be seen as the opposite of nationalism, which emphasizes national interests and values in opposition to internationalist ideas and programs that are perceived to threaten national independence. Both ideologies have rational as well as emotional qualities. Internationalism should also be distinguished from cosmopolitanism. Whereas cosmopolitanism envisages a universalistic community, internationalism takes the existing division into particularistic communities as its point of departure. Internationalists, in other words, do not share the cosmopolitan vision of transcending the state but take the division into states as a given and look for ways of aligning conflicting interests.[1]

The label "liberal" indicates one distinct variety of internationalist thought that may be distinguished from conservative and socialist internationalism. In contrast to its conservative counterpart, which views balance of power as the principal way of restraining states, liberal internationalism is more optimistic about the prospects for interstate cooperation. And against the socialist vision of the withering away of states and an ensuing classless world society, liberal internationalism posits a zone of peace and cooperation among liberal states. Another, partly overlapping typology contrasts liberal internationalism with hegemonic internationalism—the belief that the only possible and desirable way of integrating the world is on asymmetrical, unequal terms—and with radical or revolutionary internationalism.[2]

This chapter deals with *classical* liberal internationalism. It is a tradition of thought with roots in the Enlightenment. Where the classical era ends and neoliberalism takes over is debatable. For the purpose of this chapter, the border is arbitrarily drawn at World War II. The war entailed a crisis for liberal internationalism. Criticized as idealistic, naïve, and utopian, it was overtaken by realism as the prevailing paradigm. The postwar re-establishment of liberal internationalism in the form of neoliberal institutionalism, is dealt with elsewhere in this volume. It should be noted that whereas the classical tradition was primarily a prescriptive and prospective ideology with minimal empirical claims, neoliberalism offers an analytical framework for the study of historical processes rather than a remote ideal.[3]

A caveat seems called for at the outset: When we attach the label "liberal internationalism," especially with the epithet "classical," to a number of early thinkers from the eighteenth to the twentieth century, we apply a terminology of later origin: "Many thinkers are retrospectively categorized as liberal internationalists despite the fact that they would neither recognize nor identify with the term."[4]

This chapter first outlines some of the basic values and tenets associated with liberal internationalism. It then gives a brief account of the evolution of the tradition, pointing to some of its most prominent exponents. The section thereafter identifies and discusses recurrent tensions and controversies within liberalism related to international relations. The concluding remarks dwell on the legacy of classical liberal internationalism and its relevance to contemporary realities.

Basic tenets of liberal internationalism

In Michael Doyle's oft quoted words, "there is no canonical description of liberalism," only something resembling "a family portrait of principles and institutions" associated with liberal states.[5] If liberalism in general defies precise definition, liberal internationalism appears even more ambiguous. "Few political notions are at once so normative and so equivocal as liberal internationalism."[6] Yet there is a fair degree of agreement on identifying a cluster of values characterizing liberalism as a political ideology and their application to international affairs.

The most fundamental value shared by all liberals concerns individual *freedom*. Commitment to this principle entails challenging vested interests and arbitrary authority while defending human rights and promoting popularly based institutions. Power is considered legitimate only if it is based on popular consent and respects basic freedoms. Liberalism rests on confidence in the rational and moral qualities of human beings. The emphasis on the liberty and welfare of individuals over and above social structures sets liberalism apart from socialism. Another core element of liberalism is a belief in progress. Classical liberalism is thus an ideology of reform, reflecting confidence in the corrigibility and improvability of all political arrangements. Malfunctioning behavior is viewed as a product of counterproductive institutions and practices that can be remedied by reforming the system that produces it. This emphasis on progressive change sets liberalism apart from conservatism.[7]

How, then, do these core values translate into the international arena? First, it should be noted that the international dimension is not an afterthought or a later derivative, but has always been an integral part of liberal thinking. It can be argued that "liberalism is by definition international."[8] The growth of international interaction and cooperation is seen as a central element in the realization of greater human freedom. The belief in progress applies to the international arena as well. Liberal internationalism envisages a gradual transformation of international relations, which helps promote human freedom by establishing conditions of peace, prosperity and justice.[9] Thus, "liberal accounts of international politics were characteristically those of a process, not what we have today, but what we may have later if we keep to a certain course."[10] Like all liberals, internationalists celebrate the possibility of deliberate reforms, but their expectations go beyond the domestic sphere to include international relations. While not teleological, liberal internationalism offers a broad vision of an open, rule-based system where states have overcome constraints and are prepared to cooperate and pursue collective action.[11]

Other themes characteristic of classical liberal internationalism include free trade, national self-determination, nonintervention in the internal affairs of other states, and strengthened international law. Free trade is seen to generate peace and prosperity by binding people together in material interdependencies that would raise the costs of war and create an international division of labor. The belief that national self-determination promotes peace is a variant of democratic liberalism. It draws on an assumed similarity of relationships between states and international order, on the one hand, and individuals and domestic order, on the other, as does the principle of nonintervention. In the same way that morally autonomous citizens hold rights to liberty, states that represent them democratically have the right to be free from foreign intervention. Similarly, the progress of international law is measured by its increasing similarity to domestic law.

As pointed out by several observers, the classical liberal vision of international reform is built to a considerable degree on a domestic analogy: The same general principles that had led to the transformation of political life domestically were seen to apply externally as well. Stanley Hoffmann argues that "the international dimension of liberalism was little more than the projection of domestic liberalism on a world scale."[12] Critics claim that early liberals overlooked the differences between domestic and international politics. However, more nuanced accounts posit that the liberal vision did not rest on a naïve analogy but reflected "the view that the anarchic system of sovereign states can and ought to be *domesticated* in a way that resembles, however imperfectly, the liberal vision of political society within the state."[13]

Classical liberal internationalism is best characterized as an ideology, that is, a system of political thought arising out of, and reflecting, the economic, political, and cultural experience of particular social groups. As such, it is geared toward political action in a political realm where it has to struggle with the world views of other social groups. Historically bound, ideologies are constantly changing. To account for liberal internationalism as an ideology therefore requires "an engagement with its conditions of emergence and an historical account of its struggle with internal and external competitors."[14]

The origins and evolution of liberal internationalism

Liberalism originated in Europe around the turn of the seventeenth and eighteenth century, a tumultuous period in that continent's history. The feudal system had fallen; the political control of papal Christendom was broken; the Renaissance had renewed interest in the republican and cultural traditions of antiquity; a system ordered on sovereign states was emerging; and the Enlightenment introduced ideas about reforming society, using reason rather than tradition, and advancing knowledge through science. It was during this era of change that liberalism emerged to become the dominant theory of modernity. Domestically, the feudal legacy of ruling aristocracies and autocratic rule became targets of liberal criticism; internationally, the prevalence of violence and hypocrisy in a system dominated by balance-of-power thinking came under attack.

The earliest liberal intellectuals sought to use an empiricist methodology developed in the natural sciences to determine a political theory that would organize and defend the aspirations of the emergent middle class for a defense of private property, a rationalized system of laws, and a voice in lawmaking while still providing a basis for moral and ethical life consistent with deep-seated Christian values and beliefs.[15]

Although liberalism has no unequivocal founder who played the role Marx did for Marxism, John Locke is generally recognized as a pioneer in terms of drawing disparate liberal ideas together.[16] His seventeenth-century philosophy laid the foundation of modern liberal individualism. Locke believed in human rationality, which was ultimately to be embodied in government by consent and the protection of private property. Arguing that the duty of the state was to uphold the "life, liberty and property" of its citizens, Locke drew a moral parallel between external aggression and domestic oppression. Aggressive war was seen to violate the *raison d'être* of society, thus being inconceivable as a delegated power of legitimate government.[17]

Early liberal internationalists tended to believe, with Adam Smith, in the unhampered pursuit of economic interests. Government intervention needed to be minimized in order to allow the private sector to flourish. If trade and manufacture were to be conducted freely throughout the world, a pattern of cooperation and peaceful competition would ensue. In his "Plan for an Universal and Perpetual Peace," written in 1786–89 as part of his *Principles of International Law*, the British utilitarian Jeremy Bentham argued that free trade would bring the greatest economic benefits to the greatest number of people at the same time as trade relations would discourage war. Similar ideas of "commercial pacifism" based on *laissez faire* principles were developed by later British liberal thinkers, such as James Mill, John Stuart Mill, and Richard Cobden.

The role of republican governments based on liberal principles in developing peaceful international relations was highlighted by Immanuel Kant in his influential book *Perpetual Peace* (*Zum ewigen Frieden*), written in 1795. In this, he envisioned the widening acceptance of three "definitive articles" of peace. The first requires that state constitutions be republican. In contrast to the aggressive interests of absolutist monarchies, republics are not inclined to go to war because this requires the consent of the citizens, who are reluctant to accept the costs in lives and financial resources. According to Kant's second definitive article, liberal republics will progressively establish peace among themselves by means of a pacific federation (*foedus pacificum*). As more and more republics join, an expanding "zone of peace" is created. Even if Kant does not elaborate on the organizational embodiment of this pacific union, it is clearly more than a single peace treaty but less than a world state. It is not seen to acquire any power or authority over and above each autonomous state. The third definitive article outlines the idea of a cosmopolitan law "limited to conditions of universal hospitality" as a complement to the pacific union. Cosmopolitan law would guarantee access to foreigners and the flow of goods and ideas across national borders.[18]

Even if Kant himself would hardly have recognized the concept of "liberalism," his philosophy has inspired subsequent generations of liberal internationalists to the present era. For instance, contemporary theories of "democratic peace" and "cosmopolitan democracy" draw on Kant's idea of a republican zone of peace.[19] The popularity of his writings, in combination with their complexity and ambiguity, has entailed differing interpretations. By some he has been interpreted as an idealist; by others as a revolutionary: "These readings hover between two distinct forms of expectation: either they emphasize the moral aspect of the Kantian idea of peace, and end up interpreting it as a *promise*; or they emphasize the natural necessity of this idea and the inevitability of its realization, and end up interpreting it as a *prognosis*."[20]

The nineteenth century is generally considered the golden age of liberalism, especially in the United Kingdom. While beginning as an expression of middle-class industrial interests, English liberalism developed into a national political movement. It was now that a number of thinkers, such as John Stuart Mill, Richard Cobden, and Herbert Spencer, combined different liberal internationalist strands into a credo that free trade would produce international prosperity, peace, and cooperation; a vital private sector constituted the engine of progress; and this vitality depended on the freedom provided by democratic or republican government.[21]

Nineteenth-century industrialism produced a new setting "in which the implementation of ideas of equal rights and opportunities became more feasible, but only if the state were accorded a more positive role than in classical liberal theory."[22] Although much of the liberal agenda had been achieved in the advanced capitalist states, the envisaged domestic and international effects had disappointingly not appeared. In addition, liberalism now had to take up the struggle with another radical ideology, socialism. A downturn in the world economy in combination with *fin de siècle* fatalism and pessimism precipitated a crisis of liberalism around the turn of the century. The outbreak of World War I delivered a severe blow to liberal internationalism and is sometimes conceived as the end of the liberal century that had begun in 1815.[23]

The "new liberalism" that gradually emerged promoted a greater role for the state. Earlier versions had paid more attention to what states should refrain from doing than what they could positively do. Among new liberals the emphasis moved from "negative" to "positive" liberty, from "freedom from" government interference to "freedom to" enjoy work and social improvements. This entailed calls for appropriate institutional responses domestically as well as internationally, not only to problems of law and order but also to those of economic and social welfare. Increasingly suspicious of private exchanges domestically, the new liberals came to doubt their efficacy in the management of international relations. The emerging "welfare internationalism" demanded government engagement in regulating international intercourse.[24]

The liberal state, in short, was expected to uphold private property rights and free markets, while simultaneously providing politically necessary regulation to mitigate the detrimental consequences of the market.[25]

Two prominent exponents of the new liberal internationalism were Norman Angell and J.A. Hobson. Angell is best known for his argument concerning the futility of war. In *The Great Illusion*, published in 1912, he argued that modern production, transportation, and communication technologies had made national economies so interdependent that war would be disruptive to all. In his treatment, not only free trade but also the international networks of financial elites contributed to these interdependencies. Angell also believed that extensive education was necessary to overcome public ignorance and "the crowd mind," which tended to encourage war. Angell was awarded the Nobel Peace Prize in 1933.

While Hobson is usually associated with his work on imperialism, his prolific writings dealt with a number of issues that modified early liberal internationalism. Proceeding from an analogy of society to an organism, Hobson criticized the individualism of nineteenth-century liberalism. Applying the organic analogy to international relations, he envisaged expanding cooperation within an emerging world society made up not only of interacting states but also of networks of individuals and groups. Hobson suggested that the international realm was an integral part of social life, with people living in "concentric circles of association." In the same way that he argued for more interventionist government domestically, he saw the need for international control and organization—both intergovernmental and nongovernmental—to regulate and mitigate the excesses of the world market. His ideal was a loose international federation with associated functional organizations. He can be seen as a precursor of, and formed a theoretical basis for, David Mitrany's functional approach to international integration. Hobson, in short, played an important role in the transformation from nineteenth-century to twentieth-century liberal internationalism.[26]

Early twentieth-century internationalism reflected the transition domestically from old liberalism to the doctrine of the welfare state. This entailed a drift toward institutional arguments. Plans for, and the eventual performance of, the League of Nations provided foci of attention and contention. Whereas nineteenth-century liberals saw the internal reform of states inexorably leading to external reform, most twentieth-century liberals argued that external reform was integral to, or a precondition for, domestic reform. They also imagined reform, not in terms of limitations on government, but as positive engagement in international policies encouraging wealth creation and social stability. Mitrany's functionalism, for example, focused on economic and social welfare issues that were increasingly becoming issues for government policy, arguing that the national basis was inadequate. His criticism of the limits of the League is telling: "It is no use putting a policeman at the street corner to keep the traffic in order and to watch for burglars if at the same time the water and food supply for that street is being cut off."[27]

At the end of World War I, Woodrow Wilson's vision of a liberal world order became a controversial component of world politics. This was a "one-world" vision of an orderly international community of states interacting in a system of laws and international organization. Following Kant, Wilson believed that peace could be established only by a compact among inherently peaceful democracies: "Wilson had fought his war to make the world safe *for* democracy; he created his League to make the world safe *by* democracy." National self-determination, in Wilson's view, was an essential corollary of democracy: "Just as the people had a right to govern themselves within the national system, so the nations had the right to govern themselves within the global system."[28]

Taken together, the Wilsonian vision of liberal internationalism was both breathtakingly ambitious and surprisingly limited. It sought to transform the old global system based on the balance of power, spheres of influence, military rivalry, and alliances into a unified liberal international order based on nation-states and the rule of law. Power and security competition would be decomposed and replaced by a community of nations. But Wilsonian liberal internationalism did not involve the construction of deeply transformative legally binding political institutions. Liberal international order was to be constructed around the "soft law" of public opinion and moral suasion.[29]

In the United Kingdom during the interwar years, an active liberal internationalist movement launched campaigns for open diplomacy, arbitration, and disarmament. With the League of Nations Union (LNU) as a key organizational basis, liberal internationalism spread through "mainstream" UK opinion and transgressed party boundaries. Momentous changes in the international environment in the 1930s led to internal controversies. While gradually changing their conception of peace through collective security, liberal internationalists maintained a deep commitment to conflict prevention.[30]

During the interwar era liberal internationalism also became the target of much criticism, most famously in E.H. Carr's *The Twenty Years' Crisis*. Characterizing liberal internationalism as based on idealist or even "utopian" myths of a "harmony of interests" among states, Carr laid the foundation of realism as an alternative perspective on international relations. The pejorative labels of "idealists" or "utopians" have had a lasting impact. Carr's critique is echoed, for instance, by Stanley Hoffmann, who speaks of liberal internationalism's "fallacy of believing that all good things can come together." Yet recent scholarship has demonstrated that Carr painted too simplistic a picture and created a straw man out of the diverse views held by liberal internationalists. And Woodrow Wilson's Fourteen Points, which came to be seen as "something approaching an idealist Magna Carta" in the interwar period, have provided the foundation of efforts to resuscitate "neo-idealism" after the end of the Cold War.[31]

In sum, it was only in the twentieth century that international organization entered the liberal internationalist agenda in earnest. Before then, either free trade or an expanding network of liberal republics was seen as producing future prosperity and peace. As the nineteenth century drew to an end, the "domestic analogy" took on another meaning, as the proactive welfare state came to serve as a model for intensified collaboration internationally.

Tensions and controversies in liberal internationalism

We need to be reminded that "liberalism did not just enter this world as a benevolent rational force which gradually conquered ground by the authority of example, but rather as a sectarian political position which had to fight its way to the top and adjusted its goals and means to the given circumstances."[32] As the brief account of the evolution of liberal internationalism indicates, this struggle was not only with contending ideologies but included internal disagreements. One may speak of "contending liberalisms."[33] Moreover, liberalism itself contains unresolved internal tensions and contradictions.[34] In the following, some of the most prominent tensions and controversies within liberal internationalism will be identified.

At a general level, liberalism encompasses two different perspectives on human nature: One proceeding from human selfishness, defining interests in material terms, and believing that human greed may produce general benefits; the other promoting the moral aptitude, self-fulfillment, and civic virtues of human beings and emphasizing rights and duties.[35] Another recurrent general tension is that between experience and expectation. Liberal internationalism is a container of past experience as well as expectations for the future.[36] A more tangible division concerns the importance accorded to economic and political factors. The question of whether economic or political driving forces will produce international improvement and reforms has divided liberals throughout history. Moreover, within each faction there have been contentious issues.

Economic issues

One of the first liberal debates concerned the relationship between freedom and property. Whereas individual liberty and the right to private property were fundaments in early liberal thinking, the question was whether all citizens should have a voice in government or whether popular rule should be restricted to the propertied. The defense of property rights was central in the early *laissez faire* formulations of liberal internationalism. The role of the state was to be constrained to enforcing a limited set of laws, adjudicating disputes, and defending property and individual rights. State intervention in the domestic economy as well as in international economic transactions was seen as detrimental. Unconstrained activity by the private sector would contribute to a steady improvement of the material and moral condition of all people. This "liberalism of privilege" demoted or shunned the doctrine of equal rights.[37]

Although *laissez faire* liberalism continued to hold sway throughout the nineteenth century, a number of later liberal thinkers questioned the classical idea of the independence of the economy from political pressure or social concern. They had less confidence in the progressive potential of the private sector, arguing that previous liberal thought had neglected powerful political interests of industrial and financial elites. Capitalism was not necessarily a force for peace, but could be an incitement to war because of the influence of sectional interests.[38] The re-evaluation of economic actors entailed a more favorable view of the state as a vehicle for the redistribution of wealth and power and guarantor of liberal values, not only at home but abroad as well. Several liberals advocated foreign intervention for liberal ends. As early as 1849 John Stuart Mill declared that every liberal government "has a right to assist struggling liberalism, by mediation, by money, or by arms, wherever it can prudently do so; as every despotic government, when its aid is needed or asked for, never scruples to aid despotic governments."[39]

Political issues

If classical liberal internationalism harbors certain economic divergences against the backdrop of a general belief in the beneficial effects of a free private sector, there is a greater amount of contentious political issues. The common denominator is the conviction that liberal states constitute the foundation of a peaceful and prosperous world. This, however, does not exclude significant disagreements.

Related to the *laisse faire* problematic is the contrast between "negative" and "positive" freedom. Whereas the early English tradition equated liberalism with freedom from control by the state, the "new liberals" in the 1880s advanced a positive ideal of freedom as "the liberation of the powers of all men equally for contributions to a common good" and "the maximum of power for all members of human society to make the best of themselves."[40] This debate recurs as differing views of the international role of the state. Early liberals were critical of the traditional practices of power politics, mistrusted foreign policy elites, diplomats and the military, and wanted to minimize government intervention not only within but also beyond national borders. The more "positive" conceptions of self-actualization and social welfare entailed a more active role for the state in the international arena as well. Thus, the divisive issue of intervention for "positive" freedom meant that liberal internationalism might encompass a wide span from what we today label isolationism to moral crusades.[41]

Retrospective analyses have raised the question whether classical liberal internationalism was genuinely inclusive and *international*. Post-colonial scholars, in particular, have portrayed liberalism as Eurocentric, paternalist, and imperialist, insofar as it regarded Western values as universally applicable and served as a justification of Western superiority. They point out that the nineteenth century witnessed the triumph of Western liberalism at the very time that British imperialism expanded. Among liberal internationalists there were, in fact, different views concerning the "civilizing mission" of liberal states. For instance, Locke supported British colonialism and Mill believed in hierarchical relations between civilized and barbarian peoples, arguing for colonial government intervention. By contrast, Kant's principle of nonintervention, his expectation that republican constitutions would emerge through internal political processes rather than outside interference, and his emphasis on consent as the basis of republican constitutions precluded imperialist policies. Hobson, for his part, argued that a "civilizing mission" was necessary but only under the tutelage of an independent international organization.[42]

Classical liberal internationalism also exhibits a tension between *moral* and *institutional* arguments.[43] Moral arguments point to a new international consciousness as the agent of a positive transformation of international relations. The conscience of civilized humankind was to safeguard the internationalist goals of order and progress. In the words of L.T. Hobhouse: "Moral rights and duties are founded on relations between man and man, and therefore applicable to all humanity. To deny this applicability is merely to throw back civilized ethics to the savage state."[44] According to institutional arguments, international progress cannot be left to ethics alone, but requires institutional mechanisms. The aim is then to devise political institutions that can induce people to act in morally defensible ways. World War II tipped the balance in favor of institutional arguments. Humanitarian ethics had proved inadequate to avert warfare, and an international organization to promote peace and prevent the recurrence of war, a league of nations, became a cornerstone of liberal internationalism.

Another unresolved question concerns whether the sovereign state facilitates or impedes the overarching goal of individual freedom. On the one hand, the political and legal framework of sovereignty permits freedom from the coercion of others; on the other hand, it allows the state to impose arbitrary and oppressive ends on individual citizens. Kant, for instance, was ambiguous on this issue, at times considering state sovereignty as a *sine qua non* condition of freedom, on other occasions viewing sovereignty as a threat to freedom.[45] The classical liberal internationalist solution, or vision, is that "the *external* sovereignty of states will be exercised with more restraint—and anarchy will thereby be mitigated—when *internal* sovereignty is located in the people."[46]

Nineteenth-century nationalism confronted liberals with a new quandary. Eighteenth-century liberals viewed the relationship of state and society in rational terms—as a set of mutual obligations or a social contract. Nationalism drew on emotional bonds of allegiance, loyalty, and passion. The predominant liberal position was to embrace the principle of national self-determination, which was seen as an external extension of the principle of consent, a corollary of liberal self-government. Yet this entailed an incongruity, insofar as liberalism had originally been an appeal to reason. Nationalism had more to do with emotion and a common national will. By overrunning the restraints on power and creating new sources of intense conflict between states, nationalism threatened both the liberal program at home and the vision of international order and peace.[47]

Another question concerns the interstate/transnational dimension: Would national reforms establishing liberal states in and by themselves establish the desired world order, or is the formation of a transnational society, linking people across borders beyond government control, an additional precondition? Free commerce, cultural interaction, and the formation of a world public opinion were part of the classical liberal internationalist vision. Most liberals would include both national and transnational processes in their perspectives, but with varying emphasis. Some, such as Kant and Woodrow Wilson, believed in a world order created mainly by self-determining states, whereas Mitrany's functionalism saw the world of states as a constraint and envisaged transnational associations of legitimacy transforming human attachment to particular states.[48]

The location of rules and authority—how the envisaged liberal order is to be governed—is another unresolved and contested question. At issue is essentially to what extent the liberal order entails legal-political restrictions on state sovereignty. As we have seen, there have been different ideas about the need for an international organization, and those who have advocated one have not concurred on its scope and mandate. By the same token, the "rule of law" has been a significant part of the liberal vision of a peaceful world, but there has been no consensus as to the proper role of international law. Some have advocated "soft law," that is, rules and norms enforced through moral suasion and world public opinion; others have called for articulated sets of rules that prescribe and proscribe state action. The variety of liberal institutional and legal proposals have one thing in common: they have been "attempts to align an unwillingness to give up on the nation-state with a desire for peace."[49]

In sum, whereas liberal internationalists have shared a belief in international progress defined as movement toward increasing levels of harmonious cooperation between states, they have had varying views on how to achieve these goals. The "domestic analogy" pervades this debate, as "the competing liberal instruments with which to pursue individual freedom within the state have been directed outward as mechanisms for domesticating the international realm."[50] Modes of governance within and between states are interlinked in the liberal internationalist conception.

Conclusion

The evolution of liberal internationalism in its first centuries reveals a set of recurring themes and unresolved issues. In the period covered here, liberal internationalism is best characterized as an ideology, pointing to a more peaceful and harmonious international order. Based on a belief in progress, it adapted continually to new circumstances. Both world wars represented serious disappointments and exposed liberal internationalism to charges of idealism. And the liberal vision of an improved international order did indeed remain a remote ideal for centuries.

Although there were earlier international developments in directions desired and proposed by liberals, it was only after the end of World War II—with the removal of a vast number of barriers to trade, successive waves of democratization, and the proliferation of international organizations—that significant parts of the classical ideals became reality. This development meant that liberal internationalism changed character from a prospective ideology to an analytical framework challenging realism, and substituted the prefix "neo" for the epithet "classical." Yet classical liberal internationalism bequeaths a legacy of themes and issues that each new generation will relate to and recognize.

Additional reading

Carsten Holbraad, *Internationalism and Nationalism in European Political Thought* (Basingstoke: Palgrave Macmillan, 2003).

Beate Jahn, *Liberal Internationalism: Theory, History, Practice* (Basingstoke: Palgrave Macmillan, 2013).

Michael Pugh, *Liberal Internationalism: The Interwar Movement for Peace in Britain* (Basingstoke: Palgrave Macmillan, 2012).

Hans Reiss, ed., *Kant: Political Writings* (Cambridge: Cambridge University Press, 1990).

Mark W. Zacher and Richard A. Matthew, "Liberal International Theory: Common threads, divergent strands," in *Controversies in International Relations Theory*, ed. Charles W. Kegley, Jr. (New York: St. Martin's Press, 1995).

Notes

1 Carsten Holbraad, *Internationalism and Nationalism in European Political Thought* (Basingstoke: Palgrave Macmillan, 2003), 1–2; Fred Halliday, "Three Concepts of Internationalism," *International Affairs* 64, no. 2 (1988): 187–198, 187; Anthony F. Lang, Jr., "Internationalism," in *International Encyclopedia of the Social Sciences*, Vol. 4, ed. William A. Darity, Jr. (Detroit, MI: Macmillan Reference USA, 2008), 102–103; Jens Bartelson, *Visions of World Community* (Cambridge: Cambridge University Press, 2009), 1–3.

2 Holbraad, *Internationalism and Nationalism*, 7–10; Halliday, "Three Concepts of Internationalism," 192–197.

3 Duncan Bell, "Liberal Internationalism," in *Encyclopedia of Governance*, ed. Mark Bevir (Thousand Oaks, CA: Sage, 2006), 525.

4 Antonio Franceschet, "The Ethical Foundations of Liberal Internationalism," *International Journal* 54, no. 3 (1999): 468. The first recorded use of the word "internationalism" in English dates from 1851. Casper Sylvest, "Continuity and Change in British Liberal Internationalism, *c*. 1900–1930," *Review of International Studies* 31, no. 2 (2005): 263–283, 265. Halliday ("Three Concepts of Internationalism," 189) claims that the first use of the term came as late as 1877.

5 Michael W. Doyle, "Liberalism and World Politics," *American Political Science Review* 80, no. 4 (1986): 1152.

6 Jamie Munn, "Review of Antonio Franceschet, *Kant and Liberal Internationalism*," *Canadian Journal of Political Science* 37, no. 4 (2004): 1063.

7 Doyle, *Ways of War and Peace*, 207; Antonio Franceschet, "Sovereignty and Freedom: Immanuel Kant's Liberal Internationalist 'Legacy,'" *Review of International Studies* 27, no. 2 (2001): 213; Franceschet, "The Ethical Foundations," 471; Stanley Hoffmann, "The Crisis of Liberal Internationalism," *Foreign Policy* 98 (1995): 160; James L. Richardson, "Contending Liberalisms: Past and Present," *European Journal of International Relations* 3, no. 1 (1997): 8; David Long, "Conclusion: Inter-War Idealism, Liberal Internationalism, and Contemporary International Theory," in *Thinkers of the Twenty Years' Crisis*, eds. David Long and Peter Wilson (Oxford: Clarendon Press, 1995), 313.

8 Beate Jahn, *Liberal Internationalism: Theory, History, Practice* (Basingstoke: Palgrave Macmillan, 2013), 14.

9 Holbraad, *Internationalism and Nationalism*, 39; Hoffmann, "The Crisis of Liberal Internationalism," 160; Mark W. Zacher and Richard A. Matthew, "Liberal International Theory: Common Threads, Divergent Strands," in *Controversies in International Relations Theory*, ed. Charles W. Kegley, Jr. (New York: St. Martin's Press, 1995), 109–110.

10 Gal Gerson, "Review of Casper Sylvester, British Liberal Internationalism, 1880–1950: Making Progress?" *Victorian Studies* 53, no. 3 (2011): 541.

11 Jens Bartelson, "The Trial of Judgment: A Note on Kant and the Paradoxes of Internationalism," *International Studies Quarterly* 39, no. 2 (1995): 259; John Ikenberry, "Liberal Internationalism 3.0: America and the Dilemmas of Liberal World Order," *Perspectives on Politics* 7, no. 1 (2009): 72.

12 Hoffmann, "The Crisis of Liberal Internationalism," 160.

13 Franceschet, "Sovereignty and Freedom," 211 (emphasis in original); Chiara Bottici, "The Domestic Analogy and the Kantian Project of *Perpetual Peace*," *Journal of Political Philosophy* 11, no. 4 (2003): 392–410.

14 Beate Jahn, "Liberal Internationalism: From Ideology to Empirical Theory—and Back Again," *International Theory* 1, no. 3 (2009): 436.

15 Zacher and Matthew, "Liberal International Theory," 111.

16 Jahn, "Liberal Internationalism," 41.

17 Jahn, "Liberal Internationalism," 424; Lee Ward, "Locke on the Moral Basis of International Relations," *American Journal of Political Science* 50, no. 3 (2006): 702.

18 See, e.g., Michael W. Doyle, *Ways of War and Peace* (New York: W.W. Norton & Company, 1997), 253–258.

19 Antonio Franceschet, "Popular Sovereignty or Cosmopolitan Democracy? Liberalism, Kant and International Reform," *European Journal of International Relations* 6, no. 2 (2000): 277–302.

20 Bartelson, "The Trial of Judgment," 263.

21 George H. Sabine, *A History of Political Theory*, 3rd ed. (London: George G. Harrap & Co., 1963), 703; Zacher and Matthew, "Liberal International Theory," 114.

22 Richardson, "Contending Liberalisms," 13.

23 Long, "Conclusion: Inter-war Idealism," 314–316.

24 Hidemi Suganami, *The Domestic Analogy and World Order Proposals* (Cambridge: Cambridge University Press, 1989), 108; cf. Cornelia Navari, *Internationalism and the State in the Twentieth Century* (London: Routledge, 2000), 231.

25 Jahn, "Liberal Internationalism," 122.

26 On Angell, see J.D.B. Miller, "Norman Angell and Rationality in International Relations," in *Thinkers of the Twenty Years' Crisis*, eds. Long and Wilson; cf. Zacher and Matthew, "Liberal International Theory," 114–115. On Hobson, see David Long, *Towards a New Liberal Internationalism: The International Theory of J.A. Hobson* (Cambridge: Cambridge University Press, 1996); David Long, "J.A. Hobson and Economic Internationalism," in *Thinkers of the Twenty Years' Crisis*, eds. Long and Wilson.

27 Sylvest, "Continuity and Change in British Liberal Internationalism"; Navari, *Internationalism and the State*, 248; Suganami, *The Domestic Analogy*, 106–107 (including Mitrany quotation).

28 Inis L. Claude, Jr., *Swords into Plowshares*, 3rd ed. (New York: Random House, 1964), 47.

29 Ikenberry, "Liberal Internationalism 3.0," 75.

30 Michael Pugh, *Liberal Internationalism: The Interwar Movement for Peace in Britain* (Basingstoke: Palgrave Macmillan, 2012).

31 E.H. Carr, *The Twenty Years' Crisis* (London: Macmillan, 1939). Cf. Hoffmann, "The Crisis of Liberal Internationalism," 167; Franceschet, "The Ethical Foundations," 464, 466; Franceschet, "Sovereignty and Freedom," 211; Peter Wilson, "Introduction: *The Twenty Years' Crisis* and the Category of 'Idealism' in International Relations," in *Thinkers of the Twenty Years' Crisis*, eds. Long and Wilson, 14; Charles W. Kegley, Jr. "The Neoidealist Moment in International Studies? Realist Myths and the New International Realities," *International Studies Quarterly* 37, no. 2 (1993): 131–146.

32 Jahn, "Liberal Internationalism," 429.

33 Richardson, "Contending Liberalisms," 8.

34 The "contradictory and fragmentary dynamics of liberalism" is a *Leitmotiv* in Jahn, "Liberal Internationalism."

35 Hoffmann, "The Crisis of Liberal Internationalism," 174.

36 Bartelson, "The Trial of Judgment," 256.

37 Richardson, "Contending Liberalisms," 9, 13.

38 Zacher and Matthew, "Liberal International Theory," 112; Long, *Towards a New Liberal Internationalism*, 184–185.

39 As quoted in Holbraad, *Internationalism and Nationalism*, 41.

40 T.H. Green, as quoted in Richardson, "Contending Liberalisms," 11–12.

41 Hoffmann, "The Crisis of Liberal Internationalism," 162.

42 Martin Hall and John M. Hobson, "Liberal International Theory: Eurocentric but Not Always Imperialist?" *International Theory* 2, no. 2 (2010): 210–245; Beate Jahn, "Kant, Mill, and Illiberal Legacies in International Affairs," *International Organization* 59, no. 1 (2005): 177–207; Jahn, "Liberal Internationalism," 49–52.

43 Sylvest, "Continuity and Change in British Liberal Internationalism."

44 As quoted in ibid., 272.

45 Franceschet, "The Ethical Foundations," 473; Franceschet, "Sovereignty and Freedom," 218.

46 Franceschet, "Popular Sovereignty or Cosmopolitan Democracy?," 284 (emphasis in original).

47 Hoffmann, "The Crisis of Liberal Internationalism," 162–164.

48 Franceschet, "Sovereignty and Freedom," 213; Franceschet, "The Ethical Foundations," 477.

49 Ikenberry, "Liberal Internationalism 3.0," 72–73; Lang, "Internationalism," 102.

50 Franceschet, "The Ethical Foundations," 468.

CONTENTS

Liberal institutionalism

Tana Johnson and Andrew Heiss

Liberal institutionalism presumes that domestic and international institutions play central roles in facilitating cooperation and peace between states. But currently, this influential approach to thinking and practice appears to be in jeopardy. The United Kingdom seeks to be the first state ever to withdraw from the European Union (EU). The United States threatens to renegotiate or leave several international arrangements that it has recently signed or long supported. Meanwhile, China hints that it would be happy to take on greater global leadership if the United States retreats from this traditional role.

It is hardly unprecedented to see states reconsidering or rejecting cooperation. However, what is surprising is the rhetoric. Liberal institutionalism presented itself as a corrective to conventional international relations theory, which held that powerful states dominate world politics while international institutions are inconsequential. And yet today, liberal democracies—which are some of the world's most powerful states—seem to be desperate to escape the clutches of formidable international institutions that supposedly demand too much. Meanwhile, non-liberal authoritarian regimes are willing not only to stay, but also to take on greater burdens.

To fathom the irony, it is necessary to understand liberal institutionalism in tandem with historical events and competing theoretical views. Hence, the chapter begins by explaining how this theoretical approach has developed in response to both the conceptual, and the real, worlds. In doing so, it tracks major critiques of liberal institutionalism from realists, Marxists, constructivists, non-liberal governments, feminists, developing countries, and the general publics in North American or European liberal democracies. The chapter concludes with open questions about the survival of the contemporary world order—and the liberal institutionalism that has animated it.

Conceptual roots of liberal institutionalism

Liberal institutionalism selectively embraces and repudiates tenets of other theories of international relations, and therefore it cannot be understood without first grasping the broader conceptual milieu of realism, classical liberalism, and Marxism. Modern international relations theory is often traced to Niccolò Machiavelli, the Florentine diplomat whose 1513 treatise *The Prince* advised rulers about using ethically questionable means to achieve their goals.[1] Rooted in pragmatism rather than ideology, this approach to governance has become entwined with the paradigm of realism. Realism eventually developed a particular set of assumptions, including:

1 states are the primary actors
2 states interact in an anarchic system lacking any higher authority or enforcement
3 states are rational actors, selecting actions they expect will achieve their goals
4 to survive and thrive, states must accumulate power
5 accumulating power is a zero-sum game in which gains for one state necessitate losses for another.

Under these assumptions, realists consider any interstate cooperation to be only a temporary reprieve from states' general circumstances of competition, conflict, and war.

Classical liberalism, the intellectual antecedent of liberal institutionalism, is a paradigm that strongly challenges the realist premise that states are on an inevitable collision course in their quest for power. Instead, liberalism perceives high prospects for sustained cooperation. States can surmount competition, conflict, and war by forming like-minded groups and binding themselves through domestic and international institutions.

This rationale permeates Immanuel Kant's 1795 essay *Perpetual Peace*, which offers three linked prescriptions.[2] First: Internally, each state should embrace a republican form of government in which legislative power and executive power are separated. Such domestic institutions make war more difficult to wage because the citizenry, who bear much of the cost, would need to approve it. Second: Externally, these republican states should band together in a pacific federation whose members renounce the right to wage war with one another. Such international institutions facilitate trade and other linkages that would make war even more damaging for its perpetrators. Third: Universally, individual "citizens of the world" who conduct themselves peacefully should be free to travel and do business in states other than their own. Once states are restrained at the domestic and international levels, their citizens are more likely to respect the rights of other states' citizens, further reducing the impetus for interstate conflict.

In theory, the Kantian system widens over time, as more states become republican and therefore eligible to enter the pacific federation and reciprocal rights of "hospitality." And as more states subscribe to universalist values, which guide how all members of the in-group must be treated, the in-group itself grows. Thus, political institutions lie at the core of Kantian perpetual peace, for they are crucial pieces of an expanding system that discourages war.

This sunny perspective is at odds not only with realism but also with Marxism. Far from seeing capitalist institutions and economic relations as the underpinnings of peace, Marxists see them as the sites of contestation between social classes and as vehicles for exploitation at both the domestic and international levels.[3] Marxism clashes with the Kantian premise that liberal institutions can bind people together and promote peace.

This foreshadows one of liberalism's thorniest issues. Until all states reciprocate an identical set of universalist values, there will be an in-group and an out-group. Enhancements for one can be threats to the other. Hence until the system is all-encompassing, peace will be fragile, partial, and intermittent. It is difficult to know, then, how to interpret the outbreak of wars: Are they predictable bumps on the road to perpetual peace, or are they evidence that liberalism is not a viable approach to international politics?

Real-world roots of liberal institutionalism

Proponents of liberalism continually wrestled with this, especially as real-world conflicts underscored the dilemma. For instance, in his 1911 publication *The Great Illusion*, Norman Angell reacted to saber rattling in continental Europe.[4] Although this work is often misinterpreted as a positive argument for why war in Europe *could* not happen, in fact it is a normative argument for why war *should* not happen. The "great illusion" was governments' continuing faith in military power. Angell asserted that war among interdependent industrialized countries would be costly and self-immolating, because most of the material and human resources sought through conquest could be obtained much more effectively through other means.

Although World War I nevertheless ensnared states in Europe and elsewhere, liberalism would have another chance to guide international politics when US President Woodrow Wilson incorporated liberal notions into the Fourteen Points he articulated for the postwar system.[5] He called for an intergovernmental League of Nations, a remarkable manifestation of Kant's "pacific federation" in which states with shared values and linked economies could coexist. The League was created, but the United States itself never formally joined.

The League's many weaknesses—along with evidence of Japan's imperial aspirations and the renewed tensions in Europe—highlighted the ongoing conceptual tussle between the liberal and realist paradigms. In the 1939 book *The Twenty Years' Crisis*, E.H. Carr lambasted "utopians" who had trusted transnational ties or institutions to overcome states' innate attraction to power, competition, and armed conflict.[6] Carr acknowledged liberalism's normative appeal. However, he ultimately argued that in the existing milieu of jostling nation-states, the realist paradigm was a superior guide and predictor of political behavior. Indeed, later that year Hitler invaded Poland, launching World War II.

After the war, the conceptual tussle persisted. Realism's tenets seemed to explain the failure to prevent a second large-scale war among industrialized countries, and its assumptions appeared to fit the burgeoning Cold War between the United States and the Soviet Union. Nevertheless, liberalism also thrived. In his 1941 State of the

Union address, US President Franklin D. Roosevelt asserted freedom of speech, freedom of religion, freedom from want, and freedom from fear as core values that could and should spread throughout the United States and the world.[7] Traces of these "four freedoms" pervade the United Nations (UN), the intergovernmental organization that replaced the League of Nations in 1945. Similar values also gird a host of other international institutions—including the Food and Agriculture Organization (FAO), the General Agreement on Tariffs and Trade (GATT), the International Monetary Fund (IMF), and the World Bank—that the US government helped to design and fund at the end of World War II. These values and institutions are the foundations of today's liberal world order.[8]

In the middle of the twentieth century, unable to ignore the flurry of postwar institution building, realists sought to bring these institutions in conformity with their own paradigm. Some work, such as Hans Morgenthau's *Politics Among Nations*, marginalized international institutions as epiphenomenal: If institutions merely reflect the balance of power among states, then it continues to be expedient for theories to ignore institutions and look directly at states.[9] Other work, such as Charles Kindleberger's *The World in Depression*, took a more nuanced approach.[10] As an early proponent of "hegemonic stability theory" (HST), Kindleberger argued that the belligerence and economic woes of the 1930s stemmed from that period's lack of a single hegemonic state that was powerful enough to keep the international system running smoothly. After World War II, however, the United States saw that its own capabilities and aims fit the role. Hence, this powerful state built a network of international institutions to help it provide economic stability and other public goods for the international system. A confluence of liberal values was unnecessary, because peace could be achieved by a hegemon who would self-servingly enforce cooperation.

More recent work, such as G. John Ikenberry's *After Victory*, bridges realist and liberal interpretations of postwar institution-building.[11] For Ikenberry, state power is important, but international institutions and liberal values are too. Institutions are difficult to change or dismantle once they begin operating. Therefore, a hegemonic state can use institutional rules to restrain itself when it is at the height of its power but also to extend its influence into the future, when its raw power has declined. If the hegemon injects liberal values into these institutions, then the institutions themselves will perpetuate the rule of law and the sorts of universalist principles that Kant envisioned. The hegemon's initial self-restraint helps to convince other states to join—and as a greater number of states become invested in the institution, the institution is even more likely to persist and propagate. That helps to explain why the liberal world order, initiated following World War II, has expanded and still exists today.

Rehabilitation and redemption: The emergence of liberal institutionalism

Liberalism had struggled to make sense of the two world wars, but it prospered afterward. From a real-world standpoint, it aligned with the institution building and relative peace of the latter half of the twentieth century. From a conceptual standpoint, it rehabilitated and redeemed itself with the emergence of several offshoots, culminating in the refinement of liberal institutionalism from the 1970s onward. Repeatedly, the influence of liberalism has soared after its proponents are forced to wrestle with competing theoretical views or unexpected historical events.

In the decades after World War II, the construction of global and regional institutions continued, rejuvenating "functionalist" notions that had begun challenging core realist tenets in the 1930s. Promulgated through writings such as David Mitrany's 1933 book *The Progress of International Government*,[12] functionalism argues that authority is not necessarily monopolized by nation-states within sovereign territories. Instead, governance is a set of functions that can—and perhaps should—be carried out across national borders by a mix of state and non-state actors specializing in particular tasks. This becomes self-perpetuating: As entities in a variety of functional areas develop deep expertise and cooperate effectively to wield authority, states cede even more authority to international institutions. And in line with liberalism, such connectedness disincentivizes war.

Europe's incremental development of supranational governance made these abstract ideas concrete. The path began in 1951 with the European Coal and Steel Community (ECSC), which would manage coal and steel production in France, West Germany, Italy, Belgium, the Netherlands, and Luxembourg. In 1967, the ECSC merged with two sister bodies to form the European Economic Community (EEC; later the European Union). In 1973, the original six-state membership expanded to include Denmark, Ireland, and the United Kingdom. Throughout this process, numerous European policymakers expressed an Angell-like insistence on making their states so interdependent that war among them would never again be a compelling option.

The European undertaking gave credence to liberal and functionalist notions, and it also inspired a new line of "neo-functionalist" thinking about regional integration. Building on Mitrany's insights, works such as Leon Lindberg's *The Political Dynamics of European Economic Integration*[13] and Ernst B. Haas' *Beyond the Nation-State*[14] argued that the architects of European integration were strategically sequencing the delegated functions. By initially cooperating in economic matters, states were building institutions and trust that eventually could spill over into more politically sensitive areas.

Among the shortcomings of functionalism and neo-functionalism, one of the most serious was the supposition of a steady march toward supra-nationalism. By the 1970s, the US was thinking about rolling back its support for international institutions—and certainly not making them broader and deeper. US officials questioned whether they could, or should, continue to bear the largest costs for international public goods such as freer trade, collective defense, and the UN system. Nevertheless, interdependence across the world proved difficult to reverse. Not only states, but also firms, subnational governments, and civil society groups were intensifying their transnational activities.

In their 1977 book *Power and Interdependence*, Robert Keohane and Joseph Nye explored this complexity, arguing that monolithic states do not dictate international affairs. Instead bureaucrats, legislators, judges, international institutions, firms, civil society groups, and others interact with each other domestically and internationally. Consequently, states' fortunes were now tied not only through conventional economic linkages but also through novel political and societal ones.[15] Keohane and Nye flirted with liberal views, without explicitly endorsing them—and they concluded that the US government could not easily extricate itself from the institutions and networks it had helped to create.

Kenneth Waltz's 1979 realist treatise *Theory of International Politics* took a different tack.[16] According to him, the world's ostensible complexity had a very simple cause: The number of powerful states in the international system. Such structural realism contended that the existing bipolar system, in which two great powers tried but failed to dominate one another, would naturally look different from a unipolar system with a global hegemon or a multipolar system with several evenly matched states. Thus the real action was not among businesses, or international institutions, or civil society groups, or even among most states—instead, all could be traced simply to the rivalry between Washington and Moscow. Realism reasserted itself, this time with a qualifier: "Neo-realism."

Liberal notions soon rematerialized, taking on the parallel name of "neoliberalism" and building on Keohane and Nye's ideas of interdependence. In the 1980s, scholars amassed evidence about the importance of domestic institutions, a "black box" rarely opened by realists. Summarizing historical data, Michael Doyle noted that mature liberal democratic states do not go to war against one another, but they do go to war against illiberal, nondemocratic states. He posited that this "democratic peace" is not maintained via a hegemonic overseer. Rather, it results from liberal values, norms, and institutions within individual states aligning with those of fellow democracies, thus producing a modern stepping-stone to Kantian perpetual peace.[17] The findings again underscored the interim existence of in-groups and out-groups: Renouncing war as a solution to problems was a "universal" principle that worked primarily within the groups of states whose domestic democratic institutions made reciprocation of that principle more credible.

Other scholars complemented these findings on domestic institutions by showing that international institutions matter, too. Since the early 1970s, the United States had decried freeriders in global affairs and had tried retreating from its hegemonic support of international institutions and public goods. Yet institutions such as the Food and Agriculture Organization (FAO), the General Agreement on Tariffs and Trade (GATT), the International Monetary Fund (IMF), UN, and World Bank continued to facilitate aid, trade, financial stability, peace, and development. How could this be, if realists were correct that institutions merely reflected the will of the most powerful states?

John Ruggie and Robert Keohane offered somewhat different answers for why an international institution can survive even if a hegemon retreats, declines, or disappears. In *After Hegemony*, Keohane adopted the core realist assumptions of state-centrism, anarchy, and rationality, but he rejected the premise that international politics is a zero-sum quest for power. He offered a corrective to realism by harkening back to functionalism and neo-functionalism: Institutions can persist when they provide information, coordination, enforcement, or other benefits that states could not provide on their own.[18] By selectively tweaking realist tenets, Keohane demonstrated much greater prospects for cooperation, even without a hegemonic patron. In contrast, Ruggie did not work from realist tenets, and in his work on "embedded liberalism" he diverged markedly from realism by emphasizing social purpose: Institutions can endure when a larger community of states continues to share the values embodied in those institutions.[19] In a foreshadowing of future divisions in international relations theory, Ruggie presaged the emergence of constructivism, while Keohane linked the new "liberal institutionalism" with realism.

Realist or constructivist critiques of liberal institutionalism

Clearly, liberal institutionalism was not universally embraced. Instead, new strains of realism and liberalism would engage in a so-called "neo-neo" debate, which lasted for more than a decade. Joseph Grieco, for instance, argued that international cooperation could not be as easy to achieve as Keohane and others asserted. Attempting to reinstate the rejected realist premise, Grieco argued that international politics indeed is a zero-sum game, and therefore each state will inevitably fixate on relative gains rather than being satisfied with absolute gains. Presented with any arrangement from which it derives some benefits but another state derives even more, a state will refuse to participate. Grieco concluded that this dynamic would unravel international cooperation and institutions.[20]

However, a variety of formal models countered this view. Duncan Snidal and Robert Powell concluded that a fixation on relative gains occurs only under particular conditions. The fixation can dissipate in non-security issues[21] or with increases in the number of participating states,[22] thus explaining why interstate cooperation is often prevalent and lasting. Robert Axelrod acknowledged that in numerous situations international politics shares characteristics with a Prisoners' Dilemma game, in which each player's dominant strategy is to defect rather than cooperate. However, in the real world many of these situations are repeated, and this iteration makes prolonged cooperation possible through reputation building and other means.[23] The result was that formal models shored up elements of, but also delivered a further departure from, classical liberalism. It was unnecessary to aim for world government, because cooperation could be sustained through uncoordinated, self-interested reciprocity.

Despite these conceptual victories, the real-world endurance of domestic and international institutions would be tested in the late 1980s and early 1990s, after the fall of the Berlin Wall and the Soviet Union's disintegration officially ended the Cold War. Would international institutions crumble in a unipolar world in which the United States did not need their assistance in its competition with the Eastern bloc and might be disinclined to restrain newfound American dominance? Would interstate war become widespread again, since there were no longer two superpowers reining in the smaller states in their respective blocs? Would the camaraderie of liberal democracies collapse, now that their primary external antagonist had disbanded?

Europe reacted by not only deepening but also widening the region's supranational institutions. In 1993, the Maastricht Treaty transformed the European Community (EC) into the European Union (EU), an even bolder form of economic and political integration. The EU expanded its membership eastward and eventually developed a common currency for states opting into its Eurozone. Various works, such as Andrew

Moravcsik's 1998 *The Choice for Europe*, strove to determine whether realism, liberalism, or something else best accounted for this institutional phenomenon.[24] Meanwhile, policy practitioners toyed with the idea of recreating the European experiment in other parts of the world—thus far, the African Union is the most overt attempt at replication.

Although realists continued to question the importance of institutions,[25] liberal institutionalists now believed the evidentiary trail was compelling enough to stop playing defensively.[26] The interesting question was not whether institutions mattered—it was when, or how. In this vein, Jon Pevehouse, Edward Mansfield, and Bruce Russert argued that international institutions spread both peace and democracy.[27] Meanwhile, Helen Milner reasoned that democratic domestic institutions aid the diffusion of technology.[28]

Despite this progress, since the 1990s liberal institutionalism has faced a new conceptual difficulty: The rise of social constructivism. According to constructivists, actors in international affairs are socialized and influenced by their surroundings, and therefore their proclivities toward conflict or cooperation are collectively constructed.[29] Those who interact with others negatively will generate a hostile realist system; those who interact with others more positively can create a Kantian system in which self-interests meld with community interests. But as social constructions, neither realism's zero-sum game nor liberalism's value-aligned in-group is assured. Both can be undone.

Beyond this, constructivism directly disputes the realist assumptions of state-centrism, rationality, and anarchy.[30] Since liberal institutionalism also adopted these premises, it too is challenged by the constructivist confrontation with realism. In fact, some observers conjoin the two as "rationalist" views that greatly differ from constructivism. Ironically—although many liberals share constructivists' appreciation for ideas, non-state actors, and goals other than power—liberals can be painted with the same brush as the realists they had spent centuries contesting.[31]

Today, many researchers (including the authors of this chapter) eschew strict allegiance to a single paradigm and instead draw from multiple conceptual insights to investigate pressing real-world developments. For instance, Tana Johnson's 2014 book *Organizational Progeny* uses rationalist principal–agent models—but also constructivist notions about policy-related values, the pursuit for institutional legitimacy, and alliances with civil society—to examine the staff members working within the UN and other intergovernmental organizations.[32] Meanwhile, Andrew Heiss' research on "amicable contempt" considers the role of both material and ideational considerations in authoritarian governments' interactions with nongovernmental organizations that appear to promote Western norms of behavior.[33]

The spreading critiques of liberal institutionalism

As liberal institutionalism grew more prominent, its critics grew more vocal. In fact, critiques that now circulate among the general public in North American or European liberal democracies have been swirling for years among non-liberal governments, feminists, and developing countries. The highlighted problems come in at least three strains.

One strain focuses on dangerous divergences from Kant's philosophical foundations. While Kant's great hope in liberal institutions was rooted in universality, the modern democratic peace is non-universal and may even be non-Kantian. According to Kant, peace emerges naturally when states and their citizens choose to embrace similar values and institutions, domestically and internationally. Peace spreads as more people adopt these vehicles for reciprocal hospitality. However, contemporary critics note a paradox: Incomplete universalism may deter liberal states from interfering or warring with one another—but it can allow, or even embolden, liberal states to meddle or fight with non-liberal ones.

In the pursuit of peace, there has been a strong temptation to *impose* liberal values and democratic institutions on non-liberal states. Such interventions jeopardize liberal institutionalism itself. After all, spreading it through coercive means is "the propagation of particularist law under a universal guise," as "liberals disqualify non-liberals from choosing their own laws."[34] If real Kantian peace comes from states' spontaneous alignment of universal political principles, then forced adherence cannot bring real peace. Instead, it makes liberalism operate illiberally.

Besides this problem with implementation, critics also question the conceptual roots of liberal institutionalism. In particular, feminists decry its reliance on masculine perspectives. In responding to realists, liberals absorbed some of their rivals' fascination with power, nation-states, and the international system. This runs the risk of creating a body of knowledge that is based largely on the lives of power-seeking men—while neglecting other goals, actors, or communities.[35]

Non-Western critics, too, disparage the conceptual roots of liberal institutionalism. Western thinkers, generally arguing about Western states and institutions, dominated debates between realists and liberals—and later, between neo-realists and neoliberals.[36] This overlooked non-Western experiences and risked excluding states in the Global South from full participation in international affairs.[37] Many of today's domestic governance standards and major intergovernmental organizations reflect the experiences and expectations of the former Western bloc—a handful of North American and Western European states that were among the first liberal democracies. To the many additional states that willingly adopted these standards and organizations, the West still seems to have an edge, enjoying greater benefits from international institutions and greater influence over international norms. Reminiscent of Marxism, these "subaltern" critiques argue that the structures of global governance privilege a small set of transnational elites. By repackaging elite interests as a "liberal consensus," global governance structures then oppress non-elites in developing and industrialized countries alike.[38]

The future of liberal institutionalism—and liberal institutions

Liberal institutionalism's future cannot be known without examining its past, and its past cannot be understood without appreciating liberals' interactions with rival theoretical views and knotty historical events. As the discussion shows, liberals occupy a tough position. By adopting many of realism's tenets, they become vulnerable to its shortcomings. At the same time, they try to distinguish themselves: Realists simply anticipate war, while liberals anticipate war but strive for peace. Kantian perpetual peace is a goal more than a prediction; indeed, the path to such peace will be punctuated by war, because tensions arise between in-groups and out-groups as long as universalism is incomplete. Moreover, for values and institutions to generate longstanding peace, they must be embraced voluntarily, rather than foisted on unwilling populations.[39]

Grievances, now trumpeted in the West in addition to other parts of the world, are not so different from those of the 1970s, 1930s, and other periods. At times grievances were surmounted; other times they were not. Therefore, several questions arise for international relations scholars and policy practitioners. For instance, is liberal institutionalism on the cusp of collapse, or merely experiencing growing pains on the path to perpetual peace? Can civil society groups, firms, or other non-state actors bring more stability to global affairs? To what extent does the survival of international institutions depend on the preservation of democratic domestic institutions? Could the liberal world order, which was established by democratic Western states, be maintained by a powerful non-liberal state such as China?

When placed within the historical context, these questions point to a core truth. The future is fraught with danger. But for liberal institutionalism and liberal institutions, that has always been the case.

Additional reading

Amitav Acharya, "Dialogue and Discovery: In Search of International Relations Theories Beyond the West," *Millennium: Journal of International Studies* 39, no. 3 (May 2011): 619–37.

Michael Doyle, "Liberalism and World Politics," *American Political Science Review* 80, no. 4 (December 1986): 1151–69.

Tana Johnson, *Organizational Progeny: Why Governments Are Losing Control over the Proliferating Structures of Global Governance* (Oxford: Oxford University Press, 2014).

Immanuel Kant, *Perpetual Peace* (1795; reprinted, Philadelphia, PA, and Syracuse, NY: Slought Foundation and Syracuse University Humanities Center, 2010).

Robert Keohane, *After Hegemony: Cooperation and Discord in the World Political Economy* (Princeton, NJ: Princeton University Press, 1984).

Lisa Martin and Beth Simmons, "Theories and Empirical Studies of International Institutions," *International Organization* 52, no. 4 (October 1998): 729–57.

J. Ann Tickner, "You Just Don't Understand: Troubled Engagements Between Feminists and IR Theorists," *International Studies Quarterly* 41, no. 4 (December 1997): 611–32.

Notes

1 Niccolò Machiavelli, *The Prince*, eds. Quentin Skinner and Russell Price (1513; reprinted, Cambridge: Cambridge University Press, 1988).

2 Immanuel Kant, *Perpetual Peace* (1795; reprinted, Philadelphia, PA, and Syracuse, NY: Slought Foundation and Syracuse University Humanities Center, 2010).

3 Karl Marx and Friedrich Engels, *The Communist Manifesto*, ed. David McLellan (1848; reprinted, Oxford: Oxford University Press, 1998).

4 Norman Angell, *The Great Illusion: A Study of the Relation of Military Power in Nations to Their Economic and Social Advantage*, 3rd ed. (New York; London: G.P. Putnam's Sons, 1911).

5 Woodrow Wilson, *Woodrow Wilson's Fourteen Points*, 8 January 1918 (reprinted, New York: Woodrow Wilson Foundation, 1943).

6 E.H. Carr, *The Twenty Years' Crisis, 1919–1939: An Introduction to the Study of International Relations* (New York: St. Martin's Press, 1939).

7 Franklin Roosevelt, *State of the Union Message to Congress*. January 11 (Washington, DC: American Presidency Project, 1941), www.presidency.ucsb.edu/ws/?pid=16518.

8 Dan Plesch and Thomas G. Weiss, eds., *Wartime Origins and the Future United Nations* (London: Routledge, 2015).

9 Hans Morgenthau, *Politics Among Nations: The Struggle for Power and Peace* (New York: A.A. Knopf, 1948).

10 Charles Kindleberger, *The World in Depression: 1929–1939* (Berkeley: University of California Press, 1973).

11 G. John Ikenberry, *After Victory: Institutions, Strategic Restraint, and the Rebuilding of Order After Major Wars* (Princeton, NJ: Princeton University Press, 2001).

12 David Mitrany, *The Progress of International Government* (New Haven, NJ: Yale Uniervsity Press, 1933).

13 Leon Lindberg, *The Political Dynamics of European Economic Integration* (Palo Alto, CA: Stanford University Press, 1963).

14 Ernst B. Haas, *Beyond the Nation-State: Functionalism and International Organization* (Palo Alto, CA: Stanford University Press, 1964).

15 Robert Keohane and Joseph Nye, *Power and Interdependence: World Politics in Transition* (Boston, MA: Little, Brown & Company, 1977). For a more recent argument that emphasizes the importance of networks, see Anne-Marie Slaughter, *A New World Order* (Princeton, NJ: Princeton University Press, 2004).

16 Kenneth Waltz, *Theory of International Politics* (New York: McGraw-Hill, 1979).

17 Michael Doyle, "Kant, Liberal Legacies, and Foreign Affairs, Part 1," *Philosophy & Public Affairs* 12, no. 3 (1983): 205–35; "Liberalism and World Politics," *American Political Science Review* 80, no. 4 (1986): 1151–69.

18 Robert Keohane, *After Hegemony: Cooperation and Discord in the World Political Economy* (Princeton, NJ: Princeton University Press, 1984). Also see Arthur Stein, "Coordination and Collaboration: Regimes in an Anarchic World," *International Organization* 36, no. 2 (1982): 299–324; Barbara Koremenos, Charles Lipson, and Duncan Snidal, eds., *The Rational Design of International Institutions* (Cambridge: Cambridge University Press, 2004).

19 John Ruggie, "International Regimes, Transactions, and Change: Embedded Liberalism in the Postwar Economic Order," *International Organization* 36, no. 2 (1982): 379–415.

20 Joseph Grieco, "Anarchy and the Limits of Cooperation: A Realist Critique of the Newest Liberal Institutionalism," *International Organization* 42, no. 3 (1988): 485–507.

21 Robert Powell, "Absolute and Relative Gains in International Relations Theory," *American Political Science Review* 85, no. 4 (1991): 1303–20.

22 Duncan Snidal, "Relative Gains and the Pattern of International Cooperation," *American Political Science Review* 85, no. 3 (1991): 701–26.

23 Robert Axelrod, *The Evolution of Cooperation* (New York: Basic Books, 1984).

24 Andrew Moravcsik, *The Choice for Europe: Social Purpose and State Power from Messina to Maastricht* (Ithaca, NY: Cornell University Press, 1998).

25 John Mearsheimer, "The False Promise of International Institutions," *International Security* 19, no. 3 (1994/1995): 5–49.

26 Lisa Martin and Beth Simmons, "Theories and Empirical Studies of International Institutions," *International Organization* 52, no. 4 (1998): 729–57.

27 Edward Mansfield and Jon Pevehouse, "Democratization and International Organizations," *International Organization* 60, no. 1 (2006): 137–67; Jon Pevehouse and Bruce Russett, "Democratic International Governmental Organizations Promote Peace," *International Organization* 60, no. 4 (2006): 969–1000.

28 Helen Milner, "The Digital Divide: The Role of Political Institutions in Technology Diffusion," *Comparative Political Studies* 39, no. 2 (2006): 176–99.

29 Alexander Wendt, *Social Theory of International Politics* (Cambridge: Cambridge University Press, 1999).

30 Michael Barnett and Raymond Duvall, eds., *Power in Global Governance* (Cambridge: Cambridge University Press, 2005); Margaret Keck and Kathryn Sikkink, *Activists Beyond Borders: Advocacy Networks in International Politics* (Ithaca, NY: Cornell University Press, 1998); Michael Barnett and Martha Finnemore, *Rules for the World: International Organizations in Global Politics* (Ithaca, NY: Cornell University Press, 2004).

31 Stanley Hoffmann, "Liberalism and International Affairs," in *Janus and Minerva: Essays in the Theory and Practice of International Politics*, ed. Stanley Hoffmann (Boulder, CO: Westview Press, 1987), 394–417.

32 Tana Johnson, *Organizational Progeny: Why Governments Are Losing Control over the Proliferating Structures of Global Governance* (Oxford: Oxford University Press, 2014).

33 Andrew Heiss, *Amicable Contempt: The Strategic Balance Between Dictators and International NGOs*, PhD dissertation, Duke University, 2017.

34 Beate Jahn, "Kant, Mill, and Illiberal Legacies in International Affairs," *International Organization* 59, no. 1 (2005): 177, 188.

35 J. Ann Tickner, "Retelling IR's Foundational Stories: Some Feminist and Post-colonial Perspectives," *Global Change, Peace & Security* 23, no. 1 (2011): 5–13; Christine Sylvester, *Feminist International Relations: An Unfinished Journey* (Cambridge: Cambridge University Press, 2002).

36 Mohammed Ayoob, "Inequality and Theorizing in International Relations: The Case for Subaltern Realism," *International Studies Review* 4, no. 3 (2002): 27–48.

37 Amitav Acharya, "Dialogue and Discovery: In Search of International Relations Theories Beyond the West," *Millennium: Journal of International Studies* 39, no. 3 (2011): 619–37.

38 B.S. Chimni, "International Institutions Today: An Imperial Global State in the Making," *European Journal of International Law* 15, no. 1 (2004): 1–37.

39 David Lake, *The Statebuilder's Dilemma: On the Limits of Foreign Intervention* (Ithaca, NY: Cornell University Press, 2016).

Rational choice

From principal–agent to orchestration theory

Duncan Snidal and Henning Tamm

Rational choice is one of the main approaches to the study of international relations (IR), including to more specific topics such as international organizations (IOs) and global governance. It has long underpinned realist theories of peace and war, but its central role became more explicit with the development of nuclear deterrence theory, and with expected utility and bargaining models of war. Rational choice has also played a central role in international political economy and, more recently, in theories of international cooperation and explanations of the importance and design of international institutions. Even constructivist approaches, usually taken as a critique of rationalist approaches, often invoke rationality and strategic action as part of their own explanation of behavior. In short, rational choice lies at the heart of many explanations of international politics and, perhaps more than any other approach, provides a systematic framework for thinking about questions of international organization and global governance.[1]

This chapter examines the use of rational choice approaches to study international organization and global governance with special attention to principal–agent (PA) and orchestration theory. PA models investigate the circumstances under which states delegate problems to IOs. For example, the International Atomic Energy Agency (IAEA) conducts nuclear inspections, the World Bank supports economic development, and the World Health Organization (WHO) monitors global health. PA theory addresses both why states delegate such tasks to IOs and the problems inherent in that delegation. Orchestration theory builds on this approach to examine IOs as proactive agents shaping the terms of relations among states, between IOs and states, and between IOs and civil society.

This chapter begins with a discussion of rational choice as an approach to international politics, including through its use of models. The chapter then looks at PA models of state–IO relations, which represent some of the most important recent applications of rational choice to IR. We begin with a simple example of states using an IO to distribute development aid, examine the advantages and pitfalls of their doing so, and consider extensions of the model to situations involving multiple principals and/or agents as well as delegation chains. Next we canvass several leading applications of PA analysis to IOs and other non-state actors involved in global governance. Here we criticize the failure of the literature (with notable exceptions) to fully address the agency of these actors. The penultimate part of the chapter considers three prominent alternative frameworks, which envision IOs as bureaucracies, trustees, or orchestrators. We highlight orchestration theory as a particularly promising way of putting IOs at the center of the analysis. Overall, we conclude, this critical examination shows that rational choice provides a valuable and progressive framework for understanding global governance that can be adapted to the many different circumstances of international politics.

Rational choice in international relations

Rational choice theory assumes that, given their capabilities and beliefs about how the world works, actors choose their actions in order to best attain their goals. Actors can be any agents that make choices that matter—including states, IOs, nongovernmental organizations (NGOs), business firms, and individuals. Their goals need not be material and can include aesthetic and moral objectives such as preserving cultural heritages and promoting human rights; their goals also do not need to be selfish or self-interested but can include helping others, such as through development aid. This makes rational choice a very flexible framework for explaining deliberate choices of various actors; it can also be adapted to more normative questions regarding how actors *should* behave in different circumstances.

The full power of rational choice theory is unleashed when it moves beyond explaining individual choice in isolation to understanding situations where multiple actors make choices that matter. This is the realm of strategic interaction (and game theory), in which achieving the best outcome depends on finding the right combination of individual choices. If we want global aviation to be safe, for example, pilots and ground controllers must all speak the same language. If we want to gain the benefits of open international trade, states must refrain from imposing unilateral tariffs or other barriers to the free flow of commerce. Such choices become complicated when circumstances involve a mix of conflicting and coinciding considerations: No one wants airplanes to crash, but Lufthansa pilots prefer to communicate in German and Air France pilots prefer French; every state wants other states to lower tariffs but prefers to keep its own tariffs in place. To understand and resolve such tensions, we need to consider both individual and collective interests.

A particular advantage of rational choice is that many of its central arguments have been expressed very precisely in terms of models, sometimes in mathematical form, which makes it particularly amenable to exploring further theoretical implications of the argument. Because these models are fairly abstract, they are not tied to particular substantive questions and so can be transferred across different substantive topics without great difficulty. Thus, even though much rational choice was developed initially in economics—although not entirely, since some important analyses have been prompted by international relations problems such as nuclear deterrence—its arguments have been widely transferred to IR. However, the abstractness of rational choice means that its models must be supplemented by substantive analysis to apply them to any specific problem. Finally, the advantage of models rests partly in their (relative) simplicity and clarity but there are significant tradeoffs in using such simple devices to study the enormous complexity of real-world problems.

The PA model is a prime example of a simple model that helps explain seemingly diverse problems. It was originally developed to examine economic problems such as how a business firm might ensure that its employees work hard, then adapted by students of US politics to understand how Congress can control regulatory agencies, and then adapted by IR scholars to consider how states might use IOs.[2] Each application requires careful attention to the particular substantive problems—management–employee relations are different from Congress–regulatory agency relations, which are different from state–IO relations—but the PA model offers important insights across these seemingly different contexts. However, it is important not to force the analysis onto a problem that it does not fit properly and not to overlook key elements of the problem that the model does not emphasize. We illustrate these issues below with respect to the advantages and limitations of PA analysis of IOs.

While most rational choice theory in IR has focused on states as actors, the theory has been increasingly applied to non-state actors, including not only IOs but also NGOs, firms, and terrorist groups. The inclusion of terrorist groups is an instructive reminder that rational action is not necessarily desirable from all perspectives and that cooperation benefiting one group may harm another group. Of course, in many cases the interests of actors are not diametrically opposed—PA models look at situations in which the principal and agent are able to work together, albeit imperfectly.

Principal–agent theory

PA theory is based on the idea that a principal delegates authority to an agent to perform tasks on its behalf.[3] The specific terms of this relationship are defined by a contract, which, in practice, may be either a formal or an informal agreement. One central question that PA models address is how the principal can best design this contract to maximize its benefits relative to the costs of delegation. Here, we use the example of international aid to illustrate the basic logic of PA theory.

Consider a scenario in which a wealthy state wants to provide development assistance to poorer countries. Although it could do so directly, it may have several good reasons to delegate this task to an IO. First, an IO specialized in development aid (such as a multilateral development bank (MDB)) will have specific expertise and organizational capacity to manage the complex issues involved in delivering aid more effectively. Second, the state may want to convince others that it will not use aid as a foreign policy tool. Recipient countries may be concerned that donors will use aid for diplomatic leverage; public opinion polls in wealthy countries also suggest that voters favor need-based over strategic allocation of aid. By delegating this task to an MDB, which is generally considered more independent of direct state interference than are individual states' aid agencies, the state can commit to need-based policies. Third, the donor state may prefer to work through an IO to avoid political responsibility if projects fail, to avoid long-run commitments, or even to obscure its current involvement in the activity. Regardless of its motives, by acting through an IO, the state becomes a principal and the IO becomes its agent.

However, delegation also involves costs. The obvious cost is paying the agent for its services, but that is presumably offset by the benefits of the intended project. More significant but less obvious forms of *agency costs* arise because of two factors that make PA analysis vital for understanding delegation. One is that the agent's preferences may differ from those of its principal and therefore the agent may act opportunistically in pursuit of its own goals instead of the principal's goals. The other is that the agent may have information that is unavailable to the principal (hidden information) or its actions may not be fully observable by the principal (hidden action). The conjunction of these considerations creates costs for the principal because they potentially allow an agent to pursue its own interests unless it is somehow constrained or incentivized to do what the principal wants. If the principal can perfectly observe the agent, then the former can control the latter perfectly by creating the right incentives or constraints. If hidden information or hidden action pertains, then agency problems arise.

If the principal is not able to monitor every single step the agent takes, the latter can engage in its own preferred behavior rather than do what is desired by its principal. Such *agency slack* is sometimes further divided into *shirking* (minimizing the effort it exerts) and *slippage* (actively pursuing its own interests, not the principal's). In our scenario, the wealthy state will therefore seek to minimize agency slack by offering the MDB a contract that rewards good performance but also includes control mechanisms such as monitoring and reporting requirements that trigger penalties if slack is detected. Oversight procedures themselves create costs that reduce the principal's gains from the division of labor. Moreover, there is the problem of incomplete contracting: It is typically impossible to design a contract that anticipates all potential sources of agency slack. In sum, the wealthy state faces an unavoidable tradeoff. The rationalist logic of PA theory suggests that the wealthy state will only choose delegation to an MDB if the expected overall benefits exceed the overall costs.

Two special cases of agency problems are adverse selection and moral hazard. *Adverse selection* occurs if an agent can misrepresent its abilities and preferences in order to be engaged by a principal. For instance, an MDB will claim its priorities are the same as the principal's even if it intends to use donor money to expand its bureaucracy or pursue other projects; the state will therefore need to screen potential agents to be sure it selects an IO that will serve its needs. But gathering information for effective screening is costly, and screening is not always effective; the principal may only realize after the fact (if ever) that its wishes were not being fulfilled.

Moral hazard emerges when an agent takes risks whose costs fall on the principal if the risky policy fails and things go badly. For example, the IMF contributes to moral hazard through its willingness to bail out countries that experience balance-of-payments problems—which may encourage countries to behave in ways that cause such problems in the first place.[4]

Our scenario of a single state and a single IO is useful for thinking through the basics of PA models, but it does not adequately capture all IR complexities. We thus consider a more realistic scenario in which several wealthy states want to provide aid through an MDB. For simplicity, we first assume that the MDB will have separate contracts with each state, but that they all relate to the same MDB policy (action). If these multiple principals all have the same preferences, they face the same problems that we have already described in the earlier scenario. If their preferences diverge, however, the model will predict greater potential MDB autonomy (and thus greater opportunities for agency slack), as the agent will now play different principals off against each other. In contrast, if a single wealthy state faces multiple MDBs, agency slack will decrease, as each MDB would fear that its slack could lead the state principal to switch to another MDB agent. Moreover, a state might engage several MDBs each in charge of different development projects and use their comparative performance as a measure of agency slack. Finally, with multiple states and multiple MDBs, these effects offset each other so that we should expect a medium level of slack. Figure 9.1 summarizes these arguments.[5]

Some PA models incorporate further empirical complexities by studying chains of delegation. In the case of our basic scenario, one could disaggregate the wealthy state into voters (as principals) and the government (as agent), and then extend the chain of delegation with the government (as principal) to the MDB (as agent), followed by the MDB (as principal) to a recipient developing country bureaucracy (as agent).[6] The model would now include three distinct PA relationships—voters to government; government to MDB; and MDB to recipient bureaucracy. These conceptual maneuvers, which we discuss in the next section, raise the question of how much real-world complexity a good model should incorporate.

We conclude this section by highlighting two potentially problematic aspects of PA theory. First, agency problems hinge on the assumption that agents' preferences diverge from principals' preferences. If this is not the case, the models lose their power. Second, PA models focus largely on how principals can avoid agency slack; at least in their formal variants, it is the principal who acts first by offering a contract, typically on a "take-it-or-leave-it" basis. This is somewhat ironic insofar as cooperation theorists have argued that introducing PA theory to IR enables them to study IO—rather than state—agency. We address these aspects in greater detail in the following two sections.

	Single principal	Multiple principals
Single agent	Medium	High
Multiple agents	Low	Medium

Figure 9.1 Opportunities for agency slack

International organizations as agents

Here we begin with examples of PA analysis applied to international as well as supranational organizations and outline key complicating features that occur with delegation in the international context. Second, we consider why most PA models in IR concentrate on the principal rather than the agent—which is peculiar if we wish to focus on IOs—and we present efforts to alleviate this bias. Third, we review the growing literature on transnational relations that applies insights from PA theory to both states and non-state actors, thus shedding new light on global governance structures.

The first sustained IR applications of PA theory were to the European Union (EU), to which states have delegated more authority than to any other international institution. Do the EU's supranational organizations—such as the European Commission, the European Parliament, or the European Court of Justice (ECJ)—undermine the authority of member states? Mark Pollack drew on PA theory to show how states maintain control in varying degrees.[7] The ECJ provides one of the most important cases of how delegation creates autonomous power and, along with the experiences of other international courts, has led to one of the main critiques of PA models, which we address in the next section.[8]

In another important early contribution, Daniel Nielson and Michael Tierney used PA theory to explain how the World Bank exercised significant autonomy in its operations but then suddenly adjusted its behavior under pressure from member governments.[9] They highlighted three complicating features of PA relationships in the context of IOs. First, states often act as a "collective principal," designing a common contract for an agent; they first need to solve collective-action problems among themselves before interacting with that agent. Second, IOs sometimes face multiple principals from the same state—e.g., when the legislature and the executive have separate "contracts" with the agent. Third, as suggested earlier, delegation chains are often long.

These early studies culminated in the edited volume *Delegation and Agency in International Organizations*, which shows the wide applicability of PA analysis to international organizations across such diverse areas as development, finance, health, justice, security, and trade.[10] The contributors point out specific benefits of international delegation that result from the fact that it often involves collective principals. For instance, delegating to an agent may facilitate collective decision making or help resolve disputes between principals because the agent can serve as an agenda setter or arbitrator. Nonetheless, the last chapter concludes: "Delegation 'under anarchy' appears to be pretty much the same as delegation in other political forums."[11] This overlooks the greatest promise of PA theory, however, which is to show not just how states control IOs but how IOs can gain and exercise autonomy precisely because control mechanisms are not as strong under anarchy, while the need for global governance is ever growing.

PA models of IOs typically focus on the principal rather than on the agent, emphasizing why states delegate to IOs, and how they control IOs after delegating authority. These are essentially questions about institutional choice and design.[12] Pollack discusses methodological reasons for not studying agent behavior in greater detail. Because agents can rationally anticipate the reactions of their principals, they adjust their behavior in order to avoid costly sanctions; in the presence of control mechanisms, it is thus impossible to ascertain whether or not agents actually have opportunistic preferences. Moreover, the very idea of hidden action implies that it is difficult to measure agency slack directly. However, Pollack suggests that careful analysis of open conflicts between principals and agents can be revealing even if these episodes are not necessarily representative.[13] In a similar effort to study agent behavior, Hawkins and Jacoby show how agents influence contract design at the selection stage and reinterpret their mandates afterwards.[14]

So far, the agents discussed are organizations created by states and tightly constrained by them. There is, however, an emerging literature that uses PA theory to model transnational relations between states, on the one hand, and international nongovernmental organizations (INGOs), rebel groups, and terrorists, on the other hand. This pushes the boundaries of PA theory and raises interesting questions about global governance. In a study of transnationalism, for example, Alexander Cooley and James Ron model a delegation chain that involves governments as donors, INGOs as contractors, and local actors as recipients. Their main insight is that INGOs operate in a context of organizational insecurity characterized by PA problems, which creates "imperatives that promote self-interested action, inter-INGO competition, and poor project implementation."[15] Thus, even actors such as INGOs that are typically motivated by "good" normative agendas may be compelled to act opportunistically to ensure organizational survival.

Turning to less savory agendas, Idean Salehyan examines state support to foreign rebel groups as a PA relationship. Like Daniel Byman and Sarah Kreps in their analysis of state-sponsored terrorism, Salehyan highlights the benefit of plausible deniability—hence evading international condemnation—when delegating violent attacks to third party actors.[16] While Salehyan and his colleagues discuss the "resources-versus-autonomy dilemma" that rebel groups face in this context, Lucy Hovil and Eric Werker go one step further: They suggest that some rebel groups use excessive violence against civilians, even to the extent of undermining their own long-term objectives, in order to send a credible signal to their foreign patrons that they remain committed to destabilizing the target state.[17]

This research on rebel and terrorist groups suggests interesting new approaches for studying the "dark side" of global governance. It challenges scholars to analyze delegation in a context of political violence and demonstrates the strategic dimensions of transnational relations, where the strategies of the agents need to be addressed more centrally.

IOs as bureaucracies, trustees, or orchestrators

This section addresses three alternatives to PA models of global governance. Each takes issue with the assumption that IOs are best conceived purely as agents of states, instead according them a more autonomous role.

Even before PA theory took off in IR, Michael Barnett and Martha Finnemore criticized its assumptions and offered a constructivist explanation for agency slack—or, in their terminology, "pathologies"—of IOs. Drawing on sociological institutionalism, they conceived of IOs as bureaucracies that embody rational–legal authority, which gives them legitimacy and power independent of the states that created them. It is this authority, rather than the lack of control mechanisms, that enables IOs to act autonomously. At the same time, however, their internal bureaucratic culture can breed pathologies—dysfunctional behavior that is in neither the member states' nor necessarily the IO's own interest.[18]

Yet IO culture need not be dysfunctional and may promote collective values which states espouse but are themselves unable to practice. Good examples include the role of the WTO secretariat in promoting the free trade agenda or of the Intergovernmental Panel on Climate Change (IPCC) in pressing the climate change agenda despite the reluctance of state parties. Whatever the mix, IO goals need to be addressed more explicitly whenever delegation leaves significant room for agency slack. In order to theorize more specific agent preferences, however, scholars must bring in substantive considerations from outside PA theory.[19]

Karen Alter criticizes the assumptions of PA models in the specific context of delegation to international courts. Building on Giandomenico Majone's work on fiduciary relations, Alter sees international courts as "trustees" and principal–trustee relations as fundamentally different from those between principals and agents. Trusteeship aims to improve the legitimacy of decision making by harnessing the authority of the trustee. Principals deliberately give up large parts of control, for the very authority of trustees hinges on their independence.[20] Other scholars disagree, arguing that PA theory can capture the fact that different tasks require different degrees of agent discretion. Pollack, for instance, argues that a complete and irrevocable transfer of authority is unlikely in international relations and that it is more useful to study the far-reaching independence of international courts in the context of a continuum of discretion.[21]

Instead of criticizing how PA theory models delegation, Kenneth Abbott and his colleagues propose an alternative mode of governance—called "orchestration"—that leads to quite different understandings of the relations among states, IOs, NGOs, and other actors.[22] As orchestrators, IOs enlist and support like-minded intermediary actors to address target actors in the pursuit of governance goals. These intermediaries can include INGOs, business organizations, public–private partnerships, trans-governmental networks, and even other IOs. The targets can be states themselves or private actors, such as firms, which IOs have not traditionally been allowed to govern. Orchestration models thus address the complexities and reach of global governance.

We can distinguish orchestration from other governance modes and compare it to PA analysis by reference to two dimensions: Direct and indirect; hard and soft (see Figure 9.2). In both delegation and orchestration, governance is indirect since the governing actor works through a third party to achieve its goals. The difference is that, in delegation, the principal has authority to control the agent hierarchically by command whereas, in orchestration, the orchestrator does not have authority and can influence the intermediary only through softer means including ideational and material support. Orchestration shows the limits of PA theory: When goals are correlated and the third party's cooperation is voluntary, orchestrator–intermediary–target

	Direct	Indirect
Hard	Hierarchy	Delegation
Soft	Collaboration	Orchestration

Figure 9.2 Modes of governance

(O–I–T) models may have greater purchase than PA models. It also adapts and extends PA theory—treating states as principals to IOs and IOs as orchestrators of non-state intermediaries suggests a governance chain that involves both delegation and orchestration.

Most strikingly, orchestration provides a means for IOs to reverse the standard relationship by "bypassing" or "managing" states.[23] IOs can bypass states as regulators when they enlist NGOs to influence the behavior of private firms, or even to go around recalcitrant states as the WHO has in its AIDS program. IOs can manage states when they engage third parties to shape the preferences and behavior of states as the UN Security Council has through the Kimberley Process, which regulates the international trade in rough diamonds. But one should not exaggerate IOs' powers of orchestration: Collectively, states ultimately control IOs and can therefore rein them in. However, a surprising finding of orchestration theory is that states often encourage IOs to orchestrate them. The reason, perhaps, is that when states face a cooperation problem requiring central management, they would rather accept IO orchestration than actually delegate authority directly to IOs.[24]

Conclusion

Rational choice is a flexible and versatile approach for studying international politics. PA theory illustrates its particular importance for understanding international organizations and governance in terms of states, individually or collectively, as the principal in designing and controlling an IO as its or their agent. While this has the virtue of treating IOs as partially autonomous actors that have to be controlled, it does not fully capture their ability to shape relations with states and other actors. Alternative frameworks redress this limitation by conceptualizing IOs as more autonomous bureaucracies, trustees, or orchestrators. These models and extensions show how rational choice can incorporate different conceptions of international organizations and other actors to broaden our understanding of global governance.

Additional reading

Kenneth W. Abbott, Philipp Genschel, Duncan Snidal, and Bernhard Zangl, eds., *International Organizations as Orchestrators* (Cambridge: Cambridge University Press, 2015).
Daniel Byman and Sarah E. Kreps, "Agents of Destruction? Applying Principal–Agent Analysis to State-Sponsored Terrorism," *International Studies Perspectives* 11, no. 1 (2010): 1–18.

Darren G. Hawkins, David A. Lake, Daniel L. Nielson, and Michael J. Tierney, eds., *Delegation and Agency in International Organizations* (Cambridge: Cambridge University Press, 2006).

Mark A. Pollack, *The Engines of European Integration: Delegation, Agency, and Agenda Setting in the EU* (Oxford: Oxford University Press, 2003).

Duncan Snidal, "Rational Choice and International Relations," in *Handbook of International Relations*, eds. Walter Carlsnaes, Thomas Risse, and Beth A. Simmons (Los Angeles, CA: Sage Publications, 2013), 85–111.

Notes

1 Duncan Snidal, "Rational Choice and International Relations," in *Handbook of International Relations*, eds. Walter Carlsnaes, Thomas Risse, and Beth A. Simmons (Los Angeles, CA: Sage Publications, 2013), 85–111; Andrew H. Kydd, "Methodological Individualism and Rational Choice," in *The Oxford Handbook of International Relations*, eds. Christian Reus-Smit and Duncan Snidal (Oxford: Oxford University Press, 2008), 425–443.

2 On the origins in economics, see Kathleen M. Eisenhardt, "Agency Theory: An Assessment and Review," *Academy of Management Review* 14, no. 1 (1989): 57–74. For political science, see Gary J. Miller, "The Political Evolution of Principal–Agent Models," *Annual Review of Political Science* 8 (2005): 203–225; J. Bendor, A. Glazer, and T. Hammond, "Theories of Delegation," *Annual Review of Political Science* 4 (2001): 235–269.

3 Darren G. Hawkins, David A. Lake, Daniel L. Nielson, and Michael J. Tierney, "Delegation under Anarchy: States, International Organizations, and Principal–Agent Theory," in *Delegation and Agency in International Organizations*, eds. Hawkins, et al. (Cambridge: Cambridge University Press, 2006), 3–38. For delegation with particular application to international law, see Curtis A. Bradley and Judith G. Kelley, "The Concept of International Delegation," *Law and Contemporary Problems* 71, no. 1 (2008): 1–36.

4 See J. Lawrence Broz and Michael Brewster Hawes, "US Domestic Politics and International Monetary Fund Policy," in *Delegation*, eds. Hawkins, et al., 77–106.

5 Figure 9.1 extends arguments regarding the number of available agents developed in Darren G. Hawkins and Wade Jacoby, "How Agents Matter," in *Delegation*, eds. Hawkins, et al., 203–205.

6 Helen V. Milner, "Why Multilateralism? Foreign aid and domestic principal–agent problems," in *Delegation*, eds. Hawkins, et al., 107–139. See also Alexander Cooley and James Ron, "The NGO Scramble: Organizational Insecurity and the Political Economy of Transnational Action," *International Security* 27, no. 1 (2002): 14–24.

7 Mark A. Pollack, "Delegation, Agency, and Agenda Setting in the European Community," *International Organization* 51, no. 1 (1997): 99–134; *The Engines of European Integration: Delegation, Agency, and Agenda Setting in the EU* (Oxford: Oxford University Press, 2003).

8 Anne-Marie Burley and Walter Mattli, "Europe before the Court: A Political Theory of Integration," *International Organization* 47, no. 1 (1993): 41–76; and Geoffrey Garrett and Barry R. Weingast, "Ideas, Interests and Institutions: Constructing the European Community's Internal Market," in *Ideas and Foreign Policy: Beliefs, Institutions, and Political Change*, eds. Judith Goldstein and Robert O. Keohane (Ithaca, NY: Cornell University Press, 1993), 173–206.

9 Daniel L. Nielson and Michael J. Tierney, "Delegation to International Organizations: Agency Theory and World Bank Environmental Reform," *International Organization* 57, no. 2 (2003): 241–276.

10 Hawkins, et al., eds., *Delegation*.

11 David A. Lake and Mathew D. McCubbins, "The Logic of Delegation to International Organizations," in *Delegation*, eds. Hawkins, et al., 344.

12 Barbara Koremenos, Charles Lipson, and Duncan Snidal, "The Rational Design of International Institutions," *International Organization* 55, no. 4 (2001): 761–799.

13 Pollack, *The Engines of European Integration*, 69.

14 Hawkins and Jacoby, "How Agents Matter," 212.

15 Cooley and Ron, "The NGO Scramble," 14.

16 Idean Salehyan, "The Delegation of War to Rebel Organizations," *Journal of Conflict Resolution* 54, no. 3 (2010): 503; Daniel Byman and Sarah E. Kreps, "Agents of Destruction? Applying Principal–Agent Analysis to State-Sponsored Terrorism," *International Studies Perspectives* 11, no. 1 (2010): 6.

17 Idean Salehyan, Kristian Skrede Gleditsch, and David E. Cunningham, "Explaining External Support for Insurgent Groups," *International Organization* 65, no. 4 (2011): 717; Lucy Hovil and Eric Werker, "Portrait of a Failed Rebellion: An Account of Rational, Sub-Optimal Violence in Western Uganda," *Rationality and Society* 17, no. 1 (2005): 7–8.

18 Michael N. Barnett and Martha Finnemore, "The Politics, Power, and Pathologies of International Organizations," *International Organization* 53, no. 4 (1999): 699–732. For a critical appraisal, see Mark A. Pollack, "Principal–Agent Analysis and International Delegation: Red Herrings, Theoretical Clarifications, and Empirical Disputes," Bruges Political Research Papers no. 2 (2007): 15–21.

19 Erica R. Gould, "Delegating IMF Conditionality: Understanding Variations in Control and Conformity," in *Delegation*, eds. Hawkins, et al., 308. See also Andrew P. Cortell and Susan Peterson, "Dutiful Agents, Rogue Actors, or Both? Staffing, Voting Rules, and Slack in the WHO and WTO," in *Delegation*, eds. Hawkins, et al., 258–262.

20 See Karen J. Alter, "Agents or Trustees? International Courts in their Political Context," *European Journal of International Relations* 14, no. 1 (2008): 33–63; Giandomenico Majone, "Two Logics of Delegation: Agency and Fiduciary Relations in EU Governance," *European Union Politics* 2, no. 1 (2001): 103–122.

21 Pollack, "Principal–Agent Analysis," 9–12.

22 Kenneth W. Abbott and Duncan Snidal, "International Regulation without International Government: Improving IO Performance Through Orchestration," *Review of International Organizations* 5, no. 3 (2010): 315–344; Kenneth W. Abbott, Philipp Genschel, Duncan Snidal, and Bernhard Zangl, eds., *International Organizations as Orchestrators* (Cambridge: Cambridge University Press, 2015).

23 Abbott, et al., "Orchestration: Global Governance Through Intermediaries," in *International Organizations as Orchestrators*, eds. Abbott, et al., 6.

24 Abbott, et al., "Orchestrating Global Governance: From Empirical Findings to Theoretical Implications," in *International Organizations as Orchestrators*, eds. Abbott, et al., 350.

CONTENTS

Constructivism

Susan Park

Constructivism is a central approach for understanding international relations (IR), international organizations (IOs), and global governance. Emerging as a theoretical contender in the late 1980s, constructivist approaches seek to identify how and when ideas matter for shaping international politics. As this chapter outlines, constructivism flourished alongside more radical critical theories to challenge narrow IR debates over how to make the analysis of events occurring in world politics more scientific. While there are distinctions among constructivists over the scientific endeavor,[1] the major thrust of constructivism was to challenge the dominance of "rational" theories of international relations such as neorealism and neoliberal institutionalism.

Constructivists embraced the position that everything in the world is socially constructed and that many things taken as given are instead "social facts" created by shared agreement among state and non-state actors alike. Institutions such as money and gross domestic product (GDP), what constitutes a failed state, and the very nature of state sovereignty and the international system, are social constructs that endure because state and non-state actors are willing to accept them as given and to act in accordance with them. Norms that states currently take for granted include sovereignty, antislavery, antiapartheid, the chemical weapons taboo; opposing wartime plunder and piracy; opposing the use of mercenaries; opposing drug trafficking and the trade in endangered species; and prohibiting torture, among others. This approach radically challenged rational theories that assume that many of these structures were immutable and unchanging.

This chapter outlines the emergence and basic tenets of constructivist thought before detailing current debates over how and when ideas matter. A constructivist perspective, based on norms, culture, and identity counterposes rationalist theoretical accounts of change within international relations. The original point of contention was to identify when ideas rather than material factors shaped international politics. Early scholars examined the importance of norms, which are collective expectations about proper behavior for actors with a given identity for influencing the international system, absent material factors. Ideas can shape international politics both as regulative norms and constitutive ones. Regulative norms lead to norm following behavior such as agreeing to adhere to UN treaties and protocols or to act in accordance with how the World Bank classifies states as developed or developing. In order to demonstrate that norms led to change, scholars traced how norms induce compliance. Constitutive norms not only lead to norm following but the practice of following fundamentally reconstitutes state and non-state actors' identities, reshaping what they understand as their interests and preferences. Norms have constitutive power when they make certain ways of thinking and acting possible, and actors internalize the norm such that their norm-consistent behavior becomes part of who they are.

This is vital to the constructivist argument: Social interaction is constitutive in the sense that norms change actors' behavior which in turn feeds back into and reshapes the norm. While norms do not necessarily cease to exist if they are challenged, they can no longer hold structural power in influencing actors' behavior if the majority of actors no longer follow or enforce them. This means that "in all politics . . . actors reproduce or alter systems through their actions," and that "any given international system does not exist because of immutable structures, but rather the very structures are dependent for their reproduction on the practices of the actors." Change may occur in the international system when "actors, through their practices, change the rules and norms constitutive of international interaction."[2] This process of structuration shapes our world.[3]

That said, constructivist debate has increasingly cleaved between those focusing purely on norms that lead to a change in behavior (norm following or compliance) versus constitutive arguments of identity and normative contestation. Constructivists have also shifted their focus from state compliance as evidence of the importance of norms to analyze how both state and non-state actors strategically attempt to bring about normative change.[4] A significant strand of constructivist work examines how IOs often work in conjunction with non-state actors to shape the behavior of states to become norm followers.[5]

In pursuit of its aims, the chapter begins by detailing the history and basic tenets of constructivism. It then explores key criticisms of the constructivist literature. Thereafter, the chapter details how constructivist insights are being used: Not only to highlight the role of IOs in classifying and categorizing the world but also in midrange theorizing alongside rationalist approaches to explain how norms advanced by IOs and states intersect with material interests to create new categories of action.

History and development of constructivism

This section outlines the emergence of constructivist ideas before detailing five key tenets of the approach for understanding IOs and global governance. Constructivism blossomed in the 1990s to become a dominant approach in IR in the first decade of the twenty-first century. The genesis of constructivism can be found in European philosophies that opposed the very basis on which realism, liberalism, and Marxism were founded. Realism is based on states maximizing their power and ensuring their survival in the international system. Liberalism is based on the reasonable actions of individuals to ensure their freedom and rights. Neoliberalism is based on the rational actions of states to maximize their utility while arguing that states can increase their gains if they cooperate within the international system. Marxism argues that inequities between classes means that the capitalist class will use the state to enforce its position within society. Neo-Marxists such as Robert Cox argue that hegemonic transnational bloc uses the gains from the spread of capitalism across the globe to ensure the dominance of the transnational capitalist elite. All these theories build their arguments on the rational basis of the actors involved. So individuals, classes, and states generally act in rational ways to get what they want. Constructivists argue, however, that not all events occur because of rational actions, and that we can understand IR by looking at the social context in which decisions are made, which may include behavior that is not within states' national interest.

Constructivism sought to challenge the dominance of rationalist theories by emphasizing the historical, changing, and fluid nature of events, situations, and contexts in international politics. Constructivists argued that by understanding the social relations between actors and the context in which events occur can lead to better understanding of why something occurred in the way it did and not otherwise. For example, how was it possible for the International Monetary Fund (IMF) to pressure its member states to change its Articles of Agreement in the 1990s to rule out states' options to use capital controls as a viable monetary policy when it had been fundamental to the instantiation of the IMF in 1944?[6] How is it possible that we have a taboo over the use of chemical weapons but not other equally atrocious means of killing?[7] How is it possible that development is primarily understood as the level of a state's GDP but not other measures such as the Human Development Index?[8]

The early focus on "how" and not "why" questions differentiated the constructivist endeavor from other theoretical approaches. The early constructivist challenge included opposing the scientific claims of theory, or the ability of the scholar to explain the events and actions of the international system, and predict their recurrence. Perhaps even more damning was the challenge to rationalists over their ability to determine with complete certainty cause and effect. Early constructivists argued that one cannot ascribe motivations and intentions to actors from what has occurred. One can only go by how actors act and the justifications that they give for their actions.

Yet constructivism is, like all other theories, a broad church encompassing many different, often competing, and overlapping varieties. Constructivism includes both modern and postmodern as well as critical strands.[9] Modern constructivism seeks to investigate how subjects and objects are created through language relations rather than the critical theory focus on how knowledge and power determine the world in which we live. Modern constructivism therefore accepts a minimal foundation to knowledge, whereby conclusions drawn from analyzing the social world are variable and limited in time and place, rather than fixed and immutable as assumed in rationalist theorizing.[10]

Some have argued that modern constructivism diverges from rationalist perspectives in terms of ontology (the social rather than material world) but not in terms of epistemology (discussed below) and methodology.[11] Regarding the last, this means that modern constructivism can use both conventional and critical tools to understand how events unfolded in one way and not another. For example, constructivists can gather evidence, conduct interviews, engage in participant observation, use discourse analysis, use process tracing, use genealogy or undertake ethnography in order to identify how ideas can lead to change or inform actors' behavior.[12] Irrespective of the variety, all constructivists adhere to the first of the tenets set out below and situate themselves somewhere on a continuum in agreement or disagreement with the others.

First, all constructivists argue that everything in the world is socially constructed. The only way in which we can understand IR is by examining the social relations among actors. Thus everything that occurs in IR is a result of the interactions between actors whether they are states, IOs, or nongovernmental organizations (NGOs), individuals, or other social groups. Constructivism is not state centric although many do examine how state identities are constructed and how changes to the international system may induce an identity crisis.[13] Constructivism sought to challenge the ground on which contemporary IR is built by rejecting the overt material focus on power, wealth, and inequality that did not examine how power, and wealth and inequality, were constructed. How actors think about our world helps construct it. Moreover, constructivism behooves us to examine why the world is constructed in one way and not another as well as how some norms seem to trump others (such as the norm of non-interference versus the responsibility to protect (R2P)).

Second, a strong theme in constructivism is that while social and material factors matter ideas are more important for understanding IR. While realists point to military capability, liberals point to economic wealth, and Marxists point to inequality between classes, constructivists argue that material power is not as important as the ideas that we attribute to these items. As such, how we understand these factors and the function that we attribute to them is more important than the concrete nature of the thing itself. All actors are engaged in social relations that shape their reactions but also their identities. Nature is not the primary determinant. Ideas have structural characteristics in that they "define the limits of what is cognitively possible and impossible for individuals."[14]

One of the reasons for the focus on ideas in the 1990s was the rise of identity politics and the collapse of the Soviet Union, the fall of the Berlin Wall, and the implosion of Yugoslavia. The seemingly impossible suddenly became possible; the Cold War, which for decades had seemed immutable, was swept away. Yet rationalist theories had not predicted it. The field was riven with debates over why people aligned on the basis of national identities and not class, gender, or other categorizations. This helped cement the importance of constructivism.

Third, constructivists share a broad understanding of how rules and norms influence actors' identities. The social relations between actors are based on norms and rules. Norms are powerful when they are endorsed by a critical mass (or one-third of states) such that they have reached a tipping point and have cascaded throughout the international system.[15] Rules shape interactions in international politics. There are diplomatic rules of engagement for everyday bilateral and multilateral interactions as well as a significant body of rules regarding appropriate conduct in warfare including the Geneva conventions on the treatment of non-combatants and prisoners of war. There are taboos on the use of chemical and biological weapons, prohibiting their use in warfare. The latter was most prominently displayed in April 2017 when the Syrian government allegedly used chemical weapons against its own people leading to the death of eighty-nine people and harming over 500 more. Leading international outrage was the UN Secretary-General Antonio Guterres, who called it a war crime.[16]

If actors do not comply with international norms, this may lead to informal or formal sanctioning procedures. Specifically, actors' may face ideational practices such as shaming and shunning or material economic or military sanctions to bring them into line. For constructivists then, it is not only that states follow rules such as those codified in the Chemical Weapons Convention most of the time because they may face material sanctions from other states, but that states accept that there should be limits on the use of violence within war because it is right and legitimate. Moreover, if states continue to view these norms as important then they will remain so. Should the majority of states choose not to defend them then the norm is replaced by a new norm accepting in this case the use of chemical and biological weapons.

Fourth, as outlined earlier, constructivists aim to understand rather than explain IR. This is because constructivists attempt to draw out the social reasons for why states, IOs, and other non-state actors behave the way they do, rather than otherwise. They seek to examine the interactions between states and other social formations, which is based on attempting to understand how things came to be as they are, rather than attempting to identify the causal explanation of events. Thus, constructivists can tell us how states interpret the international system, or interpret particular events within IR, rather than locating the cause of specific outcomes. Scholars have examined why IOs behave the way that they do and not otherwise. For example, they have "opened the black box" of IOs to analyze how the culture and internal ideas within an organization may lead to decision making that may not seem to be in the organization's best interests, or how an IO acts against its own mandate owing to its pathological behavior.[17]

Fifth, early and critical constructivists reject the scientific basis of theory. The distinction between understanding and attempting to explain events is rooted in the divergent position of scholars on theory as a scientific endeavor. All rationalist theories have a commitment to positivist epistemology. Positivism is:

> [A] belief in the naturalism of the social world . . . a separation between facts and values, by which is meant both that 'facts' are theory-neutral and that normative commitments should not influence what counts as facts or as knowledge; a commitment to uncovering patterns or regularities in the social world . . .; and finally, a commitment to empiricism as what counts as knowledge."[18]

Positivist epistemology is used by most rationalist theoretical approaches to objectively determine the main cause of events in IR. In this vein, scholars can observe what happens in IR and make inferences as to what caused certain actions and outcomes. Like the hard or physical sciences of chemistry and physics, we can make law like generalizations about the world that are true and immutable. As with gravity, we too can have laws about international relations. The strongest law like generalization that we have is the argument that democracies do not go to war with one another. This scientific basis for theory is such that we can posit a hypothesis—that democracies do not go to war with one another. We can then observe, gather evidence, and test our hypothesis. Each result either nullifies or proves the hypothesis. Owing to the distinction between scientific, objective, and value-free theorizing and the recognition of the value-laden, subjective, and interpretive theory espoused by constructivism, early and critical constructivists rejected the rational basis of all mainstream IR theories. They argued that no theory is value free, but constructivists generally do not take the extra step that critical theorists do; that we as scholars impute our own values into what we see, and thus influence the outcome. The best that we can do is attempt to recognize this reality, and analyze how all social relations influence our understanding of the social world. Thus, constructivists can observe what is occurring within the international system and attempt to understand how the social relations between actors influences who they are and how they act.

Current debates

Significant constructivist work has been done on the role of both global and regional IOs as diffusers of norms, spreading them throughout their region or the international system.[19] IOs along with NGOs can operate to exert pressure on states to behave according to norms agreed to at the international level such as on human rights, or they can act as norm entrepreneurs to create new norms.[20] IOs can do so owing to their technical expertise and moral authority.[21] Initially constructivists attempted to demonstrate the importance of ideas in cases where material factors were absent. In reality however, there are few situations where material factors are not present in international politics. Indeed, IOs attempt to spread norms but these cannot be divorced from such material offerings as the European Union (EU). With the collapse of the Soviet Union, the EU began an enlargement project to incorporate Central and Eastern European states. Tied to entry into the EU were considerable material advantages in terms of access to the common market and the ability to move capital, goods, services, and labor across borders. Constructivists examining the EU thus identified that it was not a case of when ideas versus material factors mattered. It was not an "either/or" proposition, but a "both/and."[22] They therefore looked at how and if Central and Eastern European states were being socialized into the Western European norms on democracy, capitalism, and human and minority rights as part of the accession process. Were Central and Eastern European states beginning to adopt new norms on minority rights because they began to see the value of such ideas or were they induced to do so by the carrots offered? Could we argue that institutionalizing the norm through changing domestic laws and institutions was sufficient evidence of normative change or did we need to know that states internalized the norms, thus changing their identity?[23] The difference is discussed below.

Beyond analyzing IOs as advocates, defenders, and diffusers of norms, constructivists also began to examine what drives IOS behavior and whether they are capable of change. Here the constructivist focus remained on the identity or organizational culture of an IO. For constructivists, the organizational culture informs how an IO behaves. Scholars have attempted to examine the internal norms, rules, and ideas shaping IO behavior in terms of how this limits what policy options are available in any given situation.[24] For scholars operating in this vein, the professional orientation of most of the staff shapes internal cultures. IO actions may stem from an organization's culture or how management and staff think they should undertake their mandate. Scholars generally agree that the reason that an IO tackles its mandate in a certain way is based on the dominant professional culture of the organization. Medically trained staff at the World Health Organization (WHO), for example, imbue the organization with a radically different culture than if it were staffed by non-medically trained staff. This structure made it difficult to move beyond primary medical interventions when tasked with doing so. The policy options changed for the World Bank when it moved from being an institution predominantly staffed by engineers to one by economists, helping to facilitate the shift from bricks-and-mortar development projects to program lending.

Organizational culture can lead staff to promote norms rather than being determined by management or member states, or it may forestall the organization from changing and taking up new tasks. Much has also been made of the IMF's organizational culture based on staff's training in neoclassical economics undertaken at particular US universities in driving the institution's emphasis on capital account liberalization despite this emphasis not being within the Fund's mandate or by the demands of its powerful member states.[25] Other examples also show when member state demands for reforming its loan conditionality stalled as a result of the IMF's organizational culture.[26] Furthermore, organizational culture may lead to pathological or dysfunctional behavior as an IO follows its internal approach to problem solving rather than properly addressing an issue.[27] This can lead to organized hypocrisy as an IO attempts to continue its established practices despite pledging to change its ways to member states.[28]

Key criticisms and emerging issues

This section highlights three main criticisms of constructivism as well as important emerging issues. From the beginning constructivists have faced three key criticisms: When norms matter, the role power plays in constructivist analysis, and the predominant focus on good norms. First, critics have alleged that constructivists choose cases where norms are important but that they do not go far enough to explain when norms and ideas matter as opposed to other factors such as power, wealth, and states' national interest. This argument was leveled by rationalists against modern constructivists over the need for a clear articulation of the scope of conditions for when ideas matter. At heart was an attempt to demand the very law like generalizations about the role of ideas in international politics that early constructivists had rejected. The response for some was to articulate the need to specify better the scope of conditions for interrogating the impact of norms.[29]

In a similar attack but from critical theorists came the argument that constructivists ignore power. The focus on language and social interactions ignores how power operates through discourse to marginalize the weak and maintain a status quo. Although the continuum of constructivist work includes those more "modern" and those more "critical," the argument turns on how power is defined. Many constructivists referenced throughout this chapter have indeed examined how ideas are mediated through IOs with asymmetric power relations and where the ideas may come from materially non-powerful actors such as IO staff and management and NGOs.

Finally, constructivists have been accused of only looking at good norms particularly on human rights. This is a valid criticism, with little work done on bad norms, their emergence, development, and distribution.[30]

A key emerging issue for constructivism is how it is increasingly being blended with rationalist insights. Arguably constructivist success in the 1990s for occupying the "middle ground" of IR theory has also led to it being combined with rational theories.[31] While there are constructivists who remain focused on identifying how norms are adopted, contested, and reconstituted,[32] increasingly ideas have been combined with materialist factors to explain IO behavior. For example, scholars seeking to bridge the rationalist–constructivist divide have combined organizational culture arguments with the rationalist principal–agent (PA) model. Within the PA model, IOs are treated as agents that have been contractually tasked by the member state principals to undertake activities mandated by states. IOs have various levels of autonomy and discretion to undertake their tasks but have their own preferences and interests, which may diverge from those of their collective principals. Advocates of the blended PA model and organizational culture have argued that IO change is possible if member state "principals" ensure that their reforms are "adjacent to existing norms (i.e. they 'fit' within the existing culture)."[33]

Subsequently, scholars have increasingly moved towards the use of mid-range theorizing to argue that both ideas and material factors matter for explaining how certain norms become predominant within IOs. For example, Alexandru Grigorescu has identified how hypotheses derived from the PA model and organizational culture can help identify which IOs adopt bureaucratic oversight mechanisms and when.[34] The stripping down of constructivist insights in this manner thus contributes to the broader rationalist project for identifying law like generalizations about the world while at the same time recognizing that the process under examination also creates new categories of action.

Conclusion

This chapter provides an overview of the main tenets of constructivism as a social approach to understanding IR. Driven by the position that everything in the world is socially constructed, constructivists carved out a position between the mainstream focus on rational action that informs theorizing about realism, liberalism, and Marxism and critical theory in which there is no foundation to knowledge, and in which power and knowledge shape our world. The five key tenets of constructivism are that the world is socially constructed; that both ideas and material factors matter but ideas are more important for understanding international relations; that norms and rules influence actor's identities; that the constructivist approach is to understand not explain international relations; and that early and critical constructivists reject the positivist epistemology used by rationalist theories.

That said, there are distinct variations in and of constructivism. Arguably there are now more constructivists that seek to explain events in IR that employ a positivist epistemology rather a critical one. Moreover, there is an increasing move towards mid-range theorizing in terms of using both ideas and material factors to explain how IOs behave, including creating new categories of action. In some senses, the discipline of IR may have moved beyond theoretical grand debates; but while the middle blends ideas and material factors, critical constructivists remain committed to the five tenets highlighted herein. Where we go from here remains to be seen.

Additional reading

Amitav Acharya, *Whose Ideas Matter? Agency and Power in Asian Regionalism* (Ithaca, NY: Cornell University Press, 2009).

Michael Barnett and Martha Finnemore, "The Politics, Power and Pathologies of IOs," *International Organization* 53, no. 4 (1999): 699–732.

André Broome and Leonard Seabrooke, "Special Issue: Seeing Like an International Organisation," *New Political Economy* 17, no. 1 (2012).

Alistair Johnston, "Treating International Institutions as Social Environments," *International Studies Quarterly* 45, no. 4 (2001): 487–515.

Sarah Percy, "Mercenaries: Strong Norm, Weak Law," *International Organization* 61, no. 2 (2007): 367–397.

John Ruggie, "What Makes the World Hang Together? Neo-utilitarianism and the Social Constructivist Challenge," *International Organization* 52, no. 4 (1998): 855–885.

Alexander Wendt, "Anarchy is What States Make of it: The Social Construction of Power Politics," *International Organization* 46, no. 2 (1992): 391–425.

Antje Wiener, *The Invisible Constitution of Politics: Contested Norms and International Encounters* (Cambridge: Cambridge University Press, 2008).

Notes

1 Martin Hollis and Steve Smith, *Explaining and Understanding International Relations* (Oxford: Clarendon Press, 1990); Steve Smith, "Wendt's World," *Review of International Studies* 26, no. 1 (2000): 151–163; Colin Wight, "They Shoot Dead Horses Don't They? Locating Agency in the Agent–Structure Problematique," *European Journal of International Relations* 5, no. 1 (1999): 109–142; Friedrich Kratochwil, "Constructing a New Orthodoxy? Wendt's 'Social Theory of International Politics' and the Constructivist Challenge," *Millennium* 29, no. 1 (2000): 73–101; Alexander Wendt, *Social Theory of International Politics* (Cambridge: Cambridge University Press, 1999).

2 Rey Koslowski, and Friedrich Kratochwil, "Understanding Change in International Politics: The Soviet Empire's Demise and the International System," *International Organization* 48, no. 2 (1994): 216.

3 Alexander Wendt, "Anarchy Is What States Make of it: The Social Construction of Power Politics," *International Organization* 46, no. 2 (1992): 391–425.

4 Margaret Keck and Kathryn Sikkink, *Activists Beyond Borders: Advocacy Networks in International Politics* (Ithaca, NY, and London: Cornell University Press, 1998); Thomas Risse, Stephen Ropp, and Kathryn Sikkink eds., *The Power of Human Rights: International Norms and Domestic Change* (Cambridge: Cambridge University Press, 1999); Audie Klotz, "Transnational Activism and Global Transformations: The Antiapartheid and Abolitionist Experiences," *European Journal of International Relations* 8, no. 1 (2002): 49–76.

5 Martha Finnemore, *National Interests in International Society* (Ithaca, NY, and London: Cornell University Press, 1996); Jacqui True, and Michael Mintrom, "Transnational Networks and Policy Diffusion: The Case of Gender Mainstreaming," *International Studies Quarterly* 45, no. 1 (2001): 27–57.

6 Ralf Leiteritz, "Explaining Organizational Outcomes: The International Monetary Fund and Capital Account Liberalisation," *Journal of International Relations and Development* 8, no. 1 (2005): 1–26; Jeffrey Chwieroth, "Normative Change from Within: The International Monetary Fund's Approach to Capital Account Liberalisation," *International Studies Quarterly* 52, no. 1 (2008): 129–158.

7 Richard Price, "A Genealogy of the Chemical Weapons Taboo," *International Organization* 49, no. 1 (1995): 73–103.

8 Michael Barnett and Matha Finnemore, *Rules for the World: International Organizations in Global Politics* (Ithaca, NY, and London: Cornell University Press, 2004).

9 Peter Katzenstein, Robert Keohane, and Steven Krasner eds., *Exploration and Contestation of World Politics* (Cambridge and London: MIT Press, 1999).

10 John Ruggie, "What Makes the World Hang Together? Neo-utilitarianism and the Social Constructivist Challenge," *International Organization* 52, no. 4 (1998): 855–885.

11 Katzenstein et al., *Exploration and Contestation of World Politics*, 1999.

12 Martha Finnemore and Kathryn Sikkink, "Taking Stock: The Constructivist Research Program in International Relations and Comparative Politics," *Annual Review of Political Science* 4 (2001): 391–416.

13 Koslowski and Kratochwil, "Understanding Change in International Politics," 1994; Maja Zehfuss, "Constructivism and Identity: A Dangerous Liaison," *European Journal of International Relations* 7, no. 3 (2001): 315–348.

14 Emmanual Adler, "Seizing the Middle Ground: Constructivism in World Politics," *European Journal of International Relations* 3, no. 3 (1997): 325.

15 Martha Finnemore and Kathryn Sikkink, "International Norm Dynamics and Political Change," *International Organization* 52, no. 4 (1998): 893, 901.

16 Antonio Guterres, "UN Chief Guterres Called the Alleged Use of Chemical Weapons in Khan Shaykhun a War Crime," video clip, United Nations, 2017, www.un.org/apps/news/infocusRel.asp? infocusID=146.

17 Michael Barnett and Martha Finnemore, 1999, "The Politics, Power and Pathologies of IOs," *International Organization* 53, no. 4 (1999): 699–732.

18 Steve Smith, "The Discipline of International Relations: Still an American Social Science," *British Journal of Politics and International Relations* 2, no. 3 (2000): 383.

19 For a review see Susan Park, "Theorizing Norm Diffusion within International Organizations," *International Politics: A Journal of Transnational Issues and Global Problems,* 43, no. 3 (2006): 342–361.

20 Finnemore, *National Interests in International Society*, 1996.

21 Barnett and Finnemore, *Rules for the World*, 2004.

22 Frank Schimmelfennig, "International Socialisation in the New Europe: Rational Action in an Institutional Environment," *European Journal of International Relations* 6, no. 1 (2000): 109–139.

23 Judith Kelley, "International Actors on the Domestic Scene: Membership Conditionality and Socialization by International Institutions," *International Organization* 58, no. 3 (2004): 425–457. On this debate, see Park, 2006.

24 Severine Autessare, *The Trouble With the Congo: Local Violence and the Failure of International Peacebuilding* (New York: Cambridge University Press, 2010).

25 Leiteritz, "Explaining Organizational Outcomes," 2005.

26 Bessma Momani, "Limits on Streamlining Fund Conditionality: The International Monetary Fund's Organizational Culture," *Journal of International Relations and Development* 8, no. 2 (2005): 142–163.

27 Autessare, *The Trouble With the Congo*, 2010.

28 Catherine Weaver, *The Hypocrisy Trap: The World Bank and the Poverty of Reform* (Princeton, NJ: Princeton University Press, 2008); Michael Lipson, "Organized Hypocrisy? Peacekeeping in the United Nations," *European Journal of International Relations* 13, no. 1 (2007): 5–34.

29 Jeffrey Checkel and Andrew Moravcsik, "A Constructivist Research Program in EU Studies?" *European Union Politics* 2, no. 2 (2001): 219–249.

30 For an exception, see Bobb Clifford, "Packing Heat: Pro-Gun Groups and the governance of Small Arms" in *Who Governs the Globe?*, eds. Deborah Avant, Martha Finnemore, and Susan Sell (Cambridge: Cambridge University Press, 2010), 183–202.

31 Adler, "Seizing the Middle Ground," 1997.

32 Mona Krook and Jacqui True, "Rethinking the Life Cycles of International Norms: The United Nations and the Global Promotion of Gender Equality," *European Journal of International Relations* 18, no. 1 (2012): 103–127; Wayne Sandholtz, "Dynamics of International Norm Change: Rules Against Wartime Plunder," *European Journal of International Relations* 14, no. 1 (2008): 101–131; Amitav Acharya, *Whose Ideas Matter? Agency and Power in Asian Regionalism* (Ithaca, NY: Cornell University Press, 2009); Rebecca Adler-Nissen, *Opting Out of the European Union: Diplomacy, Sovereignty and European Integration* (Cambridge: Cambridge University Press, 2014).

33 Daniel Nielson, Michael Tierney, and Catherine Weaver, "Bridging the Rationalist-Constructivist Divide: Re-engineering the Culture of the World Bank," *Journal of International Relations and Development* 9, no. 2 (2006): 107–139.

34 Alexandru Grigorescu, "The Spread of Bureaucratic Oversight Mechanisms across Intergovernmental Organizations," *International Studies Quarterly* 54, no. 3 (2010): 871–886.

CONTENTS

Critical theory

Robert W. Cox**

The states of the world have created international organization as a means of dealing with common problems through negotiation. Global governance would be the result of this process as it develops into a regular method of reaching consensus. Critical theory is concerned with understanding and influencing how this process works. When we speak of "process," we are thinking about something that evolves over time. So critical theory is a way of thinking about development and change over time.

One perspective on the world about us is to think of how states, institutions, people and other forces are interacting in the same time, how they influence each other directly. This is a synchronic perspective, or simultaneous interactions. Critical theory is not unconcerned about this perspective but is most of all concerned with change over time and with the choices we may have to make about the kind of future we may have. Critical theory is about the making of history.

The British historian and philosopher R.G. Collingwood wrote about the "inside" and the "outside" of history.[1] The "inside" is the story of the motivations, intentions, and reactions of the historical actors. The "outside" is all that can be observed—material resources and constraints and recordable events. Critical theory is concerned with understanding the "inside"—the thought, reasoning and emotion that "makes" history.

What follows discusses the distinction between problem solving and critical theory—the synchronic and diachronic perspectives; the nature of time and of how people of different civilizations have understood time in historical change; distinguishing eras of creativity and decline; dominance and subordination among civilizations; and the problem of world order in the present world.

The term "critical theory" is used in a generic sense independently of any particular meaning that has been given it in the work of others.[2] To be critical is to examine

** This chapter is reproduced in its original form from the first edition.

something carefully so as to become aware of any flaws or weaknesses. Theory is a systematic approach to understanding and explanation. Criticism, of its nature, should seek to improve on what is criticized; so critical theory does not stop with the negative part of criticism but extends to envisage transformation of existing reality. It is reformist or revolutionary in essence.

Theory is always for some*one* and for some *purpose*.[3] All theories have a perspective. Perspectives derive from a position in time and space, specifically social and political time and space. The world is seen from a standpoint that can be defined in terms of nation or social class, of dominance or subordination, of rising or declining power, of a sense of immobility or of present crisis, of past expectations, and of hopes and expectations for the future. Of course, sophisticated theory is never just the expression of standpoint or perspective. The more sophisticated a theory is, the more it reflects on and transcends its own perspective; but the initial perspective is always contained within a theory and is relevant to its explication. There is, accordingly, no such thing as theory in itself, divorced from a standpoint in time and space. When any theory so represents itself, it should be examined as ideology so as to lay bare its concealed perspective.

Problem-solving theory and critical theory

Broadly speaking, there are two purposes that define different kinds of theory: One purpose is to make a simple, direct response to the pressure of events, to be a guide to help solve the problems presented in the realities immediately confronted. This purpose leads to the development of problem-solving theory. The other purpose is more reflective on the process of theorizing itself, namely, to search for a theoretical perspective that would comprehend how the present world has come about and what forces are at work transforming it. This is the purpose of critical theory.

Problem-solving theory takes the world as it finds it, with the prevailing social and power relationships and the institutions into which they are organized, the given framework for analysis. The general aim of problem solving is to make these relationships work smoothly by dealing effectively with particular sources of trouble. Since the general pattern of institutions and relationships is not called into question, particular problems can be considered in relation to the specific areas of activity in which they arise. Problem-solving theories are thus fragmented in dealing with a multiplicity of spheres of action, each of which assumes a certain stability in the other spheres (which enables these other spheres of activity in practice to be ignored) when confronting a problem in the particular sphere concerned. The strength of the problem-solving approach lies in its ability to fix limits or parameters to a problem area and to reduce the statement of a particular problem to a limited number of variables that are amenable to relatively close and precise examination or measurement. The *ceteris paribus* assumption, on which such theorizing is based, makes it possible to arrive at statements of conclusions or regularities which may appear to have general applicability but which imply, of course, the continuing existence of the institutional and relationship parameters assumed or taken for granted in the problem-solving approach.

Critical theory stands apart from the prevailing order of the world and asks how that order came about. Unlike problem-solving theory, critical theory does not take institutions and social power relations for granted but calls them into question by concerning itself with their origins, and how and whether they may be in process of changing. It is directed towards an appraisal of the very framework for action which problem-solving theory accepts as its parameters. Critical theory is directed to the social and political complex as a whole rather than to its separate parts.

As a matter of practice, critical theory, like problem-solving theory, takes as its starting point some aspect or particular sphere of human activity. Whereas the problem-solving approach leads to further analytical subdivision and limitation of the issue to be dealt with, the critical approach leads towards the construction of a larger picture of the whole of which the initially contemplated part is just one component, and seeks to understand the processes of change in which both parts and whole are involved. Problem-solving theory, for example, is applicable to evaluating the various policies and practices of states with regard to specific international organizations as to whether these policies and practices strengthen or weaken cooperation. Critical theory is concerned with the development of international organization as a whole and the opportunities and obstacles to its further development.

Critical theory is theory of history in the sense of being concerned not just with the past but with a continuing process of historical change. Problem-solving theory is non-historical (or ahistorical); in effect, it posits a continuing present— the permanence of the institutions and power relations that constitute its parameters. The strength of the one is the weakness of the other. Because it deals with a changing reality, critical theory must continually adjust its concepts to the changing object it seeks to understand and explain.[4] These concepts and the accompanying methods of enquiry seem to lack the precision that can be achieved by problem-solving theory, which posits a fixed order as a point of reference. This relative strength of problem-solving theory, however, rests on a false premise; social and political orders are not fixed but (at least in a long-range perspective) are changing. Moreover, the assumption of fixity is not merely a convenience of method, but is also an ideological bias. Problem-solving theories can be represented, in the broader perspective of critical theory, as serving particular national, sectional, or class interests that are comfortable within the given order. Indeed, the purpose served by problem-solving theory is conservative, since it aims to solve the problems arising in various parts of a complex whole in order to smooth the functioning of the whole.

Critical theory is, of course, not unconcerned with problems in the real world. Its aims are just as practical as those of problem-solving theory, but it approaches practice from a perspective which transcends that of the existing order, which problem-solving theory takes as its basis. Critical theory allows for a normative choice in favor of (or against) a social and political order different from the prevailing order, but it limits the choice to alternative orders which are feasible transformations of the existing world. Critical theory must reject improbable alternatives just as it rejects the permanency of the existing order. In this way, critical theory can be a guide to strategic action for bringing about an alternative order, whereas problem-solving theory is a guide to tactical actions which, intended or unintended, sustain the existing order.

The perspectives of different historical periods favor one or the other kind of theory. Periods of apparent stability or fixity in power relations favor the problem-solving approach. The Cold War was one such period. In international relations, it fostered a concentration on the problems of how to manage an apparently enduring relationship between two superpowers. A condition of uncertainty in power relations beckons to critical theory as people seek to understand the opportunities and risks of change.

Time and change in history

Thinking about the nature of time is an essential step in contemplating historical change and the goal of creating a desirable future. The *Annales* group of French historians, chief among them Fernand Braudel, have distinguished three different categories of time. The time they are thinking of is not the movement of hands on a clock but rather experienced time, the time of living and time of acting (or of failing to act). The first kind of experienced time is the time in which events happen, in which they are recorded, which the *Annales* writers call *événementiel* (events time). More complex is the convergence of forces that shape and limit what *can* happen. This, the *Annales* writers call the *conjuncture*. The third kind is long-term time in which society evolves in all its interrelated aspects, change in populations, in economic structures, in political structures, and in ways of thinking. This they call the *longue durée*. In all three cases, time is seen as lived experience, how people experience either historical change or stasis.

Beyond the experience of lived time is the way of conceiving the future. People in different civilizations and in different eras have thought about the nature of movement into the future in one of two ways. The most natural way has been to think of change in the human condition by analogy with the change in nature as a cyclical process like that of the seasons: Spring, summer, autumn, winter, and then a new spring, etc. This has been a natural way of conceiving change not only for primitive peoples who have lived close to nature but also for people in evolved civilizations who knew their own history as a heroic beginning, which led to a period of relative prosperity, to be followed by a phase of decadent decline, ultimately saved by a stimulus probably from the periphery of their civilization or from a hitherto marginal group which proved to be capable of launching a creative revival. This cyclical pattern of understanding historical time has been characteristic not only of primitive peoples but also of all the major civilizations, with one exception.

The exception has been Western civilization, which has had the peculiarity of conceiving historical time as a continuing progressive development into the future with an imagined apotheosis. We can trace the origins of this way of thinking about the future to the birth of monotheistic religion. The primitive religion everywhere, and evolved religions in most parts of Asia, saw spirituality in the many different manifestations of nature, as a multiplicity of gods, and required man to live in harmony with nature. Monotheism posited one all-powerful God, with a capital "G," who was separate from and supreme over man and nature. Nature appeared to be God's gift to be exploited by humans.

The origins of monotheism may be traced to the Middle East in the Axial Age. It may have been derived from the centralized power of the ancient hydraulic empires where everything appeared to flow from a single central source. Egypt in the age of the pyramids conveyed the idea of an all-powerful center. Everything was subordinate to and directed by the emperor and his agents. This experience of the all powerful in everyday life could be easily transferred to the idea of one all-powerful God. People who lived close to nature could not, however, so easily abandon the sense of spirituality of nature in its manifold forms. The worship of saints in medieval Christianity preserved that polytheistic element of primitive religion within the formal monotheism of their faith. St. Francis of Assisi represented that loosening in the rigidity of monotheistic doctrine. With Calvinism, however, in its simplified purity, monotheism achieved a total break with nature.

Unilinear progressive theories of history came to elaborate the monotheistic vision. The earliest version was put forward by the twelfth-century Calabrian monk Joachim of Floris who introduced a three-stage conception of historical development, which was built on the doctrine of the Trinity. History, for him, was *Christian* history. There was no other. He divided history into three periods: The reign of the Father, the rule of the unincarnate God, an authoritarian pre-Christian era; the reign of the Son or the Christian era in which political institutions were necessary to constrain people's behavior in conformity with the revelations of Christianity; and the reign of the Holy Spirit as a communitarian future in which harmony would prevail naturally without the need for political constraints.

This triadic form, entrenched in Western consciousness, was, perhaps unconsciously, taken over in a secular form by Georg Wilhelm Friedrich Hegel in his three-stage version of history as progressing from the rule of one (monarchy), through the rule of several (aristocracy), to culminate in the rule of all under the law (the republic). Karl Marx, in his turn, presented yet another secularized version of the triadic progression. His vision was of an historical movement beginning with the primitive social exchange economy followed by its displacement by the development of capitalism, which would in time collapse from its own contradictions. The third and final phase, the coming of the communist society, would not be so different in conception from the communitarian society that Joachim of Floris had forecast.

The Western sense of a unilinear history was confirmed in the popular imagination by economic expansion. Britain's economy was expanded by trade; and trade, as the saying went, "followed the flag," in other words trade and military/naval power were interrelated and mutually supporting. Other Western nations, Germany and France, followed in Britain's wake. Together they expanded European power into Asia and Africa. Meanwhile, the United States was following the British example, initially in Latin America, and ultimately during the twentieth century, following the Cold War and the collapse of the Soviet Union, becoming the single dominant world power, the global hegemon.

During the nineteenth century, the idea of "Progress," with a capital "P," became prominent in popular culture. It conveyed the sense that European economic growth and imperial expansion was both inevitable and beneficent. The word "progress" had become less current in political discourse by the early years of the twenty-first century. It had been substantially displaced by the new word "globalization" which, without actually putting it in these words, inferred the global extension of the US way in which the world was becoming organized.

Eastern civilizations never embraced the European idea of progress, which in its practical meaning put them in an inferior position. Now they are resistant to the idea of an unregulated "globalization," which can seem to them to be just a new ideology of imperialism.

Building global governance involves understanding how people in the different civilizations that coexist in the world today may understand time, in the sense of historical evolution, differently. Effective global governance requires that each party is able to understand the thought processes of the others; and differences in the way people understand the nature of historical time is fundamental in this respect.

Creativity and decline

Thinking in the time dimension—the diachronic—leads us to consider whether society, civilization, or culture is in a period of a creative movement, or whether it seems to be stalled or in a phase of decline. Production in the arts and technology and innovations in social organization are indicative of creativity. These are all activities that take time to develop. The space dimension—the synchronic—focuses on things as they are, on their interrelationships, and particularly on the means of controlling activity. At the present time finance, which functions synchronically, dominates and controls production. One can speak of the "financialization" of society, meaning the dominance of the synchronic over the diachronic. Finance operates at electronic speed. The development of production in its manifold spheres, in goods and services, in invention and innovation, and in artistic and cultural creativity, is slow and painstaking.

The struggle between the synchronic and the diachronic—put in abstract terms—is perhaps the underlying issue of our time. It will determine whether people will be able to muster the stimulus for a new creative forward movement or whether a blockage of the creative potential in society, manifested most likely by prolonged financial crisis will forestall that possibility. The issue is being fought out in Europe at the present time between the concept of financial Europe and social Europe at the level of the European Union. In the world as a whole, it is a question of whether the consequences of the global financial crisis of 2008 and its sequel will obstruct the reform of prevailing social structures and so prevent the emergence of new forms of social, economic and political organization.

The doubt that hangs over this confrontation is whether the protest movements that challenge the "inevitability" of "globalization" will have sufficient creativity to generate both the bonds of solidarity and the innovation of institutions and practices that could become the harbinger of an alternative society. There is much pessimism, the predicament of the left in the Western world. The will to resist may be there, but is the vision of a really creative alternative still missing? And if present, who has the capacity to communicate it?

Whether or not societies possess the creativity to reinvent themselves is a question that has to be asked in eras when the "inevitable" seems to overwhelm any possibility for fundamental change. Those in authority will close the discussion by saying, with

Mrs. Margaret Thatcher, that "[T]here is no alternative." Yet at other times, it seemed that people were more inspired to change.

This is not a matter peculiar to our present world. Studies of the Roman imperial period have reflected on this question of the innate creative capacity of a civilization. The Canadian historian Charles Cochrane saw the question as a matter of the balance between what, in the classical terminology, was known as virtue and fortune, *virtù* and *fortuna*, two words that have become transformed and trivialized in meaning from their Latin origins.[5] In a more modern idiom, we could render these ideas as creative collective energy, for the first, and the objective limits of the possible, for the second.

Cochrane saw the failure of the classical world in its final stage as a waning of confidence in the creative capacity of politics when confronted with the despair engendered by sheer degradation of the material conditions of existence. The balance in the classical mind had shifted from virtue to fortune, in other words from creativity to fate.

A millennium later, Machiavelli made a similar analysis of his own society: Too corrupt to restore from within itself the spirit of civic capability, or *virtù*. He looked to a prince who would be capable of arousing once again the civic spirit that in earlier times had sustained a Republic.[6] Four centuries later, Antonio Gramsci looked to the party, as a modern prince, to perform the same function. What is common is the awareness of a moral and intellectual failure and a search for a means of moral and intellectual regeneration.[7]

This problem of creativity is not a peculiarity of Western civilizations. The fourteenth-century North African Islamic diplomat and historian Ibn Khaldun confronted the same predicament. Although by all accounts a devout Muslim, he wrote history with an accent of historical materialism. He was attentive, in the first place, to the geographical and ecological constraints on human action. He was, however, primarily concerned with the presence or absence of the quality he called *'asabiya, or* the sense of solidarity through which people, in the course of their history, became capable of founding and sustaining a state.[8] The state will make possible the enjoyment of sedentary, urban civilization; but urban life and the affluence it generates proves to be corrupting and ultimately erodes the spirit of solidarity that created it.

The traditional Chinese conception of history is of a fundamental rhythm of the universe alternating between *yin*, a quiescent phase of unity and harmony, and *yang*, a phase of activity, conflict and fragmentation. History, in both Chinese and Ibn Khaldun's conceptions, is cyclical rather than progressive and unilinear.

Virtù and *'asabiya* are words that apply to something missing, something required to trigger a response to a failure of culture or civilization. They give a diagnosis, not a prescription for recovery. What would it take to generate a sufficient collective response? Where would the necessary stimulus come from?

Ibn Khaldun, Machiavelli, and others have taught us where to look: First, to an analysis of the material conditions of existence and the mental and institutional structures that delineate the conditions of civilization; and second, at the marginal and marginalized social forces from which contestation and innovation may come. Those marginal forces today, as in earlier times, are both internal and external and they are contradictory. They include those groups of people who are being adversely affected by the dominant trend of globalization; the mass migrations that are mixing traditions of civilization at the most popular level; and transformations taking place in contiguous civilizations. A primary example today is the conflict within Islam between modernizers who seek to adapt Islam to modern material and social practices and reactionary obscurantists such as the Taliban and Al-Qaeda. The challenge is to distil some coherence and common purpose out of these contradictory elements—and this challenge is directed in the first instance to marginal intellectuals, to those who work outside the mainstream. It is from that quarter, uncompromised as it is by the weight of presently dominant thought and practice, that a new vision of a possible future may come.

Dominance and subordination

A common purpose in the world today would be to resolve the problems of coexistence of contiguous civilizations. In this regard, it is necessary to deal with a lot of historical baggage in the conflicts among cultures and civilizations. Edward Said characterized the Western approach to the study of Eastern civilizations as "orientalism."[9] For him, orientalism was a form of knowledge through which Eastern civilizations were seen as subordinate to the West. Western scholarship, assuming a position of universal objectivity, has defined the characteristics of dominated civilizations and has had the power to transmit to the dominated this knowledge about themselves. The elites of the dominated could thus become absorbed into an alien universalism. Kinhide Mushakoji has used the term "occultation" to describe the manner in which the thought processes of one civilization have been displaced by those of another, more dominant one. Yet the thought processes of the dominated civilization are not totally suppressed but remain latent, ready to be aroused by some crisis.[10]

Antonio Gramsci's concept of "passive revolution" has relevance here.[11] Gramsci took the term from Vincenzo Cuocuo, the historian of Naples under Napoleonic rule, for whom passive revolution was the introduction of ideas from an alien society, which were embraced by a local elite though they did not resonate with the common people. The result was a situation Gramsci called revolution/restoration in which the newly adopted ideas and modes of behavior were never securely entrenched since they never penetrated thoroughly to the mass of the people. One might draw a parallel with British intellectual and institutional influence in India, seemingly secure in the Nehru era but subsequently contested and displaced from its dominant position in society by the Hindu nationalists when they gained power.

Oswald Spengler put forward a concept that suggests how an impetus from one civilization penetrating into another can partially transform that other civilization but be constrained by the persisting structures of the penetrated civilization. Borrowing a term from mineralogy, he called the process "pseudomorphosis."[12] He applied it to the formation of the European Middle Ages from the time of Augustus to the tenth century. A nascent Arabian spiritual energy became configured by a fixed and persistent Greco-Roman political form. Spengler discerned a similar phenomenon in the way Westernization imported into Russia by Peter the Great framed and shackled the Russian spirit. The tragedy of the Russian pseudomorphosis, in Spengler's analysis, has been the continuing dominance of Western imported thought over a suppressed and barely articulate Russian spirit. By analogy, the more recent "market reformers" coming on the heels of the collapse of the Soviet Union were but an extension of the Western-inspired Communist managers, themselves natural successors to Peter the Great's modernization. In the post-Communist débacle, opposition to the Westernizing advocates of "shock therapy" revived an anti-Western *narodnik* sentiment. One literary instance is in a revived interest in the work of Nicholas Berdyaev.[13] Those with a longer historical perspective could trace the phenomenon of an alien culture overlaying the Russian spirit back to the Varangians!

All these concepts—orientalism, occultation, passive revolution, and pseudomorphosis—evoke the phenomenon of the dominance of one civilization over another but also of the latency of the dominated culture and the potential for reaffirmation of its authenticity. A most important object of inquiry is thus to trace the evidence of linguistic and conceptual superposition, and to identify the kinds of crisis likely to precipitate a rejection of the superimposed discourse by subordinate groups.

The channels of international organization and global governance allow for a continuing dialogue of civilizations through which the creativity or decline of different civilizations becomes apparent and issues of dominance and subordination may be confronted. These channels exist to provide a means for the world to adjust to changes in the power structure of world order.

The problem of world order

The central problem for critical thinking in the world today is to understand the dynamics of world order and to give guidance towards achieving a harmonious development of world politics. On one side, for the moment the apparently dominant one, are the theorists of globalization who envisage US style capitalism absorbing the rest of the world into a single global political economy that would bring about a comprehensive global political organization, and social and intellectual habits and practices that would be consistent with that dominant politico-economic structure.

On the other side is the political and intellectual rejection of that view of the future. One can look back a century earlier to the geopolitical vision of Halford Mackinder. He envisaged a "Heartland" or "World Island," a unified force of Eurasia as the dominant central world power. A century before Mackinder, the US naval historian Alfred Thayer Mahan envisaged the strategy for US dominance as encirclement by sea power of the rest of the world. These two geopolitical constellations are taking shape. The "empire" of the United States is one. Eurasia is the other.

Russia feels the threat of encirclement by the US presence or influence in Georgia, Ukraine, and the Central Asian republics. China, the greatest and growing Eurasian power, shares the concern about encirclement, specifically US influence in Taiwan and its military presence in Japan and South Korea. The US challenge of encirclement of Eurasia is countered by the coming together of the Eurasian powers. The Shanghai Cooperation Organization, a body that has been given very little attention in the

Western media, has as its members China, Russia, and the Central Asian republics. It foreshadows the prospect of Eurasian geopolitical consolidation.

The first side has the advantage of momentum. The United States has built up an imperial constellation of power. Major allies have become so aligned with the United States as for all practical purposes to abandon their real independence from US policy in world affairs. Zbigniew Brzezinski, a realist strategic thinker and US policy advisor, in an historical analogy, referred to them as America's *vassals*.[14]

The United States leads something that might be called an empire but is different from what the word "empire" represented in the past. States retain a formal independence but are bound into the agglomeration of US power by complex bonds of dependency. Yet at the same time, US power has been sundered into a dualism at the top. Since the debacle in Vietnam, the US Army ceased to be a draft of citizens called up for exceptional military duty; it became a disciplined professional body separate and distinct from a permissively self-indulgent society.[15] The Pentagon, although formally under the command of the president, has developed as an autonomous force in the formation and application of foreign policy.[16]

This became apparent with the election of Barack Obama as president in 2008. The enthusiasm of popular mobilization for change that marked his election campaign settled months later into resignation that all was still the same. There were evident limits to the power of the president in his conduct of world affairs and those limits were fixed by what former president Dwight Eisenhower, in his valedictory warning, called the "military-industrial complex."

The Pentagon, the directing center of that complex, remained supreme in determining the strategy of American world leadership. It has divided the world into its regional spheres of control, each under the supervision of a proconsul: The Pacific Command headquartered in Pearl Harbor, Hawaii, covering the Pacific ocean and all of East Asia; the European Command, headquartered in Stuttgart, Germany, which covered all of Europe and most of Africa and part of the Middle East including Israel (it also had the command of all NATO forces); the Central Command, headquartered in Tampa, Florida, which covered the remainder of the Middle East, including the Persian Gulf, Central Asia, and the Horn of Africa; and, finally, the Southern Command, located in Miami, Florida, which covered Central and South America and the Caribbean. The proconsuls charged with these commands had resources vastly greater than those possessed by other government agencies, notably the State Department.[17]

There are two directions in which the political, military, economic, and social forces alive in the world today could move in shaping world order for the coming years. One is that the decline of US power, which is manifest in relation to a group of major countries of growing weight in world affairs, could lead to a plural world with several centers of world power engaged in a continuous negotiation for a constantly adjustable modus vivendi. This would depend very largely on US acceptance of a new role as one among several major powers.

One common threat to all the major powers would hang over this process of negotiation and adjustment of power relations. The problem of global warming and the fragility of the biosphere would put pressure on all of them, particularly if civil society had aroused public awareness, to subordinate particular interests to the common interest of saving life on the planet.

The other direction in which the world seems to be heading is towards a catastrophic confrontation of the United States with Eurasia. The trigger may well be the determination of Israeli leadership to strike Iran and the reluctance or political weakness of the US leadership to prevent it. Unfortunately, this direction is the more likely absent the arousal of public protest on a world scale.

The first scenario, a movement towards a plural world with the United States playing a role in company with other world powers, would make it possible to subordinate particular national interests to the common interest of the survival of the planet. The second would subordinate the global interest to the clash of a global cleavage.

Conclusion

Critical theory is rooted in the movement of history. It is a method both for understanding history, especially contemporary history, by seeking to know the interaction of forces unobstructed by any ideological gloss, and for thinking how the future course of events might be influenced so as to yield the optimum result for mankind. Thus, as critical theory foresees a coming collapse of the biosphere unless immediate and continuing steps are taken to curb the noxious effects produced by human activities in our present way of doing things, it must give both a warning and a guideline for a different way of doing things that would be consistent with bringing the biosphere back into a tolerable equilibrium. The possibility of approaching general agreement among the world powers on how to stop the destruction of the biosphere is, however, negated by the build-up of global military confrontation. Critical theory can lay bare the political choices the great powers have to make towards saving the biosphere. It is a question of priorities: Survival of life on the planet vs. "full spectrum dominance" and catastrophic confrontation.

International organization and the procedures of global governance would maintain the existence of a plural world in which the major powers together with the lesser powers would negotiate and seek consensus on global problems. The impetus of "globalization" towards the effective integration of an American-led "empire" would bypass the existing structures of international organization and global governance or else it would subvert them to its own purposes. A catastrophic confrontation of the US "empire" with Eurasia would utterly destroy the remnants of international organization and global governance.

Additional reading

Andrew Bacevich, *American Empire* (Cambridge, MA: Harvard University Press, 2002).
Nikolai Berdyaev, *The Russian Idea* (London: Geoffrey Bles, 1947).
Charles Norris Cochrane, *Christianity and Classical Culture: A Study of Thought and Action from Augustus to Augustine* (London: Oxford University Press, 1944).
Robin George Collingwood, *The Idea of History* (Oxford: Oxford University Press, 1956).

Robert W. Cox, "Social Forces, States and World Orders: Beyond International Relations Theory," *Millennium: Journal of International Studies* 10, no. 2 (1981): 126–155.

Robert W. Cox, *The New Realism: Perspectives on Multilateralism and World Order* (London: Palgrave Macmillan for the United Nations University, 1997).

Niccolò Machiavelli, *The Prince*, eds. Quentin Skinner and Russell Price (Cambridge: Cambridge University Press, 1988).

Notes

1 Robin George Collingwood, *The Idea of History* (Oxford: Oxford University Press, 1956).

2 The term "critical theory" has been associated with Max Horkheimer and others of the Frankfurt School.

3 This sentence is a quote from Robert W. Cox, "Social Forces, States and World Orders: Beyond International Relations Theory," *Millennium. Journal of International Studies* 10, No. 2 (1981): 126–155.

4 Edward Palmer Thompson argues that historical concepts must often "display extreme elasticity and allow for great irregularity." His treatment of historical logic develops this point in his essay "The Poverty of Theory," in *The Poverty of Theory and Other Essays*, ed. Edward Palmer Thompson (London: Merlin Press, 1978), esp. 231–242.

5 Charles Norris Cochrane, *Christianity and Classical Culture: A Study of Thought and Action from Augustus to Augustine* (London: Oxford University Press, 1944), 157–161.

6 Niccolò Machiavelli, *The Prince*, eds. Quentin Skinner and Russell Price (Cambridge: Cambridge University Press, 1988); Federigo Chabod, *Machiavelli and the Renaissance* (London: Bowes & Bowes, 1958).

7 Antonio Gramsci, *Selections from the Prison Notebooks of Antonio Gramsci*, eds. Quintin Hoare and Geoffrey Nowell Smith (New York: International Publishers, 1971), esp. 123–205.

8 Ibn Khaldun, *The Muqaddimah*, trs.l Franz Rosenthal (Princeton, NJ: Princeton University Press, 1967). See also Robert W. Cox, "Towards a Post-Hegemonic Conceptualization of World Order: Reflections on the Relevancy of Ibn Khaldun," in *Governance Without Government: Order and Change in World Politics*, eds. James Rosenau and Ernst-Otto Czemliel (Cambridge: Cambridge University Press, 1992), 132–159.

9 Edward Said, *Orientalism* (New York: Vintage Books, 1979).

10 Kinhide Mushakoji, "Multilateralism in a Multicultural World: Notes for a Theory of Occultation," in *The New Realism: Perspectives on Multilateralism and World Order*, ed. Robert W. Cox (London: Palgrave Macmillan for the United Nations University, 1997).

11 Gramsci, *Selections from the Prison Notebooks*, 105–120.

12 "In a rock stratum are embedded crystals of a mineral. Clefts and cracks occur, water filters in, and the crystals are gradually washed out so that in due course only their hollow mould remains. Then come volcanic outbursts which explode the mountain; molten masses pour in, stiffen, and crystallize in their turn. But these are not free to do so in their own special forms. They must fill up the spaces that they find available. Thus there arise distorted forms, crystals whose inner structure distorts their external shape, stones of one kind presenting the appearance of stones of another kind. The mineralogists call this phenomenon *Pseudomorphosis*. By the term 'historical pseudomorphosis' I propose to designate those cases in which an older alien Culture lies so massively over the land that a young Culture born in this land, cannot get its breath and fails not only to achieve pure and specific expression forms, but even fully to develop its own self-consciousness. All that wells up from the depths of the young soul is cast in the old moulds, young feelings stiffen in senile works, and instead of rearing up in its own creative power, it can only

hate the distant power with a hate that grows to be enormous." See Oswald Spengler, *The Decline of the West*, vol. II (New York: Knopf, 1939), 189.

13 Nikolai Berdyaev, *The Russian Idea* (London: Geoffrey Bles, 1947).

14 Zbigniew Brzezinski, *The Grand Chessboard* (New York: Basic Books, 1998). Forty states that the three grand imperatives of imperial policy, expressed in deliberately archaic terminology, are "to prevent collusion and maintain security dependence among the vassals, to keep the tributaries pliant and protected, and to keep the barbarians from coming together."

15 Andrew Bacevich, *American Empire* (Cambridge, MA: Harvard University Press, 2002), 168, writes "Vietnam had created a gulf separating the armed services from American society as a whole."

16 Andrew Bacevich, in *American Empire: The Realities and Consequences of U.S. Diplomacy* (Cambridge, MA: Harvard University Press, 2002), 215–223, gives a description of the emergence of the Pentagon's autonomy in foreign policy.

17 Bacevich, Ibid, 178, writes: "Those resources included not just military assets—carrier battle groups or fighter squadrons—but executive jets, instantly available secure communications, retinues of attentive aides, and lavish budgets for discretionary spending that no mere ambassador could even dream of."

Marxism

Julian Germann

This chapter introduces students of global governance to the resources available within Marxism for understanding an increasingly interconnected but profoundly unequal world. The first section argues that in order to appreciate what is distinct about Marxist approaches to global governance, we need to know what is new and different about capitalism as a way of organizing social life. The second section argues that Marx's conception of capitalism as a uniquely expansive and conflictive social system helps us rethink the most profound challenges—from global inequality to climate change—that the discourse and practices of global governance are meant to address. The third section argues that Marxism reveals the structural and direct forms of capitalist power that circumscribe the capacities of global governance to solve these very problems. In addition to exploring the socially biased character of global governance, the final section argues that Marxism also casts light on the particular governance problems and policy conflicts that arise from the uneven development of capitalism across an international system made up of diverse states and societies.

Foundations

The school of thought pioneered by Karl Marx and Friedrich Engels is rich and diverse, and this chapter offers one of many interpretations of their work. All of them, however, agree that the object of global governance is *capitalism*. For Marxists, capitalism is not simply another word for "the economy." Mistaking one for the other makes us think of a realm that is separate from other spheres of social life such as politics, culture, religion, and so on. Worse still, because the economy is often presented in technical jargon and experienced by many who work for a living as mindless drudgery, one might conclude that it is best left to trained economists to decipher. Instead, Marxists argue that capitalism is an entire social system that today permeates most of our human life and creates the very conditions of intensified interconnectedness that informs liberal theories of global governance. This has not always been so. Using the terms "economy" and "capitalism" as if they were the same makes capitalism seem an ancient, almost natural, feature of human history—after all, no society could exist without some form of economy to support it.[1] By contrast, Marxists insist that capitalism is both relatively recent and radically different from most of humanity's lived experience. This distinction is important because we can identify earlier episodes of what could be called globalization, based on numerous significant economic as well as social, cultural, and political exchanges that have connected different parts of the world with one another at various points in history.[2] It is only when we begin to think of our object of study in terms of a globalizing capitalism that the true novelty of what contemporary global governance is about comes into view.

It is essential therefore to build our understanding of capitalism from the ground up. Contrary to liberal philosophy, which takes the individual as the starting point for its analysis, Marxists insist that the smallest possible units of analysis are the concrete social relations between human beings. Of the numerous ways that people relate to one another, it is those activities through which they sustain their livelihoods that Marxists consider the most important. Human societies, throughout the ages, differ in innumerable ways from one another. However, what they have in common is that they must, in one way or another, produce all that is necessary to make social life possible.[3] Marxists argue that studying the specific ways societies and their members organize the material conditions of their existence holds the key to understanding how they are governed and—important for students of IR—how they interact with one another across geographical space.

Most human societies have been class-based ones divided into a majority group who directly produce the material necessities (and luxuries) of life, and a minority who appropriate most of this wealth. In most of these societies, the producing classes have been peasants who live on and work the land, and who are obliged by law, custom, and/or religion to surrender a portion of what they produce to those of superior social status. The titles and roles of the appropriating class—lords, priests, kings, emperors, and so on—differ across time and place. However, they share a claim over the fruits of the labor of others which they are able, if necessary, to enforce through violence against unruly subjects and potential rivals.

Capitalist society is unusual in that the appropriating class is able to claim parts of the social product of labor not through the threat of violence but because it privately owns the tools—land and raw materials, machinery, and technology, what is collectively known as "capital"—that individuals, their families, and communities need in order to feed, clothe, and house themselves. Unlike the peasantry in much of human history, those who produce wealth under capitalism are separated from their means of livelihood. Because they cannot make ends meet in any other way, they are compelled to sell their capacity to work (that is, their "labor power") in exchange for a wage. The owners of capital purchase this capacity and employ it to produce goods and services that they sell back to society at a premium—that is, above the costs of production. The ultimate source of profit for capitalists is the unpaid portion of the labor that workers perform during the workday—the difference between their wages that at least must keep them alive and able to work, and the value they create during the time their labor power is put to work by their employer. Because capitalists compete with one another, they regularly reinvest these profits in order to expand their enterprise, bringing about a self-reinforcing and widening cycle of accumulation that has fundamentally transformed the social and international order over the last 200 years.

Whereas liberals posit a possible harmony of interests, Marxists point to the irreconcilable differences in a society centered on the market: While workers must find employment in the labor market at a wage high enough to ensure their physical survival, capitalists must sell their commodities in consumer markets at a price low enough to keep up with their competitors. This market compulsion forces capitalists to get as much out of their workers as they can while paying as little as possible. Workers, when they can, will resist attempts to intensify exploitation and make demands (for higher wages, shorter working days, or safer working conditions) that in turn threaten capitalists' profits.

Most contemporary Marxists reject the teleological views of their predecessors that this conflict of interests will inevitably lead to communism. Some stress the fundamentally open-ended nature of social contestation under capitalism, driven by the free choices and conscious and creative actions of human beings.[4] Others adopt a more structuralist approach to the contradictions that drive capitalist development.[5] What unites these approaches is the emancipatory potential within capitalism: That working people, in seeking to reclaim control over how their time and labor is spent, will try to put the productive resources of society at the disposal of the majority.

Key issues

So far this chapter has worked with a schematic representation of what capitalism is, just as Marx did when he wrote his lifework *Capital*. It has bracketed history and geography and assumed, for the sake of simplicity, that the world consists of a single capitalist society writ large. This simplification is evidently not so, and the chapter demonstrates later just how crucial it is to acknowledge that the world consists of multiple states and societies. Even provisionally, however, we can see that Marxism differs from conventional approaches to global governance. Marxists claim that the focus on a globalizing capitalism is more precise than the popular but vague catchphrase of "globalization"—which denotes a "process of becoming worldwide" without specifying what, exactly, is being globalized.[6] At the same time, they contend that their critique of capitalism yields a far richer conception of global governance than its alleged preoccupation with the economy would suggest.

Capitalism has an inbuilt drive to produce ever more things at an ever faster rate. But because private profit rather than public decisions determine what gets produced and what does not, there is a real possibility that vital human needs will go unmet, just as there is a risk—from the point of view of capitalists—that the types and volumes of goods produced will not match the capacities (or desires) of people to consume them.[7] The lion's share of the wealth created by human labor accrues to capitalists, and their competition with one another results in its concentration among a tiny minority: In 2016, for example, the eight richest men in the world owned as much wealth as the poorest half of humanity.[8]

Unlocking the paradox of persistent poverty in a world of plenty, Marxism also casts a critical light on international development agencies that aim to bring the world's poor into the orbit of capitalism in the hope that making their labor power marketable will help them rise out of poverty. Marxists have pointed out that the exploitative nature of capitalism is bound to frustrate these aspirations, and that genuine human development can only emerge from the grassroots struggles of global laboring classes against the concrete forms of oppression and exploitation they experience.[9]

Lastly, Marxists have argued that the epochal scale of environmental degradation and climate change—for which a small number of big firms are largely responsible[10]—should be understood as the inevitable outcome of a system of endless capital accumulation. It feeds on the extraction of raw materials and the combustion of ever larger volumes of fossil fuels.[11]

In sum, Marxism reveals capitalism to be an inherently conflict-driven, crisis-prone, and earth-destroying force. Seen in this light, the promises and problems of global governance as a normative project and set of institutional practices come into view. Clearly, the humanitarian concerns of liberal advocates of global governance overlap to a considerable degree with the emancipatory project inscribed in Marxism: To empower human beings to govern collectively their common affairs. And yet, from a Marxist view, there is a danger that the liberal conception obscures the unequal power relations at the center of capitalist globalization that invariably elevate the interests of some over those of others.[12]

Who governs?

All class societies require some form of political authority to maintain, by force if necessary, existing social hierarchies that permit one group to extract the wealth produced by another. In contrast to other appropriating classes, the owners of capital generally do not need to threaten violence in order to get workers to part with the surplus that their labor produces. Deprived of other ways to make a living, working people have little choice but to offer up their labor power for a wage at or above subsistence but below the value that their labor actually creates.

Under capitalism, therefore, direct coercion is overtaken by systemic compulsion mediated by the market. The result is a differentiation of capitalist society into two domains that appear to us as distinct and even natural entities, causing the conflation of "capitalism" with "the economy" discussed above. On the one hand, a private sphere of economic exchange emerges that is free from coercion and thus ostensibly based on a voluntary contract between two equals, workers and capitalists. On the other hand, the moment of coercion is relocated to a public sphere of political authority that seems to stand above society and use force impartially to uphold the rule of law and enforce the contractual obligations of both parties.[13]

Because capitalism is unstable and inherently conflictual, some form of governance is essential to ensuring its maintenance. The state is the most important provider because it maintains a general infrastructure that capital needs in order to expand; it enforces laws and regulations to prevent the most dysfunctional forms of capitalist competition; and in countries where working people have won some forms of representative democracy, it limits the grossest forms of capitalist exploitation. In the contemporary global governance system, these roles are partly coordinated among several states, transferred to supranational authorities, and parceled out to private actors. Its regimes and institutions can thus be approached with the same set of questions that Marxists have asked about the capitalist state: How far do they manage the multiple contradictions of capitalist globalization? Do they expand the reach of capitalism or do they impose public constraints on it? Do they mitigate its worst excesses or do they deepen exploitation and inequality?

Analyzing global governance with the tools of Marxist state theories also raises questions about its socially biased nature. The capitalist state, Marxists insist, is far from a neutral arbiter between capital and labor. By using its political power to guarantee private ownership of the resources society needs, the state sanctions the economic power of capitalists to do what they want with their property and to dictate the terms under which other members of society can access this privatized wealth. There is a longstanding debate among Marxist scholars over why the capitalist state acts in such partisan ways, especially liberal-democratic ones in which those who govern need to stand for election. Is it because the owners of capital wield direct influence over state personnel—through lobbying, campaign financing or elite social networks? Or is it because an economy in which vital investment decisions are privatized forces policymakers to do what is best for business because they depend on economic growth for their tax base and popular approval?[14]

Although these questions continue to be debated and remain unanswered, they help illuminate the structural and direct forms of capitalist class power in the current era of globalization. The rise, since the 1960s, of transnational corporations (TNCs) that control production across several jurisdictions has strengthened the leverage over public authorities. When confronted with unfavorable legislation, TNCs can threaten to move their operations elsewhere. The increased ability of investors to move money for speculative gain or investment between national economies and various financial markets imposes similar pressures to pursue business-friendly policies or face outflows of capital.[15] Lastly, governments as well as international financial institutions such as the World Bank and the International Monetary Fund (IMF), need to borrow money in capital markets in order to finance operations.[16] The resulting charge is that the system of global governance and its major states and organizations are structurally predisposed to prioritize the interests of the owners and investors of internationally mobile capital over the needs of the overwhelming majority of the world's population.

In addition to these structural forms of power, some Marxists argue that an elite fraction of the capitalist class has taken a direct role in managing capitalist globalization. The activities of these global elites and the institutions under their control have been explored most exhaustively by scholars who draw on the prison notebooks of the Italian communist leader Antonio Gramsci. His central category is "hegemony," by which he meant the unique ability of capitalist classes in Western Europe and the United States (as opposed to Czarist Russia) to reinforce their power over society through the active organization of mass consent rather than through coercion. Applying these insights to the new world order constructed by the United States after 1945, Gramscian scholars have argued that its postwar leadership is best understood as an internationalized form of capitalist class rule rather than simply a relationship between states.[17] US hegemony had two consensual dimensions: It unified the capitalist classes from North America, Western Europe and Japan around a US-led project of capitalist reconstruction of their societies and the world economy. And it provided working people with a measure of economic welfare, social security, and political participation.

Building on these insights, scholars have examined a range of public and private elite forums—for instance, the G-7 summits and ministerial meetings, the World Economic Forum, and the Trilateral Commission—that enable state officials, corporate leaders, media and civil representatives to come together and develop a common outlook on global issues.[18] Most important since the crisis of the welfare state in the 1970s has been their shared commitment to free capital from social regulations and restrictions and to facilitate its unimpeded flow worldwide. Alongside national governments, international organizations such as the IMF and the World Trade Organization (WTO) have been tasked to translate this elite consensus into pro-globalization and pro-market policies that aim to roll back the power of trade unions and the state (conceived as barriers to free trade and investment), and to open up national economies to global capital searching for export markets, raw materials, and cheap labor.[19] The case of the EU in particular has brought into focus another aspect of the elite drive behind global governance. Delegating certain issues to intergovernmental decision-making bodies is one way of removing key economic decisions from the mandate of national governments and their electorates. The aim is to lock in policies favorable to global capital and insulate them against popular interference.[20]

Unevenness and the state system

Marx expected a globalizing capitalism to remake the world in its own image so that the same dynamics of competitive accumulation and exploitation that he saw at work in Victorian Britain would ultimately come to play out on a global stage. In this respect, he can rightly be considered "the first major theorist of globalization,"[21] predicting in the 1848 *Communist Manifesto* a system of universal interdependence that would replace national with global patterns of production and consumption. Contrary to the liberal architects of global governance, Marx left no doubt that this process would globalize the crises, contradictions, and class conflicts of capitalism rather than create a peaceful and prosperous global village. Like them, however, he did not pay much attention to the fact that capitalism had been born into a world made up of many different states and societies, and that this preexisting system might inflect its expansive logic in novel ways. Many of his successors have recognized that a mere scaling-up of his analysis of capitalist society would not do, and that even as capitalism became global in scope, the lines of conflict in world politics ran not simply between classes but also between states.

Marxists differ on the sources and significance of interstate conflicts. Some argue that the competition among capitalists in the world market pits their home states against one another and drives them to intervene—economically, politically, and militarily—in other regions in order to secure favorable market access and vital energy and raw material supplies.[22] Others object that capitalist globalization has long overcome such nationally based economic interests and associated rivalries. In as much as force is being deployed today, it is done collectively by the major capitalist states and directed outwards against potential rivals and recalcitrant states that refuse to open their economies to global capital.[23]

Far from a niche concern of Marxists, the concept of "imperialism" that frames this debate gave rise to the first fully formulated theories of IR even before the discipline was formally founded after WWI.[24] In fact a sanitized version of the two major positions staked out in the original exchange between Vladimir Lenin and Karl Kautsky—the inevitability of inter-imperialist rivalry or the possibility of ultraimperialist unity—also shaped the emerging subfield of international political economy (IPE).[25] Marxism shines a critical spotlight on the debate between liberalism and realism about whether and how international regimes and institutions can regulate interstate relations and prevent the disintegration of the world economy into protectionist blocs. Its main contention is that the centrifugal pressures that global governance is meant to mediate do not emerge from international anarchy but from the uneven character of capitalist development.

Thus, where mainstream IR has traditionally focused on the relations between the most powerful states, Marxism has systematically studied the underlying relations of domination and exploitation between a capitalistically developed core and a less or even underdeveloped periphery. Scholars writing from a "world-systems perspective" have cast core and periphery as the functional complements of a single, inherently unequal, capitalist world economy.[26] In this view, the principal purpose of the rules and institutions that govern it is to keep the periphery locked in place and facilitate the smooth transfer of wealth from the Global South to the Global North.

Scholars drawing on Leon Trotsky's work have proposed a more dynamic image of uneven and combined development based on the fact that capitalism first emerged in one particular corner of the globe and only belatedly spread elsewhere. Trotsky's crucial improvement on Marx's theory of capitalism was that latecomers do not simply repeat the same process of capitalist transformation as their predecessors, but rather they develop along different paths that are shaped by their particular domestic conditions and international situation. Global governance, from this standpoint, is not simply about maintaining a hierarchical division of labor between core and periphery, but about managing a complex and ever changing composite of diverse states and societies at various points on their individual trajectories.[27]

The big question, for both approaches, is whether the late but rapid rise of China and other emerging economies will close the gap in power and wealth that has characterized the interstate system, and thus whether it will fundamentally transform global politics. Skeptics object that the capitalist nature of their rise suggests that it will do little more than add new members to the core, while leaving the underlying asymmetries between core and periphery, and thus the biased nature of global governance, intact.[28]

Finally, some Marxist analysts argue that the sources of conflict within the North Atlantic core do not emerge from capitalist competition as such but from a mismatch between the transnational reach of capital and the territorial division of the world into multiple states. In other words, governing global capitalism, with its crisis tendencies and conflict potential, falls on several powerful states. This plurilateral management—in which the United States plays by far the most prominent role[29]—poses a distinct set of governance problems that have no parallel at the national level. Globally, the practical tasks facing state authorities is how to arbitrate between competing class interests while creating conditions favorable to capital accumulation. The negotiations and coordination among sovereign states may give rise to policy disagreements that cannot be resolved. Instead, they may involve attempts by some states to prod others into their preferred direction.

Lastly, it may lead states to depart from the balancing role that they play domestically, and to seek to advance the particular economic interests of capital invested in or originating from within their borders.[30] Although these policy conflicts fall well short of the inter-imperialist confrontations that some Marxists predict, they are nevertheless central to understanding the form and direction of capitalist globalization.

Conclusion

The purpose of this chapter has been to assemble a set of tools derived from Marxist thought and illustrate how they can be applied to the prevailing system of international organization. It has argued that Marxism provides critical intellectual resources to understand both the globalization of capitalism—along with its tendencies for crises and its potential for conflict—as well as its continuing unevenness within a state system that predates its emergence and refracts its globalizing logic. How these tools are put to use, and what solutions they might yield, is up to those who choose to deploy them.

This chapter ends with a series of open-ended questions. First, the Marxist critique of capitalism raises questions about the class character of global governance. A key empirical concern therefore is to examine whether the particular frameworks, rules, and procedures that define the content and conduct of global governance in specific areas empower some actors over others. Do they allow for the genuine input of citizens, or do they give priority to unelected technocrats, corporate lobbyists, and financial investors? Marxist analysis of global politics also throws light on the unequal political geography of capitalist globalization, centered in the North and governed by a small number of powerful states led by the United States. Do the rules and institutions of global governance simply reflect or potentially ameliorate this asymmetry in power and wealth? Do they help dominant and emerging powers negotiate their differences, or advance the interests of some over others?

In approaching these questions, students of global governance may find that their object of analysis is neither a liberal haven of peace and prosperity nor simply a "euphemism for the global rule of capital."[31] Rather, they encounter a complex and contested set of international political and economic processes that—while socially biased and internationally unbalanced—are shaped by a host of creative actors. Thus, such analysis leaves open the possibilities to democratize and transform global capitalism to serve better the needs of present and future generations.

Additional reading

Alexander Anievas, *Marxism and World Politics: Contesting Global Capitalism* (London: Routledge, 2010).

William Brown, Simon Bromley, and Suma Athreye, eds., *Ordering the International: History, Change and Transformation* (London: Pluto, 2004).

Ray Kiely, *Rethinking Imperialism* (London: Palgrave, 2010).

Mark Rupert and M. Scott Solomon, *Globalization and International Political Economy: The Politics of Alternative Futures* (Lanham, MD: Rowman & Littlefield, 2006).

Susan Soederberg, *Global Governance in Question: Empire, Class and the New Common Sense in Managing North–South Relations* (London: Pluto, 2006).

Notes

1 Ellen Wood, *The Origin of Capitalism: A Longer View* (London: Verso, 1999).

2 Mark Rupert and M. Scott Solomon, *Globalization and International Political Economy: The Politics of Alternative Futures* (Lanham, MD: Rowman & Littlefield, 2006), 25.

3 Karl Marx, *Capital*, vol. I. (New York: Vintage, 1977), 290.

4 Samuel Knafo and Benno Teschke, "The Rules of Reproduction of Capitalism: A Historicist Critique," *Centre for Global Political Economy*, Working Paper Series 12 (Brighton: University of Sussex, January 2017), www.sussex.ac.uk/webteam/gateway/file.php?name= rules-of-reproduction-knafo-n-teschke-w-imprint-text.pdf&site=359.

5 David Harvey, *Seventeen Contradictions and the End of Capitalism* (London: Profile, 2014).

6 Justin Rosenberg, "Globalization Theory: A Post Mortem," *International Politics* 42, no. 1 (2005): 11.

7 David McNally, *Global Slump: The Economics and Politics of Crisis and Resistance* (Oakland, CA: PM Press, 2010), 72.

8 Deborah Hardoon, "An Economy for the 99%," *Oxfam Briefing Paper*, 16 January 2017, http://policy-practice.oxfam.org.uk/publications/an-economy-for-the-99-its-time-to-build-a-human-economy-that-benefits-everyone-620170.

9 Benjamin Selwyn, *The Global Development Crisis* (Cambridge: Polity Press, 2014).

10 A study estimating the costs of environmental degradation concluded that the top 3000 corporations are responsible for one-third of all environmental damage. UNEP, Finance Initiative and Principles for Responsible Investment Association, "Why Environmental Externalities Matter to Institutional Investors", 2011, www.unepfi.org/fileadmin/documents/ universal_ownership_full.pdf.

11 Andreas Malm, *Fossil Capital* (London: Verso, 2016).

12 Susan Soederberg, *Global Governance in Question: Empire, Class and the New Common Sense in Managing North–South Relations* (London: Pluto Press, 2006); Henk Overbeek, "Global Governance: From Radical Transformation to Neo-Liberal Management," *International Studies Review* 12 (2010): 697.

13 Ellen Wood, "The Separation of the Economic and Political in Capitalism," *New Left Review* I, no. 127 (1981): 66–95.

14 Clyde W. Barrow, *Critical Theories of the State* (Madison: University of Wisconsin Press, 1993).

15 Mark Rupert, "Marxism," in *International Relations Theory for the Twenty-First Century: An Introduction*, ed. Martin Griffiths (London: Routledge, 2007), 35–46.

16 Marcia Annisette, "The True Nature of the World Bank," *Critical Perspectives on Accounting* 15, no. 3 (2004): 303–323.

17 Andreas Bieler and Adam Morton, "A Critical Theory Route to Hegemony, World Order and Historical Change: Neo-Gramscian Perspectives in International Relations," *Capital & Class* 28, no. 1 (2004): 85–113.

18 Kees van der Pijl, *Transnational Classes and International Relations* (London: Routledge, 1998).

19 Richard Peet, *Unholy Trinity: The IMF, World Bank and WTO*, 2nd ed. (London: Zed, 2009); Paul Cammack, "The Governance of Global Capitalism: A New Materialist Perspective," *Historical Materialism* 11, no. 2: 37–59.

20 Stephen Gill, "Constitutionalizing Capital: EMU and Disciplinary Neo-Liberalism," in *Social Forces in the Making of the New Europe: The Restructuring of European Social Relations in the Global Political Economy*, eds. Andreas Bieler and Adam Morton (London: Palgrave, 2001); Stephen Gill and A. Claire Cutler, eds. *New Constitutionalism and World Order* (Cambridge: Cambridge University Press, 2014).

21 Simon Bromley, "Marxism and Globalisation," in *Marxism and Social Science*, eds. Andrew Gamble, David Marsh, and Tony Tant (London: Macmillan, 1999), 280.

22 Alex Callinicos, *Imperialism and Global Political Economy* (Cambridge: Polity Press, 2009).

23 William Robinson, *Global Capitalism and the Crisis of Humanity* (New York: Cambridge University Press, 2008).

24 Benno Teschke, "Marxism," in *Oxford Handbook of International Relations*, eds Christian Reus-Smit and Duncan Snidal (London: Routledge, 2008), 163–187.

25 Julian Germann, "International Political Economy and the Crisis of the 1970s: The Real 'Transatlantic Divide,'" *Journal of Critical Globalisation Studies* 1, no. 4 (2010): 10–22.

26 Immanuel Wallerstein, *The Modern World-System: Capitalist Agriculture and the Origins of the European World-Economy in the Sixteenth Century* (New York: Academic Press, 1976).

27 Justin Rosenberg, "Uneven and Combined Development: 'The International' in Theory and History," in *Historical Sociology and World History: Uneven and Combined Development over the Longue Durée*, eds. Alexander Anievas and Kamran Matin (Lanham, MD: Rowman & Littlefield, 2016), 17–30.

28 Patrick Bond and Ana Garcia, *BRICS: An Anti-Capitalist Critique* (London: Pluto, 2015).

29 Simon Bromley, "Reflections on Empire, Imperialism and United States Hegemony," *Historical Materialism* 11, no. 3 (2003): 17–68; Leo Panitch and Sam Gindin, *The Making of Global Capitalism: The Political Economy of American Empire* (London: Verso, 2013).

30 Hannes Lacher, "Making Sense of the International System: The Promises of Contemporary Marxist Theories of International Relations," in *Historical Materialism and Globalization*, eds. Mark Rupert and Hazel Smith (London: Routledge, 2002): 147–164.

31 Henk Overbeek, "Global Governance: From Radical Transformation to Neo-Liberal Management," *International Studies Review* 12, no. 4 (2010): 697.

Feminism

Susanne Zwingel, Elisabeth Prügl, and Gülay Çağlar

Feminism is a political movement for change, and feminist theories are theories of change. Accordingly, both feminist engagements with international organizations and feminist theorizing about global governance center on identifying and combating gender discrimination, calling out and fighting various forms of subordination and the oppression of women, and problematizing entrenched heteronormativity—i.e., the tendency to treat the male–female binary and heterosexuality as naturally given. Both feminist activism and feminist theory are thus inherently political. Aware of the deep gender biases in scholarship carrying the mantle of objectivity, feminist researchers recognize that all knowledge is interested and strives for a "dynamic objectivity" that makes knowledge interests explicit.[1]

Gender is a central (and perhaps *the* central) analytical concept for feminist scholars. The concept is complex, capturing multiple facets of social reality. It designates individual identity as much as social relations, and functions as a structuring principle of discourse. Thus, at the individual level feminist scholars have explored the construction of gendered selves in processes of socialization; at the level of social relations they have analyzed gender divisions of labor and the gendered structures of institutions; and with regard to discourses they have probed the deployment of gender binaries as a way of distributing value. These different uses of gender share an important theoretical commitment: In all instances gender is treated as a social construction. That is, gender is a product of processes of socialization, structured agency, performances and/or discursive practices. It is mobile and malleable, but the continuation of gender as a structuring relation requires considerable effort.

Such gender politics is power politics. Through their politics and writing, feminists seek to destabilize existing arrangements; in so doing, they challenge existing orthodoxies and habits, and run into opposition from those benefitting from current arrangements. Multiple facets of power thus emerge as a central preoccupation of feminist activists and theorists. How can and do feminists influence agendas?

How can and do they counter backlashes, resistances, and mechanisms of power that deflect and co-opt their agendas? What is the power of international norms to impact gender relations worldwide? How does discursive power operate in the governance of gender?

In this chapter, we survey a range of approaches that feminists have put forward in order to explain why and how international organizations and processes of global governance contribute to constructing and reconstructing gender relations on a global scale. We first provide a historical overview of feminist efforts to create an agenda for gender equality and for gender mainstreaming, together with the challenges that these efforts have encountered. We then review new approaches and current issues in international feminist scholarship. Three particularly compelling areas include research that probes the continuous translation of international gender norms within and beyond global governance structures, research that analyzes the disciplinary and governmental character of international discourses in a Foucauldian sense, and research that challenges the hegemonic focus on gender as locked into a heteronormative logic. Reflecting the ways in which feminist theory and practice are intertwined, our narrative combines a review of theoretical approaches with a recounting of experiences of feminist engagements with international organizations and global governance.

History

Recent global governance literature has explored the functions of international, regional, and multilevel institutions as well as the crucial role of the reconfigured state in the regulation of an increasingly globalized world. Feminists have intervened both in the scholarly debate on and the real-life formations of such governance. In a nutshell, feminist emphasis in this context has been on making clear that "gender matters in global politics,"[2] and on critically examining the conditions as well as the obstacles for the inclusion of gendered interests into mechanisms of global governance. This focus has to be understood as part of the broader feminist endeavor in international relations (IR) of exposing the absence of female bodies and interests and debunking a supposedly disembodied discourse as derived from male-only human experiences.

Feminists have conceptualized institutions of global governance as structural configurations different from the state in which struggles against patriarchal social structures may yield some degree of transformation. Since state bureaucracies and formal political institutions are typically themselves entrenched in patriarchal norms, gender equality advocates have long been wary of engaging with the state and have preferred to organize outside of formal institutions. On the global level, women's organizations have created transnational networks in order to make collective claims for gender equality toward the international community of states. However, intergovernmental organizations have typically not integrated feminist voices in all their transformative potential; more often, feminist claims have been exploited to achieve other ends, or else were converted from an emancipatory vision into management tools added to (and buried in) bureaucratic processes. Hence, feminist literature has focused on the tension between the inclusion of gender awareness into global governance structures, on the one hand, and the preservation of core feminist goals, on the other. Increasingly, it also reflects on what exactly "gender awareness" in global governance entails: While it was originally meant to bring women into the picture and elevate them from subordinate positions, exclusions based on gender have a much broader scope, for example the marginalization of gender identities produced by heteronormativity (see section below on new approaches and issues).

We see three broad developments regarding feminist interventions in global governance: First, in virtually all global policy fields, gender equality advocates both from the nongovernmental sector and from within global governance bureaucracies have engaged in agenda setting—that is, in making gender a relevant dimension of global politics. In some areas, such claims have faced less resistance than in others. For example, women's work became understood as a crucial part of development in the 1970s, and the notion that population policies should be connected to the education of women and measures to increase their reproductive health has gained attention since the 1980s. Other areas such as security polices or macroeconomic and finance policies have proved to be more resistant. The recognition of gender as an important dimension for managing security through Security Council resolution 1325 and subsequent resolutions has been successful within a hyper-masculinized context. This is less true for macroeconomic and finance policies, where the andro-centric underpinnings of technical "expertise" are not questioned and gender equality is understood as a tool to maximize performance, but not as a goal in its own right. Thus, while gender now plays a role on diverse global agendas, gender awareness is not necessarily considered at the heart of each policy issue.[3]

Second, it has become clear that despite the difficulties of agenda setting, agenda *keeping* is the real challenge for feminist advocates. Feminist advocates have to ensure that gender equality is kept alive as an important organizational vision and that it is being consistently translated into specific policies and programs. Globally agreed language on gender equality does not automatically result in policy traction. Within historically patriarchal institutions, documents representing gender equality "successes" easily turn into paper tigers unless their legitimacy and recognition is actually produced through sustained activism, as in the case of the Convention on the Elimination of All Forms of Discrimination Against Women (CEDAW). In addition, rhetorical feminist "victories" can never be taken for granted and may come under severe attack. This was the case with the 1995 Beijing Platform for Action (BPA) in the post-9/11 period because of changes in the general political climate—here, a shift from multilateralism in the 1990s to fundamentalism and militarism in the 2000s—and more vocal governmental and nongovernmental resistance to feminist ideas, often presented as "family values."[4] Further, the organizational realization of cases of successful agenda setting often turns out to be disappointingly superficial. The strategy of "gender mainstreaming," perhaps the most widely implemented element of the ambitious BPA, has often been converted into a management tool, to the extent that its original radical intent of creating gender equal policy processes and outcomes "evaporated."[5]

Feminist literature has identified a number of factors that influence the degree of meaningful inclusion of gender equality claims, among them the nature of the policy field, the solidification or flexibility of the organizational structure, and, perhaps most importantly, the critical feedback loop between the perspectives of institutional "insiders" and autonomous "outsiders." The lack of outsider feedback— often reinforced by a construction of superior gender expertise of insiders—almost inevitably leads to cooptation of gender equality goals. Arguably, this dynamic of cooptation has strengthened gender activism that rejects global governance institutions as a meaningful site for intervention altogether.[6]

Third, thus far we have a rudimentary understanding of the connection between gendering global governance mechanisms and the state of gender relations worldwide. Two bodies of literature have started to close this gap. On the one hand is empiricist literature that measures the status of gender relations cross-nationally and correlates these with state commitments to global standards which, depending on the indicators and global standards used, concludes that the real-life impact of instruments of global governance are more or less optimistic.[7] One the other hand, literature on norm translation conceptualizes norm creation and realization as complex processes between variously contextualized agencies that produce myriad interpretations of global gender norms. We discuss this approach in more detail below.

New approaches and current issues

The focus on transformative inclusiveness in the feminist literature on international organizations and global governance has produced three particularly salient currents of debate. The first focuses on the translation of gender norms expands on the boundaries of global governance structures and draws connections between global and manifold contextualized gender norms through the analysis of translating agency. The second debate is on the transformation of gender equality norms from marginalized claims into governance tools produced and applied by resourceful bureaucracies. This transformation raises new issues of power, exclusion, emancipation and discipline. The third debate reflects on the scope of meaning of "gendering global governance." Expanding on the notion of women as marginalized subjects, this debate focuses on masculinities as the other, typically more privileged pole within the heterosexual male–female dichotomy, on the intersectional identities of women in all their diversity, and on ways to address more effectively sexual orientation and gender identity as grounds of discrimination.

Norm translation

The feminist literature on the translation of gender norms is part of the broad debate on norm diffusion within IR scholarship. However, the character of gender norms—in particular the fact that they are ubiquitously and not just internationally produced, and that a wide variety, including mutually exclusive, notions of appropriate gender orders exist—has led to particular theoretical frameworks designed to capture dynamics in a field of such deep social significance. Accordingly, these frameworks suggest that gender norms are generated in various sites and explore the ways connecting agency translates norms from one context into another. This translation process does not work automatically from global to local levels but is multidirectional and informed by various ways of engagement that range from support for, to partial or an entire rejection of the norms in question.[8]

The norm translation literature departs from a transnational perspective and entails a reconception of the global, the national, and the local as contexts that produce idiosyncratic norms and practices and which are influenced by phenomena beyond their demarcation.[9] The literature on transnational feminism has long focused on the manifold forms of contextualized women's activism as well as the border-crossing connections between them.[10] It has also produced insightful re-readings of the actors relevant for gender norm translation; in particular, international institutions do not provide a consistent, but rather a contradictory, framework in terms of gender equality norms, as many of their policies work against this goal;[11] states differ widely in terms of factual sovereignty, but also in regards to the type of national gender orders they institutionalize;[12] and nongovernmental organizations (NGOs) may be idealistic actors aiming to pressure states into compliance with globally agreed gender norms, but they may also be comparatively powerful and oppose global norms.[13]

Within this reconstructed global landscape the norm translation literature has identified two broad movements of "travelling" gender norms. The first movement is toward and within global governance institutions. A number of studies have analyzed activism that aims at influencing such institutions and activists' use of global spaces to create transnational links and strategies of action.[14] While an earlier focus of this literature was on the dimension of agenda setting, it has more recently shed light on the dynamics of continuous contestations of norms after they are "placed" on the international agenda. In other words, "global gender norms" constitute a principally unfinished discourse rather than a fixed set of ideas to be domestically implemented.[15] Works in the tradition of feminist institutionalism explain another dimension of global gender norm dynamics, namely the relatively unsuccessful translation of rhetorically accepted gender equality norms into the practice of global institutions because they are "nested" in gender-blind traditions.[16]

The second direction of norm translation is toward and within domestic contexts. The literature tracing such processes looks into agency that uses international gender norms to influence domestic gender regimes; it analyzes both actor constellations and context characteristics as these shape strategies and outcomes of norm translation processes. Peggy Levitt and Sally Merry have coined the term "vernacularization" for the process of making international gender norms understandable and acceptable in other-than global contexts.[17] This type of norm translation may result in the strengthening of a local norm through international impulses or it might introduce an entirely new norm, but it may also produce norm adaptation or rejection, for example, when domestic civil society actors think such rejection adds legitimacy to their claims.[18] Taken together, the norm translation literature conceptually stretches IR theorizing on global governance dynamics beyond the international and sheds light on the modes of connection between various contexts.

Gender politics as governmentality

A burgeoning literature in the field of feminist IR analyzes gender politics in global governance through the lens of discourse theory as well as governmentality studies.

This Foucauldian perspective implies a shift in the focus of attention. Feminist analyses on agenda setting have provided valuable insights on institutional opportunities as well as barriers; they have illustrated how feminist actors seize on political opportunities and identifies which institutional obstacles they face within male-dominated organizations and environments in the international arena.[19] Thus, they conceptualize power in global governance as something that limits agency. The focus is on identifying the gendered power asymmetries that work against the meaningful inclusion of gender issues in international policies and programs. In contrast, Foucault-inspired theorizing highlights the productive character of power. Feminist scholars drawing on Foucault are interested in the ways discourses, practices, and knowledge systems produce power effects. These discourses, practices, and knowledge systems shape actors' identities, constitute them as subjects and, thus, enable a certain kind of agency. This understanding of power is akin to what Steven Lukes calls the "third dimension" of power, which is "the power to shape, influence or determine others' beliefs and desires, thereby securing their compliance."[20]

Feminist scholars draw in diverse ways on Foucault. Some employ a discourse analytical approach, while others use the concept of governmentality. Discourse analysis puts the emphasis on the production of meaning. Feminist studies that employ a discourse analytical approach probe how both subjects and objects of knowledge come into existence through discourse. Discourse, in a Foucauldian sense, is a set of statements and practices that produce both the subjects and objects of knowledge.[21] It focuses on the norms and rules that facilitate a certain set of statements and practices, and it demarcates what gender equality means in a specific societal context and institutional setting.

Therefore, scholars drawing on Foucault do not regard an object of political intervention (such as gendered violence or economic development) as exogenously given but rather as discursively constructed.[22] They sketch the multiple ways a policy issue becomes relevant, to which gendered meanings are assigned and how it is made governable. Megan MacKenzie, for instance, examines "development policies as a source of regulation and discipline"[23] and illustrates how empowerment initiatives in the disarmament, demobilization, and reintegration process in Sierra Leone prescribe appropriate gender roles. One telling example is the design of microcredit programs as a tool to make female ex-combatants fit into the role of supportive wives within the nuclear family rather than to facilitate their economic independence.

Another concept on which feminist scholars increasingly draw is that of "governmentality." These studies probe how gendered subjectivities are spawned and what role state institutions play in this process. Feminist scholars drawing on the governmentality framework agree with Foucault's critique of the conventional conceptualization of the state as a monolithic entity that possess all power and that exerts this power over its population. Instead, state power is regarded as diverse and diffuse. These studies approach "government" to mean the "conduct of conduct," which is "any more or less calculated and rational activity, undertaken by a multiplicity of authorities and agencies, employing a variety of techniques and forms of knowledge, that seeks to shape conduct by working through the desires, aspirations, interests and beliefs of various actors."[24] Thus, governmentality is a neoliberal technology of power as it induces free subjects to control their behavior and optimize their actions through techniques of observation, calculation, and administration. The concept of governmentality has been taken up by feminist IR scholars and has mostly been applied to analyze the strategy of gender mainstreaming in international organizations.

Gender mainstreaming is an interesting example, as it comprises disciplinary practices of benchmarking, monitoring, and evaluation. Studies theorize gender mainstreaming as a technology through which gendered identities are shaped and gender relations are governed.[25] Lynne Phillips, for instance, shows how gender mainstreaming in the activities of the UN Food and Agriculture Organization (FAO) has sought to put the responsibility of food security on rural women by shaping their subjectivities as active and knowledgeable agents in regard to food and by creating the image of the "new rural woman."[26] In this way, regulatory practices of gender mainstreaming are infused with specific ways of knowing about gender roles; and new subjectivities are produced, on the basis of the idea that "women feed the world." Thus, stereotypes about gender roles remain intact.

Feminist studies drawing on Foucauldian frameworks conceptualize gender politics in international governance as discursively constructed and/or as a technique of government that reproduce and reinforce traditional gender roles. Thus, they shift the focus of attention away from androcentric power asymmetries toward the productive dimension of power inherent in gender politics themselves.

Beyond women and gender

Feminist strategies to make global governance structures more inclusive have long placed the rights and empowerment of women at the center of attention. This focus on women has become a target of critique for obscuring multiple and intersecting structures of inequality and for hiding the role of men in the continuation of women's subordination. Partially in response to this critique, feminist and gender experts in the 1980s shifted the focus from women to gender, replacing the women-in-development approach with the gender-in-development approach. The 1990s introduced gender mainstreaming in order to address the way gender was embedded in all policies and programs. The express intention of these shifts was to make visible relationships of power between women and men and to meet these power relationships head on. In addition, feminist scholars have developed a much broader understanding of gender that includes three components: A problematization of men and masculinities; a bringing into view of intersecting status positions and diversity among women; and render visible sexual orientation and gender identity (SOGI) as grounds for discrimination and with it the heteronormative foundations of international governance structures.

Gender theory puts in the center of analysis not only women, but the structured relationship between women and men, as well as the relational construction of *masculinity*. Theorists of masculinity have "gendered men"—that is, they have emphasized that what is considered manly is also an outcome of cultural and historical practices.[27] Accordingly, masculinities vary depending on cultural and institutional contexts. However, theorists of masculinity also have emphasized that these identities are always constructed in relation to femininity and—typically—in a way that subordinates femininities to masculinity. Furthermore, multiple masculinities coexist with one type of masculinity emerging as aspirational or hegemonic. The problem of patriarchy is thus reformulated as a problem of hegemonic masculinity.[28]

Pluralizing understandings of masculinity makes it possible to recognize that men are not only the problem but that they can also play a role in achieving gender equality. Accordingly, there have been efforts in recent years to recruit men as feminist allies, such as in UN Women's "HeforShe Campaign." Moreover, feminist men have organized—for example, in the White Ribbon Campaign—to help fight sexual and gender-based violence. Accompanying these new understandings of men has been a recognition that they can also be victims, including of sexual violence, as has now been documented in a number of studies from conflict zones around the world.[29] The various forms in which men are reconstructed in international gender discourses raises interesting questions about the way gender operates to both victimize and authorize men.

The notion of hegemonic masculinity has perhaps been deployed most productively in the area of security governance, an area dominated by men and masculine cultures. Feminist academics have long unveiled the privileging of masculine values and practices and the parallel denigration of femininity in foreign policy and security establishments, militaries and peacekeeping operations. They have argued that this produces a variety of dysfunctional outcomes, from sex trafficking by peacekeepers and sexual violence in wartime to the systematic exclusion of women from processes of postwar reconstruction.

While a number of Security Council resolutions in the new millennium have formulated an agenda on "women, peace, and security," they have largely failed to problematize structures of gender subordination and associated militarist masculinities. The promise of a gender approach that does not reduce gender to women and problematizes gendered power relations thus remains to be realized in the area of security governance and continues to form the basis of critical feminist strategizing and theorizing.[30]

A second reaction to the "woman-centeredness" of international gender politics has been the claim to understand women as shaped by diverse social dimensions beyond gender. Critiques in the 1980s from women in the Global South began to question whether women across the globe actually have common interests. This argument received an academic formulation in Chandra Mohanty's trenchant critique of Western feminist scholarship as colonial, exercising power by producing the "Third World woman" as a singular and monolithic subject, always already oppressed.[31] Today feminists have embraced the understanding that feminist politics must recognize the "*intersectionality*" of status positions—i.e., they must recognize that women are very differently located depending on their place in the international system, their race, class, and other markers of difference.[32] In some international organizations, such as the European Union, this new approach has led to a shift from gender mainstreaming to "diversity mainstreaming" and the effort to treat markers of difference simultaneously. While feminists value this recognition of the complexity of the politics of difference, on the one hand, they also have, on the other, been wary of tendencies to set gender equal to other status positions, thereby obscuring the profoundly constitutive character of gender for the formation of core identities.[33]

The struggle to recognize different forms of *sexual orientation and gender identity* constitutes a third frontier of feminist interventions in international governance. It resonates with feminist and queer theories that suggest that not only gender is a matter of social construction, but so are biological sex and sexual desire. Compulsory heterosexuality orients not only the direction of sexual desire but also cements the gender binary.[34] LGBTI (lesbian, gay, bisexual, transgender, intersex) activists have long drawn attention to the discriminatory consequences of heteronormativity, and organizations of the intersexed have questioned the naturalness of the gender binary. Both increasingly frame the recognition of different types of sexual orientation and gender identity as a matter of global justice.[35]

Recognizing sexual orientation and gender identity as grounds for discrimination is one of the most contested issues in current human rights politics. The issue has received some support from international courts, in particular the European Court of Human Rights, but finds considerable opposition in more political forums, such as the Human Rights Council. This is not surprising since homosexuality continues to be prohibited in more than one-third of UN member states, and in seven countries it is punishable by death.[36] Because it makes visible the link between compulsory heterosexuality and gender subordination, the claim of LGBTI activists for human rights has been particularly threatening to reactionary patriarchal ideologies that construe women's secondary status as a natural outcome of a reproductive imperative. In several UN forums and in alliance with fundamentalists of various religious shades they have fiercely contested using the term "gender," considering it a Trojan horse that makes it possible to claim rights for LGBTI persons and thus undermine what they consider the "natural family."[37] However, the issue is gaining recognition, and in 2016 the Human Rights Council approved the appointment of an Independent Expert on Sexual Orientation and Gender Identity to help combat violence and discrimination on that basis.

Conclusion

The encounter of feminist activists with international organizations and global governance constitutes a particular kind of power politics, one in which the state is the main actor but in which non-state actors seek to win over international organizations and global governance structures for their emancipatory agendas. Through their engagement with international organizations, feminists seek to change gendered power relations. Their focus is on gender as a sociopolitical construct and as an organizer of international policies and discourses. International norms in a broad range of issue areas typically have been silent on gender and in claiming gender neutrality often have inadvertently reproduced gendered power relations. From a feminist perspective, international governance in this way perpetuates masculine rule, and such masculine hegemony deserves to be radically transformed.

Successful feminist agenda setting in some issue areas has begun to shake masculine hegemony through the creation of international law, such as CEDAW, and through organizational strategies such as gender mainstreaming. In other words, feminist politics has activated the power of norms to influence international agendas and governments worldwide. In these efforts, international feminist politics, like all politics that attacks fundamental commitments of individuals and institutions, encounters resistances that provide a challenge for what we have called "agenda keeping." Feminist agendas are being co-opted for various purposes and translated into multiple contexts. While feminist discourses have thus come to pervade the antechambers of power, they sometimes have become distant from the feminist critiques that spawned their formulation.

Processes of cooptation join the logic of governmentality to generate a new type of power politics as feminism has become a part of international government in this way. A narrow focus on women has sometimes functioned to obscure the diversity of experiences of women differently located, and it has helped cement an understanding of gender as a binary between women and men. The LGBTI challenge has made visible the exclusionary effects of such politics and pushed towards a broadening of feminist agendas to encompass the fight against discrimination based on sexual orientation and gender identity. This entails an attack on heteronormativity and the associated naturalization of the gender binary.

Feminist research into international organization and global governance has as its object an exposure of the power politics in these structures. It seeks to comprehend the way international feminist commitments can generate change, the mechanisms of power that obstruct such change, and the disciplining and exclusions that are generated as feminists engage with international power structures. Feminist researchers share with movement activists an interest in emancipatory knowledge that helps overcome the seemingly endless continuation of gender subordination and gender-based violence. Their common hope is to harness power and turn institutions that perpetuate masculine rule into enablers of gender justice.

Additional reading

Gülay Çağlar, Elisabeth Prügl, and Susanne Zwingel, eds., *Feminist Strategies in International Governance* (London and New York: Routledge, 2013).

Karen Garner, *Women and Gender in International History, Theory and Practice* (London: Bloomsbury, forthcoming 2018).

Annica Kronsell and Erika Svedberg, eds., *Making Gender, Making War: Violence, Military and Peacekeeping Practices* (New York: Routledge, 2012).

Shirin M. Rai and Georgina Waylen, eds., *Global Governance: Feminist Perspectives* (Basingstoke and New York: Palgrave Macmillan, 2008).

Laura Shepherd, ed., *Gender Matters in Global Politics: A Feminist Introduction to International Relations*, 2nd ed. (London and New York: Routledge, 2015).

Jill Steans and Daniela Tepe-Belfrage, eds., *Handbook on Gender in World Politics* (Cheltenham and Northampton: Edward Elgar Publishing, 2016).

Notes

1 Sandra Harding, *The Science Question in Feminism* (Ithaca, NY: Cornell University Press, 1986).

2 Laura J. Shepherd, *Gender Matters in Global Politics: A Feminist Introduction to International Relations*, 2nd ed. (London and New York: Routledge, 2015).

3 Arvonne S. Fraser and Irene Tinker, eds., *Developing Power: How Women Transformed International Development* (New York: Feminist Press, 2004); Jutta Joachim, *Agenda Setting, the UN and NGOS: Gender Violence and Reproductive Rights* (Washington, DC: Georgetown University Press, 2007); Carol Cohn, "Mainstreaming Gender in UN Security Policy: A Path to Political Transformation", in *Global Governance: Feminist Perspectives*, eds. Shirin M. Rai and Georgina Waylen (Basingstoke and New York: Palgrave Macmillan, 2008), 185–206; Shahra Razavi, "Governing the Economy for Gender Equality? Challenges of Regulation," in *Feminist Strategies in International Governance*, eds. Gülay Çağlar, Elisabeth Prügl, and Susanne Zwingel (London and New York: Routledge, 2013), 217–232.

4 Gita Sen, "Neolibs, Neocons and Gender Justice. Lessons from Global Negotiations," *Occasional Paper No. 9* (Geneva: United Nations Research Institute for Social Development, 2005).

5 Jacqui True, "Mainstreaming Gender in International Institutions," in *Gender Matters in Global Politics: A Feminist Introduction to International Relations,* ed. Laura. J. Sheperd (London and New York: Routledge, 2010), 189–203; and Caroline Moser, "Has Gender Mainstreaming Failed? A Comment on International Development Agency Experiences in the South," *International Feminist Journal of Politics* 7, no. 4 (December 2005): 576–590.

6 Catherine Eschle and Bice Maiguashca, *Making Feminist Sense of the Global Justice Movement* (Lanham, MD: Rowman & Littlefield, 2010).

7 Mark M. Gray, Miki Caul Kittilson, and Wayne Sandholtz, "Women and Globalization: A Study of 180 Countries, 1975–2000," *International Organization* 60, no. 2 (2006): 293–333; Emilie Hafner-Burton, Kiyoteru Tsutsui, and John W. Meyer, "International Human Rights Law and the Politics of Legitimation. Repressive States and Human Rights Treaties," *International Sociology* 23, no. 1 (2008): 115–141.

8 Susanne Zwingel, *Translating International Women's Rights: The CEDAW Convention in Context* (London: Palgrave Macmillan, 2016).

9 Ulf Hannerz, *Transnational Connections. Culture, Peoples, Places* (New York: Routledge, 1996); Sally Engle Merry, "Constructing a Global Law—Violence Against Women and the Human Rights System," *Law and Social Inquiry* 28 (2003): 941–977.

10 Valentine Moghadam, *Globalizing Women: Transnational Feminist Networks* (Baltimore, MD: Johns Hopkins University Press, 2005); Amrita Basu, ed., *The Challenge of Local Feminisms. Women's Movements in Global Perspective* (Boulder, CO: Westview Press, 1995).

11 Uché U. Ewelukwa, "Centuries of Globalization, Centuries of Exclusion. African Women, Human Rights, and the 'New' International Trade Regime," *Berkeley Journal of Gender, Law and Justice* 20 (2005): 75–149.

12 Lynn Savery, *Engendering the State: The International Diffusion of Women's Human Rights* (New York: Routledge, 2007).

13 Kim D. Reiman, "A View from the Top: International Politics, Norms, and the Worldwide Growth of NGOs," *International Studies Quarterly* 50, no. 1 (2006): 45–67; and Doris E. Buss, "The Christian Right, Globalization, and the 'Natural Family,'" in *Gods, Guns, and Globalization. Religious Radicalism and the International Political Economy*, eds. Marry Ann Tétreault and Robert A. Denemark (Boulder, CO: Lynne Rienner, 2004), 57–77.

14 Devaki Jain, *Women, Development, and the UN: A Sixty-Year Quest for Equality and Justice* (Bloomington: Indiana University Press, 2005).

15 Mona Lena Krook and Jacqui True, "Rethinking the Life Cycles of International Norms: The United Nations and the Global Promotion of Gender Equality," *European Journal of International Relations* 18, no. 1 (2012): 103–127.

16 Louise Chappell, *The Politics of Gender Justice at the International Criminal Court: Legacies and Legitimacy* (Oxford: Oxford University Press, 2016).

17 Peggy Levitt and Sally Merry, "Vernacularization on the Ground: Local Uses of Global Women's Rights in Peru, China, India and the United States," *Global Networks* 9, no. 4 (2009): 441–461.

18 Anne S. Roald, "Islamists in Jordan: Promoters of or Obstacles to Female Empowerment and Gender Equality?" *Religion and Human Rights* 4, no. 1 (2009): 41–63.

19 Joachim, *Agenda Setting, the UN and NGOS: Gender Violence and Reproductive Rights*; Robert O'Brien, Anne Marie Goetz, Jan Aart Scholte, and Marc Williams, *Contesting Global Governance* (Cambridge: Cambridge University Press, 2000); Anne Winslow, ed., *Women, Politics, and the United Nations* (Westport, CT: Greenwood Publishing Group, 1995); Nüket Kardam, *Bringing Women In: Women's Issues in International Development Programs* (Boulder, CO, London: Lynne Rienner Publishers, 1991).

20 Steven Lukes, "Power and the Battle of Hearts and Minds: On the Bluntness of Soft Power," in *Power in World Politics*, eds. Felix Berenskoetter and M.J. Williams (London and New York: Routledge, 2007), 90; Jane Parpart, "Gender, Power and Governance in a Globalizing World," *Development Research Series*, Working Paper no. 126 (Aalborg: Research Center on Development and International Relations, 2004).

21 Michel Foucault (1980), "Truth and Power," in *Power/Knowledge. Michel Foucault: Selected Interviews and Other Writings 1972–1977*, ed. Colin Gordon (New York: Pantheon Books, 1980), 117.

22 Laura J. Shepherd, "Loud Voices Behind the Wall: Gender Violence and the Violent Reproduction of the International," *Millennium: Journal of International Studies* 34, no. 2 (2006), 377–401; Gülay Çağlar, "Gender Knowledge and Economic Knowledge in the World Bank and UNDP: Multiple Meanings of Gender Budgeting," in *Gender Knowledge and Knowledge Networks in International Political Economy*, eds. Christoph Scherrer and Brigitte Young (Baden-Baden, Germany: Nomos, 2010), 55–74.

23 Megan MacKenzie, "Empowerment Boom or Bust? Assessing Women's Post-Conflict Empowerment Initiatives," *Cambridge Review of International Affairs* 22, no. 2 (2009): 201.

24 Mitchel Dean, *Governmentality. Power and Rule in Modern Society*, 2nd ed. (London, Thousand Oaks and New Delhi: Sage Publications, 2010), 18.

25 Lynne Phillips, "Gender Mainstreaming: The Global Governance of Women?" *Canadian Journal of Development Studies* 26, no. 1 (2005): 651–663; Magdalena Bexell, "Global Governance, Gains and Gender," *International Feminist Journal of Politics* 14, no. 3 (2012): 389–407; Audrey Reeves, "Feminist Knowledge and Emerging Governmentality in UN Peacekeeping: Patterns of Co-optation and Empowerment," *International Feminist Journal of Politics* 14, no. 3 (2012), 348–369; Elisabeth Prügl, "Diversity Management and Gender Mainstreaming as Technologies of Government," *Politics and Gender* 7, no. 1 (2011): 71–89.

26 Phillips, "Gender Mainstreaming: The Global Governance of Women?" 656ff.

27 Jeff Hearn, *Men of the World: Genders, Globalizations, Transnational Times* (London: Sage, 2015).

28 R.W. Connell and James W. Messerschmidt, "Hegemonic Masculinity: Rethinking the Concept," *Gender and Society* 19, no. 6 (2005): 829–859.

29 Marysia Zalewski, Paula Drumond, Elisabeth Prügl, and Maria Stern, *Sexual Violence against Men in Global Politics* (London: Routledge, forthcoming).

30 Claire Duncanson, "Hegemonic Masculinity and the Possibility of Change in Gender Relations," *Men and Masculinities* 18, no. 2 (2015): 231–248; Carol Cohn, "Mainstreaming Gender in UN Security Policy: A Path to Political Transformation," in *Global Governance: Feminist Perspectives,* eds. Shirin M. Rai and Georgina Waylen (New York: Routledge, 2008), 185–206.

31 Chandra Talpade Mohanty, "Under Western Eyes: Feminist Scholarship and Colonial Discourses," *Feminist Review* 30 (Autumn 1988): 61–88.

32 Patricia Hill Collins and Valerie Chepp, "Intersectionality," in *The Oxford Handbook of Gender and Politics*, eds. Georgina Waylen, Karen Celis, Johanna Kantola, and S. Laurel Weldon (Oxford: Oxford University Press, 2013), 57–88.

33 Mieke Verloo, "Multiple Inequalities, Intersectionality and the European Union," *European Journal of Women's Studies* 13, no. 3 (2006): 211–228.

34 Judith Butler, *Gender Trouble: Feminism and the Subversion of Identity* (New York: Routledge, 1990).

35 Manuela Picq and Markus Thiel, eds., *Sexualities in World Politics: How LGBTQ Claims Shape International Relations* (New York: Routledge, 2015).

36 Joke Swiebel and Dennis van der Veur, "Hate Crimes Against Lesbian, Gay, Bisexual and Transgender Persons and the Policy Response of International Governmental Organisations," *Netherlands Quarterly of Human Rights* 27, no. 4 (2009): 485–524. Homosexuality draws the death penalty in Iran, Mauritania, Saudi-Arabia, Sudan, Yemen, and in some parts of Nigeria and Somalia. Ibid., 513.

37 Doris E. Buss, "Finding the Homosexual in Women's Rights: The Christian Right in International Politics," *International Feminist Journal of Politics* 6, no. 2 (2004): 257–284.

Post-structuralism

James Brassett

Recent years have seen a proliferation of advances in the theory and practice of global governance from a post-structural perspective.[1] While such approaches are not neatly categorized in the paradigmatic fashion still common in mainstream international relations (IR) and international political economy (IPE), there are nevertheless certain critical themes and political questions that recur. Most fundamentally, post-structural approaches to global governance often foreground the significance of discourse, in general, and the mutual entwinement between discourse and political subjects, in particular. Post-structural approaches are sensitive to how we come to know what global governance "is," and what "normative" problematics are entailed. Beyond this broad cut, however, there is a rich and productive array of theoretical and empirical agendas that can be developed under the banner of post-structuralism in global governance.

This chapter introduces and critically analyzes three significant post-structural approaches that can inform the theory and practice of global governance: Deconstruction, governmentality, and performativity. While each adopts a critical position on the idea of global governance, seeing it as either an expression of the limits of modern state-centric theorizing, or as a productive element in wider patterns of neoliberalism, they all provide a set of important political challenges for students of global governance. In particular, post-structural scholarship can be reflective of how the theory and practice of global governance is in a continual process of change and adaptation, augmenting its purposes and auspices via a range of discursive supplements. The way that global public policy debates seek to manage or recuperate discourses of justice, security, or feminism can be taken as an important signpost for the emergence and politics of new rationalities of global governance such as "fair trade," "gender mainstreaming," and "resilience."

This chapter is divided into three sections. The first section surveys the main propositions and critical dilemmas introduced by post-structural approaches to global governance. It draws out key themes that emerge from the critiques of global governance as a discourse that promotes a particular, sometimes exclusionary, vision of what politics "is." Different currents in the literature—deconstruction and governmentality—point to diverse ways this insight translates into a research program.

The second section summarizes key debates and dilemmas in post-structural approaches to global governance, particularly with regard to its ethics. Discourses of global governance can be so fully reflective of a modernist, Western conception of politics that even in its most cosmopolitan manifestation, the agenda can resemble a re-production of the very hierarchies and problematics that global governance seeks to mitigate.[2] Thus, *the way* in which discourses about global governance emerge, adapt, and change over time and across institutions and scales can be understood as a pressing question. The politics of global governance entails a forensic analysis of the logics and rationalities that are perpetuated, the systems of monitoring and surveillance that are established, and the kinds of neoliberal subject that are implemented.

The third section asks "what is at stake?" For all that we should be sensitive to the political dimensions of the apparently benign analytic of global governance, a post-structural approach can tend towards a form of nihilism or, somewhat counterintuitively, a totalizing vision of politics in which global governance is the inevitable extension of neoliberal government. This view can, in turn, generate a silence over questions of how we might contest the political limits of global governance; indeed, how we might imagine alternative ways of being political within the discursive frameworks performed in its name.[3] Ultimately, the chapter argues that a focus on performance and performativity in global governance can provide an important and reflective space for engaging—*and resisting*—the contingent politics of global governance.

Discourse, deconstruction, and governmentality

Post-structural approaches to global governance are critical of the role of discourse in framing what global governance "is." Insofar as contributions to theorizing come from a post-structural perspective, they tend to operate at the level of either a fundamental critique of the concept itself, or an elaboration of how its logics produce a set of political limits—of scale, of surveillance, of discipline. While the nature of the post-structural critique can seem like a straight rejection of global governance scholarship, we can discern an important set of theoretical and empirical dilemmas that can inform research. A focus on discourse is not an abstraction from or a denial of reality so much as a provocation to think through how the production of what we come to describe as the reality of global governance is a political process "all the way down." In this view, discourse is not just a collection of words and sentences that describe reality. Rather, discourse is a complex, evolving web of binary oppositions, signs and symbols, embodied practices, and normative logics through which meaning is produced and reproduced.[4]

What does it mean to think about global governance as a discourse? A broad suggestion of the literature on global governance is to recognize a set of empirical changes in global politics that problematize its state-centric vision. The growing importance of international organizations and non-state actors like nongovernmental organizations (NGOs) and media are understood to alter the spatial organization and substantive focus of politics. While nominally distinguished from Kantian accounts of world government, a central proposition of much global governance scholarship is that problems such as environmental degradation or financial stability necessitate forms of organization and cooperation that exceed, and therefore fundamentally problematize, the sovereign imaginary of politics. In this sense, a normative logic can be discerned that undermines methodological nationalism and seeks to explore the politics of transnational or supra-territorial communities of fate. Importantly, such politics could entail a mix of substantive alternatives from realist restatements of the role of the state to cosmopolitan arguments that support the democratization of international organizations via the inclusion of relevant NGOs. As a discourse of world politics, global governance combines an interesting and plural range of actors, levels of analysis, and normative logics. In analytical terms, it seems to carry an implicit politicizing dynamic that has been associated with a wide range of critical, participatory, and cosmopolitan agendas.[5]

Post-structural theory can provide a significant critique of global governance by questioning the broad notion of politics. One important post-structural intervention on the discourse can be drawn from the work of Rob Walker, who considers that discourses of world politics—including global governance and cosmopolitanism—can be deconstructed to reveal the fundamentally state-centric and exclusionary logics that they seek to mitigate.[6] Against a normative logic of improvement of global governance as the progressive realization of a set of supra-territorial identities or cosmopolitan values, Walker discerns a coalescence between a certain idea of the modern state-centric form of politics—through which inclusion relies on the historically violent formation of rights to property, citizenship, and voting—and a recurring myth of escape to some cosmopolitan utopia. Against this he argues:

> [T]he challenges of contemporary political life cannot usefully be posed in terms of the dangers of an anarchy whether supposedly natural or international; the dangers that are usually deployed to scare people into thinking the way forward must involve an historical shift towards universality and cosmopolitanism, or to persuade them that globalization involves a progressive shift towards an enlightened reason. On the contrary the more pressing problem is to come to terms with the forms of universality, cosmopolitanism and globalization that have already produced and enabled (and have in turn already been produced and enabled by) a specific account of the necessary relation between universality and particularity within the modern subject, the modern sovereign state and the modern system of sovereign states.[7]

In this way, Walker calls attention to the constitutive role of the formal practices of theorizing global governance in (simultaneously) defining and limiting our political horizon. While the specific details of institutions or policies will differ, a general sense about the direction of political change is shared. Across perspectives there will be many "disagreements about whether such a move is in progress or not, as well as about whether this version of progression, or Progress, is in fact possible or not, or desirable or not," however, Walker contends that these are judgments within a pre-established frame of politics. They "invite assignments of a yes or no to a reading of historical possibility that is firmly entrenched in the contemporary political imagination as a primary ground on which we might be positive or negative, progressive or reactionary, open to alternatives or locked in the necessities and ambitions of a fragmented but structurally determined array of sovereign states."[8]

While this may seem a broad or fundamental critique of the discourse of global governance, there are clear lines of extension to contemporary debates. For example, the current noise over the UK referendum to leave the European Union (EU) has been portrayed in exactly these terms: As a choice between a vision of progressive history, where EU governance is pitched as the embodiment of universalist values of peace and social welfare, and where the choice to leave is portrayed as reactionary and parochial. From a post-structural perspective, we might question how this framing of the EU downplays the export of European violence through foreign military actions, or the dependence of the European social welfare model on the absence of worker rights in the Global South (and indeed, the absence of potential migrants who are excluded by European borders). Equally, the idea that Brexit is only intelligible within a dichotomous range of political possibility ignores the significance of the largest democratic exercise in UK history, or indeed, the potential decolonial consequences of a united Ireland or an independent Scotland that could well flow from this political event.[9] The point of a deconstructive critique is not to support or defend any such specific positions but rather to encourage awareness of how such debates are limited by a set of binaries—between international and global, politics and ethics, state and non-state—that prefigure the possibility or not of taking such positions.

To foreground the discursive limits of political imagination is to render aspects of the discourse of global governance as a mere technique or technology of power. It recognizes that the substance of discursive postulates concerning, for instance, ethics or agency can only work within a prefabricated notion of what such ethics or agency can be. Power is defined not as a resource or even a capability but as a productive field of relations.[10] And this notion of power can open some interesting and provocative lines of analysis and research.

Beyond the deconstruction of global governance as a set of normative logics, political possibilities, and limits, post-structural approaches can also contribute to the empirical study of global governance as a form of government, *per se*.[11] Indeed, for a range of scholars working in the intellectual tradition of Michel Foucault, discourse is taken as a productive element in everyday social relations; as central to the formation of regimes of truth as to the production of corruption rankings by NGOs. Here the idea of power is emphasized to look at what discourses of global governance "do": What logics of interaction do they foster? What systems of surveillance do they instantiate? What practices of the individual subject do they encourage? The emphasis is less on the big picture or normative logics of global governance, and more on the practical form of disciplinary power, how it produces and is produced by a certain set of relations between discourses and political subjects.

Crucial to understanding this form of power, and how it might relate to global governance, are Foucault's reflections on the "panopticon," which was a draft for a prison based on a simple panoptic design: A central viewing tower would allow a single guard to see into all prison cells that were arranged around it. Due to the height and angles of the central viewing tower, prisoners would not know, for certain, if they were being watched at any one time, just that they could be. The idea was to make the prisoner internalize the possibility that they were being watched, and thus behave as if they were. Inmates would therefore live in accordance with prison rules on the assumption that they could be under surveillance. As Foucault described it: "He who is subjected to a field of visibility, and who knows it, assumes responsibility for the constraints of power; he makes them play spontaneously upon himself; he inscribes in himself the power relation in which he simultaneously plays both roles; he becomes the principle of his own subjection."[12]

This metaphor about the changing nature and practice of power has spurned numerous extensions within IR and IPE. For example, authors such as Paul Langley have contemplated the way that practices like credit rating work in a comparable fashion.[13] By collecting information about an individual over the course of their lifetime and using it to rate their credit worthiness ratings agencies are placed in a disciplinary relation with financial subjects. Individual borrowers are, very often, unaware of what agencies collect this information, or indeed, precisely, which information counts towards a positive or negative score. Financial subjects must discipline themselves over time in accordance with a certain set of unclearly specified expectations. They must in a sense make themselves responsible, to behave as entrepreneurs of their own financial lives.

If we now begin to imagine this idea of disciplinary power as something that can operate in such other areas of global governance as sovereign credit ratings or trade certification, democracy rankings, and university accreditation, and so on, then the potential governmental dimensions of global governance become pervasive. Indeed, some regard governmentality or the conduct of conduct as the pervasive form of power in modern liberal society. "Governmentality" refers to the various ways and means by which the conduct of a political subject is directed, managed and controlled; "to govern, in this sense, is to structure the possible field of action of others."[14] Against a vision of governance as merely bureaucratic—a benign form of administration that promotes order and ethics when compared to the alternative brute power of sovereign interest—the idea of governmentality presents a framework for thinking about how power is rephrased through such practices. Here the pervasive search for regularity through codes of conduct, processes of monitoring and checking against certain global benchmarks, or rankings can entail a system of regulation that disciplines various agents—states, populations, firms, and individuals. While this practice of power does not rely on a clear hierarchy, where the powerful impose on the powerless through instruction or punishment, there is still an emerging logic of government, reminiscent of the prisoner in Foucault's panopticon, where the rationality by which subjects should conduct themselves is internalized in certain, localized, and specific ways.

The neoliberal subject of global governance

While conventional or mainstream theoretical approaches might seek to address the politics of global governance via a focus on the interests of key states, or key sectors of capital, or through the ideological analysis of global public policy, a post-structural approach seems to work at one stage removed from such debates. Against a form of analysis that would seek to correct or improve global governance by intervening to suggest that one or other state embrace a more cosmopolitan vision or by seeking institutional reform to mitigate collective action dilemmas, a post-structural approach is more concerned with how the practices and rationalities of global governance produce a certain mode of political life. A more direct critical focus of post-structural approaches has been to diagnose the linkages between global governance and a wider set of changes in advanced liberal societies associated with neoliberal government.[15]

It is important to distinguish governmentality from another venerable tradition that has long provided a certain diagnosis of the links between global governance and neoliberalism. This approach has been to highlight how basic principles of neoliberal economics—free markets, capital account convertibility, central bank independence, floating exchange rates, and deregulation—have been progressively written into constitutional logics of global governance.[16] Here the legal entrenchment of policies that prohibit state support for industries means that a public welfare conception of political economy has been placed in tension with the political interests of multinational corporations. This neo-Gramscian argument has sometimes drawn on the same language and metaphors as post-structural theory to discuss a purported "global panopticon" as well as the rise of a form of "disciplinary neoliberalism."[17] While such debates are certainly important and interesting, there is a sense in which they simply update and nuance well-established Marxist ideas about the political power of capital in the context of globalization. Instead, the approach of governmentality is more concerned to unpick how new rationalities and subjects emerge through these logics and rationalities of global governance.

Global governance is a moving feast. Think of the discourse of global trade governance and the way it has adapted to a range of critiques that have been leveled against it.[18] For a long period, the World Trade Organization (WTO) and the multinational corporations (MNCs) that sought to benefit from global trade rules were taken as the embodiment of "all that was wrong" with globalization, with its tendency to elevate materialism and profit above wider principles and values. Indeed, the anti-globalization movement has, at various points, sought to question the ethics of a form of global governance that privileges openness and free trade at almost any cost: Environmental degradation, declining labor standards, and erosion of public services.

After certain high-profile demonstrations, a number of initiatives emerged that promoted alternative visions of "fair" or "ethical" trade. Ethical trade was intended to promote new principles such as sustainable development, fair payment for farmers, or wider practices of transparency in MNCs, which might restore trust and understanding in global trade. For example, the UN Global Compact sought voluntary commitments from MNCs to proactively foster a sense of corporate social responsibility (CSR).[19] Equally, the fair-trade certification system quickly established itself as a system for adjusting the price that small or peasant farmers were paid for their product. More broadly, a vast swathe of transnational bodies called "roundtables" emerged to bring together multiple stakeholders—MNCs, environmental NGOs, peasants—to discuss forms of ethical or environmental certification for various products, including timber and biofuels.[20]

From a neo-Gramscian perspective, it would be easy to dismiss such initiatives as an ideological smokescreen, a case of window dressing to legitimate business-as-usual, or a commodification of ethics that simply produces a new market niche in fair trade products. However, from the perspective of governmentality, this interpretation ignores the productive power that emerges from these new forms of certification and regulation. Governmentality is thus more concerned with what such practices make possible; what forms of knowledge emerge; and how they work to orchestrate global governance in new ways. For example, in her analysis of the extension of "ethical auditing" to the Kenyan cut-flower market, Alex Hughes found that the well-intentioned ideas of ethical trade advocates translated into rather convoluted practices of monitoring, which then became an end in themselves.[21] The practice of routinized monitoring and the production of metrics meant that farms began to hire people specifically for the purpose of dealing with the audit. It was thus something in which producers participated principally to qualify for the trade access it permitted, even as the audit itself became divorced from the reality of production. As Hughes concluded:

> [T]he origins of stakeholder mentalities and rituals of audit in advanced capitalist societies means that not only are ethical trading programmes themselves initiated in developed countries, but so too are the rationalities and tacit knowledges underpinning them. This therefore not only poses a practical test for workers, trade unions and NGOs working to widen Southern participation in ethical trade, but also presents a much deeper political conundrum.[22]

We might discern in the governmentality perspective, not just a diagnosis of neoliberalism, but a clear critique of how it instantiates new practices of monitoring; making certain things visible under the banner of ethics. Certain forms of knowledge and judgment are elevated, particular rituals of surveillance established.

Neoliberalism is understood as an evolving form of government and rationality a fair-trade works to produce new political subjects. For example, the consumer subject of fair-trade is typically called on to figure their consumption decision in relation to an (underspecified) ideal of ethics or fairness. One coffee shop serves fair-trade products, another "rainforest alliance." Company websites contain hundreds of pages of information about their commitment to CSR, about the various projects they fund in different developing countries. In this sense, the very act of consumption is recast as an opportunity to take ethical responsibility for the world around us. While such a situation may seem a long way from the prisoner in the panopticon, the principles are basically similar: The consumer subject takes responsibility for performing the (ethical) objectives enshrined in the wider rationality of fair trade. Global ethics is recast as something that "we do" through particular consumption choices. But again the power relations are productive. This consumption choice is an empowering act, which produces the neoliberal subject as ethically responsible for the world around them.[23]

From the point of view of neoliberal governmentality, the idea of a self-reliant, self-making, responsible market subject is an essential component of wider policies that scale back the role of the state in insuring against market failure. Thus, the responsibilization of the subject is understood as a pervasive theme in neoliberal societies that seek to accommodate subjects and make them more resilient to the potential deleterious effects of global markets. For example, in the world of healthcare provision, individuals are increasingly recast as responsible for their own lifestyle choices achieved through a combination of both, encouragements to eat healthily and exercise, along with more disciplinary policies such as the withholding of certain treatments in cases where a patient smokes or is obese. Likewise, in education, pupils are increasingly encouraged to learn through failure; competition and regular testing are intended to foster a sense of resilience that students must own their educational experiences and trajectory. Across a broad range of issue areas then, neoliberal subjects are encouraged to work on themselves to build up their resilience to cope with and adapt to the everyday challenges of market life. Indeed, Pat O'Malley argues that this turn to resilience will license new logics and techniques of the self:

> The new resilient self is . . . to be achieved rather than taken as natural . . . As with "markets" and "communities," "resilience" has shifted from being a natural given to being a technique to be applied wherever advantageous, built up, or assembled in ways that resonate with . . . advanced liberal consumers who assemble their lives from an array of commodities.[24]

Imagination and resistance

Post-structural approaches usefully critique and problematize the discourse and normative logics of global governance scholarship. By highlighting the continuity of Western reason, state-centrism, and binaries—for example, particular/universal, state/global, politics/ethics—that define a limited conception of political possibility, a post-structural approach can point to new research themes and issues. Indeed, the previous section drew out how a productive conception of power—i.e., power as proliferative and enabling of certain practices—could rephrase the study of global governance in terms of discipline and government. The way in which ethical agendas are woven into new practices of monitoring and surveillance in the global economy through trade certification, standard setting, and so forth, created unintended consequences; the politics of which are far from the original intentions of ethical trade advocates. Finally, a key challenge in the analysis of governmentality is to unpick how the political subject is produced—indeed, how subjects are encouraged to produce themselves—in terms that foster the continuation of neoliberal governance.

Here the chapter can do no more than hint at the range of issues and practices of global governance that might be rendered according to a governmental critique. While the previous section dealt with the neoliberal subject of consumption, it was suggested that the idea of empowerment through choice, indeed responsibilization, and wider trends towards resilience were rationalities of the neoliberal subject that can be discerned in other areas, including health and education. In addition, finance and most famously the entrepreneurial subject of business falls into this category. In this sense, we might be tempted to speak of global governmentality as a form of disciplinary neoliberalism that perpetuates itself across nearly all walks of modern life. However, a critical perspective on such post-structural approaches might allow for a more subtle take on this area of research. While sympathetic to the arguments and indeed the political problematics that are identified by post-structural thought, I am nevertheless mindful of a set of contradictions and a certain tendency to "Matrix-like" visions of the world.

In the post-structural critique of ethics there is sometimes a mood to turn away from ethical questions. While it is clearly edifying to promote awareness of how the public discourse of ethical progress is imbued with a set of discursive limits that enable conversations, it is equally problematic to eschew any such ethical conversation. There is a contradiction in the commitment to a form of critique that seems to have no other purpose than the perpetuation of a form of critique that questions the idea of ethical purpose. In that sense, ironically post-structural scholarship can often become more concerned with the logic of its own method than with the consequences of the politics of contingency that it identifies. In line with certain pragmatist and queer theorists, it is important to underline the ethical importance of what Richard Rorty called "imagination," or what Butler describes as "performative agency."[25] This would affirm the ethical importance of being able to open new conversations, contingent and limited on their own terms for exploring a form of politics that may be less violent and more open.

In essence, then, there is a curious tendency in post-structural scholarship to over-state the method of the critique, while understating the political consequences of that critique. In the past, this tendency has been encapsulated under the traditional philosophical dilemma of relativism, whereby the critique of ethical foundations is held to compromise any form of ethical commitment. While an interesting conundrum, there is perhaps more that can be said about the importance and empirical commitment of post-structural scholarship to reveal in a detailed manner how global governance works. A more pressing question is to understand how the critique of neoliberal governmentality allows for alternative forms of politicization and engagement. It is here that post-structural scholarship is occasionally undermined by a tendency to nihilism, indeed, a rather simplistic vision of how the world is being made (again and again) in the image of neoliberal reason and subjectivity. As such, almost any new development, event, or reform initiative can be woven into the logic of neoliberal governmentality, such that a more intriguing question might be: "What is not neoliberalism?"

In this sense, there are two ideas in post-structural theory that might be reclaimed and redeployed in further research on global governance. The first is a politics of contingency. We should think more about what is at stake, in the contingency and fragility of discourses on global governance, in general, and the subject of governance, in particular. Judith Butler talks about performative breakdown or failure: What happens when performances of certain discourses of global governance do not work? What if prisoners do not act on themselves in precisely the way that is intended? How could such contingencies and breakdowns be politicized and engaged?[26] The second and related idea speaks to the politics of this issue by recovering the idea of resistance in post-structural scholarship. For Foucault, forms of governmentality would always be met by resistances and dissent. All attempts to conduct would initiate the politics of "counter-conduct," which would, in turn, produce its own new forms of politics. Equally, in the work of Judith Butler, we can discern interest in this idea of counter-conduct, in terms of the question of how subjects can work on themselves in alternative ways; imaginative, subversive, or poetic even. Beyond the apparently sterile form of empowerment in neoliberal discipline, we should emphasize the question of resistance as a form of self-care or self-making within, or against, the logics and rationalities foretold by governmentality scholarship.[27]

Conclusion

This chapter has sought to establish theoretically and critically how a post-structural approach to global governance can elucidate new and interesting debates. From a general focus on the idea of politics contained within discourses of global governance, through to a focus on the productive power of practices of monitoring and surveillance, it was argued that post-structural thought can be regarded as an important critical voice in the literature. The approach can usher in a wide spectrum of empirical subjects and issues that seek to take account of the continual change and adaptation that accompanies the politics of global governance. In particular, the literature on governmentality points to important concerns with the way in which a form of neoliberal subject is performed and augmented to cope with the demands of market life. Finally, some critical questions were raised about the importance of recovering a politics of contingency and resistance that is central to the ideas of certain post-structural authors, but not always reflected in the wider methods of governmentality scholars.

Additional reading

Jacqueline Best, *Governing Failure: Provisional Expertise and the Transformation of Global Governance* (Cambridge: Cambridge University Press, 2014).
Mitchell Dean, *Governmentality: Power and Rule in Modern Society* (London: Sage, 2010).

Michel Foucault, *Discipline and Punish: The Birth of the Prison* (London: Penguin, 1991).

Penny Griffin, *Gendering the World Bank: Neoliberalism and the Gendered Foundations of Global Governance* (New York: Palgrave Macmillan, 2009).

Paul Langley, *The Everyday Life of Global Finance. Saving and Borrowing in Anglo-America* (Oxford: Oxford University Press, 2008).

Rob Walker, *After the Globe, Before the World* (London: Routledge, 2010).

Notes

1 Penny Griffin, *Gendering the World Bank: Neoliberalism and the Gendered Foundations of Global Governance* (New York: Palgrave Macmillan, 2009); Paul Langley, *The Everyday Life of Global Finance: Saving and Borrowing in Anglo-America* (Oxford: Oxford University Press, 2008); Rob Walker, *After the Globe, Before the World* (London: Routledge, 2010). See also James Brassett and Nick Vaughan Williams, "Crisis is Governance: Sub-Prime, the Traumatic Event and Bare Life," *Global Society* 26, no. 1 (2012): 19–42.

2 Rob Walker, "Polis, Cosmopolis, Politics," *Alternatives* 28, no. 2 (2003): 267–286. See also Heikki Patomäki, "Problems of Democratizing Global Governance: Time, Space and the Emancipatory Process," *European Journal of International Relations* 9, no. 3 (2003): 347–376.

3 James Brassett and Chris Holmes, "Building Resilient Finance? Uncertainty, Complexity and Resistance," *British Journal of Politics and International Relations* 18, no. 2 (2016): 370–388.

4 See Tom Lundborg and Nick Vaughan Williams, "New Materialisms, Discourse Analysis, and International Relations: A Radical Inter-textual Approach," *Review of International Studies* 41, no. 1 (2015): 3–25.

5 Jan Aart Scholte, "Civil Society and Democratically Accountable Global Governance," *Global Society* 39, no. 2 (2004): 211–233.

6 Rob Walker, *After the Globe, Before the World* (London: Routledge, 2010).

7 Ibid., 30.

8 Ibid., 9.

9 A similarly dichotomous logic of possibility plays out in the discursive politics of global trade governance, for instance, where liberal multilateralism of a kind associated with the WTO is often tied to a set of progressive ideas like cooperation, human rights, law, and development, whereas "protectionism" is associated with nationalist parochialism, the past, and—rhetorically at least—the kind of sovereign rivalries that lead to war. This is despite the rich set of debates that exist on the progressive role of the state in facilitating development and trade throughout history. Quintessentially, see Ha Joon Chang, *Kicking Away the Ladder: Development Strategy in Historical Perspective* (London: Anthem Press, 2003).

10 Michel Foucault, "The Subject and Power," *Critical Inquiry* 8, no. 4 (1982): 777–795.

11 Mitchell Dean, *Governmentality: Power and Rule in Modern Society* (London: Sage, 2010). See also Peter Miller and Nikolas Rose 'Governing Economic Life', *Economy and Society* 19, no. 1 190: 1–31.

12 Michel Foucault, *Discipline and Punish: The Birth of the Prison* (London: Penguin, 1991) pp. 202–203.

13 Paul Langley, "Equipping Entrepreneurs: Consuming Credit and Credit Scores," *Consumption, Markets and Culture* 17, no. 5 (2014): 448–467.

14 Foucault, "The Subject and Power": 790.

15 Mitchell Dean, *Governmentality: Power and Rule in Modern Society* (London: Sage, 2010).

16 Stephen Gill, "Globalisation, Market Civilisation, and Disciplinary Neo-Liberalism," *Millennium: Journal of International Studies* 24, no. 3 (1995): 399–423.

17 Stephen Gill, "The Global Panopticon? The Neoliberal State, Economic Life and Democratic Surveillance," *Alternatives: Global, Local, Political* 20, no. 1 (1995): 1–49.

18 Rorden Wilkinson, "Talking Trade: Common Sense Knowledge in the Multilateral Trade Regime," in *Expert Knowledge in Global Trade*, eds., Erin Hannah, Silke Trommer, and James Scott (London: Routledge, 2016), 21–40.

19 John G. Ruggie, "Reconstituting the Global Public Domain: Issues, Actors, and Practices," *European Journal of International Relations* 10, no. 4 (2004): 499–531.

20 James Brassett, Ben Richardson, and William Smith "Private Experiments in Global Governance," *International Theory* 4, no. 3 (2012): 367–399.

21 Alex Hughes, "Global Commodity Networks, Ethical Trade, and Governmentality: Organising Business Responsibility in the Kenyan Cut-Flower Industry," *Transactions of the Institute of British Geographers* 26, no. 4 (2001): 390–406.

22 Ibid., 402.

23 Clive Barnett, Paul Cloke, Nick Clarke, and Alice Malpass, "Consuming Ethics: Articulating the Subjects and Spaces of Ethical Consumption," *Antipode* 37, no. 1 (2005): 23–45.

24 Pat O'Malley, "Resilient Subjects: Uncertainty, Warfare and Liberalism," *Economy and Society* 39, no. 4 (2010): 505.

25 Richard Rorty, *Contingency, Irony and Solidarity* (Cambridge: Cambridge University Press, 1989); Judith Butler, "Performative Agency," *Journal of Cultural Economy* 2, no. 2 (2010): 147–161.

26 Ibid.

27 James Brassett, "British Comedy, Global Resistance: Russell Brand, Charlie Brooker, and Stewart Lee," *European Journal of International Relations* 22, no. 1 (2016): 168–191.

Contents

Decoloniality

(Re)making worlds

Jacquelin Kataneksza, L.H.M. Ling, and Sara Shroff

This chapter introduces decoloniality and its implications for global governance. We explain: (1) *what* decoloniality is, (2) *how* it differs from post-coloniality, and (3) *why* we should decolonize. By way of demonstration, we focus on three types of global institution that prevail in contemporary life and on which decoloniality brings much to bear: International relations (IR), liberal capitalism, and modern love. Each of these institutions conveys a colonial narrative that tells us how to act (power), what to think (knowledge), and who to be (being). Decoloniality urges greater justice, not just efficacy, in international organization and global governance.

What is decoloniality?

Decoloniality targets the modernity/coloniality complex: That is, a myth that propagates a particular understanding of progress and rationality for human emancipation but which, at the same time, rationalizes genocidal violence by the "Western Self" against all "Others" (we cease using quotation marks for these terms, including "Rest," after this point to simplify the text. But the reader should consider these terms as always contingent). Here, global capitalism plays an integral role. Its colonial undertaking begins in the fifteenth century with the *conquistadores*' so-called discovery of the so-called New World. Europe's competition for Asia's lucrative spice trade compelled various adventurers, not least Christopher Columbus, to search for alternative routes not dominated by Arabs, Chinese, Gujaratis, Jews, Khotanese, Mongols, Muslims, Persians, Sogdians, Turks, and other well-worn travelers from Central-South Asia and the Indian Ocean along the ancient Silk Roads (1–15 CE). Columbus happened on a landmass initially mistaken for "India" but soon realized it offered a whole new terrain of land, people, and resources to exploit. A duality of enlightenment and barbarity ensued and prevailed as the dominant form of global governance. Under the guise of "helping" Others, the European Self perpetrated almost five centuries of chattel slavery, colonialism/settler colonialism, and religious conversion. For the Western victors of World War II, this legacy consolidated a new system of global governance: That is, a postwar program of internationalizing liberal capitalism as "development," especially during the Cold War rivalry between American capitalism and Soviet socialism. Thereafter, the demise of the Soviet Union in 1989 projected liberal–capitalist development, now reframed as "neoliberal globalization," to universal legitimacy and the core of contemporary global governance. In sum, the twentieth century may have dismantled colonialism's juridical–political institutions but, as this chapter will show, its system of governance prevails and the power relations that come with it.

Note, for example, how dominant renditions of power, knowledge, and being internalize and institutionalize coloniality. Colonial power rationalizes a hierarchy of superiority versus inferiority whereby the West always supersedes the Rest. Erasing millennia of intellectual—not to mention substantive—interactions between these designated polarities, colonial knowledge commits "epistemicide" by training generations to think and act from a Eurocentric center only. A coloniality of being emerges: It entitles the colonizer to a certainty and completeness of Self that permits "prediction and control"—that is, the Self-proclaimed authority to predict and control Others in the colonizer's image—as a method of social science. For the subaltern, in contrast, a coloniality of being reduces subjectivity to a condition of non-being or liminality that often leads to a fractured existence (typically, through mimicry of the West like neoliberal development) and/or annihilation (today, primarily through global terrorism). In other words, coloniality does not grant the subaltern any terms of *self*-reference. The subaltern can only reflect or react to the West. Lost in this vast desert of modernity/coloniality, the subaltern parches for a sense of humanity that never comes. A trifecta of coloniality results: Identity atomizes into false enclosures of racialized identities associated with colonial classifications of gender, class, sexuality, nationality, and religion; survival depends on a capitalist economics of competition, war, occupation, exploitation, and extraction; and knowledge divides into irreconcilable binaries like Self versus Other, developed versus developing, civilized versus barbarian.

Decoloniality seeks to dismantle this complex and its form of global governance. It does so from a multidirectional/intersectional perspective articulated by, from, and for the Other. These urge a rereading of all kinds of center, margin, and border that police them, thereby dissolving the "complex discursive, historical and epistemological interventions that [have] created the present-day racialized, hegemonic, patriarchal and capitalist world order."[1] In forwarding Other thoughts, reasonings, knowledges, and imaginations, decoloniality seeks to remake the world.

A "radical exteriority" thus characterizes decolonial thought:

[It] rehumaniz[es] the world [by] breaking hierarchies of difference that dehumanize subjects and communities and that destroy nature, and [produce] counter-discourses, counter-knowledges, counter-creative acts, and counter-practices that seek to dismantle coloniality and to open up multiple other forms of being in the world.[2]

Still, decolonial thought is neither new nor uncritical of precolonial historicity. Decoloniality reflects and supports a range of Western and non-Western critiques broadly construed as subaltern studies. These include but are not limited to critical race studies, Chicana feminism, First World/Third World feminisms, indigenous studies, queer theories, trans studies, as well Asian-Andean-Afrocentric philosophies, and critical Islamic feminist studies. What is new, and far overdue, is the application of decolonial thought to forms of, and ways of thinking about, international organization and global governance.

Decoloniality as praxis furthers this momentum. Political movements include the Zapatistas in Mexico, Black Lives Matter, indigenous rights throughout the globe, and the establishment of decolonial universities in Africa. The African Leadership University in Mauritius, for example, seeks to ground its curricula and university structure in decolonial theory. The university will open source data to students by 2019; teach non-English texts as part of university curricula; engage with non-textual sources of histories, cultures, and beliefs; and foster epistemic collaborations across the global South. Global governance could learn from these endeavors.

How does decoloniality differ from post-coloniality?

Decoloniality and post-coloniality complement each other, albeit with some internal tensions. Each offers a counter-narrative to the Eurocentric hegemonic world order and its social, cultural, and structural hierarchies. Both seek another kind of knowledge production and world making that shifts from the insularity of Europe to beyond the modernity/coloniality complex.

To decolonial theorists, however, post-coloniality remains implicated in the modernity/coloniality complex. *Post*-coloniality comes into being by recognizing the role of subalterns in constructing coloniality. In so doing, post-colonialists do not just make subalterns complicit in their own subjugation, as some have charged, but rather they highlight subaltern *agency*. In recognizing that colonizers do not make the world alone, postcolonial theorists open cognitive and political space to identify "Third World difference" within and outside the West (e.g., First World/Third World feminisms), accounting for concepts like "hybridity," "gnosis," and "thirdspace."

Decoloniality expands on this postcolonial disruption. It enables subalterns to dialogue, disagree, and dismantle the old so as to reimagine and reconstruct the new. In this way, the world (re)gains access to multiple means of, and modes to, decolonized knowledge production. We discover not just the legitimacy but also relevance of ancient yet lived traditions like Andean *pachamama* or African *Ubuntu* or the subcontinent's *Bhagavad Gita* or Confucian *ren*. These worldviews no longer sit in dusty corners of "ancient philosophy," of interest only to the romantic or the eccentric; rather, they give us insight into how millions outside the West live, learn, love, and die.

Sample topics include decolonial love, Afrocentric *epistemes*, and an alternative genealogy of modernity. These address contemporary conditions such as white supremacy, antiblackness, gendered and sexual violence, orientalism and Islamophobia, neocolonialism, and settler colonialism.

A decolonial *episteme* does not, however, reject the West or seek to replace it. Rather, decoloniality by its very hybrid and interstitial nature aims to realign Eurocentric and subaltern knowledges so they can mutually engage and evolve. In this way, decolonials envision a "world of multiple worlds."

Why should we decolonize?

Decoloniality helps to achieve greater equity and justice in this world-of-worlds. To demonstrate, we draw on decolonial analyses of the three prevailing global institutions mentioned at the outset of this chapter: IR, liberal capitalism, and modern love. How we construct the world provides an overall context for global institutions and their management. Theories of IR—especially those of international organization and global governance—seek to persuade why one approach matters more than another. Here, we compare decoloniality to four main schools: Realism, liberalism, Marxism, and constructivism. These relate to the economy as well: Not only does the global economy bolster political relations but also material structures and interests *account* for them. "Development" as a program of "empowerment" and "progress" encapsulates this relationship. Without addressing the materiality of ideology, as well as the ideology of materiality, decolonial analyses cannot pinpoint the heart of the modernity/colonial complex. Towards this end, decoloniality addresses one indispensable element: Modern love. After all, what is all this colonial striving *for* were it not for a promise? That is, the modernity/colonial complex can ensure the colonizer's attainment of desire without suffering any undue taxations of conscience. And modern love fits the bill perfectly.

We begin with IR.

International relations

Conventional analysts take IR at face value. Realists view world politics as a set of billiard-ball states, constantly bumping (warring) against one another; liberals see market relations as tempering and binding political relations, thereby instituting peace through systemic equilibria; Marxists target transnational elites who gouge the world of people and resources for short-term gains and long-term revolution; constructivists examine rules and rule, in some cases, ideas and identities, that make the world what it is.

Decolonials highlight what's *behind* world politics: That is, the sociocultural and material infrastructure that enables certain kinds of power and politics, ideas and institution. For instance, a decolonial analysis of IR notes the embeddedness of world politics in hypermasculine Eurocentric whiteness (HEW). *Hypermasculinity* refers to an ideology that denigrates anything smacking of the feminine: For example, intellection, welfare, compassion. *Eurocentrism* regards all things European—people, customs, languages, institutions, philosophies, even fashions and lifestyles—as definitive of "civilization." *Whiteness* reflects a racialized order of privilege and entitlement derived from all the above. An ideology more than biology, HEW can enthrall non-Western compradors as much as the Western Self. By the same token, HEW can repel its key constituency—so-called "white males"—as much as decolonized Others who seek a more emancipated world politics.

HEW contests key IR assumptions. The very conception of states as non-cognitive, self-contained billiard balls warrants asking: Who can afford to remain so blind and for so long? Not women and other subordinates who must pick up the pieces after the "billiard balls," usually led by elite men, damage one another. Similarly, to whose "invisible hand" does the market respond? Not those who serve the market more than benefit from it. Whose racism, caste-ism, sexuality, and class remain after a revolution, especially when the revolutionaries merely replace the power elite rather than interrogate it? And even if they interrogate it, as Maoists did during the Cultural Revolution, who can afford not to pay the consequences? Not those intellectuals, critics, dissidents, or "social deviants" who would challenge the regime in any case. And whose rule and rules, not to mention ideas and identities, prevail when multiple worldviews contend? Not those that have been erased.

Recognizing HEW in world politics begins to decolonize IR and with it systems of international organization and global governance. In foregrounding the global infrastructure already in place to sustain coloniality in world politics, HEW repudiates any analytical binaries or hierarchies. It focuses on those who must pick up the pieces in addition to those who break worlds through war; those who toil for the global political economy not just command it; those who interrogate/challenge a new power elite not just populate it; and those whose *epistemes* have been erased so others could make the rules to rule. In brief, HEW highlights what IR denies yet relies on intimately to survive: That is, the marginalized, the exploited, the inconvenient, and the multiple.

Decolonial analysis of IR's longtime partner, liberal capitalism, detoxifies world politics in a similar fashion.

Liberal capitalism

A *coloniality of economics* focuses on marginalized and racialized populations (wo/men, non-normative genders, and queers). It targets the production and permeation of coloniality in economic structures, values, and lives. Drawing on queer economics and decolonial feminism, decolonial feminist economics further identifies a *coloniality of gender*. It intersects contending orders of racialized identities, gender, class and sexuality alongside an *a priori* binary of humans and non-humans. All operate within colonial hierarchies known conventionally as "economics" or "development."

Decolonial feminist economics challenges four main assumptions: Land/property as possession and consumption; development as ideal or desirable; white women's liberation as empowerment; and heterosexuality as normal and natural. In so doing, decolonial feminist economics dismantles universal, legitimate, secular, rational, and natural sites of empowerment. Property thus need not mean ownership; development, progress; empowerment, moneymaking and capitalist waged labor; and sexuality, hetero-patriarchal, nuclear familymaking and marriage.

Binaries collapse and the coproduction of value becomes apparent. Connections and complicities appear between the human and non-human, masculinity and femininity, gay/straight/trans, rich and poor, economics and affect. None could exist without its other. The affective/emotional, for example, informs how we organize our economic lives; economics, in turn, deeply structures how we perceive land, labor, love, and life.

Nowhere is this more evident than in decolonial *exposés* of modern love.

Modern love

A key subplot of the popular film *The King and I* (1956) involves modern love. This model of love refers to free choice in marital partners rather than submitting to the dictates of parents or other authority figures. In the film, a young couple falls in love but they may not marry. They are in the court of King Mongkut of Siam in the early 1860s and subject to various social prohibitions. The lovers decide to run away together one night but are soon caught. The enraged king wants to punish them for violating his court's protocol—until Anna, the English governess hired to teach his children "modern" (Western) ways, intervenes. She pleads on the couple's behalf, introducing the king and his court to the exceptional notion of modern love. They have a right, she argues, to love and marry whom they please. This is what civilized people do!, she declares. The king reconsiders. (A less racist version of this film aired in 1999 but it did not achieve the same level of commercial or critical success as the original.)

Like liberal capitalism, the film underscores the barbarity of no free choice. It does not consider the possibility that other modes of love and being loved could share equal validity or even desire. For example, different contexts may require different arrangements such as polyandry in female-scarce locations. In insisting that all peoples from all places in all types of circumstance must adhere to the "civilized" standard of free choice in love and marriage, we see the coloniality of modern love.

It's "racist love," some Asian-American scholars assert. It sets up a racialized hierarchy of a "good" Other to counter and contain its "bad" counterpart: For example, Stepin Fetchit versus the "hostile black stud"; Hollywood's Tonto and Cochise versus "savage, kill-crazy Geronimo"; the Cisco Kid and Pancho versus "mad dog General Santa Ana"; Charlie Chan and his Number One Son versus Fu Manchu and the Yellow Peril. Female stereotypes abound also: Mammy versus "the angry black woman"; Pocahontas versus "the squaw"; "the maid" versus "the Latina slut"; and "lotus blossom baby" versus "the dragon lady." Each "good" Other assimilates into white society whereas the "bad" Other fails to do so because of inadequacies of personality or will.

These juxtapositions reveal the *economics* of modern love. That is, love in general under liberal capitalism tends to colonize the Other for the benefit of the Self but this becomes especially so for racialized minorities. As many critical and post-colonial scholars have shown, people (especially women) and places (especially Third World sites) become proxies for each other. For example, *King Solomon's Mines* (1885), a popular British adventure novel, opens with a description of an African landscape that takes on features of a woman's anatomy, thereby feminizing Africa and reifying African women. Or, a woman symbolizes a place, rendering both subject to manly conquest by HEW. A notable example comes from the film *The Quiet American* (2005), based on Graham Greene's 1955 novel by the same title. When Pyle, the white American male of the title, first meets and becomes besotted with the Vietnamese mistress of his British friend, Fowler, another white male, we hear Fowler's voiceover: "I should have realized how saving a country and saving a woman would be the same thing to someone like Pyle."

Colonial love, in short, reflects its origins. Like the colonial enterprise, colonial love establishes a system of social reproduction. It centers on possession and consumption, conquest and desire, masculine privilege and feminized, sexualized exploitation. Along similar lines, colonial love shapes ideas of and for international organization and global governance.

Decolonial analysis offers alternative modes of love and loving, thought and thinking. We illustrate with three precolonial sources: *Ubuntu*, Confucianism, and Sufi Islam.

Ubuntu love

Ubuntu speaks to the very essence of being. Coming from the southern African philosophy of humanism, *Ubuntu* posits that: "I am because we are, and since we are, therefore I am." A person becomes human only through interactions with others. A dynamic co-creation between selves and others necessarily infuses *Ubuntu* subjectivity. This mutual enjoinment collapses binaries and hierarchies of dominance and deficit, knowing and unknowing, inherent in the modernity/colonial complex. *Ubuntu* motivates not just empathy for fellow human beings but also a fundamental recognition of what it takes to be human in the first place.

In this way, *Ubuntu* resists alienating others, including the non-human, natural world. As a site of decolonial love, *Ubuntu* points to an alternative, emancipatory way of being. It shifts away from antagonistic and dichotomous social relations of coloniality to a space of possibility for Afrocentric considerations and beyond. By focusing on co-constructed and jointly mediated understandings of Self and the world, *Ubuntu* disrupts and decolonizes dominant narratives that have long silenced alternative ways of being and knowing.

Confucian love

Devotion characterizes Confucian love. It spans time and space by establishing love as a *karmic* encounter across multiple, reincarnated lives. If, for some reason, the love does not succeed in one lifetime (say, one dies before the other), then Confucian love posits that the two lovers will meet and fall in love again in the next life as they had in previous ones. Confucian love manifests most distinctively in the sacrifice of oneself for the benefit of the beloved. This seemingly negative attribute stems from a positive appreciation: That is, *respect* rather than conquest or desire.

We note, for example, this dialogue from a Chinese television drama, "The Legend of Miyue" (*Miyue Zhuan*, 2014).[3] The heroine, Miyue, is beginning to recognize a more mature love for her childhood friend, Huang Xie:

> MIYUE: Why are you so good to me?
> HUANG: Because you are worthy of my being good to you.
> MIYUE: I must repay you . . .
> HUANG: There's no need.
> MIYUE: I will repay you . . . with a lifetime.
> HUANG (teasingly): A lifetime? Too short.

Far from essentializing gender relations, Confucian love's emphasis on relationality allows for multiple expressions of Self. "The Legend of Miyue," for instance, details the rise of China's first female political leader. A low-born princess (fourth century BCE), Miyue ends up commanding armies and two generations of an empire. She lays the foundations for a unified China later implemented by her great-grandson, the First Emperor (Qin Shih Huangdi).

Confucian love is not limited to men and women only. It also upholds brotherly love as an abiding and meaningful bond. The television drama, "Three Kingdoms" (*Sanguo*, 2010), based on the fourteenth-century novel *Romance of the Three Kingdoms* (*Sanguo yanyi*) about third-century Chinese politics, celebrates the fraternal bond between three warriors: Liu Bei, Guan Yu, and Zhang Fei. It contrasts starkly with the lonely isolation of the epic's villain, Cao Cao, perhaps accounting for his frequent migraines. (Sisterly love appears less often.)

At root, Confucian love stems from a sense of personal integrity. In "Nirvana in Fire" (*Langya bang*, 2015), a fictional account of sixth-century dynastic politics, the hero brings one emperor to his knees and raises another to the dragon throne based on his single-minded pursuit of truth, honor, integrity, and justice. He ultimately rights an historic wrong by demonstrating devotion not only to his family and country, but also his friends, his beloved, and especially himself. During its broadcast, *Langya bang* received half of China's viewing audience, the highest ever for a television drama.

Sufi love

Sufi love promises no less. A decolonial reading of that thirteenth-century poet of rapture, Rumi, reaps unexpected boons. Given its subtleties and nuances about human relations, Sufi love offers an open-ended model of how to act, what to think, and who to be. Sufi love disdains disciplinary boundaries by unifying the head with the heart, the immanent with the concrete, theory with action. For Rumi, love of knowledge along with the knowledge of love integrates reason and unreason, the rational and the esoteric, space and time as well as their contingent space-less-ness and time-less-ness. Instead of comprising opposed camps, normalcy and deviation *account* for one another, thereby signaling an inherent freedom within each.

Here, precolonial love and queer IR share much in common. Each springs from a spirit of exploration, especially of received wisdom, from a position that is multiple and in-between. Like precolonial love, queer IR encompasses either/or (e.g., boy or girl) *and* both/and (e.g., girl and boy) *and* more (e.g., combinations of genders, sexes, sexualities, parentage, states, civilizations). Indeed, precolonial love and queer IR transcend binaries whether these are biological and societal, or metaphysical and spatial. This quality conveys decoloniality in its fullest, queerest sense: That is, "[an] open mesh of possibilities, gaps, overlaps, dissonances and resonances, lapses, and excesses of meaning when the constituent elements of anyone's gender, of anyone's sexuality aren't made (or *can't be* made) to signify monolithically."[4] Together, precolonial love and queer IR envision a less hegemonic and therefore less violent horizon to global governance, *even when* legal protections—like gay rights—apply to those with so-called non-mainstream, plural subjectivities. Put differently, neither homonormativity nor homonationalism can replace, respectively, heteronormativity and heteronationalism. Each on its own merely reproduces the violence of another binary.

Decolonial love, in short, emancipates. Regardless of form, this substantive notion of love as a source of emotional, epistemic, and spiritual generosity enables us to arrive at solutions where none had previously existed. We also see problems in a different light. This requires another mode of learning and teaching that may include an element of "madness." As Einstein once said: "No problem can be solved from the same level of consciousness that created it."

Where do these insights take us? We now turn from decolonial critique to reconstruction.

From critique to reconstruction

Decoloniality offers reconstructive options. To explore these, we first summarize decoloniality's six key analytical features. They are: Situating identities to foreground their agency; voicing alternative ontologies, especially of love to counter colonial fear or anxiety; emphasizing fluidities of play, negotiation, engagement, and disruption in both identity and action; recognizing the complicities and connections between the material with the ideological with the affective/spiritual; targeting the global infrastructure behind contemporary world politics: That is, hypermasculine Eurocentric whiteness; and presenting a "radical exteriority" to remake the world.

Given this analytical platform, what kinds of re-visioning can we launch? Two possibilities include analogizing world politics to a barrel-of-raindrops and political healing as a means of conflict resolution.

World politics as raindrops-in-a-barrel

World politics as raindrops-in-a-barrel liquefy time, space, and being. Fluidities between what is inside and out of the barrel make these raindrops possible in the first place: For example, the sky and other environmental elements (e.g., climate change), ripples that spread horizontally across space (e.g., globalization) or evaporate vertically over time (e.g., stories and memories, prayers and traditions), and currents at the bottom of the barrel (e.g., the past, heresies, the underclass) that invariably infiltrate the top (e.g., the present, conventions, the upper class), and vice versa.

The barrel simply contains the raindrops of multiple worlds. It has no other function or impact; it is, for all intents and purposes, just an ordinary, wooden barrel. This decolonial analogy contrasts sharply with neorealist structuralism. It stipulates a closed system of anarchy and murderous competition for world politics, whereby identical pressures on identical states predetermine ways of acting and thinking, regardless of internal differences.

Within the barrel, sameness (e.g., globalities) and difference (e.g., localities) coexist *and* co-penetrate. The very multiplicity of nodes, ripples, and swirls ensures a mutual balancing that evens the flow. Like real water, the barrel must stay open to keep its content fresh and vital. Otherwise, still water (e.g., hegemony) can turn stagnant and spread life-threatening disease (e.g., global terrorism, ceaseless warfare, famine and other ecological disasters, economic depression, species extinction) through mosquitoes (e.g., corrupt bureaucracies and predatory corporate interests) or some other vermin. Equilibrium disappears, of course, when a sudden storm strikes (e.g., a tsunami or pandemic), the barrel leaks (e.g., "failed" states and other institutional breakdowns), or a cat jumps in (e.g., something totally unexpected like a worldwide refugee crisis). None is subject to prediction or control.

Still, the raindrops swirl around one centripetal force: The heart. Like *Ubuntu* or Confucian or Sufi love, these raindrops flow between a co-created intersubjectivity that cannot divide the physical from the emotional, the familiar from the alien, the Self from the Other. In world politics as a barrel of raindrops, each node represents a world that ripples from a similar heart force. Since multiple traditions and practices of intimacy pertain in multiple worlds, the heart not only makes spirituality possible in world politics but also *undeniable*.

A critical reader could ask: "Where lies the heart in a plain old barrel?" How could enlightenment take place in a system that seems devoid of biology? Here, the analogy relies on an alternative ontological resource from the fourth century BCE: Daoism. It respects water *as if* the latter has volition. That is, water's transformative qualities ("meekest in the world"/"strongest in the world") come from an inherent integrity and agency ("[water] benefits everything," "[it] dwell[s] in places loathed by the crowd"). For this reason, water not only reflects but also enables the *dao* (the way).

Like the human body, the barrel of raindrops encases a multitude of life forces operating in dynamic tension. *Ayurvedic* medicine from the Asian subcontinent refers to these energy vortices as *chakras*. Seven altogether, the deepest, most concrete *chakras* of safety, sexuality, and nourishment connect with the higher, more abstract ones of creativity, intuition, and cosmic consciousness through one linchpin: The heart *chakra*. If left alone, each *chakra* flows naturally and organically into the other, stabilizing and strengthening the whole when and where as needed. Illness arrives when the system suffers from imbalance due to a blockage or an excess when one *chakra* dominates the others.

Such realizations generate another kind of world politics. Strategies for conflict resolution serve as one example.

Implications for conflict resolution

Take, for example, current conflicts between China and Japan in the East China Sea. Both claim sovereignty to a set of uninhabited islets known in Chinese as Diaoyutai and in Japanese as Senkaku. Because conventional IR can only attend to the lower *chakras* of safety, sexuality, and nourishment, hostilities would necessarily erupt and a classic security dilemma spiral forth. Each state would seek to protect or enhance its own security (safety), usually by making hypermasculine-militaristic poses (sexuality) or allying with those who can, thereby escalating everyone's sense of insecurity. Meanwhile, the population's ability to feed itself (nourishment) would suffer, as national security consumes more and more resources, even as the state claims to protect all members of the homeland.

World politics as raindrops-in-a-barrel makes analogical reasoning possible. It would reconceive of the Sino-Japanese conflict in terms of a need for balance between the upper *chakras* of creativity, intuition, and cosmic consciousness and the lower *chakras* of physical safety, sexuality, and nourishment through the heart *chakra*. In this way, the system could regain its former health, happiness, and stability. The fifth *chakra* of creativity, for example, could inspire use of the arts and humanities to broaden, not to mention deepen, sovereign relations among peoples and states. Governments could draw on such legacies to re-appreciate what the supposed adversarial Other has meant to the Self. These re-visions would bypass colonial posturings of hypermasculine border control for *shared* traditions, philosophies, and worldviews.

China and Japan could do likewise. This would put their conflicts from the past one hundred years into a context filled with two *thousand* years of exchanges, adaptations, learning, and mutual enrichment, not least the transmigration of Buddhism. In viewing conflicts as emanating from a *common* body politic, treatment of chronic political traumas would restore a sense of systemic balance between asymmetrical, HEW-defined states, release blocked arteries so much needed flows and energies could resume, and identify mutual resonances to sustain an inter-civilizational, intersubjective love.

From this basis, binaries, hierarchies, and power politics can dissolve. With intuition and cosmic consciousness, world politics may awaken to a new level of consciousness and compassion.

Conclusion

Decoloniality resists and decenters the modernity/coloniality complex. In so doing, decoloniality brings into view erased ontologies and epistemologies, not to mention specific experiences and memories, feelings and sensibilities. These (re)constitute the power behind knowledge production, knowledge itself, and understanding who we are.

By debunking the myth of modernity/coloniality, decoloniality helps us to imagine Other possibilities. Not satisfied with critique only, decoloniality seeks also to construct a world that has never been: That is, a decolonial/post-capitalist one. This new world may learn from a precolonial past (like *ayurvedic* medicine or precolonial love); nonetheless, a decolonial world also builds on the scars of a colonial present full of violence, hierarchy, heteropatriarchy, and hegemony.

With decoloniality, dominant forms of power, knowledge, and being begin to crack. Decoloniality reveals the underlying inter-relationalities that make colonial power possible, exposing the intimate links between hegemon and subaltern, colonizer and colonized, Self and Other. To violate the Other means, essentially, violating the Self. Decolonial references to local and marginalized knowledges also confront and redress the injustice of colonial "epistemicide." The subaltern's epistemic record can now return to its *pre*colonial status with *de*colonial applications. And decoloniality turns colonial subjectivity on its head, celebrating a multiple, versatile, and rich sense of being embodied in subaltern conditions of liminality and mimicry.

We are all raindrops in a barrel. A trifecta of decoloniality appears that comprises identities across received categories of racism, gender/sexuality, class/caste, nationality, and religion; in which survival filters economic production and consumption through a "cosmic consciousness" of awakened compassion; and wherein knowledge is based on epistemic reconciliations. From this basis, decolonials can recuperate from feelings of discontent and unease, at best, and violence and alienation, at worst, induced by colonial world politics.

We conclude with a story. Japanese Zen master Eihei Dōgen (1200–1253) identifies three stages of thinking to facilitate what we would call a paradigm shift: That is, thinking (*shiryō*), not-thinking (*fushiryō*), and non-thinking (*hishiryō*). This practice helps the mind to journey from the conventional to the ineffable.

Dōgen cites this example:

> An ancient Buddha said: "Mountains mountain, waters water." These words don't say that "mountains" are mountains, they say that mountains mountain. This being the case, we should study "mountains." When we investigate mountains in this way, mountains mountain.[5]

Dōgen exhorts us, in brief, to decenter the Self when considering Others, including that which may seem inanimate or insentient. When we think of mountains as "mountains" only, we are prioritizing ourselves—that is, our preconceived notion of a mountain—in our understanding of it. To not think about the mountain, in turn, would erase something that obviously exists. Both cases would violate the mountain. When we perceive that a mountain mountains, however, we begin to relate to it on its own terms and in its own context. We are entering the realm of non-thinking. Much like falling in love, we begin to *experience* the mountain directly and viscerally. In this way, we emancipate ourselves from preconceptions or other normalized ways of thinking. We begin to realize the world as it seeks/needs to be realized—and our (minuscule) role in it.

Decoloniality offers one means of departing from the "thinking" and "not-thinking" of the modernity/coloniality complex. Through "non-thinking" or directly experiencing the world, we may *feel*, not just see, mountains mountaining and waters watering. And with this insight, we may begin the journey, at last, towards a more just world politics.

Additional reading

Sadia Abbas, *At Freedom's Limit: Islam and the Postcolonial Predicament* (New York: Fordham University Press, 2014).

Jodi Byrd, *The Transit of Empire: Indigenous Critiques of Colonialism* (Minneapolis: University of Minnesota Press, 2011).

Grace Kyungwon Hong and Roderick A. Ferguson, eds., *Strange Affinities: The Gender and Sexual Politics of Comparative Racialization* (Durham, NC: Duke University Press, 2011).

L.H.M. Ling, *The* Dao *of World Politics: Towards a Post-Westphalian, Worldist International Relations* (London: Routledge, 2014).

Walter D. Mignolo, *The Darker Side of Western Modernity: Global Futures, Decolonial Options* (Durham, NC: Duke University Press, 2011).

Sousa Santos, Boaventura de, *Epistemologies of the South: Justice against Epistemicide* (New York: Routledge, 2016).

Notes

1 Sabelo J. Ndlovu-Gatsheni, *Coloniality of Power in Postcolonial Africa: Myths of Decolonization* (Dakar: CODESRIA Book Series, 2013), xiii.

2 Nelson Maldonado-Torres, "Outline of Ten Theses on Coloniality and Decoloniality," Fanon Foundation 2016, http://frantzfanonfoundation-fondationfrantzfanon.com/IMG/pdf/maldonado-torres_outline_of_ten_theses-10.23.16_.pdf, 10.

3 "The Legend of Miyue" (*Miyue zhuan*, 2015). See (www.viki.com/tv/27800c-the-legend-of-miyue?locale=en).

4 Quoted Cynthia Weber, *Queer International Relations: Sovereignty, Sexuality and the Will to Knowledge* (Oxford: Oxford University Press, 2016), 3.

5 Quoted Koji Tanaka, "Contradictions in Dōgen," *Philosophy in East & West* 63, no. 3 (2013): 326.

PART IV
STATES AND INTERNATIONAL
INSTITUTIONS IN GLOBAL GOVERNANCE

Part introduction

Part IV comprises eight chapters designed to introduce readers to the role of "states and international institutions in global governance." State-sponsored intergovernmental organizations (IGOs) have traditionally been the main pillars underpinning the way the world is governed, so this part of the book examines the main intergovernmental aspects of international organization as well as the key powers that underpin these formations. As elsewhere, readers should not be surprised to see the prominent role that states and the institutions that they have created play in contemporary global governance. As the chapters that comprise this part of the book illustrate, states and their intergovernmental creations are and remain the central components of the contemporary global governance puzzle.

The eight chapters bring together contributions from leading analysts on the key statist aspects of global governance. As elsewhere in the book, we have designed this part to lend itself to use in a variety of courses. It moves from the largest global intergovernmental organization, through regional associations and broad "groups" of states, to the globe's most powerful singular actor, the United States, and to its chief competitor, China. All classes on international organization (IO) and global governance should take in Leon Gordenker's chapter on "The UN system" (Chapter 16)—the universal-membership and most obvious and largest intergovernmental institutional component of contemporary global governance. This most likely would be supplemented by Mônica Herz's chapter on "Regional governance" (Chapter 18); Andrew F. Cooper and Ramesh Thakur's chapter on "The BRICS in the evolving architecture of global governance" (Chapter 20); W. Andy Knight's on "US hegemony" (Chapter 22); and Shaun Breslin and Ren Xiao's on "China and global governance" (Chapter 23). More extensive investigations into the intergovernmental aspects of global governance might also then be supplemented with the chapters by M.J. Peterson ("The UN General Assembly," Chapter 17), Ben Rosamond ("The European Union," Chapter 19), and Ian Taylor ("The Global South," Chapter 21). These chapters provide important pieces in the global governance puzzle and are essential contributions to better understanding how the world is organized.

States and international institutions in global governance: Chapter synopses

Leon Gordenker, one of the founders of UN studies in the United States and whose own contributions to understanding the world organization are widely acknowledged, begins this part of the book in Chapter 16 with an incisive investigation into the "The UN system." Drawing on his own lifetime of research and analysis, Gordenker frames the so-called system as a "clan," thereby indicating the relevance of the Hatfield and McCoy clashes (a notorious nineteenth-century feud between two families on the West Virginia–Kentucky border that has since animated US folklore) to explain a dysfunctional family of intergovernmental bodies that is anything except what the appellation "system" connotes.

The closest but inadequate approximation that we have to a world parliament is one of the UN organization's six principal organs, and in "The UN General Assembly" M.J. Peterson brings to bear her career-long interest in this body. In Chapter 17, she teases out a series of lessons about the difficulties of having a conversation among 193 member states as well as the benefits of attempting such a dialogue. A talk-shop it is, but the alternative to "jaw-jaw," as Winston Churchill famously noted, is "war-war."

Chapter 18 probes the nature and varieties of "Regional governance." Mônica Herz explores the nuts and bolts of a phenomenon that has become an important building block for global governance, particularly in its economic variant but also more recently in fielding peace operations. She contrasts the idea of regional governance with actual practice, which has returned in the last two decades to the forefront of scholarly inquiry following the preoccupation with globalization. One of the future challenges will be to find a balance between globalization, driven by the private sector and transnational corporations, and the forms of regionalism, driven by governments.

The regional experiment that has advanced furthest—administratively, economically, legally, and politically—is "The European Union," which is the subject of Ben Rosamond's synthesis of the continent's experience with integration since World War II (WWII). While earlier chapters were quick to indicate that the UN is not a world government, Chapter 19 examines the intergovernmental organization that has to date the most supranational features. The award of the 2012 Nobel Peace Prize suggests that, in spite of the ups and downs with the euro and the possibility that members may—forcibly or otherwise—leave the currency or withdraw from the EU as the United Kingdom has begun to do after its 2016 Brexit referendum, there is much to learn from the European experiment that provides numerous insights into multilevel governance.

Andrew F. Cooper and Ramesh Thakur's focus in Chapter 20 is on "The BRICS in the evolving architecture of global governance." One of the key insights from global governance is the critical importance of informal arrangements and multilateralisms of various stripes that complement more formal institutions. This transformation of the map of global governance is especially marked by a new constellation of informal groupings of states without fixed physical sites or permanent secretariats and with an emphasis on intimate intergovernmental interactions. Cooper and Thakur focus on various "clubs" that pool like-minded countries, from the emerging economies in the Global South to the gathering of the world's most powerful economies in the Group of 20 (G-20). They focus particularly on the importance of the BRICs (Brazil, Russia, India, and China; and, more recently, the BRICS with the addition of South Africa), an unusual grouping in light of the diversity and spread of continents, political systems, values, and economic models.

Ian Taylor's exploration of "The Global South" in Chapter 21 sheds light on the longer standing history of developing countries in pooling their efforts to level the actual and symbolic playing fields of world politics. Among other things, Taylor probes the impact on world politics of both the Nonaligned Movement and the Group of 77 developing countries in changing the political and economic agendas of what is usually dubbed the "North–South dialogue," but which often appears to be a conversation among deaf diplomats. Given the diversity of postcolonial countries, Taylor ends with a plea to rethink the idea of the Global South in global governance.

The penultimate chapter in this part of the book deals with the proverbial elephant in the room, US power. W. Andy Knight's overview of "US hegemony" in Chapter 22 probes the role of the United States and its part in constructing an international order held in place by the intergovernmental organizations that we currently have. Drawing on the history of what he sees as earlier hegemons (the Dutch Republic in the seventeenth century and the United Kingdom in the nineteenth and twentieth centuries), Knight examines the substantial body of theory and counter-theory along with the recent historical record regarding the pluses and minuses of US power, both hard and soft, and its meaning for contemporary global governance. The 2016 election of Donald Trump makes Knight and the editors reluctant to forecast the future.

This part of the book ends with a chapter we deemed an essential addition for the second edition, Shaun Breslin and Ren Xiao's "China and global governance." Although China has certainly been a growing factor in changing world politics as a result of its unprecedented two-plus decades of double-digit growth, Chapter 23 deals with the appearance of a major power to confront the United States, hinting at the start of a multipolar rather than a unipolar moment; it explores the roles that China has played in existing international institutions as well as in those that it has sought to create.

Where to now?

As readers quickly see, each of the chapters brings together major pieces of the global governance puzzle. It is overlaying the insights of subsequent parts of this book on the insights gleaned here that enables a better appreciation of the depth, breadth, and diversity of IO and global governance in their contemporary manifestations.

The UN system

Leon Gordenker

The term "United Nations system" figures prominently in talk and reports about what the world organization does, plans, and operates. A quick search of official documents turned up some 140,000 recent uses of the phrase. That seems to imply a deliberately created, harmonious structure, based on unity of purpose, process, action, and result. In fact, those two words cover—aside from the United Nations—thirty-one formal international organizations of state participants. Their expenditures, including the UN itself, total more than $48 billion in 2015. Their staffs include tens of thousands from every land on earth.[1]

That "system" might better be understood as a clan, a loose collection that shares ancestors and goals.[2] Most of the ancestors were established during or after World War II, but a few date back to the nineteenth century.[3] All reflect the organizational needs of a world of sovereign states. Almost all are concerned with cooperative linking of governments and creation of common policies. Only rarely do some directly serve needs of individuals, such as famine victims or forced migrants—and then only with consent of the relevant governments.

Yet the scope of what is termed in shorthand here the "clan" includes all of human life from conception and from birth to old age across the UN system: Good times to social catastrophe; inherited problems to fresh headlines; illiteracy to advanced technologies; icy polar regions to using outer space; arid land to changing global climate; from trading organs of wild animals to protecting biodiversity; and much more. Its products include vast stocks of statistical data, reports and recommendations, training of specialists, and drafting of international law that is binding on governments that accept it. All of this fits with the aims of the United Nations. Almost all clan policies and programs, however, require active application by governments. Their decisions thus underlie the outcomes of clan activities.

As is usual in clans, the UN version includes triumphs; dysfunction; explicit and implicit rules; ability to reproduce; protection of territory; and adaptive mutations. What follows sketches the emergence, process, activity and inherent difficulties of the so-called UN system. So complex has that become that full exploration requires many volumes. Rather, this overview will sketch the tangle of sustained activity that seeks to deal with global issues.

Genealogy, heritage, and construction

When ancestors of the UN clan began to appear in the nineteenth century, the world had begun to use such new technology as steamships, railroads, mail services, and the telegraph. Some governments organized international agencies to set standards to improve services. Two of them, the Universal Postal Union (UPU) and the International Telecommunication Union (ITU), now are part of the UN system. Other multilateral treaties, rather than institutions, represented national commitments to join in, for example, controlling ship-borne epidemics, suppressing trade in narcotics, and prohibiting traffic in human beings.

While governments coped with such social issues, their militaries embraced ever deadlier technology. Its use in the first global war deeply rattled society and opened the way to novel international relationships. This was most clearly displayed in the League of Nations. Of vast ambition in the shadow of failed prescriptions to prevent warfare, the League was put together at the end of World War I amidst the usual political fumbling and human need after military action.[4]

The architecture of the League in 1919 set patterns that still apply in the UN system. Founded by states that claimed sovereignty, the League was no world government. Rather its basic intention was to discover and promote common interests. Its central purpose was avoiding war. Around that, national governments could cooperatively design policies that they would carry out. They pledged to apply international law and to augment it by practice and by recommending lawmaking treaties for ratification by members. The League had little to do with individuals, could not levy taxes, and had no military force. It promoted what in the late twentieth century became known as "global governance" by identifying common problems and the searching for solutions.

The initial enthusiasm for the League of Nations was short lived. Its prestige was fractured in the 1930s by national decisions that led to a war of unparalleled destruction. Despite some lasting accomplishments, governments that had founded it, soon largely ignored it.

Early in World War II, the eventual victors began thinking about the postwar world. Addressing the Congress in January 1941, US president Franklin D. Roosevelt set out broad aims for the future—freedom of speech, of want, of religion and from fear. Known as the "four freedoms,"[5] these maxims defined a wide scope for postwar cooperation. Institutionalizing these aims relied silently, but in fact, on the structural design and experience of the League of Nations, its progeny and ancestors. The ambitions, however, went beyond any earlier attempt to promote and organize cooperative international relations. The eventual victors began using the title, "United Nations," in 1942, and announcing their intentions long before the outcome of the war was certain.[6]

Institutional construction

With World War II ending, new international institutions were constructed at an unprecedented rate. By the time that the San Francisco Conference of 1945 approved the UN Charter that created the central organization of the UN system,[7] plans had already been made and some realized for other agencies.[8] Even before military operations had stilled, a short-lived international organization, the now largely forgotten UN Relief and Rehabilitation Agency (UNRRA), had stretched precedent to bring supplies, shelter and technical advice to liberated territories.[9]

This spurt of construction can be explained in several ways. To begin with, because the UN alliance had defeated Germany, Japan, and lesser allies, it could both dictate the peace and convincingly plan for the postwar world. This was a moment to shape the future, to approve far reaching global goals and to produce means to reach them. Unlike the earlier, diplomatic dances to ensure the future, for example after the Napoleonic wars, or even in constructing the League of Nations, the victors had experienced multilateral military cooperation on a global scale. They could use that in constructing a new world from the ashes of the old. The United States was ready to take the lead. Moreover, there was every reason to think that such an edifice would be popular. And it could include those global institutions that had survived the war.

As in 1919, Washington took the lead in building that new world. This time, however, the planning showed special sensitivity to US domestic politics. Much was done to avert the political divisions that later led the United States to abandon the League of Nations before it was fully organized. Roosevelt and his envoys got backing from the UN allies, especially the United Kingdom, in blueprinting what would get universal accord, notably including the US Senate. At the same time, Roosevelt's prestige supported international institutions as indispensable in maintaining peace. Furthermore, his leadership during the Great Depression of the 1930s and the onset of war powerfully argued for the use of government in building strong economic and social programs.

Yet that did not mean that US-tinted ideas envisaged, any more than those suggested in other countries, that a world government was aborning. Rather, the centuries' old doctrine that sovereign states made their decisions without outside interference would be an enduring pillar of any new international community. The UN Charter, the constitutional document of the new organization, was explicit on the point.

If some momentum propelling the postwar institutional construction rested on the hopes of the four freedoms speech, other impulses came from experience. These had most relevance for the UN specialized agencies that were conceptualized in functionalist theory.[10] It claims that the experts who deal with practical international issues, such as wartime merchant shipping, regulation of labor conditions in mines, or medical protocols to limit epidemics, must leap over international boundaries to succeed. Short-term politics could support long-term evolution.

The experts, it was said, had done so during World War I. They did so in World War II in even more complex supply problems. UNRRA, too, provided an example. Comparable examples were provided by the International Labour Organization (ILO) and some programs of the League of Nations. Moreover, relief undertaken by private transnational bodies—what the UN Charter calls nongovernmental organizations (NGOs)—had a similar character. All succeeded, it was argued, because they had common aims, technology and practice, not political whims. Their practices, it was asserted, would eventually "spill over" from their successes into yet others. Such general acceptance would broaden and reduce international conflict. In short, technologists could build patterns of cooperation that elude the political leaders and generalist diplomats.

However much functionalist notions may have affected enlarging the list of specialized agencies, it did not convince critics. The most negative criticism came from realists, who dismissed this line as neglecting the role of power in politics. The specialized agencies, they held, signified mostly the power of the United States. After all, no government would agree to hand over resources or reduce its influence if that would strengthen its competitors. Moreover, national interests so vary that even weak common denominators could seldom emerge from parliamentary-like debates among instructed delegates. The voting formulas in most of the specialized agencies ensured that majorities would only hide the competing interests. Therefore, anything adopted would not signify dependable commitment. In short, this line rejects the usefulness of searching for general interests of states. Promoting national interests, however defined, was the supreme goal.

Another line of negative criticism came not from the defenders of the state but from its skeptics. These critics argued that the issues assigned to the UN system were too complicated, important, and urgent to be submitted to processes that had already proved lacking. Real governing was what was needed, not this feeble mirroring of fuzzy images. The world needed a global government with a democratic constitution and strength enough to enforce its writ and to cope with the danger of the new nuclear weapons.[11] This government should be organized at once. Some of its advocates nevertheless saw the UN system as a way station. Along that way, the United Nations could be strengthened.

The San Francisco Conference of 1945 took little notice of theoretical criticism. It was busy with approving the UN Charter, the constitutional foundation for what came to be called the "UN system." The UN fitted with the general aims of the four freedoms and the words of the preamble of the UN Charter: The UN system would "employ international machinery for the promotion of economic and social advancement of all peoples." That would help, as the UN Charter put it, to create "conditions of stability and well-being which are necessary for peace and friendly relations among nations" [Article 55]. It presumed that the members would be "peace-loving states" [Article 3–4] that pledged to "fulfill in good faith" their obligations [Article 2(2)]. The model of sovereign states was guaranteed by a prohibition of UN action on matters "which are essentially within the domestic jurisdiction of states" [Article 2(7)].

BOX 16.1 UN SPECIALIZED AGENCIES

[Name, Founding Date, Location]

Food and Agriculture Organization of the United Nations (FAO), 1945, Rome

International Atomic Energy Agency (IAEA), 1957, Vienna

International Civil Aviation Organization (ICAO), 1947, Montreal

International Fund for Agricultural Development (IFAD), 1977, Rome

International Labour Organization (ILO), 1919, Geneva

International Maritime Organization (IMO), 1958, London

International Monetary Fund (IMF), 1945, Washington

International Telecommunications Union (ITU), 1865, Geneva

United Nations Educational, Scientific and Cultural Organization (UNESCO), 1946, Paris

United Nations Industrial Development Organization (UNIDO), 1986, Vienna

Universal Postal Union (UPU), 1875, Berne

World Bank Group, 1945, Washington

> Comprises five agencies:
>
> International Bank for Reconstruction and Development (IBRD)
>
> International Centre for the Settlement of Investment Disputes (ICSID)
>
> International Development Association (IDA)
>
> International Finance Corporation (IFC)
>
> Multilateral Investment Guarantee Agency (MIGA),

World Health Organization (WHO), 1948, Geneva

World Intellectual Property Organization (WIPO), 1970, Geneva

World Meteorological Organization (WMO), 1950, Geneva

World Trade Organization (WTO), 1995, Geneva

Source: UN Chief Executive Board: www:UNSYSTEM.ORG.

That "international machinery"—the specialized agencies that over time would be joined by the UN's own special funds and programs—would operate within a legal framework that respects their autonomy. Their relationship to the UN rests on negotiated agreements that always include reporting to the Economic and Social Council (ECOSOC). Its resolutions, to be endorsed by the General Assembly, are recommendations, not mandates. That applies, too, to the instruction of ECOSOC to promote coordination of the reporting agencies. The clear intention was governance to cope cooperatively with common problems, not mandating what states and their subjects did.

To obtain content and consent for policy recommendations directed to governments, a process is required. The clan employs rich diplomatic experience, which includes countless contacts by official representatives of governments, usually professional diplomats or specialists in international relations, to seek solutions to common problems. In principle, diplomats follow instructions of their governments in participating in international organs. They try to find and decide on cooperative responses to issues that both actors in the clan and governments could accept.

Multinational decisional organs were institutionalized in the UN system. All members would participate in a periodic, usually annual, meeting to determine priorities and give overall approval to policy recommendations. Between meetings, sub-organs with defined assignments provide continuity and topical attention. To help in housekeeping and in providing advice to facilitate the decisional process, the UN followed the precedent of the League of Nations that created the first international secretariat headed by an independent Secretary-General. He/she and staff are explicitly barred from accepting any direction from governments. The Charter gives the office the added prestige of a principal organ.

The UN employs specialized architecture for work between General Assembly sessions at which last-word decisions are made by majority voting. The ECOSOC takes up the reports from the UN system and has the power to react with recommendations, including coordination. The last word on such advice belongs formally to the General Assembly. Both ECOSOC Council and the General Assembly make decisions by majority voting.

Central as is the General Assembly, it nevertheless produces persuasion, not orders, in the form of resolutions that are approved by majority votes. The underlying political logic relies on member governments to make their own choices, developed in their own national ministries, as to how they will carry out the policies urged throughout the UN system. In actuality, such policies are not self-executing and usually require national programming. Moreover, as the UN itself does, clan agencies rely on financial contributions from members and decide on their own budgets.[12] In short, the member governments retain the ultimate, discretionary policymaking and administrative power.

The quasi-parliamentary style from which formal decisions emerge in the UN system cannot assure that recommendations, however informed by expert knowledge, will have a uniform outcome. Membership of some clan agencies exceeds the 193 of the UN itself. Not all governments—perhaps only a minority—have capacities effectively to act on or even fully consider and follow up the system's agendas. Neither is every member government equally engaged in the goals of these organizations in which they usually have equal votes.[13] Furthermore, the organizational agendas tend to grow with globalization and with changing technology.

The effect of national constraints on the UN clan tends to vary according to the specific subject matter of its specialized agencies, funds, and programs. The ultimate goal of maintaining international peace and security, including the possible use of force, connects directly to classical diplomacy. It linked rulers and now governments directly with one another by diplomats stationed on one another's territories.

In current practice, the instructions to diplomats come from their national ministries of foreign affairs, which, in the traditional ranking, are senior departments of government. Thus communications among governments are usually directed exclusively there. The League of Nations followed this traditional model with some adaptations. Recommendations on handling technical problems in, say, promoting international commerce arrived first in the foreign ministries of member governments where priority went to national security. They were then passed along by it to the financing or trade ministry for action or recommendation.

In the UN system, routine contacts between organizations and governments are, in fact, usually determined by subject matter. This echoes a central notion of the functionalist doctrine. For instance, the WHO stays in touch with the health ministries of its members while the ILO with labor ministries of its members. In all-member assemblies, analogous to the UN General Assembly, the relevant minister, usually in person, attends part or all of sessions and speaks for the government. At UN headquarters in New York, member states maintain permanent missions with an ambassador in charge, often aided by specialists. Many also maintain representation in Geneva and Vienna and other UN cities, where several important agencies have headquarters. The missions there, especially of the larger, richer countries, usually include experts familiar with specialized issues. In Washington, the World Bank Group and the International Monetary Fund (IMF) provide for continuous attendance of financial specialists representing member governments. Moreover, some clan agencies station representatives in national capitals to facilitate advocacy and fundraising.

Policies, words, and deeds

However expert the national spokesmen in UN meetings may be, their work involves many controversial choices defined by a political process. For instance, in the International Telecommunication Union, negotiations take place on the allocation of wavebands for electronic communication—the artery system of the Internet and the mobile telephone. The results affect every part of the world and all its population and need execution by all governments.

Typically, the UN system agrees on some policies that governments are *obliged* to carry out. These are formulated as international legal conventions that governments accept as part of their national law. Such agreements that impose legal obligations agreements rely on the proposition that governments will act according to what they have agreed in clan meetings. The long history of such legal obligations on technical issues supports the expectation that most will be reasonably respected and carried out by member governments.

Most decisions only *recommend* practices and policies for governments. They are expected to consider these recommendations, adapt them, and follow them. But if they do not accept the legal obligations, it is only sometimes the crucial point. Rather policy recommendations reflect the majority opinion and in many cases are highly informed by experts. Governments thus can benefit from following them or assume the costs of failing to do so. A veteran diplomat points out that "international negotiations and decision-making cannot be separated from national policy-making on issues coming up in international fora."[14]

Some of the chief officers of the UN system's secretariats, originally seen as mere helpers of the national diplomats, soon found ways to offer impartial leadership on organizational policies and outputs. Beyond providing grease for the organizational wheels, they could offer ideas and knowledge, based on the institutional memories, past practices, and new ideas. As the UN agendas expanded, some of them even originated policies applied by many member governments.[15]

With its emphasis on standard setting, research, and national execution of recommendations, the original design of the specialized agencies offered little capacity for concrete assistance and emergency help to governments. From their beginning, however, the IMF and the World Bank did provide direct assistance to some governments on economic and development issues. And even before they began to function, UNRRA had provided a suggestive model for true international assistance to displaced persons and many countries damaged during World War II. Use of this model led to another line of expansion, parallel to and sometimes overlapping with the specialized agencies.

This expansion was accomplished in the General Assembly. At first, the new agencies responded, as UNRRA had, to emergency needs. Then followed long-term services to governments for the economic and social development sketched in the Charter. This line was eventually expanded as broadly as the protection of the world environment and managing climate change.

Over decades, the General Assembly thus created new and path-breaking organizations based on its decisions, rather than following the narrower pattern of the multilateral, lawmaking conventions of the specialized agencies. Like the latter, the new design also reports through ECOSOC. Such agencies are financed mainly by voluntary contributions by governments willing to commit themselves to cooperation and by grants from private sources. They manage their programs in accordance with decisions made by their own councils of governmental representatives.

"Surviving the war was one thing," observed historian Tony Judt, "surviving the peace was another."[16] Hunger, disease, and displacement that were beyond the scope of UNRRA, which itself was on the way out, grew even while the United Nations began work. Driven by human misery, governments used the new global organization to create the UN International Children's Emergency Fund (UNICEF) and the agency from which the UN High Commissioner for Refugees (UNHCR) evolved. In 1946, these fixtures in the current UN system at first had only short-term mandates to deal with what myopically were treated as temporary needs. By now they link with other permanent organizations with global agendas, such protection of the world environment, industrial development and most recently the needs and potentials of women.[17]

Responding to the growth of the UN membership list and the rapidly accruing theoretical understanding of economic and social development, the UN system was further built up via the General Assembly. Some of these put together programs—all of them approved by the host governments—that engage international civil servants as well as local employees and private contractors. Others use occasional visiting missions or a resident advisor or two to keep in touch with programs on the ground. In particular, the UN Development Program (UNDP) has offices in most of the more than 177 states and territories to serve as coordinators of UN efforts and as what resembles a specialized diplomatic service.

The UN clan now also has a long list of emergency functions, ranging from rapid coordinating responses by the UN Secretariat to disasters, such as earthquakes and tsunamis, to provision of food to displaced persons. Massive food supplies for emergencies are handled by the World Food Programme (WFP), one of the giants of the system. Some of the specialized agencies, such as WHO and the UN Educational, Scientific and Cultural Organization (UNESCO), also provide useful counsel. UNHCR now tries to protect and help displaced persons in their own lands—well beyond the originally closely defined status of refugees. Away from emergencies, UNICEF emphasizes technical advice that reaches for long-term development to benefit mothers and children.

The notion that "politics" and the maintenance of international peace and security could be confined to the Security Council long ago disappeared. Its silent refutation came with a long list of humanitarian emergencies to which UN organizations responded. Practically every peacekeeping venture mandated by the Security Council took place adjacent to large forced migrations, hunger, disease, and social collapse. Beyond relief, demands for reconstruction followed.

Two of the organizations, UNHCR and WFP, have been especially visible in such UN operations in Bosnia-Herzegovina, Sierra Leone, Côte d'Ivoire, Sudan, and Somalia. While UNHCR organized camps and tried to protect the rights of people displaced by fighting, WFP provided substantial emergency food relief and logistics for the system as a whole. Their originally modest mandates have turned into involvement with the threatened lives of millions of people. Moreover, parts of the clan offered specialist help that engages NGO personnel. The broad mobilization of the UN system represents much direct contact with the consequences of violations by governments of human rights and of their undertakings to control the use of violence.

Interlocking agendas and coordination

The names alone of the system's organizations suggest overlaps and complexities. From the beginning the Charter provided for "consultation with and recommendations" for coordination with the other UN organizations. In addition, the Charter opened a rapidly widening door to participation by NGOs in both policy decisions and field. Furthermore, as the agencies evolved separate organizational cultures, some governments sought reduction of the resulting complexity at both national and international levels.

For some UN staff, the word "coordination" summons up visions of ignorant meddlers pushing microphones and cameras into their realms. For others, it means combining talents to achieve better results. It may also offer a channel by which some help can be made available for UN peace-maintaining tasks. Perhaps for all it signified yet more meetings and documents and at the national level more policy decisions. For none meant it hierarchical commands from somewhere on high.

Consequently, a main instrument of coordination—the UN Chief Executives Board (CEB)—came into being through efforts by the Secretary-General and the Secretariat. It brings together the top managers of the UN system with the UN Secretary-General as the presiding officer. His staff organizes the now routine gatherings. Gradually, once reluctant agencies such as the World Bank and IMF discovered utility in the consultations, thus recognizing "that the UN has legitimacy that can help those organizations."[18]

BOX 16.2 UN CHIEF EXECUTIVES BOARD MEMBERSHIP

United Nations (chair)

Food and Agriculture Organization of the United Nations (FAO)

International Atomic Energy Agency (IAEA)

International Civil Aviation Organization (ICAO)

International Fund for Agricultural Development (IFAD)

International Labour Organization (ILO)

International Monetary Fund (IMF)

International Organization for Migration (IOM)

International Telecommunication Union (ITU)

UN International Children's Emergency Fund (UNICEF)

UN Conference on Trade and Development (UNCTAD)

UN Development Programme (UNDP)

UN Educational, Scientific and Cultural Organization (UNESCO)

UN Environmental Programme (UNEP)

UN Habitat (UNHABITAT)

UN High Commissioner for Refugees (UNHCR)

UN Industrial Development Organization (UNIDO)

UN Office on Drugs and Crime (UNODC)

UN Office for Project Services (UNOPS)

UN Population Fund (UNFPA)

UN Relief and Works Agency for Palestine Refugees (UNRWA)

UN Women (UNWOMEN)

UN World Food Programme (WFP)

UN World Tourism Organization (UNWTO)

Universal Postal Union (UPU)

World Bank Group (WBG) [four agencies]

World Health Organization (WHO)

World Intellectual Property Organization (WIPO)

World Meteorological Organization (WMO)

World Trade Organization (WTO)

Source: www.unsystem.org/content/ceb

From its beginning under the spectacular bureaucratic title of Administrative Committee on Coordination, the CEB has served to dispense information, voice suggestions, and bargain about who does what and how.[19] Moreover, its stocktaking functions encouraged the penetration of such central themes as protection of human rights into the programs of individual organizational entities. It helped to inject expert arguments into unprecedented global conferences, such as on the status of women and the protection of the global environment and climate change.[20] New ventures included increasingly operational assignments, such as helping to plan and operate national and regional campaigns to control the spread of HIV/AIDS and providing food for tsunami victims. New operations included increasingly large NGO participation.

The CEB served Secretary-General Kofi Annan as an instrument for simulating the system to fulfill the Millennium Development Goals (MDG). These set pioneering quantitative goals and thus accountability for much that the UN system does. Annan's successor, Ban Ki-moon, hailed sustainable development as a central theme as the successor objectives, the Sustainable Development Goals (SDGs), were agreed in his penultimate year in office. And António Guterres began his term as the ninth secretary-general in January 2017 with the SDGs on his agenda.

All secretaries-general have assigned senior officials to supervise a host of coordination functions. CEB documents[21] increasingly provide insights about how the UN system follows up programs recommended via ECOSOC and the General Assembly as well as in conjunction with some large peacekeeping missions authorized by the Security Council.

Conclusion

The UN clan safeguards the conventional autonomy of member states while offering openings for persuasion but few for compulsion. It is demand driven but always falls short of supply of goods and services. Built around decentralized management, successfully applying advice and operations require coordination from the policy level to the specified consumer.

The history of the UN system suggests a primacy of procedures and parliamentary decisions, which involve a torrent of rhetoric, a mountain of reports, and contradictory agendas handled by a variety of participants in a non-stop whirl of meetings. Overwhelming or not, they reflect underlying global needs and adaptations in trying to meet them. Simplistic claims that the system has been imposed on the world is belied by the changes in agendas and programs accepted by member states. Granted that not all governments—possibly a minority—carry out much of what they have agreed to in one or another assembly. Nevertheless, the UN clan enables some governance—and promises more—in a world that needs organized cooperation of national governments.

Furthermore, organizational layering increasingly connects to classical diplomatic concerns with use of force. Linking UN organizations to peacekeeping missions helps with humanitarian needs and the reconstruction of fractured societies. Beyond that, with its goals of protection of human rights and of development, UN organizations and its collaborating NGOs reflect a groping towards promoting the conditions of peace. However desirable the hopes, they clearly are far from fulfilled. Official reports of the system's organizations and academic research acknowledge less than full accomplishment. Governments provide much of the budget and rail against bureaucracy, complexity, costs, and content; but none has entirely turned away, and all have declined fully to transform the system. Nevertheless, one secretary-general after another has offered reform plans and pressed hard for their adoption.[22]

The last of these major unsuccessful efforts, by Secretary-General Kofi Annan in 2005, also was preceded by agreement on the MDGs. Beside them, the UNDP's *Human Development Report* clarifies the effects of uneven national social and political backgrounds. It was clear by 2012 that the MDG goals would not be reached. But progress, mixed in term of location and depth, has been made. And with a target of 2030, a new campaign for SDGs is underway.

The UN clan obviously is constrained by the inherent complexities of its aims. By now, enough has no doubt been learned to exclude ignorance as an excuse for ignoring goals. Yet each government can add constraints. These include undermining the independence of the international civil services. Others often emerge from national politics, including ideological refusal to carry out particular policies, objections voiced in election campaigns, inability to supply financing, inadequate infrastructures and limitations on speech and enterprise. Thus, while collectively they support augmented global governance, each protects far reaching autonomy. If few show similar zeal in executing all the policies that formally they accept, nevertheless, the clan continues to evolve.

Additional reading

Kofi Annan, *Renewing the United Nations: A Programme for Reform* (New York: UN, 1997).
Mark Malloch Brown, *The Unfinished Global Revolution* (New York: Penguin Press, 2011).
Leon Gordenker, Roger A. Coate, Christer Jönsson, Peter Söderholm, *International Cooperation in Response to AIDS* (New York, Pinter, 1995).
Jeffrey A. Meyer and Mark G. Califano, *The Oil-for-Food Scandal and the Threat to the U.N.* (New York: Public Affairs, 2006).
Thomas G. Weiss, David P. Forsythe, Roger A. Coate, and Kelly-Kate Pease, *The United Nations and Changing World Politics*, 8th ed. (Boulder, CO: Westview Press, 2017).

Notes

1 www.unsystem.org/content/FS-F00–05. For expenditures of each agency, see www.unsystem.org/content/FS-F00-03.
2 Jacques Fomerand and Dennis Dijkzeul, "Coordinating Economic and Social Affairs," in *Oxford Handbook on the United Nations*, eds. Thomas G. Weiss and Sam Daws (Oxford: Oxford University Press, 2007), 561.
3 For an analytic account, see Craig N. Murphy, *International Organization and Industrial Change: Global Governance Since 1850* (Cambridge: Polity Press, 1994).
4 For detailed history, see F.P. Walters, *A History of the League of Nations*, 2 vols. (London: Oxford University Press, 1952).
5 Address to US Congress, 6 January 1941. For full text, see http://docs.fdrlibrary.marist.edu/od4freed.html.
6 At the beginning of 1942, the twenty-six governments then allied as the United Nations issued a declaration that they intended to construct a postwar organization. Other

governments later adhered to the declaration. See Dan Plesch and Thomas G. Weiss, eds., *Wartime Origins and the Future United Nations* (London: Routledge, 2015).

7 For details, see Ruth B. Russell, *A History of the United Nations Charter* (Washington, DC: Brookings Institution, 1958); Robert Hildebrand, *Dumbarton Oaks: The Origins of the United Nations and the Search for Postwar Security* (Chapel Hill: University of North Carolina Press, 1990); Stephen L. Schlesinger, *Act of Creation: The Founding of the United Nations* (Boulder, CO: Westview Press, 2003).

8 Georg Schild, *Bretton Woods and Dumbarton Oaks* (New York: St. Martin's Press, 1995).

9 George Woodbridge, *UNRRA: The History of the United Nations Relief and Rehabilitation Administration* (New York: Columbia University Press, 1950), offers details. Negative experiences are related in William I. Hitchcock, *Liberation: The Bitter Road to Freedom, Europe 1944–1945* (London: Faber & Faber, 2009), Part III. See also Thomas G. Weiss, "Renewing Washington's Multilateral Leadership," *Global Governance* 18, no. 3 (2012): 253–266, for the assertion that UNRRA still provides a model for international leadership.

10 A wartime tract published in Great Britain expertly set out the theoretical basis: Reissued as David Mitrany, *A Working Peace System* (Chicago, IL: Quadrangle Books, 1955).

11 For an argument that this approach still has relevance, see article by Thomas G. Weiss, "What Happened to the Idea of World Government," republished in his *Thinking about Global Governance* (London: Routledge, 2011), 66–86.

12 In 2015, private donors have offered $247 million contributions to the program budgets of clan agencies. www.unsystem.org/content/FS-L00–02.

13 Voting in the World Bank Group and the IMF reflects the size of contributions made by members.

14 Johan Kaufmann, ed., *Effective Negotiation: Case Studies in Conference Diplomacy* (Dordrecht: Martinus Nijhoff Publishers, 1989) 173–179.

15 For further discussion, see Leon Gordenker, *The UN Secretary-General and Secretariat*, 2nd ed. (London: Routledge, 2010), which includes bibliography. Thomas G. Weiss, Tatiana Carayannis, Louis Emmerij, and Richard Jolly, *UN Voices: The Struggle for Development and Social Justice* (Bloomington: Indiana University Press, 2005), chapters 9–10 offer insights of some direct participants in sustaining the international civil service.

16 Tony Judt, *Postwar: A History of Europe Since 1945* (London: Vintage Books, 2010), 21.

17 Articles 1.3 and 55 of the UN Charter set non-discrimination by sex as specific aims.

18 Interview with John Ruggie, scholar and erstwhile senior UN official, quoted by Weiss, Carayannis, et al., *UN Voices*, 367.

19 For revealing observations of UNDP's history and process, see Craig N. Murphy, *The United Nations Development Programme: A Better Way?* (Cambridge: Cambridge University Press, 2006).

20 See Michael G. Schechter, *United Nations Conferences* (New York: Routledge, 2005) and Michael G. Schechter, ed., *United Nations-sponsored World Conferences* (Tokyo: United Nations University, 2001).

21 A vast storehouse with analytic index tools. See www.unsystem.org for access.

22 For an overview, see Thomas G. Weiss, *What's Wrong with the United Nations and How to Fix It* (Cambridge: Polity Press, 2008).

The UN General Assembly

M.J. Peterson

In 1945 the UN was firmly anchored in the world of intergovernmental relations. Although the Preamble to the UN Charter begins with an affirmation that "We the Peoples of the United Nations" are determined to create a better world, it ends by shifting the active role to "our respective Governments," which agree to the Charter and establish the United Nations. While most of its substantive and organizational provisions are fitted to an international system in which autonomous states are the primary actors, the Charter also contains intimations of a world in which relations among states coexist with webs of transnational activity by individuals, groups, firms, and private organizations. Article 41 suggests that suspension or reduction of economic transactions, travel to or from, and communications to or from a state threatening international peace will help curb aggression; Article 71 creates the possibility of direct consultations between the UN Economic and Social Council (ECOSOC) and "non-governmental organizations [NGOs] which are concerned with matters within its competence"; and Article 87 establishes direct contact between the Trusteeship Council and the inhabitants of a Trust Territory as part of the scheme for UN supervision of state administration.

Contacts between various parts of the UN system and non-state actors have expanded considerably over the years, but the General Assembly remains relatively insulated. Non-state actors appear frequently in subsidiary bodies or at "high-level meetings" and "interactive dialogues" on particular topics, but the plenary and main committee meetings remain firmly intergovernmental. This is reflected in the composition of most delegations. Each member state may send a delegation consisting of up to five "representatives" and any number of "experts" and "advisers." Some do use the expert and adviser slots to include individuals drawn from outside government.

While some have appointed politicians, officials from outside the diplomatic service, or other prominent persons as representatives, the typical representative is a career diplomat with prior experience representing the country in UN bodies.

Its persisting intergovernmental character explains why proposals to transform the United Nations into a world government feature either replacing the General Assembly with a unicameral world legislature of popularly elected representatives or using it as an "Assembly of States" paired with an elected "Assembly of Peoples" in a bicameral world legislature.

This chapter contains four sections and a conclusion. The first section briefly examines how the General Assembly has figured in international relations (IR) theory. The second section outlines its institutional design and evolution. The third section examines the General Assembly's role and impact within the current UN structure. The fourth section takes up ongoing debate about how the General Assembly might fit into efforts to make the United Nations more relevant to contemporary global governance.[1] The final section offers some concluding thoughts about the future of the General Assembly and the principal dynamics that are likely to continue to prevail therein.

The General Assembly in international relations theory

The General Assembly has attracted relatively little attention from IR theorists because few outside its halls regard it as having important effects on world politics. Realists and Marxists, emphasizing the political dynamics among great powers or the economic dynamics of a world split into capitalist and socialist camps, have regarded it as insignificant. The post-World War II functionalists expected that international cooperation would take first hold in technical areas and eventually spread to political matters, so regarded other intergovernmental bodies as more immediately important. Similarly, world federalists looked past the existing General Assembly in anticipation of a future world legislature.

Institutionalist and rationalist theorists, including those applying principal–agent analysis to intergovernmental organizations, have focused mainly on the organizations used to manage particular international regimes. Constructivists and feminists are more attuned to Inis Claude's argument that UN bodies provide major forums for collective affirmation of shared aspirations, identification of shared aversions, and collective endorsement or condemnation of particular states' positions or actions;[2] but they pay only scattered attention to the General Assembly. While analysts of global governance might pay attention to it when tracing how new problems are identified and get added to the international agenda, their interest quickly shifts to whatever intergovernmental or private bodies become most closely engaged with addressing the problem.

Thus, most academic studies use the General Assembly as source material for other inquiries. Some focus on understanding how general diplomatic practice or hierarchies among states affect individual states' ability to secure foreign policy goals;[3] others analyze its formal votes to assess the degree of political affinity among pairs of states or track the cohesion within coalitions of states.[4]

Institutional design and evolution

A hybrid of traditional European diplomatic practices and parliamentary procedure was worked out for multilateral diplomacy in the late nineteenth century, and extended to economic and security issues by the League of Nations Assembly between 1920 and 1939. In 1946 the UN General Assembly took up where the League Assembly left off, soon inspiring discussions of "parliamentary diplomacy" or "conference diplomacy" as a distinct form of interstate negotiations.[5]

The traditional diplomatic side of General Assembly procedures manifests in its authority, composition, and distribution of votes. It makes binding decisions only on matters of internal UN organization and operation; otherwise, its resolutions are recommendations. The individuals participating in meetings are delegates chosen by the governments of their states. The principle of sovereign equality asserted in diplomatic practice supports the rule that each national delegation has one vote. Yet in a major departure from the traditional diplomatic practice of unanimity, Charter Article 18 takes the General Assembly in a parliamentary direction by specifying that agreement by a simple majority of delegations "present and voting" is sufficient to adopt resolutions on most questions, and a two-thirds majority sufficient for anything defined as an "important question." This combination of one-state-one-vote and majoritarian decision establishes the General Assembly as an "egalitarian" balancer of the Security Council with its explicit acknowledgment of great power importance in rules about membership and veto rights. However, this egalitarianism remains one of states, not of people; the boundaries of states do not partition the global population into equal sized groupings.

In 1946 when representatives of the fifty-one original UN member states met in London for its first session, it was clear that the General Assembly would have to divide up the work to get through its agenda of global issues and supervision of UN organization, budget, and staffing. Thus, it emulated national legislatures, by working mainly through committees and having rules of procedure designed to balance individual rights of expression with methods for moving the work along strongly resembling national-level parliamentary procedure.[6] Yet even in its deliberation, General Assembly practice maintained certain diplomatic traditions. Speaking time is allocated chronologically, in the order delegations sign up on the speakers' list. This generally limits delegates' ability to respond directly to different viewpoints, and has inspired some efforts to develop other discussion formats.

Historical accident, since coalesced into well-established practice, accounts for another reversion to "traditional" diplomatic technique. Beyond their alliance against the Axis powers, political alignments among UN member states were unclear in 1944–1946. This encouraged use of geographically defined regional groupings of states for allocating committee leadership positions and seats on any limited membership assembly subsidiary body. Although stable voting coalitions did appear shortly afterward—first the Cold War divisions of East and West, and then the division into South and North based on level of economic development—they never displaced the regional groupings as the device for allocating seats. The apparent need to do so was low because the Cold War-induced division of Europe into Eastern and Western groups and the general assumption that Russia and Eastern Europe were "industrialized" meant that the regional groups could be seen as consistent enough with the substantive coalitional divides to serve for allocating seats.

Delegates also shifted the balance between the parliamentary and the diplomatic through practice. After a few years of acting out the Cold War stalemate through highly formalized use of the parliamentary procedures, member governments began to converge on more flexible methods of work. For different reasons, both the Soviet bloc— interested in getting out of isolation—and the Non-aligned Movement (NAM)— needing to maintain a sprawling coalition of developing countries—supported replacing formal voting with greater adoption of resolutions by consensus. In the late 1950s twenty to thirty percent of resolutions were adopted by consensus. The proportion reached fifty to sixty percent by the mid-1980s, about seventy-five percent in the early 1990s, and is now often close to eighty percent.[7] Consensus seeking reinforced the shift towards pursuing detailed discussion of draft resolutions in various subsidiary bodies, working groups, *ad hoc* "friends of the chair" groups or other informal gatherings. Most formal plenary and main committee meetings became occasions for putting governments' views on the record and adopting the sole draft resolution put forward. General Assembly work is thus a confusing mix of a visible formal "tip of the iceberg" and a much larger set of less visible informal negotiations. The intertwining is best presented visually, as in Figure 17.1.

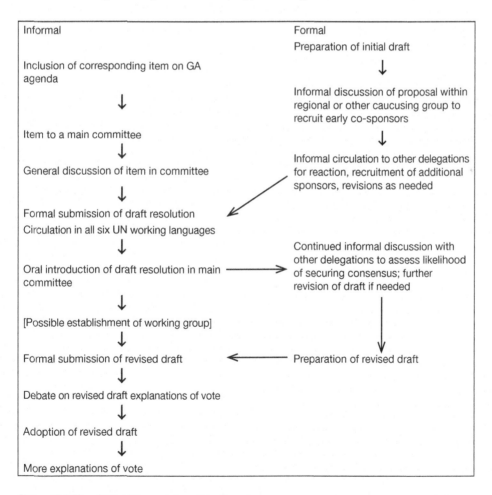

Figure 17.1 Flowchart of General Assembly discussions

A decision to request a vote rather than pursue consensus occurs in three distinct situations: A large supporting coalition wants to adopt a particular text now rather than continue negotiating with other members; one or more member states wants its own or others' individual views placed on the record; or an overwhelmingly large coalition wants to demonstrate that opponents are few and isolated. Only the first reliably indicates that supporters have decided against further efforts to seek consensus; the second and third occur when it is absent or very widespread.

When consensus does not yet exist, the likelihood of reaching it the following year depends on the type of issue. This is clear from Table 17.1, which summarizes the extent of voting in the six main committees and the plenary during the sixty-fourth through seventy-first sessions.[8] When an issue is first handled in a main committee, whether the plenary adopts by consensus or vote depends on how the committee acts. The high proportion of voted drafts in the First Committee (Disarmament), reflects stalemate on nuclear weapons issues. There is less contention in the Second (Economic) and Third (Social, Humanitarian, and Cultural) Committees, with most of the contention in the Third Committee arising over proposals to condemn particular states for human rights abuses because most abusers have supporters reluctant to see them condemned. Dissention is so high in the Fourth (Political and Decolonization) Committee because it handles the Palestinian–Israeli conflict. The Fifth (Administrative and Budgetary) Committee has long coped with the strong divergence between who has most of the votes and who provides most of the money by favoring consensus on budget-related matters, particularly when dealing with the discretionary parts of the budget because pressing for a vote "might lead to a reduction in financial contributions."[9] Delegates in the Sixth (Legal) Committee, regards consensus as essential for success in their work on refining international law. The issues handled directly by the plenary are a mix of very hot political items and very routine matters, resulting in a level of contention in the plenary well below that prevailing in the First and Fourth Committees.

The politics of voting in the Assembly is perplexing to the general public despite strong consistency within the Assembly. Although in most context "abstain" suggests having no strong opinion either way, it became almost as negative a signal as voting

Table 17.1 Proportion of draft resolutions recommended by a split vote, 2009–2016

	%
Discussed in plenary only	13–18
First Committee	40–50
Second Committee	10–20
Third Committee	20–29
Fourth Committee	52–65
Fifth Committee	0–4
Sixth Committee	0–0

Updated from the first edition, based on calculations of GA data.

"no" early in the General Assembly's history. Thus, majorities have been eager to minimize abstentions as well as negative votes when advancing general propositions. All delegates are aware that whenever the total of negatives plus abstentions rises above one-third of the membership (sixty-five of 193 members), support for the proposition under consideration is too weak to start along the path of advancing some new idea by securing adoption of a mild initial expression and then negotiating for incrementally stronger statements in future resolutions.

Conclusions about individual countries' shifts between abstention and opposition depend on their attitudes towards abstaining. Initially, the United States was like most members in preferring to avoid deep isolation by abstaining rather than voting "no" if it would be alone or nearly alone in opposition. In the mid-1970s a stream of elite opinion believing that it was better to vote against unacceptable texts became more influential.[10] This confrontational approach resonated particularly strongly in the administrations of Ronald Reagan and George W. Bush, but has influenced others as well. Today other member states are also willing to cast a sole "no" vote; in recent sessions these have included Bolivia, India, Turkey, and Zimbabwe. On the whole, however, governments prefer to avoid casting isolated no votes.

The General Assembly has grown from a body composed of fifty-one delegations adopting 113 resolutions on about that many agenda items in 1946–1947 to a body composed of 193 delegations addressing 173 agenda items and adopting 309 resolutions plus 154 decisions in 2015–2016. The resulting increase in time pressure has forced other changes in General Assembly practice. Time saved by agenda-pruning measures, including the grouping of related items and taking up some longstanding issues every other or every third year, has been modest. Some issues are raised every year because enough members insist, and this generally reflects coalition-maintenance dynamics that make it hard for the NAM and G-77 (Group of 77 developing countries) to define priorities within their own agendas.[11] This has forced the assembly to seek other remedies.

Multiple simultaneous meetings has not been one of them. The tiniest delegations, numbering four or fewer, cannot hope to cover all simultaneous meetings, but the small delegations of ten to fifteen have been able to limit how many meetings occur at the same time. Yet even with the practice that only three of the main committees meet at the same hour on any given day, the greater reliance on subsidiary bodies reporting to the main committees and informal discussions outside formal meetings increases the time pressure. This procedure gives significant advantages to those member states able to send larger delegations and assign personnel to meetings according to their individual areas of expertise. Smaller delegations typically cope by selecting a limited set of issues for constant attention while taking cues from their regional or caucusing group on others.

Time pressure has also led the General Assembly to carve out more meeting time. In the 1970s it found more time within the thirteen-week regular session by returning to a practice, lost in early sessions, of starting meetings promptly. It has also expanded meeting time by adding days to formal sessions. The UN Charter provides for convening "Special Sessions," while resolution 377(V) established a procedure for short-notice, "Emergency Special Sessions." Special Sessions continue to be convened occasionally, but there have been no Emergency Special Sessions, other than initiation and occasional continuation of the Tenth Emergency Special Session on Palestine, since 1982. The General Assembly now favors sponsoring "high-level meetings" or "global summits" coinciding either with the approximately two weeks of plenary general debate that start a regular session in mid- to late September to take advantage of the presence of heads of state, heads of government, and foreign ministers, or during the resumed sessions that have existed since 2003. Convening "regular resumed sessions" in the spring began as a way to hold an organizational meeting in June to elect the General Assembly president, vice presidents, and main committee chairs for the next regular session. In 2005, General Assembly resolution 59/313 specified that resumed sessions would include special meetings on whatever had been selected as the main theme for the session, completion of the Fifth Committee's work, a few plenary meetings, election of officers, and election of states to the Security Council and the ECOSOC.

Any stable coalition of member states holding two-thirds of the votes can control the General Assembly and use it to shape global discourse or influence the course of particular conflicts by supporting or condemning participants. Two such coalitions have existed in the assembly's history: The US-led coalition from 1947 through 1960, and the Third World coalition prevailing since the mid-1960s influx of new member states following decolonization. The US-led coalition (including at the outset states from Latin America) did not experience a dramatic falling out; it was gradually superseded as the newly independent states joining the UN in the 1960s swelled the ranks of the NAM (focused originally on political issues) and the G-77 (focused on economic issues) that constituted the "Third World" and more recently called the "South" or the "Global South." The Soviet bloc was able to escape isolation in the General Assembly by siding with the NAM and G-77 against the West. However, the revolutionary optimism of the 1970s was replaced by a loss of confidence in the 1980s as its economy stagnated and the Soviet Union found itself as mired in an unsuccessful foreign war in Afghanistan as the United States had been in Vietnam in the early 1970s. The collapse of the Soviet bloc in 1989–1991 meant that the South–North divide became the primary cleavage in the General Assembly.

Even before the Third World coalition acquired the two-thirds majority to control it, the Cold War had affected the General Assembly's position relative to the Security Council. In the original Charter design, the Security Council was the central body for coordinating responses to threats to international peace and security, while the General Assembly was the central forum for developing broad rules for the conduct of world politics. However, the Cold War meant stalemate in the Security Council. While in 1950 the US-led coalition pioneered using the General Assembly to provide a UN mandate for member action in a crisis with resolution 377 (V), "Uniting for Peace," the Soviets were equally willing to use the assembly in 1956 when British and French vetoes would have stymied Security Council action in the Suez crisis. Yet, as East and West generally preferred, the Security Council remained the primary authorizer of peacekeeping operations. Continuing disagreement among the five permanent members (P-5)—which became even more complex when the People's Republic of China replaced the Republic of China in 1971—limited Security Council approval to neutral truce observation and mediation missions.

The end of the Cold War changed dynamics in the Security Council. The unanimity with which Saddam Hussein's invasion of Kuwait was condemned and joint action to force Iraqi withdrawal endorsed in 1990 began an era when the leading powers were readier to use the Security Council as a forum for agreeing on how to deal with crises. This inspired much optimism and commentary on how collective security might be revived or the UN move from peacekeeping to peace enforcement. Even as events of the mid- and late 1990s eroded the post-Kuwait euphoria, the P-5 kept matters within the Security Council, either to settle on doing nothing, or watching while one or more member states bypassed the UN altogether. Both have helped intensify developing countries' insistence that the General Assembly become more prominent, although this has not yet resulted in G-77 or NAM use of resolution 377(V) to take charge of any situation of armed conflict.

Current role and impact

The perceived gap between what the General Assembly might be and what it is has made "revitalizing" the General Assembly a longstanding concern, one addressed by five separate *ad hoc* committees since the early 1950s.[12] Discussions in the fifth of them, the Ad Hoc Working Group on Revitalization, are now well into their second decade. Most of the current suggestions address familiar ideas like reducing the agenda by focusing on fewer issues, adopting fewer resolutions, and pruning the verbiage of those adopted. These have had little effect. Some newer ideas, like providing the assembly president with a more adequate support staff, organizing meetings in different formats to permit more interactive exchanges,[13] or finding ways to help the smallest delegations cope with the press of meetings, are useful but do not address the core question facing UN member states.

Addressing that question requires the General Assembly's place in the UN organization and in world politics more clearly. The NAM, the G-77, and the Global Governance Group[14] routinely assert that the General Assembly, as the most inclusive intergovernmental forum with the broadest agenda, is the proper place to determine the basic terms of world order. A few developing country diplomats have gone further and argued that General Assembly resolutions adopted under the current, one-state-one-vote should be regarded as legally binding.[15] However, there is much opposition to this idea; many proposals for increasing the role of the "G-193" in global governance involve creating new bodies—a Global Economic Coordination Council or an Economic Security Council—rather than using the General Assembly.[16]

By the twenty-first century, global summits were perceived as overshadowing the General Assembly's regular sessions. Efforts by some members to have the assembly attain greater prominence by sponsoring studies of and meetings about how to respond to the global financial crisis in 2008–2009 were complicated not only by serious substantive disagreements among member governments but also by strong reactions against the assembly president's efforts to steer the discussions himself by organizing a special global summit—even after postponements, few heads of state or government attended—and circulating his own proposal to create eight new global bodies to deal with economic and financial issues.[17] Nor was the assembly able to succeed in its self-assumed task of acting as the preparatory committee producing the preliminary conference document for the June 2012, Rio+20 conference; the Brazilian government ended up providing it through the Brazilian diplomat who had been selected as conference chair.[18]

More recently, however, optimists point out that the Assembly's Open-Ended Working Group on Sustainable Development Goals (SDGs) was able to formulate a set of seventeen broad goals and establish general parameters within which states will define national performance targets in 169 areas of economic development, social development, and environmental protection for the period 2015–2030 endorsed in resolution 70/1.[19] This effort has elicited mixed reactions—some praising it as setting out a common vision of the future with a planning process for attaining the goals[20] and others regarding it as an overlong muddle[21]—but it is being incorporated into UN organizations' work as a successor to the earlier Millennium Development Goals (MDGs).

Some General Assembly decisions about the UN's organizational structure reveal the continuing centrality of South–North differences to politics at the UN. The UN Human Rights Council (HRC)—established in 2006 following the 2005 World Summit's decision to make a new start on human rights issues—has disappointed its strongest supporters by resembling the supplanted Commission on Human Rights. Hopes that having the General Assembly rather than ECOSOC select the members and specifying that selection should take candidate states' human rights records into account were dashed because the seats were divided up among regions in the usual manner. Regional groups frustrated hopes of competitive election by putting forward only as many candidates as they were allocated seats.

The 2010 creation of UN Women, another result of the 2005 summit, consolidating UN activity on the position of women in society by replacing four smaller units, reflected the ongoing tensions between control of votes and possession of resources. Developing countries pressed to constrain industrialized-country influence over the agency by limiting them to less than twenty percent of the seats on the governing board.[22] After long negotiations, General Assembly resolution 64/289 approved a two-sided structure in September 2009. "Normative support functions" are coordinated through the existing forty-five member UN Commission on Women, an ECOSOC subsidiary body with all seats allocated by regional group, while "operations" are supervised by an Executive Board of forty-one members, with thirty-five seats divided among the regional groups and the other six given to four industrialized and two developing "contributing countries" (that is, "donors").

The General Assembly in a world of global governance

Although diplomats instructed to reach agreement necessarily regard attaining consensus as success, many outside regard the General Assembly's reliance on consensus as a sign of failure to move beyond lowest common denominators masked by weak or ambiguous language. The length of the agenda is creeping up again, the pattern of multiple resolutions on certain "hardy perennial issues" persists, and voting on some issues is stuck in familiar patterns because of the persisting symbolic politics, including such bellwethers as the Israeli–Palestinian conflict and elimination of racism.[23]

Some commentators suggest that agreeing to define General Assembly resolutions as legally binding commitments would encourage more focused debate and clearer resolutions. Yet in the political conditions prevailing today, a string of votes along the South–North divide would harden divisions, increase the tendency of industrialized states to cooperate elsewhere, and reduce prospects for effective implementation. Some proponents of increasing assembly authority over UN member states have sought to avoid these problems by proposing that the General Assembly also adopt a weighted voting system in which UN membership, share of world population, and share of UN assessment would be combined to give member states differing numbers of votes.[24] However, agreement to accept General Assembly resolutions as binding seems likely only as part of a more general and now very unlikely move toward world government.

Since the present trajectory of world politics is towards decentralized global governance, the immediate future of the General Assembly today depends on finding a role that makes sense in that context.[25] This search would not require any significant amendment of the UN Charter. Its provisions anticipated many features of contemporary global governance by defining the General Assembly as an intergovernmental deliberative forum overlaying a system of more specialized entities—specialized agencies and other General Assembly-created UN funds and programs—providing governments with focused process managers and sources of expert assistance in addressing problems of common concern. Article 10 gives the assembly a broad remit to "discuss any questions or any matters within the scope of the present Charter or relating to the powers and functions of any organs provided for in the present Charter." Articles 11 and 12 define its relation with the Security Council as one in which the General Assembly takes up broad principles while the council deals with particular disputes and armed conflicts. Articles 13 and 55–58 define a similar relationship with the rest of the UN system. Article 13 authorizes the General Assembly to "initiate studies and make recommendations" for "promoting international cooperation" in political, economic, social, cultural, education, and health and for "assisting in the realization of human rights and fundamental freedoms for all." Articles 55–58 indicate that the actual cooperation will be pursued through the specialized agencies and other bodies. The Charter also at least partly anticipated states organizing smaller group cooperative efforts outside the UN by referring to regional organizations in Articles 33 and 52.

It is now clear that the early references to the General Assembly as "town meeting of the world" or "parliament of man" were flights of fancy. The Charter's language suggests four roles in a world of global governance if governments broke established habits and seriously reconfigured its activity. First, the general debate, high-level meetings, and global summits could function more effectively as sounding boards where governments try out new ideas and listen for responses. These responses might not come immediately, but having some years pass between initial mention of an idea and its adoption by governments or UN organizations is entirely consistent with multilateral experience.

Second, the General Assembly could continue using its convening power to channel the work of hammering out agreements on new issues into appropriately structured bodies able to devote the time needed to assess a situation. And, when warranted, it could endorse and promote agreements that go beyond the lowest common denominator existing at the start of discussions.

Third, the General Assembly could shift more attention to reviewing the results and impacts of global governance efforts, to identify synergies or interferences among them. Although each distinct entity or network is already monitoring actions and outcomes in the cooperative processes it is managing, their horizons tend to be limited to their areas of immediate concern. Such an approach would be different from the sometimes proposed monitoring of implementation of General Assembly resolutions, an idea that is only lukewarmly supported even within the G-77;[26] rather, it would focus on areas for which states have made firmer commitments to action, such as the SDGs. The search for cross-issue spillovers also means this proposed monitoring function would need to be broader than assessing UN system efforts to provide "global public goods," popular as that notion is among advocates of energizing the UN system. Delivering public goods is only one aspect of governance; providing the common normative and operational frameworks within which actors of various types pursue their own activities is the larger part of global governance.

Fourth, the General Assembly would continue to be the supervisor of the UN system's organizations. The assembly leadership was closely involved in revision of the staff discipline system in 2007, and far more prominent than it had been earlier in defining and managing the process of selecting the Secretary-General in 2016 in resolution 69/321.

Conclusion

The political context for redefining the General Assembly's role is not promising. The South–North division—increasingly at odds with the global distribution of wealth and power—remains the primary cleavage among the UN's 193 member states. While evolving, the distribution of capability does not yet align control of votes in the General Assembly with capabilities outside. Neither do the NAM and G-77 comprise coherent coalitions. Although the West and Japan remain primary targets, NAM and G-77 rhetoric is sometimes directed against the G-20 as a whole or the most powerful of the "emerging countries." The G-77 expelled Mexico and South Korea after they joined the Organisation for Economic Co-operation and Development (OECD). Chinese leaders have said that they will not join the OECD, but at least one diplomat from a G-77 country has said that any country participating in the G-20 should also be excluded from the G-77.[27]

Maintaining NAM and G-77 influence depends on keeping the major emerging countries—particularly Brazil, China, and India—within the coalition of developing countries. Without them, the rest of the Global South lacks sufficient capacity and politico-economic importance to have significant weight in the emerging network structure of global governance. Thus, the General Assembly's future depends on whether developing countries continue to accept that the G-20 is a major venue for discussing global economic issues and maintaining ties with emerging powers in it. Alternatively, the developing countries in the remaining G-173 could heed the call of a few—most notably Bolivia, Cuba, Ecuador, Nicaragua, and Venezuela—in confronting the G-20.

The General Assembly remains an intergovernmental body, and the rising powers clearly want to keep it that way.[28] As long as independent states remain the key political units, and governments continue to possess the largest measure of administrative and enforcement capacity, that design is appropriate. The task facing reformers is finding ways to better structure the activities of that intergovernmental forum for a world of global governance. Governments and their delegates should acknowledge that the General Assembly is good for goal setting, but not for determining the precise terms of global governance. They would do well to shift the assembly's focus towards acting as a global assessor of what concerns require attention and of how well global governance is faring in all of its aspects.

Additional reading

Nassir Abdulaziz Al-Nasser, *A Year at the Helm of the United Nations General Assembly: A Vision for our Century* (New York: New York University Press, 2014).

M.J. Peterson, *The UN General Assembly* (London: Routledge, 2006).

Vincent Pouliot, *International Pecking Orders: The Politics and Practice of Multilateral Diplomacy* (Cambridge: Cambridge University Press, 2016).

Joseph E. Schwartzberg, *Transforming the United Nations: Designs for a Workable World* (Tokyo: UN University, 2013).

United Nations Association of the USA published *A Global Agenda: Issues before the General Assembly of the United Nations* each September in 1986–2006 and 2009–2012. Since 1950 Oxford University Press has published the *Annual Review of United Nations Affairs*.

Notes

1 The official record of the UN General Assembly is available in all six official languages; the English version is www.un.org/en/ga. Institutes and think tanks providing some commentary about the General Assembly and its proceedings include the Council on Foreign Relations in New York (www.cfr.org); the journal *Foreign Policy* (www.foreign policy.com); the EU-sponsored European Council on Foreign Relations (www.ecfr.eu); the Indian Council on Global Relations (www.gatewayhouse.in); and the China Institute of International Studies and the China Institutes of Contemporary International Relations.

2 Inis L. Claude, Jr., "Collective Legitimization as a Function of the United Nations," *International Organization* 20, no. 3 (1966): 367–379.

3 Diana Panke, *Unequal Actors in Equalizing Institutions: Negotiations in the United Nations General Assembly* (Basingstoke: Palgrave Macmillan, 2013); T.V. Paul, Deborah Welch Larson, and William Wohlforth, eds., *Status in World Politics* (Cambridge: Cambridge University Press, 2014); Vincent Pouliot, *International Pecking Orders: The Politics and Practice of Multilateral Diplomacy* (Cambridge: Cambridge University Press, 2016).

4 Kisuke Iida, "Third World Solidarity: The G77 in the United Nations General Assembly," *International Organization* 42, no 2. (1988): 375–395; S.Y. Kim and Bruce Russett, "The New Politics of Voting Alignments in the United Nations General Assembly," *International Organization* 50, no. 4 (1996): 629–643; Eric Voeten, "Clashes in the Assembly," *International Organization* 54, no. 2 (2000): 185–215; Michael A. Bailey, Anton Strezhnev, and Erik Voeten, "Estimating Dynamic State Preferences from United Nations Voting Data," *Journal of Conflict Resolution* 61, no. 2 (2017): 430–456.

5 Philip Jessup, "Parliamentary Diplomacy," Hague Academy of International Law *Recueil des cours* 89 (1956): 181–320; John G. Hadwin and Johan Kaufman, *How United Nations Decisions are Made* (Leiden: Sijthoff, 1961).

6 General Assembly Rules of Procedure, UN document A/520/Rev.17, April 2008, www.un.org/en/ga/about/ropga.

7 M.J. Peterson, *The UN General Assembly* (London: Routledge, 2006), 75–77; later sessions calculated from list of resolutions, www.un.org/en/ga/[session number]/resolutions.shtml.

8 John R. Mathiason, "The General Assembly: Addressing Global Problems, Incrementally," in *Annual Review of United Nations Affairs 2009/2010*, eds. Joachim Müller and Karl P. Sauvant (New York: Oxford University Press, 2011), 4.

9 John R. Mathiason, "Commentary on the Sixty-Eighth General Assembly," *Annual Review of United Nations Affairs* 1 (2015), 5.

10 Daniel P. Moynihan, "The United States in Opposition," *Commentary* (1975): 31–42; Daniel P. Moynihan and Suzanne Weaver, *A Dangerous Place* (Boston, MA: Little, Brown, 1978).

11 Lydia Swart, "The Future of the G77," in *The Group of 77: Perspectives on Its Role in the United Nations General Assembly*, eds. Lydia Swart and Jakob Lund (New York: Center for UN Reform, 2011), chapter 7.

12 Sources of proposals for improving the UN include the Center for UN Reform Education (www.centerforunreform.org); Germany's Committee for a Democratic UN (www.uno-komitee.de/en/index.php); and the South Centre (www.southcentre.org).

13 Such as the ten-hour informal interactive dialogue on Secretary-General Ban Ki-moon's report "Mobilizing Collective Action: The Next Decade of the Responsibility to Protect" (A/70/999–S/2016/620) on 6 September 2016.

14 A group of thirty smaller UN members drawn from Western Europe, Latin America and the Caribbean, Africa, the Gulf, and Southeast Asia, www.mfa.gov.sg/content/mfa/overseasmission/newyork/nyemb_statements/global_governance_group.html.

15 Such as Miguel D'Escoto Brockmann of Nicaragua in his opening speech as president of the sixty-third session, 16 September 2008, UN document A/63/PV.1.

16 *Report of the Commission of Experts of the President of the United Nations General Assembly on Reforms of the International Monetary and Financial System*, Stiglitz Commission, 21 September 2009, www.un.org/ga/econcrisissummit/docs/FinalReport_CoE.pdf; José Antonio Ocampo, "The United Nations and Global Finance," *Annual Review of United Nations Affairs 2008–2009* 1: xliv–xlv.

17 General Assembly Resolution 63/305, 31 July 2009. The distance between the Assembly president's ideas and what the members adopted can be judged by comparing the conference outcome document, given in the Annex to General Assembly Resolution 63/303 of 9 July 2009, with a president's draft dated 18 May 2009, www.un.org/ga/president/63/interactive/financialcrisis/outcomedoc.pdf.

18 Transition noted in "Rio+20: 'Encouraging Progress' Made on Outcome Document," UN News Centre, 16 June 2012, www.un.org/apps/news/story.asp?NewsID=42255&Cr=sustainable% 20development& Cr1=.

19 Report of the Open-Ended Working Group of the General Assembly on Sustainable Development Goals, UN document A/68/970, 12 Aug 2014.

20 John R. Mathiason, "Commentary on the Sixty-Eighth General Assembly," *Annual Review of United Nations Affairs* 1 (2015), 21.

21 Bjorn Lomborg, "The UN Chose Way Too Many New Development Goals," 2015, http://time.com/4052109/un-sustainable-development-goals.

22 Jakob Lund, "The G77's Limited Role in the Third Committee," in *The Group of 77*, eds. Swart and Lund, 113.

23 Raphael N. Beker, Arye L. Hilman, Niklas Potrafke, and Alexander H. Schwemmer, "The Preoccupation of the United Nations with Israel: Evidence and Theory," *Review of International Organizations* 10, no. 4 (2015): 413–437.

24 Richard Hudson, *The World Needs a Way to Make up Its Mind: The Case for the Binding Triad* (New York: Center for War/Peace Studies, 1981); Joseph Schwartzberg, *Revitalizing the United Nations: Reform through Weighted Voting* (New York and The Hague: Institute for Global Policy, World Federalist Movement, 2005), Appendix A, 60–63.

25 Wolfgang Reineke and Francis Deng, *Critical Choices, the United Nations, Networks, and the Future of Global Governance* (Ottawa: International Development Research Centre, 2000).

26 Lydia Swart, "Revitalization of the Work of the General Assembly," in *Managing Change at the United Nations,* eds. Jonas von Freiesleben, Lydia Swart, Irene Martinetti, and Nana Yeboah (New York: Center for UN Reform Education, 2008).

27 Quoted in Swart, "The Future of the G77," 154.

28 Bas Hooijmaaijers and Stephan Keukeleire, "Voting Cohesion of the BRICS countries in the UN General Assembly 2006–2014: A BRICS Too Far?" *Global Governance* 22, no. 2 (2016): 392.

CONTENTS

Regional governance and regional organizations

Mônica Herz

While global governance often focuses on activity and institutions at the global level, globalization has led to the disaggregation of the loci of governance, the dispersion of sites of authority,[1] and the willingness to explore issues with an array of different actors at different institutional levels. In Ulrich Beck's terms, such "debounded" transboundary risks[2] as terrorism, financial crises, transnational crime, infectious diseases, environmental degradation, human rights abuses, and humanitarian crises that are not contained by national boundaries must be dealt with on different levels, including regionally. As such, "regions" have acquired an enhanced significance. While the idea of regions was formerly limited largely to academic debates about alliances and economic integration, it has been revived during the last few decades as regions became key to research about governance because norms, public policies, and dispute-settlement mechanisms also occur at the regional level.

This chapter examines the idea and practice of regional governance as a component of world order during the last two decades, a contribution to the debate about the most appropriate location for tasks within a range of governance mechanisms. The chapter begins with some definitions. It then examines in depth the "idea" of regional governance before contrasting it with actual practice.

Definitions

Three definitions are helpful for this chapter: Those of regions, regionalization, and regional governance. "Regions" are the result of political processes and social actors that construct the regions that become building blocks for global governance.[3] Regions are social spaces; they are part of the interactions that generate governance, not solely the stage where this process takes place.[4] The term "region," in fact, originates from the idea of rule as in the Latin *regere* (command); regions provide the locus for the formulation of norms, public policies, and various mechanisms because of decisions by governing elites and other relevant actors. The definition of regions, although typically having a geographic element, can be politically contested.[5] This analysis is limited to geographically defined regional institutions that go beyond national boundaries, while recognizing the possibilities for other broader and narrower definitions (culture or subnational, for instance).

Regions are areas of the world formed by a number of countries that are economically and politically interdependent and are defined politically by the actors that agree to build on the definition of the region, including its institutions. But to think in terms of regions also historically implies a specific geographical space, a cognitive move initially made by geographers in the nineteen century, first by the German geographer Carl Ritter and through the search for common elements such as climate or water boundaries in order to categorize states in a given region.

Regions were relevant in world politics as a space for disputes between great powers and their spheres of influence, but today regionalization usually refers to the intensification of economic and social interactions among a limited number of independent states. The deepening of transnational production networks, the growing share of intraregional trade and investment flows, cultural manifestations, and human mobility forge this contemporary pattern. As activity increases at the regional level occurs,[6] regional awareness or identity may also develop.[7] For example, increased regional activity gave rise to "pan-Arabism" or "pan-Africanism" or to "European identity."

"Regionalism," however, can be defined as a state-led political project to promote intergovernmental collaboration within a defined space. It may involve generating regional identities and building regional political communities.[8] The phenomenon is today widespread. Both spatially and functionally, it is a major part of international relations (IR), both in theory and practice.

Finally, "regional governance" is a wider process involving state and non-state actors and several locations of authority. It is relevant to the organization of political reality, which has resulted in the establishment of regional institutions, discourse, and practice. It is also relevant to the organization of knowledge particularly regarding crucial questions of politics, conflict, and cooperation within these regions.

This chapter explores regional governance mechanisms and the functions that they perform. Governance, of course, involves an array of actors—including nongovernmental organizations (NGOs), transnational social movements, networks, coalitions, and epistemic communities—but intergovernmental regional organizations provide the focus here. They often are the hub of regional interactions and are leaders in the generation of rules, norms, and treaties.

Regional governance

Regional governance helps us to understand the complexity of the post-Cold War era. It flows from the debate about global governance in this volume as well as from diverse perspectives on regionalism and regionalization and has produced a substantial scholarly literature.[9] Governance has become more diverse and fragmented, which demands new concepts; and regional governance is part of a wider debate about who governs what, or from what social base? States, subnational governmental institutions, international organizations, nongovernmental forms of association on different levels—but especially regional—are part of this story.

Regional integration projects initiated in the 1950s and 1960s put regions at the center of public policy debates. Alternative theoretical approaches sought to understand these processes. Proponents of intergovernmentalism, liberal institutionalism, neo-functionalism, and multilevel governance examined domestic actors in order to understand regional integration;[10] meanwhile, economists focused on trade and monetary integration and free movement as factors of production. By the end of the 1980s, analyses of regional integration processes largely reflected a debate between intergovernmentalists and supra-nationalists about the role and format of regional institutions and their relations with the changing nature of sovereignty.

In the 1990s, multidimensional regionalism—involving economic, cultural, military, political, and social forms of interaction—became part of a broader discussion about regional governance.[11] Regional organizations acquired new functions; their projects for cooperation in economic, cultural, security, and other social spheres became interconnected.

As the European project became more robust in the 1990s, the concept of multilevel governance became more prominent in the analyses of this particular regional experience, vying for academic attention with older concepts such as federalism and liberal institutionalism. It was possible to focus on the European Economic Community (EEC) as a political system rather than a process of integration,[12] and to confront multiple actors, processes, jurisdictions, and layers of government. Several authors conceptualized the dispersion of authoritative decision making, which became the dominant political discourse within what became the European Union (EU). Thus, regional governance was viewed as one institutional level in a complex web of governance mechanisms.

Regional governance employs different institutional designs, both intergovernmental and supra-governmental; like global governance, it encompasses non-state actors. The concept of multilevel or multilayered governance allows us to picture the involvement of states, NGOs, informal networks, and activities among academics, researchers, and journalists participating in the production of governance.

In order to understand the idea of regional governance, it is crucial to examine three other processes: The changing nature of sovereignty; globalization; and the challenges to nationally based representative democracy. First, regional governance is closely connected to discussions about the erosion, or at least changing character, of state sovereignty. Regional governing mechanisms often deal with the debounded issues of a globalized world. State sovereignty may thus be limited by the need to comply with rules produced regionally. At the same time, cooperative decision making on a regional basis can also be seen as a way to strengthen the sovereignty of territorially bounded states because regional governance often involves the participation of national agencies in regulation.[13] The concept of meta-governance allows us to understand how, in spite of the emergence of regional rules, the state retains the ultimate decision-making capacity associated with sovereignty.[14]

At the same time, the architecture of states changes as they interact with governing mechanisms emerging at all levels, including regionally. As regional norms are agreed, states adapt to this new reality by creating new agencies, coalitions, forms of intervention, and discourses. At the same time, states need to interact with regional policy networks to build the coalitions necessary to put forward and implement governing and control mechanisms. New forms of dialogue and negotiations take place that demand new narratives and institutional designs.

Regionalism is also linked to the "re-spatialization" of the state that describes the reconstruction of the relationship between social relations and space. Regions as a space allow for the stretching of social relations that are not face to face, but still reproduce rules and resources. As Anthony Giddens writes: "[S]pace is not an empty dimension along which social groupings become structured, but has to be considered in terms of its involvement in the constitution of systems of interaction."[15] This change involves the redefinition of the locus of state power, actors exercising state power and normative-ideological justifications for state power.[16]

Second, the relationship between regionalization, regionalism, or regional governance, on the one hand, and globalization, on the other hand, has been hotly debated. Globalization concentrates on the compression of time and on social processes that transcend space, taking into account the relevance of new actors and de-territorialized networks worldwide.[17] Globalization can be traced back to the sixteenth-century European explorers or to the intensification of the trans-nationalization of production, investment, and commerce since the 1980s that generates the demand for new rules. Regional governance is one way to write new rules in the context of globalization. It reflected porous regions in contrast to earlier regional integration projects of the 1960s and 1970s, which were geared mainly towards the constitution of trade blocs of contiguous countries and protectionist policies for areas of production in order to make them more competitive internationally. In addition, this "new regionalism"[18] involves social processes of civil society and transnational corporations associated with the globalization of commerce, financial transactions, production, and technology.[19] As such, regionalism and regionalization can be understood as one feature of the contemporary neoliberal world order.[20]

Regional institutions can also be a reaction to or compensation for the market forces of globalization. For countries in the Global South, it may appear to promote national interests in a world dominated by the industrialized countries of the North. Several authors view regional groupings in the Global South, specifically after the end of the Cold War, as a positive sign of regional autonomy, facing up to the specificity of the conflicts.[21] Amitav Acharya notes that regionalism in the postcolonial world is geared towards "securing independence from colonial rule and limiting the intervention of outside powers in regional affairs."[22] Resistance to systemic processes can, in fact, be traced back to strategies against great power intervention during the Cold War, or even earlier in the case in Latin America.

Third, governance mechanisms that do not respect the boundaries of the state raise the issue of a democratic deficit. Representative democratic government is based on the notion that a national community has its voice reflected in and is affected by decisions from its duly elected government and parliaments. A very different situation exists in a globalized world in which decisions are made on many different levels with little or no democratic accountability.[23]

International and regional organizations have had great difficulty in tackling this issue. The concepts of representation, debate, and negotiation within a political community, on which modern democracy is based, have found only a torturous route into intergovernmental organizations, despite mechanisms to associate NGOs and to create regional parliaments. Democratic governance,[24] in contrast to democratic government, refers to the institutionalization of spaces for the expression of views in a context in which the state is not the sole focus, in which there is no single player with the capacity to make decisions. The technical functions of international and regional organizations, often portrayed as neutral, can exacerbate the problem of voice. Thus, the rise of the unelected bureaucrats,[25] in particular, raises questions about the accountability for democratic decision-making processes.

Regional governance can be approached through different theoretical lenses. Rationalists stress the role of regional institutions in reducing transaction costs, and in improving transparency and trust; they thus increase the incentives for cooperation in a context of complex interdependence. Liberals stress the role of economic and social interests as they are channeled towards the positions of states in governance mechanisms. Constructivists, in contrast, look to the historical processes of social interactions that change ideas, identities, interests, and preferences and that allow for the creation of regional governance mechanisms. Constructivism takes into account processes of socialization by which norms and values are diffused.[26] Realism focuses on the distribution of power within a region, on the role of hegemons, and the incorporation of regional power politics into a broader international strategy. For realists, governance mechanisms express the actual distribution of power, regionally or globally. Power relations that constitute and acquire expression in regional governance mechanisms can also be studied through critical theory, which highlights the asymmetry of power and the exclusion of un-powerful or ignored voices from governance processes. The notion of "regional worlds" captures the dynamisms of regions—within regions and between regions and the global sphere—and allows us to see regions as expressions but also forms of resistance to the existing distribution of power. It moves us towards a "pluralist conception of global order."[27]

The practice of regional governance

Some argue that regional is easier than wider (especially global) cooperation because a region often is more homogeneous, has greater awareness of collective problems, may acquire a collective identity, and seems more invested in a solution for a specific problem—for instance, migration in Europe or transnational crime in Latin America. For certain issues, it may become easier to mobilize resources or agree on a common agenda because the interests of a region's member states are on the line.

Regional governance is unequal throughout the international system. Regional governance can take place in several spheres: Security, development, trade, financial mechanisms, social development, environment, human rights, and democracy. The levels of institutionalization, the involvement of public and private actors, and the focus and content of institutional design vary immensely, as do the resources devoted to a particular organization. The contrast is striking, for instance, between Europe— where institutions exist for a wide variety of tasks and are complex, well-funded, and robust—and the Asia-Pacific region—where regional governance is far less institutionalized and there is no body for security challenges.[28] Some institutional settings were initially geared towards one sphere of interaction, before moving to other spheres. For example, the Association of Southeast Asia Nations (ASEAN) was created in 1967 to address a security agenda but then moved towards emerging forms of regional economic governance.[29]

Regional governance is intertwined with other forms of governance and, as Peter Katzenstein reminds us, regional institutions were a central part of US strategy during the Cold War, most clearly expressed in regional alliances such as the North Atlantic Treaty Organization (NATO) and Southeast Asia Treaty Organization (SEATO).[30] They were also part of the Soviet Union's foreign policy with the Warsaw Pact. The decline of superpower rivalry diminished their perceived interests in some regions; and strategic competition in distant regions became less important in some regions.[31] The door was open for greater and more autonomous interactions within regions themselves, which were no longer determined primarily by global power dynamics. Moreover, the process of decolonization, which accelerated by the 1960s, laid the basis for regionalization among the new independent countries of Africa, Asia, and the Middle East. This process continued with the end of the Soviet empire and the accompanying territorial changes in Asia and Eastern Europe.[32]

The relationship between regional and global governance also acquires additional traction when we examine the historical relations between the United Nations and regional organizations. Regions were specifically mentioned in Chapter VIII of the Charter, but better cooperation between the UN and regional organizations became part of the debate on the reform of the UN system after the end of the Cold War and the expansion of peace operations by the UN and regional organizations, individually and collectively.[33] The UN secretary-general convened high-level meetings with regional organizations involved in security operations, which produced a framework for cooperation.[34] Moreover, regions have long been the basis for representation within the UN system—for recruitment of staff and for negotiations among states. In addition, of course, there are its five regional economic and social commissions working mainly on development—for Africa, Asia and the Pacific, Western Asia, Latin America and the Caribbean, and Europe.

Regional organizations—along with states and universal UN organizations—are part of social processes through which power relations, the success and failure of previous experiences, and the internalization of rules and concepts permit their socialization and legitimation. Thus, regional governance mechanisms do not have an impact restricted to the specific geographic area that they represent. Practices and discourses developed in one region may have an impact in others or across the international system more broadly. Diffusion of regional governance experiences has an impact not only on institutional designs but also on cooperation and rule building. Thomas Risse mentions diffusion through direct promotion, coercion, positive incentives or negative sanctions, learning, and mimicking.[35] Moreover, translation of experience takes place as they are adopted in other regions or, in Acharya's terms, localization processes are crucial.[36] In addition, global governance mechanisms also function as transmission belts for diffusion processes.

Regional organizations are central to regional governance and may perform a centrifugal role, bringing together private and public actors to focus on a specific

Table 18.1 Regional organizations with multiple dimensions

Europe and North America	Americas	Africa	Asia Pacific and Middle East	Non-territorial definition
NATO	Andean Community	African Union	Arab League	Commonwealth
OSCE	Central American Common Market	South African Customs Union	Gulf Cooperation Council	Organization of Islamic Cooperation
EU European Union	Southern Cone Common Market	Economic Community of West African States	Collective Security Treaty Organization	Community of Portuguese Language Countries
EEA European Economic Area	Bolivarian Alliance for the Peoples of Our America	Economic Community of Central African States	Economic Cooperation Organization—Iran, Turkey, Pakistan	Organisation Internationale de la Francophonie
Council of Europe	Union of South American Nations	Community of Sahel-Saharan States	Commonwealth of Independent States	
	North American Free Trade Agreement	Common Market for East and Southern Africa	Association of Southeast Asian Nations	
	Organization of East Caribbean States	East African Community	Asia-Pacific Economic Cooperation	
	Caribbean Community	Southern African Development Community	Mekong-Ganga Cooperation	
	Organization of American States	West African Economic and Monetary Union	Indian Ocean Rim Association	
	Economic Community of Latin American and Caribbean States (CELAC)		Shanghai Cooperation Organization	
			South Asian Association for Regional Cooperation	

Source: Data reflect information on the official websites of the regional organizations that figure in this table.

issue. A very large number of regional integration agreements, for example, have been generated; the World Trade Organization (WTO) registers more than 500,[37] many with histories stemming back to the regional integration projects of the 1950s and 1960s. The second phase of regionalism is associated with "new regionalism" in the 1980s when the EU was re-energized, moving towards monetary union and a single market with more openness towards world markets. It is also linked to multidimensional experiences in which regional organizations expanded the range of their activities. Other regions followed the European experience, such as the Economic Community of West African States (ECOWAS) or the Common Market of the South (Mercosur), which are forums and actors in different spheres including economic integration, security cooperation, functional coordination, and technical assistance. The process of diffusion explains why these multidimensional regional organizations often perform similar tasks in the security, economic, and political spheres. Table 18.1 suggests the wide variety of such institutions.

Democratic governance is now considered a central link between domestic and international governance, and regional organizations have been since the 1990s moving towards a common agenda and institutional design for the promotion of democratic governance.[38] This process is not homogenous, and the commitment to this agenda varies immensely as well. Nonetheless, regional organizations have created normative devices, established conditions for participation in their activities and decision making, formulated assistance programs, and provided a model for the development of representative democracy and the rule of law. The agendas for human rights and humanitarian crisis management are linked to the broader democratic governance agenda. Regional organizations also have created numerous ways to cope with this new reality, and Table 18.2 lists the range of such measures in several regional organizations.

Table 18.2 Regional organizations for human rights and humanitarian action

International organization	Human rights/humanitarian institutions	Documents and conventions
African Union	African Court on Human and Peoples' Rights	African Charter on Human and Peoples' Rights
	Peace and Security Council	Protocol to the ACHRPR
	African Commission on Human Rights and Peoples'Rights	Convention Governing the Specific Aspects of Refugee Problems in Africa
	African Peer Review Mechanism	
	Coordinating Committee on Assistance and Protection to Refugees, Returnees and Internally Displaced Persons in Africa	
Arab League	Parliament Committee for Legislative, Legal and Human Rights Affairs	Arab Charter on Human Rights
	Committee of Experts on Human Rights	
Asia-Pacific Economic Cooperation	Emergency Preparedness working group	

(Continued)

Table 18.2 (Continued)

International organization	Human rights/humanitarian institutions	Documents and conventions
ASEAN	ASEAN Intergovernmental Commission on Human Rights	Agreement on Disaster management and Emergency Response (AADMER)
CAN	Work Programme for the Dissemination and Implementation of the Andean Charter for the Promotion and Protection of Human Rights	Andean Presidential Council Declaration on Democracy and Integration
		Andean Charter for the Promotion and Protection of Human Rights
		Machu Picchu Declaration on Democracy, the Rights of Indigenous Peoples and Poverty Reduction
CARICOM	Caribbean Disaster Emergency Response Agency	
Commonwealth of Independent States	Interstate Humanitarian Cooperation Fund	Convention on Human Rights and Fundamental Freedoms
Council of Europe	European Commission of Human Rights	European Convention of Human Rights
	European Court of Human Rights	European Social Charter
East African Community		East African Community Treaty
ECOWAS	Department of Humanitarian and Social Affairs	Protocol Relating to the Mechanism for Conflict Prevention, Management, Resolution, Peacekeeping and Security
	Office of the Commissioner Political Affairs, Peace and Security	
	ECOMOG	
	Disaster management unit	
	Emergency response team	
European Union	European Instrument for Democracy and Human Rights (European Commission)	Charter of Fundamental Rights
	EU Special Representative for Human Rights (European Commission)	Copenhagen Criteria
	Commission's European Community Humanitarian Office (European Commission)	
	Committee on Civil Liberties, Justice and Home Affairs (European Parliament)	
	Subcommittee on Human Rights (European Parliament)	
	Human Rights Unit (European Parliament)	
	European Union Agency for Fundamental Rights (Council of European Union)	

International organization	Human rights/humanitarian institutions	Documents and conventions
Mercosur	Institute of Public Policies on Human Rights (IPPDH)	
NATO	Civil Emergency Planning	
	Euro-Atlantic Disaster response coordination center	
Organization of American States	Inter-American Court of Human Rights	American Convention on Human Rights
	Inter-American Commission on Human Rights	Protocol of San Salvador
	Inter-American Program on the Promotion of Women's Human Rights and Gender Equity and Equality	Inter-American Democratic Charter
	Inter-American Commission of Women	Convention to Facilitate Disaster Assistance
	Inter-American Children's Institute	
	Inter-American Program and Protection of the Human Rights of Migrants, Including Migrant Workers and their Families	Cartagena Declaration on Refugees
	Inter-American Program of Judicial Facilitators	
	Inter-American Program on the Promotion of Women's Human Rights and Gender Equity and Equality	
	Demining Program	
	Committee on Natural Disaster Reduction	
Organization of Islamic Cooperation		Cairo Declaration on Human Rights in Islam
Organisation Internationale de la Francophonie	Réseaux Institutionnels de la Francophonie	
Organization for Security and Co-operation in Europe	Office for Democratic Institutions and Human Rights	Copenhagen Document
	High Commissioner on National Minorities	
Southern Africa Development Community	Disaster Risk Reduction Unit	Protocol on Politics, Defence and Security Cooperation
		Protocol on Health
		Regional Water Policy
South Asian Association for Regional Cooperation	Technical committees on gender inequalities and reduction of poverty	SAARC Convention on Combating and Preventing of Trafficking of Women and Children for Prostitution
		Convention on Promotion of Welfare of Children

Source: Data reflect information on the official websites of the regional organizations that figure in this table.

Regional institutions are particularly involved in fostering greater regional economic integration, in promoting development, and in the coordination of economic policies. Regional agreements for liberalization of trade and exchange of concessions on market access include free-trade areas, custom unions, and common markets; they form the reality of regional trade governance.[39] The post-World War II order incorporated a role for regional organizations, and this experience became intertwined with regional integration. Regional development banks provide financial and technical assistance for development, lower interest loans, and grants. Regulatory harmonization, infrastructure connectivity, energy integration, and capacity building are public goods produced by regional development governance.[40] Table 18.3 lists regional development projects currently in place, showing the diversity of initiatives across the world's regions.

Security governance has also been addressed on a regional basis,[41] and threats have been interpreted through regional socialization processes. Regional cooperative security generates confidence and may avoid the security paradox spiral of arms acquisition and deployment; they may also help build confidence. The balance of power can be managed regionally, and alliances can ensure collective defense and coordination of security policies. In some regions, security communities can be built and violence avoided. Collective security can move regions away from a strict national security logic. Conflict prevention or management can be achieved through a variety of means: Negotiation of territorial disputes; an end to intrastate conflicts; and the creation of security regimes increasingly take place within regional organizations. Moreover, regional leaders play a role in offsetting the costs of these processes and shaping their outcomes.

Obviously, there is no single model or homogeneous pattern; but all of the preceding features and roles have characterized one or more regional organizations. As indicated earlier, in some regions, institutions are very developed, and in others *ad hoc* measures are more common. Some issues, such as territorial disputes, may lend themselves to regional administration; others, such as the proliferation of weapons of mass destruction, tend to be addressed better in global forums. Nevertheless, a trend toward increased reliance on regional administration for peace and security challenges can be observed; the United States and other major powers have provided incentives and fostered this tendency, especially in Africa.

After the initial optimism regarding the new role of the UN in the post-Cold War era faded, many turned toward the regionalization of security. There were clear indications that the UN would be unable to deal with its seemingly ever expanding agenda and list of demands for peace operations. Financial limitations, political deadlock, and the problems of coordination among different UN organizations and departments became evident.

One of the responses to the crisis of UN overstretch, presented by both practitioners and specialists,[42] was sharing responsibilities and tasks with regional organizations or *ad hoc* coalitions of the willing. NATO, the Organization of American States (OAS), the OSCE, and others expanded their involvement in managing conflicts. The 1990 ECOWAS intervention in Liberia marked the beginning of greater participation by regional organizations on the continent. The coordination between regional organizations and the UN became especially evident and acute as international

Table 18.3 Regional development mechanisms and organizations

Africa	Americas	Asia, Pacific and Middle East	Europe
African Development Bank (AfDB)	Caribbean Development Bank (CDB)	ASEAN Infrastructure Fund (AIF)	Black Sea Trade and Development Bank (BSTDB)
African Energy Commission (AFREC)	Central American Bank for Economic Integration (CABEI)	Asian Development Bank (ADB)	Council of Europe Development Bank
Arab Bank for Economic Development in Africa (BADEA)	Commission for Environmental Cooperation (CEC)	Asian Infrastructure Investment Bank (AIIB)	Eurasian Development Bank (EDB)
Central African Power Pool (CAPP)	Development Bank of Latin America (CAF)	Eurasian Development Bank (EDB)	European Bank for Reconstruction and Development (EBRD)
Development Bank of Central African States (BDEAC)	Initiative for the Integration of the Regional Infrastructure in South America (IIRSA)/ UNASUR-COSIPLAN	Initiative for the ASEAN Integration (IAI)	European Investment Bank (EIB)
East African Development Bank (EADB)	Inter-American Development Bank (IDB)	Islamic Development Bank (ISDB)	European Regional Development Fund (ERDF)
Eastern African Power Pool (EAPP)	Intergovernmental Committee of Countries of the Plata Basin (CIC)	Pacific Islands Development Bank	European Union Cohesion Fund
Eastern and Southern African Trade and Development Bank/PTA Bank	Latin American Association of Financial Institutions for Development (ALIDE)	SAARC Development Fund (SDF)	Nordic Investment Bank (NIB)
ECOWAS Bank for Investment and Development	Latin American Energy Organization (OLADE)		
New Economic Partnership for Africa's Development (NEPAD)	Mercosur Structural Convergence Fund (FOCEM)		
SADC Banking Association	Mesoamerica Integration and Development Project (MP)		
Southern African Power Pool (SAPP)	North American Development Bank (NADB)		
West African Development Bank (BOAD)	South American Council of Social Development of UNASUR (CSDS)		
West African Power Pool (ECOWAS specialized agency)	South American Energy Council of Unasur (CES)		
	Caribbean Development Bank (CDB)		

Source: Data reflect information on the official websites of the regional organizations that figure in this table.

involvement in the conflict in Bosnia grew. *An Agenda for Peace*, written by Boutros Boutros-Ghali at the outset of his first term as UN secretary-general, promoted regional organizations; the so-called 2000 Brahimi report sought to regulate better the relation between the UN and regional actors.[43] Thus, regional organization became increasingly relevant to address threats to international peace and security, which led to a new vocabulary to emerge such as regionalization of security and "subcontracting."[44]

Since the 1990s, academic and policy research has focused on the need to prevent state failure and provide assistance to strengthen state institutions, often looking to regional institutions. Violence, refugees, and economic disruption that follow state failure acquire a regional dimension as they inevitably move across borders. In this context, regional actors tend to be willing to engage in action in support of internal and international governance. Countries such as Brazil and Nigeria and organizations such as the AU have taken a lead in dealing with internal conflicts and humanitarian crises.

The fight against terrorism and crime has often been tackled through regional mechanisms. The contributions of regional organizations to peace operations have increased dramatically and is a useful indication of their potential and actual contribution to global governance.[45] Their inputs range from troops for the maintenance of international peace to finance and personnel to help build or rebuild state institutions. Table 18.4 highlights the contributions of regional organizations to peace operations between 2015 and 2017.

Table 18.4 Contributions of regional organizations to peace operations, 2015–2017[1]

Multilateral operations	Country	Time period
North Atlantic Treaty Organization		
Kosovo Force	Kosovo	1999–
Resolute Support Mission	Afghanistan	2015–
European Union		
EU Advisory and Assistance Mission for Security Reform in the DRC	Democratic Republic of the Congo	2005–2016
EU Advisory Mission for Civilian Security Sector Reform in Ukraine	Ukraine	2014–
EU Border Assistance Mission for the Rafah Crossing Point	Israel/Palestinian Territories	2005–
EU Military Advisory Mission in the Central African Republic	Central African Republic	2015–2016
EU Military Operation in Bosnia and Herzegovina	Bosnia and Herzegovina	2004–
EU Monitoring Mission in Georgia	Georgia	2008–
EU Naval Force Mediterranean/ Operation Sophia	Mediterranean Sea	2015–
EU Naval Force Somalia/ Operation Atalanta	Somalia	2008–

Multilateral operations	Country	Time period
European Union		
EU Police Mission for the Palestinian Territories	Israel/Palestinian Territories	2005–
EU Police Mission in Afghanistan	Afghanistan	
EU Rule of Law Mission in Kosovo	Kosovo	2008–
EU Training Mission in the Central African Republic	Central African Republic	2016–
EU Training Mission Mali	Mali	2013–
EU Training Mission Somalia	Somalia	2010–
EUCAP Sahel Mali	Mali	2015–
EUCAP Sahel Niger	Niger	2012–
Organization for Security and Co-operation in Europe		
Mission in Kosovo	Kosovo	1999–
Mission to Bosnia and Herzegovina	Bosnia and Herzegovina	1995–
Mission to Moldova	Moldova	1993–
Mission to Montenegro	Montenegro	2006–
Mission to Serbia	Serbia	2001–
Mission to Skopje	Macedonia	1992–
Observer Mission at the Russian Checkpoints Gukovo and Donetsk	Russia	2014–
Presence in Albania	Albania	1997–
Special Monitoring Mission to Ukraine	Ukraine	1999–
Organization of American States		
Mission to Support the Peace Process in Colombia	Colombia	2004–
African Union		
AU Observer Mission in Burundi	Burundi	2015–
AU-led Regional Task Force for the elimination of the Lord's Resistance Army	LRA-Affected Areas in Africa	2011–
Human rights observers and military experts	Burundi	2015–2017
Mission for Mali and the Sahel	Mali	2013–
Mission for the Central African Republic and Central Africa	Central African Republic	2014–
Mission in Somalia	Somalia	2007–
UNAMID: AU/UN Hybrid Operation in Darfur	Sudan	2007–

(*Continued*)

Table 18.4 (Continued)

Multilateral operations	Country	Time period
Economic Community of West African States (ECOWAS)		
ECOWAS Mission in Guinea-Bissau	Guinea-Bissau	2012–
ECOWAS Mission in The Gambia	Gambia	2017–
Ad hoc coalitions of states		
Multinational Joint Task Force	Boko-Haram- affected areas	2015–
Ceasefire and Transitional Security Arrangements Monitoring Mechanism	South Sudan	2015–
International Monitoring Team	Philippines (Mindanao)	2004–
Joint Control Commission/Joint Peacekeeping Forces	Moldova (Transnistria)	1992–
Multinational Force and Observers	Egypt (Sinai)	1982–
Neutral Nations Supervisory Commission	South Korea	1953–
Office of the High Representative	Bosnia and Herzegovina	1995–
Regional Assistance Mission to Solomon Islands	Solomon Islands	2003–
Temporary International Presence in Hebron	Israel/Palestinian Territories	1997–

Source: Data reflect information on the official websites of the regional organizations that figure in this table.

[1] Includes peace operations that were active at some point between 2015 and May 2017. See Stockholm International Peace Research Institute, "SIPRI Map of Multilateral Peace Operations 2017," available at www.sipri.org/sites/default/files/2017-05/map-multilateral-peace-operations-2017.pdf; and "SIPRI Map of Multilateral Peace Operations 2016," available at www.sipri.org/sites/default/files/Map-multilateral-peace-operations-2015.pdf; and *SIPRI Yearbook 2016*, available at www.sipri.org/sites/default/files/Peace-operations-and-conflict-management.pdf.

Conclusion

This chapter has presented the concepts and practices of regional governance; it has highlighted the relations between regional mechanisms and global processes in a context of the fragmentation of authority and the diversifications of forms of governance. Historical processes, including the end of the bipolar system, led to a resurgence of interest in the possibilities for regional governance. To state the obvious, regions are different, and regional dynamics generate a diverse range of experiences and lessons. Moreover, the level of institutionalization, areas of cooperation, and strength of actors vary. This chapter has emphasized the role played by multidimensional regional organizations since the Cold War's end in the sphere of economic cooperation, political change, and security.

Regional mechanisms are part of wider processes dominated by the most powerful states and elites in the international system, but they have adapted and responded to debounded threats and challenges. Regional governance can only be understood in the context of these wider processes. The focus on regions as relevant political spaces has produced distinct political choices and generated new rules, identities, and, indeed, regions.

Additional reading

Amitav Acharya, *The End of American World Order* (Cambridge, Polity Press: 2014).
Tanja Börzel and Thomas Risse, eds., *The Oxford Handbook of Comparative Regionalism* (Oxford: Oxford University Press, 2016).
Barry Buzan and Ole Waever, *Regions and Powers: The Structure of International Security* (Cambridge: Cambridge University Press, 2004).
Andrew Cooper, Christopher W. Hughes, and Philipe de Lombaerde, *Regionalisation and Global Governance* (London: Routledge, 2008).
Mary Farrell, Björn Hettne, and Luk Van Langenhove, eds., *Global Politics of Regionalism* (London: Pluto Press, 2005).

Notes

This article was researched with the support of CNPq (National Council for Scientific and Technological Development- Brazilian government) and FAPERJ (Foundation for the Support of Research of the state of Rio de Janeiro).

1 James Rosenau, *Distant Proximities: Dynamics beyond Globalization* (Princeton, NJ: Princeton University Press, 2003).
2 Ulrich Beck, *World Risk Society* (Cambridge: Polity Press, 1999).
3 Iver Neumann, "A Region-Building Approach," in *Theories of New Regionalism: A Palgrave Reader,* eds. F. Söderbaum and Timothy M. Shaw (Basingstoke: Palgrave Macmillan, 2003), 160–178.
4 Rogério Haesbaert, *Regional-Global: Dilemas da Região e da Regionalização na Geografia Contemporânea* (Rio de Janeiro: Bertrand Brasil, 2010), 114.
5 Ibid., 238.
6 Louise Fawcett, "Regionalism from an Historical Perspective," in *Global Politics of Regionalism*, eds. Mary Farrell, Björn Hettne, and Luk Van Langenhove (London: Pluto Press, 2005), 25.
7 Andrew Hurrell, "The Regional Dimension in International Relations Theory" in *Global Politics of Regionalism*, eds. Mary Farrell, Björn Hettne, and Luk Van Langenhove (London: Pluto Press, 2005), 38–53.
8 Fawcett, "Regionalism from an Historical Perspective," 21–37.
9 Andrew Cooper, Christopher W. Hughes, and Philippe de Lombaerde, *Regionalisation and Global Governance* (London: Routledge, 2008); Mary Farrell, Björn Hettne, and Luk Van Langenhove, eds. *Global Politics of Regionalism*; the special issue of the *Australian Journal of International Affairs* 63, no. 3 (2009); Van Langehove, *Building Regions: The Regionalization of World Order* (Farnham: Ashgate, 2011); Tanja Börzel and Thomas Risse, eds., *The Oxford Handbook of Comparative Regionalism* (Oxford: Oxford University Press, 2016).
10 Tanja Börzel, "Theorizing Regionalism," in ibid., 41–63.
11 Beate Kohler-Koch and Berthold Rittberger, "The Governance Turn in EU Studies," *Journal of Common Market Studies* 44, no. 1 (2006): 27–49.

12 Gary Marks, "Structural Policy and Multi-Level Governance," in *The State of the European Community, Vol 2: The Maastricht Debates and Beyond,* eds., Alan Carfuny and Glenda Rosenthal (London: Longman, 1993).

13 Kanishka Jayasuriya, "Regulatory Regionalism in the Asia-Pacific Region," *Australian Journal of International Affairs* 63, no. 3 (2009): 335–347.

14 Bob Jessop, "Multi-level Governance and Multi-level Metagovernance," in *Multi-level Governance*, eds. Ian Bache and Matthew Flinders (Oxford: Oxford University Press, 2004), 49–74.

15 Anthony Giddens, *The Constitution of Society* (Cambridge: Cambridge University Press, 1984), 368.

16 Shahar Hameiri, "Beyond Methodological Nationalism, But Where To For The Study of Regional Governance?" *Australian Journal of International Affairs* 63, no. 3 (2009): 439.

17 Jan Aart Sholte, *Globalization: A Critical Introduction* (New York: St. Martin's Press, 2000).

18 B. Hettne, Andras Inotai, and Osvaldo Sunkel, eds., *The New Regionalism Series Vol. I–V* (London, Macmillan, 1999–2001); Finn Laursen, ed., *Comparative Regional Integration: Theoretical Perspectives* (Aldershot: Ashgate 2003).

19 Björn Hettne and Fredrik Söderbaum, *The New Regionalism Approach,* UNISA, www.unisa.ac.za/Default.asp?Cmd=ViewContent&ContentID=11583.

20 James Mittelman and Richard Falk, "Global Hegemony and Regionalism," in *Regionalism in the Post-Cold War World,* ed. Stephen C. Calleya (Aldershot: Ashgate, 2000), 3.

21 Amitav Acharya, "The Periphery as the Core: The Third World and Security Studies," in *Critical Security Studies*, eds. Keith Krause and Michael C. Williams (Minneapolis: University of Minnesota Press, 1997), 299–327.

22 Amitav Acharya, "Regionalism beyond EU Centrism," in *The Oxford Handbook of Comparative Regionalism*, eds. Borzel and Risse, 109–130.

23 David Held, *Democracy and the Global Order From the Modern State to Cosmopolitan Governance* (Stanford, CA: Stanford University Press, 1995).

24 Amit Ron, "Modes of Democratic Governance," in *Oxford Handbook of Governance*, ed. David Levi Faour (Oxford: Oxford University Press, 2012), 472–484.

25 Frank Vilbert, *The Rise of the Unelected: Democracy and the New Separation of Powers* (Cambridge: Cambridge University Press, 2007).

26 Thomas Risse, "The Diffusion of Regionalism," in *The Oxford Handbook of Comparative Regionalism*, eds. Borzel and Risse, 85–108.

27 Amitav Acharya, *The End of American World Order* (Cambridge, Polity Press: 2014), 82.

28 Yasumasa Komori, "Regional Governance in East Asia and the Asia-Pacific," *East Asia* 26, no. 4 (2009): 321–341.

29 Heribert Dieter, "Changing Patterns of Regional Governance: From Security to Political Economy?" *Pacific Review* 22, no. 1 (2009): 73–90.

30 Peter Katzenstein, *A World of Regions: Asia and Europe in the American Imperium* (Ithaca, NY: Cornell University Press, 2005).

31 Barry Buzan and Ole Waever, *Regions and Powers: The Structure of International Security* (Cambridge: Cambridge University Press, 2004), 10.

32 Ibid., 15–16.

33 Michael Pugh and Waheguru Pal Singh Sidhu, *The United Nation and Regional Security Europe and Beyond* (Boulder, CO: Lynne Rienner, 2003).

34 Ramesh Thakur and Luk Van Langenhove, "Enhancing Global Governance Through Regional Integration," in *Regionalisation and Global Governance*, eds. Cooper, Hughes, and de Lombaerde, 17–42.

35 Risse, "The Diffusion of Regionalism," 89.

36 Amitav Acharya, *Whose Ideas Matter? Agency and Power in Asian Regionalism* (Ithaca, NY: Cornell University Press, 2009).

37 World Trade Organization, *Regional Trade Agreements*, www.wto.org/english/tratop_e/region_e/region_e.htm.

38 T. Borzel and V. Van Hullen, eds., *Governance Transfer by Regional Organization: Patching Together a Global Script* (Basingstoke: Palgrave Macmillan, 2015); Emilie M. Hafner-Burton, Edward D. Mansfield, and Jon C.W. Pevehouse, "Human Rights Institutions, Sovereignty Costs and Democratization," *British Journal of Political Science* 45, no. 1 (2015): 1–27.

39 S.Y. Kim, "Deep Integration and Regional Trade Agreements" in *The Oxford Handbook of the Political Economy of International Trade*, ed. L.L. Martin (Oxford: Oxford University Press, 2015), 360–379.

40 Laszlo Bruszt and Stefano Palestini, "Regional Development Governance," in *The Oxford Handbook of Comparative Regionalism*, eds. Borzel and Risse, 374–404; Brian Frantz, Tam Robert Nguyen, and Antoni Estevadeordal, eds., *Regional Public Goods: From Theory to Practice* (Washington, DC: Asian Development Bank and Inter-American Development Bank, 2004).

41 James Sperling, "Regional Security Governance," in *Handbook of Governance and Security*, ed. James Sperling (Cheltenham: Edward Elgar, 2014); Emil J. Kirchner and Roberto Dominguez, eds., *The Security Governance of Regional Organizations* (Abingdon: Routledge, 2011), 98–119.

42 Thomas G. Weiss, ed., *Beyond UN Sub-contracting: Task-Sharing with Regional Security Arrangements and Service-providing NGOs* (London: Macmillan, 1998); Pugh and Sidhu, eds., *The United Nations and Regional Security*.

43 Boutrous Boutrous-Ghali, *An Agenda For Peace: Preventive Diplomacy, Peacemaking and Peace-keeping* (New York: United Nations, 1992); Lakhdar Brahimi, *Report of the Panel On United Nations Peace Operations*, UN document A/55/305—S/2000/809), 2000, www.un.org/peace/reports/peace_operations/docs/full_report.htm.

44 Pugh and Sidhu, *The United Nations and Regional Security*.

45 Alex Bellamy and Paul D. Williams, "Who's Keeping the Peace? Regionalization and Contemporary Peace Operations," *International Security* 29, no. 4 (2005): 157–195; and Linnea Bergholm, "Who Can Keep Peace in Africa?" *African Affairs* 106, no, 422 (2007): 147–154.

CONTENTS

The European Union

Ben Rosamond

The European Union (EU) is both a regime of regional governance and an actor within the global governance system. This relatively simple observation needs to be fleshed out to consider the relationship between these two roles. Is the EU's primary purpose to insulate its member states from global pressures while protecting and advancing a distinctive European model of society and political economy? Alternatively, does it function as a kind of cipher through which European societies are globalized? Questions like this are not easily answered. They are the sources of considerable debate within international relations and the more specialized subfield of EU studies, with discussions tending to cluster around two distinct understandings of the interplay between the nature of the EU's internal governance and its status as an actor within the global system.

The first position maintains that the EU's primary rationale is to transplant global governance norms into the European context. This line of argument tends to associate European integration with the "constitutionalization" of neoliberal global governance norms.[1] The second position treats the EU as an important intermediary between global processes and European societies. The EU thus "manages" globalization and seeks to fashion a distinctive European approach to political economy and to protect certain types of institution and values. In this second version, the EU is also an actor seeking to use its "normative power" to propagate its norms globally and/or its "market" power to fashion the global regulatory order in ways that suit its interests.[2] What the EU does matters because membership involves a significant delegation of powers from the national governments to the European level. Since member states have voluntarily ceded parts of their sovereignty to European institutions, it is important to ask why and with what purpose.

This chapter concentrates on the relationship between the EU's own character as a regime of European economic governance and its participation in global governance. It begins by summarizing the development of the EU and its institutional order from its origins in the 1950s, noting the significance of two features: The distinctive institutional design and its status as a "market order." It is suggested that these two features are important to the constitution of the EU as an actor in the politics of global governance. The chapter then considers interest-driven and "normative power" accounts of the EU's external behavior before considering some examples of the way in which it seeks to influence outcomes in global economic governance and how these relate back to its internal characteristics. The chapter closes with a few concluding comments about the sustainability of the EU in the context of a series of ongoing (potentially existential) crises.

The evolution of the EU

Two features of the EU need to be taken into account in this context: Its longevity and its complexity. The union's longevity—its direct ancestor the European Coal and Steel Community (ECSC) was created by the Treaty of Paris in 1951—means that its character may have shifted and indeed drifted over time. Nothing illustrates this point better than the controversy surrounding the award of the Nobel Peace Prize to the EU in 2012. Critics of the award were puzzled as to how an organization responsible for the imposition of punitive austerity budgeting on one of its member states (Greece) could be given an award designed to recognize the promotion of "fraternity between nations." The most typical counterargument stated that the prize was recognition of a *historic* achievement: The role of European integration in securing more than six decades of peace in Europe.

Also, by the standards of most other international organizations and forms of regional cooperation, the EU is institutionally complex. As Table 19.1 shows, it has a mix of intergovernmental and supranational institutions. The EU Commission is a supranational bureaucratic body that is formally responsible for the initiation of legislation. The commission's proposals must be compliant with the treaties and it must be able to show that EU-level action is justified. Intergovernmental interests are represented by the Council of Ministers (often known simply as the "Council"). Council meetings consist of government ministers from the member states with responsibility for the policy area under discussion. Its primary task is to legislate the proposals forwarded to it by the commission. EU legislation takes two primary forms. Regulations are directly and immediately applicable in national law, whereas directives have to be legislated into national law by national parliaments. The implementation of directives is normally allowed to take account of specific national circumstances and administrative arrangements.

When first created in the 1950s, the European Parliament (EP) consisted of delegates from national parliaments and was merely consulted for an opinion on legislative proposals. Since 1979 the EP has been directly elected and starting in the 1980s, it has gradually acquired more powers, including powers of legislative co-decision with the council. The EP formally approves the appointment of the commission and has oversight of the EU budget. The commission's agenda-setting monopoly has been progressively challenged since the 1970s by the evolution of the European Council: The regular summit meetings of member state heads of government. The EU oversees

Table 19.1 Evolution of the treaties of the EU*

Date of signing	Treaty	Purpose
1951	Treaty of Paris	Establishment of the European Coal and Steel Community
1957	Treaties of Rome	Establishment of the European Economic Community and the European Atomic Energy Community
1965	Merger Treaty	Fusion of the three existing communities into a single set of institutions
1986	Single European Act	Specification of a timetable for completion of the common market Move to qualified majority voting in matters relating to the internal market Expansion of powers of the European Parliament
1992	Maastricht Treaty on European Union	Formal creation of the EU Creation of the category of European citizenship Specification of institutional format, process, and conditions for the creation of monetary union Creation of the Common Foreign and Security Policy Creation of EU competence in "Justice and Home Affairs" Introduction of the co-decision procedure, giving the European Parliament powers of co-legislation with the Council in some areas
1997	Treaty of Amsterdam	Increased use of co-decision Incorporation of the Schengen Agreement into the Treaties Pre-enlargement institutional reforms
2001	Treaty of Nice	Institutional reforms, including changes to the composition of the Commission and recalibration of voting weights in the Council
2007 (not in force until 2009)	Treaty of Lisbon	Creation of permanent Council Presidency and a New High Representative for Foreign Affairs Creation of European External Action Service New powers to the European Parliament Changes in voting procedures in the Council Introduction of the "citizens' initiative" Legally binding "Charter of Fundamental Rights"

Source: Compiled by author. The treaties are consolidated into the Treaty on European Union and the Treaty on the Functioning of the European Union.

a large body of supranational law that is supreme over any conflicting legislation in the member states. The European Court of Justice is charged with interpreting EU law, and its jurisprudence has been very significant to advancing integration and establishing the authority of the European legal order over national systems.

The EU has competence over a large number of policy areas, primarily relating to economic governance. The commission is currently organized into thirty-four directorates general, each charged with a particular policy domain. However, the degree to which any given policy area is Europeanized varies, and each policy domain has its own distinct trajectory as well as its own institutional logic.

The EU's growth and development are perhaps most easily understood by looking through two prisms: Treaties and institutional design, and the internal market.

Treaties and institutional design

The EU's origins lie in the dilemmas confronting European states in the aftermath of World War II. The ECSC sought to integrate the coal and steel sectors of its six founding member states (Belgium, France, the Federal Republic of Germany, Italy, Luxembourg, and the Netherlands) under the auspices of a common high authority. The foundation of the ECSC matters for a number of reasons. First, although a limited project of sectoral integration, it was explicitly designed to solve Europe's major security dilemma: The historic enmity between France and Germany. Thus the second feature of lasting interest was the method selected to resolve the European security dilemma. The integration of economies, starting with the strategically important coal and steel sectors, would be used to create radical and lasting economic interdependence between the participating countries.

Following a clear commercial liberal logic, deep economic interdependence would significantly reduce (to the point of eradication) the probability of violent conflict between member states. Their economies would be bound together in welfare-enhancing ways that would make it irrational to defect from the arrangement. Interdependence would be further underscored by the institutionalization of the new regime. So the third feature of the ECSC that generates lasting interest is its institutional design. The most striking feature of this design was the creation of the High Authority, a supranational bureaucratic body charged with the strategic oversight, management of the integration process, and the initiation of relevant legislative measures in accordance with the treaty. The supra-nationalism of the High Authority (later the commission) was offset by an intergovernmental institution (the council), but the ECSC Treaty set in place the principle of policy initiation as the responsibility of a European-level bureaucratic actor. Indeed, the Treaty of Paris laid down the basic institutional pattern (illustrated in Table 19.1) that has survived into the modern incarnation of the EU.

As suggested earlier, the EU is unusually institutionalized by the standards of conventional international organizations. Moreover, the EU's institutional design—inherited from decisions taken in the 1950s—contains a much greater degree of supra-nationality than that of any other regional integration project. This observation confirms something of quite significant theoretical importance: Institutional designs can be "sticky" over time and can remain intact despite the solution or disappearance of the original dilemmas which prompted policymakers to create them in the first place. The communities of the 1950s were institutional solutions created by politicians living under the shadow of the unprecedented violence of two world wars, both fought to a large extent in the European "theater." That context and those imperatives changed, but the institutional framework and the core policy methodology (supranational initiative–intergovernmental legislation–supranational judicial oversight) remained intact. This issue also relates to a controversial analytical puzzle: Is the EU comparable to other regional organizations, or rather is it a unique case without historical precedent or contemporary parallel? There is a sizable and still growing academic literature on this problem, but it is also an international policy issue: To what degree does the EU provide a template for other regional organizations to emulate? Is there a "European model" of regionalism? And if so what does that model consist of beyond a basic institutional design?[3]

The subsequent evolution of the EU was first defined by the signing, by the original "six," of the Treaties of Rome in 1957, which created the European Atomic Energy Community (Euratom) and, most importantly, the European Economic Community (EEC). The three communities (thereafter the "European Communities," EC) were fused into a common institutional framework by the Merger Treaty of 1965. The main treaty changes in the EU's history are illustrated in Table 19.1. On the face of it, this history suggests that the EU has become more deeply integrated over time (for example, from single market to monetary union), that policy competence in an increasing number of domains has moved from national to (at least partially) supranational level, and that integration has moved decisively beyond the sphere of the economy (most notably the incursion of the EU into matters of policing and internal security and foreign policy). While this "bird's-eye view" account is undoubtedly correct, it masks the extent to which ratification of new treaties has become highly contentious. Most recently, the attempt to create a so-called "constitutional treaty" had to be abandoned after the proposal was defeated in ratification referendum in France and the Netherlands in 2005. The first serious evidence of domestic discontent with the direction of the EU came with the surprise rejection of the Maastricht Treaty on European Union by the Danish electorate in June 1992. The Brexit referendum of 2016 provides further evidence of populist resistance to integration and the EU.[4]

This tendency has been thought of in terms of a breakdown of a forty-year "permissive consensus" in which domestic publics had tolerated the advance of integration as orchestrated by their governing elites.[5] Debate exists about why that "permissive consensus" has eroded. One line of argument links the advance of integration into areas where core sovereignty concerns are raised (control of monetary policy, border management and policing, foreign policy) to the absence of EU-level mechanisms to allow proper democratic oversight. This is part and parcel of what is often called the "democratic deficit," a problem that has become amplified in public consciousness across Europe over the past quarter-century. The management of these ratification dilemmas has led to one important consequence: The proliferation of derogations and opt-outs negotiated by and granted to some member states (for example the Danish and British opt-outs from monetary union). Such derogations lead, in turn, to a much more flexible, variegated, and differentiated picture of integration than might be apparent at first sight.[6] This is important for debates about the relationship between European and global governance and the possible status of the former as a model for the latter.

The significance of the internal market

The 1957 EEC Treaty committed the member states not only to the elimination of internal customs duties, but also to the establishment of a customs union (which would levy a common external tariff on imports to the community) and to the abolition of obstacles to the free movement of goods, persons, services, and capital. In other words, from its inception the EU was a market-making project. Indeed, for some scholars this is the EU's central defining feature. It is seen from this perspective as an organization tasked with the creation, maintenance, and regulation of a liberal market order.[7] Nineteen of the current member states have moved well beyond the common market stage of integration by engaging in a monetary union and the creation of a single currency. EU membership is meant to imply willingness to adopt the euro, but member state economies need to be performing suitably in terms of a series of "convergence criteria," covering budget deficits, accumulated national debt, and exchange rate stability before transition to the single currency can be sanctioned. These performance parameters are not required for membership of the EU, which means that the union consists of three groups: Countries that have dissolved their national currencies, those that are committed to do so, but are not yet ready, and those that have either negotiated opt-outs from monetary union (Denmark and the UK) or found ways to stay out (Sweden).

In addition, the EU has significant and growing policy competences in two other areas: Justice and home affairs, and foreign and security policy. A major part of the latter is the Common Security and Defense Policy (CSDP), which allows for the EU to operate as an entity in military operations, notably in the realms of humanitarian assistance, peacekeeping, and crisis management. The emergence of this policy competence, while still limited, challenges the postwar division of labor between the EU (charged with economic integration) and the likes of NATO and the Western European Union (WEU), which organized and delivered European security through military means. Whether the EU should have extended its reach in this way is a significant political question for some member states, and for some close observers of the EU there are strong technical and normative grounds for the EU's not extending beyond the delivery and regulation of the single market.[8]

The EU's foundational commitment to its own internal market has a number of important ancillary implications. These are not usually present in regional organizations, which typically exist to deliver a less intense form of integration (recall that most regional organizations operate with nothing more that the aspiration to create a free-trade area). First, the quest for a common market requires a significant transfer of regulatory authority from the national to the European level. This is needed to secure the approximation of relevant laws and standards across the member states. While this has been made somewhat simpler following the acceptance of the mutual recognition principle (the idea that a product or service cannot be excluded from the territory of another state even if the technical or quality specifications differ between originating and receiving countries) over the past three decades, that simplicity has been offset by two facets of European integration: The enlargement to include significantly more member states (the "six" have become twenty-eight—a summary of EU enlargements is in Table 19.2); and the expansion of EU policy competence over time. The thousands of legislative acts and European Court of Justice judgments that constitute the *acquis communautaire* run to thirty-five chapters, covering—mostly— matters pertaining to the regulation of the single market. Adoption of the *acquis* is a basic requirement for new prospective member states.

The second implication of the commitment to the single market is that it spawns a need for common policies. A single market cannot operate without an active

Table 19.2 European Union enlargements

Date	New member states
1951	Belgium, France, (Federal Republic of) Germany, Italy, Luxembourg, Netherlands (six member states in total)
1973	Denmark, Ireland, United Kingdom* (nine)
1981	Greece (ten)
1986	Portugal, Spain (twelve)
1995	Austria, Finland, Sweden (fifteen)
2004	Cyprus, Czech Republic, Estonia, Hungary, Latvia, Lithuania, Malta, Poland, Slovakia, Slovenia (twenty-five)
2007	Bulgaria, Romania (twenty-seven)
2013	Croatia (twenty-eight)
	Official candidates: Albania (applied for membership in 2009), FYR Macedonia (2004), Iceland (2009), Montenegro (2008), Serbia (2009), Turkey (1987)

Source: Compiled by author from EU documents. The United Kingdom government (under Article 50 of the treaties) initiated the process of leaving the EU in March 2017 following the successful "Leave" outcome in a national referendum the previous June.

competition policy (the regulation of mergers, acquisitions, cartels, market dominance, and state aid to industry) and this has become one of the most important EU policy regimes. Likewise, the development of a common external tariff and a collective commercial (trade) policy is needed to guarantee that no single member state can acquire competitive advantage by applying differential tariffs to imports from outside the EU at the national border. The single market, even if considered straightforwardly as a set of measures to reduce barriers to factor movement, brings a number of policy domains into the purview of the EU: The regulation of banking and financial services, environmental policy, and company law, to take but three prominent examples.

This leads to a third outgrowth of the single market, which relates specifically to the free movement of persons. Labor mobility implies the freedom of a citizen of one member state to work and live in another. This brings with it a range of additional issues that would need to be resolved for the single market to function properly: Rights of access to social security and healthcare, the right of residence, the capacity of mobile workers to access banking and credit facilities, and voting rights. The 1992 Treaty on European Union's creation of the category of EU citizen showed the extent to which the requirement of a transnationally mobile workforce "spilled over" into something rather deeper (and somewhat beyond the scope of what was functionally necessarily from the point of view of economic imperatives). In addition, the incorporation of the Schengen Agreement (allowing border-free movement within the area defined by participating states) into the treaties in 1997 amounted to the moment when the free movement of persons within (large parts of) the EU was legally guaranteed.

The fourth concern is whether the commitment to complete the single market carries with it an imperative to integrate more extensively and more deeply. Scholars of the early communities together with economic theorists of the time held that this was an inherent dynamic of the integration process.[9] For example, creating conditions for free factor movement would create significant pressures for supranational involvement in social policy. A single market might be made more efficient by the adoption of a single currency to enhance transparency and reduce transaction costs in the process of cross-border economic exchange. Indeed, in the history of the EU one tactic (used principally by the commission) has been to initiate deliberation on deeper integration when progress on a more modest set of integration commitments has stalled. This might explain why the commission began work on monetary union in the early 1960s, despite there being no mention of it in the EEC Treaty. More recently, a similar dynamic seems to have been at work in initiatives designed to coordinate national fiscal policies as a way to solve deep dilemmas associated with monetary union—dilemmas that became apparently intractable after 2010 in the context of the sovereign debt crisis in the Eurozone.

The fifth and final implication of the internal market is external, and vital for broader questions of global economic governance. Because the EU is a customs union, it operates with a single voice within the WTO. This places the EU as a major force within global trade politics, but it is also important to note that the EU is one of the world's primary regulators and a major site of regulatory innovation. According to *The Economist*, it "is becoming the world's regulatory capital."[10] For example, external producers seeking access to the internal market—the largest "economy" in the world by GDP and one of the largest by population (a little over half a billion)—must conform to EU product standards. And some producers have actively chosen to adopt EU standards rather than those of other major regulatory powers, most notably the US.[11] This is an example of how the internal market is generative of the EU's "market power" and of how the single market is "nested" within the global economy.

The EU and global governance

It has been suggested already that the EU is a significant player in global governance almost by default. As a trade bloc with a common external tariff it operates formally as a collective unitary actor in international trade negotiations. Moreover, its single market means that the EU is one of the most significant suppliers of regulatory standards in the global economy. The global domains of trade and regulation are the most obvious venues for the "externalization" of EU policy competence. But they are also interesting for two other reasons. First, we might ask about the extent to which the EU actively pursues discernible (European) interests in the global governance arena. Second, we might wonder whether the EU works on behalf of a specific set of values.

Needless to say, these two questions correspond to quite different readings of the EU as an actor within global governance. These, in turn, tend to map onto respectively rationalist and constructivist understandings of world politics. A variety of rationalist understandings of the EU as an actor are possible, but all would expect the EU's preferences as a regulator or as a trade negotiator to reflect certain underlying interests that would be traceable back to the "domestic" context of intra-European integration (and in turn to, *inter alia*, the interests of particular member states, or organized interests, or particular supranational institutions). The constructivist position would expect the EU's actions in global politics to be driven by certain ideas and for its actions to seek to set certain normative standards in world politics. The ongoing debate about whether the EU is a "normative power"[12] is, in many ways, the key intellectual space for discussion between these two characterizations.

Advocates of the "normative power Europe" (NPE) position hold that the EU's external behavior is founded on a set of core values that are inscribed into the treaties. The EU's actions should be interpreted in terms of setting standards for what is "normal" in world politics, where that "normality" is the effective spread of the EU's core norms globally. Ian Manners identifies the EU's nine core norms as "sustainable peace," "social freedom," "consensual democracy," "associative human rights," "supranational rule of law," "inclusive equality," "social solidarity," "sustainable development," and "good governance." This suggests that the EU's "foreign policy" (broadly defined) might be a very distinctive presence and a quite important component in the politics of global governance. Manners, for example, argues that the EU has been a major force in struggles to spread global human rights norms such as the abolition of the death penalty—a position that marks it out very clearly from a major normative rival in the democratic world, the US.[13]

The most developed critiques of the NPE position fall into three types. The first simply maintains that it is mistaken to see the EU's behavior as value driven. The EU is seen as an interest-driven actor like any other, its normative language seen as little more than rhetorical cover for behavior that is strategically motivated and inconsistent in application. A second position does not necessarily dispute that the EU seeks to propagate and spread its norms. Rather the objection is that it—through policy frameworks such as the European Neighborhood Policy—actually promotes these norms coercively and without allowing any form of dialogue between its norms and the norms of others. A third position is yet more sympathetic to the basic claims that external behavior is internally constituted by core values and that external action is "normative" in character. But it suggests that the standard NPE account overemphasizes a set of positive civic liberal values while neglecting the importance of economic liberalism as also (and perhaps predominantly) constitutive of the EU and its behavior.[14]

The NPE account of Europe's role in global governance is a normative position in itself. In other words, those using the term are not only analyzing what the EU is, but also saying something about what they think the EU should be. The NPE position dovetails quite precisely with the self-image of the EU that is found in, for example, the commission's communicative discourse, where the term has been adopted to describe the EU's comparative advantage as the source of important values. The idea of spreading Europe's core values has been a part of the treaties since Amsterdam (1997) and the European Security Strategy is explicit in articulating that external military deployments in the name of the EU should operate on behalf of key values that closely resemble the list assembled by Manners: "The best protection for our security is a world of well-governed democratic states. Spreading good governance, supporting social and political reform, dealing with corruption and abuse of power, establishing the rule of law and protecting human rights are the best means of strengthening the international order."[15]

A few examples of the EU's engagement in global economic governance illustrate the complexities that are raised in the course of any attempt to ascertain the essence of the EU's external behavior. The fact that the picture is complex should not surprise regular students of European integration, for whom the question of what (if anything) the EU is remains an ongoing puzzle. Since the onset of debates around the concept of globalization in the mid-1990s two basic positions about the EU have taken shape in the literature (and have been, at the same time, reflected in policy discourse). For some, the EU is nothing less than an incarnation of neoliberal globalization: An institutional device for the accelerated globalization of European societies. For others, the EU is a vital buffer between the ravages of a global market order and European societies and a vital and successful "manager" of globalization.[16]

Of course, it may be that the EU's relationship to globalization is differentiated—between policy domains or over time. Some scholars draw attention to a neoliberal "drift" in certain areas of economic policy such as the EU's competition regime or company law and corporate governance, not to mention trade policy.[17] This might emerge from a dynamic internal to the EU whereby market liberal principles have become progressively "constitutionalized" at the supranational level, leaving market-correcting policies underdeveloped and largely confined to the national level,[18] but it may also reflect the continued ascendancy of neoliberal ideas within policy circles more generally.[19]

This movement has been discernible in an apparent doctrinal shift in EU trade policy over the course of the first decade and a half of this century. Between 2001 and 2006, under then commissioner for trade Pascal Lamy, EU trade policy seemed to be governed by a doctrine of so-called "managed globalization," which Sophie Meunier describes as "a broad and encompassing doctrine that subordinated trade policy to a variety of trade and non-trade objectives such as multilateralism, social justice and sustainable development."[20] For some the importance of this position was that it constituted a clear rival stance to US trade doctrine. While the EU sought to use the World Trade Organization (WTO) to regulate and manage globalization, the US approach in contrast was to involve itself in an increasing number of free-trade agreements as a means to the end of accelerating market liberalization.[21] And although the doctrinal positions of the EU and the United States may have converged over the past decade, the difference that became apparent in the mid-1990s is of particular interest to students of global governance. It raises the question of what the ends of global governance are: Market liberalization (the assumption being that the progressive removal of barriers to factor movement on a global scale will be welfare enhancing for all) or the use of market liberalization as a tool to service a broader set of social, political, security, and perhaps environmental ends.

By focusing on doctrines and their meaning, we focus on the role of ideas in global governance and the role of actors such as the EU as carriers of those ideas. The EU is complex in this regard because it seems to express at least three types of liberalism in its external actions. We have noted two of these already. The first is economic liberalism, which suggests an approach to governance that prioritizes the making and maintenance of a market order. The second is the package of positive civic liberal principles associated with human rights, the rule of law, and the propagation of political rights through the spread of democracy. The third is bound up with what is arguably the EU's greatest achievement: The delivery of a pacific international system in line with the precepts of liberal international theory.[22]

That said, there may be other reasons for diverging approaches to global economic governance among different actors. One theme that has become popular in the literature on the global politics of regulation notes the EU's affiliation with the "precautionary principle" when assessing public policy risks.[23] The idea is embedded within the treaties (Article 191 of the Treaty on the Functioning of the European Union) and presupposes a cautious approach to the management of risk, particularly in relation to matters of public health and the environment when scientific assessment of those risks is not definitive. This is often contrasted with a more relaxed attitude toward scientific certainty in the United States. Perhaps the most famous application of the precautionary principle occurred in 1999 when the EU moved to ban the import of US beef injected with growth hormones that were thought to be potentially carcinogenic. The EU ban was quickly ruled in breach of WTO rules, and some suggest that the invocation of ideas such as the precautionary principle can be used as a cover for old-fashioned protectionist policies.[24] Nevertheless, the very idea of the precautionary principle as a policy tool suggests that approaches to global economic governance may not simply be about the application of different ideas and interests, but also about divergence between different policy cultures. And while it may be true that there is actually significant sectoral and national variation within European policy cultures,[25] the fact that there is an EU approach written into the treaty provides evidence of at least the potential importance of the EU as an actor in global governance.

None of this is to suggest that interests are unimportant. Mitchell Smith argues that two important overlapping determinants of the EU's involvement in global regulatory politics are: The Commission's rational strategy of seeking to ensure that the EU's market rules become the global rules; and efforts by European firms to ensure that they are not put at a competitive disadvantage by regulations formulated in Brussels.[26] This does not mean that the EU ends up delivering and defending "lowest common denominator" regulation—far from it. Environmental policy is a pertinent example, because the EU is well known as an advocate of high regulatory standards and tough emissions targets in the global politics of climate change. How a multi-country entity in which member states have quite distinct approaches to environmental regulation became a global leader on climate change is an interesting puzzle. The original EEC Treaty did not mention environmental policy. The Communities did not possess environmental policy competence until the ratification of the Single European Act in the mid-1980s. Yet the Commission, using arguments about the utility of environmental policy for market completion, was able to establish a supranational regime of environmental rulemaking in the early 1970s.[27] Powerful environmental lobbies in EU member states ensured the upload of stringent environmental regulation to the EU level.

The constructivist argument at this point would be to suggest that the EU's external behavior in global environmental governance reflects the externalization of a set of principles that have been settled within the European context. The rationalist alternative is to suggest that, once settled, these environmental standards need to be advocated globally by the EU in order to prevent a loss of competitiveness for European business.[28] Again, it is worth noting that the determination of how the EU acts globally and the preferences it expresses cannot be separated from the internal politics of European integration, which, in turn, incorporates domestic political processes in the member states.

Environmental policy is a domain in which the EU has been reasonably successful at externalizing its internal standards. This is in part because of the existence of clear supranational environmental policy competence. As suggested, market-correcting social policy is less Europeanized, but even where there exist EU-level standards, their export into the relevant international regimes is much more problematic. A good example is core labor standards, where the EU has no obvious competence to act authoritatively in relevant international forums such as the International Labour Organization (ILO). This is not to say that the EU does not pursue this agenda, but it is instead worked into trade and development policies, where the EU's competence to act is more clear cut.[29]

Conclusion

This chapter began with the observation that the EU operates both as an actor in the global system and as a system of regional governance. The latter is clearly constitutive of the former, but as the foregoing has shown the question of how internal governance influences external behavior is not straightforwardly answered. Moreover, this question is not simply analytical; it is also normative. The factor that most obviously supplies the EU with global agency is its status as a market order. Whether the EU operates as a "manager" of globalization that subordinates the market to other priorities or as a force of economic liberalization driven by the logic of the market alone is an empirical question. In the wake of the financial crisis of 2008 that morphed into an ongoing sovereign debt crisis in the Eurozone thereafter, it is also an intensely political question.

Whether the EU can maintain a role in global governance may depend on whether it can navigate its own internal crises. Some of these, such as those linked to the Eurozone and refugees seem to be intractable and frequently provoke nationalist and populist reactions, which in turn are potentially corrosive of European integration. These tensions do not necessarily mean that the EU will collapse. What is rather more likely is a scenario where integration is more differentiated, and a more differentiated future is one where the EU's voice in global governance debates may be somewhat less coherent.

It is often said that the election of Donald Trump to the US presidency and "Brexit" were delivered by a set of common dynamics.[30] Both of these phenomena threaten to disrupt prevailing modes of geopolitics and geo-economics. The UK referendum result quickly provoked a flurry of rival future visions—from actors outside of the EU as well as within—for how diplomatic alignments would evolve and how the international economy would be ordered in a post-Brexit world.[31] We are witnessing the onset of a period of uncertainty, not only in terms of how the EU's interests and values might evolve, but also of whether the EU will still be able to assert its interests and values into the processes of global governance.

Additional reading

Chad Damro, "Market Power Europe," *Journal of European Public Policy* 19, no. 5, 682–699.
Desmond Dinan, Neill Nugent, and William E. Peterson, eds., *The European Union in Crisis* (London: Palgrave Macmillan, 2017).
Christopher Hill, Michael Smith, and Sophie Vanhoonacker, eds., *International Relations and the European Union* (Oxford: Oxford University Press, 2017).
Wade Jacoby and Sophie Meunier, eds., *Europe and the Management of Globalization* (London: Routledge, 2010).
Ian Manners, "Normative Power Europe: A Contradiction in Terms?," *Journal of Common Market Studies* 40, no. 2 (2002): 235–258.
Magnus Ryner and Alan Cafruny, *The European Union and Global Capitalism: Origins, Development, Crisis* (London: Palgrave Macmillan, 2017).

Notes

1 Magnus Ryner and Alan Cafruny, *The European Union and Global Capitalism: Origins, Development, Crisis* (London: Palgrave Macmillan, 2017), chapter 3.
2 Wade Jacoby and Sophie Meunier, "Europe and the Management of Globalization," *Journal of European Public Policy* 17, no. 3 (2010): 299–317; Ian Manners, "Normative Power Europe: A Contradiction in Terms?" *Journal of Common Market Studies* 40, no. 2 (2002): 235–258; Chad Damro, "Market Power Europe," *Journal of European Public Policy* 19, no. 5 (2012): 682–699.
3 Frederik Söderbaum *Rethinking Regionalism* (Basingtoke: Palgrave Macmillan, 2015).
4 Sara B. Hobolt, "The Brexit Vote: A Divided Nation, a Divided Continent," *Journal of European Public Policy* 23 no. 9 (2016): 1259–1277.
5 Lisbet Hooghe and Gary Marks, "A Postfunctionalist Theory of European Integration: From Permissive Consensus to Constraining Dissensus," *British Journal of Political Science* 39, no. 1 (2009): 1–23.
6 See Alex Warleigh, *Flexible Integration: Which Model for the European Union* (Sheffield: Sheffield Academic Press, 2002); Rebecca Adler-Nissen, *Opting Out of the European Union: Diplomacy, Sovereignty and European Integration* (Cambridge: Cambridge University Press, 2013).
7 Giandomenico Majone, *Dilemmas of European Integration: The Ambiguities and Pitfalls of Integration by Stealth* (Oxford: Oxford University Press, 2005).
8 David Cameron, "EU Speech at Bloomberg," 23 January 2013, www.number10.gov.uk/news/eu-speech-at-bloomberg; Giandomenico Majone, *Europe as the Would-be Super power: The EU at Fifty* (Cambridge: Cambridge University Press, 2009).
9 Ernst B. Haas, *The Uniting of Europe: Political, Social and Economic Forces, 1950–1957* (Stanford, CA: Stanford University Press, 1958); Leon N. Lindberg, *The Political Dynamics of European Economic Integration* (Stanford, CA: Stanford University Press, 1963); Bela Balassa, *The Theory of Economic Integration* (Homewood, IL: Richard D. Irwin Inc., 1961).
10 "Charlemagne: Brussels Rules OK," *The Economist*, 20 September 2007.

11 Mark Schapiro, *Exposed: The Toxic Chemistry of Everyday Products and What's at Stake for American Power* (White River Junction, VT: Chelsea Green Publishing, 2009).

12 Manners, "Normative Power Europe"; Ian Manners, "The Normative Ethics of the European Union," *International Affairs* 84, no. 1 (2008): 45–60.

13 Manners, "Normative Power Europe," 245–252.

14 Richard Youngs, "Normative Dynamics and Strategic Interests in the EU's External Identity," *Journal of Common Market Studies* 42, no. 2 (2004): 415–435; Thomas Diez, "Constructing the Self and Changing Others: Reconsidering 'Normative Power Europe,'" *Millennium: Journal of International Studies* 33, no. 3 (2005): 613–636; Owen Parker and Ben Rosamond, "Normative Power Europe Meets Economic Liberalism: Complicating Cosmopolitanism Inside/Outside the EU," *Cooperation and Conflict* 48, no. 2 (2013): 229–246; Ben Rosamond, "Three Ways of Speaking Europe to the World: Markets, Peace, Cosmopolitan Duty and the EU's Normative Power," *British Journal of Politics and International Relations* 16, no. 1 (2014): 133–148.

15 European Security Strategy, *A Secure Europe in a Better World*, 12 December 2003, www. consilium. europa.eu/uedocs/cmsUpload/78367.pdf.

16 Jacoby and Meunier, "Europe and the Management of Globalization"; and Nicolas Jabko, "The Hidden Face of the Euro," *Journal of European Public Policy* 17, no. 3 (2010): 318–334.

17 Hubert Buch-Hansen and Angela Wigger, "Revisiting 50 Years of Market-Making: The Neoliberal Transformation of EC Competition Policy," *Review of International Political Economy* 17, no. 1 (2010), 20–44; Laura Horn, *Regulating Corporate Governance in the EU: Towards a Marketization of Corporate Control* (Basingstoke: Palgrave Macmillan, 2011); Gabriel Siles-Brügge, "Resisting Protectionism After the Crisis: Strategic Economic Discourse and the EU–Korea Free Trade Agreement," *New Political Economy* 16, no. 5 (2011): 627–653.

18 Fritz Scharpf, "The European Social Model," *Journal of Common Market Studies* 40, no. 4 (2002): 645–670.

19 Colin Crouch, *The Strange Non-Death of Neoliberalism* (Cambridge: Polity Press, 2011); Mark Blyth, *Austerity: The History of a Dangerous Idea* (New York: Oxford University Press, 2013).

20 Sophie Meunier, "Managing Globalization? The EU in International Trade Negotiations," *Journal of Common Market Studies* 45, no. 4 (2007): 906.

21 Alberta Sbragia, "The EU, the US, and Trade Policy: Competitive Interdependence in the Management of Globalization," *Journal of European Public Policy* 17, no. 3 (2010): 368–382.

22 Rosamond, "Three Ways of Speaking."

23 Jale Tosun, *Risk Regulation in Europe: Assessing the Application of the Precautionary Principle* (New York: Springer, 2013); and David Vogel, "The Hare and the Tortoise Revisited: The New Politics of Consumer and Environmental Protection in Europe," *British Journal of Political Science* 33, no. 4 (2003): 557–580.

24 Giandomenico Majone, "What Price Safety? The Precautionary Principle and its Policy Implications," *Journal of Common Market Studies* 40, no. 1 (2002): 89–109.

25 Alasdair R. Young, "Confounding Conventional Wisdom: Political Not Principled Differences in the Transatlantic Regulatory Relationship," *British Journal of Politics and International Relations* 11, no. 4 (2009): 666–689.

26 Mitchell P. Smith, "Single Market, Global Competition: Regulating the European Market in a Global Economy," *Journal of European Public Policy* 17, no. 7 (2010): 936–953.

27 Christoph Knill and Duncan Liefferink, "The Establishment of EU Environmental Policy," in *Environmental Policy in the EU: Actors, Institutions and Processes*, 3rd ed., eds. Andrew Jordan and Camilla Adelle (London: Routledge, 2013), 13–31.

28 R. Daniel Kelemen, "Globalizing European Union Environmental Policy," *Journal of European Public Policy* 17, no. 3 (2010): 335–349.
29 Jan Orbie and Olufemi Babarinde, "The Social Dimension of Globalization and EU Development Policy: Promoting Core Labour Standards and Corporate Social Responsibility," *Journal of European Integration* 30, no. 3 (2008): 459–477.
30 Mark Blyth, "Global Trumpism," *Foreign Affairs*, 16 November 2016. www.foreignaff airs.com/articles/2016–11–15/global-trumpism.
31 Rebecca Adler-Nissen, Charlotte Galpin, and Ben Rosamond, "Performing Brexit: How a Post-Brexit World is Imagined Outside the United Kingdom," *British Journal of Politics and International Relations* 19, no. 3 (2017): 573–591.

The BRICS in the evolving architecture of global governance

Andrew F. Cooper and Ramesh Thakur

The architecture of global governance is made up of intergovernmental global and regional organizations as the inner core of formal multilateral machinery; informal but functionally specific and single-problem-oriented institutions like the Proliferation Security Initiative and the Nuclear Security Summits; and a "soft" layer of informal, general-purpose institutions such as myriad "G" groups that serve as sites for incubating consensus and setting general direction rather than making collective decisions. Amid the plethora of informal groupings, the initial BRICs (Brazil, Russia, India, and China) and then the BRICS (with the addition of South Africa in 2011) stand out for being important, intriguing and yet also of uncertain unity, coherence and staying power. The group is important because it brought together the big emerging markets whose economic growth—as Jim O'Neill of Goldman Sachs famously recognized in 2001[1]—was expected to outstrip and, indeed, anchor the rest of the world. That promised future gave them considerable clout—individually and collectively—in the present. It was intriguing because of the diversity and spread of continents, political systems and values, and economic models that they span between them.

Yet it attracted skepticism also precisely because the diversity attested to the lack of unifying values, principles, goals, and even interests. Is "BRICS" a construct of the social media-driven marketplace of ideas—an attention grabbing glib phrase in which speed is a substitute for and trumps quality and depth of analysis? This chapter begins with a sketch of the state of uncertainty in the international governance architecture at the time of writing. It then describes the evolution of the BRICS, followed by how it advanced global governance. Next it discusses the structural and other limitations that constrain the group's role and influence and then notes the deepening institutionalization of the grouping.

A world in flux—or disarray?

As of 2017, global governance is moving towards a visibly pluralistic future, without the traditional dominance of the West.[2] With the election of Donald Trump as US president and the retreat from liberal internationalism, world order is in transformation.[3] Even if its military power remains paramount, the capacity of "America First" to lead with ample followers is severely limited.[4] And with Brexit (Britain's exit from the European Union (EU)) and other strains of populism, the EU's ability to compensate in terms of the projection of normative power is more highly contested as well.

What the precise architecture of global governance will be in this new era remains unclear. But certain characteristics have emerged. One is that the traditional formal institutions at the apex of global governance will continue to struggle with respect to status. Although the United Nations (UN), the international financial institutions (IFIs), and the World Trade Organization (WTO) have abundant built-in legitimacy in terms of numbers of members, all face ongoing questions about their representational legitimacy and instrumental performance.[5] Another is that the "G-1" unipolar world has faded, and the G-7 (without Russia) is unlikely to regain its importance.

That said, however, there is no sign of a return to deep polarization along North/South or East/West lines found in the post-1945 years. The "rest" have become far more varied, with a sharp spread between winners and losers of globalization. Some such as the BRICS, the group of countries at the core of this chapter, have been able to shape these trends to their own advantages.[6] Although generic in some respects, the BRICS are different from other countries in the Global South. All have demonstrated an impressive reach in terms of their diplomatic profile. The stretch of China's international influence has been well documented. India has become a hub of diplomatic interaction—network as well as club diplomacy—as old and new friends alike vie for attention and deals. Brazil launched a number of high-profile diplomatic initiatives, from leadership on the G-20 developing countries via the WTO, to the proposal for a global fund against hunger, a push on biofuel diplomacy, and advocacy for independent oversight on UN-authorized interventions under the responsibility to protect (R2P) doctrine.[7]

Many other non-Western countries continue to be highly vulnerable, marginal to the core shifts in economic power whether interpreted via the dynamic of multipolarity or the deepened process of complex interdependence. Some, most notably small-island states, face existential problems relating to the environment. Others need to resort to unorthodox strategies to survive in the global political economy. Almost all except the BRICS are not big enough to escape the context of their immediate neighborhoods,[8] although some like Indonesia and Turkey are trying to carve out a niche for themselves as a bridge between small states, the big emerging markets, and the major powers.[9]

The ascendancy of informal modes of governance has benefited countries that in earlier eras were kept out of the central concerts of power. This is especially true of the BRICS countries, which continued to face the massive gaps in post-1945 and even post-1991 systems of governance. But the trend extends to an expanded cluster including many categorized in the past as middle powers. As such, no longer can global governance be visualized in exclusive terms.

The contrasts with older constructs are reinforced in turn by the ambiguity of the relationship between rising non-Western powers and the embedded global order. On the one hand, the BRICS are the major beneficiaries of both multi-polarity and deepening systemic interdependence, anticipated to match the original G-7's share of global output around 2040. Their growing economic self-confidence also finds expression increasingly in political assertiveness, and there is no hiding the declaratory message of global transition that underlies the group's policy priorities. Brazil's President Luiz Inácio Lula da Silva, host of the April 2010 summit, declared grandly that: "A new global economic geography has been born."[10] On the other hand, the BRICS remain frustrated that they are still not in a position to shape the rules of the global system. The first choice of the BRICS remained reforms of the formally mandated organizations, especially the UN with its unique legitimacy. In practice, however, these organizations fell short. Two of the BRICS (China, Russia) are permanent members of the UN Security Council, but the aspiration of the other three to that status continues to be frustrated. And some reform notwithstanding, the IFIs continue to be weighted in favor of the West.

This ambiguity calibrated the attitude of the BRICS to the G-20, the world's premier informal economic grouping.[11] In the midst of the global financial crisis all the BRICS accepted membership in the elevated G-20 at the leaders' level, which in many ways filled a major governance gap. It represents the best crossover point between legitimacy, effectiveness and efficiency. At the same time there remained a distance between the role of the old establishment and the BRICS in the ability to put their stamp on the G-20 in membership and mode of practice (including the question of hosting). The early stages of the summit were dominated by the G-7 members, and especially the United States and the United Kingdom.

The paradox of the G-20 was that, while it brought the BRICS into the hub of global governance at an institutional level, it also made the creation of an autonomous forum with membership only for the BRICS inevitable. Once the avenue of informality was opened up, at a highly visible and operationally significant level (beyond just the technically oriented G-20 made up of finance ministers and central bankers) the way was clear for a summit process made up of these countries by themselves to take form.

The BRICS' economic narrative of fast paced economic growth was necessary to grab attention in that it pointed to a different challenge from the Global South, one premised not on a sense of ideological fervor (and an emphasis on the weight of numbers), but on individual and collective material clout. By 2015 the BRICS accounted for forty-two percent of the global population, twenty-two to thirty percent of the world GDP at market exchange rates or purchasing power parity (PPP)

Table 20.1 Key statistics for BRICS countries

	Population (mn)	Total military personnel (2015, 000)	Military expenditure (2016, USD bn)	GDP (2015, USD bn) Market rate	PPP	GDP Average annual growth (%) 1990–2000	2000–2012	2016–2017
Brazil	208 (5)	729 (17)	24.5 (12)	1804 (9)	3147 (7)	2.7	3.7	0.7
Russia	144 (9)	1490 (4)	44.6 (6)	1366 (12)	3480 (6)	-4.7	4.8	1.4
India	1311 (2)	2798 (3)	51 (4)	2089 (7)	7910 (3)	6.0	7.6	7.1
China	1371 (1)	2843 (1)	161.7 (2)	11,065 (2)	19,631 (1)	10.6	10.6	6.6
South Africa	55 (25)	106 (55)	4.6 (43)	315 (32)	708 (29)	2.1	3.6	1.1
World	7347	27,437	1686	74,189	114,933	2.8	2.7	
BRICS global share (%)	42	29	34	22	30			

NB Figures in parentheses indicate world rankings.

Sources: World Development Indicators (Washington, DC: World Bank, 2017), 10–13; World Bank, http://data.worldbank.org/data-catalog/GDP-ranking table; http://data.worldbank.org/indicator/MS.MIL.TOTL.P1; World Bank, "Armed Forces Personnel, Total," http://data.worldbank.org/indicator/ MS.MIL.TOTL.P1; The Economist, 6–12 May 2017, p. 72; www.globalfirepower.com/active-military-manpower.asp; www.globalfirepower.com/defense-spending-budget.asp; SIPRI (2017), www.sipri.org/sites/default/files/Trends-world-military-expenditure2016.pdf

dollars respectively (see Table 20.1), and nineteen percent of world total trade. Their contribution to world economic growth is "estimated to exceed 50 percent."[12] Focusing attention on the four big original BRICs as the dynamic global motors of growth is appealing. On the basis of GDP/PPP China, India, Russia and Brazil are all in the top ten.

Still, this is not a sufficient theme to justify an extended analysis of the BRICS in terms of global governance. An assessment of the BRICS that only looks at economic criteria highlights the differences as much as the similarities. China's economic success has its roots in the adoption of agricultural reforms in the mid-1970s, supplemented in the 1990s with large increases of foreign direct investment (FDI) in manufacturing. Growth in India has been led by the indigenous services sector rather than exports of manufactures financed by FDI inflows. Brazil's economic fortunes are tied closely to export growth concentrated in agriculture and natural resources, a profile more exaggerated in Russia. By most standards, China is far ahead of the other BRICS in terms of economic performance. Trade is quite low among the BRICS, except for the bilateral relationship with China. Brazil's president Dilma Rousseff stated in 2015 that intra-BRICS trade had climbed from $27 billion in 2002 to $212 billion in 2010.[13] But the declared ambitious aim of doubling the volume to $500 billion by 2015 fell short by $250 billion (with this goal being moved back at the 2016 Goa summit to 2020). And there are specific tensions, above all between India and China. The question must be raised then why not only has BRICS emerged as a political forum, but how it has been able to sustain its role.

Underscoring the need to go beyond a narrow economic-driven analysis of BRICS is the uneven performance of the member countries. While all did extremely well through the immediate global financial crisis, they have fallen back since 2012. A common revised image is one of the broken BRICS.[14] Mutual funds based on the BRICS have been wound down, including the one created by Goldman Sachs. Again, however, the uniqueness of the BRICS is in its staying power. If the BRICS is explicitly a manifestation of the altered challenge from the Global South, a challenge based on a claim on strength and weakness, this strength is as much diplomatic as economic.

The most obvious example of how the construct of the BRICS as a political forum differs from their initial economic image is the addition of South Africa. Goldman Sachs not only left it out of its constellation but also out of the Next 11, the cluster of countries thought to be the next wave of up-and-coming countries. The relative weakness of South Africa in economic terms did not prove an impediment to the other incentives for South African membership. In addition to its resource endowments, infrastructure, and corporate and financial footprints into the rest of Africa,[15] South Africa retains a pivotal status as a diplomatic actor and a regional economic powerhouse—at the same time as many African countries contest the privileged treatment of South Africa as Africa's global representative, and Pretoria itself faces a constant tussle between its African and global identity.[16]

In terms of influence on the architecture of global governance, the existence of the BRICS demonstrates the degree of fragmentation and competition in the global system. The meaning of this separation remains unclear. The BRICS can be taken to be part of a hedging approach that allows its members some flexibility. It can also be analyzed as a lobby group that attempts to leverage the weight of the "rising" big powers through collective action. It can finally be interpreted as a revisionist challenge to the global order.

The evolution of the BRICS

BRICS is a rare phenomenon: A diplomatic grouping that follows an acronym coined by a private sector analyst. It is not the product of diplomatic negotiations based on shared political values or common economic interests. Moving from an analytical turn of phrase in 2001, an operational grouping was born. Looking back at its creation, it is the ability of the BRICS to play up commonalities and play down differences that stands out.

Although it faced some competition from a number of other acronyms—above all IBSA[17] (India, Brazil, and South Africa—the democratic subgroup of BRICS) and BASIC (Brazil, South Africa, India, and China), BRICS soon established a dominant position both conceptually because of its association with the key "rising states," and in terms of comparative perspective because of the translation from an artificial construct to an operational form of activity. Signs appeared that the concept of BRICS was being reconfigured as a grouping prior to the financial crisis, with some momentum built up because of a shared experience of all the BRICS except Russia in the Heiligendamm outreach process with the G-8 between 2005 and 2009.[18] In October 2007 the foreign ministers of Russia, China, and India met in Harbin, China. In May 2008 all four BRICs foreign ministers met for a day in Yekaterinburg, Russia. The global financial crisis shifted the balance more dramatically between the old establishment and the "rising" states. The first official BRIC summit was held, again in Yekaterinburg, in June 2009, with subsequent meetings in Brasilia, Brazil (April 2010), Hainan, China (April 2011), New Delhi, India (March 2012), Durban, South Africa (March 2013), Fortaleza, Brazil (July 2014), Ufa, Russia (July 2015), Goa, India (October 2016), and Xiamen, China (September 2017).

In the context of the global financial crisis, a confident BRICS resented calls for "responsible" stakeholder policies as efforts to subjugate their worldviews to the global North's priorities: "No burden sharing without benefit sharing," they countered. Instead, they take an instrumental approach to global governance. For example, China and Russia are instinctively suspicious of the very notion as a self-serving Western concept, preferring informal gatherings of big powers and regional institutions to formal multilateral machinery.[19]

Politically, the 2012 Delhi Declaration signaled a growing self-consciousness among the five BRICS that they have global weight and mean to use it. They announced the exploration of a new BRICS development bank. The statements on Syria and Iran marked out a clear "product differentiation" from the dominant trans-Atlantic policy on contemporary global controversies. To be sure, in the crucial vote on a draft Security Council resolution on Syria in July 2012, reflecting its identity as an open economy and a plural democracy, India sided with the West, while China and Russia cast a double veto. Yet: "One of the *advantages* of the BRICS process is that it remains a loose association of states with somewhat disparate interests, so no effort is made to force a common position when the BRICS states cannot agree on one. But these states have also found a way to disagree on some key issues . . . without torpedoing the entire enterprise."[20]

The most potent source of BRICS cohesion is geopolitical: The common interest in checking US/Western clout by leveraging collaboration with fellow non-Western powers. While all have an interest in an open international trading system, they "seek to adjust the way global wealth is generated and shared."[21] Several of the BRICS have an accumulating list of irritants in relations with Washington and all five have a strong vested interest in protecting strategic autonomy *vis-à-vis* the United States.[22] The Russian presidency of BRICS (April 2015–February 2016) coincided with the West's imposition of sanctions on Russia for the annexation of Crimea and thus increased Russian reliance on BRICS and other non-Western countries.[23]

On many global issues, the BRICS share a common interest in securing a broad array of economic, political, and security interests relative to the dominant industrialized states. The BRICS were among the opponents of the strikes by the North Atlantic Treaty Organization (NATO) on Serbia and the US-led invasion of Iraq in 2003. While South Africa initially voted for Security Council resolution 1973 on Libya in 2011, all five expressed unhappiness with NATO's interpretation of the 1973 mandate.

Looking at various BRICS summit declarations as well as statements from the five countries individually, their common position on a number of trouble spots can be distilled into four core elements. First, they support a rebalancing of the current global trade and financial system and are at the forefront of demanding changes to both the institutions and the rules regulating the global economic order, including greater voice and vote in writing the rules and designing and controlling the institutions. Second, they are skeptical of its morality and efficacy; and they are generally opposed to the use of sanctions as a tool of international policy both in principle (sovereignty) and on pragmatism (ineffectiveness-cum-harm to innocent civilians). Third, they are surprisingly similar in their resistance to democracy promotion and human rights monitoring and enforcement by external state, intergovernmental, and nongovernmental actors. Fourth, they reject militarization of disputes and conflicts, promote political resolutions through diplomatic talks, work to soften the West's interventionist impulse in the internal affairs of independent states (typically, developing countries), and are opposed to infringements of territorial integrity and sovereignty—but most have powerful militaries for robust defense of their own territorial claims. In part, they are motivated by historical memories of being invaded and colonized by the major European powers, and, in part, by fears of Western interference in their own internal affairs (Kashmir, Chechnya, Tibet).

On these issues, in general and over time, the BRICS positions and vote (for example in UN bodies) are more closely aligned to one another than to the G-7 (which, unlike the BRICS, are bound by common political and economic values). However, the differences between the North and Global South can be exaggerated. For example, the BRICS are sometimes portrayed as lukewarm supporters, if not closet opponents, of R2P. Yet a study of their statements and votes in the Security Council shows that their primary concern is to ensure consistent application and implementation, and to check the propensity of the North to evade norms when they prove inconvenient.[24]

Having floated the idea in Delhi in 2012, at the Fortaleza Summit in 2014 the BRICS established the New Development Bank (NDB) with an initial $50 billion fund, with equal stakes provided by each of the members.[25] They also agreed to establish a Currency Reserve Agreement (CRA), amounting to $100 billion as a buttress against financial crises. The NDB is headquartered in Shanghai (with a Johannesburg-based African Regional Centre), the inaugural president is K.V. Kamath from India; the bank became operational in February 2016. With an eye to reinforcing the image of the BRICS as an instrumental driver the first projects of the NDB were announced in 2016. The NDB and CRA initiatives represent the most significant institutional innovation to emerge from the BRICS summit process to date, countering the most common criticism of the BRICS, that it was all talk and no action.

The BRICS were increasingly tempted to exit the IFIs because of the continued failure to reform decision-making procedures, in particular to have influence commensurate with their growing global financial profile. Although competition in multilateral development banking could duplicate existing institutions and weaken loan-enforcement mechanisms, the NDB (along with the China-led Asian Infrastructure Investment Bank (AIIB)) introduced much needed choice for prospective borrowers in funding cost and modalities (especially the vexed issue of conditionality).[26]

The combination of the diversity within BRICS and the features that set them apart from other developing countries means that their viability, credibility, and relevance will depend not simply on the growth trajectories of members but also on the extent to which they can represent the worldviews, interests, and policy priorities of all developing countries. On issues with shared interests and views, the BRICS can exert more leverage in combination than separately. They can also leverage their atypical attributes of population size, market power, and geopolitical heft to cultivate the Global South as their natural constituency.[27] Many developing countries remain worried that the forces of globalization impinge adversely on their economic sovereignty, cultural integrity, and social stability. "Interdependence" among non-equals can mean the dependence of some on international markets that function under the dominance of others in norm setting and rule enforcement. On intellectual property, for example, whether it be with respect to generic life-saving drugs, seeds for agriculture, or traditional medicine, they can team up to take on the lobbying power of the "Big Pharma" (e.g., Pfizer) and global agribusiness (e.g., Monsanto) to robustly protect the rights of poor people to affordable medicines, of poor farmers to affordable seeds, and of indigenous peoples to ownership of traditional knowledge.

Limitations on the BRICS

Advances notwithstanding, some caution is warranted about the robustness of these contours of transition in global governance. One explanation of the trajectory of the BRICS points to a comprehensive process of realignment of power, with a new alternative concert of oppositional/adversarial states taking shape. Thus, even though the main deliverables from the Fortaleza summit were economic in form and content—the NDB and the CRA—their primary import was geopolitical: Rewiring the existing system of global governance so that it no longer ran through Western capitals.[28]

Equally, however, there are strong counterforces to reconfigured interstate polarization and "overt balancing."[29] In all of them, domestic priorities and problems trump club solidarity. The five are far from homogeneous in interests, values, and policy preferences, which exposes the dismissive comment that the BRICS lack the necessary cement to bind them together. They are totally different countries with separate histories, contexts, political and economic systems, needs, opportunities, and development trajectories. China, India, and Russia are in a qualitatively different category within BRICS from Brazil and South Africa with economic sluggishness and political turbulence in the last two. The G-7 spread of per capita incomes is considerably less than for the BRICS: Brazil, Russia, and South Africa export commodities; China exports manufactured goods; India exports services.

These constraints are exacerbated by the political, social, and economic problems. Since 2014 the importance accorded by China, India, and Russia to BRICS as the locus of cooperation for reforming global order has been substantially modified by parallel developments in the relations of each with the United States. Moscow and Washington's relations deteriorated sharply after the geopolitical crisis in Ukraine and Russian annexation of Crimea in 2014, sharply orienting Moscow to a consolidated relationship with Beijing. The election of the nationalist Narendra Modi government cooled India's relations with China even while those with the United States warmed as India looks for advanced technology and foreign investment to fasttrack economic development.

Of the five, only China has maintained the projections anticipated by Goldman Sachs, and even Chinese growth has slowed. It may be the case that the deceleration in their growth rates reflects the advantages of cheap labor—especially surplus from the countryside—and imported technology are leveling off as they exhaust the rapid, investment-intensive, catch-up model of growth. Systemic corruption is a chronic and deep-seated problem in all five. And political turmoil has cut into the confidence of a number of BRICS, most notably Brazil and South Africa. By contrast, Russia seems to have stabilized in its politics and India gained political stability with the election of the Modi government in 2014 with a comfortable majority in parliament not seen in thirty years.[30] China maintained political stability through the years of turmoil in the other BRICS countries.

The most serious drag on being a major force in global governance is not resistance by the old order but serious differences of values and interests among the group's members. The BRICS are riven with rivalries over borders, resources, and status. India has a longstanding serious border dispute with China. Two of the five are authoritarian states, although the three democracies have traditions of reticence in global democracy promotion. They are divided on reform of the Security Council, with China's interest lying more in a bipolar than a genuinely multipolar global order, and on the global economic effects of China's currency.

Each of the BRICS retains deep and specific ties with the pivotal countries in the North. All have a greater stake in bilateral relations with the United States for reasons of market power, investments, and high technology. Realist scholars also signal the prospect of an alternative alignment with the US-led North if one of the BRICS rises faster and in a more antagonistic manner than the others. John Mearsheimer points in particular to "China's unpeaceful rise" as a catalyst for this type of balancing response.[31] Oliver Stuenkel argues that rather than confrontation, the rising powers will continue to support the existing liberal institutional consensus while seeking to carve out their own institutional spaces within a "global competitive multilateralism."[32] Not only are the rising powers, including the BRICS, suspicious of powerful Western countries; they are equally wary of one other's intentions and therefore are flexible in pursuing international cooperation or choosing conflict partners, depending on the issue to hand.

Hence the BRICS do not always act as a concerted bloc within other institutional settings. Stefan Schirm highlights the presence of mixed coalitions within the G-20, where *ad hoc* groupings reflect a variety of arrangements comprising both developed and developing countries, and where like-minded groupings such as the established G-7 and BRICS co-mingle on a variety of issues.[33] The cohesiveness among the BRICS has not congealed to the point at which the diplomatic grouping acts as a bloc across an array of institutional settings.

China and India are the two heavyweights. Because of the sweeping expansion of its comprehensive national power, China has seen an exponential increase in its weight in the global economy, Asian and global power balances, and regional and global governance institutions. In its growing international relations to date, China has reaffirmed Westphalian norms of state sovereignty and responsible international behavior such as nonaggression, nonintervention and noninterference in internal affairs. Nevertheless, it remains reticent and reluctant on shouldering the managerial responsibilities of world order traditionally associated with being a great power.[34] China's currency manipulation has imposed significant economic costs on its fellow BRICS. Brazil has complained that China's sharp practices include damaging Brazilian prospects in third markets, dumping exports diverted from Europe in Brazil, and erecting steep tariff barriers to Brazilian imports.

Until the creation of BRICS with an activist agenda and the elevation of the G-20 to leaders' level, even the big emerging markets were essentially rule takers in global governance. The global financial crisis as the primary stimulus to the G-20 elevation gave them a seat at the table of the top global economic governance, which they used, along with their increases in quotas and voting power in the IMF and World Bank, to become partners in the collective responses of expansionary fiscal and monetary policies. Even so, they still lagged behind in the exercise of institutional soft power dominated by the North Atlantic. The real significance of the BRICS 2014 Fortaleza summit was that for the first time they staked out institutional leadership territory. But they still suffer from critical capacity deficits whereby Brazil and India, for example, remain hesitant norm shapers more than normsetters.[35] South Africa's normative reach has shrunk to disable even that, Russia seems intent more on defending the global governance system of 1945 than innovating, and only China among them seems to have gained the poise, self-confidence, and financial and geopolitical heft to take on a leading role in reshaping the global normative architecture.

China's exceptional economic and geopolitical weight means that the future of BRICS will largely be shaped by China's choices and capabilities. The creation of the NDB and the CRA were followed by the launch of the AIIB and President Xi Jinping's Belt and Road Initiative that emphasizes infrastructure and land–sea connectivity by building ports, railways and pipelines across Asia, the Middle East and Europe.[36] Only China today could conceive of a project of such scale and ambition— the largest single infrastructure project in history. More than one hundred countries attended the inaugural summit in Beijing in May 2017, including twenty-eight national leaders. The trillion dollar initiative symbolizes the expansion of China's economic, political, and strategic influence at US expense by consolidating its position at the center of global supply chains and manufacturing networks. In January at the annual Davos meeting—"the spiritual home of capitalism"[37]—President Xi defended the global trade system from attacks by the protectionist US president-elect.

Thus, the extraordinary alignment of financial and technical resources, and the political commitment and international cooperation, decisively sets apart China from the other BRICS. However, India replaced China as the world's fastest growing major economy in 2015 and 2016. India is at once a country with a large number of very poor and vulnerable people and a big emerging market with a rising global profile with many interests in common with the other rapidly industrializing countries. The G-77 is the natural home of the former and BRICS of the latter. India's international role also is hampered by the paradox of being a "premature power," one whose global reach is outstripped by national indicators of development.[38] India's ambivalent and often defensive and rarely entrepreneurial response is rooted in its transitional identity as a rising power with growing economic weight but a hugely poor and underdeveloped country with a multitude of serious policy challenges.

China and India are united in a common defense of the principle of sovereignty. However, some explicit differences have appeared. For example, India might team up with China against Europe and the United States on greenhouse gas targets but join Washington in a hedging strategy against China's growing military footprint and assertive behavior. China has made little secret of its efforts to thwart India's ambitions for permanent membership in the Security Council and the Nuclear Suppliers Group, and its efforts to have the UN list some Pakistan-based individuals as international terrorists. India, in turn, remains deeply suspicious of the China–Pakistan Economic Corridor, took advantage of being host of the Goa BRICS summit in October 2016 to invite neighboring countries sans Pakistan, instead calling the latter the "mothership of terrorism,"[39] and was conspicuously absent from the Belt and Road Initiative forum in Beijing in May 2017.

Deepening institutionalization

Still, in spite of these differences, the BRICS have hung together on key geopolitical issues. They rejected host Australia's suggestion to exclude Russia from the 2014 G-20 Brisbane summit. At Ufa, the leaders did not refer specifically to Russia's actions but only to the BRICS "deep concern about the situation in Ukraine" and the need to resolve the situation through "inclusive political dialogue." The photo-op of the leaders was used by Moscow as proof of the failure of "the West's attempts to isolate Russia."[40]

In a statement issued after the February 2017 meeting in preparation for the Chinese presidency, Russia's foreign ministry spokesperson Maria Zakharova said:

> We welcome and share our Chinese friends' commitment to strengthening the role of BRICS as a major factor in the formation of a new polycentric world order . . . to strengthen solidarity within the framework of BRICS so that the "group of five" can speak in a "single and strong voice" on topical issues of international politics and economics.[41]

BRICS continues to institutionalize as a platform for policymakers to engage one another in normative debates about the institutions of global order[42] and coordinate actions in international forums such as the UN and the IMF, and giving policymakers and officials unprecedented access in capitals. It has spawned a sprawling set of and regular ministerial meetings in sectors such as agriculture, education, energy, health, water, railways, and terrorism. The group's 2016 calendar lists 124 meetings from February (when India took over the presidency) to December 2016 on an extensive range of topics.[43] India's Finance Minister Arun Jaitley has called for a BRICS arbitration panel in order to reduce reliance on such centers located in the West whose award decisions seem to be loaded against the interests of developing countries.[44] At the eighth summit in Goa in October 2016, leaders decided to create a BRICS-led rating agency on the matching belief that the existing institutions (Moody's, Standard & Poor, Fitch) are unfairly biased in favor of Western countries and companies.

In other words, the BRICS have witnessed an unspectacular but steady growth in coordination and consultation in technical areas that do not attract headlines but facilitate an alignment of public policy. There is also a BRICS inter-parliamentary group. Some of the skepticism about the group has its roots in the misguided attempt to apply frameworks of analysis of world order derived from North Atlantic experiences.[45] BRICS is both a symptom of and a contributor to emerging multi-polarity. As Amitav Acharya has argued,[46] the decline of US primacy has produced a matching decline in the US-created and US-led global order and in the new "multiplex order" with the BRICS as one of the world's many theaters, each playing with its own simultaneous set of lead actors and storylines. And, with the Belt and Road Initiative, China is positioning itself at the center of a global economic hub-and-spoke system that mirrors the US-centric military hub-and-spoke system.

Conclusion

The BRICS are a reflection of widening global multi-polarity and are thus a challenge to the establishment. The existence of the BRICS is a function of the renewed prominence of informal multilateralism or plurilateralism, as well as the newfound agency and enhanced capacity of these countries in international politics. The consolidation into groupings has placed them in an elevated strategic position within the wider governance architecture where, at summit-level institutions, emphasis often is on

South–South solidarity. Shared frustration with the architecture and management of the existing international financial and political order does not in and by itself translate into joint initiatives and leadership to replace it. The challenge for the BRICS is in working from economic reality to a tighter sense of normative and ideational identity among the group's membership. It is easy and tempting to dismiss it as "more a way station than a summit"[47] because of the lack of commonality, the existence of tensions and squabbles, and potential serious conflicts. Yet the grouping has tried to put pressure on the West to facilitate and accommodate and not block the rise of emerging economies.

However contested a concept, BRICS has clearly notched up early successes as an agenda-shaping geopolitical grouping that has moved slowly but steadily towards growing institutionalization with an annual summit and a host of ministerial, official, and working sessions in between. It is Janus faced in being both an instrument "to dilute the dominance of the U.S.-led West"[48] and a vehicle for promoting its members' shared economic and diplomatic interests. In other words, the BRICS "brand" has become part of the national identity of the five countries in their global interactions,[49] and the agenda has expanded from the initial focus on reforming the IFIs to include international security[50] and development. The BRICS have put down markers that they intend to use their demographic and economic clout to challenge and change the way that the world is governed through formal multilateral machinery and informal groupings.

Additional reading

Cedric de Coning, Thomas Mandrup, and Liselotte Odgaard, eds., *The BRICS and Coexistence: An Alternative Vision of World Order* (London: Routledge, 2015).

Andrew F. Cooper, *The BRICS—A Very Short Introduction* (Oxford: Oxford University Press, 2016).

Ruchir Sharma, "Broken BRICs: Why the Rest Stopped Rising," *Foreign Affairs* 91, no. 6 (2012): 2–7.

Oliver Stuenkel, *The BRICS and the Future of Global Order* (Lanham, MD: Lexington, 2015).

Ramesh Thakur, "How Representative Are BRICS?," *Third World Quarterly* 35, no. 10 (2014): 1791–1808.

Notes

1 Jim O'Neill, *Building Better Economic BRICs* (Global Economics Paper No. 66, Goldman Sachs, 2001), www.goldmansachs.com/our-thinking/archive/archive-pdfs/build-better-brics.pdf.

2 G. John. Ikenberry, *Liberal Leviathan: The Origins, Crisis, and Transformation of the American World Order* (Princeton, NJ: Princeton University Press, 2011).

3 Stewart M. Patrick, "Trump and World Order: The Return of Self-Help," *Foreign Affairs* 96, no. 2 (2017): 52–57.

4 For the earlier period of followership, see Andrew F. Cooper, Richard A. Higgott, and Kim Richard Nossal, "Bound to Follow? Leadership and Followership in the Gulf Conflict," *Political Science Quarterly* 106, no. 3 (1991): 391–410.

5 Alan Alexandroff and Andrew F. Cooper, *Rising States, Rising Institutions: Challenges for Global Governance:* (Washington, DC: Brookings Institution, 2010); Ramesh Thakur, *The United Nations, Peace and Security: From Collective Security to the Responsibility to Protect*, 2nd ed. (Cambridge: Cambridge University Press, 2017).

6 Andrew F. Cooper, *The BRICS—A Very Short Introduction* (Oxford: Oxford University Press, 2016).

7 See Sean W. Burgess, *Brazil in the World: The International Relations of a South American Giant* (Manchester: Manchester University Press, 2017); Christina Stolte, *Brazil's Africa Strategy: Role Conception and the Drive for International Status* (London: Palgrave, 2015); Philip Cunliffe and Kai Michael Kenkel, eds., *Brazil as a Rising Power: Intervention Norms and the Contestation of Global Order* (London: Routledge, 2016).

8 Andrew F. Cooper and Timothy M. Shaw, *The Diplomacies of Small States: Between Vulnerability and Resilience* (London: Palgrave Macmillan, 2009).

9 See Awidya Santikajaya, "Walking the Middle Path: The Characteristics of Indonesia's Rise," *International Journal* 71, no. 4 (2016): 563–586; Emel Parlar Dal and Ali Murat Kursun, "Assessing Turkey's Middle Power Foreign Policy in MIKTA: Goals, Means, and Impact," *International Journal* 71, no. 4 (2016): 608–629.

10 Lula da Silva, "At Yekaterinburg, the BRICs Come of Age," *Hindu*, 16 June 2009.

11 Andrew F. Cooper and Ramesh Thakur, *The Group of Twenty (G20)* (London: Routledge, 2013).

12 Zhang Yan (China's Ambassador to India), "Powering the World," *Indian Express* (Delhi), 28 March 2012.

13 Dilma Rousseff, "We're All in It Together," *Times of India*, 29 March 2012.

14 Ruchir Sharma, "Broken BRICs: Why the Rest stopped Rising," *Foreign Affairs* 91, no. 6 (2012): 2–7.

15 On South Africa's motivations in the BRICS, see Chris Alden and Maxi Schoeman, "South Africa in the Company of Giants: The Search for Leadership in a Transforming Global Order," *International Affairs* 89, no. 1 (2013): 111–129.

16 Chris Landsberg and Candice Moore, "BRICS, South–South Cooperation and the Durban Summit: What's in it for South Africa?" *Portuguese Journal of International Affairs* 7 (Spring/Summer 2013): 3–14.

17 Sarah Al Doyaili, Andreas Freytag, and Peter Draper, "IBSA: Fading Out or Forging a Common Vision?" *South African Journal of International Affairs* 20, no. 2 (2013): 297–310.

18 Andrew F. Cooper and Agata Antkiewicz, eds., *Emerging Powers and Global Governance: Lessons from the Heiligendamm Process* (Waterloo, Canada: Wilfrid Laurier University Press, 2008).

19 Charles Grant, *Russia, China and Global Governance* (London: Centre for European Reform, 2012).

20 Nikolas Gvosdev, "The Realist Prism: What the US Can Learn from the BRICS," *World Politics Review*, 22 June 2012 (emphasis added).

21 George G. Gilboy and Eric Heginbotham, "Double Trouble: A Realist View of Chinese and Indian Power," *Washington Quarterly* 36, no. 3 (2013), 136.

22 Edward Luce, "How Obama Lost Friends and Influence in the BRICS," *Financial Times*, 20 April 2014.

23 Georgy Toloraya and Roman Chukov, "BRICS to be Considered?" *International Organisations Research Journal* 11, no. 2 (2016): 70–81.

24 Oliver Stuenkel, *The BRICS and the Future of Global Order* (Lanham, MD: Lexington, 2015), 125–146; Ramesh Thakur, "R2P after Libya and Syria: Engaging Emerging Powers," *Washington Quarterly* 36, no. 2 (2013): 61–76.

25 Adriana Abdenur, "China and the BRICS Development Bank: Legitimacy and Multilateralism in South–South Cooperation," *IDS Bulletin* 45, no. 4 (2014): 85–101; Andrew F. Cooper and Asif B. Farooq, "Testing the Club Dynamics of the BRICS: The New Development

Bank from Conception to Establishment," *International Organizations Research Journal* 10, no. 2 (2015): 32–44.

26 Helmut Reisen, "BRICS Contribution to Global Governance: Policy Areas," *International Organisations Research Journal* 10, no. 2 (2015): 81–89.

27 Ramesh Thakur, "How Representative are BRICS?" *Third World Quarterly*, 35, no. 10 (2014): 1791–1808.

28 Ramesh Thakur, "Not Just another Brick in the Geopolitical Wall," *Tehelka Magazine*, 2 August 2014: 36–40.

29 Andrew Hurrell, "Hegemony, Liberalism and Global Order: What Space for Would-Be Great Powers?," *International Affairs* 82, no. 1 (2006): 1–19.

30 Ramesh Thakur, "Polls Herald the Rise of Aspirational India," *Tehelka Magazine*, 31 May 2014: 38–41.

31 John J. Mearsheimer, "China's Unpeaceful Rise" *Current History* (April 2006): 160–162.

32 Oliver Stuenkel, *Post-Western World: How Emerging Powers Are Remaking Global Order* (Cambridge: Polity Press, 2016).

33 A. Stefan Schirm, "Global Politics Are Domestic Politics: How Societal Interests and Ideas Shape Ad Hoc Groupings in the G20 Which Supersede International Alliances," paper prepared for the International Studies Association Convention in Montreal, 16–19 March 2011, www.sowi.rub.de/mam/content/lsip/schirmg20 isa2011.pdf.

34 Gregory Chin and Ramesh Thakur, "Will China Change the Rules of Global Order?" *Washington Quarterly* 33, no. 4 (2010): 119–138; Andrew F. Cooper, Timothy M. Shaw, and Gregory Chin, "Emerging Powers and Africa: Implications for/from Global Governance?," *Politikon: South African Journal of Political Studies* 36, no. 1 (2008): 27–44.

35 Waheguru Pal Singh Sidhu, Pratap Bhanu Mehta, and Bruce Jones, eds., *Shaping the Emerging World: India and the Multilateral Order* (Washington, DC: Brookings Institution, 2013).

36 Peter Ferdinand, "Westward ho—the China Dream and 'One Belt, One Road': Chinese Foreign Policy under Xi Jinping," *International Affairs* 92, no. 4 (2016): 941–957; Christopher K. Johnson, *President Xi Jinping's "Belt and Road" Initiative: A Practical Assessment of the Chinese Communist Party's Roadmap for China's Global Resurgence* (Washington, DC: Center for Strategic and International Studies, 2016), https://csis-prod.s3.amazonaws.com/s3fs-public/publication/160328_Johnson_PresidentXiJinping_Web.pdf.

37 Edward Luce, "The Changing of the Global Economic Guard," *The Atlantic*, 29 April 2017, www.theatlantic.com/international/archive/2017/04/china-economy-populism/523989/.

38 Navroz K. Dubash, "Of Maps and Compasses: India in Multilateral Climate Negotiations," in *Shaping the Emerging World*, eds., Sidhu, Mehta, and Jones, 272.

39 Jon Boone, "Narendra Modi Labels Pakistan 'Mothership of Terrorism,'" *The Guardian*, 17 October 2016.

40 Alexander Gabuev, "Another BRIC(s) in the Great Wall," Carnegie Moscow Center, 7 July 2015, http://carnegie.ru/commentary/?fa=60628.

41 "Russia's priorities during China's BRICS presidency," Briefing by Foreign Ministry Spokesperson Maria Zakharova, Moscow, 2 March 2017, www.mid.ru/en/foreign_policy/news/-/asset_publisher/cKNonkJE02Bw/content/id/2664840.

42 Cedric de Coning, Thomas Mandrup, and Liselotte Odgaard, eds., *The BRICS and Coexistence: An Alternative Vision of World Order* (London: Routledge, 2015).

43 Published online by India's Ministry of External Affairs: http://brics2016.gov.in/content/calender.php.

44 PTI, "Arun Jaitley Pitches for BRICS Arbitration Platform, Does Not Want to Rely on Developed Nations," *Daily News and Analyses* (Mumbai), 28 August 2016, www.dnaindia.com/money/report-arun-jaitley-pitches-for-brics-arbitration-platform-does-not-want-to-rely-on-developed-nations-2249540.

45 Stuenkel, *The BRICS and the Future of Global Order*, is especially good on this point.

46 Amitav Acharya, *The End of American World Order* (Cambridge: Polity Press, 2016).

47 Sanjaya Baru, "BRICS in Search of Cement," *Business Standard* (Delhi), 18 April 2011.

48 Interview with Russia's President Vladimir Putin, "Putin Wants Measures to Protect BRICS Nations From U.S. Sanctions," *Moscow Times*, 15 July 2014, https://themoscowtimes.com/articles/putin-wants-measures-to-protect-brics-nations-from-us-sanctions-37305.

49 Hongmei Li and Leslie L. Marsh, "Building the BRICS: Media, Nation Branding, and Global Citizenship," *International Journal of Communication* 10 (2016): 2973–2988.

50 See Victoria Panova, "The BRICS Security Agenda and Prospects for the BRICS Ufa Summit," *International Organisations Research Journal* 10, no. 2 (2015): 90–104.

The Global South

Ian Taylor

The idea of the Global South emerged from the maelstrom of World War II as it was in this post-war period that the developing world began to "fit" into the wider international political economy in a way that had not been readily apparent in the pre-Cold War era. In normal usage, the term "South" (alongside "Third World," "developing world," and, less frequently—although more accurately—"majority world") refers to those countries in an uneven process of underdevelopment primarily located in the ex-colonial states of Africa, Asia, and Latin America. The very notion of the South implies a commonality of material and ideational interests. This shared identity may, to a greater or lesser extent, have been the case in the immediate postcolonial moment, but it has progressively become ever more problematic as this chapter makes clear. Today, it is debatable whether or not the South actually exists.

The South as a coherent bloc has long been an aspiration of various elites located in the postcolonial world. Yet the capacity for a coherent bloc to form ran contrary to economic and political developments across the South. This chapter examines some of the attempts to institutionalize what is now called the "Global South" through the creation of various organizations and forums and, in extension, explore the involvement of underdeveloped countries in global governance. As the chapter shows, attempts to formulate institutions to express a notional "Southern" position have been undermined by the diversity of interests that elites within the postcolonial territories possess and express, as well as by robust responses in the capitalist heartland to undermine and sabotage such efforts. Taking place at a variety of levels, nonetheless the result has been a progressive weakening of any putative voice from the South. This then fits with another reality that we need to acknowledge when talking of "the South:" does it actually exist?

The idea of the Global South

The idea of the Global South itself is derivative of Third Worldism, which has been described as "the universal institutionalization of national sovereignty as the representation of independence of decolonized peoples, political confrontation with European racism, and a movement of quasi-nationalist elites whose legitimacy depended on negotiating their economic and political dependence."[1] The notion of a commonality of interests that all ex-colonial states possessed was the driving force behind such expressions. This sense of community was grasped by some elites in the postcolonial world as one way new-found economic and political freedoms could be guaranteed and protected in the context of the Cold War in which a whole swathe of "new" countries were inserted.

Enjoying political power and the advantages that this confers, the elite classes who attained power once the colonial flags were lowered had no intention of surrendering it. At once then, Third Worldism was Janus faced. It sought to legitimize extant elites as representing the "poor and dispossessed" of the postcolonial world (when objectively, this was often the exact opposite of the situation) and also sought to extract as much maneuverability as possible within the global order for accumulation and regime stabilization. In other words, the South was always a domestic and externally oriented project and, in so being, was always an elite political expression. The heydays of the South were really at an historic juncture, when newly independent countries were flexing their muscles, and there was a heady optimism regarding the leverage of the postcolonial world *vis-à-vis* the industrialized North. This was when the institutionalization of the South emerged and when, momentarily, it appeared coherent.

Bandung

The Asian-African Conference in Bandung may be seen as the watershed when newly emergent postcolonial elites expressed the idea that they shared certain interests. Convened in Indonesia between 18 and 24 April 1955, the idea of such an Asian-African gathering had first been suggested at a meeting of the prime ministers of Burma, Ceylon, India, Indonesia, and Pakistan in Colombo, Ceylon (now Sri Lanka), in April 1953. Representatives from twenty-nine countries attended the conference, at a time when the United Nations had only fifty-nine member states. Bandung provided many provisional contacts between newly emerging elites from the postcolonial world; and it has since been described as "in essence a celebration of the wave of independence that had swept across Asia and was then cresting in Africa."[2]

The motives for convening such a conference varied widely as did the economic and political orientations of participants. Nonetheless, Bandung adopted a number of resolutions that have been described as "an augur of a future protest against the subordinating stays of the developing countries in the international system," and which established a set of normative values that sought to establish a more equitable world order. Such expressions from elites in the notional South found their institutional manifestation in two important organizations that have historically provided the main loci of developing countries in international affairs: The Non-Aligned Movement (NAM) and the United Nations Conference on Trade and Development (UNCTAD) within which the Group of 77 (G-77) emerged. By looking at the histories of these two organizations, the development of the South as an idea and its effective defeat by the assertive and dominant West can be traced.

NAM

Bandung was followed by the Belgrade Conference of 1961, at which the NAM was officially launched. A declaration containing the common views of delegates on international problems was issued that was in line with the general Bandung position and an agreement about triennial summits was also reached. The NAM was established as a loose multilateral project with very little formal organization, which resulted in "conference diplomacy (becoming) a specific characteristic of nonalignment."[3] By confirming the "Spirit of Bandung" in 1961, the NAM also adopted a posture that rejected the bilateralist impulses that dominated the world through the system of Cold War alliances. Yet perhaps what was the most important outcome from Belgrade, which has continued to the contemporary period, was the general establishment of behavioral norms for state activity. Although this has certainly been compromised as the NAM has evolved, it is important to remember that at that particular time such normative expressions were pioneering, even revolutionary, and consciously rejected big power domination of the global order.

The NAM committed itself to a project that privileged the role of the United Nations as the proper forum for interstate activity. The "Lusaka Declaration" of 1970 explicitly promoted the UN and aimed to strengthen the body "so that it will be a more effective obstacle against all forms of aggressive action and the threat to use force against the freedom, independence, sovereignty and territorial integrity of any country."[4] Such calls, while rhetorical to be sure, expressed a desire by a large number of states to operate in a world less beholden to the unilateralist activities of the so-called superpowers (Washington and Moscow) and other great powers as well. At the same time, the NAM's focus began to shift from issues *vis-à-vis* the East–West confrontation and towards development issues and North–South relations. Indeed, this focus on constructing a normative order to resolve developmental contradictions produced by global capitalism henceforth preoccupied the summits of the organization—in itself a reflection of changes in the international system, stimulated by the heady growth in the South's representation at the UN and other multilateral organizations.

The NAM, alongside UNCTAD became in the 1970s an important platform in the South's efforts to put forward the New International Economic Order (NIEO), which was a set of proposals to improve the terms of trade for developing countries, and to increase aid and reduce tariffs on exports from them. It was a call for a restructured global economy that would help facilitate development in the South, which symbolically culminated at the Sixth Special Session of the United Nations in 1974. Under the NAM's then leader (Algeria's Honari Boumedienne), the South deployed NAM and G-77 texts in successfully pushing for a comprehensive normative declaration detailing the aspirations of the developing world's elites. As Craig Murphy asserts:

> [F]or the first time the General Assembly approved a massive resolution covering all of the economic issues the Third World had raised since the Second World War. The resolution touched on sovereignty over natural resources, improving terms of trade through international regulation of trade based on equitable treatment, reforming the global monetary system to include an aid component, expanding concessionary multilateral aid, providing debt relief, controlling TNCs, promoting international support for industrialization, and reforming the United Nations system to give Third World governments greater control over international economic decisions.[5]

Much of this rhetoric was derivative of leading Southern elites' perceptions of their own domestic interests in light of the breakdown of the Bretton Woods system and the maneuverings of the Organization of the Petroleum Exporting Countries (OPEC). It is important here to assert that it was the leading elites of relatively developing countries that led the way. Already, there had been a tacit recognition that the Global South was a divided entity, with the nomenclature of "least developed country (LDC)" being introduced at the United Nations in November 1971 in General Assembly resolution 2768 (XXVI). LDCs were those that, according to the UN, exhibited the lowest indicators in terms of socioeconomic development. While commonsensical and obvious, what the LDC appellation officially admitted—arguably for the first time—was that the South was not monolithic.

Yet equally, negotiations regarding the future architecture to replace such a system seemed logical to many Southern elites. In short: "[T]hey took the opportunities offered by the evolving politics of international economic relations to create leadership roles for themselves," thereby bolstering their own standing at the domestic level. This was important as "their position as the ruling class at the periphery remain[ed] tenuous, hence, the imperative of external association and support"—and public posturing on the international stage.[6]

The NAM's platform

Until the Jakarta Summit in 1992, the NAM's position was fairly consistent, centering around territorial integrity, resistance to "imperialism," and a rejection of hierarchies of power and privilege in the international system. The essential aims were crystallized in the Lusaka Declaration of 1970, which stated that the NAM was committed to:

> The pursuit of world peace and (the) strengthening the role of nonaligned countries within the United Nations so that it will be a more effective obstacle against all forms of aggressive action . . . opposition to great power military alliances and pacts . . . the universality of and strengthening of the efficacy of the United Nations; and the struggle for economic independence and mutual co-operation on a basis of equality and mutual benefits.[7]

Paradoxically, although the Lusaka Declaration came as the push for liberation in southern Africa was reaching a climax, and as calls for the NIEO focused the minds of state elites in both North and South, it was also a watershed in another way. Membership of the NAM by this point was not only predominately African but also, as membership of the body expanded, the principles on which the organization was founded were compromised. The heavily dependent and poverty-stricken African states joined, but many were by no means non-aligned, being firmly within the French and hence Western capitalist camp. Yet the ongoing process of decolonization and global politics meant that by the mid-1970s the NAM had become ostensibly more "socialist" in orientation, perhaps by the Colombo summit in 1976, and certainly by the sixth summit which symbolically was held in Havana in 1979.

The reassertion over the South of Northern politico-economic dominance came, as became obvious in UNCTAD, at a historical juncture when financial indebtedness was acting to drastically undermine—if not emasculate—sovereignty and maneuverability in the developing world. At the same time, leadership fractions within the Global South were increasingly drawn into the ongoing restructuring process as promoted by the neoliberal project, and their specific class interests tended to be different from their own constituencies suffering from the liberalization of developing economies. Indeed, the call for liberalization—dressed up as it was in the rhetoric of economic "realities" and "TINA" (there is no alternative)—gave space for conservative elements within the ruling elites in the South, who had always been reluctant to commit themselves to a concrete plan of action *vis-à-vis* the NIEO.

Their seizure on the globalization discourse to help explain away unpopular policies (which concomitantly reified the positions of certain externally oriented class fractions within the domestic polity) reflected not only a minimal commitment to any major restructuring of the global economy (except where it benefited Southern elites), it also mirrored the tensions and contradictions inherent within an organization such as the NAM whose membership was so disparate. As Walden Bello succinctly put it:

> The ambivalence of the NIEO program as expressed by NAM reflect[ed] the fact that despite rhetorical unity, the alliance that advanced this program was an uneasy one, composed of conservative, radical, and liberal states with divergent objectives. For status quo states like Mexico, world economic reform along NIEO lines was seen as a means to alleviate pressures for much-needed internal economic reforms and thus solidify the position of the ruling elites. Also, waving the NIEO flag was a perfect ideological weapon to blunt criticism from forces for change within the country.[8]

Furthermore, the abandonment of "confrontational" posturing (such as the NIEO) served the interests not only of specific class fractions throughout the South, but also the specific foreign policies of particular NAM states. For example, towards the end of the 1980s, Yugoslavia became aware of the pressing need to tie its economic future to the ongoing European integrationist project, particularly in the light of the decline of the rest of the socialist world. Thus at the ninth summit in Belgrade in 1989, Yugoslavia "pleaded for the modernization of the Movement (thus) discarding the NAM's attitude of assertiveness *vis-à-vis* the two power blocs. Instead, the NAM (adopted) a more tolerant and flexible position with emphasis on co-operation and dialogue."[9] Such a position was not simply a reflection of the host country's perception, but it also reflected a playing out of the increasing integration of the world's markets and the desire by Southern elites to benefit from this process.

Combative posturing against the structural inequalities of the capitalist system were seen to be of little use in facing up to globalization, particularly when—as has been pointed out—many of the elites in the Global South subscribed to the hegemonic project of neoliberalism. Even those who did not fully accede to this "new world order" were painfully aware of the ongoing marginalization that many developing countries were enduring and, in the words of the Indonesian ambassador to South Africa, were "willing to undertake whatever was necessary to ensure that (they) could engage the rest of the international community in dialogue."[10] Yet the international community set the agenda in the new North–South dialogue; while the NAM adopted what can be seen as a "trade unionist" approach to the world economy, discussions of the structural inequalities that underpinned the global capitalist system were quietly shelved. Meanwhile, rhetoric about "economic realities," appealed to "universal standards," and claims about the "de-ideologization" of global politics became the norm.

UNCTAD

UNCTAD was established in 1964 to "create a forum in which the more prosperous member countries (of the United Nations) would come under pressure to agree to measures benefiting the less-developed countries," More specifically UNCTAD's formation was "a deliberate effort to use international bureaucracy and conference diplomacy to alter current norms affecting trade and development."[11] Its founding reflected the growth in membership of the UN of newly independent states. A large number of the elites from these new entities keenly felt the inequity of the world order, which was informed by the ideologies of the North—actually the wealthy West—and in which the new states had had no hand in crafting.

As an organization, UNCTAD was mandated to perform a variety of purposes, perhaps most importantly to formulate policies designed to create general and explicit prescriptions associated with fairer trade and development. The UNCTAD secretariat's efforts were guided by its own research or by consultants recruited by the organization. Typically painstaking negotiations followed with the entire UNCTAD membership. Agreement was dependent on consensus, a dynamic that invariably strengthened the status quo. If and when a decision was reached, UNCTAD took on an observational role to monitor compliance, while technical cooperation and assistance sought to enable member countries to follow various prescriptions agreed by the organization. That much of this process resulted in a skewed scenario in favor of the ongoing order reflected in the organizational bias inherent in UNCTAD's constitutional principles, as well as the negative perceptions of developed countries towards the organization. Historically UNCTAD was:

> The first real confrontation of North and South, symbolic of the new, fundamental structure of international politics, in which the problems of relations of industrialized rich and agricultural poor had replaced the problem of relations between western capitalist and eastern Communist. It was an occasion to redress the injustices perpetrated under colonial regimes . . . UNCTAD would begin to apply in practice what Western political theory had taught since the time of Plato, that no political community could be stable if it contained extremes of rich and poor.[12]

The West was ambivalent towards UNCTAD's establishment, preferring to rely on the General Agreement on Tariffs and Trade (GATT) to regulate global trading relations. Such a preference suited their own interests, and its reluctance to discuss substantial issues *vis-à-vis* development reflected the preferred procedure of consensus decisions.[13] This "procedure of conciliation" meant that the terms of the debate and the maneuverability of UNCTAD were constrained because developed countries had influence in line with their material power but out of proportion to their numerical strength—thus perpetuating their dominance over the South. Such structural power enabled the North to "generally confine their role (in UNCTAD) to opposing any proposals for change" while ostensible "positive proposals" of their own were invariably "of a cosmetic nature designed to conceal their underlying resistance to change."[14]

UNCTAD was not necessarily doomed from the outset. Indeed, during the epoch of the demand for the NIEO, UNCTAD had limited successes, notably in the formulation of the Generalized System of Preferences and the Integrated Program for Commodities. Yet much of the success of such formulations were sabotaged by the North's unwillingness to fully implement the agreements: "[I]t had become obvious by the late 1970s that the high expectations held in some quarters for progress towards a new order were being frustrated," symbolized by the breakdown of the Paris Conference on International Economic Cooperation in June 1977 and the failures of UNCTAD IV, V, and VI (May 1976, June 1979 and June 1983, respectively).[15] Furthermore, the inflexibility of the North *vis-à-vis* developing counties began to harden as the neoliberal counterrevolution gained momentum under Reagan and Thatcher, which was graphically illustrated by US president Ronald Reagan's response to the Brandt Commission's proposals for a meeting to overcome the deadlock in global negotiations over questions concerning trade and development. Reagan only agreed to attend provided that Cuba was excluded, that the meeting avoided substantive issues, and the gathering was not to issue any form of final *communiqué*!

The reassertion by the North over the Global South

The attitude towards the Global South was compounded by Washington's behavior at the actual summit in Cancún at which Reagan used the meeting as an "opportunity to lecture Third World leaders on Reaganomics and offer American technical assistance to

Third World governments that wanted to emulate his domestic policies . . . Afterwards, the U.S. simply refused to engage in global negotiations, forcing the North–South dialogue to a stall."[16] Such actions were applauded by Margaret Thatcher, who suggested that one of the "valuable" outcomes of Cancún was that it "was the last of such gatherings." Henceforth, "the intractable problems of Third World poverty, hunger and debt would not be solved by misdirected international intervention, but rather by liberating enterprise, promoting trade—and defeating socialism in all its forms."[17]

Throughout the 1980s, Washington (and London) actively pressured the Global South to accept the neoliberal macroeconomic policies favored by the North. In terms of global economic governance, the period witnessed the transfer of power to those international financial institutions in which the North was preponderant. In addition, the ability to withstand the liberalizing thrust promoted by the North was further weakened by the Uruguay Round of GATT, which not only sought to lock in developing countries to the increasingly globalized world economy, but also effectively and definitively ended UNCTAD's role as a negotiating forum. UNCTAD's role as purely a discussion forum was particularly clear after 1995 when the newly created World Trade Organization (WTO) took on the substantive role of agreeing on binding trade agreements. UNCTAD's previous efforts to discuss the regulation of the global economy as a means to promote development were dramatically undercut.

It was in this context that the government elites and the international staff within UNCTAD sought to repackage the organization. While the logic of neoliberalism was broadly accepted by many, the negative effects of a liberalized world were also obvious. This essential acceptance of the normative order was exemplified by the abandonment of any confrontational posturing in the final communiqué. Instead, rhetoric in the "Spirit of Cartagena" spoke about the need to "overcome confrontation and to foster a climate of genuine cooperation and solidarity."[18]

Acceptance of the hegemonic discourse while attempting to ameliorate the worst aspects of the established order became the tactic for much of the developing world. This remarkable sea-change in UNCTAD's normative posture was clear, because "until (Cartagena) UNCTAD could be viewed as a counter-hegemonic organization resisting the dominance of the Bretton Woods institutions. The restructuring of the organization (gave) it a less confrontational role in the North-South dialogue."[19]

Explaining the demise of the Global South

The reassertion by the North came within the context where high debt levels and economic stagnation in most of the postcolonial world acted to drastically undermine the Global South's maneuverability. Since formal independence and because of its continued dependence on the North, developing countries continually borrowed from the North to nurture their economies. With the recycling of petrodollars making borrowing so easy, much of the Global South indulged in massive borrowing with its external debt expanding at very rapid, and unsustainable, rates. The adventurous lending practices of the North's bankers contributed to massive debts and massive problems throughout the Global South with such debts creating a Catch-22 situation whereby funds to finance development were diverted to pay off debt. In addition, the necessity to secure foreign exchange to service the debt led to a quick depreciation of many Southern currencies accompanied by hyperinflation. Paradoxically, high oil prices, which had initially stimulated the lending/borrowing spree, exacerbated the problem, particularly for oil-importing countries.

At the same time, the call for liberalization—dressed up in the rhetoric of so-called economic realities—provided space to retreat for conservatives within the ruling elites of the Global South, which had always been reluctant to commit to the NIEO. They seized on the growing globalization discourse to help justify unpopular policies to cope with debt crises, which actually reflected their longstanding, minimal commitment to any major restructuring of the global economy—unless it directly benefited them. Thus, state elites within Southern-dominated bodies such as UNCTAD and NAM sought to repackage their organizations. Certainly, while the logic of neoliberalism was broadly accepted by most, the negative effects of globalization were equally felt. An acceptance of the normative principles of neoliberalism, while advocating ameliorating policies to cope with this "actuality," emerged to define the principles on which the two organizations operate and which characterizes other political expressions of developing countries.

The BRICS in the Global South

Both UNCTAD and the NAM have continued their broad trajectories, and neither challenges the extant global order. As the economic power of emerging economies accelerated from the start of the twenty-first century, speculation developed that some of the new powerhouses would utilize their new found status to press for major alterations in world order, but this hope has not materialized. The BRICS bloc (Brazil, Russia, India, China, and South Africa) was perhaps the centerpiece of such suppositions. Russia hosted the first formal meeting in Yekaterinburg, in May 2008, to which Moscow invited Brazil, India, and China; soon after, in December 2010, South Africa was formally invited to join.

Prior to South Africa's membership, the BRIC group's members were, according to the International Monetary Fund (IMF), projected to account for around sixty percent of global growth by 2014. Interestingly, the BRIC acronym was originally coined back in 2001 by the chief economist for Goldman Sachs, Jim O'Neill, when his global investment banking and securities firm advanced the argument that these emerging economies were likely to surpass the traditional economies by 2040. According to his report, "in less than 40 years" the states dubbed the BRICs were expected to surpass the G-6, making up the world's main "engine of new demand growth and spending power," thereby "offset(ting) the impact of graying populations and slower growth in the advanced economies."[20] The Goldman Sachs report saw the four initial BRIC states as prospective "engines of growth," arguing that stable and cumulative growth in Brazil and India alongside the sheer size of China and Russia's economies would fundamentally change the shape of the global economy and, by implication, the global balance of power away from the dominant West. Although methodologically the concept had some severe flaws—such as a linear extrapolation of growth and little research ("when O'Neill coined the term BRIC in 2001, he had never properly visited three of the four countries"),[21] the concept soon caught on and entered the global lexicon.

Its relevance for any discussion of the Global South was that for the first time in years, leading developing countries were on the global stage advocating issues pertaining to global governance. At one level, this turn radically destabilized the very notion of the Global South, given the economic power of some of these states. China has indeed grown spectacularly since the inception of its socialist modernization policies, and the other BRICS had steadily—if more gradually—grown their economies. When purchasing power parity (PPP) measures of gross domestic product (GDP) are used, Beijing's economy was already three-quarters the size of that of the United States when the BRICS entered the scene, while Brazil, Russia, and India possessed economies of similar size to Japan, Germany, Britain, France, and Italy.

What the BRICS term really captured was both anxieties and expectations within international politics regarding how these rising powers from among "developing countries" would interact with the established powers, possibly stimulating "a fundamental shift of influence away from the Western world."[22] Yet, such concerns reflected a realist understanding of the world and never properly interrogated the actual claims of these voices from the Global South. How development might be related to the WTO, for example, emerged as a subject of public statements by some BRICS leaders.

Beyond the lofty rhetoric of "change" (never defined), the motivations for the BRICS leaders revealed no coherent, identifiable project that might be associated with the Global South. For Brazil's elites, the BRICS presented an opportunity to promote the country's assumed status and solidify its self-proclaimed status as the voice of Latin America. Russia eagerly joined as a means to recover some prestige lost in the aftermath of the collapse of the Soviet Union and to balance China's rise. India used its BRICS membership to demand the international respect that its ruling classes believed their due. Meanwhile, China saw the BRICS as a useful tool to promote a stable international environment through a reformist agenda. For South Africa, membership of the BRICS fed Pretoria's long-held exceptionalism, the belief that South Africa should be the default African nation; to compensate for the decline in interest in South Africa internationally post-Mandela and after the debacle of Thabo Mbeki's tenure and then Jacob Zuma's disastrous reign. From the perspective of the ruling social forces within the BRICS countries, there were understandable reasons to take ownership of the concept. But from the perspective of the Global South, the idea was nakedly based on national interest rather than any collective good.

In the immediate postcolonial period, it was perhaps permissible to assert that the newly independent states possessed a notional set of common interests: Guarding their newfound sovereignty, the promotion of development, the aspiration to be taken seriously by the great powers, and the need to redress the structures of their economic systems. Yet as the years progressed and greater and greater differences arose in both economic and political profiles, the coherence of the category was increasingly questioned. What does China *really* have in common with Chad, or Brazil, or Brunei? Even within continents, the interests of a relatively developed export-based economy such as South Africa's has very little—if anything—in common with that of Rwanda or Togo. These sorts of problem were quite clear when the BRICS countries tried to posture themselves as somehow representatives of the Global South. As the elites of the more developed among developing countries become interested in maintaining the global status quo, what is the meaning of the Global South? Always an elite-led project, the vagaries of their changeable interests have necessarily doomed the project in terms of conceptual clarity. The term is still widely used as shorthand to indicate generically countries not of the West, hardly a useful category.

Conclusion

With the acceptance of the norms of trade liberalization goes recognition of the uneven process of globalization, which has led at times to calls for a lessening of the worst aspects of this process. This position, exemplified most recently by the BRICS but redolent in much of UNCTAD's and NAM's positions over the last half-century, has taken on board the realities of globalization and today's world order. The institutionalization of the idea of the Global South is mired there, a massive retreat from the heady days of the NIEO.

At best, some Southern elites urge the North to engage in supposedly "real" free trade rather than the "existing" free trade. The critical engagement with the North tends to be characterized as "partnership," which attempts to deal with both the positive and negative aspects of ongoing globalizing processes. Such pragmatic policies dominated the agendas of the BRICS, for example. However, the viability of these positions remains debatable. Is it actually possible to deregulate markets and roll back the state, allowing a free rein for international capital and, at the same time promote notions of equity and mutual development in both developed and developing countries? Is the generation of wealth within a global capitalist system predicated on poverty-producing principles? Must there always be dominant and dominated sectors—within countries and internationally a North and a South? Neoliberal ideas, now embraced by key elites in the Global South and enacted through such projects as the BRICS, mean that most developing countries are led by governments that clamor for economic prescriptions emanating from the North. As has been shown, institutional expressions of the Global South have progressively converged with the prescriptions of the capitalist North. The space for critical thinking as exemplified in the NIEO era have, at the time of writing, evaporated. Combined with the wide and ever growing divergences in both economic and political terms that now characterize the postcolonial world, the idea of the Global South in global governance is problematic.

Additional reading

Christopher Lee, *Making a World after Empire: The Bandung Moment and Its Political Afterlives* (Athens, OH: Ohio University Press, 2010).

Vijay Prashad, *The Darker Nations: A People's History of the Third World* (London: Verso Books, 2008).

Vijay Prashad, *The Poorer Nations: A Possible History of the Global South* (London: Verso Books, 2013).

Susanne Soederberg, *The Politics of the New International Financial Architecture: Reimposing Neoliberal Domination in the Global South* (London: Zed Books, 2004).

Ian Taylor, *Global Governance and Transnationalizing Capitalist Hegemony: The Myth of the "Emerging Powers"* (London: Routledge, 2017).

Notes

1 Rajeev Patel and Philip McMichael, "Third Worldism and the Lineages of Global Fascism: The Regrouping of the Global South in the Neoliberal Era," *Third World Quarterly* 25, no. 1 (2008): 241.

2 Roger Mortimer, *The Third World Coalition in International Politics* (Boulder, CO: Westview Press, 1984), 9.

3 Graham Evans and John Newnham, *Dictionary of World Politics: A Reference Guide to Concepts, Ideas and Institutions* (Hemel Hempstead: Harvester Wheatsheaf, 1992), 224.

4 Peter Willetts, *The Nonaligned Movement* (London: Verso, 1978), 31.

5 Craig Murphy, *International Organization and Industrial Change: Global Governance since 1850* (Cambridge: Polity Press, 1994), 114.

6 Timothy Shaw, "The Non-Aligned Movement and the New International Division of Labour" in *Africa in World Politics*, eds. Ralph Onwuka and Timothy Shaw (Basingstoke: Macmillan, 1989), 6.

7 Cited by Peter Willetts *The Nonaligned Movement* (London: Verso Books, 1978), 31.

8 Walden Bello, *Brave New Third World: Strategies for Survival in the Global Economy* (London: Earthscan, 1990), 9.

9 J.J.G. Syatauw, "The Non-Aligned Movement at the Crossroads: The Jakarta Summit Adapting to the Post-Cold War Era," *Asian Yearbook of International Affairs* 3 (1993): 129.

10 Nana Sutresna, "Speech of H.E. Mr Nana S. Sutresna at a Conference on 'South Africa and the Non-Aligned Movement' in Johannesburg on 10 June 1998," *Indonesia in Perspective* 9 (1998): 4.

11 Joseph Nye, "UNCTAD: Poor Nation's Pressure Group," in *The Anatomy of Influence: Decision–making in International Organizations*, eds. Robert Cox and Harold Jacobson (New Haven, CN: Yale University Press, 1973), 334.

12 Charles Robertson, "The Creation of UNCTAD," in *International Organisation: World Politics,* ed. Robert Cox (London: Macmillan, 1969), 258.

13 Mortimer, *The Third World Coalition*, 17.

14 Robert Ramsay, "UNCTAD's Failure: The Rich Get Richer," *International Organization* 38, no. 2 (1984): 388–389.

15 S.K.B. Asante, "The Role of the Organisation of African Unity in Promoting Peace, Development and Regional Security in Africa," in *Africa: Perspectives on Peace and Development*, ed. Emmanuel Hansen (London: Zed Books, 1987), 132.

16 Enrico Augelli and Craig Murphy, *America's Quest for Supremacy and the Third World: A Gramscian Analysis* (London: Pinter, 1988), 189.

17 Margaret Thatcher, *The Downing Street Years* (London: Harper & Collins, 1993), 170.

18 "The Spirit of Cartagena," Declaration adopted by UNCTAD at its eighth session held at the Convention Centre, Cartegena de Indias, Colombia, 8–25 February 1992, www.inro.com.my/inro/caragena.htm.

19 Marc Williams, *International Organisations and the Third World* (Hemel Hempstead: Harvester Wheatsheaf, 1994), 179.

20 Dominic Wilson and Roopa Purushothaman, "Dreaming with BRICs: The Path to 2050," Goldman Sachs Global Economics Paper no. 99 (October 2003): 2.

21 Gillian Tett, "The Story of the BRICS," *Financial Times* (London), 15 January 2010, 4.

22 Tett, "The Story of the BRICS."

US hegemony

W. Andy Knight

Prevailing wisdom has it that China is about to overtake the United States within the next few decades, ushering in a new era of Chinese international political dominance. Indeed, since the early 1970s several scholars and observers of international relations have argued that the United States has lost its hegemonic position in the world or is experiencing a decline in dominance. A recent Pew Research Study suggested that groups surveyed in fifteen out of twenty-two countries believe that China has already overtaken the United States as the global leader, or soon will. And, the US National Intelligence Council boldly forecasts that China will usurp US authority by 2030.

The late Susan Strange used to chide US academics, in particular, for perpetuating this "myth of America's lost hegemony." She was particularly critical of those who not only "unquestionably accepted" the proposition of American hegemonic decline but also took it on themselves to spread that myth in such a way that it gained credence outside the United States.[1] Similarly, other observers like Thomas White argue forcefully that reports of US hegemonic decline have been grossly exaggerated. Many of those reports rely on raw data that show a trend supporting the view that China is making important economic gains on the United States. But reliance on such data is insufficient to conclude that US hegemony is waning. For White, and others: "[I]t is international relationships that truly undergird world superpowers." He continues, "China has seen its regional influence increase substantially in recent years . . . a situation [in which] China and not the US leads a successful international coalition of allies is fantasy."[2]

Despite challenges to its hegemonic status, the United States continues to be a global hegemon. However, we need to be cognizant of the fact that there are some very real questions about the long-term sustainability of US hegemony; thus, it is important to understand hegemony in the context of the *longue durée*. Contrary to what Francis Fukuyama would have us believe, history did not come to an end with the advent of the universalization of Western liberal democracy once the Cold War thawed.[3]

In fact, during the immediate post-Cold War era, although many states embraced the Western style of liberal democracy and capitalism, we did not witness a true universalization of Western liberal democracy as a "final" form of government. China and Russia may have embraced capitalism and global markets, but neither of them is "liberal" or fully "capitalist." China is still far from being considered by the other major powers as a trustworthy ally. Domestically, China commits deeply troubling human rights violations. It censors the press and the Internet and restricts freedom of religion, expression, and political association in the country. And Russia, while seemingly trying to recapture the glory days of the Soviet Union, is unable to command the global respect required to make it a serious contender for global hegemony.

It is important to question any thesis that posits the continual superiority and progressiveness of the West and the perpetual subordination and backwardness of the rest. Similarly, it is imperative to take seriously the critiques of those who question the notion that US hegemony is here to stay.[4] The election of President Donald Trump is a clear reminder that US credibility as a global leader is not secured. In fact, many world leaders are beginning to suggest that a new world order may have to be built that is "less reliant on US leadership and less vulnerable to the vagaries of American elections."[5] At the same time, this chapter heeds Strange's caution not to accept blindly the view that the United States has lost its hegemonic status, that its hegemony is waning, or that a fundamental rupture has occurred in the systems of global governance the US put into place after World War II.

The chapter is divided into four parts. First, the concept of hegemony is explained and a distinction is drawn between hegemony and dominance. Second, a brief historical overview of US hegemony and dominance is provided. Third, some of the challenges to this hegemony are outlined, which have been used by observers to indicate a waning of American power. A brief conclusion follows that takes into consideration recent indications that the newly elected populist US president may, in fact, be taking America into unchartered waters that could eventually lead to the demise of the US as a global leader and precipitate the advent of a post-hegemonic era in which no country in the globe will be "hegemonic."

Conceptualizing hegemony

Before we can determine whether or not US hegemony is waning or has been lost—and what the impact of this might be on international organization and global governance—it is important to distinguish between hegemony and dominance. The simplistic view of hegemony postulates that hegemons are preeminent powers with material and coercive ability to control the weak. Donald Puchala notes that much of the literature on world order treats hegemony as "the institutionalization of privilege, consequent inequality in the distribution of various values, and the injustices inherent in inequality." In other words, hegemony is generally seen as "a condition in human relations to be resented, rejected, and removed."[6] Immanuel Wallerstein's take on hegemony attaches similar malevolent qualities to the term. Wallerstein defines hegemony as "that situation in which the ongoing rivalry between so-called 'great powers' is so unbalanced that one power is truly *primus inter pares*; that is, one power can largely impose its rules and its wishes (at the very least by effective veto power) in the economic, political, military, diplomatic and even cultural arenas."[7]

This malevolent interpretation of hegemony rightly evokes resistant/"anti-hegemonic" reactions, or what Robert Cox calls "counter-hegemony."[8] Randolph Persaud explains that counter-hegemony ought to be "seen as dialectically consti-tutive of the conditions of hegemonic practices on a global scale."[9] This means that whenever there is hegemony, one should expect a counter-hegemonic reaction to it. But Puchala's conception of hegemony is a bit more nuanced than those that equate it with state "dominance" and "preponderance of power." When applied to inter-national relations, a hegemon "arises when a single state attains preponderant power and elects to use its power to manage the international system." Thus, the power of the hegemon can be used in both malevolent and benevolent ways. Such a position is in conformity with hegemonic stability theory that suggests that the hegemon is a dominant power with the ability to shape norms, rules, and institutions of the inter-national system and is expected to enforce the rules it has established by rewarding compliant states while punishing the recalcitrant.

Ian Clark notes that the term hegemon is always associated with "a concentration of power." But he also acknowledges that the concept of hegemony is much richer than that of primacy or dominance. Whereas primacy focuses on "the accretion of material power," hegemony "most readily achieves its distinctive identity when it is associated with legitimacy," respect for the leader, and voluntary or non-coercive acquiescence on the part of those being led.[10] Cox, building on the work of Italian social theorist Antonio Gramsci, drills even deeper to gain a better understanding of the concept of hegemony. For him, the term refers to "a structure of values and understandings about the nature of order that permeates a whole system of states and non-state entities."[11] In a world order in which a hegemon is present, the values and understandings would be relatively stable and ostensibly unquestioned. In other words, the order created by the hegemon would be considered by most actors in the system as the "natural order."

The structure of values and understandings is always underpinned by a structure of material power in a system where the hegemon is present. That material power is what infuses the hegemon with characteristics of dominance and preponderance. But, as Cox points out, dominance is not sufficient for hegemony to be exhibited. "Hegemony derives from the ways of doing and thinking of the dominant social strata of the dominant state or states insofar as these ways of doing and thinking have acquired the acquiescence of the dominant social strata of other states."[12] Put another way, it is those social practices embedded in institutional arrangements and regimes, and the ideologies that underpin, explain, and legitimize them that, in fact, lay the foundation of any hegemonic order.[13]

Great powers "get their way most effectively by securing voluntary or even unthinking cooperation from others." Thus, a hegemon does not have to rely on costly coercion to get what it wants.[14] It can utilize "soft power" to induce cooperation.[15] Intellectual and moral leadership, framed by ideational terms of reference, is what separates hegemony from dominance. For that kind of leadership to develop in a world order setting, there has to be a convergence of interests and attitudes, especially among international elites, and the ideational elements associated with the hegemon must become embedded in the institutions of global governance.[16]

Thus, to come to grips fully with US hegemony, we must understand the extent to which the US has used its materially dominant position in the international hierarchy of states to take on the management of the international system; create institutions, regimes, and rules that lend order and predictability to the system; promote and embed within those institutions, regimes, and rules certain ideas and ideologies that favor American self-interests and purposes; induce voluntary compliance and concurrence from the international elite class; and absorb or co-opt emerging counter-hegemonic ideas and forces that have the potential to challenge the US hegemonic position.

The primary challenge for the sustainability of any hegemon, including the US, is to somehow combine both hard and soft power in such a way that induces consensus around the principles, norms, and rules that structure the institutional governance of the international system while at the same time protecting that governance apparatus by "the armour of coercion."[17] This is not an easy task, particularly if the hegemon is so predominant that its structural power (military, economic, scientific, and techno-logical) subsumes most challenges to its global role. The United States, in fact, was derisively labeled a "hyperpower" immediately following the end of the Cold War precisely because American structural power could not be matched by any other power within the international system.[18] With Washington's greatest challenger, the erstwhile Soviet Union, unraveling as a result of foreign policy overextension (e.g., the quagmire in Afghanistan) and internal leadership crises, the US was the sole superpower by 1989. Since that time, no challenger has been able to match the preponderance of the US or effectively counter its hegemony.[19]

A brief history of US hegemony and dominance

Achieving global hegemonic status is rare and transient. According to Wallerstein, hegemonic power was exercised only three times in the modern world system: By the United Provinces[20] in the mid-seventeenth century; the United Kingdom in the nineteenth century; and the United States from around 1945. In each case, the hegemon achieved its preeminent position not only because it was dominant but also because it was able to operate more efficiently than other powers in the international system in at least three economic areas—agro-industrial production, commerce, and finance.[21] Each successive hegemon's competitive edge in efficiency was so great that enterprises based in the hegemonic power could outbid those located elsewhere in the world. The political and cultural influences of each of these hegemonic powers were so pervasive that they were considered more than simply coercive powers. They were able to combine material and military advantages with intellectual and moral leadership to steer the international system in a particular direction.

US hegemony

The transition from the United Provinces' hegemony to British hegemony was a rela-tively long and drawn-out one that took about 150 years to complete. The transition from UK to US hegemony took half as long,[22] in large part because of the strategy adopted by the United Kingdom as its hegemony waned. From the late 1870s until 1940, the United Kingdom began to acquiesce to the United States, as the latter began to establish and assert its own sphere of interest in the Americas. Instead of treating the rise of the United States in a hostile manner, the United Kingdom considered American interests as complementary with its own. For its part, the United States was not yet willing to take on the full mantle of global leadership but seemed content to allow the United Kingdom to continue to rule its vast colonial Empire.

The United Kingdom ceded priority to the United States in certain areas of its sphere of influence (e.g., in South America and the Caribbean)—thus acquiescing to the 1823 Munroe Doctrine[23]—and basically took a cooperative approach with the United States in managing and maintaining the international order. But, as the US gradually assumed the mantle of global leadership from the United Kingdom, it initially acted more as a dominant power than a hegemon. For instance, in 1846–1848 the United States took California, Arizona, and New Mexico from Mexico in the Mexican–American war; in 1888 the United States intervened militarily in a civil war in Haiti; in 1895–1896 Washington intervened in a boundary dispute between Venezuela and British Guyana; between 1898 and 1932, the United States militarily intervened thirty-four times in nine Central American and Caribbean countries; in 1899, the United States occupied Cuba to protect American interests there during the Cuban independence revolution; and in 1903, after seizing Puerto Rico during the Spanish–American War, the United States declared sovereignty over the Panama Canal.[24] These were actions of a dominant power, not necessarily those of a hegemon.

World War I (WWI) proved beyond the shadow of a doubt that the United States was more than a hemispheric power and that it had the ability to emerge as the new global hegemon.[25] By this time, the United States enjoyed naval parity with the United Kingdom and was the world's leading credit nation and industrial power. Clearly, on several fronts, the United States was indeed a dominant force to be reckoned with. But it began to use its material clout to press for the creation of international institutions of governance.

On 8 January 1918, before the US Congress, President Woodrow Wilson used Washington's rising dominance to argue in one of his fourteen points for the creation of "a general association of nations formed on the basis of covenants designed to create mutual guarantees of the political independence and territorial integrity of States, large and small equally."[26] This articulation of a new type of standing international organization dedicated to fostering international cooperation and providing security and enduring peace for all of its members came at a propitious time. Europe was exhausted by the four years of WWI and wanted to avoid the devastation of another systemic conflagration. The League of Nations was created from Wilson's vision. He used his influence to ensure that the Covenant of the League would be attached to the Treaty of Versailles, which ended the war. Wilson drafted that Covenant with two other elites, Georges Clemenceau of France and David Lloyd George of the United Kingdom. Despite popular support in America for this new organization, the US Congress failed to ratify the Treaty and the Covenant, fearing that the League would be an expensive organization that would reduce its ability to defend its own interest. The United States never joined the League, and some analysts argue that its absence doomed that organization to failure. Whether or not that argument holds, the League's collective security apparatus was considerably weakened because of the absence of the emerging hegemon from its membership.

Immediately after WWI, the United States seemed unwilling to take on the global hegemonic role. In fact, Washington resorted to isolationism as the global economic problems caused by WWI led to the collapse of the international financial system by 1931.[27] With the UK's appeasement strategies and the absence of US hegemonic leadership on the world stage, both Germany and Japan began to exhibit counter-hegemonic tendencies as the world spiraled into another systemic war.[28] At this point, the United States shifted its stance from one of neutrality to one which strengthened its alliance with the United Kingdom in order to beat back the counter-hegemonic challenges from Germany and Japan during World War II (WWII). By the time that Washington joined the war effort in 1941, after its territory in Pearl Harbor was attacked by the Japanese, it was more prepared to assume the hegemonic role. But it initially did so in collaboration with the United Kingdom.

The United States joined the United Kingdom in drafting the Atlantic Charter in 1941, which laid out plans for reconstructing the international economic order when the war was over. The Atlantic Charter was a pivotal statement of US policy which hinted at the dismantling of all protected spheres of interest, including the British Empire, and the reconstruction of world order under American leadership. The Charter, negotiated in August 1941 by UK Prime Minister Winston Churchill and US President Franklin Roosevelt, reflected Washington's and, even more, Roosevelt's idealistic vision of establishing an international organization to serve as arbiter of disputes and a mechanism for protecting the peace. It paved the way for the "Declaration by United Nations," signed on 1 January 1942 in San Francisco by twenty-six governments that pledged to continue their fight against the Axis Powers. In San Francisco, on 25 April 1945, two weeks before Roosevelt's death, fifty countries met at the United Nations Conference on International Organization to draft the United Nations Charter. The UN system was initiated with the signing of the Charter on 26 June 1945.[29]

The shift from *Pax Britannica* to *Pax Americana* was one in which the United States, as emergent hegemon, pushed for as full and complete a liberalization of international economic relations as possible, while the outgoing hegemon preferred a transition period of protectionism that would allow it to relinquish gradually its sphere of influence while retaining its imperial preference system and control over large parts of its colonial empire. But the United States, through bilateral and multi-lateral negotiations, induced the United Kingdom to support its aim of recreating an open multilateral trading economy. The United States took the lead in bringing together 730 delegates from forty-four allied countries to Mount Washington Hotel in Bretton Woods, New Hampshire, to deliberate and eventually sign the agreements that brought into effect a novel system of rules, institutions, and procedures to regulate the international monetary system.[30] The Bretton Woods agreements represented an unprecedented experiment in international rulemaking and institution building for a postwar monetary and financial system that would be led by the US. That system included the International Monetary Fund (IMF), and the International Bank for Reconstruction and Development (IBRD, or the World Bank), and was intended to lay the foundations for the negotiation at a later date of the International Trade Organization (ITO). The US Congress did not support the ITO, but in its place was established a negotiating forum, the General Agreement on Tariffs and Trade (GATT): "The Anglo-American agreements established sophisticated rules that would attempt to reconcile openness and trade expansion with the commitments of national governments to full employment and economic stabilization." This blend of *laissez faire* and interventionist policies was the result of the compromise that the emerging hegemon would reach with the waning hegemon.[31]

Thus, it would seem that US elites recognized limits of coercion and chose to build the American postwar agenda around principles of multilateralism, discourse, and compromise. In so doing, they hoped to lend legitimacy to the postwar order they were constructing. Part of gaining that legitimacy was the approach of Washington in addressing the devastation in Europe caused by WWII. In 1947, a reconstruction plan to provide economic and technical assistance to the war-torn countries in Europe was devised by US State Department officials William Clayton and George Kennan. The Organisation for European Economic Co-operation (OEEC) was subsequently established to help administer the Marshall Plan. As it turned out, the Plan was used not only to rebuild war-torn European economies but also to expand US trade and economic activity and, at the same time, prevent any more European countries from being absorbed into the Soviet sphere of influence.[32]

The US approach to hegemony after World War II was one that mixed its obvious hard military power with soft power and the principles of multilateralism, discourse, and compromise in creating norms and institutions to steer the international system in a direction of its choosing. But it should be noted that the United States did so in collaboration with the United Kingdom and a concert of like-minded powers because it had to be mindful of internal political divisions over its hegemonic role, as well as the need to deal with counterhegemonic challenges.

Challenges to US hegemony

Anglo-American collaboration in the creation of institutions of the postwar world order evolved into collaboration between the United States and those European and other states not yet drawn into the Soviet Union's vortex. As noted earlier, at the global level, counter-hegemony can be viewed as dialectically constitutive of the conditions of hegemonic practice. One can see counter-hegemonic reactions to the US preponderance almost immediately after World War II ended.

Chandra Muzaffar has argued that US hegemony was never really global or total.[33] Despite the fact that Washington exhibited overwhelming military power, political power, economic power, scientific and technological power, and information and cultural power in the postwar period, there were at least five major challenges that checked US hegemony.

First, Moscow posed a stiff challenge to US hegemony almost immediately after WWII. Although both the United States and the Soviet Union were allies during the war, the ideological differences between the capitalist and communist powers were too massive to overcome. The Cold War (roughly 1945 to 1991) was characterized by bipolarity and a precarious balance of power. In 1947 US President Harry Truman devised what would be called the "Truman Doctrine" to contain communist advances. Germany was divided into the German Federal Republic (West Germany) and the German Democratic Republic (East Germany); Washington established a military alliance—the North Atlantic Treaty Organization (NATO)—to protect Western Europe from a possible Soviet security threat. The Soviets countered by creating the Warsaw Pact to protect their European satellites from a possible US threat. A bitter ideological confrontation resulted between the two nuclear-armed superpowers, fueled by a security dilemma, which was played out by proxies in different parts of the globe and within the UN Security Council. This Cold War climate, undergirded by the doctrine of mutually assured destruction (MAD), placed a check on US hegemony. But in 1991, when the Soviet Union imploded, this challenge to US hegemony subsided. Russia was brought into the Group of 7 (G-7) consortium and the world capitalist system during the post-Cold War era and was no longer considered a significant counter-hegemonic threat.

Second, in 1949 the US-backed Kuomintang regime in Beijing was overthrown by Mao Tse-Tung in a popular revolution. Although China was a US ally during WWII, it chose under Mao to embrace the communist ideology, and it posed a challenge to US hegemony by rejecting liberal capitalism. North Korea also posed a similar challenge when it separated from South Korea as a result of the Korean War (1950–1953) and embraced communism. Vietnam, which suffered huge casualties during its war with the United States, also rejected liberal capitalism. Cuba, in the American backyard, chose to align itself ideologically with the Soviets. These developments countered US global hegemony and its attempt to spread liberal capitalist ideology. But in recent years China has more or less been co-opted into embracing capitalism to save its socialist revolution and has been gradually reversing Mao's heavy emphasis on Marxism and self-reliance by joining the Western-controlled international financial institutions. Indeed, beginning in the 1980s, Washington "in effect became China's patron in encouraging more and more substantial participation by the PRC in the global capitalist system."[34] Vietnam has also embraced Western capitalism, and the communist counter-hegemonic threats from North Korea and Cuba are really insignificant.

The bellicosity of the North Korean government's rhetoric has escalated in recent years, and is an obvious concern for South Korea and the United States given the evidence of a more credible Pyongyang ballistic missile capability. Yet, it is highly unlikely that US hegemonic standing in the globe and in the Asia-Pacific region will be under serious challenge from North Korea.[35] In 2015, US President Obama restored diplomatic ties with Cuba. Combined with the death of Fidel Castro, it seems unlikely that Cuba will in the future present a challenge of any significance to US predominance in the region.[36] His successor appears to be on the cusp of reversing the opening to Cuba, which critics argue would be a regressive move "back toward Cold War-era policies designed as part of a catastrophically failed half-century attempt to foster regime change" in that country.[37] In any event, since the Soviet Union's collapse, Cuba has not been in a position to pose a credible threat to the US standing as a regional and global power.

Third, the US quest for global hegemony occurred during the 1950s and 1960s with the significant growth of nationalism in territories controlled by colonial powers. During the process of decolonization, some African, Asian, and Caribbean states decided to align themselves with Washington, and others with Moscow, but a large number preferred to stake out an independent path that would put them in neither the US nor the Soviet ambit. Beginning with the 1955 summit in Bandung, Indonesia, many of these states formed the Non-aligned Movement (NAM). It began, and continues, to use the UN General Assembly as a forum to resist Westernization and particularly Americanization. The NAM adopted resolutions in the General Assembly for the establishment of a New International Economic Order (NIEO), and in the UN Educational, Scientific and Cultural Organization (UNESCO) to establish a New International Information Order (NIIO) as a counter to US-dominated liberal capitalism and media. For a moment, aided by the high oil prices, the so-called Third World was a counterbalance to US hegemony, but by the early 1980s the coalition of what became known as the "Global South" lost steam, and resistance to US hegemony was weakened. Nothing much became of the NIEO or the NIIO, and the United States was able to co-opt many elites from the Global South.

Fourth, US hegemony was challenged by its own overstretch.[38] Today, the United States maintains a network of almost 750 military bases and other installations in more than 130 countries. Since the early 1990s, the United States has been involved in a number of wars that have drained its resources (e.g., the 1990 war with Iraq; the fiasco in Somalia; the invasion and occupation of Iraq after the 9/11 terrorist attacks; the ongoing military expedition in Afghanistan; and the "global war on terror" in Syria and Iraq.[39] In each case, financial and personnel costs have "sapped the strength of the US economy" and challenged US hegemony.[40] Military overextension could become the Achilles heel of US hegemony, as it did in the cases of the hegemonies of both the United Provinces and the United Kingdom.

Fifth, a challenge to US hegemony comes from the rise of competing states and blocs. The advent of the European Union (EU) and the economic integration of countries on the continent posed a challenge of sorts to US economic, if not military, hegemony. For instance, the adoption of the euro by seventeen EU members provided competition for the US dollar. The US trade deficit with Europe further contributed to weakening the dollar. The rise of China as an economic power and the fact that Chinese manufacturing companies are out-producing US companies is another reason for concern. Despite a slowdown, China is expected to surpass the US as the world's largest manufacturer by 2020 and is predicted to become the world's largest economy in dollar-based GDP by 2041.[41] The BRICS (Brazil, Russia, India, China, and South Africa) are also expected to out-produce the United States, the United Kingdom, France, Germany, Japan, and Italy combined by 2039.[42] In Latin America, a number of states have joined together to resist US hegemonic pressure. The Bolivarian Alternative of the Americas (ALBA), the brainchild of late Venezuelan President Chavez, was established in 2004 to counter the hegemonic idea of a Free Trade Area of the Americas (FTAA), which would have perpetuated US hegemony over Latin America.

However, there are major questions about the ability of emerging powers to convert their material power into "a distinctive, acceptable, form of order." Ian Clark points out, for instance, that "China faces a complex array of severe domestic problems that will dominate its policy priorities for many decades to come."[43] Brazil provides a different illustration and is undergoing a precipitous decline due to mismanagement of the economy. Dilma Rousseff, its last president, was removed from office following an impeachment vote in the Senate. Meanwhile, its current and former presidents are under investigation. Brazil, a nation rich in natural resources with acres of farmland, rainforest, and fourteen percent of the world's fresh water, saw its economy shrink by almost four percent in 2015, when its inflation rate was almost eleven percent and its unemployment was nine percent. Can any of the BRICS, individually or collectively, develop an institution of hegemony that would inspire widespread international consent?

Conclusion

As noted, hegemony is both rare and transient. There have been only three true hegemonic powers in our modern world—the United Provinces, the United Kingdom, and the United States. The third maintains its hegemonic position despite several counter-hegemonic challenges. But is it likely, as Earl Fry predicted, that by 2040 the United States will no longer be a global hegemon? Some have argued that its hegemony was always overstated. And with the election of Donald Trump, there is a growing sentiment that the US remains a preponderant power but may no longer possess the legitimacy to maintain its status of the global hegemon. Indeed, we may be moving towards a post-hegemonic world in which there will be no single over-arching dominant power.[44]

WWII placed the United States in the unenviable position of being the world's policeman and bearing the brunt of the economic costs of establishing norms and regional and multilateral institutions to sustain its global hegemonic position.[45] Being a global hegemon meant that the United States was pivotal to the construction of the post-WWII order and had the military and economic might to support that order. But it did so in collaboration with the waning hegemon and with a concert of states. During that period, Washington's only clear global rival, the Soviet Union, never produced more than half of US total national output. Soviet allies were "restive occupied countries" and at best "partners of convenience" and "drains on its limited resources."[46] Since the end of the Cold War, the United States has been the most powerful state in history[47] and for a decade experienced a "unipolar moment."[48] During the immediate post-Cold War era, many historians and political scientists acknowledged Henry Luce's foresight in *Life* magazine on 17 February 1941 that the twentieth century would be known as the "American Century."

Despite the recent challenges to its hegemonic position posed by emerging powers and a resurgent Russia, the United States continues to maintain a predominant position. But as Henry Kissinger warned after the first Gulf War, America's preeminence cannot last. Its preeminent military might is no longer matched by sufficient economic resources to truly dominate the globe.[49] As *The Economist* puts it, the US "knows that it no longer has the economic clout to run a hegemony."[50]

That said, hegemony is about more than military or economic dominance. Hegemony is sustained by intellectual and moral leadership—something that the Barack Obama administration seems to have provided. The United States has been able to co-opt and absorb counter-hegemonic forces over a sustained period of time. It has also been able to induce voluntary and sometimes unthinking cooperation from most of its followers. Joseph Nye uses the term "soft power" to encapsulate the notion that a hegemon can get what it wants "through attraction rather than coercion or payments." For him, soft power "arises from the attractiveness of a country's culture, political ideals, and policies." Nye continues: "When you can get others to admire your ideals and to want what you want, you do not have to spend as much on sticks and carrots to move them in your direction. Seduction is always more effective than coercion, and many values like democracy, human rights and individual opportunities are deeply seductive."[51] It is therefore in the pervasiveness of American culture and the use of its soft power that we see lingering continuing signs of US hegemony. But it has extended well beyond its cultural influences. The United States will remain hegemonic as long as its ideas are embedded in the countless regimes (principles, norms, rules, and decision-making processes) that operate in various corners of the globe, and in the current generation of institutions of global governance.

However, major questions remain at this critical historical juncture: Are we moving towards a multipolar system in which the United States will simply be *primus inter pares*? Will the Trump administration's retreat from global leadership in a number of significant areas (e.g., pulling out of the global climate compact, bullying NATO allies, withdrawing from regional trade agreements, and cutting funds to UN peacekeeping and to UN specialized agencies) result in the persistent impression that the US is in terminal decline?[52] Has the United States created a post-hegemonic world "that can no longer be dominated by any single state or its cultural fruits?"[53]

While, as Strange reminded us, it is a mistake to prophesize the imminent decline of US hegemony, "it would be just as erroneous to engage in American triumphalism."[54] Cycles of hegemony run in centuries rather than decades. Even if the United States is in decline, as Noam Chomsky argues, there is "no competitor for global hegemonic power" at least not for "the foreseeable future."[55] If Robert Cox is right, we may be witnessing the gradual disintegration of a historical structure that was created after WWII. Are we seeing a new world disorder? "Hegemony is weakened and eroded when the legitimacy of the power structure is called into question and an alternative order seems possible and desirable."[56] In the early twenty-first century, US legitimacy is being called into question. Its decline is largely self-inflicted and accelerated by the incoherence of the Trump administration.[57]

The world seems to be yearning for an alternative, more pluralist world order. Whether or not it comes to pass depends on the convergence of interests and attitudes of the existing preponderant power and the emerging powers, as well as on the willingness of the United States to accept a new role in a post-hegemonic world order.

Additional reading

Robert Keohane, "After Hegemony Cooperation is Possible," *International Spectator* 50: 4 (2015): 92–94.

Christopher Layne, "China's Challenge to US Hegemony," *Current History* 107, no. 705 (2008): 13–18.

Joseph S. Nye, Jr., *Soft Power: The Means to Success in World Politics* (New York: Public Affairs, 2004). 3.

Elaine Sio-ieng, "Putting the Chinese State in its Place: A March from Passive Revolution to Hegemony," *Journal of Contemporary Asia* 47, no. 1 (2017): 66–92.

Alan Watson, "US Hegemony and the Obama Administration: Towards a New World Order," *Antipode* 42, no. 2 (2010): 242–247.

Notes

1 Susan Strange, "The Persistent Myth of Lost Hegemony," *International Organization* 41, no. 4 (1987): 552.

2 Thomas White, "Why U.S. Hegemony Is Here to Stay," *HuffPost,* 12 November 2013, www.huffingtonpost.com/thomas-white/why-us-hegemony-is-here-t_b_4258264.html.

3 Francis Fukuyama, *The End of History and the Last Man* (New York: Free Press, 1992).

4 See, for example, Earl H. Fry, "The Decline of the American Superpower," *The Forum* 5, no. 2 (2007), www.degruyter.com/view/j/for.2007.5.2_20120105083452/for.2007.5.2/for.2007.5.2.1153/for.2007.5.2.1153.xml.

5 Adair Turner, "Trump Election and the Future of U.S. Global Leadership," *Institute for New Economic Thinking,* 28 November 2016, www.ineteconomics.org/perspectives/blog/trump-election-forces-governments-to-move-beyond-reliance-on-u-s-leadership.

6 Donald J. Puchala, "World Hegemony and the United Nations," *International Studies Review* 7, no. 4 (2005): 571. Subsequent quotes from 572.

7 Immanuel Wallerstein, *The Politics of the World Economy: The States, the Movements and the Civilizations* (Cambridge: Cambridge University Press, 1984), 3.

8 Robert W. Cox, "Gramsci, Hegemony and International Relations: An Essay in Method," *Millennium* 12, no. 2 (1983): 162–175.

9 Randolph B. Persaud, *Counter-Hegemony and Foreign Policy: The Dialectics of Marginalized and Global Forces in Jamaica* (Albany: State University of New York Press, 2001), 69.

10 See Ian Clark, "China and the United States: A Succession of Hegemonies?," *International Affairs* 87, no. 1 (2011): 1424.

11 Robert W. Cox with Timothy J. Sinclair, *Approaches to World Order* (Cambridge: Cambridge University Press, 1996), 151.

12 Cox, *Approaches to World Order*, 151.

13 See John Gerard Ruggie, "International Regimes, Transactions, and Change: Embedded Liberalism in the Postwar Economic Order," *International Organization* 36, no. 2 (1982): 379–415.

14 David P. Forsythe, "The U.S. and Trans-Atlantic Relations: On the Difference Between Dominance and Hegemony," DIIS Working Paper no. 2005/16: 4.

15 Joseph S. Nye, Jr., *Soft Power: The Means to Success in World Politics* (New York: Public Affairs, 2004).

16 On these points, see Mark Rupert, *Producing Hegemony: The Politics of Mass Production and American Global Power* (Cambridge: Cambridge University Press, 1995), 43–56.

17 William I. Robinson, *Promoting Polyarchy: Globalization, US Intervention, and Hegemony* (Cambridge: Cambridge University Press, 1996), 22.

18 *The New York Times*, "To Paris, the U.S. Looks like a 'Hyperpower,'" 5 February 1999, www.nytimes.com/1999/02/05/news/05iht-france.t_0.html.

19 See Peter Van Ness, "Hegemony, Not Anarchy: Why China and Japan Are Not Balancing US Unipolar Power," *International Relations of the Asia-Pacific* 2, no. 1 (2002): 132–134.

20 The United Provinces is another name for the Federated Dutch Republic (or the Netherlands) that emerged as a unified entity in 1581. From 1618 to 1648 the United Provinces exhibited qualities of a hegemonic power and is considered by world system theorist Immanuel Wallerstein as the first global hegemonic state. See Peter J. Taylor, "Ten Years That Shook the World? The United Provinces as First Hegemonic State," *Sociological Perspectives* 37, no. 1 (1994): 25–46.

21 Immanuel Wallerstein, "The Three Instances of Hegemony in the History of the Capitalist World-Economy," in *Current Issues and Research in Macrosociology: International Studies in Sociology and Social Anthropology* 37, ed. Gerhard Lenski (Leiden: E.J. Brill, 1984), 103.

22 Giovanni Arrighi, Po-Keung Hui, Krishnendu Ray, and Thomas Ehrlich Reifer, "Geopolitics and High Finance," in *Chaos and Governance in the Modern World System*, eds. Giovanni Arrighi and Beverly J. Silver (Minneapolis: University of Minnesota Press, 1999), 64.

23 In 1823 US President James Munroe laid claim to regional leadership in Latin America and the Caribbean by asserting, in an address to the US Congress, that any attempt by the European powers to expand their influence in the Western Hemisphere would be considered a threat to American interests and to its peace and security. See George C. Herring, *From Colony to Superpower: U.S. Foreign Relations Since 1776* (Oxford: Oxford University Press, 2008), 153–155.

24 Peadar Kirby, *Introduction to Latin America: Twenty-First Century Challenges* (London: Sage, 2003), 96–97.

25 Peter J. Hugill, "The American Challenge to British Hegemony," *Geographical Review* 99, no. 3 (July 2009): 408.

26 For Wilson's "fourteen points," see www.lib.byu.edu/index.php/President_Wilson's_Fourteen_Points.

27 Charles P. Kindleberger, *The World in Depression, 1929–1939*, rev. ed. (Berkeley and Los Angeles: University of California Press, 1986).

28 Andrew Gamble, "Hegemony and Decline: Britain and the United States," in *Two Hegemonies: Britain 1846–1914 and the United States 1941–2001*, eds. Patrick Karl O'Brien and Armand Clesse (Aldershot: Ashgate, 2002), 127–140.

29 Poland, which was not present at the founding, later signed the charter to become one of the original fifty-one member states of this organization.

30 Armand Van Dormael, *Bretton Woods: Birth of a Monetary System* (London: Palgrave Macmillan, 1978).

31 G. John Ikenberry, "The Political Origins of Bretton Woods," in *A Retrospective on the Bretton Woods System*, eds. Michael D. Bordo and Barry Eichengreen (Chicago, IL: University of Chicago Press), 179.

32 See M. J. Hogan, *The Marshall Plan: America, Britain and the Reconstruction of Western Europe, 1947–1952* (Cambridge: Cambridge University Press, 1987).

33 Chandra Muzaffer, "The Decline of US Helmed Global Hegemony: The Emergence of a More Equitable Pattern of International Relations," *World Public Forum*, Dialogue of Civilizations, 4 October 2012, http://wpfdc.org/politics/999-the-decline-of-us-helmed-global-hegemony-the-emergence-of-a-more-equitable-pattern-of-international-relations.

34 Van Ness, "Hegemony, Not Anarchy," 139–140.

35 "How Potent Are North Korea's Threats?" *BBC News*, 15 September 2015, www.bbc.com/news/world-asia-21710644.

36 Nahal Toosi, "Obama's Opening to Cuba: Here to Stay?" *Politico*, 26 November 2016, www.politico.com/story/2016/11/cuba-hardliners-castro-death-231846.

37 Miriam Pensack, "Trump to Reverse Obama's Opening to Cuba under the False Flag of Human Rights," *The Intercept*, 16 June 2017, https://theintercept.com/2017/06/16/trump-cuba-embargo-reverse-obama-opening.

38 See Paul Kennedy, *The Rise and Fall of the Great Powers: Economic Change and Military Conflict from 1500 to 2000* (New York: Random House, 1987).

39 See Muzaffer, "Decline of US Helmed Global Hegemony."

40 Fry, "The Decline of the American Superpower," 17.

41 *Financial Times*, "US to Lose Role as World's Top Manufacturer by 2020," 24 May 2007, www.ft.com/cms/s/0/25c8a88e-0958-11dc-a349-000b5df10621.html#axzz2JwGhjYkU.

42 Dominic Wilson and Roopa Purushothaman, "Dreaming with the BRICs: The Path to 2050," Global Economics Paper no. 99 (New York: Goldman Sachs, October 2003).

43 Clark, "China and the United States," 28.

44 Fry, "The Decline of the American Superpower," 1–22.

45 *The Independent*, "The Perils of Pax Americana," 6 February 1991.

46 Salvatore Babones, "American Hegemony Is Here to Stay," *The National Interest*, July–August 2015, http://nationalinterest.org/feature/american-hegemony-here-stay-13089.

47 On this point, see Bruce Russett, "America's Continuing Strengths," *International Organization* 39, no. 2 (1985): 213–214.

48 Charles Krauthammer, "The Unipolar Moment," *Foreign Affairs* 70, no. 1 (1991): 23–33.

49 *The Times*, "America Cannot Police the World Forever," 12 March 1991.

50 *The Economist*, "The World Order Changeth," 22 June 1991.

51 Nye, *Soft Power*, x.

52 Simon Reich, "The End of American Global Leadership?" *Salon*, 5 June 2017, www.salon.com/2017/06/05/the-end-of-americas-global-leadership_partner.

53 John Agnew, *Hegemony: The New Shape of Global Power* (Philadelphia, PA: Temple University Press, 2005), viii.

54 Paul MacDonald, "Rebalancing American Foreign Policy," *Daedalus* 138, no. 2 (2009): 124.

55 Noam Chomsky, "Future Global Hegemony and the US," *Global Policy Forum*, 26 August 2011, www.globalpolicy.org/challenges-to-the-us-empire/general-analysis-on-challenges-to-the-us-empire/50643-future-global-hegemony-and-the-us.html.

56 "Robert Cox on World Orders, Historical Change, and the Purpose of Theory in International Relations," *Theory Talk #37*, 12 March 2010, www.theory-talks.org/2010/03/theory-talk-37.html.

57 See Max Bergmann, "Present at the Destruction: How Rex Tillerson Is Wrecking the State Department," *Politico Magazine*, 29 June 2017, www.politico.com/magazine/story/2017/06/29/how-rex-tillerson-destroying-state-department-215319.

CONTENTS

China and global governance

Shaun Breslin and Ren Xiao

The idea that China will try and change the world to one more to its liking as soon as it has the chance (and power) to do so has adherents from among those who welcome a challenge to the status quo as well as those who fear it. There might not be any shared understanding of what this reformed world might look like, or a clearly articulated Chinese reform agenda. But the idea that we are on track for some sort of inevitable transition to a post-Western era or Chinese led global governance has nevertheless garnered a number of supporters.[1]

There are good reasons why this nonspecific general sentiment of impending transition exists. China's continued growth and increasing global reach and significance stands in contrast to a crisis of global neoliberalism that the existing structures of global governance failed to foresee and prevent. And there is dissatisfaction in China with current structures—both the distribution of power within major organizations and some of the basic principles that underpin them. Moreover, in recent years, we have seen an increasing Chinese preparedness to both push for reform of existing bodies, and also to establish new ones to meet Chinese objectives.

That said, a historical review shows that China has actually moved a long way from relative isolation and a rejection of Western-dominated institutions of global governance, to becoming an active member of many of them. China has, we suggest, been more prepared to change and align itself with the status quo than the international order has been prepared to change to accommodate Chinese interests (or reflect its power).

What this suggests is something of a tension in Chinese objectives and strategies. On the one hand, a desire to become (and to be seen as) a "responsible stakeholder" in a system that has served Chinese interests very well in recent years. On the other hand, a frustration that China's successes do not always get the respect that they deserve, and that changing power distributions in the global order (and not just towards China) remain less than fully respected and reflected in the way that governance functions are organized. This tension reveals itself in what we call a responsible reformist global governance agenda. Or in the words of Chinese Premier Li Keqiang in March 2017, China has become a participant, beneficiary, contributor, and reformer of the international system, all at the same time.[2]

In terms of formal global forms of governance, the Chinese emphasis is on empowering the United Nations system, utilizing the G-20 as a mechanism for bringing about broader global change, and working through the Word Trade Organization (WTO). However, the most significant Chinese initiatives are not those that are undertaken at the global level itself, but are instead projects and interactions at other levels that have global significance and impact. Thus, for example, what China does in terms of promoting regional forms of governance, or does bilaterally with developing nations across the world, has long-term consequences for the nature of governance across the globe that might seriously undermine the legitimacy, force, and efficacy of existing institutions and actors.

From outsider to actor

In many respects, it would be odd if China did not want to reform the existing order—it is, after all, an order that was constructed by others. The US-led embargo of China in the 1950s, combined with widespread recognition of the Republic of China (ROC) on Taiwan as the sole Chinese sovereign authority, meant that the People's Republic of China (PRC) was alienated from both emerging Western-dominated forms of governance, and those global institutions that fell under the UN system. Even though the PRC initially relied on the Soviet Union for financial and military assistance, China never joined the Warsaw Pact or the Council for Mutual Economic Assistance (or COMECON), and so did not fall under non-Western Moscow-led governance institutions either. As Sino-Soviet relations deteriorated in the late 1950s into the 1960s, and domestic Chinese politics took a radical revolutionary turn in the Cultural Revolution, China became one of the most autarkic and isolated countries in the world.

This position changed—and changed quiet dramatically—when the UN General Assembly voted to replace the ROC with the PRC as the sole representative of China in October 1971. This vote not only resulted in China becoming an actor in global governance, but its assumption of permanent membership in the Security Council immediately propelled the PRC into a leadership position of sorts; or at the very least, a position of privileged power in the UN. As we will discuss in more detail, the UN system has remained central to Chinese perceptions of how best to organize and deliver governance at the global level ever since.

A second key change came with the shift from revolutionary to developmental goals as the main challenge for the Communist Party in the post-Mao era. The perceived developmental benefits of engaging the capitalist world resulted in not only an increase in Chinese trade and inward investment but also an acceptance of the need to participate in those institutions designed to regulate and govern such international economic interactions.[3] China became a member of the World Bank and International Monetary Fund (IMF) in 1980, and became one of the world's leading recipients of financial and technical assistance from them over the next two decades.[4]

The relative ease with which China was welcomed into the Washington-based financial institutions was not repeated when it came to the fifteen-year attempt to join the WTO. After the end of the Cold War and the domestic turmoil in China in 1989, questions began to be raised over the wisdom of facilitating the further growth of a country that even in the early 1990s was being identified by some as destined to surpass the United States as the world's largest economy.[5] This external hesitancy was echoed in a vigorous debate within China over the extent to which the domestic changes that would have to be made to gain entry would harm key economic sectors through increased international competition. For some, pursuing WTO entry was akin to abandoning China's national interests, and China should "say no" and reject the West rather than try to join it.[6] Nevertheless, despite both these external and domestic misgivings, after extensive deliberations, and considerable concessions on the Chinese side, a deal was finally done that allowed China to join the third main pillar of global economic governance in December 2001.

The WTO should (in theory at least) depoliticize international economic relationships—and this in no small part explains its perceived importance for the Chinese leadership. Before joining the WTO, China was concerned that other countries might take action against it because of concerns about the consequences of China's rise, or because they disliked China's political system and human rights regime (or both). Inside the WTO, trade disputes continue; indeed, China has been subject to more antidumping actions than any other developing economy. It has also used the WTO system to bring complaints and actions against others as well. But the WTO dispute settlement system creates clear and transparent processes for settling these disputes, and decisions should be based on technical and legal criteria rather than on considerations of great power politics and power balancing.[7]

There was a widespread assumption in China that after fifteen years of membership, it would gain "market economy" status—a categorization that would change the methodology that others had to use in trying to bring antidumping cases against China (and in the process strengthen China's ability to defend itself against such cases). However, as the fifteen-year anniversary (11 December 2016) got closer, it became clear that the United States, the European Union (EU), and Japan (among others) did not share China's interpretation of the automatic granting of a status change; and so they would continue to treat China as a nonmarket economy. While the WTO system allowed for China to respond with technical legal challenges over its status and the way that antidumping cases were being established, there was a strong feeling in China that politics was once more the defining factor in its treatment. After fifteen years of negotiating entry into the rules-based world trading system, and another fifteen years of operating within it, China believed it had behaved properly; and if anything, the dispute increased Chinese commitment to play an increasingly weighty and influential role from inside the system in the future.

The global financial crisis: A power shift?

To these three important turning points we can add a fourth in the form of the global financial crisis. While China had been a member of the G-20 since its inception in 1999, the transformation of the G-20 (and China's membership of it) created the opportunity for China to increase its voice and influence when it came to debating global governance reforms—not least, but not only, when it came to hosting the annual G-20 summit in 2016. Notably, China's role in the G-20 stands in stark contrast to its continued absence from the G-7/G-8; although Chinese preferences feed into governance discussions even when there is not actually a China representative at the table.

In less tangible terms, the crisis also resulted in a shift in perceptions of the nature of the world order in China, and China's place within it. With the Western neoliberal model viewed as tainted, there was a renewed focus on the merits of the sort of strong state capitalism that had helped China to rebound quickly from a sudden and dramatic drop of exports in 2008. With a number of Western states and the EU not in financial trouble and looking to China for investment and help, the idea that a power transition had taken shape gained considerable purchase. Not a replacement of the United States by China, but a shift in relative power asymmetries beneath the still predominant United States.[8]

The idea that China has subsequently become more assertive is frequently rejected.[9] Nevertheless, in the post crisis years, there seems to have been a greater appetite to articulate Chinese dissatisfactions with the way that global governance is organized, and some of the normative preferences of previously dominant Western liberal elites (for example, the wisdom of privatization, deregulation, and neoliberal economic reform). There is also concern that Washington and the other Western powers keep moving the governance goalposts at China's expense. The above-mentioned failure to grant China "market economy" status and the promotion of the Trans Pacific Partnership without Chinese participation are two cases in point. And rather than just be dissatisfied, if change is not forthcoming (or coming quick enough), China is prepared to be proactive and provide alternative forms of governance instead.

Governance at the global level

For our purposes here, it is worth parsing further how China emphasizes the multilateral arenas within the UN system and the G-20, before the next section traces more indirect impacts.

China and the UN system

China attaches particular importance to the role of the UN system in global governance. For China, the founding of the UN—as its seventy-plus years of history has shown—was an epoch-making event, and an important milestone in humanity's cause of peace and progress. China sees the UN as the most important and most representative international organization and thus a key component of the web of global governance. The UN, as the core of the collective security mechanism, plays an irreplaceable role in international cooperation to ensure global security. China believes that such a role should only be strengthened and must not in any way be weakened by, for example, military action by powerful Western states. Because it views the UN as valuable, China invariably tries to help safeguard the UN's authority.

China maintains a rhetorically strict line on opposing external interference in the politics of sovereign states and opposes unrequested military intervention or regime change. Nevertheless it accepts that maintaining peace and security is a key part of the UN's work, and has increasingly become an active participant in UN peacekeeping operations. Between 1989 and 2016, China deployed more than 30,000 troops in twenty-nine UN peacekeeping operations. Indeed, China recently has sent more peacekeeping troops than any other permanent members of the Security Council, and at the beginning of 2017, more than 3100 Chinese peacekeepers were serving worldwide.[10]

As a result of China's economic growth (particularly since 2000), it pays higher assessed contributions than in the past. China's share of the UN budget stayed at 1.54 percent between 2001 and 2003 before rising to over two percent after 2004, and it has kept growing ever since. After the UN adopted a new controversial budget convention in 2016, Beijing's quota shares for membership dues rose from 5.148 percent to 7.921 percent. China also subsequently contributed 10.2 percent of the total peacekeeping budget. This meant that China's total UN membership dues ranked third among the 193 member states, following only the United States and Japan. Based on the new quota, China contributed $196 million to the UN's regular budget in 2016 and $199 million in 2017.[11]

China also has set up cooperation funds and taken other measures to increase its contribution and strengthen the world organization. In 2015, marking the seventieth anniversary of the UN's foundation, President Xi Jinping delivered a speech at the General Assembly in which he announced a series of decisions designed to support the UN. This included a ten-year, US$1 billion China–UN peace and development fund to advance multilateral cooperation and contribute more to international peace and security as well as to development. China also joined the new UN Peacekeeping Capability Readiness System and promoted itself as a leader in setting up a permanent peacekeeping police squad and a peacekeeping standby force of 8000 troops. China also committed a total of US$100 million of free military assistance to the African Union (AU) over five years to support the establishment of the African Standby Force and the African Capacity for Immediate Response to Crisis.[12] By the time President Xi visited the UN's Geneva headquarters in January 2017, the China–UN Peace and Development Fund was already in operation supporting a range of projects across the UN system.

China and the G-20

Participating in the G-20 is an important signal of China's return to the high table of global politics. The G-20 at both ministerial and summit levels is a relatively more informal grouping than other global institutions. However, from a Chinese viewpoint, given its aggregate weight and its incorporation of the emerging powers, it is hard for the G-20's importance to be overestimated. Rather than the G-7/G-8, the G-20 is seen as the key to world economics and politics today.

China was part of the G-20 from its establishment, first as a gathering of finance ministers and central bank governors (prompted by the Asian financial crisis in the late 1990s). Over time, China increasingly became a more powerful member in the group. When the global financial crisis broke out in 2008, the G-7/G-8 proved unable to cope with a crisis of such a magnitude; and the United States under George W. Bush attempted to change course by proposing the elevation of the G-20 to the summit level. China, a nonmember of the then G-8, readily accepted the suggestion and has participated in all subsequent summits, helping to turn the G-20 into a significant platform for global economic cooperation.[13]

The presidency for the 2016 summit provided China with an opportunity to play a larger leadership role by exercising "host diplomacy." China chose the theme for the Hangzhou summit and set agendas for future developments in key areas, including initiatives for world trade promotion and new principles for global investment. Seeing the G-20's emergence and revival as part of a multipolar world, China regarded the Hangzhou summit as a rare opportunity to promote the G-20 as a major pillar of global governance, and it was keen to provide the resources to make it succeed. After having experienced nearly four decades of far reaching reform and phenomenal economic growth, China had the necessary power—both in terms of material resources and what we might call "developmental prestige"—to call on other members to act together at the G-20 to bring about China-influenced global change.

China has also tried to make the G-20 a vehicle to fulfil the UN's new 2030 Development Agenda, and it has tried systematically to focus attention and activities on the developing world and common development. As part of the host diplomacy, China invited more representatives from the developing world than any other previous G-20 summit host. The addition of these observers increased the voice and appeal of the developing countries to be more fully made and expressed during the summit and furthered China's claims to be a proponent of greater inclusion and democracy in global governance. It also provided the opportunity to further China's credentials as a putative responsible global governance innovator. As Carrie Gracie argued:

> Put bluntly, China hopes the world will look back and identify the Hangzhou G20 as the moment when China looked like a better guardian of global economic governance than a US paralysed by poisonous politics at home and handicapped by distractions abroad.[14]

The indirect impact on global governance

As important as these formal initiatives at the global level, it is the collective consequences of what China is doing below that level that we suggest will have the most significant impact on the way that the globe is governed in future years. This impact does not entail imposing Chinese ways of doing things on other countries. On the contrary, with the exception of not recognizing Taiwan, China does not link financial measures for developing countries to political or economic conditionalities. Others may choose to adopt or adapt parts of "the China model" if they wish, but this is not something on which China insists. But by providing such a "no strings attached" alternative to dealing with the West—either individual countries or the major financial institutions—represents a significant difference from previous eras when a number of countries had little or no choice other than to accept conditionalities if they wanted external financial support. So, while not necessarily promoting a clearly identifiable and articulated Chinese global order, this Chinese alternative undermines the ability of others to impose and maintain their preferences. This approach provides "alternative" ways of pursuing development in an era when the Washington Consensus has become discredited.

Regional governance

Arguably the main focus of Chinese reform efforts have been at the regional rather than the global level. Despite initially perceiving regional institutions as largely hostile to China (or at least not supportive of Chinese objectives), from the 1990s China's leaders began to see participation in regional multilateral organizations as being in the national interest. A key driver was the impact of a number of crises (including the Asian financial crisis, avian flu, and SARS) that made clear the importance of dealing with transnational issues cooperatively. Being seen to be a good and responsible neighbor was also seen as beneficial in allaying fears in the region about the consequences of China's continued rise.[15]

As a result, China became an active regional partner with the Association of Southeast Asian Nations (ASEAN), with the ASEAN secretariat, and in a broader regional collaboration with Japan and South Korea (ASEAN Plus Three). While there is also considerable collaboration over shared environmental governance challenges, the relationship is dominated by different forms of economic cooperation. Perhaps most importantly, China and ASEAN established a Free Trade Area in 2010. This arrangement is not the sort of partnership that reflects a radical rejection of the existing global order.

China has also established a different type of regional partnership with a different set of neighbors in the former Soviet Union via the Shanghai Cooperation Organization (SCO). It started life as a body designed to increase mutual trust in a region where political formations and alliances were still taking shape in the wake of the demise of the Soviet Union, and to deal with the transnational threat of terrorism and extremism.[16] The SCO has subsequently increased both its membership and also the scope of its discussions to include the possibility of closer economic cooperation. Despite tensions in the group (not least over potential conflicting Chinese and Russian grand plans for developing regional influence)—its existence is significant as an early sign of China's willingness to establish (or co-establish) new forms of non-Western regional organizations (rather than attaching itself to existing bodies as it did in the ASEAN case).

China has subsequently become more ambitious in establishing new groupings and institutions. These include working to turn the BRICS (Brazil, Russia, India, China, and South Africa) into something more than just an acronym (including the creation of the BRICS new development bank discussed in detail by Cooper and Thakur earlier in this book) and the Asian Infrastructure Investment Bank (AIIB) launched in 2014. While the latter is regional in terms of where it is looking to focus its funding activities, it has become a global institution of sorts. After the United Kingdom announced its intention to join in March 2015, a range of other non-Asian countries followed suit, although notably not the United States or Japan. Although China retained by far the biggest percentage of shares and votes (33.34 and 26.06, respectively, compared to 8.52 and 7.51 for the next largest state, India), this does not guarantee it an automatic majority. The board of directors also has members from the United Kingdom, Germany, Saudi Arabia, Egypt, Turkey, Thailand, Russia, India, Indonesia, South Korea, and Australia. Moreover, almost as soon as it started work, the prospect of extending activities to Latin America and Africa came onto the agenda.[17]

The AIIB is an interesting test case—not just of Chinese intentions but also of how others perceive (and react to) these intentions. It is very much a China-led initiative. However, while it will follow some of the lending criteria of existing bodies (for example, legal transparency and environmental impact considerations), it will not be a force for deregulation and privatization that other development funders are often associated with. In this respect, it does indeed represent some sort of challenge to the dominant *status quo ante*. But providing development assistance is not a revolutionary activity, particularly when many traditional funders in the West are struggling with their own domestic financial problems. It is also notable that three of the first round of AIIB funded projects were co-financed by mainstays of the existing global financial architecture—the World Bank, the Asian Development Bank, and the European Bank for Reconstruction and Development. In short, the AIIB is not replacing existing governance institutions but adding to them.[18] Ultimately, whether the AIIB is primarily seen as a good or bad thing for global governance seems largely to depend on the prior question of whether China's rise in itself is seen as good and inevitable, on the one hand, or bad and something that should be resisted wherever possible, on the other.

China and the Global South

The idea (and reality) of China as an alternative to the status quo reaches far beyond its regional backyard. China has also been active in both attaching itself to existing institutions (as in the China-Community of Central American and Caribbean States forum) and taking the lead in establishing new ones. Perhaps the most high profile of these new organizations is the Forum on China Africa Cooperation (FOCAC), established in 2000. FOCAC has become something of a symbol of China's attempts to establish itself as a new type of development partner for the continent.[19]

Despite becoming the first or second largest economy in the world (depending on how it is calculated), China like other rising powers has not become a member of the Organisation for Economic Cooperation and Development (OECD). It has various forms of intensive cooperation with the OECD, and it has joined some of its bodies (such as the OECD Development Center); but Beijing remains outside the formal structure. This includes not being a formal member of the Development Assistance Committee (DAC), although it has participated in some DAC meetings since 2001.

The DAC was established as the self-defined global forum for the world's major development donors. So the absence of a country that is now one of the world's biggest sources of finance for development projects would seem problematic if the

OECD is to maintain its role in the future. Furthermore, as a nonmember, China does not report its overseas financing activities in ways that conform to those international standards and definitions as established by the DAC, so establishing comparable international statistics is problematic. Moreover, it is unclear how much Chinese financing would actually count as "official development assistance" defined by the OECD as "flows of official financing administered with the promotion of the economic development and welfare of developing countries as the main objective."[20] Chinese projects often have a commercial logic to them, with an expectation that Chinese companies will benefit from development projects overseas alongside the recipient country, through the sourcing of materials, technology, labor, and so on. But while it might not officially count as development aid, these activities have considerable developmental benefits to China's partners.[21]

Not only does the growth of Chinese finance for overseas development projects lead to questions over the efficacy and representativeness of the DAC, it also potentially changes the very definition of aid itself by blurring the distinction between aid and commercial projects. We also suggest that China has developed a different development focus. While it does provide aid for traditional development projects like health and education, there is a particularly strong focus on financing major infrastructure projects.

Conclusion

The importance of building connections through infrastructure projects is one of the key agendas of the much vaunted Belt and Road project—the twin goal of constructing a land-based Silk Road Economic Belt and a Maritime Silk Road linking China through either Southeast, Central, and South Asia or via East Africa and the Gulf to Europe. The way that the project was promoted is more important than what has actually happened (and will happen) in terms of investments. Money could and would have flowed from China into other countries along the Belt and Road without being part of the bigger project. The fact that such investments are announced as Belt and Road projects—and often with considerable fanfare—is connected to President Xi Jinping's personal interest, endorsement, and promotion. It also says a lot about the way in which Xi wants to position and identify China as a provider of global public goods.

Xi is also personally identified with the concept of a "new type of great power relations" to guide China's relations with other great powers (which often, but not always, refers simply to the United States). While this concept accepts that China is indeed a great power, most Chinese analysts qualify this status by arguing that China is also still a rising power and a developing economy at the same time. It is thus very different from others that rose to great power status in the past, and should only be expected to take on the burdens of global leadership that are commensurate with its special status.

Nevertheless, even this qualified acceptance of a special status as a global actor and power marks a significant shift from previous eras. As outlined above, China is now indeed taking a role in providing global public goods that have important governance consequences. This largely takes the form of *adding* to existing governance structures and processes, rather than fundamentally *challenging* them. Although in the example of development finance and aid, there is perhaps something of a normative challenge to the status quo as well—albeit a relatively moderate reformist rather than revolutionary challenge.

In his speech at the Davos World Economic Forum in 2017, Xi further consolidated the idea of China as a key global power by inviting the world to "join the express train of Chinese development." He also reaffirmed China's commitment to getting a fair and equal say for all countries in global governance institutions and restated the importance of connectivity. Such connectivity for Xi entailed not just building bricks-and-mortar infrastructure but also rejecting protectionism and maintaining a free and open global trade and investment regime.[22] Without mentioning any proponents of an alternative world view by name, the implication was clear that China, and not the United States under Donald Trump, was the main defender of an open global order, while others were turning inwards and trying to overturn the status quo.

Of course, what exactly an "open" system actually means is subject to debate, and Xi's version does not equate to the sort of radical liberalization and deregulation associated with the Washington Consensus. Even so, his speech shows just how far both China and the world have moved since China joined the WTO in 2001. And it is likely that China will further promote its understanding of (and preferences for) an "open" system through free trade initiatives in the Asia-Pacific as well as along the Belt and Road. It is fair to say that China's growing influence is not welcomed by all. But for some issues, a more proactive Chinese position is expected, welcomed, and desired by many members of the international community of states.

Additional reading

Gregory Chin, Margaret Pearson, and Wang Yong, eds., *International Political Economy in China: The Global Conversation* (London: Routledge, 2015).

Jaques DeLisle and Avery Goldstein, eds., *China's Global Engagement: Competition and Influence in the 21st Century* (Washington, DC: Brookings Institution, 2017).

Scott Kennedy, ed., Global Governance and China: The Dragon's Learning Curve (London: Routledge, 2018).

Samuel Kim, *China, the United Nations and World Order* (Princeton, NJ: Princeton University Press, 2015).

John Kirton, *China's G20 Leadership* (London: Routledge, 2016).

Notes

1 Thomas Christensen, *The China Challenge: Shaping the Choices of a Rising Power* (New York: Norton, 2015).

2 Li Keqiang, *Report on The Work of Government*, http://english.gov.cn/premier/news/2017/03/16/content_281475597911192.htm.

3 Harold Jacobson and Michel Oksenberg, *China's Participation in the IMF, the World Bank, and GATT: Toward a Global Economic Order* (Ann Arbor: University of Michigan Press, 1990).

4 Nicholas Lardy, "China and the International Financial System," in *China Joins the World: Progress and Prospects*, eds. Elizabeth Economy and Michel Oksenberg (New York: Council on Foreign Relations, 1999), 206–230.

5 William Overholt, *The Rise Of China: How Economic Reform Is Creating a New Superpower* (New York: W.W. Norton & Company, 1993).

6 Song Qiang, Zhang Zangzang and Qiao Bian, *Zhongguo Keyi Shuo Bu [China Can Say No]* (Beijing, China: Zhonghua Gongshang Lianhe Press, 1996).

7 Kong Qingjiang, "China in the WTO and Beyond: China's Approach to International Institutions," *Tulane Law Review* 88, no. 5 (2014): 959–980. Also James Scott and Rorden Wilkinson, "China Threat? Evidence from the WTO," *Journal of World Trade* 47, no. 4 (2013): 761–782.

8 Wu Xinbo, "Understanding the Geopolitical Implications of the Global Financial Crisis," *Washington Quarterly* 33, no. 4 (2010): 155–163.

9 Alastair Iain Johnston, "How New and Assertive is China's New Assertiveness?" *International Security* 37, no. 4 (2013): 7–48.

10 See http://mt.sohu.com/20160603/n452809926.shtml. For a good study, see Bates Gill and Chin-Hao Huang, *China's Expanding Role in Peacekeeping: Prospects and Policy Implications*, SIPRI Policy paper no. 26, November 2009.

11 http://news.163.com/15/1226/03/BBNTLA0O00014Q4P.html.

12 Speech by Xi Jinping at 70th UN General Assembly, 28 September 2015, www.voltairenet.org/article188880.html.

13 Ren Xiao, "A Reform Minded Status Quo Power? The G20, and Reform of the International Financial System," *Third World Quarterly* 36, no. 11 (2015): 2023–2043.

14 Carrie Gracie, "Hangzhou G20: China's Ambitions for Global Leadership," *BBC Online*, 2 September 2016, www.bbc.co.uk/news/world-asia-china-37241315.

15 Shaun Breslin, "Understanding China's Regional Rise: Interpretations, Identities and Implications," *International Affairs* 85, no. 4 (2009): 817–835.

16 Originally established as the Shanghai Five in 1996 (China, Russia, Kazakhstan, Kyrgyzstan, Tajikistan), the grouping became the SCO in 2001 when Uzbekistan also joined. India and Pakistan were approved to become full members in 2015.

17 Each director acts on behalf of a constituency of other member states. For example, Germany represents the other Eurozone member states but not all are on a regional basis. Egypt, for example, represents Brazil and South Africa. For details see www.aiib.org.

18 Ren Xiao, "China as an Institution-builder: The Case of the AIIB," *The Pacific Review* 29, no. 3 (2016): 435–442.

19 Ian Taylor, *The Forum on China Africa Cooperation (FOCAC)* (London: Routledge, 2012).

20 www.oecd.org/dac/stats/officialdevelopmentassistancedefinitionandcoverage.htm.

21 Shaun Breslin, "China and the South: Objectives, Actors and Interactions," *Development and Change* 44, no. 6 (2013): 1273–1294.

22 Full text of Xi Jinping's Keynote at The World Economic Forum, 17 January 2017, https://america.cgtn.com/2017/01/17/full-text-of-xi-jinping-keynote-at-the-world-economic-forum.

PART V
NON-STATE ACTORS IN
GLOBAL GOVERNANCE

Part introduction

The proliferation of actors and the scope of their activities have been central to the burgeoning field of global governance. This part of the book introduces readers to some of the most significant non-state actors that make the study of global governance both more interesting but inevitably more unwieldy than focusing simply on international organizations.

The eight chapters contained in Part V of the book move well beyond state-centrism to address the major aspects of the pluralism that is a feature of the way that the world is currently governed. As with each of the parts in this book, the chapters are arranged to cover as much ground as possible while allowing classes to choose contributions that best suit their purposes. The chapters are arranged so that they flow from the largest and most obvious non-state actors through to the darker and more subversive end of the global governance spectrum. Taking in the full run of chapters would give readers the best insights into this arena of global governance. That said, introductory courses may wish to emphasize Jan Aart Scholte's chapter on "Civil society and NGOs" (Chapter 25) and Michael Moran's on "Global philanthropy" (Chapter 29). Classes seeking to investigate civil society groups in more depth may then explore James G. McGann's chapter on "Think tanks and global policy networks" (Chapter 28). Relations among corporate actors are explored by Chris May in his chapter on "Global corporations" (Chapter 24). Non-state economic actors are also the core focus on Timothy J. Sinclair's chapter on "Credit rating agencies" (Chapter 27), and Nigel Haworth and Steve Hughes' on "Labor" (Chapter 26). The security aspects of non-state actors—what some see as "uncivil" society—are explored in chapters by Peter J. Hoffman on "Private military and security companies" (Chapter 30) and Frank G. Madsen on "Transnational criminal networks" (Chapter 31). Together these chapters add additional pieces to the evolving mosaic of contemporary global governance.

Non-state actors in global governance: Chapter synopses

This part begins in Chapter 24 with "Global corporations," Chris May's perceptive account of the role of transnational businesses as global governance actors in their own right. He shows that global corporations govern significant aspects of world order as individual agents as well as in conjunction with other institutions. He suggests that to appreciate fully how global corporations exercise governance we need to understand the supply chains in which they are engaged, the processes and practices of governance that play out therein, and the opportunities that exist to pursue strategies for better corporate social responsibility.

The expansive and oftentimes unmanageable topic of "Civil society and NGOs" is masterfully parsed by Jan Aart Scholte in Chapter 25. Scholte opens readers' eyes to the fact that a prominent explanation for the move from international organization (IO) to global governance is the growth in the numbers, scope, and impact of civil society and nongovernmental organizations (NGOs). He outlines many of the strengths of involving different voices and energies in global governance, but he also does not shy away from presenting their obvious shortcomings, including their questionable legitimacy—that is, many are self-appointed representatives for particular peoples and issues.

In Chapter 26, Nigel Haworth and Steve Hughes explore the role of organized labor in global governance. They seek to highlight the ups and downs of labor's capacity to defend its interests and shape a measure of the way the world is organized. Integral to their analysis is a prominent international institution—both a physical structure and a web of conventions, practices, and guidelines—the International Labour Organization (ILO). Yet, its importance lies in more than just its record in keeping working conditions and worker rights in the global spotlight. This unusual institution was ahead of the curve in making room for a variety of non-state actors. From its inception in 1919, it has embodied a three-pronged partnership among labor, business, and government. For many this tripartite structure lends the ILO great strength, while for others it weakens labor's global capacity to defend itself. What is clear, however, is that this form of partnership has now found expression elsewhere, including in such institutions as the UN Global Compact.

Timothy J. Sinclair's exposition of the role of "Credit rating agencies" in Chapter 27 gives a dramatic insight into the hidden power exercised by those financial bodies. Moody's Investors Service and Standard & Poor's Ratings Group render judgments that are authoritative enough to cause substantial global market responses. Hence, the role of these private agencies is essential in order to understand the nature of order, stability, and predictability in the world economy. Moreover, the spread globally of an essentially US practice has become the general one in all developed country markets and increasingly in "emerging" ones as well. Recurrent episodes of ratings failure and criticism of these agencies suggest the limits of non-state forms of global governance as well as the need for government regulation.

The adage that "knowledge is power" takes on a new flavor in Chapter 28—"Think tanks and global policy networks." James G. McGann, who directs a center that studies the phenomenon, paints a portrait of worldwide research efforts to influence elite opinion and policy- and decision making. In a complex, interdependent, and information-rich world, governments and a variety of policy- and decision makers confront the common challenge of bringing expert knowledge to bear. He describes yet another manifestation of globalization, here the race to produce applicable knowledge. The growth of public policy research organizations, or "think tanks," over the last few decades has been nothing less than explosive—not only have their numbers increased, but the scope and impact of their work have also expanded dramatically at the national, regional, and global levels.

In Chapter 29, Michael Moran examines the importance of "Global philanthropy" in contemporary global governance. The weight and visibility of the Bill and Melinda Gates Foundation—unparalleled in modern private global governance—is the most recent installment of the use of private monies to finance public goods. Moran shows how private fortunes have been invested in projects ranging from the Green Revolution to IR scholarship and human rights. While criticisms abound—a reflection of its salience—global philanthropy should be placed in context. Comparatively marginal in relation to other non-state actors, nonetheless its unique attributes—an endowment and associated financial agency as well as a close association with actors from across sectors—at important junctures has helped develop the institutional architecture of global governance.

A growing part of the privatization puzzle consists of "Private military and security companies" (PMSCs), which became (in)famous especially with their expanded and visible presence in the twenty-first-century's wars in Afghanistan and Iraq. In Chapter 30, Peter J. Hoffman investigates why governments as well as intergovernmental and nongovernmental organizations find paying contractors for protection to be not only a cost-effective but also a palatable approach to improving security. Hoffman points out the long history of mercenaries as a feature of world politics; he disrupts conventional state-centric readings of world politics; he exposes just how influential these non-state actors are; and he illustrates how much of the high politics of security has been outsourced.

Chapter 31 explores another dark side of globalization, namely "Transnational criminal networks." In this chapter, Frank G. Madsen evaluates the far-flung and intricate worldwide criminal networks that exist and benefit from modern technologies and pathologies. He also spells out those forms of intergovernmental cooperation, ranging from INTERPOL to financial tracking by banks, which endeavor to improve global criminal governance. In short, in many substantive areas of global problem solving, but especially in criminology, understanding global crime governance requires taking into account not only the operation of criminal networks but also of the networks created by governments to neutralize them. Drawing on illustrations ranging from human trafficking to money laundering and drugs, Madsen views criminal networks as consisting of several subnetworks, which makes the network concept even more concrete for viewing the range of actors and issues detailed elsewhere in this volume.

Where to now?

This overview of non-state actors is essential, not peripheral, to IO and global governance. All too often they are adjuncts in texts that are otherwise mainly about intergovernmental organizations (IGOs). What each of these chapters illustrates clearly is how non-state actors play a key role on the global governance stage. They are serious and substantial components of contemporary world order, not merely a little extra spice to mix into the usual IO casserole.

Global corporations

Christopher May

This chapter does not discuss how various corporations have influenced global governance, or how (global) governance institutions have sought to regulate corporations.
These two common approaches might be best regarded as seeing the relationship
between corporations and global governance as either an input (helping shape the
agendas of global governance institutions) or as an output (corporations impacted by
institutional decisions). On the input side, there is significant evidence of corporations
having successfully lobbied and shaped the agenda of various global governance
institutions and other globally focused organizations.[1] Likewise, most analyses of
global governance discuss the varying levels of regulation and (lack of) compliance
by corporations across a range of issue areas, from environmental protection to labor
rights. Let me be clear: Both these aspects of the relationship between global governance and corporations are important, but they also are clearly visible in the debates
about global governance.

However, this chapter proposes a third and additional perspective: The global corporation itself has a significant governance role within its own international networks,
and as such it is an institution of global governance in its own right. Given that
"governance" is often presented as the importation of business values and processes
into politics,[2] it is perhaps surprising that corporations' (extra-economic) governance of their own networks has remained under-remarked. This chapter is therefore
concerned with the wider realm of relations on which global governance analyses
should focus—specifically including but not limited to, the supply chain assembled
and governed by contemporary globally active corporations.

Patterns of organization vary widely between corporations,[3] but limitations of
space mean the focus here is on the question of governance in general rather than
looking at actual corporate networks (as would be required to further develop this
approach through specific cases). Thus, while recognizing that not all major global
enterprises are corporations (Ikea and Zara, for instance, are privately owned and not

therefore incorporated), organizational practices are not so varied by this (different) legal character as to suggest that the approach here does not apply. The challenges and practices of governance of supply chains do not likely differ significantly depending on the ownership structure of the enterprise, although further research is required to test such a proposition.

Therefore, this chapter, rather than adopting an analytical perspective that focuses on the process of management, instead employs the lens of a *governance* function undertaken by corporations, which is characterized by explicit and implicit power relations. It is thus concerned with more than the technical management of efficiency in network interactions. Hence, our understanding both of global governance and the political economy of the global corporate sector can be enhanced by adding this third, complementary view.

The next section briefly sets out what the global corporation is, highlighting some important legal and political issues. Thereafter, it explores the forms of power that it can deploy across its production and supply networks before examining some current debates about the impact of the corporation's governance of its network. This approach underpins the argument that we can gain extra traction on the political economy of the global corporation by understanding it as an institution of global governance itself. The conclusion highlights some key issues that this approach helps illuminate.

The political economy of the global corporation

There is a wide and distinguished literature looking at the role of corporations in the global system; here they are referred to as "global" corporations, but they have also been called "multinational" and "transnational" corporations or enterprises. These accounts are often broadly focused on the relations between relatively independent corporations operating across a number (sometimes a large number) of state jurisdictions, and their varying relations with these states.[4] There are various ways these relations are conceptualized, but the key point is that they treat the corporation (or enterprise) as a singular unit (or often a black box). Although there are other forms of company or private commercial enterprise, it is almost always the case that those active at the global level are incorporated in a national jurisdiction (or constituted through parallel legal forms). Thus, while accepting differences, the similarities are more important.

Although corporations are organizations made up of groups of people, various social and internal institutions with capital and other assets mobilized toward a set of economic (and sometime extra-economic) ends, they are usually treated as having a single personality for legal purposes. This legal fiction pays clear organizational dividends within contract law—for instance, the corporation can be dealt with as an effective signatory to agreements and undertakings. Although there are other modes of corporate organization, the central aspects of the Anglo-Saxon legal form—corporate personality; limited liability; specified modes of corporate governance—have become increasingly influential and widespread in the new millennium, especially as regards the corporation's legal personality. Moreover, for many corporations the desire or need to compete to raise capital in London or New York, and thus seek stock market listings in the United Kingdom or United States, has driven the adoption of the legal arrangements to deliver specified accounting and financial reporting requirements required in these jurisdictions. Through compliance with such regulations, a particular legal form has been exported to countries with differing legal traditions and practices.

This partial convergence of corporate forms has not necessarily been beneficial for the accountability of business; for instance, the increasing adoption of Anglo-Saxon modes of limited liability within the governance of subsidiaries has shielded companies and their shareholders from accountability across their international networks. In the Anglo-Saxon corporate legal form, corporations have the ability to hold stock or own other companies as they are treated as single legal persons with similar rights to ownership to "natural persons" (that is, people). This allows the corporation itself to benefit from the protection of limited liability (originally formulated to protect individuals from excessive risk not to safeguard corporations themselves), in its role as a holding company. Possibly the most important aspect of legal personality is the extension of the benefits of limited liability. This is the formal limitation of the investor's exposure to loss to the amount of the original investment; once the shares have been purchased, their value may plunge to zero, but there can be no further demands on the investor for funds whatever the plight of the (failing) corporation.

Originally, the extension of legal personality through incorporation to business enterprises was a grant of authority by the state to carry out certain purposes for the public good. One of the key shifts in the modern political characterization of incorporation has been a move from a conception of delegation of certain powers from the state, to seeing incorporation as a mode of protection *from* the state. Thus, now the multinational corporation occupies a social space where its supporters argue that its forms and practices are not political but merely technical; we are confronted with the question of how far such corporations actually fulfil their side of any (now largely forgotten) bargain.[5]

While corporations remain outside the scope of international law (like other persons, they are subjects only of national law), corporations' recourse to legalized personality is a relatively internationalized legal norm even if it remains a national jurisdictional matter. While corporations may be influenced by international "soft law" (regulations that have the appearance of law but not the capacity to sanction non-compliance), little regulation at the international level has been solidified into hard, positive law to hold them firmly to account outside national jurisdictions. This has the advantage of offering corporations opportunities for organizational convergence with its posited associated efficiency benefits, but with few of the accountability costs of formal legislative development.

This legal situation does mean that multinational corporations are exposed to a significant legal tension; they are constituted under the laws of their home country, and as such this has some impact on their character and practices. However, equally most countries require the local subsidiary operation of any corporation to be incorporated or registered under national law, and as such frequently a global multinational's legal form is highly diversified. Sometimes, governments of multinational's home/ headquarters seek to extend their legal reach though the extraterritoriality of their regulatory focus to demand that subsidiaries should be governed by the regulations of the home country even if they conflict with those of the subsidiary's host jurisdiction.

Conversely, host states may also seek to hold multinational corporations accountable through national legal mechanisms that may be in tension with how a corporation expects to manage its affairs in its headquarters country. Where bilateral investment treaties (BITs) have been negotiated, the host state may end up constricting its own ability to so regulate as a way of "encouraging" inward investment as well as subjecting itself to often potentially contentious international investor-state dispute settlement or arbitration.[6]

Corporations seek to navigate this international legal terrain with its variable rules by establishing an inner governance function that builds on these legal requirements, but that establishes network-wide norms and rules to enable the network to function as a single (albeit complex) organization. This practice of governance is the subject of the rest of this chapter.

Supply chains and governance

The complexity of the organization of supply chains has become an ever more serious issue for globally active corporations as their networks have become more internationalized. These extended networks have been developed to gain cost and functional advantages for the overall production of goods and services across a global market; but corporations not only need to utilize these networks, they need to govern them as well. Indeed, among institutions and global policy organizations, we might identify as producing global governance outputs, such as the United Nations Global Compact (UNGC) or the Extractive Industries Transparency Initiative (EITI), there is a growing recognition that improving the governance function of corporations can have beneficial effects. However, there has been much less discussion of how this governance function might be best understood as a political economic issue.

Neil Coe and Henry Yeung's work on global production networks maps out much of this space and offers a dynamic account of supply/value chain development.[7] The realm of interactions where corporations seek to achieve their ends through forms of governance can be described across four dimensions: Intrafirm coordination, interfirm control, interfirm partnership, and extra-firm bargaining. In each, corporations' strategies are likely to be dynamic and responsive to both internal shifts but also external factors that have an impact and shape the micro-context of the relations between the core corporation and its connected entities, whether they are contractors or subsidiaries. Extending and developing that approach requires that a governance analysis move beyond seeing immediate profit maximization and efficiency gains as the only explanations for the specifics of these dynamic actions and decisions about how the global production network is organized.

The decisions made by a corporation within its supply chain or production network are not necessarily directly concerned with efficiency or profits but rather with the perpetuation of control and the values stressed by the central management groups.[8] Moreover, these values are likely to vary from sector to sector: Corporations in the pharmaceutical or high-technology sectors, for instance, will undoubtedly have considerably more interest in the manner in which their networks treat, use, and protect intellectual property rights (IPRs) than a corporation in the food sector.[9]

Likewise, corporations in capital intensive industries such as energy generation will confront different governance issues from clothing retailers with extensive and complex buyer-led supply chains. Thus, a high-technology corporation will be concerned not just with the manner in which partners use specific IPRs but also the national legal context, such as a state's government's willingness to enforce such rights. Of note is that Chinese unwillingness to enforce IPRs has been identified as an issue for the development of some supply chain relations. However, for clothing and assembling networks, brand impact of labor relations will be a larger concern for contractors seeking to either distance themselves from unwelcome developments (such as the Rana Plaza fatal building collapse) or by seeking more direct control of labor standards in the supply chain through forms of relational contracting.

As these examples begin to suggest it is likely that the corporation may be effectively managed by a coalition of stake-holding groups focused on myriad outcomes including immediate profitability but by no means limited to it. As corporations have become embedded in more fragmented supply chains, so, too, these coalitions have often needed to resolve internal conflicts over various competing outcomes.[10] Thus, we immediately should differentiate between the politics of control across the corporation's network and a focus just on its beneficial ownership structures; perhaps more importantly this points towards the centrality of governance in these networks.

When we think of global corporations' governance function, the key issue is not necessarily the ownership of assets and resources but rather the ability and abiding interest in controlling access to those resources.[11] While significant parts of the supply chain network are usually outside the ownership structures of any particular global corporation, the ability to control access to the central resources of the network, and also—for instance, through noncompetition clauses in contracts—an ability to constrain access by competitors to key "independent" elements of the network is an important part of corporations' governance function.[12] Although the ownership structures of global corporate networks are often complex, the management and control of these networks produce identifiable governance effects.

This management interest is not limited to the issue of prices or market conditions; but rather given their network character, it is also crucially an issue of managing time and space; a global corporation's managers seek to control its own political geography to maximize its returns and remain a going concern.[13] As Lynne Dallas contends, the chief and perhaps only really effective lever of corporations is their ability to mobilize and allocate resources across the space that they seek to control. Here we should understand "resources" widely to include "social products" including influence, legitimacy, and preferences that the central managerial coalition governing the supply chain can deploy to shape more micro-level decision making.[14] This can also be seen as the institutionalization of specific network-specific relations, habits, and socialized knowledge about what would be regarded as normal activity. Furthermore, a key outcome of corporations' governance of their networks is the transfer of risk away from the central corporation and onto other stakeholders and partners in the supply chain. Seeing corporations as governance institutions requires a focus on ongoing relations within these networks and not merely on a series of periodic intra-network transactions.

For example, global corporations set standards and rules in many market sectors directly via the contracts that are used to pattern the supply chain. As Katharina Pistor points out, corporations "have increasingly assumed a role as regulators of their suppliers and producers. The latter have little choice but to tailor their production to [these] demands."[15] Moreover, as many global sectors actually function as effective oligopolies,[16] and as such are controlled by a small group of corporations whose managers, even if not colluding with one another, share a broad set of interests, the acceptable and normal practices in these often quite closely bounded market segments are set by a small number of corporations. The corporations at the center of these supply chains seek to perpetuate their position by re-creating this environment as change and innovation are required, to maximize their capture of any associated advantages or benefits.[17] At the same time, they shift the risks associated with change into the supply chain—costs of transition are often borne by contracting partners not the core corporation itself.

Within these networks, corporations effectively construct regimes of private law to govern the relations between the various elements, while also seeking to influence public law. Private law can be manifest through standard setting as well as through contract law more generally. The use of private law—that is, contract provisions and arbitration agreements—often utilizes public international law as a background justification but equally is crafted to serve the needs of the particular corporate network in which it is deployed.[18] This approach becomes an important part of that corporation's governance functionality as Dan Danielsen has pointed out:

> [T]he decisions and actions of corporations have social consequences largely indistinguishable from those created by public regulators, but . . . corporate decision-making [i]s largely insulated from public participation, engagement or scrutiny . . . If corporations are significant institutions in the transnational governance regime, then policymakers and activists will need to find ways to affect the decision-making of these corporate institutions.[19]

The democratic deficit often identified as compromising the legitimacy of global governance is likely more serious when corporations by their very actions are regulating economic interactions, even if these are also shaped by various other regulatory regimes and to a large extent internal to contracted networks across their global supply chains. The choice between competing standards, differential corporate governance regimes, and the incorporation of national rules into standard corporate practices open a number of options. Corporations can decide which regimes they might use, how they interpret them, and if, as in the face of no acceptable standards or rules, they can and need to set their own for their network's internal relations.

A further challenge for governance for many corporations is that theirs may be only one among a number of supply chains serviced by a particular supplier, and their ability to govern the actors involved is therefore incomplete. Moreover, there is much less clarity than for states, for instance, about the legitimate reach of corporations' jurisdiction as regards the other organizations in the supply chain, and hence their need to work to maintain legitimacy within the network. One might expect that the more any subcontracting network partner was dependent on the core corporation, the more compliant it would be, although there is also an issue of specificity of their own technology and other assets that might mitigate the asymmetry of power prompted by a narrow range of network engagements. For complex supply-chain relations for which considerable (if different) points of leverage exist on both sides, the establishment and maintenance of legitimacy of core corporation regulatory and practical requests is key to holding the network together.

This leads Kate Macdonald to characterize the governance of supply chains as exhibiting "decentralised, non-hierarchical dynamics, without established deliberative processes or other norm- or procedure-governed mechanisms to determine outcomes or resolve conflict."[20] Thus, for instance, where the governance of labor standards has become an issue for the core corporation, there may be a political need for the governance function, and the regulations to which it is applied, to become a more collective or "democratic" endeavor among a number (sometimes quite a large number) of corporations, contractors, and civil society actors. Here the internal governance function of the corporation and the realm of private authority, as exemplified by civil society organizations and civil regulation interact.

Governance from this central point is seldom entirely hierarchical but is more often a process of negotiation and engagement. The central corporation may have distinct advantages; but subsidiaries, contractors, and others may also have forms of leverage that can be deployed within supply-chain decision making. Thus, where the core corporation is contracting with partners to access particular technologies, or localized resources or knowledge, the contractor may have significant opportunities to shape the contractual relation. The central corporation may also seek to benefit from "reverse diffusion" of practices and innovations for which they have been developed in one part of the network; here governance is concerned with how to establish the new practice/approach around the network.

Additionally, the corporation at the center of the network may have multiple interests and thus present competing positions to partners, shifting and changing the focus of potential leverage. For instance, particular subcontracting partners in the network may get a very different steer from the corporate social responsibility (CSR) team that visits their plant to ascertain their compliance with various standards and requirements, than they will from the buying team, whose emphasis is likely to be on price and quality. Focusing on corporations as institutions of global governance suggests the reasons for differences between high-level commitments and what happens within the supply chain itself. Like other governance institutions, global corporations have complex bureaucratic managerial arrangements, which produce difficulties of coordination between policy and practice. This is to say, like all complex organizations, there is an element of bureaucratic politics that analysis needs to place and recognize.

Therefore it makes some sense to follow David Ciepley and posit that "within its jurisdiction, the business corporation exercises powers analogous to those of government, if more limited, including the right to command, regulate, adjudicate, set rules of cooperation, allocate collective resources, educate, discipline and punish."[21] Indeed, as Florian Wettstein argues, corporations "are now perpetuating competitive advantage not through superior efficiency or their innovative strength but first and foremost through their use of political power."[22] Global markets are largely governed by corporations that are able to exercise power over the character of, access to, and reach of markets that are largely encompassed by their networks. As such these "markets" are essentially planned and mostly unlike spot markets with issues of supply and demand not settled via the price mechanism,[23] but rather by the priorities of the main corporation enacted via its governance function. These priorities cannot merely be determined by an account of efficiency or profitability, but they need to be understood as the results from political deliberation within the governance function.

When compared to the sovereign state, there may be considerable difference in the scope and range of such legitimate capabilities.[24] When a global corporation is compared to the typical institution of global governance, however, these differences are considerably less significant. The corporation can actually be in a stronger position as regards its network than a globally focused institution in relation to its issue area or constituent state members. Corporations may well be able to more effectively sanction and govern network members than some international organizations can govern state members.

Moreover, global corporations have developed processes that often mimic legal structures. This situation negates many unwelcome consequences of globalization. In the absence at the supranational laws of property or contract, the global corporation's network of subsidiaries and affiliates respond to the internalized, law-like rules and regulations that the core corporation puts in place[25] and less to differences in national legislation. Within its own network or effective jurisdiction, the corporation is a form of governing body. It adopts, as Ceipley suggests, many of the attributes of government; the authority that it mobilizes, however, is not completely separate from government, but rather flows from the legal mechanisms (such as incorporation and property law) that facilitate corporations' operational modes in specific jurisdictions. The corporation's governance function is not against the state, but rather it is partly facilitated by the state.[26] Where differences in national legislation are to the corporation's advantage, the relationship between globalized internal rules and national laws is finessed to ensure that both serve the corporation's needs. A governance analysis is useful because it points to the need to develop and maintain legitimacy in relations between governing and governed, and it also points to its micro-political relations.

Conclusion

Although global corporations certainly interact with the other institutions of global governance, they also govern significant realms of the global political economy themselves, sometimes in conjunction with the regulations and guidelines of other institutions, sometimes as single governing authorities. While using forms related to, and indeed constituted by states, their character and effect within the corporation's "internal" relations—that is within its networked supply chain not only within its incorporated core—are defined by the corporation not the state.[27] Where corporations are constituted differently from the dominant Western model, perhaps incorporated in states across the Global South or are state owned, the formal, legal issues may vary considerably. In some cases, considerably different governing principles may arise, but the underlying requirements for efficacy are likely to lead to similar practices. To be effective, even if state sanctioned forms of supply chain or network governance should be regarded as legitimate by network partners, contractors, and participants.

Accepting this analysis suggests that rather than seek to understand supply chains primarily on the basis of profit maximization, cost reduction, or resource acquisition, analyzing the processes and practices of governance—most importantly around the issue of the establishment of legitimate authority within corporate networks—allows for a hitherto under-recognized realm of global governance to be illuminated. It highlights the supply chain network as a terrain of global politics, which in turn allows researchers to deploy a rich and well-established set of conceptual tools developed to understand global governance. The express intent of appreciating how these networks are governed and the opportunities and impediments that such practices imply permit defining better strategies for corporate social responsibility.

Additional reading

Centre for Research on Multinational Corporations (SOMO), www.somo.nl.
Neil M. Coe and Henry Wai-Chung Yeung, *Global Production Networks: Theorizing Economic Development in an Interconnected World* (Oxford: Oxford University Press, 2015).
CorpWatch, www.corpwatch.org/index.php.
Doris Fuchs, *Business Power in Global Governance* (Boulder, CO: Lynne Rienner Publishers, 2007).
IGLP Law & Global Production Working Group, "The Role of Law in Global Value Chains: A Research Manifesto," *London Review of International Law* 4, no. 1 (2016): 57–79.
Kate Macdonald, *The Politics of Global Supply Chains* (Cambridge: Polity Press, 2014).
Richard Whitely, "The Institutional Construction of Firms," in *The Oxford Handbook of Comparative Institutional Analysis*, eds. Glenn Morgan, John L. Campbell, Colin Crouch, Ove Kaj Pedersen, and Richard Whitley (Oxford: Oxford University Press, 2010).
World Economic Forum, www.weforum.org.

Notes

1 Doris Fuchs, *Business Power in Global Governance* (Boulder, CO: Lynne Rienner Publishers 2007); Susan George, *Shadow Sovereigns: How Global Corporations are Seizing Power* (Cambridge, MA: Polity Press, 2015).
2 Matthew Eagleton-Pierce, "The Concept of Governance in the Spirit of Capitalism," *Critical Policy Studies* 8, no. 1 (2014): 5–21.
3 Peter Dicken, *Global Shift: Mapping the Changing Contours of the World Economy* (London: Sage, 2015), 54–67.
4 Mats Forsgren, *Theories of the Multinational Firm: A Multidimensional Creature in the Global Economy* (Cheltenham: Edward Elgar, 2013); Fuchs, *Business Power*; Sol Picciotto, *Regulating Global Corporate Capitalism: International Corporate Law and Financial Market Regulation* (Cambridge: Cambridge University Press, 2011); John

Stopford and Susan Strange, *Rival States, Rival Firms: Competition for World Market Shares* (Cambridge: Cambridge University Press, 1991).

5 Joel Bakan, *The Corporation: The Pathological Pursuit of Profit and Power* (London: Constable, 2005).

6 Kyla Tienhaara, "Investor-State Dispute Settlement," in *Regulatory Theory: Foundations and Applications*, ed. Peter Drahos (Acton: Australian National University Press).

7 Neil M. Coe and Henry Wai-Chung Yeung, *Global Production Networks: Theorizing Economic Development in an Interconnected World* (Oxford: Oxford University Press, 2015).

8 Katharina Pistor, "Multinational Corporations as Regulators and Central Planners: Implications for Citizens' Voice," in *Corporations and Citizenship*, ed. Greg Urban (Philadelphia: University of Pennsylvania Press, 2014): 242.

9 Christopher May, "The Corruption of the Public Interest: Intellectual Property and the Corporation as a Rights Holding 'Citizen,'" in *The Challenges of Global Business Authority: Democratic Renewal, Stalemate or Decay*, eds. Tony Porter and Karsten Ronit (Albany, NY: SUNY Press, 2010): 179–203.

10 Lynne L. Dallas, "Two Models of Corporate Governance: Beyond Berle and Means," *Journal of Law Reform* 22, no. 1 (1988): 40–42.

11 Raghuram G. Rajan and Luigi Zingales, "Power in a Theory of the Firm," *Quarterly Journal of Economics* 113, no. 2 (May 1998): 387–432.

12 Mark P. Dallas, "'Governed' Trade: Global Value Chains, Firms, and the Heterogeneity of Trade in an Era of Fragmented Production," *Review of International Political Economy* 22, no. 5 (2015), 880; Pistor, "Multinational Corporations," 233.

13 Adam D. Dixon, *The New Geography of Capitalism: Firms, Finance and Society* (Oxford: Oxford University Press, 2014), 62–63.

14 Dallas, "Two Models," 83–84.

15 Pistor, "Multinational Corporations," 238.

16 Jeff Harrod, "The Century of the Corporation," in *Global Corporate Power*, ed. Christopher May (Boulder, CO: Lynne Rienner, 2006), 25.

17 Dallas, "Two Models," 98.

18 Volkmar Gessner, "Enabling Global Business Transactions: Relational and Legal Mechanisms" in *Capitalisms & Capitalism in the Twenty-First Century*, eds. Glenn Morgan and Richard Whitley (Oxford: Oxford University Press, 2012), 158–159.

19 Dan Danielson, "How Corporations Govern: Taking Corporate Power Seriously in Transnational Regulation and Governance," *Harvard International Law Journal* 46, no. 2 (2005): 424.

20 Kate Macdonald, *The Politics of Global Supply Chains* (Cambridge: Polity Press, 2014), 179.

21 David Ciepley, "Beyond Public and Private: Toward a Political Theory of the Corporation," *American Political Science Review* 107, no. 1 (2013): 142.

22 Florian Wettstein, *Multilateral Corporations and Global Justice: Human Rights Obligations of a Quasi-Governmental Institution* (Stanford, CA: Stanford Business Books, 2009), 225.

23 Pistor, "Multinational Corporations," 239.

24 Andrew Crane, Dirk Matten, and Jeremy Moon, *Corporations and Citizenship* (Cambridge: Cambridge University Press, 2008), 72–76.

25 Gessner, "Enabling Global Business Transactions," 151.

26 Jean Philippe Robé, "Multinational Enterprises: The Constitution of a Pluralistic Legal Order," in *Global Law Without a State*, ed. Gunther Teubner (Aldershot: Dartmouth Publishers, 1997).

27 Robé, "Multinational Enterprises", 66–67.

Civil society and NGOs

Jan Aart Scholte

A prominent development in the move over recent decades from "international organization" to "global governance" has been the growing involvement of nongovernmental organizations (NGOs) and civil society actors more generally. Civil society participation goes back to the earliest days of global regulation; however, the scale and intensity of contemporary interactions are in a different league. As of 2017 almost 5000 NGOs have consultative status with the United Nations Economic and Social Council (ECOSOC).[1] Since the 1990s hundreds of civil society associations attend the Annual Meetings of the International Monetary Fund (IMF) and the World Bank, Ministerial Conferences of the World Trade Organization (WTO), annual gatherings around the United Nations Framework Convention on Climate Change (UNFCCC), and meetings on the Nuclear Non-Proliferation Treaty (NPT). Summits of the Group of 7/8 (G-7/8) and the Group of 20 (G-20) can attract thousands of street protesters. Questions of global governance have also figured prominently in civil society spaces such as the World Social Forum and Occupy, as well as a variety of populist and religious movements. In some cases, such as the Forest Stewardship Council (FSC) and the World Fair Trade Organization (WFTO), NGOs themselves are making and implementing the rules of global governance.

As global institutions have gained more importance in regulating contemporary society, civil society associations have, not surprisingly, turned more attention to these regimes. Modern political theory has generally conceived of civil society as a counterpart of the state.[2] However, these state-centric conceptions must now be adjusted to reflect altered circumstances in which civil society actors also substantially engage with global regulatory processes, sometimes bypassing national governments altogether.

This chapter examines forms, consequences, and challenges of civil society involvement in contemporary global governance. The first section considers definitions of civil society. The second maps the various involvements of civil society actors in global regulatory processes. The third section assesses the substantive impacts of civil society interventions in global governance—that is, how NGOs and other civil society groups affect institutional developments, agendas, decisions, discourses, and deeper structures of global governance. The fourth section considers the relationship between civil society and legitimacy in global governance. The conclusion includes several suggestions for future enhancement of civil society engagement of global-scale regulation.

Space constraints prevent an elaboration about how the various explanatory theories of world politics depict the role of civil society in global governance. Realist, liberal, constructivist, Marxist, poststructuralist, post-colonialist, feminist, ecological, and other theories interpret the relationship of civil society to global governance in highly divergent ways. Moreover, a study of civil society and global governance could combine inspirations from several theories to form its own synthesis. The selection of a theoretical framework is a matter for each researcher and tends to involve political as much as intellectual choices.

What is civil society?

As with any key analytical concept, "civil society" is open to multiple and often conflicting interpretations. These debates begin with the very definition of the term. What sorts of activity and circumstance does the term "civil society" cover?

Many researchers as well as practitioners of global governance treat civil society as synonymous with NGOs. From this perspective, civil society is a collection of formally structured, legally registered, and professionally staffed organizations outside official and commercial sectors that undertake a variety of advocacy and service delivery operations. This is the civil society of Amnesty International, Disabled Peoples' International, Focus on the Global South, Friends of the Earth, the Internet Society, the Nuclear Threat Initiative, Oxfam, Tax Justice Network, Women's Environment and Development Organization, and so on.

Yet the equation of civil society with NGOs can be overly narrow. Such a conception tends to ignore many informal and grassroots engagements of global governance.[3] These might occur, for example, through social media groups, paramilitary cells, and spontaneous street demonstrations. In addition, conceptions of NGOs often overlook the activities of social movements such as faith groups, labor unions, nationalist fronts, and peasant mobilizations. Discussions of NGOs also generally neglect the important role in contemporary global governance of business lobbies such as chambers of commerce, employer federations, and industry associations. Foundations and research institutes arguably occupy the civil society field as well. Thus, while NGOs are certainly an important part of civil society, the net can be cast more widely in order to encompass a fuller scope of nonofficial voices and influences in global regulatory processes.

That said, in another sense the equation of civil society with NGOs can be overly broad, particularly when the range of activities in question is extended to include service delivery. Many NGOs are today involved in global governance as implementers of projects under contract with bodies such as multilateral development banks and the Office of the UN High Commissioner for Refugees (UNHCR). Yet "civil society" has traditionally been about overtly political concerns, such as relations between authorities and subjects, the dynamics of obtaining and exercising social power, and processes of constructing and embedding norms and rules. Of course, the provision of services such as humanitarian relief, healthcare, schooling, and policing has political dimensions. However, service delivery by NGOs is often mainly assessed for its efficiency and effectiveness as outsourced policy execution, without explicit attention to the politics of these activities. In such cases, treating civil society as synonymous with NGOs can have a depoliticizing effect that underplays the workings of power in global governance.[4]

In order both to widen and to narrow the field relative to NGOs, civil society might be conceptualized as "a political space where associations of citizens seek, from outside political parties, to shape societal rules." Such a definition emphasizes the centrality of politics to civil society. Moreover, reference to a "space" treats civil society less as an organization and more as an arena where people congregate to deliberate, strategize, and mobilize. Reference to "associations" indicates that civil society involves group activities, whether through formal bodies or informal networks. Reference to "citizens" signifies that people enter civil society to exercise their rights and fulfill their obligations as members of a political community. The exclusion of political parties is specified in order to underline that civil society operations do not normally aspire to occupy positions of official authority. However, civil society activities do aim "to shape societal rules": That is, to influence the principles, norms, laws, and standards that govern the collective lives of human beings.

Note also what this conception of civil society does *not* imply. It does not say that civil society is always wholly and neatly distinguishable from commercial, official, and political party activities: In practice these sectors can somewhat overlap. In addition, this conception does not restrict civil society to a Western-liberal-modern cultural frame: One can also find civil society among clans, religious revivalists, and movements of indigenous peoples.[5] Neither does the phrase "civil society" imply anything about ideological outlook: These spaces can be filled with mainstream, reactionary, reformist, or transformational visions. Civil society is not necessarily "civil" either: This space can be as crowded with arrogance, fraud, greed, and violence as any other realm of society.[6] The mafia and the Ku Klux Klan also inhabit civil society. Neither is civil society necessarily a level playing field: Both the overall arena and many individual associations are marked by hierarchies of age, caste, class, gender, geography, race, sexual orientation, and other inequalities.[7]

Civil society—with its various promises as well as perils—has become increasingly relevant to global governance as more and more societal rules in contemporary history emanate from institutions and processes of worldwide, trans-planetary proportions. For several hundred years prior to the middle of the twentieth century, societal regulation was achieved almost exclusively through states. Hence, in such contexts civil society engaged almost exclusively with individual country governments, and political theorists related civil society wholly and solely to the state. Yet today, when much governance comes from global quarters, considerable civil society activities are now understandably directed at sites such as the UN system, the G-7 or G-20, the

Asia–Europe Meeting (ASEM), and institutions of private global governance such as the Internet Corporation for Assigned Names and Numbers (ICANN) and the Global Fund to Fight AIDS, Tuberculosis and Malaria (GFATM). So a twenty-first-century textbook on global governance definitely needs a chapter on civil society.

Civil society involvements in global governance

NGOs, social movements, business forums, research institutes, and other civil society associations engage with global governance in many ways, both direct and indirect. Modes of direct participation include accreditation, membership of government delegations, policy consultations, seats on official committees and boards, evaluation exercises, and actual global regulation itself. With indirect engagement civil society groups seek to shape global governance institutions via third parties such as governments, political parties, and the mass media. In other cases, civil society associations involve themselves in global governance by openly resisting it through street demonstrations and other defiance.

Direct participation

Direct participation by civil society actors in global governance processes dates back to the early "international organizations."[8] For example, employer federations and trade unions have worked alongside governments in the International Labour Organization (ILO) since its beginnings in 1919. The Conference of Non-Governmental Organizations in Consultative Relationship with the United Nations (CONGO) was set up in 1948. Some 250 NGOs assembled around the Stockholm Conference on the Human Environment in 1972.[9]

However, the main growth of civil society participation in global governance has occurred since 1990. This period has seen most major public global regulatory bodies establish offices for liaison with civil society groups. The World Bank has the largest such provision, with over 200 designated staff for civil society engagement.[10] Several private global governance bodies such as ICANN have also created civil society liaison bureaus within their organization. In addition, many global governance agencies have in the past two decades articulated official guidelines for their staff's relations with civil society organizations.

One formalized way that civil society associations can be involved in global governance is through accreditation. In this case, a global regulatory institution accords approved citizen groups official recognition and related possibilities to observe and intervene in policy processes. The most elaborate civil society accreditation scheme exists in respect of the United Nations. NGOs apply and, if accepted, obtain different degrees of access to UN buildings and deliberations, depending on whether they hold "general consultative status," "special consultative status," or "roster status."[11]

In other cases civil society associations can apply for short-term accreditation with a global governance body in order to attend a particular meeting. An accreditation badge gives approved civil society actors entry into official meeting areas and, in some instances, also a right to speak in the proceedings. The UN operates such arrangements in respect of global gatherings such as the annual Conference of the Parties (COP) on climate change and other summits on food, health, population, social development, and further issues. Likewise the IMF and the World Bank have civil society accreditation schemes for their Annual and Spring Meetings, while the WTO permits vetted civil society groups entry to its Ministerial Conferences. Hundreds of civil society associations typically obtain accreditation for such global governance events.

Sometimes certain civil society actors are invited to be members of government delegations to global governance meetings. In these situations, civil society activists have a formally equivalent status with government officials. For example, a number of small island states have invited NGO advisers onto their official teams in global conferences on ecological matters. Officers from business associations and development NGOs have regularly joined the delegations of some governments to WTO meetings.

Much additional civil society participation in global governance occurs through ongoing policy consultations in between the big conferences. For this purpose, the UN maintains a Department of Public Information (DPI) and a Non-Governmental Liaison Service (NGLS). Since the 1990s the so-called Arria Formula has opened space for civil society associations to brief members of the UN Security Council, particularly on issues of human rights and humanitarian intervention.[12] Among specialized agencies the UN Environment Programme (UNEP) has convened a Global Major Groups and Stakeholder Forum since 2000, and the UN Development Programme (UNDP) has had a Civil Society Advisory Committee also since 2000. The World Bank consults civil society groups on the design and implementation of most of its projects and programs. IMF teams normally meet with some local civil society groups during their country visits to advise governments on macroeconomic policy. Since 1998 the WTO has accepted some submissions from civil society groups in its dispute settlement process. The Organisation for Economic Co-operation and Development (OECD) maintains regular consultations, *inter alia*, through its Business and Industry Advisory Committee (BIAC) and Trade Union Advisory Committee (TUAC). ICANN does the same through its At-Large Advisory Committee (ALAC) and Noncommercial Users Constituency (NCUC). Since 1965 the Commonwealth Foundation has assembled civil society groups, while the Commonwealth Secretariat has focused on the member governments. The GFATM engages local civil society for its country activities and also holds a biennial Partnership Forum with civil society actors from around the world. The Organisation of Islamic Cooperation (OIC) also holds some informal interactions with NGOs. Through these numerous formalized and *ad hoc* practices consultation with civil society has become a norm of contemporary global governance.[13]

To be sure, global governance consultations of civil society have not always gone far and deep. Indeed, the preparation, execution, and follow-up of these dialogues can be wanting. For example, "consultation" of civil society may occur late in the policymaking process, after important decisions have already been taken. In addition, global governance officials can undermine consultations with negative attitudes of arrogance, inflexibility, reluctance, and secrecy. For their part, civil society associations can neglect opportunities to engage global governance and/ or can bring to the table inaccurate information and underdeveloped analysis. The quality of global governance engagement of civil society has also suffered, both democratically and substantively, when the consultations disproportionately involve associations from elite quarters, marginalizing disadvantaged geographical and social circles.

Beyond consultation, in certain cases civil society associations have obtained formal representation at the decision table in global governance. In addition to the already mentioned ILO tripartism, the International Organization for Standardization (ISO) involves trade associations, professional societies, and universities in its technical committees. Civil society actors have also held several seats on the board and committees of ICANN and on the global board and the country coordinating mechanisms of the GFATM.[14] NGOs and social movements figure prominently in the Committee on World Food Security (CFS), which channels policy recommendations into the UN system.[15] The Global Reporting Initiative (GRI) is one of several schemes for corporate social responsibility (CSR) that involve business, labor, and NGOs along with government. To be sure, civil society membership of official boards and committees remains far from the norm in contemporary global governance; nevertheless, the spread since the late 1990s of so-called "multi-stakeholder" arrangements is striking.[16]

Civil society associations also participate in global governance through performance evaluations. For example, think tanks have conducted commissioned official policy reviews for ICANN, and NGOs have contributed to investigations by the IMF's Independent Evaluation Office, established in 2001. Civil society groups have also brought various cases to the World Bank's Inspection Panel since its creation in 1994. In addition, civil society organizations are continually publishing their own (often critical) assessments of global governance institutions and policies, thereby serving an important external monitoring function and contributing to public awareness and debate.

Finally among modes of direct participation in global governance, certain civil society bodies act as regulatory bodies. In these cases, it is the civil society associations themselves who do the formulation and administration of global rules, without direct involvement by official actors. For example, the FSC regime for sustainable forestry involves collaboration between business, environmental, indigenous, and labor groups. The WFTO framework of fair trade standards assembles consumer and producer associations. Other examples of global governance by civil society organizations include the Marine Stewardship Council (MSC, providing sustainability standards in fisheries) and the Worker Rights Consortium (WRC, suggesting labor codes in the sourcing of university and college apparel).

Indirect involvement

In countless other instances, civil society associations pursue involvement in global governance indirectly, through third parties. For example, business forums, trade unions, and NGOs commonly bring their concerns about global governance to member states, in hopes of influencing the positions that governments take in global institutions. In this vein, civil society groups have engaged foreign ministries regarding the UN, finance ministries regarding the G-7, communications ministries regarding ICANN, and so on. Indeed, some governments actively solicit civil society inputs before attending major global conferences. Sometimes states (especially the major states) are targeted on global governance matters not only by civil society associations from their own country, but also by transnational organizations. Thus, for instance, Global Unions and Oxfam International maintain offices in Washington, DC, in order to engage US government departments as well as the Bretton Woods institutions.

In other cases, civil society groups take questions of global governance to the legislative branch of government, e.g., the French National Assembly, the Japanese Diet, and the US Congress. Civil society groups in these situations seek to shape parliamentary debates on global governance and/or to engage parliamentary committees that scrutinize government policy on global governance. Occasionally, as in Malawi, civil society associations have sponsored workshops and other activities to raise the capacities of national parliamentarians to address issues of global regulation. In respect of the European Union (EU), civil society associations have also gone to a regional parliament on global governance matters, particularly in the area of trade, where the EU is a member of the WTO in its own right.

More generally, too, regional institutions can be indirect channels to global governance for civil society. The European Commission continually addresses global issues, and civil society groups have engaged with various directorates-general. In Latin America, Mercosur (Common Market of the South) has an Economic and Social Consultation Forum in which civil society representatives *inter alia* discuss global issues. Similarly, civil society has been involved with the Southern African Development Community (SADC) on global governance questions such as debt, HIV/AIDS, and trade.[17]

Engagement with sub-state authorities, as well, can be a mode of indirect civil society involvement in global governance. For example, ecology campaigners have urged hundreds of "greening cities" in the United States to back the 1997 Kyoto Protocol and the 2015 Paris Agreement on climate change when the Bush and Trump administrations rejected these global instruments. Other civil society groups have engaged global organizations of cities, including United Cities and Local Governments (UCLG) and Metropolis, which in turn relate to intergovernmental institutions through agencies like the Commonwealth Local Government Forum and the UN Global Compact Cities Programme.

Multiple nonofficial channels for indirect civil society engagement of global governance are also available. Outside government, citizen associations can take concerns about global institutions to political parties, the mass media, companies, online social networks, and other deliberative spaces such as the World Economic Forum and the World Social Forum. NGOs have sometimes also called on celebrities to publicize global issues, as when Bob Geldof and Bono amplified civil society demands for debt relief *vis-à-vis* global financial institutions. Noteworthy, too, is the rise in the 2010s of online petitions and hashtag initiatives on global issues through platforms such as Avaaz, Jhatkaa, and MoveOn.[18]

Resistance

In addition to the direct participation and indirect pressures reviewed above, civil society actors have also related to global governance by refusing it. Rejectionist groups decline overtures to interact with global institutions. Alternatively, these challengers so disrupt global governance proceedings that officials do not invite them again.

Resistance movements have on various occasions taken to the streets to protest against what they regard as harmful, undemocratic, and unjust global governance arrangements. In the so-called "Battle of Seattle" in 1999, street demonstrations severely disrupted a Ministerial Conference of the WTO. G-7/G-8 and G-20 summits and IMF/World Bank meetings have also drawn mass protests, particularly in the early 2000s.

In another resistance tactic, NGO-inspired boycotts of several major multinational companies have promoted the growth of CSR as an informal global governance of production and investment. Street theatre, videos, and monuments are other mediums through which civil society groups have expressed renunciation of some or all global governance.

In multiple ways, then, civil society engagement of global governance has become widespread since the 1990s. This is not to suggest that business forums, NGOs, and social movements are displacing states in global governance. However, understandings of contemporary politics which restrict civil society to the domestic sphere are clearly obsolete.

Civil society impacts on global governance

Yet does all the civil society activity just surveyed in respect of global governance actually matter? This section explores various possible effects of citizen activism on concrete situations of global regulation. The record shows many correlations between circumstances in civil society, on the one hand, and developments in global governance, on the other. The following paragraphs identify five general types of possible civil society impact on global governance, namely, in relation to institutions, agendas, decisions, discourses, and deeper structures.

Of course, it is one thing to observe a concurrence of phenomena and quite another to establish a causal connection between them. How can one demonstrate that it was specifically civil society that affected a given situation of global governance? Different theories and methodologies yield different interpretations of whether, in what ways, and how far civil society has influenced a particular scenario of global regulation. Moreover, it is generally difficult to disentangle the influence of civil society from other forces (e.g., states, capitalism, etc.) that might shape the course of global governance. Greater exploration of these theoretical and methodological issues lies beyond the scope of the present chapter, but it is important to underline here that "proving" civil society impacts on global governance is anything but straightforward.

Regarding the first of the five types of impact named above, civil society can shape the institutional evolution of global regulation. Citizen associations have often advocated for the establishment, reform, and/or dissolution of one or the other global governance agency. For example, numerous internationalist groups urged the creation of first the League of Nations and later the United Nations. Some 200 NGOs were present at the San Francisco Conference that founded the UN in 1945, forty-two of them as consultants to the US government delegation.[19] Proposals to launch the Uruguay Round negotiations that spawned the WTO emanated initially from the World Economic Forum, a high-profile business association. A major civil society campaign in the 1990s propelled the establishment of the International Criminal Court (ICC). Civil society groups have also figured prominently in drives for various institutional reforms of global governance, such as the establishment of the Human Rights Council at the UN, reallocations of quotas at the IMF, and the inclusion of a vote for affected communities on the board of the GFATM. True, rejectionist voices in civil society have not succeeded in their aims to close certain or all global governance agencies. However, these movements have severely disrupted some official proceedings, such as the WTO Ministerial in Seattle. Moreover, the challenge of radical opposition has perhaps made global governance bodies more amenable to institutional reform.

A second general area in which civil society can impact on global governance is the agenda. In other words, citizen activism can influence what issues are considered in global regulatory processes and with what relative priorities. Indeed, civil society associations have highlighted a number of global problems that might otherwise have received (considerably) less attention. The many examples include arms control, corruption, debt, democracy, disability, ecological degradation, gender, HIV/AIDS, human rights, humanitarian intervention, indigenous peoples, labor standards, land grabs, poverty, and the use of non-Western scripts on the Internet. It seems unlikely that—without civil society pressure—global governance would have addressed such questions, or at any rate given them as much prominence.

In addition to institutional change and agenda formation, civil society pressure can be linked to a host of policy decisions taken in global governance. For instance, the WTO move in 2003 to relax intellectual property provisions on essential medicines followed a concerted NGO campaign. Persistent civil society mobilization likewise fed into the reduction and cancellation of many debts of low-income countries in the 1990s and 2000s, as well as the adoption of the Paris Agreement on climate change in 2015. Civil society associations have arguably also contributed to ratifications of global human rights instruments, initiatives to undertake humanitarian intervention, adjustments to many World Bank projects, and countless other policy decisions in global governance.

In a fourth type of impact, civil society involvement can go beyond individual decisions to shape the discourses of global governance. By "discourse" is meant here the overarching concepts, language, and analytical framings that are employed in political discussions. Civil society associations have arguably furthered innovations in the core vocabulary of global governance by promoting notions such as "fair trade," "human security," "sustainable development," and "global public goods." More generally, civil society critiques have encouraged shifts in discourses of global economic governance from a *laissez faire* neoliberalism that prevailed in the late twentieth century to the contrasting rhetoric of both responsible capitalism and anti-globalism in the early twenty-first century.

Fifth and finally, civil society impacts can reach still deeper to influence the underlying social structures—the primary ordering principles—of global governance.

To give one example, by circumventing states to engage directly with global regulatory institutions civil society associations have promoted a shift in the overall mode of governance from statism (where societal rules emanate more or less entirely from the state) to polycentrism (where governance transpires through multi-actor networks). In addition, civil society involvement in global governance has, by mobilizing multiple types of political community besides nations (e.g., solidarity on lines of caste, class, faith, gender, race, sexual orientation, etc.), encouraged a shift in the primary structure of identity in world politics from nation-centrism to greater pluralism. Also, inasmuch as citizen activism on global governance has enlarged political space for indigenous peoples and religious revivalists, civil society has facilitated challenges to the predominant modern-rationalist knowledge structure in today's world.

Considering in sum these five types of impact—on institutional evolution, agenda formation, policy decision, discourse construction, and deeper structure—is civil society a force of continuity or change in global governance? Moreover, to the extent that civil society brings changes to global governance, do these alterations have more of an incremental reformist character or more of a systemic revolutionary quality? In Gramscian terms, is civil society on the whole a hegemonic force that reinforces and legitimates established interests in global governance; or does civil society play a counter-hegemonic role of subversion and transformation?

Clear and definitive answers to these questions are not available. The picture is messy partly because evidence from civil society involvement in global governance often points in several directions. In addition, different theories emphasize different kinds of evidence and/or interpret the same data in highly different ways. Cumulative experience certainly suggests that civil society has an impact in contemporary global governance, but the precise significance is and will remain debated.

Civil society and legitimacy in global governance

In addition to the substantive impacts considered above, it is important also to assess the attitudinal consequences that civil society might have for the legitimacy of global regulation. Legitimacy refers to a condition under which people believe that a governance arrangement exercises its authority appropriately. With legitimacy, political subjects accord a given regime a normative right to rule. As a result of having such support, a governing institution can attract more resources, take more decisions, obtain more compliance, and generally have greater impact. Without legitimacy a governance apparatus collapses—or survives only through trickery, coercion, and/or violence towards its subjects.

Shortfalls in legitimacy are a major problem for much contemporary global governance. Challenges such as climate change, financial instability, and humanitarian crises demand enlarged and strengthened global regulation. However, on the whole, citizens have not ascribed legitimacy to global governance organizations in the way that people have generally endorsed the authority of (most) national and local governments. As a result, global institutions have often struggled to acquire the necessary mandates, resources and influence to deliver effective global public policy.

Many cosmopolitan commentators hope that civil society might enhance the legitimacy of global governance and thereby promote more effective responses to urgent planetary problems.[20] As an arena of public deliberation and mobilization, civil society offers major possibilities to link citizens with global issues, global organizations, and global rules. Indeed, at a time when global political parties, global parliaments, and global plebiscites seem remote prospects, civil society could provide some of the greatest available potential for a democratization of global governance.[21]

Certainly many civil society associations have highlighted democratic frailties that afflict most existing global governance arrangements, and have urged corrective action. NGOs and social movements have also furthered democratic global governance when they provide channels of voice and influence for affected people, including in particular constituencies (for example, indigenous peoples and sexual minorities) that tend otherwise to be silenced in global politics. Civil society groups have often worked to make global governance institutions more transparent and more consultative *vis-à-vis* implicated publics. Many civil society organizations have in addition promoted learning and debate about global issues and their regulation, so that people can undertake more informed and empowered actions in respect of global governance. Civil society actors have moreover often served as watchdogs who scrutinize global governance in the public interest. Advocacy groups have also regularly demanded redress for harmed people when global regulatory agencies have caused damage. And numerous civil society initiatives have urged, on social-democratic lines, a progressive redistribution of world resources, so as to create a more level playing field in global politics.

That said, the relationship between civil society and democracy in global governance is not unconditionally positive. For one thing, civil society could do much more to advance democracy in global regulation. So far the scale of these democratizing activities has remained quite modest, especially relative to the need. Moreover, civil society interventions in global governance have to date disproportionately involved already privileged circles of society, such as the Global North, urban professional classes, and white men. Also, civil society contains some decidedly undemocratic elements, such as secretive clubs of corporate capital and terrorist cells. Even "progressive" civil society groups often show shortfalls of democratic accountability in their own practices.[22] Hence, civil society engagement of global governance does not automatically generate greater democratic legitimacy: This outcome has to be deliberately and concertedly nurtured.

Democracy is not the only basis for legitimacy, of course. Civil society activism can also bolster public confidence in global governance by lending it moral force. In this vein, citizen group initiatives have prodded global regulatory agencies to promote just ends like decolonization, gender equity, human rights, poverty eradication, fair trade, anticorruption, peace, and ecological integrity. True, civil society also comprises "uncivil" groups of fundamentalists, militarists, racists, and ultranationalists; so its interventions in global governance do not always and inherently bolster moral legitimacy. However, civil society pressures have often helped to persuade global regulatory authorities to champion just causes, and this has raised the moral standing of global governance in the public eye.

On other occasions, civil society has enhanced the legitimacy of global governance by improving its technical performance. In this case, people believe that global authorities exercise rightful rule because the institutions deliver operational efficiency and desired outcomes—e.g., a working Internet, food security, disease control, solvent banks, etc. Civil society can contribute to this problem-solving aspect of legitimacy by providing global governance institutions with valuable information, insights, methods, and advice. In addition, civil society associations can, with challenges to established policies, provoke a global governance agency to sharpen its thinking and improve its instruments. Moreover, sometimes subcontracted NGOs can execute global governance policies more effectively than official bureaucracies. Needless to say, when civil society inputs undermine technocratic performance— e.g., with faulty information or flawed execution—they sooner contribute to a delegitimation of global governance.

Moreover, some elements of civil society seek deliberately to delegitimize authority beyond the state. So-called "anti-globalization movements" have opposed particular global governance institutions or indeed the very principle of suprastate authority. These challenges are not by definition "left wing" or "right wing," but they have come from various positions on the political spectrum, including certain environmentalists, populists, and socialists. Such movements amply demonstrate that civil society does not inherently support global authority and, on the contrary, can in some cases be a significant force for its delegitimation.

Thus, the record of civil society consequences for the legitimacy of global governance is mixed. On the one hand, considerable evidence suggests that civil society can bolster important sources of legitimacy for global governance, such as democracy, fairness, and problem solving. On the other hand, civil society also includes unaccountable, morally dubious, and incompetent elements. Moreover, some strains of civil society oppose global governance. And there may be situations where coopted civil society forces can serve to legitimate global governance arrangements that in practice undermine human dignity and a good society.

Conclusion

This chapter has considered the place of civil society in contemporary global governance. The discussion has identified multifarious involvements by NGOs, social movements, and other citizen groups in global regulation. As seen throughout the chapter, assessments of these activities are much contested: Definitions, explanations, evidence, and evaluations go in many directions.

Quite undeniable, however, is that civil society has acquired considerable presence in contemporary global governance. This involvement looks likely to increase still further in the future. Such greater engagement can be welcomed in principle, given that civil society offers some of the best possibilities currently available to connect global regulation with affected people on the ground.

Yet, as repeatedly seen in this chapter, civil society practices *vis-à-vis* global governance have not always lived up to optimistic expectations. Significant upgrades are required if civil society relations with global regulation are more fully to realize their potential contributions in the future. Five broad suggestions can be briefly mentioned in closing here. First, both sides—civil society as well as global governance—could raise their capacities for meaningful interaction, with greater mutual comprehension, improved institutional arrangements, etc. Second, better coordination of campaigns could allow civil society groups to increase their impact, as witnessed in the wide-ranging networks that pursued debt relief and the prohibition of landmines. Third, all parties to civil society relations with global governance institutions could make deliberate and sustained efforts to increase voice and influence for geographically and socially marginalized groups, who have so far had limited opportunities for participation and impact. Fourth, civil society associations could more strenuously resist co-optation and reinforce their role as critical watchdogs of global governance. Finally, civil society interlocutors with global governance could turn the searching spotlight also onto themselves, with more rigorous attention to their own account-abilities. In the words of one human rights activist: "When you point a finger, you need to do it with a clean hand."[23]

Additional reading

Donatella Della Porta and Sidney Tarrow, eds., *Transnational Protest & Global Activism* (Lanham: Rowman & Littlefield, 2005).

John Gaventa and Rajesh Tandon, eds., *Citizen Engagements in a Globalising World* (London: Zed Books, 2010).

Mary Kaldor, *Global Civil Society: An Answer to War* (Cambridge: Polity Press, 2003).

Margaret E. Keck and Kathryn Sikkink, *Activists Beyond Borders: Advocacy Networks in International Politics* (Ithaca, NY: Cornell University Press, 1998).

Robert J. O'Brien, et al., *Contesting Global Governance: Multilateral Economic Institutions and Global Social Movements* (Cambridge: Cambridge University Press, 2000).

Jan Aart Scholte, ed., *Building Global Democracy? Civil Society and Accountable Global Governance* (Cambridge: Cambridge University Press, 2011).

Jonas Tallberg, et al., *The Opening Up of International Organizations: Transnational Access in Global Governance* (Cambridge: Cambridge University Press, 2013).

Peter Willetts, *Non-Governmental Organizations in World Politics: The Construction of Global Governance* (Abingdon: Routledge, 2011).

Notes

1 UN DESA, "Consultative Status with ECOSOC and other accreditations," http:// esango.un.org/civilsociety/displayConsultativeStatusSearch.do?method=search&session Check=false.

2 Jean Cohen and Andrew Arato, *Civil Society and Political Theory* (Cambridge, MA: MIT Press, 1992).

3 Donatella Della Porta, et al., *Globalization from Below* (Minneapolis: University of Minnesota Press, 2006).

4 William Fisher, "Doing Good? The Politics and Antipolitics of NGO Practices," *Annual Review of Anthropology* 26, no. 1 (1997): 439–464.

5 Chris Hann and Elizabeth Dunn, eds., *Civil Society: Challenging Western Models* (London: Routledge, 1996).

6 Petr Kopeck and Cas Mudde, eds., *Uncivil Society?* (London: Routledge, 2002).

7 Jan Aart Scholte, "A More Inclusive Global Governance? The IMF and Civil Society in Africa," *Global Governance* 18, no. 2 (April–June 2012): 185–206.

8 Steve Charnovitz, "Two Centuries of Participation: NGOs and International Governance," *Michigan Journal of International Law* 18, no. 2 (1997): 183–286.

9 Carolyn Stephenson, "Women's International Nongovernmental Organizations at the United Nations," in *Women, Politics, and the United Nations*, ed. Anne Winslow (Westport, CT: Greenwood, 1995), 139.

10 World Bank, "Civil Society," www.worldbank.org/en/about/partners/civil-society#2.

11 Kerstin Martens, "Civil Society and Accountability of the United Nations," in *Building Global Democracy? Civil Society and Accountable Global Governance*, ed. Jan Aart Scholte (Cambridge: Cambridge University Press, 2011), 42–57.

12 "Arria and Other Special Meetings between NGOs and Security Council Members," www.globalpolicy.org/security/mtgsetc/brieindx.htm.

13 Scholte, *Building Global Democracy*.

14 Garrett Brown, "Multisectoralism, Participation, and Stakeholder Effectiveness: Increasing the Role of Nonstate Actors in the Global Fund to Fight AIDS, Tuberculosis and Malaria," *Global Governance* 15, no. 2 (April–June 2009): 169–178.

15 Josh Brem-Wilson, "Towards Food Sovereignty: Interrogating Peasant Voice in the United Nations Committee on World Food Security," *Journal of Peasant Studies* 42, no. 1 (2015): 73–95.

16 Mark Raymond and Laura DeNardis, "Multistakeholderism: Anatomy of an Inchoate Global Institution," *International Theory* 7, no. 3 (2015): 572–616.

17 Andréas Godsäter, *Civil Society Regionalization in Southern Africa: The Cases of Trade and HIV/AIDS* (Abingdon: Routledge, 2016).

18 W. Lance Bennett and Alexandra Segerburg, *The Logic of Connective Action: Digital Media and the Personalization of Contentious Politics* (Cambridge: Cambridge University Press, 2013).

19 Bill Seary, "The Early History: From the Congress of Vienna to the San Francisco Conference," in *"The Conscience of the World." The Influence of Non-Governmental Organisations in the UN System*, ed. Peter Willetts (London: Hurst, 1996), 25.

20 Jan Aart Scholte, "Civil Society and the Legitimation of Global Governance," *Journal of Civil Society* 3, no. 3 (December 2007): 305–326.

21 Jan Aart Scholte, "Civil Society and Democratically Accountable Global Governance," *Government and Opposition* 39, no. 2 (2004): 211–233.

22 Lisa Jordan and Peter van Tuijll, eds., *NGO Accountability* (London: Earthscan, 2006).

23 Perry Arituwa, Uganda Joint Christian Council, cited in Jan Aart Scholte, *Democratizing the Global Economy: The Role of Civil Society* (Coventry: Centre for the Study of Globalisation and Regionalisation, 2004), 95.

Labor

Nigel Haworth and Steve Hughes

Labor's world has been subject to constant upheaval since the Industrial Revolution. As mass labor forces were created in capitalist economies, and as labor forces politicized and mobilized, periods of political accommodation, particularly between the 1930s and 1970s, seemed to provide a degree of political stability and legitimacy for labor and its organizations. But, even then, the emergent labor movements of the developing world faced the upheavals of colonization and postcolonial development. Since the 1970s, labor has confronted the twin challenges of globalization and neoliberalism, which have substantially undermined established political accommodations, while introducing new challenges as a result of integrated global production systems. In the early twenty-first century, the institutional and political challenges confronting labor are as grave as at any other time in modern history. Nevertheless, labor activism, coupled with political concerns at national and international levels, has placed issues such as the promotion and regulation of labor standards at the heart of contemporary global governance and in the forefront of debate around the social costs of globalization. Labor standards are an important issue in the agendas of international organizations, and in the boardrooms of global companies. As a result, public opinion and interest mobilization around labor standards have become critical considerations in global governance arrangements.[1]

This chapter assesses the contemporary challenges facing labor and its status in global governance. It begins by providing a context for contemporary labor. It then analyzes briefly the modes and practices of global governance as they engage with labor before addressing the institutional and political approaches adopted by labor in the modern period. Finally, it asks whether the continuing defense of labor's interests requires a major institutional and political reorientation.

We should be clear what we mean by "labor." The focus is on the activities of labor in the formal sector—that is, wage labor in "modern" sector employment. However, in terms of political and institutional challenges, and in terms of global governance arrangements, it is no longer possible, if indeed it ever was, to establish a clear dividing line between formally employed labor, and the many and complex forms of "informal" and rural labor practices. The erosion of barriers between these different categories is an important and underdeveloped aspect of the account that follows. We also note that in the International Labour Organization (ILO) and in other international agencies, these categories are being eroded by growing international interest in labor standards for informal and peasant workers. The adoption by the ILO in 2011 of Convention 189 on Domestic Workers is a good illustration.

Labor's context

The transcendent processes that define modern labor are globalization in its many forms, and the post-1970s power of neoliberalism and its global vehicle, the Washington Consensus. We must be brief in our discussion of these phenomena; but, in our view, their impact cannot be underestimated. A third, lesser context is that engendered by the global financial crisis (GFC) of 2008. We argue "lesser" because the GFC was a product of globalization and neoliberalism.

Globalization, understood broadly as systemic global economic integration, often beyond formal political control by national governments, has had four major impacts on labor: The "Great Doubling"; the emergence of globally integrated production systems; the emergence of complex regional geopolitical and trade relations; and the expansion and reconfiguration of labor migration.

The Great Doubling refers to the period in the 1990s when, with the entry of China, Russia, and the ex-Soviet bloc into the global market, the global workforce available to the market grew from 1.5 to three billion.[2] Simultaneously, the global capital-to-labor ratio nearly halved. As a consequence, developed economies feared the "hollowing out" of their productive sectors, in which work might be undertaken more cheaply using these new supplies of cheaper labor. Such fears either could drive a high road model of high-quality, niche production (for example, the Mittelstand model of small and medium sized companies in Germany, often cited as key to explaining Germany's contemporary economic success),[3] or could result in a competitive drive downwards based on competitive wage cost reductions (the feared "race to the bottom").[4] For our purposes, the Great Doubling signals an increase of power for the employer and investor as capital mobility allows the integration of new workforces into global production. That increase in power is reflected in the difficulty created for trade unions to organize in this new global environment.

The second relevant characteristic of globalization is the emergence of global production systems. Four main streams of global production thinking have been identified.[5] Initially, there developed the idea of the "commodity chain," defined as the network of labor and production processes giving rise to a finished commodity. Subsequently, the "global commodity chain" emerged as a more developed concept, focusing on interfirm networks and the organization of global production and on production upgrading. Thereafter, the idea of the "global value chain" (GVC) emerged as a third tradition, emphasizing the creation and appropriation of value, the structure and role of governance within global production systems, and, again, system upgrading.[6] Finally, the idea of "global production networks" (GPN) emphasizes the entirety of network relationships (that is, beyond the linear relationships argued to be key to GVC analysis) and focuses on the full range of networking relationships between actors in the network, rather than on narrower interfirm governance arrangements.[7]

For labor, such production systems involve systemic integration into the production process across time, space, and technical functions, under the governance of large, internationally based companies. Global production systems are, in many ways, the embodiment of globalization, able, for example, to link seamlessly the peasant primary producer in a developing economy with the affluent consumer of a sophisticated, transformed commodity in the developed world. Power within such production systems often lies in the governance process, in which the voice of labor is not guaranteed, and work may sometimes be low paid, sweated, and hazardous. There is, in relation to such systems, discussion of "social upgrading," that is, the incorporation of labor standards into these networks at the behest of the buyers and consumers, or their incorporation as a result of supplier strategy, or of government intervention.[8] These standards are most frequently the core labor standards defined by the ILO, reflecting its key role and status in labor-standards setting.

Third, as globalization has developed since the 1970s, there has been a commensurate development of supranational regional arrangements, designed at once to manage and benefit from global economic integration. They tend to differ from the preexisting forms of regionalism such as the European Union (EU), founded on a broad commitment to economic, political, and social integration. In contrast, modern regional arrangements tend to be narrower, trade and investment-driven agreements, in which the interests of investors and exporters are paramount, and in which the voice of labor is again muted. Interestingly, such arrangements have adopted, on the whole, orthodox economic explanations for free trade and free movement of capital, yet eschew the logical commitment to the promotion of free movement of labor. Indeed, where labor is addressed at all, it is usually in one of several marginalizing fashions—labor understood as skilled, mobile, and highly desirable, for example, or as a politico-social problem that cannot be ignored formally, but is in practice, for example ill-monitored and poorly implemented "labor clauses" attached to trade agreements.[9] Yet, despite this marginalization, there is pressure on supranational regional or international arrangements as a result, for example, of the political and organizational pressures imposed by migrant labor, or global skills shortages, or pressure from the developed economies and their consumers for the implementation of labor standards in developing countries, as was seen in the "social clause" debate in the World Trade Organization (WTO) in the 1990s.[10]

Fourth, the issue of labor and migration has gained momentum. We have already alluded to the inconsistency in an economic orthodoxy that in general favors free trade and the free movement of capital. Yet both ignore, or deliberately exclude, the free movement of labor across national borders. The orthodoxy accepts that labor migration, although perhaps a desirable principle, is politically unachievable. In practice, labor migration is emerging as a matter of major political and policy importance in several ways. First, global skill shortages have been identified by many economies for at least a generation, leading to advanced economies seeking to absorb high-skilled labor from relatively low-pay nations. Qualification, recognition, and portability have become key in the movement of skilled labor, as has the rise of international education provision. Second, demographics—especially ageing populations—have raised the specter of policy shifts in favor of larger scale labor migration. For example, we note the debate in Japan about the future domestic workforce, the needs of which are unlikely to be met from traditional sources.[11] Third, control of mass migration–whether across the US–Mexico border or across the Mediterranean from North Africa to the EU, or Southeast Asian boat people into Australia—raises policing and human rights issues. Global economic integration inevitably drives increased migration pressures.

The second major process is neoliberalism. In myriad guises, at international and national levels, neoliberal thinking has promoted a package of economic settings—for example individualism, economic liberalization, privatization, corporatization, the "small state," reduced welfare provision, a single metric focus on inflation, free trade, and investment flows—which dominated policymaking from the 1970s to the early twenty-first century. Neoliberalism, in principle, does not favor minimum standards or platforms of labor standards, for it prefers wages and conditions to be settled on market terms—that is, by agreement between the employer and the individual employee. Ideologically, neoliberalism also rejects pluralist notions of social partnership. In particular, it rejects corporatist arrangements and the status accorded to organized labor (that is, trade unions) in such arrangements.

This thinking on minimum standards and trade unions was "globalized" in the Washington Consensus that promoted a global, neoliberal approach to economic development and which became a generation of policymakers' blueprint for labor markets. It particularly delegitimized collective employee voice at all levels—workplace and national policymaking included—resulting in that voice being excluded from supranational trade and investment and other international framework setting arrangements. Only after the GFC in 2008 did unemployment and political stability issues reverse that trend a little.

Globalization and neoliberalism—as a mechanism for greater global integration, especially across the financial sector, and as a purveyor of "light" or minimal regulation, respectively—came together in the 2008 GFC, a global crisis preceded by a series of more localized crises, such as the Asian Crisis of the late 1990s. The consequences of the crisis for labor were immediate and sustained. Depression led to rapidly increasing unemployment levels internationally, often compounded by immediate pressure on welfare provision. Moreover, medium-term economic policy responses to the crisis frequently reinforced downward pressure on wages and welfare provision, whilst the specter of "jobless growth" began to haunt policymakers. It was in this context that finance ministers and central bank governors from the world's most dominant twenty economies (meeting together as the G-20) turned to the ILO for input into pro-growth policies in which employment creation played a significant role.[12]

Summarizing the global context in which labor must act, it has been defined by major global integration, often beyond the control of states and their legislation, a policy framework generally inimical to labor as an organized presence, and a series of economic crises, culminating in the 2008 GFC, in which increased unemployment and reduced welfare provision have usually been immediate consequences. It has been in general a bleak generation for labor, in which increased standards of living for many workers in rapidly developing economies are the one great positive.

Labor: Modes of global governance

Labor and governance engage at multiple levels—workplace, sector, nation, region, and globe. Here we focus primarily on the global aspects of labor and governance. In particular, while the national level of governance—the way in which labor movements are formed and organized, and the way in which they act within national industrial relations systems—is important, we do not address it in detail. However, as is clear from the previous discussion, how labor is represented, and the extent to which it is empowered and given voice at national level, is in part an effect of supranational pressures, be they the impacts of, for example, integration into global production systems, of the GFC, or of the Washington Consensus. National industrial relations systems are inevitably subject to external intervention and consequent adaptation.

Here we focus on the firm (especially in terms of global production systems, corporate social responsibility, and labor standards); the supranational regional level (contrasting the EU with the North American Free Trade Agreement (NAFTA) and Asia-Pacific Economic Cooperation (APEC); the global level, focusing on the ILO, particularly since the GFC of 2008. The interrelated nature of these levels of analysis underpins our understanding of the global governance of labor standards. Regulation crosses and integrates the different levels of analysis in the universal recognition of core labor standards established by the ILO, such as freedom from forced and child labor, freedom from discrimination in the workplace and the right to join a union and bargain collectively. Adherence to these standards is promoted primarily on the basis of moral suasion, dialogue, and cooperation rather than by hard law. It is a system of governance informed by ethical voluntarism, with institutions at each level playing a role in promoting and monitoring adherence to core labor standards.

The firm

At firm level, there are three primary initiatives in operation around labor-related standards—codes of practice, such as the 2000 UN Global Compact, the introduction of corporate social responsibility (CSR) measures by both domestic and international companies, and the "social upgrading" of global production systems. Framework agreements—agreements struck by international unions with international companies— are discussed below in relation to Global Unions.

The Global Compact is a UN initiative and is designed to align businesses with ten universally accepted principles in the areas of human rights, labor, environment, and anti-corruption. In terms of labor, the principles are that businesses should uphold the freedom of association and the effective recognition of the right to collective bargaining; there should be the elimination of all forms of forced and compulsory labor; the effective abolition of child labor should be prioritized; and the elimination of discrimination in respect of employment and occupation.

These are the core labor standards of the ILO, brought into the Global Compact as essential principles of good business practice. The Global Compact is a voluntary arrangement, governed by a board of business, labor, and civil society representatives, appointed by the UN secretary-general in their personal capacity. The purpose of the compact is to mainstream these ten principles, including core labor standards, across global business.[13]

While the impact of the Global Compact is questioned, the signal to business from the UN has been that, when it comes to appropriate labor market behavior, the standards expected are those laid down by the ILO. The corporate signatories to the Global Compact may be "delisted" for not abiding by the annual requirement of Communication on Progress (COP), a report made public to stakeholders detailing progress in implementing the Global Compact's ten principles. By 2010, 1693 signatories had been delisted as stakeholders and pressure groups keep a watchful eye on those who view compact membership more as a marketing exercise than a commitment to its principles.

Modern CSR measures by companies have developed since the 1960s. Their current form proposes a positive view of CSR, in which value is added to company performance as a result of the internal (for example workforce buy-in, productivity improvements) and external (for example customer recognition and loyalty) impacts of responsible company practice in environmental, social, labor, human rights, and other dimensions. The contemporary view supersedes the earlier, somewhat defensive view, which suggested that CSR was primarily a risk assessment and avoidance measure, predicated on the identification and avoidance of company practices with adverse public and market consequences. From the perspective of labor, a standard CSR approach has been for companies to commit unilaterally to the ILO's core labor standards across their operation and on into their subcontracting activities. Internal and external monitoring often follows, with large companies establishing a CSR team within the company, and external agencies, such as the Fair Labor Association, conducting audits of labor practices. The debate about the impact of such measures is fierce.[14] Companies point to changed practices and behaviors. Opponents argue that CSR is adopted insofar as it helps the value-add, but no further, or that it is a sham. Other opponents take a quite different line, arguing that it is not the responsibility of the company to second-guess the market by introducing noncommercial criteria into business decision making.

In terms of global production systems, there exists a burgeoning discussion of "social upgrading"—that is, the incorporation of labor standards into the operation at the behest of the buyers and consumers, or their incorporation as a result of supplier strategy, or of government intervention. These standards are most frequently the core labor standards defined by the ILO, reflecting its role and status in labor standard setting.

The debate around social upgrading has a number of dimensions. First, there are important strategic dimensions of these chains in relation to social upgrading. Traditionally, network strategies might be placed on a continuum between "low-road" strategies, in which the advantages offered by global production arrangements derive from access to pools of cheap labor, and "high-road" strategies, in which skill and quality outputs combine to produce higher value outputs. Social upgrading might traditionally be expected in high-road approaches, but not in low-road ones.

However, there is also evidence that some sectors traditionally associated with low-road approaches—e.g., apparel—are also being required to upgrade on both social and environmental fronts, with the drive to social upgrading coming from the buyers in the chain or network, or from consumers.[15]

Second, there is an interesting discussion of "learning" in these chains. Learning, and the transfer of knowledge, within chains is argued to be uneven and an effect primarily of the different governance arrangements that exist. However, it is agreed that different types of learning and transfer take place, particularly in terms of product, functional, and process arrangements. Recently, it has been argued that transfers and learning associated with both environmental and social upgrading have been undertheorized and the focus of growing empirical study.[16]

Third, there is the "pull–push" mechanism that promotes social upgrading in these networks. Producer firms may adopt improved labor standards as a means to achieve improved deals with buyers and to command associated rents. Equally, buyers, with an eye on consumer expectations, may require social upgrading as a component of a contract. Another aspect of the "push" component is the role of national governments, which are likely to be working with the ILO and other international agencies, and therefore may favor a national "upgrading" of labor standards as part of a broader development strategy.

Supranational regional arrangements

We illustrate supranational regional dimension of labor and governance with three contrasting arrangements—the EU's "social dialogue" model, NAFTA's "labor clause" model, and APEC's refusal to address labor issues in any serious fashion.

One of the defining characteristics of the EU is social dialogue—that is, meetings between the social partners—employers (private and public) and employees, with or without the participation of member state or EU representatives. Social dialogue was reasserted at the 2000 Lisbon summit as one of the fundamental pillars of the "European Social Model," which combines good economic performance and high skills with a high level of social protection. It is in this social dialogue that trade union representation and power within the EU are protected and displayed.

The origins of social dialogue are rooted in European social and political traditions, which gave rise in 1991 to a Social Protocol, created by the social partners, which was eventually adopted at the EU's 1991 Maastricht summit. The social partners therefore were instrumental in defining the emerging EU industrial relations system. When the Social Protocol was adopted as an annex to the Maastricht Treaty of February 1992, the social partnership model became a central theme of the social dimension of European integration and social dialogue increased in importance thereafter. The result was a powerful role for the European Trade Union Council (ETUC) across the EU decision-making process. The social dialogue approach is unusual and provides the most comprehensive engagement by labor in supranational regional arrangements, although the future of that engagement has been brought into question as EU member states seek to counteract the impact of the GFC.

The case of the North American Agreement on Labor Cooperation (NAALC), a "side agreement" of NAFTA (a trade and investment agreement between Canada, the United States, and Mexico effective from 1 January 1994), presents an example of an intermediate labor standards governance regime. The expressed intention of the side agreement was to allow any failure to sustain appropriate labor standards as an effect of trade and investment arrangements under NAFTA to be subject to investigation and, where proven, sanctions. The efficacy of the side agreement approach has been much questioned. In particular, unions have pointed to a consistent unwillingness to take cases of poor labor standards beyond bureaucratic discussions. Unions believe that the side agreement is cosmetic, rather than a fully supported and implemented arrangement. Canadian unions have pointed to US Democratic presidential candidates, who have recognized this weakness and called for binding obligations on labor (and environmental) standards, to be central to the NAFTA process rather than marginal. Versions of side agreements or similar "distanced" arrangements are common in contemporary trade and investment deals. All suffer the same weakness: They are secondary to the main issues of trade and investment, lack teeth, and provide limited support for strong labor standards.

APEC is an example of a trade and investment arrangement that has long avoided active engagement with labor standards issues. Founded in the late 1980s, APEC became a powerful trans-Pacific force for free trade and investment. It cast itself as the vanguard of the VITO, pressing for ever deeper and wider trade and investment liberalization. Although it also developed a modest development agenda, member state politics resulted in a deliberate marginalization of labor as an interest group (except, rarely, when individual members chose to include trade union members in delegations) and avoided assiduously any of the social clause discussions that took place in the WTO. This approach contrasted strongly with the powerful business lobby in APEC, which is given high status and privileged access to the top of the APEC process. Only after the 2008 GFC was there some relaxation of this position, at the instigation of China, but APEC remains a major regional trade and investment arrangement without formal labor representation and with an aversion to labor-related matters.

The attitude of APEC to labor-related issues also raises an important question about "who" is responsible for labor standards. The default position, illustrated by APEC, is that labor standards are either a domestic matter, to be regulated at the level of the nation-state, or a matter for specialist agencies such as the ILO. In other words, there remains a strong belief in agencies such as APEC that global action on labor standards is "someone else's problem."

The ILO

The ILO is at the center of contemporary global labor governance, as has been the case since its establishment in 1919. The ILO is the institutional core and epistemic community at the heart of the International Labor Standards Regime. Its tripartite model of convention and recommendation creation, established on the principle of dialogue, cooperation, and equal voting between government, employer, and labor representatives to the ILO, remains the most powerful institutional location for labor's global voice.

However, the ILO entered the 1990s in search of a response to both globalization and neoliberalism, both of which raised challenges to the ILO's traditional standard-setting model. In particular, neoliberal policy hegemony in the 1980s challenged the tripartite model on which the ILO was founded. Trade union density was declining in many economies as free market policies rejected corporatist arrangements and frequently marginalized union voice. The relevance of the ILO was being questioned, as was its very survival.

Director-General Francis Blanchard recognized the new challenges facing the ILO in the 1980s. His response was to encourage proactive engagement with the Bretton Woods institutions in search of a niche for the ILO in a "structurally adjusted" global economy. Blanchard's initiatives were carried forward by his successors. Michel Hansenne, director-general between 1989 and 1999, significantly reformed the ILO's mission. The 1998 ILO Declaration on Fundamental Principles and Rights at Work centered ILO activities on a much contested definition of "core" labor standards, which were to be a fundamental dimension of a "fair" globalization, providing better targeted, more effective labor standards.

Hansenne's successor, Juan Somavía, continued the redirection of the ILO in response to globalization and its impacts. In particular, he addressed three issues: Globalization; the engagement with other international organizations, especially the WTO, the World Bank, and the IMF; and the ILO's message and organizing principles. The 2008 "Declaration on Social Justice for a Fair Globalization" brought together ILO thinking on globalization, in turn based on a 2004 ILO report—*A Fair Globalization: Creating Opportunities for All*. Renewed efforts to work with other international agencies were supported strongly. The Decent Work agenda became the organizing principle for the ILO, captured in the ILO's four strategic objectives:

- Creating jobs—an economy that generates opportunities for investment, entrepreneurship, skills development, job creation, and sustainable livelihoods.

- Guaranteeing rights at work—to obtain recognition and respect for the rights of workers. All workers, and in particular disadvantaged or poor workers, need representation, participation, and laws that work for their interests.

- Extending social protection—to promote both inclusion and productivity by ensuring that women and men enjoy working conditions that are safe, allow adequate free time and rest, take into account family and social values, provide for adequate compensation in case of lost or reduced income, and permit access to adequate healthcare.

- Promoting social dialogue—involving strong and independent workers' and employers' organizations is central to increasing productivity, avoiding disputes at work, and building cohesive societies.

The comprehensive reforms under Hansenne and Somavía have gone some way towards a successful repositioning of the ILO in a globalized world. This is particularly evident in the high-profile activities undertaken by the ILO as a result of the GFC. Hence, labor's global presence remains strong in areas of activity in which it plays an important role. However, stresses remain within the ILO, as was seen in employer attempts in 2012 to undermine some important procedures and institutions (such as the Committee of Experts).[17] Moreover, threatening both EU and ILO traditions of social dialogue, social partnership has been shown to be fragile in EU economies seeking a way through the GFC (especially in the case of Greece). While the ILO remains a vital global institution for labor, its status and influence are not assured, requiring labor to consider complementary institutional and organizational measures.

Labor's institutions

The challenges created for labor by the global environment are reflected also in the changing institutional configuration of the global labor movement. Once again, we do not address the changing conditions and structures of domestic labor movements in any detail, while recognizing that such movements are important constituent elements of international labor organizations, and also recognizing that there are synergies between the international and the domestic. Here, we concentrate on three levels—supranational regional arrangements, the central global organization (the International Trade Union Confederation, ITUC), and the Global Unions network, including the Global Union Federations.

Supranational regional organizations

A variety of supranational regional labor institutions exist. *Primus inter pares* in terms of power and status is the ETUC, a union presence in the EU defined by the social dialogue mechanisms discussed above. However, there are other supranational regional institutions, primarily linked to the ITUC. These include, for example the ITUC-Africa, the Trade Union Confederation of the Americas (TUCA), and the ITUC-Pan European Regional Council (ITUC-PERC). We discuss these in relation to the ITUC.

The contrast between the organizational presence of labor in the EU and in NAFTA is telling. In the EU, the ETUC is a social partner, recognized by the Council of Europe and the European Free Trade Association (EFTA), in addition to the EU, as the representative trade union organization. As such, it is consulted consistently on key aspects of European integration. It has a status guaranteed by treaty and an ability to represent trade union issues at all levels of discussion. This is in contrast to the operation of the NAALC. The operating principles of the NAALC are intergovernmental, with national administration offices established in government departments in the three member countries. Complaints relating to labor standards (described as "public communications") are initially dealt within an administrative process, which may lead to ministerial consultations, an evaluation by an expert committee, and independent arbitration. Progress beyond the first stage is rare. Hence, in the EU, trade unions are in principle fully consulted about the design and implementation of policy, and in its subsequent monitoring and evaluation, under the NAALC, labor's voice is reduced to that of one actor among others operating in a predetermined intergovernmental arrangement. Needless to say, NAFTA-based unions are both critical of, and cynical about, the impact of the NAALC.

Even in the EU, however, the challenge to social dialogue raised by post-GFC policy developments in members such as Greece suggests that the institutionally privileged status of the ETUC is not a guarantee of power or influence. In terms of presence and influence, supranational regional labor representation is at best a mixed success.

The ITUC

The ITUC was formed in Vienna in 2006, following the merger of the International Confederation of Free Trade Unions (ICFTU) and the World Confederation of Labour (WCL). Its emergence as the single dominant global trade union organization also reflected the demise of the Eastern bloc-backed World Federation of Trade Unions (WFTU) in the late 1980s and 1990s. As of 2015, the ITUC claims a membership of 176 million in 328 affiliates in 162 countries. The ITUC is a major international agency active not only in the ILO but also a frequent attendee of meetings involving the range of UN and other bodies; it enjoys considerable global status as the legitimate voice of labor on issues that consider work and workers—from traditional labor standards issues to contemporary questions such as climate change and human rights. However, presence and size do not ensure influence and power, and question marks remain about the impact of ITUC's voice in international discussions.

Many saw the creation of the ITUC as a great success in comparison with the Cold War clashes that gave rise to the division between the ICFTU and the WFTU, in particular. However, the ITUC has not avoided significant criticism from within labor, primarily in relation to its stance on globalization and neoliberal policies. Critics argue that the ITUC has tempered its political stance on globalization and neoliberalism in order to be accepted as a legitimate body by other international agencies. A key element of this critique is that the ITUC responds mainly to the views of developed world unions, and that the needs of the Global South are marginalized. Contemporary "social movement" analysis is frequently invoked as the antidote to a developed world hegemony. The critics argue for a far more political and radical global organization, often believing that the origins of the ITUC will not allow it to become such a force.

Supporters of the ITUC reject the criticism. They point to progress in creating a single global union body, and in gaining access for labor in global governance arrangements. They argue that the ITUC must be a pluralist agency in that it represents many strands of union thinking—politically, spatially, and experientially. They reject an adventurism that suggests that there are gains to be made by radicalizing the ITUC and taking it out of the global governance networks in which it operates.

A balanced judgment suggests that the ITUC represents a significant step forward by labor in global governance, yet its impact and status cannot yet be established. In particular, its capacity to influence the direction of globalization, and the outcomes of the GFC, to the sustained advantage of workers remains unclear.

Global Unions

Global Unions is a network including the ITUC, the Trade Union Advisory Committee to the OECD (TUAC), and what were for many years known as the International Trade Secretariats (ITS); it remains global sectoral union bodies (for example for engineers, the public sector, education, and so on). The ITS tradition reaches back to the late nineteenth century. The ITS transformed themselves into Global Union Federations (GUFs) in the 1990s.

GUFs are in general seen as successful. They are focused and have a long history of effective international reach and have grown since the 1990s, especially as the Cold War ended and new membership bases opened up. Growth has also exacerbated a traditional resource constraint, as many affiliates are not resource rich. Some GUFs also have a tradition of greater radicalism and have been the source of creative thinking about global trade union activities. Their members may also belong to the ITUC, yet, through GUF campaigns, express difference from ITUC positions. Equally, however, GUFs are expected to deliver benefits to members, often in the form of campaigns, solidarity actions, and the promotion of "framework agreements," which are agreements to abide by agreed labor standards, struck across an international company by its management and the relevant GUF. Framework agreements are in many ways the leitmotif of the GUFs.

Conclusion

Labor has a significant institutional presence in global governance. Its institutions draw on experience that reaches back to the late nineteenth century, and take advantage, where possible, of tripartite traditions (as, for example, in the EU and ILO). Labor's global institutions have undergone significant change over the last generation, driven by a combination of factors—the end of the Cold War, globalization, the GFC, and a pressing need to have labor's voice "at the top table" of global governance. Yet the power of that voice remains uncertain, for the role of labor as a social partner in globalization is still to be confirmed, and remains under attack from neoliberalism. And while that uncertainty remains, it also creates an opportunity for traditions within labor to argue for a far more radical stance against capitalism in its modern form, a perennial debate—but one given new vitality by the GFC and pressures from the Global South.

The pressing concern for labor is the grounding of its voice in global governance. There is a strong comparison to be made with the epoch which saw the creation of the ILO and the first international legitimation of that voice in 1919. Then, the threat of Bolshevism, coupled with the rise since the nineteenth century of worker militancy, helped to establish the tripartite model of the ILO, which was also a reflection of concerns about protectionism in the global trading system. In sum, there were pressing reasons to create a role and voice for labor in the global governance arrangements of the day. Until the GFC, such arguments had lost much of their force. Neoliberalism had sought to destroy unions. Globalization was apace, with little interest in hearing the voice of labor. The reform of the ILO under Hansenne and Somavía was a direct consequence of that marginalization of labor. The GFC has partly halted the marginalization, at least in global governance terms, as fears about political instability and jobless growth have grown. Still, the evidence for cases such as Greece suggests that when hard decisions must be made, the voice of labor is marginalized from formal decision making and must make itself heard on the streets.

Labor's institutions comprehend these pressures and have reformed themselves. However, they also face challenges, not only from marginalization, but also from more radical internal traditions. They are forced to steer a nuanced and at times contradictory course as they seek, on the one hand, to represent labor in the upper reaches of global governance, and, on the other, meet the aspiration of a widely differentiated membership. It is an unenviable task.

In rising to this challenge, labor's response has long been multilayered and multi-faceted. From official structures such as the ITUC to loose coalitions of industry or company-focused shop steward committees, labor has sought to represent its interests, frame its goals, and influence policymaking internationally. The multilayered analysis we have provided in this chapter underlines the complexity of global governance, the diffuse articulation of institutional power, and the role of labor standards in framing debate around a social dimension to globalization.

The emergence of a multi-actor system with power exercised at different levels has been one of the enduring legacies of postwar economic planning. Our understanding of this system is challenged by the diversity of the institutional and political actors that govern it and the complexity of policy responses it represents. However, the problem for labor has often been framed in terms of local labor versus global capital, the globalization of production and the localization of the wage bargain. International activity has, in these terms, been no more than an addendum to a tradition that empha-sizes nationally based accounts of labor rights. The establishment of a set of core labor standards that are deemed universal across national boundaries has provided an organizing platform on which labor is able to mobilize beyond national regimes of labor regulation and into the system of global governance.

Within and across our different levels of analysis, labor has sought to reframe the rules and norms of an international regime to reflect its interests. This reframing has taken different forms with different outcomes, depending on the level of governance and the nature of institutional and political power. Nonetheless, the ability of labor to articulate its voice within the institutions of global governance has been instrumental in developing different frameworks in the regulation of labor standards. While the recognition of core labor standards is at the heart of these activities, the willingness and ability of governmental, labor, and private actors to accommodate their interests within the institutions of global governance provide the political and social where-withal for regulatory action elsewhere.

Additional reading

Verity Burgmann, *Globalization and Labour in the Twenty-First Century* (London: Routledge, 2016).

ILO, Workplace Compliance in Global Supply Chains (Geneva: ILO, 2017), www.ilo.org/sector/Resources/publications/WCMS_540914/lang—en/index.htm.

ILO, *World Employment and Social Outlook* (Geneva: ILO, 2017).

Rob Lambert and Andrew Herod, eds., *Neoliberal Capitalism and Precarious Work: Ethnographies of Accommodation and Resistance* (Cheltenham: Edward Elgar, 2016).

Francis Maupain, *The Future of the International Labour Organization in the Global Economy* (Oxford: Hart, 2013)

Notes

1 Nigel Haworth and Stephen Hughes, "International Political Economy and Industrial Relations," *British Journal of Industrial Relations* 41, no. 4 (2003): 665–682. See also Nigel Haworth and Stephen Hughes, "Internationalisation, International Relations and Industrial Relations," *Journal of Industrial Relations* 42, no. 2 (2000): 195–213.

2 Richard Freeman, "The Great Doubling: The Challenge of the New Global Labor Market," 2006, http://emlab.berkeley.edu/users/webfac/eichengreen/e183_sp07/great_doub.pdf.

3 Federal Ministry of Economics and Technology, *German Mittelstand: Engine of the German Economy. Facts and Figures about Small and Medium-Sized German Firms*, (Berlin: FMET, 2013).

4 Edward Whitfield, "China and the Great Doubling: Racing to the Top or Bottom of Global Labour Standards?" *Global Policy* 7 (2016): 37–45.

5 Leonhard Plank, Cornelia Staritz, and Karin Lukas, *Labour Rights in Global Production Networks* (Vienna: Kammer für Arbeiter und Angestellte für Wien, 2009), 14–15.

6 Gary Gereffi and Joonkoo Lee, "Economic and Social Upgrading in Global Value Chains and Industrial Clusters: Why Governance Matters," *Journal of Business Ethics* 133 (2016): 25–38.

7 Neil Coe and Henry Yeung, *Global Production Networks: Theorizing Economic Development in an Interconnected World* (Oxford: Oxford University Press, 2015), 1–32.

8 Christina Stringer, Steve Hughes, Hugh Whittaker, Nigel Haworth, and Glenn Simmons, "Labour Standards and Regulation in GVCs: The Case of the New Zealand Fishing Industry", *Environment and Planning* 48, no. 10 (2016): 1910–1927.

9 Liam Campling, James Harrison, Ben Richardson, and Adrian Smith, "Can Labour Provisions Work Beyond the Border? Evaluating the Effects of EU Trade Agreements," *International Labour Review* 155, no. 3 (2016): 357–382.

10 Nigel Haworth, Stephen Hughes, and Rorden Wilkinson, "The International Labor Standards Regime: A Case Study in Global Regulation," *Environment and Planning A* 37, no. 12 (2005): 1939–1953. See also Nigel Haworth and Stephen Hughes, "From Marrakesh to Doha and Beyond: The Tortuous Progress of the Contemporary Trade and Labor Standards Debate," in *The Politics of International Trade in the Twenty-First Century*, eds. Dominic Kelly and Wyn Grant (London: Palgrave, 2004), 130–143.

11 The Japan Institute for Labor Policy and Training, *Labor Situation in Japan and Its Analysis General Overview 2015/2016* (Tokyo: JILP, 2016).

12 Nigel Haworth and Steve Hughes, "The ILO, Greece and Social Dialogue in the Aftermath of the Global Financial Crisis," in *After '08: Social Policy and the Global Financial Crisis*, eds. Stephen McBride, Gerry Boychuk, and Rianne Mahon (Vancouver: University of British Columbia Press, 2015), 121–139.

13 Andreas Rasche and Dirk Ulrich Gilbert, "Institutionalizing Global Governance: The Role of the United Nations Global Compact," *Business Ethics: A European Review* 21, no. 1 (2012): 100–114.

14 Shawn Pope and Arild Wæraas, "CSR-Washing is Rare: A Conceptual Framework, Literature Review, and Critique," *Journal of Business Ethics* 137 (2016): 173–193.

15 Amira Khattak, Nigel Haworth, Christina Anne Stringer, and Maureen Benson-Rea, "Is Social Upgrading Occurring in South Asia's Apparel Industry?" *Critical Perspectives on International Business* 13, no. 3 (2017): 1–36.

16 Stephanie Barrientos, "Contract Labor: The 'Achilles Heel' of Corporate Codes in Commercial Value Chains," *Development and Change* 39, no. 6 (2008): 977–990.

17 Janice Bellace, "Back to the Future: Freedom of Association, the Right to Strike and National Law," *Kings Law Journal* 27, no. 1 (2016): 24–45.

Credit rating agencies

Timothy J. Sinclair

Credit rating agencies have become a focus of political and media attention since the Asian financial crisis of 1997–1998, as people have repeatedly questioned the accuracy and timeliness of their ratings with successive episodes of rating "failure." The global financial crisis that started in 2007 has greatly heightened these concerns, while the European sovereign debt crisis that began in 2010 has demonstrated the continuing importance of the agencies despite persistent concerns about their competence.[1]

Moody's Investors Service and Standard & Poor's (S&P), both headquartered in New York City, are the two most important agencies. Fitch Ratings, with headquarters split between New York and London, has risen in importance in the last twenty years so that now analysts often refer to Moody's, S&P, and Fitch as the "Big Three." They are blamed for inflating the ratings of exotic financial products such as subprime securities before 2007. Many of these financial instruments were dramatically downgraded by the agencies in 2008 as problems emerged. Although criticized for accuracy, the views of the agencies were closely followed again as governments in southern Europe increasingly found themselves in financial trouble as the global financial crisis affected their income (reducing their tax take) and expenditure (greatly increasing expenditure for bank bailouts).

Few have linked the increasing importance of the agencies to the problem of global governance.[2] Although the Commission on Global Governance endorsed a central role for private market agents of governance in its vision of managing world affairs,[3] the broader implications of the growing role of rating agencies are more significant.

This chapter argues these agencies have become increasingly important non-state actors with the shift from a world of mainly intergovernmental organization to a more complex world of global governance. Rating agencies have acquired greater salience because they fit with the predominantly managerial objectives of global governance institutions. The rating agencies are private and turn such political problems as funding a bridge's construction into technical issues. This transformation reduces the scope for political debate. But recurrent episodes of rating failure and the associated criticism of the agencies also highlight the fragility of non-state forms of global governance.

This chapter begins with a discussion of the history and growth of these agencies, which is followed by discussion of competing perspectives. It then explores the current debate about the efficacy and challenges facing the agencies linked to the aftermath of the global financial crisis.

History

Credit rating is a process of determining the probability of default by a borrower or potential borrower. Increasingly, we all have a credit rating and these assessments of our ability to repay our debts are used by credit card companies when we apply for a new card, and by mortgage lenders when we want to buy a house. Corporations and governments also have credit ratings. It is these wholesale credit rating agencies that form the focus in this chapter.

Rating agencies emerged after the US Civil War.[4] Between 1865 and 1914, US financial markets experienced an explosion of private information provision in the absence of good, reliable, publicly gathered statistics. The transition between issuing collections of information and actually making judgments about the creditworthiness of debtors occurred after the 1907 financial crisis and before the end of World War I. The 1907 crisis demonstrated the heightened volatility of finance. Ratings looked useful in such an uncertain world. By the mid-1920s, the entire US municipal bond market was rated by Moody's. The growth of the bond rating industry subsequently occurred in a number of phases. Up to the 1930s, and the separation of the banking and securities businesses in the United States with the 1933 passage of the Glass–Steagall Act, bond rating was a fledgling activity. Rating entered a period of rapid growth and consolidation with this separation and institutionalization of the securities business after 1929, and rating became a standard requirement to sell any debt issue in the United States after many state governments incorporated rating standards into their prudential rules for investments by pension funds. Securities, like bank loans, are debts; but, unlike bank loans, securities such as bonds can be traded in the market. The price at which they trade is affected by the rate of inflation and a judgment about the creditworthiness of the corporation or government that issued them. A series of defaults by major sovereign borrowers, including Germany, made the bond business largely a US one from the 1930s to the 1980s, dominated by US blue-chip industrial firms and municipalities.[5] The third period of rating development began in the 1980s, as a market in junk or low-rated bonds developed. This market—a feature of the newly released energies of financial speculation—saw many new entrants participate in the capital markets.

Moody's and S&P are headquartered in the lower Manhattan financial district of New York City. Fitch is run from New York and London. Moody's was sold in 1998 as a separate corporation by Dun and Bradstreet, the information concern, which had owned it since 1962, while S&P remains a subsidiary of McGraw-Hill, which bought S&P in 1966. Fitch is majority owned by the Hearst Corporation. The agencies have numerous branches in the United States, other developed countries, and several emerging markets. S&P is famous for the S&P 500, the benchmark US stock index listing around $1 trillion in assets. Other agencies include the Dominion Bond Rating Service based in Toronto. All the agencies use rating symbols like those listed in Table 27.1 to indicate the relative creditworthiness of bond issues and issuers. "Aaa" or "AAA" is the best, with the lowest probability of default or failure to repay by the issuer or borrower. Just as people with better credit pay lower interest rates on their credit card borrowings, borrowers such as governments and corporations pay lower interest on AAA bonds than, say, BB ones. Governments tend to get upset when their creditworthiness is downgraded by the agencies.[6]

In the late 1960s and early 1970s, rating agencies began to charge fees to bond issuers to pay for ratings. The firms have fee incomes of several hundred million dollars a year. Ratings comprise an important part of the infrastructure of capital markets. They are key benchmarks in the marketplace, which form the basis for subsequent decision making by participants. In this sense, rating agencies are important not so much for any specific rating they produce, but for the fact that they are a part of the internal organization of the market itself. So, we find that traders may refer to a company as an "AA company," or some other rating category, as if this were a fact, an agreed and uncontroversial way of describing and distinguishing companies, municipalities, or countries.

Rating agencies operate in a specific context. The New Global Finance (NGF) is a social structure in which rating agencies and other reputational intermediaries assume a new and greater importance. Bank lending is familiar to us. Banks traditionally acted as financial intermediaries, bringing together borrowers and lenders of funds. They borrowed money, in the form of deposits, and lent money at their own risk to borrowers. However, in recent years disintermediation has occurred on both sides of the balance sheet. Depositors have found more attractive things to do

Table 27.1 Credit rating scales

Moody's Investors Service	Standard & Poor's
Aaa	AAA
Aa	AA
A	A
Baa	BBB
Ba	BB
B	B
Caa	CCC
Ca	CC
C	C
N/A	D

with their money at the same time as borrowers have increasingly borrowed from nonbank sources. The reasons for this development seem to lie in the heightened competitive pressures generated by globalization, and the high overhead costs of the bank intermediation infrastructure.

Disintermediation is at the center of the NGF. This process is changing what banks are, and creating what economists call an "information problem" for suppliers and users of funds. In a bank-intermediated environment, lenders depend on the prudential behavior of banks, which are regulated and required to maintain a certain level of reserves. Traditionally, banks lend money, assuming the risk of lending themselves. But this business model is less competitive today as cheaper alternatives exist. Borrowers such as corporations and governments have increasingly sought funds in the capital markets, where costs do not include the cost of running a bank and its infrastructure, and the bad loans that a bank has made in the past. In a dis-intermediated financial environment like the bond market, those with funds must make their own judgments about the likelihood of repayment by borrowers they contemplate lending money to—no bank is there to assume this risk for them. Given the high costs of gathering suitable information with which to make an assessment by individual investors, it is no surprise that institutions have developed to solve the information problem in capital markets by providing centralized judgments on creditworthiness.

Before the mid-1990s, most European and Asian companies relied on their market reputations alone to secure market financing for securities. But this situation changed when the pressure of globalization led to the desire to tap the deep US financial markets and to a greater appetite for higher returns (and thus risk). In these circumstances, the informality of "old boys' networks" was no longer defendable to shareholders or relevant to pension funds halfway around the world. What was essentially a US approach to market organization and judgment has become the global norm in the developed world, and, increasingly, in emerging markets as well.

The growth of rating has a number of central features. Globalization is the most obvious characteristic. As noted, cheaper, more efficient capital markets now challenge the commercial positions of banks everywhere. The New York-based rating agencies have grown rapidly to meet demand for their services in newly disintermedi-ated capital markets. Second, innovation in financial instruments is a major feature. Derivatives and structured financings, among other things, place a lot of stress on the existing analytical systems and outputs of the agencies, which are developing new rating scales and expertise in order to meet these changes. The demand for timely information is greater than ever. Third, competition in the rating industry has started to accelerate, for the first time in decades. The basis for this competition lies in niche specialization (for example, Fitch Ratings in municipals and financial institutions) and in the "better treatment" of issuers by smaller firms. The global rating agencies, especially Moody's, are sometimes characterized as highhanded, or in other ways deficient, in surveys of both issuers and investors.

Over the century or so of their existence, rating agencies have become more important in the world of global finance as the bond markets have grown in import-ance. Their position has made them increasingly significant non-state actors in the system of global governance, which is very much organized around market principles and the value of market-based actors like the agencies. This is in contrast to the state-centric system of international organization which was so characteristic of the world order prior to the 1990s. Unlike the International Monetary Fund (IMF), the judgments by agencies have tended to be seen as nonpolitical, enhancing their effectiveness. The growth in the global governance significance of the agencies is matched by increasing recognition in official agencies, development banks, and governments, including of the United States, which agencies are, at times, useful promoters of market norms as their reach grows worldwide.

Current debates

We can identify three competing ways of thinking about these agencies. Two emerge from business schools and law, while the third reflects thinking in the social sciences more broadly. The first is the rationalist approach, which means that what rating agencies do is seen as serving a "function" in the economic system. In this view, rating agencies solve a problem in markets that develops when banks no longer sit at the center of the borrowing process. Rating agencies serve as what Peter Gourevitch calls "reputational intermediaries," like accountants, analysts, and lawyers, who are "essential to the functioning of the system," monitoring managers through a "constant flow of short-term snapshots."[7] Another way to think about this function is to suggest that rating agencies establish psychological "rules of thumb" that make market decisions less costly for participants.[8] As banks have changed their nature, becoming a less significant part of the governance of markets, the rating agencies have become more significant. Looking at the process of capital market growth around the world, the developing role of the handful of rating agencies seems strategic in character.

The second approach, the regulatory license view, sees whatever power the agencies have in the capital markets as a reflection of delegation from government.[9] Because governments, especially Washington, have used ratings as a way of promoting prudential requirements for pension funds and have designated specific agencies as suitable for this purpose, whatever power the agencies have is simply a reflection of the power of government, not what the agencies offer. This is a much more limited conception of the global governance potential of the credit rating agencies, which views them merely as a reflection of delegated power from sovereign states.

The third approach is the social foundational approach, which has much in common with constructivist ways of thinking about international organization and global governance. Proponents see that purely functional explanations for the existence of rating agencies are deceptive. Attempts to verify or refute the idea that rating agencies must exist because they serve a purpose have proved inconclusive. Rating agencies have to be considered important actors because people view them as important, and they act on the basis of that understanding in markets, even if it proves impossible for analysts to actually isolate the specific benefits that agencies generate for these market actors. Investors often mimic other investors, "ignoring substantive private information."[10] The fact that people may collectively view rating agencies as important—irrespective of whatever "function" the agencies are thought to serve in the scholarly literature—means that markets and debt issuers have strong incentives to act as if participants in the markets take the rating agencies seriously.

In the social foundational view, the significance of rating cannot be estimated like a mountain or national population, as a "brute" fact that is true (or not) irrespective of shared beliefs about its existence, neither is the meaning of rating determined by the "subjective" facts of individual perception.[11] What is central to the status and consequentiality of rating agencies is what people believe about the agencies, and then act on collectively—even if those beliefs are clearly false. Indeed, the beliefs may be quite strange to the observer, but if people use them as a guide to action (or inaction) they are significant.

Dismissing collective beliefs misses the fact that actors must take account of the existence of social facts in considering their own action. Reflection about the nature and direction of social facts is characteristic of financial markets on a day-to-day basis. Whether rating agencies actually add new information to the process does not negate their significance, understood in these terms. This third approach to understanding the agencies suggests that the source of their power as agents of global governance is not just their immediate coercive effect on the cost of borrowing money, but rather on their broader impact on the ideas and confidence in the markets, institutions, and governments.

Key criticisms and emerging issues

Recurrent episodes of rating failure and the associated criticism of the agencies highlight the fragility of non-state forms of global governance. The subprime crisis that began in 2007 caused dismay and panic throughout governing circles in developed countries as efforts to reignite confidence in the financial markets failed. The crisis revolved around mortgage lending for housing purchases by buyers with weaker than "prime" personal credit ratings. The financial markets developed a series of exotic financial instruments associated with these housing loans to allow lenders to reduce their balance sheet risk. Other institutions traded in these derivatives to make money. Given that the subprime securities market was worth only $0.7 trillion in mid-2007, out of total global capital markets of $149 trillion, the impact of subprime assets was out of proportion with its actual weight in the financial system.[12]

The subprime crisis is not a direct consequence of subprime mortgage delinquencies. The paralysis that came over global finance in 2007–2009 is a consequence of the nature of markets themselves, rather than the logical result of relatively minor problems with lending to the working poor. But this analysis of the subprime crisis is difficult to incorporate in a rationalist view, in which events must have material causes. In a rationalist world, panics, crises, and collapses are explained as a result of specific failures rather than as a consequence of the social interactions in markets.

Since the 1930s, financial crises have almost always been accompanied by public controversy over who was at fault. Before then, governments were not generally held responsible for economic conditions; but since the 1930s the public has expected governments to manage the financial system. Inevitably, efforts to defuse or redirect blame develop. During the Asian financial crisis (1997–1998), corruption in Asian governments and among their business leaders was held responsible, even though just a few years before "Asian values" were supposedly responsible for the unprecedented growth in the region. During the Enron scandal of 2001–2002 auditors were blamed for not revealing the financial chicanery of the corporation. The subprime crisis was no different, with rating agencies, mortgage lenders, "greedy" bankers, and "weak" regulators all subject to very strong attacks for not doing their jobs.

The rating agencies have been subject to unprecedented criticism and investigation. US Congressional committees, the Securities and Exchange Commission (SEC), the European Parliament and Commission, and the Committee of European Securities Regulators have all conducted investigations. The crisis over subprime ratings was the biggest threat to date for these agencies in a century of activity. This effort to blame the agencies is curious given that the rating agency business is now open to greater competition since passage of the Credit Rating Agency Reform Act by the US Congress in 2006. It suggests that the movement from regulation to self-regulation—from "police patrol" to "fire alarm" approaches—has not eliminated the role of the state. Governments are still expected by their citizens to deal with market failure, and when necessary act as lenders of last resort, and governments know it. What we see is a disciplining of the agencies by a regulatory state, intent on improving their performance.[13] Although this is a US debate in the first instance, it has global consequences because the internationally respected agencies are US based. It shows how concerns about regulation in a specific domestic context can have transnational implications.

The activities of rating agencies have been largely free of regulation until recently. Starting in the 1930s, the ratings produced by the agencies in the United States have been incorporated into the prudential regulation of pension funds so as to provide a benchmark for their investments. This required pension funds to invest their resources in those bonds rated "investment grade" and avoid lower rated, "speculative grade" bonds. Regulation of the agencies themselves only started in 1975 with the SEC's Net Capital Rule. This gave a discount or "haircut" to issuers whose bonds are rated by "Nationally Recognized Statistical Rating Organizations" (NRSRO). No criteria were established for them at the time, and standing was determined by the SEC informally. NRSRO designation acted as a barrier to entry until the Rating Agency Reform Act of 2006, passed in the wake of the Enron scandal, created criteria and a recognized path to NRSRO recognition.

The impulse is to regulate the agencies by creating a framework of regulative rules that are "heavier" or "harder" or somehow more "serious." The impulse to regulate is derived from a failure to understand what it is the rating agencies did that was actually in error, and a failure to accept the social nature of finance and the circumstances that brought the crisis into being in the first place. The prevailing understanding behind the impulse to punish and regulate seems to be that the people involved were doing things wrong. It is as if the mechanic fixing a car has downloaded the wrong software updates to the car's computers. But this auto analogy will not do for global finance. Finance is not a natural or physical phenomenon. While financial markets may display regularities in normal times, these regularities are not law like because change is an ever present feature of all social mechanisms.

John Searle made a useful distinction between regulative rules that "regulate antecedently or independently existing forms of behavior" and more architectural forms of rule.[14] The latter, or "constitutive rules, do not merely regulate, they create or define new forms of behavior." He goes on to suggest that chess and football are only possible with rules. In short, the rules make the game. His point is that public and elite panic has focused on regulative rules (or the lack of them) and those who allegedly broke them. But the rules themselves are not the problem with rating agencies, or what has brought about the global financial crisis. The problem is that deep, constitutive rules were damaged by the panic, and thus why the crisis was so challenging.

In the case of the rating agencies, regulative issues are insubstantial and no more than a useful rhetorical device to address poor forecasting. What are important and little commented upon are the constitutive issues. The major problem arose in the early 1980s with the rise of structured finance. Structured finance is important because it has been the principal means through which financial innovation has made illiquid debts like credit-card receivables, car loans, and mortgages into tradable, liquid securities. In a context of low interest rates and the hunt for yield, structured finance grew to around $10.7 trillion or 7.17 percent of the total in 2007.

When people think of financial innovation, they inevitably think of computers and highly educated "rocket scientists" developing quantitative techniques for managing risk. But that is not at the heart of this matter. *Lawyers* are the key to the problem. The essence of structured finance is to be found in the legal rights to revenues organized in the contracts and trusts that underpin the securities. This documentation can run to thousands of pages. These legal underpinnings give different rights to different tranches of a security. Some, such as the AAA tranche, have the right to be paid first, while others have to wait in line. This is how a mass of not very creditworthy subprime mortgages could produce some AAA bonds. The AAA investors had first right to revenue, and the expectation was that even if some subprime mortgage holders defaulted as expected, enough would pay so that those with the highly rated securities would be paid in full. Unfortunately, when expectations are upset and people are uncertain, as in 2007–2009, this model does not work. When recession is added to the mix, the result is a wholesale write-down of the global market in securities.

As disastrous as this situation was, the rating agencies' real failure was something else, namely, their own move into the markets. For decades Moody's and Standard & Poor's had played the role of a judge or referee, standing back from the action and making calls as necessary. They were valued for this role, which allowed them to build up substantial reputational assets. Structured finance is only possible with the active involvement of the rating agencies in designing the financial instruments. The agencies and their ratings actually created the distinct tranches or levels of specific structured finance issues. Some of them were rated AAA, while others were rated lower. Because of the complexity of the legal documentation and protection necessary for these tranches, the raters did not stand back as neutral judges as they normally do. In structured finance, the raters acted more like consultants, helping to construct the securities themselves, indicating how they would rate them if they were organized in ways that offered specific legal protection to investors.

In addition to these concerns, two major sets of issues dominate discussions about the rating agencies in the wake of the global financial crisis. The first relates to the competence of the agencies and the effectiveness of their work. The second set concerns broader, structural issues. Critics have frequently attacked the timeliness of rating downgrades, suggesting that the agencies do not use appropriate methods and fail to ask the sort of forensic questions needed to properly investigate a company. Concerns about staffing, training, and resourcing are associated with these problems. Recently and increasingly stridently, critics have attacked what are perceived to be broader, structural problems in how the agencies do business. These problems, suggest the critics, create poor incentives and undermine the quality of the work the agencies undertake.

The first of these broader structural issues is the legacy of weak competition among rating agencies as a result of the introduction of the NRSRO designation. Although several new agencies were so designated after passage of the Rating Agency Reform Act, many critics would like NRSRO status to be abolished, removing any reference to ratings in law. The view is that weak competition has led to poor analysis, as the rating agencies have had few incentives to reinvest in their product. In this view, the revenues flowing to rating agencies are rents from a government-generated oligopoly.

Concerns about how the agencies are funded became widespread with the onset of the subprime crisis. The idea was that there was something wrong with "issuer pays." Although this worked for forty years, the scandal was based on latent conflict of interest in that the agencies have incentives to make their ratings less critical than they would if they were paid by investors, the ultimate users of ratings. Like NRSRO status, many critics called for an end to the issuer pays model of rating agency funding.

A vigorous—if often poorly informed—debate about the merits of regulating rating agencies has taken place since the onset of the crisis in spring 2007. Behind the rhetoric, it is very clear that both US SEC and European Commission officials were reluctant to regulate either the analytics of the rating process itself or the business models of the major rating agencies (the issuer pays model). In amendments to NRSRO rules announced in February 2009, the SEC enhanced required data disclosures on performance statistics and methodology, and it prohibited credit analysts from fee setting and negotiation or from receiving gifts from those they rate.[15] How ratings are made and who pays for them are materially unaffected by these changes. This is also the case with the Dodd–Frank Act, 2010, which mandated further SEC reporting. The Dodd–Frank Act was the major US legislative response to the global financial crisis that started in 2007—named after the two congressional leaders, Representative Barney Frank and Senator Chris Dodd.

Much the same can be said for European efforts. Hampered by the reality that Moody's and S&P are both headquartered in the United States, for many years rating agencies were little more than "recognized" in European states by local regulators who were freeriders on US regulatory efforts. With the Enron crisis, which led to the bankruptcy of the Texas-based energy trading firm, concerns about rating agencies grew and the International Organization of Securities Commissions (IOSCO) code of conduct was increasingly referred to in Europe as a useful form of self-regulation. With the onset of the global financial crisis European Commission officials have sought to regulate the agencies in Europe.[16] This legislation, which is premised on local enforcement, creates a registration process like the NRSRO system, and addresses the limited issues of transparency, disclosure, and process.[17] But it does not change rating analytics or challenge the issuer pays model of the rating business.

Despite the worst financial crisis since the 1930s and the identification of a suitable culprit in the rating agencies, the proposed regulation following the 2007–2008 crisis was so insubstantial as to do little to alter the rating system that has been in place in the United States since 1909 and in Europe since the 1980s. Part of this can be put down perhaps to a lack of confidence on the part of regulators and politicians in the efficacy of traditional solutions to market failure. It may also recognize the palpable weakness of ostensibly heavily regulated institutions such as banks and an understanding that the financial system is, despite the rating crisis, likely to continue to move in a more market- and rating-dependent direction in future. Indeed, the rating agencies have been major beneficiaries of the US bailout program, reporting substantial returns during the crisis.[18]

The global financial crisis exists at the constitutive level. This crisis reflects a deep loss of confidence in the basic infrastructure of the capital markets. This loss of confidence is a social rather than a technical process, and tinkering with regulative rules, while tempting and politically distracting, will not address the heart of the matter. It is tempting to prescribe a simple fix, but institutions develop over time and do not heal instantly. Encouraging institutional diversity and restraining hubris about alleged cures is advisable. For the rating agencies, attending to the relationships and the expectations that built their reputations in the first place is their best course of action. The extent of substantial change is likely to be limited. Thus, seeing the rating agencies as the brave new way forward for a market-centric form of global governance is risky, to say the least. The global financial crisis has not been kind to anyone, but it has highlighted the necessary and vital role of government in times of upheaval.

Conclusion

Ratings have become increasingly central to the regulatory system of modern capitalism and therefore to governments. Getting credit ratings "right" therefore seems vitally important to many observers. But in pursuing improvement in the rating system, we need to appreciate the challenges and limits to rating. The increasingly volatile nature of markets has created a crisis in relations between the agencies and governments, pushing politicians and regulators to seek to monitor their performance and stimulate reform in their procedures. Given the inherent challenges in rating, it must seem paradoxical that it is growing in importance as an approach to information problems in a variety of contexts outside the financial markets. This form of governance is increasingly important in health care, education, and many commercial activities.

Credit rating agencies serve a useful purpose on most accounts in an increasingly capital market-based financial system. This form of market institutionalization is growing around the world, slowing displacing traditional bank lending. The main agencies have a good track record rating corporations and governments over extended periods of time. But the current reliance on credit rating agencies is problematic. They serve narrow interests; and in times of crisis, such interests can make crises worse as they seek to exit a country or a company because of a rating downgrade. This "pro-cyclical" quality of the agencies makes them troubling as key sources of global governance. In good times, they may appear to offer a neat market-based way of managing future risks. But when things go bad, as they invariably do, are credit rating agencies equipped with the sort of wider responsibility and systemic regard that we expect and require of the institutions of global governance?

Additional reading

Andreas Kruck, "Resilient Blunderers: Credit Rating Fiascos and Rating Agencies' Institutionalized Status as Private Authorities," *Journal of European Public Policy* 23, no. (2016): 753–770.

Frank Partnoy, "The Siskel and Ebert of Financial Markets? Two Thumbs Down for the Credit Rating Agencies," *Washington University Law Quarterly* 77, no. 3 (1999): 619–719.

Lena Rethel and Timothy J. Sinclair, *The Problem with Banks* (London: Zed Books, 2012).

Timothy J. Sinclair, *The New Masters of Capital: American Bond Rating Agencies and the Politics of Creditworthiness* (Ithaca, NY: Cornell University Press, 2005).

Dimitrios Soudis, "Credit Rating Agencies and the IPE: Not as Influential as Thought," *Review of International Political Economy* 22, no 4 (2015): 813–837.

Notes

1 Daniel Inman, "Spain Downgrade Hits Asian Shares," *Wall Street Journal*, 11 October 2012.

2 Timothy J. Sinclair, *Global Governance* (Cambridge: Polity Press, 2012), 23–24.

3 Commission on Global Governance, *Our Global Neighbourhood* (Oxford: Oxford University Press, 1995).

4 This history is based on Timothy J. Sinclair, *The New Masters of Capital: American Bond Rating Agencies and the Politics of Creditworthiness* (Ithaca, NY: Cornell University Press, 2005).

5 Alvin Toffler, *Powershift: Knowledge, Wealth, and Violence at the Edge of the 21st Century* (New York: Bantam, 1990), 43–57.

6 Reuters, "Argentina Slams Credit Agencies for 'Terrorist' Reports," 16 October 2012, http://uk.reuters.com/article/2012/10/16/uk-argentina-ratings-minister-idUKBRE89F10 B20121016.

7 Peter Gourevitch, "Collective Action Problems in Monitoring Managers: The Enron Case as a Systemic Problem," *Economic Sociology—European Electronic Newsletter* 3, no. 3 (2002): 1 and 11.

8 Jeffrey Heisler, "Recent Research in Behavioral Finance," *Financial Markets, Institutions and Instruments* 3, no. 5 (1994): 78.

9 Frank Partnoy, "The Siskel and Ebert of Financial Markets? Two Thumbs Down for the Credit Rating Agencies," *Washington University Law Quarterly* 77, no. 3 (1999): 619–719.

10 David S. Scharfstein and Jeremy C. Stein, "Herd Behavior and Investment," *American Economic Review* 80, no. 3 (1990): 465.

11 John Gerard Ruggie, *Constructing the World Polity: Essays on International Institutionalization* (New York: Routledge, 1998), 12–13.

12 Bank of England, *Financial Stability Report* (London, October 2007), 20.

13 Michael Moran, *The British Regulatory State: High Modernism and Hyper-Innovation* (Oxford: Oxford University Press, 2003), 1–11.

14 John R. Searle, *Speech Acts: An Essay in the Philosophy of Language* (Cambridge: Cambridge University Press, 1969), 33.

15 Securities and Exchange Commission, "17 CFR Parts 240, 243, and 249b Re-Proposed Rules for Nationally Recognized Statistical Rating Organizations; Amendments to Rules for Nationally Recognized Statistical Rating Organizations; Final Rule and Proposed Rule," *Federal Register* 74, no. 25 (9 February 2009): 6456–6484.

16 Commission of the European Communities, "Proposal for a Regulation of the European Parliament and of the Council on Credit Rating Agencies" (Brussels, 11 November 2008); European Parliament, Committee on Economic and Monetary Affairs, "Draft Report on the Proposal for a Regulation of the European Parliament and of the Council on Credit Rating Agencies" (Strasbourg, 13 January 2009).

17 Oliver Kessler, "Towards an Economic Sociology of the Subprime Crisis?," *Economic Sociology: The European Electronic Newsletter* 10, no. 2 (2009): 11.

18 Serena Ng and Liz Rappaport, "Raters See Windfall in Bailout Program," *Wall Street Journal*, 20 March 2009.

CHAPTER 28

Think tanks and global policy networks

James G. McGann

In an age when smartphones facilitate a constant stream of news and notifications, the average young adult is training for jobs that do not yet exist, and regular commercial travel to space is a reality, information surges often raise more questions about reliable intelligence than they answer. In this increasingly complex and information-rich world, governments and individual policymakers face the common problem of applying expert knowledge to decision making. In response, the growth of public policy research organizations, or think tanks, over the last few decades has been explosive. Not only have they increased in number, but their scope and impact have expanded dramatically at the national, regional, and global levels. In 1993 at the first global meeting of such groups in Barcelona, Spain, many scholars believed that the term "think tank" did not travel well across borders. Today, the term is an accepted transnational concept.[1]

This chapter discusses their dramatic growth over the last quarter-century, and their increasing influence in global governance. As think tanks have developed, so too has analysis and understanding of their current influence and their future potential. Just as it is now difficult for one state to solve problems on its own, so too are think tanks finding that they must expand globally to further their own research, development, and credibility. Think tanks can use their knowledge to assist policymakers and other actors who are immersed in the daily affairs of governing and have less time for analysis. The progress and problems of think tanks are discussed later in this chapter.

A short history

Think tanks undertake research, analysis, and engagement that generate policy advice on domestic and international issues, enabling policymakers to make informed decisions and bridging the gap between the government and the public. Think tanks serve as "go-to" institutions when experts on specialized topics are needed. These organizations are classified in one of the following categories: for profit; autonomous and independent; quasi-independent; university affiliated; political party affiliated; quasi-governmental; or governmental. However, a finer line gets drawn when separating international think tanks with a domestic focus from those that are truly global or transnational.

"International" does not necessarily mean "global." Many think tanks conduct research on international issues, but they are not global. Like multinational corporations, global think tanks have operational centers on two or more continents, along with field offices with local staff and scholars, research findings shared with global audiences, and a variety of international funding sources. Some think tanks are regional or merely transnational, meaning they operate in two or more countries. There are just a dozen or so think tanks that truly are global. But the numbers are growing. If we count both global and transnational organizations, there are now approximately sixty think tanks that have cross-border operations.[2] There are currently ninety-two global think tanks in Table 28.1.

Table 28.1 Global think tanks

Region	Global think tank	Date of establishment
Asia (six)		
Asia	Asian Institute for Policy Studies	2008
Asia	Chinese Academy of Social Sciences	1977
Asia	Gateway House	2009
Asia	Institute of Developing Economies	1958
Asia	Japan Institute of International Affairs	1959
Asia	United Nations University	1975
Central and Eastern Europe (seven)		
Central and Eastern Europe	Albanian Institute for International Studies	1997
Central and Eastern Europe	Centre for Liberal Strategies	1994
Central and Eastern Europe	Institute for Public Affairs	1997
Central and Eastern Europe	Institute of World Economy and International Relations	1956

Central and Eastern Europe (seven)		
Central and Eastern Europe	Moscow State Institute of International Relations	1944
Central and Eastern Europe	Polish Institute of International Affairs	1947
Central and Eastern Europe	Prague Security Studies Institute	2002
Central and South America (four)		
Central and South America	Centro de Analisis y Difusion de la Economia Paraguay	1969
Central and South America	Comision Economica para America Latina	1951
Central and South America	Consejo Latinoamericano de Ciencias Sociales	1967
Central and South America	Fundación Global Democracia y Desarrollo	2000
North America (thirty-four)		
North America	Aspen Institute	1950
North America	Arctic Institute	2011
North America	Atlantic Council	1961
North America	Atlas Network	1981
North America	Brookings Institute	1916
North America	Carnegie Endowment for International Peace	1910
North America	Carter Center	1982
North America	Center for Global Development	2001
North America	Center for International Private Enterprise	1983
North America	Center for Strategic and International Studies	1962
North America	Center on International Cooperation	1996
North America	Center for European Policy Analysis	2006
North America	Council on Foreign Relations	1921
North America	East West Institute	1980
North America	Freedom House	1941
North America	German Marshall Fund of the United States	1972
North America	Hoover Institution	1919
North America	Human Rights Watch	1978
North America	Institute for Policy Studies	1963
North America	International Development Research Center	1970
North America	International Food Policy Research Institute	1975
North America	International Institute for Sustainable Development	1990
North America	International Peace Institute	1970
North America	Migration Policy Institute	2001

(*Continued*)

Table 28.1 (Continued)

Region	Global think tank	Date of establishment
North America (thirty-four)		
North America	National Democratic Institute	1983
North America	Open Society Foundations (FKA Open Society Institute)	1979
North America	Peterson Institute for International Economies	1981
North America	RAND Corporation	1948
North America	Stimson Center	1989
North America	Tinker Foundation, Inc	1959
North America	Woodrow Wilson International Center for Scholars	1968
North America	Worldwatch Institute	1974
North America	World Bank Institute (FNA Economic Development Institute)	1955 (EDI) 2006 (WBI)
North America	World Resources Institute	1982
Sub-Saharan Africa (two)		
Sub-Saharan Africa	Center for Conflict Resolution	1968
Sub-Saharan Africa	South African Institute of International Affairs	1934
Western Europe (eleven)		
Western Europe	Alexander Von Humboldt Stiftung	1860
Western Europe	Atlantic Community	2004
Western Europe	Barcelona Centre for International Affairs	1973
Western Europe	Bertelsmann Stiftung	1977
Western Europe	Bruegel	2005
Western Europe	Chatham House	1920
Western Europe	Center for Economic Policy Research	1983
Western Europe	Centre d'Etudes Prospectives et d'Informations Internationales	1978
Western Europe	Club of Rome	1968
Western Europe	Demos	2003
Western Europe	Deutsche Forschungsgemeinschaft	1920
Western Europe	Ecologic Institute	1995
Western Europe	European Council on Foreign Relations	2007
Western Europe	Fondazione Eni Enrico Mattei	1989
Western Europe	Frankfurt Institute	1922
Western Europe	Fraunhofer-Gesellschaft	1949
Western Europe	French Institute of International Relations	1979
Western Europe	Friedrich Ebert Stiftung	1925
Western Europe	Friedrich Naumann Stiftung für die Freiheit	1958
Western Europe	Hanns-Seidel-Stiftung	1967

Western Europe (eleven)

Western Europe	Helmholtz Gemeinschaft	1958
Western Europe	Institut de Relations Internationales et Strategiques	1991
Western Europe	Institute for International Economics Studies	1961
Western Europe	Institute of International Affairs	1965
Western Europe	Italian Institute for International Political Studies	1934
Western Europe	International Crisis Group	1995
Western Europe	International Institute for Strategic Studies	1958
Western Europe	International Relations and Security Network	1994
Western Europe	Kiel Institute for the World Economy	1914
Western Europe	Konrad-Adenauer-Stiftung	1955
Western Europe	Leibniz Gemeinschaft	1969
Western Europe	Overseas Development Institute	1960
Western Europe	Peace Research Institute Oslo	1959
Western Europe	Real Instituto Elcano	2001
Western Europe	Royal United Services Institute	1831
Western Europe	Stockholm International Peace Research Institute	1966
Western Europe	TEPAV	2004
Western Europe	Transparency International	1993
Western Europe	World Economic Forum	1971

Source: Data based on author's own research in the Think Tanks and Civil Societies Program, Lauder Institute for Management and International Studies, Wharton School and School of Arts and Sciences.

One of the most successful think tanks to employ a truly global strategy is the International Crisis Group (ICG). With field offices worldwide, staff representing forty-nine nationalities and forty-seven languages, and fifty percent of its funding coming from governments of twelve different countries, the ICG is a pacesetter but not alone in its endeavor. The Carnegie Endowment for International Peace (CEIP) has set goals and has already come a long way in terms of global operations with the opening of its sixth office in New Delhi. Think tanks can go global in other ways. The Brookings Institution and RAND have a number of operational centers outside the United States and have expanded their brands globally through the Internet, collaborative projects, and scholar exchanges. BI has made a big investment in its website in the last decade, including adding select content in Arabic, Chinese, and Spanish. Today, about one-third of the visitors to it are from outside of the United States. A third approach is the franchise model by which a think tank will transfer its name, strategy, structure, and philosophy to groups operating in other countries. German political foundations have created what can be described as "political-party, think-tank franchises" worldwide. Think tanks are clearly globalizing, multiplying, and increasing. There are currently 6486 think tanks, fifty-five percent of which are based in North America and Europe (see Figure 28.1). But, this scene is dramatically changing year by year. The greatest surge in the number of think tanks is in Asia, Africa, and the Middle East. However,

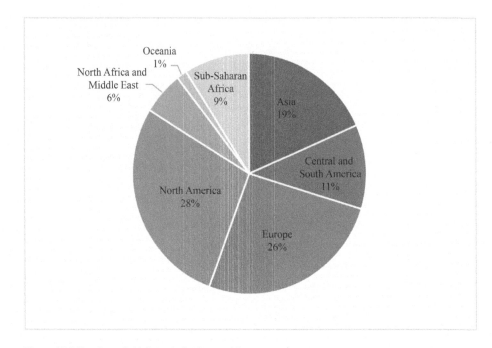

Figure 28.1 Number of think tanks in the world

Source: Data based on author's own research in the Think Tanks and Civil Societies Program, Lauder Institute for Management and International Studies, Wharton School and School of Arts and Sciences.

their institutional capacities, civil societies, and sources of funding remain weak and underdeveloped. A recent trend is the number of emerging power countries that are opening offices in Washington, London, Berlin, and Paris.

Primary reasons for the dramatic growth of think tanks are democratization, globalization, and development. Democratization inspires demands for analysis and information independent of government influence. It also allows for a more open debate about government decision making, an environment in which think tanks thrive. In addition, think tanks can no longer be armchair analysts sitting in Brussels, Paris, or Washington; they must be in country and on the ground covering events if they want to have credibility and influence on the major issues of the day. The growth of international actors and the pressures of globalization have led many think tanks to expand their operations. Both the ICG and the CEIP cite the end of the Cold War and the emergence of US supremacy as inspiration for going global. Figure 28.2 shows the emergence of global think tanks with the most significant growth since 1950. Others, such as BI and the German Marshall Fund, use development and advances in technology and communications to globalize for added convenience.

There is undoubtedly a large potential for positive global policy impact. Global think tanks have the opportunity to provide a constructive forum for the exchange of information between key stakeholders, or a "neutral space" for debate. In a globalizing, fast paced, information-rich world, think tanks can also provide important field research and efficient, quality responses to time-sensitive foreign policy problems. The Carnegie Endowment for International Peace and the BI both attempt to fill

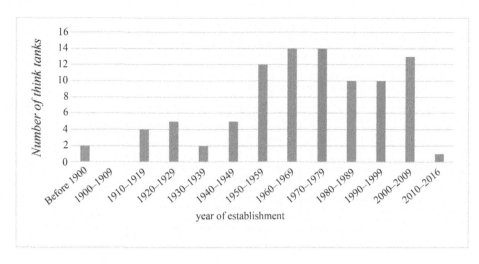

Figure 28.2 Development of global think tanks

Source: Data based on author's own research in the Think Tanks and Civil Societies Program, Lauder Institute for Management and International Studies, Wharton School and School of Arts and Sciences.

this role by having offices in key cities and countries, including Doha, New Delhi, Moscow, Beirut, Beijing, and Brussels—each specializing in regionally important economic and security issues. Additionally, when think tanks become global and form networks, it is more likely that they will pool their efforts and aggregate resources. Some issues, like carbon emissions, healthcare, and financial systems, are inherently global because they require cross-national coordination and may only take second place to domestic issues and agendas within any individual country.

Think tanks are not necessarily passive research organizations. Some have taken quite an active role when it comes to lobbying for or articulating and implementing policy in distinct areas. They are contractors, trainers, and media outlets. The International Peace Institute, for example, trains military and civilian professionals in peacekeeping strategies. Brookings' Internally Displaced Persons project, operating in tandem with the United Nations in partnership with the London School of Economics, seeks to help populations uprooted by violent conflict and civil unrest. These examples stand in sharp contrast to the days when think tank scholars would sit in their "universities without students" and come up with great ideas, and policymakers would beat a path to their door to seek advice. The six different categories of think tanks are depicted in Table 28.2. Their importance cannot be understated. In US foreign policy in particular, the ideas coming from think tanks have reshaped conventional wisdom and changed the direction of strategic issues.[3]

With such a broad range of functions, the global think tank of tomorrow will continue to gain in importance. However, some key obstacles remain. First, the lack of research institutions in developing countries should be addressed. Building up research institutions in those areas is actually an explicit goal of BI's Africa Growth Initiative, which seeks to partner with many different African think tanks and organizations. Global think tanks and policy networks will increase in utility when expansion is encouraged, a framework for knowledge transfer is provided, and independent and

Table 28.2 Functions of global think tanks

Category	Definition
R	Research and policy analysis
P	Project work or advocacy work
F	Field research/data gathering
D	Dialogue/information sharing
T	Training and education
L	Liaison function/relationship building with governments or international organizations

Source: Data based on author's own research in the Think Tanks and Civil Societies Program, Lauder Institute for Management and International Studies, Wharton School and School of Arts and Sciences.

Table 28.3 Categories of think tank affiliation

Category	Definition
Autonomous and independent	A public policy research organization that has significant independence from any one interest group or donor and autonomous in its operation and funding from government
Quasi-independent	A public policy research organization that is autonomous from government but controlled by an interest group, donor, or contracting agency that provides a majority over operations of the think tank
University affiliated	A public policy research center at a university
Political party affiliated	A public policy research organization that is formally affiliated with a political party
Government affiliated	A public policy research organization that is part of the structure of government
Quasi-governmental	A public policy research organization that is funded exclusively by government grants and contracts but not a part of the formal structure of government
For profit	A public policy research organization that operates as a for-profit business

Source: Data based on author's own research in the Think Tanks and Civil Societies Program, Lauder Institute for Management and International Studies, Wharton School and School of Arts and Sciences.

effective management is cultivated. There are governments that try to create what are known as "phantom think tanks" designed to appear nongovernmental when they are, in fact, arms of the government that are used to oppose legitimate civil society organizations. Funding also tends to exert direct or indirect influence over research agendas; problems arise if think tanks fail to put the policies and procedures in place to safeguard integrity and independence. A wide variety and large number of donors helps prevent subservience to government or narrow special interests; they are shown in Table 28.3.

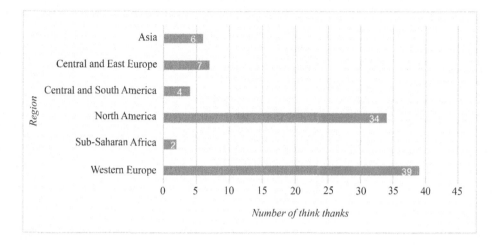

Figure 28.3 Global think tanks

Source: Data based on author's own research in the Think Tanks and Civil Societies Program, Lauder Institute for Management and International Studies, Wharton School and School of Arts and Sciences.

Ultimately, global think tanks and policy networks will be crucial in helping policymakers manage the "Four Mores" on a global scale: More issues, more actors, more competition, and more conflict. To do so, they need to master the "Four Rs": Rigor, relevance, reliability, and reach (national, regional, and global). All think tanks face the need to balance academic-quality research with information that is understandable and accessible for policymakers and the public. This becomes even more critical on a larger scale. The surge and spread of global think tanks is exactly that attempt to keep up with globalization and distill avalanches of information down to manageable and understandable analyses. As different countries continue to form more global networks and closer relationships, the think tanks of the future that manage to address obstacles inherent in expansion will continue to grow in both numbers and influence, as indicated in Figure 28.3.

They are also ideally suited to help us respond to a new trend that could be labelled "policy tsunamis" (economic, political, social, and health crises): Issues and events that will appear in one region and then sweep rapidly across the globe with increasing intensity and devastating impact. The 2008 economic meltdown, the rise of ISIS, and the Syrian refugee crisis are examples. A global network of think tanks could track issues and events and try to understand them before they reach the crisis stage, to harness the vast reservoir of knowledge, information, and associational energy that exist in public policy research organizations in every region of the world for public good. Clearly, one of the drivers of think tanks "going global" is to be on the ground in critical countries and capitals worldwide.

Past, current, and future challenges

Although both global think tanks and policy networks have the potential to be effective agents for social change, they face a series of internal and external challenges.

They are plagued by inadequate funding and need for sponsorship. They find it extremely difficult to raise funds for independent policy research, and donors often find it difficult to continue to sponsor an operation that does not produce immediate, quantifiable results. Attracting donors who do not have an immediate or direct interest in a project also proves challenging.[4] Even if funding is secured, think tanks face the additional obstacles of finding a niche in the "global marketplace of ideas" and translating the ability to gather information or consult on policy into the ability to affect or implement policy change. Once they have distilled valuable ideas from the plethora of available information available, they must work to get government actors and those in positions of official authority to utilize these ideas and produce results. This means getting their research and analysis in the right form, at the right time and in the right hands. Creating objectives and defining an agenda can be a potential complication for both think tanks and policy networks; a subsequent loss of focus are potential issues that inevitably arise due to the considerable startup costs and the time required to produce and promote viable and visible results.[5] Global think tanks in particular face distinctive challenges apart from funding and policy changes. They must overcome the substantial hurdle of finding a balance between communication and research competencies. Although the greatest surge in the number of think tanks being established is taking place in the Global South, these regions face a specific set of challenges, particularly an acute lack of resources. Not focusing enough on research could undermine think tank missions in such countries. Furthermore, although committing significant resources to research is important, it is also important that these institutions work to increase their visibility. Without a certain amount of legitimacy, credibility and influence are lost. Finally, it is important for global think tanks to identify competitors and scale up. For example, protestors and advocacy groups often have the same mission as think tanks—i.e., having an impact on policy.[6]

Policy networks face additional challenges because often they function in the absence of a formal organizational structure because they tend to operate on an *ad hoc* basis. Among these challenges are a lack of consensus resulting from poor communication, an underdeveloped organizational structure and leadership, difficulties recruiting and retaining members, and questionable legitimacy. In terms of operations, policy networks often lack the intellectual and scholarly resources that many global think tanks have.[7] Instead, they work to influence policy by attracting media attention, political patronage, and government support and resources. Furthermore, consistent commitment, especially investment in strengthening management capacity, as well as sustained monitoring from all participating members within a network, are critical to remaining effective.

Their evolutionary nature and their flexible structures create a sense of malleability and fluidity, allowing for the entry of new players and the exit of old ones as issues and agendas change.[8] Networks can be organized as "open assemblies,"[9] in which admission for prospective members is easy to obtain or as networks that admit members according to given criteria. Policy networks can also arise with a different time frame than global think tanks, taking the form of temporary "issue networks" to influence a very specific policy issue. While think tanks are concerned with bringing knowledge to bear on public policymaking, policy networks are organized to mobilize stakeholders on a specific policy issue in an effort to influence the policy process and achieve policy results that are in the interest of its stakeholders.

However, these results—like the network as a whole—are highly contingent on the continued existence of trust among the network members, the level of transparency, and equitable power symmetries among the network members.[10] Since a defining aspect of a policy network is its adaptability and open structure, establishing and maintaining high levels of sustainable trust as new links are added and old ones are removed can be difficult. Power asymmetries are yet another critical issue confronting policy networks, especially those that are unable to gain access to financial or other resources and are thus severely disadvantaged. Moreover, the volatility of policy networks necessitates careful and constant management and attention in order to maintain and promote their effectiveness. Policy networks tend to be fluid by nature because they are often defined by the policy issue they coalesce around. So unless the issue is an enduring one, the network tends to dissipate after the policy objective is achieved.

Perhaps the most difficult challenges faced by both global think tanks and policy networks are producing concrete results and measuring their impact. Although think tanks and policy networks certainly have political and social influence, they operate externally from existing power structures. As a result, their impact is difficult to quantify. Furthermore, many are still in the primary phase of their development, which makes it premature and virtually impossible to measure their effectiveness and judge their influence.

Implications for global public policy

What do the challenges and opportunities facing global think tanks and structurally independent public policy networks mean for the creation of truly global public policy? How can they incorporate opinions and analysis from actors across multiple geographical and functional orientations, draw on evidence from the locations in which policy is implemented, and provide solutions that are appropriate for the society and political structure of distinct and disparate locations? These include global warming and carbon emissions concerns; natural and manmade disasters; health crises; global terrorism; and financial regulatory architecture. In addition to being complex and global in scale, these issues often have specific effects on individual areas and regions. Tailored rather than uniform policy solutions have the highest possibility of succeeding. Familiarity with the perspectives and aspects of each particular region must be incorporated into potential solutions, which means that no institution, entity, or state could possibly propose and implement alone.

Various global think tanks have proved particularly successful in influencing global policy. There is no absolute, uniform method of going global. Each of the following global think tanks approaches and engages opportunities differently, often reacting and adapting to the specific regional, cultural, or societal aspects. Just as there are a diverse number of global think tanks, so too are there numerous means of going global.

With the increasing use of technology, even online global think tanks have been established, with various researchers from around the world meeting on an online platform to discuss progress and individual field work. For example, the Climate Scorecard Project was started out of the Conference of the Parties (COP21) to assess and rating the top twenty-five carbon-emitting countries based on their reductions. Its staff hails from around the globe, often from the country that a staff member is assessing. The staff meets online to discuss their countries' progress and provide updates to the website to hold accountable COP21 signers to their pledges. This Internet-based group holds no offices, but its members establish operations in their assigned country through communication and collaboration with private entities and civil society working on climate change in a country. The Internet facilitates trans-border collaboration and knowledge sharing so that more online global think tanks may develop to bring together many different people without the requirement that they leave the place that they are analyzing.

Arguably, the best and most powerful opportunity for think tanks and policy networks to affect or influence global policy is their ability to provide policymakers with important field research and up-to-the-minute information on critical issues or on geographically and socioeconomically disparate populations. Subsequently, these organizations should focus on increasing the efficacy of response to time-sensitive policy issues. For example, since 1995 the ICG has reported on conflict hotspots and proposed preventive and remedial policies. It has a flexible focus that responds to the scope of current global crises. It produces a bulletin, *CrisisWatch*, distributed to subscribers, that provides up-to-the-minute information on various global conflicts. Its 145 staff members on five continents issue reports that are directed at governments and intergovernmental bodies such as the UN, European Union (EU), and World Bank. ICG's sophisticated ability to gather and disseminate information, combined with a high-level advocacy, provides a "model."

Global think tanks also provide important entry points into authoritarian countries. The Brookings Institution (BI), for example, has established global centers in Beijing and Doha, and is creating dialogue forums. BI has entered into funding or research partnerships with government agencies in both areas, signaling its ability to create relationships with governments in countries in which think tanks have little independence. Its partnerships abroad help demonstrate to these countries that think tanks can be useful, thereby facilitating a more widespread acceptance of a functioning civil society governed by authoritarian regimes.

Friedrich Naumann Institute für die Freiheit is a German foundation and think tank with numerous offices worldwide that conduct project work and gather information on democratic transitions. This institution has an ideologically liberal leaning, and its work provides an important model for a means of bridging the space between democracy and autocracy through the provision of basic services, technical training, education, and policy design. As an independent organization providing essential benefits to the local population through its project work, this global think tank perhaps can avoid more easily the "Western imperialist" label that an international organization or government agency might receive. Undertakings carried out by think tanks, by being more "unofficial," can also be more flexible and work in areas where more formal national presences are impossible. As Richard N. Haass notes, the Carnegie Endowment's work in the 1980s brought leading South

African citizens together, creating gatherings which "helped establish the first dialogue and built understanding on South Africa's future during a delicate political transition."[11]

Carbon emissions and energy security is another area in which global think tanks can become heavily involved and assume a position of importance in affecting global policy. For example, the International Institute for Strategic Studies (IISS) is structurally independent and autonomous, a UK limited company and a registered charity but with offices in Bahrain, Singapore, and the United States. It conducts policy-oriented research and promotes dialogue on peace and security policy through an international member network at the same time that its research and dialogue-facilitating functions foster solutions to global security problems. The IISS is notable for its expansion beyond traditional security and defense. For instance, its Transatlantic Dialogue on Climate Change and Security suggest the way that established networks can utilize their membership toward finding solutions in new discipline areas. Since energy security varies widely and often requires tailored solutions for each region, IISS's structure is at least partially responsible for its success.

Health issues are another area in which global think tanks have become powerful voices of advocacy. The Global Alliance for Vaccination and Immunization (GAVI) is a health-based global public policy network. It was used as a model for the establishment of related networks such as the Global Fund to Fight against AIDS, Tuberculosis, and Malaria and the Global Alliance for Improved Nutrition (GAIN).[12]

The Heritage Foundation was established in 1973 as an educational institute, and its conservative-leaning research agenda includes healthcare policy. It is an example of a traditional think tank that includes health issues as part of its research and advocacy-based agenda, in contrast to the GAVI model of network establishment for the primary purpose of bringing stakeholders together to address health issues.

Global think tanks can also influence the shape of international financial architecture. The Center for Financial Studies is a think tank based in Germany with a global network of researchers and members. As one of the only global think tanks with a focus on financial innovation and regulatory policy, it performs a much needed research and dialogue function. In the area of international organization, the Center on International Cooperation (CIC) is a public policy research institution affiliated with New York University that focuses on enhancing international responses to humanitarian crises and global security threats. The CIC specifically targets multilateral organizations and UN reform to improve peace operations and post-conflict peacebuilding. In contrast, the Friedrich Ebert Stiftung (FES) is quasi-governmental but calls itself a private foundation. Founded in 1925, it focuses on political education and consultations. Its research priorities include globalization process, public sector reform, EU, democratic development and civic society, social politics in Germany and Europe, international politics, conflict management, and UN reform. Its policy work is complemented and strengthened by some eighty-five offices worldwide and projects with partners in over one hundred countries.

By providing a constructive forum for the exchange of information and negotiations between key stakeholders, independent and nonpartisan think tanks can create "neutral space" for public policy discussion, in which research findings are presented to the wider community and key experts debate them.[13] For example, the Aspen

Institute believes that the development of good leadership values and open-minded dialogue will lead to better policy decisions. Its mission is to "foster values-based leadership, encouraging individuals to reflect on the ideals and ideas that define a good society, and to provide a neutral and balanced venue for discussing and acting on critical issues." The Aspen Seminar is its primary "neutral space." The promotion of dialogue can lead to greater policy innovation; it also creates an opportunity for policymakers to mingle with staff from these institutions, thereby increasing civil society sector input in the overall policymaking process.

Networks and think tanks have several qualities and functions that distinguish them from other civil society organizations and entities. Networks have "boundary transcending" qualities that allow them to act as mediators.[14] In this sense, they can explain complicated topics and processes to policymakers and the public. Networks can place issues of global importance on the agenda and demand accountability from formal government structures. Global policy networks facilitate the transfer and use of knowledge in the public sphere, preventing governments from having a monopoly of information on policy. As discussed earlier, think tanks can do so as well, but the inherent nature of networks—specifically their ability to incorporate a wide array of perspectives, voices, and actors—lends itself to this function. At the same time, a very specialized function that think tanks can perform at the global level is the translation of international governance codes and laws for domestic applications.[15] In other words, such organizations as the World Bank and WTO can interpret, analyze, and adapt the various details of the international codes and laws to fit the specific contexts in which they must operate at the national or legal level.

Criticisms

As think tanks and their influence have expanded globally, they have received increased scrutiny. Perhaps the most difficult aspect is measuring impact and effectiveness. As government policy paralysis has increased, think tanks have been criticized as part of the problem instead of the solution. This criticism stems from decreasing general operating support, the rise of specialized think tanks, project-specific funding, and a narrowing set of policy options—problems that have led think tanks to support the status quo and not challenge conventional wisdom by providing alternatives.

One example is the policy gridlock that gripped Washington long before the elections of either Barack Obama or Donald Trump. The US think tank domain, in particular, has become increasingly politicized. Robert K. Landers believes that the influence of politics has led to a new breed of think tank: Unabashedly partisan and ideological with an emphasis on "spinning" information instead of producing original research or mediating discussion and debate. Several scholars have asked if the think tank model is broken, maintaining that the value of academic freedom is disappearing at all levels. It remains to be seen, however, if such politicization has created overly partisan organizations and denatured the traditional institutional form so that academic integrity is compromised. There is much variety in the think tank sphere, with several prominent institutions focusing substantial resources on moderating debate and promoting detailed analysis. One such example is the Woodrow

Wilson Center in Washington, where scholars research national topics and engage in global outreach through public meetings and events, with an aim of enhancing bipartisan cooperation. Think tanks that are able to bridge political, economic, cultural, and social divides are the best placed to produce original and exciting content that is relevant for a range of actors.

The key question is: "What works?" The complexity of international issues, their overlap, and the turmoil in which they surface make theorizing and reconciling points of view challenging, as there are many points of view and interests to be reconciled, as well as shifting politics and uncertainties about the efficacies of policy alternatives. Think tanks have the potential to help policymakers and the public meet those challenges because of their unique role in the policymaking process and their capacity to engage in interdisciplinary, policy-oriented research. Politicization and gridlock are serious issues in governments in Europe, the United States, and elsewhere; but think tanks can maneuver outside these issues. They can, indeed, be part of the solution.

Conclusion

Democratization, globalization, and development have led to new approaches to and thinking about global governance; these forces have also contributed to the dramatic growth of think tanks playing a role in international affairs. Think tanks can bridge the gap between academics and policymakers, generating policy advice and new ideas. They are a prominent illustration of the strong and growing influence of non-state actors in global governance; they also illustrate some of the challenges inherent in global expansion, such as adapting to different national and cultural contexts. In an increasingly connected world, states cannot solve problems alone, and international cooperation is necessary.

Think tank networks are facilitating such cooperation. Networks allow scholars from different institutions with expertise to come together in collaborative research. A disease, disaster, or conflict can easily spill over borders and require various groups—governments, intergovernmental and nongovernmental organization, and the private sector—to come together. Similarly, think tanks and policy networks are going global. They can no longer have offices only in Washington or Brussels; they must increasingly move to put experts on the ground in various regions and build their global presence. Moreover, technology and increased communications permit collaboration within and between think tanks, even without a physical presence. They may benefit from a legitimacy that a government lacks, when they are considered more reputable sources for information and analysis.

Independence is crucial to a think tank's legitimacy; but it is also difficult to maintain, reflecting both how much funding is received and from which sources. Without adequate and diverse funding, an institution may be forced to cater to the interests and ideologies of the donors or be perceived as doing so thereby undermining the integrity of research products. Sustainable funding is an especially serious challenge in much of the Global South, where funding options are limited and likely to come from less diversified sources.

As think tanks proliferate and increase in strength and influence on the world stage, a key challenge is to measure their effectiveness and impact. As political gridlock deepens, some scholars have called into question the effectiveness of think tanks, moving away from analysis and towards lobbying for their own interests and those of their donors. This issue reflects the increased presence of think tanks and policy networks, many of which are moving away from the distant and traditional passive stance toward advocacy. The most successful global think tanks are single-issue and nonpartisan think tanks.

The necessity to invest in larger, worldwide issues serves as a check against ideological bias; it can serve to prevent global think tanks from catering to their donors. This chapter has detailed the valuable role of think tanks in addressing democratic transitions as well as environmental, global health, and financial problems. As more issues, actors, competition, and conflict are on their agenda, global think tanks and policy networks will be increasingly relevant for policymakers managing a changing world order. However, if nativism and extreme nationalism continue—spurred by Brexit and the election of Donald Trump in the United States—the influence of global think tanks could wane as partisan "facts" come to the fore.

Think tanks and policy networks have grown in both scope and depth, especially during the last quarter-century. Such non-state actors play an essential role in moderating debate, generating advice, and influencing policymakers. They have a vast reservoir of knowledge, information, and energy that, if harnessed properly, will improve global public goods and global governance.

Additional reading

James G. McGann, *The Fifth Estate: Think Tanks, Public Policy, and Governance* (Washington, DC: Brookings Institution, 2016).

James G. McGann and Richard Sabatini, *Global Think Tanks: Policy Networks and Governance* (New York: Routledge, 2011).

James G. McGann, Anna Viden, and Jillian Rafferty, eds., *How Think Tanks Shape Social Development Policies* (Philadelphia: University of Pennsylvania Press, 2014).

David Shambaugh, "China's International Relations Think Tanks: Evolving Structure and Process," *China Quarterly* 171 (2002): 575–596.

Diane Stone, "Global Public Policy, Transnational Policy Communities, and Their Networks," *Policy Studies Journal* 36, no. 1 (2008): 19–38.

Diane Stone, "The Group of 20 Transnational Policy Community: Governance Networks, Policy Analysis and Think Tanks," *International Review of Administrative Science* 81, no. 4 (2015): 793–811.

Raymond J. Struyk, "Management of Transnational Think Tank Networks," *International Journal of Politics, Culture, and Society* 15, no. 4 (2002): 625–638.

Notes

1 James G. McGann, "Think Tanks and the Transnationalization of Foreign Policy," *U.S. Foreign Policy Agenda* 7, no. 3 (2002): 5–8.

2 James G. McGann and Richard Sabatini, *Global Think Tanks: Policy Networks and Governance* (New York: Routledge, 2011).

3 Roland D. Asmus, "The Role of Think Tanks in U.S. Foreign Policy," *U.S. Foreign Policy Agenda* 7, no. 3 (2004): 29–31.

4 Diane Stone, "Knowledge Networks and Global Policy," in *Global Knowledge Networks and International Development*, eds. Simon Maxwell and Diane L. Stone (New York: Routledge, 2004): 89–105. For funding opportunities, see Julie Kosterlitz, "Going Global," *National Journal* (29 September 2007), 67; Jan Martin Witte, Wolfgang H. Reinicke, and Thorsten Benner, "Global Public Policy Networks: Lessons Learned and Challenges Ahead," *Brookings Review* 21, no. 2 (2003): 18–21.

5 Raymond J. Struyk, "Management of Transnational Think Tank Networks," *International Journal of Politics, Culture, and Society* 15, no. 4 (2002): 625–638.

6 James G. McGann, "The Global Go-To Think Tanks: What Works Where?" Overseas Development Institute, 10 March 2009.

7 Raymond J. Struyk, "Management of Transnational Think Tank Networks," *International Journal of Politics, Culture, and Society* 15, no. 4 (2002): 625–638; Stella Theodoulous, *Policy and Politics in Six Nations: A Comparative Perspective on Policy Making* (Boston, MA: Pearson, 2001); Ines Selvood and Vanesa Weyrauch, *Weaving Global Networks: Handbook for Policy Influence* (Buenos Aires: Fundación CIPPEC, 2007); James G. McGann with Richard Sabatini, *"Global Think Tanks: Policy Networks and Governance* (New York: Routledge, 2011).

8 Charlotte Streck, "The Role of Global Public Policy Networks in Supporting Institutions: Implications for Trade and Sustainable Development," Institute for International and European Environmental Policy, 23 June 2009, www.agro-montpellier.fr/sustra/research_themes/global_governance/papers/Charlotte_Stre ck.pdf.

9 Struyk, "Management of Transnational Think Tank Networks," 627.

10 Streck, "The Role of Global Public Policy Networks in Supporting Institutions," 2009.

11 Richard N. Haass, "Think Tanks and US Foreign Policy: A Policy-Maker's Perspective," *U.S. Foreign Policy Agenda* 7, no. 3 (2002): 5–8.

12 Diane Stone, "Transfer Agents and Global Networks in the 'Transnationalization' of Policy," *Journal of European Public Policy* 11, no. 3 (2004): 560.

13 David M. Malone and Heiko Nitzschke, "Think Tanks and the United Nations," *Magazine for Development and Cooperation*, Jan. 2004.

14 Stone, "Knowledge Networks and Global Policy," 13.

15 Diane Stone, "Think Tanks and Policy Advice in Countries in Transition," in *How to Strengthen Policy-Oriented Research and Training in Viet Nam*, ed. Asian Development Bank Institute Symposium, Hanoi, 31 August 2005.

Global philanthropy

Michael Moran

The Rockefeller Foundation, established a century ago, was one of the earliest modern non-state actors to exert its influence on the institutional structures that emerged in the early to mid-twentieth century to govern international development. Its material resources and deep and extensive networks into domestic and international politics, among other factors, made it one of the most formidable players in the development of the nascent international aid architecture. While there are now over 80,000 grantmaking foundations registered in the United States, an expanding sector in Europe, and embryonic but growing development in East Asia, the number of foundations with substantive international activities is comparatively small. They remain dwarfed in numbers by transnational corporations, international nongovernmental organizations (INGOs), and the resources of official development assistance agencies and international organizations. Still, actors such as the Bill and Melinda Gates Foundation (hereafter the Gates Foundation), as with the Rockefeller and the Ford Foundations before it, while lacking formal authority (and legitimacy), can command significant influence by virtue of their material resources and role in nurturing, developing, structuring, and shaping international public policy.

At the same time, new types of philanthropic actors, for example the Acumen Fund, are growing in importance, bringing with them a focus on cultivating social enterprise in developing states. In contrast to the Acumen Fund, which is structured as a nonprofit, other new actors, such as Omidyar Network, avoid the nonprofit form. What unites these actors is focus on moving away from grantmaking toward social impact investment—providing investments that generate both a social and financial return.

Collectively these trends have contributed to a shift in the global governance of development—or what can be described as the "philanthrocapitalist" turn. Controversially, this has led to creeping marketization of philanthropy. It also reveals tensions that have long accompanied "big" philanthropy: the power of the wealthy to shape public policy; concerns regarding the accountability and legitimacy of private actors; and the type of development interventions favored by foundations, which, according to some critics, have tended toward the top down and technical (and more recently the market oriented) at the expense of the social and the political. These tensions have resurfaced in recent years, with the ever present Gates Foundation extending its influence and the "new philanthropy" altering the dynamics of international development.

BOX 29.1 WHAT ARE PRIVATE FOUNDATIONS?

Private foundations are the most common institutional form in global philanthropy and remain the principal philanthropic actors within global governance. While the term varies across different regions, a private foundation is defined by five features: (1) nonprofit and nongovernmental status; (2) tax exemption; (3) a board of trustees/ directors; (4) an endowment and/or fund capitalized by a single individual, institution, or family; and (5) distribution of funds, principally through grants, for charitable, educational, or religious purposes.[1] In the US, they are registered as tax-exempt organizations under 501(c)(3) of the tax code and precluded by the Internal Revenue Service from directly operating programs or undertaking service delivery. Instead, they typically act as *intermediaries* between their funders (individual and/or institutional) and recipients (usually but not exclusively nonprofits and state agencies) in order to obtain defined charitable goals.

How much do they give?

Despite an increasingly high profile, giving by foundations from the US remains principally domestically focused. The numbers, however, are not small and the peak body for research on philanthropy in the US notes that while international grantmaking is dominated by a relatively small number of large funders, in 2012 these funders distributed nearly 27% of total foundation grants (domestic and international) to international causes.[2] In 2014 US grantmaking foundations gave $6.9bn to international causes, of which $4.7bn was directly to developing countries.[3] This constituted 11% of private giving from the US.[4] The Gates Foundation is by far the largest funder. In 2014 it gave approximately $3.2bn to international causes including global development ($1.9bn); global health ($1.4bn) and global policy and advocacy ($200m).[5] While the Gates Foundation total includes grants to US-based organizations with a development focus as well as other recipients in the developed world, the $3.2bn figure places it just outside the top ten rich countries on the OECD's development assistance committee for 2014. The next largest funder was the Ford Foundation, which gave $138m in grants outside the US in 2016. However, the Foundation Center observes that "as the many thousands of

continued

newer foundations established by younger, more globally focused foundations come of age, the number of foundations that incorporate an international focus in their work will undoubtedly continue to grow".[6]

1 Foundation Center, "Foundations Today," http://foundationcenter.org/getstarted/tutorials/ft_tutorial/what.html.
2 Foundation Center, *Key Facts on U.S. Foundations: 2014 Edition* (New York: Foundation Center, 2014), 6.
3 The Center for Global Prosperity, *Index of Global Philanthropy and Remittances 2016* (Washington, DC: Hudson Institute, 2017), 34.
4 The Center for Global Prosperity, *Index of Global Philanthropy and Remittances 2016*, 35.
5 The Bill & Melinda Gates Foundation, *Annual Report 2014* (Seattle: Bill & Melinda Gates Foundation, 2014).
6 Foundation Center, *Key Facts on U.S. Foundations: 2014 Edition* (New York: Foundation Center, 2014), 6.

This chapter begins by charting the activities of foundations in the interwar era through to the present via an examination of areas in which private foundations have been most active. The subsequent section examines key criticisms and controversies before the chapter moves to providing a brief overview of emerging issues and future trends in global philanthropy.

Private foundations: From international organization to global governance

Foundations surfaced in the late nineteenth and early twentieth centuries during what was known in the United States as the "Progressive Era"; they were by and large a product of the country's rapid industrialization and emergence as a center of production, consumption, and population growth. The American tradition was driven by wealthy businessmen, known popularly as the "robber barons," who were encouraged by Scottish-born industrialist Andrew Carnegie to distinguish their giving from charity. They argued that conventional charity was ameliorative, while philanthropy should tackle the root causes of deprivation. This was premised on a belief that scientific reason would fuel progress, and rationality became "the guiding principle for grant-making once new foundations were chartered."[1] The term *scientific philanthropy* was coined to describe this philosophy, which fused with a range of concurrent ideas, including the liberal internationalism espoused by President Woodrow Wilson, the positivism of the Progressive Era, established American Protestant and Calvinist beliefs, and the associated emphasis on self-help and self-reliance.

The domestic orientation of many foundations notwithstanding, they emerged as some of the most important international actors of this period. Indeed, prior to the emergence of official development assistance as a mainstream function of foreign policy of the industrialized states and the establishment of the major international organizations, foundations were some of the most well-resourced and influential actors in international affairs. This was particularly pronounced in the first decades of the twentieth century, in which the United States exhibited an isolationist approach to foreign policy.

Public health was the first area in which foundations became significant players internationally. The focus on health can be traced to the early programs of the Rockefeller Foundation, which had three major components. First, the Foundation played a significant role in the development of medical education and physician training. Its programs began in the United States with, among other things, the creation of medical schools, including the fledging Johns Hopkins University, which was used as a laboratory for "transforming medicine through a closer association with science."[2] In 1914 the focus was extended to China, with the founding of the China Medical Board and the Peking University Medical College, the objective of which was to extend Western-style medical education and disseminate Western approaches to public health into the developing world.

Second, the Rockefeller Foundation sought to combat communicable diseases, "single-handedly creat[ing] American tropical medicine research"[3] by confronting three diseases in consecutive order: Hookworm, yellow fever, and malaria. The hookworm program began first and grew out of the work of the Rockefeller Sanitary Commission in the United States, and was initially extended to Mexico. The Foundation then instigated a yellow fever campaign that expanded the Foundation's reach into South America and then Africa, ending in the development of a vaccine. Finally, attention was turned to malaria and to the eventual eradication of the disease in many regions of the world.

Third, the foundation played a seminal role in the early expansion of the international health architecture, providing substantial financial and in-kind support for the League of Nations Health Organization (LNHO) and backing for its successor, the World Health Organization (WHO). The foundation contributed almost half the LNHO's fiscal needs, while also giving technical assistance and making "its own staff available for special purposes."[4] While not a model of success due to its short-lived mandate, Rockefeller's support for a nascent international institution—the LNHO—played a vital role in linking weak domestic health systems with rapidly improving international standards.[5]

Similar approaches were replicated in agriculture in perhaps the most celebrated (and controversial) foundation-initiated project, the "Green Revolution." Like public health, this also began as an intervention in the nearest and strategically significant southern neighbor, Mexico, and in a context of strained interstate relations between the two countries. Acting at the request of the US government, concerned that shortfalls in staple crops were causing food shortages, which was, in turn, leading to political and social instability, the Rockefeller Foundation, in direct partnership with the Mexican government, instigated a program to develop high-yield varieties. The objective was to replicate the advances that had occurred in industrialized states in staple crops, notably wheat, by using a combination of inorganic pesticides, fertilizers, and selective plant breeding to increase yields per hectare. To achieve this goal, Rockefeller created the Office of Special Studies within the Mexican Ministry of Agriculture; established experimental stations across the country; and trained agricultural scientists, with a series of scholarships, training facilities, and international exchanges to transfer Western scientific knowledge to newly industrializing Mexico.

The program was perceived by its supporters to be a success. Mexico went from being a net importer of wheat in the early 1940s to a net exporter within less than a generation, despite a dramatic increase in population.[6] Efforts were made to replicate the program in other national contexts, including Colombia, Chile, India, and the Philippines, in partnership with the Ford Foundation. In 1960, Rockefeller and Ford collaborated with the Filipino government to establish the International Rice Research Institute.

The chief objective was to apply rapidly evolving gene technologies to the Asian region,[7] which was expected to reach a state of food crisis by the mid-1960s, with

---

BOX 29.2 FOUNDATIONS AND INTERNATIONAL RELATIONS THEORY

Foundations have played a role not only in international relations, but also in the development of international relations theory, providing significant individual and institutional support to scholars and fostering research communities. The Ford Foundation, for example, is acknowledged as one of the chief protagonists in the shift toward behavioralism in American political science that began in the 1950s. While this did not initially emerge as the dominant mode of inquiry in IR, it had later ramifications with the drift of rationalism and public choice into American IR. In contrast, the Rockefeller Foundation, under the leadership of Kenneth Thompson, a classical realist scholar and student of Hans Morgenthau, took a different tack, favoring realism and "theory" over the new empirics. To this end the Rockefeller Foundation in 1954 organized the apparently shambolic but nonetheless influential Conference on International Politics. In attendance were luminaries including Hans Morgenthau, Reinhold Niebuhr, Paul H. Nitze, Walter Lippman, and Arnold Wolfers; a young Kenneth Waltz was note taker. While the conference did not achieve its ambitious aims, Guilhot credits Thompson as central in establishing his mentor Morgenthau as a key figure in the emerging field as well as in IR's (and realism's) ascendency in the post-war era as a discipline distinct from the more empiricist political science.[1] On the other side of the Atlantic, Rockefeller also funded the British Committee on International Relations, whose members included, among others, Herbert Butterfield, Martin Wight, and Hedley Bull, laying the basis for the English School of IR.

1 Nicolas Guilhot, "Introduction: One Discipline, Many Histories," in *The Invention of International Relations Theory: Realism, the Rockefeller Foundation, and the 1954 Conference on Theory*, ed. Nicolas Guilhot (New York: Columbia University Press, 2011), 15.

widespread famine predicted should productivity not improve. The broader intervention was therefore framed as an "emergency" and was extended to the Indian subcontinent, which had experienced famine with increasing frequency, to the point that some commentators now, somewhat ominously, saw it as a "natural" product of "population pressure."[8] The early successes in Mexico were repeated and, at least in aggregate terms, the project's extension to Asia succeeded in dramatically lifting food production, although this was not evenly spread.

Although technical, the programs nonetheless required significant interagency coordination and were as much a suite of agricultural development policies as an apolitical project designed to enhance agricultural productivity. After developing these *national* programs, concurrently with the project's spread into Asia, Rockefeller and Ford *internationalized* the Green Revolution and, in partnership with governmental and intergovernmental bodies, established the Centro Internacional de Mejoramiento de Maíz y Trigo, and the umbrella Consultative Group on International Agricultural Research, which formed the backbone of a global network of agricultural research institutes. This international architecture remains operational today and continues to be the primary institutional hub for agricultural research across the Global South, a lasting legacy of foundation activity.

Foundations in global governance: Advocacy networks and public–private partnerships

Congressional scrutiny, shifting granting priorities, and global recession had an adverse impact on endowments and led foundations to enter a period of relative caution in their international activities in the 1970s. The international system was also radically changed. New state, intergovernmental, and non-state actors, for example the United States Agency for International Development (USAID), the international finance institutions such as the World Bank, and development NGOs, had emerged as important players and the relative importance of the major foundations waned. Additionally international philanthropy remained a comparatively small component of the otherwise rapidly growing development finance mix. For instance, in 1982, international grants comprised less than five percent of all US foundation grants, with international philanthropy dominated by Rockefeller and Ford, whose grants between 1975 and 1995 comprised almost half of all grants given by the largest fifty foundations.[9] Nonetheless, with the rise of new foundations in the 1990s from the burgeoning technology and finance industries, the sector began to diversify.

With the Green Revolution under way and supported by the Consultative Group on International Agricultural Research network, the Ford Foundation moved away from agriculture. Building on earlier support for the civil rights and new social movements of 1960s' America, which had attracted some controversy from conservatives as well as the Ford family, in the 1970s the Foundation shifted its focus to civil society development and democratization abroad, a process that began with funding of human rights organizations in Latin America. After employees in its social science program identified threats to academic freedom from authoritarian regimes, they managed, despite resistance from USAID and some internal wrangling, to engender a shift toward funding "activist human rights groups" and dissidents.[10]

This acted as a catalyst for the dissemination of human rights norms throughout Latin America and by the 1980s the foundation's influence extended across the whole gamut of transnational human rights networks: From antiapartheid to women's rights. Ultimately the Ford Foundation became "the principal funder of almost all major human-rights NGOs," including Helsinki Watch, the forerunner to Human Rights Watch.[11] The foundation was therefore integral in financing what Margaret Keck and Kathryn Sikkink would later term "transnational advocacy networks"—intrinsically economical, albeit powerful, modes of political advocacy, but nonetheless modes of actions in which the primary non-state actors—international and domestic NGOs and social movements—are often dependent on external funding. Foundations, particularly MacArthur and Ford, performed an integral pecuniary function in this respect.

While the Rockefeller Foundation's priorities also became increasingly diverse, perhaps its most important contribution to global governance occurred in the 1990s, when it acted as a catalyst for the development of global health partnerships. Specifically it became one of the central players behind product development partnerships (PDPs) for tackling neglected and communicable diseases that disproportionately impact poor communities in the Global South. From the 1970s onwards, the Rockefeller Foundation remained one of the few funders of basic research into such diseases, as rich country governments as well as the transnational pharmaceutical companies that had become integral players in the political economy of drug development shifted funding toward diseases of lifestyle, such as diabetes and cancer, predominantly affecting the rich world. By the late 1980s the dearth of funding for tropical diseases such as malaria through to neglected diseases such as dengue fever was at crisis level. In response, the foundation, along with a range of other players in the emerging global health community—which coalesced around a range of NGOs and international organizations, including the WHO, the World Bank, Médecins sans Frontières, the International Federation of Pharmaceutical Manufacturers and Associations, as well various European and North American official development assistance agencies—determined that new institutional and policy responses were required to tackle the crisis and both stimulate research and development (R&D) into these diseases as well as develop financing mechanisms to ensure their distribution to those in need.

Work toward this was facilitated by a number of critical meetings at Rockefeller's Bellagio Center in Northern Italy, as well as in New York, during which the foundation and its partners focused on tackling the lack of support for an HIV/AIDS vaccine.[12] What emerged was the International AIDS Vaccine Initiative, which became one of the first PDPs to bring together public, civic, and private actors in a partnership to incentivize pro-poor product development. Between 1994 and 2000 the Rockefeller Foundation provided seed funding and in-kind support to incubate a further four global health partnerships, including the Global Alliance for TB Drug Development (TB Alliance), the International Partnership for Microbicides, the Pediatric Dengue Vaccine Initiative, and the Centre for the Management of Intellectual Property in Health R&D, as well as lent its support to the Global Call to Stop Cervical

Cancer. While the success of PDPs has been mixed, they nonetheless played a role in reshaping global governance and show how foundations can act as important players in influencing policy outcomes.

Yet, while the Rockefeller Foundation punched above its weight, as it no longer commanded the resources of earlier epochs, the most influential philanthropic actor in contemporary global health is, without doubt, the Gates Foundation—a private actor whose material influence remains unparalleled in global governance. The emergence of the Gates Foundation has been as rapid as it has been transformational, but its rise also coincided with global health partnerships, to which it quickly attached itself in the early 2000s. Following the lead of its intellectual and institutional antecedent, the Rockefeller Foundation, Gates became the major funder of almost all PDPs.

Nonetheless, the grants with perhaps the most far reaching implications for global health governance have been the Gates Foundation's $750 million to launch the GAVI Alliance in 2000 and an equal commitment in 2002 for the Global Fund to Fight AIDS, Tuberculosis and Malaria (hereafter the Global Fund). GAVI is a health partnership that brings together the major bilateral donors, recipient countries, the WHO, the World Bank, UNICEF, the pharmaceutical industry, and Gates, in a multisectoral partnership to finance and facilitate vaccine coverage—for example diphtheria, hepatitis B, and yellow fever, etc.—to the poorest regions of the globe. It was established as a response to the diminishing effectiveness of earlier multilateral initiatives and the abrupt arrival of Gates funds. The Global Fund brings together these same actors with a focus on extending prevention and treatment for the big three communicable diseases: AIDS, tuberculosis, and malaria. Since they were established the two partnerships have emerged as critical players in the governance of global health, and along with the Gates Foundation are part of the informal grouping, the Health 8, in which they, along with the health-related international organizations (World Bank, WHO, UNAIDS, etc.), meet to lobby for, and coordinate, global health aid.

There are three noteworthy features of these funds that illustrate the behaviors of foundations as transnational actors as well as wider shifts within global governance. First, while they retain the trappings of conventional international organizations, including a large staff, secretariat, and regionally based offices, they are not considered institutions, but public–private partnerships that sit outside intergovernmental structures and, although intertwined, outside the UN system. This organizational structure has been adopted to differentiate them from existing UN bodies seen as bound by bureaucratic inertia and institutional inefficiencies.

Second, in contrast to most international organizations, with a few notable exceptions such as the International Labour Organization (ILO), they operate a hybrid governance framework that vests significant decision-making power in private actors, including the Gates Foundation, which has a renewable seat alongside traditional international organizations such as the WHO, as well as on advisory committees.

Third, there is a strong emphasis on adopting private sector approaches and, in alignment with GAVI's original mission, acting as a "businesslike partnership for health aid." It has changed its mission but describes its "unique public–private business model" as its defining feature. For example, GAVI's "business model" leverages the competences of the alliance's partners to pool demand; facilitate long-term funding; to shape vaccine markets; and ultimately improve access to vaccines. This model echoes the approach of earlier eras in which foundations can be seen as some earliest brokers of cross-sectoral partnerships. It also represents a shift from focusing primarily on building the capacity of state actors to nongovernmental actors (including business).

These three attributes are innately connected to the Gates Foundation's initial provision of philanthropic risk capital that seeded the partnership, with its continuing support reaffirmed in mid-2015 when the Gates Foundation committed another $1.55 billion, bringing its total commitment to $4.1 billion to GAVI [13] and approximately $1.7 billion to the Global Fund since the initial seed grant.[14]

Controversies and criticisms

Despite its benevolent meaning—from the Greek "love of humankind"—philanthropy is not without controversy. In the field of international relations in particular, philanthropy has been the subject of periodic scrutiny that spikes during periods in which foundation influence is seen as significant, or indeed excessive. The main critiques can usefully be discussed under three headings: Northern dominance, legitimacy and accountability, and technical and market orientation.

"Billanthropy," soft power, and Northern influence

Philanthropy is an act that virtually everyone participates in, whether it takes the form of volunteering or cash donations to charitable causes. Yet few have the resources to influence public policy, let alone international public policy. Unsurprisingly, then, perhaps the most frequent and enduring criticism pertains to the perception that philanthropy accords some institutions—and individuals—undue and sometimes unchecked power.

Recently these concerns have been underlined by the growth of "billanthropy" or "philanthrocapitalism" and the rise of a generation of often highly engaged billionaire philanthropists who have scaled up their philanthropic activities. Examples range from financier George Soros' extensive network of civil society-building organizations through the Open Society Institutes to the influence that Bill, Melinda, Bill Sr., and Warren Buffett exert through the comparatively lean governing board that comprises the Gates Foundation. While few question the humanitarian intention behind these efforts, there is concern among some commentators that big philanthropy can accord a select group agenda-setting power in international public policy that is at worst inconsistent with democratic values or at best contra to participative policy processes.[15]

These are not new arguments. Taking a cue from the work of Antonio Gramsci, scholars have long linked this exercise of elite power with the consolidation of hegemony. Certain initiatives, such as the Green Revolution were viewed by critics within the context of the Cold War, with some seeing foundations as acting as a surrogate or proxy for the US government. These interventions, it is asserted, assisted in shoring up capitalism as well extending US "soft power" and nurturing a favorable image for the ascendant hegemon.[16]

More recent research and commentary has highlighted the influence of the Gates Foundation in global health governance. For example, over the past decade it has become the second largest donor to the WHO after the United States, contributing approximately one-quarter of its annual budget.[17] As Sophie Harman has observed, donations by public or private actors can be allocated at donor discretion to specified priorities.[18] As the relative weight of state-based and voluntary donations has shifted in the latter's favor, it is argued that this shift has increased the agenda-setting influence of the Gates Foundation's influence in the key institutional organ in global health.

Related criticisms have focused on foundations' role in the continuing dominance of global health by the North. For example, the Gates Foundation's grantmaking practices have been scrutinized. David McCoy and colleagues have identified an apparent bias to North American and European-based research institutes, international organizations and INGOs, as well as increasingly Northern-based and dominated public–private partnerships.[19] Whether intended or not—grantmaking may reproduce geographies of wealth and the scientific research infrastructure in the North—grantmaking patterns of foundations do appear to exhibit an intrinsic bias for actors who share foundations' geographic origin. When combined with the Gates Foundation's influence through the global health partnerships referenced above it plays a central role in international health policy outcomes—but without the legitimacy of other actors.[20]

Legitimacy and accountability

Underlying these concerns is another common criticism, namely that foundations suffer from a legitimacy deficit and lack adequate accountability. As with other private actors, foundations lack the claim to legitimacy that democratic states derive from electoral processes as well as the periodic accountability of the ballot box. International organizations, also the subject of anxiety associated with a perceived democratic deficit, nonetheless derive some forms of legitimacy from a type of "popular sovereignty" that is delegated to them by member states; they are, in theory, also accountable to their members through voting mechanisms and budgetary allocations. Even firms are accountable to their stockholders when publicly listed and also subject to the discipline of market forces, which acts as a constraint on their behavior, as well as remaining targets for public scrutiny when they partake in activities seen to exert influence on international public policy. These act as a check on their power, albeit an imperfect and limited one. INGOs are also occasionally seen as lacking legitimacy but remain accountable to their donors (including individuals, foundations, and states) and can derive legitimacy from their loose association with social movements and civil society when they are community driven, grassroots, and participative.

The perceived legitimacy deficit of foundations is compounded by the existence of a perpetual endowment—or with a limited-life foundation a defined but generally very large pool of capital—that relieves foundations of the financial pressures that affect and check other actors in global governance. Moreover, philanthropists almost always acquire a tax benefit from their donations, which means that their capital is, in effect, public monies as it is forgone taxation. Therefore, foundations have an obligation for both accountable and transparent use of funds.

Technical and market-oriented interventions

Another criticism that is often leveled at foundations pertains to their approach to development activities, which some critics deem to be overly technical in focus, top down in orientation, and increasingly market oriented. The technical focus is generally portrayed as a legacy of philanthropy's emergence in the Progressive Era when confidence in the ability for science to resolve complex social problems was at a high point. Despite foundations gradually moving toward more participatory approaches in line with broader trends in development assistance, the tradition has remained fairly resilient. The global health partnerships above are a case in point. They operate as what are known in development policymaking circles as "vertical funds," with a focus on attainment of narrow sectoral goals. Health partnerships, for instance, are often disease-specific, highly targeted funding mechanisms, with tightly measurable objectives. This contrasts with "horizontal" health financing, in which aid is channeled directly through primary-care systems. Critics assert that global health partnerships do not always focus sufficiently on strengthening health systems or on building local capacity. These criticisms are extended to other like modalities, for example in agriculture, which are also seen to be overly technical and to be operating in a relative social and political vacuum.

More pointed criticism concerns two levels of the increasing market orientation of the major foundation-financed projects with relevance for global governance.[21] At the organizational level, the private sector disposition of funders is said to extend to the institutional culture of organs established by foundations. From this perspective, a results orientation, a focus on performance measurement, and a businesslike disposition are seen as a donor-driven process. At the broader structural or system level, this is seen as advancing an, albeit moderated, form of neoliberal global governance. Evidence can be found in the prevalence of market mechanisms for financing public goods such as vaccines through, for example, the GAVI Alliance or emulating private sector practices for product development in PDPs.

BOX 29.3 THE NEW GLOBAL PHILANTHROPY

The past decade has seen a perceptible internationalization and marketization of philanthropy. New organizational types, modes, and vehicles for philanthropy, as well as new philanthropists, from celebrities such as U2's Bono through to former politicians such as Bill Clinton, have emerged as important actors in development finance. These changes have affected the major foundations, which have, to varying degrees, both adapted to and at times driven these sectoral shifts. The most significant developments are occurring among entities, primarily with linkages to the technology sector in California's Silicon Valley and, to a lesser extent, global finance.

New organizational types

New funders have emerged that are defined by an emphasis on technology and entrepreneurialism.[1] Often they select former private sector employees over nonprofit managers in leadership roles (not just as trustees); have a heavy focus on program evaluation, particularly quantitative-based metrics; increasingly use social impact investment strategies, that utilize the endowment for debt and equity investments, and are high engagement, preferring deep, rather than passive, interaction with grantees (or so-called "investees"). Foundations, for example the Skoll Foundation, funded by former eBay CEO Jeff Skoll, and venture philanthropy funds, such as the Acumen Fund, are exemplars of this organizational type. Other variations on this model include eBay founder Pierre Omidyar's Omidyar Network and the Chan Zuckerberg Initiative, established by Facebook co-founder, Mark Zuckerberg, and his physician wife, Patricia Chan. Neither of these entities has taken the traditional nonprofit form of private foundations or charitable entities. Instead the Omidyar Network is a hybrid—consisting of a 501(c)(3) that like a traditional foundation makes grants—and a limited liability company (LLC)—that invests in for-profit entities with a social environmental mission. The Chan Zuckerberg Initiative has opted to follow the LLC path thus opening a path to investment in for-profits, engaging in political activities such as lobbying, and without the disclosure requirements of nonprofits. At this stage, little is known about how the Initiative will integrate into global governance but it points to a shift among philanthropists toward for-profit forms and strategies.

What they fund

These organizations channel resources toward social entrepreneurship and; extending the sectoral blending that characterizes more traditional partnerships, while blurring the increasingly fuzzy lines between nonprofit and for-profit models. Early examples include microfinance schemes, originally developed by Muhammad Yunus, which extend financial services, principally credit, to individuals and firms that struggle accessing capital. Although an established poverty reduction tool, supported by traditional foundations such as Ford, which was an early backer of Yunus, foundations and philanthropists increasingly invest in large microfinance funds, which mediate capital from rich world investors to developing world borrowers. At the other end of the scale are peer-to-peer lending organizations, for example Kiva.org, which facilitates direct small-scale lending between individuals, usually in the rich world, to other individuals, usually in the developing world.

Other examples include the proliferation of activity at the base of the pyramid (BoP) by social venture funds. Although heavily contested, the BoP concept posits that there

continued

is a largely untapped market among the world's 2.5 billion poorest people who subsist on less than $2 a day and are overlooked by mainstream firms. Instead of tackling poverty through, for example, providing cash grants for the construction of a water well, social venture funds, such as the Acumen Fund or Root Capital, finance businesses that provide essential products and services—housing, clean water, health care, etc.—to the poor. This is part of a broader shift from the provision of grants with no expected return, to the use of investments, in which return is generally below that which would normally be expected or market related, but in which investors receive a compensatory social return.

1 Raj M. Desai and Homi Kharas, "The California Consensus: Can Private Aid End Global Poverty?" *Survival* 50, no. 4 (2008): 155–168.

Are these criticisms warranted?

Despite well-founded concerns, there is a tendency to overstate foundation power in three ways. First, foundations as actors in global governance have structural limitations, which are often overlooked. Grantmakers are legally precluded from delivering programs, which renders foundations highly dependent on other actors: They must "work through third parties . . . through grant-making," acting as "facilitators rather than operators."[22] Consequently, despite foundations remaining, in theory at least, one of the most flexible organizational forms in contemporary global governance, they are constrained by their function as grantmakers, which often act as funders of networked-type arrangements. Foundations are therefore highly dependent on other actors to attain their goals, which constrains and limits their influence, sometimes to the provision of funds.

Second, as with other aspects of global governance, relational and structural imbalances are pervasive, and certain actors (for example, foundations) without doubt retain a privileged position within decision-making processes. Nonetheless, collaborative governance arrangements (for example, partnerships) are also sites of diffuse power in which influence is dispersed. Moreover, foundations are often dependent on the intelligence and field knowledge of partner entities for new ideas, projects, and field knowledge. Therefore because of a combination of limits on staff, the need to be across diverse areas of technical specialization, and the need for innovative ideas, foundations are arguably as dependent on demand-side actors (for example, INGOs) as demand-side actors are on foundation resources.

Third, obvious questions remain for the accountability and legitimacy of states and international organizations.[23] Moreover, while foundations lack the *input* or procedural legitimacy of public actors for the reasons sketched above, that deficiency may arguably be offset through *output* legitimacy or their efficacy in problem resolution.[24] Indeed, concerns regarding the criticisms of foundations sometimes seem inflated, particularly if contrasted with other private actors, as foundations are subject to the same domestic regulatory, legal, and governance requirements as INGOs, as well as extraterritorial legislation that keeps a check on their actions.

Conclusion

Private foundations have historically played a significant, if often obscure, part in world politics. While comparatively marginal in relation to many other non-state actors, they have deployed their unique attributes—an endowment and associated financial agency, as well as a close association with actors from across sectors— to exercise influence at important junctures in the development of the institutional architecture. Such influence has been especially obvious during the interwar and early postwar eras, as well as from the 1990s in the period of accelerated globalization.

Not surprisingly, perceived influence has led in turn to upsurges in scrutiny, which can be observed in the literature on the "big" foundations, which during the middle decades of the twentieth century attained almost state-like status in international politics. The Gates Foundation, similarly state like in its scale and influence in global health governance, as well as the growth in philanthropy among private actors and individuals more broadly, has renewed interest in evaluating the mechanics of foundation power. The continuing growth of philanthropy with a global focus shows no sign of diminishing. The new philanthropy point to new directions in philanthropic practice also likely to have significant, although as yet difficult to predict, ramifications for the future of global governance.

Additional reading

Lael Brainard and Derek Chollet, eds., *Global Development 2.0: Can Philanthropists, the Public, and the Poor Make Poverty History?* (Washington, DC: Brookings Institution, 2008).

Michael Edwards, *Small Change: Why Business Won't Save the World* (San Francisco, CA: Berrett-Koehler Publishers, 2010).

Nicolas Guilhot, ed., *The Invention of International Relations Theory: Realism, the Rockefeller Foundation, and the 1954 Conference on Theory* (New York: Columbia University Press, 2011).

Linsey McGoey, *No Such Thing as a Free Gift: The Gates Foundation and the Price of Philanthropy* (London: Verso, 2015).

Michael Moran, *Private Foundations and Development Partnerships: American Philanthropy and Global Development Agendas* (London: Routledge, 2017).

Inderjeet Parmar, *Foundations of the American Century: Ford, Carnegie, and Rockefeller Foundations in the Rise of American Power* (New York: Columbia University Press, 2012).

Notes

1 Barbara Howe, "The Emergence of Scientific Philanthropy, 1900–1920: Origins, Issues and Outcomes," in *Philanthropy and Cultural Imperialism: The Foundations at Home and Abroad,* ed. Robert Arnove (Boston, MA: G. K. Hall & Co., 1980), 33.

2 Ann Westmore and David Penington, "Courting the Rockefeller Foundation and Other Attempts to Integrate Clinical Teaching, Medical Practice, and Research in Melbourne," *Health and History* 11, no. 2 (2009): 63.

3 Peter J. Hotez, "Vaccines as Instruments of Foreign Policy," *Science and Society* 2, no. 10 (2001): 862.

4 Kelly Loughlin and Virginia Berridge, *Historical Dimensions of Global Health Governance* (Geneva: World Health Organization, 2002).

5 Paul Weindling, "Philanthropy and World Health: The Rockefeller Foundation and the League of Nations Health Organisation," *Minerva* 35, no. 3 (1997): 269–281.

6 Kenneth W. Thompson, "The Green Revolution: Leadership and Partnership in Agriculture," *Review of Politics* 34, no. 2 (1972): 174–189.

7 Norman E. Borlaug, "Sixty-Two Years of Fighting Hunger: Personal Recollections," *Euphytica* 157, no. 3 (2007): 292.

8 Eric B. Ross, *The Malthus Factor: Poverty, Politics and Population in Capitalist Development* (London: Zed Books, 1998), 150.

9 Robert W. Herdt, "People, Institutions, and Technology: A Personal View of the Role of Foundations in International Agricultural Research and Development 1960–2010," *Food Policy* 37 no. 2 (2012): 185.

10 Margaret Keck and Kathryn Sikkink, *Activists Beyond Borders: Advocacy Networks in International Politics* (Ithaca, NY: Cornell University Press, 1998), 101.

11 William Korey, *Taking on the World's Repressive Regimes: The Ford Foundation's International Human Rights Policies and Practices* (New York: Palgrave Macmillan, 2007), ix, 93.

12 Michael Moran, "Philanthropic Foundations and Global Health Partnership Formation: The Rockefeller Foundation and IAVI," in *Health for Some: The Political Economy of Global Health Governance*, eds. Sandra J. MacLean, et al. (New York: Palgrave Macmillan, 2009).

13 GAVI Alliance, "Donor Profiles: The Bill & Melinda Gates Foundation," http://www.gavi.org/funding/donor-profiles/bmgf.

14 The Bill & Melinda Gates Foundation, "Grant Database," www.gatesfoundation.org/How-We-Work/Quick-Links/Grants-Database.

15 Michael Edwards, *Just another Emperor? The Myths and Realities of Philanthrocapitalism* (London: Demos/The Young Foundation, 2008).

16 Ross, *The Malthus Factor*.

17 Natalie Hunt and Carmen Paun, "Meet the World's Most Powerful Doctor: Bill Gates," *Politico,* 4 May 2017, www.politico.eu/article/bill-gates-who-most-powerful-doctor.

18 Sophie Harman, "The Bill & Melinda Gates Foundation and Legitimacy in Global Health Governance," *Global Governance* 22, no. 3 (2016): 349–368.

19 David McCoy, et al., "The Bill & Melinda Gates Foundation's Grant-Making Programme for Global Health," *Lancet* 373, no. 9675 (2009): 1645–1653.

20 Natalie Hunt and Carmen Paun, "Meet the World's Most Powerful Doctor: Bill Gates."

21 Linsey McGoey, *No Such Thing as A Free Gift: The Gates Foundation and the Price of Philanthropy* (London: Verso, 2015).

22 Helmut K. Anheier and Siobhan Daly, eds., *The Politics of Foundations: A Comparative Analysis* (London: Routledge, 2006), 160.

23 Simon Rushton and Owain Williams, "Private Actors in Global Health," in *Partnerships and Foundations in Global Health Governance*, eds. S. Rushton and O. Williams (New York: Palgrave Macmillan, 2011), 19.

24 Michael Moran and Michael Stevenson, "Illumination and Innovation: What Philanthropic Foundations Bring to Global Governance," *Global Society* 27, no. 2 (2013): 117–137.

CHAPTER 30

Private military and security companies

Peter J. Hoffman

Private military and security companies (PMSCs) and contractors raise quintessential issues of global governance—they have become both subjects and objects of administration as international organizations endeavor to regulate them and use them as tools to impose order. There is a chicken-and-egg relationship between governance and force; force can be a cornerstone of governance to coerce obedience from those who resist it, and governance can structure the conditions under which force is deployed. In this way, PMSCs can enforce global governance but are also constrained by it. Consequently, an analysis of PMSCs illuminates authority and power in global governance and, where formalized into rules, in international organization.

PMSCs are confounding to conventional, state-based international politics because they underscore not only that non-state actors are influential, but also that the foundations of world order may be grounded in economics and that security can be outsourced. This chapter unpacks this peculiar form of market-based violence, explaining what it is and how it is governed. First, it examines the configuration of economic, military, and political factors that explain the genesis and evolution of PMSCs. Second, it surveys the contemporary characteristics of the private military and security sector, including examples of major companies and the range of customers. Third, it reviews relevant core principles and regulatory schema that shape usage of PMSCs and the behavior of armed contractors. Lastly, it considers the preeminent issues that inform or should inform pivotal debates regarding PMSCs.

From mercenaries to military and security contractors

Private military and security contractors are the most recent iteration of market-based force, and while they possess unique features that distinguish them from other forms of this phenomenon, their origins should be situated with reference to mercenaries. Although most military organizations were oriented toward, if not intrinsically connected to political authorities, mercenaries were not. Indeed, the very term "mercenary" comes from the Latin *mercenarius*, which is rooted in the word *merces*, or "pay or wages," and highlights the prominence of their economic agendas. The lack of political encumbrance allowed these armed actors to sell their skills on the open market, and this position inspired the language associated with independent contractors under modern capitalism; these "lances" were "free" to work for whomever, hence the term "freelancer" in other contexts.

Mercenaries arose due to both military needs and economic logic. First, mercenaries provided crucial capabilities. Producing effective military power is not simply a matter of collective will or organization, but a synergy of manpower, technology, and strategy. Mercenaries furnished the skilled and experienced military labor that has often been in high demand by those who seek to deploy coercion. Second, from an economic point of view, hiring mercenaries was a means of acquiring military power without the costly and time-consuming practice of building and maintaining standing forces. In other words, mercenaries were readymade forces that could be swiftly deployed and then, after military objectives were achieved, dismissed, thereby no longer draining financial resources. Accordingly, there are numerous instances of mercenaries from antiquity to the modern period.

However, starting in the seventeenth century mercenaries began to be displaced because of the ascendance of the state as the supreme source of political governance (i.e., sovereignty) and its role in organizing warfare. States sought a monopoly on the use of force not only to defend against and dispatch opponents but also because supplying security was a primary means of generating revenues (i.e., taxes) and legitimacy. Initially states did not eradicate mercenarism but rather harnessed it to state interests; mercenaries continued to operate but only at the behest of states.[1] For instance, in the fourteenth and fifteenth centuries "military companies" (or mercenary armies) were commonly employed by Italian city-states. There were also "mercantile companies," large commercial enterprises that were authorized by a state to facilitate trade and colonialism, and these entities often contained a military component. Although mercenaries remained a fixture of warfare into the eighteenth century, use of them declined appreciably throughout the nineteenth century, when during the Napoleonic Wars (1803–1815) the model of national armies demonstrated that armed forces composed of citizens and motivated solely by politics could be capable military actors.

In comparison with mercenaries, the benefits of national military forces were viewed as threefold.[2] First, they fought for less money, which was economically advantageous. Second, they were more disciplined in refraining from plunder, which was important to achieving political popularity in conquered areas. Third, they were more dependable because they were far less likely to switch sides purely for economic gain. Therefore, during the remainder of the nineteenth century and into the twentieth, the use of mercenaries dwindled greatly as most states transitioned to citizen-based armies. Furthermore, the concern that mercenaries based within a state might entangle that state in foreign wars also prompted prohibiting the practice. Although mercenarism persisted into the twentieth century, the practice was of minor importance and essentially only by individuals.

In the 1990s a new form of for-profit armed actor came to the fore, private military and security companies. Although rudiments of this sector originated long before the Cold War ended—defense industries providing arms and maintenance, or guards for hire—it was not until after this period that PMSCs coalesced and materialized as significant standalone purveyors of force. The expansion of PMSCs was propelled by factors of supply (providers) and demand (consumers).[3]

On the demand side, states and businesses sought to hire PMSCs for three reasons. First, access to quality military and security personnel, particularly special proficiencies, had been dictated by Cold War rivalries and former colonial powers. Weaker states desired more highly skilled military labor than they themselves produced and businesses sought protection in operating in volatile environments. Moreover, the speed of PMSC deployments is usually much faster. Second, a belief in the efficiency of the market to allocate resources opened the floodgates for the private sector to provide military and security services. The neoliberal school of thought popularized in the 1980s and spread widely in the 1990s, embraced a new public management agenda that called for a reduced role for governments and greater privatization of public goods, including war making and protection.[4] Third, during the 1990s it had become apparent that states were sensitive to, if not outright exhausted by, the political, military, and economic costs associated with the use of force. The "body bag" factor—the political fallout for governments of soldiers killed in missions that they authorized—created political momentum to decrease the exposure of militaries to the dangers of using force when it was not paramount to national security interests. Moreover, given that PMSCs are not government employees, they are not subject to legal restrictions or oversight and usually do not receive the level of scrutiny that soldiers do, thus enabling states to pursue their interests under the political radar and even officially deny responsibility.

With respect to the supply side, corporations and contractors that produce violence also sought to open the marketplace for force, which is usually ascribed to purely a profit motive, as force is a lucrative, non-substitutable commodity. But more than that, for those who have military training but lack other marketable skills, military and security contracting may be the optimal, if not only viable, source of income—this was a position many former soldiers found themselves in during the early 1990s, when following the Cold War many militaries were downsized. The economic benefits and "soldiers of fortune" narrative often receives the most attention but contractors also may have ideological grounds for selling their wares. Contractors may sympathize or identify with the ideas of the party that hires them. In short, PMSCs fight not just for pay; they also frequently fight for politics.

The organizational and functional elements of PMSCs resemble the military and mercantile companies of the medieval and early modern periods more than the individual and bands of mercenaries that endured into the twentieth century. These new entities are organized as formal corporations—they have or seek legal standing as legitimate businesses. Furthermore, while some PMSCs are like their predecessors in being directly involved in the production of violence, others play a more indirect role by encouraging, facilitating, and enabling.

The label "PMSC" has been applied to various firms with a wide assortment of services; three basic types can be seen, although many companies often provide a combination of services. First, military and security forces require considerable infrastructure and mission support activities to carry out their operations and this type of PMSC furnishes these vital underpinnings. The work of PMSCs that offer support and supply logistics includes serving meals, doing laundry, providing transportation, building bases, and engineering. A good example of this sort of PMSC is KBR, which builds military bases and has become one of the top contractors for the US Army and Department of Defense.

Second, the intricacies of modern warfare and contemporary dangers have spurred interest in receiving guidance from professionals on the best means to understand threats, conduct military operations, and manage security. Consulting PMSCs provide analysis and training to militaries, businesses, and intergovernmental (IGOs) and nongovernmental organizations (NGOs), as well as offer command and control services. Less skilled and experienced military forces require situational assessments and instruction, if not real-time mentoring, in strategy and tactics. Typifying this type of PMSC is Engility, a conglomerate offering an array of tactical and technical services—such as intelligence and explosive ordnance disposal—conducive to operating in non-permissive environments.

Third, "trigger pullers" are by far the most controversial type of PMSCs and are the primary focus of concern about the phenomenon. However, some armed contractors, it should be noted, concentrate on combat and specifically offensive actions (i.e., *private military companies*), whereas others are devoted exclusively to defensive tasks and the provision of safety (i.e. *private security companies*), although this is a blurry line. An illustration of force providing PMSCs is Aegis. This company furnishes protective services for operating in high-threat situations— e.g., guarding convoys, coordinating movements in theaters of operation, and securing locations.

Most analyses of PMSCs revolve around what these companies do, but it should not be overlooked that, like other global corporations, they are influenced by economic globalization, which has an impact on what labor they employ. Contractors vary not only by function but also according to training and nationality; three categories can be seen. Those contractors from industrialized countries are usually considered the best, as they tend to be experienced veterans from top militaries, primarily American and British. While these contractors have valuable specialized skills (such as counterinsurgency) and advanced high-tech equipment, they are frequently the most expensive. Local contractors, by contrast, are prized for their ability to blend into their operating environs as well as for their contacts, and their lesser training may make them a cheaper alternative. However, some PMSCs have reservations about hiring "host-country nationals" (HCNs) because their loyalty to their communities may render them unreliable security providers to foreign elements. Lastly, there are "third-country nationals" (TCNs), who are neither from wealthy countries nor locals. This hodge-podge of armed contractors tends to come from one of three sorts of country: Those that downsized their military forces due to the end of the Cold War (e.g., Belarus); those that disbanded oppressive forces (e.g., South Africa); or those that simply have international experience in peacekeeping or other operations and exchanges (e.g., Fiji): "Third-country nationals often have more training than locals and are less expensive than 'First World' contractors. Although the high-end contractors tend to capture the headlines, HCNs and TCNs are far more prevalent—perhaps constituting 90 percent of all armed contractors."[5]

PMSCs are routinely painted with a broad brush that invariably invokes the specter of mercenaries. Critics lament that PMSCs are illegal, violate human rights, and profit from violence. However, such a one-dimensional portrayal of avaricious "hired guns" neglects the wider political, security, and economic context that gave birth to PMSCs and sustains the sector. PMSCs may recall mercenaries but their identity as formal corporations, their evolving status under international law (see below), and the variety and complexity of the tasks associated with modern battlefields that they have taken up distinguish them.

The private military and security sector in the world today

Since the private military and security sector surfaced in high-profile activities in the 1990s, it has skyrocketed and been present in a multitude of contemporary armed conflicts and precarious areas, from post-Hurricane Katrina New Orleans to Pakistan. The growth of this industry is remarkable: Estimates gauge that it earned $55.6 billion in 1990 and around $100 billion in 2003.[6] By 2012 it surpassed $200 billion and with a current annual growth rate of near six percent, it is projected to reach $240 billion by 2020.[7] In addition to a burgeoning of revenues, there are a mounting number of people working in this field. In 2011, there were between 19.5 and 25.5 million personnel around the world in the private military and security sector, which represents a doubling, if not tripling, over the last ten to twenty years.[8]

PMSCs can be seen in many recent and current wars and zones of instability, particularly where Western states or businesses have an interest. Two illustrations of post-US interventions are telltale—in Afghanistan since the terrorist attacks of 9/11 and in Iraq after the overthrow of Saddam Hussein in 2003. In both instances, the United States has intervened with a modest force footprint relative to what is necessary to defeat all armed opposition and instill a stable state, and PMSCs were hired to not only supplement US troops but gradually takeover the provision of security as well as training forces of new governments. Indeed, as US forces have dwindled in Afghanistan and relatively few remain in Iraq, PMSCs are present in far larger numbers.

Another prototypical case of PMSC use is Somalia, where an escalation in piracy compounded by a large-scale insurgency, has besieged a fragile state, fostered regional instability and threatened key shipping lanes. Few states have the political will and the military resources necessary to truly address the circumstance. Consequently, there has been a marked expansion in private maritime security, which is viewed as less expensive than tackling governance in Somalia, changing commercial routes, higher insurance premiums, or paying ransoms. Overall, in places that lack order but are not at the top of the military agendas of any large military powers, PMSCs are expanding into such vacuums.

While a vast majority of the consumers of private military and security services are governments and businesses, the sector has its eye on expanding its customer base by seeking to work for IGOs and NGOs. Such arrangements will not yield contracts of a magnitude comparable to those with states and other corporations, but they would normalize their use as well as improve the reputation of PMSCs.[9] Some argue that the approach and capabilities of PMSCs enable a quicker response than international bureaucracies and that they are adept at providing peacekeeping or protecting humanitarian operations. Therefore, many PMSCs have increasingly developed and sold packages of services designed to suit the specific needs of this clientele, including meeting United Nations (UN) requirements in equipment, training, and logistics.[10] In fact, the UN has been hiring PMSCs since the early 1990s, and in recent years usage has been soaring—there was a 250 percent increase in the value of contracts between the UN and PMSCs over the period 2006–2011.[11] While a handful of humanitarian NGOs, such as Médecins Sans Frontières (MSF) and Save the Children, have made strong and public efforts in refusing to work with PMSCs, virtually all other agencies have "hardened" themselves by employing armed contractors at least once.[12]

There are far too many PMSCs to list them all, and they often operate out of the spotlight, although those actively involved in prominent armed hostilities clearly stand out. The first to receive great attention was Executive Outcomes, a South Africa-based firm that used surprisingly small contingents in routing guerilla groups in Angola and Sierra Leone during the mid-1990s. These operations set a precedent for the large-scale privatization of military and security affairs and ignited a boom in hiring PMSCs.

However, by far the most notorious PMSC is the company formerly known as Blackwater, which in 2009 changed its name to Xe Services LLC, in 2011 changed it to Academi, and in 2014 was acquired by Constellis. This company prided itself on taking on the most hazardous operations and providing the most professional, robust forces. However, several incidents in Iraq soured perceptions of Blackwater, especially those that resulted in civilian casualties with no legal accountability for its personnel. In a similar fashion, DynCorp has garnered attention for episodes of corruption and its lack of liability. For instance, the company was implicated in a sex trafficking scandal in Bosnia in the late 1990s while working for the UN and yet DynCorp has remained a staple tool of US foreign policy.

Yet, the single largest firm in the sector, and the third largest private employer in the world, G4S, which presently has near 600,000 employees and annual revenues approaching $10 billion, is mostly ignored. This company has provided a variety of security services to the British government, among other clients, including protection at the 2012 Summer Olympics in London. G4S's subsidiary ArmorGroup has been hired by the UN in Afghanistan but has been criticized for essentially subcontracting its work to local warlords, although the company continues to receive contracts from many governments and businesses.

Two other illustrations substantiate how PMSCs can be largely unknown because they do not undertake offensive combat operations and work for IGOs and NGOs. In the middle of the 1990s Defense Systems Limited was hired to guard the facilities of the International Committee of the Red Cross (ICRC) in the eastern part of the Democratic Republic of the Congo (DRC) while it was engaged in humanitarian relief. At roughly the same time but in the northern part of country, the World Wildlife Fund considered hiring Saracen to stop poaching in Garamba National Park, although ultimately no contract was signed.

Lastly, like any other modern industry, PMSCs have formed trade associations to publicize their prowess, court opportunities, and build legitimacy. Examples include the US-based International Stability Operations Association, the British Association of Private Security Companies, and the Private Security Company Association of Iraq. At present the sector is thriving because the norm of armed contractor usage has been well established, with states, businesses, IGOs, and NGOs readily employing them and PMSC interest groups striving to further embed this practice.

Global governance and PMSCs

To those who champion and those who reject PMSCs, the key issue hinges on governance. Supporters look at legal and ethical parameters for realizing contracts and tackling malfeasance. Opponents have traditionally searched for legislative tools to ban the practice outright, but in recent years some from this perspective have instead turned to regulating the sector. For the most part, PMSCs inhabit a netherworld of legality; currently there are essentially no binding international agreements that directly address their legal status, and therefore much of the jurisprudence applied to them is by way of extrapolation and interpretation. There are three main controversies regarding private military and security contractors. First, are they, in effect, soldiers—i.e., legal combatants representing a state—and thus entitled to the protections afforded to formal armed forces? Second, if armed contractors are lawful combatants, what activities are they permitted to engage in (conduct)? Third, what procedures are in place to ensure they are accountable for illegal activities?

Ten major normative frameworks and legal instruments guide or influence the global governance of PMSCs.[13] The first is the Hague Convention V, Articles 4 and 6 (1907). The first widely recognized international treaty with direct implications for for-pay militarized forces is built on the principle of neutrality. Although this treaty does not use the term mercenary, let alone PMSC, it effectively prohibits the recruitment of mercenaries in states that are neutral. However, it does not prevent individuals from crossing borders to become mercenaries.

The second is Geneva Convention III, Article 4 (1949). The four Geneva Conventions of 1949 do not discuss either the conduct or place of private military and security contractors under international humanitarian law. Indeed, PMSCs would seem to fall in the gaps—Geneva I and II refer to the formal combatants of states, meaning soldiers and sailors. Geneva IV addresses civilians, but private military and security contractors would not qualify because they are armed and join in hostilities. Geneva III, however, refers to the treatment of the captured and detained in conflict, including the conditions under which they are officially "prisoners of war" (POWs). But according to the criteria enumerated, such as being directly under the command of soldiers or wearing uniforms, PMSCs are likely not covered. Paragraph 4 refers to "supply contractors," which may pertain to support or consulting PMSCs but clearly not those who use force. Overall, the Geneva Conventions do not criminalize armed contractors, but they do not explicitly grant them the privileges of lawful combatants.

The third consequential framework is Additional Protocol I to the Geneva Conventions, Article 47 (1977). An upsurge in non-state actors engaging in armed conflicts in the post-World War II period inspired a reformulation of and additions to the laws of war, including a provision that defines and bans mercenaries, and this is often invoked in regard to PMSCs. Article 47 states that it is fundamentally illegal to fight for pay and results in forfeiting the protections granted under international humanitarian law. In other words, captured mercenaries are to be treated as criminals, not defeated soldiers. But the criteria for this category are extensive—recruited abroad; directly involved in hostilities; motivation is compensation beyond what other combatants receive; neither a national nor resident of territory party to conflict; not acting on official duty from a state—and few armed contractors would seem to meet them all. Moreover, it would be difficult to verify given that there is little formal documentation of PMSCs. Thus, although this agreement delineates mercenaries it has limited applicability in clarifying the status of PMSCs.

The fourth salient structure is the Organization of African Unity Convention for the Elimination of Mercenarism (1977). The use of mercenaries in support of colonial regimes and to undermine independent nationalist governments in Africa during the Cold War prompted the Organization of African Unity (now the African Union) to criminalize the practice. This treaty bears much resemblance to Additional Protocol I to the Geneva Conventions, but it goes further in that it also considers states that enable or allow mercenaries to operate from their territory as liable.

The fifth is the United Nations' International Conventions against the Recruitment, Use, Financing and Training of Mercenaries (1989). This agreement simplifies the definition of mercenary to the "desire for private gain" and broadens the scope of activities that are illegal to encompass recruiting, using, financing, and training. Furthermore, this convention requires states to take measures to prevent mercenarism. However, it also somewhat softens the treatment of captured mercenaries as it calls for allowing the ICRC to contact them and to monitor how they are treated.

The sixth standard-setting agreement is the Montreux Document (2008). The steady increase in PMSC usage sparked the Swiss government and the ICRC to devise regulations for the sector. After soliciting views from states, scholars, IGOs, NGOs, and PMSCs, the Montreux Document on the Pertinent International Legal Obligations and Good Practices for States Related to Operations of Private Military and Security Companies during Armed Conflicts was signed by "contracting states" (which hire armed contractors), "home states" (in which PMSCs are based), and "territorial states" (in which they operate). The agreement essentially distills the Geneva Conventions, the ICRC Study on Customary International Humanitarian Law, the UN Basic Principles on the Use of Force and Firearms by Law Enforcement Officials, the UN Code of Conduct for Law Enforcement Officials, and a variety of national regulatory frameworks.

The Montreux Document deems that armed contractors are "civilians" unless they are incorporated into military forces, in which case they are to be treated as soldiers, and, if they directly participate in conflicts, they are to be considered as combatants. This means that PMSCs do not qualify for the protections granted civilians and may lawfully be attacked. Additionally, the document sets out "good practices," which involve a licensing system to strengthen control and oversight as well as a tracking system of PMSCs to encourage the contracting state to only hire those that respect human rights and international law. However, this agreement is not legally binding; it is merely designed to clarify the rights and responsibilities associated with PMSC use. Although there is a statement within it that contends this initiative is not intended to legitimize PMSCs or otherwise take a position on the issue, this agreement does seem to imply an imprimatur of legality. In sum, the Montreux Document fundamentally identifies a way for armed contractors and their users to heed international standards—that is, it is a vehicle for demarcating the status of PMSCs under international humanitarian law.

The seventh normative and legal framework is the International Code of Conduct for Private Security Providers (2010). Whereas the Montreux Document called on states to uphold their responsibilities under international humanitarian law, there remained a lack of clear and formal commitment by PMSCs themselves to comply. To address this shortcoming the Swiss Department of Foreign Affairs, along with the Geneva Centre for the Democratic Control of Armed Forces and the Geneva Academy of International Humanitarian Law and Human Rights, and in conjunction with members of the PMSC industry, developed the International Code of Conduct for Private Security Providers. This agreement requires signatories to respect human rights and to adhere to humanitarian legal obligations in their operations with regards to their clients and the populations in the areas where they work, as well as their own personnel. Provisions cover rules for the use of force; standards for recruiting, vetting, and training personnel; and procedures for reporting violations (field auditing and a method for filing complaints). Moreover, should companies commit human rights abuses, under the Code, those that hire the offending company could fire them on the grounds of breach of contract. However, this agreement is somewhat limited in terms of its applicability and enforcement as it only governs companies that formally sign on, not the smaller local security providers that have also come to play more pronounced roles in armed conflicts.

The eighth framework can be discerned in a set of United Nations documents that establish and clarify the legality of PMSCs and address UN usage: The UN Draft Convention on Private Military and Security Companies (2011) and policies and guidelines found in the 2012 manuals of the UN Security Management System (UNSMS). The spread of PMSC utilization coupled with a belief in the inadequacy or inapplicability of legislation proscribing mercenaries initiated concern among many member states of the United Nations and its staff. Since 1987 the UN had appointed a special rapporteur to examine issues relating to mercenaries, but by 1997 this office recognized that laws against mercenarism did not strictly cover PMSCs. In 2005, the special rapporteur was succeeded by a new entity, the Working Group on the use of mercenaries as a means of violating human rights and impeding the exercise of the right of people to self-determination. It was tasked with the same responsibilities and intended to develop new principles to coax PMSCs to respect human rights.

A 2010 report by the UN Working Group on Mercenaries served as the basis for a new treaty proposed in 2011 that demands states take responsibility for PMSCs in their jurisdiction; international and national laws hold armed contractors accountable; restrictions on the use of force to protect state sovereignty and civilian populations; prohibitions on PMSCs undertaking combat, police, or intelligence work; and constraints on arms intended to prevent illegal trafficking. It also requires vetting personnel and training them in human rights and international humanitarian law; proper identification that distinguishes them from civilians; methods for reporting incidents, field audits and complaint procedures; and means for prosecution when laws are broken. This list of principles embodies current norms on the use of PMSCs. Most importantly, this treaty would not criminalize armed contractors, but instead regulate them.

The latest rules issued by the UNSMS in November 2012 exemplify this development. At an elementary level, its statements could be characterized as capstones of the normative and legal shifts toward normalizing PMSC usage by the organization in that they bring together and elaborate upon previous international agreements. The instructions and directives they lay out set forth the conditions under which PMSCs may be used: When security measures by host states, other member states, or the UNSMS are inadequate or inappropriate; the under-secretary-general for safety and security has approved a request based on a thorough security risk assessment; the company and its personnel have been screened; the company's "use of force" policy is as, or more, restrictive than the UN's own "use of force" policy; the company has signed and is in compliance with the International Code of Conduct for Private Security Providers; the company is licensed in its home state as well as the state where it operates as per the Montreux Document; and the company has registered with the UN Procurement Division. Therefore, the UN has not only played a part in sanctioning PMSC usage, the world organization has itself become a user.

A ninth instrument is the product of a collaboration between the American National Standards Institute (ANSI) and ASIS International (formerly the American Society for Industrial Security). ANSI/ASIS have devised a mechanism for private security companies that outlines their obligations and good practices identified by the International Code of Conduct for Private Security Providers and the Montreux Document. In addition, it details an audit system, evaluations of auditors, and measures for adherence to criteria. Basically, it depicts how companies are performing as per established metrics.

The tenth framework has been constructed through the International Organization for Standardization (ISO) and its policies for "security management systems for the supply chain" (ISO28000) (2007). In considering security as merely another part of the production process, it has formulated "Guidelines for Private Maritime Security Companies providing private contracted armed security personnel on board ships" (ISO28007) (2015). Among IOS criteria is respect for various international legal obligations, including the UN Guiding Principles on Business and Human Rights (2011), a benchmark of uniting state duties and corporate social responsibility. This agreement thus potentially opens paths for addressing abuses, although compliance is voluntary and there is no specific enforcement.

Although the beliefs and bans regarding mercenaries provide some direction for interpreting ideas about private military and security companies, PMSCs represent a different form of market-based force where the norms and laws are still unfolding. At present, practice seems to have tilted toward considering PMSCs as combatants that can legally be attacked and, if they accompany soldiers, may be granted POW status. However, this has not been set unambiguously under international humanitarian law. The most recent frameworks on PMSCs demonstrates just how far the norm of their usage has come. While there are still stalwart opponents of any sort of marketization of force, the goalposts of the debate have moved such that international deliberations are no longer centered on whether such actors are legal or legitimate, but rather how to use market rationalities and modalities to best influence their conduct.

Conclusion

The use of force in international affairs is customarily riddled with a dilemma of means and ends—is violence a solution or does it merely metastasize the problem?—and the uncertain nature of and tensions surrounding PMSCs add new twists to recent debates. Are armed contractors innately dangerous and inherently illegitimate? Are they the next logical and justifiable step in a globalizing world? Are they an imperfect actor reflecting an imperfect world? The answers to these questions are still open and changing, but five aspects are worth consideration in deliberating the costs and benefits of PMSCs: Role and position; norms and jurisdiction; commodification and markets; knowledge and expertise; and sacrifice and justice.

The first aspect derives from the growth of the sector and the decline of the state's monopoly on the use of force.[14] PMSCs have grown not only in size and scope but also in terms of the roles they play relative to national armed forces. Although some contend that state control over violence may never have been an unadulterated monopoly, by the twentieth century governments were clearly the only major players in the international use of force. However, in the past twenty years armed contractors have fundamentally challenged this as power and authority over violence have shifted thereby presenting the prospect that force is governed by "contract culture." PMSCs started by supplementing national armed forces and operating as "public–private partnerships," but now they are increasingly positioned to entirely supplant them.

The second issue regards questions of legality and legitimacy that suggest changing norms on the status of PMSCs. The growing use of and dependence on them by states and businesses is likely to sap the political will to outlaw armed contractors despite the protests of some human rights groups. For that reason, whether PMSCs are legal increasingly seems moot. New regulations governing PMSCs effectively suggest that their use is lawful and palatable—indeed, NGOs that once opposed the use of PMSCs now focus on regulation and security governance. However, the lines of authority for using PMSCs and acceptable modes of conduct need to be drawn more clearly to ensure transparency and accountability. The political blowback from usage is also a factor as many people in places where PMSCs operate are resentful, sometimes to the point that their use exacerbates armed conflicts. There must be consequences for wrongdoing, or there is no legitimacy to the use of PMSCs. Additionally, labor relations are of concern as the treatment of contractors by companies can potentially also undermine the lawfulness and propriety of PMSCs and the actors that hire them.

The third matter of interest is based on economics and efficiency, which reveals the trend of commodification. Supporters claim that the market allocates military and security resources more cost effectively, but the empirical answer is not readily apparent when considering other economic facets such as the loss of investment when personnel trained by states move to the private sector or the expenditures in renting forces rather than owning them. Moreover, the criticism that what may begin as an issue of efficiency becomes a form of extortion or exploitation must addressed. Outsourcing may result in dependency and PMSCs have no incentive to attend to the source of threats. What's more, it appears the market does not regulate behavior because even when there is a deviation from standards (such as human rights), consumers do not stop using services.[15]

The fourth area exposes the power of PMSCs as producers of knowledge.[16] PMSCs define security problems for clients through risk analysis and then prescribe solutions that commonly entail using the services of PMSCs—"permanent risk management" generates an endless stream of revenues.[17] This situation often articulates security as purely a technical issue and avoids understanding political mechanics. Additionally, it also builds and reinforces contractors as possessing expertise, and furthermore, may also habitually steer toward inflammatory force-based approaches. In fact, the UN's use of PMSCs has resulted in an embrace of the perceptions of contractors, which has not necessarily enhanced peacekeeping as much as it has cemented commercial interests.[18]

The final point of contention relates to the notion of sacrifice and justice. Part of the popularity of PMSCs with governments is it caters to a casualty-adverse mindset, but severing the sense of sacrifice associated with participating in armed conflicts subverts the conversation about the human toll of war. Historically, states and societies bargained: States respected the rights of citizens in exchange for societies providing resources to states, including manpower for military service. Contracting undercuts this arrangement; states do not draw on their citizenry to fight and thus may not be beholden to them to ensure rights. Furthermore, without directly experiencing loss from war, citizens may not concern themselves with where states are making war or why. In a world where PMSCs alone bear the burden of sacrifice, debates on the justness of force and the price of order are obscured.

In thinking and talking about PMSCs and the ubiquitous need for security, there is no panacea—sometimes force is required and no other actor is available. However, we are better off in being candid about what drives the phenomenon, how it interacts with the nature of governance, and what is at stake.

Additional reading

Rita Abrahamsen and Michael C. Williams, *Security Beyond the State: Private Security in International Politics* (Cambridge: Cambridge University Press, 2011).

Deborah D. Avant, *The Market for Force: The Consequences of Privatizing Security* (Cambridge: Cambridge University Press, 2005).

Simon Chesterman and Chia Lehnardt, eds., *From Mercenaries to Market: The Rise and Regulation of Private Military Companies* (Oxford: Oxford University Press, 2007).

Emanuela-Chiara Gillard, "Business Goes to War: Private Military/Security Companies and International Humanitarian Law," *International Review of the Red Cross* 88, no. 863 (September 2006): 525–572.

International Stability Operations Association, www.stability-operations.org/.

James Pattison, *The Morality of Private War: The Challenge of Private Military and Security Companies* (Oxford: Oxford University Press, 2014).

Notes

1 Sarah Percy, *Mercenaries: The History of a Norm in International Relations* (Cambridge: Cambridge University Press, 2007), 90–91.

2 Deborah Avant, "From Mercenary to Citizen Armies: Explaining Change in the Practice of War," *International Organization* 54, no. 1 (2000): 41–72.

3 Peter W. Singer, *Corporate Warriors: The Rise of the Privatized Military Industry* (Ithaca, NY: Cornell University Press, 2003), 49–72; David Shearer, *Private Armies and Military Intervention*, Adelphi Paper 316 (Oxford: Oxford University Press, 1998).

4 Carlos Ortiz, "The New Public Management of Security: The Contracting and Managerial State and the Private Military Industry," *Public Money & Management* 30, no. 1 (2010): 35–41.

5 Katherine E. McCoy, "Civil–Military Relations: Reflections on Civilian Control of a Private, Multinational Workforce," *Armed Forces & Society* 36, no. 4 (2010): 671–694.

6 Cited in Alex Vines, "Mercenaries and the Privatization of Security in Africa in the 1990s," in *The Privatization of Security in Africa*, eds. Greg Mills and John Stremlau (Johannesburg: South African Institute for International Affairs Press, 1997), 47; Peter W. Singer, "Peacekeepers, Inc.," *Policy Review* 119 (June 2003): 60.

7 The Freedonia Group, *World Security Services* (January 2017), 2.

8 Nicolas Florquin, "A Booming Business: Private Security and Small Arms," in *Small Arms Survey 2011: States of Security* (Cambridge: Cambridge University Press, 2011), 101.

9 Jutta Joachim and Andrea Schneiker, "NGOs and the Price of Governance: The Trade-offs Between Regulating and Criticizing Private Military and Security Companies," *Critical Military Studies* 1, no. 3 (2015): 185–201.

10 Malcolm Hugh Patterson, *Privatizing Peace: A Corporate Adjunct to United Nations Peacekeeping and Humanitarian Operations* (New York: Palgrave Macmillan, 2009), 73.

11 Lou Pingeot, *Dangerous Partnership: Private Military & Security Companies and the UN* (New York: Global Policy Forum, July 2012), 47.

12 Abby Stoddard, Adele Harmer, and Victoria DiDomenico, *Providing Aid in Insecure Environments: Trends in Violence against Aid Workers and the Operational Response—2009 Update*, HPG Briefing Paper 34 (April 2009), 8.

13 There are also national regulations and bans on mercenaries—for instance the US Neutrality Act (1797), the UK's Foreign Enlistment Act (1870), and South Africa's Foreign Military Assistance Act (1998)—but the multinational properties of PMSCs and nebulous pertinence and antiquated character of these laws usually hampers them from playing a role with respect to armed contractors.

14 Elke Krahmann, "Private Military and Security Companies, Territoriality and the Transformation of Western Security Governance," in Stefano Guzzini and Iver B. Neuman, eds., *The Diffusion of Power in Global Governance. International Political Economy Meets Foucault* (Basingstoke: Palgrave Macmillan, 2012), 38–70.

15 Elke Krahmann, "Choice, Voice, and Exit: Consumer Power and the Self-regulation of the Private Security Industry," *European Journal of International Security* 1, no. 1 (2016): 27–48.

16 Anna Leander, "The Power to Construct International Security: On the Significance of Private Military Companies," *Millennium* 33, no. 3 (2005): 803–825.

17 Elke Krahmann, "Beck and Beyond: Selling Security in the World Risk Society," *Review of International Studies* 37, no. 1 (2011): 349–372.

18 Åse Gilje Østensen, "In the Business of Peace: The Political Influence of Private Military and Security Companies on UN Peacekeeping," *International Peacekeeping* 20, no. 1 (2013): 33–47.

Transnational criminal networks

Frank G. Madsen

There is an almost infinite variety of theoretical attempts to understand how our world is governed, commencing with the international relations (IR) triad of realism, liberal institutionalism, and constructivism. As, however, global governance is increasingly no longer seen as being fully described as an interaction between and among states, sociology and anthropology have offered a plethora of understandings from their respective fields.

International illicit traffics, for example, in organs for transplantation, narcotic drugs, and prostitutes, have in common that they are caused by denied demand, and that the various traffics are made possible by networks. Thus, cocaine trafficking from the farmer in Colombia to the user in a Western country is made possible by several subnetworks of finance and corruption, apart from the more obvious ones of transportation and sales. Other transnational crimes, however, rely heavily on the operation of networks, for example human trafficking and environmental crimes, both of which are used as exemplars in this chapter. Likewise, the corresponding interdiction efforts reflect the use of networks of diplomats, prosecutors, and law enforcement personnel

Indeed, interrelation of powers in a very wide sense of this term is often best understood if seen as network interactions, referred to as "power circuits" by Adam Edwards.[1] Although network theory as an explanatory and illustrative model has gained importance with the progress of computing studies, the origin of the concept is far from recent. Networks and networking are as old as organized society, and network theory can conveniently be dated from the beginning of the nineteenth century with Henri de Saint-Simon, who in 1813 developed "organism-network theory" based on his observation of the human organism in extensive dissection studies.

The network has now developed into an important or some would argue *the* most important theory to enhance scholarship's understanding of the illicit flows of goods and services, which are the major constituent feature of transnational organized crime. The application of network theory is examined further later; but to end these short more theoretical remarks, it is worth noticing that the term "theory" was defined in 1905 by Ludwig Boltzman as: "A depiction of the organization of a domain and of the connections among its parts." Kenneth Waltz, however, noted: "The infinite materials of any realm can be organized in endlessly different ways."[2]

The chapter contains three main sections. The first examines global governing and notes the presence of both visible and less visible actors. The second section identifies the flowing or dynamic nature of the global governance of crime; it highlights the flexible, ever changing, protean networks that make up the dark side of our world—that is, transnational organized crime (TOC). The attempts at interdicting or limiting the transnational flows of illicit nature, be they of humans, merchandise, or services, are considered in the third section, which also examines how judicial and enforcement authorities have formed networks.

Governing

Yuliya Zabyelina observes that TOC has never been central to IR theory. Nevertheless, as TOC is having an ever increasing impact on international security, world politics, international trade, and human rights, she suggests that TOC should be understood both theoretically and empirically within the IR framework.[3] In this sense, the realist view of crime viewed in the context of a struggle for the actors' hierarchical location within society ignores the power of non-state actors.[4] Liberal institutionalism adopts the labeling priority—i.e., whatever the state defines as crime is crime, extending this exercise to human rights.[5] Finally, constructivists "identify zones of ambiguity" since they see crime as constituted of elements of the social process and of "grounded reality."[6]

The gradual realization that more or less invisible actors play important roles in global governance has led scholars to adopt a less state-centric understanding of the causal and dispositional characteristics of the development and exercise of power. Indeed, recent scholarship has emphasized "multi-centered governance" and "circuits of power." Adam Edwards also observes that liberal democracies have decentered power from the state downwards, upwards, and outwards—moving them, respectively, to local and regional authorities, supranational authorities, and commercial enterprises.[7] Such decentralization causes observers to question the state's ability to deliver on one of its most central obligations: Security within its territorial boundaries. Likewise, an alleged crime globalization is seen to subvert state sovereignty. David Garland notes that citizens must adapt to the normality of crime and to the incapacity of states to "deliver on their self-legitimating 'punitive display' through various narratives of warfare on crime, drugs and terror."[8]

Economic globalization, especially new communications and transportation technologies, have led over the last quarter of the twentieth century to a paradigm shift in organized crime. TOC itself, however, has not changed fundamentally. It is still in its vast majority based on satisfaction of denied demand, but it has adopted the networked business models of transnational enterprises. As such it concentrates on production in low-risk and commerce in high-income areas, strategic alliances, subcontracting, and joint ventures.[9] This aspect of organized crime, and of TOC in particular, may be seen to erode state sovereignty. It shifts from territorial and partially ethnicity-based modes of operations to functioning as a subset of a chain of connected networks. One only needs to consider the importation of huge quantities of bulky, counterfeit products into the United States and the European Union (EU) to understand that a number of networks must cooperate to manufacture, transport, import, and commercialize such products; and that under these circumstances any formerly existing exclusivity in the organization as a whole is no longer viable. A number of the subnetworks are family, clan, or ethnically limited. Thus, after the difficult years 1992–1996, the reconstruction of the Sicilian mafia entailed much tighter blood relationship criteria for election to join and concurrently a shift from subversion to submersion. At least that part of TOC has understood the powerful message of postmodern society: "What does not exist in the media, does not exist."[10]

From the point of view of IR and public policy, the most distressing aspect of organized crime is the creation of states that are controlled by criminal groups, working in layered and intersecting networks. Moisés Naím uses the term "mafia states" for states with three characteristics: The national interest and the interests of organized crime are inextricably intertwined; the conceptual divide between state and non-state actors is blurred; and their behavior is difficult to predict.[11] Examples are legion, but it is useful to illustrate with allegations about Venezuela. In January 2012, the US media reported that the recently appointed minister of defense, Henry Rangel Silva, was not only suspected of drug trafficking but had also been placed on the list of Specially Designated Narcotics Traffickers (SDNT).[12] Likewise, in January 2015, the bodyguard of the National Assembly president, Diosdado Cabello, deserted his position in the Venezuelan armed forces; and with the assistance of the Drug Enforcement Administration, DEA, traveled to the United States to testify that Cabello was the head of the corruption and drug-smuggling Cartel of the Suns, composed largely of political and military officials.[13]

The rapid expansion of crime networks in the former Soviet Union led to, or was partially responsible for, a somewhat distorted transition from a communist to a market economy. An essay in *Foreign Affairs* almost prophetically predicted that such a state of affairs (unchecked economic chaos and gang violence) "could foster the rise of a hostile, totalitarian power on the Eurasian continent, instead of the prosperous partner the West requires for a stable 21st century world."[14]

In order to understand briefly the role played by transnational criminal networks within IR theory, it is necessary to see such networks in context. The scholar who developed the most helpful understanding was Susan Strange. She elaborated the "symbiosis paradigm."[15] In abbreviated form, it observes the existence of many, not one, markets; they should be analyzed as power systems, thus joining Hedley Bull's concept of neo-medievalism.[16] Her analysis of the global power structures led to the recognition of the power of numerous actors, which in a symbiotic mode erodes public confidence, in particular in the delivery of public services and security by the state accompanied by the rise of civil society attempting to provide such services. The gap between "declining political authority and an insufficiently developed civil society is filled by the covert world," which, according to Robert Cox, includes organized crime as well as "the intelligence services, money-laundering banks, the arms trade, drug cartels, and terrorist organizations." Although they have conflicting goals, they develop symbiotic relationships.[17] Strange's analysis of global power networks is helpful in understanding TOC, but Cox goes on to provide an additional insight that "it is necessary to examine the whole milieu and not just some of its component actors."[18]

The concept of "convergence" expresses the fear that illicit networks and terrorism may come together or even converge. One might define convergence as the point at the fulcrum of the terrorism-organized crime continuum, where "a single entity simultaneously exhibits criminal and terrorist characteristics."[19] This observation leads to the logical, but not universally accepted, realization that: "The old paradigm of fighting terrorism and transnational crime separately, utilizing distinct sets of tools and methods, may not be sufficient to meet the challenges posed by the convergence of these networks into a crime-terror-insurgency nexus."[20]

This chapter emphasizes transnational as opposed to international crime. Although the use of these terms is fluid, there is nevertheless a tendency to speak of "international" crimes when one refers to war crimes, crimes against humanity, genocide, torture, aggression, and some parts of international terrorism. These crimes are, according to Antonio Cassese, characterized by the cumulative presence of four elements: Violation of international customary rules (including treaties that explicitly refer to customary law as their basis); rules are intended to protect values considered important by the whole international community of states; universal interest in their prosecution; and, if such crimes are committed by state officials, these cannot invoke immunity.[21]

Other crimes are most often referred to as "transnational"—for instance, piracy, illicit traffic in narcotics, unlawful arms trade, smuggling of nuclear and other dangerous material, money laundering, the slave trade, and traffic in women. These crimes are not considered international crimes because their international interdiction is treaty based and not based on customary international law. Moreover, they usually are perpetrated by private individuals or organizations, and they are committed against states rather than by states. Finally, if committed by state officials, they are pursuing their own personal interests rather than national interests.

Flowing

This section has two parts. The first is an examination of the concept of network theory; its origin, development, and use with regard to criminality lead to the suggestion that more emphasis should be placed on the observation of flows rather than of operators and human interactions. The second part considers in more detail the application of the concept to TOC, based on case studies from the transnational traffic in humans and transnational environmental crime.

Networks and network theory were introduced to the study of organized crime in the 1990s by such scholars as Phil Williams and Malcolm Sparrow and it became *the* preferred aspect under which to analyze such crime.[22] This use of network theory reflects dissatisfaction with the hitherto predominant theory of organized crime as hierarchies. A helpful definition is provided by Daniel Parrochia, who defines network as a coherent and ordered distribution in space of a plurality of relations; he also suggests that a network is the theater of circulation.[23]

Three characteristics of criminal networks are: They are ordered, self-repairing, and examples of self-organized criticality. Criminal networks are ordered or coherent, meaning that the members of the network must be in agreement about the scope and purpose of the network; in a criminal network, agreement concerns a desirable and profitable position in the future. Such networks are self-repairing or, to use another term, "resilient." Their ability to bounce back is the result not only of redundancy but also of the ease of actor replacement. Low entrance requirements in educational and capital investment are paired with the absence of opportunities in the communities from which such actors are recruited.[24]

Criminal networks are self-organized critical systems. The abundance of possible neural pathways from a given point to another developed to ensure information and communications survival after an attack on the United States led to the development of the Internet. A similar description applies to criminal networks, their national and international modes of cooperation, the functioning of money-laundering structures, and the operation of terrorist networks. Criminal networks are critical systems because of the tension between the elements in the system itself, between the system and similar systems, and between the system and its legal and sociopolitical environment. The lack of an external conflict-resolution mechanism means that the magnitude of almost any disturbance can be absorbed by the self-repairing quality which characterizes such systems. One participant is replaced by another as a new balance is struck between networks. As good business sense demands that solutions be found, solutions are, indeed, found.

Network theory assists in the understanding TOC but does not, at least at this stage, enhance enforcement. Indeed, perusal of the case studies elaborated by two of the major scholars of criminal networks, Phil Williams and Carlo Morselli, shows that their more than a dozen cases have all been successfully investigated by well-known, traditional techniques: The infiltration of informants into the networks, and the use of physical and electronic surveillance.[25]

As a means of a better visual understanding of networks in their traditional function as social networks, the so-called Olympic Rings representation is found in Figure 31.1. The individual circles represent networks while the totality represents *the* network. Each network in the overall network is self-organized, which tallies very well with observations made of organized crime, where substantial independency apparently is accorded individual, more or less amorphous groups. The points, where the circumferences of the circles intersect with each other are called *nodes*. These are the points where one finds power brokers, i.e., agents, who manipulate information rather than product or clients.

Two examples of criminal network are good illustrations. The first shows the network structure and the law enforcement consequences of the realization by competent authorities that the trade in ivory is not the result of a more or less haphazard meeting between traveling business persons and famished poachers. The second is

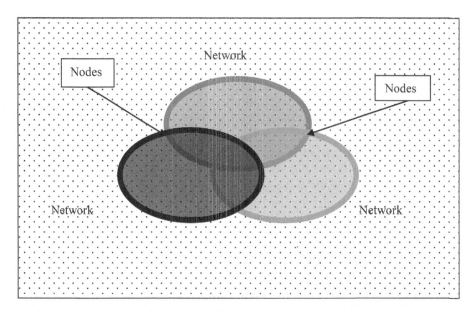

Figure 31.1 Networks, Olympic rings

an important manifestation of the characteristics of invisible, but highly resilient and self-organizing, self-repairing, and self-protecting criminal networks that constitute the little known—almost global—structure of trafficking in humans.

The killing and subsequent mutilation of rhinoceros and elephants in order to nurture the international trade in tusk has now reached what can be called "species-threatening dimensions." When international law enforcement first turned their attention to the subject matter, local authorities in Africa were laboring under the misconception that the trade was of the simplest structure possible. Traveling Chinese or Malay business persons purchased the tusk from independently operating poachers. In other words, there was no underlying network, which, in practical terms, meant that the conditions for the application of the 2000 United Nations Convention on Transnational Organized Crime were not met.

With time, however, local investigations showed that the reality of the ivory traffic from sub-Saharan Africa is highly organized by individuals who reside in major cities from where they manage the contacts with poachers and with shippers in the main export locations, as well as with the corruption network, and the wholesale clients in Southeast Asia.[26] The urban organizer constitutes a perfect illustration of a node in Figure 31.1.

Likewise, the network behind the smuggling of migrants into Europe is an enlightening example, which extends from migrant-generating countries such as Pakistan and Somalia to final point of delivery in, say, Italy. Extensive interviews of "people smugglers" now allow a better understanding of their simple, but at the same time efficient networks.[27] Although this particular trade necessitates the intervention of a large number of operatives, on different levels and with different functions, the main underlying principle remains the characteristic that, to the extent possible, in the organization there is a "first operator" and a "second operator" and a third. The first knows the second, but not the third and so on.

A typical organized human trafficking network consists of three entities: Clients, organizers, and recruiters (see Table 31.1). The clients are mostly made up of Syrians, Kurds, Afghans, and Pakistanis. They are here referred to as "migrants," a term that covers illegal immigrants (who enter a state without permission but cannot apply for asylum); migrants (who enter legally, via a tourist or student visa, and then remain within the confines of the state in question, without permission); and migrants (who enter the state illegally, but once entered may apply for asylum).

The organizer resides in Istanbul, which is a major hub for the traffic. Under different identities, he will also have residences in other countries—typically, around the Black Sea—allowing for temporary retreat from direct presence in the trade, for example after a capsizing involving loss of life, which may lead to increased law enforcement. The organizer uses a multitude of names and is personally known to

Table 31.1 Human trafficking

Prices per migrant: Transportation and illicit entry		
From	*To*	*US$ x 1000*
Afghanistan	Iran	0.7
Afghanistan	United Kingdom (London)	25
Sub-Saharan Africa	North Africa	2.5
Asia	Europe	3–10
Asia	United States	25
Bangladesh	Brazil	10
China	Italy	15
China	United Kingdom	41.8
China	United States	40–70
Cuba	United States	10
Guatemala	United States	7
Iraq	Germany	7–14
Iraq	United Kingdom	10.5
Mexico	United States	1–4
North Africa (coast)	Italy	1.5–3
North Korea	South Korea	6
Pakistan	United States	22
Somalia	United States	10
South America	United States	8.5
Turkey	Italy	2.5–5
Vietnam	Europe	28.5

Source: Global Black Market Information, available at www.havocscope.com; and Di Nicola and Musumeci, *Confessioni di un trafficante di uomini*, 40–41.

very few members of the organization, who each knows him under a different name. In the navigable season, he concurrently may employ some thirty-five captains.

The recruiter is typically a Turkish national of Kurdish origin. When business is slow, he travels to the countries from which migration originates (e.g., Pakistan) and offers the organization's services; otherwise, he relies on local "agents," who provide information about the organization, prices, and *modus operandi* to potential migrants. The last must be in possession of $5000–7000, of which $2000 is paid immediately to the recruiter. The rest is deposited with a trusted, irregular "banker" in Istanbul (typically, a money changer or a jeweler). This sum—minus the amount paid as a fee to the money changer—is only disbursed to the organization when the client has arrived safely in the target country. Also the recruiter's main residence is in Istanbul, but he (not usually she) travels extensively, both to the migration-generating countries and to the southeast of Turkey to meet new clients on arrival. It is likewise part of the recruiter's function to rent abandoned industrial sites or unused hostels as staging posts for the clients awaiting transportation.

There are additional elements in the network. Guards are local; they feed the clients and keep them in the staging area, indoors, to avoid their presence being known. They receive $20–30 per client but are paid by the organization, not directly by the client. Observers provide counter-surveillance from staging area to embarkation site on the Turkish coast (typically near Bodrum). They are not in contact with the transport itself, but observe from behind and from the front to ascertain if the transport is under surveillance. They are paid $700–800 each per trip. The smuggler is a sea captain, typically from the Black Sea, who rents or buys a vessel. A rental may be $3000/week; a purchase in less than perfect shape may be $50,000. The smuggler is paid $10,000 per trip. The trafficker is a figure who is not always present but exploits migrants after arrival in target country—e.g., Nigerian organized crime.[28]

The overall economy of a human smuggling operation is difficult to estimate. One well-known trafficker, Musharaf, based in Rome, Italy, is known to traffic 200–300 clients per month or at least 3000 per year with an annual turnover of some $18–30 million.[29] The United Nations estimates that the annual profit to the smugglers, who traffic migrants from Africa to Europe, at $150 million, while those who bring migrants to the United States have a gain of $6 billion a year.

Interdicting

These two examples from transnational environmental crime and from human trafficking illustrate the covert organization of TOC. The authorities charged with opposing such traffics have formed themselves into networks; the interdiction network is the subject of this last part of the chapter.

We have seen that the transnational criminal world now consists of dynamic, self-repairing networks, the nodes of which are occupied by actors, in particular brokers, while the flows consist of goods, services, and monetary instruments. Interdiction efforts, public and private, have formed into somewhat less dynamic but still close-fitting networks worldwide. Known as "the global crime governance network," the meshes are finer in such areas as money laundering and terrorism, and coarser in others such as human trafficking. The global crime governance network at present represents a complex interplay of interests, actors, policies, and processes. Nevertheless, underlying all general and topical areas is information and trust; trust occupies the nodes, and information travels along the many connections. Indeed, without trust, the flows of information would soon cease because law enforcement and, more generally, judicial cooperation between countries on all levels are based on goodwill ("comity"). Applying the premise that it takes a network to defeat a network, law enforcement and somewhat later prosecutorial authorities have forged cooperative networks.

The latter offer the advantage that they allow a quicker, informal way of cooperation than the use of letters rogatory. They are demands for judicial assistance issued by a court in one country and transmitted to a court in another. The process ensures legal control but suffers from a reputation for tardiness. A request must be transmitted from a court to a ministry of justice and from there to a ministry of foreign affairs in one country; and then, in the other, the same process occurs in reverse. The answer from the requested court must then travel by the same route back to the requesting court.

The interdiction network consists of international and intergovernmental organizations, transnational extensions of states' executive functions, and private or quasi-private initiatives. The result has been the establishment of another, formal interdiction network of treaties and memoranda of understanding between states, and between states and international and intergovernmental organizations. The sum of these treaties and memoranda is important, but the network consisting of extradition treaties is more impressive. In fact, it can be considered one of the most tightly knit of networks, that often, but not always, is also one of the most efficient.

The United Nations Office of Drug Crime (UNODC) in Vienna, Austria, is an overarching think tank in the interdiction network, a repository for related statistics, and an active generator of international law. Interpol—or more correctly the International Criminal Police Organization (ICPO)—in Lyon, France, has both educational and think tank functions. From its inception in 1923, the main task remains operational, namely the exchange of actionable data on criminal activity, now via the Interpol Criminal Information System (ICIS), created in 1998. An important milestone in the organization's history was reached in 2005, when Interpol issued the first Interpol–United Nations Special Notice for individuals subject to UN sanctions, based on determination by the UN Security Council.

The Organisation for Economic Co-operation and Development (OECD) is another vital link in the network. Of particular note is its anticorruption efforts as witnessed by its Convention on Combating Bribery of Foreign Public Officials in International Business Transactions, which entered into force in 1999.

Likewise, a number of national enforcement, criminal intelligence, and judicial entities have formed more formal international cooperative organizations to increase the flow of information. Various financial intelligence units (FIUs) in 1997 created the Egmont Group and exchange information through a secure website. Some scholars would postulate a clear democratic deficit with regard to the operation of such networks. Ironically, the anti-money-laundering network is extremely developed, allegedly investigating the proceeds of crime; but, in reality, more likely it concentrates on revenue violations. Similar structures, apart from Interpol, do not exist for such crimes as the commercial sexual exploitation of children or, counterfeit pharmaceuticals. Counterfeit and substandard antimalarial drugs alone are responsible for some 200,000 deaths a year, while thirty percent of drugs purchased at random in Southeast Asia and thirty-five percent in sub-Saharan Africa fail testing for their pharmaceutical ingredient.[30]

The propagation of, in particular US, transnational enterprises across the planet led to the concurrent dissemination of forensic accounting and corporate investigations (FACI). In order to appreciate their financial status, transnational enterprises had to streamline recordkeeping in their domestic and nondomestic branches by imposing uniform accounting regulations throughout each individual transnational enterprise. They also established worldwide auditing functions consisting of teams who inspect and audit each branch office in an unending cycle according to centrally determined accounting and auditing guidelines. Commonly accepted, understandable, and transparent accounting and auditing rules have slowly been established worldwide. They were backed by quasi-uniform training of personnel and their professionalization—for example, through specialized associations such as the American Society for Industrial Security. Likewise, and based on the central corporate authority, internal corporate investigations have imposed, step by step, US concepts of corporate governance. They have become widespread—for instance, in matters as disparate as the prevention of corruption of foreign officials and of sexual harassment. The influence of transnational enterprises and the dissemination of FACI have led over the last three decades to changes in corporate culture and altered rules, regulations, and laws in a quasi-legislative process referred to by Gunther Teubner as "global law."[31]

Anne-Marie Slaughter argues that problems of democratic accountability could be overcome by ensuring that international cooperation through networks was the prerogative of "politically accountable government officials" rather than a "hodge-podge" of "experts, enthusiasts, international bureaucrats, and transnational business-people."[32] Clearly, today's interconnected world requires new means of governance, including for criminal law. Nevertheless, information being exchanged through such networks as one FIU to another is often about persons and actions that are vaguely "suspect" rather than the subject of a definable criminal investigation. Such inquiries presumably would not even pass the "probable cause" test in front of a judge. It may be that this kind of exchange is valid in maintaining citizen security, but as long as these initiatives are not parts of a global rule of law with appropriate, nonexecutive overview, the concern for misuse remains.

A fitting way to conclude this final section is to refer to Michael Bayer's 2010 book, *The Blue Planet*.[33] He examines a truly global interdiction network, the full potential of which is not reached, namely, that of transnational informal law enforcement. He is correct in pointing out that time is of the essence in criminal and terrorist investigations. Therefore, although the formal methods of cooperation are both professional and legally necessary, they must, by the very nature of international criminal justice cooperation, take time, whereby the investigative momentum may be lost. It is quite common that cooperation between enforcement officials in two Interpol member countries, for example, may first be undertaken informally (typically by telephone between officials who already know each other and therefore have developed a high level of trust, the *sine qua non* condition), and then later confirmed by formal exchange of messages or documents via the Interpol or similar systems.

A number of countries have created networks of so-called liaison officers (criminal police officers) stationed worldwide. Such a network is more or less extensive, the most active of which are the United States, Germany, and France. A liaison officer maintains good relations between his or her home country's law enforcement and that of the host country. But these officials also play an active role in ongoing investigations by obtaining direct access to investigators in both countries and thus to information that is not, or not yet, available via such customary communication channels as Interpol. For example, US agencies have substantial outreach: DEA has ninety-six offices overseas and the FBI seventy-nine, while the Secret Service and the Bureau of Alcohol, Tobacco, Firearms and Explosives have a number of foreign offices.

Conclusion

The notion of networks is widespread in contemporary social science, ranging from criminology to international relations, from anthropology to public administration. Both criminal networks and the concomitant creation of judicial and enforcement networks are best seen as part of a more generalized use of networks in global governance in the sense proposed by Slaughter. This chapter has also pointed out that the development of government official networks might raise concerns about democratic and judicial control.

However, networks undoubtedly will continue to develop, as they have intrinsic qualities that render them "unstoppable," to use a term from a recent work on leaderless organizations.[34] Ori Brafman and Rod Beckstrom stipulate a number of characteristics of leaderless organizations, which they term "starfish" because when attacked, a decentralized organization tends to become even more open and decentralized like a neural network. Moreover, intelligence is spread throughout the system and is not centralized, which explains the concept of resilience. Leaderless systems can easily mutate, and mutate quickly; therefore they can also grow quickly. These observations echo those of Moisés Naím: "Networks behave like mercury. Once one tries to grab it, it slips through one's fingers, forming many smaller droplets." This obviously leads to the conclusion regarding enforcement that often "government interference is nothing more than another cost of doing business, and as often it just serves as a price-boasting intervention."[35] A discouraging, but accurate, observation that echoes Anja Jakobi: "[T]he rise of global crime governance does not necessarily imply that crime has decreased."[36]

The chapter has reviewed the use of network theory as a useful explanation of and illustration to analyze TOC, while noting its development within the framework of global governance. A reticular methodology has a number of advantages that permit a better understanding of the interactions among actors in networks. Seeing a criminal network as consisting of several subnetworks makes the concept even more effective, an insight for interpreting the range of actors and issues that are detailed throughout this volume.

Additional reading

Peter Andreas and Ethan A. Nadelmann, *Policing the Globe: Criminalization and Crime Control in International Relations* (New York and Oxford: Oxford University Press, 2006).

John Aquilla and David Ronfeld, eds., *Networks and Netwars: The Future of Terror, Crime, and Militancy* (Santa Monica, CA: RAND, 2001).

Pierre Hauck and Sven Peterke. *International Law and Transnational Organised Crime* (Oxford: Oxford University Press, 2016).

Barry A.K. Rider, ed., *Research Handbook on International Financial Crimes* (London: Edward Elgar, 2015).

Notes

1 Adam Edwards, "Multi-centred Governance and Circuits of Power in Liberal Modes of Security," *Global Crime* 17, no. 3–4 (2016): 240–263.

2 Kenneth N. Waltz, *Theory of International Politics* (Reading, MA: Addison-Wesley, 1979), 8.

3 Yuliya Zabyelina, "Transnational Organized Crime in International Relations," *Central European Journal of International and Security Studies* 3, no. 1 (2009): 11–22.

4 Waltz, *Theory of International Politics*.

5 Rob White and Fiona Haines, *Crime and Criminology: An Introduction* (Oxford: Oxford University Press, 1996).

6 Zabyelina, "Transnational Organized Crime in International Relations," 12; see also Mats Berdal and Mónica Serrano, eds., *Transnational Organized Crime and International Security: Business as Usual?* (Boulder, CO: Lynne Rienner Publishers, 2002), 15.

7 Edwards, "Multi-centred Governance," 240–253.

8 David Garland, "The Limits of the Sovereign State: Strategies of Crime Control in Contemporary Society," *British Journal of Criminology* 36, no. 4 (1997): 445–447.

9 Manuel Castells, *End of Millennium*, 2nd ed. (Oxford: Blackwell, 2000), 171.

10 Antonio Balsamo, "Organised Crime Today: The Evolution of the Sicilian Mafia," *Journal of Money Laundering Control* 9, no. 4 (2006): 375.

11 Moisés Naím, "Mafia States: Organized Crime Takes Office," *Foreign Affairs* 91, no. 3 (2012): 100–111.

12 Geoffrey Ramsey and Jeremy McDermott, "Is Venezuela's Military Playing a Role in Drug Trafficking?" *Christian Science Monitor*, 31 January 2012.

13 "Venezuela Confirms Desertion of Ex-agent from Armed Forces," *Associated Press*, 28 January 2015.

14 Stephen Handelman, "The Russian 'Mafiya'," *Foreign Affairs* 73, no. 2 (1994): 83–96.

15 Susan Strange, *The Retreat of the State* (Cambridge: Cambridge University Press, 1996).

16 Robert W. Cox, "The Retreat of the State?" *International Journal* 52, no. 2 (1997): 366–369; Hedley Bull, *The Anarchical Society: A Study of Order in World Politics* (New York: Columbia University Press, 1977), 254–255.

17 Cox, "The Retreat of the State?," 366–369.

18 Cox, "The Retreat of the State?," 369.

19 Tamara Makarenko, "The Crime-Terror Continuum: Tracing the Interplay Between Transnational Organised Crime and Terrorism," *Global Crime* 6, no. 1 (2004): 131.

20 Michael Miklaucic and Jacqueline Brewer, eds., *Convergence: Illicit Networks and National Security in the Age of Globalization* (Washington, DC: National Defense University Press, 2013), xv.

21 Antonio Cassese, *International Criminal Law*, 2nd ed. (Oxford: Oxford University Press, 2008), 11.

22 Phil Williams, "The Nature of Drug Trafficking Networks," *Current History* 97, no. 618 (1998): 154–159; see, in particular, his "Transnational Criminal Networks" in *Networks and Netwars: The Future of Terror, Crime and Militancy*, eds. John Arquilla and David Ronfeld (Santa Monica, CA: RAND, 2001), 61–97.

23 Daniel Parrochia, "La rationalité réticulaire" in *Penser les Réseaux*, ed. Daniel Parrochia (Seyssel: Editions Champs Vallon, 2001), 13, 17.

24 Williams, "Transnational Criminal Networks," 72; Frank G. Madsen, "International Narcotics Law Enforcement: A Study in Irrationality," *Journal of International Affairs* 66, no. 1 (2012): 123–144.

25 Williams, "Transitional Criminal Networks," 84–90; Carlo Morselli, *Inside Criminal Networks* (New York: Springer, 2009), chapters 2–8.

26 "Kenyan, Tanzanian Rangers Trained on Ivory Detection," *Xinhua*, 24 July 2015.

27 Andrea Di Nicola and Giampaolo Musumeci, *Confessioni di un Trafficante di Uomini* (Milan: Chiarelettere, 2014).

28 Ibid., 10.

29 Ibid., 39.

30 Gaurvika M.L. Nayyar, Joel G. Breman, Paul N. Newton, and James Herrington, "Poor-Quality Antimalarial Drugs in Southeast Asia and Sub-Saharan Africa," *Lancet Infectious Diseases Journal* 12, no. 6 (2012): 488–496.

31 Gunther Teubner, ed., *Global Law Without a State* (Aldershot: Dartmouth, 1997), 87; see also Thomas Mathiesen, "Lex Vigilatoria: Global Control Without a State?," in *Surveillance and Governance: Crime Control and Beyond*, ed. Mathieu Deflem (Bingley: Emerald, 2008), 101–127.

32 Anne-Marie Slaughter, *A New World Order* (Princeton, NJ: Princeton University Press, 2004), 262.

33 Michael D. Bayer, *The Blue Planet: Informal International Police Networks and National Intelligence* (Washington, DC: National Defense Intelligence College Press, 2010).

34 Ori Brafman and Rod A. Beckstrom, *The Starfish and the Spider: The Unstoppable Power of Leaderless Organizations* (New York: Portfolio, 2006).

35 Moisés Naím, *Illicit* (New York: Doubleday, 2005).

36 Anja P. Jakobi, *Common Goods or Evils? The Formation of Global Crime Governance* (Oxford: Oxford University Press, 2013), chapter 1.

Part introduction

Part VI of this book contains ten chapters addressing "Securing the world, governing humanity." One of the main explanations for human efforts to better govern the world has been the need to foster international peace and security. Wars have typically led to experiments with different generations of international organization (IO)—the Congress of Vienna after the Napoleonic wars; the League of Nations after World War I; and the United Nations after World War II.

We have arranged this part of the book to flow from the global governance of conflict management and prevention through to the reconstruction of war-torn societies and the human aspects of global security governance. This order is arranged not by political salience, financial commitments, or success; but it structures discussion and reading around familiar topics. All courses on IO and global governance could, for instance, use Paul D. Williams and Alex J. Bellamy's chapter on "The UN Security Council and peace operations" (Chapter 32)—the most familiar and high-profile aspect of global security governance. "Regional organizations and global security governance"—as S. Neil MacFarlane shows in Chapter 33—are also an increasingly salient part of the story, which advanced or specialist classes on global security would also likely take in. Thereafter, Part VI offers readers a suite of chapters dealing with specific issues—"Weapons of mass destruction" (Waheguru Pal Singh Sidhu, Chapter 34); "Counterterrorism cooperation and global governance" (Peter Romaniuk, Chapter 35), "Human rights" (David P. Forsythe, Chapter 36); "The pursuit of international justice" (Richard J. Goldstone, Chapter 37); "Humanitarian intervention and R2P" (Simon Chesterman, Chapter 38); "Crisis and humanitarian containment" (Fabrice Weissman, Chapter 39); "Post-conflict peacebuilding" (Graciana del Castillo, Chapter 40), and "Human security as a global public good" (Mark Raymond and Stefanie Neumeier, Chapter 41)—that can be explored as courses of study and interest allow. They cover a large swath, if not all, of the global security governance tapestry.

Securing the world, governing humanity: Chapter synopses

Various forms of military force are often the products of decisions made by, and provide the background for, the "UN Security Council and peace operations." One of six UN "principal organs," the council is the only part of the world organization's machinery that makes binding "decisions" rather than mere "recommendations" that states can even more easily ignore. In Chapter 32, Paul D. Williams and Alex J. Bellamy provide an historical overview and analysis of traditional UN peacekeeping in addition to scrutinizing the contemporary debates related to the relationship between the UN and regional arrangements, questions about who provides UN soldiers, and controversial issues related to the use of military firepower by the international community of states. UN peace operations have always been a testimony of adaptation and learning, seeing what works in practice not in theory.

In Chapter 33, S. Neil MacFarlane explores "Regional organizations and global security governance" as essential building blocks for contemporary world order. While regional economic cooperation has long been the subject of scholarly theorizing and analysis, MacFarlane demonstrates the extent to which regional security organizations are a growing reality that requires more understanding if we are to improve global security governance. While always seen as potential partners for the universal UN by Chapter VIII of the Charter, regional organizations have assumed an unprecedented role in peace operations since the end of the Cold War. Both the UN's overstretch and some comparative advantages made regional organizations more central to international conflict management and resolution—sometimes on their own, sometimes in "hybrid" operations with the United Nations. The fabric of global security governance has many regional strands, but the diversity in capabilities means that many regions actually have no real organization to help improve security while others are well heeled. Experience suggests a substantial potential for a division of labor between the UN and regional organizations in global security governance, but that potential is far from being realized.

In Chapter 34, Waheguru Pal Singh Sidhu explores "Weapons of mass destruction" (WMD) by parsing the nuclear, chemical, and biological threats whose proliferation constitutes a major challenge to contemporary global security governance. Sidhu spells out the existing regimes that govern each of the WMD. He argues that they should not be lumped together but unpacked individually to understand how far we have come and how far we have to go for to develop appropriate governance regimes. The task has taken on increased urgency lest they fall into the hands of "rogue" states and non-state actors. Sidhu indicates the hypocrisy of the Security Council's permanent five members pointing fingers at various states that possess or are trying to procure WMD but without taking significant steps to move forward by reducing their own obscenely large arsenals of all types.

In Chapter 35—"Counterterrorism cooperation and global governance"—Peter Romaniuk deals with a topic that seems omnipresent since 9/11, and also since the label is increasingly used as a convenient moniker to describe any dissident that is fighting an entrenched regime. Romaniuk spells out growing but fledgling intergovernmental efforts to improve the prospects for minimizing the damage from terrorism, if not halt every instance. He demonstrates the utility of using global governance as a concept in interpreting counterterrorism cooperation over time because capturing "process" and "activities" among a range of state and non-state actors is the essence of exercising authority and influence in various forms to fight this plague. There are multiple routes to effective action, including the flexible use by states of UN machinery.

In most texts, the previous topics would clearly be among "security" institutions. But contemporary notions of the topic require a broader scope. Thus, we asked members of our distinguished team to explore issues that provide a more complete and complex depiction of how important components underlying international peace and security, namely human rights and humanitarian affairs, are governed. In Chapter 36, David P. Forsythe addresses "Human rights in global governance," which perhaps are the most subversive and revolutionary element in the UN Charter—Eleanor Roosevelt used the image of a "grapevine" to indicate that human rights would take on a life of their own. Forsythe explores how both public international law and an increasing number of organizations—governmental, intergovernmental, and nongovernmental (NGOs)—are working in international vineyards. His emphasis is on intergovernmental machinery, but NGOs are a key part of his analysis as well, in a never ending battle to get governments to respect the letter of the norms, declarations, conventions, and treaties that they have approved.

In Chapter 37, Richard J. Goldstone examines "The pursuit of international justice." Tracing the advance of international criminal justice from the carnage of Solferino and the founding of the International Committee of the Red Cross, through the Nuremberg trials to today's frequent media reports on the prosecution of war criminals, Goldstone demonstrates how much these developments are indicators of advances in global governance. Of particular interest was the institutionalization of international criminal justice through the courts that were established in the last decade of the twentieth century—namely, the two United Nations *ad hoc* tribunals for the former Yugoslavia and for Rwanda, the various hybrid or mixed tribunals, and the International Criminal Court.

No topic has moved more quickly in the international normative arena than the "responsibility to protect" (R2P), and few people are better placed than Simon Chesterman to analyze the international legal and political implications of that advance. In Chapter 38—"Humanitarian intervention and R2P"—he details the history of the contested moniker "humanitarian intervention" and its replacement by the more palatable, at least to many, norm of "R2P." The international rules governing the use of force and the attempts—largely unsuccessful—to fit humanitarian intervention into those rules are examined. So too are the moral, legal, political, and military challenges that come to the fore in discussing post-Cold War applications of the use of military force for human protection purposes, from the spectacular interventions in northern Iraq at the beginning of the last decade of the twentieth century to Libya in the second decade of the twenty-first century.

Chapter 39 addresses the fallout from such interventions and the politicization of life-saving succor for war victims. Fabrice Weissman's "Crisis and humanitarian containment" reflects his views as a field practitioner whose analytical skills have been honed within one of the more reflective NGOs, Médecins Sans Frontières (MSF). The politicized arena for contemporary humanitarian action involves considerable material and symbolic stakes. Coming to the rescue is not necessarily on the side of the angels in today's fraught world of IO and global governance. Tough decisions and countless political transactions are the daily bill-of-fare, but they often are concealed by legal and moral rhetoric. Distinguishing between "new" (politicized engagement) and "autonomous" humanitarianism, Weissman indicates the costs and benefits of decisions by aid agencies to align themselves with international military forces and to participate in humanitarian and peacebuilding efforts determined by donor priorities. He makes a plea for future global humanitarian governance to return to the tradition of impartial relief; and he questions the wisdom of aid agencies that have solidified an alliance with liberal democracies and the UN based on neutralizing and punishing war criminals as well as establishing a liberal peace in dysfunctional societies torn apart by "new wars."

Picking up the pieces after wars is not new, but the number of civil wars beginning in the late 1980s and their devastation led to a dramatic expansion of such efforts. Theorizing about the challenges ensued, as did the establishment of new UN "architecture" devoted specifically to such efforts—the Peacebuilding Commission, the Peacebuilding Support Office, and the Peacebuilding Fund. In Chapter 40, Graciana del Castillo traces the evolution of the idea of "Post-conflict peacebuilding" and its application to the real-world environment in which it takes place, in particular the clash between the economics of war and of whatever follows. She examines why peacebuilding has been contested over time, especially because of interference in domestic affairs. Adaptation is part of the story of both IO and global governance. Like "peacekeeping," which does not figure in the Charter but is generally considered a creative UN invention, so too has peacebuilding become a (increasingly *the*) major task, although only implicitly figuring in the UN's constitution.

Chapter 41 concludes Part VI of the book. Mark Raymond and Stefanie Neumeier survey "Human security as a global public good." The move from the obsession of international security specialists with bombs, bullets, and other hardware to a concern with the welfare and empowerment of individuals as the ultimate way to measure "security" is a conceptual and operational leap for students of IO and global governance. Perhaps the biggest challenge for governing the world is the lack of global public goods. Raymond and Neumeier's approach is ambitious: The provision and protection of basic human liberties, certain key political and civil rights, and basic standards of equity and social justice for all peoples regardless of their ethnic or national origins, socioeconomic status, religious creed, or political persuasion. Admitting that all are underprovided, they argue for a portfolio diversification to the provision of global public goods related to human security in which different combinations of actors and institutions and networks are required to maximize the comparative advantages of each.

Where to now?

This part of the book provides an extensive overview of efforts to attenuate insecurities and the geopolitics behind them. Together these chapters complete a large part of the global governance puzzle. Once they have been consulted, their wisdom needs to be overlaid with an understanding of how the economic and social world is governed, and how institutions and mechanisms have evolved to address global environmental degradation—issues to which the final part of the book turns.

CONTENTS

UN Security Council and peace operations

Paul D. Williams and Alex J. Bellamy

The UN Security Council has never possessed a monopoly on either the authorization or conduct of peace operations. But it has become the predominant source of authority for legitimizing such operations, and the UN's "blue helmets" have conducted more than any other entity—seventy-one missions as of May 2017. By this stage, the UN was fielding approximately 100,000 uniformed personnel (i.e., soldiers, police officers, and security experts) and another 14,000 civilians in its peacekeeping operations. They were deployed by about 120 member states at a cost of about $8 billion per year.

Particularly since the end of the Cold War, the Security Council has authorized and conducted increasing numbers of peace operations. It has also tended to give them broader mandates, sometimes encompassing everything from assisting the implementation of peace agreements, supporting the rule of law, protecting civilians, disarming and reintegrating combatants, supporting electoral processes, reforming security sectors, facilitating humanitarian assistance, and extending state authority. A major reason why these mandates broadened was because they were often conducted in the complex theaters of intrastate armed conflicts, and because the Security Council displayed an unprecedented level of interest in the internal governance structures of the host state. Not surprisingly, as these operations have increased in number and scope, so too did the number of peacekeepers required and the bill to support them.

Although UN peace operations have received their fair share of criticisms, overall they have had positive effects on many of the world's conflict zones. As one analyst put it: "The answer to the question of whether peacekeeping works is a clear and resounding yes."[1] Some have credited peace operations with helping to lower the number of armed conflicts from the global peak in the early 1990s.[2] Others have noted that peace operations significantly reduce the likelihood of wars reigniting after peace agreements have been concluded. Specifically, where UN peacekeepers are deployed, the likelihood of war reigniting fell by at least seventy-five to eighty-five percent compared to cases in which no peacekeepers were deployed.[3] Peace operations have also significantly increased the probability that genocide and mass killing can be slowed or stopped.[4] Similarly, peace operations can help protect civilians in civil wars.[5] It is also thought that peace operations can make a positive contribution to building stable, democratic peace in the medium and long term, although they are often rushed and asked to complete such tasks "on the cheap."[6] This is important because while enforcement operations can stop violence, they cannot sow the seeds of long-term peace. At the same time, consent-based operations may struggle to stop violence but are quite effective in helping belligerents build long-term, democratic peace when they choose to put down their arms.[7] If deployed effectively, therefore, enforcement operations can lay the foundations for a subsequent consensual peace operation which can make a significant contribution to building long-term, stable peace.

This chapter provides an historical overview and analysis of the development of peace operations as well as three key contemporary debates concerning the relationship between the UN and regional arrangements; participation in peace operations and who provides UN peacekeepers; and the use of military force.

History and development

Peace operations involve the expeditionary use of uniformed personnel (police and/or military) with a mandate from an international institution or at the invitation of parties to a peace agreement to assist in the prevention of armed conflict by supporting a peace process; serve as an instrument to observe or assist in the implementation of ceasefires or peace agreements; or enforce ceasefires, peace agreements, or the will of the Security Council in order to build stable peace. Although this definition encompasses a wide range of operations—approximately 200 missions since the end of World War II—it does not include the UN's special political missions, of which there are currently about two dozen, usually run by the UN's Department of Political Affairs (DPA).

In theoretical terms, the story of the Security Council and its relationship to peace operations is best captured through a constructivist lens because the UN Charter did not define or even contain the term "peacekeeping." As a result, the world organization and its member states have developed and legitimized certain norms and practices related to peace operations over time. In short, peace operations are what international society, and particularly the Security Council, make them.

Since the creation of the UN in 1945, the universe of peace operations can be divided into three broad types, depending on the source of authority that established the mission and the type of actor that conducted it. First, there are UN-led operations. These "blue helmet" missions are authorized under Chapters VI and VII of the Charter but are also commanded and conducted by the UN. Second, there are UN-authorized operations. These missions are authorized by the UN with reference to Chapters VI, VII, or VIII, but the command and control of mechanisms are delegated to other actors, such as coalitions of states or other international organizations such as the European Union (EU) and African Union (AU). Finally, there are non-UN operations. These missions perform the tasks associated with peace operations but do so without a mandate from the Security Council and are conducted by non-UN actors. Most UN-authorized and non-UN peace operations have been conducted by regional organizations. Between 1946 and 2016, thirteen regional organizations conducted sixty-five peace operations, of which forty-eight—roughly seventy-four percent—took place after the end of the Cold War in 1989, most of them in Africa.[8] Some examples of these different types of peace operation are displayed in Table 32.1. The rest of this chapter focuses on the first category of UN-led, "blue helmet" peace operations.

The history of peacekeeping is a prime example of constructivism in action—i.e., the rules have been made up as the UN went along. The vision of the UN as the "world's policeman" was severely circumscribed by the Cold War and the organization became more of an instrument of crisis management tasked with maintaining "international peace and security" than an institution concerned with policing international law. Employed first as an *ad hoc* tool in response to individual crises, peacekeeping became one of the UN's principal instruments for crisis management. Indeed, this has been a constant theme whereby the key characteristics of peacekeeping have evolved in line with the political circumstances in which peacekeepers found themselves.

In 1947 the General Assembly dispatched an observation mission (UNSCOB) in response to a complaint from the Greek government that its Yugoslav neighbor was actively assisting communist rebels engaged in a civil war against the government. The following year, the Security Council began its engagement in two of the world's most pressing crises, the Israeli–Palestinian conflict and the struggle over

Table 32.1 Peace operations: A typology with examples

Actor	UN operations	UN-authorized operations	Non-UN operations
UN blue helmets	UNEF, UNFICYP, UNMIL, MONUSCO, MINUSMA etc.	N/A	N/A
Other international organizations	N/A	ECOWAS in Liberia (2003) EU in DR Congo (2003) AU in Somalia (2007–)	ECOWAS in Liberia (1990–97)[†] AU Operation Democracy in the Comoros (2008)
Coalition of the willing	N/A	UNITAF in Somalia (1992–93)[††] INTERFET in East Timor (1999) ISAF in Afghanistan (2002–14)	Helpem Fren in Solomon Islands (2003–)[†]
Individual government	N/A	No examples	UK in Sierra Leone (2000)[†] South Africa in Burundi (2001–03)[†]

Notes: [†] Missions subsequently welcomed by the UN Security Council in either a resolution or presidential statement. [††] Missions conducted without host government consent.
Source: Adapted from Alex J. Bellamy and Paul D. Williams, "Who's Keeping the Peace? Regionalization and Contemporary Peace Operations," *International Security* 29, no. 4 (2005): 172.

Kashmir. In the Middle East, the UN's Ralph Bunche secured a ceasefire agreement that would be overseen by a UN Truce Supervision Organization (UNTSO), which played an important role in helping to constitute peacekeeping as a distinct practice in international security. A similar model was pursued in Kashmir, where the council authorized the creation of a mission (UNMOGIP) to observe a ceasefire and write periodic reports. In the space of a few months in 1948, the Security Council had begun to carve out a role for itself in the promotion of international peace and security and to lay the foundations of modern peace operations.

These *ad hoc* missions began to be seen as an opportunity for the UN to play a coherent role in what was called "preventive diplomacy"—a concept articulated by Secretary-General Dag Hammarskjöld, although his predecessor as secretary-general, Trygve Lie (1946–1952), laid the groundwork. Hammarskjöld described "preventive diplomacy" as the "main field of useful activity of the UN in its efforts to prevent conflicts or to solve conflicts." He saw the UN's primary role as intervening in crises to prevent the escalation of local conflicts into regional or global wars.[9] However, it was the need to develop operational guidelines for the UN's first self-styled peace-keeping operation, the UN Emergency Force (UNEF I)—deployed to the Sinai to help defuse the Suez Crisis of 1956—and not conceptual thinking about the UN's role that prompted the organization to further refine its thinking on peacekeeping.

What became the core principles of consent, impartiality, and minimum use of force were first developed in response to the Suez crisis and were framed by the twin goals of developing a proposal that could make a positive difference while being acceptable to member states. At the time, there was little recognition outside the UN Secretariat that important precedents were being established. Nonetheless, the UN went on to conduct several more similar operations before the end of the Cold War. It is important, however, not to fall into the trap of thinking that Cold War peacekeeping was exclusively concerned with ceasefire monitoring and supervision. During this period, the UN also undertook peace enforcement action through the UN Operation in the Congo (ONUC), and embarked on complex missions in the Congo and Dutch West New Guinea (West Irian) that had comprehensive mandates for, among other things, helping to build state institutions and promote human rights.

The ONUC (1960–1964) was a larger, more complex, costly, and multifaceted operation than anything the organization had attempted previously. Although it accomplished much of its mandate, ONUC proved highly controversial, divided the Security Council, and helped create a financial crisis for UN peace operations. At its height, almost 20,000 troops were deployed alongside a significant civilian com-ponent, and the mission was mandated to fulfill a number of different roles. ONUC was mandated to maintain law and order during the Congo's turbulent decolonization after Belgian rule. However, the rapid disintegration of the security situation forced ONUC away from Hammarskjöld's vision of preventive diplomacy (as reflected in the UNEF I mission) towards peace enforcement to help defend the Congo's terri-torial integrity. The political fallout from ONUC had a profoundly negative effect on UN peace operations. In the twenty-three years that followed ONUC, the UN conducted only five new missions, four of which were continuations of previous UN engagements in the Middle East and Kashmir, while the fifth, the UN Peacekeeping Force in Cyprus (UNFICYP), was aided by a unique set of circumstances that saw the United Kingdom keen to divest itself of its colonial responsibilities there.

As the Cold War wound down between 1988 and 1993, peace operations underwent a transformation driven by a combination of demand-side factors (notably the resolution of Cold War proxy conflicts which generated requests for UN support) and supply-side factors which made it easier for the Council to reach a consensus and take a proactive stance. The key aspects were:

- a *quantitative transformation* which saw the number of UN-led peacekeeping operations grow rapidly, such that in a five-year period the UN launched more peace operations than it had in its previous 40 (see Figure 32.1)
- a *normative transformation* catalyzed by a growing belief among some member states that peacekeepers should be at the forefront of defending and extending liberal values
- a *qualitative transformation* which led to peacekeepers being asked to deliver humanitarian aid, protect vulnerable populations, deter violations of Security Council mandates, oversee elections, and assist in the building of state institutions.

In short, not only did the Security Council authorize more peacekeeping missions, these missions were much larger and more expensive than anything that the UN had attempted previously, with the important exception of ONUC.

Problems emerged, however, as it became clear—just as it had during the ONUC mission in the 1960s—that the principles and guidelines for peacekeeping were not suited to the operational demands of large and complex missions deployed in situations of ongoing violence. In September 1992, the UN Angola Verification Mission (UNAVEM II) was unable to prevent the slide back into civil war in Angola or to protect civilians as approximately 300,000 people died when violence resumed.

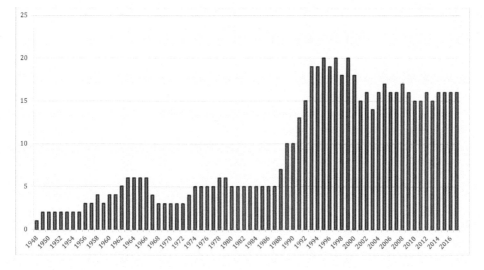

Figure 32.1 Number of active UN-led peacekeeping operations, 1948–2016

Source: Compiled from the authors from the information on the DPKO: www.un.org/en/peacekeeping/operations/[un.org].

A little over a year later, in October 1993, US attempts to arrest the Somali warlord Mohamed Farah Aidid resulted in the notorious "Black Hawk Down" incident and the eventual withdrawal of the UN Operation in Somalia (UNOSOM II). Then in April 1994 the Arusha peace process in Rwanda collapsed as Hutu militia and coup plotters unleashed genocide on the country that the UN Assistance Mission for Rwanda (UNAMIR) was unable to prevent or stop and which killed an estimated 800,000 people. In July 1995, around 8000 boys and men were taken from the UN-protected "safe area" of Srebrenica in Bosnia and killed by Bosnian Serb forces.

Both the traditional approach to UN peacekeeping and the resources made available by member states proved badly insufficient to accomplish the increasingly ambitious mandates handed down by the Security Council. In environments in which peace and ceasefire agreements were often precarious, peacekeepers were repeatedly confronted with an awful dilemma: Soldier on with the limited resources, authority, and political support offered by international society, or advocate withdrawal. Although the UN received much of the blame for what happened—some of it rightly so—it is important to note the crucial roles played by member states. They, not the UN Secretariat, crafted the mandates and determined resources for these four operations. Moreover, the bungled operation in Mogadishu in October 1993 that marked the beginning of the end for UNOSOM II was conducted by US soldiers (not UN peacekeepers); the UN Department of Peacekeeping Operations (DPKO) had warned the Security Council that without adequate resources the so-called "safe areas" in Bosnia would be vulnerable to attack; and the decision to stand aside during Rwanda's genocide in 1994 was taken against the advice of the UN's force commander on the ground.

These catastrophes prompted many states to reassess the value of peace operations and how they would contribute to them. Some senior UN officials also questioned whether the organization should go "back to basics" and focus only on conducting operations in benign conditions and with the consent of the host parties.[10] The number of UN peacekeepers deployed around the world fell dramatically as member states expressed a preference for working through regional organizations and alliances, such as the Economic Community of West African States (ECOWAS) and the North Atlantic Treaty Organization (NATO); and the Security Council became reluctant to create new missions. A period of introspection occurred at the UN which resulted in some important reforms, not least those outlined in four important reports examining various aspects of its peace operations: The inquiries into the failings at Srebrenica (1999) and Rwanda (1999), the "Brahimi Report" on UN peace operations (2000), and the report on the failure of the UN sanctions regime against UNITA rebels in Angola (2000).

One of the most significant was the 2000 report of the UN Secretary-General's Panel on United Nations Peace Operations. The so-called Brahimi Report, named after its chair the former Algerian foreign minister and veteran UN troubleshooter Lakhdar Brahimi, called for steps to ensure that peacekeeping operations have the resources, training, and operational guidance needed to complete their work; that missions be deployed rapidly; and that peacekeepers are capable of operating effectively. The phrase "robust peacekeeping" was coined to refer to the idea that, at a minimum, UN peacekeepers should be able to defend themselves, other members of the mission and associated international staff, and protect civilian populations within the area of operations. To achieve this, peacekeepers should be presumed to have permission to use force in defense of the mission's mandate at the operational and tactical levels, while maintaining the consent of the major parties at the strategic level. The report thus ushered in a decade-long process of reform at the United Nations, which has fundamentally changed the way in which peacekeeping is managed.

The world organization also made major strides in terms of professionalizing its operations. "Professionalization" here refers to the development of a cadre of competent bureaucrats, relevant doctrine, guidelines and procedures for peacekeeping, and the capacity to engage in systematic reflection on the UN's failures and successes.[11] Institutionally, key developments were the establishment of DPKO in early 1992, its gradual strengthening and then its separation from the provision of peacekeeping logistics by the establishment of the Department of Field Support (DFS) in 2007. Among other things, the UN has developed operational guidelines for peacekeeping, basic requirements for national contingents, a stronger system for logistics support, and improved support for training. The DPKO has also become much more cautious in its advice to the Security Council in relation to what can be achieved through peacekeeping. As a result, an informal division of labor has begun to emerge, with peacekeeping activities being conducted by the UN and regional arrangements or *ad hoc* coalitions of the willing taking primary responsibility for higher intensity military operations. Often, these two types of operation have worked in unison, whether sequentially (for example, in East Timor, where the UN deployed after the conditions

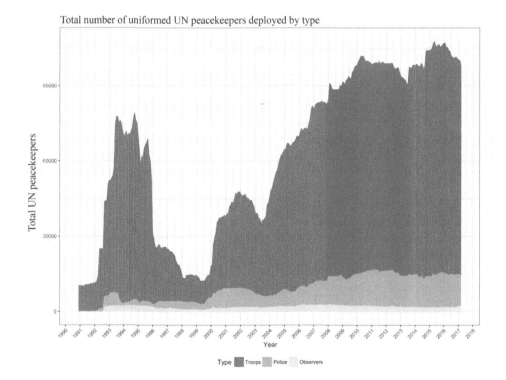

Figure 32.2 Number of uniformed personnel in UN-led peacekeeping operations, 1990–2017

Source: Based on information compiled by the authors from providingforpeacekeeping.org/peace keeping-data-graphs/. The complete database can be found at www.providingforpeacekeeping.org/ contributions/[providingforpeacekeeping.org].

had been created by an Australian-led intervention force, the International Force for East Timor, INTERFET) or simultaneously (for example, the 2003 French-led intervention in eastern Democratic Republic of the Congo (DRC) conducted alongside the UN Organization Mission in the DRC, MONUC, or the 2013 French Operation Serval in Mali that operated alongside the AU's African-led International Support Mission to Mali, AFISMA, and then later the UN Multidimensional Integrated Stabilization Mission in Mali, MINUSMA) (Figure 32.2).

In the first two decades of the twenty-first century there were significant changes in how the Security Council conducted its peacekeeping business. At the strategic level, the politics of decision making concerning peace operations takes place in informal settings. Informal interaction between Council members—whether in the form of external retreats, corridor discussions, seminars, or informal meetings—now occurs very regularly, making it easier for the council to find consensus on most peacekeeping mandates and to consult on its periodic reviews of ongoing operations. To deal with the increasing complexities of peace operations and the demand for specialized knowledge and expertise, the Security Council has established various mechanisms to support its decision making. For instance, it utilizes Groups of Friends, "Arria formula" meetings, sanctions committees, monitoring groups, and panels of experts, as well as making fact-finding visits outside of New York. The Military Staff Committee has also, from time to time, provided the Security Council with military advice on peacekeeping issues. The council also has a dedicated Working Group on Peacekeeping Operations, which is supposed to act as a forum for private expert debate among its members.

The growing sophistication and professionalism of UN peacekeeping facilitated a partial return of confidence in the twenty-first century. Rising demand for peacekeepers saw the United Nations operate at a historically unprecedented tempo, with increases in the number and size of missions as well as in the scope and complexity of their mandates. Among other things, peace operations are now regularly mandated to protect civilians, assist in the rebuilding of state institutions and the extension of state authority, assist in the reestablishment of the rule of law, assist or supervise elections, provide assistance to refugees and internally displaced persons, monitor borders and compliance with embargoes and sanctions regimes, assist with disarming, demobilizing and reintegrating militia members, assist security sector reform, protect visible individuals, promote human rights, protect and empower women, and support the provision of humanitarian assistance—all of which extends well beyond the original remit of peacekeeping. Faced with big and complicated new missions, notably in the Sudan—the African Union/ UN Hybrid Operation in Darfur (UNAMID), UN Mission in the Republic of South Sudan (UNMISS) in South Sudan—along with two others—MINUSMA and the UN Multidimensional Integrated Stabilization Mission in the Central African Republic (MINUSCA)—advances in the conceptual development of UN peacekeeping and its management structures have helped to avoid a repeat of the calamities of the 1990s.

Nevertheless, these missions have generated some major practical and conceptual challenges and dilemmas. One major challenge revolved around the issue of host state consent and what to do when the hosts were uncooperative. Sometimes, hosts changed their mind and ejected UN missions, as in Burundi, Chad, Eritrea, and Sudan; and sometimes they gave their official consent but threw up all sorts of practical obstacles to restrict the peacekeepers, as occurred in Darfur, DRC, and South Sudan. Sometimes, the supposed hosts refused to consent to the mission's deployment in the first place, as occurred in 2016 with Burundi and South Sudan following Security Council resolutions 2303 and 2304, respectively. Faced with several missions that were struggling to make political headway and develop a successful exit strategy, particularly in Africa, the secretary-general assembled another expert panel on peace operations which reported in mid-2015. The High-level Independent Panel on Peace Operations (HIPPO) stressed a few central recommendations to strengthen the performance of peace operations. They revolved around the need to give greater emphasis to conflict prevention and sustaining peace; the primacy of politics by tying peace operations to a viable political strategy and identifying a pathway to end the conflict in question; more effective capabilities in the field by enhancing mission support elements, bureaucratic structures, and establishing effective means of evaluating peacekeeper performance; effective and accountable leadership teams; and effective partnerships with other institutions engaged in peace operations. The numerous proposed HIPPO reforms are still working their way through the UN system. Some progress has occurred but significant challenges remain, which are examined next.

Current debates, key criticisms, and emerging issues

This section analyses three key debates that have prompted new thinking and practices as well as criticism of UN peacekeeping. They relate to participation, regionalization, and the use of military force.

Participation

One major debate revolves around the question of which countries contribute uniformed personnel to UN missions.[12] Today, the task of providing UN peacekeepers continues to be met in a highly unequal manner, with well over two-thirds of all UN uniformed personnel coming from just 20 or so countries. Among the top contributors of uniformed personnel to UN missions in the twenty-first century were several from South Asia (Pakistan, Bangladesh, India, and Nepal) and from Africa (Nigeria, Ethiopia, Ghana, and Rwanda). Over the same period, the world's most stable and prosperous governments in the Western world—which also possessed most of the world's high-tech military capabilities—significantly reduced the numbers of their troops contributed to UN-led peace operations.[13] In addition, developing countries, especially from Africa, have sustained high casualties from robust peace operations, whereas their Western counterparts have publics with virtually no tolerance for casualties in peace operations.[14] European countries subsequently made a partial return to UN missions in the two operations in Lebanon (the UN Interim Force in Lebanon, UNIFIL, after 2006) and Mali (MINUSMA after 2013). By early 2011, this had created a disquieting situation acknowledged by then UN Secretary-General Ban Ki-moon: "Securing the required resources and troops [for UN peacekeeping] has consumed much of my energy. I have been begging leaders to make resources available to us."[15]

The other dimension of this debate was whether countries should provide their peacekeepers to the United Nations or deploy them under the auspices of other international organizations or coalitions of states. While the twenty-first century saw a significant increase in the overall number of peacekeepers deployed by various coalitions of states and international organizations—the UN's main competitors were NATO, EU, and AU—the range of alternative institutional vehicles for conducting peacekeeping operations meant that the UN competed for personnel.

It was in this context that the DPKO and DFS launched their "New Horizon" initiative, which in 2009 called for "an expanded base of troop- and police-contributing countries . . . to enhance collective burden-sharing and to meet future requirements."[16] The following year, the General Assembly's Special Committee on Peacekeeping Operations (C34) also emphasized the need to "expand the available pool of capabilities" for UN peacekeeping. To achieve this goal, the committee called upon the UN Secretariat to analyze "the willingness and readiness" of contributing countries and "to develop outreach strategies" in order to strengthen contacts and longer term relationships with current or potential contributing countries, encourage further contributions from existing contributors, and provide practical support to emerging contributors.[17]

Expanding the pool of available capabilities for UN-led operations involves four main tasks: Persuading more countries to become major contributors of UN peacekeepers, namely, being able to provide sustained contributions of, say, two or more battalions of troops/police; persuading Western (and other) states with relevant specialist and enabling capabilities such as medical, aviation, and engineering units to deploy them in order to fulfill key UN peacekeeping functions; convincing current major contributors to sustain or expand their contributions while also improving the performance capabilities of their deployed forces; and persuading some contributors to purchase or develop relevant specialist/niche capabilities that they either do not currently possess or do not have in surplus, and to contribute them to UN peacekeeping operations. Each of these areas presents its own challenges, not least as states tend to privilege their own perceived strategic interests and more states come to view UN peacekeeping as one among many forms of crisis management.

Regionalization

In debates about peace operations, "regionalization" is commonly understood in two senses.[18] Empirically, it is often used as a label to describe the increased level of activities undertaken by regional organizations with regard to conflict management in general and peace operations in particular. Normatively, regionalization refers to the idea that each region of the world "should be responsible for its own peacemaking and peacekeeping, with some financial and technical support from the West but few, if any, military or police contingents from outside the region."[19] With the high demand for peacekeepers and the UN's capacity to deliver straining, some policymakers and analysts see regionalization as a potential solution.

As a descriptive label for the contemporary peacekeeping landscape, however, "regionalization" is rather misleading in several respects. First, regional organizations are not the only important actors in relation to peace operations: The UN, *ad hoc* coalitions, individual states, and private military companies all play significant roles. Second, regionalization has occurred unevenly around the globe. While some parts of the world have regional organizations that are willing and able to conduct peace operations, others have the will but lack the relevant capabilities. Some dislike the idea of conducting military operations but are keen to undertake political and observer missions. Still other regional organizations have no desire to engage in collective peace operations of any sort. And some parts of the world have no significant regional arrangements that deal with conflict management issues at all. Third, not all regional arrangements have confined their activities to their own region. Some (Western) regional organizations, NATO and the EU for instance, have operated well beyond their own neighborhood.

The starting point for understanding the challenge of regionalization is two fundamental characteristics of the UN system. The first is that Chapter VIII of the UN Charter encourages "regional arrangements" to be proactive in peacefully resolving conflicts that occur within their neighborhood, but they must gain Security Council authorization to use force. The Charter thus created a system flexible enough not to grant the Security Council a monopoly of authority on issues of international peace and security. The second fundamental characteristic is the UN's lack of standing armed forces, which has meant that it must sometimes delegate to other actors the conduct of peace operations, especially those involving large-scale enforcement. The growing number of regional arrangements that have taken an explicit interest in conflict management has thus provided the UN with an expanding set of options. As noted above, thirteen regional arrangements have deployed peace operations since the late 1940s. Since 2004, all new regional peace operations have taken place in Africa.

Despite these caveats, the normative debate about the place of regional organizations in peace operations and their relationship to the UN remains on the agenda. This old debate has become more prominent since the end of the 1990s after NATO's intervention in Kosovo/Yugoslavia in 1999. As then UN Secretary-General Kofi Annan put it in 2002, "multilateral institutions and regional security organizations have never been more important than today."[20] In 2009, for the first time ever, the Security Council established a new mission funded by using the UN's assessed peacekeeping budget to provide logistical support for a regional peace operation, the UN Support Office for the African Union Mission in Somalia (UNSOA).

The contemporary challenge is thus for the UN to find an appropriate working relationship with those regional organizations that are in the business of conducting peace operations. So far, the key practical debates have played out with a focus on Africa, where since 2005 the UN has embarked on a major capacity-building program to enhance the ability of Africa's regional organizations to conduct peace operations. So have a variety of bilateral (primarily Western) donors and the European Union. This project has made progress, and the African Union has become a more capable partner.[21] The most recent focus has been on how to ensure successful transitions from AU to UN-led operations, as occurred in Burundi (2004), Darfur (2008), Mali (2013), and Central African Republic (2014).

The use of military force

There have been at least three major strands to debates about the use of military force in UN peace operations—debates that stretch back to ONUC in the 1960s. The first relates to humanitarian military intervention; the second to "robust" peacekeeping that emerged with the Brahimi Report; and the third to the emergence of the protection of civilians (POC) as a mandated goal.

The most controversial issue has been the question of when it is legitimate for the UN to conduct humanitarian military intervention as a form of peace enforcement. The Security Council has authorized its peacekeepers to use force on numerous occasions—notably it has since 1999 frequently authorized the use of "all necessary means" to protect civilians in DRC, Sudan, and Côte d'Ivoire, among others. Nonetheless, such authorizations are all undertaken with the consent of *de jure* state authorities and thus represent a use of force at the operational and tactical levels rather than at a strategic level. To date, outside the context of interstate aggression, the Security Council has authorized force to protect civilians against the consent of the *de jure* state authorities only once—the March 2011 resolution 1973 that authorized the use of force to protect civilians against the wishes of the Libyan authorities. One of the principal lessons from the peacekeeping disasters of the 1990s was that a clear line should be drawn between peacekeeping and peace enforcement, and that situations requiring the use of force to achieve strategic goals (such as creating a safe environment, or disarming belligerents) were not a UN comparative advantage. In such situations, the DPKO typically advised that the Security Council should consider deploying a multinational force capable of high-intensity operations. In the Libyan case, the operations were conducted by a NATO-led coalition of states not UN peacekeepers.

The second set of issues relating to the use of military force stems from the notion of "robust" operations developed by the Brahimi Report. "Robustness" referred to the idea that peacekeepers might use tactical force in order to defend themselves or other UN personnel, defend the mission mandate from spoilers and not cede the initiative to them, and protect civilians threatened with physical violence. The concept won widespread support from some, especially Western member states, which argued that robust peacekeeping had largely succeeded in East Timor (1999 and 2006), Sierra Leone (after the 2000 British intervention), and eastern DRC in 2003. However, many traditional peacekeeping nations expressed concerns about its potential impact on consent and impartiality. In practice, the concept has been difficult to operationalize in environments in which peacekeeping forces lack the resources to be credibly robust, where operations depend on local and national consent, and in which building sustainable peace demands political solutions. As a result of these and other challenges, the DPKO became more reticent about employing the term.

There has been much greater support for the idea that UN peacekeepers should use force to protect civilians, not least because the moral imperative is clearer. The Security Council has, at times, been enthusiastic. The 1999 resolution 1265 expressed the council's "willingness" to consider "appropriate measures" in response "to situations of armed conflict where civilians are being targeted or where humanitarian assistance to civilians is being deliberately obstructed," and to explore how peacekeeping mandates might be reframed to afford better protection to endangered civilians. The Brahimi Report earlier had argued that peacekeepers who witness violence against civilians should "be presumed to be authorized to stop it, within their means." Starting in 1999 with the UN Mission in Sierra Leone (UNAMSIL), the Security Council has regularly invoked Charter Chapter VII to create civilian protection mandates, albeit while inserting some important geographical, temporal, and capabilities-based caveats. Gradually the Security Council has become more relaxed about imposing them. For example, in 2011 it granted the UN Mission in Côte d'Ivoire (UNOCI) a broad mandate to use "all necessary means" to "protect civilians" in resolution 1975. But this too has raised some fundamental questions about the UN's impartiality as well as operational headaches for peacekeepers tasked with implementing such mandates in the field. Debates intensified during 2013 when resolution 2098 authorized a force intervention brigade of South African, Tanzanian, and Malawian troops within the UN Organization Stabilization Mission in the DRC (MONUSCO) to undertake "targeted offensive operations" against a rebel group known as "M-23."[22] Similarly, the 2016 resolution 2095 authorized the UN soldiers in Mali, MINUSMA, "to anticipate and deter threats and to take robust and active steps to counter asymmetric attacks against civilians or United Nations personnel" perpetrated by several named "terrorist organizations."

However, moves towards "robust" peacekeeping and the protection of civilians have undoubtedly improved the effectiveness and professionalism of UN peace-keeping operations and prevented a repeat of past calamities. But these advances have come at a cost. First, the use of force remains controversial. Second, the demands of robustness, protection, and expanded mandates have led to rising costs for equipment and numbers of required peacekeepers. Indeed, adjusted for inflation, approximately three-quarters of all UN peacekeeping costs incurred since 1948 were spent between 2004 and 2017. However, questions remain about whether UN peace operations have the resources required to use force effectively. For example, the capacity of UN peacekeepers to collect intelligence is widely deemed essential for the effective use of force, but UN peacekeepers have traditionally been denied

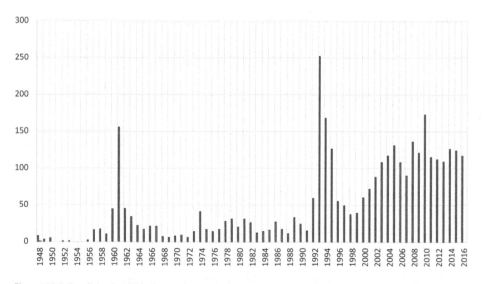

Figure 32.3 Fatalities in UN-led peacekeeping operations, 1948–2016

Source: Data drawn from Marina Henke, *Has UN Peacekeeping Become More Deadly?* (New York: International Peace Institute, 2016).

access to intelligence-gathering capabilities. Debates are currently ongoing about how UN peacekeepers can utilize modern monitoring and surveillance technologies to overcome some of these problems at a reasonable cost.[23] Third, a more proactive approach to the use of force raises the risk of higher casualties among UN peacekeepers. So far at least, this has not led to a large increase in deaths by malicious attacks on peacekeepers, although over 3500 peacekeepers have now died on mission and some operations, notably MINUSMA, have faced unprecedented forms of asymmetric attacks, including improvised explosive devices (IEDs) (see Figure 32.3). Fourth, debate persists over whether the UN is structurally well suited to using military force. There is clearly a consensus that it is not well suited to high-intensity combat missions, but in some tactical situations UN peacekeepers have occasionally used force effectively against non-state actors who threaten civilians.

Conclusion

UN peacekeeping is an example of constructivism in action—what started out as a series of *ad hoc* practices have over time developed their own operating guidelines, standard procedures, professional standards, and methods of evaluation. Peacekeeping institutions, doctrine, and methods have all come *after* peacekeeping practice. As a result, both the history of UN peacekeeping and its current operations are made up of field experiments and lesson learning. Throughout its history the key lessons have focused not just on what might work in theory but what works within the political and material limits set by international society. Sometimes, as in the early 1990s and more recently with the agenda for the protection of civilians, the Security Council has played a proactive role in driving peacekeeping forward and expanding its scope and mandates. In both cases, the UN Secretariat was left with the challenge of achieving complex mandates with limited resources. That UN peacekeeping has generally avoided the calamities of the mid-1990s is testament to the growing professionalization of the UN and its peacekeepers. At the same time, serious questions remain about how the UN will find the necessary resources, how it will partner with regional organizations, and how it will employ force in effective and sustainable ways. But thus it has ever been: UN peacekeeping is, and will remain, a work in progress.

Additional reading

Alex J. Bellamy and Paul D. Williams, *Understanding Peacekeeping*, 2nd ed. (Cambridge: Polity Press, 2010).

Michael W. Doyle and Nicholas Sambanis, *Making War and Building Peace: United Nations Peace Operations* (Princeton, NJ: Princeton University Press, 2006).

William J. Durch, ed., *Twenty-First Century Peace Operations* (Washington, DC: United States Institute of Peace Press, 2006).

Virginia Page Fortna, *Does Peacekeeping Work? Shaping Belligerents' Choices after Civil War* (Princeton, NJ: Princeton University Press, 2008).

Joachim Koops, et al., eds., *The Oxford Handbook of United Nations Peacekeeping Operations* (Oxford: Oxford University Press, 2015).
Providing for Peacekeeping project at www.providingforpeacekeeping.org.

Notes

1 Virginia Page Fortna, *Does Peacekeeping Work? Shaping Belligerents' Choices after Civil War* (Princeton, NJ: Princeton University Press, 2008), 173.
2 For example, Andrew Mack, *Global Political Violence: Explaining the Post Cold War Decline* (New York: International Peace Academy, 2007).
3 Fortna, *Does Peacekeeping Work?* 171.
4 Matthew Krain, "International Intervention and the Severity of Genocides and Politicides," *International Studies Quarterly* 49, no. 2 (2005): 363–387. See also Taylor Seybolt, *Humanitarian Military Intervention* (Oxford: Oxford University Press for SIPRI, 2007).
5 Lisa Hultman, Jacob Kathman, and Megan Shannon "United Nations Peacekeeping and Civilian Protection in Civil War," *American Journal of Political Science* 57, no. 4 (2013): 875–891.
6 Roland Paris, *At War's End* (Cambridge: Cambridge University Press, 2004).
7 Michael W. Doyle and Nicholas Sambanis, "International Peacebuilding: A Theoretical and Quantitative Analysis," *American Political Science Review* 94, no. 4 (2000): 795. See also Michael W. Doyle and Nicholas Sambanis, *Making War and Building Peace: United Nations Peace Operations* (Princeton, NJ: Princeton University Press, 2006).
8 Paul D. Williams, "Global and Regional Peacekeepers: Trends, Opportunities, Risks and a Way Ahead," *Global Policy* 8, no. 1 (2017): 124–129.
9 Brian Urquhart, *Hammarskjöld: A Life in War and Peace* (New York: Croom Helm, 1972), 265. See also Bertrand G. Ramcharan, *Preventive Diplomacy at the UN* (Bloomington: Indiana University Press, 2008).
10 Shashi Tharoor, "Should UN Peacekeeping Go 'Back to Basics?,'" *Survival* 37, no. 4 (1995): 52–64.
11 Thorsten Benner, Stephan Mergenthaler, and Philipp Rotmann, *The New World of UN Peace Operations* (Oxford: Oxford University Press, 2011).
12 This section draws from Alex J. Bellamy and Paul D. Williams, eds., *Providing Peacekeepers: The Politics, Challenges, and Future of United Nations Peacekeeping Contributions* (Oxford: Oxford University Press, 2013). More and updated details can be found at www.providingforpeacekeeping.org/.
13 Alex J. Bellamy and Paul D. Williams, "The West and Contemporary Peace Operations," *Journal of Peace Research* 46, no. 1 (2009): 39–57.
14 Thomas G. Weiss and Martin Welz, "The UN and the African Union in Mali and Beyond: A Shotgun Wedding?" *International Affairs* 90, no. 4 (2014): 889–905; "Military Twists and Turns in World Politics: Downsides or Dividends for UN Peace Operations?" *Third World Quarterly* 36, no 8 (2015): 1493–1509.
15 Ban Ki-moon, Cyril Foster Lecture, University of Oxford, 2 February 2011, www.un.org/News/Press/docs/2011/sgsm13385.doc.htm.
16 United Nations, *A New Partnership Agenda: Charting a New Horizon for UN Peacekeeping* (New York: UN DPKO/DFS, July 2009), vi.
17 UN, *Report of the Special Committee on Peacekeeping Operations 2010 Substantive Session (22 February–19 March 2010)*, General Assembly Official Records 64th Session, Supplement No. 19, UN document A/64/19, 2010, para. 75.
18 See Williams, "Global and Regional Peacekeepers."
19 Marrack Goulding, *Peacemonger* (London: John Murray, 2002), 217.

20 Kofi Annan, "Regional Security Organizations Never More Important Than Today," UN document SG/SM/8543, 9 December 2002.
21 Paul D. Williams and Solomon Dersso, *Saving Strangers and Neighbors: Advancing UN–AU Cooperation on Peace Operations* (New York: International Peace Institute, 2015).
22 UN, "Letter Dated 24 December 2015 from the Chair of the Security Council Working Group on Peacekeeping Operations Addressed to the President of the Security Council," UN document S/2015/1040, 28 December 2015.
23 Walter K. Dorn, *Keeping Watch: Monitoring Technology and Innovation in UN Peace Operations* (Tokyo: UN University Press, 2011).

CONTENTS

Regional organizations and global security governance

S. Neil MacFarlane

The end of the Cold War brought considerable enthusiasm concerning the potential role of regional organizations in generating peace and security in a very promising, but also very uncertain, post-Cold War landscape. As Secretary-General Boutros Boutros-Ghali declared in 1992: "In this new era of opportunity, regional arrangements or agencies can render great service if their activities are undertaken in a manner consistent with the Purposes and Principles of the Charter, and if their relationship with the United Nations, and particularly the Security Council, is governed by Chapter VIII."[1] This enthusiasm reflected a widespread view in the Global South that postcolonial states ought to be allowed to resolve their own problems without interference from the major powers.[2] It followed that regions should take the lead in managing regional security.

From the perspective of the Euro-Atlantic states, the end of bipolar competition in the Third World removed the structural interest in direct engagement in regional disputes. The major Western states were looking forward to a peace dividend. The United Nations was in serious financial difficulty; operational burden shifting was attractive. If things did not go well, blame could be shifted too.

There were other reasons for enthusiasm. In principle, actors closer to a regional security problem had a stronger interest in resolving it, since it was likely to affect them more directly. Regional actors were arguably more familiar with the factors producing regional armed conflicts. Their knowledge advantage presumably favored more nuanced and informed approaches to conflict resolution and management. Regional leaders were more closely acquainted with one another, enhancing predictability and, possibly, trust. Regional bureaucracies were accustomed to dealing with each other. These personal and bureaucratic connections could facilitate mediation. Arguably, decisions taken by regional multilateral organizations would enjoy greater legitimacy than decisions taken by outsiders.

In short, there was a substantial case for empowering regional organizations to address security matters within their geographical area. In the post-Cold War era, this approach has been amply explored, with substantial encouragement from the United Nations.[3] Regional organizations have been engaged as mediators and facilitators, peacekeepers, confidence builders, peace enforcers, and guarantors of settlements. They have adopted and implemented preventive development programs and have been heavily involved in reconstruction and institution building. In other words, they have together constituted a central pillar in international efforts to achieve peace and security since 1991.

This case was contested. Critics suggested that, although regional actors might have a greater interest in engagement in local conflict, the interests of neighboring countries might conflict. Their particular interests in the outcome of a regional dispute might outweigh their collective interest in conflict resolution and stability. Likewise, although regional actors might be more familiar with the intricacies of a regional dispute, that was no guarantee of impartiality or legitimacy. In regions where a locally dominant state existed, the organization could become its vehicle for asserting hegemony. In addition, many regional organizations lacked both the capacity and the experience for effective intervention in regional disputes.[4]

This chapter examines the contribution of regional organizations to global security governance since the end of the Cold War.[5] Is there regionalization of security governance? If so, how should one view the relationship between growing regional activity and the role of the United Nations and its Security Council as the locus of global security governance? Are regional powers and regional organizations supplanting global security governance? The chapter begins with conceptual, legal, and historical background to the issue. It continues with an overview of regional organizations' engagement with peace operations and broader governance of security in the twenty-seven years since the end of the Cold War. This is followed by consideration of the interface between regional and global security governance.

Concepts and definitions

This chapter revolves around two concepts: Security and regional organization. Concerning the former, there is a broad consensus on the core meaning of security: The absence of threats to core values (survival, welfare, identity). However, that definition raises more questions than it answers. Whose security are we talking about—individual human beings, minority groups, states, regions, the international system, the global community? What threats are we talking about—military, criminal, terrorist, cultural, economic, ecological? Where do security threats come from—other states, individuals, non-state political, economic, or religious actors, or from the natural environment?

The degree of contestation is evident, for example, in the evolution of the notion of "human security," which questions both the traditional privileging of the state and the conventional focus on military threats in security studies.[6] While recognizing the importance of the wider conversation, this chapter focuses on threats associated with the existence, or the threat, of organized violence within or between states. Managing, if not eliminating, these threats has been a core function of the United Nations since its establishment in 1945.

Regions are geographically limited spaces linked by notions of shared history, culture, custom, or threat. Regional organizations are groups of states that purport to share common objectives regarding their area.[7] They may cover the entire expanse of a region, for example the Organization of African Unity (OAU; later the African Union, AU) or sub-regional parts of that space, for example the Association of Southeast Asian Nations (ASEAN). They may be inclusive of all states within a space, for example, the Organization for Security and Co-operation in Europe (OSCE) or they may not, for example, the North Atlantic Treaty Organization (NATO). Regional organizations may be institutionalized or not; for example, the Conference on Security and Cooperation in Europe was not a formal organization until it was transformed into the OSCE in 1993. They may be permanent or they may be *ad hoc* and focused on a particular challenge, for example the Contadora Group during Central America's wars of the 1980s.

Their objectives may include peace and security, but that is not a necessary attribute. The North American Free Trade Area (NAFTA) has never had a security function. In other cases, security was, and is, the reason that they exist—e.g., the OSCE. Organizations without a security role in their initial mandate may adopt such a role over time. The European Economic Community (EEC) passed its first thirty-five years or so without acknowledging any direct security role. Then, it developed a Common Foreign and Security Policy (CFSP) within what was renamed the European Union (EU). Some regional organizations continue to have no explicit security role, but their activities may overlap with a broad security agenda, for example the Council of Europe, whose basic purposes comprise the protection and promotion of human rights and the rule of law.

Early history

Coming together to address a shared threat or to mitigate insecurity has been a common regional practice throughout international history, classical Greece's alliance against the Persians being an early case in point. The League of Nations Covenant made provision for contribution by "regional arrangements" to international peace. The UN Charter devoted an entire chapter to the "regional arrangements and agencies." Chapter VIII was an attempt not only to legitimate regional arrangements but also to define their relationship to UN security governance. Article 52 notes that members of regional arrangements should seek pacific resolution of disputes before referring them to the Security Council. Article 53 provides for the council to use regional arrangements in enforcement actions, while prohibiting enforcement action by regional actors without Security Council authorization. Article 54 obliges regional agencies and arrangements to inform the council of activities that are related to international peace and security.[8]

The Cold War period witnessed four relevant developments. One, and specific to Europe, was development of regional agencies to foster reconstruction and regional economic integration (the OEEC, the ECSC, the EEC). A second was the emergence of regional organizations outside Europe that were linked to decolonization. The third was the creation of numerous Western-sponsored treaty organizations to assist in containment (the Baghdad Pact and the Central Treaty Organization, NATO, and the Southeast Asian Treaty Organization). The communist countries engaged in similar institution building, for example the Warsaw Treaty Organization. These organizations had, by and large, little to do with the promotion of international peace and security, except through their deterrence and collective defense functions. A fourth was the creation of regional and sub-regional organizations for specific (often hegemonic) purposes by major regional powers (the Organization of American States—OAS—as successor to the Pan-American Union, and the Southern African Development and Coordination Conference).

The Cold War alliances outside Europe amounted to very little. In Europe, however, NATO and the Warsaw Pact became significant security adversaries. NATO emerged as the multilateral military arm of Western defense and deterrence strategy in Europe. The Warsaw Pact was an instrument of the Soviet Union in the effort to coordinate Soviet and allied military posture *vis-à-vis* NATO, and also as a means to implement and to legitimize Soviet efforts to control its satellite states, as in Hungary and Czechoslovakia.

Peace or other military operations by regional organizations during the Cold War were extremely rare. They include the Warsaw Pact interventions just mentioned, the role of the OAS in the Dominican Republic in 1965–1966, and an abortive operation by the OAU in Chad's civil war in 1980.

The post-Cold War era

There has clearly been a step-change in the role of regional organizations in security governance after the Cold War. It is useful to analyze this expansion in terms of organizational mandates and of operations.

Organizational mandates

One element of this transformation was organizational, the expansion of institutional mandates by existing regional organizations—for example, the transformation of the European Community into the European Union in 1993. The EU embraced a foreign and security policy.[9] This evolution culminated in the acceptance of a mandate for humanitarian and peacekeeping operations and combat tasks associated with crisis management (the Petersberg tasks), elaboration of a European Security Strategy, agreement on the formation of rapid deployment forces, and the creation of EU foreign and security policy institutions.

The 2003 EU Security Strategy acknowledged that, as an "inevitable" global power, the security role was not limited to the territory of its members but extended to the European neighborhood and beyond.[10] Although the EU's original focus was regional, it broadened its notion of security responsibility to the world as a whole, reflecting its aspiration (or at least the aspiration of some of its member states) to become a great power in its own right.

A second example would be the CSCE. The conference was initially a mechanism to manage security (and in particular "soft security") in Cold War Europe. When the Soviet Union collapsed, the question of how to approach its successor states and those of the former Yugoslavia arose. The CSCE took an inclusive approach, sooner or later admitting all the new successor states in Europe, with the exception of Kosovo and the various breakaway sub-states in the former Soviet republics. In addition, it established itself as a formal international organization with a focus on softer security issues. Responding to the evolving conceptualization and practicalities of security, the organization adopted a human dimension that focused on the rights of individuals within member states.

The end of the Cold War also posed challenges for NATO. Founded as a defensive alliance, the original mandate did not envisage peacekeeping and peacebuilding. Its operational responsibilities extended to the NATO Treaty Area, but no further.[11] In 1990–1991, the threat NATO was designed to deter or to resist evaporated. Its major members took the view that its substantial institutional capacity could be adjusted to address security challenges in the post-Cold War era. NATO readjusted its strategic concept to emphasize the organization's role in confidence building, conflict prevention, crisis management, as well as humanitarian and disaster response. It loosened the alliance's area of operations to allow engagement out of area.[12] It created institutions for dialogue and cooperation with former communist states in order to forge a single cooperative security space across Europe and then embraced enlargement.[13] By 2012 NATO had grown from sixteen to twenty-eight states, taking in all of the members of the defunct Warsaw Pact, the Baltic Republics, Slovenia, Croatia, Albania, and Montenegro.

The NATO commitment to crisis management in the European area as a whole implied a willingness to act outside the traditional alliance's area of operations. The "global war on terrorism" (GWOT) expanded NATO threat assessment beyond the European arena. Africa witnessed analogous expansion of mandates. The OAU was founded in 1964 with a multidimensional mandate, including an underspecified security function. The organization had little presence or effect during the Cold War in addressing regional security issues. The end of the Cold War coincided with an increase in civil violence in the region. One consequence was the transition of the OAU into the AU. At its first assembly in 2002, it adopted a protocol establishing a Peace and Security Council whose objectives comprised conflict prevention, management, and resolution. The functions included peacemaking, peace support operations, intervention, peacebuilding, humanitarian action, and disaster assistance. The protocol envisaged the creation of an African Standby Force and a Military Staff Committee.[14] At the sub-regional level, both the Southern African Development Community (SADC) and the Economic Community of West African States (ECOWAS) adopted mandates to produce and maintain peace and security in their sub-regions, and created security organs.[15]

In a limited number of cases, new regional organizations were established. One was the Commonwealth of Independent States (CIS), formed by the majority of the Soviet Union's successor states to maintain functional and political integration after the Soviet collapse.[16] The CIS agreement envisaged close military integration (joint command structures, a general staff, and a headquarters). Some members supplemented the CIS agreement with a Treaty on Collective Security in 1992. Signatories accepted the obligation to eschew the use of force between states within the treaty area and to assist any treaty member attacked by another state. The treaty acknowledged the primacy of the UN Charter in security matters, referring to the right of individual and collective self-defense under Article 51.[17] Both the Collective Security Treaty (implicitly) and the CIS Charter include provisions for peace operations within the membership space.

Implementation of mandates

What have these institutions done to implement their new mandates? NATO has developed extensive programs for training both members and partners in peace and disaster operations, through the Partnership for Peace (PfP). More significantly, it led an intervention in Bosnia in 1995 under a Security Council mandate that ended the civil war. It then maintained the peace for nearly a decade before withdrawing. In Kosovo in 1999, NATO attacked Serbia without a UN mandate (China and Russia would have vetoed it) and forced its military to withdraw from the region; but NATO then cooperated with the UN to stabilize the internal situation to allow reconstruction and state building. Ten years later, most NATO members recognized the independence of Kosovo. Recalling discussion of NATO's "going global," in 2003—operating under a UN mandate—NATO took on the leadership of the International Security Assistance Force in Afghanistan (ISAF), which was tasked to stabilize the country and to control the threat from terrorism. NATO ended the ISAF mission in December 2014, although some member states retain military capacity and roles in the country.

The EU has been involved in all dimensions of international response to conflict. Nonmilitary security responses include conflict prevention (e.g., Macedonia), humanitarian action (the Balkans and the Caucasus), mediation (the council presidency's negotiation of a ceasefire agreement between Russia and Georgia in 2008), ceasefire monitoring (in Georgia since 2008) and post-conflict reconstruction, state capacity building, and strengthening the rule-of-law (Kosovo and Georgia), and policing (Bosnia and Macedonia).

Outside the European area, the EU has repeatedly launched missions into conflicts or potential conflicts in Africa and Asia. In general, the organization has taken niche roles with small numbers of personnel involved.[18] However, in rare cases, it has taken on stabilization missions involving combat forces, as, for example, in the case of Operation Artemis in Ituri in the DRC in 2003. Overall, the European Union has embarked on more than thirty-five, and has completed more than eighteen, missions.

In the meantime, the OSCE has provided considerable assistance on soft security issues. One dimension has been observing and certifying elections by the Office for Democratic Institutions and Human Rights. Another is the deployment of "missions of long-term duration" in transitional states to monitor and report on potential conflicts, to assist in the stabilization of ceasefires, and to promote human rights. A subsidiary unit of the OSCE—the High Commissioner for National Minorities— has mounted an extensive program to monitor minority problems and to suggest policy changes that might mitigate the potential for violence.

In Africa, ECOWAS, SADC, and the AU conducted peace operations within their regions and sub-regions, including in Liberia, Sierra Leone, Guinea-Bissau, the Ivory Coast, Lesotho, the Democratic Republic of the Congo, Burundi, Sudan, Somalia, and Mali. In a number of instances, sub-regional organization acted prior to authorization from the Security Council under Chapter VIII of the Charter.

In the former Soviet Union, the CIS mounted a peacekeeping operation in Georgia (concerning the conflict in Abkhazia) and peace enforcement in Tajikistan. In the first instance, a CIS contingent interposed itself between Georgian government and Abkhaz secessionist forces, policing a demilitarized zone and controlling heavy weapons cantonments. In Tajikistan, the Russian army and border forces stationed in the country supported the incumbent government against a challenge from a democratic and Islamic opposition. In both instances, engagement of Russian forces preceded authorization by the CIS, with UN approval coming considerably later still.

In short, there has been a large change in security governance in the international system since the end of the Cold War. Where regional actors (organizations, *ad hoc* coalitions) were rarely active during the Cold War, there is now a multitude of security-related initiatives at this level. The growing operational role of regional organizations both within their regions and (in the case of the EU and NATO) outside their regions produced a substantial "force multiplier," physically in terms of boots on the ground for peacekeeping and peace enforcement, and, metaphorically, through conflict prevention, mediation, peacekeeping, peace enforcement, and post-conflict peacebuilding and state building.

Many of the organizations discussed above have embraced to varying degrees the UN's global principles of human rights, democracy, and the rule of law, and the responsibility to protect as normative underpinnings of their activities. In other words, not only are they lined up with the UN on the need to contribute to the production of peace and security but they share many aspects of the broadening of the concepts of security and threat characteristic of the UN's discourse on the management of international security. On some occasions (for example, the AU in Sudan), regional forces act in close coordination with UN contingents.

Diversity in capacity, performance, and discourse

The general observations above conceal great diversity in the capabilities and competence of regional organizations to contribute to global security governance. First, the coverage of regional organizations is not universal. Some regions (e.g., Europe) are heavily institutionalized. Others either lack institutionalized regional organizations completely (e.g., Northeast Asia) or, where such institutions exist, they face strong regional normative and political constraints on multilateral efforts to address threats to peace and security. For example, in South Asia, while there is a shell of regional cooperation (South Asian Association for Regional Co-operation, or SAARC), the shell is empty in terms of security cooperation and management. That reflects a fundamental bipolarity in the region between India and Pakistan, and the concerns of smaller states that their more powerful neighbors would dominate regional initiatives. The lack of any significant regional conflict management of the civil war in Sri Lanka is a blatant illustration of the absence of regional capacity or will. SAARC has also been passive during periodic exacerbation of Indo-Pakistani relations. The relationship is managed, or mismanaged, bilaterally.

The Association of Southeast Asian Nations (ASEAN) has adopted a very cautious approach to security issues. The prevailing security norms among members are noninterference in internal affairs and the resolution of interstate disputes by peaceful means. The consequences are evident in the minimal role of the association in efforts to resolve the dispute in East Timor in 1999, and also in the absence of any regional response to widespread ethnic and religious violence with significant humanitarian consequences in Indonesia at the end of the 1990s, the conflicts in Aceh and Western New Guinea, endemic insurgency in the Philippines, chronic human rights abuse and low-level conflict in Myanmar; and potential conflict with China in the South China Sea. Instead, where security issues are engaged, the focus is on informal consultation and mediation (the "ASEAN Way"). Such responses are useful, but they highlight the limits for a global security safety net of relying on regional solutions to regional problems in this region, particularly where such solutions might involve engagement in the internal affairs of member states. Asia's overall deficit in regional security multilateralism contrasts sharply with Europe, where there is arguably a surplus. Most other regions fall between the two.

In the Middle East, there is no evidence of serious willingness on the part of the region's states to engage directly and proactively in the management of security issues. There is no region-wide organization. The Arab League, by definition, excludes the most capable military actor in the region, Israel, as well as Iran. Subregional organizations such as the Gulf Co-operation Council also exclude key players (notably Iran). The region's states have long been divided by significantly different understandings of legitimacy and community. The Arab Spring exacerbated these differences. The net effect is that the region needs bailing out by larger nonregional organizations. An example would be the Arab League's request for a UN response to the meltdown in Libya in 2011. The Security Council subcontracted to a NATO-led coalition of the willing. However, extra-regional bailouts are uncertain. When a civil war broke out in Syria in 2011–2012, there was no substantial multilateral response, despite an appeal by the Arab League for "deterrent measures" from the UNSC. The two cases share a number of problems. One is that although regional organization agreement may facilitate Security Council action by providing a degree of legitimacy, it does not guarantee a robust UN response, as the request regarding Syria suggests. Disagreements among the permanent members of the council about implementation of the NATO mandate in Libya have made consensus on action under Chapter VII significantly more problematic. The two cases are similar also on outcome: State weakness, protracted conflict, terrorism, humanitarian crisis, and competitive behavior by interested states.

Even where there may be the will to engage in the regional management of security issues, there is a wide variation in the capacity to do so. NATO has the largest and best established multilateral peace enforcement capacity. The EU and the OSCE, with a smaller brief, draw on the substantial resources of member states for soft security missions. In contrast, the AU has accumulated considerable experience of regional peace operations, but the funding base and military capacity are substantially lower. In Latin America, experience of participation in UN operations is far more developed than that of regional multilateral response. The same is true in much of Asia.

In other words, if there is a regionalization of peacekeeping, it is uneven and incomplete. The regional embrace of the emerging UN normative framework on security governance is also uneven. As seen earlier, it appeared that the normative embrace of wider conceptions of security, including human rights, democratization, and the rule of law, was spreading. That spread suggested a wider embrace of the responsibility of outsiders to engage in the domestic jurisdiction of states where those states' practices are inconsistent with the preferred normative agenda.

However, regional discourses around this matter fall into at least two categories. One is acceptance of sovereignty as responsibility, and the attenuation of sovereignty where a state is perceived not to be fulfilling its responsibility (e.g., EU and AU). A second is a focus on sovereignty and nonintervention (e.g., ASEAN and CIS). Others fall in the middle, where discursively there is an embrace of international standards but practice suggests a lingering attachment to traditional sovereignty and nonintervention norms. Where there are no organizations actively engaged in regional security (e.g., Northeast and South Asia), largely because of reluctance to engage in the internal affairs of member states, the issue does not even arise. In short, there is significant variation in the extent to which purportedly universal norms are accepted in principle or pursued in practice.

Normative variability points to a third issue: Response to regional threats to peace and security is highly politicized. The Syrian example suggests that the UN's capacity to manage international security is highly affected by political conflict. So too is the capacity of regional organizations. The ASEAN normative lowest common denominator mentioned above is a product of political and cultural cleavages. The impotence of regional multilateralism in South Asia reflects the mutual suspicion of India and Pakistan, in addition to the concerns of smaller states in the region with regard to Indian primacy. In West Africa, the regional security role of ECOWAS was hampered by differences of view between Francophone and Anglophone members regarding the conflicts in which ECOWAS engaged and, to a lesser extent, the concerns of smaller states regarding the regional asymmetry of military and economic power favoring Nigeria.[19] In effect, ECOMOG actions in the region involved engagement by a subset of like-minded members operating under a regional multilateral umbrella, while other members (e.g., Burkina Faso and Côte d'Ivoire) materially supported the opposing side.

Similarly, the CIS served as a cover for Russian unilateralism in Georgia. Although the CIS mandated the 1993–2008 peace operation there, the forces were purely Russian and the deployment served to draw Georgia back into Russian-dominated multilateral structures. It also impeded Georgia's adoption of a Western foreign policy orientation. In 2008, Russia responded to a more substantial Georgian effort to leave its sphere of influence by invading Georgia, detaching Abkhazia and South Ossetia and recognizing them status as sovereign states. There was no CIS condemnation of this flagrant violation of its charter, of OSCE norms, and of

UN Charter law concerning the use of force. By the same token, despite Russian diplomatic efforts, the organization was unwilling to endorse Moscow's action or to recognize the breakaway territories. The Security Council was paralyzed by the veto power. The result was that the first aggressive use of force and violation of the principle of territorial integrity in Europe since 1945 met no effective governance response at all.

The ability of regional organizations to contribute to global security governance is strongly affected by the degree of normative consensus among member states and also the degree to which they see common purpose in the multilateral management of regional security. In this sense, the unevenness is not only interregional but also intraregional, with the CIS as a good example. In the Southern Caucasus, the CIS deployed to keep the peace on the *de facto* boundary between Georgia and Abkhazia, and to create the peace in Tajikistan. It did not do so in South Ossetia, where Russia deployed a peacekeeping force without multilateral authorization. In Moldova also, Russia deployed on a bilateral basis without authorization from the regional organization. In Azerbaijan's Nagorno-Karabakh, Russia mediated a ceasefire, but no peacekeeping force was deployed. The dominant factor in these cases appears to be Russia's perception of its own interest. There are also many threats to peace and security in Africa where regional or sub-regional organizations have not engaged.

The problem of politicization is linked to the matter of authority and legitimacy. The UN Charter is fairly clear on this point. Article 24 indicates that the Security Council has primary responsibility for international peace and security. This is elaborated in Chapter VII, Articles 39–42. Chapter VIII suggests that regional arrangements should address security threats within their spaces (Article 52.2), but that they should seek authorization from the Security Council to do so (Article 53.1).

The Charter establishes the *locus* of authority in law. However, this does not resolve issues of legitimacy in practice. What happens when the Security Council finds it impossible to agree on a Chapter VII response? It is a stretch to suggest that nonresponse is legitimate when peace is threatened and innocents are dying, as in Syria. What happens if the Security Council mandates a UN-based action, but the response fails to ameliorate the situation to which it is responding (for example, UNAMSIL in Sierra Leone prior to British unilateral intervention or UNAMIR observing Rwanda's genocide)?

In considering the "responsibility to protect" (R2P), the International Commission on Intervention and State Sovereignty suggested that "right" authority lay in the first instance with the Security Council. In conditions where the council failed to act, then regional multilateral response might be justifiable on grounds that action through formal multilateral organizations or informal coalitions of the willing conferred a degree of legitimacy. It concluded by noting that in circumstances where there was no multilateral response, it was a real question whether the "greater harm" in the event of unauthorized action was the erosion of Security Council authority through acting without approval, or the damage to that authority resulting from mass slaughter while the Security Council ducked. The 2005 World Summit decision that makes Security Council authorization a *sine qua non* for R2P only exacerbates the problem, as the Syria case amply demonstrated.

In practice, in some instances regional arrangements or informal coalitions have sought and obtained the authorization of the Security Council under Chapter VII or

VIII prior to intervention—NATO's Implementation Force (IFOR) in Bosnia, ISAF in Afghanistan, and intervention in Libya in 2011. Some have sought, but have been refused, authorization (the US-led coalition in Iraq in 2003). Some have sought authorization, but after the fact (the CIS in Georgia and Tajikistan, and ECOWAS in Liberia and Sierra Leone). Some, finally, have neither sought nor obtained UN authorization (e.g., SADC in Lesotho). Cases in the last two categories often reflect the use of the regional multilateral brand by a regionally dominant state. In such cases, the authorizing function of the United Nations is in some doubt. By extension, the contribution of regional arrangements to global security governance needs further interrogation.

Conclusion

Mention of the UN's authorizing function raises the larger question of the relationship between regional organizations and the UN in global security governance, and of possible global–regional synergies. The pluralistic character of the international system intrinsically limits the global governance of security. As discussed, the Charter provides an authoritative definition of the relations between the UN and regional arrangements in security, focusing on notification and authorization. There are numerous instances in which regional organs have failed to notify or seek authorization in their forceful responses to what they deem to be regional threats to peace and security.

Practice also suggests that there is potential for fruitful division of tasks on the basis of comparative advantage between regional organizations and the world organization. The Yugoslav experience involved NATO heavy lifting in enforcement and deterrence with substantial UN engagement in civilian stabilization and reconstruction. The EU has provided force effectively in Ituri, where UN peacekeepers could not address a particular threat. In addition, regional organizations can legitimize UN action as in Libya, where the Arab League request for action was useful in overcoming objections from some Security Council members about the impact on nonintervention norms of coming to the rescue of civilians.

The two decades since the end of the Cold War have witnessed a sea-change in the engagement of regional organizations in global security governance. This increase has involved the retooling of alliance systems to address general regional and global security interests, and the acceptance of stronger security mandates by regional multilateral organizations.

This evolution is, however, far from complete. Some regions do not have organizations that engage in efforts to enhance security. Some do not embrace the potential derogation of sovereignty associated with robust international response to internal crises. Regional engagement in local peace and security issues has been uneven; in some areas, it has been absent, in others it has been substantial. In the last cases, some has been consistent with global norms, and some not. In some cases, regional multilateralism provides a cover for the preferences of regionally dominant powers. Regional organizations vary significantly in their capacity to produce security, whether or not that is their intention, and in the extent to which their versions of security conform to UN norms.

Recent experience suggests some potential for a division of labor between the UN and regional organizations in global security governance. This involves not only the multiplication of assets available for responses to threats to international peace and security, but also a contribution to the legitimacy of international peace operations. At the same time, cooperation between regional organizations and the UN involves substantial coordination problems. They have different norms, interests, and institutional cultures; they compete for roles, credit, and resources. Moreover, engagement by regional organizations in security issues raises substantial and unresolved issues about authority and legitimacy. To what extent do these organizations accept the primacy of the Security Council in the context of Chapter VIII? If they do not, what should be the global perspective on their independent activities?

The risk is that the relationship may not evolve towards effective subsidiarity but fragmentation of global governance. As regional powers such as China and India grow relative to the Euro-Atlantic area, and as leading states in several regions (China in East Asia, Russia in the former Soviet Union) contest the allegedly universal principles underpinning global governance, that fragmentation may accelerate.

Additional reading

Amitav Acharya, "How Ideas Spread: Whose Norms Matter? Norm Localization and Institutional Change in Asian Regionalism," *International Organization* 58, no. 2 (2004): 239–275.

Alex J. Bellamy and Paul D. Williams, "Who's Keeping the Peace? Regionalization and Contemporary Peace Operations," *International Security* 29, no. 4 (2005): 157–195.

Shaun Breslin and Stuart Croft, eds., *Comparative Regional Security Governance* (London: Routledge, 2012).

Benedikt Franke, *Security Cooperation in Africa: A Reappraisal* (Boulder, CO: Lynne Rienner, 2009).

T. V. Paul, ed., *Regional Transformation in International Relations* (Cambridge: Cambridge University Press, 2012).

Thomas G. Weiss, ed., *Beyond UN Subcontracting: Task-Sharing with Regional Security Arrangements and Service-Providing NGOs* (Basingstoke: Macmillan, 1998).

Notes

1 Boutros Boutros-Ghali, *An Agenda for Peace* (New York: United Nations, 1992), para. 63.

2 For a more detailed discussion, see S. Neil MacFarlane and Thomas G. Weiss, "Regional Organizations and Regional Security," *Security Studies* 2, no. 1 (1992): 6–7.

3 Boutros-Ghali, in *An Agenda for Peace*, devotes a full chapter (paras. 60–65) to the role of regional organizations in building global peace. See also the General Assembly's *2005 World Summit Outcome*, UN document A/Res/60/1 (24 October 2005), para. 93.

4 MacFarlane and Weiss, "Regional Organizations and Regional Security," *passim*. See also *A More Secure World: Our Shared Responsibility. Report of the High-Level Panel on Threats, Challenges, and Change,* UN document A/59/565, 2 December 2004, 60, para. 220, www.un.org/secureworld/report.pdf.

5 The regional organizational element is only one part of a larger set of regional actions that includes *ad hoc* coalitions of regional actors, or single states within a region. These fall outside the focus of this analysis.

6 S. Neil MacFarlane and Yuen Foong Khong, *The UN and Human Security: A Critical History* (Bloomington: Indiana University Press, 2006).

7 This analysis takes a broad view of regional organizations, following the UN Charter. See United Nations, *Charter of the United Nations* (San Francisco: UN, 1945), art. 52. The UN's flexible approach follows that of the League of Nations Covenant, which speaks of "regional arrangements." See League of Nations, *Covenant of the League of Nations* (League of Nations, 1919), http://avalon.law.yale.edu/20th_century/leagcov.asp.

8 Article 51's reference to collective self-defense has also been seen to legitimize regional security arrangements.

9 See Title I (Common Provisions), Article B, and Title V (Provisions on a Common Foreign and Security Policy) of *The Maastricht Treaty: Treaty on European Union* (7 February 1992), www.eurotreaties.com/maastrichteu.pdf.

10 EU, *A Secure Europe in a Better World: European Security Strategy* (12 December 2003), www.consilium.europa.eu/uedocs/cmsUpload/78367.pdf.

11 See *The Washington Treaty* (Washington, DC, 4 April 1949), www.nato.int/cps/en/natol ive/official_texts_17120.htm.

12 See "The Alliance's New Strategic Concept" (7–8 November 1991), www.nato.int/cps/en/natolive/official_texts_23847.htm.

13 "Study on NATO Enlargement" (3 September 1995), www.nato.int/cps/en/natolive/offi cial_texts_ 24733.htm.

14 "Protocol Relating to the Establishment of the Peace and Security Council of the African Union," Durban, 9 July 2002, www.au.int/en/sites/default/files/Protocol—peace and—security.pdf.

15 See, in respect of ECOWAS, the revised treaty of 1993, which permits conflict prevention, peacekeeping, and peacebuilding; and *The Protocol Relating to the Mechanism for Conflict Prevention, Management, Resolution, Peacekeeping and Security* (10 December 1999), which replaced the Protocol on Mutual Defense Assistance of 1981. See www.comm.ecowas.int/sec/index.php?id=ap101299&lang=en. In respect of the SADC, see *The Treaty of the Southern African Development Community* (17 August 1992), art. 10A, www.sadc.int/documents-publications/show/865.

16 For the text of the agreement, see http://cis.minsk.by/reestr/ru/index.html#reestr/view/text?doc=1. In January 1993, the original agreement was supplemented by a CIS Charter. See http://cis.minsk.by/reestr/ru/index.html# reestr/view/text?doc=187.

17 For the treaty text, see: www.dkb.gov.ru/start/index_aengl.htm.

18 European Council, *Peace Operations*, October 2012 and April 2017, http://consilium.europa.eu/eeas/securitydefence/eu-operations?lang=en.

19 See Linus Malu, "Background Note on ECOWAS," World Bank Headline Seminar on the Global and Regional Dimensions of Conflict and Peacebuilding, Addis Ababa, 10–12 October 2009, 1–2.

Weapons of mass destruction

Waheguru Pal Singh Sidhu

The term weapons of mass destruction (WMD) was defined by the Report of the United Nations General Assembly's Commission on Conventional Armaments in 1948 as:

> [A]tomic explosive weapons, radioactive material weapons, lethal chemical or biological weapons, and any weapons developed in the future which have characteristics comparable in destructive effect to those of the atomic bomb or other weapons mentioned above.[1]

In doing so the commission made two clear distinctions: Between conventional arms and WMD; and between atomic (nuclear), chemical, and biological weapons. The commission's definition also tacitly sets apart atomic weapons as *primus inter pares* among WMD and underlined a central role for the United Nations in managing them. Although traditional literature tends to club nuclear weapons with biological and chemical weapons into a convenient but specious category of WMD, this chapter deliberately focuses on nuclear weapons separately for a number of reasons, which are explained in the first section.

This chapter begins with a brief historical overview of the evolution and development of the various international institutions and regimes to deal with nuclear, chemical, and biological weapons. It then looks at the role of informal and *ad hoc* arrangements and their relationship to the formal treaty-based institutions. The following sections identify the challenges ahead and explore the prospects of the regimes in addressing them.

Differences among WMD

Biological, chemical, and nuclear weapons do not belong to the same conceptual category. The lethality of chemical weapons is not significantly different from that of conventional explosives and a variety of masks, suits, and procedures, albeit cumbersome, can be used to protect against the effects of chemical weapons. Similarly, a variety of prophylactic measures exist to mitigate the effects of a biological attack. In addition, victims of some chemical and biological weapons can be effectively treated. In contrast, apart from some deep underground concrete bunkers, there are no effective preventive or protective measures that can alleviate a nuclear attack and as of now there is no known treatment for the effects of nuclear radiation. Indeed, so horrific are the effects of a nuclear blast that experts opine that in any nuclear exchange the survivors will envy the dead.[2]

Despite their cataclysmic nature, nuclear weapons were until July 2017 not forbidden by a treaty or international law (as is the case with biological and chemical weapons).[3] Indeed, during the Cold War they emerged as the ultimate currency of power and the basis for world order, evident in the fact that all the five permanent UN Security Council members (P-5) possess them. Even in the post-Cold War period, the possession of and protection by nuclear weapons, remains the ultimate guarantor of security, evident from the continued dependence on nuclear weapons by states already possessing them and the acquisition of these weapons by new states.[4]

In contrast, neither chemical nor biological weapons are regarded as either significant symbols of power or underpin international security as do nuclear weapons. Given the fact that chemical weapons are relatively easier and cheaper to make, they are sometimes disparagingly referred to as the "poor man's nuclear weapons." Although some states have sought to equate chemical weapons to nuclear weapons, this has not been universally accepted; nuclear weapons remain unique. Evidence is that while all P-5 members of the Security Council continue to resist calls for nuclear disarmament, they have either already given up or are in the process of dismantling their chemical weapons. This is also the case with biological weapons.

Despite these fundamental differences in the characteristics, nature, concepts, and relative value of nuclear, chemical, and biological weapons, the arrangements designed to deal with them are built around three key international treaties and share three common objectives. In the first instance the three regimes seek to collectively get rid of all WMD. These are, in chronological order, the 1968 Nuclear Non-proliferation Treaty (NPT), the 1972 Biological Weapons Convention (BWC) or Biological and Toxin Weapons Convention (BTWC), and the 1992 Chemical Weapons Convention (CWC). Second, the regimes aim to prevent proliferation—both vertical (the qualitative and quantitative enhancement of these weapons among present possessors) and horizontal (the qualitative and quantitative spread of these weapons to new states)—of all WMD. Finally, to varying degrees the regimes also seek to unfetter, if not encourage, the use of nuclear, chemical, and biological technology for peaceful uses. More recently the WMD regimes have also sought to prevent these weapons being acquired by non-state actors.

Historical overview

Chemical and biological weapons, which have been around for centuries, predate nuclear weapons, which only made their appearance in 1945. Consequently, serious multilateral efforts to deal with chemical weapons date back to at least the nineteenth century.[5] Similar efforts for biological weapons date back to the 1925 Geneva Protocol for the Prohibition of the Use of Asphyxiating, Poisonous or Other Gases, and Bacteriological Methods of Warfare, which focused on chemical and biological weapons.[6] These efforts were prompted by the extensive use of chemical weapons during World War I. It was only around 1970 that multilateral attempts to manage biological and chemical weapons diverged. In contrast, efforts to address the multi-faceted threats posed by nuclear weapons began in earnest in 1946. Ironically the present institutions to deal with nuclear weapons have actually preceded those for biological and chemical weapons.

The nuclear weapon regime

Disarmament of nuclear weapons was the subject of the very first General Assembly resolution in January 1946 and called for:

(b) the elimination from national armaments of atomic weapons and all other major weapons adaptable to mass destruction

(c) effective safeguards by way of inspection and other means to protect complying States against the hazard of violations and evasions.

The fact that this resolution was passed a mere five months after the first and only use of nuclear weapons by the United States on Hiroshima and Nagasaki indicates the expectations that these weapons needed to be dealt with on a global, multilateral scale by the brand new United Nations.

On 14 June 1946, at the inaugural meeting of the United Nations Atomic Energy Commission (also created by the General Assembly's first resolution), the United States, which was still the world's only nuclear weapon state, presented the Baruch Plan[7] to the United Nations. In effect, the plan called for international ownership and control of all production of uranium-235 and plutonium, the ending of all nuclear weapons programs, opening the way for destroying all existing nuclear weapons and thus leading to their complete elimination. The Soviet Union, which had still not built its own nuclear weapon, did not accept this proposal. On 19 June 1946, Moscow presented a plan of its own, named after Andrei Gromyko, who would later become the Soviet foreign minister. The Gromyko Plan[8] proposed the reverse of the US approach: Disarm first (within three months) according to the terms of an international convention prohibiting nuclear weapons, and then set up an international system of supervision. Washington rejected the Gromyko Plan and conducted two nuclear tests in July 1946—the first tests since the bombing of Nagasaki on 9 August 1945. Following the first nuclear test by the Soviet Union on 29 August 1949 any hopes that these early efforts to eliminate nuclear weapons would succeed vanished.[9] Indeed, the UN Atomic Energy Commission itself was dissolved in January 1952.

By 1964 three other countries—Britain, France, and China—had also conducted nuclear tests. With five states possessing nuclear weapons and the prospect of at least a dozen other countries joining the club, the emphasis of the two superpowers shifted from futile disarmament efforts to trying to prevent further proliferation of these weapons. The result was the 1968 Nuclear Non-proliferation Treaty (NPT), which sought to prevent proliferation while also giving the existing possessors the status of nuclear weapon states.[10] The NPT entered into force in March 1970, and is now near universal, with 190 members: Only nuclear-armed India, Israel, and Pakistan are non-signatories while the Democratic People's Republic of Korea (DPRK) withdrew from the Treaty in 2003 and built nuclear weapons.[11] It also has provisions related to the peaceful uses of nuclear energy and nuclear disarmament, which along with nonproliferation make up the "three pillars" of the Treaty. Peaceful uses was first proposed in US president Dwight Eisenhower's famous Atoms for Peace[12] address to the General Assembly on 8 December 1953, which led to the establishment of the International Atomic Energy Agency (IAEA) in Vienna in 1957—over a decade before the NPT was opened for signature.

The NPT neither specifies detailed provisions for verification of compliance nor sets up an inspectorate or verification organization. Instead, it relies on the IAEA to work out the scope, frequency, intrusiveness, and procedures of inspections with member states and also carry them out. Thus, the IAEA has the objective of both promoting peaceful uses of nuclear energy and preventing the proliferation of nuclear weapons; a challenging task, given that the wherewithal for peaceful uses can easily be converted to produce nuclear weapons.

Although the NPT is the cornerstone of the nonproliferation regime, the regime itself is much broader and is considered to comprise of the following elements: The Partial Test Ban Treaty (PTBT) and the Comprehensive Test Ban Treaty (CTBT), both of which sought to prevent nuclear proliferation by banning nuclear tests; the proposed Fissile Material Cutoff Treaty (FMCT), which seeks to ban the production of fissile material; bilateral negotiations and agreements to limit nuclear arsenals, particularly of the US and the Soviet Union/Russian Federation such as the Anti-Ballistic Missile (ABM) Treaty; START I, II and III; Intermediate-Range Nuclear Forces (INF) Treaty; the Strategic Offensive Reductions Treaty (SORT); ensuring compliance of the NPT provisions through the safeguards of the IAEA; and Nuclear Weapon Free Zones (NWFZs).

In addition to these multilateral institutions, individual states (notably the United States) and groups of like-minded countries (mostly Western industrialized states) have also established national instruments and/or collective plurilateral export control and other arrangements against countries suspected of nuclear weapons proliferation.

Perhaps the most prominent national instrument is the 1978 Nuclear Non-proliferation Act passed by the US Congress. Similarly, the Nuclear Suppliers Group (NSG), the Zangger Committee, and the Missile Technology Control Regime (MTCR) sought to prevent nuclear weapon proliferation by restricting export of nuclear and missile technology.[13] Most of these were prompted by the 1974 Indian nuclear test. While these arrangements have contributed somewhat to slowing down, if not curbing proliferation, the *ad hoc*, exclusive, and nontransparent nature of these regimes has laid them open to accusation of being technology-denial regimes, preventing countries from developing peaceful uses of nuclear energy.

The biological weapons regime

The 1925 Geneva Protocol was the first serious international effort to ban the use of biological weapons and drew on the horrendous experience of World War I. However, it had two major weaknesses: It banned the use of these weapons only during war but did not ban their development, production, or possession; and some countries that joined the Geneva Protocol reserved the right to retaliate if they were attacked with biological weapons.[14] Consequently, several countries built biological weapons particularly during the Cold War. Among them the Soviet Union and the United States had the biggest programs.

International efforts to rid the world of these deadly weapons gained momentum in the late 1960s when in 1969 US President Richard Nixon unilaterally decided to dismantle its biological weapons program. These efforts culminated in the Convention on the Prohibition of the Development, Production and Stockpiling of Bacteriological and Toxin Weapons and on their Destruction, or simply the Biological Weapons Convention, which opened for signature on 10 April 1972.[15] It was the first multilateral disarmament treaty to ban the development, production, stockpiling, acquisition, retention, or transfer of an entire category of weapons. Unlike the NPT, the BWC does not recognize any weapon possessors. The BWC does not explicitly prohibit the use of biological weapons; the assumption is that if possession itself is banned, then their use is not possible. It entered into force in March 1975, five years after the NPT. Presently there are 179 states parties to the convention, including all five Security Council permanent members. However, some states with potential biological weapons capability have either not signed the convention (such as Israel) or have signed but not ratified it (such as Egypt and Syria). Moreover, some states (such as Russia and Iraq) were found to have had undeclared biological weapons programs, despite being signatories and it is suspected that some other members might also have clandestine weapons programs.

The BWC also suffers from several other drawbacks: Unlike the NPT, which has the IAEA, the convention has no organization or implementing body. Consequently, there is no systematic monitoring of implementation or treaty compliance and there is no mechanism for investigating alleged violations. Indeed, the lack of a verification mechanism, akin to that provided by the IAEA is, perhaps, the biggest weakness of the BWC. Although parties to the BWC have met regularly at five-yearly intervals to review the operation of the BWC and also between some of these review conferences to strengthen the effectiveness and improve the implementation of the convention, they have not been able to resolve the vexing issue of how to verify treaty compliance and investigate alleged violations. Nonetheless, the BWC has established a norm against these weapons and has also used confidence-building measures to increase confidence and transparency among its members.

Like the NPT, the formal BWC is supported by the informal forum called the Australia Group (AG), "which, through the harmonisation of export controls, seeks to ensure that exports do not contribute to the development of chemical or biological weapons."[16] The AG with a majority of Western industrialized countries as members are all members of the BWC and "serve to support the objectives of the BWC by enhancing the effectiveness of national export licensing measures."[17] However, as with the NSG, the MTCR, and the Zangger Group, the AG's rules are not legally binding. Finally, the absence of key BWC signatories with significant biological capabilities from the Group, such as India, has led to charges that the AG is merely a technology-denial cartel.

The chemical weapon regime

The extensive and indiscriminate use of chemical weapons during World War I, which reportedly caused 100,000 deaths, was the primary impetus that led to the 1925 Geneva Protocol.[18] However, as noted earlier, the protocol did not prevent the use of these weapons: Italy employed chemical weapons against Abyssinia/Ethiopia in 1935–1936 and Japan followed suit in China in 1937–1938. Nazi Germany extensively used chemical weapons in their concentration camps and gas chambers. During the Cold War, at least twenty-five countries were suspected of having chemical weapons programs, including the United States and the Soviet Union, which had the largest stockpiles. In addition, in the 1980s Iraq used chemical weapons not only against Iran but also its own population.

Against this backdrop, the 1975 BWC paved the way for a similar convention related to chemical weapons. Article IX of the BWC noted that each signatory:

> [A]ffirms the recognised objective of effective prohibition of Chemical Weapons and, to this end, undertakes to continue negotiations in good faith with a view to reaching early agreement on effective measures for the prohibition of their development, production and stockpiling and for their destruction.[19]

Despite this affirmation multilateral negotiations remained tortuously slow until the mid-1980s. The revelations of a chemical attack on civilians in northern Iraq in March 1988 followed by the 1990 bilateral agreement on chemical weapons between the United States and the Soviet Union under which the two countries agreed not to produce chemical weapons, to reduce their stocks to twenty percent and to begin destruction in 1992 provided the impetus. Although the US–Soviet treaty never entered into force, the Chemical Weapons Convention was finally concluded by January 1993 and entered into force in April 1997—nearly a century after the 1899 Hague Convention first sought to ban the use of chemical weapons.

Although the CWC was the last multilateral instrument established to deal with WMDs, it has three unique characteristics when compared to the NPT and the BWC. First, it aims to eliminate an entire category of weapons of mass destruction under strict international verification, which is distinct from both the NPT (which is weak on the elimination aspect) and the BWC (which lacks an international verification mechanism). The CWC categorically prohibits the development, production, stockpiling, transfer, and use of chemical weapons. It even prohibits any military preparations for the use of chemical weapons as well as the use of riot control agents as a method of warfare. Second, the CWC is comprehensive—the text itself is some fifty pages in length, and the annexes on verification and confidentiality bring the total to nearly 200, making it the longest WMD-related treaty; non-discriminatory—it does not recognize any state as a legitimate possessor; and with 192 countries having ratified or acceded to the Convention, including the P-5 and almost every country with significant chemical industries, it is truly multilateral. Finally, the CWC also established a dedicated international organization to ensure the implementation of its provisions, including verification: The Organization for the Prohibition of Chemical Weapons (OPCW).

There are four distinct "pillars" of the CWC: Disarmament—the destruction and elimination of chemical weapons stockpiles and their associated production facilities; nonproliferation—ensure that toxic chemicals and their precursors are developed, produced, transferred, or used only for peaceful purposes; protection and assistance— provide assistance through the OPCW in case of chemical weapon use or threat of use against a signatory; and facilitate international cooperation in the peaceful application of chemistry.

Eight countries declared that they possessed chemical weapons when they signed the CWC, including the United States and Russia—the two largest holders of such weapons. As per their agreements all the declared chemical weapon stocks (about 71,000 metric tons) should have been destroyed by 2012. In 2013, following chemical attacks in Syria, the revelation of an arsenal, and subsequent international pressure led by Washington and Moscow, Damascus was forced to declare its stockpile, sign, and ratify the CWC, and agree to an expeditious timetable for the elimination of its stash of weapons.[20] However, chemical attacks in 2017 revealed that the Syrian regime might not have declared its entire cache of chemical weapons. Moreover, by mid-2017, only ninety-six percent of all declared global stocks had been verifiably destroyed. Even if all the current declared stockpiles are destroyed, the world will not be rid of chemical weapons; three countries, with suspected chemical weapons or chemical weapons capabilities have either not signed the CWC, including Egypt and North Korea or, as in the case of Israel, have signed but not ratified the CWC, and remain outside its ambit.

As in the case of the BWC, the AG is the *ad hoc* plurilateral forum that seeks to support the nonproliferation pillar of the CWC. In fact, the AG was established in response to the 1984 UN findings of chemical weapons use by Iraq and that at least some of the precursor chemicals and materials for Baghdad's weapons had been sourced through legitimate trade channels.[21] However, the exclusive nature of the AG and its nonbinding nature render its impact limited.

Current challenges

All the regimes designed to deal with nuclear, chemical, and biological weapons face three sets of challenges. The first is posed by states within the existing regimes. Here states that either withdraw from the regime and build weapons or violate the regime through clandestine weapons programs pose as much of a challenge as states that, on the one hand, are dragging their feet over disarming their existing arsenals while, on the other, are seeking to improve the quality of weapons. In the nuclear realm, while much attention has been devoted to Iran and North Korea, not as much effort has been focused on the huge arsenals and the modernization plans of the five NPT nuclear weapons states. In the chemical realm, the continued use of weapons by Syria, even after joining the CWC, poses a critical challenge to the regime.

The second set of challenges comes from states without the existing regimes. In the nuclear arena, this includes India, Israel, and Pakistan (non-signatories of the NPT) but also states such as China, the DPRK, Egypt, Iran, Israel, and the United States, which have still to ratify the CTBT. This shortcoming also applies to the CWC and the BWC, which are still missing key countries with weapons capabilities (and, possibly, stocks) as members. There are a variety of reasons why some states either never join the treaties, or having joined decide to opt out or secretly violate them. These reasons could vary from domestic political, technological, or economic factors to regional security concerns to prestige and the desire to have a greater say in global governance.

The third and, perhaps, the most formidable challenge comes from non-state actors, including, but not limited to, terrorist groups. All three WMD-related regimes were conceived and designed to deal with state-based nuclear, chemical, and biological weapons and therefore stipulate obligations for state parties and not non-state entities or individuals. Thus, at best they address the threat from non-state actors only indirectly. According to Security Council resolution 1540 of 28 April 2004, a non-state actor is defined as an "individual or entity, not acting under the lawful authority of any State in conducting activities which come within the scope of this resolution." This would include the quest of transnational or subnational fundamentalist or cult groups, such as Aum Shinrikyo, Al-Qaeda, and the Islamic State to develop WMDs as well as the antics of scientists and entities, such as Abdul Qadeer Khan, to hawk their materials and expertise.[22]

In addition, each of the WMD regimes described above faces unique challenges. For instance, the NPT has been more successful in preventing new states from acquiring nuclear weapons than it has been in either slowing down or disarming states that already possess nuclear weapons.[23] In contrast, the CWC and the OPCW, which have constituted the most successful WMD disarmament arrangement until now, faces the challenge of transitioning to strengthening its nonproliferation capabilities; keeping up with the rapidly evolving science and technology; and preserving and strengthening the norm against chemical weapons possession and use. For the BWC, there are two critical challenges. First, given the rapidly growing biotech capabilities, technological advances (such as synthetic biology), shrinking costs, and widely expanding interest, participation, availability, and access there is a concern that the assessment and management of these risks is lagging far behind. The five-yearly review conferences and even the intersessional meetings might not be frequent enough to keep pace with the evolving threats. Second, in the absence of a dedicated organization to undertake compliance verification there are doubts whether the present "network approach" might be adequate to assure compliance.

Way forward

These challenges from state parties, states not parties, as well as non-state actors to the WMD regimes, coupled with the rapid diffusion of the technology to make these weapons, have led the international community of states to follow at least three different approaches to address them. First, there is the traditional multilateral institutional approach anchored in negotiated treaty-based regimes, such as the NPT (1970), the BWC (1975), and the CWC (1997). All these treaties were concluded after a long-drawn-out negotiating process. In the case of the CWC, for instance, the idea was first proposed in 1899 but reached fruition only in 1997. Given the complexity of negotiating treaties, such treaties are also not amenable to amendments and cannot be altered to adjust to the new realities. They are invariably strong in setting norms and principles and in international law, but they tend to be relatively weak on enforcement. For instance, the NPT is as incapable of dissuading states from exercising the right to withdraw under Article X as it is of enforcing nuclear disarmament under Article VI.[24] If the treaty-based regime is ineffective in holding member states to their commitments, it is even weaker in its efforts to deal with both nonmember states as well as non-state actors.

Despite these drawbacks, the post-Cold War period was regarded as one of opportunity to strengthen the treaty-based regime. Yet, in the period of transition to a multipolar world this optimism was dashed. For instance, while the CTBT, the latest attempt to address nuclear weapons, was successfully negotiated in 1996, it has still not entered into force and is unlikely to do so in the foreseeable future. A similar fate is likely for the proposed FMCT. One key factor for this is the paralysis that has beset the Geneva-based Conference on Disarmament (CD). The CD has not been able to negotiate any treaty over the past twenty years primarily on account of its consensus rule, which allows just a single country to effectively block any treaty from being negotiated or adopted.

Second, partly on account of these inherent weaknesses in the CD and treaty-based regimes, in the post-Cold War world the international community of states embarked on a series of nontreaty-based multilateral approaches, such as the various declarations and resolutions of the General Assembly. This approach had been tried earlier. In the 1960s the assembly passed several resolutions supporting the NPT and, after further revision—concerning mainly the preamble and Articles IV and V, it commended the draft text of the NPT, which is annexed to resolution 2373 (XXII). Similarly, it was the General Assembly that resurrected the CTBT (after it had been blocked at the CD) by adopting a resolution 50/245 in September 1996. In April 2005, the assembly also adopted the "International Convention for the Suppression of Acts of Nuclear Terrorism," which addresses non-state actors.

In 2017 one of the most significant developments under the aegis of the General Assembly was the successful negotiation of the Treaty to Prohibit Nuclear Weapons.[25] Some 120 countries—or nearly two-thirds of UN member states—that do not possess nuclear weapons participated in this UN conference. The treaty, which was concluded in July 2017, is unlikely to disarm a single nuclear weapon. Yet, it has put the concept of nuclear weapons-based deterrence on notice. Unsurprisingly, all the states with nuclear weapons plus a number of countries that live under the nuclear umbrella—fewer than forty UN members—boycotted the conference, which underlined a real chasm between nuclear haves and nuclear have nots.

In contrast, the Security Council which was in a debilitating paralysis during the Cold War became active on the issue of WMD proliferation thereafter. The first indication of this was the various resolutions related to Iraq's invasion of Kuwait, which also established the UN Special Commission (UNSCOM) to disarm Iraq's nuclear, biological, and chemical programs. Another significant step was the Security Council Presidential Statement of 31 January 1992, which stressed that "proliferation of all weapons of mass destruction constitutes a threat to international peace and security" and with specific reference to nuclear weapons noted "the decision of many countries to adhere to the [NPT] and emphasise the integral role in the implementation of that Treaty." Ironically, this statement also highlighted the failure of the NPT nuclear states (including the P-5) to keep their commitments to the NPT. Subsequently, the council passed several other resolutions related to state actors.[26] In addition, it also passed several resolutions related to non-state actors including 1373 (2001), 1540 (2004), 1673 (2006), 1810 (2008), 1977 (2011), and 2055 (2012).

The last sets of resolutions are particularly innovative for two reasons: They seek to deal with non-state actors, and they aim to provide stopgap arrangements to plug existing loopholes in the present treaty-based regime. Security Council resolution 1540 in particular is far reaching because it calls on all UN member states to "adopt and enforce appropriate effective laws which prohibit any non-State actor to manufacture, acquire, possess, develop, transport, transfer or use nuclear, chemical or biological weapons and their means of delivery" as well as to "take and enforce effective measures to establish domestic controls to prevent the proliferation of nuclear, chemical, or biological weapons and their means of delivery." While the resolution has been generally welcomed given that present treaty-based regimes do not address this aspect of proliferation, there is concern that this approach of using the Security Council to legislate, if exercised often enough, would circumvent the negotiated approach to developing treaty-based regimes.

Third, and of even greater concern to some member states, are the *ad hoc*, non-institutional, nonconventional approaches led by individual states or a group of states to address the immediate challenges of nonproliferation. These include the so-called preventive war against Iraq's nuclear, chemical, and biological weapons in 2003, which was probably the first and perhaps last nonproliferation war (although Iran might still emerge as another potential future target); the US-led Proliferation

Security Initiative (PSI); the P5+1 negotiations with Iran, leading to the Joint Comprehensive Plan of Action (JCPOA); the six-party talks to address the DPRK's nuclear ambitions; the Indo-US civilian nuclear initiative as well as India's efforts to join the AG, the MTCR, the NSG, and the Wassenaar Group; and the Nuclear Security Summits (NSS).

These arrangements tend to be stronger on the enforcement aspect but relatively weak in both international law as well as establishing norms and principles. Indeed, all of these initiatives are discriminatory and, predictably, do not enjoy universal adherence. Although the states behind these initiatives—primarily the NPT nuclear weapons states—have attempted to seek greater legitimacy by having these initiatives endorsed by the Security Council, there is concern that these initiatives might deal a fatal blow to the already weakened treaty-based nonproliferation regime. Nonetheless, given the inability of the existing formal regime to address many of the proliferation challenges of today, these *ad hoc* initiatives are likely to flourish.

For instance, the NSS process—to prevent non-state actors, particularly terrorists, from acquiring nuclear material—was launched with fanfare in 2010 by US President Barack Obama with the ambitious objective "to secure all vulnerable nuclear material in four years." Six years and four summits later—the last of which concluded in 2016—this aim has not been reached, despite substantial progress being made. Similarly, the July 2015 JCPOA to curb Iran's potential nuclear weapon program is regarded as a successful effort to curb proliferation through diplomatic means, though the agreement's effective implementation remains formidable.

Finally, among the *ad hoc* approaches there are several independent commissions and nongovernmental initiatives that also endeavor to eliminate WMDs. Prominent among these are the International Commission on Nuclear Non-proliferation and Disarmament; The Weapons of Mass Destruction Commission; Global Zero; and the series of op-eds written by four senior US statesmen.[27] However, unlike the International Commission on Intervention and State Sovereignty (ICISS), which led to the "Responsibility to Protect" (R2P) norm, none of the efforts related to nuclear weapons or WMD in general have had a similar impact.

Conclusion

Liberal institutionalists would prefer strengthening the multilateral treaty-based institutions to address WMD challenges rather than opt for *ad hoc* and military options. In contrast, realists would be inclined towards the *ad hoc* and unilateral or "coalition-of-the-willing" approaches, including the use of force, to ensure the security of the state *vis-à-vis* other states as well as non-state actors. However, *ad hoc* approaches alone are unlikely to be considered legitimate or likely to be effective either in the short or the long term unless they are intrinsically linked to the universally applicable treaty-based regime. Similarly, such regimes by themselves, despite their solid legal and legitimate credentials, are unlikely to be effective in their objectives unless they are nondiscriminatory and universal as well as have a strong verification and enforcement mechanism. In short, liberal institutionalists and realists need to bridge their differences and find a middle ground. The CWC is, perhaps, the model treaty that builds on such middle ground. Is a similar compromise possible in the case of nuclear and biological weapons?

Additional reading

Arms Control Association website (www.armscontrol.org) is a very useful source for the basic facts of the various WMD regimes as well as the ongoing current challenges, debates and responses.

M. Bothe, et al., eds., *The New Chemical Weapons Convention: Implementation and Prospects*, (Leiden: Brill, 1998).

Bulletin of Atomic Scientists, www.thebulletin.org. The oldest (founded in 1945 by atomic scientists involved in the Manhattan Project) and most respected journal on all things nuclear, especially nonproliferation. Its data on nuclear arsenals of nuclear states (prepared by the Natural Resources Defense Council) are regarded as some of the most reliable.

Melissa Gillis, *Disarmament: A Basic Guide*, 3rd ed. (New York: United Nations, 2012).

Filippa Lentzos and Gregory D. Koblentz, "It's Time to Modernize the Bioweapons Convention," *Bulletin of Atomic Scientists*, 4 November 2016, http://thebulletin.org/it%E2%80%99s-time- modernize-bioweapons-convention10128.

Piers Millett, ed., *Improving Implementation of the Biological Weapons Convention: The 2007–2010 Intersessional Process* (Geneva: UNIDIR, 2011).

Nuclear Threat Initiative (NTI) at www.nti.org is a one-stop website for nuclear, biological, and chemical weapon programs of different countries. The website also hosts an innovative online tutorial (WMD 411), which provides essential information on nuclear weapons and efforts to disarm them.

Waheguru Pal Singh Sidhu, "The Nuclear Disarmament and Non-profliration Regime" in *Security Studies: An Introduction*, 3rd ed., ed. Paul D. Williams (New York: Routledge, 2017).

Weapons of Terror: Freeing the World of Nuclear, Biological and Chemical Arms (Stockholm: EO Grafiska, 2006).

Notes

1 See Commission for Conventional Armaments, *Resolution Adopted by the Commission at Its Thirteenth Meeting*, 12 August 1948.

2 See, for instance, *Nuclear Explosions and their Effects* (New Delhi: Government of India, Ministry of Information and Broadcasting, 1958); S. Glasstone and P.J. Dolan, *The Effects of Nuclear Weapons*, 3rd ed. (Washington, DC: U.S. Government Printing Office, 1977); Jonathan Schell, *The Fate of the Earth* (New York: Alfred A. Knopf, 1982); Melissa Gillis, *Disarmament: A Basic Guide*, 3rd ed. (New York: United Nations, 2012), 17.

3 In 2017 nearly 120 UN members that did not possess or were not under the protection of nuclear weapons began negotiations to create a "legally binding instrument to prohibit nuclear weapons, leading towards their total elimination." See United Nations Conference to Negotiate a Legally Binding Instrument to Prohibit Nuclear Weapons, Leading Towards their Total Elimination, 16 February, 27–31 March, 15 June–7 July 2017, www.un.org/disarmament/ptnw/background.html.

4 Waheguru Pal Singh Sidhu, "The Nuclear Disarmament and Non-proliferation Regime," in *Security Studies: An Introduction*, ed. Paul D. Williams, 2nd ed. (New York: Routledge, 2013), 410.

5 The 1899 Hague Convention was the first serious attempt to prevent the use of the chemical weapons and called on signatories to "abstain from the use of projectiles the object of which is the diffusion of asphyxiating or deleterious gases." See http://avalon.law.yale.edu/19th_century/dec99-02.asp.

6 The text of the Geneva Protocol is available at https://unoda-web.s3-accelerate.amazonaws.com/wp-content/uploads/assets/WMD/Bio/pdf/Status_Protocol.pdf.

7 See www.atomicarchive.com/Docs/Deterrence/BaruchPlan.shtml.

8 See Randy Rydell, "Going for Baruch: The Nuclear Plan that Refused to Go Away," *Arms Control Today*, June 2006, www.armscontrol.org/act/2006_06/LookingbackBaruch.

9 See www.ctbto.org/the-treaty/history-1945-1993/1945-54-early-efforts-to-restrain-nuclear-testing/.

10 Jozef Goldblat, *Nuclear Non-proliferation: A Guide to the Debate* (Stockholm: SIPRI, 1985); Gillis, *Disarmament: A Basic Guide*, 31–37.

11 The newly established state of South Sudan is the only country without nuclear weapons that has not signed the NPT so far.

12 The original speech can be found at www.iaea.org/about/history/atoms-for-peace-speech.

13 For the NSG, see www.nuclearsuppliersgroup.org/en/; for the Zangger Committee, see www.zanggercommittee.org/; for the MTCR, see http://mtcr.info/. In addition, see the Arms Control Association fact sheets on the Nuclear Suppliers Group (NSG) at a glance at: www.armscontrol.org/factsheets/NSG and Missile Technology Control Regime at a glance at www.armscontrol.org/factsheets/mtcr. See also Waheguru Pal Singh Sidhu, "Looking Back: The Missile Technology Control Regime," *Arms Control Today*, April 2007.

14 Gillis, *Disarmament: A Basic Guide*, 43.

15 For details of the BWC, see www.unog.ch/bwc and the unofficial www.opbw.org/. In addition, see the Arms Control Association fact sheet on the Biological Weapons Convention at a glance at www.armscontrol.org/factsheets/bwc.

16 See www.australiagroup.net/en/index.html.

17 See www.australiagroup.net/en/bwc.html.

18 Gillis, *Disarmament: A Basic Guide*, 39.

19 See www.opcw.org/chemical-weapons-convention/genesis-and-historical-development/; Julian Perry Robinson, "The Negotiations on the Chemical Weapons Convention: An Historical Overview," in *The New Chemical Weapons Convention: Implementation and Prospects*, eds. M. Bothe, et al. (Leiden: Brill, 1998), 17–36.

20 Waheguru Pal Singh Sidhu, "Weapons of Mass Destruction: Managing Proliferation," in *The UN Security Council in the 21st Century*, eds. Sebastian von Einsiedel, David M. Malone, and Bruno Stagno Ugarte, (Boulder, CO: Lynne Rienner, 2015), 323–345.

21 See the Origins of the Australia Group at www.australiagroup.net/en/origins.html.

22 Sidhu, "The Nuclear Disarmament and Non-proliferation Regime," 417–418.

23 See, for instance, W. Pal Sidhu, "Overview: Challenges and Prospects of Monitoring," in *The 2010 NPT Action Plan Monitoring Report* (Geneva: Reaching Critical Will, 2012), 3–9.

24 Article X of the NPT gives each signatory the "right to withdraw from the Treaty if it decides that extraordinary events . . . have jeopardised the supreme interests of its country" while Article VI calls on members to "pursue negotiations in good faith on effective measures relating to the cessation of the nuclear arms race at an early date and to nuclear disarmament."

25 United Nations Conference to Negotiate a Legally Binding Instrument to Prohibit Nuclear Weapons, Leading Towards their Total Elimination, 16 February, 27–31 March, 15 June–7 July 2017, www.un.org/disarmament/ptnw/background.html. and *Treaty on the Prohibition of Nuclear Weapons*, https://treaties.un.org/doc/Treaties/2017/07/20170707%2003-42%20PM/Ch_XXVI_9.pdf.

26 These include Security Council resolutions 1172 (1998), 1696 (2006), 1718 (2006), 1737 (2006), 1747 (2007), 1803 (2008), 1835 (2008), 1887 (2009), 1929 (2010), 1984 (2011), and 2049 (2012). Although not all of them dealt with chemical and biological weapons, they were about WMD.

27 For the Report of the International Commission on Nuclear Non-proliferation and Disarmament titled *Eliminating Nuclear Threats: A Practical Agenda for Global Policymakers*, see http://icnnd.org; the report of the Weapons of Mass Destruction Commission is titled *Weapons of Terror: Freeing the World of Nuclear, Biological and Chemical Arms*; for details of Global Zero, see www.globalzero.org; Henry Kissinger, Sam Nunn, Bill Perry, and George Shultz penned their vision in four prominent *Wall Street Journal* op-eds: "A World Free of Nuclear Weapons" (4 January 2007), "Towards a Nuclear Free World" (15 January 2008), "How to Protect out Nuclear Deterrent" (19 January 2010), and "Deterrence in the Age of Nuclear Proliferation" (7 March 2011).

CONTENTS

Counterterrorism cooperation and global governance

Peter Romaniuk

In June 2016, a gun and bomb attack at Istanbul's Atatürk International Airport claimed more than forty victims. In his response, Turkish President Recep Tayyip Erdoğan recalled the global nature of the terrorist threat. His prescription was clear: "Unless all government and the entire mankind [sic] join forces in the fight against terrorism, much worse things than what we fear to imagine today will come true."[1] In June 2014, some two months after the abduction by Boko Haram extremists of 276 girls from a government school, Nigerian president Goodluck Jonathan editorialized in the *Washington Post* on the need to, "establish an enduring, worldwide commitment to destroying terrorism and those who finance or give safe haven to the terrorists." He undertook to use his speech to the UN General Assembly that September to call for a, "UN-coordinated system for sharing intelligence and, if necessary, special forces and law enforcement to confront terrorism wherever it occurs."[2] A decade earlier, following the three-day hostage crisis at a school in the town of Beslan, North Ossetia, that yielded more than 330 fatalities, Russian president Vladimir Putin called on his security services to step up international cooperation.[3] In the short term, that led to increased cooperation between Russia and, of all institutions, the North Atlantic Treaty Organization (NATO).[4] Two months after the attacks in the United States on 11 September 2001 ("9/11"), then UN Secretary-General Kofi Annan accompanied US president George W. Bush to the site of the World Trade Center. Expressing sympathy, Annan called the UN a "New York institution" that was also directly affected by the tragedy. But the attacks, he said, did not simply target New York or the United States. Rather, they were a strike against the world. "That's why we all need to come together" to fight terrorism, he affirmed.[5]

Such statements from elites reflect a strong demand for global governance on counterterrorism. This chapter describes the extensive efforts that have been made to supply it. Those efforts follow a distinctive pattern. For most of the last century, counterterrorism did not lend itself to global governance. States disagreed about the legitimacy of non-state actors using violence for political purposes and about how to respond. While states concluded twelve international legal instruments, and despite an increase in cooperation after the end of the Cold War, multilateralism remained the "mood music" to counterterrorism until 2001.[6] The record changed quickly after 9/11. Those attacks and subsequent incidents across the globe have elicited a sustained burst of multilateralism. Today, more than thirty-five UN entities are engaged on counterterrorism. UN Secretary-General António Guterres has proposed the creation of a new under-secretary-general position, to head an office on counterterrorism.[7] A similar uptick in activity can be observed among regional and specialist organizations, and across civil society. Outside of the UN, several new, high-profile multilateral mechanisms have been initiated. Less than two decades ago, global governance on counterterrorism barely existed. But it is now a crowded field, with multiple actors pursuing multiple mandates across multiple forums.

"Global governance" is an apt conceptual entry point for interpreting these developments. "Governance," here, refers to the "sum of the many ways individuals and institutions, public and private, manage their common affairs. It is a continuing process through which conflicting or diverse interests may be accommodated and cooperative action may be taken."[8] It is a deliberately broad concept that "encompasses the activities of governments, but . . . also includes the many other channels through which 'commands' flow in the form of goals framed, directives issued, and policies pursued."[9] In this regard, "global governance"—a concept initiated in the post-Cold War period—is generally understood to subsume the study of formal international organizations. Recent trends in global governance include increasing diversity in forms of multilateralism over time,[10] as well as greater complexity in institutional arrangements in certain issue domains, resulting in fragmentation and overlaps.[11] Certainly, global governance on counterterrorism manifests these trends.

The next three sections describe the evolution of global governance on counterterrorism in the pre- and post-9/11 periods, demonstrating the proliferation of cooperation over time. While the growth of cooperation in this field has often been contested, challenges to global governance have tended to yield more, not less, multilateralism. The subsequent section reflects on the causes and consequences of these developments. To some extent, changing patterns of cooperation are derivative of the changing threat environment. But global governance and counterterrorism occur within a political context, and states use international organizations (IOs) to advance and protect their interests, and influence others. Just as an understanding of global governance is necessary to interpret counterterrorism cooperation, the chapter concludes that the achievements and challenges of multilateral counterterrorism today contribute much to our knowledge of IOs and global governance.

Before 9/11: Barriers to global governance

The record of counterterrorism cooperation in the twentieth century illustrates well the barriers to its global governance. While states' interests occasionally aligned, the form and substance of those interactions reflected a fundamental political cleavage among them. As such, the engagement of IOs was relatively limited and it is a stretch to talk about global governance in any robust form in this period.

The deepest origins of global governance on counterterrorism lie in the 1890s, when police officials in Europe convened a series of conferences to discuss the anarchist threat that took the lives of several heads of state. In 1904 these meetings brought to fruition the first international counterterrorism instrument of the modern era, when ten states signed an anti-anarchist protocol. However, despite the effort to institutionalize cooperative mechanisms at the operational level, anarchist terrorism could not sustain states' attention as the world moved towards war.[12] A second attempt to advance counterterrorism cooperation was made in the interwar years, through the International Association of Penal Law and then the League of Nations. The latter eventually concluded the "Convention for the Prevention and Punishment of Terrorism" in 1937. That convention defined terrorism as "criminal acts directed against a state and intended or calculated to create a state of terror in the minds of particular persons, or a group of persons, or in the public." Despite the apparent circularity of this definition (i.e., it defines "terrorism" by referring to "state of terror"), the League's achievement was unique as no consensus definition has emerged since. Still, the convention attracted only twenty-four signatories and one ratification. It never entered into force, and terrorism again disappeared from the agenda in the march to war.

The creation of the United Nations in 1945, in the aftermath of such a bloody conflict, might have given rise to a demand for cooperation to suppress the use of terrorism. Within a few decades of its founding, however, the UN was divided. On one side were states of the Global South that sought to preserve the legitimacy of "national liberation movements," while labeling others as "state terrorists." This coalition brought together the postcolonial states of the Nonaligned Movement as well as the Soviet Union. On the other side was the West, which rejected the notion that violence by non-state actors should be accommodated. The sharp end of this disagreement was the politics of the Middle East. In his 1974 speech to the UN General Assembly, the Palestinian Liberation Organization's Chairman Yasser Arafat proclaimed: "The justice of the cause determines the right to struggle."[13] The legitimacy of such violence is often summarized in the cliché "one man's terrorist is another man's freedom fighter." And so it was in the UN throughout the 1970s and into the 1980s, especially in the General Assembly, which produced no comprehensive response to terrorism.

What are the possibilities for global governance under conditions of such fundamental political disagreement? States identified some convergent interests and found a workaround. Over this period, we see the emergence of a "piecemeal" approach to counterterrorism through IOs. Between 1963 and 1999, twelve international legal instruments emerged, each with a specific topical focus, including in the domains of aviation security, maritime security, the protection of diplomats, nuclear security, and terrorist financing. The conventions often provided exceptions, thereby permitting the forms of violence that they otherwise sought to eradicate; ratification rates remained modest. But this body of international law reflects the UN's principal contribution to global governance on counterterrorism prior to 9/11.

As states grew frustrated with the relative stalemate at the UN, they shopped for other forums in which they could advance their counterterrorism objectives. This "spillover effect" meant that specialist organizations—such as the International Civil Aviation Organization (ICAO), International Maritime Organization (IMO), and the International Atomic Energy Agency (IAEA)—began to discuss counterterrorism. Similarly, regional organizations—including the Arab League, the Organization of American States (OAS), the Council of Europe, and the European Commission—elaborated counterterrorism measures, as did limited-membership bodies such as NATO and the Group of Seven (G-7).

So, despite political dissension, global governance began to emerge. In this regard, the post-Cold War record of the Security Council is worth noting. Over the course of the 1990s it imposed sanctions against Libya, Sudan, and the Taliban for terrorism-related reasons. Among them, the financial sanctions, travel ban, and arms embargo imposed on the Taliban would attain a much higher profile after 9/11. Further, in resolution 1269 of October 1999, the Security Council came as close as was possible to a general statement on terrorism. Sponsored by Russia, it condemned terrorism in general terms and called on states to take a range of counterterrorism measures and to become parties to the conventions.

In sum, prior to 2001, global governance on counterterrorism was constrained. Politics precluded a comprehensive response through IOs. But in the interstices of these disagreements, cooperation emerged.

After 9/11: Embracing global governance

In his address on the evening of 9/11, President Bush stated: "America and our friends and allies join with all those who want peace and security in the world and we stand together to win the war against terrorism."[14] Today, the Bush administration is more likely to be remembered for its willingness to act unilaterally in pursuing its "global war on terrorism" (GWOT). However, the record suggests that the United States has consistently viewed multilateralism as an important, if imperfect, tool of counterterrorism. In turn, US leadership has often elicited more consensus than contention, especially in the immediate post-9/11 period.

A critical example in this regard is Security Council resolution 1373, adopted within two weeks of 9/11. It broadened and deepened global governance on counterterrorism in a previously unimaginable fashion. Passed under Chapter VII of the UN Charter, it requires states to implement a wide range of counterterrorism measures in such areas as financial regulation, migration and customs control, and arms transfers. The resolution calls for bilateral, regional, and international cooperation on law enforcement, extradition, administrative and judicial matters, and as regards exchange of information relating to terrorism. Drafted and introduced by Washington—but attracting unanimous support—1373 effectively consolidated and extended preexisting UN measures and made them mandatory. Moreover, the resolution created a mechanism—in the form of a subsidiary organ of the Council, the "Counterterrorism Committee" (CTC)—to oversee implementation. While subsidiary organs had been established to monitor the implementation of the Security Council's sanctions regimes in the 1990s, the CTC had a higher profile; by May 2003, all member states had submitted to it at least one implementation report, as required. Experts were seconded to the CTC to review and respond to member state reports. They also began identifying "best practices" to implement 1373, engaging regional and specialist organizations, more than sixty-five of which met in New York in March 2003.

The initial record of the CTC was promising. But it was ambitious to think that a subsidiary organ of the Security Council, supported by a small staff of experts, could fulfill the functions delegated to it. Between 2001 and 2003 the consensus of the immediate post-9/11 period dissipated, as council members fell out over the Bush administration's decision to go to war in Iraq. The CTC's role in monitoring implementation of 1373 was soon viewed as too intrusive, leading to the claims that the Security Council was acting as a global legislature. Further complicating its role, the sanctions in place on the Taliban since 1999—which had been expanded to include Al-Qaeda and others—became a lightning rod for controversy. After 9/11, the list of targets subject to the sanctions grew rapidly, which raised concerns about due process and clashed with privacy laws in several jurisdictions. European states, in particular, faced legal challenges in domestic courts from their own citizens, who argued that their assets had been frozen without an opportunity to be heard or to appeal the decision.

Yet even as the optimism attached to the Security Council's response to 9/11 began to wane, global governance on counterterrorism continued to advance. A kind of "spillover effect" can be seen, with specialist and regional organizations pursuing counterterrorism-related measures in new and innovative ways. For example, after 9/11 the IMO advanced a new regime on ship and port security, and the ICAO developed new rules on travel document security, incorporating biometric data and computer chips in international standards for passports. Similarly, after 9/11 Interpol developed a database on lost and stolen passports, and that the world's leading anti-money-laundering body, the Financial Action Task Force (FATF), extended its mandate to countering terrorist financing. Indeed, if acronyms are a proxy for the vitality of multilateralism, then global governance positively flourished as we were introduced to the CTAG (the then-G-8's Counterterrorism Action Group), the CTAP process (APEC's Counterterrorism Action Plan), the ACSRT (the African Union's African Center for Study and Research on Terrorism), the ICPAT (the Intergovernmental Authority on Development's, IGAD, Capacity-building Program Against Terrorism), and RATS (the Regional Antiterrorism Structure of the Shanghai Cooperation Organization), as well as SEARCCT (the Southeast Asian Regional Centre for Counterterrorism in Kuala Lumpur) and JCLEC (the Jakarta Centre for Law Enforcement Cooperation, in Semarang), among many others (and these all outside of the UN system). There has been much variation in the scope and impact of such initiatives over time, but their volume alone is striking.

The leadership role of the Security Council on counterterrorism addressed in a proposal for the CTC's "revitalization" in 2004. CTC experts were replaced by a

"Counterterrorism Executive Directorate" (CTED), established as a special political mission. Subsequent resolutions expanded the mandate of the CTC and CTED, and the latter carved out a role facilitating their implementation through identifying "best practices" (drawn from a wide range of IOs active in the functional domains covered by the CTC's mandates), disseminating them (through workshops, meetings, and outreach), and monitoring their implementation. The CTED participates in country visits to observe firsthand member states' response to Security Council resolutions. The CTED is joined in these visits by other organs, such as the committee over-seeing the sanctions on the Taliban and Al-Qaeda, and the "1540 Committee" (the committee established to oversee the implementation of the 2004 resolution 1540 on the proliferation of nuclear, chemical, or biological weapons to non-state actors).

The General Assembly, so often a forum for dissension on this issue, contributed its most important statement on counterterrorism in 2006, in the form of the Global Counterterrorism Strategy. It comprises four pillars. Two of these (preventing and combating terrorism, and building state capacity to counter terrorism) essentially repeat Security Council resolutions. But the other two pillars, which refer to "conditions conducive to terrorism" and the importance of human rights while countering terror-ism, cover issues elided in the council's response. Further, seven legal instruments relating to terrorism have been concluded since 9/11, effectively extending the "piece-meal approach." Still, there remain familiar constraints on the assembly as a forum for advancing global governance on counterterrorism. For example, efforts in the Sixth Committee (Legal) to negotiate a Comprehensive Convention on International Terrorism remain stalled on the question of a definition, among other issues.

More broadly, having birthed global governance on counterterrorism in this way, the perennial challenges of implementation and coordination arose. Both the strategy and relevant Security Council resolutions have been reviewed periodically.[15] These documents provide evidence of activities pursuant to post-9/11 but do not address effectiveness, prompting criticism of "paper compliance," alongside concerns that the uptick in activity has come to be seen as an end in itself.

Regarding coordination, it is no surprise that horizontal integration is a challenge in the UN system, more so in the context of a historically contentious issue. The Counterterrorism Implementation Taskforce (CTITF) was established in 2005 in the Secretariat's Department of Political Affairs (DPA), with the specific mandate of coordinating UN entities. Some members of the Task Force include counterterror-ism among their core mission. For example, the UN Office on Drugs and Crime (UNODC) maintains a Terrorism Prevention Branch that has a longstanding program to assist states in implementing the international conventions. But others have been wary about framing their work in terms of "counterterrorism." When CTITF was tasked with an oversight role in coordinating strategy implementation, it endeavored to pursue some programmatic activities alongside its core coordination function. In practice, it has mastered neither.

Recent developments: Proliferating global governance

Ten years after the passage of resolution 1373, the limits of UN-led counterterror-ism cooperation loomed. By that time, the comparative advantages of the UN were clear—as a norm setter, convener, capacity builder and monitor of norm implementation.[16] But the ability to deliver on these seemed to have stagnated. Despite the reference to human rights in the strategy, advocates criticized UN measures for enabling repressive state counterterrorism practices.[17]

Rather than returning to the past, four developments served to extend cooperation on counterterrorism. First, states showed their willingness to further adapt existing institutions and to create new ones within the UN system. A "Special Rapporteur on the promotion and protection of human rights and fundamental freedoms while countering terrorism" was appointed by the then Commission on Human Rights in 2005. Reforms to the processes for listing and delisting individuals subject to Security Council counterterrorism sanctions proceeded in several stages. In 2011, the "UN Counterterrorism Centre" (UNCCT) was launched within CTITF. Funded by Saudi Arabia, to the tune of an initial $10 million over three years, its mandate is to aid strategy implementation. All the while, practitioners debated how best to organize the UN's counterterrorism activity.

More significant was the 2011 creation of an entirely new multilateral organization, the Global Counterterrorism Forum (GCTF). Comprising thirty member governments and the European Union (EU), the GCTF was designed to fill gaps in cooperation. It initiated a series of thematic and geographically focused working groups and crosscutting initiatives, enabling closer cooperation on new and emerging issues. Further, the GCTF spawned three related mechanisms. In 2012, the Hedayah International Center of Excellence for Countering Violent Extremism (CVE) was launched in Abu Dhabi. Its role includes convening stakeholders, facilitation and capacity building, and some research and analysis, in the service of implementing GCTF measures. In 2013, the formation of the Global Community Engagement and Resilience Fund (GCERF) was announced, with a mandate and donor support to advance community-level initiatives to prevent terrorism. In 2014, the International Institute for Justice and the Rule of Law (IIJ) was inaugurated in Valletta, Malta, to provide rule-of-law-based training to criminal justice professionals in counterterrorism and related fields. Despite the appearance of overlap with UN measures, practitioners view the GCTF and related entities as being complementary. However, the emergence of the GCTF confirms the view that the UN alone was unable to supply states' demand for global governance on counterterrorism.

Second, the threat environment changed. It is a well-worn cliché to note the evolution of the terrorist threat in the post-9/11 years. Al-Qaeda and its affiliates were the primary concern over this period. But the rapid territorial advances made by the so-called Islamic State in Iraq and the Levant (ISIL or ISIS or Da'esh) in the summer of 2014—including the declaration of a caliphate by ISIL leader, Abu Bakr al-Baghdadi, in Mosul that June—prompted a swift multilateral response. ISIL had been listed pursuant to Security Council counterterrorism sanctions as an alternative name for Al-Qaeda in Iraq in May 2013. Resolution 2170 of August 2014 was the first to mention ISIL directly. It yielded a series of reports and resolutions, including the renaming of the sanctions committee to include a reference to ISIL, the expansion and extension of the sanctions, and a separate Security Council workstream on foreign terrorist fighters (FTFs)—that is, volunteers who left their home countries to join ISIL or other extremist groups in Syria and Iraq.

Overall, the UN—and particularly the council and its counterterrorism organs—have demonstrated a renewed sense of purpose. Beyond the UN, cooperation against ISIL has taken the form of a "Global Coalition against Da'esh," formed in September 2014. The coalition comprises some seventy members, who collaborate on a range of measures with the goal of degrading and defeating ISIL. This includes military cooperation as well as measures to stem its financing, counter its propaganda, staunch the flow of FTFs, and stabilize areas liberated from ISIL.

Third, among the most important developments in counterterrorism *per se* in recent years has been the pivot to terrorism prevention. In short order, "countering violent extremism" (CVE), sometimes known as "preventing violent extremism" (PVE), has emerged as a field of policy and practice in its own right. "Violent extremism" is understood to be broader than terrorism alone, referring more generally to ideologically motivated violence. To counter it, states have evolved a range of tools designed to work non-coercively and preventively, to dissuade vulnerable individuals and others from adopting extremist views and acting violently. In practice, this range of tools is quite vast and includes counter-narrative measures (especially online), intervention programs, community engagement and capacity building, and initiatives in the fields of social, economic, cultural, development, education, youth and women's policy. The shift to such "soft power," PVE measures represents a conscious departure from the tactile, coercive counterterrorism tools favored both domestically and multilaterally after 9/11.

In several states, domestic PVE initiatives had been in train for some time before they began to trickle up to the multilateral level. From its inception, the GCTF established a working group on CVE and produced in September 2013 the "Ankara Memorandum on Good Practices for a Multi-Sectoral Approach to Countering Violent Extremism." Its related entities, Hedayah and GCERF, define their mandates with reference to CVE. In February 2015, US president Barack Obama hosted a high-profile three-day summit, bringing together practitioners and experts from across the globe. In December 2015 under the aegis of the UN secretary-general, the UN released a "Plan of Action to Prevent Violent Extremism."[18] It identifies a wide range of possible causes of violent extremism and furnishes a long list of possible responses, while asking member states to develop their own national plans. Insofar as it signals a departure from the overemphasis on kinetic counterterrorism, the plan is a welcome development, but it also has elicited criticism. Its account of the drivers of violent extremism is broad and vague, and the scope of its prognoses gives rise to the perception that it, "makes for an agenda so expansive that it risks offering everything but nothing."[19] Critics fear that the plan may have a permissive effect, reinforcing the kinds of counterterrorism practices that states ought to be revisiting.

In the short term, the plan has provided the impetus for several UN entities to initiate or increase their engagement on counterterrorism, under the guise of PVE. For example, the UN Development Programme (UNDP) has been a member of CTITF but was reticent to participate so as not to dilute its core development mandate. It has now followed the lead of national and regional development actors, which have undertaken programmatic activities under the rubric of PVE. The plan enables entities such as the UN Alliance of Civilizations and the UN Educational, Scientific and Cultural Organization (UNESCO) to frame their work in terms of PVE. The plan notes the links between PVE and recent high-level reports on peace operations and the peacebuilding architecture. It asserts the relevance of PVE to the agendas on women, peace and security, and sustainable development. The broad framing of PVE has the potential to bring multiple, related domains into the orbit of global governance on counterterrorism. In May 2017, the Security Council extended its role on PVE in resolution 2354, which advances a comprehensive international framework to counter terrorist narratives, setting out guidelines for states to follow and mandating further work from CTED and CTITF.

Fourth, global governance on counterterrorism has thrived outside of the UN system and beyond the GCTF. A full account is beyond the scope of the present chapter, but regional and sub-regional organizations have mobilized on counterterrorism. From the OAS to the Organization for Security and Co-operation in Europe (OSCE), from the Asia-Pacific Economic Cooperation (APEC) to the Economic Community of West African States (ECOWAS), existing institutions have been adapted, and new mechanisms initiated. For its part, EU action on counterterrorism alone has prompted several, book-length treatments.[20] Here, too, the rise to prominence of PVE has extended global governance. Among numerous recent examples, the IGAD Center of Excellence in Preventing and Countering Violent Extremism, based in Djibouti, held its inaugural meeting in October 2016. Several governments have supported the development of transnational networks of researchers, who have documented and analyzed the turn to PVE. For example, as a result of the Radicalisation Awareness Network (supported by the European Commission) and the Resolve Network (housed at the United States Institute of Peace), and other mechanisms, the professional community of PVE practitioners has advanced rapidly and is, potentially at least, better informed on a range of increasingly specialized issues in the field (such as the role of women in PVE, how to evaluate PVE measures, PVE in a prison context, and so on).

Developments in civil society are similarly noteworthy. Since 2001, the growth of multilateral counterterrorism has been tracked by human rights advocates, who have highlighted the ways in which global governance has contributed, directly or indirectly, to human rights abuses. In some cases, this has involved the formation of transnational advocacy networks on specific issues, such as that formed in response to FATF-led efforts to suppress terrorist financing through the nonprofit sector, which had the unintended consequence of inhibiting civil society space in many countries.[21] Again, the emergence of PVE has had a mobilizing effect within civil society. By its nature, PVE posits an important role for civil society actors, especially those at the community level who may have the ability to identify vulnerable individuals, and the legitimacy to act against radicalization. Some such actors have questioned the premises and implementation of PVE programs.[22] In turn, some governments have supported the adaptation of existing civil society networks and the development of new networks, with the aim of building consensus and sharing experience on PVE.[23] As a result, a growing number of civil society actors across the world are joining the multitude of stakeholders in global governance on counterterrorism.

Counterterrorism's lessons for global governance

Global governance on counterterrorism is more dynamic today than ever. Beyond the volume of cooperation alone, the above patterns remind us that there are multiple multilateral routes. Cooperation here includes prominent roles for IOs, as well as regimes, trans-governmental networks, epistemic communities, and other institutional forms. Consistent with the emerging literature on "international regime complexity" (which analyzes the "presence of nested, partially overlapping, and parallel international regimes that are not hierarchically ordered"),[24] global governance on counterterrorism is characterized by fragmentation and overlaps. Specific issues within this broader domain—say, countering terrorist financing, PVE, border control, and law enforcement cooperation—are pursued among multiple actors in multiple forums, with varying degrees of coordination. This gives rise to questions about both the causes and consequences of such arrangements.

A relatively benign explanation can be offered for causes. If we view counterterrorism cooperation simply as a response to threats, we should expect that global governance tracks changes in the threat environment, which this account confirms. Multilateralism, and the UN in particular, is often perceived as clunky and bureaucratic. But it has shown itself to be relatively nimble in this case, adapting to such new threats as ISIL and addressing such issues of concern as the procedures for listing and delisting individuals subject to sanctions. Beyond responsiveness, one might even observe a measure of policy learning here.

But counterterrorism always occurs within a political context. Elite appeals for international action cited at the outset have a dual purpose. On the one hand, they are intended for a domestic political or institutional audience to demonstrate leadership in times of crisis. On the other hand, they serve as a reminder that, among those demanding cooperation, interests and preferences vary. States have different motives in advancing global governance, and the pattern that has emerged attests to competing viewpoints regarding whether and how cooperation should proceed. In turn, the fragmentation of cooperation suggests that global governance is permissive and, through its proliferation, can accommodate different preferences. Different explanations of the dynamics of regime complexity are emerging, but power-based accounts provide compelling insights here.[25] As in world politics generally, there are relative "winners" and "losers" in multilateral counterterrorism. The former are those powerful states that have been able to set the agenda and launder their preferences through multilateralism. The latter are those less powerful states for which terrorism may not even rank as a priority but who have been increasingly called to account on this issue.

Regarding the consequences of complexity, part of the emerging debate asks whether institutional overlaps have a positive or negative impact on compliance, cooperation, and outcomes. Too little effort has gone into understanding the effects and effectiveness of global governance on counterterrorism. Evaluative exercises within the UN, including that which yielded the current proposal to establish a new under-secretary-general, have tended to focus narrowly on documenting outputs and debating the institutional architecture to deliver relevant mandates.[26] It is unrealistic to expect that multilateralism can have a direct, measurable impact in diminishing specific threats; but systematic attempts to evaluate the contribution of multilateralism to counterterrorism—or at least to gauge whether intended consequences prevail more often than those unintended—are rare.[27] In light of this gap, it's tempting to retreat to the shibboleth that if global governance on counterterrorism did not exist, we would have to invent it. Under these conditions, readers should expect that complexity will beget more complexity, and that the now established pattern of expanding multilateral counterterrorism cooperation will continue. The evolution of global governance on counterterrorism to this point will inform future efforts to supply whatever demands for cooperation may emerge in the future.

Conclusion

Donald Trump is a remarkably unconventional US president, but there is one way in which he resembles his predecessors. On his first stop of his first trip abroad, in Saudi Arabia, he was eager to be seen to be advancing the cause of counterterrorism cooperation. Together with the Egyptian president and Saudi king, he helped launch the Global Center for Combating Extremist Ideology in Riyadh. Readers will judge for themselves whether this triumvirate is best placed to advance this cause. But their endeavor is utterly typical.

Prior to 9/11, the presence of a chapter on counterterrorism in a volume about international organization and global governance would not have been warranted. But today, counterterrorism cooperation furnishes lessons for scholars and students of international organization and global governance. The forms of multilateralism are diversifying over time, producing complexity, fragmentation and overlaps, but satisficing the demand for global governance among states that might otherwise disagree. This reality should prompt questions about the proportionality and effectiveness of multilateral counterterrorism in responding to existential threats. How much global governance on counterterrorism is the right amount, and in what form? To what extent does multilateral counterterrorism "work"? In the world of counterterrorism, they are difficult questions to address. But researchers would be well advised to focus their energies in this direction.

Additional reading

Chris Bordeleau, Jeff J. Chalifoux, and Karina Sangha, "The Global Fight Against Terror: An Evaluation of Counter-Terrorism Governance," Canadian Network for Research on Terrorism, Security and Society, Working Paper Series No. 15–01, January 2015.

Capability of the United Nations System to Assist Member States in Implementing the United Nations Global Counter-Terrorism Strategy, Report of the Secretary-General (General Assembly document A/71/858), 3 April 2017.

Christian Dorsch, "A New Barometer for the Evolution of Multilateral Counterterrorism: Introduction to the Materials, Methods, and Results of the UN Security Council and Terrorism Dataset (UNSC-TDS)," *Terrorism and Political Violence* 27, no. 4 (2015): 701–721.

Hendrik Hegemann, *International Counterterrorism Bureaucracies in the United Nations and the European Union* (Baden-Baden: Nomos Verlagsgesellschaft, 2014).

Barak Mendelsohn, *Combating Jihadism: American Hegemony and Interstate Cooperation in the War on Terrorism* (Chicago: University of Chicago Press, 2009).

Peter Romaniuk, *Multilateral Counterterrorism: The Global Politics of Cooperation and Contestation* (London: Routledge, 2010).

Notes

1 Statement by President Recep Tayyip Erdoğan on the Terror Attack on Istanbul Atatürk Airport, 28 June 2016, www.tccb.gov.tr/en/speeches-statements/558/45540/statement-by-president-recep-tayyip-erdogan-on-the-terror-attack-on-istanbul-ataturk-airport.html.
2 Goodluck Jonathan, "Nothing Is More Important than Bringing Home Nigeria's Missing Girls," *Washington Post*, 26 June 2014.
3 "Putin Widens Kremlin Powers for Terror Fight," *The Australian*, 14 September 2004.
4 Andrei Kelin, "NATO-Russia Cooperation to Counter Terrorism," *NATO Review*, 1 September 2005, www.nato.int/docu/review/2005/Combating-Terrorism/NATO-Russia-Cooperation-Terrorism/EN/index.htm.
5 "Annan, President Bush Visits 'Ground Zero' of Terror Attacks in New York," UN News Centre, 11 November 2001.
6 Paul R. Pillar, *Terrorism and US Foreign Policy* (Washington, DC: Brookings Institution, 2003).
7 *Capability of the United Nations System to Assist Member States in Implementing the United Nations Global Counter-Terrorism Strategy, Report of the Secretary-General*, UN document A/71/858, 3 April 2017.
8 Commission on Global Governance, *Our Global Neighborhood: Report of the Commission on Global Governance* (Oxford: Oxford University Press, 1995), 2.
9 James N. Rosenau, "Governance in the Twenty-First Century," *Global Governance* 1, no. 1 (1995): 14.
10 Shepard Forman and Derk Segaar, "New Coalitions for Global Governance: The Changing Dynamics of Multilateralism," *Global Governance* 12, no. 2 (2006): 205–225.
11 For example, note the special sections on "regime complexity" in: *Perspectives on Politics* 7, no. 1 (2009); *Global Governance* 19, no. 1 (2013).
12 Richard Bach Jensen, "The International Campaign Against Anarchist Terrorism, 1880–1930s," *Terrorism and Political Violence* 21, no. 1 (2009): 89–109.
13 Address by Yasser Arafat to the General Assembly of the United Nations, 13 November 1974.
14 www.nytimes.com/2001/09/12/us/a-day-of-terror-bush-s-remarks-to-the-nation-on-the-terrorist-attacks.html.
15 www.un.org/counterterrorism/ctitf/un-global-counter-terrorism-strategy. Implementation surveys, and summaries of member state reporting under relevant Council resolutions, are available at www.un.org/sc/ctc/resources/assessments.
16 James Cockayne, Alistair Millar, David Cortright, and Peter Romaniuk, *Reshaping United Nations Counterterrorism Efforts: Blue-Sky Thinking for Global Counterterrorism Cooperation 10 Years after 9/11* (New York: Center on Global Counterterrorism Cooperation, 2012); Naureen Chowdhury Fink, Peter Romaniuk, Alistair Millar, and Jason Ipe, *Blue Sky II: Progress and Opportunities in Implementing the UN Global Counterterrorism Strategy* (New York: Center on Global Counterterrorism Cooperation, 2014).
17 Amnesty International, *Security and Human Rights: Counter-terrorism and the United Nations* (London: Amnesty International, 2008).
18 *Plan of Action to Prevent Violent Extremism, Report of the Secretary-General*, UN document A/70/674, 24 December 2015.
19 Richard Atwood, "The Dangers Lurking in the U.N.'s New Plan to Prevent Violent Extremism," International Crisis Group, 8 February 2016, www.crisisgroup.org/global/dangers-lurking-u-n-s-new-plan-prevent-violent-extremism.
20 Oldrich Bures, *EU Counterterrorism Policy: A Paper Tiger?* (Burlington, VT: Ashgate, 2011); Raphael Bossong, *The Evolution of EU Counter-Terrorism: European Security Policy After 9/11* (New York: Routledge, 2013).

21 Peter Romaniuk and Tom Keatinge, "Protecting Charities from Terrorists . . . and Counterterrorists: FATF and the Global Effort to Prevent Terrorist Financing Through the Non-profit Sector," *Crime, Law and Social Change* (forthcoming, 2017).

22 For example, Humera Khan, "Why Countering Extremism Fails: Washington's Top-Down Approach to Prevention is Flawed," *Foreign Affairs*, 18 February 2015, www.foreign affairs.com/articles/united-states/2015-02-18/why-countering-extremism-fails.

23 The Prevention Project, www.organizingagainstve.org.

24 Karen J. Alter and Sophie Meunier, "The Politics of International Regime Complexity," *Perspectives on Politics* 7, no. 1 (2009): 13.

25 Daniel W. Drezner, "The Power and Peril of International Regime Complexity," *Perspectives on Politics* 7, no. 1 (2009): 65–70; "The Tragedy of the Global Institutional Commons," in *Back to Basics: State Power in a Contemporary World*, eds. Martha Finnemore and Judith Goldstein (Oxford: Oxford University Press, 2013).

26 *Capability of the United Nations System.*

27 Chris Bordeleau, Jeff J. Chalifoux, and Karina Sangha, "The Global Fight against Terror: An Evaluation of Counter-Terrorism Governance," Canadian Network for Research on Terrorism, Security and Society, Working Paper Series No. 15-01, January 2015.

Contents

Human rights

David P. Forsythe

As the introduction to this book suggests, the management of international relations is inseparable from the subject of international organization. This has been evident especially since 1919 when reflections on the dangers of an almost pure nation-state system after World War I led to the creation of the League of Nations. Yet its inability to prevent World War II (WWII) did not lead to the abandonment of the effort to better organize international relations but rather to improving international governance. The resulting United Nations system from 1945, supplemented especially by regional organizations, again tried to restrain in particular the excesses of national psychology and power. While the UN has lasted longer than the League, it and other contemporary international organizations struggle to manage destructive nationalist views and power maneuvers. The process is complicated by certain sub-national actors, some with economic global range such as Royal Dutch Shell or with transnational political goals such as the Islamic State.

One of the striking aspects of this historical process is the increased attention given to human rights. The League's Covenant made no mention of human rights, even if in the interwar years state representatives debated the subject and gave considerable attention to "social" matters including refugee affairs or slavery. In 1945 the UN Charter obligated all member states to take action to "promote" human rights (Articles 55 and 56). With the 1948 Universal Declaration of Human Rights, adopted as a nonbinding resolution by the UN General Assembly, and then with the negotiation and coming into legal force of numerous human rights treaties, a normative revolution occurred. What had been a national matter in some states became universalized with derivative implications for non-state actors like transnational corporations, armed non-state actors, and even for international organizations themselves as legal persons. Regional organizations followed similar if distinctive patterns especially in Europe, the Americas, and Africa.

The explanations are still debated. For some, protection of human rights correlates with peace; gross human rights violations correlate with aggression and war. UN Charter Article 55 calls on member states to promote human rights and create the conditions of stability and wellbeing that are necessary for peaceful and friendly relations. For others, a focus on human rights is the right thing to do. Appealing perhaps to a sense of moral intuition, they believe in categorical imperatives: Torture is always wrong; genocide is always prohibited, as are crimes against humanity and major war crimes. In this view, human rights are a necessary part of good governance. Still others believe that what started as propaganda during WWII took on a life of its own as especially Western leaders were trapped by their own rhetoric. US President Franklin Roosevelt and UK Prime Minister Winston Churchill issued the Atlantic Charter in 1941 to give principled meaning to the struggle against fascism and militarism. They promised a future characterized by peace, freedom, and self-determination. Having made that promise and won the war, they and their subsequent political heirs found it difficult to renounce what had been endorsed. Finally, some academics looking back see the attention to human rights through international organizations as either Western cultural imperialism or another utopian crusade.[1]

For whatever reason, universal human rights became a prominent feature of international relations and global governance after 1945. There were ups and downs in the salience of human rights along with a good deal of state hypocrisy. Many if not most states supported the idea of human rights, or at least appeared cooperative with the major Western states that championed them, but many states also wanted to retain their sovereignty to take expedient decisions. Numerous autocrats, of course, did not really believe in most human rights, but they also often wanted to avoid the pressures of critics. So they went through the motions of supporting diplomatic agreements on human rights, ratifying loosely worded treaties, and generally trying to deflect attention from their own shortcomings.

The subsequent analysis in this brief chapter will take this historical pattern and break it down into some component parts. Above all, these sections will show that the normative revolution in international relations that has produced a vast international law of human rights has *not*, in general, been accompanied by a complete behavioral and policy revolution. Narrow or parochial nationalism remains strong in many parts of the world. The quest for national power likewise remains strong in many places. Some armed non-state actors are so committed to revolutionary violence that attacks on civilians, beheading of prisoners, and systematic rapes are all seen as legitimate tactics. There is a persistent reluctance by many powerful states to delegate national authority to international organizations for the purpose of effectively protecting internationally recognized human rights in an evenhanded way. Yet at the same time, the human rights normative revolution has made some difference in international relations. The political game is not played the same way as before 1945. Some action, including action through international organizations, is indeed taken to protect universal human rights, and some progress in this matter can be documented. But in the last analysis, the glass is not close to being full, with much remaining to be done to achieve effective management of serious human rights violations around the world.

The normative revolution

However much Roosevelt may have believed in a broad range of human rights, along with national self-determination, early drafts of the Charter prepared in the United States did not mention human rights. Human rights language was added in subsequent drafts, with uncertain paternity.[2] Unsurprisingly, the Charter's language on human rights was general and aspirational, without legally enforceable specifics. In 1945 the United States was still characterized by its version of apartheid and legal discrimination against African-Americans, the United Kingdom was still committed to empire and an inferior status for individuals living in its nonwhite colonies, and the Soviet Union still had its gulags—led by Josef Stalin, one of the twentieth- century's great mass murderers.

By 1948 the UN's Commission on Human Rights (CHR) moved to correct a major anomaly: Member states were obligated to promote human rights, but there was no international definition. Made up of state representatives and chaired by Eleanor Roosevelt, there was superficial agreement in the CHR on the abstract notion of human rights but not full agreement on their origins or exact content. Avoiding sources (e.g., God or natural law), it constructed a list of thirty human rights principles including civil, political, social, economic, and cultural rights—basically an endorsement of social democracy.[3] States were obligated to advance not only civil and political rights designed to protect a "negative freedom" from external interference of personal liberty, but also a "positive freedom" designed to allow individuals to maximize their potential by guaranteeing such things as adequate education and healthcare. Without negative vote (but with eight abstentions), the General Assembly approved the Universal Declaration of Human Rights (UNDHR) that was greatly shaped by social democrats such as René Cassin speaking for France, and John P. Humphrey of Canada on the UN staff. Mrs. Roosevelt's role was not one of substantive intervention in debates but rather in greasing the wheels of personal interaction, cooperation, and compromise. She may have lobbied US President Harry Truman to throw the weight of the United States behind the Declaration—which he did.[4]

Even as a nonbinding General Assembly resolution, the UNDHR became the cornerstone for subsequent UN action. It also generated a broad influence on many national constitutions and bills of rights in new states emerging from colonialism. Regardless of which human rights treaties a state had ratified, a state could be criticized for failing to implement parts of the UNDHR in various UN organs and agencies. However, the emergence of the Cold War power struggle between NATO and the Warsaw Pact overshadowed UN developments for a time, including on human rights.

The eclipse of human rights at the UN occurred despite the horrors of the Holocaust and other mass atrocities, and despite other rights developments such as a new treaty on genocide in 1948 and various war crimes trials in Nuremberg and Tokyo. Hence the terrible fate of some individuals linked to the war of 1939–1945 had some effect on subsequent international relations, and certainly on the human rights norms debated at the UN in the mid- and late 1940s. But UN developments were weakened by the Cold War between Washington and Moscow as to what political economy and associated values would prove decisive in the world—democratic capitalism or auto-cratic socialism.[5] The Cold War, in turn, generated fears—sometimes paranoia—in the United States that international influences would alter traditional arrangements; the Eisenhower administration backed away from internationally recognized human rights especially at the United Nations and sacrificed US leadership in this area.[6]

Nevertheless, while Samuel Moyn is correct that there was no simple and direct path from the Holocaust and war atrocities to the new UN diplomacy on behalf of human rights,[7] states continued to try to translate the 1948 Declaration, referred to as "aspirational" by Mrs. Roosevelt, into treaties. The core effort ran from 1948 to 1966. By the latter date UN member states had negotiated the International Covenant on Civil and Political Rights (ICCPR) and the International Covenant on Economic, Social, and Cultural Rights (ICESCR). These two multilateral treaties, combined with the UNDHR, comprised an international bill of rights. It was clear that states were in no hurry to complete this task of building the core corpus of international human rights law. And it took until 1976 to obtain sufficient ratifications for the two core treaties to come into legal force. The United States, as close to a global hegemon as one could find, did not consent to the ICCPR until 1992 and then with serious and controversial reservations.[8] It has never fully accepted the ICESCR. Nonetheless, parts of the UNDHR have become legally binding, based on becoming part of cus-tomary international law.[9]

The international bill of rights was supplemented by other treaties covering the more specific subjects of apartheid, torture, discrimination against women, racial discrimination, slavery and slave-like practices, enforced disappearance, migrant workers, and the rights of the child. Already mentioned was the convention against genocide. Treaties on refugees and also on labor rights were usually also considered to be important parts of international human rights law.[10]

Even with the adoption of the two core covenants, some states or other actors believed there was insufficient attention to some continuing problem. This was true of many nongovernmental organizations (NGOs) active on rights, such as Amnesty International and later Human Rights Watch, which became increasingly important to global human rights governance. Often the solution was seen in negotiating a new human rights treaty on a specific subject. Such a process spotlighted a problem and generated new pressures on offending parties. But the result was a proliferation of human rights standards that troubled any number of observers. The international law of human rights came to encompass numerous rights, many of which were largely ignored by many states.

These and related developments at the UN were supplemented by considerable human rights diplomacy in regional international organizations. The most interest-ing was in Europe, where the Council of Europe produced in 1950 the European Convention for the Protection of Fundamental Rights and Freedoms. Unlike the 1948 UNDHR, this regional document was produced in large part in opposition to social democracy and in support of a more conservative or libertarian version of human rights that was limited only to civil and political rights.[11] The European Convention was eventually characterized by a supranational European Court of Human Rights at Strasbourg with the authority to rule on claims of rights violations by private individuals in any of the forty-seven member states.

In addition to the Council of Europe, the European Union evolved as an international organization to be twenty-eight states, largely for economic matters. But it too manifested a supranational court, the European Court of Justice at Luxembourg, which occasionally ruled on human rights matters associated with economic integration such as right of free movement of persons and various labor rights. So Europe wound up with two international courts with mandatory jurisdiction and the authority to issue binding rulings on states.

The two supranational regional courts were swamped with cases and regularly ruled against governments and in favor of individuals, which helped produce the 2016 British decision via referendum to exit the European Union. Brexit was a vote to depart the EU and reflected resentment against foreign elites and workers; but some British opinion felt that regional human rights developments were also undesirable. Brexit, however, did not change British legal obligations under the global international law of human rights, neither will withdrawal from the EU change legal obligations within the Council of Europe.

Regional human rights developments also flourished in the Americas, where the Organization of American States (OAS) adopted the Inter-American Declaration of the Rights and Duties of Man in April 1948—that is, even before the UN General Assembly adopted the UNDHR. Also known as the "Bogota Declaration," it also took the approach of social democracy, with attention to socioeconomic as well as civil–political rights. This was also true of the subsequent American Convention on Human Rights adopted by the OAS in 1969. Like Europe, the Americas eventually manifested a regional human rights court that came to exercise supranational authority—making binding judgments on about twenty states (some states acceded to the court's jurisdiction but later withdrew, and thus the number varied).[12] There was also an active Inter-American Commission on Human Rights.

Unlike in Europe, some important states in the Americas did not ratify the regional human rights treaty and did not accept the authority of the regional human rights court. This was true of the United States and Canada, and also most English-speaking states of the Caribbean. Washington might endorse some international human rights norms in vague terms, but it was unwilling to submit to an authoritative international review of its human rights record.

Briefly, one can note that what is today the African Union (AU) adopted the African Charter (or Banjul Charter) on Human and Peoples Rights in 1995. At the time of writing thirty states had consented to the jurisdiction of the related regional human rights court, created in 1998, and several cases were underway as initiated by the African Commission on Human Rights. An optional protocol allowed for petitions to the court directly from individuals and certain NGOs. The controlling norms not only reflected the values of social democracy but also several collective or people's rights such as protection of the family and the right of a national people to self-determination and disposal of its natural resources. Proposals to fold this regional human rights court into a more general AU court with jurisdiction over broad subject matter has yet to occur.

There also were minor developments pertaining to human rights in the Arab League, Association of Southeast Asian Nations (ASEAN), Commonwealth, and the Francophonie (the French equivalent of the Commonwealth). The general point is that in regional and non-global international organizations, including the North Atlantic Treaty Organization (NATO), attention to human rights was pervasive. Human rights norms were obviously constructed in a diplomatic and political process and varied across time and place. In some regions (Europe, the Americas, and Africa) developments went beyond those at the United Nations in the sense of supranational courts for enforcement. The Middle East, South Asia, and East Asia showed the weakest institutional developments. Europe and then the Americas showed the most impressive developments. But by the time of writing, parochial nationalism especially in Europe has called into question whether and for how long many states would tolerate authoritative international organizations in the human rights domain with deep impact on nations.

Before moving to that conversation, a brief discussion is in order about the laws of war. In addition to the international law of human rights with its related international organizations, developed mostly since 1948, there is the international law of armed conflict or international humanitarian law (IHL), developed mostly since 1864. The 1949 Geneva Conventions for Victims of War contain many of the important norms. Whereas the United Nations and regional organizations have been centrally important in the former, the International Committee of the Red Cross (ICRC) and Switzerland have demonstrated leadership in the latter. This bifurcation arose by happenstance or historical accident.[13]

Two points are noteworthy for present purposes. First, much (but not all) of IHL is concerned with protecting the wellbeing of individuals in armed conflict. They are now said to have rights. Second, the precise distinction between laws of war and human rights law becomes blurred in the scrum of international relations. Increasingly, there is much talk about protecting or advancing human dignity in this or that situation, which may entail lawyerly reference to either branch of international law, or both. Actors including the UN Security Council may refer to both types of law when, for instance, trying to protect civilians endangered by some kind of violence.

As for the substantive norms of IHL, the original purpose of developments from 1864 was to improve the fate of individuals affected by armed conflict—roughly, first the wounded combatant, then the detained combatant, then civilians including those under military occupation, and so on. As for the means and methods of warfare, the prohibition of certain weapons such as dum-dum bullets and poisonous gases was intended to spare persons from superfluous suffering, however difficult to implement. The norms were developed for international war but extended in reduced form to civil war. One of the central normative themes was to neutralize, and thus make off limits to attack, medical facilities and medical personnel and those in need of medical attention. In order to develop and help implement these norms, one found the evolution of the network that is now called the International Red Cross and Red Crescent Movement, which is comprised of the ICRC in Geneva; national Red Cross or Red Crescent societies (or their equivalent) in some 190 states; the association of these national societies, the RC Federation; and other organs and agencies.

More space would allow more discussion of some interesting norms found within IHL. For example, the private ICRC, with an all-Swiss governing board, has been given the right to visit detainees, whether civilian or combatant, in international armed conflict. This is to ensure that such detainees are provided a humanitarian quarantine for the duration of captivity. This is one example of IHL's attempt to interject a modicum of humanitarian concern into what belligerents consider military necessity. While fighting parties have obligations and the ICRC has procedural rights, detainees have a right to speak in confidence with ICRC representatives in places of detention. In addition, states have self-interested reasons for supporting the laws of war, which include maintaining domestic support, military discipline in following rules, and protection of their own personnel.

As for the meshing of norms from the two distinct bodies of law, some human rights norms remain applicable in armed conflict. Prohibitions on murder, torture and cruelty, enforced disappearance, and certain other rules remain binding in armed conflict. So while human rights law is said to be general, and IHL said to be specific to armed conflicts (whether international or non-international), some of the rules of the former still apply to the latter.

The structure of IHL can lead to disagreement as to triggering conditions. For varying reasons, there is often disagreement as to when war is international or internal. There is often dispute as to whether one faces an internal armed conflict or a riot or rebellion or unrest or internal troubles and tensions. In short, the "legal boxes" of international or internal war are often difficult to superimpose on the complexity of a violent situation. Moreover, governments often have their self-serving reasons for denying that an international or internal armed conflict exists.

Thus, there is much room for debate in various international organizations as how best to protect the welfare of persons in situations of violence. Should one refer to human rights law, IHL, both, neither? Should one bypass both human rights law and IHL by referring to "complex emergencies" or "human security?" Should one use the notion of "human dignity" in order to bypass legalistic debates that might impede progress in actually helping persons in a concrete or pragmatic way?

A limited revolution

Some seven decades after the start of the normative revolution on behalf of human rights and humanitarian affairs in international relations, one could find many observers who question the importance of the subject. If we use as major benchmarks the 1948 UNDHR and the 1949 Geneva Conventions, decades later it was easy to see a yawning gap between the law on the books and the law in action. One can compile a short list of the reasons for this disparity.[14]

The treaties often display loose wording that allows consenting states much "wiggle room" in avoiding human rights obligations. Moreover, treaties alone cannot resolve human rights problems any more than a national constitution can resolve legal problems without accompanying independent courts to issue judgments in complicated situations.

There is no human rights court in the UN system to resolve disputes about proper interpretation of UN human rights treaties.

States do not often give their consent for important human rights issues to reach the International Court of Justice (ICJ). A case here or there might concern something like genocide in the western Balkans or whether a sitting state official can be individually prosecuted for some atrocity, but at the end of the day the ICJ has not been able to have a profound effect on protecting human rights. States do not allow independent judges serving in their personal capacity to have the ultimate authority to rule on such sensitive matters as the gassing of civilians in Syria or the torture of prisoners under the control of US authorities. As a general matter, states have to give their consent for a legal dispute to be handled by the ICJ. They have not done so to an extent that permits the court to have persistent and profound impact on human rights violations.[15]

Regional courts have indeed proved important, which explains why there has been a backlash against them for intruding into what many still consider to be the domestic affairs of member states. For Britain in Europe as for in Brazil in the Americas, there is growing opposition to having international judges on regional courts decide sensitive subjects such as freedom of movement for foreign workers. This trend is a brake on assertiveness by these courts.

Likewise, as the International Criminal Court (ICC) has begun to have a concrete effect on African leaders, convicting a warlord here or there, investigating leading officials in this or that state, some African leaders have demonstrated second thoughts about accepting the court's jurisdiction. Some charge the court with being neocolonial in focusing disproportionately on African cases. But the real reason behind the considerable African criticism of and noncooperation with the ICC is that it was having an impact on bad governance in that region. Moreover, many important military powers refused to be bound by the court: The United States, India, Israel, Russia, China, Iran, Iraq, and North Korea, etc. They did not want independent, authoritative reviews of what might be a war crime or crime against humanity (systematic attack on the civilian population). Ironically, the UN Security Council might refer a situation to the ICC, which occurred regarding Sudan and Libya, but the three most powerful permanent members (the United States, China, and Russia) have refused to consent to the Rome Statute creating that court.[16]

Beyond the matter of various international courts in applying international human rights law and IHL, other organized efforts at implementation remain weak. About half a dozen of the UN human rights treaties provided a diplomatic "monitoring mechanism" to supervise implementation of the treaty norms. Such bodies as the UN Human Rights Committee, created under the ICCPR, primarily evaluated periodic reports from ratifying states and were given the authority to raise questions and make summary judgments. The questions by its independent members might prove temporarily embarrassing to the state representative who had to defend a state record, but it was unclear that such questioning often led to a major change in that state's policy on human rights under the treaty. Conclusions or "general comments" by the international body were nonbinding. The process clarified a number of legal points; but when a state's violation of the norms was calculated rather than accidental, the process constituted weak pressure.

Something similar could be said about the UN Human Rights Council (HRC), which replaced the UNCHR in 2006. This body, comprised of states as already noted, moved from primarily drafting norms to trying to supervise state performance around 1970, which can be seen as progress. But the resulting record of the CHR was such that states replaced it with the HRC. From 2006, the latter proved to be essentially old wine in a new bottle. States continued to be elected to the HRC that manifested quite serious human rights problems, although no UN member state had totally clean hands. Even longstanding democracies sometimes engaged in torture or cruel treatment of detainees (e.g., the United States, Israel, and India). There was a persistent singling out of Israel. There were indeed violations of human rights and IHL there, but other countries had worse records but escaped comparable criticism. States fought hard to avoid critical resolutions, but if they lost that procedural struggle they did not necessarily conform to what the HRC demanded.

Likewise, its "special procedures" constituted a diplomatic process that many advocates for human rights wanted to maintain, especially the human rights NGOs. Consisting of an independent person or persons focusing on particular themes—e.g., disappeared persons, or countries (e.g., Iran), or problems (e.g., civilian deaths in the fighting in Gaza)—these arrangements generated some pressure on states to respect human rights. Like the UN monitoring mechanisms or HRC meetings in Geneva, these special procedures sometimes led to media coverage—which generated further pressure on targeted states. Again in the last analysis, the conclusions and recommendations were nonbinding. They seemed to have little effect on states committing major violations of human rights and IHL.

Underlying these developments was a reluctance by many states to pay high sovereignty costs to see that human rights and IHL standards proved controlling. Most states are simply reluctant to delegate ultimate authority to international organizations to have the last say about when and how to implement human rights norms. The major exception to this pattern was in Europe until Brexit in 2016, because states consented to the jurisdiction and authority of two regional international courts, one dealing exclusively with human rights. Globally, especially the most powerful states, i.e., the United States, China, and Russia, want to maintain almost total national independence and almost always reject international authoritative review of their human rights policies. In the case of autocratic states with poor human rights records, one can at least understand why they reject international jurisdiction; but for the United States and other democracies such as Israel and India, the reasons for assertive unilateralism rather than authoritative multilateralism are somewhat different.[17] Indeed, the United States sees itself exceptional regarding human rights and this leads to considerable unilateralism.[18]

In addition, such armed non-state actors as the Islamic State Movement and Boko Haram believe that the past and present are so offensive that no human rights or humanitarian law restrictions should be observed in their revolutionary activities. So, in addition to the staying power of narrow nationalism, we observe the phenomenon of total rejection of human rights and humanitarian norms in favor of a new world order rationalized in terms of a new set of norms—in the case of jihadists, a twisted version of militant Islam.

Suffice to say here that these types of violent non-state actor reinforced the desire of many states to have a free hand in suppressing them. Should one respect human rights norms if that might result in serious damage to existing states and their citizens?

Conclusion

The weaknesses of many internationally organized efforts to protect human rights should not blind us to the positive changes. When Imperial Germany engaged in genocide in what is now Namibia in the early twentieth century, the world took no notice. When the Ottoman Empire engaged in repeated atrocities against resident Christian Armenians from more or less 1895 to the end of World War I, there was no internationally organized response. In contemporary times one can certainly debate the adequacy of international responses in Rwanda in 1994 and Syria from 2011. But there is no doubt but that the international pressures for attention to various human rights and IHL are far greater. Even regarding Rwanda, after the fact there was public admission that the response should have been otherwise, with apologies from US President Bill Clinton and others.

One of the major achievements is the renaissance in attention to international criminal justice and the possible prosecution of individuals who authorize atrocities such as genocide, crimes against humanity (including ethnic cleansing), and war crimes.[19] Facilitated by the end of the Cold War, starting in 1993 one saw international criminal courts mandated by the UN Security Council—for the western Balkans, then Rwanda, and later for Lebanon. Other international or hybrid criminal courts were approved by various UN organs pertaining to Sierra Leone (expanded in some ways to include Liberia), East Timor, Cambodia, and in complicated ways in other cases, such as Bosnia and Kosovo. We have already mentioned the ICC since 2002 when it began to operate.

Simultaneously, states themselves have utilized the principle of universal jurisdiction to open their courts to prosecution for such heinous crimes as genocide and torture. Using international law as developed through international organizations, then incorporated into national law, many states have allowed the prosecution of individuals for gross violations of internationally recognized human rights.[20]

In general, after the end of repressive rule or atrocities, there was always a debate about transitional justice: Whether and how to pursue internationally approved prosecutions, or truth commissions, or formal apologies, or reparations, or construction of memorials. One might argue that had there been proper international intervention to end gross violations, one could pre-empt this debate. Nevertheless, there was indeed considerable attention to universal human rights in general, even in cases when timely enforcement had been defective.[21]

Here one should note the UN General Assembly's adoption of the principle of the responsibility to protect (R2P) in 2005. Without opposition, the assembly agreed that if a state were unwilling or unable to prevent atrocities or conduct the appropriate investigation and prosecution, other states had the duty to get involved in keeping with international law. Much remains to be done to translate this principle into effective protection, but this principle and its intent reflects a sea-change in thinking about state sovereignty and domestic jurisdiction.[22]

Space limitations prevent a further discussion about examples of progress for universal human rights, and the boundaries of such progress. For example, much can be said about double standards involved in the practice of international criminal justice. If one is a leader in a weak state without powerful patrons, one may indeed wind up having to answer in some court for gross violations. For leaders of powerful states or states with powerful patrons, the prospects are different.

So for universal human rights, we have witnessed a normative revolution along with a sizeable gap between the norms on paper and their effective translation into consistent protection—and a mixed record in the role of international organizations in moving from adopting norms to guaranteeing new policies based on new behavior.

Additional reading

David P. Forsythe and Patrice C. McMahon, *American Exceptionalism Reconsidered: US Foreign Policy, Human Rights, and World Order* (New York: Routledge, 2016).

Emilie M. Hafner-Burton, *Making Human Rights a Reality* (Princeton, NJ: Princeton University Press, 2009).

Philippe Sands, *East West Street: On the Origins of "Genocide" and "Crimes Against Humanity"* (New York: Knopf, 2016).

Thomas G. Weiss, *Humanitarian Intervention*, 3rd ed. (Cambridge: Polity Press, 2016).

Notes

1 For an introduction to this subject including its history, see David P. Forsythe, *Human Rights in International Relations,* 4th ed. (Cambridge: Cambridge University Press, 2017). For two revisionist views, see Stephen Hopgood, *The Endtimes of Human Rights* (Ithaca, NY: Cornell University Press, 2013) and Samuel Moyn, *The Last Utopia: Human Rights in History* (Cambridge, MA: Harvard University Press, 2010).

2 The traditional starting point is Ruth B. Russell, *A History of the UN Charter: The Role of the United States 1940–1945* (Washington, DC: Brookings Institution, 1958).

3 The definitive treatment is by Johannes Morsink, *The Universal Declaration of Human Rights: Origins, Drafting & Intent* (Philadelphia: University of Pennsylvania Press, 1999).

4 Mary Ann Glendon, *A World Made New: Eleanor Roosevelt and the Universal Declaration of Human Rights* (New York: Random House, 2001).

5 Moyn, *The Last Utopia.*

6 McCarthyism as a witch hunt for communists in the State Department and other places is well known. Brickerism was a nativist movement against human rights treaties (and executive agreements) and the power of the president to negotiate them. On the latter subject, see David L. Sloss, *The Death of Treaty Supremacy: An Invisible Constitutional Change* (New York and Oxford: Oxford University Press, 2016).

7 Moyn, *The Last Utopia.*

8 William A. Schabas, "Spare the RUD or Spoil the Treaty: The United States Challenges the Human Rights Committee on Reservations," in *The United States and Human Rights: Looking Inward and Outward*, ed. David P. Forsythe (Lincoln: University of Nebraska Press, 2000), 110–130.

9 Brian D. Lepard, *Customary International Law: A New Theory with Practical Applications* (Cambridge: Cambridge University Press, 2010) gives an overview of the process whereby a nonbinding norm can become binding.

10 For details and information on ratifications, see Thomas G. Weiss, et al., *The United Nations and Changing World Politics*, 8th ed. (Boulder, CO: Westview Press, 2017), chapter 6.

11 Marco Duranti, *The Conservative Human Rights Revolution: European Identity, Transnational Politics, and the Origins of the European Convention* (New York and Oxford: Oxford University Press, 2017). It should be noted that the Council of Europe adopted the European Social Charter in 1961, devoted mainly to labor rights but also other socioeconomic rights, but without an attached court. So, over time Europe as a network of regional organizations was characterized by the values of social democracy.

Civil and political rights received the most authoritative attention, but there was also—if weaker—attention to socioeconomic rights.

12 See Courtney Hillebrecht, *Domestic Politics and International Human Rights Tribunals: The Problem of Compliance* (Cambridge: Cambridge University Press, 2014).

13 Caroline Moorehead, *Dunant's Dream: War, Switzerland and the History of the Red Cross* (New York and London: HarperCollins, 1998); David P. Forsythe, *The Humanitarians: The International Committee of the Red Cross* (Cambridge: Cambridge University Press, 2005).

14 A short summary can be found in David P. Forsythe, "Hard Times for Human Rights," *Journal of Human Rights* 16, no. 2 (2017): 242–253.

15 For one view, see Gentian Zyberi, "Human Rights in the International Court of Justice," in *International Human Rights Law: Six Decades after the UDHR and Beyond*, eds. Mashood Baderin and Manisuli Ssenyonjo (Burlington, VT: Ashgate, 2010), 289–304.

16 Triestino Mariniello, ed., *The International Criminal Court in Search of its Purpose and Identity* (New York and London: Routledge, 2015).

17 The United States is a member of the World Trade Organization (WTO) whose dispute panels might strike down a US trade law. There was no comparable US membership in a human rights organization. WTO sanctions for violations were imposed by states, not the organization.

18 David P. Forsythe and Patrice C. McMahon, *American Exceptionalism Reconsidered: US Foreign Policy, Human Rights, and World Order* (New York: Routledge, 2016).

19 Out of many sources one might start with William A. Schabas, ed., *The Cambridge Companion to International Criminal Law* (Cambridge: Cambridge University Press, 2016).

20 For a concise introduction, see "Factsheet: Universal Jurisdiction," Center for Constitutional Rights, December 7, 2015, https://ccrjustice.org/home/get-involved/tools-resources/fact-sheets-and-faqs/factsheet-universal-jurisdiction.

21 Peter Malcontent, ed., *Facing the Past: Amending Historical Injustices through Instruments of Transitional Justice* (Cambridge: Intersentia, 2016).

22 From a wealth of sources, see Gareth Evans, *The Responsibility to Protect: Ending Mass Atrocity Once and for All* (Washington, DC: Brookings Institution, 2009).

The pursuit of international justice

Richard J. Goldstone

In the past 25 years, the pursuit of international justice has reinvigorated international humanitarian law (or the law of war as it used to be called). The prosecution and threatened prosecution of war criminals has now become the subject of daily news reports. It is that pursuit that forms the thrust of this essay.[1]

The origins of international humanitarian law are to be found in some early battlefield rules and limitations placed on the manner in which armies were allowed to behave, especially toward those of the enemy who were injured or captured. These laws were founded in religion and chivalry. They were based also on reciprocity—if you treat my soldiers in a humane manner I will reciprocate and treat yours similarly. Such humane treatment has unfortunately been the exception rather the rule and the more common approach was that in war there was no legal limit to the pursuit of victory. In the words of Thucydides in the fifth century BCE: "[T]o a king or commonwealth, nothing is unjust which is useful."[2] The thrust of this chapter is not the history of international humanitarian law. It is rather to examine and consider the major issues relating to the present day pursuit of international justice.

This chapter traces the history of modern international humanitarian law beginning with the 1945 Nuremberg Trial of the major Nazi war criminals. It considers the courts that were established in the last decade of the twentieth century—namely, the two United Nations *ad hoc* tribunals for the former Yugoslavia and for Rwanda, the various hybrid or mixed tribunals, and the International Criminal Court (ICC). It describes the major current debates around these tribunals and concludes with a brief consideration of likely future developments.

The origins

As World War II drew to a close, it was famously agreed by the victorious nations (France, the Soviet Union, the United Kingdom, and the United States) that the rule of law should be applied at the international level of criminal justice. It was agreed that the Nazi leaders should not be summarily executed but afforded the benefit of a fair trial.

The Nuremberg Trial had a profound influence on both lawyers and politicians of the time and it was widely anticipated that a permanent international criminal court would be established to prosecute the most serious war crimes. One finds reference to such a court in Article 6 of the Genocide Convention of 1948 where it is provided that genocide could be prosecuted "by such international penal tribunal as may have jurisdiction with respect to those contracting parties which shall have accepted its jurisdiction."[3] It was thought that such an international court would be established by treaty. That did not happen and the endeavor foundered on the sea of the Cold War and was not to be revived for almost half a century.

Modern international criminal courts

It took a European catastrophe, the Balkan war of the early 1990s, to move the United Nations Security Council in 1993 to set up the first ever truly international criminal tribunal. It had not done so in light of even more egregious war crimes committed not too long before in Cambodia and Iraq. It was the politics and the political will of the most powerful Western nations that determined that something had to be done in the face of the war crimes being committed in pursuance of a policy of ethnic cleansing in Central Europe. That "something," was the unanimous 1993 Security Council resolution 827 setting up the International Criminal Tribunal for the former Yugoslavia (ICTY). This development had become politically possible after 1989 with the disintegration of the Soviet Union and the end of the Cold War. The terrible genocide perpetrated in Rwanda in the middle of 1994 led the Security Council in resolution 955 to establish the International Criminal Tribunal for Rwanda (ICTR). These two tribunals are often referred to as "the *ad hoc* tribunals."

In establishing both tribunals the Security Council relied on its peremptory powers under Chapter VII of the Charter of the United Nations. It is there that one finds the only authority vested in the Security Council to pass resolutions binding on all member States. Charter Article 39 provides that the Security Council may determine that a situation constitutes a threat to the peace, breach of the peace, or act of aggression. Having made such a determination, the council may make recommendations, or decide what measures shall be taken in accordance with Article 41 and 42, to maintain or restore international peace and security. Under Article 41 it may decide on measures "not involving the use of armed force are to be employed to give effect to its decision. Such measures may include complete or partial interruption of economic relations and of rail, sea, air, postal, telegraphic, radio, and other means of communication, and the severance of diplomatic relations." If those measures are or prove to be inadequate, under Article 42 the Security Council may take "such action by air, sea, or land forces as may be necessary to maintain or restore international peace and security. Such actions may include demonstrations, blockade, and other operations by air, sea, or land forces of Members of the United Nations." Those provisions of the Charter are silent on the establishment of a criminal tribunal. The council held, however, that the establishment of a criminal court as a peacekeeping tool was impliedly included in the powers conferred on it by the provisions of Article 41—i.e., a measure not involving the use of force. The power to establish the two tribunals thus depended on the council's making the connection between justice and peace.

The two *ad hoc* tribunals were sufficiently successful to encourage the establishment of the so-called hybrid or mixed tribunals. These are criminal courts established by agreement between a national government and the United Nations. This method led to the establishment of criminal courts in Sierra Leone, Cambodia, and Lebanon. At the same time, efforts were being made to establish a permanent international criminal court. The statute for such a court was agreed by 120 nations at a diplomatic conference held in Rome in the middle of 1998.[4] The ICC began its operations on 1 July 2002. Some 124 countries have since ratified the Rome Statute. They comprise the supervising body of the ICC called the Assembly of States Parties (ASP). With the *ad hoc* tribunals and hybrid or mixed tribunals having completed their work or soon to complete it, the ICC will in the coming few years become the only international criminal court in the global community.

The *ad hoc* tribunals, as sub-organs of the Security Council, were given primacy and could determine which cases they would investigate. National jurisdictions were obliged to defer to decisions made in this regard by the *ad hoc* tribunals. In the first trial before the ICTY, that of Dusan Tadic, the defendant had been arrested and indicted by a court in Germany. When the ICTY decided that he should be tried before it in The Hague, the German authorities somewhat unhappily accepted that position, promulgated enabling legislation, and transferred Tadic to the ICTY for trial. The ICC works on the converse principle that it is a court of last and not first resort. The philosophy underlying this approach is that war criminals should preferably be investigated and tried by the courts of their own nations. Only if such courts are unable or unwilling to do so will the ICC have jurisdiction. Part of the duty of the ICC prosecutor is to assist and enable national courts to act against war criminals who are physically within their areas of jurisdiction.

Situations may come before the ICC in three ways. Article 13 specifies that they may be referred by the government of a state that has ratified the Rome Statute; by the Security Council; or by the prosecutor relying on his own powers. The exercise of the last mentioned power is subject to their approval of a pretrial chamber of the court.

The politics of international criminal courts

The tribunals of the 1990s owed their very existence to political decisions reached by the United Nations. In other words, those tribunals were established not solely with regard to the seriousness of the crimes committed, but also for political reasons.

Other humanitarian crises that escaped scrutiny under the system of *ad hoc* tribunals were overlooked not necessarily because the atrocities were less heinous, but because of the crass political realities of international relations. The ICC operates on a fundamentally different basis—prosecution is not contingent on an extraordinary moment of political will by the Security Council. That said, however, the reality is that major powerful countries have failed to ratify the Rome Statute and their nationals are not subject to its jurisdiction unless they commit a war crime in a country that has ratified the Statute. In particular, the United States, China, Russia, and India remain outside the Rome Statute. The first three, as permanent members of the Security Council, are also able to veto the reference of a situation to the ICC by the council. This effectively places nations that have not ratified the Rome Statute, and receive protection from a permanent member of the UN, beyond the jurisdiction of the ICC. In this way, Syria has been protected by Russia, Sri Lanka by China, and Israel by the United States. That this is a defect in the ICC system cannot be denied. The only solution is to continue to pressure all governments to ratify the Rome Statute.

We should also take notice of complaints coming from many African quarters at the fact that of the ten situations presently before the ICC all but one relate to African countries. The exception is Georgia. The African Union (AU) and a number of African political leaders have caviled at this and make allegations to the effect that the ICC is an instrument created by the West to judge Africans. The criticism is based more on perception than fact. It is rather unfair if one takes into account that of the nine situations only three have resulted from the prosecutor exercising his own powers (Kenya, the Ivory Coast, and Georgia). Of the remaining six, four were referred by African governments themselves (Uganda, Democratic Republic of the Congo, the Central African Republic, and Mali) and two by the Security Council (Sudan and Libya). This notwithstanding, the perception cannot be wished away and the ICC will have increased credibility in Africa when more situations from other continents come before it. The situation might also be alleviated by the fact that since July 2012 the Chief Prosecutor, Fatou Bensouda, is an African and former minister of justice of Gambia.

Towards the end of 2016, three African states (Burundi, Gambia, and South Africa) gave formal notice of their withdrawal from the Rome Statute. A subsequently elected government in Gambia has stated that it intends to reverse that decision; and the constitutionality of the South African notice of withdrawal has been held in a decision of the High Court to be unconstitutional and invalid.[5]

This chapter now discusses the successes and failures of these international criminal courts and tribunals, the major issues that are currently being debated, and finally assesses the prospects of the ICC.

Success and failure

What are the major successes of international criminal courts? When the first international criminal courts were established, many questioned their ability to hold fair trials. Doubts were founded on the potential problems that might emerge from having judges, prosecutors, defense lawyers and investigators coming from diverse and disparate legal systems. Would they be able to work together and find a common legal language? This was a serious concern to me in 1994 as effectively the first chief prosecutor of the ICTY. The Office of the Prosecutor was a United Nations office and accordingly was justifiably required to reflect both global geographic and gender balance. It was our experience that the different legal cultures have more in common with one another than differences. All of them have at their core the need to seek the truth and to convict defendants on appropriately gathered and rigorously tested evidence. The ICTY and the international criminal courts that followed have by and large held fair trials. This is in no small measure to the credit of the judges and prosecutors who recognized and acted on their responsibility to ensure the fairness of the proceedings. The conduct of trials before these courts has certainly not been as efficient as it might have been and lessons have been learnt and applied. In the result, there have been many convictions and acquittals and the global community no longer questions the ability of these courts and tribunals to hold fair trials. This is a signal success and one that is too frequently left out of account in the debates on international criminal justice.

Another important success of international criminal courts is the way in which they have substantially advanced and developed international humanitarian law. In my opinion, the most important single area of advance is that in relation to gender crimes and especially systematic mass rape as a war crime. Prior to the establishment of these courts international humanitarian law all but ignored rape as a war crime. In consequence of imaginative lawyering by some of the judges, prosecutors and with important contributions from academic and practicing lawyers, judgments were handed down by the *ad hoc* tribunals that recognized the importance of gender-related war crimes. The high watermark was the holding by the ICTR in the *Akayesu* case that mass rape can constitute a form of genocide.[6] The legacy of this work by the *ad hoc* tribunals is to be found in the holistic and broad definitions of gender-related crimes in the Rome Statute that establishes the ICC.[7] Other important areas of international humanitarian law that have been advanced include decisions on the legality of the *ad hoc* tribunals,[8] defining culpability under command responsibility,[9] extending command responsibility to civilian enterprises,[10] holding that an individual can be personally responsible for the commission of genocide,[11] and that members of the media can be held responsible for genocide.[12]

There can be no doubt that the work of the ICC will continue along these lines. Its first conviction was for the recruitment of child soldiers and has focused international attention on a neglected and egregious war crime.[13] More recently, in the first case of its kind, the ICC convicted Ahmad Al Faqi Al Mahdi of intentionally attacking historic monuments in Timbuktu, Mali, during the period between June and July 2012. Al Mahdi pleaded guilty to the charges and on 27 September 2016 was sentenced to imprisonment for nine years.[14]

Of course, that 124 states have ratified the Rome Statute is a success well beyond the anticipation of the most ardent supporters of the ICC. Indeed, the Rome Statute required sixty ratifications before it became operative. In 1998, it was anticipated that it might take a decade or more to reach that number. In the end, it took under four years and the number has doubled since then. As already indicated, leading powerful and populous nations have not ratified the Rome Statute and this remains a major problem for the court.

The legitimacy of the ICC also depends on the limits of its scope. Only the most serious international crimes fall within the jurisdiction of the ICC. The crimes are genocide, crimes against humanity, war crimes, and aggression. However, in the absence of agreement at Rome on a definition of "aggression," the inclusion of this crime was held in abeyance for nine years after the inception of the jurisdiction of the ICC. Only crimes committed after 1 July 2002 fall within the jurisdiction of the Court. In the case of nations ratifying the Rome Treaty after the date the ICC became operative, the treaty becomes effective with regard to them only prospectively—i.e., *from* the date of such ratification.

The crime of aggression was taken up at the first ICC Review Conference held in the middle of 2010 in Kampala, Uganda. The members of the ASP agreed by consensus on a definition of the crime. An "act of aggression" is committed by military action by a state against the territory of another state or an attack by the armed forces of a state on the land, sea, or air forces of another state. The crime of aggression is defined to include the planning, preparation, or execution by someone who holds control over the political or military action of a state of an act of aggression. By its character, gravity, and scale, it must constitute a manifest violation of the UN Charter. In short, the crime of aggression can only be committed by someone in a leadership position and only if there is a manifest violation of the prohibition on the use of force contained in the Charter. Under its Article 52, legitimate self-defense would not constitute aggression. This crime of aggression could not fall within the jurisdiction of the ICC until the beginning of 2017 and then only after at least thirty states ratify these provisions and two-thirds of the members of the ASP have adopted the relevant amendments to the statute. By the beginning of 2017, more than thirty states parties had ratified the provisions. There is no indication as to when, if ever, the amendments will come into operation. Even if they do, individual states will be entitled to opt out of the provisions.

The fact that universal impunity for the commission of serious war crimes has been ended is another success of international justice. The extent to which this acts as a deterrent is difficult to establish and anecdotal evidence is difficult to obtain. Yet the threat of criminal prosecution and being labeled as a war criminal must weigh on the minds of at least some political and military leaders when they determine their military strategies.

The work of the international criminal courts has brought important benefits to the people of the countries that have been the focus of investigation. In particular, fabricated denials of the commission of war crimes have been made more difficult in light of the evidence of many hundreds of witnesses. The ICTY has brought to trial every one of the defendants indicted by it. This feat appeared impossible a few short years ago. The major defendants indicted by the ICTR have appeared in Arusha, the seat of the tribunal. Proof of the true facts and circumstances that resulted in extreme violence and massive war crimes is an important benefit for societies that wish to repair the fractured relationships between formerly antagonistic ethnic or religious groups. It has proven to be beneficial in countries such as Rwanda, Bosnia and Herzegovina, and Sierra Leone to mention but three. No price tag can be placed on those benefits. The real bottom line is that the world must be a better place without impunity for war criminals and in which there is a court that is empowered to bring such war criminals before them and, if found guilty, to be appropriately punished. That many victims demand this acknowledgement and justice and may benefit from it has been demonstrated by their reaction to the work of these courts.

One has to recognize that the deterrent effect of a criminal justice system will always be unpredictable. It is no different in a domestic situation. In any country, the crime rate will depend directly on the efficiency of the criminal justice system. The more effective it is the lower will be the crime rate. The converse is also true—in countries with inefficient or ineffective criminal justice the higher the crime rate will become. No matter how efficient the system, some criminals will still anticipate escaping justice and crimes will continue to be perpetrated. And some unbalanced people, sadly, will never be deterred. It is no different in the international community of states. If political and military leaders anticipate being brought before a court and facing possible conviction and punishment, this may deter some of them from committing war crimes. It will not deter them all. But, just as the imperfect deterrence of even the most efficient domestic criminal justice systems does not undermine their purpose or legitimacy, the fact that some war criminals will never be deterred should not blind us to the important reality that some war criminals will be deterred. And the many thousands of innocent civilians who are spared as a result must not be forgotten.

The current debate

What of the criticisms of the international criminal courts? It cannot be denied that international courts are expensive. At their height of operations the ICTY and ICTR together accounted for about ten percent of the UN's total operating budget. The question that has to be asked is whether it has been worth it. Criminal prosecutions by their nature are expensive endeavors. If the proceedings are to be fair they cannot be rushed. In particular, the defendant has to be given sufficient time to prepare his or her defense and this includes the unfettered right to receive all relevant evidence in the possession of the prosecutor. If justice is to be done—and be seen to be done—then there are no financial shortcuts. The alternative to such prosecutions is to continue the effective regime of impunity for egregious war crimes that obtained prior to the establishment of these courts.

Another criticism relates to the punishments that are imposed by these courts. This is a problem without a solution and it must be admitted that there is no punishment that is commensurate with the serious war crimes that these tribunals are prosecuting. The maximum punishment is life imprisonment and that has been reserved by the judges for the leaders who are most responsible for the commission of the offenses. One cannot impose the same sentence for the negligent yet unlawful killing of 1000 innocent civilians during a battle as for the murder of some tens of thousands of innocent civilians in the execution of planned genocidal acts. This problem has understandably brought grief to many victims and survivors who feel that some sentences have been too lenient. It is exacerbated by the fact that some of the worst war criminals who are convicted by international tribunals serve their sentences in prisons that are more "comfortable" than the prisons in their home countries. This is also a problem without a solution. International courts cannot be party to incarceration in prisons that do not meet internationally acceptable prison conditions.

The most difficult criticism to meet is that international justice too frequently works against and not in favor of peace. Clearly, in some situations, a war crimes investigation and the issuing of indictments and arrest warrants might retard peace negotiations or otherwise endanger policy goals. Tribunals do not operate in a vacuum, and their actions undoubtedly have an impact on the ground. For instance, it has been much debated why the ICTY prosecutor issued the second indictment against Radovan Karadzic and Ratko Mladic during the week in which the Dayton peace talks were being held. The prosecutor was accused by some of using the indictment to ensure that the ICTY was not used as a "bargaining chip" in the negotiations. Similar arguments were raised when the ICTY indicted Slobodan Milosevic during the NATO bombing over Kosovo and at a time when talks were being held with Milosevic aimed at stopping the war. This argument was also raised with regard to the arrest warrant issued against Sudan's President Omar Al-Bashir. The AU expressed its displeasure at the move and unsuccessfully requested the Security Council to suspend the ICC proceedings.

The experience of all the war crimes courts to date have been such that their work does not appear to have prejudiced the peace or imperiled the lives of people in the countries in which they have operated. The little anecdotal evidence to date points in the opposite direction. It was the agreement reached by the warring parties at Dayton in November 1995 that brought the war in the former Yugoslavia to an end. That meeting could not have taken place if Radovan Karadzic, the Bosnian Serb leader and commander-in-chief of the Bosnian Serb Army, had been able to attend it. This was only four months after the Bosnian Serb Army had massacred some 8000 civilian men and boys at Srebrenica. That was held by both the ICTY and the International Court of Justice to constitute an act of genocide. It would not have been morally or politically possible at that time for the leaders of Bosnia and Herzegovina to attend a meeting with Karadzic. In September 1995, as prosecutor, I had issued a second indictment against Karadzic and his army chief, Ratko Mladic, based on events in Srebrenica. That effectively prevented Karadzic from attending the Dayton meeting—he would have been arrested by the United States and transferred to The Hague for trial. He had no option but to accept being represented at Dayton by the President of Serbia, Slobodan Milosevic. In effect, the indictment facilitated the Dayton meeting and the end of the war in the former Yugoslavia followed from it. This is a clear illustration of justice assisting peace. While an arrest warrant might have the opposite consequence and make peace negotiations more difficult, that has not happened thus far.

Even though some political leaders whose arrest is sought by the ICC remain at large, their capacity to carry out their duties has been curtailed by the issue of arrest warrants. For President Al-Bashir, it has had serious consequences. There are now 124 nations that are obliged by the terms of the Rome Statute to arrest him should he visit their shores. The fact that some African states have been in violation of that obligation does not make it comfortable for a head of state to be constrained in this way. It was no doubt for that reason that President Uhuru Kenyatta of Kenya voluntarily appeared before the ICC. It did not prevent his government from white-anting the prosecution by failing to cooperate with the prosecutor. Eventually, for lack of sufficient evidence the prosecution against Kenyatta was withdrawn by the ICC.

I have attempted to discuss the major benefits and disadvantages of international criminal courts. That there is merit on both sides of the argument cannot be denied. However, in the end the benefits considerably outweigh the disadvantages. The bottom line is that impunity for war criminals is in the process of being universally withdrawn and we are the better for that.

The future

What of the future of the ICC? International criminal justice has developed a strong forward momentum. The number of nations that have ratified the Rome Statute is impressive. At the same time, the absence of leading powerful nations is certainly retarding the endeavor. Never has international criminal justice been more in the news and there are daily references in the print and electronic media to it. It was entirely unexpected that the Security Council would refer any situations to the ICC.

The progress of international criminal law has undoubtedly furthered the application of the recently developed doctrine called the "responsibility to protect" (R2P). This doctrine was born out of egregious examples of nations failing to intervene in the face of the most serious violations of the human rights of innocent civilians by their own governments. For instance, the world stood by when, in the middle of 1994, over 800,000 innocent children, women, and men were slaughtered in the Rwandan genocide. A military force well within the peacekeeping capabilities of the United Nations could effectively have prevented much of the killing. There are other examples. One thinks, of course, of the killing fields in Cambodia.

In 2001 the International Commission on Intervention and State Sovereignty recommended the recognition by all governments of a responsibility to protect their own citizens. If they are unwilling or unable to do so, the responsibility shifts to the international community of states. This doctrine was endorsed by the 2005 World Summit. Then Secretary-General Kofi Annan emphasized that, in such an event, states must use a range of measures designed to protect endangered populations, including diplomatic and humanitarian efforts and, only as a last resort, the use of military force.

Of course, politics will play a determinative role in whether or when this doctrine of R2P will be implemented. There was a signal failure in the case of Syria where Russia and China vetoed Security Council resolutions that would have enabled the Council to become seized of the situation there. Those two nations argued that it was not for the Security Council to become involved in the internal affairs of Syria let alone to bring about regime change. Yet, at the end of 2016 the General Assembly passed resolution 248 by 105 votes to fifteen with fifty-two abstentions in terms of which a mechanism was established to assist in the investigation of the commission of war crimes in Syria. It did so in light of a deadlocked Security Council. At the very least, this mechanism is expected to collect evidence that might be used in possible future war crimes prosecutions.

There are considerable challenges facing the ICC. Perhaps the most serious arises from its complete reliance on governments for its ability to function. The ICC has no means to execute its arrest warrants or to compel compliance with its orders or requests. It requires the consent and cooperation of governments to send its investigators into their jurisdictions; it requires the cooperation of governments to have its requests and orders recognized and implemented; and, most important, it requires governmental cooperation to have its arrest warrants executed. When that assistance is withheld its work is completely frustrated. This problem has been compounded by the supine attitude of the Security Council even in respect of the two situations it has referred to the ICC. The willful ignoring of the ICC by the Sudanese Government and the Transitional Government of Libya has hardly appeared on the radar screen of the Security Council. That is regrettable for the Court and also for the Council itself. After all, it is its peremptory and binding resolutions that are being ignored.

Conclusion

International justice and particularly the ICC have brought about a distinct change in international relations and in some domestic situations. It is now more widely accepted that impunity for war criminals should be withdrawn and that, as a general rule, war crimes should be investigated and prosecuted. That the most powerful states (and especially China, Russia, and the United States) exempt themselves from this international oversight weakens but certainly does not destroy its potency. Even those countries, from time to time, support international criminal justice; and, in the case of Libya, they voted in favor of Security Council resolution 1970 referring the situation there to the ICC. Warnings by political leaders about the commission of war crimes and the ICC have become almost a daily occurrence.

It is too frequently forgotten that the main beneficiaries of any justice system are the victims, the survivors of egregious criminal conduct. It is for this reason that the Rome Statute has devoted much attention and conferred many innovative rights on victims. Those rights of intervention, from the stage of investigation to the trial and appeal, are being slowly and carefully worked out by the ICC judges. They have consistently recognized that those rights should not impact negatively on the fair trial rights of defendants.

It should have become apparent to readers that the pursuit of international justice is still in its early years. It has not yet matured into a settled and universally accepted system. That huge strides have been made cannot be doubted and neither can the tremendous challenges that still face the ICC. An international rule of law has also developed in recent years and international criminal justice is very much a part of that enterprise. The potential is there. Much work remains to be done to make it a reality. That work rests not only with the ICC but also with political leaders and above all with civil society.

Additional reading

Coalition for the International Criminal Court, available at www.iccnow.org.

Robert Cryer, Hakan Friman, Darryl Robinson, and Elizabeth Wilmshurst, *An Introduction to International Criminal Law and Procedure*, 3rd ed. (Cambridge: Cambridge University Press, 2014).

Richard J. Goldstone and Adam M. Smith, *International Judicial Institutions: The Architecture of International Justice at Home and Abroad*, 2nd ed. (London: Routledge, 2015).

International Criminal Court, available at www.icc-cpi.int.

William Schabas, *An Introduction to the International Criminal Court* (Cambridge: Cambridge University Press, 2011).

David Scheffer, *All the Missing Souls: A Personal History of the War Crimes Tribunals* (Princeton, NJ: Princeton University Press, 2012).

Notes

1 This essay draws on Richard J. Goldstone and Adam. M. Smith, *International Judicial Institutions: The Architecture of International Justice at Home and Abroad*, 2nd ed. (London: Routledge, 2015); Richard J. Goldstone, "The Fifth Maha Chakri Sirindhorn Lecture," Bangkok on 13 June 2011.

2 Henry Wheaton, *International Law* (Cambridge, MA: Harvard University Press, 1836), 18.

3 Convention on the Prevention and Punishment of the Crime of Genocide, UNTS no. 1021, vol. 78 (1951), art. 6.

4 Rome Statute for the International Criminal Court, UN document A/CONF. 183/9, 17 July 1998.

5 *Democratic Alliance v Minister of International Relations and Cooperation and Others (Council for the Advancement of the South African Constitution Intervening)*, February 22, 2017, available at www.saflii.org/za/cases/ZAGPPHC/2017/53.html.

6 *Prosecutor v Akayesu*, Case No. ICTR-96-4-T.

7 Rome Statute of the International Criminal Court, (UN document A/CONF.183/9), 17 July 1998, arts. 7 and 8.

8 *Prosecutor v Tadic*, Case No. IT-94-1-AR72.

9 *Prosecutor v Blaskic*, Case No. it-95-14.

10 *Prosecutor v Musema*, Case No. ICTR-96-13-A.

11 *Prosecutor v Kambanda*, Case No. ICTR-97-23-DP.

12 *Prosecutor v Barayugwiza*, Case No. ICTR-97-19-1.

13 *Prosecutor v Lubanga*, Case No. ICC-01/04.

14 *Prosecutor v Ahmad Al Mahdi*, Case No. ICC-01/12-01/15.

Humanitarian intervention and R2P

Simon Chesterman

Which is more important: Protecting sovereignty or protecting human rights? That is the stark manner in which some frame the question posed by humanitarian intervention. When a government attacks its own people, or is unable or unwilling to protect them, should the international community of states merely stand by and watch? An alternative framing of the question is whether one country should be allowed to determine unilaterally that a threat to human rights in another country justifies military action. If that were the case, how would we ensure that such a right of humanitarian intervention is not abused? Between these extremes, the UN Security Council has the power to authorize the use of military force. But Article 39 of the UN Charter specifies that the council can only do this in response to a "threat to the peace, breach of the peace, or act of aggression." When can a threat to human rights be said to reach the level of a threat to the peace?

This chapter first sets out the international rules governing the use of force and the attempts—largely unsuccessful—to fit humanitarian intervention into those rules. It then examines the claim that certain cases of alleged humanitarian intervention might best be seen as "exceptions" to the rule, or situations in which the rule can be disregarded. Third, it considers the emergence of the doctrine of responsibility to protect (R2P) as an attempt at a new framing of these old questions.[1]

International law

The status of humanitarian intervention in international law is, on the face of it, simple—the Charter clearly prohibits the use of force. The renunciation of war must be counted among the greatest achievements of international law in the twentieth century; that this was also the bloodiest of centuries is a sober warning as to the limits of law's power to constrain the behavior of states.

The passage in Article 2(4) agreed by states at the San Francisco conference of 1945 was broad in its scope: "All Members shall refrain in their international relations from the threat or use of force against the territorial integrity or political independence of any state, or in any other manner inconsistent with the Purposes of the United Nations." The prohibition was tempered by only two exceptions. First, Article 51 preserves the "inherent right of individual or collective self-defense." Second, the newly established Security Council was granted the power to authorize enforcement actions under Chapter VII. Although this latter species of military action is sometimes considered in the same breath as unilateral humanitarian intervention, council authorization changes the legal questions to which such action gives rise.

Both exceptions provide examples of how legal rights concerning the use of force have tended to expand. Self-defense, for example, has been invoked in ever wider circumstances to justify military actions such as a preemptive strike against a country's nuclear program, and in "response" to a failed assassination attempt in a foreign country. It also provided the initial basis for the extensive US military actions in Afghanistan in late 2001. Security Council-authorized actions have expanded even further, mandating actions in Somalia and Haiti in the 1990s that would never have been contemplated by the founders of the United Nations. Nevertheless, neither exception encompasses humanitarian intervention, meaning the threat or use of armed force in the absence of a Security Council authorization or an invitation from the recognized government with the object of protecting human rights.

A third possible exception concerns the role of the General Assembly, which dates back to the Korean War and fears that a Soviet veto would block the Security Council from acting. For some months in 1950 the ambassador from what was then the Union of Soviet Socialist Republics (USSR) boycotted the Security Council in protest at the UN's continuing recognition of the recently defeated Kuomintang regime in China. In his absence, three resolutions were passed that, in effect, authorized the United States to lead a military operation against North Korea under the UN flag. The return of the Soviet delegate precluded any further council involvement. At the initiative of Western states in 1950, the General Assembly adopted resolution 377A(V), "Uniting for Peace," which provided that it would meet to recommend collective measures in situations where the veto prevented the Security Council from fulfilling its primary responsibility for the maintenance of international peace and security. In the case of a breach of the peace or act of aggression, the measures available were said to include the use of armed force.

The legality of the General Assembly's doing more than authorizing peacekeeping with the consent of parties is dubious, but a resolution was passed recommending that all states lend every assistance to the UN action in Korea. Uniting for Peace was used again in relation to the Suez crisis in 1956 and in the Congo in 1960. The procedure has fallen into disuse, however. In particular, it appears not to have been seriously contemplated during the Kosovo crisis—reportedly because of fears that the North Atlantic Treaty Organization (NATO) would have been unable to muster the necessary two-thirds majority support of the member states.

At first glance, then, traditional international law does not allow for humanitarian intervention. There have, however, been many attempts to bring humanitarian intervention within the remit of this body of law. These have tended to follow two strategies: Limiting the scope of the prohibition of the use of force, or arguing that a new customary norm has created an additional exception to the prohibition.

As cited above, Charter Article 2(4) prohibits the use of force in very broad language. Nevertheless, it has sometimes been argued that certain uses of force might not contravene this provision. For example, it has been argued that the US invasion of Panama in 1989 was consistent with the UN Charter because "the United States did not intend to, and has not, colonialized [sic], annexed or incorporated Panama."[2] As Oscar Schachter archly observed, this demands an Orwellian construction of the terms "territorial integrity" and "political independence."[3] It also runs counter to various statements by the General Assembly and the International Court of Justice (ICJ) concerning the meaning of nonintervention, as well as the practice of the Security Council, which has condemned and declared illegal the unauthorized use of force even when it is "temporary." This is consistent with the drafting history of the provision, which, the US delegate to the San Francisco conference (among others) emphasized, left "no loopholes."

Is it possible, however, that a new norm might have developed to create a separate right of humanitarian intervention? Customary international law allows for the creation of such norms through the evolution of consistent and widespread state practice when accompanied by the necessary *opinio juris*—the belief that a practice is legally obligatory. Some writers have argued that there is evidence of such state practice and *opinio juris*, typically pointing to the Indian action to stop the slaughter in East Pakistan in 1971, Tanzania's actions against Idi Amin in neighboring Uganda in 1978–1979, and Vietnam's intervention in Kampuchea in 1978–1979. In none of these cases, however, were humanitarian concerns invoked as a justification for the use of force. Rather, self-defense was the primary justification offered in each case, with humanitarian (and other) justifications being at best secondary considerations.

Such justifications are important, as they may provide evidence of change in the law. As the ICJ has observed:

> The significance for the Court of cases of State conduct prima facie inconsistent with the principle of nonintervention lies in the nature of the ground offered as justification. Reliance by a State on a novel right or an unprecedented exception to the principle might, if shared in principle by other States, tend towards a modification of customary international law.[4]

The fact that states continued to rely on traditional justifications—most notably self-defense—undermines arguments that the law has changed.

The international response to each incident is also instructive. In relation to India's action (which led to the creation of Bangladesh from what had been East Pakistan), a Soviet veto prevented a US-sponsored resolution calling for a ceasefire and the immediate withdrawal of armed forces. Tanzania's actions were broadly tolerated and the new regime in Kampala was swiftly recognized, but states that voiced support for the action typically confined their comments to the question of self-defense. Vietnam's successful ouster of the murderous regime of Pol Pot, by contrast, was met with positive hostility. France's representative, for example, stated that:

> [T]he notion that because a régime is detestable foreign intervention is justified and forcible overthrow is legitimate is extremely dangerous. That could ultimately jeopardize the very maintenance of international law and order and make the continued existence of various régimes dependent on the judgment of their neighbors.[5]

Similar statements were made by the United Kingdom and Portugal, among others. Once again, only a Soviet veto prevented a resolution calling on the foreign troops to withdraw; Pol Pot's delegate continued to be recognized as the legitimate representative of Kampuchea (later Cambodia) at the United Nations until as late as 1990. Even if one includes these three "best cases" as evidence of state practice, the absence of accompanying *opinio juris* fatally undermines claims that they marked a change in the law.

Subsequent examples of allegedly humanitarian intervention without explicit Security Council authorization, such as the no-fly zones in protection of the Kurds in northern Iraq from 1991 and NATO's intervention in Kosovo in 1999, raised slightly different questions. Acting states have typically claimed that their actions have been "in support of" Security Council resolutions, although in each case it is clear that the council did not decide to authorize the use of force. Indeed, it is ironic that states began to claim the need to act when the Security Council faltered in precisely the same decade that its activities expanded so greatly. At a time when there was a far stronger argument that paralysis of the UN system demanded self-help, the ICJ considered and rejected arguments that "present defects in international organization" could justify an independent right of intervention.[6]

Despite the efforts by some legal scholars to argue for the existence of a right of humanitarian intervention, states themselves have continued to prove very reluctant to embrace such a right—even in defense of their own actions. This was particularly true in the case of NATO's intervention in Kosovo. Such reluctance appears to have stemmed in part from the dubiousness of such a legal argument, but also from the knowledge that if any right were embraced it might well be used by other states in other situations.

Unusually among its member states, in October 1998 Germany referred to NATO's threats against the Federal Republic of Yugoslavia as an instance of "humanitarian intervention." The Bundestag affirmed its support for the Western Alliance—provided that it was made clear that this was not a precedent for further action. This desire to avoid setting a precedent was reflected in statements by NATO officials. US secretary of state Madeleine Albright later stressed that the air strikes were a "unique situation *sui generis* in the region of the Balkans," concluding that it was important "not to overdraw the various lessons that come out of it."[7] UK Prime Minister Tony Blair, who had earlier suggested that such interventions might become more routine, subsequently retreated from this position, emphasizing the exceptional nature of the air campaign. This was consistent with the more sophisticated UK statements on the legal issues.

This trend continued in the proceedings brought by the Federal Republic of Yugoslavia against ten NATO members before the ICJ. In hearings on provisional measures, only Belgium presented an elaborate legal justification for the action, relying variously on Security Council resolutions, a doctrine of humanitarian intervention (as compatible with Article 2(4) of the UN Charter or based on historical precedent), and the argument of necessity. The United States, by contrast, emphasized the importance of Security Council resolutions, and, together with four other delegations (Germany, the Netherlands, Spain, and the United Kingdom), made reference to the existence of a "humanitarian catastrophe." Four delegations did not offer any clear legal justification (Canada, France, Italy, and Portugal). The phrase "humanitarian catastrophe" recalled the doctrine of humanitarian intervention, but some care appears to have been taken to avoid invoking the doctrine by name. The formulation was first used by the United Kingdom as one of a number of justifications for the no-fly zones over Iraq, but no legal pedigree had been established beyond this. The court ultimately ruled against Yugoslavia for technical reasons concerning its jurisdiction, never discussing the merits of the case.

Such reticence to embrace a clear legal position was repeated in two major commissions that investigated the question of humanitarian intervention. The Kosovo Commission, headed by Richard Goldstone, concluded somewhat confusingly (from an international legal perspective) that NATO's Kosovo intervention was "illegal but legitimate."[8] The International Commission on Intervention and State Sovereignty (ICISS), chaired by Gareth Evans and Mohamed Sahnoun, acknowledged that, as a matter of "political reality," it would be impossible to find consensus around any set of proposals for military intervention that acknowledged the validity of any intervention not authorized by the Security Council or the General Assembly:

> But that may still leave circumstances when the Security Council fails to discharge what this Commission would regard as its responsibility to protect, in a conscience-shocking situation crying out for action. It is a real question in these circumstances where lies the most harm: in the damage to international order if the Security Council is bypassed or in the damage to that order if human beings are slaughtered while the Security Council stands by.[9]

Key elements of the ICISS report *The Responsibility to Protect* were adopted by the UN World Summit in a 2005 resolution of the General Assembly, which acknowledged that a state's unwillingness or inability to protect its own population from genocide, war crimes, ethnic cleansing, or crimes against humanity may give rise to an international "responsibility to protect." This was limited to peaceful means, however, except in extreme circumstances where the provisions of Chapter VII of the UN Charter may be invoked.[10] The report and the UN resolution were carefully silent about what happens if the council does *not* agree.

What do international lawyers make of all this? It seems fairly clear that there is no positive right of humanitarian intervention without authorization by the Security Council. Neither, however, does it appear that a coherent principle is emerging to create such a right. Rather, the arguments as presented tend to focus on the non-application of international law to particular incidents. The next section will explore the implications of such an approach to international law, and where it might lead.

An exception to the rule?

James Rubin provides a graphic illustration of the debates between NATO capitals on the question of the legality of the Kosovo intervention:

> There was a series of strained telephone calls between [US Secretary of State Madeleine] Albright and [UK Foreign Secretary Robin] Cook, in which he cited problems "with our lawyers" over using force in the absence of UN endorsement. "Get new lawyers," she suggested. But with a push from Prime Minister Tony Blair, the British finally agreed that UN Security Council approval was not legally required.[11]

Such equivocation about the role of international law in decision-making processes is hardly new; the history of international law has often been the struggle to raise law above the status of being merely one foreign policy justification among others. As indicated earlier, however, most of the acting states appear to have taken some care to present the Kosovo intervention as an exception rather than a rule.

Various writers have attempted to explain the apparent inconsistency by reference to national legal systems. Ian Brownlie, for example, likened this approach to the manner in which some legal systems deal with the question of euthanasia:

> [I]n such a case the possibility of abuse is recognized by the legal policy (that the activity is classified as unlawful) but . . . in very clear cases the law allows mitigation. The father who smothers his severely abnormal child after several years of devoted attention may not be sent to prison, but he is not immune from prosecution and punishment. In international relations a difficulty arises in that "a discretion not to prosecute" is exercisable

by States collectively and by organs of the United Nations, and in the context of *practice* of States, mitigation and acceptance in principle are not always easy to distinguish. However, the euthanasia parallel is useful since it indicates that moderation is allowed for in social systems even when the principle remains firm. Moderation in application does not display a legislative intent to cancel the principle so applied.[12]

As the demand for any such violation of an established norm increases, so the need for legal regulation of the "exception" becomes more important. This seems to be occurring in the case of euthanasia, as medical advances have increased the discretion of doctors in making end-of-life decisions. In many jurisdictions, continued reliance on the possibility of a homicide charge is now seen as an inadequate legal response to the ethical challenges posed by euthanasia. In relation to humanitarian intervention, however, such demand remains low and it is widely recognized that legal regulation of any "exception" is unlikely in the short term.

For this reason, an alternative analogy is sometimes used: That of a person acting to prevent domestic violence in circumstances where the police are unwilling or unable to act. The analogy is appealing as it appears to capture the moral dilemma facing an intervener, but is of limited value as such acts are typically regulated by reference to the existing authority structures. An individual in most legal systems may defend another person against attack, and in certain circumstances may exercise a limited power of arrest. In the context of humanitarian intervention, this analogy merely begs the question of its legality.

The better view, then, appears to be that humanitarian intervention is illegal but that the international community of states may, on a case-by-case basis, tolerate the wrong. In such a situation, claims that an intervention was "humanitarian" should be seen not as a legal justification but as a plea in mitigation. Such an approach has the merits of a basis in international law. In the *Corfu Channel* case, the United Kingdom claimed that an intervention in Albanian territorial waters was justified on the basis that nobody else was prepared to deal with the threat of mines planted in an international strait during World War II. The ICJ rejected this argument in unequivocal terms, but held that a declaration of illegality was itself a sufficient remedy for the wrong.

Similarly, after Israel abducted Adolf Eichmann from Argentina to face criminal charges for his role in the Nazi Holocaust, Argentina lodged a complaint with the Security Council, which passed a resolution stating that the sovereignty of Argentina had been infringed and requesting Israel to make "appropriate reparation." Nevertheless, "mindful" of the concern that Eichmann be brought to justice, in its 1960 resolution 138, the Security Council clearly implied that "appropriate reparation" would not involve his physical return to Argentina. The governments of Israel and Argentina subsequently issued a joint communiqué resolving to "view as settled the incident which was caused in the wake of the action of citizens of Israel which violated the basic rights of the State of Argentina."[13]

This is also broadly consistent with current state practice. During the Kosovo intervention, some suggested that the action threatened the stability of the international order—in particular the relevance of the Security Council as the Charter body with primary responsibility for international peace and security. In fact, the

Security Council became integral to resolution of the dispute (despite the bombing of the embassy of one permanent member by another). In its 1999 resolution 1244 under Chapter VII, the Council welcomed Yugoslavia's acceptance of the principles set out in the 6 May 1999 meeting of G-8 foreign ministers and authorized member states and "relevant international organizations" (in other words, NATO) to establish an international security presence in Kosovo. The resolution was passed within hours of the suspension of bombing, and its preamble contained a half-hearted endorsement of the role of the Security Council: "*Bearing in mind* the purposes and principles of the Charter of the United Nations, and the primary responsibility of the Security Council for the maintenance of international peace and security." More importantly, the resolution reaffirmed the commitment "of all Member States to the sovereignty and territorial integrity of the Federal Republic of Yugoslavia" even as it called for "substantial autonomy" for Kosovo. The tension between these provisions left the province in a legal limbo, and continues to complicate the independence it declared in early 2008.

Later in 1999, military action in East Timor affirmed more clearly the continued role of the Security Council, with authorization being a condition precedent for the Australian-led INTERFET action. This authorization, in turn, depended on Indonesia's consent to the operation. Although it was presented at the time as evidence that the international community was prepared to engage in Kosovo-style interventions outside Europe, the political and legal conditions in which the intervention took place were utterly different. The view that they were comparable reflected the troubling assumption that, when facing a humanitarian crisis with a military dimension, there is a choice between doing something and doing nothing, and that "something" means the application of military force. This narrow view was challenged by then UN Secretary-General Kofi Annan, who has stressed that "it is important to define intervention as broadly as possible, to include actions along a wide continuum from the most pacific to the most coercive."[14] Similarly, the ICISS sought to turn this policy question on its head. Rather than examining at length the right to intervene, it focused on the responsibility of states to protect vulnerable populations at risk from civil wars, insurgencies, state repression, and state collapse.

A similar dynamic could be seen when the United States engaged in unilateral airstrikes against Syria in April 2017. Ostensibly in response to a chemical weapons attack on Syria's own population, the airstrikes were regarded as illegal by virtually all commentators. However, very few states took this position (Russia was a significant exception). For the most part, states cautiously welcomed the action without proclaiming it legal, or emphasized that responsibility—if it lay anywhere—lay with the Syrian government that had attacked its own people. As in the case of Kosovo, some commentators interpreted this as an indication that states viewed the airstrikes as "illegal but legitimate."

R2P

Implicit in many arguments for a right of humanitarian intervention is the suggestion that international law currently prevents interventions that should take place, which is difficult to prove. Interventions tend not to take place because states choose not to undertake them. On the contrary, states have frequently intervened for a great many reasons, some of them more humanitarian than others. For those who would seek to establish a law or a general ethical principle to govern humanitarian intervention, a central question must be whether it could work in practice. Do any of the incidents commonly marshaled as examples of humanitarian intervention provide a model that should be followed in future? Should Kosovo or Syria, for example, be a model for future negotiations with brutal regimes?

On closer analysis, it becomes clear that the real problem confronting human rights is not how to legitimize questionable actions such as the Kosovo and Syria, but how to respond to situations like Rwanda—where genocide did take place, and where no action was taken at all. Put differently, the problem is not the legitimacy of humanitarian intervention, but the overwhelming prevalence of inhumanitarian nonintervention. Addressing that problem requires mobilizing the political will of member states as much as it does the creation of new legal rules. In this context, the ICISS rhetorical shift—from a *right* of intervention to the *responsibility* to protect—may mark the most significant advance in this contested area of international relations.

The move from right to responsibility is more than wordplay. In particular, shifting the debate away from a simple question of the legality of humanitarian intervention, in the strict sense of the word, serves two distinct policy goals. First, the legal debate is sterile. It is unlikely that a clear and workable set of criteria could be adopted on a right of humanitarian intervention. Any criteria general enough to achieve agreement would be unlikely to satisfy any actual examples of allegedly humanitarian intervention. Indeed, it is clear from the statements of NATO leaders during and after the Kosovo campaign that they did not want the air strikes to be regarded as a model for dealing with future humanitarian crises. The alternative— a select group of states (Western liberal democracies, for example) agreeing on criteria among themselves—would be seen as a vote of no confidence in the United Nations and a challenge to the very idea of an international rule of law. Such problems echo the troubled history of just war theory: In particular, concerns that the criteria for military action were arbitrary and that the power to act was limited to the privileged few.

More importantly, however, the focus on a responsibility to protect highlights the true problem at the heart of this ongoing debate. The problem is not that states are champing at the bit to intervene in support of human rights around the globe, prevented only by an intransigent Security Council and the absence of clear criteria to intervene without its authority. Rather, the problem is the absence of the will to act at all.

Responsibility to protect, as a result, has achieved considerable traction in a short time. Nevertheless, the case of Libya suggests the wariness of the Security Council in embracing R2P—even in what one might regard as a perfect case for its application. State leaders are usually more circumspect in the threats they make against their population than was Muammar el-Qaddafi; impending massacres are rarely so easy to foresee. Combined with the support of African states and the Arab League for intervention, most states on the council were unwilling to allow atrocities to occur—and others unwilling to be seen as the impediment to action.

Even then in 2011, Security Council resolution 1973 authorized the use of all necessary measures to protect civilians but was vague about what might happen next. As in many previous cases, the commitment of leaders to confining their countries' involvement to air strikes alone and for a limited duration was transparently a political rather than military decision. The commencement of military action, as in many previous cases, swiftly showed that air strikes alone were unlikely to be effective. The potential tragedy of Benghazi soon devolved into farce as the Libyan rebels were revealed to be a disorganized rabble.[15]

Do something, do *anything*, is not a military strategy. How these conflicts play out will have consequences that reach far beyond the countries themselves. The doctrine of the responsibility to protect may have made it harder to say "no," but what happens next will clearly affect the likelihood of whether future leaders will say "yes."

Conclusion

In the aftermath of the 9/11 terrorist attacks on New York and Washington, DC, the United States swiftly sought and received the Security Council's endorsement of its position in resolution 1368 that this was an attack on the United States and that action taken in self-defense against "those responsible for aiding, supporting or harboring the perpetrators, organizers and sponsors of these acts" was justified. Self-defense does not require any form of authorization (although measures taken should be "immediately reported" to the Security Council), but the fact that the United Nations was involved so quickly in a crisis was widely seen as a welcome counterpoint to the unilateralist impulses of the George W. Bush administration.

Nevertheless, the decision to seek Security Council approval also reflected a troubling trend through the 1990s. Military action under its auspices has taken place only when circumstances coincided with the national interests of a state that was prepared to act, with the council in danger of becoming what Richard Falk described as a "law-laundering service."[16] Such an approach downgrades the importance of authorization to the point where it may be seen as a policy justification rather than a matter of legal significance. A consequence of this approach is that when authorization is not forthcoming a state or group of states will feel less restrained from acting unilaterally. This represents a fundamental challenge to the international order established at the conclusion of World War II, in which the interests of the powerful would be balanced through the exercise (real or threatened) of the veto.

In the context of humanitarian intervention, many appeared to hope that such a departure from "traditional" conceptions of sovereignty and international law would privilege ethics over states' rights. In fact, as we have seen, humanitarian intervention has long had a troubled relationship with the question of national interest. Most attempts by scholars to formulate a doctrine of humanitarian intervention require that an acting state be disinterested or "relatively disinterested." By contrast, in one of the few articulations of such a doctrine by a political leader, then UK Prime Minister Blair proposed his own criteria, one of which was whether "we" had national interests involved.[17]

The global war on terror reduced the probability of "humanitarian" interventions, but it also raised the troubling prospect of more extensive military adventures being undertaken without clear legal justification. President George W. Bush's 2002 State of the Union speech, in particular, in which he referred to an "axis of evil," suggested a preparedness to use ethical arguments (and absolute ethical statements) as a substitute for legal—or, it might be argued, rational—justifications. The 2003 Iraq War is often invoked as an example of the pernicious consequences that might follow.

All such developments should be treated with great caution. A right of humanitarian intervention depends on one's acceptance that humanitarian ends justify military means. As the history of this doctrine shows, the ends are never so clear and the means are rarely so closely bound to them. In such a situation in which there is no ideal, where Kosovo presents the imperfect model (and lingers today as a testament to NATO's imperfect victory), it may be better to hold that humanitarian intervention without Security Council authorization remains both illegal and morally suspect, but that arguments can be made on a case-by-case basis that, in an imperfect world, international order may yet survive the wrong.

When the Security Council *does* provide a clear authorization for the use of force—or an ambiguous one, as it did in the case of Libya—this simplifies the legal issues. By 2017, it appeared that the R2P doctrine offered a lens through which the council viewed a problem.[18] Yet diplomatic agreement to adopt a resolution does not always come with a coherent political or military strategy. In this context, the responsibility to protect has certainly made it harder for states to stand by silently when confronted by a humanitarian catastrophe. It has not simplified the question of what they should do.

Additional reading

Gareth Evans, *The Responsibility to Protect: Ending Mass Atrocity Crimes Once and for All* (Washington, DC: Brookings Institution, 2008).

J.L. Holzgrefe and Robert O. Keohane, eds., *Humanitarian Intervention: Ethical, Legal and Political Dilemmas* (Cambridge: Cambridge University Press, 2003).

Rama Mani and Thomas G. Weiss, eds., *Responsibility to Protect: Cultural Perspectives in the Global South* (New York: Routledge, 2011).

Anne Orford, *International Authority and the Responsibility to Protect* (Cambridge: Cambridge University Press, 2011).

Ramesh Thakur, *The United Nations, Peace and Security: From Collective Security to the Responsibility to Protect*, 2nd ed. (Cambridge: Cambridge University Press, 2017).

Thomas G. Weiss, *Humanitarian Intervention: Ideas in Action*, 3rd ed. (Cambridge: Polity Press, 2016).

Notes

1 This chapter draws on ideas explored at greater length in Simon Chesterman, *Just War or Just Peace? Humanitarian Intervention and International Law* (Oxford: Oxford University Press, 2001); "Violence in the Name of Human Rights," in *Cambridge Companion to*

Human Rights Law, eds. Conor Gearty and Costas Douzinas (Cambridge: Cambridge University Press, 2012).

2   Anthony D'Amato, "The Invasion of Panama Was a Lawful Response to Tyranny," *American Journal of International Law* 84, no. 2 (1990): 520.

3   Oscar Schachter, "The Legality of Pro-Democratic Invasion," *American Journal of International Law* 78, no. 3 (1984): 649.

4   *Case Concerning the Military and Paramilitary Activities in and Against Nicaragua (Nicaragua v. United States of America)*, International Court of Justice, 27 June 1986, ICJ Rep, www.icj-cij.org, 109.

5   S/PV.2109 (1979), para. 36 (France).

6   *Corfu Channel (United Kingdom v. Albania) (Merits)*, 1949, ICJ Rep 4, www.icj-cij.org, 35.

7   "Madeleine Albright, Press Conference with Russian Foreign Minister Igor Ivanov, Singapore, 26 July 1999."

8   Independent International Commission on Kosovo, *The Kosovo Report* (Oxford: Oxford University Press, 2000), 4.

9   ICISS, *The Responsibility to Protect* (Ottawa: International Development Research Centre, 2001), 54–55.

10 2005 World Summit Outcome Document, UN document A/RES/60/1, 16 September 2005, paras. 138–139.

11 James Rubin, "Countdown to a Very Personal War," *Financial Times*, 30 September 2000.

12 Ian Brownlie, "Thoughts on Kind-Hearted Gunmen," in *Humanitarian Intervention and the United Nations*, ed. Richard B. Lillich (Charlottesville: University Press of Virginia, 1973), 146 (emphasis in original).

13 Joint Communiqué of the Governments of Israel and Argentina, 3 August 1960, reprinted in 36 ILR 59.

14 "Kofi A. Annan, Address to the General Assembly," UN press release SG/SM/7136, New York, 20 September 1999.

15 See further Simon Chesterman, "Leading from Behind: The Responsibility to Protect, the Obama Doctrine, and Humanitarian Intervention after Libya," *Ethics and International Affairs* 25, no. 3 (2011): 279.

16 Richard A. Falk, "The United Nations and the Rule of Law," *Transnational Law and Contemporary Problems* 4, no. 2 (1994): 628.

17 Michael Evans, "Conflict Opens 'Way to New International Community': Blair's Mission," *The Times*, 23 April 1999. The five criteria were: Are we sure of our case? Have we exhausted all diplomatic options? Are there military options we can sensibly and prudently undertake? Are we prepared for the long term? And do we have national interests involved?

18 See Security Council resolutions 2339, 27 January 2017, and 2348, 31 March 2017, recalling the responsibility of the Central African Republic and the Democratic Republic of the Congo, respectively, to protect civilians within their jurisdictions.

Contents

Crisis and humanitarian containment

Fabrice Weissman

The World Humanitarian Summit took place between 23 and 24 May 2016 in Istanbul, Turkey. Initiated by UN Secretary-General Ban Ki-moon with the purpose "to improve global humanitarian action," the summit was ambitious. In his *Agenda for Humanity* released in February 2016, the Secretary-General had urged world leaders to adopt concrete measures to prevent and end conflicts, enforce humanitarian norms, reach out to all those in need, strengthen local and national disaster response systems and "invest in humanity."[1]

Presented as the first conference of its kind since the UN's creation, the Istanbul summit attracted some 9000 participants. Among them were representatives of 173 UN member states, the private sector, and nongovernmental organizations (NGOs). Although skeptical about its outcome, the major international humanitarian NGOs welcomed the initiative—all except one that is, because two weeks before the event Médecins Sans Frontières (MSF) announced it would not attend. In a somewhat muddled statement, the organization argued that the summit was "a fig leaf of good intentions," that "threaten[s] to dissolve humanitarian assistance into wider development, peace-building and political agendas."[2] According to the MSF, the issues to be discussed (crisis prevention, international law enforcement, strengthening of local response mechanisms, etc.) were in essence political and, as such, should not be included on the agenda of what was supposed to be a humanitarian conference. This "blurring of lines" would serve only to "politicize" further humanitarian action and weaken the humanitarian enterprise;[3] hence, MSF decided to part ways with the rest of the humanitarian sector and pull out of the summit.

While anecdotal, this controversy illustrates the aid world's longstanding debate on the objectives of humanitarian action and its relationship with international and local politics. Humanitarian actors present themselves as "apolitical." Referring to the widely signed *Code of Conduct for the International Red Cross and Red Crescent Movement and NGOs in Disaster Relief*, they claim to pursue a single objective: Saving lives and alleviating suffering whenever and wherever it is found. They argue that such an endeavor "is not a partisan or political act and should not be viewed as such." In return for their conspicuous avoidance of politics, they require from governments and local authorities "unimpeded access to affected populations."[4]

Yet, all humanitarian workers are only too aware that there is no consensus as to how or whose suffering is to be alleviated first, and that access is never "unimpeded." The goals and room for maneuver of humanitarian organizations are unfailingly subject to negotiations that reflect power relationships and incessant deal brokering with local authorities and states. Ultimately, the objectives and operational space of humanitarian actors are framed by the diplomatic and political support that they can rally and hence by the potential benefits of emergency assistance to those wielding the power. In other words, the so-called politicization of humanitarian aid (that is, its instrumentalization for political purposes) appears the primary condition for successful deployment. The main challenge for aid agencies is not to shield themselves from politics but to negotiate the best compromise possible between their interests and those of the political powers.

As a result, humanitarian organizations face two main dilemmas. From the ethical standpoint, they have to define their view of what constitutes acceptable compromise— a morally decent policy of assistance. At what point do they consider that the deals reached with political powers crosses the blurred but very real line beyond which humanitarian assistance delivered to victims imperceptibly becomes support for their tormenters? From the political standpoint, they must determine how to increase their leverage and bargaining power. How useful is it for them to attend, for instance, a high-level conference such as the World Humanitarian Summit?

The chapter begins with an overview of the actors in the political–humanitarian arena and their various interests. It then describes how humanitarian institutions—i.e., UN organizations, nongovernmental organizations (NGOs), and Red Cross entities distributing aid in the name of humanitarian principles, to the victims of war and natural disasters—have sought since the end of the Cold War to position themselves in the ethical and political dilemmas arising from their inevitable participation in global and local politics.[5]

The political–humanitarian arena

An overview of the arena can be understood by examining key actors as well as material and symbolic resources.

Actors

The power relationships circumscribing relief agencies involve many players—from the narrowly local to the broadly global. In armed conflict, humanitarian organizations must first reach an understanding with local armed forces: From the defense ministry in a country's capital to the young soldier controlling a checkpoint on a provincial road; from the exiled rebel leader to field commanders in the bush; from gang bosses holding sway over a territory to bandits who hold none. Humanitarian actors must also reach agreement with civil administrations: Interior, health, agriculture, water, labor, immigration and customs ministries and their provincial, district and village representatives, as well as governors, prefects, mayors, village and family chiefs, religious leaders, influential businessmen, refugee camp and slum representatives, political parties, local NGOs, unions, and activist groups. In crises, all of these entities participate at various levels in relief operations as part of local response programs or solidarity networks; they usually have different perceptions of the benefits and risks stemming from the deployment of a foreign humanitarian organization.

Aid agencies, whatever their stripe, also have to negotiate space with a host of other international actors. The list includes UN political and military missions, foreign military forces, donor representatives, UN relief agencies, and NGOs. There can be profound disagreements and fierce competition.[6]

The resources that humanitarian actors are able to mobilize in their many negotiations with these actors are of two kinds, material and symbolic. The material ones are the goods and services that they deliver to populations as well as the economic resources that they indirectly inject into the local economy. The symbolic ones relate to the (good or bad) publicity that they can generate for the various stakeholders.

Material resources

It is useful to have in mind the size of the global humanitarian enterprise and its growth in the post-Cold War era. Budgets of humanitarian agencies registered a thirty-five fold increase from about $800 million in 1989 to some $28 billion in 2015.[7] Equal to about one-third of the global arms trade (estimated at $65 billion in 2015),[8] international humanitarian funding mainly finances food distribution, material relief (shelter, tools, basic household items), and essential services (health care, water, and sanitation); the remainder (about fifteen percent) is dedicated to "protection," "coordination," "reconstruction," and "disaster prevention and preparedness."[9] The past fifteen years have also witnessed a sharp increase in the number of people assisted by UN agencies and their NGO partners. Varying between thirty and forty million people in the first decade of the twenty-first century, it regularly surpassed eighty million people by the middle of the second decade.[10]

Whatever the sums, public services delivered by humanitarian actors (food and water distribution, healthcare, shelter, camp and urban planning) are invaluable to governments and armed groups seeking to mobilize, displace, encamp, or detain populations.[11] Refugee camps, where humanitarian organizations perform two roles, are a prime example. On the one hand, they unintentionally support mechanisms designed to control and contain populations considered undesirable by governments.[12] On the other hand, they indirectly help to reinforce political and military groups that frequently re-form inside camps—for instance, the leaders of the genocide who took control of a number of Rwandan refugee camps in Zaire between

1994 and 1996,[13] or the people-smuggler networks that infiltrated the transit camp set up for refugees attempting to cross to the United Kingdom in Grande-Synthe in northern France.[14]

Camps for internally displaced persons (IDPs) experience similar dynamics, as illustrated by the many camps in Darfur in Sudan, which between 2004 and 2009 transformed into bastions of opposition to the Khartoum regime.[15] Conversely, from 2006 to 2009, the Sri Lankan government proved remarkably skillful at using humanitarian organizations to serve its policy of internment and surveillance of civilians evacuated from rebel-held areas—a policy aimed at suppressing any attempt at independent political reorganization by IDPs.[16] And more recently, the Nigerian Army has been relying on international humanitarian assistance to sustain the population that it forcibly displaced into internment camps in rural areas of Borno state in its efforts to defeat Boko Haram.[17]

Public services such as health care, food, housing, and water provided outside camps by humanitarian organizations are key resources for any rebel movement, government, or occupying army seeking to administer a territory and meet a population's social expectations. Aid projects implemented by the international forces in Afghanistan with the help of various for-profit and not-for-profit organizations have certainly not had the desired stabilizing effect.[18] In the 1980s, however, guerrilla movements such as the Eritrean and Tigrean People's Liberation Fronts successfully incorporated international humanitarian aid into selective redistribution policies, which enabled them to control and mobilize a significant portion of the population.[19] Such jihadist movements as Al-Qaeda in the Islamic Maghreb, al-Shebab in Somalia, and the Taliban in Afghanistan have also learned how to manipulate international relief assistance to garner support from local populations and implement their reactionary projects for society—at least during the period immediately following their accession to power.[20]

Humanitarian action can also be of indirect economic value to a region's authorities. In addition to the various humanitarian resources appropriated through taxes, diversion, theft, or looting, aid agencies inject significant funds into the economy via salaries, rents, service contracts, and local procurement. Such expenditures have a ripple effect on the local economy, with the authorities usually first in line to benefit because of the stranglehold that they exert on the most profitable markets (e.g., rent of land, houses, offices and warehouses, transportation, and private security services).[21] Indeed, competition to appropriate this revenue is one of the main sources of insecurity for aid workers in countries such as Somalia (where the majority of security incidents are related to the negotiation of employment and service contracts) and Democratic Republic of the Congo (DRC).

Symbolic resources

NGOs and UN organizations are a favorite source of information for journalists. They may also engage directly in public debate and make use of the media to alert public opinion and mobilize financial and political support. In so doing, they help to portray crisis situations and put them on media and diplomatic agendas. They contribute to constructing an international public space where the conduct of political actors—both within and beyond their borders—is described and subjected to public scrutiny.

In their public communications, humanitarian organizations usually employ a standard narrative whose ideal type is "humanitarian crisis."[22] Designed to mobilize public opinion by appealing to people's emotions, they present situations of violence as moral fables centered round the suffering of victims. According to sociologist Luc Boltanski, two narratives are generally used to render the spectacle of distant suffering morally and psychologically tolerable,[23] with one appealing to public opinion's pity (topic of sentiment) and the other to its indignation and anger (topic of denunciation).

The topic of sentiment superimposes onto a spectacle of pain an image of humanitarians in action (a nurse at a malnourished child's bedside; logisticians organizing food distributions in the middle of a desperate mob; a doctor dressing an injured patient's wounds). Extolling the gratitude of victim to benefactor, this representation shifts the viewer's sympathy to the humanitarian worker, erasing any considerations as to the source of the disaster that is blamed on some impersonal cause (like the madness of war thus relegating to the ranks of natural disaster). By narrowing the drama to the humanitarian–victim pair, politics is elided. For example, French television coverage of the July 1994 exodus to east Zaire (now the DRC) of nearly two million Rwandan Hutu refugees—which included many of those who perpetrated the genocide—was a perfect example of the narrative's power to conceal. It portrayed people who had participated in the genocide as much "victims" as the refugees, and as "saviors" the governments that had refused to intervene to halt the extermination in the first place. The spectacle of foreign armies and NGOs coming to the rescue of cholera victims as an epidemic raged through the refugee camps effectively expunged the world's passive consent to the earlier annihilation of the Tutsi.[24]

The topic of denunciation introduces two other figures: The persecutor and the savior. The spectacle of suffering is used to stir up feelings of indignation and anger among spectators thus prompted to urge the potential savior (powerful nations or multilateral organizations) to track down, neutralize, and punish the persecutor. As Boltanski points out, this narrative relies inevitably on a more or less explicit political interpretation of each situation, which is essential to attribute blame through causal links that connect the fate of the victim to the action of a persecutor and lack of action on the part of a savior. Exploiting anger, and thus violence, this narrative lends itself particularly well to war propaganda. It is frequently used by the United Nations or Western governments mobilizing "humanitarian war" to justify the use of force—as the North Atlantic Treaty Organization (NATO) in Kosovo, Afghanistan, and Libya. The topic of denunciation is also used by humanitarian organizations demanding international military intervention to protect civilians—in Darfur, in Chad, and in the DRC, to cite just a few examples from the past decade.[25]

By reducing crises to a morality fable with a cast of two (the victim and benefactor) or four (the victim, the persecutor, the humanitarian, and the savior), the narrative of a "humanitarian crisis" makes it possible to both obscure the political (topic of sentiment) and exalt it in its most extreme form—that is, moral war (topic of denunciation). In both cases, aid workers assume two roles: They are mediators, allowing the distant spectators to feel affected by the suffering of others, and experts, attesting to a person's status as victim, persecutor, benefactor, or savior. The legitimacy of the judgment made by humanitarians is based on an assumption of disinterestedness and impartiality as well as on the special expertise that allows them to discriminate between "true" and "false" victims and assess their "degree of victimization."[26]

They do so by counting the dead and sick, quantifying the severity of the privation ("shortage," "food crisis," or "famine"), documenting the psychological and physical trauma or characterizing any collective or individual violence (using such labels as "massacre," "ethnic cleansing," "genocide," "sexual violence," "torture," and "war wounds.")

When confronted with competing demands from victims or denials from persecutors, humanitarians help validate internationally the status of victim, persecutor, or savior. The ensuing political consequences result despite pleas of being "apolitical."

The controversial role of humanitarian actors

Although these political transactions are the daily lot of aid practitioners, they are regularly masked by the legal and moral rhetoric of humanitarian principles. Such interactions are, however, the subject of abundant institutional and academic literature primarily focused on the "perverse effects" of aid. The few essays of the 1980s[27] were followed by a profusion of insightful studies in the following decade.[28] Several events raised questions about the roles and responsibilities of humanitarians in armed conflicts and on what constituted fair humanitarian compromise with political powers: The war crimes committed by UN troops mandated to protect relief operations in Somalia (1992–1993); the impotence of aid actors in the face of the policies of extermination seen in Rwanda and the Great Lakes (1993–1998); the appropriation of humanitarian aid by perpetrators of the Rwandan genocide in Zaire (1994–1996) and armed factions in Liberia and Sierra Leone (1990–1997); the participation of the UN and NGOs in forced population displacements in the former Yugoslavia (1991–1995); or the containment policies implemented by Western governments in the Balkans and Central Africa where the humanitarian crisis narrative was used to justify limited engagement to the public.

In this regard, at least two concepts took shape at the beginning of the twenty-first century. The first, sometimes called the "new humanitarianisms,"[29] asserts that the only acceptable compromise available to humanitarian actors is to join in the fight for human rights. Alongside their relief operations, humanitarians must apply pressure and help the UN and liberal democracies to neutralize and punish war criminals and build liberal peace in war-torn societies. The second, often dubbed the "Dunantist approach"—named after the ICRC's founder, the Swiss businessman Henri Dunant— argues for the legitimacy of action, the primary aim of which is to save lives here and now. Both views are to varying degrees present within all aid institutions.

The new humanitarianism: Gambling on liberal peace

By the end of the 1990s, the vast majority of officials from NGOs, UN agencies, and donors as well as networks of experts and academics subscribed to the so-called new humanitarianism. This approach has its roots in a radical critique of aid policies whose sole purpose is to save lives. As Michael Barnett and Jack Snyder argue, such assistance programs did not just save lives: Their direct and indirect fallout "fueled conflict and repression."[30] On the one hand, material resources brought by humanitarian actors feed the war economy of governments and rebel groups. On the other hand, the "humanitarian crisis" narrative used by the media and world leaders masked the political origin of suffering and allowed "outside states to appear to be doing something about a crisis without having to intervene in more effective ways" than funding relief. In other words, believing that they are helping populations in danger, aid workers actually help to prolong their suffering. Hence, humanitarian organizations cannot limit themselves to treating the symptoms of crises but must also tackle their "root causes"—or at least pressure Western governments and multilateral institutions to do so.

According to the new humanitarians, the causes of the crises of the 1990s were rooted in the emergence of "new wars."[31] Subscribing to Mary Kaldor's views, most aid officials viewed post-Cold War armed conflicts as more absurd and brutal than ever. The so-called new wars were said to be motivated solely by ethnic bigotry and greed, predominantly financed by illegal trade and predation, and to kill far more civilians than combatants.[32] Widespread in the world of humanitarian aid, this view of war as generalized crime led NGOs and UN agencies to advocate a law enforcement and judicial approach to armed conflicts. Under the label of "protection," humanitarian organizations embraced the fight against impunity, supported the creation of the International Criminal Court (ICC), and campaigned for the adoption of the "responsibility to protect" (R2P), a commitment enjoining governments to use sufficient means (including military) to halt mass atrocities in states declared failing or criminal.

Reducing political violence to everyday crime necessitating a law enforcement and judicial approach, this paradigm was complemented by a more reformist one that portrayed armed violence as the symptom of dysfunctional societies incapable of self-regulation. Hence, "tackling the root causes of humanitarian crises," meant going beyond a purely law enforcement and judicial approach to a radical transformation of the institutions, behaviors, and mindsets deemed responsible for the perpetuation of violence in the first place. According to this reformist—not to say revolutionary stance—humanitarian action was to contribute to the transformation of failed states and broken societies into pacified liberal democracies based on the rule of law, human rights, and a free market economy.

As Mark Duffield points out, this broadening in the late 1990s of the humanitarian agenda from lifesaving objectives to law-enforcement and then transformative ambitions coincided with the redefinition by liberal states of their security concerns. After the fall of the Berlin Wall, conflicts and instability on the perimeters of the North were seen as breeding grounds for the proliferation of global threats, such as migration, mass refugee movements, pandemics, transnational crime, terrorism, and impediments to international trade. The transformation of war-torn societies into stable, representative states became the objective of the more ambitious development policies advocated at the turn of the twenty-first century by the World Bank, Organisation for Economic Co-operation and Development (OECD), European Union (EU), and many foreign aid ministries, including the UK's Department for International Development (DfID) and the US Agency for International Development (USAID).[33] NGOs were viewed as a preferred instrument for this "transformational diplomacy,"[34] particularly in the role of mediator with crisis-riddled societies being asked to adopt—via participatory methods—market democracy. Like Claire Short, UK Minister for International

Development (1997–2003), donors encouraged humanitarian organizations to "work with states and international organisations that are seeking to establish a democratic, law-abiding, rights-observing, market-oriented, economically rational state that provides improved conditions for all of its citizens."[35]

As Mark Duffield says, it became challenging for NGOs to "separate their own development and humanitarian activities from the pervasive logic of the North's new security regime."[36] The growth of new humanitarianisms was accompanied by a proliferation of international armed interventions. Military operations officially aimed at protecting civilians in Kosovo (1999), East Timor (1999), and Sierra Leone (2000) were followed by the invasions of Afghanistan (2001) and Iraq (2003). There were also more UN peace operations with ever broader mandates. These included ceasefire monitoring, distributing humanitarian aid, disarming and reintegrating former combatants, repatriating IDPs and refugees, organizing elections, reforming armies and national police forces, restructuring judicial institutions and public services, developing market economies, promoting good governance, and defending human and women's rights.

With the exception of Iraq, where European and US NGOs were divided on the legitimacy of going to war, the vast majority of humanitarian organizations aligned with international forces engaged in peace- and state-building policies in Kosovo, East Timor, Sierra Leone, Afghanistan, DRC, and the Sudan that were managed from New York or Washington. While considerable institutional funding was an incentive, humanitarians also believed that they were contributing to the "only truly humanitarian objective—hastening the end of a war" and "replacing a murderous regime with a civilised government as quickly as possible"—in the words of a humanitarian volunteer as the Taliban fell in Afghanistan in 2001 at the height of the new humanitarianism.[37]

By the turn of the twenty-first century, with the exception of the International Committee of the Red Cross (ICRC) and a small number of NGOs, humanitarian organizations had formed an alliance with liberal democracies and the UN based on common goals: Punishing war criminals and transforming dysfunctional societies into peaceful and prosperous democracies. The alliance appeared to be the only acceptable compromise to contend with the dilemmas stemming from humanitarian action's inescapable involvement in murky national and international politics.

However, this special relationship was not without its tensions, as humanitarian organizations reproached Western governments for neglecting them when allocating funding and failing to devote enough military resources to peacebuilding. In Afghanistan, for example, a coalition of humanitarian NGOs called for strengthening NATO troops "so that democracy can flourish";[38] then for a redirection of foreign funding to them because there were "links between development and security," and through their activities they contributed to "stability in the country."[39] NGOs also criticized Western governments for their reluctance to get involved in countries where their national interests were not directly at stake,[40] or for encroaching on their own humanitarian territory when delivering aid in campaigns to win "hearts and minds."[41]

Dunantist humanitarianism—or the policy of survival

Although widely supportive of the new humanitarianisms during the Cold War,[42] in the mid-1990s MSF was among the organizations that began to seek greater distance.

Seeing conflicts as the continuation of politics by other means, rather than generalized crime or societal dysfunction, MSF's leadership saw the project of transforming war-torn societies into the image of market democracies as a form of revolutionary messianism.[43] Not only was this ambition rooted in a colonial belief in the West's "civilizing mission," it also reflected a hubristic confidence in all powerful human control over people and societies. "The shared faith and universal illusion of modern societies" were the words of Raymond Aron, who saw the source of the "excessive ambitions from which totalitarian regimes emerge."[44] The limited success of UN peace operations and the invasions of Afghanistan and Iraq in achieving their objectives served at least to demonstrate that a liberal peace project was riskier and more costly—in terms of human lives—than its supporters acknowledged.[45]

The infatuation of the new humanitarianisms with criminal justice and humanitarian intervention also sustained criticism. As one MSF representative commented:

> [A] faction head in Congo, or an American officer in Afghanistan, indeed all those who might have a concern, founded or not, that they may one day have to account for their actions in front of a court, will see in the provision of the ICC a powerful incentive to remove any humanitarian presence.[46]

Coupled with this argument was fierce condemnation of the intrinsic virtues of the international criminal justice system[47] and the responsibility to protect.[48] Research about foreign interventions conducted in Kosovo, Sierra Leone, Timor, and Libya showed that deploying international armed forces and protecting civilians were two different things. Offering military protection is an act of war in its own right because it means engaging in hostilities with no guarantee of success or of avoiding a civilian bloodbath. No technical or legal riposte to the violence of war can ensure that those who are supposed to be helped will be protected and assisted. Calling for the military protection of a population signals the desire for a "just war" and the advent of a new political order through violence—an undertaking that never has a certain outcome and which inevitably creates victims among the very people it seeks to save.

Under these conditions, Dunantist organizations defend the legitimacy of relief action whose goal, limited in appearance, is not to police or resolve conflicts but to ensure the cost in human lives is as low as possible. Yet, as some MSF officials recognize, there is always a risk that the material and symbolic resources that aid actors bring to a theater of war will be used against the very people whom they are intended to assist. This unintended consequence is why humanitarian workers must demand a degree of freedom of action and assessment (i.e., to be allowed to move around and communicate with the population so as to plan and monitor their operations) to ensure that their work is not completely diverted from its objective. If they are unable to keep the diversions and instrumentalization of relief within acceptable limits by rallying political support—from the most local to the most global—they must abstain. Hence, MSF took the decision in 2014 not to operate in territory under the control of the Islamic State of Iraq and the Levant (ISIL or ISIS or Da'esh), citing the impossibility of being able to assess needs independently and exercise a minimum of control over its resources.

Yet establishing the circumstances in which humanitarian action reaches a "rotten compromise" with political powers, to the point of benefiting the oppressors more than their victims—requiring humanitarian actors to enter into public confrontation or to abstain—prompts heated debate within and among Dunantist organizations.[49] For example, the manner in which humanitarian aid has been delivered in Syria since 2013 has been the focus of a public controversy between MSF and the ICRC, with both organizations making mutual accusations of lack of impartiality and complacency regarding the restrictions imposed by the Syrian government and the opposition.[50]

Conclusion

Closer to the new humanitarianisms than the Dunantism, the World Humanitarian Summit concluded with over 1500 commitments. One of the most debated was the "Grand Bargain," whereby fifteen donors pledged (among others) to channel twenty-five percent of their funding directly to local and national operators by 2020 (compared to the current 0.4 percent).[51] While some NGOs praised the measure as a way to empower local actors, others expressed the fear that relying on domestic institutions supposedly more vulnerable to political pressures might further politicize humanitarian assistance and jeopardize its impartiality. Yet, there is no reason to believe *a priori* that local actors, who are the primary responders in disaster situations, will necessarily arrive at worse—or better—compromises than their international colleagues.

Additional reading

Michael Barnett and Thomas G. Weiss, eds., *Humanitarianism in Question: Politics, Power, Ethics* (Ithaca, NY: Cornell University Press, 2008).

Mark Duffield, *Global Governance and the New Wars: The Merging of Development and Security* (London: Zed Books, 2001).

Michel Feher, ed., *Nongovernmental Politics* (New York: Zone Books, 2007).

Claire Magone, Michaël Neuman, and Fabrice Weissman, eds., *Humanitarian Negotiations Revealed: The MSF Experience* (London: Hurst & Co, 2011).

David Rieff, *A Bed for the Night. Humanitarianism in Crisis* (New York: Simon & Schuster, 2003).

Thomas G. Weiss, *Humanitarian Business* (Cambridge: Polity Press, 2013).

Notes

1 UN, *Agenda for Humanity. Annex to the Report of the Secretary-General for the World Humanitarian Summit*, UN document A/70/709, 2 February 2016.

2 Médecins Sans Frontières, *MSF to pull out of World Humanitarian Summit*, 5 May 2016, www.msf.org/en/article/msf-pull-out-world-humanitarian-summit.

3 Marc Dubois, "Don't Blur the Lines between Development and Humanitarian Work," *The Guardian*, 12 May 2016.

4 *Code of Conduct for the International Red Cross and Red Crescent Movement and NGOs in Disaster Relief* (Geneva: ICRC, IFRC, 1994), 3.

5 Dorothea Hilhorst and Bram J. Jansen, "Humanitarian Space as Arena: A Perspective on the Everyday Politics of Aid," *Development and Change* 41, no. 6 (2010): 1117–1139.

6 Thomas G. Weiss, *Humanitarian Business* (Cambridge: Polity Press, 2013).

7 *Global Humanitarian Assistance Report 2016* (Bath: Development Initiatives, 2014), hereafter GHA, 4–5, http://devinit.org/wp-content/uploads/2016/06/GHA-Report-2016_Executive-summary.pdf.

8 "Record-breaking $65 Billion Global Defence Trade in 2015 Fueled by Middle East and Southeast Asia, IHS Jane's Says", *Business Wire*, 13 June 2016, www.businesswire.com/news/home/20160613005501/en/Record-breaking-65-Billion-Global-Defence-Trade-2015.

9 *GHA 2015* (Bath: Development Initiatives, 2015),79–92, http://devinit.org/wp-content/uploads/2015/06/GHA-Report-2015_-Interactive_Online.pdf.

10 OCHA, *World Humanitarian Data and Trends 2016*, 3, www.unocha.org/sites/unocha/files/World% 20Humanitarian%20Data%20and%20Trends%202016_0.pdf.

11 François Jean, "Aide humanitaire et économie de guerre," in *Economie des Guerres Civiles*, eds. François Jean and Jean-Christophe Rufin (Paris: Hachette Littérature, 1996), 543–589.

12 Michel Agier, *Managing the Undesirables: Refugee Camps and Humanitarian Government* (Cambridge: Polity Press, 2011).

13 Jean-Hervé Bradol and Marc Le Pape, *Humanitarian Aid, Genocide and Mass Killings: The Rwandan Experience of Médecins Sans Frontières* (Manchester: Manchester University Press, 2017).

14 "Un an après son ouverture, les passeurs ont pris la main au camp de migrants de Grande-Synthe," *Europe 1*, 08h04, le 07 mars 2017, modifié à 08h16, le 07 mars 2017, www.europe1.fr/societe/un-an-apres-son-ouverture-les-passeurs-ont-pris-la-main-au-camp-de-migrants-de-grande-synthe-2996195.

15 Clea Kahn, *Conflict, Arms, and Militarization: The Dynamics of Darfur's IDP Camps* (Geneva: Small Arms Survey, 2008).

16 Claire Magone, Michaël Neuman, and Fabrice Weissman, *Humanitarian Negotiations Revealed: The MSF Experience* (London: Hurst & Co, 2011), 23–49.

17 International Crisis Group, *North-eastern Nigeria and Conflict's Humanitarian Fallout*, Commentary/Africa, 4 August 2016.

18 Geert Gompelman, *Winning Hearts and Minds? Examining the Relationship between Aid and Security in Afghanistan's Faryab Province* (Medford, MA: Feinstein International Center, 2011).

19 Mark Duffield and John Prendergast, *Without Troops & Tanks: The Emergency Relief Desk and the Cross Border Operation into Eritrea and Tigray* (Lawrenceville, NJ: Red Sea Press, 1994).

20 Jean-Hervé Bradol, "Comment les humanitaires travaillent face à Al-Qaïda et l'Etat islamique," Médiapart, 1 February 2015. ODI-HPN has refused to publish the English version of this article after pressure from MSF in the United Kingdom fearing security and reputational risks.

21 Karen Büscher and Koen Vlassenroot, "Humanitarian Presence and Urban Development: New Opportunities and Contrasts in Goma, DRC," *Disasters* 34, Supplement s2 (2010): 256–273.

22 René Backmann and Rony Brauman, *Les Médias et l'humanitaire* (Paris: Victoires, 1998).

23 Luc Boltanski, *Distant Suffering: Morality, Media and Politics* (Cambridge: Cambridge University Press, 1999).

24 Bradol and Marc Le Pape, *Humanitarian Aid*.

25 See, for example, CARE International, Christian Aid, Concern Worldwide, Islamic Relief, IRC, Oxfam, and Tearfund, "Joint Agency Statement Following Tuesday's Darfur Donor

Conference," press release (more funding for the African Union force), 19 July 2006; Oxfam, "Tchad: Les Etats membres de l'Union européenne tardent à prendre une décision sur l'envoi d'une force au Tchad alors que 400 000 vies sont en jeu," press release, December 9, 2007; ACAT France/CARE/COSI/FIDH/HRW/LDH/Secours Catholique Caritas France, "RD Congo: La France doit montrer l'exemple," press release, December 10, 2008.

26 Sandrine Lefranc and Lilian Mathieu, eds., *Mobilisations des victimes* (Rennes: Presses Universitaires de Rennes, 2009).

27 William Shawcross, *The Quality of Mercy: Cambodia, Holocaust and Modern Conscience* (New York: Simon & Schuster, 1984); François Jean, *Éthiopie, du bon usage de la famine* (Paris: Médecins Sans Frontières, 1986); Jean-Christophe Rufin, *Le Piège: Quand l'Aide humanitaire remplace la guerre* (Paris: Jean-Claude Lattes, 1986).

28 Among the most influential academic works are David Keen, *The Benefits of Famine: A Political Economy of Famine and Relief in Southwestern Sudan, 1983–1989* (Princeton, NJ: Princeton University Press, 1994); Mary B. Anderson, *Do No Harm: How Aid Can Support Peace—Or War* (Boulder, CO: Lynne Rienner, 1999); Fiona Terry, *Condemned to Repeat? The Paradox of Humanitarian Action* (Ithaca, NY: Cornell University Press, 2002); Peter J. Hoffman and Thomas G. Weiss, *Sword & Salve: Confronting New Wars and Humanitarian Crises* (Lanham, MD: Rowman & Littlefield, 2006); *War, Politics, and Humanitarianism: Solferino to Syria and Beyond* (Lanham, MD: Rowman & Littlefield, 2017).

29 Fiona Fox, "New Humanitarianism: Does it Provide a Moral Banner for the 21st Century?" *Disasters* 25, no. 4 (2001): 275–289.

30 Michael Barnett and Jack Snyder, "The Grand Strategies of Humanitarianism," in *Humanitarianism in Question*, eds. Barnett and Weiss, 148.

31 Mary Kaldor, *New and Old Wars* (Stanford, CA: Stanford University Press, 1999).

32 Roland Marchal and Christine Messiant, "Les Guerres civiles à l'ère de la globalisation: Nouvelles réalités et nouveaux paradigme," *Critique Internationale* 18 (2003): 91–112.

33 Ibid.

34 Condoleezza Rice, "Transformational Diplomacy," *Comments Delivered at Georgetown University*, 18 January 2006, http://merln. ndu.edu/archivepdf/nss/state/59306.pdf.

35 Cited in Barnett and Snyder, "The Grand Strategies," in *Humanitarianism in Question*, eds. Barnett and Weiss, 151.

36 Duffield, *Global Governance*, 16.

37 Michael Barry, "L'Humanitaire n'est jamais neutre," *Libération*, 6 November 2001.

38 International Council of Voluntary Agencies, "Afghanistan: A Call for Security," 17 June 2003, www.icvanetwork.org/system/files/versions/Afghanistan-A%20Call%20for%20Security%20%28Joint% 20NGO%20Letter%29.pdf.

39 "Falling Short: Aid Effectiveness in Afghanistan," 28 March 2008, www.oxfam.org/sites/www.oxfam.org/files/ACBAR_aid_effectiveness_paper_0803.pdf.

40 Oxfam, *Protection of Civilians in 2010: Facts, Figures, and the UN Security Council's Response* (Oxford: Briefing Paper, 2010), 28.

41 CARE, "On World Humanitarian Day, CARE Asks: Why Is It More Dangerous to Be an Aid Worker than a Peacekeeper?" 19 August 2009, http://care.ca/world-humanitarian-day-care-asks-why-it-more-dangerous-be-aid-worker-peacekeeper.

42 Magone, Neuman, and Weissman, *Humanitarian Negotiations Revealed*, 233–262.

43 Rony Brauman, 'Les Nouveaux Lénines de l'humanitaire', *Alternatives Internationales*, June 2011, www.alternatives-internationales.fr/les-nouveaux-lenines-de-l-humanitaire_fr_art_1095_54590.html.

44 Raymond Aron, *Essai sur les libertés* (Paris: Hachette, Pluriel, 1998), 41–42 and 213–214.

45 Jean-Hervé Bradol, "The Sacrificial International Order and Humanitarian Action," in *In the Shadow of Just Wars: Humanitarian Action, Violence, and Politics*, ed. Fabrice Weissman (London: Hurst & Co, 2004), 1–22.

46 Éric Dachy, "Justice and Humanitarian Action: A Conflict of Interest," in *In the Shadow of Just Wars*, ed. Weissman, 318.

47 Fabrice Weissman, "Humanitarian Aid and the International Criminal Court: Grounds for Divorce' "*Making Sense of Sudan*, http://africanarguments.org/2009/07/20/humanitarian-aid-and-the-international-criminal-court-grounds-for-divorce-1/, July 2009.

48 Fabrice Weissman, "Not in Our Name: Why Médecins Sans Frontières Does Not Support the 'Responsibility to Protect,'" *Criminal Justice Ethics* 29, no. 2 (2010): 194–207.

49 http://speakingout.msf.org/. For an illustration of the controversies between MSF and the ICRC, see Rony Brauman, "Médecins Sans Frontières and the ICRC: Matters of Principle," in *International Review of the Red Cross* 94, Number 888 (2012): 1523–1535.

50 Pierre Krähenbühl, "There Are No 'Good' or 'Bad' Civilians in Syria—We Must Help All Who Need Aid," in *The Guardian*, 3 March 2013; Marie-Noëlle Rodrigue and Fabrice Weissman, "Syrie: Briser l'embargo humanitaire contre les zones rebelles," in *Le Temps*, 13 March 2013.

51 Ben Parker, "Is the Grand Bargain a Big Deal?" *IRIN*, 24 May 2016, www.irinnews.org/analysis/2016/05/24/grand-bargain-big-deal.

CONTENTS

Post-conflict peacebuilding

Graciana del Castillo

This chapter analyzes how the system of global governance has largely failed in supporting peacebuilding efforts in war-torn countries in their transition to peace, stability, and prosperity since the end of the Cold War. The term "peacebuilding"— both in the preventive and post-conflict contexts—means different things to different academics and practitioners, as well as to the international organizations and to the many other actors involved in supporting it. However, peacebuilding is a complex and challenging political process, which has resulted in multiple and overpowering operational challenges.

In the early 1990s, then UN Secretary-General Boutros Boutros-Ghali believed that civil wars and other internal conflicts in the developing world would soon "become the UN's bread and butter and that it would require comprehensive action rallying various parts of the UN system over prolonged periods of time."[1] Indeed, one of the notorious operational challenges to peacebuilding activities on the ground is precisely the large number of "foreign interveners."[2] Having these and the host government working, under the best of circumstances, without a clear vision or integrated strategy, and, at worst, operating at cross-purposes, has frequently led to failures. Lack of local ownership on the part of national governments has also been a major problem.

As the Thomas G. Weiss and Rorden Wilkinson note in the introduction to this volume, "Few things point to the importance of understanding international organization and global governance more than their stark failings . . . The term global governance . . . [captures] the pluralization of the world political stage." The operational experience of the last twenty-five years with post-conflict peacebuilding, with its numerous state and non-state actors (legal and illicit), regional and international organizations (intergovernmental), complex military–civilian relationships, and multiple objectives—each with budgetary implications that often clash with each other—illustrate all kinds of failing.

Inspired in the case of El Salvador, Boutros Boutros-Ghali attached the "post-conflict" qualification to the term "peacebuilding." The qualification was apposite for such a case where: "The UN-sponsored peace accords negotiated through 1990 and 1991 brought the decade-long war in [the country] to an end in an impeccably observed cease-fire."[3] The qualification was used to distinguish it from "preventive diplomacy," one of the three ongoing UN activities on which the Security Council had asked the Secretary-General's recommendations. While "post-conflict peace-building" was defined as "action to identify and support structures which will tend to strengthen and solidify peace to avoid a relapse into conflict," efforts at "preventive diplomacy" focused on helping countries to avoid lapsing into conflict in the first place.[4] Although many of the policies and actions to avoid lapsing or relapsing into conflict are similar, the post-conflict context requires some specific activities that are conflict related—including demining, disarming, demobilization, and reintegration—that have proved challenging.

To emphasize the common ground, his 1995 *Supplement to An Agenda for Peace* specifically referred to "peace-building, whether preventive or post-conflict," making clear that peacebuilding is necessary in the preventive context as well.[5] In the post-conflict context, it is not often possible to distinguish policies that cause countries to relapse into old conflicts or lapse into new ones. At any rate, all conflict-insensitive policies need to be avoided for peacebuilding efforts to succeed on the ground.

Boutros-Ghali warned that, to be truly successful: "Peacemaking and peace-keeping operations . . . must come to include comprehensive efforts to identify and support structures which will tend to consolidate peace and advance a sense of confidence and well-being among people."[6] Thus, peacebuilding activities must take place continuously throughout the implementation of other UN actions to minimize the risk of relapsing into violent conflict, or preventively to avoid falling into new conflicts.

Although this was true in the case of El Salvador, where the UN mediated the peace agreement and ONUSAL (United Nations Observer Mission in El Salvador) had a mandate to monitor its compliance, it was particularly true in later operations such as those in the Democratic Republic of the Congo (DRC), Afghanistan, and Iraq. In all these cases, important armed groups had been excluded from the peace process and/or large parts of the territory remained outside the control of the government. In such countries, peacekeeping operations (PKOs) coexisted with a combination of peacebuilding and peacemaking efforts, efforts that had to be combined differently in different parts of the country. For example, because of instability in eastern DRC, the Security Council decided to strengthen MONUSCO's (UN Organization Stabilization Mission) military, police, and civilian presence in that region and to reduce its presence in other regions.[7]

Two major reports on peacebuilding are critical of the state of affairs with respect to peacebuilding. The first one, entitled *The Challenge of Sustaining Peace*, emphasized the need to take a "fresh look not only at the specialized architecture [for peacebuilding] itself [for which the Group of Experts had been mandated], but at the whole approach to peacebuilding taken by the United Nations at large."[8] The second one, *Peacebuilding Challenges for the UN Development System*, noted: "It is crucial for the UN to tackle the actual situation on the ground and not worry endlessly about 'UN plumbing and configurations'." It recommends re-examining the UN's field presence in conflict-prone states to strengthen UN's operational capacity.[9] Based on such recommendations, this chapter begins with a cursory review of some of the peacebuilding issues that have affected its implementation on the ground. It then addresses the multidimensional nature of peacebuilding efforts. The third section discusses the many interrelationships between the different aspects of peacebuilding and argues for the need to address peacebuilding with an integrated approach, rather than with the silo one usually found in existing operations.

Peacebuilding in context: Terminology, foreign intervention, coverage, financing

There is extensive literature on the conceptual, theoretical, and institutional aspects of peacebuilding.[10] This section thus discusses only a few issues that have been particularly problematic for its analysis and actual practice on the ground.

Terminology itself has often been a problem. Different analysts and institutions use different terms for the same purpose. While the UN uses the term "peacebuilding" to refer to activities encompassing the security, political, and socioeconomic dimensions of the war-to-peace transition, the press and many analysts—as well as some politicians in donor countries—use interchangeably the terms "reconstruction," "nation building" (the construction of a national identity), or "statebuilding" (the construction of a functioning state).[11] They often also refer to the link between "security and development" as encompassing peacebuilding.[12] The US Department of State prefers the term "reconstruction and stabilization" (or vice versa), and so does the US Agency for International Development (USAID). Even the Bretton Woods Institutions (BWIs) use different terminology. While the World Bank Group uses the term "post-conflict reconstruction," the International Monetary Fund (IMF) refers to the transition as "reconstruction and growth" or "recovery and reconstruction." Other UN agencies use a variety of terms to indicate their own comparative advantage.[13]

Because this book focuses on global governance, we assume that all peacebuilding takes place under foreign intervention. The first column in Figure 40.1 shows the context in which peacebuilding takes place. These are not necessarily sequential: They interact and overlap in various ways, including in different parts of the country. The second to fifth columns describe domestic conditions and the challenges of the post-conflict multidimensional transition (the subject of the next section). Columns on the right (shaded in gray) assume that foreign intervention takes place in the form of UN-led activities/operations—including peacemaking, peacekeeping, and peacebuilding operations, and simultaneously in the form of humanitarian and development assistance. Although the UN leads, a variety of actors—many of which are mentioned above—are involved. We focus on post-conflict peacebuilding in war-torn countries in which the risk of conflict is high. Hence, we exclude the shaded/patterned areas at the top and bottom of Figure 40.1, where there is no violent conflict, or the risk of such conflict is low—and hence peacebuilding in these contexts is preventive rather than post-conflict.

	Domestic conditions/challenges					Foreign intervention: UN-led activities/policies						
						HA	DA	Political				
Context	Security	Political	Social	Economic				PBPC	PM	PK	PO/IO	PCPB
Pre-conflict				Development as usual		✓	UNDG/BWIs	✓				✓
Conflict: civil war or other internal chaos	Violence and insecurity	Lawlessness and political exclusion	Ethnic/sectarian, religious, ideological, or class confrontation	Economics of war/ruined and underground economies, state-controlled policies, and large macroeconomic imbalances		✓			✓			✓
Conflict resolution: peace agreement/ military intervention	Improving security	Participatory, fair, and inclusive government; respect for rule of law and human rights	Promoting national reconciliation and rebuilding the social fabric of communities	Economics of conflict resolution/NRP		✓						
Post-conflict	Security sector reform (SSR)	National elections	Developing institutional framework to address differences through peaceful ways	Economics of peace; establishing a basic macro/microframework; rehabilitating infrastructure and services; creating conditions for rural development and entrepreneurship; eradicating illicit activities		✓	UNDG/BWIs			✓		✓

Stabilization	Improved security/security transition (PKOs and foreign forces leave)	Political reform continues	Social reform continues	Economics of peace continues	UNDG/BWIs			
No conflict/low risk	Security risk is low and does not affect the economy significantly	Sovereignty and ownership in the hands of national political leaders	Individuals and communities address grievances through institutional means	Return to development as usual	UNDG/BWIs	✓	✓	✓

Figure 40.1 Post-conflict peacebuilding under foreign intervention

Notes:

HA = humanitarian assistance

DA= development assistance

PBPC = peacebuilding in a preventive context

PM = peacemaking

PK = peacekeeping operations led by an SRSG (special representative of the secretary-general)

PO/IO = peace office/integrated office led by an ERSG (executive representative of the secretary-general)

PCPB = post-conflict peacebuilding or peacebuilding in a post-conflict context

UNDG/BWIs = UN Development Group/Bretton Woods Institutions

NRP = national reconstruction plan

Contrary to the Marshall Plan after World War II, most countries embarking in peacebuilding and reconstruction activities since the end of the Cold War have been at low levels of development and destroyed by civil war or other internal chaos. For these reasons, countries required major efforts at economic reconstruction and national reconciliation for which they did not have either the resources or the technical expertise. Such financing is critical to peacebuilding: Countries coming out of war find it particularly difficult to foster domestic savings, or to attract foreign investors. They rely on foreign assistance, which often makes them aid dependent. Moreover, under misguided policies and misplaced priorities of both national governments and foreign interveners[14] war-torn countries have found it difficult to create the productive base necessary for them to satisfy the basic needs of their populations, promote reconciliation, and reduce instability. Not surprisingly, such situations have often led to conflict relapse. In some cases, large and expensive PKOs or foreign forces had to remain in place for extended periods to sustain the peace. The UN Mission in Liberia (UNMIL) is a useful illustration.

As John Maynard Keynes argued following World War I, like war, peace has economic consequences.[15] For war-torn countries in the post-Cold War context, moving from war to a path of peace on their own was not an option. After the twentieth-century's two world wars, countries had a large "peace dividend" by reducing military expenditure and redirecting it to nonmilitary sectors. After the Cold War, however, countries have not had that option since conflict had been foreign financed and financing withered as conflicts winded down.

Multidimensional nature of peacebuilding

In efforts to build societies in the image of the advanced countries, foreign interveners have tried to convert—practically overnight—insecure and destitute societies into liberal democracies with free market economies, predominant private sectors, and independent central banks. Imposing such an unrealistic agenda could reflect the ideological belief that only societies based on principles of democracy and free markets—the so-called "liberal peace"—are able to achieve peace and to generate prosperity.[16] This model may also represent efforts, particularly in countries rich in natural resources, to create the adequate conditions where companies, contractors, and experts from donor countries can flourish.

The recipe has invariably been a combination of centralized government with early and relatively free national elections, together with PKOs or counterinsurgency operations (COIN) to keep the peace, humanitarian assistance to save lives and provide minimum levels of consumption, and a few large and relatively productive investment projects requiring new and expensive infrastructure that takes time to build. This recipe has benefitted mostly foreign investors[17] and domestic elites to the detriment of the large majority of the population. But it has led to food insecurity, new grievances, and/or aid and import dependencies.[18]

Despite the peculiarities of each case, countries face the difficult challenge of addressing the root causes and consequences of the armed conflict when war ends. Contrary to earlier experiences in Korea and Vietnam, foreign interveners in the post-Cold War context pressured countries to embark on a multidimensional transition to peace. All aspects of this complex transition are interrelated and reinforce one another. They also compete for scarce resources: Crime and violence must surrender to improved security ("security"). Lawlessness, political exclusion, and violations of human rights must give way to the rule of law ("political"). Ethnic/sectarian, religious or ideological/class confrontations must give in to national reconciliation ("social"). In addition, war-ravaged, mismanaged, and largely illicit economies must transform into functioning economies ("economic"). Failure in any one of these areas puts the others at risk—as indeed it has in too many countries over the last quarter of a century.

Much attention has been given in public debate and in the academic literature to the security, political, and social aspects of the transition to peace, to the neglect of the economic one.[19] Failure to create viable economies and to give former combatants and other groups affected by the war a stake in the peace process, however, has been a major reason for the dismal record: More than half of the countries that have embarked in such transition with support from UN-led operations relapsed into conflict within a decade.[20] A peace dividend in terms of better living conditions, a rewarding occupation, and reconciliation with neighbors and former enemies has proved a *sine qua non* to sustain the peace.

The security transition is critical. As Secretary-General Kofi Annan noted in 2004: "Unlike inter-states war, making peace in civil war requires overcoming daunting security dilemmas. Spoilers, factions who see [peace] as inimical to their interest, power, or ideology, use violence to undermine or overthrow settlements."[21] UN PKOs or occupying forces from regional organization often provide basic support to enforce ceasefires and to carry out disarmament and demobilization of former combatants. Yet, for stabilization to be lasting indigenous actors must ultimately bear the responsibility for providing security.

To establish minimum security requires legislation, a reformed military force under civilian control, an active and well-trained civilian police force, and an effective judiciary. Although such reforms take a long time, without a rapid move in this direction, addressing the problems of violence, impunity, and human rights violations will be difficult. The financial costs of these reforms are often large and hard to secure. Afghanistan provides the most striking example, where foreign interveners created security forces that the country will not be able to finance on its own.[22]

Despite such reforms, security conditions in the transition are normally far from ideal, including by having large parts of the territory outside the control of the national authorities. Nevertheless, efforts to improve security should always be at the top of the post-conflict policy agenda and be a priority for national leaders and foreign interveners alike.

Whatever the security situation is, the political transition involves the passage from oppressive, autocratic, and exclusionary regimes to more inclusive, pluralistic, and participatory systems based on the rule of law and respect for human, property, and gender rights. War-torn countries, as any other, choose their political leaders and develop their institutions, policies, and governance influenced by historical, cultural, religious, ethnic, or other local idiosyncrasies. Contrary to others, however, war-torn countries are mostly dependent on outside aid and PKOs or foreign troops. Hence, the transition will normally take place amid large foreign intervention and donor-imposed political and economic conditionalities, under which issues of sovereignty and ownership frequently becomes blurred.

As Nobel Laureate Roger Myerson has noted,[23] bright hopes for new democracies in Afghanistan and Iraq soon faded and peacebuilding efforts collapsed. Myerson's work on game theory is important for any effort to improve political reform and economic reconstruction in war-torn countries. Some of his points are particularly relevant. While most analysts have questioned whether countries might have moved too quickly into presidential elections, Myerson posits that the more relevant issue may well be that the move to introduce democratic local government was too slow. Foreign interveners often promote a centralized system of government that facilitates their assistance but which is often alien to local societies. As a result, foreign interveners may effectively be choosing the long-term leader of the nation by appointing interim authorities (as indeed it happened with Hamid Karzai). Moreover, insurgencies often take root in communities where responsible local leadership is lacking.

In his view, successful democratic development depends on the availability of leaders that can use public funds responsibly in providing services and good governance. For peacebuilding to take root, foreign interveners must create opportunities for political and economic decentralization so that local leaders can develop a good reputation to get elected not only at the local but also at national levels. By creating a broad class of local leaders, a decentralized system would emerge that would reduce the government's reliance on foreign interveners.

In the centralized Afghan system, lack of local political leadership and insecurity in many provinces, allowed warlords to continue controlling customs revenue and drug profits in areas under their control. Central government's domestic revenue averaged only five percent of GDP in the first five years of the transition, which seriously affected efforts at economic reconstruction and national reconciliation.[24]

The social transition involves a process of national reconciliation in societies divided by ethnic, religious, sectarian, political, ideological, and economic cleavages that were root causes of the war. After committing atrocious acts against each other, former adversaries are expected to return to the same communities and learn to live together in peace. As former UN Under-Secretary-General Alvaro de Soto has noted: "It cannot be taken for granted that fraternal reconciliation will follow fratricidal confrontation."[25] Thus, an institutional framework needs to be created to help overcome the trauma of the war. This often includes the creation of civil society organizations, national ombudsmen, and human rights prosecutors. In El Salvador and Rwanda, among others, "truth commissions" were established to examine the most notorious human rights violations, not only as a catharsis but also to make recommendations aimed at preventing the recurrence of such abuses. Experts argue that transitional justice to redress legacies of massive human rights abuses and other ways to ease the suffering of the past are key ingredients of peacemaking and peacebuilding.[26]

To sustain the peace, building trust and improving social cohesion is necessary but not sufficient. Former combatants and other militia, as well as returnees, displaced populations, and other war-affected groups must be reintegrated not only into society in general, but also into productive activities so that they can have dignified livelihoods—a critical task of the economic transition. Economic and social reintegration is necessary for national and local reconciliation. It requires the inclusive and effective reactivation of stagnant and mismanaged war economies and the prompt rehabilitation of basic services and infrastructure. Furthermore, reintegration programs require advanced planning, bold and innovative solutions, large financial resources, and staying the course with the right policies, frequently for many years. The contrasting experiences of El Salvador and Afghanistan provide stark evidence on how reintegration can help or hinder peacebuilding efforts.[27]

The economic transition—also referred to as "economic reconstruction" or "the economics of peace"—is an intermediate and distinct phase in between the "economics of war" and long-term "development." Although typical development activities interrupted by war must restart during this period, they have to take place amid critical peace-related tasks (humanitarian assistance, rehabilitation, reintegration, demining), which should always take priority during this phase. The overriding short-term objective must be to avoid relapse into conflict, which makes this phase fundamentally different from development as usual. Given that the main objective of this intermediate phase is sustaining the peace, first-best or optimal economic policies are not generally attainable or even desirable during this phase.

As Michael Doyle and Nicholas Sambanis have pointed out, "reconstruction" needs to succeed before "development" can take root. Conflating the two has been a major factor in peacebuilding failures.[28] In connection to peacebuilding and the economics transition in particular, the BWIs refer to "reconstruction" and not to "development." The latter takes place in a context where there is no violent conflict or the risk of such conflict is low. Thus, during this period, post-conflict peacebuilding is not needed and it is the UN Development Group, rather than PKOs that leads UN operations in the country (look back to Figure 40.1).

Lack of inclusive domestic policies, misplaced priorities, together with fragmented and wasteful use of aid for the reactivation of investment and the provision of basic services and infrastructure, have been major impediments to effective transitions.[29] Suffice it to say that most foreign-supported economic policies and infrastructure development have been targeted to foreign investors and domestic elites, depriving the large majority of a level playing field leading to unsustainable dependencies. Moreover, in some countries, most notoriously in Afghanistan but also in Haiti and Liberia, as much as seventy to eighty percent of total aid has been channeled outside the government budget and hence according to donors' own agendas, which has precluded an integrated reconstruction and peacebuilding strategy according to the countries' own priorities.[30]

From a "silo" to an "integrated" approach to peacebuilding

Not only have the economic aspects of peacebuilding been neglected but also the different dimensions of peacebuilding on the ground operated as what Gillian Tett of the *Financial Times* described as a "curse of silos." Each operates within its own expertise and objectives rather than with the "integrated approach to human security," which Boutros-Ghali first advocated for post-conflict situations.[31] Figure 40.2 depicts the reality of complex relationships; rather than silos, there are feedback loops, both positive and negative.

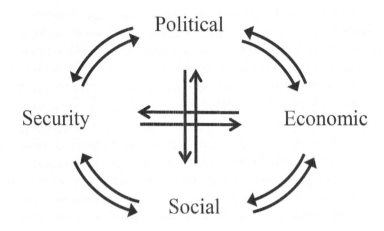

Figure 40.2 Dimensions of post-conflict peacebuilding

Source: Graciana del Castillo, *Obstacles to Peacebuilding* (London: Routledge, 2017), 39.

Indeed, although security may well be a precondition for the success of the overall transition to peace,[32] the effect works both ways: Political reform, national reconciliation, and economic reconstruction may prove futile without security; but security cannot take root without progress in those three areas. This two-way process has proved to be critical to a successful transition to peace, stability, and improved welfare.

As *The US Army and US Marine Corps Counterinsurgency Field Manual* notes, government failures at providing security and basic services, infrastructure and basic livelihoods to its population leaves a vacuum that is often filled by insurgencies. To remedy such failures is expensive and insurgencies finance themselves by "kidnapping, extortion, bank robbery, and drug trafficking—four favorite insurgent activities—[which] are very lucrative."[33] Thus, it is difficult but critical to move out of the economics of war—that is, the underground economy in which illicit activities thrive—to the economics of peace—in which the inclusive reactivation should ensure that the large majority gets a peace dividend to lure them into the peace process. Such measures are needed to minimize the risk of relapse and maximize the chances of creating good governance and effective peacebuilding.

"Expeditionary economics"[34]—using foreign military forces for economic reconstruction, improved governance, and peacebuilding in chronically insecure areas in Iraq and Afghanistan—was expensive and largely futile. Peacebuilding, or what the US military called "gaining hearts and minds," while at the same time bombing the populations has not proved to be a good recipe. Operating under the expeditionary economics mode, the US government created provincial reconstruction teams (PRTs)—consisting of a mixture of civilian experts and military officers—to provide humanitarian and reconstruction support in those areas. Military commanders had plenty of money to spend and, as one commander put it: "[W]e thought that by throwing as much money as possible to the problem, we would get it solved." This created serious price distortions and promoted corruption. Moreover, it created the resentment of inhabitants of more secure areas that, due to their good behavior, received much less support.[35]

Political legitimacy at the national level affects economic policymaking options and uncertainty surrounding the sustainability of economic reform and property rights have been major deterrents to sustainable investment. Interim governments—and even more so UN transitional authorities (Kosovo and East Timor) or an occupying force (Iraq)—should abstain from economic reforms whose sustainability investors may question. This applies to privatization of state-owned enterprises in general, and to liberalization of critical sectors such as oil in Iraq or the Trepca mines in Kosovo, in particular. Both were unrealistic, which never materialized. Indeed, one of the tragic errors of the US-led occupation was the early indication that the US authorities intended to privatize Iraqi assets, including in the oil sector. Although they soon backtracked, the insensitivity of the announcement incensed Iraqis and entailed a high security cost.[36]

The lack of an integrated approach to different phases of peacebuilding has been a problem as well. Different phases do not always take place on the ground and are often led by different actors, but they certainly affect each other. Peacebuilding during peacemaking takes place in different places and is led by UN mediators (El Salvador, Guatemala) or some other mediator or organization (the Roman Community of Sant'Egidio in the case of Mozambique).

As envisaged by Boutros-Ghali, peacebuilding in the post-conflict context must be led at the "political" and "operational" level by the special representative of the secretary-general (SRSG), as the official head of the PKO on the ground. In the case of Mozambique, although the UN was not involved in peacemaking, it was in peacekeeping and peacebuilding, with ONOMUZ (United Nations Operation in Mozambique) overseeing the implementation of the peace agreement.[37]

The *Challenges of Sustaining Peace* report rightly notes that: "[O]vercoming socio-economic grievances, offering populations the means to earn livelihoods and creating the foundations for inclusive, broad-based economic growth are integral to any transition from conflict to normalcy."[38] This shortcoming, however, has affected most transitions and a major obstacle to peacebuilding efforts since the end of the Cold War.

Much has been said about how the IMF in El Salvador "sacrificed the government's ability to implement the UN-mediated peace agreement on the altar of budgetary discipline and placed the country at the brink of relapsing into war."[39] Despite some major changes in the way in which the BWIs support war-torn countries in transition to peace, sharing of information with UN operations on the ground by itself does not suffice to have the impact that the report recommends. As de Soto and the author have argued, what has been lacking is for the SRSG to be equipped with the economic expertise necessary to take an active role in discussions with the minister of finance and the IMF. This is essential to ensure that peace-related needs are included in the economic program through appropriate budgetary allocations, and that economic policies are inclusive and conflict sensitive so that the risk of returning to war is minimized. To ensure a truly integrated approach, the UN Development Programme (UNDP) as the lead of the UN's country team and the World Bank's representatives should join in as observers so that the development institutions understand and support the top political priorities.

Because of the UN's reluctance to openly criticize governments, UN officials often publicly identify a problem when it is too late to be addressed. The result is that national governments and UN operations often work at cross-purposes as was the case, for example, in Liberia. Karin Landgren, the departing SRSG and head of UNMIL waited until her departure from the UN to bluntly tell the PBC on 5 May 2015 that the main sources of potential instability were "structural factors including Liberia's economic model." In her view, the continuation of the "growth without development model" [which had led to war in the first place], made the country vulnerable to popular resentment and future shocks.[40]

Conclusion

Analysts and scholars must examine large numbers of case studies[41] written by experts who have often been closely involved in them, since they provide good and bad lessons on peacebuilding. Mozambique, for example, illustrates two important points with regard to post-conflict peacebuilding. The first point is that peace agreements as well as mandates from the Security Council do not always reflect reality, making thinking outside the box essential to solve constraints throughout the peace process. This requires that UN operations be led by competent and innovative SRSGs, who can maintain a fluid and productive relationship with the government, with the diplomatic community in the country and in New York—including with members of the Peacebuilding Commission (PBC)—with high-level officials of BWIs, and with other stakeholders as needs may arise.

At present, most peacebuilding in the post-conflict context takes place under the aegis of the Security Council (Guatemala was an exception led by the General Assembly) with SRSGs leading PKOs. In some cases, political or integrated operations are led by Executive Representatives of the Secretary-General (ERSGs) who provide political leadership to the entire UN country team. Although the PBC has no operational capacity and hence no representation on the ground, it supports and often duplicates functions that are clearly in the purview and mandate of the SRSGs/ERSGs. Among the countries on the PBC's agenda, the exception has been the Republic of Guinea, a country that has not had a PKO. The PBC can play a useful role in countries such as Guinea that are not in the Security Council's agenda, in those exiting the council, and in "aid orphans," by keeping alive peacebuilding efforts and marshalling resources for them. In the case of Liberia, however, one of two largest recipients of economic aid and which for seven years was both in the Security Council's agenda and that of the PBC, the decision was hard to justify and it certainly duplicated functions within the mandate of the SRSG.[42]

To have a sense of the insignificant impact of the PBC on concrete peacebuilding efforts, it should perhaps be mentioned that the six countries on its agenda—Burundi, Sierra Leone, Guinea-Bissau, Central African Republic, Liberia, and Guinea—represent slightly over half of one percent of the world's population (0.56 percent) and only 0.025 percent of global GDP. For example, the DRC where a PKO in the agenda of the Security Council is located is twice as large as all six countries in terms of GDP and population.[43]

The UN Charter identifies the maintenance of international peace and security as the first purpose of the United Nations. Since the Security Council is the principal organ responsible for that mission, it is hardly surprising that it plays the key role in peacebuilding—ensuring that a conflict does not occur in the first place, or, after the guns have gone silent and tensions have eased, that it does not recur. Thus, to improve post-conflict peacebuilding going forward, the Security Council should improve the capacity of UN missions on the ground, and particularly the expertise in SRSGs/ERSGs teams so that socioeconomic grievances can be overcome and the foundations for inclusive, broad-based economic growth can be achieved. In this way, the "transition from conflict to normalcy," as recommended by *The Challenges to Sustaining Peace* report, can become a reality rather than an unattainable dream.

Additional reading

Stephen Browne and Thomas G. Weiss, eds., *Peacebuilding Challenges for the UN Development System* (New York: Future United Nations Development System Project, 2015).

Graciana del Castillo, *Obstacles to Peacebuilding* (London: Routledge, 2017).

Cedric de Coning and Eli Stamnes, eds., *UN Peacebuilding Architecture* (London: Routledge, 2016).

Roger MacGinty, *Routledge Handbook of Peacebuilding* (London: Routledge, 2013).

Roland Paris and Timothy D. Sisk, *The Dilemmas of Statebuilding: Confronting the Contradictions of Post-War Peace Operations* (London: Routledge, 2009).

UN, *The Challenge of Sustaining Peace*, Report of the Advisory Group of Experts, 29 June 2015, available at www.un.org/en/peacebuilding/pdf/150630%20Report%20of%20the%20AGE%20on%20the%202015%20Peacebuilding%20Review%20FINAL.pdf.

Notes

1 Alvaro de Soto, "Prologue" in Graciana del Castillo, *Obstacles to Peacebuilding* (London: Routledge, 2017), xv.

2 The term "foreign interveners" is preferable to "international community" in this context since not all UN member states participate directly in supporting war-torn countries.

3 Alvaro de Soto and Graciana del Castillo, "Implementation of Comprehensive Peace Agreements: Staying the Course in El Salvador," *Global Governance* 1, no. 2 (1995): 189.

4 Boutros Boutros-Ghali, *An Agenda for Peace* (New York: UN, 1992), 11. The hyphen in the word "peace-building" was dropped over time.

5 Boutros-Ghali, *A Supplement to 'An Agenda for Peace'* (New York: UN, 1995), 10.

6 Boutros-Ghali, *An Agenda for Peace*, 32.

7 See MONUSCO's web page.

8 UN, *The Challenge of Sustaining Peace*, Report of the Advisory Group of Experts, 29 June 2015, 11, www.un.org/en/peacebuilding/pdf/150630%20Report%20of%20the%20AGE%20on%20the%202015%20Peacebuilding%20Review%20FINAL.pdf.

9 Stephen Browne and Thomas G. Weiss, eds., *Peacebuilding Challenges for the UN Development System* (New York: Future United Nations System, 2015).

10 The conceptual and institutional issues were recently analyzed by the author in *Obstacles to Peacebuilding*. See also Elizabeth M. Cousens, "Introduction," in *Peacebuilding as Politics: Cultivating Peace in Fragile Societies*, eds. Cousens and Chetan Kumar (Boulder, CO: Lynne Rienner Publishers, 2001); Tom Keating and W. Andy Knight, "Introduction," in *Building Sustainable Peace* (Tokyo: UNU Press, 2004); Rob Jenkins, *Peacebuilding: From Concept to Commission* (London: Routledge, 2013); Mats Berdal, "Peacebuilding and Development," in *International Development*, eds. Bruce Currie-Alder, Ravi Kanbur,

David M. Malone, and Rohinton Medhora (Oxford: Oxford University Press, 2014); Cedric de Coning and Eli Stamnes, eds., *UN Peacebuilding Architecture* (London: Routledge, 2016). Roger MacGinty, *Routledge Handbook of Peacebuilding* (London and New York: Routledge, 2013) also discusses the more theoretical aspects of peacebuilding.

11 See, for example, Jenkins, *Peacebuilding*, 21–22; Mats Berdal and Dominik Zaum, eds., *Political Economy of Statebuilding: Power After Peace* (London: Routledge, 2013); Roland Paris and Timothy D. Sisk, *The Dilemmas of Statebuilding: Confronting the Contradictions of Post-War Peace Operations* (London and New York: Routledge, 2009).

12 See, for example, Neclâ Tschirgi, Michael S. Lund, and Francesco Mancini, *Security and Development: Searching for Critical Connections* (Boulder, CO: Lynne Rienner Publishers, 2010).

13 Michael Barnett, et al., "Peacebuilding: What is in a Name?" *Global Governance* 13, no. 1 (2007): 35–58.

14 For a detailed discussion on issues of inappropriate timing and sequence, see Arnim Langer and Graham K. Brown, eds., *Building Sustainable Peace: Timing and Sequencing of Post-Conflict Reconstruction and Peacebuilding* (Oxford: Oxford University Press, 2016). For a discussion on ineffective and fragmented aid, see del Castillo, *Guilty Party: The International Community in Afghanistan*, 2nd ed. (Bloomington, IN: XLibris, 2016), 217–230, 243, 262, 288–289, 406.

15 John M. Keynes, *The Economic Consequences of the Peace* (New York: Harcourt, Brace & Howe, Inc., 1920).

16 There is an extensive bibliography on this issue. See, for example, Roland Paris, *At War's End: Building Peace after Civil Conflict* (New York: Cambridge University Press, 2004).

17 Investors from emerging markets—particularly China, India, and Brazil—have shown increasing interest in these countries. For some of the issues involved with this type of investment, see del Castillo, "War-Torn Countries, Natural Resources, Emerging-Power Investors and the UN Development System," in *Emerging Powers and the UN: What Kind of Development Partnership?*, eds. Thomas G. Weiss and Adriana Erthal Abdenur (London: Routledge, 2016), 1911–1926.

18 del Castillo, *Obstacles to Peacebuilding*, 107–108.

19 There are, of course, exceptions. See, for example, del Castillo, *Rebuilding War-Torn States* (Oxford: Oxford University Press, 2008), 15–20; Paul K. Davis, ed., *Dilemmas of Intervention* (Santa Monica, CA: RAND, 2011).

20 del Castillo, *Obstacles to Peacebuilding*, 100–116.

21 UN, *A More Secure World: Our Shared Responsibility*, Report of the Secretary-General's High Level Panel on Threats, Challenges and Change, General Assembly document A/59/565, 2 December 2004, 70.

22 del Castillo, *Guilty Party*, 288.

23 See Roger Myerson, "Rethinking the Fundamentals of State-Building," *PRISM* 2, no. 2 (2011), 91; "Decentralized Democracy in Political Reconstruction," presentation at a High Level Meeting of Experts (Syracuse, Italy, September 2014); "Standards for State-Building Interventions," in *Economics for the Curious: Inside the Minds of 12 Nobel Laureates*, ed. Robert M. Solow (London: Palgrave Macmillan, 2014).

24 del Castillo, *Guilty Party*, 17, 148, 197, 286 and author's data bank on Afghanistan.

25 de Soto, "Prologue" in *Political Economy of Statebuilding*, xviii.

26 See, for example, Helena Meyer-Knapp, *Dangerous Peace-Making* (Olympia, DC: Peace-Maker Press, 2003), 192.

27 In addition to earlier references, see also del Castillo, "Peace Through Reconstruction: An Effective Strategy for Afghanistan," *Brown Journal of World Affairs* 16, no. 2 (2010): 195–211.

28 See Michael W. Doyle, and Nicholas Sambanis, *Making War and Building Peace* (Princeton, NJ: Princeton University Press, 2006), 132.

29 The problems with aid and aid dependency have been discussed in detail by the author in *Guilty Party*, 170–291.

30 Ibid., 160.

31 Gillian Tett, "The Danger of Silo Thinking," *Financial Times*, 15 December 2009.

32 As Persson argues, security is almost always considered the priority. See Anders Persson, "Building a State or Maintaining the Occupation? International Support for Fayyad's State-building Project," *Journal of Conflict Transformation and Security* 2, no. 1 (2012): 101–119.

33 David H. Petraeus and James F. Amos, *Counterinsurgency Field Manual* (Washington, DC: Department of the Army, 2006), Chapter 1, 11.

34 del Castillo, *Guilty Party*, 173, 232, 236, 300–303, 343–344.

35 Ibid., 220.

36 del Castillo, *Rebuilding War-Torn States*: 43, 151–153, 207–208.

37 For details, see Aldo Ajello and Patrick Wittmann, "Mozambique," in *The UN Security Council: From the Cold War to the 21st Century*, ed. David M. Malone (Boulder, CO: Lynne Rienner, 2004), 437–450.

38 UN, *The Challenge of Sustaining Peace*, 20.

39 de Soto and del Castillo, "Obstacles to Peacebuilding Revisited," 209.

40 UN, "PBC Liberia Configuration Meeting: Chair's Summary," New York, 5 May 2015, 2.

41 For references, see tables in del Castillo, *Obstacles to Peacebuilding*, 111–114.

42 Ian D. Quick, "Searching for a Niche: UN Peacebuilding in the Republic of Guinea," in *UN Peacebuilding Architecture*, eds. Cedric de Coning and Eli Stamnes (London: Routledge, 2016), 196–213.

43 Author's calculations using UN data for PKOs cost and IMF data bank for GDP.

Human security as a global public good

Mark Raymond and Stefanie Neumeier

In the second decade of the twenty-first century, there has been renewed focus on human security.[1] It is driven by developments surrounding the Arab Spring, especially events in Libya and Syria that have underscored the continuing importance of the responsibility to protect (R2P) doctrine when dictators turn their guns against their own people. But as the forces of globalization transform the world, some also argue that income inequalities between the world's richest and poorest countries are widening, as trade and investment flows intensify between those countries that can compete in the global economy and those in the Global South that cannot. This point is convincingly argued in the World Bank's 2007 *Global Economic Prospects*, which points out that although globalization will contribute to rapid growth in average incomes, it is also being accompanied by growing income inequality and potentially severe environmental pressures. As a result, the probability of civil unrest in a number of poor and middle-income countries is also rising.[2]

The concept of human security remains a central element of the discourse in international relations. This discourse also points to a new paradigm, which asserts that the provision of human security (defined in terms of the protection of basic human liberties, certain key political and civil rights, and basic standards of equity and social justice) should be viewed as not just national but also global public goods. In this paradigm, human security should reach across borders to all peoples regardless of their ethnic or national origins, socioeconomic status, religious creed, or political persuasion.

However, human security is an underprovided public good. Many states are their citizens' own worst enemy and deliberately threaten their lives and rights. Other states suffer incapacities of various kinds (e.g., administrative, fiscal, governance related) and are wracked by conflict, which limits their ability to provide for the basic needs and human security of their citizens. To the extent that human security in all its various dimensions is enjoyed as a public good, it is one that bears the hallmark of a club good—that is, its benefits are confined in large measure to citizens in rich democracies; some people in poor countries are also secure, but they are a distinct minority.

This chapter explores some of the arguments advanced to explain the human security "deficit" in contemporary international relations. This deficit is best explained by disaggregating the concept to distinguish three public goods that contribute to the realization of human security: Equity, intervention for the purposes of humanitarian protection, and peacebuilding. Doing so provides insight into the reasons that these goods are often undersupplied and demonstrates, further, that they may be most susceptible to provision by different combinations of actors and institutions. We demonstrate the sources of undersupply for each of the three public goods by using the case of the Syrian civil war, raging since 2011. Finally, we conclude by advocating a portfolio diversification approach to the provision of global public goods related to human security.

Different conceptions of human security

Despite significant research and interest in human security over the past two decades, there is no real consensus on what can or should constitute the focus of what is still loosely termed "human security studies."[3] There remains considerable methodological, definitional, and conceptual disquiet about the real meaning of human security, and about the implications of the human security paradigm for the study and practice of international relations. This reality should come as no surprise, given the nature of the academic enterprise and the different disciplinary and methodological backgrounds informing the work of scholars engaged in human security research. Even so, the evident inability of scholars to advance beyond theoretical debates over definitions toward practical policy recommendations understandably frustrates practitioners in the policy community.

There are arguably three distinct conceptions of human security that shape current debates, which are distinguishable according to their understanding of the nature of the threat. One view emphasizes direct physical harm to vulnerable populations, often but not always committed by states or their agents. It informs international efforts to prevent and respond to genocide and war crimes, and to abolish weapons that are especially harmful to civilians and noncombatants.[4] It lies at the heart of humanitarian interventions directed at improving the basic living conditions of refugees, and anyone uprooted by conflict from their homes and communities. On those rare occasions in which military force has been used ostensibly to avert genocide or ethnic cleansing, it has also been justified usually on rather specific humanitarian grounds such as the need to restore basic human rights and dignity. Another group takes a slightly more expansive view, including systematic violations of the fundamental liberal package of basic individual rights to "life, liberty, and the pursuit of happiness," and positing an obligation on the part of the international community of states to protect and promote these rights.[5]

These two views stand in sharp contrast to a broader view, which suggests that human security should be widely construed to include economic, environmental, social, and other forms of harm to the overall livelihood and wellbeing of individuals. There is a strong social justice component in this broader conception of human security, as well as a wider consideration of threats (actual and potential) to the survival and health of individuals. According to this third and considerably more controversial view, the state of the global economy, the forces of globalization, and the health of the environment (including the world's atmosphere and oceans) are all legitimate subjects of concern in terms of how they affect the "security" of the individual.[6]

The "broadeners" have attracted sharp criticism. Yuen Foong Khong, for instance, warns that making everything a priority renders nothing a priority—raising false hopes in the policy realm and obscuring real trade-offs between rival human security objectives.[7] Similarly, Andrew Mack makes the sound methodological point that overly broad definitions of human security can block investigation of the very phenomena that need to be understood.[8]

Examining the relationship between poverty and violence, for example, requires us to treat them as separate variables. A definition that conflates dependent and independent variables will confound analysis of causal connections between them. However, as a practical matter many human security initiatives, such as the international campaign to ban trafficking in small and light weapons, fall between the narrower and the broader definitions. Accordingly, these views should not be understood as mutually exclusive; rather, they are best thought of in terms of concentric circles. Nevertheless, as is illustrated below, the choice of conceptual emphasis is consequential in that it leads to concern with different underprovided global public goods related to human security—and thus also to different policy approaches for providing them.

Public goods and human security

Underlying much of the human security literature is a common belief that human security is critical to international peace and security, the primary purpose for the establishment of the United Nations after World War II.[9] To the extent that this is true, human security is not simply a private good with benefits accruing to specific individuals; rather, it may also have widely enjoyed positive spinoffs. However, many regions experience chronic shortages of human security. This reality raises the question, who responds when basic rights are threatened and citizens are subjected to further privations in their daily lives? And like all so-called public goods, the real question is who provides it and at what cost? Resolving collective-action problems are inherent to the provision of public goods.

In traditional liberal democratic theories of the state, property rights, and the safety and security of citizens are public goods that are provided by nonmarket mechanisms, typically the state. For example, the ultimate responsibility for maintaining law and order in domestic civil society rests with the state that provides this public good. Early liberal theorists like Thomas Hobbes recognized that allowing private citizens to look after their own security was a recipe for social and political anarchy. Hendrik Spruyt has argued convincingly that the comparatively greater ability of the sovereign state to guarantee property rights, relative to its synchronic competitors, helps explain the historical emergence of a homogeneous system of states.[10] The state and the provision of public goods are thus closely linked in theory and in practice. The large body of law that has developed, for example, in the area of contracts constitutes a kind of public good.[11]

The legal rules and instruments of contract law not only guarantee reciprocity, but also permit private transactions to take place in an orderly and businesslike manner. As noted by Inge Kaul, Isabelle Grunberg, and Marc Stern: "Public goods are recognized as having benefits that cannot easily be confined to a single 'buyer' (or set of 'buyers'). Yet, once they are provided, many can enjoy them for free. Street names for example. A clear environment is another. Without a mechanism for collective action, these goods can be underproduced."[12]

Public goods can be broken into two main categories: So-called pure public goods and joint goods. Pure public goods are characterized by jointness and non-excludability.[13] Their benefits are consumed by all members of a community as soon as any one member produces them and consumption does not reduce the quantity or quality of available supply. Relevant examples of the polar case of pure public goods are hard to find; but one such example is knowledge, a public intermediate input into the production function of all firms.

"Club" goods are defined by their jointness and excludability characteristics. Since the benefits from club goods are excludable, often through the price mechanism, they can be provided through the private sector (e.g., cable and pay television, movie theaters, recreational facilities). Club goods, by definition, can be extended or provided to somebody else without raising marginal costs. When jointness extends to the international level but benefits remain excludable, the optimal club size is international.[14] The remainder of this section disaggregates human security into three distinct goods; each can be best understood as club goods.

"Sustainable human development" proponents of human security argue that most current international economic governance arrangements and abstract arguments about why such institutions are needed—whether they take the form of formal international regimes or some other institutional form—lack mechanisms and instruments that address the serious distributional inequities that arise from the operations of the global markets and the forces of globalization. These inequities ultimately have an adverse impact on human welfare and human security at the local level. Allowed to become sufficiently serious in magnitude, these local inequalities may threaten regional or even global peace and security.

The sustainable human development school thus argues that equity should be considered as a global public good, and that equity and social justice must play a key role in international order.[15] The approach thus has an explicit normative agenda. Although some attention has been given over the years to income differences between the rich, developed market economies and the poor, less developed countries,[16] these advocates argue that many of these efforts have been largely ineffective.

The core problem is that the normal operation of the global economy perpetuates highly unequal income distribution, despite ameliorative mechanisms. The question, then, is how to more effectively meet the needs and rights of the disadvantaged. According to Amartya Sen, new concepts of distributive justice will only be widely adopted when "national particularism"—where distributive justice is conceived exclusively in national terms and within a national policy context—gives way to more plural affiliations involving direct "*interpersonal* sympathies and solidarities across borders." Such affiliations must have "a cogency that can substantially transcend national particularism of the estranged polities" such that fairness and distribution are seen in more global but nonetheless interpersonal terms.[17] As Sen further notes: "The freedom-efficiency of the market mechanism, on the one hand, and the seriousness of freedom-inequality problems, on the other hand, are worth considering *simultaneously*. The equity problems have to be addressed, especially in dealing with serious deprivations and poverty."[18]

The value in a public goods approach to explaining the equity deficit is its focus on the sources of undersupply—in this case, of equity—rather than on the sources of demand. The question, from this perspective, is the extent to which equity at the international level is characterized by jointness of supply and non-excludability. It is clear that equity is generally excludable—that is, it can be provided to some without the benefits accruing to all. The provision of redistribution can be done on a very granular basis, for example through development grants and charitable giving directed to particular villages or even particular families. While addressing the undersupply of equity may well generate positive social externalities such as reductions in violence (making the benefits of equity partially non-excludable), these too will tend to remain relatively localized in accordance with the patterns of direct redistribution.

The situation with respect to jointness of supply is more complex. To the extent that increased equity produces positive externalities such as peace and a reduction in levels of violence, these are likely to be enjoyed on a joint basis at least in the affected geographic area. If equity is understood in terms of reducing the differential between the highest and lowest quintiles in the global distribution of annual income, then it may also be a joint good in the sense that a reduction in the income differential between France and Indonesia does not preclude a reduction in income differential between Zimbabwe and South Korea. However, understanding equity in this manner requires accepting that citizens in advanced industrial economies would be receiving more equity (making them better off in this sense), even as their incomes declined as a result of global redistribution of resources. It is unlikely that such a view will be politically tenable in the short term. Increasing equity ultimately entails distribution either of current resource stocks or future resource flows in favor of the disadvantaged. Thus, global equity is best described, at least under currently prevailing social rules and institutions (sovereign states, free markets, and individual property rights) as blending characteristics of club goods and private goods.

Whereas sustainable development proponents of human security tend to focus on distributional failures in the international system to explain why human security is an underprovided public good (at least in terms of its equity and social justice components), analysts who see human security primarily in relation to physical safety and basic civil rights argue that the key failures are primarily *political* as opposed to economic or market based.

In the physical safety and basic rights conceptions of human security, the principal threats to international peace and security come instead in the denial of human security to the citizens in one or more states as a result of civil conflict and strife, and/or from transnational economic forces that have marginalized certain groups in the world economy. Thus, in the human security paradigm the problem of international order is redefined and shifted downwards from the systemic (i.e., international) to the sub-systemic (i.e., intrastate) level.

This argument rests on the fundamentally changed nature of international conflict in the twentieth century. Most of the wars since the second half of the twentieth century have been wars within states, and the result of ethnic, religious, or horizontal inequalities (i.e., the inequitable distribution of wealth and income among different groups within society).[19] These conflicts are fought not by regular armies but between militias, armed civilians, guerrillas, and ethnic groups. These groups arm themselves through the large international market for small arms.

This particular view of human security stresses the rule of law and liberal norms as key ingredients in the establishment of a "just" political order both domestically and internationally. Accordingly, it has its own unique view of the kinds of intervention strategy that may be required to contribute to a peaceful political order. In contrast to realism—which sees a role for force and the balance of power in the management of communal or ethnic conflict—humanitarian and rights/rule of law approaches to human security see the challenges of peacebuilding and third party involvement largely in terms of the creation of participatory governance structures, the development of new social norms, and the establishment of the rule of law and democracy. Thus, in arguing that "failed" or "failing" states are the principal source of mayhem in contemporary international politics, these human security advocates also look to a very different set of institutional responses and mechanisms for addressing these kinds of "political" failure.

Unlike Immanuel Kant, who was essentially noninterventionist when it came to promoting democracy and human rights in those states where such institutions were lacking, the human security paradigm is much more inclined to be proactive and to favor interventionist approaches to defend and secure human rights, broader human security needs, and democracy. Even so, there is considerable disquiet among participants in these debates about when intervention is desirable or the conditions under which force and other instruments of intervention should be used.[20] In the human security view of international politics, however, most of these reservations disappear; intervention, including the use of force, is sanctioned because human security is privileged over international order as a basic public good. In contrast to the focus on equity as a global public good that stems from the sustainable development view of human security, narrower political conceptions of human security focus instead on public goods such as humanitarian protection and intervention, as well as state-building measures that seek to instill and internalize cultures of human rights.

To what extent can humanitarian interventions and peacebuilding efforts be accurately understood as pure or impure public goods? As with equity, humanitarian intervention is in most respects excludable. This is true at the strategic level, as evidenced by the selective nature of such efforts. The international community of states can, and does, opt not to intervene in many humanitarian emergencies. It is also true at the tactical and operational levels, at which the rules of engagement can restrict the kinds of operation that are conducted and thus determine which civilians enjoy the protection of the intervention force and which do not. A plausible case can also be made for jointness. An intervention in one case does not preclude an intervention in another, especially if time horizons are relaxed to permit the possibility of significant additional investment in relevant military and other humanitarian capacities. Relative to the overall size of the global economy, such investments are not out of reach, especially if present military spending were diverted. The possibility of exclusion and joint (in principle) nature of supply suggest that humanitarian intervention is a club good. The key question is whether club members with the capacity to pay can be induced to do so; that is, the problem is one of political will, and the solution may rest on the availability of selective incentives of sufficient value to states (or potentially other actors) with the means to pursue them.

Peacebuilding efforts that focus on establishing and consolidating respect for human rights are non-excludable in particular state-level contexts. Short of situations of institutionalized discrimination, such as apartheid, that are clearly incompatible with modern understandings of human rights, it is difficult to imagine potential cases where rights would be understood and applied in a systematically unequal fashion. It is even more difficult to imagine a case in which such a situation is an intended outcome of a peacebuilding effort. To the extent that human rights cultures have been established above the state level, in regional human rights courts or the International Criminal Court (ICC), they are non-excludable in the sense of providing equal protection. However, legal regimes are typically excludable in the sense of applying to particular geographic jurisdictions. The genocide convention, various major human rights treaties and declarations, and the ICC arguably provide at least a thin layer of genuinely universal protection, but human rights still remain enforceable in practice primarily via domestic courts. The ICC was similarly designed according to the principle of complementarity, as well as with Security Council oversight.[21] The major consequence of these significant vestiges of sovereignty is that enjoyment of the human security public good of human rights remains patchwork in practice and is likely to do so for the foreseeable future.

If the public good is defined in terms not of the rights culture itself but rather of measures and programs to foster and maintain such cultures, these programs are likely to remain excludable for practical reasons—training workshops and other related activities can only involve finite numbers of participants. Modern information and communications technologies, including streaming video, may potentially relax this constraint; but it is unclear that online education of this kind is fully as effective as in-person instruction. This may be especially true of attempts to create emotional capacities such as tolerance and empathy that are critical to functional rights cultures. Thus, peacebuilding and the rights cultures that they create are at best club goods, though perhaps with relatively low costs of provision in contrast with equity and humanitarian intervention.

The situation with respect to jointness of supply is also more tractable regarding efforts to strengthen respect for human rights, mainly because the adoption of such beliefs and accompanying institutions in one political community does not diminish the stock of beliefs and institutions available to other communities. In fact, there are likely opportunities to leverage socialization mechanisms involving both back patting and social opprobrium, and other means of social influence.[22] Thus, the adoption of such beliefs may encourage further adoption, under the right conditions, leading to virtuous cycles.

Application to the Syrian conflict

The international response to the conflict in Syria exemplifies the shortage—one might say "absence"—of human security. Considering equity, humanitarian intervention, and peacebuilding, it becomes apparent that benefits remain excludable and that jointness of supply varies but is generally not an insurmountable problem, at least for humanitarian intervention and peacebuilding.

An examination of the Syrian civil war demonstrates the excludability of benefits from equity. It also reveals that problems associated with the absence of joint supply are more severe for equity than for humanitarian intervention or peacebuilding. With respect to excludability, there has been an undersupply of equity in terms of ensuring human security through official development assistance (ODA) to Syria. Before the war, the international community of states did too little to alleviate the escalating humanitarian crisis, which was a result of several droughts between 2006 and 2011. Syria was one of the lowest recipients of ODA in the Middle East prior to 2011.[23]

Throughout the armed conflict, providing assistance to Syria has been highly politicized. While Russia criticizes that the majority of UN humanitarian aid is channeled to anti-regime areas, Moscow mostly supplies aid to regions under control of its ally, Bashar al-Assad.[24] This distributional inequality in the region and the failure of the international community of states to provide assistance relative to needs are obvious. In regard to jointness of supply, focusing humanitarian assistance on some Middle Eastern countries does not automatically produce collective benefits neither does it ensure joint supply of ODA for all countries in the region. Even though in 2017 the international community of states increased its budget for humanitarian assistance to Syria,[25] such help was still not sufficient to ensure overall human security. Benefits enjoyed remain localized at best and might vary greatly within a particular geographic area. Global equity also appears to be a low-priority good from the perspective of the economically most advantaged societies.

With respect to humanitarian intervention in Syria, we can identify both excludability and lack of jointness of supply. With regard to the former, international actors have limited their military involvement to situations that cater to their strategic interest. The United States has prioritized arming the Syrian opposition, whereas Russia has supported regime operations.[26] Washington and its allies continue their campaign against the Islamic State of Iraq and the Levant (ISIL, or ISIS or Da'esh) and other terrorist groups and direct airstrikes towards the north and east of Syria. The majority of Russian airstrikes are conducted on opposition-held territory rather than ISIL-controlled areas.[27] The EU's inaction in terms of humanitarian intervention is also a result of political tensions and varying interests of individual member states.[28]

While all actors have framed their actions as a means to reduce overall human suffering, evidence suggests a large part of the population is excluded from benefits. President Donald Trump's reasoning in 2017 for initiating an attack following the use of chemical weapons illustrates this interpretation. The decision to intervene reflects a self-interested move to reinforce US power rather than a moral act. The lack of joint supply in terms of humanitarian intervention is moderate. While intervening in the Syrian conflict might limit resources available for interventions in similar crises elsewhere, the absence is more a result of political will rather than lack of economic capacity. Instead of devoting resources to humanitarian interventions, countries prefer to spend resources on other military and nonmilitary goods. Global military spending has increased since 2014, while multilateral peace operations have declined.[29]

Indeed, the cost of intervening in the Syrian conflict represents a fraction of American and Russian military budgets, and these costs become even more insignificant when compared to global military spending. Humanitarian interventions and other US war-related activities are part of the overseas contingency operations (OCO) spending. The OCO budget accounts for roughly ten percent of overall US military spending. The Department of Defense estimates that the operations in Syria and Iraq will only represent fifteen percent of the 2017 OCO request.[30] While the Russian Defense Ministry has not published information on the costs of its operations in Syria, IHS Jane's and *Financial Times* have estimated that even if Russia were to continue its air strikes at the current level for a full year, the country would still use less than three percent of its overall national defense budget of 2016.[31]

While capacity for interventions may be limited in the short term because of fixed resources, global military capacity is sufficient and unlikely to be exhausted. This reality is even less of a problem in the long term as the international community of states could redirect resources to future humanitarian interventions.

Although the Syrian conflict remains unresolved, it is possible to contemplate subsequent peacebuilding. As long as the war continues, the United States and Russia will support actors and carry out attacks that advance their national interests, a trend that will continue in prospective peacebuilding efforts. With regards to excludability, international actors are expected to direct their attention to groups that have previously received support. The peace talks in 2017 illustrate the continuation of strategic, exclusionary behavior as some rebel groups were invited to the meetings while others, such as the Syrian Kurds, were not.[32]

Therefore, the benefits of future peacebuilding efforts are likely to be at least partially confined to a minority. In respect of jointness of supply, missions to secure a truce in Syria do not preclude peacebuilding missions in other countries. In more localized terms, peacebuilding in conflict zones within Syria might result in an overall joint supply throughout the country, as long as the conflict is brought to an end in a manner that minimizes reprisals and ensures respect for human rights. Peacebuilding has the least severe problems in terms of both excludability and jointness of supply. However, the prospects of a just peace appear remote.

Conclusion: Providing for human security

If human security in all of its various dimensions is an underprovided public good, which international institutions, mechanisms, and actors are best equipped to provide it and to help address the different kinds of political and market failure that are experienced at both the national and international levels? Proponents of human security argue that international and intergovernmental institutions are unable to provide for human security for a variety of reasons. First, they are paralyzed or hamstrung by conflicts of interest among their most powerful (typically state) members. Second, many suffer from the corrosive logic of collective-action problems, to which there are no effective or readily available institutional remedies. Third, financial and other resourcing problems have effectively thwarted or hindered the ability of these organizations to provide public goods in the realm of human security. Fourth, formal institutional and organizational mandates cannot readily be modified or changed to address the human security agenda and provide for this public good.

Despite these shortcomings, formal international organizations still have a role to play in the provision of global public goods. Their legitimacy endows them with the capacity to identify and praise good behavior from other actors, thus encouraging public good provisions. They can also assist in coordinating the efforts of various national governments and private groups, reducing the chance of duplication.[33] Further, their roles in directly providing global public goods could often be enhanced by the provision of additional resources.

Global public goods can also be provided by groups of states. This model of provision is referred to either as "middle-power multilateralism" or as "minilateralism." Such *ad hoc* coalitions are often more able to act quickly and may be more effective in marshaling the needed capacity since powerful states can more easily be assured the resources they provide will be effectively employed in a manner consistent with their values and interests. States can also cooperate more easily with other states they have previously learned to trust.[34]

Others argue on balance that it is preferable that human security be provided on a voluntary basis and through the voluntary sector. Proponents suggest that such an approach is more efficient, and that it lends greater accountability and legitimacy to decision making. To the extent that sovereignty stands in the way of the delivery of these public goods, nongovernmental organizations working with their counterparts in other societies are best able to circumvent and work around state actors.

Current patterns of provision of the three human security-related public goods identified in this chapter (equity, intervention, and peacebuilding) vary in ways that reflect both their different characteristics as well as the related norms and rules that apply to their provision. Attempts to supply global equity involve states, but both voluntary and private sectors as well as formal international organizations play key roles in actual resource provision. To the extent that substantially increasing equity requires successful promotion of the view that the advantaged have ethical obligations to trade resources for equity, industrialized countries also have a key role to play in fostering normative change. In contrast, humanitarian intervention is typically provided via a combination of formal intergovernmental organizations and state-based coalitions of the willing.[35] This pattern reflects both the need to balance capacity and legitimacy and the desire on the part of states to retain their monopoly on the legitimate use of force. Finally, peacebuilding efforts aimed at strengthening human rights cultures involve a broad range of actors including the voluntary sector, individual governments, and international organizations. This diversity reflects the lower provision costs of this public good compared to the other two, and the strong reputational benefits accruing from being seen to engage in what is broadly understood as prosocial behavior.

Given that all three goods resemble club goods (albeit to varying degrees), the key to addressing undersupply is providing selective incentives to actors with relevant capacity. Doing so requires a realization that, while states remain vital players, they are not the only relevant potential club members—at least for the provision of equity and for peacebuilding. Further, encouraging greater provision of these goods is made significantly easier because the incentives provided to suppliers need not always be costly. Charitable giving and peacebuilding both demonstrate that social recognition and conformity with recognized group norms often provide motivation. Michael Barnett argues that donors are often motivated by intangible payoffs from giving.[36]

Even so, there is perhaps no single mode of delivery and no "preferred" path in the provision of human security. Rather, a diversified approach to human security in which states and non-state actors provide public goods to promote human security may ultimately be best suited to meeting the multidimensional aspects of human security itself.

Additional reading

Michael Barnett, *Empire of Humanity: A History of Humanitarianism* (Ithaca, NY: Cornell University Press, 2011).

Shannon D. Beebe and Mary H. Kaldor, *The Ultimate Weapon Is No Weapon: Human Security and the New Rules of War* (New York: Public Affairs, 2010).

David R. Black, et al., *A Decade of Human Security: Global Governance and New Multilateralism* (New York: Routledge, 2016).

David Chandler, "Resilience and Human Security: The Post-interventionist Paradigm," *Security Dialogue* 43, no. 3 (2012): 213–229.

Denise Garcia, *Disarmament Diplomacy and Human Security: Regimes, Norms, and Moral Progress in International Relations*. (New York: Routledge, 2011).

International Commission on Intervention and State Sovereignty, *The Responsibility to Protect* (Ottawa: International Development Research Centre, 2001).

S. Neil MacFarlane and Yuen Foong Khong, *The UN and Human Security: A Critical History* (Indianapolis: Indiana University Press, 2006)

Notes

1 Fen Osler Hampson and Mark Raymond authored this chapter in the first edition; the current authors gratefully acknowledge his contribution.

2 Frances Stewart and Graham Brown, "Motivations for Conflict: Groups and Individuals," in *Leashing the Dogs of War: Conflict Management in a Divided World*, eds. Chester A. Crocker, Fen Osler Hampson, and Pamela Aall (Washington, DC: United States Institute of Peace, 2007), 197–219; Geoffrey Gertz and Lawrence Chandy, *Two Trends in Global Poverty* (Washington, DC: Brookings Institution, 2011).

3 Mary Kaldor, *Human Security* (Cambridge: Polity Press, 2007); Derek S. Reveron and Kathleen A. Mahoney-Norris, *Human Security in a Borderless World* (Boulder, CO: Westview Press, 2011); Richard A. Matthew, Jon Barnett, Bryan McDonald, and Karen L. O'Brien, eds., *Global Environmental Change and Human Security* (Cambridge, MA: MIT Press, 2009); George Kent, *Freedom from Want: The Human Right to Adequate Food* (Washington, DC: Georgetown University Press, 2005); Osler Hampson, et al., *Madness in the Multitude: Human Security and World Disorder* (Toronto: Oxford University Press, 2002).

4 Kaldor, *Human Security*; Shannon D. Beebe and Mary H. Kaldor, *The Ultimate Weapon Is No Weapon: Human Security and the New Rules of War* (New York: Public Affairs, 2010); Samantha Power, *A Problem from Hell: America and the Age of Genocide* (New York: Harper Perennial, 2003); Boutros Boutros-Ghali, *An Agenda for Peace: Preventive Diplomacy, Peacemaking and Peacekeeping* (New York: UN, 1995); Jonathan Moore, *The United Nations and Complex Emergencies: Rehabilitation in Third World Transitions* (Geneva: United Nations Research Institute for Social Development, 1996).

5 Richard Pierre Claude and Burns H. Weston, *Human Rights in World Community: Issues and Action*, 3rd ed. (Philadelphia: University of Pennsylvania Press, 2006); Johannes Morsink, *The Universal Declaration of Human Rights: Origins, Drafting and Intent*

(University Park: University of Pennsylvania Press, 1998); Paul G. Lauren, *The Evolution of Human International Rights: Visions Seen* (University Park: University of Pennsylvania Press, 1998); Philip Alston, ed., *The United Nations and Human Rights: A Critical Appraisal* (Oxford: Oxford University Press, 1992).

6 Paul Battersby and Joseph M. Siracusa, *Globalization and Human Security* (Lanham, MD: Rowman & Littlefield, 2009); H. Richard Friman and Simon Reich, eds., *Human Trafficking, Human Security, and the Balkans* (Pittsburgh, PA: University of Pittsburgh Press, 2007); Kent, *Freedom from Want*; Matthew, et al., eds., *Global Environmental Change and Human Security*; United Nations, *The Copenhagen Declaration and Programme of Action* (New York: Oxford University Press, 1995); UNDP, *Human Development Report 1994* (New York: Oxford University Press, 1994); UNDP, *Human Development Report 1997* (New York: Oxford University Press, 1997); Jorge Nef, *Human Security and Mutual Vulnerability: An Exploration into the Global Political Economy of Development and Underdevelopment* (Ottawa: International Development Research Centre, 1999).

7 Yuen Foong Khong, "Human Security: A Shotgun Approach to Alleviating Human Misery?" *Global Governance* 7, no. 3 (2001): 231–236.

8 Andrew Mack, *Human Security Report 2005: War and Peace in the 21st Century* (New York: Oxford University Press, 2005).

9 S Neil MacFarlane and Yuen Foong Khong, *The UN and Human Security: A Critical History* (Indianapolis: Indiana University Press, 2006).

10 Hendrik Spruyt, *The Sovereign State and Its Competitors* (Princeton, NJ: Princeton University Press, 1994).

11 Mancur Olson, *The Logic of Collective Action: Public Goods and the Theory of Groups*, 2nd ed. (Cambridge, MA: Harvard University Press, 1971).

12 Inge Kaul, Isabelle Grunberg, and Marc A. Stern, "Defining Global Public Goods," in *Global Public Goods: International Cooperation in the 21st Century*, eds. Inge Kaul, Isabelle Grunberg, and Marc A. Stern (New York: Oxford University Press, 1999), 2–19.

13 Duncan Snidal, "Public Goods, Property Rights, and Political Organizations," *International Studies Quarterly* 23, no. 4 (1979): 532–566.

14 Robert O. Keohane, *After Hegemony: Cooperation and Discord in the World Political Economy* (Princeton, NJ: Princeton University Press, 1984); Barbara Koremenos, Charles Lipson, and Duncan Snidal, "The Rational Design of International Institutions," *International Organization* 55, no. 4 (2001): 761–799.

15 Mohan J. Rao, "Equity in a Global Public Goods Framework," in *Global Public Goods*, eds. Kaul, Grunberg, and Stern, 28–87.

16 Thomas Piketty, *Capital in the Twenty-First Century* (Cambridge, MA: Harvard University Press, 2014).

17 Amartya Sen, "Global Justice and Beyond," in *Global Public Goods*, eds. Kaul, Grunberg, and Stern, 120.

18 Amartya Sen, *Development as Freedom* (New York: Alfred A. Knopf, 2000), 119.

19 International Commission on Intervention and State Sovereignty, *The Responsibility to Protect* (Ottawa: International Development Research Centre, 2001); Margareta Sollenberg, Peter Wallensteen, and Andrés Jato, "Major Armed Conflicts," in *SIPRI Yearbook 1999: Armaments, Disarmament, and International Security* (Oxford: Oxford University Press), 15–33; Mack, *Human Security Report 2005*.

20 Kaldor, *Human Security*; Beebe and Kaldor, *The Ultimate Weapon Is No Weapon*; Power, *A Problem from Hell*.

21 Jo Stigen, *The Relationship between the International Criminal Court and National Jurisdictions: The Principle of Complementarity* (Leiden: Martinus Nijhoff, 2008).

22 Alistair Iain Johnston, "Treating International Institutions as Social Environments," *International Studies Quarterly* 45, no. 4 (2001): 487–515; Margaret E. Keck and Kathryn Sikkink, *Activists Beyond Borders: Advocacy Networks in International Politics*

(Ithaca, NY: Cornell University Press, 1998); Martha Finnemore and Kathryn Sikkink, "International Norm Dynamics and Political Change," *International Organization* 52, no. 4 (1998): 887–917.

23 UNDP, *Syrian Arab Republic: Third National MDGs Progress Report* (New York: UNDP, 2010), www.undp.org/content/undp/en/home/librarypage/mdg/mdg-reports/arab-states.html.

24 Martin Russell, *At A Glance: Russia's Humanitarian Aid Policy* (Brussels: European Parliament, 2016), www.europarl.europa.eu/RegData/etudes/ATAG/2016/582039/EPRS_ATA(2016)582039_EN.pdf.

25 The World Bank, "Net Official Development Assistance Received (Current US$)," last modified 2017, http://data.worldbank.org/indicator/DT.ODA.ODAT.CD?locations=SY.

26 "Syria Crisis: Where Key Countries Stand," *BBC News*, September 30, 2015, www.bbc.com/news/world-middle-east-23849587.

27 Ibid.

28 Marc Pierini, "In Search of an EU Role in the Syrian War," Carnegie Europe, 18 July 2016, carnegieeurope.eu/2016/08/18/in-search-of-eu-role-in-syrian-war-pub-64352.

29 Timo Smit, "Trends in Multilateral Peace Operations—New SIPRI Data," Stockholm International Peace Research Institute, 28 May 2017, www.sipri.org/commentary/topical-backgrounder/2017/trends-multilateral-peace-operations-new-sipri-data; Stockholm International Peace Research Institute, "World Military Spending: Increases in the USA and Europe, Decreases in Oil-exporting Countries," SIPRI, 24 April 2017, www.sipri.org/media/press-release/2017/world-military-spending-increases-usa-and-europe.

30 Katherine Blakeley, *Analysis of the FY 2017 Defense Budget and Trends in Defense Spending* (Washington, DC: Center for Strategic and Budgetary Assessments, 2016), http://csbaonline.org/research/publications/analysis-of-the-fy-2017-defense-budget-and-and-trends-in-defense-spending; Lynn M. Williams and Susan B. Epstein, *Overseas Contingency Operations Funding: Background and Status* (Washington, DC: Congressional Research Service, 2017), https://fas.org/sgp/crs/natsec/R44519.pdf.

31 Kathrin Hille, "Russia Defies Recession to Fund Syria Conflict," *Financial Times*, 25 October 2015, www.ft.com/content/8f9c21fa-7957-11e5-933d-efcdc3c11c89.

32 John Irish, "Syrian Kurdish Groups Say Not Invited to Peace Talks," *Reuters*, 10 January 2017, www.reuters.com/article/us-mideast-crisis-syria-kurds-idUSKBN14U1NY?il=0.

33 Kenneth W. Abbott, Philipp Genschel, Duncan Snidal, and Bernhard Zangl, eds., *International Organizations as Orchestrators* (Cambridge: Cambridge University Press, 2015).

34 On multilateralism, see John Gerard Ruggie, "Multilateralism: The Anatomy of an Institution," *International Organization* 46, no. 3 (1992): 561–598. On minilateralism, see Fen Osler Hampson and Paul Heinbecker, "The 'New' Multilateralism of the Twenty-First Century," *Global Governance* 17, no. 3 (2011): 299–310.

35 Ibid.

36 Michael Barnett, *Empire of Humanity: A History of Humanitarianism* (Ithaca, NY: Cornell University Press, 2011).

PART VII
GOVERNING THE ECONOMIC
AND SOCIAL WORLD

Part introduction

The final part of this book turns to manifestations of international organization (IO) and global governance in what we have labeled "Governing the economic and social world." For us, this terrain is extensive and seemingly boundless; the scale of the forms of institutionalization, actors, and sources of authority ensures that we could not hope to cover their full range. The longest part of this book contains thirteen chapters that individually and collectively offer an incisive yet extensive examination of global economic and social governance as it is manifest today.

The chapters cover most of the "big issues"—finance, trade, development, environment, poverty, hunger, health, and migration and refugees. They also analyze the principal intergovernmental institutions—the International Monetary Fund (IMF), World Trade Organization (WTO), World Bank, Global Environment Facility (GEF), UN development system, Food and Agriculture Organization (FAO), and World Health Organization (WHO), to name some of the most familiar—involved in each area along with the host of non-state actors that also play a role therein.

The chapters in this part are arranged to flow from substantive areas of institutionalization—in finance, trade, development, and environment—to pressing crises and key issues—climate change, sustainable development, energy, poverty, hunger, health, migration and refugees, and the Internet. This arrangement is not only convenient but also allows readers to select chapters as they see fit or as their interest takes them. Introductory classes on IO and global governance, for example, would most likely turn to prominent issues in the global economy and their respective institutions by exploring "Global financial governance" (Bessma Momani, Chapter 42), "Global trade governance" (Bernard Hoekman, Chapter 43), "Global development governance" (Katherine Marshall, Chapter 44), and "Global environmental governance" (Elizabeth R. DeSombre and Angelina Li, Chapter 45).

Thereafter, generalist, specialist, and advanced readers might consider surveying more specific areas. "Climate change" (Matthew J. Hoffmann, Chapter 47), "Sustainable development governance" (Roger A. Coate, Chapter 48), and "Global energy governance" (Harald Heubaum, Chapter 49) combine to flesh out more fully key issues behind the governance of the environment. "Regional development banks" (Jonathan R. Strand, Chapter 46) and "Poverty reduction" (David Hulme and Oliver Turner, Chapter 50) add further color to the global governance of development. "Food and hunger" (Jennifer Clapp, Chapter 51), "Global health governance" (Sophie Harman,

Chapter 52), "Refugees and migrants" (Khalid Koser, Chapter 53), and "Global governance of the Internet" (Madeline Carr, Chapter 54) provide further insight into the precariousness of the human condition and the global efforts seeking to improve it.

Governing the economic and social world: Chapter synopses

Bessma Momani begins this final part of the book with an exploration in Chapter 42 of the changing role of the IMF as the centerpoint of "Global financial governance." She notes how its role has been transformed over its almost seventy-five-year existence from macroeconomic assistant and exchange-rate stabilizer to global financial governor. She also details the effects of this transformation on changing the economic complexion of borrowing and lending states alike—with the economies of the latter often being much more congruous with global economic orthodoxy than the former because of IMF intervention. Momani also spells out the pressing need for more dramatic reform of the institution itself and the global financial system to reflect changing economic geography.

Bernard Hoekman continues to fill in the story of the triumvirate at the heart of global economic governance with his exploration, in Chapter 43, of the WTO as the centerpiece of "Global trade governance." He details the evolution of the multilateral trading system from General Agreement on Tariffs and Trade (GATT) to the 1995 creation of the WTO; he explores its key features; he examines the principal debates in, and the thorny nature of, global trade governance; and he identifies issues that are at the heart of the contestation over further multilateral trade liberalization and the failure of the WTO's last round of talks, the Doha round.

Global financial and trade governance, while arenas populated by a range of actors, are most easily identified with a core institution—the IMF and WTO, respectively. "Global development governance" also has a comparable core institution—the World Bank—but it is also an arena that is more heavily populated and has a range of other central actors, including but not limited to the UN Development Programme (UNDP) and UN development system, the Organisation for Economic Co-operation and Development (OECD), regional development banks, major national aid agencies such as USAID and the UK's Department for International Development (DfID), and such large nongovernmental organizations as BRAC, Oxfam, and Care International. In Chapter 44, Katherine Marshall guides readers through this densely populated realm of "Global development governance," exploring, among other things, the features and functions of key institutions, highlighting pressing issues, and setting global development efforts in their appropriate historical context. She also examines the tensions underpinning efforts to renew global development "promises" after the 2015 expiry of the Millennium Development Goals (MDGs) and their replacement with the Sustainable Development Goals (SDGs) to fix the UN's agenda until 2030.

In Chapter 45, Elizabeth R. DeSombre and Angelina Li confront an equally diverse constellation of actors in their exploration of "Global environmental governance." They begin with an examination of the history of global environmental governance, locating its emergence in conservation agreements and global *ad hoc* conferences beginning with the Stockholm gathering in 1972. DeSombre and Li then consider the principal institutions at the heart of the contemporary global governance of the human environment that we actually have, before looking at the role of non-state actors, key debates, and emerging issues. The promising yet uncertain future for the December 2015 Paris Agreement provides a *Leitmotif*.

Jonathan R. Strand completes the book's exploration of the major intergovernmental aspects of global economic and social governance with an examination, in Chapter 46, of "Regional development banks and global governance." They are often miscast as mini-World Banks, and Strand shows the diverse histories, roles, and operating principles that these relatively hidden but crucial intergovernmental actors play in shaping development outside of the Western European and North American core. Among many insights, he shows the utility of comparing and contrasting the different approaches to development that each of the regional development banks has, as well as situating and contrasting them in relationship to the major sub-regional development banks.

The remaining chapters in the book track global governance as it is manifest in distinct policy areas. In Chapters 47, 48, and 49, Matthew J. Hoffmann, Roger A. Coate, and Harald Heubaum add further color to the various shades of global environmental governance. Hoffmann deals specifically with "Climate change," setting out the urgency of the problem, detailing the almost comic (as well as tragic) fashion with which it has been dealt at the global level while also pointing out more hopeful initiatives and setting out the key debates and future scenarios. Coate's task is different. He explores the coming together of two distinct and sometimes conflicting ideas—about the imperative to conserve the human environment for future generations, and to pursue economic and social development for the current generation—to become the foundation on which all human industry and activity ought to take place, "Sustainable development governance." He includes the pursuit of the MDGs and SDGs as part of his story. Heubaum explores "Global energy governance," an important component of the environmental puzzle that was absent from the first edition but provides an essential input here. Alternative sources of energy and the evolving views of energy producing countries and firms are part of his analysis. All three contributors emphasize the role of various institutions in coming together to create and nourish a distinct concept; they also concentrate on the political underpinnings of past and current debates and speculate about the future.

In Chapters 50 and 51, David Hulme and Oliver Turner examine "Poverty reduction" and Jennifer Clapp "Food and hunger" to help reveal still other crucial dimensions of the global governance of development. Both chapters deal with destitution, and both have as a central concern the need to redouble efforts to address entrenched and enduring poverty and the precarious existence of an unacceptably large number of the globe's denizens. Hulme and Turner explore the problem of global poverty, examining historical efforts targeted at its reduction—including such laudable but problematic global initiatives as the MDGs and SDGs—along with where and why it persists, and debates about how it might be reduced and who is involved in governance initiatives designed to bring about its alleviation. Likewise, Clapp maps out the extent of the global food problem, illustrating how food insecurity persists and is growing for sections of the world's population. She covers, among other things, the role of financialization in the production of greater precarity, the reforms that have been put in place but also those areas wherein action is urgently required, and what the future of alleviating global hunger holds.

In Chapters 52 and 53, Sophie Harman examines "Global health" and Khalid Koser "Refugees and migrants." These two contributors further examine additional issues of precarity and efforts to mitigate their most egregious manifestations. Harman argues that efforts to address pressing health concerns have been in place since the nineteenth-century beginning of the modern system of IO and global governance. While this ensures a jumpstart of sorts for public health at the global level, problems persist that undermine the capacity of the existing apparatus to eliminate human ill health at a time when the knowledge and resources exist but when the international community of states has been unable or unwilling to apply that knowledge and those resources appropriately. Koser explores the existing institutional architecture for dealing with the insecurities arising from the pull of economic migration but mainly the push of war and violence that result in forced migration. He sets out key debates and emerging issues that have a heavy bearing on migrants and refugees (including the looming challenges posed by climate change), and considers the prospects for a more formal union between the refugee and migration regimes.

This part—and the book—ends with a topic that was absent from the first edition but could not be ignored this time, namely "Global governance and the Internet." In addition to the obvious benefits of communications technologies, in Chapter 54, Madeline Carr also points to a different kind of precariousness in the dependence of modern societies for their guaranteed smooth functioning on computer networks. Hence, rapid technological advances and concrete threats to international peace and security have pushed this formerly somewhat esoteric topic closer to the top of the international security agenda as well as being essential to a discussion of governing the economic and social world. Yet, it is not only that the efforts have been applied to govern the Internet that matters. It is also how the Internet has been used as a device of governance itself that shapes a measure of world order.

Where to now?

What the chapters in this part, as well as in the volume as a whole, show is the multiple actors, institutions, and mechanisms at work in contemporary global governance. We also see some problematic aspects along with those areas that represent genuine achievements in making the world a more peaceable place. The most visible elements of this picture are international organizations, and precisely their visibility draws attention and the lion's share of criticism. Yet, what we also observe is a host of other actors and networks that are part of the problem as well as of possible solutions.

Global financial governance

Bessma Momani

From its creation in July 1944, the International Monetary Fund's (IMF) role was one of observer and functionary in the international economic system. However, with the onset of the world debt crisis, the fall of the Soviet Union, and the European financial crisis, the IMF's role as crisis manager deepened. Moreover, as the world has continued to experience economic and political crises, the IMF further institutionalized its influence in governing the global economy. It is during this period of turmoil that the IMF emerged as an institution tasked with striking the delicate balance between financing and adjustment and acting as a provider of economic policy norms.

Particularly in the aftermath of the 2008 global financial crisis, which witnessed the collapse of financial institutions, prolonged downturns in world markets, and the massive bailouts of banks and companies by national governments, the deepening institutionalization of the IMF manifested itself in its movement from international organization (the IMF as a lender of last resort) to global financial governor (the IMF as an organization capable of governing the world economy) given the need to coordinate economic reform to bring about enhanced worldwide macroeconomic growth. This new period in its history will most likely come to be viewed as one in which it has responded to great criticism and performed its pivotal role as a norm-setting crisis manager. The direction the G-20 chooses to set for the IMF will lay the groundwork for the institution's relevance within the global financial architecture in the coming decades.

The chapter begins with an overview of the history of the IMF. It then moves on to an in-depth discussion of current debates regarding the organization's expanding global role before considering the key criticisms and challenges it faces today, as well as stakeholders' attempts to push reforms to improve its legitimacy. The chapter concludes that without continued reforms, the IMF will struggle to fulfill its mandate, to the detriment of global economic growth and financial stability.

IMF: From Bretton Woods to crisis manager

This section provides an overview of the history of the IMF, and a breakdown of its basic governing structure as well as the organization's evolution from a post-war institution to its current and often controversial role as global financial crisis manager.

In response to the Great Depression of the 1930s and the calamities of World War II, the international community of states devised the IMF and the International Bank for Reconstruction and Development (IBRD, or the World Bank) at the 1944 Bretton Woods Conference in New Hampshire. The conference arose from the need to create a system of monetary exchange and financial relations that would prevent crises like those that had rocked the industrialized world in the post-World War I period from happening again. In this new system of fixed exchange rates, world currencies were adjusted to match—or became "pegged to"—the value of gold to protect against market fluctuations. The IMF was imbued with the power to intervene in economic policy when a country could not maintain its balance of payments.

The highest ranking body in the IMF is its Board of Governors, comprising one governor (typically the head of a central bank or a finance minister) and one alternative governor from each member country. The Board of Governors controls the admittance of new members into the IMF and the withdrawal of existing members. It also retains the right to amend the IMF's Articles of Agreement and By-Laws, as well as the right to approve quota increases and allocations of Special Drawing Rights (see below). The Board of Governors is advised by the institution's Development Committee and the International Monetary Financial Committee.

With its twenty-four members, the IMF's Executive Board is responsible for the day-to-day workings of the Fund, for example, overseeing policy relevant to global economic issues. The Executive Board represents all 189 member states, most of which are grouped into constituencies of four or more. Larger states, in particular China and the United States, have their own seats on the Executive Board. Executive Board decisions are made by consensus, but there are times when formal votes are taken, after which a report summary of the decision is issued.

The IMF operates on a quota system, which is key to the management of the Fund's financial resources. Member countries are each assigned a quota determined by their relative position in the world economy—that is, countries that join the IMF are assigned a quota in the same range as the existing members with similar economic traits (i.e., size). This quota, in turn, determines a member country's maximum financial commitment to the IMF and its access to IMF funds. Quotas are denominated—or expressed in—Special Drawing Rights (SDRs), the IMF's unit of account through which a country may obtain currency via the voluntary exchange of SDRs between members, or an IMF designation through which member states with strong external positions are directed to purchase SDRs from those with weaker positions. IMF quotas are an important factor in determining a member state's voting power in IMF decisions, with votes being made up of basic votes plus an additional vote for each SDR 100,000 of quota that each member possesses.

The IMF quota formula used to assess a member's position comprises the following criteria: A weighted average of that country's gross domestic product (fifty percent),[1] degree of openness (thirty percent), its economic variability (fifteen percent), and its international reserves (five percent). Currently—with its quota of SDR 82.99bn (about $113 billion)—the United States remains the IMF's largest member, while the smallest, with a current quota of SDR 2.5 million (about $3.4million), is Tuvalu.

With forty-four countries present at Bretton Woods, the decision to establish the IMF and World Bank was an achievement of functionalist cooperation. The IMF, as designed by British economist John Maynard Keynes and US economist Harry Dexter White, was crafted to ensure the conditions necessary for stability and growth in the global economy, which, according to Keynes, would help foster a more peaceful and prosperous world. However, the two organizations were relatively ineffective and ceremonial. The World Bank, with its mandate to provide loans to countries for development projects, was the busier organization, assisting in the rebuilding of war-torn Europe.

Things changed for the IMF in the late 1950s with the return to the free exchange of local and foreign currencies in Western Europe (an exchange otherwise known as current account convertibility), and in the 1960s as the Fund responded to fluctuations in global commodity prices with short-term loans for IMF members from the industrialized world. In 1971, when US President Richard Nixon announced the abandonment of the gold standard—the monetary standard established through which world currencies could be exchanged for the fixed rate of gold—it seemed as though the collapse of the Bretton Woods system would severely damage the IMF's organizational strength. Yet, Nixon's announcement had the unintended consequence of creating a new role for the IMF which strengthened its involvement in the global economy. Coupled with an energy crisis in the early 1970s and rising commodity prices, the end of the gold standard turned the IMF's attention away from assisting industrialized developed states and toward short-term lending to developing countries. Moreover, the increasing globalization of capital during this time pushed the IMF to shift from managing small balance-of-payment crises to large and expectations-dependent capital account driven crises.

With the threat of Mexico's bankruptcy in 1982, the world's attention focused on assisting developing countries to deal with the debt crisis. Here, the IMF relished its newfound purpose of providing structural reform advice to developing countries. With rescue packages and staff trying to protect crisis-prone countries from gyrations in the global economy, the IMF, and to a lesser extent the World Bank, were labeled as promoters of the "Washington Consensus" (1989), a set of ten policy reforms designed to fix ailing economies in the developing world (see Table 42.1). These policies were no doubt influenced by neoliberal ideas about the importance of markets, criticism of statist policies adopted by developing countries, and the value of individual entrepreneurship.

Table 42.1 The ten policies of the Washington Consensus

Policy	Content
Fiscal discipline	Strict criteria should be implemented to avoid large budget deficits relative to GDP
Reordering public expenditure priorities	Moving away from subsidies and government administration towards neglected fields that promise high economic returns
Tax reform	Broadening the tax base and cutting marginal tax rates
Liberalizing interest rates	Allowing interest rates to be determined by the market
Ensuring competitive exchange rates	Allowing interest rates to induce economic growth
Trade liberalization	Including the elimination of trade protectionism and the encouragement of low tariffs
Liberalization of inward foreign direct investment (FDI)	Via the reduction of FDI barriers
Privatization	Including the privatization of state enterprises
Deregulation	Elimination of regulations that restrict the entry of new firms or those that impede financial competition, with exceptions in the areas of safety, environment, and finance
Property rights	Enhanced legal security for property rights and a reduced role of the state in such matters

Source: Data inspired by John Williamson, "Speeches, Testimony, Papers: Did the Washington Consensus Fail?," *Institute for International Economics* (2002).

In the mid-1980s, as it became increasingly clear that the information gaps in the globalized economic system created inherited vulnerabilities, the IMF also played a key role in promoting policy coordination among developed countries' currencies and exchange rate systems. The Plaza Accord (1985), the Louvre Accord (1987), and the Brady Plan (1989) were key moments of international negotiation that depended on IMF intervention. This trend continued as the fall of the Soviet Union in 1991 ushered in new members to the liberal global economy. Here, the IMF found its greatest role yet: Reengineering socialist countries into liberal market-based economies. During this time, as tectonic shifts in the global economy solidified, the Fund embraced its influence as a provider of global ideas in times of crisis.

Financial crises continued to rock the international economy throughout the 1990s and 2000s. The interconnected nature of the global economy produced financial attacks in many Asian countries that spread to Russia, Brazil, Argentina, and Turkey. Of these, the 1997–1998 Asian Financial Crisis—in which shortages of foreign exchange, falling currency values, and waning investor confidence in countries such as Thailand, Indonesia, and South Korea threatened to spread to economies the world over—played the greatest role in stoking fears of worldwide economic meltdown, and underscored the need for a new approach to global financial management. The IMF responded with financial resources and its now infamous and often detested economic advice, or "conditionality." The painful adjustment caused by IMF conditionality came under the scrutiny of many IMF member governments. In particular, the IMF and the World Bank were criticized for their continued involvement in heavily indebted poor countries (HIPCs), and their repeated recycling of debt in these countries. As nongovernmental organizations (NGOs) and civil society stepped up global campaigns in industrial countries in the mid-2000s regarding debt recycling and their low chance of debt repayment, the global effort toward debt forgiveness mounted for HIPCs.

IMF criticism also came from emerging market economies. These economies had been subjected to IMF conditionality in past decades and now called for reform. Emerging market economies were emboldened in the 2000s as the global economic wealth shifted from the "West to the rest." The call for internal governance changes to reflect this shift in global economic wealth persisted, and soon the IMF found itself in an existential crisis: The developed economies, which had most of the IMF's decision-making power, were increasingly cash strapped and incapable of increasing IMF liquidity. Meanwhile, capital-surplus countries of the emerging market economies, especially in Asia, distanced themselves from the IMF and began self-insuring against speculative currency attacks (increased market volatility caused by the sudden acquisition of currency by previously inactive investors) by swelling their own currency reserves.

In the eyes of emerging market economies, this global imbalance of savings was now coupled with the loss of IMF legitimacy as well as with attempts by developed economies to preserve their remaining power in global economic governance. Moreover, it was during this period of IMF decline that dynamic emerging economies began to consider regional alternatives to the Fund. The IMF was deemed by influential actors as irrelevant. At one point in the mid-2000s, there were even fears that the interest earned on IMF lending would no longer cover its operational costs. The IMF's apparent irrelevancy was further emphasized by many countries' abilities to bypass the organization and raise funds on capital markets without having to comply with IMF conditionality. Financial policies and reform efforts previously funded by it, such as emergency financing to correct trade imbalances, could now be funded by a country's ability to attract global investment, thus eliminating the need to borrow from the IMF.

This crisis of confidence in the IMF was, however, short lived. The international financial crisis of 2007–2008 reenergized the IMF as the provider of ideas, policy coordination, surveillance, and catalytic financing. Moreover, the newly established G-20 reaffirmed the central place of the IMF in governing the global economy. Originally gathered in 1999 as a meeting of finance ministers from the world's most powerful states (i.e., United States, China, and Germany), the G-20 was convened in Washington as a leader's summit during the onset of the 2008 financial crisis by US President George W. Bush, and today continues its work of coordinating global regulatory reform and economic stimulus. The G-20 recognized the need for improved global economic surveillance, and it reinvigorated the IMF with an expanded mandate, new resources, and a renewed governance reform agenda. It was asked to facilitate the coordination of the macroeconomic policies of the world's preeminent economies, and the accountability of these countries to agree on norms and policy commitments. Further, the IMF extended its surveillance role in developed countries, in accordance with the newly empowered Financial Stability Board via its Financial Sector Assessment Program.

The institutionalization of the IMF emboldened it to monitor the pulse of the global economic system. Its once backseat role in observing the workings of the global economy has developed into that of a rule-making and norm-setting crisis manager entrusted with promoting economic growth, foreseeing global economic instability, and being a first responder to global economic crises.

Ongoing debates

With great power, however, comes immense responsibility, and the IMF is currently grappling with a number of critical issues that may influence its current role and mandate. The IMF must balance the needs of member states, best practices found in the economic discipline, and the hard economic realities that challenge global economic stability. At the forefront of current debates facing the IMF are issues of capital account liberalization and flows; surveillance and crisis prevention; and transparency and its relationship with civil society. This section reviews each of these debates.

Capital liberalization—the process whereby government regulation on inflows and outflows of capital is relaxed or eliminated in order to stimulate economic growth—has become prevalent in the globalized market economy. With the IMF at the helm of the global norm-setting system, states have been advised to liberalize the entry and exit of capital to spur savings, promote investment, and diversify economic growth. Yet, the question remains: How to effectively govern capital flows given their lack of regulation and governance? As Rawi Abdelal argues, a tension existed, first, between US views of *ad hoc* globalization that preferred to see private markets and actors shaping the future course of financialization (White's legacy) and, second, the European view of entrusting the IMF and other international organizations with managing the influx of capital in globalized financial systems (Keynes' legacy).[2]

For analysts and policymakers, the global financial system became more complex and difficult to navigate. Nonetheless, despite the rising influence of private market actors, the IMF remained the locus of debate on the worthiness of capital controls and on mapping the ebbs and flows of capital. With each subsequent financial crisis, the IMF increasingly became the central node of managing capital flows and of providing solutions to the debilitating effects of "hot money" (capital that is transferred regularly between financial institutions by investors seeking to maximize interest from short-term gains) as well as financial contagion (the transition of financial shocks and crises from one economy to another). With the rise of global imbalances, the Fund was also tasked with coordinating macroeconomic and exchange-rate policy between the world's key economies in an attempt to unwind potentially destabilizing imbalances.[3] Its failure to do so is still being felt today.

In short, the growth in IMF access to data on capital flows and to policymakers and market actors has increased its role in governing capital flows. Ironically, however, the pressure to liberalize capital came, in part, from the IMF itself: In its loan conditionality with developing countries and emerging market economies, and, to a lesser extent, from the dominant neoliberal economic discipline and its emphasis on free markets and trade liberalization. Moreover, as the economic crises of the late 1990s and 2000s continued to cripple countries experiencing rapid capital outflows and massive capital inflows of "hot money," the IMF attempted to take a middle road approach. Yet, there is a feeling that the IMF still prefers to endorse the concept of capital liberalization, even for countries in which such measures may not be appropriate, and that it only grudgingly accepts government attempts to regulate capital flows if the latter can withstand IMF pressure.[4]

Surveillance and crisis prevention are frequently viewed as areas that are the cornerstone of IMF work. IMF members are obliged to meet the terms of its Articles of Agreement, which require IMF staff surveillance annually and periodically in the interest of preventing crises, limiting crisis spillover, and advising corrective measures to promote global economic growth and financial stability. The IMF conducts consultations with all its members and, with their consent, releases bilateral surveillance reports to the public. Moreover, the IMF composes regional surveillance reports, called *Regional Outlooks*, which are meant to provide an integrated snapshot of regional economic dynamics. Last, the IMF produces a global report, the *World Outlook*, which attempts to assess the opportunities and challenges of the global economy.

For the IMF, the work of surveillance and crisis prevention is tremendous and not without difficulty. Yet, despite the abundance of information that staff have at their disposal, the IMF has effectively failed to predict and warn of looming crises. In some cases, small warning bells had rung, but these failed to alert economic systems in time to cope with often drastic changes of events. Again, in failing to predict imminent crises through its surveillance mechanisms, the legitimacy of the IMF is undermined.

Its surveillance function and role in global financial governance have also been confined by political capture. The challenge, historically, has been that advanced industrial economies have often ignored IMF surveillance advice, while weaker, indebted countries seeking funding were mandated to adjust their policies to suit conditions. Powerful IMF members also remain the primary benefactors of the organization, given their contribution of the largest share of financial deposits to the Fund. Moreover, these members provide the largest national contingency of IMF staff and the strongest ideological support for its paradigms. Most importantly, they hold the greatest decision-making weight on the Executive Board, although the entrenchment of these powerful IMF players has recently been put to the test, and not all may emerge unscathed (discussed below).

With the onset of the international financial crisis in 2008, it became clear that the advanced industrial economies were not as stable as previously thought. Similarly, it became apparent that financial markets were subject to market failures to an extent not previously believed. More importantly, core industrial states' policies had enormous ramifications on other economies such that contagion became a reality of globalized banking and financial markets. Advanced economies were now seen as "systemically important" countries that could potentially undermine the global economy, and therefore, despite not being traditional IMF borrowers, many argued that these economies should not escape oversight. To address these concerns, the G-20 strengthened the IMF surveillance mechanism by requiring all members to complete Financial Sector Assessment Programs (FSAPs), supervised by the IMF. The G-20 also created the Financial Stability Board (FSB) to coordinate with IMF advice on weaknesses in the financial, banking, and economic system. While strengthening surveillance has been a process in the making, the 2008 financial crisis cemented the necessity for the Fund's continued presence on the global economic scene, working in coordination with other multilateral organizations to ensure a systemic approach to governing the flow of capital, banking systems, and exchange-rate policies.

Finally, the IMF is grappling with determining how deeply it should engage with member states. While it is accountable to governments, it must also be sensitive to the fact that state governments ought to be accountable to their people. Although such accusations seem exaggerated, the Fund has been repeatedly criticized for dealing with corrupt and undemocratic governments. Indeed, many of the IMF's borrowing clients were also autocratic regimes, especially from the 1970s to the 1990s. It soon realized that member governments that failed to implement its policies were also unable to implement IMF programs for lack of country ownership. This meant that many of these members were in perpetual IMF loan rescheduling cycles and remained heavily indebted. As more countries within the global community, influenced by NGOs and civil societies, realized that debt relief for its poorest members could be an opportunity to call for political accountability, the IMF began calling for good global governance and applying its own advice to internal good governance and corporate best practices.[5]

Moreover, IMF calls for transparency in member states pushed civil society to call for transparency in dealings with member states. The IMF has responded by opening its doors to civil society at its annual meetings, in its support for the Independent Evaluation Office (an internal, but independent watchdog), and in its regular consultation with civil society in member countries on its relationship with member states. While some critics argue that this is window dressing, at the very least it can be said that the IMF is changing its access to information policies and its rhetoric on the role of civil society in order to enhance its accountability measures; arguably its interactions with borrowing states have expanded to include a variety of new actors or new working relationships with them. These include parliamentarians, NGOs, media, academics, think tanks, and labor organizations.[6]

Key criticisms and emerging issues

This section discusses the key criticisms and emerging issues currently facing the IMF, all of which involve the central problems with efforts to achieve effective global financial governance: How should the IMF reform in order to keep pace with the changing realities of the global economic system? And how should the Fund contend with the proliferation of actors and sites of authority that have emerged on the global scene?

As global economic power has shifted from the industrialized Group of Seven (G-7)[7] toward the emerging market economies—including Brazil, Russia, India, and China (the BRICs and sometimes including South Africa, or the BRICS) and expanded membership of the G-20—the question of how to reform the IMF such that it better reflects this shift in global economic power is a key concern of stakeholders.

This question raises another tension evident in the IMF itself—namely, that even as the organization's power as a key knowledge actor increases in the realm of global economic governance, it is also generating ideas on policies that are no longer under the complete control of its powerful member states.

One key criticism concerns its close relationship with certain member states, despite more recent attempts at accountability and transparency. Shortly after its inception, the G-20 encouraged the IMF to meet the short-term liquidity needs of the emerging market economies with a fast disbursing credit line that had no conditionality attached. In response, the Fund created a new flexible credit line (FCL) and the new precautionary credit line (PCL) to provide uncapped access to IMF resources to countries that had been preapproved for financing. Much like when countries affected by the 1997 Asian crisis resorted to using contacts in the US Treasury Department to pressure the IMF to expedite its loan process, the countries seeking FCL arrangement were, notably, US geopolitical allies.

Moreover, while the IMF should be commended for reacting quickly to the 2008 international financial crisis with the FCL and PCL, the question remains as to whether the IMF has learned from its past failures. Specifically, throughout the Asian crisis, it failed to instill confidence in Asian economies and precipitated the crisis further via its strict conditionality requirements. Indeed, many Asian countries have asked the IMF to acknowledge its past failure in Asia as an important confidence-building measure toward the organization's reform. This apology, however, was never formally made, although assessing the needs of Asian countries and renewing their good faith in the IMF should be a top priority given its mandate of global financial governance. As it stands, the question of whether the damage done is so deep that only a regional fund will meet the needs of the Asian countries—for example the Chiang Mai initiative—remains an open one.

In addition to new credit lines, the IMF was also tasked with coordinating the newly transformed FSB. By drawing on its universal membership, the IMF helped the FSB to expand its membership base to include the G-20. Unlike the IMF, the FSB lacks an organizational structure and a sizeable support staff. However, the FSB's interaction with senior policymakers and regulatory supervisors serves as part of a useful feedback loop into IMF surveillance exercises, including the above-mentioned *World Economic Outlook* and *Regional Economic Outlook* reports, and bilateral Article IV Consultations. Nonetheless, noting the parallels between FSB and IMF functions, the G-20 has asked both organizations to promote further cooperation and interorganizational communication. The FSB and the IMF could then, for example, work to develop early warning exercises against financial systemic risk and develop a regulatory standard that would keep financial institutions in check. We now turn to an in-depth discussion of the IMF's expanding mandates.

Perhaps the greatest endorsement of increased institutionalization of its mandate occurred when the G-20 entrusted the IMF with the role of determining whether sound macroeconomic policies were being followed by its members, and "naming and shaming" those who failed to implement such standards in order to achieve compliance. Expanding on the IMF's traditional surveillance function, the G-20 proposed a Framework for Strong, Sustainable, and Balanced Growth. This loose agreement gave the IMF an added hand in independently intervening in countries that put the international economic system at risk by mismanaging their economic policies. To operationalize the framework, the G-20 created the Mutual Assessment Process (MAP)—an innovative part peer-review, part multilateral surveillance governance mechanism. IMF staff were tasked with helping the MAP to deepen global macroeconomic policy coordination. This process was designed to bypass the IMF's Executive Board to prevent an added layer of politicization of the staff's research and recommendations, and represents a significant increase in the IMF's independence and authority.

Following this move for G-20 cooperation on shared policy objectives and medium-term policy frameworks, G-20 leaders also allowed IMF staff to assess countries' progress against an agreed-upon set of "indicative guidelines."[8] Moreover, G-20 members must now submit themselves to the IMF–World Bank FSAP, a move that expands existing FSAP purview to encompass all of the G-20, notably the United States, which prior to the international financial crisis had not accepted FSAP reviews.

Given its renewed mandates, the international community of states is trusting that the IMF will play its intended role as a "ruthless truth-teller," in the words of John Maynard Keynes. Yet, this arrangement is problematic to say the least. For example, while G-20 and IMF staff agreed in April 2011 to set policy targets that members could strive for and that the IMF could assess and monitor, they remained shielded from the public and market actors such that there was no external monitoring of the process. Thus, the politicization of the IMF remains an issue.

The second means of reinvigorating the IMF came with a series of decisions beginning in 2009 to drastically increase the Fund's lending capacity. The first of these was a one-time allotment of SDR 250bn—by far the largest ever such allotment—designed to boost global liquidity at a time of severe malfunctioning in global money markets. The G-20 and other prominent economies also moved to bolster the Fund's short-term lending capacity by agreeing to an expanded New Agreement to Borrow (NAB). Finally, in April 2012 the G-20 announced its commitment to add an additional SDR 277 billion to the IMF's capital structure. It is important to note, however, that throughout this process of increased lending capacity, the BRICs have been reticent about providing funds directly into the IMF coffers without first receiving guarantees of meaningful voice and governance reforms.

Given that among the G-20 the consensus has been to keep IMF quotas as a reflection of contribution to the world economy, the case remained that rising economic powers were still underrepresented in quota strength and, therefore, in political strength. IMF governance reform therefore involved reallocating quotas to give rising powers more decision-making power by reconfiguring the Executive Board. Voice and governance reforms began in 2008 with the decision to implement quota increases for fifty-four emerging economies, as well as reforms aimed at improving the participation of low-income countries in the Fund's decision-making process.

However, unsatisfied by such modest gains, the BRIC nations demanded that any further expansion of IMF resources be tied to additional governance reform. For example, China's assistant finance minister, Zhu Guangyao, recommended rebalancing the IMF by transferring voting weight from the developed countries (which had fifty-seven percent of voting rights at the IMF and fifty-six percent of voting rights at the World Bank) to developing countries (which had forty-three percent and forty-four percent of voting rights at the IMF and World Bank, respectively). The BRICs also proposed that the IMF transfer seven percent of traditional powers' quota share to the emerging powers. In response, the G-20 offered a shift of six percent of quotas from overrepresented countries to underrepresented countries—in effect setting in motion a movement of quotas from the European countries to the emerging economies.

More recent IMF reforms have also been put in place to help remedy the Fund's problematic representation. In December 2015, the US Congress authorized the 2010 IMF quota and governance reforms, conditions for which were met in January 2016. According to IMF Managing Director Christine Lagarde, the implementation of these reforms will help create "[a] more representative, modern IMF."[9]

These reforms include: Increasing the quotas of all IMF members via an increase of the Fund's quota resources (from SDR 477 billion to SDR 238.5 billion); shifting more than six percent of quota shares from overrepresented to underrepresented members and emerging market and developing countries; a commitment by advanced European countries to reduce their combined Executive Board representation by two chairs; a commitment by the IMF to protect the voting power and voting shares of its poorest members; and placing the BRICs among the IMF's largest, top ten members (along with the United States, Japan, France, Germany, Italy, and the United Kingdom). Notably, IMF Executive Board seats will now be elected by IMF member countries, rather than following the previous system in which five Executive Board states were appointed by IMF members with the five largest quotas.[10]

The new dynamic created by this shift in IMF governance warrants future research as its impact remains to be seen. Nevertheless, reforming the IMF Executive Board and the underlying quota system seems likely to help improve IMF legitimacy and, ultimately, global financial governance.

Conclusion

In the aftermath of the worst global economic downturn since the Great Depression, the IMF has been restored to its previous position as the jewel in the crown in the international financial architecture. Moving forward, the health of the international monetary system and the global economy will be tied to the effectiveness of the public goods provision provided by the G-20: The promotion of enhanced public goods, including environmental protection, technological development, and international security. Effectiveness will, in turn, be tied to the legitimacy of the institution that the G-20 relies most heavily on to generate good governance in dealing with crises and promoting macro-economic stability: The IMF.

This chapter has reviewed the key historical and contemporary challenges faced by the IMF. The institution's legitimacy has ebbed and flowed as it has dealt with persistent critiques of its policy prescriptions, ideological leanings, and internal governance practices—critiques that today are being made by an ever broadening constituency of stakeholders. The IMF has finally begun to address these critiques and has made efforts to reform itself. However, much remains to be done. Sustained reform is a necessity; and if history is any guide, the IMF will continue to institutionalize its role in governing the global economic system.

At the same time, as its authoritative power and its role as a key knowledge actor in global economic governance increase, many IMF ideas on policies can no longer be controlled by powerful member states. The recent empowerment of IMF staff through the G-20 MAP—a framework through which G-20 members seek to identify, evaluate, and craft policy so that shared objectives for economic governance can be implemented—is an important example. The policy and political outcomes of an increasingly autonomous IMF and a more complex global system of power remain to be seen and merit greater academic study. This chapter has attempted a preliminary start to such a project.

Additional reading

Mark Copelovitch, *The International Monetary Fund in the Global Economy: Banks, Bonds, and Bailouts* (Cambridge: Cambridge University Press, 2010).

Reuben Lamdany and Leonardo Maritnez-Diaz, *Studies of IMF Governance: A Compendium* (Washington, DC: International Monetary Fund, 2009).

Bessma Momani and Mark Hibben, *What's Wrong with the IMF and How to Fix It* (Cambridge: Polity Press, 2017).

Susan Park and Antje Vetterlein, eds., *Owning Development: Creating Global Policy Norms in the IMF and the World Bank* (Cambridge: Cambridge University Press, 2010).

James R. Vreeland, *The International Monetary Fund: Politics of Conditional Lending* (New York: Routledge, 2007).

Ngaire Woods, *The Globalizers: The IMF, World Banks and Their Borrowers* (Ithaca, NY: Cornell University Press, 2006).

Notes

1 With GDP measured as a blend of a member country's market exchange rates (sixty percent) and its purchasing power parity exchange rates (forty percent), defined as exchange rates that take into account the prices of goods in each country's economy in order to obtain prices unaffected by financial market fluctuations.

2 Rawi Abdelal, *Capital Rules: The Construction of Global Finance* (Boston, MA: Harvard University Press, 2007).

3 Mark Copelovitch, *The International Monetary Fund in the Global Economy: Banks, Bonds and Bailouts* (Cambridge: Cambridge University Press, 2010).

4 Pardee Center, *Regulating Global Capital Flows for Long-run Development* (Boston, MA: Boston University Press, 2012).

5 Ngaire Woods, "Making the IMF and the World Bank More Accountable," *International Affairs* no. 77 (2001): 83–100.

6 Jan Aart Scholte, *Building Global Democracy? Civil Society and Accountable Global Governance* (Cambridge: Cambridge University Press, 2011).

7 Or G-7, comprised of finance ministers from the powerful industrialized nations of the United States, Japan, Germany, Britain, France, Canada, and Italy.

8 International Monetary Fund, *Review of the Fund's Involvement in the G20 Mutual Assessment Process* (Washington, DC: International Monetary Fund, 2011).

9 International Monetary Fund, *Press Release: IMF Managing Director Christine Lagarde Welcomes U.S. Congressional Approval of the 2010 Quota and Governance Reforms*, www.imf.org/external/np/sec/pr/2015/pr15573.htm.

10 Ibid.

CONTENTS

Global trade governance

Bernard Hoekman

The 1995 establishment of the World Trade Organization (WTO) was the capstone of a gradual process of global trade liberalization that started after World War II. Average tariffs for many countries in 1950 were in the twenty to thirty percent range, complemented by a wide variety of nontariff barriers (NTBs). As of 2015, the average level of import protection had dropped to about five to ten percent in most countries, reflecting a process of economic liberalization that accelerated in the 1980s. In conjunction with technological changes that greatly reduced trade costs—telecommunication advances, the Internet, containerization, and other improvements in logistics—these reforms led to a boom in world trade. The value of global exports of goods and services was some $21 trillion in 2015. Taking imports and exports together, the ratio of global trade to world output (measured as gross domestic product, GDP) was about fifty-three percent in 2015, up from thirty-nine percent in 1990.

The global trade regime played an important role in supporting globalization by providing a framework for countries to exchange trade policy commitments and establishing a mechanism to make these enforceable. The trade regime has proved to be quite effective in sustaining cooperation among members. The scope and coverage of policy disciplines expanded steadily from the creation of the General Agreement on Tariffs and Trade (GATT) in 1947, as did the membership. The dispute settlement mechanism has been particularly noteworthy: Over 500 disputes have been adjudicated since the establishment of the WTO in 1995, most of which resulted in the losing party bringing its measures into compliance. The regime proved resilient during the 2008 financial crisis; recourse to the type of protectionist policies that characterized the interwar period and the global recession of the late 1970s/early

1980s was limited. Some thirty countries have acceded to the WTO since 1995—including China and Russia.

Most observers agree that the WTO has been relatively effective in fostering transparency, and that the dispute settlement system has worked rather well. However, following the successful conclusion of the Uruguay Round in 1994, members proved unable to bring the Doha Development Round, launched in 2001, to closure. Efforts to include new disciplines on investment, public procurement, and competition policies failed, and the WTO has been subject to frequent criticism by a variety of civil society groups. Concerns were raised by developing country governments about the unbalanced nature of the Uruguay Round, which extended the trade regime into new areas such as intellectual property protection (including for medicines) and investment measures. Ministerial meetings of the WTO in Seattle (1999) and Cancún (2003) were accompanied by large demonstrations.[1] But business—a core constituency—also became less enamored with the WTO in the twenty-first century as it became clear that issues of concern to them could not be addressed. This helps explain why many governments increasingly pursued bilateral and regional trade agreements in the post-1995 period. Over 500 such agreements have been notified to the WTO, raising obvious questions regarding its efficacy and relevance.

This chapter starts with a brief summary of major milestones and features of the institutional framework governing global trade. It then discusses some of the key debates of the governance of the multilateral trade regime. And it outlines the major challenges and emerging issues that confront the WTO.

History and development of the trading system

The genesis of the multilateral trading system was the interwar experience of beggar-thy-neighbor protectionism and capital controls put in place by governments as they sought to stimulate domestic economic activity and employment. Following the adoption of the so-called Smoot–Hawley Tariff Act, which raised average US tariffs from thirty-eight to fifty-two percent, US trading partners imposed retaliatory trade restrictions. A domino effect resulted: As trade flows were diverted to other markets, protectionist measures were taken there, and further retaliation ensued. Even before World War II was over, political leaders sought to establish international institutions to reduce the probability of a repeat performance. New international organizations were created with a mandate to help manage international relations and monetary and exchange-rate policies—in the UN and the International Monetary Fund (IMF)—and to assist in financing reconstruction and promoting economic development—in the World Bank. An international organization was also envisaged to manage trade relations, the International Trade Organization (ITO). Greater trade was expected to support an increase in real incomes, and nondiscriminatory access to markets was expected to reduce the scope for political conflicts or trade disputes spilling over into other domains.[2]

The ITO Charter, negotiated immediately after the war, regulated trade in goods and commodity agreements, as well as subjects such as employment policy and restrictive business practices. In parallel to the ITO negotiations, a group of twenty-three countries—twelve developed and eleven developing—pursued negotiations on the GATT and an associated set of tariff reduction commitments. The GATT entered into force on January 1948, on a provisional basis, pending the conclusion and the entry into force of the ITO Charter. However, the ITO was never established, the result of the unwillingness of the US Congress to ratify the Charter. Thus, the only outcome of the trade negotiations was the GATT, which applied on a "provisional" basis for over forty years until it became part of the WTO in 1995. While formally never more than a treaty, the GATT gradually evolved into an international institution. Over time more countries acceded to the GATT, and the coverage of the treaty was expanded and modified. Some major milestones are noted in Table 43.1.

Table 43.1 From GATT to WTO: Key events

Date	Event
1947	Tariff negotiations between twenty-three founding parties to the GATT concluded
1948	GATT provisionally enters into force on 1 January 1948, pending ratification of the Havana Charter establishing an ITO
1950	China withdraws from GATT. The US Administration abandons efforts to seek Congressional ratification of the ITO
1960–61	Dillon Round of tariff negotiations
1962	Long-term Arrangement on Cotton Textiles agreed, permitting quota restrictions on exports of cotton textiles as an exception to GATT rules
1964–67	The Kennedy Round
1965	Part IV (on Trade and Development) is added to the GATT, establishing new guidelines for trade policies of—and towards—developing countries
1973–79	The Tokyo Round results in a set of "codes of conduct" on a variety of trade policy areas that countries could decide to sign on a voluntary basis
1986	The Uruguay Round is launched in Punta del Este, Uruguay
1993	Three years after the scheduled end of negotiations, the Uruguay Round is concluded on the basis of a "single undertaking" including new rules on services and intellectual property, and agreement to create a World Trade Organization
1995	The WTO enters into force on 1 January with 128 founding members
1997	Forty governments agree to eliminate tariffs on computer and telecommunication products on a most favored nation (MFN) basis (the Information Technology Agreement)
1999	Ministerial meeting in Seattle collapses amid large-scale demonstrations and fails to launch a new "Millennium" round
2001	The Doha Development Agenda round of negotiations is launched in Qatar
2003	The "mid-term" Ministerial review meeting in Cancún fails to agree to start negotiations on investment and competition policies and ends in disarray
2006	The Doha Round is declared to be in a state of suspension

(*continued*)

Table 43.1 Continued

Date	Event
2008	After a concerted effort to overcome the stalemate, Doha talks break down again
2013	Ministers conclude talks on the Agreement on Trade Facilitation—the first new set of multilateral disciplines negotiated under the WTO
2015	Agreement obtained at the Nairobi ministerial meeting to eliminate scheduled export subsidies Ministers formally recognize differences in views on continuing the Doha talks and the call by some members for new negotiation modalities Fifty signatories to the Information Technology Agreement commit to extend free trade to an additional set of IT products on a MFN basis

Source: Updated from Bernard Hoekman and Michel Kostecki, *The Political Economy of the World Trading System*, 3rd edn (Oxford: Oxford University Press, 2009) and the WTO website.

The Contracting Parties to the GATT conducted eight rounds of multilateral negotiations between 1947 and 1993. Up to the Kennedy Round, negotiators were essentially preoccupied with the reduction of tariff barriers. Starting in the mid-1960s, recurring negotiating rounds expanded the scope of the GATT to cover nontariff barriers (NTBs), such as antidumping measures, quantitative restrictions, and product standards. An Agreement on Technical Barriers to Trade was negotiated in the Tokyo Round (1979), followed by agreements on sanitary and phytosanitary measures, intellectual property rights, and measures affecting trade in services in the Uruguay Round (1993). The result has been a gradual extension of the trading system to cover a number of domestic policies that affected the conditions of competition prevailing on markets and that could impede "market access" abroad, even if the measures concerned did not necessarily aim at discriminating against foreign industries.

The evolution of the GATT/WTO is the result of political bargaining, with the terms of the bargain at any point in time influenced by both governmental and nongovernmental actors. Initially largely a tariff agreement, as average tariffs fell over time, and attention shifted to nontariff policies affecting trade, the set of interest groups/stakeholders expanded. Thus, the extension of the WTO to include agreements on services and intellectual property rights reflected the interests of industry groups in the countries of the Organisation for Economic Co-operation and Development (OECD)—telecom providers, banks, and pharmaceutical firms—to improve access to foreign markets for their products. The interest that these groups had in negotiating new disciplines allowed developing and other countries to demand a *quid pro quo* in areas that were important to them, including trade in agricultural products and textiles and clothing. These were sectors with above average levels of protection in many OECD countries because in the 1960s and 1970s they were to a large extent removed from the ambit of GATT rules and disciplines—reflecting not just the political power of the workers and farmers employed in these sectors in the industrial countries but also the negotiating strategies that were pursued by developing countries during that period. Rather than engage in reciprocal exchanges of liberalization commitments, developing countries as a group demanded special and differential treatment and less than full reciprocity. As a result, OECD countries had little incentive to remove high trade barriers in sectors of export interest to developing nations.[3]

For much of the GATT period (1947–1994), the United States acted as a hegemon, with limited concern for freeriding or noncooperative behavior by developing countries—which were mostly small players in the trading system.[4] The focus of rulemaking and negotiations revolved primarily around OECD nations, in particular the "Quad"—Canada, the European Community (EC; later European Union, EU), Japan, and the United States. This began to change in the late 1980s as a result of the growing economic significance of a number of developing countries in Asia and Latin America. An important development was the emergence of US unilateralism in the 1980s, as reflected in provisions such as Section 301 of the 1974/1988 US Trade Act, which required the US Trade Representative (USTR) to identify and potentially retaliate against countries that maintained policies that were detrimental to US exports, which was defined to include inadequate protection of intellectual property rights. While such exploitation of differences in size, or "market power," is an important feature of the operation of the trading system, the rapid increase in the national products of emerging market economies—most notably China—since the mid-1980s means that there are today more players in the WTO that can and will block efforts to push the system into a direction that they do not support. An illustration is the 2003 failure of EU and US efforts to obtain agreement to launch talks on WTO disciplines for investment, procurement, and competition policies.

Key features of the WTO

The WTO has five major functions: To facilitate the implementation, administration, and operation of the Agreement; to provide a forum for negotiations; to administer the Dispute Settlement Understanding; to administer the Trade Policy Review Mechanism; and to cooperate with the IMF and World Bank Group to achieve greater coherence in global economic policymaking.

Decision making in the WTO operates by consensus. Voting is technically possible but does not, in practice, occur. Consensus implies that any motion or decision can be blocked if any member objects. While, in principle, this ensures that no country can be steamrollered into accepting decisions or agreements it objects to—giving it leverage to seek either concessions to agree to a matter or to refuse to consent to a change in the rules of the game—in practice, the largest players carry more weight than do small ones. One way small countries seek to increase their weight in decision making is through coalitions. Examples include the G-20, an alliance that includes Brazil, China, and India, and the G-11, a group of developing countries that were active in the nonagricultural market access talks in the Doha Round.[5]

In negotiations the analogue to consensus is the single undertaking: "Nothing is agreed until everything is agreed," that is, the results of a multilateral round are treated as a package deal. Both the consensus principle and the single undertaking are practices, not formal rules. The consensus practice has a long history in the GATT/WTO, whereas the single undertaking was first employed successfully in the Uruguay Round and was central to the creation of the WTO—that is, the WTO was a package, take it all or leave it deal. The Doha round was conceived as a single undertaking, but could not be concluded as such. A number of WTO agreements foresee periodic negotiations to revisit and expand disciplines that do not entail package deals (cross-issue linkages). As discussed below, a number of standalone deals have been negotiated under WTO auspices and this approach may become more prevalent in the future.

The nondiscrimination principle—what in trade parlance is called most favored nation (MFN)—requires that any concession or commitment be accorded to all members. WTO members may not grant a subset of countries with which they have negotiated concessions better treatment than countries that have not offered such concessions. The only exceptions are if members conclude free trade agreements with each other or negotiate a so-called plurilateral agreement. The latter is a mechanism for a subset of WTO members to agree to specific disciplines that apply only to them, and need not apply the associated benefits to non-signatories. However, a plurilateral agreement can only be appended to the WTO on the basis of consensus (and unanimity if there is recourse to voting). Thus, the plurilateral option is conditional on the membership as a whole perceiving a proposed deal among a subset of members not being detrimental to their interests. To complicate matters further, a group of WTO members may agree to liberalize trade in a sector and apply this on a nondiscriminatory basis to all WTO members without requiring reciprocity. Plurilaterals are not without contention. Their use during the Tokyo Round was one of the reasons why the single undertaking was pursued in the Uruguay Round, as many countries were of the view that the Tokyo Round plurilateral agreements had led to excessive fragmentation of the trading system.

The management of the WTO is collective. It is governed by a ministerial conference of all members that is scheduled to meet, but has not always done so, at least once every two years. Between such meetings the WTO is managed by a General Council. This meets about twelve times a year, with WTO members usually represented by heads of delegations based in Geneva. The General Council turns itself, as needed, into a body to adjudicate trade disputes (the Dispute Settlement Body) and to review trade policies of the member countries (the Trade Policy Review Body). Three subsidiary councils operate under the guidance of the General Council: The Council for Trade in Goods; the Council for Trade in Services; and the Council for Trade Related Aspects of Intellectual Property Rights. Separate committees, working parties, and subcommittees deal with specific subject areas covered by multilateral agreements.

All councils, committees, and so forth, as well as all negotiating groups, are chaired by a representative of a WTO member state. The only exception is the Trade Negotiations Committee, the body that oversees multilateral trade talks, which is chaired by the director-general. The latter does not have a defined role in the agreement establishing the WTO. This was left to the ministerial conference to determine, which to date it has not done.

The main actors in day-to-day activities of the WTO are the officials affiliated with the delegations of members. The member-driven and network nature of the organization puts a considerable strain on the delegations in Geneva and officials in capitals. There are thousands of meetings in the WTO every year. This level of activity makes it very difficult, if not impossible, for citizens of members to keep track of what is happening. At the time of writing, there are 164 members. Few, if any, members participate in all meetings and activities, but all committees are open to all members. WTO practice is for members to organize in informal small groups to develop proposals that may subsequently be put forward to the broader membership, either formally through existing bodies and committees or informally to other members/groups. In WTO-speak, this process is described as the "concentric circles" approach to agenda setting.

The Secretariat provides technical and logistical support when requested by committees or councils. It has very little formal power of initiative; is prohibited from identifying potential violations of WTO rules by members and may not interpret WTO law or pass judgment on the conformity of members' policies. These matters are the sole prerogative of members. Similarly, dispute settlement panels are staffed by members of WTO delegations or outside experts drawn from a roster that has been pre-approved by the membership, not the Secretariat, although the latter has an important support function.

WTO dispute settlement aims at maintaining the balance of negotiated concessions. If a member is found to have violated a commitment, the remedy is *prospective*: The offending member is simply called on to bring its measures into compliance. How this should be done is left to the member to determine. If it does not comply with the ruling of the dispute settlement bodies, retaliation may be authorized in an amount equal in effect to the action taken by the country that violated a commitment. This introduces a significant asymmetry: Small countries cannot exercise much effective pressure through retaliation against large countries that continue to violate their commitments.

Current debates

The one-member, one-vote, consensus-driven *modus operandi* of the WTO, combined with a binding dispute settlement mechanism that works well, helps explain why it is difficult to amend the organization—its rules, norms, practices, and procedures—or to conclude multilateral negotiations on a timely basis. The failure of the Doha negotiations is a major negative for the WTO as an institution as it is the first multilateral round to have been held under its auspices. Not surprisingly, current debates on the WTO often focus on the reasons for—and implications of—the difficulty of "getting to yes."[6] There are many strands of argument and analysis. Is it because of the governance of the WTO—the consensus rule? Is it a consequence of the negotiating modalities that are employed—such as the single undertaking? Or is disagreement more a function of the (rapid) shifts in relative economic fortunes—the "rise of the rest" and in particular the explosive growth in China's share of world trade? Or, related, that the membership has been expanding rapidly—164 today compared to "only" 128 in 1995—with the resulting heterogeneity in interests, social preferences, and capacities across members making agreement difficult to obtain?

Some proposals to address the failure to conclude a Doha deal have centered on the single undertaking practice and consensus-based decision making. One of the premises of the single undertaking approach in multilateral trade negotiations is that it ensures that all participants obtain a net benefit from an overall deal. By allowing for issue linkages and requiring a package deal, countries can make tradeoffs across issues and increase the overall gains from cooperation. However, the approach also creates potential "hold-up" problems and can have the effect of inducing negotiators to devote (too) much time to seeking exceptions and exemptions. This has led to proposals that WTO members shift towards "variable geometry" and approaches that permit a subset of the membership to move forward on an issue, while allowing others to abstain. Two types of approach have been suggested, with some advocating that agreements apply only to signatories (as in the case of plurilateral agreements) and others arguing that any agreements between a smaller group of WTO members should abide by the MFN principle, implying that any such deals would need to be so-called critical mass agreements (i.e., that a sufficiently large number of countries participate so as to address potential concerns about freeriding by nonparticipants).[7]

While agreements among a subset of the membership would allow countries to move forward on issues that are not yet the subject of WTO rules, it is not clear that pursuit of either of these options would have made much of a difference in addressing the problems that held up a Doha Round agreement. The lack of progress in the Doha Round reflected the assessment of the major players that what was on the table was not of sufficient interest—it was not that a small group of small countries were holding up a deal. Trade agreements are self-enforcing treaties: If the large players do not see it in their interest to make a deal, they will not—whether the proposed deal involves just a small number of countries or all of the WTO membership. Any outcome, even if endorsed by a majority, will not be implemented if one or more of the large countries finds it unacceptable. Because the WTO is an incomplete contract, governments have a revealed preference for maintaining tight control over the functioning of the organization. There are good reasons why there seems to be a "consensus on consensus." Indeed, economic analysis suggests that the effects of moving away from the status quo on the incentives to cooperate may be perverse—reducing the willingness to agree to rules and to make commitments.[8]

Another factor explaining the difficulty in adding to the rulebook is the increasing complexity of the policy agenda confronting countries.[9] As tariffs have fallen, the policies that create negative pecuniary spillovers for trading partners are increasingly "behind-the-border" and regulatory in nature. Agreeing on ways to reduce the market-segmenting effects of policies that are aimed at achieving social objectives or addressing market failures is inherently a more complex endeavor than negotiating down tariffs or agreeing to abstain from using quantitative trade restrictions. Related to this are arguments that some of the policy areas that are critical for international business are not on the WTO table, and that the very slowness of the processes used in the WTO makes the negotiations (and the organization) less relevant. In the fourteen-year period following the launch of the Doha Round, for example, technologies changed dramatically. The use of mobile telephone networks and mobile broadband exploded, for example, giving rise to new policy issues that were not on the original agenda, including data security, privacy of cross-border flows of information, and the governance of e-commerce transactions.

Another subject of debate concerns the implications of the pursuit by virtually every WTO member of preferential trade agreements (PTAs). According to the WTO, as of early 2017 there were 274 PTAs in force. There is a longstanding scholarly debate whether PTAs are good or bad for the trading system—building blocks or stumbling blocks.[10] Much of the relevant literature tends to focus on agreements liberalizing trade in goods, but the practice in the last decade has been for PTAs to deal with the very issues that have proved to be controversial in the WTO such as liberalizing access to markets for services and investment (foreign direct investment, FDI) and to agree on rules of the game for policies that are not subject to WTO disciplines. Fears of large-scale trade diversion and discrimination against nonmembers of PTAs have not materialized—in large part because countries often have implemented reforms on a nondiscriminatory basis. But the proliferation of PTAs generates significant transactions costs for businesses as provisions differ across agreements. So far the largest trading nations/blocs—the EU, United States, and China—have yet to negotiate PTAs between themselves and it is not clear whether such agreements will materialize in the future. Noteworthy in this regard is increasing civil society opposition to trade agreements in the EU, reflected in campaigns against a Transatlantic Trade and Investment Partnership (TTIP) with the United States and a PTA with Canada, as well as the decision of the US government not to proceed with ratification of the Trans-Pacific Partnership (TPP) agreement that had been successfully concluded in 2016.

Yet another area of vigorous debate concerns the appropriate approach in the WTO to economic development. Historically, differences in size and power were addressed through "special and differential treatment" (SDT) of developing countries.[11] This approach involved an agreement that developing countries were not expected to reciprocate fully in trade negotiations and a promise by rich countries to provide preferential access to their markets. As a result, developing countries have greater legal latitude to use trade policies (sometimes called "policy space"). An example is the rule banning use of export subsidies, from which the poorest countries were exempted. A major motivation for SDT was a perception that trade policy can be a useful instrument to promote industrial development by sheltering nascent ("infant") industries from international competition. Technical and managerial changes have greatly increased the importance of international production chains and created opportunities for firms in low-income countries to specialize in a specific part of a supply chain. These developments have greatly reduced the effectiveness of border protection as an instrument of industrial policy because firms need to be able to import materials that they process into what they export. This has led to greater emphasis on other instruments to assist developing countries, including "aid for trade"—development assistance that is targeted towards enhancing trade capacity—and a greater focus on trade facilitation. The entry into force in 2017 of the Bali ministerial Trade Facilitation Agreement will help pave the way for a more effective linkage between trade disciplines and aid for trade as a result of the innovative features of the agreement that link implementation of many of its provisions by developing countries to the provision of assistance by high-income countries. The design and impact of WTO provisions and trade-related development assistance in low-income nations is a subject of active debate.[12]

Challenges and emerging issues

The economic theory of trade agreements is premised on the notion that the motivation for governments to negotiate trade agreements is to improve access to export markets. The objective is to "level the playing field" for exporters. Numerous policies can affect access to markets, not just tariffs and quotas that are applied at the border. A major challenge confronting the WTO looking forward is what policies should remain sovereign and what should be subject to agreed rules. The WTO has established a good track record when it comes to providing a framework for disciplines on border measures, but has done less to agree on rules of the game for other policies. Examples include climate change-motivated policies, subsidies of varying types, and the market segmenting effects of regulatory regimes more generally. Increasingly this is an agenda that involves services activities. In most countries upwards of sixty percent of GDP is generated in services sectors, where competition is often affected by regulation that may have disproportionate effects on foreign providers. This confronts policymakers and polities with the challenge of how best to proceed in ensuring that markets are contestable, while attaining social and economic regulatory objectives.

The lack of progress in the Doha Round raised the question of whether the political economy dynamics that generated large-scale merchandise trade liberalization in recent decades could carry over to cooperation on the "new(er)" agenda of "behind-the-border" regulation of product markets. In the 1980s and 1990s, engagement in trade agreements reflected domestic political economy forces. Multilateral trade negations were primarily used as a vehicle to support and lock in national trade reforms. It is not clear when it comes to services sectors and regulatory areas whether a similar dynamic will prevail. The mechanics of trade negotiations—a process of bargaining on *quid pro quo* "concessions" may create perverse incentives by inducing governments to make what would be welfare-enhancing policy changes conditional on actions by trading partners. Even if these eventually can be agreed, the history of the Doha Round illustrates that such an approach will take much time and thus can give rise to potentially large opportunity costs of delay. More fundamentally, a process of negotiating regulatory reforms simply may not be appropriate given the large differences in country circumstances and social preferences.

Given the complexity of many of the regulatory issues that are becoming the subject of discussion in trade agreements, a greater effort is needed to build an understanding at the national level of the effects of prevailing policies and the likely impacts of alternative proposed reforms. Many regulatory reforms do not require—and should therefore not be made conditional on—actions by other governments (trading partners). This does not mean that there are no gains from multilateral cooperation or that negotiations cannot be used as a mechanism to improve access to foreign markets. International cooperation can be a mechanism to harness the potential for greater services in trade and investment to support more inclusive growth. But it appears that this requires a shift away from a focus on reciprocal negotiations and towards a process that centers attention much more on the potential gains from unilateral (autonomous) action by governments.

Different approaches can be envisaged in pursuing cooperation on regulatory policies. Binding international law—the standard *modus operandi* of the WTO—is one option. Others include "soft law" forms of cooperation and delegation to independent entities that are given a transparency and analysis mandate—for example, tasked with assessing whether and how large are negative spillovers created by national policies. In many cases, there will be a significant degree of uncertainty as to what the net effects of policies are, taking into account the overall impact of the relevant policy measures. A key precondition for agreement on binding international rules is a shared recognition that the negative spillovers associated with a policy (set of policies) are significant and that binding disciplines will result in greater efficiency (lower costs). At present there is no such recognition when it comes to important policy areas that are argued to generate negative competitiveness spillovers. This suggests that countries need to work towards putting in place the preconditions for stronger forms of international cooperation—by improving the transparency of applied policies; supporting independent analysis of the effects of policies; and establishing mechanisms through which governments can consult and exchange information.

The importance of policy coherence has already been noted. Much of the literature on policy coherence in the WTO context has focused on the extent to which the activities of other international organizations (IOs) promote the objectives of the WTO, and that allow countries to exploit the policy space that is provided by WTO rules. Other dimensions of policy coherence are likely to become increasingly prominent looking forward. An example is the consistency of the macroeconomic policies pursued by countries with their trade policy commitments. A perennial issue in this regard—going back to well before the creation of the WTO—is the concern regarding the potential for manipulation of exchange rates to affect trade competitiveness and undermine negotiated market access commitments. Another example concerns climate change-related policies and their direct and indirect impact on trade policies and trade and investment flows.

A final challenge to the trading system that must be mentioned is the proliferation of PTAs. As mentioned, the pursuit of PTAs implies that the trading system is increasingly fragmented—the famous spaghetti bowl analogy.[13] While PTAs are a challenge for the WTO, they are also an opportunity as they reflect a willingness by governments to make binding commitments on trade matters, even if they are not able or willing to do so in the WTO. The proliferation of PTAs offers the WTO membership as a whole an opportunity to learn from the many experiments and approaches that are being pursued. This includes lessons from failures—such as Washington's abandonment of the TPP in 2017. PTAs are in some sense laboratories. Over time the best of what is pursued in specific PTAs may be transferable to the WTO. A precondition for such learning is transparency: WTO members need to have information on what is being done in the PTA context, suggesting an important role for the WTO is to provide this information through monitoring and facilitation of regular discussion of the experiences of different PTAs.

Conclusion

The WTO, and the GATT as its predecessor, is in many ways a unique international organization. It has played an important role in supporting global economic growth and poverty reduction by creating a framework of rules of the game for trade policies. Since its creation in 1995 the WTO membership has confronted major difficulties in agreeing on where the institution should go. Many developing countries want to see the rules and processes adapted to better support development objectives. Many high-income countries are of the view that the emerging market countries need to do more to open their markets and offer greater reciprocity than in the past. The disagreements among the membership are leading to ever more PTAs and splintering of the trade regime. At the same time, it is important to recognize that WTO members have been willing and able to conclude "critical mass" agreements to liberalize trade—for example, for information technology products—where a group of countries remove tariffs on a nondiscriminatory basis—that is, to all WTO members including those that refuse to participate. They also demonstrated that multilateral agreements that apply to all members can be concluded. The 2013 Agreement on Trade Facilitation, which entered into force in 2017, is innovative in allowing for flexible, country-by-country, self-defined implementation schedules and including provisions that assure developing countries of obtaining the assistance they may need to be able to apply agreed good practices.

Additional reading

Jagdish Bhagwati, Pravin Krishna, and Arivind Panagariya, eds., *The World Trade System: Trends and Challenges* (Cambridge, MA: MIT Press, 2017).

Manfred Elsig, Bernard Hoekman, and Joost Pauwelyn, eds., *Assessing the World Trade Organization: Fit for Purpose?* (Cambridge: Cambridge University Press, 2017).

Petros C. Mavroidis, *The Regulation of International Trade* (Cambridge, MA: MIT Press, 2016).

Amrita Narlikar, Martin Daunton, and Robert Stern, eds., *The Oxford Handbook on the World Trade Organization* (Oxford: Oxford University Press, 2012).

Rorden Wilkinson, *What's Wrong with the WTO and How to Fix it* (Cambridge: Polity Press, 2014).

Notes

1 Joseph Stiglitz, "Two Principles for the Next Round, or, How to Bring Developing Countries in from the Cold," *The World Economy* 23, no. 4 (2000): 437–454; John S. Odell, "Growing Power Meets Frustration in the Doha Round's First Four Years," in *Developing Countries and Global Trade Negotiations*, eds. Larry Crump and S. Javed Maswood (London: Routledge, 2007), 7–40; J. Michael Finger and Philip Schuler, "Implementation of Uruguay Round Commitments: The Development Challenge," *The World Economy* 23 no. 4 (2000): 511–525; Amrita Narlikar and Rorden Wilkinson, "Collapse at the WTO: A Cancun Post-mortem," *Third World Quarterly* 25, no. 3 (2004): 447–460.

2 Bernard Hoekman and Michel Kostecki, *The Political Economy of the World Trading System*, 3rd ed. (Oxford: Oxford University Press, 2009).

3 Robert E. Hudec, *Developing Countries in the GATT Legal System* (London: Trade Policy Research Centre, 1987).

4 Rorden Wilkinson and James Scott, "Developing Country Participation in the GATT: A Reassessment," *World Trade Review* 7, no. 3 (2008): 473–510.

5 Amrita Narlikar and Diana Tussie, "The G20 at the Cancun Ministerial: Developing Countries and their Evolving Coalition in the WTO," *The World Economy* 27, no. 7 (2004): 947–966.

6   See, for instance, Kent Jones, *The Doha Blues: Institutional Crisis and Reform in the WTO* (Oxford: Oxford University Press, 2010); Rorden Wilkinson, Erin Hannah, and James Scott, "The WTO in Nairobi: The Demise of the Doha Development Agenda and the Future of the Multilateral Trading System," *Global Policy* 7, no. 2 (2016): 247–255.

7   Robert Wolfe, "The WTO Single Undertaking as Negotiating Technique and Constitutive Metaphor," *Journal of International Economic Law* 12, no. 4 (2009): 835–858; Peter Gallagher and Andrew Stoler, "Critical Mass as an Alternative Framework for Multilateral Trade Negotiations," *Global Governance* 15, no. 3 (2009): 375–392.

8   Bernard Hoekman, "WTO Reform: A Synthesis and Assessment of Recent Proposals," in *The Oxford Handbook on the WTO*, eds. Amrita Narlikar, Martin Daunton, and Robert Stern (Oxford: Oxford University Press, 2012), 744–775.

9   Hoekman and Kostecki, *The Political Economy*.

10 Jagdish Bhagwati, "Regionalism and Multilateralism: An Overview," in *New Dimensions in Regional Integration*, eds. Jaime De Melo and Arvind Panagariya (Cambridge: Cambridge University Press, 1993), 22–57.

11 Hudec, *Developing Countries in the GATT Legal System*; and Hoekman and Kostecki, *The Political Economy*, ch. 12.

12 Bernard Hoekman, "Operationalizing the Concept of Policy Space in the WTO: Beyond Special and Differential Treatment," *Journal of International Economic Law* 8, no. 2 (2005): 405–424; Dani Rodrik, "Industrial Policy for the Twenty-First Century," CEPR Discussion Paper 4767 (2004); Faizel Ismail, *Mainstreaming Development into the WTO: Developing Countries in the Doha Round* (Jaipur: Consumer Unity & Trust Society, 2007); Dominique Njinkeu and Hugo Cameron, eds., *Aid for Trade and Development* (Cambridge: Cambridge University Press, 2008).

13 Jagdish Bhagwati, *The World Trading System at Risk* (Princeton, NJ: Princeton University Press, 1991).

Global development governance

Katherine Marshall

The deadline for the Millennium Development Goals (MDGs) that world leaders blessed in 2000 arrived in 2015. Following extensive consultations, papers, meetings, and negotiations, a new architecture for global development, the Sustainable Development Goals (SDGs), emerged, also with a fifteen-year time frame.[1] They cover a broader range of topics than the MDGs and apply to all, not just poorer, nations. Recognizing that seventeen goals and 169 targets were indigestible, framers highlighted five unifying themes: Peace, prosperity, people, planet, and partnership. The tight linking of conflict, environment, and economic and social progress mirrors challenges and changes in understandings of "development," also apparent as the World Bank concluded that the term "developing" countries was obsolete.[2]

The SDG framing reflects stunning changes that have reshaped world economies, societies, politics, religions, and cultures since World War II. Transformations include demography—the world's population has increased from 2.3 to 7.5 billion people, the majority now living in cities—and technological changes that have revolutionized communications. A world seen as irretrievably divided into three: The wealthy capitalist core, the Communist/socialist bloc, and the large majority "underdeveloped" is no more. The messy contemporary configuration of countries and communities fits uncomfortably with the inherited categories and divides, although the notions of sharply dividing cleavages of rich and poor, North and South persist. Even so, these changes upend understandings of development and the institutions associated with it.

The core vision of the 1948 Universal Declaration of Human Rights still anchors development ideals, its buffeting over the years notwithstanding: All people are truly born equal, entitled to a decent life and opportunities. True and full equality is an elusive ideal, but various notions of equity, meaning fairness and balance, provide ethical foundations for contemporary international relations, at least as an aspiration and principle. Poverty, long seen as inevitable, is today a scourge to be conquered; and because ending poverty is not only just but attainable, it becomes a common responsibility. The SDGs are, however, complicated by looming climate change, sharp inequalities, financial fragility, and security threats in a world where tensions spread across the world with stunning speed.

This chapter explores the global architecture of international development against the backdrop of global transformations. It sketches ideas that gave rise to the complex array of institutions—multilateral and national, public and private—working to end poverty and advance social justice; and it explores how this "system" of institutions and efforts to govern works. The chapter introduces the actors involved in development and asks how their interventions shape and are shaped by evolving systems as global challenges and forces call into question underlying assumptions and institutions. The chapter concludes by returning to the fundamental challenge that development represents, and whether and how "global governance" aptly describes either the ends involved or the means in place to meet them.

Development ideas and challenges

The MDGs and SDGs hammered out in 2000 and in 2015 (see Box 44.1) represent something approaching a scaffold for international development work. Designed to guide (and goad) action by UN member countries, they reaffirm the United Nations' vision of a peaceful, prosperous, and more just world. They are to bolster a global social compact through commitments to new, disciplined, and bolder forms of partnership.

This implicit global development "architecture" reflects sea-changes in thinking and action about development over the years. Intensive scrutiny of development progress in the year 2000 and again in 2015 found much to applaud but also to bemoan. Many countries that were barely a gleam in patriots' eyes in 1945 thrive. Great strides could be claimed in fighting hunger, disease, and ignorance. But wars and misery persist, albeit in new forms. New technologies make the sufferings of conflict, displacement, and persistent poverty and inequalities instantly visible and a source of acute shame or blame.

After World War II, notions of development were embryonic, both as to goals and what it would take to get there. The notion that the world was divided into "haves" and "have nots" was generally, if implicitly, accepted. Few truly envisioned as a reality the idea embedded in the lofty documents that launched the United Nations: A world, if not equal, at least equitable and fair, where every human being has opportunities to thrive. Poverty was still seen as an inevitable if regrettable condition.

Development took form first as an idea and an ideal, then as a set of institutions, practices, and programs. With strong leadership South Korea and Singapore were transformed from seemingly hopeless societies into thriving ones. China, India, and

BOX 44.1 GLOBAL VISIONS FOR DEVELOPMENT

The 2000 Millennium Declaration (signed by 189 heads of state)

We will spare no effort to free our fellow men, women and children from the abject and dehumanizing conditions of extreme poverty, to which more than a billion of them are currently subjected. We are committed to making the right to development a reality for everyone and to freeing the entire human race from want.

. . . We resolve therefore to create an environment—at the national and global levels alike—which is conducive to development and to the elimination of poverty.

The 2015 Sustainable Development Goals

1 No poverty

2 Zero hunger

3 Good health and wellbeing

4 Quality education

5 Gender equality

6 Clean water and sanitation

7 Affordable and clean energy

8 Decent work and economic growth

9 Industry, innovation, and infrastructure

10 Reduced inequalities

11 Sustainable cities and communities

12 Responsible consumption and production

13 Climate action

14 Life below water

15 Life on land

16 Peace, justice, and strong institutions

17 Partnerships for the goals

Brazil defied pessimists who bemoaned their intractable problems. Development plans, in the sense of deliberate strategies and programs, proliferated. Some succeeded, some failed spectacularly. Thinking about what drove change and how policy and investment could affect it evolved. Simplistic recipes centered on capital investment gave way to healthy respect for the complexity of social and economic change and instruments that could bring them about. What was considered development expanded in scope: Health and education were not directly associated with development at first but are now central. The idea that women deserved special focus was scoffed at, but integrating women into mainstream development strategies is now (at least rhetorically) vital for successful social transformation. Science and technology as well as ports, power, and roads became part of the development venture. And a growing awareness of the actual and potential impact of climate change and environmental degradation changed both language and approaches.[3]

There are grounds for optimism about what development efforts have achieved. Vast changes in poverty statistics and in how poverty is perceived reflect deliberate efforts by the community of nations, pressured by ideals but also by processes of shaming and competition. Development, in short, has been the result not only of economic and social forces but also an array of institutions and programs, transnational and national, public and private, aimed deliberately at global transformation.

In 2017, the notion of development can be said to include virtually every dimension of social and economic life. In today's mosaic of development, a multitude of institutions are involved; indeed, few global institutions are not part of the venture broadly defined. Trade and investment were long seen as the central planks that would ensure growth and progress. Today the digital divide and technology, microfinance, nutrition, legal systems, security apparatuses, and scientific research are part of the development canvass. The same applies for academic and professional disciplines. Initially largely a matter for economists and diplomats, today virtually every discipline, from engineering and anthropology to psychology and medicine, is involved.

What works and what does not, who is responsible, and the ethics of action are topics of continuing debate. From an enterprise where strategies were concocted in (literally) smoke-filled rooms by white men, today citizens and leaders in every corner of the world are involved. Few governments do not accept at least in principle that they—individually and as part of the United Nations—have a responsibility to advance global development or at least to fight abject poverty through appropriate policies. Global social movements—for example, the Jubilee Debt Campaign and Make Poverty History—have transformed development from technocratic, poorly understood territory into a complex array of global campaigns and continuing exchange and action.

Six key challenges-cum-changes stand out. Motivations for foreign aid for development are complex. Support by richer countries for international development was initially quite baldly justified by a blend of interests and charity. Interests involved a recipient's fit with the donor's diplomatic, strategic, and commercial interests. Especially where humanitarian emergencies were involved, compassion and charity built on ancient religious traditions and nineteenth-century traditions of social welfare. Today, human rights and the "right to development" (embedded, however hazily, in human rights) are a central justification, although interests, charity, and fear also play their parts.[4]

Most early development programs were the domain of "experts." Well-paid professionals from wealthier countries provided "technical assistance," compensating for human capacity shortages and calling many shots. Gradually the folly of designing programs without heeding voices of those who were to benefit became apparent and "consultation" emerged as a norm. This progressed to "participation" and then to "empowerment," a contemporary development norm. More fundamentally, the essential right of a country to manage its own destiny is reflected in basic understand-ings of "country ownership." What ownership and empowerment mean is subject to plenty of debate, but the shifting vocabulary reflects a vital change in understandings of the ethics of development work as well as its practice.

Much early development work assumed rather simplistically that either market forces or economic planning and direction would transform societies, propelling modernization through growth. Reality soon intervened, as did academic research and the wise insights of such leaders and thinkers as Julius Nyerere, Luis Ignacio Lula da Silva, Amartya Sen, Sadako Ogata, Robert McNamara, James D. Wolfensohn, and many others. Far more than investment and free trade were needed. The sticky poverty that kept the poorest in societies from benefiting from progress drew attention to poverty's complexities, which involved culture, religion, psychology, and above all institutions. Development became an increasingly multidisciplinary, multisectoral venture. The notion of human capabilities—developing human capital through edu-cation, health, and opportunity, moved from the periphery to the center.

The respective roles of public and private sectors, and the civil society organiza-tions that have exploded in complex mosaics, have changed radically. The proper role of the state is debated, both globally and in many countries, but simplistic notions that governments could "pick winners" and steer progress in specific directions have been shattered by the growing dominance of private enterprise in resource flows and the witness of dynamic market-led progress in many settings, often astounding policy gurus and politicians who thought they were in control. Sharp attention focuses on financial sectors, trade reform, and, above all, proper regulation and the perils of predatory corruption. Social entrepreneurship, galvanizing the energies of often small-scale actors to bring transformation, and microfinance, small-scale lending that can unleash the potential energies of poor people, especially women, today are essential parts of what is understood to bring development. As civil society organizations have multiplied, transparency and citizen engagement take on greater importance. *Why Nations Fail*, a thought-provoking analysis by Daron Acemoglu and James Robinson, was published in 2012 and draws the central lesson that inclusive institutions matter most.[5] Strong institutions that go beyond the interests of elites are what make for development success.

Monitoring and evaluation entered the vocabulary fairly early on because public financial resources were involved, but the importance of accountability and working to achieve specific results now has an unshakable grip on development thinking. Measuring and setting targets has achieved the level of an art. Growing awareness of the reality of corruption and massive losses of development resources to illicit private gain is one driver. Transparency (to shed light on decision making and actual spending) and anticorruption strategies as part of good governance are indispensable aspects of development thinking and action today.

Finally, states that are, for various reasons, fragile (poorly governed, facing insur-mountable development challenges, or riven by conflict) need different, tailored treat-ment. This group of some thirty-five to fifty countries demands external support yet defies traditional development approaches, because leadership and institutions are so weak. In late 2011, a "New Deal" was launched for this group of countries. Similar appreciations apply for the poorest communities, even those located in affluent societies and countries. New approaches, institutions, and financing mechanisms are emerging to deal with stubborn situations at the bottom of socioeconomic ladders.[6]

Development institutions

Institutions involved in international development and humanitarian work have multiplied in quite stunning ways since the late 1940s. Today an elaborate array of formal development institutions alongside a host of other institutions with varying degrees of formality are engaged in the development enterprise (here termed development actors). Various institutions and mechanisms work to coordinate and guide the "system" of institutions. However, while the terms "development architecture," "international system," and "international community" are fairly commonly used, institutions in practice have evolved organically, without a grand design or strategy. This historical reality is clearly reflected in how institutions work and how they emerged.

Chronologically, the first transnational development institution, created while World War II still raged and the United Nations was on the drawing board, was the International Bank for Reconstruction and Development, the World Bank, born in 1944 at the Bretton Woods Conference in New Hampshire. Its name reflects the reality that development was almost an afterthought. The International Monetary Fund (IMF) was the primary focus of the Bretton Woods negotiations and was designed to hammer out some kind of order in global financial systems to avoid the crises that had dogged the interwar period. The World Bank worked alongside the United Nations Relief and Rehabilitation Agency (UNRRA), founded in 1943, with a similar concern and focus on postwar reconstruction. It began operating in 1946, but the US Marshall Plan essentially displaced both the World Bank and UNRRA in their postwar relief and rehabilitation work. "Development" then took a more prominent spot. Reflecting understandings that development was primarily about capital and trade, a series of multilateral development banks and institutions followed suit, with the first being the Inter-American Development Bank (IDB) founded in 1959. Today some twenty institutions operate at global and regional levels with varying sources of capital and differing governance systems. They include new institutions such as the Asian Infrastructure Investment Bank and the New Development Bank.

The World Bank plays a special (if contested) role as a leader in the field because of its long history of engagement, its large commitment to intellectual leadership (for example, through annual World Development reports), and its capacity to mobilize financial resources through borrowing on private markets, capital shares, and gifts from wealthier nations.

The United Nations includes a wide range of core and specialized agencies with important development roles. These took shape, and multiplied over time. The lead institution within the UN system is the United Nations Development Programme (UNDP), looked to as both intellectual leader and coordinator for development. It was created in 1965, merging the United Nations Expanded Program of Technical Assistance and the United Nations Special Fund. Both the United Nations General Assembly and the Economic and Social Council (ECOSOC) take up development issues. The United Nations International Children's Emergency Fund (UNICEF), the Food and Agriculture Organization (FAO), the United Nations Population Fund (UNFPA), and virtually all the other specialized agencies as well as UN funds and programs are directly and actively involved in development work.

The European Union (EU) is the most significant regional institution. Its development focus and mandate date from the 1957 Treaty of Rome with activities expanding over the years. At first confined to territories (colonies and independent states) linked directly to European Community members, the EU today is one of the largest sources of development assistance. The Islamic Development Bank, active in many of the fifty-six member nations of the Organization of Islamic Cooperation (OIC), is a significant player.

Various global programs focus on what are termed vertical programs. A prominent example, that builds in efforts to involve private actors and those directly affected, is the Global Fund to Fight AIDS, Tuberculosis and Malaria. Another is the Global Vaccine Initiative (GAVI).

Many countries have bilateral development programs, increasing from five or six in the mid-1940s to at least fifty-six today (with numbers ever increasing).[7] Among the best known are the United States Agency for International Development (USAID) and the UK's Department for International Development (DfID). Most bilateral programs had multiple rationales and origins, ranging from humanitarian objectives (responding to disasters) to commercial interests. Bilateral concerns tend to figure prominently in these aid programs and aid takes many and increasingly complex forms. In the United States, for example, at least twenty-six federal government departments are involved in international development, and state governments run various programs. Activities vary from explicit trade promotion to programs like the Peace Corps and university support for training and research.

The bilateral aid system (if it can properly be so termed) has an institutional support mechanism, the Development Assistance Committee (DAC) of the Organisation for Economic Co-operation and Development (OECD). Created in 1960, it is considered "the venue and voice of the world's major bilateral donors." Products include statistics on official development assistance (ODA) and compilations of principles and best practices.[8] DAC has broadened its scope over the years and seeks to include newer development players. It leads efforts to harmonize aid and establish norms for development work.[9]

Development actors

In the early decades of international development work, the prevailing assumption was that governments were the leaders both of development processes in poorer countries and in providing and orchestrating development assistance. This has changed radically. Both in numbers of actors and overall aid flows, a far more diverse picture prevails. The volume and proportion of financial flows to developing countries from private sector actors has increased sharply as have roles of widely varied civil society entities. Also significant are private philanthropy and foundations (notable among them the Ford and Rockefeller Foundations, with the Bill and Melinda Gates Foundation today dwarfing the growing array of foundations, large and small). Finally, the roles of academic institutions and the media—as shapers of ideas and a source of expertise—have expanded. Many universities have training programs targeted at development leaders and research programs— the University of Sussex, Harvard, Columbia, Georgetown, London School of Economics, Singapore's Lee Kuan Yew program, CERDI (Center for Studies and Research on Development at the University of Auvergne), and the Dutch Institute of Social Studies are examples.

From the earliest days the private sector was seen as the principal driver for investment and thus progress. The International Finance Corporation (IFC) was established in 1956 within the World Bank Group so that riskier investments and joint ventures could be encouraged. A variety of investment guarantee mechanisms have emerged. Governments have developed mechanisms to encourage their companies to invest and operate overseas, and private companies look to emerging economies. Dramatic increases in private aid flows today dwarf official development assistance.

The creative energies of the wide range of private actors are an engine not only for investment but also for innovation. Large transnational companies are major investors, in infrastructure and mining, for example, but social entrepreneurs operate at a smaller scale and in mechanisms like the "patient capital" promoted by Acumen Fund. Consulting firms play central roles. Microfinance and support for small and medium sized enterprises are popular avenues for development. A growing appreciation for the market power of poor people at the "bottom of the pyramid" has prompted a host of new mechanisms to mobilize and channel private capital and energies towards development ends.

Private sector roles do not always sit easily with public development approaches. Microfinance has potential downsides if it is seen as a panacea, and insufficient attention is paid to solid institutional and financial practices. A rash of suicides in India, for example, brought welcome sobriety to microfinance circles, but unleashing the energies of poor people is a vital path and important mechanisms have emerged. Likewise, the potential for large transnational companies to spur development and create jobs is enormous, although global giants can dwarf the capacities of many poor country governments to regulate. Altruistic motives, centered on development and poverty alleviation, are rare, with the exception of growing corporate social responsibility (CSR) programs. The nature of partnerships involving private companies and other actors pose live issues: How to ensure effective regulatory measures that do not stifle innovation and investment, how to benefit from the undoubted skills and verve of the private actors. Creating a positive investment climate at the policy, legal, and practical level is a central development concern, to remove barriers to investment and correct obvious market distortions. Large-scale land purchases in Africa and aggressive natural resource extraction are critical topics, although who can and should act to check excesses and channel energies in positive directions is far from clear.

"Global civil society" is one of the more contested terms used today because it involves so many different kinds of institution, but this loosely defined group has taken an increasingly important place among development actors. The field includes ancient actors, notably churches, missions, temples, and the like that for centuries ran schools and clinics and promoted community development projects. After World War II, such organizations as CARE, Oxfam, Catholic Relief Services (CRS), and several Jewish organizations emerged with essentially humanitarian, relief objectives. Their numbers have multiplied with mandates shifting from short-term relief towards longer term development.

Today many thousand transnational organizations (most commonly termed non-governmental organizations, or NGOs) operate in every sector and virtually every country worldwide. Some, like World Vision and CARE, are enormous organizations, often with a franchise-type organization that gives increasing weight to country-based affiliates. Islamic Relief, a transnational entity that emerged in response to droughts and state collapse in the Horn of Africa, exemplifies newer entities in the development field; it operates (from a base in Birmingham, in the UK) with a growing number of national affiliates. These organizations engage in advocacy, for policies and development assistance, and in operations, especially at the community level. Many work closely with bilateral aid programs and UN organizations. With the proliferation of civil society entities, coordinating and support bodies, for example InterAction in the United States, and Civicus globally, have emerged as voices and practical networks for support.

Nonetheless, the question of how civil society is represented in development circles is a lively issue. A common complaint is that "If you are not at the table, you end up on the menu." Which tables, however, and which representatives? Which voice? The broad realm of civil society was especially visible during the 1980s and 1990s. Protests and demands for action centered on environmental issues and norms that international development institutions followed in making investments. Specific concerns broadened, and for a time what one actor termed a "swarm" of NGOs came close to paralyzing development operations in some sectors. The era of sharp protests and conflicts culminated in the late 1990s in violent demonstrations in Seattle in 1999, during World Trade Organization (WTO) meetings, and during 2001 G-8 meetings in Genoa. Virtually every large development gathering at the time involved hordes of security forces and chain link fences separating "delegates" from civil society actors eager to make their voices known.

Various terrorist attacks and especially those of September 11, 2001 (9/11), changed the picture; new security concerns took precedence and the energies of what had always been a highly diverse grouping of protesters turned towards more decentralized targets and forms of action. Various governments challenge "civil society space" today. The years of tension, however, were significant, indeed transformative, for the development world. Enduring changes include the opening up of operations of development institutions (transparency), with far more information available today than several decades ago, a raft of new accountability mechanisms, and sharpened emphasis on results. Inspection panels created for the World Bank and the regional banks, where those who argue that development actions have brought them harm have the right to appeal, are examples. The Jubilee Debt Campaign citing ancient Biblical ideas of a periodic "jubilee" of debt forgiveness, was instrumental in changing long-set policies on debt, taking the year 2000 as an inspiration. Large public mobilizations under loose banners such as "make poverty history," engage both civic groups and celebrities like Bono and Angelina Jolie to make development a public moral call and cause. Civil society actors are a clear and active presence in most policy forums today.

Large transnational foundations like the Rockefeller and Ford Foundations have long played dynamic roles in development work. Their independence from both domestic and international politics and fungible resources allow them to support innovation and to intervene in areas such as human rights where political leaders tread reluctantly. The enormous resources of the Bill and Melinda Gates Foundation focus admiration and hope, as well as some fears, on this group of institutions and actors. A host of smaller foundations and private philanthropists (institutional and individual) are players in the development field, though often under the radar of both attention and resource counting. Again, they can support important innovations and ensure that support goes to communities where people are in need. The drawback is that uncoordinated efforts can diffuse impact.

Remittances from people living overseas are a vital source of development finance and ideas. These actors were long ignored despite their fairly obvious relevance, in part because they were hard to measure and track, much less to direct. The energy and resources of both diaspora communities and remittances they send home are an important resource, estimated at some $430 billion in 2015.

Falling in all categories are a varied and dynamic group loosely termed "new actors." China has been engaged in development support for decades. The fact that China's government was rarely part of the formal development "clubs" means that it is sometimes seen as a "new" actor. The group of countries known as the BRICS (Brazil, Russia, India, China, and South Africa) and Indonesia are finding new voice and taking on new roles in the development world, transmitting ideas and finance. Wealthy Arab countries are witnessing an explosion of bilateral programs as well as new private foundations. "South–South" cooperation has long been an important idea, deflating the notion that all technical expertise and support flows from the "rich West" to the "poor South," but in the complex geopolitical configurations of today such partnerships are taking on greater prominence. An illustration among many is advice flowing between Malaysia and South Africa (in both directions) on land reform, development of smallholder agriculture in relation to large farm sectors, and mechanisms to encourage and empower local business.

Development governance?

The development world sometimes seems like something from the *Sorcerer's Apprentice*, with ever multiplying institutions, amid rising concern for strategic focus, accountability, and consistent, higher quality effort towards development results. But is this a development system? Is it in any manner governed? Indeed, is it at all governable?

The current array of institutions involved in international development in no way constitutes a planned, organized, rational system. Institutions have emerged as a product of many forces and development today is intertwined with virtually every dimension of international social, political, economic, and cultural affairs, every discipline, and all countries. So lack of coherence is hardly surprising. That said, international development is set within broad global objectives, most prominently those set out by the United Nations, including the international humanitarian system, with its norms and coordinating mechanisms, and covenants and implementation mechanisms that support international human rights.

Several purposeful mechanisms support more coherent approaches to global development. Deliberate efforts to address well-known weaknesses of international development governance include aid harmonization initiatives, starting with the OECD's DAC meeting in Rome in 2003, followed by successive efforts in Paris in 2005, Accra in 2008, and Busan in 2011. Not all development actors are part of these efforts by any measure, and not all issues are addressed; but they constitute a deliberate effort to bring more coherence into what is recognized as an imperfect system. Aid harmonization and related efforts address the longstanding proliferation of aid practices, mechanisms for conditionality, procurement, tied aid, and other issues. Efforts to align foreign aid with national public investment programs, often through budget support, and to promote learning, include drives to increase girls' education, health programs, and agricultural investment. An aid transparency initiative to improve the quality and timeliness of information about development programs was a Busan product.[10]

The governance of development is a leading topic for the United Nations, and especially the General Assembly. Almost from its inception practical and ethical concerns of global inequality and development have featured on UN agendas. Issues such as HIV and AIDS, gender justice, food security, and maternal mortality are the subject of countless international conferences and feature regularly on the General Assembly's agenda as well as those of ECOSOC and other UN bodies. Since 2000, a series of special conferences and regular assembly meetings aim to make the principles of accountability enshrined in the MDGs and SDGs a living reality.

Other important global forums where development priorities and issues are sometimes at the center are the array of the "Gs"—that is, the G-7 (the group of the wealthiest nations), G-8, G-77, G-24, and, most significant in the present era, the G-20. The last includes countries that represent some eighty percent of the world's population and, when economic crises do not drive them from the agenda center, they take up development priorities. A new grouping is the G-7+, fragile states led by Afghanistan and Timor Leste, behind the "New Deal" initiative.

Other significant mechanisms, some formal, others informal, include the Paris Club, an informal mechanism run by the French Treasury that leads processes underlying bilateral debt negotiations. The London Club, now largely in abeyance, was a similar mechanism directed towards commercial bank debt.

Regional forums, for example the Southern African Development Community (SADC), ASEAN (Association of Southeast Asian Nations), and the African Union (AU), play roles in development advocacy and, less often, leadership and coordination of specific development programs. They can play significant roles where post-conflict abuts with development, in resolving barriers that block development (security issues, financial arrears, or investment disputes, for example) and mobilizing resources.

The most important, pragmatically grounded development governance in practice takes place at the country level. Time-honored mechanisms, some now largely in abeyance, include Aid Consortia for India, Pakistan, and Bangladesh. The World

Bank and the UNDP have led many country aid coordination mechanisms that are increasingly giving way to country-led mechanisms.

The multilateral banks, and especially the World Bank, play critical roles in situations where extraordinary resource mobilization is urgent, especially in post-conflict or post-disaster situations but also in crises like that with Ebola. Meetings termed, for example, the "Friends of 'X country'" seek consensus on strategic frameworks for assistance, priorities, and modalities.

With the financial pinch in many wealthier countries, continuing bilateral and multilateral aid flows are always in question, with constant concerns about erratic and unpredictable aid flows that make the job of development managers especially difficult. The very general, unrealized—except for a handful of Western donors—pledge that wealthier countries will devote 0.7 percent of their gross national income to development assistance offers little comfort.

New realities include the "flattening" and broadening of development actors, hearing and engaging marginalized groups, fighting corruption with greater passion and effectiveness, terrorism and security, and ensuring true commitment to rule of law. With dramatic increases in forced migration, the ills of the humanitarian system and its links to development present operational challenges. The rapprochement, if not the merging, of climate change and development agendas is a new, complicating reality. Ideals for balanced partnerships built on mutual respect and a development philosophy grounded in rights, not charity, take on greater prominence, especially where the poorest, most fragile nations and communities are concerned.

Conclusion

Challenges to development governance touch fundamental challenges for global governance overall. Development cannot be a segmented effort through which richer countries "help" poorer countries. It presents the far broader challenge of how the international community sees the ideal society and economy. What are responsibilities, the proper means, the measures of success and accountability, and of appropriate conditionality? In discussions about development paradigms, the idealistic vision of the Kingdom of Bhutan captivates imaginations and academic and political attention; Bhutan's articulation of a search for "Gross National Happiness" suggests where we should be going.

The international development constellation is not a system that can be readily defined, far less governed in its entirety. It is far too complex and dynamic, with its vast number of independent actors. Various mechanisms aim to increase the system's coherence and ensure better accountability, an important priority given that unequal power is the essence of the development challenge. Some, like OECD/DAC aid harmonization initiatives, yield encouraging results. Country-led coordination mechanisms show increasing rigor and impact. Norms and standards for development work, ways to measure achievements, and innovative ideas that integrate, for example, environmental concerns with social policies, are clearer than before. Much wisdom has emerged from seven decades of experience with directed development efforts. Important success stories justify the conviction that ending poverty is indeed a possible dream.

Nonetheless, stepping back from the specifics of aid harmonization, accountability measures, and UN assessments of progress or lack thereof towards the SDGs, systems are challenged and changing, reflecting major forces that are transforming the geopolitical landscape. Systems in place, such as they are, largely reflect political and economic realities of past decades. They are predicated on a system of "donors" and "recipients," public aid flows to support development projects designed to address identified needs, centered in the countries that held power after World War II. They assume a world divided into two or three categories of country. Development institutions have adapted to changing realities. They have opened tightly held documentation and data to public scrutiny, and invited new actors to "clubs." Civil society, long exiled from tables where policies were made, is more welcome. Women are part of the discussion. Corruption is openly, even constantly, discussed. Climate change is seen as an integral part of the development agenda.

Yet formal institutional structures still reflect power and social realities of a fading era, with the shape of new structures emerging slowly. It is obvious that future mechanisms will be more complex and will move and change faster than those slowly shaped by consensus. They will involve far more actors, be messier, and, if anything, harder to govern and to assess. That is the reality of global development governance today.

Additional reading

Daron Acemoglu and James Robinson, *Why Nations Fail: The Origins of Power, Prosperity, and Poverty* (London: Profile Books, 2012).

Stephen Browne, *United Nations Development Programme and System* (London: Routledge, 2011).

Paul Collier, *The Bottom Billion: Why the Poorest Countries Are Failing and What Can Be Done about It* (Oxford: Oxford University Press, 2008).

William Easterly, *The Tyranny of Experts: Economists, Dictators, and the Forgotten Rights of the Poor* (New York: Basic Books, 2015).

Katherine Marshall, *The World Bank: From Reconstruction to Development to Equity* (London: Routledge, 2008).

Jeffrey D. Sachs, *The Age of Sustainable Development* (New York: Columbia University Press, 2015).

Rorden Wilkinson and David Hulme, eds., *The Millennium Development Goals and Beyond: Global Development After 2015* (London: Routledge, 2012).

Notes

1 www.undp.org/content/undp/en/home/sustainable-development-goals.html.
2 The reasoning for the shift is laid out in a 2015 blog on the World Bank website: https://blogs.worldbank.org/opendata/should-we-continue-use-term-developing-world.
3 Katherine Marshall, *The World Bank. From Reconstruction to Development to Equity* (London: Routledge, 2008), provides a fuller history.
4 Katherine Marshall, "Climbing up to the Light," *Reflections. A Magazine of Theological and Ethical Inquiry* 97, no. 2 (2010): 5–7.

5 Daron Acemoglu and James Robinson, *Why Nations Fail: The Origins of Power, Prosperity, and Poverty* (London: Profile Books, 2012).

6 Paul Collier helped to shift paradigms towards fragile states in *The Bottom Billion: Why the Poorest Countries Are Failing and What Can Be Done about It* (Oxford: Oxford University Press, 2008).

7 The World Bank, "Aid Architecture: An Overview of the Main Trends in Official Development Assistance Glows," Update, May 2008, http://siteresources.worldbank.org/IDA/Resources/Aid_Architecture-May2008.pdf. *From Billions to Trillions: Transforming Development Finance. Post-2015 Financing for development*, http://siteresources.world bank.org/DEVCOMMINT/Documentation/23659446/DC2015-0002(E)Financing forDevelopment.pdf.

8 OECD, *DAC in Dates: The History of the OECD's Development Assistance Committee*, www.oecd.org/dac/1896808.pdf.

9 J. Brian Atwood, "Creating a Global Partnership for Effective Development Cooperation," Center for Global Development, October 2012, www.cgdev.org/files/1426543_file_Atwood_BusanFINAL.pdf.

10 Aid Transparency Initiative, www.aidtransparency.net.

Global environmental governance

Elizabeth R. DeSombre and Angelina H. Li

Environmental issues require global governance. Many environmental problems arise in areas, such as the oceans or the atmosphere, that are outside state jurisdiction. Often, action in one state contributes to environmental problems in another, and resources in one area are frequently of significance to people around the world. Resources with these traits cannot be managed without some level of international coordination.

The governance of these issues is fragmented and diffuse, taking place across many different issue-focused institutions, which leads to new or renewed negotiations as unforeseen complications arise. This multiplicity of institutions can lead to duplication of effort, "convention fatigue," and sometimes even conflicting mandates, but it also enables the creation of nimble institutions responsive to emerging issues. Over time institutions in similar issue areas have learned to coordinate to increase their joint efficiency and manage potential conflicts.

This governance also involves important action by non-state actors, which have emerged as intergovernmental institutional processes have encountered difficulties. Global environmental issues are thus currently governed through a cacophony of coordinated (and sometimes uncoordinated) governance efforts that make incremental progress towards addressing environmental problems as they arise. This chapter discusses the UN system, other international institutions, the contribution of non-state actors, and funding mechanisms for supporting global environmental governance.

United Nations

Unlike some other areas of global governance, there is no central institutional structure for global environmental governance. The closest approximation to such a framework is the United Nations Environment Programme (UNEP) and a series of global environmental conferences held under the auspices of the United Nations. While these institutions play a significant role in facilitating and catalyzing action, they fall short of creating a centralized governance framework. Understanding both the achievements and shortcomings of these UN entities is crucial to understanding the structure of global environmental governance as a whole.

UN global conferences on the environment have played a prominent role in intergovernmental approaches to environmental governance. The United Nations Conference on the Human Environment was the first, held in Stockholm in June 1972. This conference recommended a more formal structure under the UN's mandate for addressing environmental issues. This recommendation ultimately prompted UNEP's creation and laid the groundwork for several other agreements protecting endangered species and cultural heritage, and preventing marine pollution and acid rain.

Twenty years later, the United Nations Conference on Environment and Development, the largest gathering of world leaders in history up to that point, was held in Rio de Janeiro, Brazil, in June 1992. States negotiated the UN Framework Convention on Climate Change (UNFCCC) and the Convention on Biological Diversity in time to be signed at the conference. The conference declaration included support for the "polluter pays" principle and reiterated support for states in the exercise of sovereignty over their natural resources.

Two additional global conferences of note followed: The World Summit on Sustainable Development in 2002 in Johannesburg, South Africa; and a conference called Rio+20, held in 2012 in Brazil. The 2002 conference asked states for voluntary (and often vague) commitments to improve water and sanitation, energy, health, environment, and biodiversity. It also focused on business, with a set of public–private partnerships called "Type II agreements" reached to advance conference goals.[1] The 2012 conference resulted in no major new commitments or initiatives, although many states made individual pledges about environmental behavior, and side-agreements were concluded between individual corporations and governments.

Opinions differ on the usefulness of these global gatherings. At minimum, the 1972 and 1992 conferences appear to have attracted public attention and focused governmental and intergovernmental action. The pressure of finalizing treaty negotiations in advance of the 1992 conference may have pushed states toward agreement, and the principles elaborated in the Stockholm and Rio declarations and action plans have been taken up in local, national, and international regulations since then. However, these conferences have often led to vague, nonbinding agreements and weak statements of intent from individual states. At worst, these events may detract attention and resources from more serious efforts at governance, and may even provide public cover for inaction, with public statements from high-ranking officials garnering more attention than the lack of action that follows.

UNEP plays a more central role in governance. It was founded in 1972 as a specialized UN agency to coordinate environmental aspects of UN operations and catalyze further environmental action. It is funded through voluntary donations. In recent years, to boost resources, it has created a "voluntary indicative scale of contributions," which suggests to countries what their contributions should be.[2] Its headquarters are located in Nairobi, Kenya, making it the first major UN entity to be based in a developing country. UNEP also convenes and runs negotiations of major international environmental agreements, provides secretariat functions to a number of the institutions created to oversee these agreements, coordinates monitoring and scientific research, and works to build the capacity of states (and other non-state entities) to protect the environment.

One of UNEP's biggest successes is its Regional Seas Programme. This programme oversees the creation of joint action plans and treaties among states around a regional sea, to protect and manage the common body of water. To date, this program involves 143 countries in protecting thirteen regional seas. It has seen some impressive successes in political cooperation, although in recent years these programs have suffered from weakened monitoring and a lack of funding. It is difficult to ascertain the environmental results these agreements have achieved, although they have likely slowed increases in pollution.

UNEP has helped create and support some significant international environmental agreements. At the same time, it is routinely criticized for having a confused mandate—it is not the only source of assessment and monitoring, funding, coordination, or secretariat services, so it may not be clear what entity will provide which services for international negotiations. It also faces a chronic problem with underfunding, which on occasion has significantly threatened the continuation of the environmental agreements it oversees, and has certainly hampered its ability to successfully coordinate a growing number of environmental agreements and institutions. Ultimately, although UNEP faces structural problems with its efficacy, many of its problems can most accurately be attributed to the unwillingness of individual states to engage in stronger environmental action or to give it more resources and influence.

Agreements and institutions

One of the most notable things about global environmental governance is simply how many institutions exist to carry it out. Most intergovernmental cooperation to address environmental problems begins with the negotiation of issue-specific treaties, many of which create organizations to oversee and implement the obligations to which states agree. Although UNEP coordinates the negotiation of many of these agreements, the initiative to begin the negotiation frequently comes from one or more states that are especially concerned about the issue. International cooperation thus often begins at the initiative of states that have already undertaken domestic action; the global nature of the problem means that they cannot fully address the problem without multilateral cooperation and so they push for international negotiation.

Once these institutions have been created, they contribute to the further deepening of cooperation. They generally include scientific processes that gather or assess information to make recommendations about further actions, and political decision-making processes empowered to change obligations as new information deems further action necessary. The most important of these institutions are discussed below, by exploring four issue areas: Oceans, biodiversity, atmosphere, and toxic materials.

Ocean resources and pollution

Since the oceans do not belong to any one particular state, issues concerning maritime resources and standards are all governed through international cooperation. The two main types of ocean environmental issues are fisheries conservation and ocean pollution. Ocean resources are addressed by a variety of regional fisheries management organizations (RFMOs) along with other institutions that address marine mammal harvesting. Ocean pollution is regulated primarily by the International Maritime Organization (IMO) and the set of international agreements it oversees.

Fisheries resources present a natural incentive for international management: Successful management of these resources can lead to abundant stocks of fish for all states to profit from, whereas failure to cooperate can quickly deplete fisheries and eliminate a vital source of revenue and food that many states rely on. RFMOs were among the earliest organizations working to protect natural resources internationally. Currently, there are approximately nineteen RFMOs with regulatory capacities, which manage by species, by region, or a combination of the two. Most have a scientific commission, charged with making recommendations on what a sustainable catch for the stocks in question would be, and a fishery commission, composed of member state representatives, that makes political decisions that include actual restrictions on fishing. In order to expedite decision-making processes, most commissions impose catch restrictions by majority vote, changing rules annually or biennially in response to new scientific information about the health of stocks. Because states would be reluctant to agree to processes in which they can be subject to rules they vote against, many of these agreements allow states to opt out of regulations within specified constraints, in fear that without this option states would refuse to join RFMOs in which they could be outvoted.

The success of the various RFMOs has been mixed: Nonparticipation in regulation is easy, and compliance, even among states that do accept regulation, has varied. A larger problem arises from the fact that catch limits are not directly coordinated between different regional institutions, and thus catch limits set by institutions in one area sometimes result in increased fishing pressure in other areas; a failure of management of fish stocks as a whole.[3] Nevertheless, some RFMOs, like the Commission for the Conservation of Antarctic Marine Living Resources and some of the tuna commissions, have done a reasonably good job at managing the fish stocks they control, in part through setting catch limits while taking into consideration the overall functioning of the ecosystems in which they operate.

The IMO is a broad and independent UN specialized agency, currently consisting of 171 member states. It addresses both environmental and non-environmental issues related to ships. It currently oversees over fifty international agreements and protocols, some of which were negotiated within the organization and others that were negotiated separately and only later brought under the IMO umbrella. Besides agreements, the IMO also issues nonbinding codes that offer substantial recommendations on maritime operations. Some of these provide specific guidelines on how to implement associated agreements.

One of the most important IMO agreements is the 1973/1978 International Convention for the Prevention of Pollution from Ships (known as MARPOL), which established equipment standards that meant all new ships had to be built (and old ones retrofitted) in ways that made intentional oil pollution nearly impossible and discharges from accidents less likely.[4] This agreement has significantly changed ship construction, and it has substantially decreased the extent of oil pollution in the ocean. Other agreements the IMO oversees include efforts to regulate the dumping of certain toxics, as well as of pollutants from ballast water and fouling systems.

Evaluations of the IMO's effectiveness are mixed. On the one hand, the IMO has received an impressively high degree of participation in its agreements—for instance, the states party to MARPOL represent about ninety-eight percent of the world's registered tonnage.[5] On the other, there has been a mixed level of implementation of conventions even when states adopt them, and some suggest the organization could do more to push its member states towards further implementation.[6] The growing phenomenon of states allowing ship registrations by non-nationals has also shifted political power within the IMO away from European and North American states and towards so-called "flag of convenience" states, which may benefit from keeping regulatory standards low. Ultimately, domestic resistance to shipping governance is the strongest impediment to IMO's effectiveness; since international trade strongly depends on the availability of cheap shipping, many states have powerful incentives to avoid costly regulation.

Species and biodiversity

While early species governance focused largely on the conservation of species (including fisheries resources) to ensure their sustainable use, recent institutions take several different approaches towards the management of endangered species. Some institutions still focus on conserving specific categories of species, whereas others focus on protecting the diversity of species and genetic material as a whole, or even on preserving natural habitats or ecosystems for their own merits. Most institutions reflect multiple approaches towards species management, which, in turn, reveals the ongoing evolution of ideas about what constitute acceptable human interactions with the natural world.

One of the earliest conservation agreements that still functions today is the 1973 Convention on International Trade in Endangered Species of Wild Fauna and Flora (CITES), which restricts trade in endangered species. Species are categorized into three appendices with tiered levels of restriction that range from almost absolute bans on trade in some species to requirements for permits to ensure sustainable use in others. Member states are required to create scientific authorities and national management authorities to oversee the permit process and generate annual reports containing export and import data on species passing through their borders.

Some of the difficulties CITES faces are inherent in the types of problem it seeks to address: Many species of concern involve trade with states with weak governance or significant corruption, and many countries (particularly those in the developing world) lack the capacity to monitor species trade or maintain sufficient control over their borders to implement the agreement's provisions. Additionally, since implementation information is self-reported, low levels of reporting make it difficult to monitor actual levels of compliance with trade restrictions. Despite these inherent problems, CITES has seen some notable successes in decreasing trade in restricted species, and, in particular, has almost certainly improved the situation for African elephants, which originally faced huge population pressures from poaching activities and international demand for ivory in places far away from Africa.

The Convention on the Conservation of Migratory Species (CMS) protects species that migrate internationally. In addition to listing species requiring protection on appendices that mandate level and type of protection, its institutional processes negotiate species-specific agreements and memoranda of understanding (MOU) among range states (not all of which are members of the CMS) for a given species, to conserve and restore habitats that listed endangered species migrate through. As of 2017 these include seven binding agreements and nineteen MOU. While many species are not yet subject to protection by agreements or MOU, in recent years CMS has significantly increased the number of agreements negotiated. While there are some protected species under the CMS whose populations have rebounded, many agreements are sufficiently recent that their impact cannot yet be meaningfully gauged.

A significant shift in species management toward a broader concept of conservation came from the 1992 United Nations Convention on Biological Diversity (CBD). The CBD was created as a framework convention to conserve biodiversity, ensure the sustainable use of biological resources, and promote the "fair and equitable sharing" of benefits from using such genetic resources. States party to the agreement subsequently negotiated two protocols to implement different aspects of the agreement's broader goals. The Cartagena Protocol on Biosafety attempts to avoid possible harms to developing countries from the genetic modification of organisms by allowing states to determine whether living modified organisms can cross their borders. The Nagoya Protocol on Access and Benefit Sharing attempts to prevent wealthier states or corporations from utilizing the genetic resources of developing states without permission for economic gain. Both protocols rely heavily on the idea of obtaining prior informed consent (although this goes by "advanced informed agreement" under the Biosafety Protocol), and both have created clearinghouses to transmit relevant information about each problem area between parties to the protocols.

While the CBD framework reflects an ambitious departure from previous conservation agreements, it is less successful at stipulating specific obligations that result in direct biodiversity conservation. One major impediment to the CBD's work is simply the lack of scientific knowledge about the vast array of species that make up the world's biodiversity. The Biosafety Protocol may nevertheless have led to an increase in the scientific capacity of developing states, and future CBD measures may tackle conservation more directly.

Several other institutions also involve the protection of ecosystems as a whole. The Convention on Wetlands of International Importance (the Ramsar Convention), especially, works to protect the wetland habitats of migratory bird species. Participating states designate one or more wetland within their territory to protect. In addition to increasing the number of protected wetlands, the agreement has contributed to a long-term shift in the perception of the benefits of wetlands.

Another agreement, the Convention Concerning the Protection of World Cultural and Natural Heritage (WHC), takes an even broader approach to nature protection, protecting sites of particular cultural or natural importance. Overall, the number of species institutions may occasionally lead to problems of institutional overlap and poor centralized management, but may also ensure that some species and ecosystems receive more protection than they would have otherwise because they fall under the mandate of several institutional structures.

Air and atmospheric pollution

There are three prominent problems of the atmospheric commons: Acid rain and related transboundary pollution, ozone depletion, and climate change. These problems exemplify classic traits that make environmental problems particularly difficult to resolve: States cannot be kept from polluting the atmosphere, and any one state's input of pollution decreases the quality of the atmosphere for others. States are thus not able to protect their own atmospheric resources without international cooperation. Institutions addressing atmospheric pollution include those representing both the great successes and notable failures of global environmental governance.

The first major international air pollution agreement was the Convention on Long-Range Transboundary Air Pollution, negotiated within the United Nations primarily among Western and Eastern European states in the Cold War context of 1979. Over time, across different separately negotiated protocols, it has required different approaches to reductions of a variety of air pollutants that move directionally across borders, taking into consideration the sources and effects of the pollutants, and eventually coming to focus on the interaction among pollutants. As with many environmental institutions, it required states to monitor and report on conditions within their states; this monitoring caused several states to realize that they were more severely affected by air pollutants than previously thought, and thus improved the willingness of some states to cooperate with binding emissions reductions.[7] Other institutions regulating transboundary air pollution have generally been regionally focused, as air pollutants typically travel on the scale of hundreds of kilometers.

The interconnected institutions protecting the ozone layer, which shields the earth from excess UV radiation, have constituted some of the most successful attempts at global environmental governance to date. The primary agreement addressing the depletion of the ozone layer is the Montreal Protocol on Substances that Deplete the Ozone Layer, which was signed in 1987 and built on the institutional structure created by the Vienna Convention for the Protection of the Ozone Layer of 1985. The Montreal Protocol initially required states to freeze and then, after modification, gradually phase out the consumption of ozone-depleting substances. As scientific research increasingly demonstrated the magnitude of the problem, the reductions were deepened to complete phasedown, the timeline for these reductions compressed, and new substances restricted. The consumption of these ozone-depleting substances dramatically slowed—and is starting to contribute to a turnaround in—the depletion of the ozone layer.[8]

The Montreal Protocol is widely regarded as a significant success both in terms of global cooperation (as of 2009 it became the first set of treaties in the world to be ratified by all UN member states) and its actual environmental impact. One reason for its success was its ability to lure reluctant states into the agreement via both negative (trade restrictions in controlled substances with anyone outside the agreement) and positive (assistance in meeting obligations) inducements. The protocol allowed developing states additional time before having to meet phasedown requirements, and ultimately created a multilateral fund to help these states meet the "incremental costs" of the treaty's obligations. These concessions came about in part because of strong negotiation power on the part of developing states, without whose participation the agreement would be ineffective. The agreement created a precedent of granting developing countries special consideration and economic assistance that has now become the norm within global environmental agreements.

One of the most difficult global environmental issues to address has been climate change, which has been regulated, since its signing in Rio in 1992 through the UNFCC. There have been two prominent agreements under its auspices. The first was the Kyoto Protocol in 1997, which required reductions in the emissions of greenhouse gases (GHGs) by developed countries but ran into difficulties when the United States, then the largest emitter of greenhouse gases, refused to ratify. The second was the Paris Agreement in 2015, which uses individual pledges by states with an overall goal of keeping the global average temperature from increasing by more than 1.5°C. Unlike the Kyoto Protocol, the Paris Agreement involves both developing and developed states in nationally determined pledges to reduce emissions of GHGs; and it has had greater success than the Kyoto Protocol in engaging prominent emitters like China and, at least initially, the United States. The future of US involvement, however, has become uncertain under the Trump administration.

Underpinning scientific collaboration on climate change is the Intergovernmental Panel on Climate Change (IPCC), created in 1988 by UNEP and the World Meteorological Organization (WMO) to assess the state of the global scientific understanding of climate change. Over time this multinational group of scientists has demonstrated increasing confidence in human effects on the global climate system and predicted increasingly severe impacts.

Toxic materials

The movement of hazardous materials across borders accounts for another set of environmental governance structures.[9] Hazardous materials fall broadly into three categories: Byproducts of economic activity that are unintentionally transported across borders; byproducts that are deliberately traded between countries; and useful substances that nevertheless cause under-anticipated harms to human or ecological health. The institutions that attempt to regulate hazardous waste share connected histories and common approaches, and they have begun to collaborate in their efforts. As a whole, they regulate the movement of hazards through trade restrictions and other domestic measures, and they work to create informed consent in trade between developing and developed states.

While most hazardous waste trade still occurs largely between industrialized countries, as waste disposal in developed countries has become more expensive, it can be cost effective for companies to send hazardous waste to developing states. On the face of it, these trades are voluntary. In practice, states with high poverty levels frequently do not have the ability to control what crosses their borders, or may only be willing to accept dangerous materials because of economic need.

In this context, the Basel Convention on the Transboundary Movement of Hazardous Wastes and Their Disposal was negotiated in 1989. The agreement established the requirement that states must be notified before hazardous waste is shipped to them, and enumerates their right to refuse such shipments either individually or categorically. The most important development since the creation of the convention is the negotiation of a protocol that would ban all export of hazardous waste from developed to developing states, but its entry into force has been stalled for decades. African states had called for a stronger regulatory system under Basel than was ultimately agreed on. In response to these failed efforts, African states negotiated the Bamako Convention on the Ban of Import into Africa and the Control of Transboundary Movement and Management of Hazardous Wastes Within Africa in 1991; it entered into force in 1998 and held its first conference of parties in 2013; Bamako convention parties refuse all imports of hazardous waste.

Other governance structures address additional ways that toxic materials move internationally. One such process concerns chemicals and pesticides in international trade. Substances that have been deemed to be too toxic to use, or dispose of, in one state could be sold to another without its knowledge of the risk. This issue was initially addressed through the creation of a nonbinding "prior informed consent" procedure. The nonbinding nature of this process increased the initial willingness of states to adopt this procedure. There was nevertheless pressure to make these provisions binding, which led to the negotiation of the Rotterdam Convention for the Prior Informed Consent Procedure for Certain Hazardous Chemicals and Pesticides in International Trade in 1998.

This process essentially formalized the previous nonbinding procedure. The secretariat maintains a list of chemicals and pesticides whose use has been restricted by two states in different regions. If a chemical appears on this list, all states must indicate whether they refuse to accept any shipments of this substance generally, are willing to accept shipments, or agree to accept shipments under certain circumstances. States may only export a listed chemical if they have received prior informed consent from the state to which they are sending it, and must abide by any conditions (including a complete refusal) indicated by receiving states.

A different mechanism addresses persistent organic pollutants (POPs), a type of bio-accumulating pollution (frequently pesticides or byproducts of industrial pollutants) that can cause cancer and other health problems. The governance process for addressing them was created by the Stockholm Convention on Persistent Organic Pollutants in 2001. Under this agreement, pollutants are listed in annexes that determine whether their use and production is scheduled to be eliminated or not. Trade in these substances is prohibited except for reasons of "environmentally sound disposal" unless states have registered exemptions. The most controversial of controlled substances is the pesticide DDT, which is environmentally problematic but is considered important for malaria control in parts of the developing world. For this reason, many states have registered exemptions for this substance.

A recently negotiated agreement tackles the movement of mercury across borders. Mercury is released naturally through geological processes, but intentional and unintentional human activities, such as coal burning, goldmining, and even use in dentistry, have dramatically increased its release into the environment. Mercury bio-accumulates, and causes damage to both human and animal health. The Minamata Convention on Mercury, negotiated in 2013, sets restrictions on both permitted trades and permitted uses of mercury, with an aim to phase out selected uses of mercury completely and reduce other uses significantly through targeted action plans on a state-by-state basis. Controversially, mercury emissions from small-scale gold mining and atmospheric emissions—two of the biggest sources of mercury globally—have the least stringent restrictions in the agreement. The convention entered into force in August 2017.

Funding

Addressing global environmental problems requires funding. At least initially, taking action to prevent environmental degradation costs more than "business-as-usual." Particularly affected are developing countries, whose participation in global environmental governance is necessary for preventing or addressing problems. These states are often reluctant to take on obligations that preclude development options that had been available to already industrialized states.

One key institution was created as the primary standing mechanism for funding for addressing global environmental issues. The Global Environment Facility (GEF) was established as a collaboration between the World Bank, UNEP, and other development organizations. It currently serves as the official funding mechanism for five treaties: The Convention on Biological Diversity, the UNFCC, the United Nations Convention to Combat Desertification, the Stockholm Convention, and the Minamata Convention. It also provides funding for other projects relating to global or transboundary environmental protection, particularly in the areas of climate change, biodiversity, landuse, and international waters. Unlike the Washington-based international financial institutions and regional development banks, contributions in the GEP do not determine voting power, and developing states thus have significant decision-making influence.

Non-state environmental governance

Intergovernmental institutions, the primary focus of this chapter, are created and governed by their member states. But states are not and have never been the only relevant actors for governing the global environment. Non-state actors—nongovernmental organizations (NGOs), scientific organizations, industry, and even individuals—play important roles in influencing efforts to address global environmental issues.

Among the many governance roles played by non-state actors are an increasing participation in formal roles within intergovernmental institutions, and the creation of fully non-state international collaboration mechanisms that influence globally relevant environmental behavior. Non-state governance processes addressing global environmental issues have taken on growing prominence, especially in contexts such as climate change where traditional intergovernmental processes have fallen short.

One type of non-state environmental governance involves NGOs performing governance-like roles within broader intergovernmental governance processes. The IPCC is one such institution; although the organization was created by intergovernmental organizations, the scientists who comprise it serve as individuals rather than as representatives of states. Another such entity is the International Institute for Applied Systems Analysis (IIASA). It is an international scientific institute, which conducts both environmental and non-environmental policy-oriented research. Its Regional Acidification INformation and Simulation (RAINS) model provided technical expertise to teams negotiating the 1979 LRTAP Convention. IIASA was later given responsibility for conducting integrated assessment modeling under the agreement.[10] The organization's other environmental models and research have also influenced UNEP reports on carbon emission reductions and other intergovernmental processes.

A second approach involves non-state institutions working across borders collaboratively to influence the actions of actors (often from industry) that contribute to global environmental problems. One such effort involves creating environmental standards and awarding certification to processes or products that are environmentally friendly. In these instances, an international NGO sets standards that must be met for industry actors worldwide to receive certification that their products are sustainable. This process, used effectively for both forestry operations (via the Forest Stewardship Council) and fisheries (via the Marine Stewardship Council), calls attention to environmentally friendly products that consumers can choose to purchase, and motivates foresters or fishers to ensure that their actions allow them to meet the certification requirements. This practice has the greatest effect when intermediate actors—such as major retailers or governments—agree to only provide certified products.

Other non-state governance processes with effect on the global environment include a wide variety of collaborative measures to manage GHGs in a context in which global efforts have been weak or nonexistent.[11] For example, the Cities for Climate Protection program guides cities around the world in making greenhouse gas emissions reductions commitments and implementing and reporting on them. Other NGOs have worked to create the accounting standards businesses and governments use to calculate and report their greenhouse gas emissions, or to set up emissions trading systems that allow different entities to collaborate in reducing emissions cost effectively. What is notable are the many efforts with international effect that have arisen to fill a gap left by inadequate intergovernmental governance.

Conclusion

Global environmental problems are complex and multifaceted, as are the institutions that address them. Most global environmental governance is conducted via a diffuse set of institutions created to oversee the implementation of issue-specific treaties. These governance processes tackle difficult problems that require widespread participation by states in order to improve environmental conditions. One of the hallmarks of this governance is the deepening cooperation made possible as scientific evidence shows the need for increasingly serious action. Furthermore, successful early cooperative efforts make states willing to expand their collective efforts. At the same time, as institutions proliferate and their mandates expand, additional efforts are needed to ensure coordination across institutional structures.

As environmental problems grow more complex and more connected to broader aspects of human behavior—and especially as some countries, such as the United States under the Trump administration, have become more reluctant to participate in intergovernmental cooperation—the focus of global environmental governance has shifted to include more non-state and other informal governance processes. Ultimately, some combination of intergovernmental and non-state governance processes is likely beneficial in figuring out how to best govern issues of the global environment.

Additional reading

W. Bradnee Chambers and Jessica F. Green, eds., *Reforming International Environmental Governance: From Institutional Limits to Innovative Reforms* ((Tokyo: United Nations University Press, 2005).

Pamela S. Chasek, *Earth Negotiations: Analyzing Thirty Years of Environmental Diplomacy* (Tokyo, New York, and Paris: United Nations University Press, 2001).

Elizabeth R. DeSombre, *Global Environmental Institutions*, 2nd ed. (New York: Routledge, 2017).

Sebastian Oberthür and Olav Schram Stokke, *Managing Institutional Complexity: Regime Interplay and Global Environmental Change* (Cambridge, MA: MIT Press, 2011).

Henrik Selin, *Global Governance of Hazardous Chemicals: Challenges of Multilevel Management* (Cambridge, MA: MIT Press, 2010).

Notes

1 Pablo Gutman, "What Did WSSD Accomplish? An NGO Perspective," *Environment* 45, no. 2 (2003): 20–26.

2 David L. Downie and Marc A. Levy, "The UN Environment Program at a Turning Point: Options for Change," in *The Global Environment in the Twenty-First Century: Prospects for International Cooperation*, ed. Pamela S. Chasek (Tokyo: United Nations University Press, 2000).

3 J. Samuel Barkin and Elizabeth R. DeSombre, *Saving Global Fisheries: Reducing Fishing Capacity to Promote Sustainability* (Cambridge, MA: MIT Press, 2013).

4 Ronald B. Mitchell, *Intentional Oil Pollution at Sea* (Cambridge, MA: MIT Press, 1994).

5 IMO, "Summary of Status of Conventions," 2017, www.imo.org/en/About/Conventions/Status OfConventions/Pages/Default.aspx.

6 Piers Campbell, Judith Hushagen, and Dipanwita Sinha, "Challenges, Opportunities and Evolution: Review of the Secretariat of the International Maritime Organization," Switzerland: MANNET, 21 March 2001, 13.

7   Henrik Selin and Stacy D. VanDeveer, "Mapping Institutional Linkages in European Air Pollution Politics," *Global Environmental Politics* 3, no. 3 (2003): 14–46.

8   Edward A. Parson, *Protecting the Ozone Layer: Science and Strategy* (Oxford: Oxford University Press, 2003).

9   Henrik Selin, *Global Governance of Hazardous Chemicals* (Cambridge, MA: MIT Press, 2010).

10 Selin and VanDeveer, "Mapping Institutional Linkages."

11 Matthew J. Hoffmann, *Climate Governance at the Crossroads: Experimenting with a Global Response After Kyoto* (Oxford: Oxford University Press, 2011).

Regional development banks and global governance

Jonathan R. Strand

Even casual observers of world politics recognize the significance of the International Monetary Fund (IMF) and World Bank as major players in global economic governance. These two organizations make headlines daily and are often cast as heroes or villains in analyses of their roles in governing the global political economy. Along with the World Trade Organization (WTO), the IMF, and World Bank are among the most studied formal organizations. However, to understand global economic governance more completely, it is necessary to move beyond this triad to include other formal institutions that play essential roles in governing the global economy.

This chapter examines the place of regional development banks (RDBs) in global economic governance, which are multilateral development banks that engage in lending and other activities designed to foster economic growth in developing countries. Like the World Bank, RDBs provide various types of loan as well as policy advice to member governments but should not be viewed as miniature versions of the World Bank. While the RDBs occupy much of the same global governance terrain as the World Bank, they differ from the World Bank in important ways and have their own organizational cultures and historical contexts. These differences highlight critical doctrinal disputes between governments as well as the unfolding of new norms.

There are five major RDBs and several others that operate at a sub-regional level. The four older, "legacy" ones are the African Development Bank (AfDB), Asian Development Bank (ADB), Inter-American Development Bank (IDB), and the European Bank for Reconstruction and Development (EBRD). The AfDB, ADB, and IDB were created during the Cold War, while the EBRD was created at its end. The newest RDB is the Asian Infrastructure Investment Bank (AIIB), which began operations in 2016 and has generated a lot of policy and scholarly commotion as it was created by a non-Western power: China.

Sub-regional development banks (SDBs) have narrower scopes of operation than the larger RDBs. The most important SDBs are the Caribbean Development Bank (CDB), the Central American Bank for Economic Integration (CABEI), the East African Development Bank (EADB), and the West African Development Bank (BOAD). They have limited geographic range; notably the United States is not a member of any SDB. The RDBs and SDBs operate at the regional and sub-regional levels, but because of the roles they play in world politics in general, and development policy in particular, they should be viewed as pieces of global economic governance. For instance, RDBs and SDBs have been involved in political debates about development economics and have responded to changing global norms such as the incorporation of "good governance" in lending policies.[1]

The chapter begins with a brief history of the RDBs and SDBs. It then asks, who controls these institutions? A discussion follows of the three main activities of the RDBs: Project lending, policy-based lending, and policy advice. This section highlights how the RDBs are often focal points for discord between powerful states as well as pressures from civil society organizations. This last substantive section explores how RDBs and SDBs have responded to changing norms and shifts in the relative power of member governments. The conclusion reflects on the future of the RDBs in light of changes to ideas and material power in the world political economy.

RDBs in historical context

Developing countries have many sources of capital available, including private capital markets, bilateral aid, and aid offered through multilateral institutions. After World War II, many developing economies could not qualify for loans from private capital markets because of concerns about their ability to repay them. Bilateral foreign aid was also (and remains) problematic as it was often seen as politically motivated since donor governments have control over the disbursement and use of such capital. Multilateral aid was (and continues to be) viewed by many as less political since money from multiple donors is pooled together and individual donors have less firsthand oversight of how the aid is distributed.

The World Bank is the foremost multilateral development institution; given its size and expertise, the need for regional development institutions might be questioned. The World Bank was created, in part, to promote economic development, which began after European reconstruction. From the perspective of the twenty-first century, an observer might ask, why create smaller regional banks? To understand the establishment of RDBs and SDBs, the historical context of each institution needs to be explored.

The creation of international organizations was not methodical, and the ideational linkage of the RDBs and SDBs to the World Bank was less continuous than it appears today. Early in its history, the World Bank failed to approve most loan applications from poorer countries because of concerns about borrowers' creditworthiness. It was also the case that the primary focus of the World Bank during its early years was on reconstruction of Europe—indeed, its official name is the International Bank for Reconstruction and Development (IBRD). World Bank lending to the poorest borrowers was meager until the 1960 creation of a "soft loan" window, the International Development Association (IDA). In other words, the World Bank was not satisfying all of the demand for multilateral development assistance, which, in part, explains the formation of RDBs. There were also specific political reasons for the creation of each of the RDBs. The establishment of the legacy RDBs involved varying degrees of great power interests within the changing global context of the Cold War and American leadership. The AIIB, by way of contrast, reflects the leadership ambitions and development policy priorities of a rising power, China.

In addition to the practical need for capital, the Cold War context was important in the creation of the legacy RDBs. The United States, which was instrumental in creating the World Bank and IMF, sought other means to promote US foreign policy and views on desirable development pathways to follow—that is, that they should be market-oriented rather than socialist. For instance, US foreign policymakers were concerned that Soviet influence in the Western hemisphere could increase, and that the IDB would be viewed as one vehicle to support allies. The IDB was the first of the RDBs, starting operations in 1959.

The interests of middle-income and lower income countries were vital in the creation of the RDBs. Immediately after its creation, the World Bank concentrated on reconstruction projects in Western Europe, before turning its attention to newly independent—that is, decolonized—countries. Some non-Western independent countries were concerned that the World Bank would not pay enough attention to their needs. Smaller, regionally focused multilateral institutions were viewed as more amenable to regional and individual country interests. In short, interest in creating the IDB and ADB came from middle-income countries. Also, in the case of the ADB, Japan was keen to have opportunities to positively reengage regional countries, many of which suffered immensely during Japan's decades of occupation and imperialism.

The ADB began operations in 1966 and made its first loans in 1968. Early lending by the ADB was influenced by American military concerns in Southeast Asia and Japan's efforts to rebuild its economy. Throughout the ADB's history, Japan has played a particularly significant role in the management of the bank as well as the ideas underpinning the ADB's views on economic development.

The Cold War played a different role in the creation of the AfDB and IDB. The AfDB was shaped by a political movement that sought to increase solidarity and cooperation among sub-Saharan African countries.[2] The United States and other developed countries were not as instrumental in the AfDB's formation. Several members had been unable to qualify for World Bank and private banking loans and therefore looked to the AfDB for assistance. When it began operations, the AfDB was expected to be a development bank controlled by, and for the benefit of, African governments. The agreement creating the AfDB was finalized in 1963, and the bank opened its doors in 1964.

A difficulty for the AfDB was that it was undercapitalized at the outset since it excluded wealthy, non-regional governments. Eventually regional member governments forwent some control over the AfDB in order to receive contributions from wealthier countries. Today the AfDB has some eighty member governments, including twenty-six from outside the region. For most of its history, the AfDB was based in Abidjan, Côte d'Ivoire, but in 2003 political instability caused the bank to move to Tunisia, where its headquarters remained until moving back to Abidjan in 2014. In 2017 the annual meeting of the AfDB was hosted by India, which is notable as it was the first time the meeting was held outside Africa and reflected the growing importance of non-Western powers in the organization.

The EBRD was created in 1991 at the end of the Cold War with a mandate to assist economies in Central and Eastern Europe in transitioning to a market-oriented system. Unlike the negotiations to create earlier RDBs, there was widespread consensus about the need for a new development organization. The EBRD's different historical context than the other three legacy RDBs helps explain why it engages in more political activity than other RDBs. The EBRD often is thought of as a political bank not only because it has an obligation to build political institutions but also because there has often been a political divide between the United States and the United Kingdom, on one hand, and France and other continental European governments, on the other hand.[3] Today the EBRD has over sixty-five governments and two other European agencies as members.

The AIIB, first proposed by Chinese leaders just after the Great Recession (2007–2009), is the most recent RDB and, along with the New Development Bank (NDB)—together undoubtedly the most significant change to global economic governance in over twenty years. For many observers, the AIIB suggests attenuation to the US-centered world order and a challenge to legacy RDBs and the World Bank. It is too early to fully assess whether it will complement or contest with legacy RDBs. Thus far the AIIB has adopted an institutional design and issued policies on lending practices that are similar to legacy RDBs and the World Bank.

Like the RDBs, SDBs have distinct histories and need to be understood against the backdrop of the stakeholders that created and control them. Of the SDBs, the CDB is the most widely studied. In 1970 the CDB began operations with a mandate to engage in lending and other assistance to promote economic growth in the Caribbean. Its membership includes most countries with water access to the Caribbean, except for the United States and Cuba. There are also five members from outside of the region: Canada, China, Germany, Italy, and the United Kingdom. While the United States is not a member, it was involved in the bank's creation and contributes capital to special funds and projects. China joined the CDB in 1998, and soon after those Caribbean governments that had previously recognized the Republic of China (Taiwan) as the legitimate sovereign changed their recognition to Beijing.

Founded by four Central American governments in 1960, CABEI has thirteen members and began operations in 1961. CABEI has concentrated on projects that enhance investment opportunities, "giving precedence to the export, basic services (infrastructure, electricity, communications), and agricultural sectors."[4] The bank is based in Tegucigalpa, Honduras, and primarily promotes projects in Belize, Guatemala, Panama, Dominican Republic, El Salvador, Honduras, Nicaragua, and

Costa Rica. In addition to these eight members, there are five members from outside the region that contribute to the bank. The only members from outside the Western hemisphere are Spain and Taiwan. In addition to loans, CABEI engages in efforts designed to promote educational programs and environmental projects with a focus on biodiversity.

The EADB was originally created in the late 1960s but was dissolved in 1977 because of the failure of the East African Cooperation (EAC) Treaty. In 1980, the EADB was relaunched with its own charter separate from the EAC Treaty. The EADB has four primary members (Kenya, Rwanda, Tanzania, and Uganda) and several associated members, which include other global institutions such as the AfDB. In recent years, the largest share of loans issued by the EADB has been for construction and real estate development. While the four primary governments control the bank, the EADB also has such private sector shareholders as Barclays Bank.

In 1973, BOAD was established by eight governments as an organ of the West African Monetary Union. The bank began operations in 1976 and in recent years has focused on facilitating private investment and promoting deeper economic integration. BOAD is largely controlled by member governments but it also includes among its membership the Export and Import Bank of India.

These smaller institutions have specialized missions. While they do not lend as much capital as the larger RDBs, they have mobilized capital and served as agents of regional integration. While they are less conspicuous than the RDBs, the relatively small size of the SDBs can make them better equipped to grapple with local problems. Together, RDBs and SDBs are significant parts of global economic governance. They were not created to supplement or complement the World Bank but rather to reflect specific historical contexts for particular political purposes. While it may be tempting to view the RDBs as "mini" World Banks, doing so clouds their significantly different origins.

Inside out: Internal governance

RDBs and SDBs were created by governments to engage in lending and other activities designed to promote economic development. As formal intergovernmental organizations, their members agree to adhere to each organization's foundational treaty. These treaties provide guidance regarding how the banks will be organized, how they will make decisions, and their substantive mandates. The rules used for internal governance can influence the lending and other activities of the banks. In addition to the role played by member governments, these institutions comprise large and distinct bureaucracies, which also shape the way they operate. The literature on the RDBs and SDBs—as well as other international organizations (IOs)—often debates whether governments or bureaucrats matter more in understanding the behavior of IOs. Some scholars emphasize the power bestowed by governments and the rules for decision making. Other scholars point out that bureaucracies have their own vested interests and can at times undermine the intent of decisions made by governments. Most studies agree that within IOs there is a complex interplay of power, ideas, and rules that require a nuanced approach to recognize essential actors, ideas, and forces.

At first glance, it seems these IOs are controlled by member governments since they are "shareholders" and are assigned voting rights. RDBs have complex voting rules that include weighted voting and selective representation. While uncommon in UN organizations, weighted-voting systems are fairly common in domestic and other international settings and usually rationalized as necessary in instances where some voters have an empirical claim to more votes than others. The RDBs use weighted voting to apportion influence on the assumption the governments which contribute more money should have more influence over decisions. Since most of the votes in the RDBs are held by the wealthiest members, there is concern that their poorer borrowers have little voice over the terms. Weighting votes based on the size of a country's contributions can give the perception that the RDBs are controlled much like private corporations, where the largest shareholders have the most votes. To surmount this view, most RDBs assign some votes without regard to contributions. Referred to as "basic votes," they are used by all the RDBs except the EBRD. In the ADB, basic votes are assigned to all members as an equal share of twenty percent of total votes. The IDB and AfDB assign a set number of votes to each member: 135 for the IDB and 625 for the AfDB. In the AIIB, basic votes are set as a percentage and founding members receive an additional share of votes.

As "regional" organizations, several of the RDBs make an effort to maintain a regional flavor in the allocation of votes. For example, in the IDB, at least half of all votes must be held by regional borrowing members but there is a "basement" limit on the votes held by the United States and Canada. This leaves only approximately sixteen percent of the votes to be allocated to lending non-regional members like Italy, Japan, and Norway. When China joined the IDB in 2009, it meant the relative share of votes held by other non-regional members declined.

A more extreme rule, once used by the AfDB, barred wealthy countries from joining and holding votes, although they could contribute money to special funds. In an effort to obtain more capital, in the early 1980s the AfDB began to allow wealthy countries to become full members; but it also put in place a rule limiting the percentage of votes held by non-regional countries.

In the ADB, at least sixty percent of all votes must be allocated to regional members. While the EBRD does not use the regional/non-regional dichotomy, there is a complex nesting of European agencies. The European Investment Bank and the European Union (EU) are also members of the EBRD and they have more votes than some member states.

Like the legacy RDBs, the AIIB uses weighted voting but also provides additional influence for first governments that joined. Given China's leadership role in establishing the AIIB it is no surprise that it holds the most votes at just over thirty-two percent; more than three times that of the second largest vote holder India.

Weighted voting, while the most obvious aspect of internal governance, is not the only factor determining which members have the most influence. Through the process of selective representation, all members have a seat on a general voting body but there is a smaller, more important voting body in each RDB that make major decisions and carry out daily business. On the executive boards, there are some governments with individual seats, but most are aggregated into voting groups and each group selects a representative. The IDB has only two individual seats, held by Canada and the United States, while the remaining forty-six members are aggregated into twelve voting groups. This form of selective representation makes meetings of the executive boards more manageable but also results in the majority of members not directly representing themselves.

The complex, formal elements of internal governance and associated emphasis on the representation of governments can lead to the conclusion that the wealthier countries which contribute the bulk of resources have more influence. Borrowing governments have only a handful of votes and are usually not guaranteed seats on the executive boards. This has been described as a polarization of members into wealthy "rulemakers" and poorer "ruletakers," with the former rarely required to live by the rules they make. Such state-centric claims are not without foundation, but there are other influential stakeholders within RDBs that at times are more important than member governments.

As noted above, RDBs are large bureaucracies comprised of leadership and rank-and-file staff, all of whom exert a degree of influence. Even if governments vote to implement a policy, it is left to the bureaucracies to operationalize and interpret the policy. In this activity, there are opportunities for staff members and the structure of the bureaucracy itself to have an impact on policymaking. The RDB with the largest number of staff is the ADB, with about 3000. Most of the ADB's staffers are from the Philippines, but only a few hold high-level posts. There are about 150 employees from Japan, including several in key leadership positions. In fact, the president of the ADB has always been a citizen of Japan with a close affiliation to Japan's Ministry of Finance. There are also about 150 Americans working at the bank, and at least one of the four vice-presidents has always been an American.

Headquartered in Washington, DC, the IDB has around 2000 employees. Given its physical proximity to the US Treasury Department, the IDB has long been viewed as dominated by US foreign policy interests. Most of the IDB's employees are based in Washington, DC; while the head of the IDB has always been from a developing country, at least one other key position has always been held by an American. Almost all the AfDB's leadership and 2000 staff members are from developing countries.

The Beijing-based AIIB has fewer than 125 employees although as it continues to expand its lending operations there will be growth to the size of its bureaucracy. The presidency of the AIIB is held by a Chinese national while several senior positions are held by other members, including key posts currently filled by French and UK nationals. The RDB with the least emphasis on the nationality of leadership and staff is the EBRD.

Consideration of the national origin of staff members only goes so far in defining the internal culture of the RDBs. Nevertheless, the norms that have developed regarding leadership positions influence the policies and ideas pursued by the banks. For instance, in the ADB, the number of Japanese staffers and Japan's monopoly on the presidency give the appearance of conspicuous Japanese influence. Early on in the bank's history, however, the United States often had more influence over key decisions.[5] But this relationship changed by the 1980s as Japan sought a more assertive role. More recently, Japan and the United States have openly differed over the lending goals of the ADB.

One shortcoming of the norms of national origin—that is, a person from X country would normally be expected to hold Y post—is that the best person may not be selected for key leadership positions. It is instructive to ask: "Is the president of the

ADB a Japanese citizen because s/he is the most qualified person for the position, or because Japan has more influence over the selection of the president?" This question can be asked of the other key leadership positions. Additionally, there is a tendency within the RDBs for policy inertia generated by an institutional path dependency. The RDBs, like other organizations, change slowly and can be insular from shifting norms and alterations in material power relations.[6] In sum, the organizational cultures of the RDBs as well as internal governance place special emphasis on the role of regional members, but the RDBs remain grounded in economic ideas stemming from the prevailing neoliberal paradigm. Even the Chinese-led AIIB has put in place policies and protections, such as an accountability mechanism and environmental impact assessments, which mirror those of other RDBs and the World Bank.

Discord over ideas and lending activities

The RDBs engage in three main activities. First, from the outset they were designed to promote economic development through project lending. To this end, the RDBs receive capital contributions from all members and pool these resources for lending purposes. These contributions can be either paid-in capital where the funds are placed under the control of an RDB or merely commitments by members to provide capital if needed to guarantee loans. The majority of capital committed to the RDBs is in this latter form of "callable capital." Project loans are the most common type of lending activity undertaken by the RDBs. As the name implies, these loans are designed to fund specific projects. Over the years, the RDBs have developed themes to guide project lending. Many of the projects are a result of private sector firms identifying a need and convincing a developing country and other stakeholders to facilitate RDB funding.

The second mission of the RDBs is to provide capital to help governments facing financial crises, such as during the Latin American debt crisis of the 1980s. Policy-oriented lending is often controversial since borrowing governments are required to change public policies, and often the effects of policy changes are not proportional on all domestic sectors and populations. Usually associated with IMF lending, the legacy RDBs have also participated in conditional lending. Loans made for such purposes are designed to assist governments facing budgetary or other emergencies. Policy lending requires the borrowing government to commit to economic reforms such as increasing economic openness, reducing budget deficits, and privatizing state-owned enterprises.

In addition to high-profile lending activities, the RDBs have a third mandate to provide policy advice. Such counsel often goes hand in hand with lending, especially for crises. The RDBs undertake regular evaluations of members' economies, and such surveillance activities can influence the views of private investors and other IOs.

These three activities are not unconnected from one another; as received wisdom regarding governance and development has changed over the past fifty years, discord among stakeholders has followed. We should recall that the bureaucracies of the RDBs are subject to the influence of member governments; but those governments rely on staff to implement policies. During crises, or moments when discord occurs between powerful members, the organizational culture of an RDB can have an impact on the outcome of disagreements. There have been high-profile disputes about the mandates of the RDBs in response to changes in ideas about development policies and the rising influence of emerging markets.

Two areas in particular have resulted in major debates within the RDBs. The first area is the introduction of—and adoption by—IOs of new ideas about accountability and "good governance." The RDBs followed the World Bank's lead in defining good governance and developing their own accountability mechanisms. The second area involves debate about the development mandates of the RDBs. In particular, governments have conflicts over ideas and these ideational clashes are concomitant with changes to relative material power of stakeholders as they try to influence key concepts underpinning the lending policies of the RDBs.

The RDBs emulated the World Bank and have set standards for so-called good governance, which is often defined with reference to transparency, accountability, and adherence to rules.[7] Since the late 1990s, each RDB has formulated procedures associated with good governance and has established independent evaluation offices. These new agencies have varying degrees of independence and responsibilities; but in general they take stock of the impacts of RDB lending and allow groups adversely affected to file complaints. Skeptics view good governance and evaluation offices as window dressing that results in little tangible change to RDB activities because the "independent" agencies are not completely free from the influence of the bureaucracies; more importantly, these agencies do not possess the ability to dictate changes to RDB policies and procedures.

In addition to the adoption of good governance and creation of independent evaluation agencies, the RDBs have been institutional battlefields for debates about development policies. For example, Japan and other East Asian governments have attempted to have their post-World War II development experiences accepted by the World Bank and the RDBs as suitable options for developing countries to emulate. Japan and other East Asian economies pursued state-centric economic growth strategies labeled "export-led growth," the "development-state model," or the "East Asian development model." Regardless of the name, the set of policies associated with it do not fit neatly into neoliberal orthodoxy. The United States and the World Bank have both resisted efforts to have such state-centric views of development accepted as alternatives to market-oriented policies. Japan was successful in getting the World Bank to explore the development experiences of Asian economies but was not able to have these illiberal policies systematically incorporated into World Bank practices. Perhaps not surprisingly, given its influence within the ADB, Japan was more successful in obtaining support for its ideas about East Asian development within the ADB. The East Asian Financial Crisis of 1997–1999, however, undermined the credibility of the "miracle," and there was little change to the tenets of ADB lending.

There has been disagreement between the United States and Japan on the ADB's strategic plan. The ADB's *Strategy 2020* report outlined its vision for changing its lending doctrine.[8] It proved controversial and was not supported by the United States. In addition to US resistance, civil society organizations were also critical. One nongovernmental organization (NGO), for example, asserted that *Strategy 2020* had a clear "corporate bias."[9] In addition, there was political disagreement over the direction of the bank, with Japan and other regional members seeking "to strike out in new directions and help weld Asia together physically and in terms of policies." Meanwhile, the United States and some European members wanted the ADB "to stick to policies designed to reduce poverty and increase social well being."[10] In an unusually public display of discord, when *Strategy 2020* came up for approval, the United States voted against it.[11] Some borrowing members also were concerned about the shift away from traditional projects aimed at poverty reduction. Despite US resistance to *Strategy 2020*, an ADB senior staff member claimed there was no real impact on bank operations, with the implication that US opposition had only a nominal impact.[12]

The AIIB, with its genesis in Chinese leadership, is perhaps the most prominent example of policy and political discord in global economic governance in the twenty-first century. Unlike discord in the legacy RDBs, many observers claim the AIIB challenges longstanding US influence in global governance. Washington engaged in diplomatic attempts to stymie the AIIB by trying to convince allies to not join. Part of the US argument rested on the idea that Asia already had an RDB, the ADB. Despite pressure, most of Washington's allies nonetheless joined and have become active in the AIIB. That many European countries joined may indicate that US influence in global governance is waning. Japan is one close ally that has not joined the AIIB, although Japanese officials have not ruled out joining in the future. A major question is the extent to which the AIIB reflects Chinese efforts to increase soft power and contest US-dominated IOs.[13] Many see the AIIB part of a broader Chinese effort to create a global order reflecting Beijing's understanding and vision for global economic governance. The AIIB only has been making loans since 2016, but there are concerns that it will operate diametrically opposed to prevailing development practices, duplicate the ADB, and undercut extant global institutions. Despite such concerns, the internal governance of the AIIB is very similar to that of the legacy RDBs, with one major exception: The United States is not a member.

In sum, the RDBs are at the confluence of battles among powerful actors in global governance over ideas and world order. The RDBs do not merely reflect the doctrines on development pursued by the World Bank because they have different organizational and historical contexts as well as allowing for a greater role for regional members. The RDBs are vital instruments of global economic governance; for students of IOs, they provide additional examples of institutional design and development practices.

Conclusion

The RDBs have formal rules that determine how decisions are made on loans and important policy matters. The role of their administrations, including the leadership staffs as well as the foundational ideas about development, also explains which players have power in specific contexts. In other words, observers should not point to one aspect of RDB governance and behavior, such as their weighted-voting systems or nationalities of leadership, in order to understand their role. The RDBs as organizations exist in an environment in which they are subject to material pressures and ideational conflicts from global society as well as from within their own bureaucratic structures.

Often overlooked in studies of global governance, the RDBs and SDBs provide important lessons in how economic ideas are operationalized into practice. Moreover, lending does not occur divorced from politics, and these IOs are at the center of great debates about development. While the RDBs and SDBs have regional flavors, they are still subject to the influence of great powers and the ideas behind pro-globalization neoliberal economic policies. With the rising status in the world economy of emerging markets, such as China, Brazil, and India, questions loom about how the legacy RDBs will adjust to such systemic political change, and whether China and other rising powers will seek to create additional IOs to better express their political and economy interests.

Additional reading

Sarah Babb, *Behind the Development Banks: Washington Politics, World Poverty, and the Wealth of Nations* (Chicago, IL: University of Chicago Press, 2009).

Tamar L. Gutner, *Banking on the Environment* (Cambridge, MA: MIT Press, 2002).

Susan Park and Jonathan R. Strand, eds., *Global Economic Governance and the Development Practices of the Multilateral Development Banks* (London: Routledge, 2016).

Jonathan R. Strand, *Regional Development Banks: Lending with a Regional Flavor* (London: Routledge, 2018 forthcoming).

Notes

1 Tina M. Zappile, "'Sub-regional Development Banks' Development as Usual?," in *Global Economic Governance and the Development Practices of the Multilateral Development Banks*, eds. Susan Park and Jonathan R. Strand (London: Routledge, 2016), 187–211.

2 Karen A. Mingst, *Politics and the African Development Bank* (Lexington: University of Kentucky Press, 1990).

3 Stuart Shields, "The European Bank for Reconstruction and Development as Organic Intellectual of Neoliberal Common Sense in Post-Communist Transition," in *Global Economic Governance*, eds. Park and Strand, 167–186.

4 Daniel Titelman, "Subregional Financial Cooperation: The Experiences of Latin America and the Caribbean," in *Regional Financial Cooperation*, ed. José Antonio Ocampo (Baltimore, MD: Brookings Institution Press and United National Economic Commission for Latin America and the Caribbean, 2006), 208.

5 Dennis T. Yasutomo, *The New Multilateralism in Japan's Foreign Policy* (New York: St. Martin's Press, 1995), 83.

6 Jonathan R. Strand and Michael W. Trevathan "Implications of Accommodating Rising Powers for the Regional Development Banks," in *Global Economic Governance*, eds. Park and Strand, 121–142.

7 Thomas G. Weiss, "Governance, Good Governance, and Global Governance: Conceptual and Actual Challenges," *Third World Quarterly* 21, no. 5 (2000): 795–814.

8 Asian Development Bank, *Strategy 2020: The Long-Term Strategic Framework of the Asian Development Bank, 2008–2020* (Manila, Philippines: ADB, 2008).

9 Bank Information Center, "ADB's 2020 Strategy Confirms Corporate Bias," 11 April 2008, www.forum-adb.org/BACKUP/pdf/PDF-LTSF/LTSF%20PR-final.pdf.

10 *Business Times Singapore*, "ADB Divided over Future Direction: Asian Members Want New Course, Advanced Nations Remain Traditional," 8 May 2006.

11 Ralph Minder, "US Shoots Down ADB's Strategic Plan," *Financial Times*, 9 April 2008, 3.

12 Ragu Gopalakrishnan, "U.S. and Asia Development Bank Split over Lending Policies," *International Herald Tribune*, 25 April 2008, 11.

13 Gregory T. Chin, "Asian Infrastructure Investment Bank: Governance Innovation and Prospects," *Global Governance* 22, no. 1 (2016): 11–26.

Climate change

Matthew J. Hoffmann

Climate change may be *the* governance challenge of our time and may remain so for the next century. Climate change is truly global in multiple senses—the climate system is global and the energy and economic systems that are causing the problems are global. Yet, in important ways, climate change is a profoundly local problem—the anthropogenic greenhouse gas emissions at the heart of the problem are produced everywhere, and the effects of climate change will be felt differently in different locales. The governance task is thus enormous. The latest climate science tells us that we are already on track for significant planetary warming, and that to hold this warming to 2°C (a level that may allow us to avoid some of the most dire ramifications of climate change), global emissions of greenhouse gases must peak in the next decade and fall off from there rapidly, moving the world towards de-carbonization by the end of the century.

Governing climate change is unlike other global governance challenges that humanity has previously faced because of how pervasive its causes and effects are and how deeply embedded fossil fuels are in the global economy and energy systems. To be effective, global climate governance needs to put the world on a path of massive transformation. In many ways, climate change has become the keystone issue in global environmental politics. It is directly connected to many other issues, like deforestation, biodiversity loss, and desertification, as a cause or consequence, and it is impossible to conceive of pursuing the agenda of sustainable development, like the world attempted in the Rio+20 meetings in 2012 and the agreement on the Sustainable Development Goals (SDGs) in 2015, without also addressing climate change.

This chapter chronicles the global response to climate change, and the evolution of the global governance of this issue. The first section outlines the scope of the problem, in terms of both its causes and effects. The chapter then discusses the first phases of the UN-based multilateral governance of climate change that emerged in the late 1980s and reached a nadir in the Copenhagen negotiations of 2009. Multilateral governance is not the sum total of the global response to climate change, however. The discussion of governance therefore must also explore transnational governance efforts that emerged in the twenty-first century. With the signing of the 2015 Paris Agreement, the global response to climate change entered a new phase, and the penultimate section explores the possibilities and challenges in this new era. The chapter concludes with some of

---

BOX 47.1 ORIENTING TERMS AND DYNAMICS

Greenhouse effect

Ironically, the greenhouse effect is actually something that allows humanity to thrive on Earth. The atmosphere acts as a greenhouse, holding in solar radiation that would otherwise reflect off the Earth and be sent into space. Without this *greenhouse effect*, the planet would be too cold to support life as we know it.

Greenhouse gases

There are a number of *greenhouse gases* both naturally occurring and human made (and some are both): Water vapor, carbon dioxide, methane, nitrous oxide, and hydro-fluorocarbons. Of the anthropogenic gases, carbon dioxide is by far the most prevalent, although some other gases, such as methane, have larger warming effects. The gases have different sources as well. Carbon dioxide results from the combustion of fossil fuels (coal, gasoline, oil) while methane is produced by the decay of organic matter.

Global warming (anthropogenic)

Since the Industrial Revolution, concentrations of human-produced greenhouse gases, especially carbon dioxide, have increased dramatically compared to natural baseline concentrations of these gases. Because most of the world's energy and economic systems are tied closely to the burning of fossil fuels (for energy production, transportation, agriculture, and industrial processes), we have caused large increases in the amount of greenhouse gases in the atmosphere. This increasing concentration of greenhouse gases leads to global warming. Climate scientists tell us that the Earth is already warming and that we could expect to see global average temperatures increase anywhere from two to six degrees centigrade in the course of this century.

Climate change

Climate change is the broad term for the ramifications of global warming. Atmospheric warming alters the dynamics of the climate. Possible changes include altered precipitation and drought patterns, changing storm frequencies and strengths, transformed seasons and incidences of extreme heat and even cold, rising sea levels, glaciers and polar ice caps melting, species migrations/extinctions, altered disease vectors and trajectories.

the key debates that currently animate the academic and policy discussions around global climate governance, especially and the recent ways in which multilateral and transnational governance approaches are coming together.[1]

Climate change as a problem to be governed[2]

The 2007 report from the Intergovernmental Panel on Climate Change (IPCC) found consensus in the scientific community that greenhouse gas emissions have significantly increased because of human activity and, further, that the modest temperature increases we have already experienced are "very likely due to the observed increase in anthropogenic greenhouse gas concentrations" and we could expect significant warming and climatic changes because of it.[3] This understanding has not wavered since 2007, and, if anything, the consensus in the scientific community has strengthened and its warnings about climate change have become more serious.

The current political consensus expressed in the Paris Agreement of 2015 is that constraining global temperature increases to 2°C is crucial, and that humanity should even seek to limit warming to 1.5°C.[4] Time is rapidly running out to undertake the changes necessary to meet these goals. In 2009 a prominent gathering of climate scientists and policymakers declared what is still a relatively taken for granted understanding: "If global warming is to be limited to a maximum of 2°C above preindustrial values, global emissions need to peak between 2015 and 2020 and then decline rapidly."[5]

Knowledge about expected warming from current and anticipated concentrations of greenhouse gases (GHGs) is increasingly troubling, even frightening, as the climate science community learns more about the kind of impacts to expect. The possible impacts of climate change are well known, but it appears as though at least some impacts are coming sooner than anticipated in earlier models and with greater magnitude. A steady stream of scientific reports detail how climate change has already begun and that the impacts, like the melting of glaciers polar ice caps, are coming more quickly than anticipated. The warmest year on record was 2016, which also was "the third year in a row to set a new record for global average surface temperatures."[6]

While scientific consensus has generated urgency in many corners of the world, it has not yet generated political consensus and will to take significant global action. Some of this disconnect can be traced to uncertainties in climate science. The climate system is enormously complex, and there are inherent uncertainties in climate change that we may never unravel entirely. There are a number of intervening factors between concentrations of GHGs, temperature increase, and climatic changes like increased severity and frequency of storms, cycles of droughts and floods, and patterns of precipitation, and climate science has yet to figure them all out. In addition, natural variability in the climate can mask and/or exacerbate the effect of anthropogenic greenhouse gas emissions. Finally, even though the warming of the atmosphere is a global phenomenon, the magnitude and geographic extent of the effects of climate change are uncertain—in other words, we do not necessarily know how bad it will be, where, and when.

The problem, at one level, is thus fairly clear and relatively simple. Increasing concentrations of GHGs raise global temperatures. Increased global temperatures lead to a number of serious consequences that could have a severe impact on much of humanity, especially the most vulnerable. Heading off these consequences is a matter of emitting fewer greenhouse gases, especially less carbon dioxide, and thus substantially decarbonizing our economies and energy systems. The mechanics of climate change are simple, but governing the global response to this problem is not.

Development and evolution of multilateral climate governance, 1990–2009

When climate change was put on the international political agenda in the late 1980s, there was no question as to the mode of governance that would be employed to respond to this problem. Multilateral treaty making, supervised by the United Nations, was taken for granted and essentially synonymous with climate governance. It was understood that climate change was a global problem, not solvable by the actions of individual states, and that it would require a global solution. This made a great deal of sense from certain perspectives. Climate change is often characterized as a classic public goods problem—a stable climate is non-excludable and non-rivalrous and thus ripe for under-provision. The solution was to be a global treaty that would forge cooperation to address the problem. The story of global climate governance, therefore, has to begin with the multilateral negotiation process, its emergence, achievements, and challenges over the first twenty years of the climate regime.

The early climate negotiations saga

In the late 1980s, climate change transitioned from a scientific issue to an international policy problem when the UN General Assembly created the Intergovernmental Panel on Climate Change (IPCC) to provide a firm scientific foundation for taking action on climate change. It was to gather and report on the science of climate change (its causes, effects, and possible policy options). Since that time, the periodic IPCC reports (1990, 1997, 2007, and 2014) have served as benchmarks for the consensus on climate change. It should be noted that IPCC reports are a combination of scientific literature review and political messaging—states have a good deal of say about what goes into the reports.

The first set of global climate negotiations produced the 1992 UN Framework Convention on Climate Change (UNFCCC). It did not mandate any legally binding reductions of greenhouse gas emissions—this was a bridge too far at this stage of the climate regime given US reluctance to such measures and the bargaining positions of other major states and blocs that are discussed below. What the UNFCCC laid out, however, were aspirational goals to take actions that would maintain the stability of the climate and return emissions to 1990 levels, along with strictures for states to report their emissions and to develop means of technology transfer of climate-friendly technology. The UNFCCC also had within it commitments and provisions for continuing the negotiations and moving towards protocols that would take up specific actions. These negotiations have been undertaken annually since the UNFCCC came into force in 1994.

The transition from a broad aspirational climate change response to a treaty that would mandate action began in earnest in 1995, when the United States signaled its willingness to consider binding emissions reductions in a global accord. This opened the way for the negotiations that produced the Kyoto Protocol in 1997. This landmark treaty was the result of intense bargaining along both North–North and North–South dimensions. The breakthrough was an agreement by the North to collectively reduce their greenhouse gas emissions five percent below 1990 levels by 2012. In addition, the international community of states agreed to a number of "flexibility" mechanisms that states could use to reach their reduction commitments. These included a global emissions trading system and the Clean Development Mechanism, whereby actors in the global North could pay for projects in the global South and receive the emissions reductions credits that resulted. While almost everyone acknowledged that the Kyoto Protocol, alone, would be insufficient to stave off climate change, it was considered to be a decent start.

The signing of the Kyoto Protocol would prove to be the high point of the first phase of climate regime, but very quickly it became apparent that bringing the protocol into force would be a challenge and that its prospects for being effective were dim. The US Senate pledged to not ratify any agreement that did not include commensurate mandates for large developing countries (which the protocol did not have). This immediately called into question whether the single largest emitter at the time would participate. In addition, because the protocol could only come into force if states representing fifty-five percent of global emissions were represented, Washington's withdrawal effectively meant that almost every other Northern state would have to ratify.

In 2001, a difficult situation became almost impossible, as the United States "unsigned" the Kyoto Protocol under the new president George W. Bush. Even as the rest of the international community of states moved ahead with negotiations to flesh out the details of ratifying and implementing the Kyoto Protocol, the largest player withdrew. It came into force in 2005 but under a pall. Even though the states that ratified the Kyoto Protocol ultimately reached their goal of a five percent reduction from 1990 levels, it is often considered a failure because it was not the *global* agreement that most deemed necessary.

After 2005, the climate regime descended to its nadir as states floundered in their attempts to build a replacement for the Kyoto Protocol. There was renewed optimism around the 2009 negotiations in Copenhagen with hopeful signs coming from Washington after the election of Barack Obama and from China in terms of willingness to consider significant action raised expectations. Yet the international community of states was not able to achieve a legally binding replacement for the Kyoto Protocol. The "Hopenhagen" negotiations began with hope for the possibility of achieving a comprehensive, legally binding agreement to combat global warming. They ended as "Brokenhagen," achieving only a maligned Copenhagen Accord that failed to commit major greenhouse gas emitters to a new binding agreement. Instead, a system of voluntary pledges of emissions reductions along with an unspecified process of reviewing progress on those pledges was agreed in the Danish capital and reaffirmed in the Cancún negotiations of 2010.

Two decades of international climate negotiations returned the international community to where they began in 1990—aspirational goals with no effective, legally binding international treaty. The first phase of multilateral climate governance ended up with very little concrete action to show for all of the "governing."

Explaining the frustrations of multilateral climate governance

It is important to understand why this governance mechanism unfolded over its first two decades in the way that it did—especially why it failed to produce an effective response to climate change. This brief discussion examines crucial principles that underpinned the negotiations and the bargaining dynamics of major players in the first phase of the multilateral response.

In 1990 the international community of states began negotiating over climate change in earnest. Two key principles marked the trajectory of the negotiations. The first was universal participation, the idea that all states should have a voice and role in the negotiations over a global problem like climate change.[7] The response to climate change would not be formulated in the rarefied air of the UN Security Council or the G-7, or among a group of the largest producers of GHGs. On the contrary, over one hundred states attended the initial climate negotiations and from the beginning the "global" in global climate change governance referred both to the geographic extent of the problem *and* the level of political participation. The climate change negotiations began as, and remain to this day, a process encompassing essentially all states. This principle served to enhance the legitimacy of the governance process because it ensured that all states would have a voice in this most pressing of problems. However, it also has made the negotiations unwieldy at times and multiplied the number of competing interests that are represented in the bargaining.

The second foundational principle of multilateral climate governance was the idea of common but differentiated responsibilities (CBDR). This principle, developed in the course of the ozone depletion negotiations in the 1980s, was a means to navigate thorny South–North issues that arose over a policy issue as significant as climate change, with both economic development and environmental dimensions. This compromise principle ensured some middle ground, because Northern states were concerned to have a broad response to climate change given the knowledge that states from the Global South would, in the near future, be the source of the majority of GHG emissions. China in fact passed the United States in terms of absolute emissions in the middle of the first decade of the twenty-first century to become the world's most prolific emitter of GHGs.

The Global South wanted recognition that action on climate change would be expensive, and that not all states were in a position to take the same kind of action; this argument was bolstered by the fact that the historical responsibility for GHG concentrations lay overwhelmingly with the North. Thus, the negotiations were framed by the notion that every state has a responsibility to act, but that responsibility differs by development level. Differing interpretations of this principle—what is common, what is differentiated, who should have responsibilities, when, and what kind—were at the core of some of the toughest debates in the first two decades of negotiations.

These underlying principles structured the first phase of the UN-led negotiations, defining stable bargaining dynamics. The basic issues that held up the negotiations remained virtually unchanged. The political economy of state-centric, multilateral climate governance looked pretty much the same in 2009 as it did when the negotiations began in 1990 for the UNFCCC.[8]

The negotiation faultlines were evident in North–North, North–South, and South–South dimensions. The North–North debate was perennially engaged by the European Union (EU), which, for a number of reasons, has been a leader on climate action throughout, and by the United States/Canada/Japan/Russia, which have always taken a more cautious or even obstructionist stance in the multilateral negotiations. The North–South debate tended to be over participation, timing, and resources. While CBDR is an accepted principle, states in the North pushed especially large states from the Global South to move more quickly and take on commensurate responsibilities with those of the North. The global South tended to take the position that their actions should be delayed, and that any action should be compensated. The Global South is not homogeneous, and there were both groups of states at the forefront of progressive action—especially small-island developing countries that face an existential threat from climate change—and others, like oil producers, that were among the most recalcitrant in the negotiations. These faultlines were stable, so stalemate dominated the bargaining environment for the first two decades.

Beyond multilateral climate governance?[9]

The stalemate that forestalled progress on climate change was in some ways over-determined. Setting aside the scientific uncertainty, climate change is an unbelievably thorny political problem, with a host of obstacles to the kind of cooperation sought in the multilateral negotiations towards a binding legal treaty. Three stand out. First, the global economy is almost entirely dependent on the use of fossil fuels and there are vastly different interests across the diverse states about how to approach transformation in this situation. Second, states are very different in both their absolute and per capita emissions along with their historical and current emissions, making it difficult to find common ground on responsibility for addressing climate change. Third and most simply, an international agreement on emissions reductions would have to impose short-term concentrated costs (i.e., the treaty would identify who would have to cut) that promised long-term diffuse benefits (i.e., future generations would benefit more from our action on climate change than we will).

These characteristics point toward a difficult, perhaps an insoluble, collective action problem. Fortunately, the state-centric governance mode of multilateral treaty making was not equivalent to climate governance and other mechanisms emerged into the void left by stalemate in the negotiations.

From the beginning of the 1990s, the multilateral approach along with the con-comitant principles of universal participation and CBDR were conceived of as the way to govern climate change. But even given the global dimensions of the problem, universal multilateral negotiations are not necessarily a natural governing approach. In fact, climate change is a problem that has both local and global effects, and causes of the problem are found everywhere. Thus, not only is multilateral governance aimed at a collective, legally binding agreement not necessarily the only governance mechanism that could be imagined, it may not even be the best one. Decades of stalemate led those interested in responding to climate change both to question the multilateral approach and to imagine different ways of governing climate change.

Specifically, since the early part of this century, we have witnessed an explosion of transnational climate governance initiatives.[10] Community, local, state, regional, and global initiatives working on different aspects of climate change have not only emerged but also proliferated. These initiatives have been working to develop the technological, institutional, economic, and political capacity to move quickly on climate change. Organizations such as the Climate Group[11] are bringing together local governments and corporations to do large-scale pilot projects of climate-friendly technology. Initiatives including the Regional Greenhouse Gas Initiative[12] bring together northeastern US states in an emissions trading system that is demonstrating how a price can be put on carbon. Networks of municipalities like the C-40 group of large cities and the Cities for Climate Protection are demonstrating how local, municipal action on climate change can have an effect beyond the borders of individual cities.

These initiatives entail a different kind of global climate governance. It is decentralized and bottom-up as opposed to the top-down centralized UN treaty negotiations. It is the product of actions by multiple kinds of political actor instead of being state centric. Where the multilateral governance process is concentrated on negotiating emissions reductions, transnational climate governance initiatives are focused on multiple kinds of goal such as energy efficiency, smart grids, smart transportation systems, renewable energy, carbon markets, cultural change, and many more.

The emergence of transnational climate governance also signaled a major transition in how non-state actors participate in global climate governance. NGOs and corporations certainly played a role in the multilateral climate governance processes outlined.[13] Their goals, however, were oriented toward the multilateral treaty-making process, attempting to influence state negotiating positions and the treaty outcomes. In transnational governance processes, non-state actors are, in important ways, governing climate change themselves. They have been seizing the authority to make rules for other actors to follow in responding to climate change, becoming active governors of climate change on their own.

A number of these initiatives are partnerships between corporations, NGOs, and cities around the world. Cities are motivated to explore climate-friendly technologies for the economic benefits they promise, while corporations find cities ideal places to experiment with or pilot new technologies, and NGOs bring the two together. Working in concert makes it possible to demonstrate to cities that climate-friendly technology can work to reduce emissions, enhance transportation and energy delivery systems, and benefit them economically, and to demonstrate to corporations that there will be a demand for their products. The Climate Group's LED (light-emitting diode) lighting project is an example of this process. Large-scale demonstration projects facilitated by the Climate Group have shown that the technology can be beneficial for cities, and demand is now growing. Lighting accounts for ten percent of global GHG emissions. By networking municipal governments and corporations, the Climate Group has been able to facilitate a global pilot program to bring LED street lighting (fifty to seventy percent lower emissions than traditional lighting) to major global cities (e.g., New York, London, Hong Kong, Mumbai, and Calcutta), engaging a dozen corporations that manufacture LED lighting.[14]

Such efforts look very different than climate governance through the negotiation of a legally binding instrument, but they are comparable in that both are processes of authoritative rule making that is designed to shape or guide the behavior of actors in the global response to climate change. Transnational governance initiatives are smaller and more dispersed, but they are also nimble and innovative, and they provide a very different element to the global response to climate change.

The current context: New multilateral hope and evolving transnational governance

The 2009 Copenhagen negotiations were both the nadir for multilateral climate governance and the beginning of a new phase. The failure to achieve a legally binding agreement was devastating to most observers. Yet, in Copenhagen the international community of states essentially abandoned the traditional notion of what the multilateral negotiations should produce—legally binding, collectively agreed on emissions reductions commitments. Instead, the Copenhagen Accord ushered in a pledge and review system of multilateral governance. From this point forward, the multilateral negotiations would focus on developing collective goals and collective monitoring procedures, but commitments for emissions reductions would be identified and developed by individual states—nationally determined contributions (NDCs). From 2009–2014, it was unclear that this tactic would bear fruit. The negotiations in this phase were hamstrung by the same dynamics that made the post-Kyoto years so frustrating.

In 2015 the international community of states was able to reach agreement in Paris, the first major breakthrough in multilateral climate governance since the Kyoto Protocol. The Paris Agreement laid out a collective goal of avoiding 2° of warming and an aspiration of keeping it to 1.5°. It also includes funding pledges to help those states most vulnerable to climate change adapt, requirements for reporting on emissions reductions measures, and plans for collective monitoring of action and efforts to ratchet up activity over time. All of this is based, however, on each state determining its own commitment to emissions reductions individually.[15]

The shift from debilitating stalemate to breakthrough agreement had many sources. Two are particularly relevant. First, the United States and China forged a bilateral agreement in advance of the Paris Summit in which they laid out their intended national contributions and for the first time both leading states committed to significant emissions reductions.[16] This broached a longstanding North–South divide and paved the way for agreement in Paris. In addition, the increase in urgency around climate change and the surge in transnational climate governance activity provided political momentum for a global agreement.[17]

While the Paris Agreement provides hope, the effectiveness of this new agreement is yet to be demonstrated, and it faces a number of challenges. First, the NDCs pledged at Paris do not add up to enough emissions reductions to meet the 2° goal (and so certainly not the 1.5° goal).[18] Second, the effectiveness of the agreement relies to a large extent on the international community of states agreeing to monitoring measures and ratcheting up individual commitments. These ongoing elements will be difficult to negotiate. Third, the election of Donald Trump in 2016 threw US leadership on climate change, a key factor in the success of the Paris negotiations, into serious doubt. The apprehension became reality in June 2017, when Trump announced the US withdrawal from the Paris Agreement.

However, the surge of transnational initiatives that helped spur the Paris Agreement may also provide a means for countries to achieve their NDCs and collective goals. Indeed, the transnational and multilateral spheres of governance are becoming more intertwined and the transnational approach is being recognized as important in the multilateral process for the first time. There are now efforts to catalogue initiatives and to orchestrate transnational efforts at the international level in order to catalyze momentum for the Paris Agreement's goals.[19]

Conclusion

This chapter does not have a definitive conclusion because global climate governance is still unfolding in ways that are likely to surprise in coming decades. The global response to climate change is currently in flux following a brief period of guarded optimism, which is driven by political tumult in the United States. The international community of states has rallied around the Paris Agreement, and there is real momentum around developing transitions to a low-carbon world. Transnational climate governance is also expanding apace with thousands of initiatives being developed to attempt to catalyze de-carbonization in many contexts. Profound challenges remain, but the potential for an effective global response to climate change is more tangible than it has been in in many years.

In this context, there remain key questions driving the academic study of climate governance. On the multilateral side, the switch from a top-down, centralized approach to a bottom-up, decentralized process certainly enhanced the flexibility of multilateral governance and provided countries with the ability to better control their own climate responses. The conditions under which countries will now ratchet up their commitments become a crucial area of inquiry, especially with the current US administration. On the transnational side, the key question is whether and how diverse, experimental initiatives can contribute to national level goals and whether they can be usefully orchestrated at the international level to maximize their impact.[20] When we have those answers, we may have some hope that the global response to climate change is likely to be effective.

Additional reading

Harriet Bulkeley, Liliana Andonova, Michele Betsill, Daniel Compagnon, Thomas Hale, Matthew Hoffmann, et al., *Transnational Climate Change Governance* (Cambridge: Cambridge University Press, 2014).

Stephen Gardiner, *A Perfect Moral Storm: The Ethical Tragedy of Climate Change* (New York: Oxford University Press, 2011).

Matthew Hoffmann, *Climate Governance at the Crossroads: Experimenting with a Global Response* (New York: Oxford University Press, 2011).

Mike Hulme, *Why We Disagree about Climate Change: Understanding Controversy, Inaction, and Opportunity* (Cambridge: Cambridge University Press, 2009).

David Victor, *Global Warming Gridlock* (Cambridge: Cambridge University Press, 2011).

Notes

1 This chapter draws on research and text from a number of prior publications, including Matthew Hoffmann, *Ozone Depletion and Climate Change: Constructing a Global Response* (Albany, NY: SUNY Press, 2005); Matthew Hoffmann, *Climate Governance at the Crossroads: Experimenting with a Global Response* (New York: Oxford University Press, 2011).

2 This section draws on research and text from Matthew Hoffmann, "Global Climate Change," in *Handbook of Global Climate and Environment Policy*, ed. Robert Falkner (Oxford: Wiley Blackwell, 2013).

3 Intergovernmental Panel on Climate Change, *Contribution of Working Groups I, II and III to the Fourth Assessment Report of the Intergovernmental Panel on Climate Change* (2007), www.ipcc.ch/publications_and_data/ar4/syr/en/contents.html.

4 *Paris Agreement*, UN document UNFCCC FCCC/CP/2015/10/Add.1, November 2015.

5 Ian Allison et al., *The Copenhagen Diagnosis: Updating the World on the Latest Climate Science* (2009), www.copenhagendiagnosis.com/.

6 National Aeronautics and Space Administration *NASA, NOAA Data Show 2016 Warmest Year on Record Globally*, www.nasa.gov/press-release/nasa-noaa-data-show-2016-warmest-year-on-record-globally.

7 Hoffmann, *Ozone Depletion and Climate Change*.

8 Susan Sell, "North–South Environmental Bargaining: Ozone, Climate Change, and Biodiversity," *Global Governance* 2, no. 1 (1996): 93–116; David Victor, *Global Warming Gridlock* (Cambridge: Cambridge University Press, 2011); Scott Barrett, *Environment and Statecraft* (Oxford: Oxford University Press, 2003).

9 This section draws on ideas and text from Hoffmann, *Climate Governance*.

10 Hoffmann, *Climate Governance*; Harriet Bulkeley, et al., *Transnational Climate Change Governance* (Cambridge: Cambridge University Press, 2014).

11 www.theclimategroup.org.

12 www.rggi.org.

13 Michele Betsill and Elisabeth Corell, eds., *NGO Diplomacy: The Influence of Nongovernmental Organizations in International Environmental Negotiations* (Cambridge, MA: MIT Press, 2008).

14 www.theclimategroup.org/programs/led.

15 Robert Falkner, "The Paris Agreement and the New Logic of International Climate Politics," *International Affairs* 92, no. 5 (2016): 1107–1125.

16 The White House, "U.S.–China Joint Announcement on Climate Change," 11 November 2014, https://obamawhitehouse.archives.gov/the-press-office/2014/11/11/us-china-joint-announcement-climate-change.

17 Thomas Hale, "'All Hands on Deck': The Paris Agreement and Nonstate Climate Action," *Global Environmental Politics* 16, no. 3 (2016): 12–22.

18 Umair Irfan, "Climate Pledges Will Fall Short of Needed 2 Degree C Limit," *Scientific America*, 3 November 2016, www.scientificamerican.com/article/climate-pledges-will-fall-short-of-needed-2-degree-c-limit.

19 Angel Hsu, et al., "Track Pledges of Cities and Companies," *Nature* 532, no. 7599 (20176): 303–306.

20 Sander Chan, et al., "Reinvigorating International Climate Policy: A Comprehensive Framework for Effective Nonstate Action," *Global Policy* 6, no. 4 (2015): 466–473.

CHAPTER 48

Sustainable development governance

Roger A. Coate

An ever increasingly important place on the global agenda has come to be occupied by sustainable development governance. It now shares center stage with the UN's work in peace and security. How and why has the international community of states come to focus on sustainable development as the organizing principle for global action? Who have been the main players in the evolution of sustainable development? What have been the institutional arenas in which these politics have been played out? Where do we stand now and what are the current debates and prospects for the future?

This chapter explores the evolutionary and dialectical processes by which two originally distinct concepts—development and environment—have become integrated in this one overarching principle. Attention is played to the dynamic interplay of governmental, intergovernmental, and non-state actors. Both the development and environment areas have been distinctive in the extraordinary degree to which civil society actors have been actively engaged. The intent is to focus on the most relevant, benchmark events and actors rather than to try to be all inclusive. The main focus is on the nature and evolution of governance structures and processes and how they have played themselves out on the global political scene.

The emergence of ecodevelopment and sustainability thinking

As early as 1960, the notion of sustainability creaked its way into UN development discourse. General Assembly resolution 1701(XVI) designated the 1960s as the "[First] United Nations Development Decade." The goal was: "[T]o mobilize and to sustain support for the measures required on the part of both developed and developing countries to accelerate progress toward self-sustaining growth of the economy of the individual nations and their social advancement." Yet, at the international governmental level, the sentiment ended there. It would take another ten years—the Second UN Development Decade—for ecodevelopment to begin the integration process in the global agenda.

However, in various corners of civil society, action was breaking onto the surface and garnering important attention. The notion of the existence of a living envelope surrounding the Earth—the biosphere—began to take hold in scientific circles in the 1920s and 1930s. Along with this concept came the realization the humans possess the capacity to do much damage to this vital life-enabling system. In response to this and other concerns, the first international environmental nongovernmental organizations (NGOs), the International Union for the Conservation of Nature and Natural Resources (IUCN), was formed in 1948. In 1962, for example, Rachel Carson's *Silent Spring* helped bring public attention in the Global North to environmental health hazards caused by human actions. In 1968, Paul Ehrlich's *Population Bomb* and Garrett Hardin's classic essay "The Tragedy of the Commons" helped to further galvanize concern over the future of Planet Earth. *Only One Earth* by René Dubos and Barbara Ward came out in 1971, and the Club of Rome added to awareness raising with the publication in 1972 of *Limits to Growth*.

Other NGOs with an international scope began springing up, such as Friends of the Earth (1969), the International Development Research Centre (IDRC, in 1970), the Natural Resources Defense Council (1970), Greenpeace (1971), the International Institute for Environment and Development (IIED, in 1971), and Environnement et Développement du Tiers-Monde (ENDA, in 1972). Worldwatch Institute joined the growing chorus in 1975.

The United Nations Educational, Scientific, and Cultural Organization (UNESCO) was the first UN specialized agency to move energetically on the environmental front. In 1965, it launched a ten-year program, the International Hydrological Decade, to promote the study of hydrological resources, including water pollution. The following year, the UNESCO General Conference took note of the possible detrimental impacts of human actions on the living envelope surrounding the Earth and called for an international conference to consider the issue. Then in 1968, UNESCO hosted the International Conference of Experts on the Biosphere. The Food and Agricultural Organization (FAO), the IUCN, the World Health Organization (WHO), and the United Nations (UN) cosponsored the event. One outcome of the conference was the conceptual linking of the human social order with nature and the environment. Building on the concept "biosphere," conferees discussed the concept of ecologically sustainable development.

UNESCO, which by this time had become largely a development agency, moved forward on several other environmental fronts. It established an interdisciplinary research program, "Man and the Biosphere," to investigate relations between humans and nature. Significant early UNESCO programs include the International Hydrological Decade and International Oceanographic Commission (IOC). UNESCO headquarters in Paris serves as the host for the NGO International Council of Scientific Unions (ICSU). ICSU, in turn, facilitates a number of international environment-related scientific programs that were established during this early period, including the International Biological Program; the International Geosphere-Biosphere Program (IGBP); and the Scientific Committee on the Problems of the Environment (SCOPE).

In 1968, the UN General Assembly passed Resolution 2398(XXIII), calling for convening a global conference on the environment, the UN Conference on the Human Environment (UNCHE). It was in the preparatory work for this conference that the first significant merger of environment and development occurred. At the UNHCE Preparatory Committee meeting in Founex, Switzerland, the concept of "ecodevelopment" was proposed by the conference's Secretary-General, Maurice Strong, to move beyond a logjam between participants from the North and Global South. Strong suggested that long-term development depended on dealing with shorter term environmental problems, which appeased negotiators from the North. He furthermore argued that Northern donor countries should provide additional financial resources to countries of the Global South for them to undertake relatively more expensive environmentally sound development policies. This concept, "additionality," caught on, and a crucial bargain was struck. While environmental sustainability played a central role, sustainable development remained quietly in the background.

Well over 200 NGOs were engaged in some aspect of the UNCHE process. Some of these, such as the IUCN and ICSU played rather important roles as consultants to Strong. The conference final document, the "Declaration on the Human Environment," laid out twenty-six principles for environmental governance and 109 recommendations for action. One of the most significant recommendations coming out of the conference was the creation of the UN Environment Programme (UNEP). The UN General Assembly seized on this recommendation and formally created it in 1973. After UNEP was formed, a special liaison mechanism was established, the Environment Liaison Centre International (ELCI), by which NGOs could systematize civil society relations with the UN agency.

The UNCHE was followed by several other conferences in the 1970s in which development issues were infused in the debate over other issues. These included: the UN Conference on the Law of the Sea (UNCLOS, 1974–1981); World Population Conference (1974); World Food Conference (1974); UN World Conference of the International Women's Year (1975); the UN Conference on Human Settlements (Habitat, 1976); the Conference on Desertification (1977); and the World Climate Conference (1979). As one looks at the concept of sustainable development as manifest today, the linkages with these earlier global forums and the debates therein becomes apparent.

The decade of the 1980s is often referred to as the "lost development decade." Yet it bore witness to some of the most important ecodevelopment events and activities. As the decade began, the ICUN launched its *World Conservation Strategy* report. It called for a new international development strategy, based on "sustainable development," and discussed the roles of poverty, rapid population growth, social inequities, and international trading systems in environmental degradation. The report of the

Independent Commission on International Development Issues (the Brandt Report) was published in 1980, calling for a new political economic relationship between the North and South. In 1981, WHO launched the Global Strategy for Health for All by the Year 2000. The following year, UNCLOS adopted the UN Convention on the Law of the Sea. The Second World Population Conference (1984), the Third World Conference on Women (1985), Vienna Climate Change Conference (1985), and the follow-up adoption of the Montreal Protocol on Substances that Deplete the Ozone Layer (1987) added momentum regarding ecodevelopment. As the decade was drawing to a close, General Assembly resolution 43/53 created the Intergovernmental Panel on Climate Change (IPCC) to be managed by UNEP and the World Meteorological Organization (WMO) "to provide internationally coordinated scientific assessments of the magnitude, timing and potential environmental and socio-economic impact of climate change and realistic response strategies."

The cornerstone, however, was the publication of *Our Common Future*, the report of the World Commission on Environment and Development. The so-called Brundtland Commission was named after its chair, Norwegian prime minister Gro Harlem Brundtland, and provided a nominal definition of sustainable development that, although exceedingly general and somewhat wooly, has stood the test of time: "Sustainable development is development that meets the needs of the present without compromising the ability of future generations to meet their own needs. It contains within it two concepts: the concept of needs, in particular the essential needs of the world's poor, to which overriding priority should be given; and the idea of limitations imposed by the state of technology and social organization on the environment's ability to meet present and future needs."[1] The conceptualizations provided by the report served to cementing sustainable development as an integrating concept that would underpin the work of both multilateral institutions and civil society for decades to come. One indication of its breadth of impact was the formation of the Business Council for Sustainable Development, which in 1992 published *Changing Course*, arguing that business indeed does have an interest in sustainable development.

The Earth Summit and beyond

In important ways, the Brundtland Commission laid the foundation for what was to become an even greater benchmark, the UN Conference on Environment and Development (UNCED or the "Earth Summit"), hosted in Rio de Janeiro in 1992. Similar to UNCHE, the preparatory work for UNCED is where the action was centered, not at the conference itself. The Rio process last for nearly three years, and as UNCED Secretary-General Maurice Strong commented, "the process was the policy."[2] Strong understood well the importance of building a consensus from the ground up and having all critical decisions made before the actual gathering itself.

Yet, qualitative and quantitative targets and acceptable limits still eluded negotiators as they rushed to finalize agreement on the conventions, statements of principles, and plan of action. As twenty years earlier, North–South tensions also reflected competing worldviews and interests. Governments from the Global South tended to view ozone depletion, hazardous waste pollution, and global warming as products of industrialization and overconsumption in the North. Why should they bear the costs of these new Northern priorities? If Northern governments wanted the active partnership of the South in dealing with such problems, then Northern donors should make available additional financial and technical resources. Again, the concept of "additionality" came to the fore.

Resolving the debate over deforestation was particularly difficult because these North–South tensions were brought into particularly sharp focus. Southern governments forcefully resisted any incursion into the principle of sovereignty over natural resources. Tensions also prevailed in drafting the Rio Declaration, which was to guide governments and nongovernmental actors in implementing the many provisions of Agenda 21. The final compromise incorporated many of the most important elements of the development and environment perspectives of both sides. The twenty-seven principles embodied in the Rio Declaration was one stating that the cost of pollution should be borne at the source and should be reflected in product cost at all stages of production. Agenda 21 comprised over 600 pages and covered a large variety of issues, many of which were quite contentious, including issues related to biodiversity, biotechnology, deforestation, and institutional and procedural issues involving financing, technology transfer, and institutional arrangements for carrying out the elements of the action agenda.

Two legally binding international conventions—on biodiversity (Convention on Biodiversity) and on climate change (UN Framework Convention on Climate Change, UNFCCC)—were incorporated as part of the larger Rio process. The final draft documents emerging from the Earth Summit represented "framework conventions." These conventions designated general principles and obligations, but specific timetables and targets were left to be specified at future negotiations over protocols.

Many of these issues remained unresolved at the close of UNCED. Foremost among them was how to generate the financial resources needed to implement the program of action and associated activities. Governance issues were linked to the issue of financing. Who was to decide when and how such resources are to be spent? Participants from the Global South proposed the creation of a new "green fund," which would operate on more egalitarian voting principles. A partial compromise was achieved to enhance the Global South's participation while retaining for donor states elements of control. Interim financing for Agenda 21 implementation would be provided under the aegis of the World Bank Group. The Global Environmental Facility (GEF) would be expanded and its rules altered to provide for decision making by consensus among equally represented groupings of donors and recipients.

One of the most significant outcomes of the Earth summit was the creation of the UN Commission on Sustainable Development (CSD), under the jurisdiction of the UN Economic and Social Council (ECOSOC). The CSD was mandated to oversee the implementation of the provisions of Agenda 21 and coordinating the sustainable development activities of the various organizations within the UN system. It was also mandated to strengthen and integrate the role of major societal groups and civil society actors as effective participants in sustainable development decision making at all levels. The text of Agenda 21 specifically addressed the roles of eight major groups: NGOs, indigenous peoples, local governments, workers, businesses, scientific communities, farmers, and women, children, and youth.

However, the matter of how the CSD was to be empowered to fulfill its mandate effectively was left unspecified. This vagueness was especially problematic given the CSD's mandated role of being the primary mechanism within the UN system for coordinating sustainable development, especially regarding UNEP, the World Bank, the Committee of International Development Institutions on the Environment, and other intergovernmental bodies. Despite such shortcomings, the CSD and its counterpart in the Secretariat's Division of Sustainable Development, serve as focal points for coordinating UN implementation activities for sustainable development. In its Multiyear Program of Work, the CSD systematically reviews progress and makes recommendations for further action on specific clusters of issues.

Following on UNCED, the decade of the 1990s witnessed an almost unending series of global conferences on social and economic matters. These included the: World Conference on Human Rights, 1993; International Conference on Population and Development (ICPD), 1994; UN Global Conference on Sustainable Development of Small Island Developing States, 1994; World Summit on Social Development, 1995; Fourth World Conference on Women, 1995; Second UN Conference on Human Settlements, 1996; and World Food Summit, 1996. In addition, the World Conference on Education for All, the Second World Climate Conference, and the World Summit for Children had all been held in 1990 prior to UNCED. What was clear at each of these gatherings and the preparatory processes that led to them was that the concept of sustainable development and its evolving meanings was increasingly occupying center stage.

In the context of all this, UN Secretary-General Boutros-Ghali in May 1994 presented the General Assembly with his *An Agenda for Development*,[3] a companion volume to his earlier and oft cited *An Agenda for Peace*. This new "agenda" declared development to be a fundamental human right and presented a general framework within which the Secretary-General highlighted the interdependent nature of peace, economy, civil society, democracy, social justice, and environment as indispensable components of the development process. Development increasingly came to be viewed in human, as opposed to exclusively national economic, terms.

In the mid-1990s, the UNDP/UNFPA Executive Board decision 94/14 adopted "sustainable human development" as a new mission for technical assistance. Moreover, in its 1993 *Human Development Reports*, the UNDP provided a basic framework for focusing discourse. It suggested that the UN's development work should be based on at least five "new pillars": New concepts of human security, new models of sustainable human development, new partnerships between states and markets, new patterns of national and global governance, and new forms of international cooperation. Each *Human Development Report* has served to elaborate, extend, and clarify specific aspects of the development–human security nexus. Participation and empowerment have been two of the priority themes running throughout these annual reports.

The Millennium Development Goal process

A centerpiece of the UN's emerging sustainable development agenda was the Millennium Development Goals (MDG) process, evolving around the UN secretary-general's March 2000 report: *We the Peoples: The Role of the United Nations in the 21st Century*[4] and the Millennium Summit in September that year. The report specified a number of development goals and targets that made their way into the

Summit Outcome Document, the *Millennium Declaration*, as General Assembly resolution 55/2. As Stephen Browne points out, however, these goals remained rather ambiguous and had been generated by a team of international experts and international civil servants rather than from intergovernmental negotiations.[5] It was not until February 2001 that UNDP picked up the ball and devised the notion of the MDGs and began to give them form and substance.

Over the course of the year, this UNDP-led initiative resulted in consultations among various UN funds and programs, which specified eight time-bound goals and associated targets and measurable indicators to be achieved by 2015 for eradicating poverty and promoting sustainable human development and security. Seven of the eight main goals focus on substantive objectives: Eradicating extreme poverty and hunger; achieving universal primary education; promote gender equality and empower women; reduce infant mortality; improve maternal health; combat HIV/AIDS, malaria and other diseases; and better ensure environmental sustainability. The eighth MDG, global partnership, deals with creating the capacity to achieve the other seven. While the first seven MDGs targeted actions to be undertaken by the developing countries, MDG 8 targeted donor countries and stress their responsibilities to provide the resources needed to accomplish the other seven. Cumulatively, the MDGs are both mutually reinforcing and intertwined. A UN system-wide strategy has been designed for mobilizing support and monitoring progress toward achieving the MDGs.

The summit-level UN-sponsored Conference on Financing for Development in Monterrey, Mexico, in March 2002, picked up the initiative and donor countries in general conveyed an increased commitment to provide resources. The Monterrey meeting brought together stakeholders representing governments, business, civil society, and international institutions for a formal exchange of views. The "Monterrey Consensus," as that conference's outcome document was called, recognized the need to increase ODA significantly to meet the MDGs.[6] The importance here was not an actual commitment and delivery of needed financing, but the growing consensus that such a commitment was needed to fight poverty.

A decade after the Earth Summit in Rio, the United Nations convened the World Summit on Sustainable Development in Johannesburg in fall 2002, which attempted to reinvigorate sustainable development activities in the wake of deepening poverty and environmental degradation. In this regard, the summit's outcomes are questionable. However, again "process was the product." The summit reflected a new approach to conferencing and to sustainable development more generally. It represented a dialogue among major stakeholders from governments, civil society, and the private sector. Participants focused primarily on the creation of new partnerships to bring additional resources to bear for sustainable development.

Member states tried again in mid-decade to reinvigorate the MDG process during the 2005 World Summit on the UN's sixtieth anniversary. And again, the outcome was marginal. In the ecodevelopment area limited steps were agreed, including: A restated but ambiguous commitment to achieve the MDGs; a commitment by developing countries to adopt national initiatives for achieving the MDGs; agreement to move toward ensuring long-term debt sustainability through the cancellation of one hundred percent of official multilateral and bilateral debt of the heavily indebted poor countries (HIPCs) and increased grant-based development financing; a commitment to move toward innovative sources of development financing; an agreement to create a worldwide early warning system for natural hazards; and, in regard to climate change, a commitment to provide assistance to small-island developing states and other highly vulnerable states. The remainder of the decade witnessed fits and starts and failures regarding ecodevelopment, as forward progress basically stagnated on most fronts such as the annual UNFCCC Conferences of the Parties (COPs) meetings.

After being elected for a second term, Secretary-General Ban Ki-moon in January 2012 laid out his agenda for the upcoming five years.[7] Sustainable development was at the top of the agenda and focused on three priority goals: Accelerate progress on the MDGs; address climate change; and forge consensus around a post-2015 sustainable development framework and implement it. The last goal would entail defining "a new generation of sustainable development goals building on the MDGs and outline a road map for consideration by member states." He cautioned that to achieve sustainable development goals "the most important tool will be energy. Energy is the golden thread."[8]

Forty years after UNCHE and twenty years after UNCED, the Government of Brazil hosted the UN Conference on sustainable Development (UNCSD or Rio+20) in June 2012. This summit-level meeting had an associated civil society forum, Sustainable Development Dialogues, preceding the actual summit as well as a Partnerships Forum. The conference outcome document, *The Future We Want*, summaries the results.[9] It stressed the dynamic nature of three interdependent dimensions of sustainable development: economic, social, and environmental aspects.

From MDGs to SDGs

Rio+20 launched a process to develop the Sustainable Development Goals (SDGs), which would build on the MDGs and constitute the post-2015 development agenda. The conference adopted a general set of guidelines on green economy policies. It also adopted the ten-year programmatic framework on sustainable consumption and production patterns and invited the General Assembly to designate a member state body to take any necessary steps to fully operationalize the framework. It called on the General Assembly to: Establish an intergovernmental process to prepare options on a strategy for sustainable development financing; create a high-level political forum for sustainable development; establish an intergovernmental process under the General Assembly to prepare options on a strategy for sustainable development financing; and strengthen UNEP. Finally, the conference took several decisions on various thematic areas, including energy, food security, oceans, and cities.[10]

The conference outcome document called for the creation of a set of "sustainable development goals." They were to be "action-oriented, concise and easy to communicate, limited in number, aspirational, global in nature and universally applicable to all countries while taking into account different national realities, capacities and levels of development and respecting national policies and priorities."[11] Building on this, the secretary-general appointed a special High-Level Panel of Eminent Persons on the Post-2015 Development Agenda. The panel's report identified five main pillars to drive the SDG process: No one left behind; sustainable development at the core;

transform economies for jobs and inclusive growth; build peace for effective, open, and accountable institutions for all; and forge a new global partnership.[12]

While building on the MDGs, the SDGs were to be universally applicable.

As Browne points out, from this point on, however, the governance process for creating the SDGs diverged considerably from the MDG process, which had been almost exclusively dominated by the "second UN" of UN secretariats: "Even before the high-level panel had reported, the General Assembly took a decision to establish an 'open working group' (OWG) in January 2013 to devise the definitive set of goals for the post-2015 era, presided over by two local ambassadors. This committee comprised 30 members formally, but both membership and timetable were open-ended, the only constraint being the need for agreement during 2015—in almost two years' time."[13]

The OWG process was novel in that it was comprised of thirty "seats" for participants around the table, which were shared among some seventy countries. This sharing of seats created political space for breaking with traditional geostrategic coalitions. Also, the first eight rounds of negotiations were conducted as open sessions in which participants rather freely present and discuss options and ideas. Civil society organizations and private sector bodies—the "third UN"[14]—also found ways to engage. This process took the full two years, mainly because the representatives of the "first UN" (member states) had decided to start again from first principles, largely ignoring the high-level panel report and the detailed and comprehensive declarations of previous summits. The process also lacked the kind of strategic guidance from the second UN—in this case the UN's Department of Economic and Social Affairs (DESA)—to help the local mission representatives (most appointed by their foreign ministries) to assign priorities and make choices. "The intellectual firepower of the UN secretariat in New York—or elsewhere—was much diminished compared with earlier decades."[15]

By mid-2015, the SDG process had been concluded and was finalized at the 2015 UN Sustainable Development Summit. The "2030 Agenda for Sustainable Development" was approved in General Assembly resolution 70/1 and enumerated of a whopping seventeen SDGs, 169 targets, and 230 indicators.[16] The seventeen SDGs are to:

1 End poverty in all its forms everywhere
2 End hunger, achieve food security and adequate nutrition for all, and promote sustainable agriculture
3 Attain healthy life for all at all ages
4 Provide equitable and inclusive quality education and lifelong learning opportunities for all
5 Attain gender equality, empower women and girls everywhere
6 Secure water and sanitation for all for a sustainable world
7 Ensure access to affordable, sustainable, and reliable modern energy services for all
8 Promote strong, inclusive and sustainable economic growth and decent work for all

9 Promote sustainable industrialization

10 Reduce inequality within and among countries

11 Build inclusive, safe and sustainable cities and human settlements

12 Promote sustainable consumption and production patterns

13 Promote actions at all levels to address climate change

14 Attain conservation and sustainable use of marine resources, oceans and seas

15 Protect and restore terrestrial ecosystems and halt all biodiversity loss

16 Achieve peaceful and inclusive societies, rule of law, effective and capable institutions

17 Strengthen and enhance the means of implementation and global partnership for sustainable development.

While the SDGs built on the MDGs, they added an important emphasis on environmental as well as social and economic dimensions. In fact, seven of the seventeen SDGs related to the environment and energy. In addition, the SDGs stressed the principle of universality and the reciprocal responsibility of both developing and developed countries. Langsford suggests that:

> [M]any of the universal targets focus on issues that have traditionally been considered "domestic" or outside the domain of sustainable development. The reduction of income inequality and death rates, the elimination of discriminatory laws and domestic violence, the management of urbanization, and the facilitation of "orderly, safe, regular, and responsible" migration are cast as challenges for all states to address.[17]

Even as the SDG process was getting underway, UN member states were seeking a venue to replace the CSD for overseeing and monitoring sustainable development activities, initiatives, and country-level progress. At the 2012 Rio+20 conference, the High-level Political Forum (HLPF) was established to fulfil this function. It began its work in 2013 and continues as the UN's central platform for follow-up and review of the 2030 Agenda for Sustainable Development and the SDGs. It provides for the full and effective participation of all 193 member states and members of specialized agencies. The process began in 2013 with the first topic: "Building the future we want: from Rio+20 to the post-2015 development agenda." This was followed in 2014 with "Achieving the MDGs and charting the way for an ambitious post-2015 development agenda, including the SDGs." In 2015, the theme was "Strengthening integration, implementation and review—the HLPF after 2015," followed by "Ensuring that no one is left behind" in 2016. Beginning in 2017, the HLPF began a systematic three-year focus on the SDGs: "Eradicating poverty and promoting prosperity in a changing world," focusing on SDGs 1, 2, 3, 5, 9, 14, [and 17] (2017); "Transformation towards sustainable and resilient societies, focusing on SDGs 6, 7, 11, 12, 15, [and 17] (2018); and, in 2019, "Empowering people and ensuring inclusiveness and equality," examining progress on SDGs 4, 8, 10, 13, 16, [and 17].

The politics of sustainable development governance

The political dynamics of sustainable development governance have transformed markedly over the decades. As the sustainability concept slowly gained traction after the Rio "Earth Summit," it was mostly dominated by the "second" and "third" UNs. Much heavier concentration was generally given by member states from the North to environment over development in the political discourse. It was the UNDP and "second UN" that brought focus to social and economic dimensions, especially with a human security and human development face. This trend continued with the advent of the MDGs.

A downside of the predominant role of UN staff, especially New York-based bodies, was that active engagement of and support from the political bodies and specialized agencies was marginalized. By the conclusion of the MDG process, however, specialized agencies and developed countries were by and large on board. Browne has summarized the situation well: "Even by 2015 . . . the MDGs were largely unknown in developing countries. The UN secretariat had done little initially to broadcast the results of the 2000 Summit and the MDGs, a task which was taken up by field-based agencies like UNDP and UNICEF. Even developing country governments were not active proselytizers of goals and targets for which they might be held accountable."[18]

To the contrary, the SDG process was primarily a political process carried out via negotiation among member states. This process, however, was not as contentious as one may assume, given the history of UN political debates. Langsford helps to shed light on the nature of the political dynamics underlying this process with a specific illustration of inequality:

> Western states prioritized political inclusiveness and the removal of discrimination at the domestic level; the G-77, led by China, prioritized equality for developing countries at the international . . . When the deal was done in mid-2014 almost all states decried the number of goals and targets, yet none expressed willingness to trade off its own favored goals and targets.[19]

The tradeoffs inherent in the different political dynamics involved in the MDG versus SDG processes are perhaps greater awareness, legitimacy, and commitment regarding the SDGs versus the greater specificity, precision, and measurability of the MDGs. Of course, both sets of goals failed to include many dimensions thought crucial by many experts and commentators, even some critical ones, such as human rights and good governance.[20]

The way forward

In large measure, the way forward for the SDGs and sustainable development governance depends on providing the resources and enabling an environment necessary for their success. Financial resources are, of course, of fundamental importance. The July 2015 UN Financing for Development Conference in Addis Ababa represented an important step in this direction. The forum focused on the need to draw on many sources, especially domestic public and private finance.[21] Browne and Weiss stress the critical importance of moving beyond foreign aid as the primary mechanism for generating the needed resources: "The biggest change in the aid and development relationship, therefore, results from the diminishing importance of ODA as a develop-ment resource. What matters more than ever to development progress is the capacity of individual countries to attract and manage responsibly the full range of resources at their disposal, within an 'inclusive' rather than an 'extractive' context."[22]

The financial requirements for attaining the SDGs are staggering. A study pro-duced by the African Development Bank, the Asian Development Bank, the European Bank for Reconstruction and Development, the European Investment Bank, the Inter-American Development Bank, the International Monetary Fund, and the World Bank Group concluded: "To meet the investment needs of the Sustainable Development Goals, the global community needs to move the discussion from 'Billions' in ODA to 'Trillions' in investments of all kinds: public and private, national and global, in both capital and capacity."[23] The study went on to argue that:

> Globally, achieving the proposed SDGs will require the best possible use of each grant dollar, beginning with some US$ 135 billion in ODA. Yet flows for development include philanthropy, remittances, South–South flows and other official assistance, and foreign direct investment—together these sources amount to nearly US$ 1 trillion . . . This is the trajectory from billions to trillions.[24]

Yet, it is wise to heed the warning by Browne and Weiss that finance alone is not a panacea to guarantee sustainable development or anything else. They argue that: "[N]o evidence exists about aid having created sustainable results without the presence of the other critical conditions: inclusive institutions and ownership of the process."[25]

Conclusion

Sustainable development entails coping with and overcoming a nexus of complex, dynamically interdependent, contradictory, and seemingly overwhelming problems and issues. Some crucial sustainable development issues—climate change and the green economy to name just two—are some of the most highly divisive polit-ical issues and are linked inherently to conflicting ideologies and self-interests—illustrated by the decision in June 2017 by the Trump administration to withdraw from the 2015 Paris Agreement. Other factors that make sustainable development impossible, continue to be left out of the picture all together, including such essential problems as corruption, religious intolerance, internal civil strife, capital flight, denial of fundamental human rights, patrimonialism, and poor governance.

The world's current sustainable development governance models are simply inadequate to incorporate diverse interests and make meaningful the necessary contributions of the vast array of different types of stakeholder. Not all interests are equal, and most do not go far beyond individual or group perceptions of their self-interests. Unless new models of governance at all levels can be found and put in place with reasonably quickness, Worldwatch has suggested that it may be "how the world will end: in the face of protracted inaction."[26]

Additional reading

Stephen Browne, *Sustainable Development Goals and UN Goal-Setting* (London: Routledge, 2017).

Stephen Browne and Thomas G. Weiss, eds., *Post-2015 UN Development: Making Change Happen* (London: Routledge, 2014).

Lorraine Elliott, *The Global Politics of the Environment* (New York: New York University Press, 1998).

Malcolm Langsford, "Lost in Transformation? The Politics of the Sustainable Development Goals," *Ethics & International Affairs* 30, no. 2 (2016): 167–176.

United Nations, *Report of the United Nations Conference on Sustainable Development*, UN document A/CONF.216/16, 20–22 June 2012.

Thomas G. Weiss, et al., *The United Nations and Changing World Politics*, 8th ed. (Boulder, CO: Westview Press, 2016), chapters 9–11.

Rorden Wilkinson and David Hulme, eds., *The Millennium Development Goals and Beyond: Global Development After 2015* (London: Routledge, 2012).

World Commission on Environment and Development, *Our Common Future* (Oxford: Clarendon Press, 1987).

Notes

1 World Commission on Environment and Development, *Our Common Future* (Oxford: Clarendon Press, 1987).
2 Maurice Strong, *Where on Earth Are We Going?* (New York: Norton, 2001).
3 Boutros Boutros-Ghali, *An Agenda for Development* (New York: United Nations, 1995).
4 UN, *We the Peoples: The Role of the United Nations in the 21st Century*, Report of the Secretary-General (New York: UN, 2000).
5 Stephen Browne, *Sustainable Development Goals and UN Goal-Setting* (London and New York: Routledge, 2017), 84–85.
6 Barry Herman, "Civil Society and the Financing for Development Initiative at the United Nations," in *Civil Society and Global Finance*, eds. Jan Aart Scholte and Albrecht Schabel (London: Routledge, 2002), 162–177.
7 Ban Ki-moon, *The Secretary-General's Five-Year Action Agenda* (New York: UN, January 2012), www.un.org/sg/priorities/index.shtml.
8 UN, "Sustainable Development," New York: United Nations, 25 January 2012, www.un.org/sg/priorities/sustainable_development.shtml; "Sustainable Development Goals," New York: United Nations, http://sustainabledevelopment.un.org/index.php?menu=1300.
9 "Report of the United Nations Conference on Sustainable Development," United Nations document A/CONF. 216/16, June 2012.

10 UN, *United Nations Conference on Sustainable Development, Rio+20,* New York, http://sustainabledevelopment.un.org/rio20.html.

11 UN, *The Future We Want, Outcome Document of the UN Conference on Sustainable Development* Document, UN document A/RES/66/288, June 2012, paras. 247, 246.

12 UN, "A New Global Partnership: Eradicate Poverty and Transform Economies through sustainable Development, The Report of the High-Level Panel of Eminent Persons on the Post-2015 Development Agenda" (New York, 2012), chapter 2.

13 Browne, *Sustainable Development Goals,* 91.

14 Thomas G. Weiss, Tatiana Carayannis, and Richard Jolly, "The 'Third' United Nations," *Global Governance* 15, 1 (2009): 123–142.

15 Browne, *Sustainable Development Goals,* 91.

16 https://sustainabledevelopment.un.org/post2015/transformingourworld.

17 Malcolm Langsford, "Lost in Transformation? The Politics of the Sustainable Development Goals," *Ethics & International Affairs* 30, no. 2 (2016): 167–176.

18 Browne, *Sustainable Development Goals,* 99.

19 Malcolm Langsford, "Lost in Transformation?" 171.

20 Browne, *Sustainable Development Goals,* 92–101. See also Stephen Browne and Thomas G. Weiss, eds., *Post-2015 UN Development: Making Change Happen* (London: Routledge, 2014), 25–27; Bertrand G. Ramcharan, "Human Rights and the SDGs: A Sidelined Priority?" *FUNDS Project Briefing no. 31*, July 2015, www.futureun.org/media/archive1/briefings/FUNDS_Brief31_Human_Rights_SDGs_July2015.pdf.

21 UN, *Addis Ababa Action Agenda of the Third International Conference on Financing for Development,* (New York: UN, 2015), available at www.un.org/esa/ffd/wp-content/uploads/2015/08/AAAA_Outcome.pdf.

22 Browne and Weiss, eds., *Post-2015 UN Development,* 29.

23 African Development Bank, et el., "From Billions to Trillions: Transforming Development Finance Post-2015. Financing for Development: Multilateral Development Finance," Development Committee Discussion Note, April 18, 2016, 1.

24 Ibid.

25 Browne and Weiss, eds., *Post-2015 UN Development,* 16.

26 Worldwatch Institute, "The Future We Need: Reflections on Rio+20," Road Logs RIO+, Rio de Janeiro, 7 July 2012, http://roadlogs.rio20.net/the-future-we-need-reflections-onrio20.

Global energy governance

Harald Heubaum

The world economy is heavily reliant on the uninterrupted flow of energy. Without its mass production and consumption, there would be no modern economic growth and prosperity, no global trade in goods and services, no modern warfare, and no climate crisis threatening to undermine decades of human progress in health and development. Few countries are blessed with sufficient energy resources to fully meet the needs of their citizens, businesses, and industry. Establishing a degree of energy security by gaining reliable and affordable access to these sources, especially fossil fuels, has come at a price. So have the impacts produced by fossil-fuel combustion since the Industrial Revolution, which can only be effectively addressed through a fundamental restructuring of the global economy.

In short, energy as a policy issue cuts across a number of different dimensions and has been described as "among all policy fields exhibiting externalities of a global scale, by far the most complex, path dependent, and embedded."[1] Given its critical position at the very heart of global economics, politics, and society, energy naturally lends itself to be governed at the global level. Yet such governance has so far remained largely elusive, with states jealously guarding their autonomy over energy policy and intergovernmental organizations operating in this field only recently starting to cooperate more closely.

This chapter begins by charting the emergence of the existing global energy governance architecture, understood here as the "overarching system of public and private institutions that are valid or active" in the energy field.[2] This architecture is fragmented and consists of different parts with often only little interaction, let alone integration, among them.

The first section focuses on intergovernmental energy organizations that trace their origins to the post-World War II (WWII) emergence of producers in what is now called the "Global South," their challenge to the then dominant western oil majors, and the impact on oil-consuming advanced economies in the North of the former's clout in world politics of the 1970s. However, there are also other intergovernmental energy organizations, among them the International Renewable Energy Agency (IRENA), which form part of the architecture of global energy governance and are discussed here briefly. The chapter then proceeds to take a closer look at the United Nations and the role of several of its constituent parts in governing energy. The world organization is often mistakenly overlooked in energy governance research as it does not have a dedicated energy program. However, the climate negotiation process coordinated by the 1992 United Nations Framework Convention on Climate Change (UNFCCC), the 2015 Sustainable Development Goals (SDGs), and the activities of the World Bank have direct and meaningful implications for energy policymaking and investment worldwide. The third section examines the benefits and challenges of building a global energy governance architecture that is more integrated internally while at the same time better able to capitalize on overlaps and synergies with other global policy domains, especially those in climate change and international development. The chapter concludes with an assessment of the future of global energy governance, including the prospects for a World Energy Agency.

The landscape of global energy governance

The governance of energy encompasses multiple actors in both the public and private spheres, operating on different levels from the international to the local. States determine the legal and regulatory environment within which energy markets operate. Both states and private companies cooperate across borders, for example in the trade of oil and natural gas via pipelines, and the construction of renewable or nuclear power plants. At the international level, however, there are governance problems, and effective coordination has proved problematic. Since the 1960s and 1970s, the architecture of global energy governance has evolved in a way that is marked by horizontal fragmentation, with the establishment of a number of intergovernmental organizations set up to address different sets of concerns over the supply and demand of energy.

Unlike the global climate governance architecture, which revolves around the UNFCCC, there is currently no single, core institution in the field of global energy governance that incorporates all countries and has the power to help set binding rules and principles for its members. Instead, a division between the oil-consuming, industrialized economies in the North and oil-producing, developing economies in the Global South has troubled global energy governance from the beginning, with the former dominating in the International Energy Agency (IEA), and the latter in the Organization of the Petroleum Exporting Countries (OPEC). The antecedents of this split reach back to the early years of the twentieth century. In what became one of the major turning points of global history, oil was discovered in 1908 in southwest

Iran by William Knox D'Arcy—later director of the newly founded Anglo-Persian Oil Company—putting the Middle East on the energy map.

Oil producers in the Global South

Together with Royal Dutch Shell and the five largest American oil companies to have emerged from the breakup of Standard Oil in 1911, Anglo-Persian Oil (later renamed "British Petroleum" (BP)) formed a powerful cartel of multinational oil companies commonly referred to as the Seven Sisters.[3] These seven companies came to dominate the global petroleum industry in the first half of the twentieth century, controlling the vast majority of global oil reserves as well as mid- and downstream assets. The five American Sisters had built their power not on exploring and developing oilfields in the Middle East but on operations in the United States, then the world's largest oil producer. From their home base, they used their wealth and political influence to fend off unwanted competition and deepen control over petroleum projects elsewhere.

WWII fundamentally reshaped global geopolitics, laying the groundwork for a global energy governance architecture to emerge in the decades that followed. The rapid decline of the British Empire, in particular, had far reaching consequences, with a large number of developing countries gaining their independence, among them many of the oil-rich states of the Middle East. OPEC was founded by Iran, Iraq, Kuwait, Saudi Arabia, and Venezuela in 1960 in Baghdad. Its goal was to coordinate and unify the petroleum policies of the five founding members and support their economic interests on an international stage. In 1960, the Seven Sisters were still the key players in the global oil game; but by the end of the decade, OPEC and especially Saudi Arabia with its large spare capacity had replaced the United States as the global swing producer.

The Sisters were in for trouble when in 1968, the OPEC cartel, now counting ten members, published a declaratory statement underlining the right of states to fully control their domestic resources.[4] This move towards resource sovereignty culminated in a wave of nationalizations of domestic oil industries beginning in the 1970s. Within years it would end the dominant position of Western multinational oil companies, putting OPEC states firmly in charge of their own energy affairs. For many years afterwards, the organization's influence derived from its ability to quickly curb or ramp up oil production and, due to its large share of global supplies, help determine oil prices.

In 1973, Arab members of OPEC used this "oil weapon," declaring an embargo against the United States and other western countries in response to their support of Israel in the Yom Kippur War.[5] The resulting cut in oil production and increased costs had dramatic effects on oil-importing western economies, pushing many of them into recession. Since the 1990s, however, relations between oil producers in the Global South and consumers in the North have been less contentious, despite seismic events such as the 1990–1991 Persian Gulf War and the 2003 invasion of Iraq.

OPEC today counts thirteen members, representing the major oil-producing countries in the Middle East, Africa, and Latin America; it is faced with a range of new challenges, among them the rise of non-OPEC oil producers, including the re-emergence of the United States as a leading shale-oil producer. A period of high oil prices that began with a sudden spike—followed by an equally sudden temporary drop—at the height of the global financial crisis in 2008–2009 incentivized increased production around the world. This revived the fortunes of previously uneconomic projects, made new exploration economically viable, and provided additional volumes to the global oil market.

It is, in large measure, because of these developments that OPEC's ability to influence oil prices is today much reduced compared to the height of its power. The growing urgency of addressing global climate change and the resulting need to shift energy systems away from a reliance on emissions-intensive hydrocarbons, too, is putting increasing pressure on the organization's members.

Oil consumers in the Global North

The International Energy Agency (IEA), widely considered the key organization in the fragmented landscape of global energy governance, was established in 1974 as an autonomous organization within the framework of the Organisation for Economic Co-operation and Development (OECD), membership of which is a precondition for membership in the agency. Its founding was a reaction to the 1973–1974 oil crisis and the inability of the world's major oil consumers in the OECD to effectively counter its impacts on their respective economies. OECD members initially failed to react in a coordinated fashion, engaging instead in a panicked stockpiling of oil reserves which drove costs up even further.[6]

The IEA's original role was, thus, to prevent similarly problematic behavior in the face of future oil supply crises. The IEA's founding document lists the aims of the Agency as helping OECD countries develop self-sufficiency in oil in case of an emergency, establish oil demand limitation measures, gather and share information on developments in the international oil market, coordinate effective collective long-term responses to oil import dependence, and build closer relations between oil-consuming and oil-producing countries.[7] Today, the twenty-nine members are required to hold sufficient oil reserves to maintain consumption for at least ninety days without further oil imports.[8] In the years since the IEA's founding, oil from this strategic reserve has been released three times: At the outset of the 1991 Persian Gulf War; after Hurricane Katrina had wreaked havoc in the Gulf of Mexico, destroying critical oil production infrastructure in the process; and in 2011 in response to the civil war in Libya and the bombing campaign led by the North Atlantic Treaty Organization (NATO) under a UN mandate.

However, the global energy landscape has changed considerably since the early 1970s, with oil retaining its critical importance for transportation but falling out of favor in the power sector. OECD members increasingly pursued policies aimed at incentivizing a greater diversity of energy sources and addressing new threats and opportunities beyond the petroleum industry. The IEA responded to these changes by broadening its approach, incorporating into its portfolio such issues as natural gas, nuclear power and, more recently, renewable energy sources, energy efficiency, sustainable development, and environmental protection. In parallel, the agency's senior management has become more vocal, voicing strong support for greenhouse gas (GHG) emissions reductions in line with the targets spelled out in the Paris Agreement on climate change.[9] But while these developments provide evidence for the IEA exercising its organizational autonomy in a fast changing global policy environment, there are limits to what it can effectively achieve. Apart from its coordination during oil supply emergencies, the agency's main role is of an advisory, training, and information-gathering nature. For example, it does not have authority over the domestic energy policies of its members on whom it also depends for the bulk of its budget—limitations that it shares with other intergovernmental organizations populating the landscape of global energy governance. Further, the restrictions imposed on the IEA by its OECD-only membership risk leaving many of the world's biggest energy consumers, including China and India, outside emerging governance arrangements, making it harder to move towards a more integrated architecture.

Beyond the IEA–OPEC divide

The global energy governance landscape also comprises a number of other, less well-known intergovernmental organizations, some of which straddle the divide between major oil producers in the Global South and oil-consuming advanced economies in the North. These include the Latin American Energy Organization (OLADE) founded in 1973; the Energy Charter Treaty (operational since 1998); and the Gas Exporting Countries Forum (GECF) established in 2001. With its focus on renewable energy, IRENA joined the group of intergovernmental organizations working on energy in 2009; it has the broadest membership, with 150 full state members and a further thirty candidates (as of June 2017). Headquartered in Abu Dhabi, it is the intergovernmental energy organization that most clearly transcends the North–South divide. It is the only major international forum exclusively addressing renewable energy sources.

Unlike the IEA which, by virtue of a broad-based portfolio, does not pick and choose particular energy technologies over others, IRENA was founded with the express goal of promoting the increased adoption of renewables around the world.[10] This focus was in large part due to a sense of frustration among some of the founding states—Germany, Denmark, and Spain—that the IEA, of which they are members, remained too closely wedded to fossil fuels and did not sufficiently acknowledge the growth and future potential of renewables such as wind and solar photovoltaics (PV).[11] However, compared to the more established intergovernmental energy organizations, IRENA has fewer staff and resources at its disposal, limiting its ability to play a greater role in the debate and make a more powerful case for a renewable energy transition.

In addition, a number of intergovernmental organizations have emerged as important actors in global energy governance, even though they were not founded to specifically address energy issues. For example, the Shanghai Cooperation Organization (founded in 2001), whose primary focus is on strengthening mutual trust and friendship among its members and enhancing regional security, brings together a number of Asian energy-producing and consuming countries such as China, Russia, and Kazakhstan. Its members have cooperated on a range of energy issues, particularly regarding fossil fuels. The Asia-Pacific Economic Cooperation (APEC) established its Energy Working Group in 1990, which has since met almost fifty times. APEC has also convened twelve meetings of energy ministers since 1996 to discuss a range of issues such as energy infrastructure investment, oil prices, low-carbon sustainable energy development in the Asia-Pacific, or energy security and resilience—the focus of the most recent, the twelfth Energy Ministerial Meeting held in Cebu, the Philippines. The Association of Southeast Asian Nations (ASEAN) has been involved in energy issues since the late 1990s, when it created the Centre for Energy to improve coordination and cooperation among its members in the energy field. The European Union (EU) has worked on the supranational level to coordinate energy policies among its member states through the Common Energy Policy and the 2015 Energy Union Strategy. Finally, the landscape of global energy governance is further populated by summit processes such as the G-7/G-8 and the G-20, both of which have provided vital high-profile forums for the discussion of issues such as energy efficiency, the phasing out of fossil fuel subsidies, and cutting carbon dioxide emissions.

The large number of organizations in global energy governance makes a truly global approach to energy production and consumption—uniting producers and consumers in North and South under a shared set of rules and principles—next to impossible. A highly fragmented energy governance architecture also hinders moves to integrate and effectively coordinate responses to the intertwined challenges of energy security and climate change. Global energy governance is further complicated by vertical fragmentation, which plays an important role, notably regarding the often uneasy relationship between actors operating in global and regional energy markets and governments' attempts to regulate their behavior at the domestic or supranational level.

United Nations

While without a dedicated energy program, the UN nonetheless addresses energy with regards to economic, social and environmental sustainability through a number of different organizations and programs, including the United Nations Industrial Development Organization (UNIDO), the United Nations Development Programme (UNDP), and the United Nations Environment Programme (UNEP). The UN Statistics Division (UNSD) gathers energy statistics from over 190 countries, with a database reaching back to the 1950s. The International Atomic Energy Agency (IAEA) has been the focal point for international cooperation in the nuclear field since its founding in 1957, preceding the creation of OPEC and the IEA. As an autonomous intergovernmental forum within the UN family, the IAEA reports to both the General Assembly and the Security Council; it has played a critical role with regards to the safe and peaceful use of nuclear energy technologies and nuclear non-proliferation.[12]

With the 2004 establishment of UN-Energy as a mechanism for interagency collaboration on energy issues, the UN has attempted to connect its various internal activities. In theory, the creation of such a mechanism is useful to avoid duplication of efforts by different parts of the UN family and save scarce resources. However,

UN-Energy has so far lacked the sustained high-level support to enable it to live up to its full intended purpose. Similarly, the Sustainable Energy for All (SE4ALL) initiative launched in 2011 by then Secretary-General Ban Ki-moon with the goal of achieving universal sustainable energy access had only little tangible impact until the adoption of the SDGs in 2015.

Climate change negotiations

International climate change negotiations take place under the auspices of the UNFCCC, one of the outcomes of the 1992 UN Conference on Environment and Development in Rio de Janeiro. Most accounts of global energy governance make no direct mention of the UNFCCC and the results the negotiation process has produced over the last two decades. Yet the Paris Agreement on climate change, as an international agreement within the UNFCCC, is, in its implications, the most profound and far reaching energy—and economic—treaty the world has seen. Staying well below a 2°C rise in global average surface temperatures above preindustrial levels, as prescribed by the agreement,[13] requires a swift de-carbonization of energy systems around the world; major changes in the production and consumption not just of energy but of goods more generally; and the mobilization of large amounts of public and private capital to achieve the necessary changes. The actions parties intend to take under the Paris Agreement, referred to as nationally determined contributions (NDCs), begin to spell out domestic pathways to collectively achieve global carbon neutrality by 2050, with a strong focus on transitioning away from emissions-intensive fossil fuels towards renewables and other low-carbon energy technologies such as carbon capture and storage (CCS) and nuclear power. This, in turn, has direct implications for all other aspects of global energy governance, emphasizing the need to understand energy and climate change as interconnected challenges.

The guarded optimism about this multilateral agreement, however, was dampened by the Trump administration's June 2017 announcement that the United States would withdraw from the Paris Agreement. The decision will not go into effect until 2021, leaving the possibility for a return should a new US president be elected prior to that date.

Sustainable development

With the adoption of the SDGs, the UN has sought not only to continue and build on unfinished work of the preceding Millennium Development Goals (MDGs), but also to expand the scope of measures needed "to free the human race from the tyranny of poverty and want and to heal and secure our planet."[14] While the MDGs failed to mention energy, SDG 7 concerns itself exclusively with affordable energy access, energy efficiency, and clean energy infrastructure. Goal 13, with its focus on climate action, addresses energy as the main source of GHG emissions and reiterates earlier calls for a further development of renewables.

It has been argued that the majority of the SDGs are now either "wholly or partially concerned with managing resources, energy or climate change" given the strong environmental connotations of "sustainability."[15] Beyond semantics, however, the emphasis on energy and climate change is logical and consequential, as success in addressing many of the development goals and targets is directly dependent on the reliable provision of sufficient amounts of energy at affordable prices, and on whether or not the growth in global carbon dioxide (CO_2) emissions can be sufficiently reined in to slow the rise in global average surface temperatures.

With its focus on development support and poverty reduction in the Global South, the World Bank may not seem, at least initially, to be a key player in global energy governance. Yet due to the interconnection between energy provision and economic development, one of its biggest budget lines has long been lending for energy infrastructure projects. Together with the closer integration and expansion of the climate change portfolio into its core agenda, the World Bank, as a *de jure* if not always *de facto* part of the UN system, is a powerful player in supporting countries' efforts to build greater domestic power generation capacity while transitioning towards a sustainable, low-carbon energy future.

The SDGs are a reflection of a new reality in international development, which acknowledges climate change and energy as key dimensions that need to be jointly addressed if there is to be meaningful progress. In this same vein, the activities of the World Bank are now unthinkable without a significant focus on the two interconnected issues. This change is a departure from past World Bank policy, which was widely criticized because of investments in unsustainable high-emissions energy infrastructure, especially coal-fired power generation. But in a sign of the changing times, in 2016 World Bank President Jim Yong Kim warned of the construction of further coal-fired power plants if GHG targets were to be met. The World Bank Group published a Climate Change Action Plan designed to help countries meet their NDCs and invest more heavily in low-carbon energy solutions in the period up to 2020.[16] The Bank shares this new approach with other international financial institutions such as the Asian Development Bank (ADB), whose lending has shifted from support for fossil fuel projects towards renewables, energy efficiency, and sustainable transport in line with new global priorities spelled out in the Paris Agreement and the SDGs.[17]

Towards an integrated architecture?

For global energy governance to be more effective, two main challenges should be addressed. First, the various intergovernmental organizations populating the energy landscape need to be integrated into a more coherent architecture. Second, the remaining divides between energy governance and other global governance fields, such as those in climate change and international development, need to be bridged in order to capitalize on existing overlaps and synergies.

Given the diversity of energy sources and technologies and the varied energy interests of states in the international system, a further integration and potential unification of the fragmented landscape of global energy governance can only occur around an intergovernmental organization or group of organizations that addresses the breadth and scope of energy policy today. This rules out OPEC as a suitable conduit for integration, because its important but narrow focus on high-carbon petroleum products fails to adequately reflect the low-carbon direction of travel for the world's energy systems. But while global power generation is diversifying and transitioning towards renewable sources in many countries, fossil fuels and nuclear power will continue to play an important role for some time to come, especially if technological innovations such as CCS can be cost effectively applied at industrial scale. Therefore, even though IRENA will have a vital part to play in the global energy governance architecture, it, too, cannot currently serve as its main pillar. This leaves the IEA as the only widely respected and distinctly energy-focused organization with a broad enough issue portfolio to potentially take on such a role.

Integration within global energy governance

One of the keys to unlocking greater integration within global energy governance is greater cooperation between the IEA and IRENA. The "salutary shock" provided by the creation of IRENA as a potential rival organization in 2009 had an undeniable impact on the IEA and led it to pay closer attention to renewable energy sources.[18] Renewables play a much bigger role in the IEA's issue portfolio today than ten years ago. Renewable technology reports acknowledging the rapid scaling up and increasing cost competitiveness of wind and solar PV are now issued on a regular basis. In early 2012, the two organizations signed an official partnership agreement, targeting the development and publication of the IEA/IRENA Global Renewable Energy Policies and Measures Database, cooperation in technology and innovation, and the sharing of renewable energy statistics. Both organizations have also held joint workshops and co-published a number of energy technology briefs. In early 2017, the IEA and IRENA published their first joint report focused on a global decarbonization of the energy sector.

Since the 1990s there has also been an improvement in relations between the IEA and OPEC. The organizations and their members cooperate via the International Energy Forum (IEF). Both the IEA and OPEC were founding members of the Joint Organizations Data Initiative that was created as a permanent mechanism by the IEF to arrive at more reliable statistics for petroleum and natural gas; it also includes APEC, OLADE, the Statistical Office of the European Communities (EUROSTAT), GECF, and UNSD.

There are, however, limits to the partnership between the IEA and OPEC, as demonstrated in 2011. As the war in Libya drove up global oil prices, there was a failure to coordinate a joint response to the events. Attempts by consumer countries to get OPEC to increase its oil-production quotas failed, prompting the IEA to release sixty million barrels from emergency stocks over the period of thirty days. In response, OPEC Secretary-General Abdullah al-Badri complained that strategic oil reserves should not be "used as a weapon against OPEC."[19] The dispute threatened the rapprochement between the organizations and served as a reminder of the potential for conflict in the fragmented global governance architecture.

Although membership of the IEA is limited to OECD countries, the organization has recently stepped up cooperation with major non-member energy producers and consumers around the world, particularly its seven partner countries in the G-20 that are not OECD members—China, India, Brazil, Mexico, Indonesia, South Africa, and Russia—as well as with selected member states of the Association of Southeast Asian Nations (ASEAN). This cooperation has gone beyond issuing occasional reports. The seven G-20 partner countries actively participate in the IEA Ministerial Meeting, which takes place every two years and sets broad strategic priorities for the agency. The IEA's data modelling and statistics courses are designed for and attended by government representatives from nonmember countries.

In late 2013, the IEA and its partner countries (with the exception of Mexico) issued a Joint Declaration on Association which stated their mutual interest "to pursue closer cooperation on the basis of a common understanding that global energy challenges and energy security require shared solutions by producer, consumer and transit countries."[20] Since 2015, China, Indonesia, Thailand, Singapore, Morocco, and India have become association countries in an important further step towards expanding the IEA's reach beyond its traditional OECD membership and bridging the North–South divide. However, while ties have deepened with several major countries, they have threatened to break with others. The political fallout of the Ukraine crisis in 2014, the resulting sanctions imposed by Western countries on Russia, and the heated debate over the EU's continued dependence on Russian gas have all undermined the growing relationship.

Integration between different governance architectures

While climate change was not an issue occupying international policymakers' attention in the infant days of global energy governance, it has since become a key determinant of policymaking worldwide, reaching far beyond its more obvious environmental and energy policy implications. The intergovernmental organizations making up the global energy governance architecture have had to adjust to this new reality and address climate change as an integral part of their activities. The consequence has been greater interactions and growing integration between global energy and global climate governance. With its focus on renewable energy technologies and advocacy for a sustainable, low-carbon energy future, IRENA has been a natural partner for the UNFCCC and the wider climate change field since its creation in 2009.

In contrast, the IEA, as the significantly older and more established intergovernmental energy organization, underwent a period of transition to arrive in a similar place. The IEA significantly expanded its focus on climate change following the 2005 G-8 summit at Gleneagles and now gathers CO_2 emissions statistics, maintains a database on GHG emissions policies undertaken by member states, and has devoted substantial and growing attention to the issue in all its World Energy Outlooks (WEO)—the organization's annual flagship publication—since 2008. The IEA's leadership of Executive Director Fatih Birol and his predecessor, Maria van der Hoeven, became more outspoken on climate change, making the case for an aggressive reduction of global GHG emissions in line with the 2°C stabilization target spelled out in the Paris Agreement. The IEA now officially supports the UNFCCC in a number of its functions, including expert review of emissions data and climate policy measures, technical examination of de-carbonization efforts, and the mobilization of private capital for clean energy projects in developing countries. Like IRENA, the IEA is represented at Conferences of the Parties (COPs) to the UNFCCC and is a respected go-to for the kind of energy policy knowledge often lacking among many of the environmental experts supporting the climate convention process.

In the sustainable development arena, too, the cooperation between inter-governmental energy organizations and the UN system has increased over time, which is logical considering IRENA's global membership and the countries working with the IEA on an association basis. As a UN observer, IRENA works closely with UNDP and the World Bank, among others, with regards to financing of renewable energy projects and widening energy access in the developing world. The IEA has cooperated with UN actors on issues of energy poverty and universal energy access for years, drawing on its substantial work in the field since the 1990s, a cooperation that was boosted by the proclamation of the SDGs and their emphases on energy and climate change. In addition, the heads of the IEA and the World Bank have both repeatedly called for an end to fossil-fuel subsidies, following a number of joint reports on the issue prepared for the G-20 since the forum's 2009 commitment to phase out such subsidies over the medium term.

Conclusion

The future of global energy governance remains uncertain. Since the 1960s, a frag-mented landscape comprising a variety of different intergovernmental organizations has emerged, which has lately shown movement towards greater cooperation and integration. Yet how far these developments may lead cannot yet be determined. Should there be a *de facto* or *de jure* "World Energy Agency," either by adding new members (fully or on an association basis) to the IEA, or should it open up to all nonmember countries, turning itself into a universal international organization? Would this improve the integration of the different organizations within the global energy governance architecture? Would it improve the integration of the global energy and climate governance architectures? Would such a World Energy Agency need the power to set binding rules for its members and associated partners? Would countries willingly abide by those rules? Should a World Energy Agency be part of the UN system?

Powerful obstacles currently impede the establishment of a World Energy Agency. These include membership in the OECD as a legal precondition for full membership in the IEA; continuing conflicts of interest between energy consumer and energy producer countries, with the latter continuing their cooperation in organizations such as OPEC; and the requirement for IEA member states to maintain and finance a costly strategic oil reserve. They also include the political rifts between major energy producers such as Russia and consumer countries in the OECD, which have surfaced in the last few years.

However, it is not inconceivable that a World Energy Agency, for example as the result of a future merger between the IEA and IRENA, could be placed on a new legal footing with updated statutes and organizational structures adjusted for the twenty-first century. But doing so would be dependent on sufficient political will among current IEA and IRENA members to accept the newly created body's new role, and contribute to its success. In sum, from an aspirational perspective of effective global energy governance, it seems desirable to have a single organization that includes all states, and that integrates all sources of energy. Yet given the various obstacles, path dependencies, and lock-ins in current global energy governance, this logical recommendation seems unrealistic. The IEA's current strategy of slowly moving in this direction and adjusting its approach in response to a fast changing global policy environment, forging partnerships with other intergovernmental organizations as well as with nonmember states, appears to be the next best option, possibly leading to further integration and reform in the years to come.

However, as the chapter has illustrated, the key players in global energy governance are not just intergovernmental organizations specifically focused on energy but also treaty processes such as the UNFCCC and internationally agreed agendas such as the SDGs. The Paris Agreement on climate change would not normally be studied as an important part of the global energy governance architecture, and yet its implications for energy systems and energy policymaking—with or without the participation of the United States—reach far beyond the impact currently enjoyed by any of the major intergovernmental energy organizations. Likewise, the SDGs and, by extension the multilateral development banks working to deliver the ambitious new agenda, are critically important if energy security and low-carbon energy transitions are to become a reality in the poorer states of the Global South as much as in the wealthier North.

Therefore, a more holistic view of global energy governance is required. It should incorporate the various key actors and agreements that shape outcomes in this field regardless on which governance architecture they may be built.

Additional reading

Andreas Goldthau, *The Handbook of Global Energy Policy* (Chichester: Wiley-Blackwell, 2016).

Caroline Kuzemko, Andreas Goldthau, and Michael E. Keating, *The Global Energy Challenge: Environment, Development and Security* (Basingstoke: Palgrave Macmillan, 2015).

Thijs Van de Graaf, *The Politics and Institutions of Global Energy Governance* (Basingstoke: Palgrave Macmillan, 2013).

Daniel Yergin, *The Quest: Energy, Security and the Remaking of the Modern World* (London: Allen Lane, 2011).

Notes

1 Andreas Goldthau and Benjamin K. Sovacool, "The Uniqueness of the Energy Security, Justice, and Governance Problem," *Energy Policy* 41 (2012): 232–240.

2 For a more complete definition, see Frank Biermann, et al., "The Architecture of Global Climate Governance: Setting the Stage," in *Global Climate Governance Beyond 2012: Architecture, Agency and Adaptation*, eds. Frank Biermann, Philipp Pattberg, and Fariborz Zelli (Cambridge: Cambridge University Press, 2010), 15–24.

3 Standard Oil of California, Standard Oil of New Jersey, Standard Oil of New York, Texaco, Gulf Oil, Royal Dutch Shell, and the Anglo-Iranian Oil Company (the later BP). The American members of the group would later merge into the Chevron Corporation and ExxonMobil, respectively.

4 Organization of the Petroleum Exporting Countries, "Guidelines for Petroleum Policy in Member Countries," *International Legal Materials* 7, no. 5 (1968): 1183–1186.

5 Rüdiger Graf, "Making Use of the 'Oil Weapon': Western Industrialized Countries and Arab Petropolitics in 1973–74," *Diplomatic History* 36, no. 1 (2012): 185–208.

6 Ann Florini and Benjamin K. Sovacool, "Who Governs Energy? The Challenges Facing Global Energy Governance," *Energy Policy* 37, no. 12 (2009): 5239–5248.

7 Organisation for Economic Co-operation and Development, *Decision of the Council establishing an International Energy Agency of the Organisation* (Paris: OECD, 1974).

8 As net-exporter members, Canada, Denmark, and Norway are currently exempt.

9 Harald Heubaum and Frank Biermann. "Integrating Global Energy and Climate Governance: The Changing Role of the International Energy Agency," *Energy Policy* 87, (2015): 229–239.

10 International Renewable Energy Agency, *Statute of the International Renewable Energy Agency* (Bonn: IRENA, 2009).

11 Thijs Van de Graaf and Dries Lesage, "The International Energy Agency After 35 Years: Reform Needs and Institutional Adaptability," *The Review of International Organizations* 4, no. 3 (2009), 293–317.

12 International Atomic Energy Agency, *Statute of the IAEA* (Vienna: IAEA, 2016), www.iaea.org/about/statute.

13 United Nations Framework Convention on Climate Change, *Paris Agreement* (Bonn: UNFCCC, 2015), http://unfccc.int/files/essential_background/convention/application/pdf/english_paris_agreement.pdf.

14 UN, "Transforming Our World: The 2030 Agenda for Sustainable Development," General Assembly resolution (A/RES/70/1), 21 October 2015.

15 Stephen Browne and Thomas G. Weiss, "The UN's Post-2015 Development Agenda and Leadership," *Great Decisions 2016* (New York: Foreign Policy Association, 2016), 63–74.

16 Suzanne Goldenberg, "Plans for Coal-fired Power in Asia are 'Disaster for Planet' Warns World Bank," *The Guardian*, 5 May 2016. See also World Bank, *World Bank Group Climate Change Action Plan 2016–2020* (Washington, DC: World Bank, 2016).

17 Asian Development Bank, *2015 Clean Energy Investments Project Summaries* (Manila: ADB, 2016).

18 Thijs Van de Graaf, "Fragmentation of Global Energy Governance: Explaining the Creation of IRENA," *Global Environmental Politics* 13, no. 3 (2013), 14–33.

19 Barbara Lewis, "OPEC, IEA Clash Over Oil Reserves Weapon," *Reuters*, 23 June 2011.

20 International Energy Agency, *Joint Declaration by the IEA and Brazil, China, India, Indonesia, Russia and South Africa on the occasion of the 2013 IEA Ministerial Meeting expressing mutual interest in pursuing an association* (Paris: IEA, 2013).

Poverty reduction

David Hulme and Oliver Turner

In today's affluent world almost one-third of the human population experiences some form of poverty. Around 795 million people—only a little less than the populations of the United States and European Union (EU) combined—suffer from chronic hunger[1] and nearly 663 million people have no access to safe drinking water.[2] More than 300,000 women die every year during pregnancy or childbirth.[3] In the thirty minutes it takes to read this chapter, approximately 330 children under the age of five will have died, mostly from readily preventable causes.[4] Every day around the world hundreds of millions of people are denied the opportunity to lead a secure and productive life, but it does not have to be this way. Humanity has developed the technology and accumulated the resources to satisfy the basic needs of all. Food, education, healthcare services, and others could be provided if our world were organized differently. In short, poverty can be reduced if tackled more effectively through the structures of global governance.

As this chapter shows, key international organizations along with myriad additional actors have long been involved in the challenge of alleviating global poverty. The United Nations, the World Bank, civil society groups, and even celebrities have been, and remain, variously active in this regard, with mixed degrees of success. At times poverty reduction has been elevated towards the top of the global agenda, attracting focus and investment from heads of state and other political elites. At others it has been relegated to the sidelines so that issues including national security and economic stability have drawn attention and resources away from the world's poor, often with predictably lamentable results.

This chapter's brief examination of how the mechanisms of global governance have approached the issue of world poverty aims to demonstrate that resolving the problem will require those mechanisms to function more effectively. It begins with a short historical and contemporary overview of how global poverty has been conceived and approached within the international arena, particularly since the mid-twentieth century when the first multilateral institutions capable of providing leadership on the matter were established. It then asks why poverty persists and where in the world it is most pervasive, before exploring the various arguments which have been advanced over time as to how the problem may be solved. The chapter then describes the multitude of actors who make up the vast framework of global governance structures active in attempted poverty alleviation. It ends by exploring potentially critical future issues and developments which are likely to have an impact on world poverty, as well as on efforts to reduce its severity. The seemingly unattainable feat of consigning poverty to history may not be as unrealistic as commonly believed.

Global poverty: Historical and contemporary contexts

The idea that the most basic needs can be provided to all is relatively recent. Throughout history, the majority of humanity has been materially poor, with hunger and food insecurity the norm, life expectancies short, epidemic disease levels and mortality high, and exposure to the elements a daily experience. Between 1 CE and 1000 CE, world per capita economic growth rates were around zero or even negative for some areas, including Western Europe.[5] Between then and 1820, global life expectancy rose only from twenty-four to twenty-six years and per capita income (in 1990 US$) increased from just $453 to $667.[6] From around 1820 things changed dramatically. Average life expectancy rose from twenty-six years to sixty-six years and average per capita income increased from $667 to $5709 by 2000. Advances in the human condition, however, became very unevenly spread. Many were left behind and global inequality steadily increased.

Importantly for poverty as an issue of global governance, US President Franklin D. Roosevelt's "four freedoms" speech of 6 January 1941 identified freedom from want as an international priority. The United Nations was founded in 1945 with the aim of ensuring peace and preventing international warfare, creating economic stability and, more broadly, promoting human betterment. UN agencies such as the Food and Agriculture Organization (FAO), the World Health Organization (WHO), and the International Labour Organization (ILO) led on improvements in global agriculture, health, education, and science, among many other things, with the collective aim of supporting the needs of people as well as states. In 1947 the UN produced the first global consensus on eradicating poverty: The Universal Declaration of Human Rights. The key articles in relation to poverty are 25 and 28:

> Everyone has the right to a standard of living adequate for the health and well-being of his family, including food, clothing, housing and medical care . . . Everyone is entitled to a social and international order in which the rights and freedoms set forth in this Declaration can be fully realised.

These grand ideals, however, did not produce the desired results. Throughout the 1950s, development, human rights, and the nascent idea of alleviating poverty were sidelined as Cold War security concerns dominated international meetings. The environment changed briefly in the 1960s with the election of US President John F. Kennedy.[7] Yet, for the most part it was left to academics and social activists to raise awareness of global poverty and push for corresponding action. The period 1950–1973 has been described as a "golden age" for economic growth.[8] Average GDPs per capita in Africa, Asia, and Latin America increased alongside significant improvements in life expectancy and other social indicators. Yet the patterns were complex and prosperity for all did not follow.

During the 1980s, then US President Ronald Reagan and UK Prime Minister Margaret Thatcher promoted neoliberal ideas and a shift of intellectual authority for development from the UN to the International Monetary Fund (IMF) and World Bank (often referred to as the Bretton Woods institutions, or BWIs). The BWIs pursued neoliberal policies which assumed that if the state could be rolled back through deregulation and privatization, and if the market was allowed to determine resource allocations—collectively thought of as "structural adjustment"—rapid economic growth would ensue. This "Washington Consensus," in which free market forces rather than state intervention were relied on as the primary driver of growth and prosperity, dominated development thinking in the 1980s and early 1990s. It is now widely judged to have produced "a lost decade" for Africa and others.

In many ways, 1990 marked a tipping point for ideas about poverty. As the Cold War ended and doubts circulated about structural adjustment, the World Bank's *World Development Report* chose poverty as its main theme and acknowledged the need for economic reform to be accompanied by social policies. It introduced the "dollar-a-day" global poverty line and estimated that around 1.1 billion people around the world lived in extreme poverty. The UNDP's first *Human Development Report* also promoted an alternative to neoliberal economic growth, making the ideas of human development and multidimensional poverty reduction accessible to professionals and the media. Key UN conferences were held, including the World Summit for Children in 1990, the Women's Conference in Beijing in 1995, and the Food Summit in 1996. In 1995 117 heads of state and government attended the World Summit on Social Development (WSSD) in Copenhagen where a form of global consensus was first reached that poverty reduction was the priority goal for development.[9] The aim of eradicating "dollar-a-day" poverty was also approved. These events raised public awareness but foreign aid from rich countries as a share of GDP continued its long-term decline.

In 1998 control of the global poverty agenda returned to the United Nations. Its new Secretary-General, Kofi Annan, prioritized poverty and in May 1999 he identified "development, including poverty eradication," a central issue.[10] The ideas that had emerged in Copenhagen were now being institutionalized as international development became synonymous with global poverty reduction. Shortly after the UN Millennium Summit in 2000, eight Millennium Development Goals (MDGs) to be achieved by 2015 were agreed. The first was a pledge to halve extreme poverty and hunger. Ominously, however, data at the time confirmed the enormous scale of global poverty. The *World Development Report 2000/2001* explained that: "Of the world's 6 billion people, 2.8 billion . . . live on less than $2 a day, and 1.2 billion . . . live on less than $1 a day. In . . . rich countries fewer than 5 percent of all children under five are malnourished, in poor countries as many as 50 percent are."[11]

Yet once again dire need was not met with appropriate action. The World Bank was ambivalent towards the goals and the IMF paid them only lip service. They were informally approved at the 2002 Financing for Development Summit in Monterrey, Mexico, at which the United States and EU pledged additional resources for poverty reduction. Nonetheless, keeping poverty on the international agenda since then has been difficult as national self-interest and other priorities have dominated. The 2005 meeting of G-8 countries in Gleneagles, Scotland, and the UN high-level event of 2008—both led by the United Kingdom—were designed to refocus states towards poverty, but with marginal effect. Even worse, the economic crises of 2007–2008 put poverty reduction into reverse. The FAO, for example, estimated that an additional 100 million people fell into hunger over 2008 and 2009.[12]

It could be argued that the graduation of global poverty onto the international agenda is evidence of progressive social change on the grandest scale. Alternatively, it could be seen as the world's most successful confidence trick, with rich and emerging nations, and global elites retaining the existing structures of power and resource access while pretending to be concerned about poor people. Strong economic growth in selected developing countries between 1990 and 2015, particularly in China and India, has meant that the MDG goal of halving extreme poverty was achieved. The aim of halving the proportion of people with no access to safe drinking water was also met. In addition, and although falling short of the initial MDG targets, maternal mortality was cut by nearly fifty percent over the same period; child mortality declined by more than fifty percent, and primary school enrolment rates in developing countries reached ninety-one percent.[13] Despite these achievements however, for the majority of member states the years since 2000 have been "business as usual" at the UN General Assembly—that is, making grand statements about the eradication of poverty without demonstrating commitment through action. Nevertheless, in 2015 the UN General Assembly agreed to replace the MDGs with an even more ambitious set of Sustainable Development Goals (SDGs) (see Table 50.1).

Table 50.1 The Sustainable Development Goals, 2015–2030

Goal 1	End poverty in all its forms everywhere
Goal 2	End hunger, achieve food security and improved nutrition and promote sustainable agriculture
Goal 3	Ensure healthy lives and promote wellbeing for all at all ages
Goal 4	Ensure inclusive and equitable quality education and promote lifelong learning opportunities for all
Goal 5	Achieve gender equality and empower all women and girls
Goal 6	Ensure availability and sustainable management of water and sanitation for all
Goal 7	Ensure access to affordable, reliable, sustainable and modern energy for all
Goal 8	Promote sustained, inclusive and sustainable economic growth, full and productive employment and decent work for all
Goal 9	Build resilient infrastructure, promote inclusive and sustainable industrialization and foster innovation
Goal 10	Reduce inequality within and among countries

(Continued)

Table 50.1 (Continued)

Goal 11	Make cities and human settlements inclusive, safe, resilient and sustainable
Goal 12	Ensure sustainable consumption and production patterns
Goal 13	Take urgent action to combat climate change and its impacts
Goal 14	Conserve and sustainably use the oceans, seas and marine resources for sustainable development
Goal 15	Protect, restore and promote sustainable use of terrestrial ecosystems, sustainably manage forests, combat desertification, and halt and reverse land degradation and halt biodiversity loss
Goal 16	Promote peaceful and inclusive societies for sustainable development, provide access to justice for all and build effective, accountable and inclusive institutions at all levels
Goal 17	Strengthen the means of implementation and revitalize the Global Partnership for Sustainable Development (Finance, Technology, Capacity Building, Trade, Systemic Issues)

Source: www.un.org/sustainabledevelopment/sustainable-development-goals/.

Why does poverty persist, and where?

In the first instance, we can say that poverty persists because those of us doing well—powerful countries, corporations, political and economic elites, middle-class people in rich and poor countries—simply "don't care" or "don't care enough." We place a low priority on the welfare of the "distant needy," while maintaining, or increasing, our control over resources and carbon emissions, technology, and organizational capacities. Second, debates about poverty and development are often unbalanced and likely to favor the better off. It is they who finance and shape knowledge-creating institutions such as schools, universities, and think tanks that work primarily for their benefit. Third, the institutional framework tasked with addressing global poverty is in many ways unfit for purpose. The UN struggles on but is in need of major reform. The General Assembly, for instance, makes big promises but member states do not deliver; and its numerous agencies remain poorly coordinated and sometimes ineffectual. The governance structures of the World Bank and IMF also remain largely inappropriate and arguably illegitimate, as both are dominated by the United States and Western Europe, despite the reforms of 2010 that increased the voting power of developing countries. At the same time, non-state institutions have made only limited progress. While nongovernmental organizations (NGOs, or nonprofit agencies usually registered as charities) and civil society groups (among others) promote public awareness and concern about global poverty, a coordinated social movement demanding its eradication seems unlikely to emerge.

Disappointment with action to reduce global poverty since 2000 does not mean that nothing has been achieved. The MDGs were partially achieved; debt cancellation has been unprecedented; aid flows have increased; the EU has ensured that new members commit to foreign aid; countries such as Ghana, Rwanda, Mozambique, and Tanzania have improved their capacity to plan and program poverty reduction; and the SDGs have been approved. Global poverty is now on the international agenda, but it remains a secondary priority in relation to terrorism and national security, energy security, financial stability, economic growth in richer nations and others. The grand promises made by national leaders in 2000 and 2015 have made a difference, but they have not been fully honored. Neither have those leaders been held accountable.

While income poverty is vast in both Africa and South Asia, the analytical focus of global poverty has increasingly shifted towards sub-Saharan Africa. Given the continent's lost decade of the 1980s, followed by economic stagnation and the HIV/AIDS pandemic of the 1990s, this is no surprise. However, if one maps the data for Asia and disaggregates them for Indian states and Chinese provinces—which is not unreasonable given that most of these subnational units have populations much bigger than those of the average African country—a second poor continent emerges: Sub-Siberian Asia. This is a virtually contiguous area that stretches across northern India and Nepal to Bangladesh, Myanmar, and Laos, takes in much of central and western China with Mongolia, includes Central Asia (Kazakhstan, Kyrgyzstan, Uzbekistan, Turkmenistan, and Tajikistan), and completes in Afghanistan and Pakistan.

This is not to argue that Africa does not require special attention, but that the global geography of extreme poverty needs to be understood as "sub-Saharan Africa and sub-Siberian Asia plus some other countries." Assuming that poverty in China and especially India will steadily fall because both their average growth rates are currently high fails to recognize that these are continental-scale countries. The lights in Bangalaru and Hangzhou may be shining 24/7, but it is hard to find the money to buy a candle in rural Tripura and Guizhou.

Debates over reducing poverty

There is no clear "solution" to the problem of global poverty. Poverty reduction, like its intellectual and policy antecedent rural development, is about trying "to change the functioning of a complex, dynamic system in order to make progress in attaining multiple objectives."[14] Examined here are theories of why mass poverty occurs through the sequence of ideas that have dominated the history of international development, across three historical eras.

Modernization theory in the 1950s and 1960s posited that a lack of development (and associated mass poverty) across what was then called the "Third World" but is now the "Global South" was the result of economic backwardness and traditional social structures. Once these countries "caught up" with the industrialized world—technologically, institutionally, socially—mass affluence would eradicate poverty everywhere. The modernization account was attractive but by the late 1960s there was mounting evidence that it was not delivering on its promises. Neo-Marxists and dependency theorists explained that the Third World had been integrated into the world economic system in a way that permitted its exploitation through "unequal development."[15] The poor were kept poor so that the elites of wealthy countries could have high material living standards. This analysis demanded radical actions, including peasant revolution and strategies of autonomous development. These arguments played out well in the academic realm, but most countries that pursued such strategies (such as Sri Lanka in the early 1970s and Nicaragua and Tanzania in the 1970s and 1980s) did not fare well.

Neoliberal ideas became dominant intellectually in the late 1970s and politically by the early 1980s. They posited that countries were poor because of public policies that distorted prices and incentive systems and public institutions that were wasteful and rent seeking. Once economies were liberalized and opened up to international trade, the theory stated, competition would promote efficiency and a country could pursue its comparative advantages. Economic growth would ensue and with increased demand would follow job creation and prosperity. These policies following the Washington Consensus were pursued to varying degrees by countries in Africa, Asia, and Latin America. The early results were generally weak and often harmful to poor people (especially with the introduction of fees for health and education). A rapid shift in Russia after the Cold War from centralized economic planning to free market forces was catastrophic for its people. Economic growth and poverty reduction occurred in the 1990s in China and India, but in both cases the state retained a key role and pursued heterodox economic policies.

As the millennium approached, the sweeping policy narratives of the second half of the twentieth century faltered. More pluralist frameworks such as the post-Washington Consensus, which promotes a more context-specific approach to poverty reduction began to fill the global policy space. These frameworks recognized major roles for the market, the state, and civil society and emphasized a range of goals, including strengthening institutions. Growth, in short, is not enough. There was an increased recognition of the complexity of poverty and the breadth and variety of policies needed to reduce it in different countries and for different groups. Thinking since that time has become increasingly nuanced, and social policy in developing countries has moved beyond health and education to include social protection policies, such as cash transfers for the poor and noncontributory old age pensions.[16]

Poverty and global governance: Who is involved?

The institutional landscape for tackling global poverty lacks clear boundaries, and is constituted by a wide range of multilateral, national, subnational, and local institutions across the public sector, private business, and civil society. The multitudinous actors involved often have differing interests and visions of "what should be done," and the institutions, associations, and networks involved are not elements of a rationally designed international institutional architecture. In short, no one is "in charge" of global poverty eradication. It is important, nonetheless, to make sense of this architecture, beginning with the most influential multilateral institutions.

As we have seen, the UN's MDGs and now SDGs have constituted the centerpiece of efforts for global poverty reduction. Yet, within the vast UN system, a bewildering array of organizations promotes, analyzes, implements, and monitors global poverty reduction.[17] They include the UNDP, FAO, WHO, ILO, UNESCO, UNAIDS, and many others. Within the wider UN system, the World Bank is arguably the most influential in terms of setting the agenda on global poverty because of its monetary lending and its capacity to shape thinking. It has the largest concentration of development economists in the world, meaning its "analytical machine has more intellectual juice"[18] than other multilaterals and development agencies. In contrast, the IMF's commitment to poverty reduction remains shallow. The World Trade Organization (WTO) is not formally part of the UN system or a "development" organization and operates principally as a forum in which states negotiate trade deals. It has been tasked with helping to reduce global poverty through the declaration of its Doha Round of trade negotiations as a "development round."[19] However, the Doha Round has stalled.

The move from the MDGs to the SDGs has led to increasing recognition of the links between poverty and climate change, and the Intergovernmental Panel on Climate Change and the annual meetings of the Conference of Parties on climate change have become increasingly important for global action to tackle poverty.

Beyond these organizations, states meet in a variety of formal and informal associations which are to varying extents committed to reducing global poverty. For rich countries the key formal grouping is the Organisation for Economic Co-operation and Development (OECD), whose interests in international development and global poverty are articulated through its Development Assistance Committee. The African Union has particular significance because of its potential role in improving governance and policies across the continent and reducing poverty and conflict. The EU struggles to find a common external position but has reached an internal agreement to focus on the SDGs, increase aid, and induct new member states into international development. The emergence of the G-20 in 2009, reflecting the restructuring of the global economy from West to East, led to a burst of optimism in development circles, but this new association has shown little commitment to poverty reduction. A new set of global financial institutions are being established: The Asian Infrastructure Investment Bank, New Development Bank and others, led by China and the BRICS (Brazil, Russia, China, South Africa). These new institutions focus on economic growth and view that as the main strategy for poverty reduction.

Despite the importance of multinational organizations and collectives of states, national governments remain the most important institution for reducing poverty. It is the governments of the poorest countries which create conditions for economic growth and oversee the delivery of basic services. Rich governments largely determine the volume of international finance allocated for global poverty reduction and have most influence over international institutions. In addition, when subnational governments such as district councils and municipal authorities function well the conditions for health and education provision and increased productivity, among other things, become available. When they do not work well—which is common in many poor countries—poverty is more likely to persist.

Since the end of the Cold War, non-state actors have become increasingly influential in international affairs, with significance for global poverty. Civil society groups promote the idea of tackling poverty around the world and have been granted formal recognition at the United Nations. NGOs are now far more numerous and some, such as BRAC, which employs more than 110,000 staff in Bangladesh and has a budget of around $1 billion per annum, are enormous. Social movements are also gaining increasing prominence, although, as noted earlier, an organized antipoverty movement has not emerged. In addition, a new generation of "philanthrocapitalists" use their fortunes to engage in poverty reduction. While Bill Gates is the most highly publicized, this phenomenon is also established in India, China, Africa, and Latin America. The private sector is another important component of poverty reduction efforts. Indirectly it can create jobs for poor people, and more businesses are now directly active through social responsibility and fair trade programs. Public–private partnerships include the Global Fund for HIV/AIDS, Malaria, and TB (Global Fund) and the Global Alliance for Vaccines and Immunization, a partnership involving UNICEF, WHO, the World Bank, and the Gates Foundation. Finally, epistemic communities—"network[s] of professionals with recognized expertise and competence in a particular domain"[20]—are significant. They include orthodox liberal ("Chicago School") economists who, during the 1970s, formed an epistemic community that dominated thinking about international development. Recently, leading interventionist liberal economists such as Dani Rodrik and Joseph Stiglitz have challenged orthodox liberal prescriptions, although they have found it hard to establish a focused epistemic community.

The future of global poverty

The main prediction underpinning present-day thinking about global poverty is that it will steadily decline. Given humanity's vast material capabilities this assumption does not seem unreasonable. A number of emerging issues, however, may force us to rethink both the processes that cause poverty and the policies we adopt to reduce it.

One issue area is that projections of future global poverty reduction are based on the assumption that relatively high levels of global economic growth, especially in China and India, will continue. However, China's growth rate has slipped from fourteen percent in 2007 to less than seven percent in 2016. Growth influences poverty in three ways. First, poverty within these countries may be reduced via the domestic impact of economic growth, although most effectively if the benefits are distributed more evenly than at present. Second, the growth of these countries could encourage development elsewhere. Notably, China's demand for natural resources has generated more intensive bilateral relations with, and increased investment in, Africa. These links are also argued to have had negative effects, however, such as providing support for dubious regimes such as that of Robert Mugabe in Zimbabwe and Bashir Ahmed in Sudan, and the possibility that Chinese loans and deals for Africa's resources will create a new wave of highly indebted poor countries. Third, China and India may play a greater role in global public policy as both are expanding their foreign aid activities and both have the potential to lead on poverty eradication and/or poverty-reducing economic growth.

Away from Asia, three other issues merit attention. The first is the hope that the economies of at least one of Africa's slumbering giants—Ethiopia, Nigeria, or South Africa—will grow significantly. This would help increase material capabilities across the continent, provide an African economic model for emulation, and improve the image of Africa for investors. Second is the issue of climate change. The three most significant changes for human populations are likely to be rises in sea levels, changes in temperature and precipitation, and the increased frequency of extreme weather events. Most predicted scenarios indicate that poor people will suffer most, for two main reasons. First, wealthy people and countries have more resources to devote to adapting to climate change than do their poorer counterparts. Second, the parts of the world with the highest concentrations of poverty, in sub-Saharan Africa and sub-Siberian Asia, will likely experience a greater share of the negative consequences of climate change than middle to high latitude regions, such as Europe, North America, and Japan. These negative predictions make the question of "what can be done" to prevent radical climate change pressing, but the arrival of the Donald Trump administration in the United States may lead to the "Paris Agreement" of 2015 stalling.

A final key issue area is the changing nature of poverty itself, with two especially pertinent considerations. The first is the urbanization of poverty. Until recently most research, and most policy initiatives, focused on rural poverty. There were good reasons: The numbers and proportions of poor in rural areas were much higher than in urban areas; and economic and social indicators were almost universally lower for rural people. However, today more than half the world's population lives in towns, cities, or megalopolises. Poverty is the issue, and so it must be understood and tackled across the rural–urban continuum, in villages, rural centers, towns, cities, and hyper-cities. Ultimately then, while the World Bank's predictions for extreme global poverty are that it will continue to gradually decline in the medium and long term (once a recovery from the recent fuel, food, and credit crunches has been completed), there are no grounds for complacency. Geopolitically and environmentally, we are moving into a different world, and future strategies to address the planet's widespread poverty must evolve.

The second consideration is rising within-country inequality in many parts of the world. This has meant that large numbers of people who have moved out of absolute poverty (currently defined at \$1.90 a day) are still relatively poor; that is, their income is insufficient to let them participate fully in their society. In the EU, households with an income of less than sixty percent of national median income are classed as relatively poor. Martin Ravallion and Shaohua Chen have computed a "truly global poverty measure," which includes people living in \$1.90 a day poverty and those experiencing relative poverty at the national level (see Figure 50.1). This depiction shows that while absolute poverty has dropped dramatically since 1990, 'truly global poverty' has declined much less.

For example, since implementing dramatic economic reforms in the late 1970s, Beijing has lifted around 650 million Chinese out of poverty—an astonishing achievement. During that time, however, China has gone from being among the world's most equal societies to among its most unequal, with many citizens now living in relative poverty. This is important because inequality has negative consequences for all. Indeed, Richard Wilkinson and Kate Pickett found that across relatively wealthy societies the populations of those with the highest rates of economic inequality experience more crime, lower educational attainment, and elevated health and social problems, among others.[21] SDG Goal 10 explicitly seeks to "reduce inequality" but, to date, very few countries have developed plans for doing so. A key test for the SDG agenda will be whether tackling inequality moves from rhetoric to action. As ever, disparities between rhetoric and action are likely to represent one of the biggest obstacles to tackling global poverty in the future.

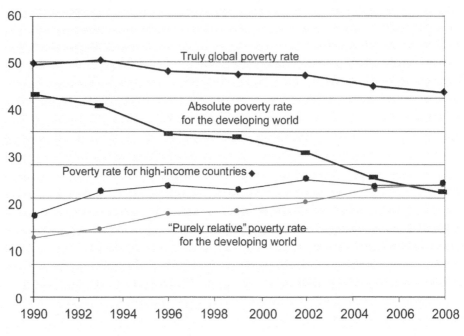

Figure 50.1 Truly global poverty rates, 1990–2008

Source: David Hulme, *Global Poverty: Global Governance and Poor People in the Post-2015 Era*, 2nd ed. (London: Routledge, 2015), 139; printed with permission adapted from M. Ravallion and S. Chen, "A Proposal for Truly Global Poverty Measures," *Global Policy* 4, no. 3 (2013): 258–265.

Conclusion

This chapter has assessed the world's appalling scale of poverty. The World Bank estimates that 767 million people currently live beneath the US$1.90-a-day extreme poverty line[22] and 2.6 billion people beneath the US$2-a-day line.[23] While this represents relative progress, with the proportion of extreme poor in the developing world down from 42 to 10.7 percent between 1981 and 2013,[24] the absolute figures are unacceptable in a world with an average GDP per capita of US$27.6 a day. A redistribution of less than one percent of global income to the poorest would eradicate extreme poverty. Clearly, the overriding constraint to solving the most serious problems of global poverty is not a lack of resources. What is missing is political commitment. Perhaps above all else, a meaningful transformation of ideas about poverty is required to establish a new set of norms.

Norms are commonly accepted understandings about "the way the world is," and when international norms change, previously accepted phenomena can become unacceptable. In 1800, for example, most British people thought of slavery as unobjectionable. By 1850, however, it was widely considered unreasonable and immoral. Ideas about slavery had changed and as a norm it came under attack. During the nineteenth century, slavery fell out of favor across Europe and North America; and, by the twentieth century, it was declared illegal across the world. Similar shifts can be traced over international norms about the roles of women, the conduct of war, and racial segregation. During the 1990s a type of global norm emerged around the need to eradicate poverty,[25] culminating in 2000 with the MDGs, and subsequently reaffirmed in the SDGs. There was an international cascade, with most states signing nonbinding agreements that the goals would be pursued. However, the internalization of the norm and implementation have been slow, and it remains to be seen whether commitment to the SDGs will improve this situation.[26]

Historical evidence indicates that the human condition is improving, and that in proportional terms poverty it is being reduced. Yet levels remain high and the absolute numbers involved have increased in recent years. Feeling angst has little value; action is required. In the short term, practical moves are required by national leaders and relevant agencies to maintain pressure on rich governments to honor the SDGs; to encourage developing countries to improve domestic governance; and to lobby for useful reform in the World Bank, IMF, and elsewhere. We can all contribute to, or volunteer for, a development NGO, buy fair trade products, and reduce our carbon footprints. In the longer term, we are required to become part of a process that facilitates a change in international social norms, ensuring recognition among the people of rich, emerging, and poor countries that extreme poverty is morally unacceptable. Progress may seem slow, but poverty can be eradicated if enough people take the necessary small steps to achieve this goal.

Additional reading

Daron Acemoglu and James Robinson, *Why Nations Fail: The Origins of Power, Prosperity and Poverty* (New York: Crown, 2012).

Jennifer Clapp and Rorden Wilkinson, eds., *Global Governance, Poverty and Inequality* (London: Routledge, 2010).

Angus Deaton, *The Great Escape: Health, Wealth and the Origins of Inequality* (Princeton, NJ: Princeton University Press, 2013).

David Hulme, *Global Poverty: How Global Governance Is Failing the Poor*, 2nd ed. (London: Routledge, 2015).

Charles Kenny, *Getting Better: Why Global Development Is Succeeding – and How We Can Improve the World Even More* (New York: Basic Books, 2011).

Martin Ravallion, *The Economics of Poverty* (Oxford: Oxford University Press, 2016).

Notes

1 World Hunger Education Service, "2016 World Hunger and Poverty Facts and Statistics," www.worldhunger.org/2015-world-hunger-and-poverty-facts-and-statistics.

2 UNICEF and WHO, *Progress on Sanitation and Drinking Water* (Geneva: WHO, 2015).

3 Leontine Alkema, Doris Chou, Daniel Hogan, Sanqian Zhang, Ann-Beth Moller, Alison Gemmill, et al., "Global, Regional, and National Levels and Trends in Maternal Mortality between 1990 and 2015, with Scenario-based Projections to 2030: A Systematic Analysis by the UN Maternal Mortality Estimation Inter-Agency Group," *Lancet* 30, no. 387 (2016): 462–474.

4 UNICEF, WHO, World Bank and UN, *Levels and Trends in Child Mortality Report 2015* (New York: UNICEF, 2015).

5 Angus Maddison, *The World Economy: A Millennial Perspective* (Paris: OECD, 2001), 28.

6 Ibid., 27–31.

7 John Toye and Richard Toye, "From Multilateralism to Modernisation: US Strategy on Trade, Finance and Development in the United Nations, 1945–63," *Forum for Development Studies* 32, no. 1 (2005): 140–144.

8 Maddison, *The World Economy*, 125.

9 UNDP, *Human Development Report 1997* (Oxford: Oxford University Press, 1997), 108.

10 James Traub, *The Best Intentions: Kofi Annan and the UN in the Era of American World Power* (London: Bloomsbury, 2006), 147.

11 World Bank, *World Development Report 2000/2001* (Washington, DC: World Bank, 2001), 3.

12 FAO, *The State of Food Insecurity in the World* (Rome: FAO, 2009), 4.

13 UN, *The Millennium Development Goals Report 2015* (New York: UN, 2015).

14 Bruce Johnston and William Clark, *Redesigning Rural Development: A Strategic Perspective* (Baltimore, MD: Johns Hopkins University Press, 1982), 26.

15 Neo-Marxists and dependency theorists apply Karl Marx's concepts to international development, but in a way that differs from Marx's analysis.

16 Armando Barrientos and David Hulme, eds., *Social Protection for the Poor and Poorest: Concepts, Policies and Politics* (London: Palgrave, 2008).

17 Stephen Browne and Thomas G. Weiss, *Making Change Happen: Enhancing the UN's Contributions to Development* (New York: World Federation of United Nations Associations, 2012).

18 Sebastian Mallaby, *The World's Banker: A Story of Failed States, Financial Crises, and the Wealth and Poverty of Nations* (New York: Penguin, 2004), 3.

19 Rorden Wilkinson and James Scott, eds., *Trade, Poverty and Development: Getting beyond the WTO's Doha Deadlock* (London: Routledge, 2013).

20 Peter Haas, "Epistemic Communities and International Policy Coordination: Introduction," *International Organization* 46, no. 1 (1992): 1–35.

21 Richard Wilkinson and Kate Pickett, *The Spirit Level: Why More Equal Societies Almost Always Do Better* (London: Allen Lane, 2009).

22 World Bank, "Poverty-Overview," www.worldbank.org/en/topic/poverty/overview.

23 Shaohua Chen and Martin Ravallion, "The Developing World Is Poorer Than We Thought, But No Less Successful in the Fight Against Poverty," World Bank Policy Research Working Paper no. 4703 (Washington, DC: World Bank, 2008).

24 World Bank Poverty Data-Poverty Headcount Ratio at $1.90 a day, http://data.worldbank.org/topic/poverty.

25 Sakiko Fukuda-Parr and David Hulme, "International Norm Dynamics and the "End of Poverty": Understanding the Millennium Development Goals," *Global Governance* 17, no. 1 (2011): 17–36.

26 David Hulme, *Global Poverty: How Global Governance Is Failing the Poor*, 2nd ed. (London: Routledge, 2015); Rorden Wilkinson and David Hulme, eds., *The Millennium Development Goals and Beyond: Global Development after 2015* (London: Routledge, 2012).

CONTENTS

Food and hunger

Jennifer Clapp

In the 2014–2016 period, almost 800 million people in the world were under-nourished, meaning they did not consume enough food to maintain a healthy life. That number represents around eleven percent of the world's population. The preva-lence of hunger in the developing world in this period was higher, at around thirteen percent of the population, or approximately one in eight people. These figures show some improvement from the early 1990s, when there were 1 billion hungry people, representing around nineteen percent of the world's population.[1] While these numbers indicate some improvement in the global battle against hunger over the past twenty-five years, they still raise concern and show that much remains to be accomplished to improve world food security. The most recent figures on undernourishment, for example, mask huge disparities across different regions. The percentage of those experiencing hunger has declined sharply in East and Central Asia, Latin America, and North Africa, while progress in reducing hunger in sub-Saharan Africa, South Asia, and Oceana has been much less dramatic. Current measures of undernourish-ment are also based on caloric needs for a sedentary lifestyle, something that we cannot easily assume meets the basic food needs for poor people in developing countries who are typically engaged in strenuous work. For this reason, these figures risk underestimating the number of people experiencing hunger.[2]

The forces that contribute to hunger are wide ranging and complex. They include, for example, poverty, high and volatile food prices, nutritional inadequacy of available foods, and agricultural production shortfalls, among others. Our understanding of these forces, and how they contribute to food insecurity, has also evolved over the years. In this context, it is not surprising that the global governance architecture for addressing hunger—the institutions as well as the legal and normative frameworks that shape the global response to food insecurity—is also highly complex. Governance in this area covers an array of functions that address different aspects of hunger and food insecur-ity. The institutions and actors involved include international organizations dedicated to a variety of tasks such as food aid, assistance to improve agricultural production, and interventions to improve nutrition, as well as nongovernmental organizations and private actors who also take on important roles in these areas.

This chapter details the ways our evolving understandings of food security have been reflected in the mandates and agendas of the key international institutions that have addressed hunger and food insecurity over the past seventy-five years. The global governance of food and hunger has been highly fragmented in practice, and characterized by poor coordination of tasks, which limits the ability to address issues that cut across the mandates of organizations or that fall between the cracks. The 2007–2008 food crisis, and subsequent period of food price volatility from 2009 to 2012, illustrated this fragmentation, and has signaled a need to improve the global governance of food security. Some reforms have taken place since that time, and important steps have been made toward improving coordination. But ongoing fragility in the global food security situation indicates that much work remains to be done.

The chapter begins by mapping the history of global food security governance and shows how changing definitions of food security have influenced the contours of the global governance architecture that has addressed hunger over time. Next, it outlines the challenges presented by the 2007–2008 food crisis and subsequent food price volatility, illustrating that fragmentation in global food security governance has hindered the global response to the economic shocks that exacerbate world hunger. It concludes by discussing some of the more recent revisions to the global food security governance framework and their implications.

The evolving landscape of global food security governance

Many definitions of food security have been put forward over the years. The most commonly cited definition is the one first adopted at the 1996 World Food Summit and refined by the Food and Agriculture Organization of the United Nations (FAO) in 2001 to add the word "social": "Food security exists when all people, at all times, have physical, social and economic access to sufficient, safe and nutritious food which meets their dietary needs and food preferences for an active and healthy life."[3] This current conceptualization of food security is the product of an evolution of our understanding of the term. In the 1930s to 1940s, it was widely assumed that food availability, that is, the amount of food produced, was the key to ensuring that people consumed enough food.

Since that time, important breakthroughs in the analysis of what determines people's ability to obtain enough food to provide a sufficient diet has helped to widen how we view, and address, food insecurity. The understanding of the concept now considers a range of factors, as well as the complex relationship between them.[4] The above definition, for example, brings out four main dimensions of food security that the FAO has stressed in recent years as foundational pillars: Availability (sufficient food), access (physical, economic, and social access), utilization (safe and nutritious food that meets dietary needs), and stability (at all times).[5] The way in which the global food security governance architecture has changed and grown over the years has reflected the evolution in our understanding of food security from one based primarily on food availability to one that recognizes multiple dimensions.

The FAO was established in 1945 and is located in Rome.[6] It was initially focused primarily on the availability pillar of food security, with activities centered on ways to increase food production through the modernization and improvement of agriculture. Other governance bodies also supported the focus on food production over the years through the promotion of the so-called "Green Revolution." This entailed the development and dissemination of high-yielding seed varieties and agricultural input packages in developing countries that were explicitly aimed at bringing about massive increases in food production. As part of this broader Green Revolution initiative, various regional and crop-specific agricultural research centers were established in the 1960s and 1970s, including, for example, the International Rice Research Institute (IRRI) in the Philippines and the International Maize and Wheat Improvement Center (CIMMYT) in Mexico. These research institutes were brought together in 1971 under a coordinating umbrella known as the Consultative Group on International Agricultural Research (CGIAR), overseen by the World Bank. Today there are eighteen CGIAR food and agriculture research institutes worldwide.[7]

The access, or distribution, dimension of food security gained more attention globally in the 1950s and 1960s. In this period, a number of key donor countries, including the United States, Canada, and the European Community (EC; later European Union, EU), institutionalized programs for international food aid. Early food aid provided a means by which donor countries could provide assistance to developing countries by giving a portion of their own agricultural surpluses, which resulted from policies to modernize and industrialize their agricultural sectors in previous decades.[8] Although it drew its fair share of criticism because of its politicized nature and its tendency to be self-serving on the part of donors, food aid was considered a key policy tool in the fight against world hunger in the early days.

In the 1960s, for example, food aid made up around one-quarter of all international development assistance, and the 1963 establishment of the UN's World Food Programme (WFP) provided a multilateral delivery channel for international food aid. The WFP, also located in Rome, initially delivered only a small proportion of international food aid alongside the bilateral aid delivered by the major donor countries. Today, the WFP delivers some seventy-five percent of all food aid. The Food Aid Convention (FAC)—a treaty among donor countries that pledges amounts of aid and maps out norms for food aid practice—was first agreed in 1967 and has been periodically updated ever since. The latest version of the FAC, agreed in 2012, has been renamed the Food Assistance Convention to take into account a wider array of food-related assistance activities, including cash donations that allow for the purchase of locally produced foods.[9]

By the early 1970s, major global governance initiatives to improve both availability and access to food were in place, as noted above. These initiatives, however, were soon revealed to be inadequate in the face of the major food crisis that erupted in the mid-1970s. Food prices increased dramatically between 1973 and 1975, with prices for food staples such as wheat, corn, and soy tripling from their 1971 levels. The rapid price increases caused havoc in the global food system. Food stocks reached record lows in 1974, and widespread panic ensued, driving prices up further. The crisis illustrated all too clearly that the global food system was highly fragile and prone to major disruptions that could result in a spike in levels of hunger around the world.[10]

The food crisis of the 1970s, the product of multiple complex factors, prompted a rethink of our conceptualization of food security and how to promote it through global cooperation. Availability and access were certainly important, as world food production declined over the 1972–1974 period in part because of poor weather, causing a disruption to food aid deliveries. But the crisis also revealed the importance of other dimensions, including market stability and nutrition. The more industrialized agricultural production systems that were promoted by agencies such as the FAO, the World Bank, and the CGIAR, for example, were heavily reliant on fossil fuels, and when oil prices spiked in this same period, food prices followed suit. There were also major shifts in global grain markets at this time, with the Soviet Union buying up massive quantities of grain as prices rose, leaving little for developing countries to receive as aid, and what was left on the market was largely out of their reach because of its higher price.[11] Increased hunger in this period also highlighted the need to pay more attention to the nutritional quality of food.

The 1970s food crisis prompted a number of reforms to the institutional framework for global food security governance. Most of these reforms emerged from recommendations made at the 1974 World Food Conference, which was convened to address the crisis. The reforms that emerged from this gathering bolstered the pillars of food security that were already supported by the governance framework—production and distribution—and also expanded that framework in a number of ways.

There was an attempt to bolster the availability pillar of food security, especially in the world's poorest countries that were hardest hit by the crisis. The International Fund for Agricultural Development (IFAD) was created to increase agricultural production and improve rural livelihoods in developing countries through investment in agricultural projects.[12] The incorporation of rural livelihoods into its mandate expanded the understanding of food security to include the integration of production and consumption through a livelihood perspective to development. There were also other reforms to the food security governance framework that addressed the access pillar, such as efforts to improve food aid practices among donors. Donors were requested to increase their commitment to food aid, and to follow better practices to target the neediest countries. These requests came about because of widespread criticism in the 1960s and 1970s that donors were channeling most of their food aid donations to political allies, rather than to the world's hungriest people.[13]

The conceptualization of food security was also widened at this time, along with the creation of new accompanying food security governance institutions. Several new international governance bodies were established following the World Food Conference, which gave weight to the emerging understanding of the significance of the stabilization and utilization pillars of food security. For example, in the UN system, a new intergovernmental body under the FAO, the UN Committee on World Food Security (CFS), was established in 1974 to serve as a forum for reviewing food security policy that would have an impact on the stability of food markets. The initial work of the CFS was primarily focused on grain production and the stabilization of grain markets.[14] The UN Standing Committee on Nutrition (SCN) was established in 1977 to monitor nutritional programs across the UN system to improve utilization.[15] The World Food Council (WFC) also came out of the World Food Conference; it was set up to serve as a body to coordinate national agriculture ministries on issues of hunger and malnutrition.[16] In 1975, an additional institution was established, the International Food Policy Research Institute (IFPRI), with an explicit focus on policy research for agricultural development, including economic and nutrition policy. IFPRI joined the CGIAR system in 1980, reflecting a growing recognition of the need to incorporate policy dimensions into agricultural research activities.

The four pillars of food security that are highlighted today were thus supported through various governance initiatives at the international level by the early 1980s. The significance of these different components was solidified with the publication of leading economist Amartya Sen's important research findings in the early 1980s, which demonstrated that food supply alone was not sufficient to ensure food security, and that other forces, including well-functioning markets, enabling livelihoods, and public policy, were also important.[17] This work helped to reinforce the broader-based approach to food security, which eventually led to the adoption at the 1996 World Food Summit of the definition of food security, noted above.

Throughout the 1980s and 1990s, other actors also began to play an increasingly important role in shaping international food security governance norms and practices. Nongovernmental organizations (NGOs) that focused on food security and development took on both operational and advocacy roles as governments increasingly began to rely on these organizations to operationalize their food security policies and programs. NGOs such as CARE and World Vision, for example, took on roles as food aid delivery agencies, while others, including Oxfam and the World Development Movement, took on an advocacy role regarding international food policy. At the same time, corporate actors began to take on a greater role in global food security governance through public–private partnerships. The Global Alliance for Improved Nutrition (GAIN), for example, was established in 2002 as a partnership between international organizations, the agrifood industry, and civil society organizations to promote initiatives in the areas of nutrition and food fortification.[18] In the early 2000s, the WFP also began to make more linkages with private donors and developed partnerships with agrifood firms and other corporations to support its food assistance work.

The 1980s and 1990s were a period of relatively low agricultural commodity prices compared to the spikes experienced in the 1970s. This period nonetheless saw episodes of severe hunger in some parts of the world, such as the 1983–1985 Ethiopian famine that led to 600,000 deaths. The tragedy in Ethiopia unfolded in the context of domestic conflict and drought, and highlighted the complexity of addressing hunger in a world of plenty. The Ethiopian government was slow to ask for international assistance, and private fundraising, through initiatives like the 1985 Live Aid concert, raised public awareness about the issue in industrialized countries.[19] Yet despite this elevation of concern about hunger, by the early 1990s, the World Food Council was disbanded and its activities were absorbed by the FAO and WFP. Renewals to the Food Aid Convention in 1995 and 1999 saw donors reduce their overall commitments to providing food aid, and aid provision declined. The World Trade Organization's (WTO) Agreement on Agriculture (AoA) also came into place on 1 January 1995, and included new rules on the international trade in agricultural products. These rules, designed to reduce trade distortions in the sector, had important implications for food security, as will be discussed below.[20]

Although some downsizing of activity took place during this period, some progress was also made in new directions on the food security front. In 2000, the UN created the post of the UN special rapporteur on the right to food, whose mandate is to promote the realization of the right to food through measures taken at the national, regional, and international levels. The creation of this post recognizes the significance of the need to promote the human right to food, first articulated in the 1948 Universal Declaration of Human Rights, within the UN system. The special rapporteur works with UN agencies, other international organizations, NGOs, and governments in raising awareness of right to food issues and promoting policy changes.[21]

The challenges presented by the 2007–2008 food crisis

According to FAO figures, from 1990 to 2006 there had been some steady, albeit slow, progress in reducing the number and proportion of food-insecure people in the world. But after 2006, the world went from a situation of low agricultural and food commodity prices to one of high and volatile food prices, with enormous consequences for food security. In late 2007 and early 2008, world food prices rose sharply, with prices for key staple crops doubling within months. These rapid price increases occurred under conditions that many characterized as a "perfect storm"—a combination of high energy prices, soaring investment in agricultural commodities and biofuels, drought in some parts of the world, rising demand in rapidly industrializing countries, and a global financial meltdown. The 2007–08 global food crisis slowed progress toward addressing world hunger, and highlighted yet again that food insecurity is extremely difficult to address, even with a wide-ranging set of specialized institutions and arrangements focused on ending hunger. The crisis revealed the limits of the existing governance framework and pointed to the need for further refinements.

The 2007–2008 crisis and the subsequent volatility on food markets in the 2009–2012 period demonstrated the extent to which food security is deeply intertwined with global economic forces. It also highlighted the extent to which the existing food security governance framework was not empowered to fully address the complex contributors to the crisis. The global food governance framework is characterized by fragmentation that results in the separation of governance tasks not only among the food-related institutions, but also between the food agencies and other institutions in the global economy that have relevance for food security. Some have characterized this framework as a "regime complex," referring to the multiple and separate bodies that govern various aspects of food security.[22]

The food security pillars of access and stability in particular have been affected by turmoil on global food markets. When those markets are disrupted by shifting trade patterns and rising prices, people's ability to access food, and to do so on a consistent basis, can become severely compromised. In such situations, it is typically the most vulnerable people in the world's poorest countries—those who spend some fifty to eighty percent of their income on food—who are affected most profoundly. The linkages between the global economic situation and food security are acknowledged in the governance work on the four pillars of food security, but the existing food governance agencies have little authority to address broader economic arrangements that affect food security.

Broader economic forces impeded food security during the crisis in two important ways. First, the world's poorest countries had become highly vulnerable because global trade and investment patterns over a period of thirty to forty years encouraged a growing dependence on food imports. The inclusion of agriculture into global trade rules in the WTO's AoA led to rules which provided little incentive, and, in fact, were a disincentive, to produce food in developing countries. Developing countries complain that they have been forced to open up their markets to food imports under these rules, but rich countries were allowed to continue to subsidize their own farmers, making it hard for developing country farmers to compete. The AoA was widely recognized as being unfair to developing countries from the start, and the WTO itself even built in an agenda that required that the AoA be revisited in the subsequent round of trade negotiations. Throughout the course of the WTO's Doha Round (which started in 2001 and was set aside in 2015),[23] a serious overhaul of agricultural trade rules had been on the agenda. Yet, very little progress has been made, leaving the world stuck with uneven and—many developing countries would say—unfair rules governing agricultural trade.[24]

Also contributing to vulnerability in the world's poorest countries was a marked decline in agricultural investment from the World Bank and bilateral donors. During the period of low agricultural commodity prices from the 1980s to the early 2000s, there was a steady drop in agricultural investment in developing countries. The share of overseas development assistance targeted at agriculture in the late 1970s was twenty percent. This number fell to just four percent in 2005, and has only increased marginally since that time.[25] This drop in international assistance was accompanied by a decline in developing countries' own investment in the sector. Lower levels of investment mean that agriculture is largely under-resourced in the world's poorest countries. Under these conditions, developing countries became increasingly vulnerable to market disruptions as their dependence on imported food rose. Meanwhile, new foreign investment after 2008 has been largely from investors interested in acquiring large tracts of agricultural land. It is unlikely that this kind of investment will be useful for food security, as much of the acquired land is being cultivated with biofuel crops or with food crops intended for export to the investor country.[26]

The second major way in which the broader economic context affected food security during the crisis was through volatility of agricultural markets and food prices. When agricultural commodity prices rose sharply and became highly volatile after 2007, the situation became intolerable for the world's poorest countries that had come to rely on food imports because their own agricultural production capacity had been weakened. The food price spikes, as noted above, were the product of many factors in the global economy. Two factors in particular deserve mention because they originated in the rich industrialized countries, yet had enormous impact on the world's poorest countries. One is speculation by financial investors on commodity futures markets. Investors engage in speculation when they buy into agricultural commodity markets purely for the purpose of making a profit, and they have no real interest in using the products they are buying and selling. Relaxed financial market legislation over the past decade in the United States in particular enabled banks and other financial institutions to sell financial products to investors that are based on prices and movements in agricultural commodity markets. The demand for these products has soared since the early 2000s, thereby driving up demand and hence prices for food.[27]

Rising investment in biofuels has also been associated with more volatile food prices. Biofuels affect food prices by taking food crops such as maize out of food markets and putting them into fuel markets instead. In the United States, for example, the largest producer and exporter of maize, some forty percent of the maize crop went into biofuel production in 2012, which left less maize on global grain markets. This shortage drove up prices for the maize that was available as a food grain. A study of the US National Academy of Sciences estimated that some twenty to forty percent of food price increases during the 2007–2008 food crisis were attributable to the boom in biofuel production.[28] According to another study, increased diversion of maize into biofuel production has added an estimated $6.6 billion to the cost of food imports in developing countries over the 2006–2011 period.[29]

When the sudden volatility in world markets was overlaid with the vulnerability in the world's poorest countries, it had profound implications for food security. The changes in the global economic landscape affected both the access and stability pillars of food security in important ways. Yet the economic forces that contributed directly to vulnerability and volatility—trade policy, declining agricultural investment, financial speculation in agricultural commodities, and increased diversion of food crops into biofuel production—are ones that the UN food governance agencies are not authorized to address in any direct way. Although the global food institutions can recommend policy direction for their member governments on these important issues, it is ultimately governments that have the most control over these broader forces.

Under these circumstances, the views of some of the world's most powerful governments tend to prevail, and their interests tend towards keeping the status quo. Food governance institutions do not have the authority to hold these governments to account on economic issues. The institutions responsible for the global governance of food security are instead relegated to providing largely scientific solutions for food production and nutrition, food assistance, and policy advice. Moreover, although the various agencies within the food security governance framework address the four food security pillars in different ways, their coordination with each other when issues cut across those pillars is not particularly strong. Overall, this lack of authority on some issues, and lack of coordination on others, has resulted in weak responses to food crises.

What future for global food and hunger governance?

The 2007–2008 food crisis sparked further reforms in the global food security governance framework. An emergency meeting was held in mid-2008 and the UN established a High-level Task Force on the Food Security Crisis (HLTF) to assess the situation. The HLTF—comprised of representatives from over twenty UN agencies and funds, as well as from the World Bank, International Monetary Fund (IMF), and

WTO—produced the Comprehensive Framework for Action (CFA) document in 2008 that aimed to provide a single process for coordination of food crisis response across the UN system.[30] This document provides an analysis of the various dimensions of the food crisis and possible actions that could be taken. A World Summit on Food Security was held in Rome in late 2009 to assess the broader situation, at which the Rome Principles for Sustainable Global Food Security were adopted. These principles outline the guiding norms for addressing food insecurity, and emphasize the need for strategic coordination of action across multiple agencies and levels of governance as well as a comprehensive approach to food security.[31]

A key recommendation of the HLTF was to reform the UN Committee on World Food Security (CFS), one of the UN bodies set up after the 1970s food crisis, but which had largely failed to operate as an effective forum for global policy coordination. Negotiations on reform of the CFS took place over the course of 2009. The reformed CFS now includes not just governmental inputs into the policy process, but also civil society voices, and a new body, the High-level Panel of Experts (HLPE), was created to provide advice on different aspects of food policy to the CFS.[32] In this context, some of the expert reports have called for bold policy changes, such as new globally managed food reserves; stepped-up policy reforms such as an overhaul to biofuel regulations in producing countries; more stringent regulation on financial speculation in commodities; and an overhaul of agricultural trade rules. The CFS has adopted a global strategic framework for food security and nutrition, which it regularly updates. With these various reforms in place, the CFS now functions much more effectively as a forum for debating these issues, but the body itself still lacks teeth to implement policy changes.[33] Part of the reason for the continued weakness of the CFS as a governing body is that it only provides advice, and many of its member governments have vested interests in certain policy frameworks and approaches.

Even as the CFS has taken on a greater role, governments have worked to tackle certain food security-related issues through other intergovernmental forums as well as through public–private partnerships that do not have the same degree of participation and transparency as the CFS.[34] In 2010, for example, the G-20—originally established to address financial and economic issues—began to develop a food security agenda. With its economic focus and membership of the world's most powerful governments, the G-20 could have made progress by pressing its members—which are home to most of the commodity markets where speculation takes place, the largest producers of biofuels, and the source of most international agricultural investment—on key issues related to food security that stem from the global economic forces. But the G-20 has thus far failed to recommend regulatory action on these issues.[35]

However, in 2012 the G-8 countries launched the New Alliance for Food Security and Nutrition (NAFSN), a public–private partnership focused on addressing rural poverty in sub-Saharan Africa. This initiative aims to leverage donor funding pledges with private sector investment and policy reform from African governments. Civil society organizations, however, have critiqued the NAFSN for what they see as demands for policy change that primarily benefit transnational corporations, rather than small-scale farmers.[36] These types of initiative will likely continue to proliferate outside of the direct oversight of the CFS. But at the same time, the legitimacy of the CFS as a key body on food security issues has grown remarkably since its reform in 2009.

Conclusion

This chapter shows that the key global institutions that address hunger and food insecurity have evolved over time with our changing understanding of what constitutes food security. As our conceptualization of food security has expanded beyond a focus on food availability to also incorporate access, stability, and utilization, the food security governance framework at the international level has responded by adding new institutions and activities aimed at addressing all four of these pillars of food security, albeit in different ways. While the current global food governance framework does cover the main components of current thinking on what contributes to enhanced food security, in practice this framework has been fragmented, leading at times to poor coordination on key issues that cut across the pillars or fall between them.

The fragmentation of the institutional landscape for global food security was highlighted in the aftermath of the 2007–2008 food crisis and ongoing episodes of food price volatility. This episode illustrated the tight linkages between broader forces in the global economy and food security. Economic problems such as unbalanced trade rules and declining agricultural investment in developing countries have contributed to vulnerability to food crises in the world's poorest countries. On top of this vulnerability has been ongoing volatility, spurred in large part by speculative financial investments in agricultural commodities and the biofuel boom.

Addressing these contributors to food insecurity requires a broad and comprehensive approach not only across the different food agencies that tackle specific pillars of food security, but also between the food agencies and the broader economic governance frameworks that address trade, investment, and finance. The need for a more comprehensive and coordinated approach to food security at the global level is well understood among analysts and policymakers. Bringing about that change, however, has been difficult in practice because of the lack of authority over economic issues held by the CFS.

Recent reforms to the broader food security framework, including the creation of the HLTF and the reforms to the CFS, show movement in the right direction. However, much work remains to make the global food security framework more comprehensive and effective. Achieving such a goal would require deeper structural reforms, particularly those that tackle the broader economic forces affecting food security. For such reforms to happen, a broader consensus across all countries on how to best restructure the global economy in ways that support, rather than hinder, food security will need to be forged.

Additional reading

Jennifer Clapp, *Food*, 2nd ed. (Cambridge: Polity Press, 2016).
Matias Margulis, "The Regime Complex for Food Security: Implications for the Global Hunger Challenge," *Global Governance* 19, no. 1 (2013): 53–67.
Bryan McDonald, *Food Security* (Cambridge: Polity Press, 2010).
Nora McKeon, *Food Security Governance* (London: Routledge, 2015).
John Shaw, *World Food Security: A History Since 1945* (London: Palgrave Macmillan, 2007).

Notes

1 FAO, *The State of Food Insecurity in the World 2015* (Rome: FAO, 2012).
2 Frances Moore Lappé, et al., "How We Count Hunger Matters," *Ethics & International Affairs* 27, no. 03 (2013): 251–259.
3 See FAO, *Trade Reforms and Food Security* (Rome: FAO, 2003), www.fao.org/docrep/005/y4671e/y4671e00.htm#Contents; FAO, *State of Food Insecurity in the World 2001* (Rome: FAO, 2001), www.fao.org/docrep/003/y1500e/y1500e00.htm.
4 Christopher Barrett, "Measuring Food Insecurity," *Science* 327 (2010), 825–828.
5 FAO, *An Introduction to the Basic Concepts of Food Security*, www.fao.org/docrep/013/al936e/al936e00.pdf.
6 John Shaw, *World Food Security: A History Since 1945* (London: Palgrave Macmillan, 2007).
7 CGIAR, "Our Research Centers," www.cgiar.org/about-us/research-centers.
8 Jennifer Clapp, *Hunger in the Balance: The New Politics of International Food Aid* (Ithaca, NY: Cornell University Press, 2012).
9 Edward Clay, *Trade Policy Options for Enhancing Food Aid Effectiveness* (Geneva: ICTSD and FAO, 2012).
10 Emma Rothschild, "Food Politics," *Foreign Affairs* 54, no. 2 (1976): 285–307.
11 Jennifer Clapp, *Food*, 2nd ed. (Cambridge: Polity Press, 2016).
12 IFAD website, www.ifad.org.
13 John Shaw, *The UN World Food Programme and the Development of Food Aid* (London: Palgrave, 2001).
14 Committee on World Food Security, *Coming to Terms with Terminology* (CFS 2012/39/4), 2012.
15 Richard Longhurst, "Global Leadership for Nutrition: The UN's Standing Committee on Nutrition (SCN) and its Contributions," Institute of Development Studies Discussion Paper no. 390 (2010), www.ids.ac.uk/files/dmfile/dp390.pdf.
16 Shaw, *The UN World Food Programme*, 81–82.
17 Amartya Sen, *Poverty and Famines* (Oxford: Oxford University Press, 1981). See also Jean Drèze and Amartya Sen, *Hunger and Public Action* (Oxford: Oxford University Press, 1989).
18 Christopher Kaan and Andrea Liese, "Public Private Partnerships in Global Food Governance: Business Engagement and Legitimacy in the Global Fight against Hunger and Malnutrition," *Agriculture and Human Values* 28, no. 3 (2011): 385–399.
19 On the Ethiopian famine of the 1980s, see Peter Gill, *Famine and Foreigners: Ethiopia since Live Aid* (Oxford: Oxford University Press, 2010).
20 See Jennifer Clapp, "WTO Agriculture Negotiations: Implications for the Global South," *Third World Quarterly* 27, no. 4 (2006): 563–577.
21 Olivier De Schutter, "Reshaping Global Governance: The Case of the Right to Rood," *Global Policy* 3, no. 4 (2012): 480–483.
22 Matias Margulis, "The Regime Complex for Food Security: Implications for the Global Hunger Challenge," *Global Governance* 19, no. 1 (2013): 53–67.
23 Rorden Wilkinson, Erin Hannah, and James Scott, "The WTO in Nairobi: The Demise of the Doha Development Agenda and the Future of the Multilateral Trading System," *Global Policy* 7, no. 2 (2016): 247–255.
24 Olivier De Schutter, "The World Trade Organization and the Post-Global Food Crisis Agenda: Putting Food Security First in the International Trade System," Briefing Note of the UN Special Rapporteur on the Right to Food (2011); Jennifer Clapp, "Food Security and the WTO," in *Trade, Poverty, Development: Getting Beyond the Doha Deadlock*, eds. Rorden Wilkinson and James Scott (London: Routledge, 2012), 57–71.
25 Jennifer Clapp, *Food*, 2nd ed. (Cambridge: Polity Press, 2016).

26 Olivier De Schutter, "How Not to Think of Land-grabbing: Three Critiques of Large-scale Investments in Farmland," *Journal of Peasant Studies* 38, no. 2 (2011): 249–279.

27 Jayati Ghosh, "The Unnatural Coupling: Food and Global Finance," *Journal of Agrarian Change* 10, no. 1 (2010): 72–86; Jennifer Clapp and Eric Helleiner, "Troubled Futures? The Global Food Crisis and the Politics of Agricultural Derivatives Regulation," *Review of International Political Economy* 19, no. 2 (2012): 181–207.

28 Cited in Tim Wise, *The Cost to Developing Countries of US Corn Ethanol Expansion*, Global Development and Environment Institute Working Paper 12–2 (2012), 2.

29 Ibid.

30 UNHLTF, *Elements of a Comprehensive Framework for Action* (New York: United Nations, 2008).

31 World Summit on Food Security, *Declaration of the World Summit on Food Security* (Rome: FAO, 2009), www.fao.org/fileadmin/templates/wsfs/Summit/Docs/Final_Declaration/WSFS09_Declaration.pdf.

32 Nora McKeon, *Global Governance for World Food Security* (Berlin: Heinrich-Boll-Stiftung, 2011); Timothy A. Wise and Sophia Murphy, *Resolving the Food Crisis: Assessing Global Policy Reforms Since 2007* (Minneapolis, MN: Institute for Agriculture and Trade Policy (ITAP) and Global Development and Environment Institute (GDAE), 2012), www.ase.tufts.edu/gdae/Pubs/rp/ResolvingFoodCrisis.pdf.

33 Nora McKeon, *Food Security Governance* (London: Routledge, 2015).

34 David Barling and Jessica Duncan, "The Dynamics of the Contemporary Governance of the World's Food Supply and the Challenges of Policy Redirection," *Food Security* 7, no. 2 (2015): 415–424.

35 Jennifer Clapp and Sophia Murphy, "The G20 and Food Security: A Mismatch in Global Governance?" *Global Policy* 4, no. 2 (2013): 129–138.

36 On the G-8 Alliance for Food Security and Nutrition, see New Alliance for Food Security and Nutrition website: https://new-alliance.org/about; on critiques, see Mark Curtis, *New Alliance, New Risk of Land Grabs: New Evidence from Malawi, Nigeria, Senegal and Tanzania* (Johannesburg: Action Aid International, 2015); Nora McKeon, *The New Alliance for Food Security and Nutrition: A Coup for Corporate Capital?* (Amsterdam: Terra Nuova and Transnational Institute, 2014).

Global health governance

Sophie Harman

In 2014 images of clinicians, cleaners, and carers in personal protective equipment (PPE) scared those they came into contact with and the world who feared the spread of Ebola, a virus first found in 1976 that had begun to devastate three West African countries. It is this image that many now think of when they think about global health governance—something to fear, be secured, and protected against. The other image is that of a new mother with a child born with microcephaly in poor urban dwellings in Brazil. This image shows how health and access to health can be shaped by structural inequalities, and the individual and global vulnerability to new health threats. Together the two images reveal the underpinning concerns of global health governance: Health security, inequality, and inequity.

From the first International Sanitary Conference in 1851 to the formation of partnerships such as the GAVI Alliance (previously the Global Alliance for Vaccines and Immunization), global health has set the model for many forms of global governance. Health—commonly defined as the state of physical and mental wellbeing—goes to the heart of questions of justice, equality, and liberty. The health of a population, a community, or an individual is a key indicator of wellbeing, wealth, and security. How health is provided or understood, as the responsibility either of the individual to take care of their minds and bodies or of the state to manage the structural determinants of ill health and redistribute wealth in a way to allow individuals to do so, has been at the crux of contemporary political debate on welfare provision and personal liberty for centuries. Health concerns have the ability to prevent the trade of goods, shut down airports, exacerbate poverty, engender fear, and destabilize armies. Yet health is often seen as a soft topic in international politics and a side issue to security and economic concerns.

The purpose of this chapter is twofold: First, to provide an introduction to what global health governance is, the mechanisms of governing, and the core debates and issues therein; and, second, in so doing, to situate health at the center of questions of global governance and international organization. The chapter begins by providing a brief sketch of the emergence of global health governance from the golden age of the 1800s to the contemporary era of new pandemics, health security, and the Sustainable Development Goals (SDGs). It then explores current debates in global health governance on pandemic preparedness and emergency response in the wake of Ebola and Zika and reform of the World Health Organization (WHO). Thereafter, the chapter reviews some of the emerging issues in global health governance with regard to leadership and the threat of antimicrobial resistance (AMR). The chapter concludes with some comments about the future of global health governance.

The development of global health governance

Global health governance has undergone several phases of development and change. The first phase began in the "golden age" of biomedical discovery of the 1800s that not only set the framework for scientific breakthrough but laid the foundations for the institutions of global health. This phase ended with the consolidation of institutions such as the League of Nations Health Organization and Office International d'Hygiène Publique (OIHP) into the WHO in the aftermath of World War II. The second phase, understood broadly as lying between the 1970s and 1990s, saw the eradication of one disease (smallpox) and the devastating impact of another (HIV/AIDS), and the emergence of a neoliberal paradigm in how global health policy was understood and practiced. The third phase laid the foundation for much of contemporary global health governance: New partnerships and philanthropy, goalsetting that focused on specific diseases and issues, and increased interest in the relationship between health, security, and pandemic preparedness.

Notable about these periods of change is the shift from international health to global health governance. International health governance often refers to state-based interaction and intergovernmental institutions that were established in two phases. Accelerated economic, social, and political globalization from the second phase onwards increased the globality and supranational nature of decision making in new and old institutions, and opened up space for the presence of private actors and partnerships in global health. Globality in decision making and the plethora of state and non-state-based actors thus generated a shift from international to *global* health governance in the third phase. These periods are discussed below.

Phase 1: 1850s–1950s, the institutional foundations of global health

The "golden age" of global health primarily refers to the mid-1800s and the discovery of x-rays, the stethoscope, and, crucially, the finding that disease is caused by microbes (germs). Scientists such as Robert Koch and Louis Pasteur and their scientific breakthrough of germ theory made them celebrities. However, this age was also notable because of the institutions formed to prevent the global spread of germs across trade routes and migratory patterns, and to promote hygiene across populations. Efforts to standardize and regulate global systems to monitor and control the spread of germs came into being through the creation of the International Sanitary Regulations in 1903 and the OIHP in 1907.

During the same period, private philanthropy took great interest in funding medical research and treatment; for example, the American oil philanthropist John D. Rockefeller established the Rockefeller Institute for Medical Research in 1901 and the Rockefeller University Hospital in 1910. The International Sanitary Regulations and the OIHP provided the basis for the League of Nations Health Organization of 1920, designed to address postwar health concerns such as influenza and typhus, and funded by a combination of state commitments and private philanthropy. That organization was to reflect the need to establish peace through healthy populations and to provide an arena in which to coordinate and monitor new threats or issues pertinent to the health of the world's population. As with the League of Nations, the progress of the Health Organization in its initial stages was limited by the onset of World War II; however, the need to link health and peace was an idea that remained central to questions of global coordination.[1]

Three clear implications for global health resulted from the institution building beginning at the end of World War II. The first was that health was going to be addressed by a broad array of UN organizations, including the United Nations International Children's Emergency Fund (UNICEF, for child famine and disease), United Nations Population Fund (UNFPA, for reproductive health), and the United Nations Development Programme (UNDP, for the right to health, for tuberculosis, and HIV/AIDS). The second was that health was to be intrinsically linked to development, economic reform, and postwar infrastructure building and thus covered by the mandate of financial institutions such as the World Bank. Third, a standalone institution was required to prevent the spread of disease and promote better health around the world; and in 1948 the WHO was established as *the* global health institution.

The WHO built on and drew together existing International Sanitary Regulations, the OIHP, and the remnants of the League of Nations Health Organization to become the lead UN and international body to promote health for all; monitor threats to the health of the world's population; and offer advice, guidelines, and recommendations to states on health matters. Underpinning the formation of the WHO were two prominent ideas: That health is a global public good—it is non-rivalrous in consumption and non-excludable, or in other words everyone should have access to it and one person's consumption should not prevent another's; and that health is a human right.[2]

The WHO has a decentralized structure, operating from its Geneva headquarters and six regional offices. The annual World Health Assembly (WHA), made up of states, sets the agenda and approves the budget of the organization; and the secretariat, headed by the director-general, is responsible for the day-to-day operations of the institution in collaboration with the regional and country offices. The WHO is responsible for leadership, coordination and partnership, research agendas and knowledge dissemination, standard setting, institutional support, and monitoring and evaluation of its own and state practice. The WHO has established two key sources of international law: The International Health Regulations (based on the International Sanitary Regulations) that bind all states to monitor and report disease outbreaks with mixed results; and the Framework Convention on Tobacco Control (FCTC) that has seen a revolution in tobacco labeling, advertising, and public smoking.[3] Member states have obligatory assessed contributions, but they only make up a small and decreasing proportion of the WHO's budget (now about twenty percent); but the remaining funds come from voluntary contributions for specific projects.[4] On the one hand, this funding formula has made the WHO more entrepreneurial and larger. On the other hand, as the specialized agency in the UN system that is most heavily reliant on noncore funding, the WHO has experienced periodic funding shortfalls and a loss of autonomy, as discussed below.

Phase 2: 1970s–1990s, disease eradication and emergence and the rise of neoliberalism

The late 1970s saw two highlights for the WHO and global public health. The first was the eradication of smallpox by 1980: The only disease ever to be eradicated. The second was the adoption of the Alma Ata Declaration of 1978 that reaffirmed the WHO's and its member states' commitments to health for all. However, this commitment to health for all and the notion of health as a public good was to be challenged by the increasingly market-based approaches to health policy, commonly labeled neoliberalism, adopted in the 1980s.

Definitions of neoliberalism are well rehearsed, but for the purposes of health they refer to opening up health delivery to competition in provision, the privatization of aspects of public health, reduced government provision and regulation, and the adoption of a market for deciding who provides a range of healthcare needs, who pays for them, and how. The stated, but contested, benefits of neoliberal policies are increased expertise, efficiency, and plurality of choice in the health system. Neoliberal reform of health systems was a key component of a number of structural adjustment loans of the IMF and World Bank in the 1980s and early 1990s. Reforms of this type were also evident in the increased privatization of the National Health Service (NHS) in the United Kingdom and remain at the heart of debates over socialized and publicly provided healthcare in European and North American politics.

The impact of neoliberal reforms in developing countries was particularly acute: Cuts to public financing of health systems were often not met by an influx of private investment or fully adopted. The result was health systems—hospitals, health professionals, and drug provision—that were underfunded. There was little money for public health campaigns, and the cost of healthcare was put onto the individual through payment of user fees.[5] At the same time these policies were being pursued, an unknown disease was killing gay men, intravenous drug users, and hemophiliacs in the United States and Europe.[6] Formally identified as acquired immune deficiency syndrome (AIDS), caused by the human immunodeficiency virus (HIV), in 1981, this disease was to go on to kill 30 million people, infect 60 million, and orphan 16 million children by 2011.[7]

The simultaneous rise of HIV/AIDS and neoliberal approaches to governing global health is particularly pertinent for understanding global health. Both confronted what constituted public health privately provided, both happened at a time of rapid economic change, and both placed strains on existing health systems, particularly in developing countries. It is important to note that neoliberal approaches to health challenged the provision of treatment and funding for a range of other health issues, such as tuberculosis, malaria, maternal health, and neglected tropical disease. However, what is specific—or, for some, "exceptional"—about HIV/AIDS is the stigma surrounding it, the silence and ignorance of political leaders, misinformation about how self-protection can be enacted, the gendered dimensions of how people are infected and affected, and the link between the disease and poverty and inequality.[8]

What is notable about HIV/AIDS is the widespread transnational activism it generated from highly organized gay community groups caring for and educating people about the spread of HIV, to young children such as Nkosi Johnson in South Africa advocating for the government of Thabo Mbeki to provide treatment for people living with HIV/AIDS. Such activism, institutional leadership, and guilt of state denial saw the creation of the first standalone UN agency for a specific health issue—the Joint United Nations Programme on HIV/AIDS (UNAIDS)—and the rise of partnerships and multiple actors wanting to address the disease.

Phase 3: 2000–2015: Millennium Development Goals (MDGs), partnerships, pandemic preparedness, and security

The new century was to be the era of unprecedented global health financing and partnership building. The millennium began with the launching of the eight Millennium Development Goals (MDGs), three of which were directly related to health: Goal 4—Child Health; Goal 5—Maternal Health; and Goal 6—Combat HIV/AIDS and other diseases. The purpose of the goals was to provide measurable markers for progress in combating poverty and generating global political will and support for key areas. The sixth goal in particular generated an upsurge in public–private partnerships with the aim of developing new drugs and vaccines, low-cost treatment, and access to treatment and new models of prevention. Partnerships such as the International AIDS Vaccine Initiative (IAVI) were reinvigorated, and the GAVI Alliance and UNITAID were created to, respectively, provide investment in vaccine research and reduce the market price of treatment for AIDS, tuberculosis, and malaria. Celebrities acted as advocates for health concerns and endorsed product development partnerships to benefit health campaigns. The G-8 and the G-20 both prioritized health in communiqués and summits.[9] The culmination of the trend towards partnership, celebrity endorsement, G-8 interest, and the prioritization of goal-oriented strategy was the creation of the Global Fund to Fight AIDS, Tuberculosis and Malaria (hereafter the Global Fund) in 2002.

The Global Fund is one of the first institutions of global health governance to have a board made up of both states and non-state representatives from civil society, campaign groups, and the private sector with equal voting power. The purpose of the Global Fund is to provide funding for countries to address AIDS, tuberculosis, and malaria. It is based in Geneva and has no in-country presence, preferring to work with partners inside countries. Since its creation it has positioned itself as one of the key providers of antiretroviral treatment for people living with HIV (alongside the US government's President's Emergency Plan for AIDS Relief—PEPFAR—project), and is seen as a model of partnership and funding that could be replicated in other areas of governance such as the environment.

The biggest game-changer during this phase of governance was the creation of the Bill and Melinda Gates Foundation and its Global Health Program in 2000. The Gates Foundation is the biggest source of private wealth for global health, with an annual budget exceeding that of the WHO.[10] The Gates Foundation is financed by the private wealth of the Gates family and donations from investors such as Warren Buffet. A key focus is on innovation, principally scientific and technology-based solutions to some of the world's biggest health problems. Hence, it has invested substantially in polio eradication and the development of vaccines to combat HIV, guinea worm, and malaria. The foundation gives money to new partnerships such as the Global Fund and GAVI, and also old institutions such as the World Bank. Representatives of the foundation attend the WHA and both Bill and Melinda Gates have a large media presence in shaping debates on global health through social media, TED talks, and newspaper opinion pieces.

The governance of global health in 2000 also became defined by a security agenda in which health issues were framed as security threats or risks to the global population. A particular area in which this played out was in response to the two pandemic flu outbreaks: H1N1 "swine flu" in 2009 and H5N1 "bird flu" in 2003.[11] For many this was particularly the case with H5N1, which generated the stockpiling of the drug Tamiflu, raised concerns (but not restrictions) about the relationship between travel and contraction and the spread of the disease, and stoked fear among the global population. Fear in particular served as a tool to generate public interest toward an array of health concerns as well as public finance and political attention towards different health issues.

A common explanation as to why diseases such as HIV/AIDS have attracted so much attention is that the disease was framed as an issue of international security in the 2000 UN Security Council resolution 1308.[12] HIV/AIDS became seen as exceptional and warranting extraordinary measures by playing on people's fears and highlighting the threat of the disease on armies and thus state security;[13] the health of people living in developing countries and thus development outcomes; the threat of risk perception and individual security; and the movement of people and international security. For some, the framing of HIV/AIDS as a security threat was a deliberate ploy to get money and attention to address the disease and less about the promotion of public health.[14] And, to an extent, this has worked.

However, "securitizing" a disease, those suffering from it, and the people, such as orphans or vulnerable children, affected by it can also be seen as problematic when thinking about how to secure these people, and the manipulation and control of people's bodies this may entail.[15] Seeing people living with HIV/AIDS as a threat to a population's security may lead to quarantine, exclusion, and, most commonly, embed problems of stigma that are so endemic to the spread of the disease.[16] Moreover, seeing individuals as security threats can directly impact on the rights of those individuals as citizens of particular states and wider claims to human rights.

The early 2000s was thus an era marked by rapid institutionalization, the targeted funding of particular health concerns, and the increased use of the language of security. During this time less attention was paid to strengthening the health systems in low- and middle-income countries that underpin the successful delivery of health. Instead of directly financing health systems, the goal-oriented and security agenda skewed global health to establish or replicate new structures of health financing at the global and national levels. The result of these "vertical" interventions that tackle specific diseases is, on the one hand, positive, because it heightens global awareness of the issue, galvanizes political support and generates money to support endeavors to address it, and shows what coordinated mass action can do to address health concerns. For many high-profile opinion formers in global health, such as the medical journal *The Lancet*,[17] vertical spending on specific disease has somewhat distorted the global health agenda and led to neglect in health systems. On the other hand, the perverse result is that the targets of vertical interventions cannot be met as they rest on the horizontal aspects of health systems such as well-staffed and equipped hospitals. The nub of this argument is that horizontal interventions are costly, long term, and often beyond the remit of health specialists. Vertical interventions, by contrast, show results and are an easier sell in getting governments and their tax-paying citizens behind an issue.

The vertical and horizontal debate has been addressed to an extent for the Sustainable Development Goals. Goal 3 of the SDGs is part an extenuation of Goals 4 (child mortality), 5 (maternal mortality) and 6 (HIV/AIDS and other diseases) of the MDGs and part commitment to health systems with a focus on universal health coverage. However SDG 3 is in many respects a shopping list of global health's needs, mixing the MDG agenda, universal health coverage, and global health laws around pandemic preparedness and tobacco control with new pertinent issues such as road traffic accidents and drug abuse included. The risk is therefore that a hierarchy of preferences will be established within the goal and universal health coverage and health systems potentially sidelined as a consequence.

The new structures of governance that emerged in 2000 have not addressed *global* health but specific diseases in developing countries. These two factors—neglect of health systems and skewed financing agendas—were to have disastrous consequences at the end of 2014 with the world facing the biggest outbreak of Ebola in West Africa.

Current debates

The 2014/15 Ebola outbreak and response is a microcosm of all that is flawed with the system of global health governance that developed at the start of the millennium. Cases of Ebola are not uncommon and are often contained by effective health systems and communications between domestic and global health institutions. The most recent outbreak became a public health emergency of international concern leading to the death of 11,300 people because of a "perfect storm" of weak health systems and corruption at the domestic level and a failure to act in a timely manner at the global level.[18] As such, Ebola highlighted two key flaws in global health governance. The first is the lack of funding and investment in health systems in low- and middle-income countries, as discussed above. The second flaw is the system of emergency preparedness within the WHO that depends on states having the capacity and will to report outbreaks, *and* for the institution to act in a timely manner to call an outbreak a public health emergency of international concern (PHEIC), thereby raising the issue up the political agenda and releasing funds to address it. For some, the WHO got this right by following the epidemiology of Ebola before declaring a PHEIC, for others the WHO acted too late and then provided too little while people died.[19]

In addition to the causal explanations for the severity of the Ebola outbreak, the global response to the outbreak raises key questions for debate in global health governance. The role of the militaries of Sierra Leone, the United Kingdom, United States, France, and Cuban medical brigades and the security forces in Liberia in responding to Ebola raise questions as to their future role in global health governance. The role of militaries in response to medical humanitarian crises is nothing new and militaries have significant and much needed capabilities in emergency response. However, for some, the militarization of global health is problematic because of how they work, the potential risks of global health actors being associated with militaries in different contexts, and the history of conflict in particular states. In many respects, militaries were actors of last resort in the Ebola response and their role was symptomatic of the inability of global and national health actors to respond in a timely and effective manner.[20]

The final issue that the Ebola response demonstrated, and the outbreak of Zika in the Americas compounded, was the role of *women* in global health. The Ebola response failed to initially disaggregate data on number of male and female incidence and deaths and did not even consider questions of gender in the emergency response. For some, this is because, in crisis situations, gender is irrelevant. Gender in global health is often reduced to just women's sexual and reproductive health needs and therefore not seen as an issue in pandemic emergency response. However, this is a significant problem given the gendered nature of formal and informal care roles, particularly in states with weak health systems, and the way in which outbreaks and responses to outbreaks can impact on men and women differently because of gender.[21]

Zika starkly reveals the problem of gender in global health. Declared a PHEIC in February 2016, the response to Zika differed to Ebola in that women were the primary focus of the response because of the relationship between Zika as the cause of microcephaly. The response focused on women's health needs in relation to sexual and reproductive health and public health solutions to such needs. The main message of the response was that women avoid pregnancy. However, such advice was given in states where contraception is not freely available to the majority of poor women affected by Zika, abortions are legally restricted resulting in a high number of unsafe terminations, and the socioeconomic position of women frame their ability to negotiate contraception use with partners.[22] The response to Zika was therefore to focus on women's public health needs with little engagement with how gender and inequality frames such needs. With both Ebola and Zika, gender was a challenge that framed both cause and response but remains unaddressed by global health governance.

Both the causes and the response to Ebola have led to new questions being asked as to the actors, systems, and priorities of global health governance particularly with reference to the future of global health financing, the role of the military, the relationship between medical humanitarianism and global health, and future emergency response planning. These questions have highlighted the tensions and flaws inherent to global health governance but have also presented an opportunity for renewal of institutions such as the WHO.

In 2011 the then WHO Director-General Margaret Chan initiated a reform agenda for the institution with three pillars: Managerial reform, governance reform, and program reform.[23] Arguments for WHO reform have both predated 2011 and emerged during the reform process. First, the organization lacks the resources to fully fulfill its core functions, and the way it is funded—where states contribute a core amount and then offer additional funds for specific health topics—limits its ability to plan operations, establish priorities independently, and undertake key initiatives. Second, the WHO is too decentralized to take a clear leadership role for the globality of health. Its decentralized structures make the WHO flexible in responding to local concerns but also hard to govern in a coherent manner, confusing budgeting and planning further. Third, the WHO is active in a crowded terrain comprising multiple different actors and partnerships, all of which have to compete for financial contributions. For some the WHO has been at the forefront of partnerships, whereas for others it has failed to adapt to the changes in who governs global health and the nature of how global health policy is financed. In addition, the sources of funding, and not the WHO, are in charge of setting the agenda and priorities for eighty percent of the organization's expenditures, which means flexibility but also often a lack of autonomy. Fourth, the WHO is only one site of policy knowledge, advice, and expertise. While the WHO maintains its advisory role to states on virus outbreaks, pre-qualifications of drugs, and multiple aspects of health policy, its legitimacy for doing so is challenged by alternative sources of knowledge funded by partnerships and private philanthropy. Finally, the Ebola outbreak in 2014/15 was for some a critical point in the WHO's history. Critics of the institution's response suggested the WHO was too slow to declare Ebola a public health emergency of international concern (PHEIC) or provide the type of emergency assistance the affected states required.[24] This led to frustration among the global health community over the WHO's perceived inability to provide global health security and thus heightened the need for reform.

However, despite this criticism there is also an argument to suggest the outbreak *strengthened* the institution as there was a recognition that the problem was not with the institution itself but the lack of core financing and member state support to equip the WHO to do its job properly. The consequence of which was an increase in the WHO's total budget following the Ebola outbreak and a commitment to house the Health Emergencies Programme[25] within the institution rather than creating a separate entity. The arguments for reform may be many, but for many of the central institutions of global governance, a credible alternative to the WHO does not exist; and little consensus exists on how it ought to be reformed.

Emerging issues

While current debates over pandemic preparedness and the future of the WHO continue to shape much of the future of global health governance, the success of global health will depend on the ability to govern emerging issues such as antimicrobial resistance (AMR) and new expressions of the old problem of financing health. This will require commitment, cooperation, and strong leadership in global health governance.

AMR is an emerging issue that will shape the future of global health govern-ance and the relationship between global health and international security. AMR occurs when microorganisms change or adapt to antimicrobial drugs, meaning a range of antimicrobial drugs used in treatments for a variety of health inter-ventions such as surgery, cancer chemotherapy, and diabetes will no longer be effective. This has serious repercussions for everyday forms of health preven-tion and treatment delivery. Everyday procedures such as organ transplants, hip replacements, and childbirth through caesarean section will become high risk.[26] The issue is that microorganisms adapt and change to drugs has been known for a long time, however, given the magnitude of the problem, little has been done about it. A full response to AMR requires collaboration between private phar-maceutical companies who need incentives to invest in new drugs; public sector actors to enact political will, develop public education on sanitation and hygiene, incentivize private innovation, and regulate the outcomes; coordination between different sectors of government (public health, agriculture, education, business and innovation, and foreign relations) and with different states; and multisectoral forums for effective global cooperation and regulation of who provides, accesses, and pays for new forms of health treatment and prevention. In 2015, the WHO published the Global Action Plan on AMR alongside a number of high-profile national reports and initiatives throughout the world culminating in the 2016 UN General Assembly high-level meeting on AMR.[27] This reflects the growing attention towards the issue. However, for a full response to AMR to be effective, global health governance has to draw on its multisectoral strengths while working through its limitations on incentivizing everyday public and private action and lack of long-term planning for future health problems.

The ability of global health to manage emerging issues such as AMR depends on the future financing and political will towards global health. These factors are common concerns in contemporary global governance as international organiza-tions struggle to contend with anti-globalist sentiments among influential member states, budgetary constraints, and a growing number of emergencies as well as protracted humanitarian crises. Financing towards global health is in better shape than other areas of global governance, with increased financing towards the WHO in response to Ebola and the need for greater emergency preparedness, the ongoing financial commitment of the Bill and Melinda Gates Foundation, and the emergence of new philanthropic actors such as the Chan Zuckerberg Initiative. In this sense, the health-humanitarian crisis of Ebola led to increased resources rather than a strain on resources as we see in other areas of global governance.

However, financing of global health governance is increasingly dependent on three factors. First, the sustained investment of such large-scale philanthrop-ists and their ability to convene other donors around particular diseases. The convening power is becoming more evident, for example Bill Gates has been instrumental in maintaining US government financing for global health under the Donald Trump administration. Second, and related, is the future commitment of member states to both new and old institutions of global health governance and whether such distinctions will split, dilute, or duplicate financial allocations. Finally, the future finance of global health will depend on the ability of governance to deliver on the SDGs and provide an adequate response to any emergent health crisis or pandemic threat. The solution to the perceived failings in the Ebola response was greater investment in emergency preparedness, however should global health governance be seen to fail in response to a future pandemic such finances will come under added scrutiny and justification. This particular issue is especially pertinent for the WHO.

The future of global health governance will have to grapple with issues of leadership. Effective leadership is often stated as a panacea to address the current and emerging issues of global health governance. This is because it is often seen as either lacking in global health governance or is spread among a range of actors from nongovernmental actors such as Joanna Liu of Médecins sans Frontières (MSF) to prominent philanthropists such as Bill Gates. The latter's role in global health has expanded from donor and research advocate to spokesperson for a range of global health and international development issues. This role is in part the clearest sign of prominent leadership in global health as Gates is unencumbered by the sovereignty constraints of institutions and can command the world's attention. However, such a prominent role also raises questions of legitimacy in global governance when an unelected leader is able to express such power. Whatever the outcome of the reform process of the WHO, the institution and its director-general will have to think of new ways of expressing leadership beyond the institutional mandate it has from the United Nations and member states. The problem of leadership is not necessarily to overcome the challenges outlined in this chapter, but rather how to provide strategic direction and guidance that generate support from global health policymakers, practitioners, and advocates, and to do so in a way that is bold, transparent, and accountable. In the current arrangements of global health governance, such leadership is lacking and is badly needed.

Conclusion

Global health is often seen as an effective model of global governance. It is relatively well resourced. It has shown progress in key areas such as infant mortality and HIV/AIDS treatment. And there is a general collective political will among member states of the WHO to provide global health security.

Ebola and Zika have highlighted the flaws and tensions in the current structures of global health governance. However, despite sustained criticisms of institutions such as the WHO, those structures have reinvigorated rather than undermined the WHO and global commitments to health. Questions remain as to the role of the military, financing for WHO, the growing leadership of the Bill and Melinda Gates Foundation, and how global health can remain relevant in the mixed agendas of the SDGs and anti-globalist populism. How global health governance responds to these questions—known threats such as AMR, and the known unknowns of a future pandemic outbreak—will test the sustainability of political will and whether lessons have been learned since Ebola. Whatever the outcome, global health governance requires effective political leadership, strategy, and convening power to address these and other challenges.

Additional reading

Sara E. Davies, *Global Politics of Health* (Cambridge: Polity Press, 2010).

Sara E. Davies, Adam Kamradt-Scott, and Simon Rushton, *Disease Diplomacy: International Norms and Global Health Security* (Baltimore, MD: Johns Hopkins University Press, 2015).

Sophie Harman, *Global Health Governance* (London: Routledge, 2012).

Linsey McGoey, *No Such Thing as a Free Gift: The Gates Foundation and the Price of Philanthropy* (London: Verso, 2015).

Colin McInnes and Kelley Lee, *Global Health and International Relations* (Cambridge: Polity Press, 2012).

Jennifer Prah Ruger, *Global Health Justice and Governance* (Oxford: Oxford University Press, 2017).

Notes

1 Sophie Harman, *Global Health Governance* (London: Routledge, 2012).

2 David Woodward and Richard Smith, "Global Public Goods and Health: Concepts and Issues," in *Global Public Goods for Health: Health Economics and Public Health Perspectives*, eds. Richard Smith, Robert Beaglehole, David Woodward, and Nick Drager (Oxford: Oxford University Press, 2003), 3–29; United Nations General Assembly, *The Right to Health: Note by the Secretary General*, UN document A/63/263, 2008.

3 WHO, *International Health Regulations 2005*, www.who.int/ihr/en; WHO, *Framework Convention on Tobacco Control* (2012), www.who.int/fctc/en/.

4 WHO, *Investing in the World's Health Organization: Taking Steps towards a Fully-funded Programme Budget 2016–17* (2015), www.who.int/about/finances-accountability/funding/financing-dialogue/Programme-Budget-2016-2017-Prospectus.pdf?ua=1.

5 Harman, *Global Health Governance*.

6 For detailed accounts of the emergence of HIV/AIDS in Europe and the United States, see Randy Shilts, *And the Band Played On* (New York: St. Martin's Griffin, 1988); Virginia Berridge, *AIDS in the UK: The Making of Policy, 1981–1994*, 2nd ed. (Oxford: Oxford University Press, 2002).

7 WHO, *Global Health Observatory: HIV/AIDS* (2012), www.who.int/gho/hiv/en/index.html; AVERT, *AIDS Orphans* (2011), www.avert.org/aids-orphans.htm #content Table0.

8 Franklyn Lisk, *Global Institutions and the HIV/AIDS Epidemic: Responding to an International Crisis* (London: Routledge, 2009); Fantu Cheru, "Debt, Adjustment and the Politics of Effective Response to HIV/AIDS in Africa," *Third World Quarterly* 23, no. 2 (2002): 299–312; Tony Barnett, "HIV/AIDS and Development Concern Us All," *Journal of International Development* 16 (2004): 943–949; Maria deBruyn, "Women and AIDS in Developing Countries," *Social Science and Medicine* 34, no. 3 (1992): 249–262.

9 John J. Kirton and Jenevieve Mannell, "The G8 and Global Health Governance," in *Governing Global Health: Challenge, Response, Innovation*, eds. Andrew F. Cooper, John J. Kirton, and Ted Schrecker (Aldershot: Ashgate, 2007), 115–146.

10 Harman, *Global Health Governance*.

11 Stefan Elbe, *Security and Global Health* (Cambridge: Polity Press, 2010); Stefan Elbe, "Pandemics on the Radar Screen: Health Security, Infectious Disease, and the Medicalisation of Insecurity," *Political Studies* 59, no. 4 (2011): 848–866.

12 Colin McInnes, "HIV/AIDS and Security," *International Affairs* 82, no. 2 (2006): 315–326.

13 Peter W. Singer, "AIDS and International Security," *Survival* 44, no. 2 (2001): 145–158.

14 Colin McInnes and Kelley Lee, "Health, Security and Foreign Policy," *Review of International Studies* 32, no. 1 (2006): 5–23; Colin McInnes and Simon Rushton, "HIV, AIDS, and Security: Where Are We Now?" *International Affairs* 86 (2010): 225–245.

15 Stefan Elbe, "Should HIV/AIDS Be Securitized? The Ethical Dilemmas of Linking HIV/AIDS and Security," *International Studies Quarterly* 50 (2006): 121–146.

16 Elbe, "Should HIV/AIDS Be Securitized?" Recent incidents of quarantining people with HIV/AIDS can be seen in Cuba and the Philippines.

17 Phyllida Travis, Sara Bennett, Andy Haines et al., "Overcoming Health-Systems Constraints to Achieve the MDGs," *Lancet* 364 (2005): 900–906.

18 Peter Piot, "Editorial: Ebola's Perfect Storm," *Science* 345, no. 6202 (2014): 1221; Peter Piot, et al, "Ebola in West Africa: From Disease Outbreak to Humanitarian Crisis," *Lancet Infectious Diseases* 14, no. 11 (2014): 1034–1035; Jeremy Youde, "The World Health Organisation and Responses to Global Health Emergencies," *Political Science and Politics* 48, no. 1 (2015): 11–12; Joshua Busby and Karen A. Grepin, "What Accounts for the World Health Organisation's Failure on Ebola?" *Political Science and Politics* 48, no. 1 (2015): 12–13.

19 Youde, "The World Health Organisation."

20 Adam Kamradt-Scott, et al, *Saving Lives: The Civil-military Responses to the 2014 Ebola Outbreak in West Africa* (Sydney: University of Sydney, 2015).

21 Sophie Harman, "Ebola, Gender, and Conspicuously Invisible Women in Global Health" *Third World Quarterly* 37, no 3 (2016): 524–541.

22 Sara Davies and Belinda Bennett, "A Gendered Human Rights Analysis of Ebola and Zika: Locating Gender in Global Health Emergencies," *International Affairs* 92, no 5 (2016): 1041–1060.

23 Sophie Harman, "Is Time up for WHO? Reform, Resilience and Global Health Governance," *Future United Nations Development System Briefing* 17, www.futureun.org/media/archive1/briefings/FUNDSBriefing17-WHO-Harman.pdf.

24 Busby and Grepin, "What Accounts?"

25 WHO, "Health Emergencies Programme," www.who.int/about/who_reform/emergency-capacities/emergency-programme/en/.

26 WHO, "Antimicrobial Resistance," www.who.int/mediacentre/factsheets/fs194/en/.

27 WHO, *Global Action Plan on Antimicrobial Resistance*, http://apps.who.int/iris/bitstream/10665/193736/1/9789241509763_eng.pdf?ua=1.

Refugees and migrants

Khalid Koser

In legal, normative, and institutional terms, refugees and international migrants comprise quite distinct categories. There is a widely ratified international convention on refugees that defines clearly who refugees are, provides a legal and normative framework for protecting and assisting them, and that forms the basis of the mandate for a specific United Nations organization devoted to refugees. In contrast, the legal and normative framework pertaining to international migrants cannot be found in a single document; but it is derived from customary law, a variety of binding global and regional legal instruments, nonbinding agreements, and policy understandings reached by states at the global and regional level. While the International Organization for Migration (IOM) became a related organization to the United Nations (UN) in 2016, it forms part of a network of intergovernmental organizations within and outside the world organization that focus on specific aspects of international migration.

The New York Declaration for Refugees and Migrants, adopted unanimously by UN Member States on 19 September 2016, reinforces this distinction, by setting in process negotiations for two separate "global compacts," one on "refugees" and the other on "safe, orderly and regular migration." The processes themselves are also divergent, with the Refugee Compact the responsibility of the Office of the UN High Commissioner for Refugees (UNHCR) and focusing on implementing a predetermined Comprehensive Refugee Response Framework, while the negotiations on the Migration Compact are less institutionalized and more open ended.

At a sociological level, the distinction between refugees and migrants is not as clear as implied by the separation of the regimes that govern them. Focusing on individual decision making, for example, reveals that most refugees and migrants move because of mixed motivations that combine political, economic, and social reasons.[1]

The categories of "refugee" and "migrants" are themselves also diverse. They cover a wide range of people, some of whose circumstances may be closer to those of people in the alternative category—for example the victims of human trafficking are defined as a type of migrant but certainly require specific assistance and protection.[2] The prospect of displacement across international borders as a result of the effects of climate change will further blur the traditional distinctions between migrants and refugees. Growing interaction can also be observed at the institutional level, with the evolution of a range of dialogue processes between agencies variously responsible for migration and refugees, as well as operational partnerships, for example during the ongoing Syrian crisis.

This tension between divergent legal, normative, and institutional frameworks and convergent practical realities is a theme that runs through this chapter. It starts by explaining the history and development of the three types of framework for refugees and migrants. The chapter then analyzes current debates pertaining to the refugee and migration regimes. The final substantive section turns to emerging issues, with a particular focus on climate change, before briefly concluding by considering prospects for a more formal union between the refugee and migration regimes.

The refugee and international migration regimes

Given the separation of the regimes governing refugees and international migrants, this section considers each in turn, describing the legal, normative, and institutional frameworks pertaining to refugees and international migrants, and how they have evolved over time.

Refugees

By the end of 2016 there were an estimated 21.3 million refugees worldwide.[3] This total included 5.2 million Palestinian refugees, who, as explained below, are registered by a different international organization than other refugees. Fifty-three percent of the world's refugees (excluding Palestinians) came from just three countries: Syria, Afghanistan, and Somalia. The top hosting countries for refugees were Turkey (2.5 million), Pakistan (1.6 million), and Lebanon (1.1 million). Despite political and public attention to Europe's "refugee crisis," about eighty-five percent of the world's refugees are hosted in the Global South.

An international regime to define and provide legal protection for refugees started to emerge only after World War I. In 1921 the League of Nations created the Office of the High Commissioner for Refugees; an office with a limited geographical scope that has been characterized as neither effective nor enduring.[4] In response to massive displacement during World War II, the Allied powers established the intergovernmental United Nations Relief and Rehabilitation Agency (UNRRA) in 1943, with a narrow mandate to oversee the repatriation of people displaced in Europe. UNRRA was abolished in 1947 and the International Refugee

Organization (IRO) created in its place, with a more comprehensive mandate but also focused exclusively on resolving the displacement arising from the war.[5] In parallel, a separate UN agency was established in 1948 to provide relief and works programs for Palestinian refugees; and the UN Relief and Works Agency (UNRWA) began operations in 1950.

In part because of the emergence of new refugee flows, as a result of the partition of India in 1947 but also arising from events in Korea and China, consensus grew that a new UN refugee agency was required, culminating in the creation of UNHCR in 1951. When he was appointed the first UN High Commissioner, Gerrit Jan van Heuven Goedhart received a mandate that was expected to last for only three years and controlled virtually no funds.[6] The current High Commissioner, Felippo Grandi, leads an agency with 10,500 staff present in over 120 countries and an annual budget of about $7.5 billion. It is arguably the leading humanitarian organization in the world.

The 1951 UN Convention relating to the Status of Refugees provides the legal foundation and basic statute for UNHCR's work. It defines a refugee as someone who, "owing to a well-founded fear of being persecuted for reasons of race, religion, nationality, membership of a particular social group or political opinion, is outside the country of his nationality, and is unable to, or owing to such fear, is unwilling to avail himself of the protection of that country."[7] This definition focuses only on people who have been displaced across borders, and does not therefore include an estimated 40 million internally displaced persons (IDPs) around the world in 2016.

The original definition covered only those who were displaced as a result of "events occurring before 1 January 1951," and thus focused mainly on Europe. This time constraint—and by extension geographical limitation—was removed, along with other changes to bring the unlimited and universal UNHCR statute into line with the 1951 Convention, by the 1967 Protocol relating to the Status of Refugees. In 2011 there were 142 states parties to both the Convention and Protocol.

Besides the legal definition of a refugee, the 1951 Convention also elaborates a normative framework, by identifying a number of specific obligations on states parties. Foremost is the principle of *non-refoulement*, which prescribes that a refugee may not be returned to any country where he or she would be at risk of persecution. Other important principles included the prescription of freedom from penalties for illegal entry; and a series of social, economic, and political rights, including employment, education, freedom to practice religion, access to courts and legal assistance, and the freedom of movement.

In addition to protecting and assisting refugees, the UNHCR mandate also extends to identifying durable solutions for them, of which there are three. Voluntary repatriation describes the return to their country of origin of refugees, once it is safe to do so—in 2015 around 200,000 refugees returned home. Local integration describes the permanent settlement of refugees in their country of asylum. This is hard to measure, but it is estimated that over the last decade about 900,000 refugees have been given citizenship in the country in which they sought asylum—two-thirds of them in the United States. Resettlement describes a process whereby refugees are moved from their country of asylum for permanent resettlement in another country. The most significant countries of resettlement worldwide are the United States, Canada, and Australia. In 2015 about 107,000 refugees were resettled worldwide.[8]

International migration

There were an estimated 244 million international migrants in the world in 2015, representing an increase of almost 70 million in the first fifteen years of the twenty-first century, and over double the number of international migrants in 1980. This figure does not include irregular migrants, currently estimated to number between 20 and 30 million.[9]

In contrast to refugees, there is no single document consolidating the legal and normative framework on migration. International migrants have rights under two sets of international instruments. The first are the core human rights treaties currently in force, namely the International Covenant on Civil and Political Rights (ICCPR), the International Covenant on Economic, Social and Cultural Rights (ICESCR), the Convention Against Torture (CAT), the Convention on the Elimination of All Forms of Racial Discrimination (CERD), the Convention on the Elimination of All Forms of Discrimination Against Women (CEDAW), the Convention on the Rights of the Child (CRC), and the Convention on the Rights of Persons with Disabilities (CRPD).

The second instrument is the UN Convention on the Protection of the Rights of All Migrant Workers and Members of Their Families, adopted by the UN General Assembly in 1990. This convention is intended to reinforce the international legal framework concerning the human rights of migrant workers by adopting a comprehensive instrument applicable to the whole migration process and regulating the legal status of migrant workers and their families. It protects the basic rights of all migrant workers and their families and grants regular migrants a number of additional rights on the basis of equality with nationals. It has not been widely ratified, and certainly not when compared with the 1951 Refugee Convention. There are currently forty-six states parties, although none is a major destination country for migrants.

Nevertheless, the convention has recently received further endorsement within the UN system. In particular the September 2016 New York Declaration calls for those states that have not yet done so to ratify or accede to the convention.

Migrant workers are also provided rights under international labor law, which includes two specific International Labour Organization (ILO) conventions, 97 and 143, concerned with the protection of migrant workers. The trafficking and smuggling protocols supplementing the UN Convention against Transnational Organized Crime also make reference to protecting the human rights of trafficked victims and smuggled migrants. ILO labor standards have also had a significant impact, especially on domestic law in ILO member states. Migrants' rights are also protected under regional treaties (e.g., under the European Court of Human Rights and the Inter-American Court of Human Rights). In addition, national courts are increasingly applying international human rights law and case law and advisory opinions from regional treaties to cases that come before them.

Also in contrast to refugees, there is no single UN organization responsible for safeguarding the legal and normative framework on international migration. Instead responsibility is divided across a whole range of institutions at the international, regional, and national levels.

The most prominent international agency working on international migration is the International Organization for Migration, which became a "related organization" of the UN after the September 2016 UN decision.[10] It does not have a specific mandate for migrant protection. Nonetheless, its guiding principle is to promote humane migration, and it supports numerous projects aimed at protecting the rights of migrant workers around the world. IOM was founded in 1951 as the Provisional Intergovernmental Committee for the Movement of Migrants from Europe (PICMME) and has gone through a series of name changes: PICMME to the Intergovernmental Committee for European Migration (ICEM) in 1952; the Intergovernmental Committee for Migration (ICM) in 1980; and the International Organization for Migration in 1989. Over this time period the agency has evolved from a small members' organization for migrant receiving states to a global agency with 166 member and eight observer states. It has also evolved from a largely technical and service-oriented agency to a more holistic migration agency. How coordination will be achieved between IOM and other UN agencies with a mandate on migration remains to be seen.

The ILO is the only UN organization with a constitutional mandate that applies to migration, but it is focused only on migrant workers, and specifically on their employment rights. The protection of migrant workers is also a significant focus for regional organizations and regional consultative processes on international migration around the world. They are addressed through provisions in numerous bilateral labor agreements between sets of states (although these provisions are not always effectively implemented). At the national level, numerous government agencies are dedicated to promoting the legal rights of migrants and protecting them in the workplace. Civil society organizations are also very active in this arena.

Current debates

There are numerous policy debates concerning refugees and migrants. UNHCR has spelled out a policy on urban refugees, who may now outnumber refugees in camps. It is concerned with finding new durable solutions for refugees in protracted refugee situations; and it remains conflicted about its role in protecting and assisting IDPs. IOM is currently focusing significant attention on migrants in transit countries; migrants caught up in conflicts and political crises; and on so-called mixed migration, which it describes as "complex population movement including refugees, asylum seekers, economic migrants and other migrants." While cognizant of these policy issues, this section focuses on current debates concerning the global governance of refugees and international migration.

Refugees

Probably the most significant debate with direct implications for the refugee regime concerns the relevance to contemporary realities of a legal definition written in a specific geographical and historical context over sixty years ago. As explained above, the time limitation and implied geographical scope included in the original definition was removed by the 1967 Protocol. Still, it is often argued that the definition risks excluding contemporary refugees, for example, who are fleeing situations of ethnic violence, or escaping the threat of gender-based persecution or persecution on the basis of sexual orientation. The 1951 Convention definition also does not include persecution by non-state actors as the basis for a claim.

Most commentators agree that it is unlikely that the 1951 Convention definition of a refugee will be renegotiated. Certainly, a new convention or protocol would be unlikely to gain the near universal ratification currently enjoyed if it included a more generous and inclusive definition of a refugee. Three broad responses have therefore developed to bring refugee status determination into line with current realities.

First, there have emerged several regional instruments pertaining to the assistance and protection of refugees that adapt the legal definition to the regional context. The Organization of African Unity (OAU, now African Union, AU) Convention Governing the Specific Aspects of Refugee Problems in Africa (adopted in 1969), for example, added to the definition that a refugee is: "Any person compelled to leave his or her country owing to external aggression, occupation, foreign domination or events seriously disturbing public order in either part or the whole of his country of origin or nationality."[11] In 1984, the Organization for American States (OAS) adopted the Cartagena Declaration, which determined that the definition of a refugee also includes: "Persons who have fled their countries because their lives, safety or freedom have been threatened by generalized violence, foreign aggression, internal conflicts, massive violation of human rights or other circumstances which have seriously disturbed public order."[12] In Europe, the 1950 European Convention on Human Rights has led to the adoption in the European Union (EU) of provisions on "subsidiary" or "complementary" protection for displaced people who do not fall within the legal definition of a refugee but are still recognized as in need of protection. These provisions were widely adopted in response to displacement from the Bosnian and Kosovo crises during the mid-1990s.

Second, there are significant regional variations in the way that refugee status is determined. In general, in most industrialized countries, refugee status is granted on the basis of an individual assessment. Thus, the cases of claimants are assessed against the criteria of the 1951 UN Convention, and any other criteria defined in national laws or policies. In contrast, in many emerging or developing countries, and especially in the poorest, refugee status is mainly granted on a *prima facie* basis, in particular where large numbers of people cross a border from a conflict zone and the host state lacks the capacity to undertake individual determinations. It has been estimated that at least two-thirds of the world's refugees have not been subject to individual refugee status determination.[13] The relatively small numbers of these refugees who are subsequently resettled in more developed countries are subject to an individual screening process.

Third, in reality most states that do rely on individual assessments increasingly apply a wider interpretation of the criteria than those determined in the 1951

Convention, although they are not required to in law. Thus, in some countries someone fleeing persecution as a homosexual may be recognized as a refugee, and, in others, not; furthermore, the way that individual states interpret the criteria varies over time.

International migration

Turning to international migration, perhaps the principal debate as regards the legal and normative framework is how it should be implemented. Certainly the framework for protecting the rights of migrant workers is far from perfect, and the institutional infrastructure for its implementation has definite weaknesses. It is generally agreed, however, that a sufficient legal framework exists to protect the rights of most migrant workers and sufficiently robust institutional responsibility. Nevertheless, many migrant workers continue to experience violence, abuse, exploitation, and discrimination.

One problem relates to the ratification of existing instruments. There is a particularly vigorous debate surrounding the UN Convention on the Protection of the Rights of All Migrant Workers and Members of Their Families. Some of the main reasons provided for non-ratification, especially by major migrant destination countries, include the convention's breadth and complexity, the technical and financial obligations it places on states that have ratified, the view that it contradicts or adds no value to existing national migration legislation, concerns that it provides migrants—and especially those with irregular status—rights that are not found in other human rights treaties, and claims that it generally disallows for differentiation between regular and irregular migrants.

Significant problems persist in making the rights guaranteed in the convention a reality, even for those states that are party to it, arising at times from a lack of political will but also from a lack of capacity and resources. Neither is there a sufficient infrastructure for monitoring or enforcing state compliance. To help fill this gap, it has been suggested that capacity building is especially required among civil society to increase its effectiveness in lobbying for the rights of migrants and migrant workers, monitoring and reporting on conditions for migrant workers, and providing migrant workers with services. Effective practice also stresses empowering migrants by providing them with information about their rights in the labor market, giving them the identification and rights needed to access banks and other institutions abroad, and developing incentives to encourage migrants to report the worst abuses of their rights.

For those states that are not yet party to the convention, the emphasis has been on trying to ensure that domestic law and regulations conform to international human rights standards. It has been suggested that one way to facilitate this is to articulate the dispersed legal and normative framework in a single compilation of all treaty provisions and other norms that are relevant to international migration and the human rights of migrants.[14]

A second current debate starts with the observation that in contrast to many other cross-border issues of our time—e.g., trade, finance, and the environment—international migration lacks a coherent institutional framework at the global level. The case for a more integrated international institutional arrangement rests on five main arguments.[15] First, contemporary international migration is now occurring at unprecedented levels and has a truly global reach. Second, the forces that drive international migration are powerful, and national migration policies alone can no longer effectively manage or control migration. Third, there are growing numbers of migrants around the world who are vulnerable and exploited, and insufficiently protected by either states or international institutions. Fourth, as discussed below, the effects of climate change on migration are likely to present new management and protection challenges. Fifth, momentum for change is slowly accumulating—for instance, there has been greater collaboration between global institutions with an interest in international migration in recent years.

As convincing as these arguments may be, the obstacles to better global international migration governance should not be underestimated. In particular, the reluctance of most states to yield national control over international migration is understandable. Sovereign states have the right to determine who enters and remains on their territory, and international migration can also have an impact on other essential aspects of state sovereignty, including economic competitiveness, national and public security, and social cohesion. States are likely to remain the principal actors in migration governance.

Emerging issues

The highest profile emerging issue, with implications both for the refugee and international migration regimes, concerns the prospects of climate change displacing people from their homes. There is very little consensus about even some of most of the basic questions. The nature of the relationship between climate change and migration remains unclear. There are likely to be direct effects, for example where natural disasters destroy homes, or rising sea levels make coastal areas uninhabitable; and there are also likely to be indirect effects, for example, where increased global warming and drought disrupt agricultural production, or competition over natural resources is intensified, potentially resulting in conflict. Estimates of the number of people likely to be displaced vary widely, as do the time horizons.[16] There also is no consensus about where those affected will move. Most experts think that the majority of displacement as a result of the effects of climate change will be internal, but the prospects of significant cross-border movements cannot be discounted.[17]

People moving inside their own country as a result of the effects of climate change would fall within the definition of IDPs as described in the "1998 Guiding Principles on Internal Displacement," although it is important to note significant gaps in IDP protection.[18] There are important gaps in the legal and normative framework for people who cross an international border. These people would not qualify as refugees under the 1951 Convention definition, but neither would they be economic migrants. Thus, their status remains unclear in international law. The same is the case for people who may have to leave low-lying island states that become uninhabitable as a result of the effects of rising sea levels. They would be in a legal limbo as neither migrants nor refugees. It is also unclear whether they would be legally defined as stateless, as under international law statelessness means to be without nationality, *not* without state.

Proposals to fill legal gaps are currently being discussed at a variety of levels. The prospects for a new international treaty or a protocol to the 1951 Refugee Convention are slim, as indicated earlier, and also have significant shortcomings. Obstacles include resistance by UNHCR and its member states; the length of time it takes to negotiate international conventions in the field of human rights; and the reality that many states would refuse to ratify a protocol or new convention. These legal and political obstacles are compounded by a lack of empirical evidence on the numbers of people expected to be displaced across borders by the effects of environmental change, the time horizon involved, and the extent to which this is likely to be a regional or truly global issue.

Instead, efforts at the multilateral level are focusing on the development and consolidation of normative principles that can inform regional or national laws and policies on environmental migration. One example is the Nansen Principles. These principles were developed at a conference cohosted by the Government of Norway and UNHCR in Oslo in June 2011; and they were adopted by over 200 delegates, including representatives of UN and civil society organizations. They recommend building on existing norms in international law, and identify the responsibility of local, national, and international actors. The Nansen Initiative was subsequently established to build consensus at the state level around the Principles. Now the Platform on Disaster Displacement has been established to follow up on the work of the Nansen Initiative.

A range of proposals is also being considered at the level of national policy in various countries. One is to develop a new humanitarian category for environmental migrants. This is what was proposed in a bill introduced to parliament by the Australian Greens in 2007, which calls for a "climate refugee" visa category for people fleeing:

[A] disaster that results from both incremental and rapid ecological and climatic change and disruption, that includes sea level rise, coastal erosion, desertification, collapsing ecosystems, fresh water contamination, more frequent occurrence of extreme weather events such as cyclones, tornados, flooding and drought, and that means inhabitants are unable to lead safe or sustainable lives in their immediate environment.[19]

The debate that followed in the Australian Senate was, however, largely critical of the proposed bill. A particular concern was that by becoming the first country to develop a specific visa category for environmental migrants Australia might become a magnet for environmental migrants from around the world.

A second model is to amend existing legislation to provide temporary protection or refugee-like protection. In the United States, Temporary Protected Status (TPS) was introduced as part of the 1990 Immigration Act to provide at least limited protection to people who are fleeing, or reluctant to return to, potentially dangerous situations in their home country. Between 1995 and 1999 the status was extended to people from Montserrat following volcanic eruptions there, and more recently to Haitians following the 2010 earthquake. Some analysts have suggested that the EU Temporary Protection Directive of 2001 may be interpreted to apply to mass influxes of people from natural disasters.[20] Within Europe, Sweden and Finland have both amended their asylum and human rights laws to incorporate some element of "environmental migration." The 2005 Swedish Aliens Act provides for the possibility to provide subsidiary protection on environmental grounds; while the Finnish Aliens Act of 2004 explicitly acknowledges that unusual environmental circumstances can produce mass influxes of migrants who require temporary protection.

None of these examples of national policies and legislation is comprehensive. An important reservation in the United States is that TPS can only apply to people already resident in the country at the time of the natural disaster, and not to people fleeing the event. Invoking the EU Temporary Protection Directive would require agreement by a majority of member states, which most commentators deem unlikely; and the focus of the directive on "mass influxes" would probably not cover most migrants from environmental change effects who will actually arrive in Europe, as they are likely to be moving over a period of time because of slow onset events such as desertification in the Middle East and North Africa. Neither of the relevant provisions in Sweden or Finland has ever been tested, and there are reservations about how they would function in practice—for example, it is unclear whether the protection envisaged is temporary or permanent.

A third model is to use existing labor migration programs to extend migration opportunities to people vulnerable to or affected by environmental change. There is some debate about whether the New Zealand Pacific Access Category visa may evolve into a migration policy for environmental migration, although that is not its intention. It is conceived as a traditional labor migration program rather than an instrument for humanitarian protection.[21] Thus, for example, it is based on a ballot system and stipulates age restrictions for applicants, who must have a job offer in New Zealand, a minimum income requirement, and a reasonable level of English. This is an important caveat as the scheme does not necessarily target those most vulnerable to or adversely affected by environmental change. Furthermore, the scheme targets a limited number of countries only, and thus represents a limited response to environmental migration. Nevertheless, the scheme does target Pacific islands at risk, including Tuvalu, Kiribati, and Tonga, and arguably provides a basis for admitting people at risk from these islands. For example, the small quota could be extended, or the ballot system and criteria for selecting candidates revised, or the target countries increased, without significant legislative changes.

Conclusion

Environmental migration is a good example of a new migration reality that will challenge the traditional legal, normative, and institutional distinctions that separate the regimes on refugees and international migration. Various proposals have been made for consolidating these regimes—for example, by creating a new World Migration Organization with responsibility for both refugees and international migrants; designating a lead agency from among existing agencies.[22] There are significant political, technical, and financial obstacles to all these proposals, and their implementation seems unlikely in the foreseeable future. Instead, cooperation on the global governance for refugees and migrants is likely to continue on an *ad hoc* and needs-defined basis, and to take the form of informal partnerships and dialogues.

The risk is that vulnerable migrants may be ignored. Criticizing the two "distinct, separate and independent" global compacts that only reify an increasingly artificial distinction between migrants and refugees, the UN secretary-general's special representative on migration has provided his own suggestions, which serve as a fitting end to this chapter:

> The most urgent task is to clarify the responsibilities of states towards migrants who are in vulnerable situations and may not be able to return home, but do not qualify for protection under the 1951 Refugee Convention. We need to overcome the facile binary approach that treats refugees as "good" (i.e., deserving help because they are forced to leave their country and deprived of its protection) and irregular migrants as "bad" (because they have made their own decision to move, without due regard for legal process). Reality is far from being so clear-cut and there is a large grey area between those who flee literally at gunpoint and those whose movement is entirely voluntary.[23]

Additional reading

Alexander Betts, ed., *Global Migration Governance* (Oxford: Oxford University Press, 2011).
Alexander Betts, Gil Loescher, and James Milner, *UNHCR: The Politics and Practice of Refugee Protection*, 2nd ed. (London: Routledge, 2012).
Khalid Koser, ed., "Special Issue on International Migration and Global Governance," *Global Governance* 16, no. 3 (2010).
Khalid Koser and Susan Martin, eds., *The Migration–Displacement Nexus: Patterns, Processes, and Policies* (Oxford: Berghahn, 2011).
Etienne Piguet, Antoine Pecoud, and Paul Guchteneire, eds., *Migration and Climate Change* (Cambridge: Cambridge University Press, 2011).

Notes

1 Anthony Richmond, "Reactive Migration: Sociological Perspectives on Refugee Movements," *Journal of Refugee Studies* 6, no. 1 (1993): 7–24.
2 Susan Martin and Amber Calloway, "Internal Displacement and Internal Trafficking: Developing a New Framework for Protection," in *The Migration–Displacement Nexus: Patterns, Processes, and Policies*, eds. Khalid Koser and Susan Martin (Oxford: Berghahn, 2011), 216–238.
3 UNHCR, *Global Trends 2011* (Geneva: UNHCR, 2012).
4 Alexander Betts, Gil Loescher, and James Milner, *UNHCR: The Politics and Practice of Refugee Protection*, 2nd ed. (London: Routledge, 2012).
5 Claudena Skran, *Refugees in Inter-war Europe: The Emergence of a Regime* (Oxford: Oxford University Press, 1995).
6 Gil Loescher, *The UNHCR and World Politics: A Perilous Path* (Oxford: Oxford University Press, 2001).
7 UNHCR, *Convention Relating to the Status of Refugees*, Chapter I, Article I (1951), www.unhcr.org/3b66c2aa10.html.
8 UNHCR, *Global Trends 2011* (Geneva: UNHCR, 2012).

9 International Organization for Migration, *World Migration Report 2011* (Geneva: IOM, 2012).

10 Nicholas R. Micinski and Thomas G. Weiss, "International Organization for Migration and the UN System: A Missed Opportunity," Future UN Development System Project Briefing 42, September 2016, www.futureun.org/media/archive1/briefings/FUNDS_Brief42_IOM_UN_Migraton_Sept2016.pdf.

11 UNHCR, Refugee Act (1989), www.unhcr.org/refworld/docid/3ae6b4f28.html.

12 UNHCR, Cartagena Declaration on Refugees, Colloquium on the International Protection of Refugees in Central America, Mexico and Panama (1984), www.unhcr.org/refworld/docid/3ae6b36ec.html.

13 Matthew Albert, *Prima Facie Determination of Refugee Status: An Overview and Its Legal Foundation*, Refugee Studies Centre Working Paper Series no. 55 (Oxford: Refugee Studies Centre, 2010).

14 Global Commission on International Migration, *Migration in an Interconnected World: Final Report of the Global Commission on International Migration* (Geneva: GCIM, 2005).

15 Khalid Koser, "Introduction: International Migration and Global Governance," *Global Governance* 16, no. 3 (2010): 301–316.

16 Oliver Brown, "Migration and Climate Change," Migration Research Series no. 31 (Geneva: IOM, 2008).

17 Susan Martin, "Climate Change, Migration, and Governance," *Global Governance* 16, no. 3 (2010): 397–414.

18 Khalid Koser, "Gaps in IDP Protection," in *Migration and Climate Change*, eds. Etienne Piguet, Antoine Pecoud, and Paul Guchteneire (Cambridge: Cambridge University Press, 2011), 289–305.

19 The Parliament of the Commonwealth of Australia, *A Bill for an Act to Recognise Refugees of Climate Change Induced Environmental Disasters, and for Related Purposes* (2007), www.comlaw.gov.au/Details/C2007B00149.

20 William Somerville, *Environmental Migration* (Washington, DC: Migration Policy Institute, 2011).

21 Jane McAdam, "Environmental Migration Governance," University of New South Wales Faculty of Law Research Series, Paper 1 (Sydney: University of New South Wales, 2009).

22 Kathleen Newland, "Global Governance of International Migration: A Fragile Evolution," *Global Governance* 16, no. 3 (2010): 331–344.

23 UN, *Report of the Special Representative of the Secretary General on Migration*, UN document A//1/218, February 2017.

Global Internet governance

Madeline Carr

Over the past quarter-century, the world has developed a dependence on an open, relatively insecure computer network for a whole range of critical infrastructure and functions. In the early years of the Internet, there was an assumption that the organization and governance of this network was simply an issue of technical coordination. Over time, it became evident that Internet governance, situated as it is at the interface of a whole range of global resources, is, in fact, deeply political. Internet governance raises many of the same fundamental questions that animate the concerns in this volume with international organization and global governance. What and who governs the Internet? Where does global Internet governance take place? And what is understood to be the purpose of global Internet governance, its structures and its practices? The answers to these questions reveal a complex, multidimensional matrix of actors, institutions, mechanisms, and interests—sometimes conflicting and competing with one another.[1]

Early Internet-savvy politicians, business leaders, and engineers could not have anticipated how extensively this technology would come to be integrated into the global financial system, military doctrines, human rights practices, and political conflict of the twenty-first century. Neither could they have been expected to anticipate the range of technical, social, and political problems that would arise. Somehow, despite the enormity of the task and the rapidity with which the Internet grew in scale and scope, these people managed to establish workable mechanisms for the organization and governance of this global critical infrastructure. How this happened, the problems that arose along the way, and the debates that persist now (and will into the future) are quite compelling. It has not been an entirely smooth path and there are many issues that have yet to be resolved. At the same time, Internet governance can be regarded as an extraordinary success—an accelerated governance process with little precedent in terms of the timeframe, scale, and criticality.

There are positive and negative lessons that we might take from the evolution of Internet governance and apply them to thinking through how other future global governance problems might be addressed. There are some unique features that should be evaluated for usefulness in other domains. Beyond that kind of problem-solving lens, however, looking carefully and critically at global Internet governance allows us to get more closely in touch with some of the less obvious mechanisms of global governance—some of which look set to play an increasingly important role in the next decade of technological development. Understanding these nuanced factors, as well as the currents of power and interest that flow beneath the surface of Internet governance now, will be essential to understanding it in the future.[2]

This chapter provides a brief overview of the background to Internet governance, which is essential to understanding how some of the less orthodox elements came to be. It is particularly interesting because Internet governance developed in an organic fashion—prior to any real comprehension of its future significance. The relatively apolitical bubble, in which these governance practices and mechanisms grew, allowed for some innovation that could potentially be applied elsewhere. There follows a discussion of contemporary debates to show how actors and interests jostle for prominence through the promotion of ideological and normative positions. Finally, the chapter touches on some of the emerging issues that are likely to shape Internet governance in the coming years. It is not possible to provide anything like a comprehensive account here—this is not the purpose of the chapter. Instead, significant factors are used here to illustrate these broader questions about international organization and global governance.

Background

To some extent, the history of global Internet governance is the history of US Internet governance. Over the course of the Cold War, the United States invested heavily in research and development of computer technology. Alarmed by Moscow's successful launch of the Sputnik satellite in 1957, which many felt signaled a shift in power and technological momentum, there was a concentrated effort to restore US leadership and advantage. The belief that computers would be integral to solving complex problems necessary for that advancement led to an injection of resources through the Defense Advanced Research Projects Agency (DARPA). The aspiration to connect computers which were, at that time expensive and rare, was prompted by the desire to maximize their potential among the scientific and research communities. Consequently, investigation into networking technology was also funded by DARPA. However, from the mid-1970s to mid-1980s, the personal computer market in the United States grew exponentially, which had the effect of engaging the private sector that saw the commercial potential in networking millions of PCs. By the mid-1990s, the Internet infrastructure and services (the vast majority of which were in the United States) had been privatized and commercialized. These developments, coupled with the invention of the world wide web in 1989 by Tim Berners Lee and Robert Cailleau, were significant. They helped establish the 1990s as birth of the digital age or the "third industrial revolution."

During this time, although the US government played a strategic role,[3] the technical community had taken primary responsibility and initiative for coordination and decision making about the Internet. Various collaborative arrangements established a number of bodies to manage the expansion of the network. The Internet Assigned Numbers Authority (IANA) was established to ensure that there was no duplication of unique domain names and numbers, the combination of which are essential to locating resources on the Internet. Bodies like the Internet Engineering Task Force (IETF) and the World Wide Web Consortium (W3C) played (and continue to play) a leading role in developing the standards and protocols necessary for interoperability.

Central to the ethos of these groups was a bottom-up, consensus-based decision-making model including mechanisms such as the "Requests for Comment" (RfC) process—a form of participatory democratic dialogue—a kind of "marketplace of ideas." Also central were ideas of openness, minimal government control, and a borderless cyberspace.[4] Without realizing the full spectrum of implications for what they were doing, these technical actors laid the foundations for the global governance of the Internet through the assertion of certain norms and the establishment of universal standards. Mark Raymond and Laura DeNardis have described this as the "power of epistemic communities to shape governance."[5]

Following the commercialization and privatization of the Internet in the mid-1990s, the uptake of Internet services and the development of websites grew exponentially. In turn, this growth produced pressure on processes for allocating domain names and IP addresses—the Domain Name System (DNS). The governance mechanisms put in place by the technical community were no longer adequate and delays in processing requests were regarded as a hindrance to fully exploiting the vast economic potential of Internet technology—a key goal of the US government.[6] After a period of stakeholder consultation, Washington established what many regard as the first formal global Internet governance institution to take over the IANA function and manage the DNS, the Internet Corporation for Assigned Names and Numbers (ICANN).

In addition to the initial governance processes handled by the technical community and the more formal, institutionalized, and international ICANN, some aspects of global Internet governance are taken up in the International Telecommunication Union (ITU), a specialized agency of the United Nations. Initiated to manage global telegraph standards in 1865, the ITU now coordinates the production of a range of international telecommunications standards and it has a normative agenda to improve access to ICTs in the developing world. Although the ITU has a broad membership (193 countries and almost 800 private sector entities and academic institutions),[7] in terms of decision making and negotiations on relevant treaties, it is a conventional international organization managed through multilateral processes. The ITU's role in Internet governance is a source of considerable dispute, which will be discussed further below.

This realization that Internet governance was much more than a technical coordination issue happened quite quickly over the course of the late 1990s and early 2000s. As awareness developed of the broader implications of the Internet, governments became increasingly engaged. However, in the short time that had already elapsed, Internet governance processes and practices had developed outside of more conventional multilateral channels. Thus, state actors found themselves entering into a governance landscape that had developed largely without their input, but that had very clear implications for their national interests. This set the stage for some of the ongoing debates that have characterized global Internet governance for the past two decades.

Current debates

Given that Internet technology intersects with the interests of many stakeholders, both public and private, it is unsurprising that it raises complex and contentious governance issues. Many current debates and criticisms of global Internet governance revolve around competing ideas about *who* should govern the Internet and through which mechanisms, organizations, or institutions. In a sense, at the heart of all of these debates is a power dynamic that revolves around the extent to which actors are able to voice their preferences. The following section provides an overview of two major debates that have shaped, and will continue to shape global Internet governance: Who should govern (multi-stakeholder and multilateral models)? And what constitutes legitimacy in an Internet governance body?

Who should govern? Multi-stakeholderism and multilateralism

Multi-stakeholderism emerged from the world of environmental governance and refers to the practice of involving a range of relevant actors in decision making so as to agree on sustainable outcomes that will not have to be revisited once they are implemented.[8] As is clear from this brief history, Internet governance matured through and into a multi-stakeholder model, beginning with the efforts of the technical community and then the gradual incorporation of the private sector, governments (in addition to the US government), and civil society. Multi-stakeholderism was further enshrined in the 2005 report from the UN Working Group on Internet Governance, which defined Internet governance as "the development and application by Governments, the private sector and civil society, in their respective roles, of shared principles, norms, rules, decision-making procedures, and programs that shape the evolution and use of the Internet."[9]

Multi-stakeholderism has been regarded as a deeply important principle by some and as a mechanism for sidelining state actors by others. While most observers would agree that there are sound reasons why multiple stakeholders should be involved in Internet governance, there are different views over who exactly should be included and especially, whether they should participate as equal to state actors or whether they should be consulted at a domestic level and then represented by state actors in global forums. Over time multi-stakeholderism has taken on a flavor much like other "isms"—that is, it has developed an ideological significance. Recognizing this allows us to identify the power dimension within it when analyzing both positions.[10]

Those who support the multi-stakeholder model argue that it is essential that a wide range of stakeholders are involved in decision making about Internet technology because of its complexity and its broad implications. Extensive private sector ownership of Internet infrastructure and services, they argue, means that these actors must be involved in governance and decision-making processes. Sometimes this is framed in the necessity of drawing on technical knowledge and sometimes it is based on market arguments—that, if Internet governance becomes overly politicized, the opportunities it offers for innovation and economic growth will be stymied. In addition, it is argued that broader stakeholder representation is essential to balance against the tendency for political machinations that might otherwise dominate. Finally, the broad implications of the Internet for people's everyday wellbeing suggests that civil society should be represented to ensure that the interests of human beings are given equal voice alongside those of governments and commercial actors. This balance of participatory and forced dialogue was anticipated to deliver the kind of equity and positive benefit that many saw possible with the advent of this new technological age.[11]

For others actors, although a range of stakeholders must be consulted (preferably at the domestic level), Internet governance is ultimately the responsibility of governments and it cannot be divested to the private sector, the technical community, or civil society. Furthermore, some regard the multi-stakeholder model as a mechanism for amplifying US power rather than redistributing it among stakeholders. For these actors, even if the private sector is to be included, the participants too often tend to be US multinationals that share so much with US government interests that they are unable to bring diversity of views to the negotiations. In addition, the inclusion of civil society can be contentious as some states see this as another veiled injection of US or Western ideology. NGOs that engage in Internet governance are very often self-selected, and they therefore lack legitimacy or are funded by the United States and focus on a liberal human rights agenda.[12] They amplify US concerns about freedom of expression online—an issue that is of less concern to those states that are preoccupied with the challenge of maintaining internal cohesion. Also for many newly independent states that have only recently come to enjoy the benefits of self-rule, ceding sovereign authority to a foreign private actor sits uncomfortably with newly established nationalist sentiment. Problematically for these actors, states with genuinely poor human rights records and oppressive political cultures also oppose the multi-stakeholder model in order maintain control. Consequently, any valid concerns or objections to multi-stakeholderism tend to be equated by its proponents with a position of illiberal autocracy.

There are two important observations about these disputes over who should be involved (and at what level) in global Internet governance. First, as Mark Raymond and Laura DeNardis have pointed out, in the complex range of processes and functions that comprise global Internet governance, the multi-stakeholder model cannot be regarded as either "right" or "wrong." Rather, it is appropriate for some of these processes and functions and clearly not for others.[13] Second, as Miles Kahler and David Lake argue, actors have no intrinsic preference for one governance arrangement over another—they are attracted to the one that they feel will best promote or protect their interests.[14] Essentially, those actors that see multi-stakeholderism as a mechanism for promoting their interests in a particular dimension of Internet governance are likely to support it while those that regard it as undermining their interests will be unlikely to.

While it would be difficult to argue against the suggestion that some degree of multi-stakeholderism is essential to global Internet governance, an awareness of the ideological power highlights the need to be clear about when, where, and why it is necessary. It also suggests that in those situations where the multi-stakeholder model is appropriate, more will need to be done to facilitate broader and more meaningful representation so that the expectations of the model—namely, the establishment of sustainable decisions, can actually be achieved. Those lessons are important for global Internet governance but they may also provide important learning for other global governance issues.

A return to geopolitics: The United States and ICANN

In addition to questions about which actors should participate in global Internet governance, ICANN has been at the center of an ongoing debate about what actually constitutes a legitimate Internet governance institution. Although it is responsible for the *global* DNS, ICANN is a private, nonprofit corporation registered in the state of California and (until September 2016) accountable to the US Department of Commerce. It may seem strange that this global governance institution would be set up in such a way but given that the DNS was initially perceived as simply a technical function and given the prominent role the US government, technical community, and private sector played in developing the Internet, it was not particularly contentious to create a secretariat when ICANN was established in 1998. Milton Mueller's comprehensive history of Internet governance details the awareness within the small Internet community of the early to mid-1990s that this could very well become contentious but there was little understanding or awareness of either the functions or the possible implications beyond that community.[15] Also, the US government was clear at that time that once ICANN was properly established and functioning well, it would transition fully from US oversight to the private sector. However, a number of factors prevented this from happening as quickly and smoothly as was anticipated.

A complicating factor was ICANN's hybrid nature which falls somewhere between: A private corporation run by a board to manage a commercial resource, a global regulatory institution which should represent stakeholders through some kind of legislative arrangement, and a forum for facilitating bottom-up consensus policy development. However, ICANN lacked the shareholders that provide accountability in private corporations, it did not have the transparency expected of a global regulatory institution, and neither did it adequately provide a platform for diverse actors and minority voices. As far back as 2004, John Palfrey described ICANN as a body that lacked the "legitimacy, authority or effectiveness of any of its component parts."[16]

As it became clear that ICANN's functions intersected with global power and the international political economy, some actors became increasingly dissatisfied with ICANN as a governance mechanism. The disgruntled included those states that had also reacted against multi-stakeholderism and felt that once again, the US government and private sector played a disproportionate role. It also included some commercial operators that were dissatisfied with the lack of transparency around issuing valuable new top-level domains (travel, museums, etc.). Perhaps surprisingly, given their role in establishing it in the first place, concern was also expressed by the US government, which found ICANN's lack of accountability and transparency inconsistent with expectations of democratic governance. Each of these groups had different preferred remedies; the US government's response was to continue to exercise oversight through the Department of Commerce for as long as necessary until ICANN's governance credentials were fully developed. Some commercial operators preferred ICANN to be disaggregated from the US government and transition to a more conventional private organization that would be guided by the predictability of market principles. The disaffected states began to argue that global Internet governance should come under the purview of the ITU. This proposal was firmly and consistently opposed by the US and many other states, ostensibly because it was believed that the ITU could not be nimble enough to respond to Internet governance challenges but possibly also because the prospect of "one flag, one vote" would not suit those that already enjoyed relative power under the existing arrangements.

Although ICANN lacked "input legitimacy"—that is, its processes and decision making did not satisfy widely held expectations, it did enjoy significant "output legitimacy." With very few exceptions, and in an extraordinary feat of global coordination, the DNS (and therefore, the Internet) succeeded: It worked consistently through exponential growth; it worked across borders, languages, and political cultures; and it worked with no roadmap or precedent. In this way, despite any weaknesses or flaws that might be attributed to it, ICANN was a remarkable global governance success story. For many actors whose interests had become dependent on a resilient and reliable Internet, any changes to ICANN needed to be very carefully considered and would have to be justified against the risk of destabilizing an effective institution and by extension, a critical infrastructure.

Tension over ICANN's structure and relationship to the US government played out through a number of pressure points. With some regularity, calls for Washington to loosen its grip were met by ICANN seeking to improve its structure and practices, and by the US government making incremental concessions but never fully relinquishing control. In 2013, this pattern of staged compromise was disrupted by the Snowden leaks, which undermined US leadership on Internet governance because it was seen to violate values of privacy, freedom of speech online, and government restraint—values that the United States had argued forcefully were a prerequisite for participation in global Internet governance. Actors opposed to the status quo used this moment to strengthen calls for ICANN to be decoupled from Washington. As a means to reaching that end, institutional reform of ICANN was implemented. Transparency measures and other key indicators of input legitimacy were developed and implemented through the stakeholder community. Once these had reached a satisfactory level, the final transition of ICANN from US oversight took place in September 2016.

This balance of input and output legitimacy could usefully be considered when future global governance challenges emerge—particularly in a very rapidly changing context such as new technology. It is difficult to ascertain the degree to which the unusual structure and lack of accountability and transparency that characterized ICANN in the early years were, in fact, key to its durability. ICANN was nimble and able to react quickly and adapt to changing circumstances; because it was a nonprofit organization and effectively managed the DNS, it enjoyed a degree of legitimacy despite these problems. Perhaps one lesson that can be taken from this unconventional governance institution is that where the international community feels that output legitimacy cannot be compromised, it is possible to develop input legitimacy over time.

Emerging issues

In addition to the debates outlined above, global Internet governance is made even more challenging because of the rapid development of technology. This growth raises questions about whether existing global governance mechanisms will continue to be fit for purpose or, alternatively, whether demand on the system will outpace the structures in place as was the case when the market for new domain names and numbers outgrew the governance mechanisms put in place by the technical community. While this is difficult to predict with any certainty (now as much as it was in the 1990s), there are some issues that look set to test global Internet governance over the next five to ten years. One of these will likely be demands from the Global South for a more equal voice and the resulting strain that may put on multi-stakeholder-led processes if they lean toward multilateral forums such as the ITU to achieve this. The second is the increased challenges of governing the "Internet of Things," which will amplify the need for standards coordination and raise new human rights and cyber security problems.

Making global Internet governance more global

As more state actors have come to realize the link between decisions about the Internet and their own national interests, they have sought a more prominent voice in that decision making. The imbalance of power in the multi-stakeholder model has led some states to regard multilateral forums like the UN as an attractive forum to operate on a more equal footing. Building on this sentiment, states including China and Russia have galvanized developing countries to exercise and project their influence into these multilateral forums—which has the effect of counterbalancing those of the West.

One stark example took place at the World Conference on International Telecommunications (WCIT) in 2012, when the ITU proposed a review and update of the International Telecommunication Regulations (ITRs). The ITRs "serve as the binding global treaty designed to facilitate international interconnection and interoperability of information and communication services."[17] The United States and the EU campaigned strongly against this update on the grounds that the ITU was overstepping its mandate and attempting to move into a realm of technology governance in which it was neither needed nor qualified. The divide between developed and the developing countries played out during a contentious vote on whether or not to update the treaty with eighty-nine countries (predominantly from the Global South, China and Russia) voting for the changes and only fifty-five voting alongside the United States and the EU to reject them. Although an impasse resulted, and the treaty remained as it was, the unprecedented alignment against Washington suggested that perhaps power in global Internet governance had shifted away from the industrialized North more significantly than previously had been understood.

The extent to which multi-stakeholderism must feature in global Internet governance will continue to be debated and negotiated. It seems clear, however, that unless the international community of states finds a way to address the growing expectations of the Global South, pressure will continue to mount for greater representation and influence in multilateral forums. And the outcome of that for the resilience and stability of the Internet is uncertain.

Governing the Internet of Things

While the emergence of digital technologies in the 1990s was understood as the third industrial revolution, the Internet of Things (IoT) is increasingly being referred to as the fourth. It is a significant shift in technology that will amplify governance challenges over the coming decade. The IoT can be understood as comprising three key elements: The proliferation of sensors (both visible and obscured) that collect vast amounts of data, the analysis of "big data," and actuators that can have effects in the physical world. An example might be a medical system that takes systemic data generated by an ingestible sensor in a person's body, sends it for analysis, and generates dosage instructions for an automated drug pump to release medication into that patient.

IoT applications like this are rapidly coming to market—indeed, estimates are that by 2020, there will be a hundred billion of these devices connected to the Internet.[18] IoT applications offer huge potential for generating wealth, creating efficiencies, and improving the human condition. However, they also raise a whole range of security and governance issues that will need to be coordinated internationally.

In a climate remarkably reminiscent of the early years of Internet technology, IoT governance is seen as a means to extract maximum value (especially but not exclusively economic value) while minimizing considerable security challenges. Once again, technical standards are fundamental to establishing how the technology will continue to develop; how it will be incorporated into existing structures and processes; and how it will shape the future. And somewhat alarmingly, just as was the case in the 1980s and 1990s, these technical standards are predominantly regarded as devoid of political implications.

Partly as a consequence of the exponential growth in data (which is being likened to the petroleum of the twenty-first century) that will be generated, shared, and analyzed, and partly as a consequence of the physical dimension of IoT, the current global Internet governance system will have to accommodate significant change. However, both the market and the technology of the IoT is already outpacing governance. New devices and applications are being introduced without adequate guidelines or standards. Problematically, unsecured devices introduce points of vulnerability, which leads to concerns that unless governance catches up, the IoT will have a negative impact on the resilience and reliability of the Internet.

Conclusion

In some ways, Internet governance revolves around perennial questions of global governance. Which actors, institutions, and mechanisms are involved? How and why did they emerge? And crucially, how can we understand the power dynamics that flow through them all? The dominant thread that runs through this particular domain of global governance is that the distribution of power in the international system more broadly has been reflected in both the evolution and more recent changes in Internet governance. Powerful states and their private sectors have been able to shape both the technology itself and the governance of that technology in ways that best promote their own interests. There is good reason to suppose that this pattern will continue to be the case and, consequently, global power transitions need to be factored into any future governance arrangements that we might anticipate emerging.

Equally, there are ways in which Internet governance provides new ground to mine for ideas about how the world can be organized—especially in such an interconnected domain. The hybrid nature of ICANN as a global governance institution as well as the relative tolerance required to let it mature over time should be carefully considered in the context of future challenges. Some of the innovations in governance practices and processes that developed in the technical community have proved remarkably durable. Nonhierarchical, consensus-based models may not be directly transferrable to other issue areas; indeed, they do not necessarily work perfectly in all dimensions of Internet governance. There is, nonetheless, a certain rationale to the argument that if the world is to continue to build on digital technology, state actors will need to be willing to share control with other stakeholder communities. Although technology and politics are intimately entwined, working out how to accommodate competing interests, balance power dynamics, and govern with legitimacy while facilitating technological innovation will require continued close dialogue between and well beyond state actors.

Ultimately, there is little alternative to global Internet governance. Our world is too dependent on the technology already to tolerate failure; and it will only become more so. Perhaps it is the realization of this dependence that maintains the complex equilibrium of actors, interests, and power that constitute today's global Internet governance. But that dependence also makes it ripe for continued contestation and challenges, which is why understanding the currents that flow beneath the surface is so important to future stability.

Additional readings

Madeline Carr, "Power Plays in Global Internet Governance," *Millennium-Journal of International Studies* 43, no. 2 (2015): 640–659.

Madeline Carr, *US Power and the Internet in International Relations: The Irony of the Information Age* (Basingstoke: Palgrave Macmillan, 2016).

Laura DeNardis, *The Global War for Internet Governance* (New Haven, CT: Yale University Press, 2014).

Jovan Kurbalija, *An Introduction to Internet Governance* (Geneva: DiploFoundation, 2014).

Milton Mueller, *Ruling the Root* (Cambridge. MA: MIT Press, 2004).

Mark Raymond and Laura DeNardis, "Multistakeholderism: Anatomy of an Inchoate Global Institution, " *International Theory* 7, no. 3 (2015): 572–616.

Notes

1 Mark Raymond and Laura DeNardis, "Multistakeholderism: Anatomy of an Inchoate Global Institution," *International Theory* 7, no. 3 (2015): 572–616.

2 Thomas G. Weiss and Rorden Wilkinson, "Rethinking Global Governance? Complexity, Authority, Power, Change," *International Studies Quarterly* 58 (2014): 207–215.

3 Carr, *US Power*, 117–148.

4 Lawrence Lessig, *Code Version 2.0* (New York: Basic Books, 2006).

5 Raymond and DeNardis, "Multistakeholderism," 585.

6 Carr, *US Power*, 124–126.

7 ITU website, www.itu.int/en/join/Pages/default.aspx.

8 Minu Hemmati, *Multi-stakeholder Processes for Governance and Sustainability beyond Deadlock and Conflict*, (London: Earthscan Publications, 2002), 1.

9 "Report of the Working Group on Internet Governance," (Château de Bossey: WGIG, June 2005), 4.

10 Madeline Carr, "Power Plays in Global Internet Governance," *Millennium-Journal of International Studies* 43, no. 2 (2015): 640–659.

11 Bertrand de la Chapelle, "Towards Multi-Stakeholder Governance – The Internet Governance Forum as Laboratory," in *The Power of Ideas: Internet Governance in a Global Multi-Stakeholder Environment*, ed. Wolfgang Kleinwachter (Berlin: Marketing for Deutschland GmbH, 2007), 260.

12 Claudia Padovani and Elena Pavan, "Diversity Reconsidered in a Global Multi-Stakeholder Environment: Insights from the Online World," in *The Power of Ideas*, ed. Kleinwachter, 109.

13 Raymond and DeNardis, "Multistakeholderism," 572–616.

14 Miles Kahler and David Lake, "Economic Integration and Global Governance: Why So Little Supranationalism?," in *The Politics of Global Regulation*, eds. Walter Mattli and Ngaire Woods (Princeton, NJ: Princeton University Press, 2009), 248.

15 Milton Mueller, *Ruling the Root* (Cambridge, MA: MIT Press, 2004).

16 John G. Palfrey, "The End of the Experiment: How ICANN'S Foray into Global Internet Democracy Failed," *Harvard Journal of Law & Technology* 17, no. 2 (2004): 425.

17 International Telecommunication Union, "World Conference on International Telecommunications (WCIT-12)," www.itu.int/en/wcit-12/Pages/default.aspx.

18 The Internet Society, *The Internet of Things (IoT): An Overview*, 15 October 2015, 4, www.internetsociety.org/sites/default/files/ISOC-IoT-Overview-20151022.pdf.

INDEX

Note: bold indicates tables; italics indicate figures.